The Breedon Book of

Scottish Football Records

Includes all League, SFA Cup and League Cup Results and League Tables

The Breedon Book of

Scottish Football Records

Includes all League, SFA Cup and League Cup Results and League Tables

GORDON SMAILES

Breedon Books
Publishing Company
Derby

First published in Great Britain by
The Breedon Books Publishing Company Limited
44 Friar Gate, Derby, DE1 1DA.
1995

Photographic Acknowledgements:
Most of the photographs in this book have been supplied by
Caledonian Newspapers Ltd of Glasgow, and EMPICS of
Nottingham

ISBN 1 85983 020 X

Printed and bound by Butler & Tanner, Frome, Somerset.
Cover printed by Premier Print, Nottingham.

Contents

Looking for the Right Result

by Andrew Ward

WHAT follows is a complete record of Scottish first-class football results. Add in the intonation of a voice, picture the scenes at the final whistle, recollect an image of where the news was first heard, and football results turn into vivid memories. Somewhere in this book you may be able to trace the first top-class game you ever saw, the moment you realised your team was relegated or promoted, the day of the wedding when you missed a game, the time you were on holiday and telephoned from a public call-box, and, if you've been really lucky, the eighth draw that brought your fortune.

When people are a long way from home, hearing a score takes on special significance. The bare details of 'the result' can spark such speculation, such pride, such longing and such identification. I often think of soldiers overseas. During World War Two, men of the 15th Scottish Division huddled round their *Tam o' Shanter* newsletters in France, Belgium, Holland and Germany. They read aloud the results of the Scottish Southern League – "Clyde five Hearts one, Motherwell two Celtic one" – and made them stretch as far as they possibly could.

Part of football's history concerns the various ways that results have been sprung upon us. In the early part of the century it was done by telegraph, newspapers and pigeon post. Pigeon fanciers would take three or four birds to the match and let them off at regular intervals in order to relay the score to a waiting village or newspaper offices. The results service has come a long way from those days, to Ceefax, club calls and Internet. Successive generations of fans have relied on wirelesses, transistors, televisions, teleprinters and frantic telephone calls to friends. Or they have stopped their car at a set of traffic-lights, rolled down a window and asked a passer-by who is wearing the right scarf, "What was the score?" Sometimes there was no need – the result was written across faces.

The story of official Scottish results begins in 1873, when 15 clubs subscribed towards the purchase of the Scottish Cup. The trophy and a full set of medals cost £56 12s 11d. Queen's Park won the Cup that year, and went on to dominate the early years with ten Scottish Cup wins in the first 20 seasons.

The Scottish Cup was soon providing us with some wonderful statistics. There is the well-chronicled tie on 5 September 1885 when Arbroath beat Bon Accord 36-0 with Petrie scoring thirteen. On the same day Dundee Harp thrashed Aberdeen Rovers 35-0 in the same competition, a result that has not been accorded the glamour it deserves. It must have been like Elisha Gray and Alexander Graham Bell turning up on the same day to file patent accounts dealing with the invention of the telephone.

Aside from Scottish Cup matches, clubs in the 1880s relied on friendlies and matches in minor competitions. The games could hardly be called 'fixtures' – there were too many late cancellations for that. Inevitably, the idea of a more organised fixture list was discussed, and this led to the formation of the Scottish League, on 30 April 1890. The League was based on the English model and had 11 founder members: Abercorn, Celtic, Cowlairs, Cambuslang, Dumbarton, Hearts, Rangers, St Mirren, Renton, Third Lanark and Vale of Leven. Reporters were quick to analyse the motivation behind the organisation. Said *Scottish Sport*: "Our first and last objection to them is that they exist. The entire rules stink of finance – money making and money grabbing."

Unlike clubs in the English League, their Scottish counterparts were bound to amateur status. In the League's first season, Celtic, Third Lanark and Cowlairs each had four points deducted for infringements of registration rules, and Renton were banned by the Scottish FA after only five League matches. Renton's crime was playing a friendly against a new club called Edinburgh Saints (which was really a hastily reformed St Bernard's after the latter had been banned by the authorities for 'concealed professionalism'). Renton and Edinburgh Saints were turfed out of the Scottish FA and both sets of players suspended.

That first season, 1890-91, was a wonderful start for the statistically minded. Dumbarton and Rangers finished level on points and drew 2-2 in their play-off match. In the absence of goal average – it wasn't introduced until 1922 – they were declared joint champions, the only time it has happened.

The Renton case was not an isolated instance of clubs violating the amateur rules. Many players were being paid, and the authorisation of professionalism, in 1893, was a sign that the Scottish Football Association had accepted the inevitable. When Celtic's John McLaughlin, secretary of the League, spoke at the 1893 Scottish FA annual meeting, he put it succinctly: "You might as well attempt to stop the flow of Niagara with a kitchen chair as to endeavour to stem the tide of professionalism."

Queen's Park had initially declined the opportunity for League soccer, but when their major fixtures disappeared they accepted the necessity of progress and joined the Scottish League in 1900. Although they won the Scottish Cup for the tenth (and last) time in 1893, Queen's Park were slipping away as a national force. Thereafter, the history of top-class Scottish soccer became irretrievably linked with the history of 'the Old Firm' – Rangers and Celtic. Rangers first qualified for a Scottish Cup Final in 1877, but, two years later, failed to turn up for the replay with Vale of Leven after being incensed at a decision in the first game. Celtic were formed later, in 1887, but had the edge in the period before the World War One.

In 1893, the year professionalism was legitimised, Division Two was formed. There was no automatic promotion and relegation between the two divisions – that wasn't introduced until 1921 – and clubs in the lower division relied on the First Division 'electing' new members. Hence, in 1905, Falkirk (second) and Aberdeen (seventh) were elected to Division One, whereas Clyde (Division Two's champions) had to stay down. Meanwhile, clubs like Port Glasgow and Queen's Park retained their Division One status despite poor placings in the higher division in the 1900s and 1910s.

There are some startling statistics from those early years: Celtic's unbeaten season of 1897-98; Rangers' 100 per cent record of 1898-99; Kilmarnock's unbeaten Division Two season of 1898-99; Third Lanark's championship of 1904 and Scottish Cup win of 1905; Celtic's astonishing defensive record of 1913-14 when they conceded only 14 goals in 38 games; Celtic's two games in a day at the end of 1915-

Soon after their election to Division One, Aberdeen in 1907-08. Back row (left to right): J.McIntosh, D.Colman, R.Macfarlane, J.Hulme, P.Simpson (trainer). Middle row: J.Muir, W.Low, A.Halkett, C.O'Hagan, W.Lennie. Front row: J.Macdonald, T.Murray.

16 season (against Raith Rovers in the afternoon and Motherwell in the evening); and 76 points out of 84 for Rangers in 1920-21. In other instances, however, statistics disappear from the records, like the abandoned Scottish Cup tie of 1905, when Rangers led ten-men Celtic 2-0 and fans invaded the pitch.

Already, Celtic and Rangers had begun their dominance, and the Scottish League became near enough an Old Firm monopoly. Between 1904, when Third Lanark were champions, and 1948 (Hibernian), only Motherwell, in 1931-32, wrested the League flag from the two premier Glasgow teams. That period began with Celtic winning six consecutive League titles (1904-05 to 1909-10). Manager Willie Maley shrewdly satisfied the first golden rule of management – get good players. He had Alec McNair at full-back, a half-back line of Young, Loney and Hay, the powerful Jimmy Quinn at centre-forward, the zippy Alex Bennett on one wing and Jimmy McMenemy and Peter Somers orchestrating from inside-forward.

During World War One, football was largely insignificant when compared with the brutal conflict which brought the deaths of many footballers. Players of some teams, like Queen's Park and Hearts, had enlisted en bloc. The Scottish Cup was abandoned, and, although the Scottish League continued, it was a shadow of itself, some of the events resembling those of local amateur soccer. In November 1915, for instance, Rangers fielded nine players against Falkirk; and, on 20 January 1917, Partick Thistle fielded a substitute against Rangers.

After World War One a rebel Central League caused disruption, and a number of clubs broke away from Division Two. These clubs were lured back with the

promise of automatic relegation and promotion. The Second Division was reformed in 1921 after a gap of seven years, and it included 11 new clubs. A First Division of 22 clubs was deemed to be too large, which led to three clubs being relegated and only one promoted at the end of 1921-22. Alloa Athletic were the first Scottish team to be automatically promoted on merit.

The following season 'goal-average' was introduced to separate teams on the same number of points. It was a curious name to describe 'the number of goals scored divided by the number of goals conceded' but the calculation managed to reach parts of the brain that whole education systems have sometimes failed to reach. Another dramatic change came with the new offside law, in 1925, when the Scots put forth a proposal at a meeting of the International Football Federation. With only two defenders, rather than three, needed behind the ball when it was last played, the game became easier for attackers, and 1925-26 saw the return of high scores.

If Celtic came out on top in the period leading up to World War One, Rangers were undoubtedly the more successful during the inter-war period, winning the League 15 times in 20 seasons under the stewardship of manager Willie Struth. This was during the heyday of players like Alan Morton, Davie Meiklejohn and Bob McPhail. Surprisingly, Rangers did not win the Cup between 1903 and 1928, although that did not stop Bob McPhail ending up with seven Scottish Cup winners' medals (including one for Airdrie in 1924). It was a man associated with Celtic, however, who set goalscoring standards that will never be equalled. Jimmy McGrory scored a British record 550 goals in first-class football, including eight in one match against Dunfermline in 1928.

Although Rangers dominated the inter-war years, there was enough excitement and competition to sustain interest outside Glasgow. Airdrieonians, for instance, were runners-up in four consecutive seasons (1922-23 to 1925-26) and Motherwell finished in the top three eight times in succession (1926-27 to 1933-34). A number of new names appeared on the Scottish Cup in the 1920s – Kilmarnock (1920), Partick Thistle (1921), Morton (1922), Airdrie (1924) and St Mirren (1926). Then, after the Old Firm had seemingly regained its grip on the competition, there came two more surprises – Second Division East Fife (1938) and Clyde (1939).

In the League, the most bizarre 'achievements' came from Edinburgh City, an all-amateur team known as 'the Queen's Park of the east'. Elected to Division Two in 1931, they showed remarkable consistency over the next eight seasons, conceding 981 goals in 276 games, an average of 3.62 per game. They finished bottom of Division Two no fewer than six times, and were responsible for one unenviable statistic: East Fife 13 Edinburgh City 2. On a clear day City could see no higher than 15th place in the League table.

After a few games of 1939-40, the Scottish League was suspended for the duration of World War Two. The following season, the Southern League began as a separate organisation, and clubs in the north and the east followed suit in 1941-42 with their own league. The North-Eastern League was unusual in awarding extra points for draws and victories away from home.

When football returned to something more normal, in 1945-46, the divisions were lettered 'A' and 'B' rather than numbered '1' and '2'. Soon, in 1946-47, a 'C' Division arrived, and Stirling Albion made an immediate impact, racing through the three divisions in three seasons. This third division, however, like its three-year predecessor in the early 1920s, was not to prove a permanent addition to the League's structure. It lasted from 1946 to 1955.

The wartime period also saw the birth of the League Cup model. It began with four sections, each section consisting of four teams playing each other home and away on a league basis. The winners of each mini-league qualified for the semi-finals. These additional fixtures served to extend the meagre wartime programme. The League Cup became an official competition in 1946-47, and this brought a new target for Scottish clubs – 'the treble'.

The first club to achieve the treble were Rangers, in 1948-49. The Ibrox club had maintained their pre-war momentum with a team known for their 'Iron Curtain' defence – Bobby Brown, George Young, Jock 'Tiger' Shaw, Ian McColl, Willie Woodburn and Sammy Cox – and two magnificent attackers in Willie Waddell and Willie Thornton. But, in those post-war years, clubs other than Rangers and Celtic showed that they, too, could attract large attendances. Good players stayed longer than usual with provincial clubs and teams were settled enough to challenge the Glasgow duo. Between 1946-47 and 1952-53, Hibernian won the League three times and were runners-up on three other occasions. In the late 1950s and the early 1960s, other clubs reached new heights of League success – Aberdeen, Hearts, Dundee and Kilmarnock – and the Cup competitions proved to be exciting and unpredictable.

Hibernian's great post-war team had Tommy Younger in goal and the 'Famous Five' forward line of Gordon Smith, Bobby Johnstone, Lawrie Reilly, Eddie Turnbull and Willie Ormond. Gordon Smith went on to win League winners' medals with three different clubs (Hibernian, Hearts and Dundee), an astonishing achievement for someone who didn't play with either Rangers or Celtic. The Hearts team of 1957-58, scorers of 132 goals to win the League, could field the 'Terrible Trio' of Alfie Conn, Willie Bauld and Jimmy Wardhaugh.

By the time Dundee won the League, in 1962, provincial clubs were beginning to sense the impact of the removal of the maximum wage in England. It became very difficult for clubs other than Rangers and Celtic to hang on to good players, and a succession of stars left Scotland at the start of the 1960s – George Mulhall (Aberdeen), Jim Storrie (Airdrie), Eddie Connachan (Dunfermline), George Herd (Clyde), John McLeod and Joe Baker (Hibs), Bobby Kennedy (Kilmarnock), Alex Young, Gordon Marshall and Bobby Blackwood (Hearts), Jimmy Gabriel and Ian Ure (Dundee), Ian St John and Pat Quinn (Motherwell), Dave Hilley, Matt Gray and Alex Harley (Third Lanark), Tommy Bryceland and Gerry Baker (St Mirren), Ron Yeats (Dundee United) and Bertie Auld (Celtic).

After this exodus, power reverted almost exclusively to the Old Firm, with the exception of 1964-65, when Kilmarnock won the title on goal-average after beating nearest-rivals Hearts by the required 2-0 on the final day of the season. In 1963-64 Rangers launched their new strength by winning the treble again. Manager Scot Symon's team included Bobby Shearer, Ron McKinnon and John Greig in defence, Willie Henderson and Davie Wilson on the wings, Jim Forrest and Ralph Brand up front and Jim Baxter all over the place. At the other end of the spectrum, Third Lanark faded into obscurity. They folded in 1967 and were lost to the League.

The most dramatic watershed came in February 1965 when Jock Stein took over as Celtic manager. Captained mainly by Billy McNeill, Celtic won the championship for nine successive seasons from 1965-66 to 1973-74, and became the first British team to win the European Cup. The 'Lisbon Lions', who beat Internazionale 2-1 in Lisbon to take the European Cup, are indelibly etched on many a mind: Simpson, Craig, Gemmell, Murdoch, McNeill, Clark, Johnstone, Wallace, Chalmers, Auld, Lennox.

The advent of the 1970s brought more changes to the Scottish soccer scene – the Texaco Cup, the Drybrough Cup, goal-difference, two substitutes – but Jock Stein's Celtic just went on and on. Without paying transfer fees of any great note, Stein was able to call on a new generation of players – McBride, Hughes, Hay, Williams, Hood, Macari, Connelly, McGrain, Dalglish, Deans, etc – and his team became hungry for more and more trophies. The stranglehold was finally broken in 1974-75, when Jock Stein was incapacitated after a horrific car accident and Rangers won the treble.

Between 1970-71 and 1978-79, every Scottish League and Scottish Cup competition was won by one of the Old Firm. Fortunately, for lesser mortals, the League Cup retained some of its unpredictability, especially in 1972 when Partick Thistle smacked four early goals past Celtic in the Final. And to prove there was still open competition, Hibernian and Dundee won the next two League Cup Finals.

In 1975 the Scottish League was restructured – a ten-club Premier Division, a 14-club Division One and a 14-club Division Two. The new structure gave a chance to Ferranti Thistle (later known as Meadowbank Thistle), an Edinburgh works team called in to extend the numbers to a more manageable 38. However, the new structure was to benefit clubs at the top rather than those at the bottom. Premier Division clubs played each other four times a season, a better prospect for high attendances, especially with four Rangers-Celtic derbies instead of two. But the Premier League, like so many Premier Leagues, initially created a fear of relegation rather than a quest for winning championships.

The new system's first casualty was the Spring Cup, which lasted only one season. This competition was open to First and Second clubs, who were split into seven groups of four for the qualifying competition. Sixteen teams – the top two in each group plus the two third-placed teams with the best records – went forward to the knock-out stage. When Airdrie beat Clydebank 4-2 in the Final at Firhill Park, after extra-time, there were only 5,000 present, so the competition was doomed. Thereafter, to make up for the loss of fixtures, the First and Second Division teams played each other three times a season instead of twice.

The first four seasons of the Premier League brought a familiar ring to the names on the trophy – Rangers, Celtic, Rangers, Celtic – and a Rangers team managed by Jock Wallace twice won the treble (1975-76 and 1977-78). Wallace's team was built around John Greig, Tom Forsyth, Colin Jackson, Alec MacDonald, Derek Johnstone and Tommy McLean. But Celtic, with the likes of Kenny Dalglish, Danny McGrain and a young Roy Aitken, were always in contention.

Then, in the 1980s, came a big challenge from the east of the country. In that decade, Aberdeen won the League championship three times, the Scottish Cup four times and the League Cup twice. Managed by Alex Ferguson, the club could field players like Alex McLeish and Willie Miller in defence, and Gordon Strachan, Mark McGhee and Peter Weir in attack. In 1982-83 Aberdeen won the European Cup-winners'

Two months after the arrival of manager Jock Stein, Celtic lift the Scottish FA Cup with a victory over Dunfermline to embark on an amazing dominance of Scottish football with nine successive League titles and many Cup wins, including the European Cup.

Cup by beating Real Madrid 2-1 in Gothenburg. Their team that night was: Leighton, Rougvie, Miller, McLeish, McMaster, Cooper, Strachan, Simpson, Weir, McGhee, Black (Hewitt).

That same season, 1982-83, Dundee United took the League title, and the balance of power continued to shift eastwards. It didn't last for long, though. After Hearts had failed on goal-difference to win the League in 1985-86 – on the last day of the season they lost at Dundee while Celtic were scoring five against St Mirren at Love Street – the next run of League champions had that familiar Old Firm ring.

The arrival at Rangers of Graeme Souness, as player-manager in 1986, began a sustained period of success for the Ibrox club. The traditional Scotland-England exodus was now reversed. Star players like Terry Butcher, Trevor Steven, Gary Stevens, Mark Hateley, Trevor Francis and Chris Woods moved across the border, but this time it was from England to Rangers. The most sensational signing was that of Maurice Johnston from Nantes in 1989, when Rangers broke with its Protestant tradition by signing a Catholic.

Meanwhile, the authorities were still experimenting with the structure of Scottish soccer. In 1986-87, a League system with two 12-club divisions at the top

Manager Alex Ferguson celebrates with his Aberdeen team after they won the Scottish League championship in 1979-80. They were to lift the title a further twice during the 1980s as well as four Scottish Cup and two League Cup wins. A victory over Real Madrid in Gothenburg gave them the European Cup-winners' Cup in 1983.

created an arduous programme of 44 Premier League games. This lasted only two seasons before a return to the 10-14-14 divisional structure. Another three seasons and a mid-season decision increased the Premier League from ten to 12 again, saving two clubs from relegation. In 1994-95, the next format – four ten-club divisions – came in. This provided opportunities for two Highland League clubs, Ross County and Caledonian Thistle (themselves an amalgam of two clubs), who were elected to the new Division Three.

Penalty competitions arrived in the Skol Cup (the sponsored League Cup) and the Scottish Cup. It wasn't too long before the Finals were settled by such means, spectacularly so in 1990, when Aberdeen won the Scottish Cup by beating Celtic 9-8 on the 20th penalty. And then, in 1994-95, Raith Rovers stressed the uncertainty of the Skol Cup by winning on penalties from Celtic. Raith Rovers were the first team outside the top flight to win a major trophy since East Fife won the League Cup in 1947-48.

The success of Raith Rovers is a reminder that the Scottish League stretches far beyond the confines of the Old Firm, or even the Premier League. This book captures not only moments of brilliant success but also times of glorious failure. Not only can you trace how Rangers won the treble in 1992-93, but you can relive the last 13 League games of Stirling Albion's 1980-81 season, when they failed to score a goal. They played 1,293 goalless minutes, and 500 or so fans still turned up to watch the last game of the season. Like all fans – and managers and players – they were still looking for 'the right result'. This book has thousands of them.

Ally McCoist joins in the celebrations as Rangers beat Aberdeen in the 1992-93 Skol Cup Final.

Scottish League & FA Cup Results

During this earlier period there are occasions where either the date or score is missing, this is due to being unable to trace these details. Where the italicised W and O appears instead of the score, the result was a walk-over. For the first few years of the Scottish FA Cup byes were often awarded, resulting in clubs missing out certain rounds.

Season 1873-74

SFA Cup
1st Round

Oct 18	Alexandra A	2	Callander	0
Oct 25	Clydesdale	6	Granville	0
	Dumbarton	*W*	Vale of Leven	*O*
	Eastern	4	Rovers	0
Oct 25	Queen's Park	7	Dumbreck	0
Oct 18	Renton	2	Kilmarnock	0
	T Lanark	*W*	Southern	*O*
	Western	0	Blythswood	1

2nd Round

	Alexandra A	0	Blythswood	2
Nov 8	Clydesdale	1	T Lanark	1
	Dumbarton	0	Renton	0
Nov 22	Queen's Park	1	Eastern	0

Replays

Nov 16	T Lanark	0	Clydesdale	0
Nov 29	Renton	1	Dumbarton	0

Dec 6	Clydesdale	2	T Lanark	0
	played at Kinning Park			

Semi-finals

Dec 20	Clydesdale	4	Blythswood	0
Dec 13	Queen's Park	2	Renton	0

Final

Mar 21	Clydesdale	0	Queen's Park	2
	played at Hampden Park			

Season 1874-75

SFA Cup
1st Round

Oct 24	Clydesdale	0	Vale of Leven	0
Oct 17	Dumbarton	3	Arthurlie	0
Oct 24	Dumbreck	5	Alexandra A	1
Oct 17	Eastern	3	23rd Renfrew R	0
Oct 17	Helensburgh	3	3rd Edinburgh R	0
Oct 17	Kilmarnock	4	Vale of Leven R	0
Oct 24	Queen's Park	1	Western	0
	Rangers	2	Oxford	0
	Renton	*W*	Blythswood	*O*
	Rovers	*W*	Hamilton	*O*
Oct 17	T Lanark	0	Barrhead	0
	West End	3	Star of Leven	0

Replays

	Clydesdale	*W*	Vale of Leven	*O*
Oct 24	T Lanark	1	Barrhead	0

2nd Round

	Clydesdale	2	Dumbreck	0
	Dumbarton	1	Rangers	0
Nov 21	Kilmarnock	0	Eastern	3
Nov 21	Queen's Park	7	West End	0
	Renton	2	Helensburgh	0
Nov 21	Standard	0	T Lanark	0

Replays

Nov 28	T Lanark	2	Standard	0

3rd Round

	Dumbarton	1	T Lanark	0
	Queen's Park	*W*	Rovers	*O*
Dec 26	Renton	1	Eastern	0

Semi-finals

Mar 20	Clydesdale	0	Queen's Park	0

Mar 27	Renton	1	Dumbarton	1

Replays

Mar 27	Queen's Park	2	Clydesdale	2
	Dumbarton	0	Renton	1
Apr 3	Clydesdale	0	Queen's Park	1
	played at Kinning Park			

Final

Apr 10	Queen's Park	3	Renton	0
	played at Hampden Park			

Season 1875-76

SFA Cup
1st Round

Oct 9	Arthurlie	0	Levern	0
Oct 23	Caledonian	0	Western	0
Oct 16	Clydesdale	1	Eastern	0
	Drumpellier		Barrhead	
	Dumbarton	1	Lennox	0
	Dumbreck	*W*	Vale of Leven R	*O*
	Hamilton	1	Airdrie	0
Oct 9	Hearts		3rd Edinburgh	
	Helensburgh	1	Star of Leven	0
Oct 16	Kilbirnie	1	Ayr T	0
Oct 9	Kilmarnock	8	Ayr E	0
	Mauchline	*W*	Ardrossan	*O*
	Northern	4	Ramblers	0
Oct 16	Queen's Park	3	Alexandra A	0
	Rangers	7	1st Lanark R.v.	0
	Renton	1	Alclutha	0
	Renton T	*W*	Queen's Park J	*O*
	Rovers	*W*	Oxford	*O*
	Sandyford		23rd Renfrew Rv	
	St Andrew's	1	Telegraphists	0
Oct 16	Towerhill	2	Lancelot	0
	T Lanark	2	Havelock	0
	Vale of Leven	*W*	Vale of Leven R	*O*
	West End		Partick T	

Replays

Oct 16	Levern	4	Arthurlie	0

Oct 16	3rd Edinburgh R	0	Hearts	0
	Both Qualified			
Oct 23	Barrhead	0	Drumpellier	1
Oct 30	Western	3	Caledonian	0
	Partick T		West End	
	Both Qualified			
	23rd Renfrew Rv		Sandyford	
	Both Qualified			

2nd Round

Nov 13	3rd Edinburgh R	1	Edinburgh T	0
	Clydesdale	6	Kilmarnock	0
	Drumpellier	2	Hearts	0
	Dumbarton	2	Renton T	1
	Dumbreck	2	St Andrew's	0
	Helensburgh	1	23rd Renfrew Rv	0
Nov 6	Kilbirnie	0	Mauchline	0
Nov 13	Levern	3	Hamilton	0
	Partick T	2	Towerhill	0
Nov 6	Queen's Park	5	Northern	0
Nov 13	Rangers	1	T Lanark	2
	Rovers	6	West End	0
Nov 13	Vale of Leven	3	Renton	0
	Western	3	Sandyford	0

Replay

	Mauchline	*W*	Kilbirnie	*O*

3rd Round

Nov 27	Dumbarton	5	Drumpellier	1
Nov 27	Dumbreck	5	Partick T	0
Nov 27	Levern	0	T Lanark	3
Nov 27	Mauchline	0	Vale of Leven	6
	played at Victoria Park			
Nov 27	Queen's Park	2	Clydesdale	0
Nov 27	Rovers	4	3rd Edinburgh R	0
Nov 27	Western	2	Helensburgh	0

4th Round

Dec 18	Queen's Park	2	Dumbreck	0
Dec 18	T Lanark	5	Western	0
Dec 18	Vale of Leven	2	Rovers	0

Semi-finals

Jan 8	T Lanark	1	Dumbarton	1
Jan 8	Queen's Park	2	Vale of Leven	1

Replays

Jan 15	Dumbarton	1	T Lanark	1
	played at Alexandria			
	Dumbarton	0	T Lanark	3

Final

Mar 11	Queen's Park	1	T Lanark	1
	played at Hamilton Cres			

Replay

Mar 18	Queen's Park	2	T Lanark	0
	played at Hamilton Cres			

Season 1876-77

SFA Cup
1st Round
Sep 30	1st Lanark R.v.	0	South Western	1
	23rd Rrv	2	Thornliebank	0
Sep 30	Arthurlie	3	Drumpellier	0
	Ayr T	1	Beith	0
Oct 7	Barrhead	4	Hamilton A	0
	Blythswood	2	Possilpark	1
	Busby	2	Renfrew	0
Sep 30	Caledonian	2	Standard	1
Oct 7	Clydesdale	6	Craig Park	0
	Crosshill	2	Hyde Park	1
Sep 30	Cumnock	1	Portland	2
Sep 30	Dumbarton	1	Renton	1
	Dumbreck	3	Dennistoun	1
	Dunfermline	W	Hearts	0
Sep 30	Eastern	1	Alexandria A	1
Sep 30	Edinburgh St A	1	Bonnybridge G	0
Sep 30	Edinburgh Swifts	2	Lenzie	1
Sep 30	Edinburgh T	5	Hanover	0
	Girvan	3	Dean	2
	Govan	W	Western	0
	Hamilton	2	Thornhill	0
Sep 23	Kilbirnie	5	Maybole Carrick	0
Sep 30	Lancefield	2	Parkgrove	0
	Lennox	3	Alclutha	0
Sep 30	Levern	0	Airdrie	1
	Mauchline	5	Winton	0
	Northern	12	Telegraphists	0
	Partick T	3	Havelock	1
	Queen of S'th	W	Ardrossan	0
Sep 30	Queen's Park	7	Sandyford	0
	Rangers	4	Queens Park J	1
Sep 30	Renton T	0	Vale of Leven R	0
	St Andrew's	W	Ayr E	0
Sep 30	St Clements	1	3rd Edinburgh Rv	0
	Star of Leven	4	10th Dumbarton	0
	Stonelaw	3	Shotts	0
	Towerhill	2	Rovers	1
Sep 30	T Lanark	6	Ramblers	0
Sep 30	Vale of Leven	1	Helensburgh	0
	West End	2	4th Rrv	0

Replays
Oct 7	Alexandria A	1	Eastern	0
Oct 7	Renton	0	Dumbarton	2
Oct 7	Vale of Leven R	1	Renton T	1
	Both Qualified			

2nd Round
Oct 21	Barrhead	4	Airdrie	0
Oct 21	Clydesdale	0	T Lanark	0
	Dumbreck	2	South Western	0
Oct 21	Edinburgh Swifts	1	Edinburgh T	0
	Girvan	4	Dumfries	0
	Hamilton A	2	Dunfermline	1
Oct 21	Kilbirnie	0	Ayr T	1
	Lancefield	2	Crosshill	0
	Lennox	5	Renton T	1
	Mauchline	2	Kilmarnock	1
	Northern	4	Alexandria A	0
Oct 21	Partick T	5	Blythswood	1
Oct 21	Portland	2	Edinburgh St A	0
Oct 28	Queen's Park	7	Caledonian	0
Oct 21	Rangers	8	Towerhill	0
	St Clements	1	St Andrew's	1
	St Andrew's Scratched			
Oct 21	Star of Leven	0	Dumbarton	4
Oct 21	Stonelaw	0	Arthurlie	4
Oct 21	Vale of Leven	7	Vale of Leven R	0
	West End	1	Govan	0

Replay
Oct 28	T Lanark	4	Clydesdale	0

3rd Round
	Ayr T	1	Dumbreck	0
Nov 18	Edinburgh Swifts	1	West End	1
	West End Disqualified			
	Hamilton		Busby	
	Lancefield	3	Girvan	0
	Lennox	1	Dumbarton	0
Nov 11	Mauchline	7	Portland	0
	Northern	2	St Clements	1
Nov 18	Partick T	2	Barrhead	0
Nov 18	Queen's Park	7	Arthurlie	0
Nov 18	Vale of Leven	1	T Lanark	0

Replay
Nov 25	Busy	0	Hamilton	0
	Both Qualified			

4th Round
Dec 23	Ayr T	W	Partick T	0
	Partick T Disqualified			
Dec 2	Lancefield	2	Hamilton	0
	Lennox	4	Edinburgh Swifts	0
Dec 2	Queen's Park	4	Northern	0
Dec 9	Rangers	3	Mauchline	0
Dec 2	Vale of Leven	4	Busby	0

5th Round
Dec 23	Lancefield	2	Ayr T	2
Dec 30	Queen's Park	1	Vale of Leven	2
	Rangers	3	Lennox	0

Replay
Ayr T	1	Lancefield	0

Semi-finals
Jan 13	Ayr T	0	Vale of Leven	9
	played at Kinning Park			

Final
Mar 17	Rangers	1	Vale of Leven	1
	played at Hamilton Cres			

Replays
Apr 7	Rangers	1	Vale of Leven	1
	played at Hamilton Cres			
Apr 14	Rangers	2	Vale of Leven	3
	played at Hampden Park			

Season 1877-78

SFA Cup
1st Round
Sep 29	10th Dumbarton	1	Star of Leven	0
	1st Lanark R.v.	1	Blythswood	0
	23rd Renfrew R	1	Levern	0
Sep 29	3rd Edinburgh R	0	Edinburgh Swifts	0
Sep 29	Alexandria	0	Milngavie	2
Sep 29	Alexandria A	2	Lancefield	0
	Arthurlie	3	Busby	0
	Ayr A	4	Vale of Calder	1
	Ayr T	W	St Andrew's	0
	Barrhead	7	Morton	0
	Beith	1	Catrine	0
	Blackfriars	W	Hyde Park	0
Sep 29	Clifton	2	Shaugraun	1
Sep 29	Clyde	0	T Lanark	1
Sep 29	Clydesdale	3	Dennistoun	1
	Derby	W	Dumbreck	0
Sep 29	Dumbarton	4	Waverly	0
	Glenkilloch	2	Wellington Park	0
	Govan	6	Albatross	0
Sep 29	Hanover	1	Edinburgh T	0
	Havelock	6	Craigpark	0
Sep 29	Hearts	0	Hibernian	0
Sep 22	Jordanhill	1	Queen's Park J	0
	Kelvinbank	3	Petershill	2
Sep 29	Kilbirnie	6	Dean	0
	Kilmarnock	5	Hurlford	1
	Kilmarnock C&FC	4	Maybole T	0
	Lennox	2	Helensburgh	0
	Lenzie	2	Ailsa	0
	Mauchline	6	Girvan	0
	Maybole C	3	Tarbolton	0
	Northern	3	Pollokshields A	0
Sep 22	Oxford	0	Sandyford	1
	Parkgrove	W	Winton	0
	Partick T	2	Union	0
Sep 29	Portland	1	Cumnock	0
Oct 6	Queen of S'th W	6	Stranraer	0
Sep 29	Queen's Park	1	Whiteinch	0
Sep 29	Ramblers	0	Stonefield	1
Oct 6	Rangers	13	Possilpark	0
	Renfrew	2	Pollokshaws	0
	Renton	W	Vale of Leven R	0
Oct 6	Renton T	2	Alclutha	0
	Rovers	0	John Elder	0
Oct 6	Shaftesbury	2	Roselyn	3
Sep 29	South Western	8	Our Boys	0
	St Clements	W	Dunfermline	0
	Strathclyde	5	West End	1
	Telegraphists	1	4th Rrv	0
	Thornliebank	1	Port Glasgow	0
	Vale of Leven	W	Kilmarnock T	0

Replays
Oct 6	Edinburgh Swifts	2	3rd Edinburgh R	1
Oct 6	Hibernian	2	Hearts	1
Oct 6	Rovers	2	John Elder	2
	Both Qualified			

2nd Round
	1st Lanark R	4	Telegraphists	0
Oct 20	Arthurlie 1	17	Renfrew R	0
	Ayr A	1	Kilmarnock	0
	Ayr T		Kilbirnie	
	Beith	1	Portland	0
Oct 27	Blackfriars	2	Rovers	2
	Caledonian	1	Rosslyn	0
Oct 20	Clydesdale	0	Queen's Park	2
	Glengowan	3	Stonelaw	1
	Govan	1	John Elder	0
	Grasshoppers	3	Clifton	0
Oct 20	Hanover	1	Hibernian	1
	Jordanhill	2	Lenzie	1
	Lennox	9	Milngavie	0
	Mauchline	1	Kilmarnock C&FC	0
	Maybole C	2	Queen of S'th W	0
	Parkgrove	2	Kelvinbank	1
Oct 20	Partick T	8	Strathclyde	1
Oct 27	Rangers	8	Alexandria A	0
	Renfrew	2	Glenkilloch	1
	Renton	3	10th Dumbarton	0
	Sandyford	2	Northern	1
Oct 20	South Western	2	Havelock	2

	St Clements	3	Dunmore	0
	Thornliebank	1	23rd Renfrew R	0
Oct 27	T Lanark	11	Derby	0
	Uddingston	3	Hamilton	0
Oct 27	Vale of Leven		Dumbarton	

Replays

Oct 27	Havelock	0	South Western	2
Oct 27	Hibernian	3	Hanover	0
Oct 27	Kilbirnie	3	Ayr T	1
Oct 27	Vale of Leven	4	Dumbarton	1
	Rovers	0	Blackfriars	0
	Both Qualified			

3rd Round

Nov 10	Arthurlie	0	Thornliebank	0
	Barrhead	2	Renfrew	1
	Barrhead Disqualified			
	Beith	3	Maybole C	0
Nov 10	Drumpellier	2	Glengowan	2
	Govan	5	Stonefield	2
Nov 10	Hibernian	2	Edinburgh Swifts	0
	Jordanhill	4	Grasshoppers	0
	Mauchline	3	Ayr A	1
	Parkgrove	3	Sandyford	2
	Partick T	3	Caledonian	0
	Rangers	13	Uddingston	0
Nov 17	Renton	2	Renton T	0

Nov 10	Rovers	1	Blackfriars	0
	South Western	4	1st Lanark Rv	0
Nov 10	T Lanark	1	Queen's Park	0
Nov 10	Vale of Leven	3	Lennox	0

Replay

Nov 17	Thornliebank	2	Arthurlie	0
	Glengowan		Drumpellier	
	Both Qualified			

4th Round

Dec 8	Barrhead	1	Partick T	0
	Barrhead Disqualified			
	Beith	W	St Clements	0
Dec 1	Kilbirnie	1	Mauchline	2
Dec 8	Parkgrove	3	Drumpellier	1
Dec 1	Rangers	0	Vale of Leven	0
Dec 8	Renton	4	Rovers	0
Dec 1	South Western	5	Glengowan	0
Dec 8	Thornliebank	1	Hibernian	2
Dec	A Draw			
Dec 1	T Lanark	7	Govan	0

Replays

Dec 8	Hibernian	2	Thornliebank	2
	Both Qualified			
Dec 15	Vale of Leven	5	Rangers	0

5th Round

Dec 29	Parkgrove	2	Partick T	1
Jan 5	Renfrew	0	Mauchline	2
Dec 29	Renton	2	Thornliebank	1
	South Western	3	Hibernian	1
	T Lanark	4	Beith	0
Dec 22	Vale of Leven	10	Jordanhill	0

6th Round

Jan 19	Renton	3	Mauchline	1
Jan 12	T Lanark	0	South Western	1
Jan 19	Vale of Leven	5	Parkgrove	0

Replay

| Jan 19 | South Western | 1 | T Lanark | 2 |
| | After Protest | | | |

Semi-finals

| Mar 9 | Renton | 1 | T Lanark | 1 |

Replay

| Mar 16 | T Lanark | 1 | Renton | 0 |

Final

| Mar 30 | T Lanark | 0 | Vale of Leven | 1 |
| | played at Hampden Park | | | |

Season 1878-79

SFA Cup
1st Round

Sep 28	1st Lrv	0	Parkgrove	0
	3rd Edinburgh R	3	Brunswick	1
	Airdrie	7	Avondale	0
Sep 28	Alexandria	2	Renton T	2
	Alexandria A	3	Jordanhill	1
Oct 5	Annan	0	Queen of S'th W	3
Sep 28	Arbroath	3	Our Boys	0
	Arthurlie	4	Cartvale	1
	Ayr A	4	Cumnock	1
	Ayr T	2	Auchinleck	0
Sep 21	Barrhead	2	Wellington Park	0
	Beith	1	Hurlford	0
	Busby	3	Morton	1
Oct 5	Caledonian	0	South Western	2
	Catrine	W	Girvan	0
	Clyde	W	Blythswood	0
	Clydesdale	W	Dennistoun	0
	Cree R	W	Stranraer	0
Sep 28	Dumbarton	8	10th Dumbarton	1
	Edinburgh T	2	Hanover	1
	Falkirk	1	Campsie Glen	0
	Glengowan	4	Mount Vernon	3
	Govan	7	Ailsa	0
	Govanhill	W	Wellpark	0
	Hamilton A	3	Uddingston	1
Sep 28	Havelock	1	T Lanark	7
	Hearts	3	Swifts	1
	Helensburgh	4	Kilmarnock T	0
	Hibernian	5	Dunfermline	2
Sep 21	Jamestown	3	Lenzie	1
	John Elder	7	Blackfriars	2
	Kilbirnie	2	Kilmarnock	0
	Kilmarnock A		Lanemark	
Sep 28	Lenzie	3	Milngavie T	0
	Levern		23rd Rrv	
	Mauchline	W	Maybole C	0
	Maybole Ladywell	3	Tarbolton	0
	Oxford	0	Derby	0
	Partick T		Northern	

	Petershill	4	Albatross	2
	Portland	9	Dean	0
Sep 21	Possil Bluebell	8	19th Lrv	0
Sep 21	Queen's Park	8	Kelvinbank	0
Sep 28	Rangers	3	Shaftesbury	0
	Renfrew		17th Rrv	
	Renton	W	Star of Leven	0
	Rob Roy	1	Coupar Angus	0
Oct 5	Shotts	3	Drumpellier	0
	Stonefield	W	4th Rrv	0
	Stonelaw	4	East Kilbride	0
Oct 5	Strathblane	8	Grasshoppers	1
Sep 21	Thistle	2	Possilpark	0
	Thornliebank	3	Glenkilloch	0
Sep 28	Union	1	Rosslyn	0
Sep 28	Upp'r Clydesd'le	12	Newmains	0
	Vale of Leith	1	Clifton	0
Sep 21	Vale of Leven	6	Alclutha	0
Sep 28	Whitefield	10	Telegraphists	0
	Whiteinch	3	Pollokshields	3

Replays

Oct 5	Parkgrove	6	1st Lrv	2
Oct 5	Renton T	1	Alexandria	1
	Both Qualified			
Oct 5	17th Rrv	1	Renfrew	2
	Derby		Oxford	
	Both Qualified			
	Lanemark	0	Kilmarnock A	4
	Northern	0	Partick T	2
	Pollokshields	3	Whiteinch	3
	Both Qualified			
	23rd Rrv	0	Levern	1

2nd Round

	Alexandria A	3	Burnside	0
	Arbroath	W	St Clements	0
	Arthurlie	3	Busby	1
Oct 19	Barrhead	6	Port Glasgow	2
	Beith	3	Ayr T	1
	Catrine	3	Maybole Ladywell	1

	Derby	3	Whiteinch	1
Oct 26	Glengowan	2	Airdrie	0
	Both Disqualified			
Oct 12	Govan	2	Oxford	1
Oct 19	Hearts	1	Thistle	0
	Helensburgh	4	Alexandria	1
Oct 19	Hibernian	3	3rd Erv	0
	Jamestown	7	Upper Clydesdale	0
	John Elder	4	Stonefield	0
Oct 19	Kilbirnie	0	Kilmarnock A	2
Oct 19	Levern	1	Renfrew	2
	Mauchline	5	Ayr A	1
Oct 19	Parkgrove	1	Union	0
	Partick T	2	Possil Bluebell	1
	Portland	4	Thornliebank	1
	Queen of S'th W	3	Cree R	0
Oct 19	Queen's Park	6	Pollokshields A	0
	Rangers	6	Whitefield	0
Oct 19	Renton	1	Dumbarton	6
	Rob Roy	3	Vale of Teith	1
Oct 19	Shaugran	1	Lenzie	0
Oct 19	Shotts	1	Clarkston	1
Oct 19	South Western	5	Petershill	0
	Stonelaw	2	Hamilton A	0
Oct 19	Strathblane	1	Falkirk	0
	Thistle	4	Clyde	1
	T Lanark	8	Wellpark	1
Oct 26	Vale of Leven	11	Renfrew T	0

Replays

Oct 26	South Western	8	Petershill	0
	After Protest			
	Clarkston	W	Shotts	0

3rd Round

	Alexandria A	2	John Elder	0
Nov 9	Beith	7	Barrhead	1
Nov 9	Dumbarton	5	Strathblane	0
Nov 16	Edinburgh Univ	2	Hibernian	5
	Govan	4	Derby	0
Nov 9	Hearts	2	Arbroath	1

	Helensburgh	...2	Shaugran	...0
	Kilmarnock A	...5	Queen of S'th W	.0
	Mauchline	...4	Arthurlie	...1
	Portland	...3	Catrine	...0
	Queen's Park	...W	Glasgow Univ	..0
Nov 9	Rangers	...8	Parkgrove	...2
	Stonelaw	...1	Clarkston	...0
	Thistle	...2	Partick T	...1
	Thistle Disqualified			
Nov 2	T Lanark	...2	South Western	...1
Nov 9	Vale of Leven	...15	Jamestown	...0

4th Round

	Beith	...9	Kilmarnock A	...1
Nov 30	Helensburgh	...2	Hearts	...1

	Hibernian	...9	Rob Roy	...0
Nov 30	Portland	...	Dumbarton	...
Nov 30	Queen's Park	...5	Mauchline	...0
Nov 30	Rangers	...3	Alexandria A	...0
Nov 30	Renfrew	...0	T Lanark	...4
	Stonelaw	...W	Thistle	...0
Nov 30	Vale of Leven	...11	Govan	...1

Replays

Dec 7	Dumbarton	...6	Portland	...1

5th Round

	Dumbarton	...9	Stonelaw	...1
Mar 8	Hibernian	...1	Helensburgh	...2
Mar 8	Queens Park	...5	T Lanark	...0
	Rangers	...4	Partick T	...0

Mar 8	Vale of Leven	...6	Beith	...1

6th Round

Mar 22	Queen's Park	...0	Rangers	...1
Mar 22	Vale of Leven	...3	Dumbarton	...1

Semi-finals

Mar 29	Helensburgh	...0	Vale of Leven	...3

Final

Apr 19	Rangers	...1	Vale of Leven	...1

played at Hampden Park

Rangers refused to replay Cup
awarded to Vale of Leven

Season 1879-80

SFA Cup
1st Round

	17th Renfrew Rv	..4	Levern	...1
	19th Lanark Rv	..W	Wellpark	...0
	Ailsa	...W	Burnside	...0
	Airdrie	...1	East Kilbride	...0
	Alexandria A	...4	Albatross	...0
	Arbroath	...5	Our Boys	...1
	Arthurlie	...3	Busby	...0
	Atholl	...W	Blythswood	...0
Sep 20	Ayr	...0	Kilmarnock A	...6
Sep 20	Barrhead	...0	Renfrew	...5
Sep 6	Beith	...	Kilbirnie	
Sep 20	Brunswick	...5	Edinburgh Swifts	...0
	Cambuslang	..W	Uddingston	...0
Sep 20	Campsie	...3	King's Park	...1
Sep 27	Campsie Glen	..4	Milngavie T	...1
	Cartvale	...5	Wellington Park	..2
Sep 20	Clarkston	...2	Stonelaw	...1
	Clyde	...W	1st Lanark Rv	...0
Sep 20	Cree R	...0	Stranraer	...2
	Cumnock	...W	Irvine	...0
Sep 6	Dumbarton	...4	Vale of Leven	...3
Sep 20	Dunfermline	...2	Edinburgh T	...0
	Dunfermline	...2	Thistle	...0
	Excelsior	...2	Clydebank	...1
Sep 20	Falkirk	...4	Grasshoppers	..2
Sep 20	Govan	...2	Caledonian	...1
Sep 20	Hamilton A	...2	Glengowan	...0
	Harmonic	...W	Stonefield	...0
	Havelock	...W	4th Renfrew Rv	..0
	Hearts	...W	3rd Erv	...0
	Helensburgh	...4	Alclutha	...2
Sep 20	Hibernian	...5	Hanover	...1
	Hurlsford	...2	Catrine	...0
Sep 20	Jamestown	...2	Star of Leven	...1
	Later Disqualified			
	John Elder	...W	Derby	...0
	Johnstone A	...W	Port Glasgow	...0
	Jordanhill	...2	Kelvinbank	...1
	Kennishead	...2	Glenkilloch	...1
	Kilmarnock	...W	Ayr A	...0
	Ladywell	...2	Auchinleck	...1
	Lennox	...W	Renton T	...0
	Mauchline	...3	Dean	...1
	Maybole C	...W	Girvan	...0
	Netherlee	...	Morton	
	Newmilns	...W	Avondale	...0
	Northern	...3	Thistle	...0
	Parkgrove	...W	Clydesdale	...0
Sep 27	Partick T	...2	Petershill	...0
	Pollokshields A	..4	Oxford	...0

	Portland	...W	Lanemark	...0
	Possil Bluebell	..W	Telegraphists	...0
	Possilpark	...	City	...
	Queen of S'th W	...W	Annan	...0
Sep 20	Rangers	...0	Queen's Park	...0
	Renfrew R	...W	23rd Renfrew Rv	..0
Sep 20	Renton	...2	Kilmarnock T	...2
	Rob Roy	...2	Coupar Angus	...1
	Rosslyn	...W	Blackfriars	...0
Sep 27	Shotts	...2	Drumpellier	...1
	South Western	.W	Whiteinch	...0
	Strathblane	...1	Lenzie	...0
Sep 20	Thornliebank	...4	Yoker	...0
	T Lanark	...W	Union	...0
	Upper Clyd'dale	.W	Mount Vernon	..0
	Vale of Teith	...W	Clifton	...0
Sep 27	Whitefield	...7	Govanhill	...0

Replays

Sep 27	Kilnbirnie	...2	Beith	...2
	Both Qualified			
Sep 27	Kilmarnock T	...0	Renton	...3
Sep 27	Queen's Park	...5	Rangers	...1
Oct 4	Campsie Glen	..4	Milngavie	...0
	After Protest			
	Morton	...7	Netherlee	...4
	Possilpark	...3	City	...1

2nd Round

Oct 18	Ailsa	...3	Rosslyn	...1
Oct 11	Alexandria A	...5	Harmonic	...0
Oct 11	Arthurlie	...8	Morton	...3
Oct 11	Barrhead R	...2	Renfrew R	...1
	Cambuslang	...4	Airdrie	...1
Oct 11	Campsie	...0	Campsie Glen	..4
	Clyde	...2	Govan	...1
	Cumnock	...W	Tarbolton	...0
Oct 11	Dumbarton	...7	Helensburgh	...0
	Excelsior	...2	Bellshill	...1
	Hamilton A	...3	Upper Clydesdale	.0
	Hearts	...2	Brunswick	...1
Oct 11	Hibernian	...4	Dunfermline	...0
Oct 11	Johnstone A	...6	Cartvale	...0
Oct 25	Jordanhill	...1	John Elder	...2
	Kennishead	...5	Cartvale	...0
Oct 18	Kilmarnock A	...0	Kilbirnie	...0
Oct 11	Kirkintilloch	...	Jamestown	...1
	Later Disqualified			
	Kirkintilloch A	..5	Star of Leven	...2
	Ladywell	...6	Stewarton	...1
	Mauchline	...6	Kilmarnock	...2
Oct 11	Maybole C	...1	Hurlford	...8

Oct 11	Northern	...3	Whitefield	...1
	Partick T	...3	Havelock	...1
	Plains Bluebell	..2	Newmilns	...0
	Pollokshields A	..5	Dennistown	...1
	Portland	...2	Beith	...1
	Possilpark	...4	High School	...1
	Queen of South	..6	Stranraer	...0
Oct 11	Queen's Park	...14	19th Lrv	...1
	Renton	...	Lennox	...
	Rob Roy	...3	Vale of Teith	...0
Oct 11	Shotts	...0	Clarkston	...2
Oct 11	South Western	...9	Atholl	...0
Oct 11	Strathblane	...1	Falkirk	...0
	Strathmore	...W	St Clements	..0
Oct 11	Thornliebank	...6	17th Rrv	...1
Oct 11	T Lanark	...0	Possil Bluebell	..0

Replays

	Lennox	...	Renton	
	Both Qualified			
	T Lanark	...1	Possil Bluebell	..0

3rd Round

	Arbroath	...6	Strathmore	...1
Nov 1	Arthurlie	...1	Renfrew	...2
	Cambuslang	...4	Clarkston	...2
	Clyde	...6	Ailsa	...1
Nov 1	Dumbarton	...5	Renton	...0
Nov 8	Hamilton A	...7	Excelsior	...1
Nov 15	Hibernian	...2	Hearts	...1
	Hurlford	...1	Cumnock	...1
Nov 1	Jamestown	...5	Lennox	...1
	Jamestown Disqualified			
Nov 1	Johnstone A	...3	Kennishead	...1
	Kilbirnie	...W	Ladywell	...0
	Kirkintilloch	...6	Lennox	...2
	Lennox Reinstated			
Nov 1	Mauchline	...0	Portland	...0
Nov 1	Parkgrove	...6	Alexandria A	...2
	Plains Bluebell	.W	Queen of S'th W	..0
Nov 1	Pollokshields A	..2	Northern	...1
Nov 1	Queen's Park	...5	Partick T	...1
Nov 8	Rob Roy	...1	Edinburgh Univ	...1
Nov 1	South Western	...2	John Elder	...1
	Strathblane	...2	Campsie Glen	...1
Nov 1	Thornliebank	...1	Barrhead R	...0
Nov 8	T Lanark	...1	Glasgow Univ	...1

Replays

Nov 8	Portland	...0	Mauchline	...1
Nov 15	T Lanark	...6	Glasgow Univ	...0
	Edinburgh Univ	...	Rob Roy	...

4th Round

	Cambuslang	...3	Plains Bluebell ..0
Nov 22	Dumbarton	11	Clyde 0
Nov 22	Hibernian	2	Parkgrove 2
Nov 29	Hurlford	1	Kilbirnie 1
	Both Qualified		
Nov 22	Johnstone A	...2	Rob Roy 4
	Mauchline	...2	Hamilton A ...0
Nov 22	Queen's Park	...10	Strathblane ...1
Nov 22	Renfrew	...1	Pollokshields A ..2
Nov 22	South Western	...4	Arbroath 0
Nov 22	Thornliebank	...12	Possilpark 0
Nov 29	T Lanark	5	Kirkintilloch A ...1

Replays

Parkgrove	2	Hibernian 2
Both Qualified		

5th Round

Dec 20	Dumbarton	6	Kilbirnie 2
Dec 20	Mauchline	0	Hibernian 2
	Pollokshields A	..4	Cambuslang 0
Dec 20	Queen's Park	...15	Hurlford 1
Dec 20	South Western	...1	Parkgrove 1
Dec 20	Thornliebank	...12	Rob Roy 0

Replay

Dec 27	South Western ...3	Parkgrove 2

6th Round

Jan 3	Dumbarton	6	Hibernian 2
	Pollokshields A	..6	South Western ...1
Jan 3	Thornliebank	1	T Lanark ...1

Replay

Jan 10	T Lanark 1	Thornliebank 2

Semi-finals

Jan 17	Queen's Park 1	Dumbarton 0
Jan 17	Thornliebank 2	Pollokshields A ..1

Final

Feb 21	Queen's Park 3	Thornliebank 0
	played at Cathkin Park	

Season 1880-81

SFA Cup
1st Round

	17th Rrv	6	Wellington Park ..1
	5th KRV	....W	Cree R 0
Sep 18	Abercorn	7	Barrhead 1
	Airdrie	3	Bellshill 0
	Airdriehill	....W	Airdrie Bluebell ..0
Sep 18	Alexandria A	4	Kelvinbank 1
	Arbroath	....W	Vale of Teith ...0
Sep 4	Arthurlie	2	Johnstone 0
	Atholl	....W	Whitefield 0
	After Protest		
Sep 18	Auchinleck	1	Cumnock 7
	Ayr	2	Catrine 0
Sep 11	Beith	4	Irvine 1
Sep 18	Caledonian	1	Clyde 2
	Cambuslang	...W	Upper Clydesdale 0
	Campsie	2	Grasshoppers ...1
Sep 18	Cartside	6	Kennishead 2
	Cartvale	....W	Levern 0
	Central	2	Bridge of Allan ..0
	City	....W	19th Lanark Rv ..0
Sep 4	Clarkston	1	Plains Bluebell ..0
Sep 18	Coupar Angus	..4	Strathmore Dun ..1
	Cowlairs	4	Petershill 3
Sep 11	Dumbarton	7	Victoria 0
Sep 18	Dunfermline	5	Hanover 3
	Dunkeld	....W	St Clements 0
Sep 11	Excelsior	3	Drumpellier 0
	Falkirk	....W	Campsie A 0
	Hamilton A	....W	Stonelaw 0
	Harmonic	....W	Ailsa 0
Sep 11	Hearts	3	Brunswick 1
	Helensburgh	....W	Lennox 0
	After Protest		
	Hurlford	....W	Ayr T 0
Sep 11	Jamestown	6	Alclutha 0
	Jordanhill	1	Windsor 0
Sep 18	Kilbirnie	3	Lanemark 0
	Kilmarnock	....W	Stewarton 0
	Kilmarnock A	..W	Girvan 0
	King's Park	1	Strathblane 0
	Larkhall	5	Uddingston 0
	Lenzie	....W	Thistle 0
	Mauchline	....W	Dean 0
	Maybole	....W	Rankinston 0
	After Protest		
	Morton	3	Glenkilloch 2
	Netherlee	....W	Oakfield 0
Sep 11	Northern	3	T Lanark 1
Sep 11	Oxford	6	Maxwell 0
	Partick T	....W	Dennistoun 0
Sep 18	Pilgrims	4	Lancefield 2
Sep 4	Pollok	5	Johnstone R 0
Sep 11	Pollokshields A	..0	Partick T 4
	Portland	8	Coylton Coila ..0
	Possilpark	....W	High School ...0
Sep 11	Queen's Park	7	John Elder 0
Sep 11	Rangers	4	Govan 1
Sep 4	Renfrew	1	Abercorn 5
	Renton	....W	Kilmarnock T ...0
	Rob Roy	2	Our Boys 1
	Shawlands	....W	Clydesdale 0
Sep 11	Shotts	4	T Lanark 0
Sep 11	South Western	7	Ingram 0
Sep 4	St Mirren	3	Johnstone A 0
Sep 18	Star of Leven	3	Kirkintilloch A ...2
Sep 11	Stranraer	3	Queen of S'th W .0
	Thistle	5	Tollcross 0
Sep 18	Thornliebank	3	Renfrew 0
	Yoker	....W	Renfrew R 0

2nd Round

	5th KRV	4	Stranraer 3
Oct 2	Abercorn	4	Morton 2
Oct 2	Airdrie	3	Excelsior 2
Oct 2	Alexandria A	1	Atholl 0
Oct 2	Arthurlie	1	Cartvale 1
	Cambuslang	...3	Hamilton A 1
Oct 2	Campsie C	5	Campsie 5
Oct 2	Clarkston	2	Airdriehill 1
Oct 2	Coupar Angus	...1	Arbroath 2
Oct 9	Cowlairs	4	Oxford 3
Oct 2	Dumbarton	2	Jamestown 1
Oct 2	Falkirk	2	King's Park 1
	Glengowan	1	Thistle 1
Oct 2	Harmonic	1	Clyde 0
Oct 2	Helensburgh	5	Star of Leven 1
Oct 9	Hibernian	3	Dunfermline 1
	Hurlford	2	Cumnock 1
Oct 16	Kilbirnie	2	Kilmarnock A ...1
Oct 9	Kilmarnock	6	Ayr 3
	Larkhall	1	Shotts 0
	Mauchline	6	Maybole 1
Oct 2	Netherlee	0	Yoker 2
	Partick T	1	Jordanhill 0
Oct 9	Pilgrims	7	City 0
Oct 2	Portland	0	Beith 1
Oct 2	Queen's Park	..5	Possilpark 0
	Rangers	1	Northern 0
Oct 9	Renton	0	Vale of Leven 1
	Rob Roy	4	Dunkeld 0
	Shawlands A	...W	Possil Bluebell ..0
Oct 9	South Western	..2	Partick T 0
Oct 2	St Mirren	3	17th Rrv 2
Oct 2	Thornliebank	0	Pollok 3

Replays

Oct 9	Cartvale	1	Arthurlie 2
Oct 9	Clyde	1	Harmonic 0
Oct 9	Campsie	1	Campsie C 3
	Thistle	6	Glengowan 1

3rd Round

Oct 23	Abercorn	1	St Mirren 4
Nov 6	Alexandria A	1	Cowlairs 2
	Arbroath	2	Rob Roy 1
Oct 23	Arthurlie	2	Pollok 0
Oct 23	Beith	17	5th KRV 2
Oct 30	Cartside	4	Yoker 3
	Central	6	Lenzie 1
Oct 23	Clyde	3	Shawlands A ...0
	Dumbarton	7	Falkirk 1
Oct 23	Hearts	5	Hibernian 3
Oct 23	Helensburgh	1	Vale of Leven 4
Oct 30	Kilbirnie	0	Hurlford 2
Oct 23	Larkhall	0	Cambuslang 5
	Mauchline	....W	Kilmarnock 0
	After Protest		
Oct 23	Queen's Park	8	Pilgrims 1
Oct 23	Rangers	3	Partick T 0
	Thistle	......W	Airdrie 0

4th Round

Nov 13	Arthurlie	4	South Western ...3
Nov 20	Cartside	1	Hurlford 3
Nov 13	Dumbarton	9	Glasgow Univ ...0
Nov 13	Edinburgh Univ	..0	Campsie C 1
Nov 13	Hearts	3	Cambuslang ...0
	Mauchline	....W	Clarkston 0
	After Protest		
Nov 13	Queen's Park	11	Beith 2
Nov 13	Rangers	11	Clyde 0
Nov 13	St Mirren	1	Cowlairs 0
	Vale of Leven	..W	Arbroath 0

Replays

Nov 27	Arthurlie 1	South Western ...1
	Tie To Arthurlie	

5th Round

Dec 11	Arthurlie	4	Hearts	0
	Hurlford	0	Rangers	3
Dec 11	Queen's Park	2	Mauchline	0
Dec 4	St Mirren	1	Dumbarton	5
Dec 4	Vale of Leven	7	Thistle	1

6th Round

Dec 25	Arthurlie	0	Vale of Leven	2
Dec 25	Rangers	1	Dumbarton	3

	Queen's Park	10	Campsie C	0

Semi-final

Feb 5	Dumbarton	2	Vale of Leven	0
	played at Alexandria			

Final

Mar 26	Dumbarton	1	Queen's Park	2
	played at Kinning Park			
	Replay Ordered			

Replay

Apr 9	Dumbarton	1	Queen's Park	3
	played at Kinning Park			

Season 1881-82

SFA Cup

1st Round

Sep 17	1st Lrv	0	Cowlairs	7
Sep 10	5th KRV		Moffat	
Sep 10	Abercorn	3	Arthurlie	3
	Airdrie	W	Tollcross	0
	Airdriehill	W	Bellshill	0
	Alexandria A	W	Possil Bluebell	0
	Auchinleck	W	Dean	0
Sep 10	Barrhead	0	Glenkilloch	2
Sep 10	Battlefield	1	Northern	3
	Beith	W	Coylton	0
Sep 10	Blairgowrie	0	Coupar Angus	4
Sep 17	Bridge of Allan	1	Thistle A	1
Sep 10	Cambuslang	5	Royal Albert	0
Sep 17	Cartvale	4	Renfrew	2
	Clarkston	W	T Lanark	0
	Clyde	W	Clydesdale	0
	Cumnock	1	Mauchline	1
Sep 10	Dumbarton	9	Alclutha	1
	Eastern A	W	Annfield	0
Sep 10	Falkirk	3	King's Park	0
	Grasshoppers	W	Campsie C	0
Sep 10	Hamilton A	1	Plains Bluebell	0
Sep 10	Hanover	1	Brunswick	2
	played at Tynecastle			
	Harmonic	W	Govan	0
	Hibernian	7	Addiewell	0
	Hurlford	W	Irvine	0
	Jamestown	W	Renton	0
	John Elder	W	Shawlands A	0
Sep 10	Johnstone	9	Greenock S	1
Sep 10	Kilbarchan	8	Ladyburn	1
	Kilbirnie	W	Catrine	0
	Kilmarnock	6	Largs A	0
	Kilmarnock	2	Helensburgh	6
	Kilmarnock A	7	Ayr	1
	Kinning Park A	W	Kelvinbank	0
	Lenzie	W	Campsie A	0
Sep 10	Levern	4	Morton	2
Sep 10	Lugar Boswell	3	Lanemark	0
Sep 17	Maybole	7	Rankinston	0
Sep 10	Mousbank	1	Partick T	3
	Our Boys	2	Arbroath	1
Sep 17	Paisley A	6	Port Glasgow A	1
Sep 17	Partick T	5	Possilpark	1
	Pilgrims	W	Oxford	0
	Pollok	W	Cartside	0
Sep 10	Pollokshields A	1	Petershill	3
	Portland	10	Stewarton	0
Sep 17	Queen's Park	14	Caledonian	0
Sep 10	Rangers	2	T Lanark	1
	Rob Roy	W	Dunkeld	0
Sep 10	Shotts	5	Drumpellier	1
	South Western	W	Jordanhill	0
Sep 10	Southfield	0	Campsie	3
Sep 10	St Bernard's	1	Hearts	0
Sep 3	St Mirren	5	Johnstone R	1
	Star of Leven	W	Kirkintilloch	0
	Stranraer	W	Cree R	0

	Strathblane	7	Dunipace	0
	Strathmore	W	St Clements	0
	Thistle	W	Stonelaw	0
Sep 10	Thornliebank	5	Johnstone A	0
	Uddingston	W	Upper Clydesdale	0
	Vale of Leven	W	Lennox	0
	Vale of Teith	W	Aberfeldy	0
	Wellington Park	4	Netherlee	1
	West Benhar	4	Glengowan	2
Sep 17	West Calder	5	Kinleith	1
	Whitefield	W	Windsor	0
	Yoker	W	Kennishead	0

Replays

Sep 17	Arthurlie	4	Abercorn	0
Sep 17	Moffat	0	5th KRV	1
Sep 24	Thistle A		Bridge of Allan	
	Mauchline	5	Cumnock	1
Oct 1	Thistle A	8	Bridge of Allan	0

2nd Round

Oct 1	Airdrie	1	Airdriehill	1
Oct 1	Alexandria A	4	Whitefield	1
Oct 1	Arthurlie	3	Pollok	1
Oct 1	Beith	3	Hurlford	3
Oct 1	Cambuslang	6	Airdrie	2
Oct 15	Campsie	2	Lenzie	0
	Clyde	W	John Elder	0
Oct 8	Cowlairs	2	Queen's Park	2
	Glenkilloch	2	Yoker	0
Oct 8	Grasshoppers	0	Falkirk	5
	Helensburgh	W	Victoria	0
Oct 8	Hibernian	2	St Bernard's	1
Oct 8	Jamestown	5	Star of Leven	0
	Kilmarnock	7	Auchinleck	1
	Kilmarnock A	5	Maybole	0
Oct 1	Levern	3	Thornliebank	4
Oct 8	Lugar Boswell	3	Annbank	1
Oct 8	Mauchline		Portland	
Oct 1	Northern	9	Luton	1
Oct 15	Our Boys	5	Dundee H	3
Oct 8	Paisley A	3	St Mirren	1
	Partick FC	3	Kinning Park	0
Oct 1	Partick T	3	Pilgrims	1
	Queen of S'th	W	25th KRV	1
	Rangers	W	Harmonic	0
Oct 1	Rob Roy	3	Coupar Angus	1
Oct 8	Shotts	2	Hamilton A	1
	South Western	W	Eastern A	0
Oct 1	Thistle	10	Uddingston	0
	Thistle	3	Strathblane	2
Oct 1	Vale of Leven	0	Dumbarton	2
	Vale of Teith	6	Dunblane	2
Oct 8	Wellington Park	3	Kilbarchan	4
Oct 1	West Benhar	2	Clarkston	0
	West Calder	W	Dunfermline	0

Replays

Oct 8	Hurlford	4	Beith	4
	Both Qualified			

Oct 15	Partick T	7	Pilgrims	1
	After Protest			
Oct 15	Portland	1	Mauchline	5
Oct 15	Queen's Park	9	Cowlairs	0
	Airdrie	3	Airdriehill	2

3rd Round

Oct 29	Airdrie	4	Shotts	4
Oct 29	Arthurlie	7	Paisley A	1
	Cambuslang		West Benhar	
Oct 22	Dumbarton	5	Jamestown	0
Oct 29	Glenkilloch	0	Catvale	3
Oct 29	Kilbarchan	1	Johnstone	1
	Kilmarnock	2	Kilbirnie	0
Oct 22	Lugar Boswell	0	Beith	1
Oct 22	Mauchline	0	Hurlford	0
Oct 22	Northern	1	Clyde	2
Oct 22	Partick FC	1	South Western	2
Oct 22	Petershill	2	Partick T	2
Oct 22	Rangers	3	Alexandria A	1
	Stranraer	4	Queen of S'th W	1
Oct 29	Strathmore	1	Our Boys	4
Oct 22	Thistle	0	Falkirk	2
	Vale of Teith	6	Rob Roy	1
Oct 22	West Calder	4	Brunswick	1

Replays

Oct 29	Mauchline	2	Hurlford	0
Oct 29	Partick T	2	Petershill	0
Nov 5	Kilbarchan	2	Johnstone	2
Nov 5	Shotts	5	Airdrie	0
Nov 5	South Western	1	Partick T	0
Nov 5	West Benhar	3	Cambuslang	2
	After Protest			
Nov 5	Partick T	3	Petershill	2
	After Protest			
Nov 12	Johnstone	3	Kilbarchan	0

4th Round

	Cartvale	5	Glasgow Univ	4
Nov 12	Edinburgh Univ	2	Clyde	3
Nov 12	Falkirk	3	Campsie	1
Nov 12	Helensburgh	1	Arthurlie	1
	Kilmarnock	9	Our Boys	2
	Kilmarnock A	3	Mauchline	2
Nov 12	Queen's Park	3	Johnstone	2
Nov 12	Thistle	0	Partick T	1
Nov 12	Thornliebank	0	Rangers	2
Nov 19	West Benhar	4	Hibernian	4
	West Calder	W	Stranraer	0

Replays

Nov 19	Arthurlie	1	Helensburgh	0
Nov 26	Hibernian	8	West Benmar	0

5th Round

Dec 10	Arthurlie	4	Kilmarnock	1
Dec 3	Clyde	4	Cartvale	5
Dec 3	Hibernian	2	Dumbarton	6
Dec 3	Kilmarnock A	2	Beith	0

Dec 3 Queen's Park ... 10 — Partick T ...0
Dec 3 South Western ..1 — Rangers ...2
Dec 3 Vale of Teith ....0 — Shotts ...5
Dec 10 West Calder ....4 — Falkirk ...2

Replays
Dec 24 Hibernian ...2 — Dumbarton ...6
After Protest
Dec 24 Rangers ...4 — South Western ...0
After Protest

6th Round
Jan 28 Dumbarton ...2 — Rangers ...1

Jan 14 Kilmarnock A ....5 — Arthurlie ...1
Jan 7 Queen's Park ..15 — Shotts ...0
Dec 31 West Calder ....3 — Cartvale ...5

Replay
Feb 4 Dumbarton ...5 — Rangers ...1
After Protest

Semi-finals

Feb 18 Dumbarton .....11 — Cartvale ...2
Feb 18 Kilmarnock A ....2 — Queen's Park ...3

Final
Mar 18 Dumbarton ...2 — Queen's Park ...2
played at Cathkin Park

Replay
Apr 1 Dumbarton ...1 — Queen's Park ...4
played at Cathkin Park

Season 1882-83

SFA Cup
1st Round

1st Dumfries Rv W — Dumfries A ...0
Sep 16 1st Lrv ...0 — Northern ...4
Sep 16 5th KRV ...8 — Thornhill ...0
Sep 9 Abercorn ...10 — Ladyburn ...1
Addiewell W — Dunfermline ...0
Sep 9 Airdrie ...5 — Plains Bluebell ...1
Sep 16 Airdriehill ...0 — Shotts ...7
Sep 9 Airdrieonians ...3 — Royal Albert ...3
Sep 9 Angus ...1 — Balgay ...2
Annbank ...7 — Langs A ...0
Arbroath ...4 — East End ...3
Sep 9 Arthurlie ...7 — Bute R ...0
Ayr ...5 — Stewarton ...3
Sep 9 Battlefield ...2 — Partick T ...4
Sep 9 Beith ...4 — Beith T ...2
Clarkston — Drumpellier
Sep 9 Clippens ...2 — Glenpatrick ...4
Sep 9 Clyde ...4 — Luton ...0
Sep 16 Coupar Angus ...1 — Dunblane ...3
Sep 9 Cowlairs ...4 — Whitefield ...1
Dumbarton W — Kilmarnock T ...0
Dundee H ...7 — Perseverance ...2
Sep 16 Dunipace ...1 — Falkirk ...5
Sep 16 Hamilton A ...0 — Cambuslang ...5
Sep 9 Hearts ...1 — St Bernard's ...1
Hibernian ...8 — Brunswick ...0
Sep 9 Jamestown ...7 — Vale of Leven ...1
Sep 9 Johnstone ...6 — Paisley A ...2
Sep 16 Johnstone A ...0 — Cartvale ...4
Sep 9 Jordanhill ...0 — Rangers ...4
Kilmarnock ...2 — Mauchline ...0
Kilmarnock A ...2 — Cumnock ...1
Sep 9 Lugar Boswell ...4 — Kilbirnie ...1
Mavisbank ...3 — Granton ...1
Maybole W — Rankinstone ...0
Milngavie ...2 — E Stirling ...1
Sep 16 Moffat ...9 — Dumfries R ...0
Morton ...2 — Johnstone R ...1
Our Boys ...2 — Dundee H ...1
Sep 16 Partick T ...5 — Petershill ...2
Sep 16 Pollok ...3 — Renfrew ...2
Sep 9 Pollokshields A ...6 — Alexandria A ...5
Port Glasgow A ...3 — Lochwinnoch ...2
Sep 9 Portland ...1 — Hurlford ...1
Sep 9 Possilpark ...0 — Pilgrims ...6
Sep 9 Queen's Park ..12 — Thistle ...1
Renton ...3 — Alclutha ...1
Sep 9 South Western ...0 — T Lanark ...3
Southfield W — Aberfeldy ...0
Sep 9 St Mirren ...8 — Yoker ...0
Strathblane ...1 — Lenzie ...0

Sep 16 Thornliebank ...7 — Southern ...1
Sep 16 Vale of Atholl ...0 — Vale of Teith ...1
West Benhar ...2 — Belshill ...1
West Calder W — Kinleith ...0
West End ...1 — Strathmore ...1
Winshaw ...2 — Holytown ...0
Sep 9 Woodland ...1 — John Maxwell ...1
Sep 16 Woodside ...0 — Kilbarchan ...6

Replays
Sep 16 Hurlford ...3 — Portland ...2
Sep 16 Royal Albert ...3 — Airdrieonians ...3
Sep 16 John Maxwell ...5 — Woodford ...3
Sep 16 St Bernard's ...3 — Hearts ...4
Sep 23 Coupar Angus ...1 — Dumblane ...6
After Protest
Sep 23 Drumpellier ...2 — Clarkston ...5
Airdrieonians — Royal Albert
Strathmore — West End

2nd Round
Sep 30 5th KRV ...5 — Moffat ...3
Sep 30 Abercorn ...2 — Pollok ...2
Oct 7 Addiewell ...0 — Hearts ...14
Airdrie ...1 — Wishaw ...2
Cambuslang ...3 — Airdrieonians ...1
Sep 30 Cartvale ...2 — Arthurlie ...1
Sep 30 Cowlairs ...13 — Apsley ...0
Sep 30 Dumbarton ...8 — King's Park ...1
Dunblane ...3 — Arbroath ...1
Dundee H ...3 — Aberdeen ...1
Oct 7 Jamestown ... 12 — Strathblane ...1
Sep 30 John Maxwell ...5 — Port Glasgow A ...3
Sep 30 Kilbarchan ...0 — Johnstone ...7
Sep 30 Kilmarnock ...2 — Hurlford ...6
Kilmarnock A ...5 — Annbank ...4
Sep 30 Lugar Boswell ...6 — Beith ...1
Maybole ...6 — Ayr ...3
Sep 30 Morton ...1 — St Mirren ...5
Sep 30 Northern ...0 — Pollokshields A ...0
Our Boys ...5 — Balgay ...3
Sep 30 Partick T ...2 — Pilgrims ...1
Sep 30 Partick T ...1 — Mavisbank ...2
Oct 7 Queen of S'th W ...5 — 1st Dumfries Rv ...3
Sep 30 Queen's Park ...3 — Rangers
Sep 30 Royal Albert ...3 — Clarkston ...5
Sep 30 Southfield ...1 — Renton ...14
Sep 30 Thornliebank ...7 — Glenpatrick ...2
Sep 30 T Lanark ...2 — Clyde ...0
Sep 30 Vale of Leven ..16 — Milngavie ...0
Oct 7 West Banhar ...10 — Shotts ...1
Oct 7 West Calder ...2 — Hibernian ...3
Sep 30 West End ...1 — Vale of Teith ...5

Replays
Oct 7 Cartvale ...1 — Arthurlie ...3
After Protest
Oct 7 Pollok ...2 — Abercorn ...2
Both Qualified
Oct 7 John Maxwell ...2 — Port Glasgow A ...6
After Protest
Oct 7 T Lanark ...3 — Clyde ...0
After Protest
Pollokshields A ...4 — Northern ...0

3rd Round
Oct 28 Abercorn ...8 — Maybole ...0
Oct 28 Arthurlie ...0 — Thornliebank ...0
Oct 21 Cambuslang ...3 — Partick T ...3
Oct 21 Dumbarton ...8 — Jamestown ...1
Dunblane ...5 — Dundee H ...0
Oct 21 Falkirk ...1 — Renton ...1
Oct 28 Johnstone ...2 — Morton ...1
Oct 21 Lugar Boswell ...6 — Pollok ...0
Oct 21 Partick T ...4 — Cowlairs ...0
Oct 21 Pollokshields A ...3 — West Benhar ...0
Oct 28 Port Glasgow A ...2 — Kilmarnock A ...5
Oct 28 Queen of S'th W ...3 — 5th KRV ...2
Oct 21 Queen's Park ...13 — Clarkston ...0
Oct 21 T Lanark ...3 — Airdrie ...0
Oct 21 Vale of Leven ...8 — Hearts ...1
Oct 28 Vale of Teith ...6 — Our Boys ...4

Replays
Oct 28 Partick T ...3 — Cambuslang ...3
Both Qualified
Oct 28 Renton ...4 — Falkirk ...1
Nov 4 Thornliebank ...0 — Arthurlie ...0
Both Qualified

4th Round
Nov 18 Arthurlie ...3 — Queen of S'th W ...1
Nov 11 Dunblane ...1 — T Lanark ...7
Nov 11 Hibernian ...2 — Partick T ...2
Nov 11 Johnstone ...1 — Pollokshields A ...3
Nov 11 Kilmarnock A ...5 — Abercorn ...2
Partick T W — Glasgow Univ ...0
Nov 11 Queen's Park ...5 — Cambuslang ...0
Nov 11 Renton ...3 — Lugar Boswell ...5
Nov 11 Thornliebank ...0 — Dumbarton ...3
Vale of Leven ...2 — Edinburgh Univ ...0
Nov 11 Vale of Teith ...2 — Hurlford ...3

Replays
Nov 18 Partick T ...1 — Hibernian ...4

5th Round
Dec 2 Hibernian ....3 Arthurlie 4
Abandoned Bad Light
Dec 2 Lugar Boswell ...1 Vale of Leven 1
Dec 23 Queen's Park ....7 Hurlford 2

Replays
Dec 23 Arthurlie ....6 Hibernian 0
Dec 23 Vale of Leven ....5 Lugar Boswell ...1

6th Round
Dec 30 Arthurlie ....1 Kilmarnock A 1
Feb 3 Dumbarton .....3 Queen's Park 1
Feb 10 Partick T ....0 Vale of Leven 4
Dec 23 T Lanark ....1 Pollokshields A ..1

Replay
Feb 3 Kilmarnock A ....1 Arthurlie 2
Feb 3 Pollokshields A ..5 T Lanark 2
Feb 10 Arthurlie ....1 Kilmarnock A 1
After Protest
Feb 17 Arthurlie ....0 Kilmarnock A 1
played at Cathkin Park

Semi-finals
Feb 24 Pollokshields A ..0 Dumbarton 1
Feb 24 Vale of Leven ....1 Kilmarnock A 1

Replays
Mar 17 Dumbarton .....5 Pollokshields A ..0
After Protest

Mar 17 Kilmarnock A ....0 Vale of Leven 2

Final
Mar 31 Dumbarton .....2 Vale of Leven 2
played at Hampden Park

Replay
Apr 7 Dumbarton .....2 Vale of Leven 1
played at Hampden Park

Season 1883-84

SFA Cup
1st Round
Sep 8 Abercorn ....7 Levern 0
Sep 8 Airdrie ....1 Tollcross 0
Sep 8 Alloa ....0 Falkirk 5
Sep 8 Arbroath ......2 Aberdeen 2
Sep 8 Arthurlie ......3 Pollok 0
Sep 8 Balgay ....2 Strathmore Arb ..2
Sep 8 Battlefield ....8 South Western ..1
Sep 8 Benhar ....2 Drumpellier 2
Bute R ......W Glenpatrick 0
Sep 8 Cambuslang ...8 Belshill 0
Sep 8 Cartvale ....8 West End A 0
Clarkston .....W Plains Bluebell ..0
Sep 8 Clippens ......3 Johnstone A 2
Sep 8 Dumbritton ....1 Vale of Leven W .1
Sep 8 Dunblane ......2 Vale of Teith 1
Sep 8 Dundee H ......9 Angus 0
Sep 15 Dunfermline ....1 St Bernard's 13
Sep 8 Dunipace ......2 Campsie 1
East End R ....W Newton Stewart .0
Sep 8 E Stirling ......3 Tayavalla 0
Sep 8 Granton ....3 Glencairn 1
Sep 8 Hamilton A .....4 Airdrieonians ...1
Sep 8 Hearts ....8 Brunswick 0
Sep 8 Hibernian ......5 West Calder 0
Hurlford ......W Beith T 0
Jamestown ....W Kilmarnock T ..0
Sep 8 Johnstone .....3 Thornliebank 4
Sep 8 Kilbarchan .....3 Paisley A 4
Kilmarnock ....W Kilbirnie 0
Kilmarnock A ..W Beith 0
Sep 15 King's Park .....11 Lenzie 0
Sep 8 Kinleith ....1 Edina 2
Sep 8 Linwood ....1 Woodland 4
Sep 8 Lugar Boswell ...3 Ayr 1
Sep 8 Lyle A ....2 Johnstone R 4
Sep 8 Mauchline .....3 Annbank 1
Sep 8 Mavisbank .....2 Dean Park 1
Sep 8 Maybole ....0 Cumnock 4
Sep 8 Morton ....1 Renfrew 0
Sep 8 Northern Greenoc .5 John Maxwell ...3
Sep 8 Northern ....0 Rangers 1
Sep 8 Our Boys ......3 West End 2
Sep 8 Partick T ......0 Queen's Park 8
Partick T ......W Pilgrims 0
Sep 8 Pollokshields A ..4 Thistle 0
Port Glasgow A .W Lochwinnoch ..0
Sep 8 Possilpark ......2 Orchard 4
Sep 8 Queen of S'th W ..7 5th KRV 7
Sep 8 Renton ....2 Dumbarton 1
Sep 8 Royal Albert ....8 Shettleston 0
Sep 8 Southern ....5 Netherlee 2
Sep 8 St Mirren ......6 Caledonian 0
Sep 8 Stenhousemuir ...3 Strathblane 2

Stewarton C ...W Portland 0
Sep 8 Strathmore Dun ..1 East End R 0
Sep 8 T Lanark ....5 Clyde 2
Vale of Atholl ..W Aberfeldy 0
Sep 8 Vale of Leven ...12 Leverndale 0
Sep 8 Vale of Nith ...2 Moffat 4
Whitefield ....W Luton 0
Sep 8 Whitehill ....3 Alexandria A ...1
Sep 8 Yoker ....0 Olympic 2

Replays
Strathmore Arb ..1 Balgay 1
Both Qualified
Vale of Leven ....0 Dumbritton 4
Sep 15 Arbroath ....7 Aberdeen 0
Sep 15 Benhar ....12 Drumpellier 0
Sep 15 5th KRV ....3 Queen of S'th W .1
Sep 22 Edina ....4 Kinleith 0
After Protest
Sep 22 Tollcross ....4 Airdrie 3
After Protest

2nd Round
Sep 29 Abercorn ......2 Paisley 0
Arbroath .....W Perserverance ..0
Sep 29 Balgay ....1 Strathmore Dun ..3
Sep 29 Battlefield .....7 Whitefield 2
Benhar ....W Vale of Avon ...0
Sep 29 Cambuslang ....7 Tollcross 0
Sep 29 Cartvale ....6 Southern 2
Sep 29 Cowlairs ....3 Granton 2
Sep 29 Drumlanrig R ....1 East End R 3
Sep 29 Dunblane ......4 Coupar Angus ...1
Dundee H .....W Vale of Atholl ...0
Sep 29 E Stirling ......2 Dunipace 2
Sep 29 Falkirk ....9 Stenhousemuir ..1
Sep 29 Hibernian ......10 Edina 1
Sep 29 Jamestown ....7 Dumbritton 1
Sep 29 Johnstone R ....6 Northern 1
Sep 29 Kilmarnock .....3 Hurlford 0
Sep 29 Kilmarnock A ...9 Stewarton C 1
Sep 29 Mauchline .....3 Lugar Boswell ...1
Sep 29 Moffat ....2 5th KRV 3
Sep 29 Newcastleton ...1 Hearts 4
Sep 29 Olympic ....5 Clippens 0
Sep 29 Our Boys ......2 Strathmore Arb ..0
Sep 29 Partick T ......2 Orchard 1
Sep 29 Pollokshield A ...6 Mavisbank 2
Sep 29 Port Glasgow A ..1 Arthurlie 3
Sep 29 Rangers ....14 Whitehill 2
Sep 29 Renton ....6 King's Park 1
Sep 29 Royal Albert ....8 Clarkston 1
Sep 29 Thornliebank ...14 Bute R 0
Sep 29 T Lanark ....2 Queen's Park 4
Sep 29 Woodland .....0 St Mirren 7

Replays
Oct 6 Dunipace ....1 E Stirling 2

3rd Round
Oct 20 Abercorn ......7 Johnstone R 0
Oct 20 Arbroath ......1 Dundee H 1
Oct 20 Arthurlie ......3 St Mirren 1
Oct 20 Battlefield .....4 Jamestown 2
Oct 20 Cambuslang ....6 Hamilton A 0
Oct 20 Cartvale ....4 Cumnock 1
Oct 20 Cowlairs ....0 Queen's Park 5
Oct 20 East End R .....1 5th KRV 6
Oct 20 Hearts ....1 Hibernian 4
Oct 20 Morton ....1 Kilmarnock A 2
Oct 20 Olympic ....0 Mauchline 5
Oct 20 Partick T ......6 E Stirling 0
Oct 20 Rangers ....5 Falkirk 3
Oct 20 St Bernard's ....7 Benhar 0
Oct 20 Strathmore Dun ..2 Our Boys 2
Oct 20 Thornliebank ...... Kilmarnock ....
Oct 20 Vale of Leven ....4 Renton 1

Replays
Oct 27 Dundee H ......2 Arbroath 1
Oct 27 Our Boys ......5 Strathmore Dun ..1
Nov 3 Morton ....0 Kilmarnock A 4
After Protest
Nov 3 Thornliebank ...2 Kilmarnock 1
After Protest

4th Round
Nov 10 5th KRV ....1 Hibernian 8
Battlefield ....W Edinburgh Univ .0
Nov 10 Cartvale ....4 Abercorn 2
Nov 10 Dunblane ......0 Rangers 6
Nov 10 Kilmarnock A ...2 Cambuslang 3
Nov 10 Mauchline .....4 Royal Albert 0
Nov 10 Partick T ......0 Queen's Park 4
Nov 10 Pollokshields A .11 Our Boys 0
Nov 10 St Bernard's ....2 Thornliebank ...0
Nov 10 Vale of Leven ....6 Dundee H 0

5th Round
Dec 1 Arthurlie ......0 Vale of Leven 0
Dec 1 Mauchline .....2 Pollokshields A ..3
Dec 1 St Bernard's ....0 Rangers 3

Replays
Dec 8 Vale of Leven ....3 Arthurlie 1

6th Round
Dec 22 Cambuslang ....1 Rangers 5
Dec 22 Hibernian ......6 Battlefield 1
Dec 22 Queen's Park ....6 Cartvale 1
Dec 22 Vale of Leven ....4 Pollokshields A ..2

Semi-finals
Feb 2 Hibernian ....1 Queen's Park 5
Jan 19 Vale of Leven ....3 Rangers 0

Final
Queen's Park .... Vale of Leven .....
Awarded To Queen's Park
Vale of Leven Did Not Appear

Season 1884-85

SFA Cup
1st Round
Sep 13 Airdrie ....4 Shettleston 6
Airdriehill .....W Vale of Avon ...0
Albion ......W Dumbritton 0
Sep 13 Alloa ....0 King's Park 4
Sep 13 Angus ....1 Strathmore Dun ..5
Sep 13 Arbroath ....3 Dundee H 2
Sep 13 Arthurlie ......2 Olympic 0
Sep 13 Battlefield ....8 Kinning Park ...0
Sep 13 Boness ......0 Hibernian 2
Sep 13 Cartvale ... 12 Greenock Rangers ..1
Sep 13 Clarkston .....1 Hamilton A 4
Sep 13 Clippens .....3 Greenock Rovers .1
Sep 13 Clyde ....1 Cowlairs 2
Sep 13 Cumnock .....3 Mauchline 2
Sep 13 Dalry ....0 Annbank 4
Sep 13 Drumpellier ....0 Airdrieonians ...6
Dumbarton ....W Leverndale 0
Dumbarton A ..W Lenzie 0
Sep 13 Dunblane ......8 Crieff J 0
Sep 13 Dunfermline ...10 Newcastleton ...2
Sep 13 East End ......8 Coupar Angus ...1
Sep 13 E Stirling .....4 Campsie 2
Falkirk ......W Strathblane 0
Sep 13 Glengowan ....2 Albion R 1
Sep 13 Granton ....1 Shawlands 0
Sep 13 Grasshoppers ...4 Dunipace 0
Sep 13 Jamestown ....1 Vale of Leven 1
Sep 13 Johnstone .....9 Lyle A 1
Sep 20 Kilmarnock ....6 Hurlford 1
Kilmarnock A ...14 Stewarton C 0
Sep 13 Lindertis ....1 Aberdeen 4
Sep 13 Lugar Boswell ...1 Ayr 4
Sep 13 Moffat ....2 5th KRV 5
Sep 13 Morton ....2 Abercorn 2
Sep 13 Northern ......6 Glasgow Univ ..4
Sep 13 Paisley A ......2 Southern 3
Sep 13 Partick T ......9 Eastern A 1
Pollokshaw ....W Kilbarchan 0
Sep 13 Pollokshields ...0 Queen's Park 4
Sep 13 Pollokshields A ..6 Pilgrims 2
Sep 13 Port Glasgow A ..6 1st KRV 1
Sep 13 Possilpark ......7 Cyrus 0
Sep 13 Rangers ......11 Whitehill 0
Sep 13 Renfrew ....1 Johnstone R ...0
Sep 13 Renton ....2 Vale of Leven W .1
Sep 13 Royal Albert .....1 Cambuslang 4
Springburn H ..W Orchard 0
Sep 13 St Bernard's ....6 Edina 0
Sep 13 St Mirren ......4 Neilston 3
Sep 13 Stenhousemuir ..1 Tayavalla 2
Sep 13 Strathmore Arb ...1 Our Boys 4
Sep 13 Thornhill ......0 Queen of S'th W ..13
Sep 13 Thornliebank ....6 Northern 0
Sep 13 T Lanark ......3 Partick T 2
Sep 13 Vale of Teith ....7 Breadalbane ...0
Sep 13 Volunteer A .....1 Vale of Nith 4
Sep 13 West Benhar ...8 Chryston 1
Sep 13 West Calder ....3 Norton Park ...0
West End .....W Perserverance ..0
Sep 13 Westburn ......6 Tollcross 2
Sep 13 Whitefield .....3 Thistle 3
Sep 13 Wishaw S .....2 Dykehead 1
Sep 13 Yoker ....2 Rock 0

Replays
Sep 20 Abercorn ....3 Morton 4
After Protest
Sep 20 Thistle ....3 Whitefield 1
Sep 20 Vale of Leven ....4 Jamestown 1
Sep 27 Dykehead ......2 Wishaw S 5
After Protest
Sep 27 Hurlford ....3 Kilmarnock 1
Hurlford Disqualified
Sep 27 Neilston ......1 St Mirren 4
After Protest
Sep 27 Abercorn ......2 Morton 2
Both Qualified

2nd Round
Oct 4 5th KRV ....3 Queen of S'th W .4
Oct 4 Aberdeen ......1 Arbroath 7
Oct 4 Airdrieonians ....2 Cambuslang ...2
Oct 4 Annbank ......4 Kilmarnock 1
Oct 4 Arthurlie ......1 Abercorn 0
Oct 4 Ayr ....5 Cumnock 0
Oct 4 Clippens ......1 Renfrew 7
Oct 4 Cowlairs ......1 Pollokshields A ..2
Oct 4 Dean Park .....2 Springburn H ..0
Oct 4 Dumbarton .....2 Albion 0
Oct 4 Dumbarton A ...3 King's Park 1
Oct 4 Dunfermline ....1 Hearts 11
Hearts Disqualified
Oct 4 E Stirling ......2 Renton 10
Oct 4 Glengowan .....4 Westburn 1
Oct 4 Granton ....1 Northern 3
Oct 4 Grasshoppers ...1 Falkirk 4
Oct 4 Hibernian ......5 Vale of Teith ...1
Oct 4 Maybole ....1 Kilmarnock A ...4
Oct 4 Our Boys ......8 West End 1
Oct 4 Pollokshaws ....2 Southern 2
Oct 4 Possilpark ......0 Battlefield 3
Oct 4 St Mirren ......2 Johnstone 0
Oct 4 Strathmore Dun ..1 East End 1
Oct 4 Thistle ....1 Queen's Park 4
Oct 4 Thornliebank ....1 Port Glasgow A ..0
Oct 4 T Lanark ......2 Rangers 2
Oct 4 Vale of Leven ... 14 Central 0
Oct 4 West Benhar ....9 Shettleston 1
Oct 4 West Calder ....0 Dunblane 1
Oct 4 Wishaw S .....8 Airdriehill 3
Oct 4 Yoker ....17 Tayavalla 0

Replays
Oct 11 Cambuslang ....10 Airdrieonians ...2
Oct 11 East End ......2 Strathmore Dun .5
Oct 11 Rangers ......0 T Lanark 0
Both Qualified
Oct 11 Southern ......3 Pollokshaws ...3
Both Qualified
Oct 18 Port Glasgow A ..2 Thornliebank ...2
After Protest
Oct 18 West Benhar ....4 Shettleston 1
After Protest
Oct 25 Thornliebank ....2 Port Glasgow A ..1

3rd Round
Oct 25 Arthurlie ....3 Cartvale 0
Oct 25 Ayr ....4 Kilmarnock A ...2
Oct 25 Cambuslang ....3 Hamilton A 0
Oct 25 Dean Park .....2 Dumbarton 2
Oct 25 Dunblane ......2 Arbroath 4

Oct 25 Hibernian ....5 Glengowan 1
Oct 25 Morton ....5 Southern 0
Oct 25 Our Boys ......5 Strathmore Dun ..1
Oct 25 Partick T ......4 Falkirk 2
Oct 25 Pollokshields A ..4 Dumbarton 1
Oct 25 Queen's Park ....2 Battlefield 3
Oct 25 Renton ....9 Northern 2
Oct 25 St Mirren ......1 Renfrew 0
Nov 1 Thornliebank ....4 Pollokshaws ...0
Oct 25 T Lanark ......0 Rangers 3
Oct 25 Vale of Leven ....4 Yoker 1
Oct 25 Vale of Nith ....0 Queen of S'th W .6
Oct 25 West Benhar ....5 St Bernard's 1
Nov 1 Wishaw S ......7 Dunfermline 1

Replays
Nov 1 Dumbarton A ....3 Deans Park 1
Nov 8 St Mirren ....3 Renfrew 0
After Protest
Nov 13 St Mirren ....6 Renfrew 3
After Protest

4th Round
Nov 15 Annbank ......5 Queen of S'th W .2
Nov 15 Arbroath ....4 Rangers 3
Nov 15 Arthurlie ......1 Vale of Leven ...2
Nov 15 Cambuslang ...2 Thornliebank ...2
Nov 15 Dumbarton A ...6 Partick T 3
Nov 15 Hibernian ......5 Ayr 1
Nov 15 Our Boys ......2 West Benhar ...2
Nov 15 Pollokshields A ..0 Battlefield 3
Nov 15 Renton ....2 St Mirren 1
Nov 15 Wishaw S ......1 Morton 2

Replays
Nov 22 Thornliebank ....0 Cambuslang 0
Both Qualified
Nov 22 West Banhar ....8 Our Boys 3
Dec 20 Arbroath ......1 Rangers 8
After Protest

5th Round
Dec 6 Annbank ......5 West Benhar ...1
Dec 6 Cambuslang ....4 Dumbarton A ...1
Dec 6 Hibernian ......4 Morton 0

6th Round
Jan 10 Cambuslang ....3 Battlefield 1
Dec 27 Hibernian ......5 Annbank 0
Dec 27 Renton ....5 Rangers 3
Dec 27 Thornliebank ....3 Vale of Leven ...4

Semi-finals
Jan 24 Hibernian ......2 Renton 3
Jan 31 Vale of Leven ...0 Cambuslang 0

Replay
Feb 7 Cambuslang ....1 Vale of Leven ...3

Final
Feb 21 Renton ....0 Vale of Leven 0
played at Hampden Park

Replay
Feb 28 Renton ....3 Vale of Leven 1
played at Hampden Park

SFA Cup
1st Round

Sep 12	5th KRV	4	Vale of Nith	0
Sep 19	Abercorn	2	St Mirren	0
Sep 26	Airdrieonians	4	Royal Albert	2
Sep 12	Albion	4	Jamestown	4
Sep 12	Albion R	6	Drumpellier	2
Sep 12	Alpha	6	Cambuslang H	8
Sep 12	Arbroath	36	Bon Accord	0
	Arthurlie	W	Olympic	0
Sep 12	Ayr	7	Maybole	0
Sep 12	Ayr R	0	Dalry	8
	Battlefield	0	Cowlairs	2
Sep 12	Broxburn S	1	Boness	1
Sep 12	Cambridge	3	Southern A	1
Sep 12	Camelon	1	Falkirk	3
Sep 12	Cartvale	2	Morton	1
Sep 12	Clyde	1	Rangers	0
Sep 12	Clydevale	2	Tollcross	4
Sep 12	Coupar Angus	2	Our Boys	8
	Cowdenbeath	W	Aberfeldy	0
Sep 12	Crieff	0	Dunfermline A	7
Sep 19	Dumbarton	3	Vale of Leven W	1
	Dunblane	W	Dunfermline	0
Sep 12	Dunipace	4	Campsie C	2
Sep 12	East End	3	Strathmore Dun	3
Sep 12	E Stirling	6	Campsie	1
Sep 12	Forfar	3	Angus	1
	Glasgow Univ	W	Eastern	0
Sep 12	Granton	0	Partick T	11
Sep 12	Grasshoppers	2	Grahamston	2
Sep 12	Greenock S	1	Neilston	10
	Hamilton A	W	West Benhar	0
Sep 12	Harp	35	Aberdeen R	0
Sep 12	Hearts	5	St Bernard's	2
Sep 26	Helensburgh	2	Dumbarton A	3
Sep 12	Hibernian	9	Edina	0
Sep 12	Hurlford	5	Cumnock	1
Sep 12	Johnstone	5	Greenock R	1
Sep 12	Kilmarnock	7	Annbank	1
Sep 12	King's Park	3	Armadale	1
Sep 12	Kirkintilloch A	0	Renton	15
Sep 26	Lanemark	0	Monkcastle	2
Sep 12	Lenzie	1	Bonhill	1
Sep 12	Mauchline	2	Lugar Boswell	3
Sep 12	Northern	4	Linthouse	1
Sep 12	Norton P	6	Glencairn	2
Sep 12	Paisley H	2	Thornliebank	2
	Pollokshields A	W	Partick T	0
Sep 12	Port Glasgow A	4	1st Rrv	1
Sep 12	Queen's Park	16	St Peters	0
Sep 12	Renfrew	1	Greenock N	0
	Rock	W	Levendale	0
Sep 12	Shettleston	1	Cambuslang	7
	St Andrew's	W	10th Lrv	0
Sep 12	Strathmore Arb	7	Aberdeen	0
Sep 12	Thistle	11	Westbourne	1
	Thornliebank	W	Moffat	0
	Vale of Leven	W	Dunbritton	0
Sep 12	Vale of Teith	9	Oben	1
	West Calder	W	Newcastleton	0
Sep 12	West End	3	Broughty	3
Sep 12	Whitefield	3	Dennistoun A	1
Sep 12	Wishaw S	2	Rutherglen	0
Sep 12	Woodvale	3	Mearns A	2
Sep 12	Yoker	5	Union	1

Replays

Sep 19	Boness	5	Broxburn S	1
Sep 19	Bonhill	6	Lenzie	0
Sep 19	Broughty	3	West End	3
	Both Qualified			
Sep 19	Grahamston	2	Grasshoppers	4
Sep 19	Jamestown	0	Albion	1
Sep 19	Strathmore Dun	1	East End	4
Sep 19	Thornliebank	2	Paisley H	0
Sep 26	Hearts	1	St Bernard's	0
	After Protest			
Sep 26	Southern A	1	Cambridge	2
	After Protest			
Sep 26	Yoker	0	Union	1
	After Protest			
	Monkcastle	2	Lanemark	0
	After Protest			

2nd Round

Oct 3	5th KRV	3	Queen of S'th W	1
Oct 3	Airdrieonians	15	Cambuslang H	2
	Albion	W	Rock	0
Oct 3	Albion R	2	Wishaw S	2
Oct 3	Arbroath	9	Forfar A	1
Oct 3	Arthurlie	2	Woodvale	0
Oct 3	Boness	8	Norton Park	1
	Cambuslang	W	Hamilton A	0
Oct 3	Clyde	2	Thistle	3
Oct 3	Cowlairs	3	Pollokshields A	2
Oct 3	Dalry	6	Lugar Boswell	2
Oct 3	Dumbarton	7	Union	0
Oct 3	Dumbarton A	2	Renton	7
Oct 3	Dunblane	10	Dunfermline A	0
Oct 3	Dykehead	3	Tollcross	1
	Dykehead Disqualified			
Oct 3	East End	2	Broughty	2
Oct 3	Falkirk	0	Alloa	4
Oct 3	Glasgow Univ	1	T Lanark	8
Oct 3	Grasshoppers	1	E Stirling	6
Oct 3	Harp	4	Our Boys	1
Oct 3	Hibernian	2	Hearts	1
Oct 3	Johnstone	1	Thornliebank	2
Oct 3	Kilmarnock	3	Hurlford	4
Oct 3	King's Park	7	Dunipace	1
Oct 3	Monkcastle	2	Ayr	4
Oct 3	Northern	7	Whitefield	2
Oct 3	Port Glasgow A	1	Neilston	1
Oct 3	Queen's Park	1	Pilgrims	0
Oct 3	Renfrew	0	Abercorn	3
Oct 3	St Andrew's	6	Cambridge	0
Oct 3	Vale of Leven	10	Bonhill	0
	Vale of Teith	W	Cowdenbeath	0
Oct 3	West End	4	Strathmore Arb	5

Replays

Oct 10	Broughty	3	East End	8
	After Protest			
Oct 10	Neilston	0	Port Glasgow A	2
Oct 10	Wilshaw S	5	Albion R	0
Oct 17	Broughty	1	East End	2
	After Protest			
Oct 17	Kilmarnock	1	Hurlford	1
	After Protest			
Oct 17	Queen of S'th W	4	5th KRV	3
	After Protest			
Nov 7	Hurlford	2	Kilmarnock	2
Nov 14	Kilmarnock	1	Hurlford	5

3rd Round

Oct 24	Airdrieonians	8	Tollcross	2
Oct 24	Albion	0	Renton	1
Oct 24	Alloa	0	Partick T	12
Oct 24	Arbroath	7	East End	1
Nov 21	Arthurlie	5	Hurlford	0
Oct 24	Cartvale	1	Port Glasgow A	1
Oct 24	Cowlairs	2	Northern	1
Oct 24	Dalry	1	Ayr	6
Oct 24	Dumbarton	3	Thistle	0
Oct 24	E Stirling	0	Queen's Park	3
Oct 24	Harp	8	Vale of Teith	1
Oct 24	Hibernian	6	Boness	0
Oct 24	Strathmore Arb	3	Dunblane	1
Oct 24	Thornhill	0	Queen of S'th W	8
Oct 24	Thornliebank	1	Abercorn	5
Oct 31	T Lanark	11	St Andrew's	0
	Vale of Leven	W	King's Park	0
Oct 24	Wishaw S	3	West Calder	0

Replays

Oct 31	Port Glasgow A	4	Cartvale	2

4th Round

Nov 14	Abercorn	7	Strathmore Arb	2
Nov 14	Cambuslang	9	Wishaw S	0
Nov 14	Dumbarton	3	Partick T	0
Nov 14	Hibernian	5	Arbroath	3
Nov 28	Queen of S'th W	1	Arthurlie	3
Nov 14	Queen's Park	1	Airdrie	0
Nov 14	Renton	4	Cowlairs	0
Nov 14	T Lanark	3	Ayr	2
Nov 14	Vale of Leven	6	Harp	0

Replays

Nov 28	Ayr	3	T Lanark	3
	After Protest			
Dec 5	T Lanark	5	Ayr	1

5th Round

Dec 5	Abercorn	0	Cambuslang	1
Dec 5	Arthurlie	1	Queen's Park	2
Dec 5	Dumbarton	2	Hibernian	2
Dec 5	Renton	2	Vale of Leven	2
Dec 12	T Lanark	1	Port Glasgow A	1

Replays

Dec 12	Hibernian	4	Dumbarton	3
Dec 12	Renton	3	Vale of Leven	0
Dec 19	T Lanark	1	Port Glasgow A	1
Dec 26	T Lanark	4	Port Glasgow A	1

6th Round

Jan 16	Hibernian	3	Cambuslang	2

Semi-finals

Jan 23	Hibernian	0	Renton	2
Jan 16	T Lanark	0	Queen's Park	3

Final

Feb 13	Queen's Park	3	Renton	1
	played at Cathkin Park			

SFA Cup
1st Round

	5th KRV	W	Thornhill	0
	Aberdeen	W	East End	0
Sep 11	Airdrie	5	Airdriehill	0
Sep 11	Albion	5	Rutherglen	1
Sep 11	Annbank	3	Kilbirnie	4
Sep 11	Arbroath	20	Orion	0
Sep 11	Armadale		Slamannan	
Sep 11	Ayr	2	Hurlford	3
Sep 11	Battlefield	0	Cowlairs	2
Sep 11	Bonhill	8	Kirkintilloch C	1

Sep 11 Broxburn S .....1 Mossend S 2
Sep 11 Broxburn T .....2 Bellstane 2
        Burntisland T ..W Dunfermline ...0
Sep 11 Cambuslang ...6 Motherwell 1
Sep 11 Campsie ......10 Dunipace 0
Sep 11 Carrick ....0 Westbourne 2
        Clyde ....5 St Peters 1
        Coupar Angus ..W Fair City A ...0
Sep 11 Dalry ....5 Ayr R 2
Sep 11 Dumbarton .....5 Vale of Leven H ..0
Sep 11 Dumbarton A ....8 Duntocher ....
Sep 11 Dunblane ....12 Crieff 0
        Dunbritton ....W Lenzie 0
Sep 11 Dundee W .....2 Broughty 7
Sep 11 Dunfermline A ..4 Alloa 8
Sep 11 Edina ....1 Hearts 7
Sep 11 E Stirling ......6 Camelon 3
Sep 11 Grahamston ....0 Lawrieston 2
Sep 11 Grasshoppers ...3 Vale of Bannock .3
Sep 11 Greenock R .....3 1st Rrv 4
        Awarded To Greenock
        Hamilton A ....W Wishaw S 0
Sep 11 Hibernian ......6 Durhamstown R .1
Sep 11 Johnstone ......6 Cartvale 2
Sep 11 Kelvinside A .....1 Whitefield 2
        Kilmarnock ....W Cumnock 0
Sep 11 King's Park .....1 Falkirk 3
Sep 11 Lindertis ......3 Harp 4
Sep 11 Linthouse ......4 Southern A 0
Sep 11 Lochwinnoch ....0 Morton 6
        Lugar Boswell ...W Maybole 0
Sep 11 Monkcastle .....1 Lanemark 3
        Newcastleton ..W Norton Park 0
Sep 11 Northern ......1 T Lanark 4
        Oban ....W Our Boys 0
Sep 18 Our Boys ......2 Forfar 5
Sep 11 Partick T ......2 Queen's Park ...3
Sep 11 Port Glasgow A .10 Johnstone H 1
        Queen of S'th W ..W Nithsdale W 0
Sep 11 Rangers ....9 Govan A 1
Sep 11 Renfrew ......3 Abercorn 3
        Renton ......W Kirkintilloch H ..0
Sep 11 Rutherglen .....2 Dumpellier 0
Sep 11 Shettleston ....3 Carfin S 3
Sep 11 Slananann .....4 Avondale 3
Sep 11 St Andrew's ....2 Pollokshields A ..5
Sep 11 St Bernard's ....3 Boness 2
Sep 11 St Johnstone ...3 Erin R 3
Sep 18 St Mirren ......5 Arthurlie 3
Sep 11 Strathmore Arb ..3 Strathmore Dun .0
Sep 11 Thistle ....13 Blairvaddick 0
Sep 11 Thornliebank ...3 Neilston 2
Sep 11 Tollcross ......0 Royal Albert ...3
        R.Albert Disqualified
Sep 11 Vale of Leven ....9 Kirkintilloch A ..0
Sep 11 Vale of Leven W ..6 Jamestown 3
        Vale of Leven W Disqualified
        Vale of Nith ...W Vale of Annan ..0
Sep 11 West Calder .....1 Armadale 3
        Woodvale ....W Pollokshaws A ..0

Sep 11 Yoker ....4 Union 2

Replays
Sep 18 Abercorn ....9 Renfrew 0
Sep 18 Broxburn T .....4 Bellstane 1
Sep 18 Carfin S ....3 Shettleston 0
Sep 18 Erin R ....7 St Johnstone ...1
Sep 18 Vale of Bannock ..2 Grasshoppers ...0
Sep 25 St Andrew's ....4 Pollokshields A .1
        After Protest

2nd Round
Oct 2 Abercorn ....8 Greenock R 2
Oct 2 Airdrie ....3 Carfin S 2
       Airdrie Disqualified
Oct 2 Albion ....7 Dykehead 0
Oct 2 Bonhill ....1 Jamestown 2
Oct 2 Broxburn T .....1 Hearts 2
Oct 2 Caledonian R ...4 Erin R 4
Oct 2 Cambuslang H ..3 Hamilton A 1
Oct 2 Clyde ....4 Cowlairs 3
Oct 2 Cowdenbeath ...3 Burntisland 3
Oct 2 Dumbarton .....4 Yoker 0
Oct 2 Dunblane ....8 Oban 1
Oct 2 East End ....5 Broughty 4
       E Stirling .....W Vale of Bannock .0
Oct 2 Falkirk ....3 Laurieston 1
Oct 2 Forfar ....3 Arbroath 5
Oct 2 Hurlford ....3 Kilbirnie 5
Oct 2 Johnstone ......4 Pollokshaws A ...0
Oct 2 Kilmarnock ....10 Lanemark 2
Oct 2 Lenzie ....0 Vale of Leven ..13
Oct 2 Linthouse ......1 T Lanark 4
Oct 2 Lugar Boswell ...3 Dalry 2
Oct 2 Moffat ....3 5th KRV 5
Oct 2 Mossend S .....1 Hibernian 1
Oct 2 Newcastleton ...1 Armadale 5
Oct 2 Queen of S'th W .12 Vale of Nith 2
Oct 2 Queen's Park ...7 Whitefield 0
Oct 2 Rangers ....5 Westbourne 2
Oct 2 Renton ....2 Dumbarton A ...0
Oct 2 Rutherglen ......1 Cambuslang 1
Oct 2 Slanannan .....0 Campsie 3
Oct 2 St Mirren ......2 Port Glasgow A .3
Oct 2 Strathmore Arb ..3 Harp 3
Oct 2 Thistle ....12 St Andrew's 0
Oct 2 Thornliebank ...0 Morton 2

Replays
Oct 9 Cambuslang ....6 Rutherglen 1
Oct 9 Erin R ....6 Caledonian R 1
Oct 9 Harp ....3 Strathmore Arb ..3
       Both Qualified
Oct 9 Hibernian ......3 Mossend S 0
Oct 16 Cowdenbeath ...3 Burntisland 1
Oct 16 Lugar Boswell ...6 Dalry 1
       After Protest

3rd Round
Oct 23 Abercorn ....1 Port Glasgow A ..5

Oct 23 Albion ....4 Thistle 2
Oct 23 Cambuslang H ..5 Jamestown 1
Oct 23 Cowdenbeath ...6 Alloa 1
       Dumbarton ...W Tollcross 0
Oct 23 East End ....3 Dunblane 3
       East End Scratched
Oct 23 Erin R ....3 Coupar Angus ..2
Oct 23 E Stirling ......1 Clyde 3
Oct 23 Falkirk ....3 Queen's Park ...8
Oct 23 Hibernian ......5 Hearts 1
Oct 23 Johnstone ......0 Hurlford 5
Oct 23 Kilmarnock .....7 Lugar Boswell ..2
Oct 23 Queen of S'th W .6 5th KRV 3
Oct 23 Rangers ....0 Cambuslang 2
Oct 23 St Bernard's ....5 Armadale 2
Oct 23 Strathmore Arb ..1 Harp 8
Oct 23 T Lanark ....3 Renton 1
Oct 23 Vale of Leven ....7 Campsie 4

4th Round
Nov 13 Albion ....1 Cambuslang 6
Nov 13 Cowdenbeath ....0 Cambuslang H ..3
Nov 6 Morton ....11 Carfin S 0
Nov 13 Queen of S'th W .8 Arbroath 2
Nov 13 St Bernard's ....5 Erin R 1

5th Round
Dec 4 Clyde ....0 T Lanark 0
Dec 4 Harp ....2 Dumbarton 2
       Harp Scratched
Dec 4 Hibernian ......7 Queen of S'th W .3
Dec 4 Hurlford ....5 Morton 1
Dec 4 Kilmarnock .....6 Dunblane 0
Dec 4 Port Glasgow A .6 St Bernard's 2
Dec 4 Queen's Park ...1 Cambuslang 1
Nov 27 Vale of Leven ....2 Cambuslang H ..0

Replays
Dec 11 Cambuslang ....4 Queen's Park ...5
Dec 11 T Lanark ....4 Clyde 2

6th Round
Dec 25 Hurlford ....0 Dumbarton 0
Dec 25 Kilmarnock .....0 Queen's Park ...5
Dec 25 Port Glasgow A ..1 Vale of Leven ...3
Dec 25 T Lanark ....1 Hibernian 2

Replays
Jan 8 Dumbarton .....1 Hurlford 2
Jan 22 Dumbarton .....3 Hurlford 1
       After Protest

Semi-finals
Jan 22 Hibernian ......3 Vale of Leven ...1
Jan 29 Queen's Park ....1 Dumbarton 2

Final
Feb 12 Dumbarton .....1 Hibernian 2
       played at Hampden Park

Season 1887-88

SFA Cup
1st Round
Sep 3 1st Rrv ....1 Renfrew 8
Sep 3 5th KRV ....5 Thornhill 0
Sep 3 Abercorn ......9 Johnstone H 0
Sep 3 Aberdeen ......4 Our Boys 9
Sep 3 Airdrie ....8 Dykehead 0
Sep 3 Albion ....12 Airdriehill 0
Sep 3 Alloa ....6 Cowdenbeath ...2
Sep 3 Arbroath ......18 Orion 0

       Ayr ....W Monkcastle 0
Sep 3 Boness ....4 Leith A 1
Sep 3 Bonhill ....1 Dumbarton A ...6
Sep 3 Broughty ....5 Montrose 7
Sep 3 Broxburn S .....0 Mossend S 4
       Mossend Disqualified
Sep 3 Burntisland ....4 Dunfermline A ..2
       Burntisland Disqualified
Sep 3 Caledonian R ....1 Crieff 7
       Cambuslang ...W Hamilton A 0

Sep 3 Cambuslang H ..5 Hamilton 4
Sep 3 Carfin S ....4 Shettleston 0
       Both Qualified
Sep 3 Carrick ....0 Thistle 10
Sep 3 Clyde ....0 Queen's Park ...7
Sep 3 Clydesdale ......1 Rutherglen 4
Sep 3 Coupar Angus ...9 Our Boys 0
Sep 3 Drumpellier .....2 Motherwell 3
Sep 1 Dumbarton ....10 Dunbritton 0
Sep 3 Dunblane ....2 Fair City A 3

Sep 3 Dundee W ....7 Lochee 0
Sep 3 Dunfermline A ....3 Lassodie 2
Dunfermline Disqualified
Sep 3 Dykebar ....5 Morton 2
Sep 3 Erin R Bath .....5 Bellstane 0
Sep 3 Erin R Perth ....3 St Johnstone ...9
Sep 3 Falkirk ....4 Kilsyth W 1
Sep 3 Grahamston ....4 Redding A 3
Grahamston Disqualified
Sep 3 Grangemouth ...2 E Stirling 5
Sep 3 Hearts ....4 Norton Park 1
Sep 3 Hibernian ......5 Broxburn T 0
Hurlford ......W Annbank 0
Sep 3 Jamestown .....3 Vale of Leven ..2
Sep 3 Kelvinside A ....6 St Andrew's 3
Sep 3 Kilbarchan ....0 Arthurlie 4
Kilbirnie ......W Lanemark 0
Sep 3 Kilmarnock ....8 Ayr T 1
Sep 3 King's Park .....1 Camelon 5
Sep 3 Kirkintilloch A ..5 Kirkintilloch C ..1
Sep 3 Lindertis ....1 Harp 2
Harp Disqualified
Sep 3 Linthouse .....3 Whitefield 3
Sep 3 Lochgilphead ...1 Oban 9
Sep 3 Lochwinnoch ...5 Pollokshaws 1
Sep 3 Lugar Boswell ..9 Dalry 0
Sep 3 Maybole ......3 Newmilns 2nd ARV .3
Sep 3 Moffat ....7 Newcastleton 1
Neilston ......W Paisley A 0
Sep 3 Northern ......5 Govan A 1
Sep 3 Partick T ......10 Westbourne 0
Plains ......W Tollcross 0
Sep 3 Pollokshields A ..4 United Abstainer ..1
Aug 27 Port Glasgow A .11 Greenock R 0
Sep 3 Queen of S'th W ..6 Vale of Nith 0
Sep 3 Rangers ....4 Battlefield 1
Sep 3 Shananann .....5 Laurieston 4
Sep 3 St Bernard's ....3 Armadale 2
Sep 3 Strathmore Arb ...1 East End 13
Sep 3 Strathmore Dun ..6 Forfar 3
Sep 3 Thornliebank ....1 St Mirren 2
Sep 3 T Lanark ....1 Cowlairs 2
Sep 3 Uddingston ....2 Royal Albert 5
Sep 3 Union ....0 Renton 6
Sep 3 Vale of Bannock ..3 Campsie 4
Vale of Leven ..W Kirkintilloch H ..0
Sep 3 Vale of Leven W ..7 Methlan Park ...2
Sep 3 West Calder .....9 Athenian 0

Replays
Sep 10 Motherwell .....2 Drumpellier 0
After Protest
Sep 10 Newmilns 2nd ARV .4 Maybole 6
Sep 10 Whitefield ......2 Linthouse 1
Sep 10 T Lanark ....1 Cowlairs 4
After Protest
Sep 10 Vale of Leven ..2 Jamestown 2
After Protest
Sep 25 Jamestown .....3 Vale of Leven H ..1

2nd Round
Sep 24 Abercorn ....6 Neilston 0
Sep 24 Airdrie ....3 Cambuslang H ..0
Sep 24 Alloa ....0 Dunfermline 1
Sep 24 Arbroath ......3 Strathmore Dun ..1
Sep 24 Arthurlie ......3 St Mirren 3
Sep 24 Boness ....5 West Calder 1
Sep 24 Cambuslang ....2 Royal Albert ...0
Sep 24 Carfin S ....3 Motherwell 1
Coupar Angus ..W Crieff 0
Sep 24 Cowlairs ....9 Southern A 1
Sep 24 Dumbarton .....1 Vale of Leven ...5
Sep 24 Dundee W .....10 Aberdeen R 0
Sep 24 Erin R Bath .....0 Hibernian 6
Sep 24 Fair City A .....3 St Johnstone ...0
Sep 24 Falkirk ....2 Campsie 2
Sep 24 Hurlford ....9 Lugar Boswell ..1
Jamestown .....7 Kirkintilloch A ..1
Sep 24 Kilbirnie ....3 Mauchline 0
Sep 24 Lindertis ....3 East End 2
Sep 24 Lochwinnoch ...2 Dykebar 5
Sep 24 Maybole ....0 Ayr 13
Sep 24 Moffat ....4 Queen of S'th W .4
Sep 24 Nithsdale W .....2 5th KRV 9
Sep 24 Northern ......6 Shettleston 3
Sep 24 Our Boys ......5 Montrose 3
Sep 24 Partick T ......2 Rangers 1
Sep 24 Queen's Park ...9 Kelvinside A 0
Sep 24 Redding A ......0 Camelon 17
Sep 24 Renfrew ....3 Port Glasgow A ..3
Sep 24 Renton ....4 Dumbarton A ...2
Sep 24 Rutherglen .....3 Albion R 6
Sep 24 Slanannan .....1 E Stirling 6
Sep 24 St Bernard's ....1 Broxburn S 1
Sep 24 Thistle ....6 Glasgow Univ ...0
Sep 24 Whitefield .....2 Pollokshaws A ..0

Replays
Oct 1 Campsie ....2 Falkirk 2
Both Qualified
Oct 1 Port Glasgow A ..5 Renfrew 3
Oct 1 Queen of S'th W ..7 Moffat 4
Oct 1 St Bernard's .....4 Broxburn S 1
Oct 1 St Mirren ....4 Arthurlie 1

3rd Round
Oct 15 5th KRV ....2 Queen of S'th W .6
Oct 15 Ayr ....4 Port Glasgow A ..0
Oct 15 Camelon ....0 Renton 8
Oct 15 Cowlairs ....9 Campsie 1
Oct 15 Dundee W ......8 Coupar Angus ..0
Oct 15 Dykebar ....2 Kilmarnock 2
Oct 15 E Stirling ......0 Cambuslang 0
Oct 15 Fair City A .....0 Our Boys 5
Oct 15 Falkirk ....2 Carfin S 2
Oct 15 Hearts ....1 Hibernian 1
Oct 15 Hurlford ....2 St Mirren 4
Oct 15 Kilbirnie ....1 Abercorn 3
Oct 15 Lassodie ....1 Boness 3
Oct 15 Northern ....3 Albion R 4

Oct 15 Oban ....1 Arbroath 5
Oct 15 Queen's Park ...3 Jamestown 0
St Bernard's ...W Dunfermline ...0
Oct 15 Thistle ....2 Whitefield 0
Oct 15 Vale of Leven ...3 Airdrie 0
Oct 15 Vale of Leven W ..9 Plains 0

Replays
Oct 22 Cambuslang ....4 E Stirling 2
Oct 22 Carfin S ....3 Falkirk 0
Oct 22 Hibernian ......1 Hearts 3
Oct 22 Kilmarnock .....9 Dykebar 1

4th Round
Nov 5 Ayr ....3 Vale of Leven ...2
Nov 5 Dundee W ......4 Queen of S'th W .3
Nov 5 Hearts ....1 St Mirren 1
Nov 5 Lindertis ....1 Renton 13
Nov 5 Partick T ......2 Kilmarnock 2
Nov 5 Vale of Leven W ..2 Boness 0

Replays
Nov 12 Kilmarnock .....1 Partick T 4
Nov 12 St Mirren ......2 Hearts 2
Nov 19 Hearts ....2 St Mirren 2
played at E Stirling
Nov 26 Hearts ....2 St Mirren 4
played at Cathkin Park

5th Round
Nov 26 Abercorn ......9 St Bernard's 0
Nov 26 Arbroath ......5 Cowlairs 1
Nov 26 Cambuslang ....10 Ayr 0
Nov 26 Dundee W ......5 Carfin S 2
Nov 26 Our Boys ......4 Albion R 2
Nov 26 Queen's Park ...2 Partick T 0
Dec 3 St Mirren ......2 Renton 3
Nov 26 Thistle ....2 Vale of Leven W .9

6th Round
Dec 17 Abercorn ....3 Arbroath 1
Dec 17 Cambuslang ....6 Our Boys 0
Dec 17 Queen's Park ...7 Vale of Leven W .1
Dec 17 Renton ....5 Dundee W 1

Semi-finals
Jan 14 Abercorn ....1 Cambuslang 1
Jan 14 Renton ....3 Queen's Park 1

Replay
Jan 21 Cambuslang ....10 Abercorn 1

Final
Feb 4 Cambuslang ....1 Renton 6
played at Hampden Park

Season 1888-89

FA Cup
1st Round
Abercorn .....W Kilbarchan 0
Sep 1 Aberdeen ......3 Arbroath 4
Albion ......W Belshill 0
Sep 1 Alva ....6 Kilsyth W 2
Sep 1 Annbank ......5 Britannia 1
Sep 1 Armadale .....12 Champfleurie ...0
Sep 1 Beith ....2 Irving 3
Sep 1 Bellstane ......2 Norton P 3

Sep 1 Bo'ness ....0 Hearts 1
Sep 1 Broxburn S .....3 West Calder 2
Sep 1 Cambuslang H ..5 Coatbridge 0
Sep 1 Campsie ....5 Camelon 1
Sep 1 Carfin S ....6 Whifflet S 1
Sep 1 Celtic ....5 Shettleston 1
Sep 1 Clydebank ......3 Vale of Leven W .4
Sep 1 Clydesdale .....1 Rutherglen 1
Sep 1 Coupar & Angus ..6 Bridgend A 1
Sep 1 Cowdenbeath ...3 Lassodie 1

Sep 1 Cowlairs ....18 Temperance A ...2
Sep 1 Crieff ....10 Vale of Atholl ...2
Sep 1 Dumbarton .....13 Kirkintilloch C ...1
Sep 1 Dumbarton A ...15 Dumbarton U ...0
Sep 1 Dunblane ......6 St Johnstone 3
Sep 1 Dundee OB .....5 Dundee East End .4
Dundee W ....W Aberdeen R 0
Dunfermline A ..W Dunfermline ...0
Sep 1 Erin R Bathgate ..6 Leith H 0
Sep 1 Erin R Perth ....8 Blairgowrie OB ..2

Sep 1	E Stirling 10	Stenhousemuir ..1	
Sep 1	Fair City A 5	Caledonian R 0	
Sep 1	Falkirk 5	Dunipace 0	
Sep 1	Forfar 14	Lindertis 1	
	Gairdoch .....W	Redding A 0	
Sep 1	Hamilton A 5	Airdrie 0	
Sep 1	Hurlford 7	Ayr 0	
Sep 1	Johnstone H 4	Woodvale 5	
Sep 1	Kelvinside A ...16	Govan A 0	
Sep 1	Kilbirnie 3	Dalry 1	
Sep 1	King's Park 4	Alloa 3	
Sep 1	Kirkcaldy W 3	Townhill 0	
Sep 1	Lanemark 7	Stevenston T 0	
Sep 1	Linlithgow A ...2	Adventurers 6	
Sep 1	Linthouse 2	Clyde 4	
Sep 1	Lochgilphead ...15	Balaclava R 1	
Sep 1	Lochwinnoch 0	Dykebar 5	
Sep 1	Lugar Boswell ..0	Kilmarnock 5	
	Maybole .....W	Kilmarnock T ...0	
Sep 1	Methian P 5	Kirkintilloch A ..0	
	Nov dale .....W	Moffat 0	
Sep 1	Montrose 8	Brechin C 1	
Sep 1	Mossend S 2	Hibernian 1	
Sep 1	Motherwell 3	Royal Albert 3	
Sep 1	Neilston 3	St Mirren 4	
	Newmilns .....W	Ayr T 0	
Sep 1	Newton Stewart .13	Nithsdale W 0	
Sep 8	Northern 2	Queen's Park 3	
	Oban ....W	Campbeltown A ..0	
Sep 1	Pollokshaws 14	Carlton 0	
	Pollokshaws H .W	Greenock R 0	
Sep 1	Port Glasgow A .3	Morton 7	
Sep 1	Queen of South .9	5th KRV 4	
Sep 1	Rangers 4	Partick T 2	
Sep 8	Renfrew 0	Arthurlie 0	
Sep 1	Renton 8	Bowling 0	
Sep 1	Slamannan 5	Grangemouth 3	
Sep 1	Southern A 1	Battlefield 9	
Sep 1	St Bernard's ...7	Leith A 0	
Sep 1	Stewarton C 4	Rosebank 3	
Sep 1	Strathmore Dun ..3	Harp 4	
Sep 1	Thistle 3	Maryhill 1	
Sep 1	Thornhill 2	Vale of Nith 2	
	Thornliebank ...W	Paisley 0	
	T Lanark .....W	Whitefield 0	
Sep 8	Union 2	Lochee 3	
Sep 1	United Abstainer .2	Pollokshields A ..1	
Sep 1	Vale of Bannock .3	Laurieston 2	
Sep 1	Vale of Leven ...6	Jamestown 1	
Sep 1	Wishaw 2	Cambuslang 4	

Replays

Sep 8	Arthurlie 3	Renfrew 1	
Sep 8	Royal Albert 1	Motherwell 2	
Sep 8	Rutherglen 2	Clydesdale 2	
	Both Qualified		
Sep 8	Thornhill 0	Vale of Nith 1	
	After Protest		
Sep 15	West Calder 2	Broxburn S 1	
	After Protest		
	Vale of Nith ...W	Thornhill 0	

2nd Round

	1st Rrv ......W	Woodvale 0	
Sep 22	Albion R 9	Rutherglen 1	
Sep 22	Alva 0	Campsie 6	

Sep 22	Arbroath 6	Montrose 2	
Sep 22	Arthurlie 3	Pollokshaw 2	
Sep 22	Battlefield 11	United Abstainer ..0	
Sep 22	Broughty 2	Harp 4	
Sep 22	Broxburn 9	Adventurers 3	
Sep 22	Cambuslang 4	Carfin S 2	
Sep 22	Celtic 8	Cowlairs 0	
Sep 22	Clyde 2	Rangers 2	
Sep 22	Clydesdale 1	Uddingston 5	
Sep 22	Coupar Angus 1	Erin R Perth 3	
Sep 22	Cowdenbeath 2	Dunfermline A ...4	
Sep 22	Dumbarton A 4	Vale of Leven ...2	
Sep 22	Dundee OB 4	Lochee 2	
Sep 22	Dykebar 1	St Mirren 6	
Sep 22	E Stirling 11	Vale of Bannock .2	
Sep 22	Fair City A 7	Crieff 1	
Sep 22	Falkirk 8	Gairdoch 3	
Sep 22	Forfar 6	Dundee W 5	
Sep 22	Hearts 4	Erin R Bathgate ..0	
Sep 29	Hurlford 5	Annbank 4	
Sep 22	Kelvinside A 0	T Lanark 8	
Sep 22	Kilmarnock 1	Kilbirnie 3	
Sep 22	Morton 1	Abercorn 4	
Sep 22	Motherwell 5	Hamilton 1	
Sep 22	Newmilns A 4	Maybole 4	
Sep 22	Oban 4	Lochgilphead ...2	
Sep 22	Pollokshaws H ...2	Thornliebank ...5	
Sep 22	Queen of S'th W .14	Newton Stewart ..2	
Sep 22	Queen's Park 6	Thistle 0	
Sep 22	Slamannan 3	King's Park 3	
Sep 29	St Bernard's 3	Norton P 1	
Sep 22	Vale of Leven H ..1	Methlan Park 3	
Sep 22	Vale of Leven W ..2	Renton 10	
Sep 22	Vale of Nith 3	Mid-Annandale ..1	
Sep 22	West Calder 1	Mossend S 6	

Replays

Sep 29	Clyde 3	Rangers 0	
Sep 29	King's Park 13	Slamannan 1	
Sep 29	Maybole 6	Newmilns 2	
Oct 6	Hurlford 2	Annbank 2	
	After Protest		
Oct 13	Annbank 2	Hurlford 3	

3rd Round

Oct 13	1st Rrv 3	Kilbirnie 4	
Oct 13	Arthurlie 0	St Mirren 7	
Oct 13	Battlefield 1	Dumbarton A 3	
Oct 13	Broxburn 2	Hearts 2	
Oct 13	Celtic 4	Albion R 1	
Oct 13	Clyde 4	Cambuslang H ...0	
Oct 13	Dunblane 4	Erin R Perth 4	
Oct 13	Dundee OB 2	Harp 1	
Oct 13	E Stirling 4	King's Park 0	
Oct 13	Falkirk 2	Campsie 2	
Oct 13	Forfar 1	Arbroath 2	
Oct 20	Hurlford 4	Irvine 2	
Oct 13	Kirkcaldy W 1	St Bernard's 3	
Oct 13	Lanemark 4	Maybole 2	
Oct 13	Mossend S 5	Armadale 2	
Oct 13	Motherwell 2	Dumbarton 6	
Oct 13	Queen of S'th W .11	Vale of Nith 1	
Oct 13	Renton 4	Cambuslang 1	
Oct 13	Thornliebank ...0	Abercorn 8	
Oct 13	T Lanark 2	Queen's Park 1	
Oct 13	Uddingston 4	Glasgow U 0	

Replays

Oct 20	Campsie 2	Falkirk 2	
	Both Qualified		
Oct 20	Erin R Perth 0	Dunblane 6	
Oct 20	Hearts 2	Broxburn 0	
Oct 27	T Lanark 4	Queen's Park ...2	
	After Protest		

4th Round

Nov 3	Abercorn 11	Dundee OB 1	
Nov 3	Campsie 3	Hearts 1	
Nov 3	Dumbarton 9	Methlan P 0	
Nov 3	Dumbarton A ...W	Dunfermline A ..0	
Nov 3	Dunblane 4	E Stirling 4	
Nov 3	Fair City A 1	Arbroath 3	
Nov 3	Kilbirnie 1	St Mirren 6	
Nov 3	Lanemark 0	Renton 8	
Nov 3	Oban 0	Clyde 6	
Nov 3	Queen of S'th W .10	Falkirk 2	
Nov 3	St Bernard's 1	Celtic 4	
Nov 3	T Lanark 7	Hurlford 1	
Nov 3	Uddingston 1	Mossend S 4	

Replays

Nov 10	E Stirling 4	Dunblane 0	

5th Round

Nov 24	Arbroath 3	Renton 3	
Nov 24	Celtic 0	Clyde 1	
Dec 1	Dumbarton 3	Mossend S 1	
Nov 24	St Mirren 3	Queen of S'th W .1	
Nov 24	T Lanark 5	Abercorn 4	

Replays

Dec 1	Renton 4	Arbroath 0	
Dec 8	Celtic 9	Clyde 2	
	After Protest		
Dec 8	T Lanark 2	Abercorn 2	
	After Protest		
Dec 15	Abercorn 2	T Lanark 2	
Dec 22	Abercorn 1	T Lanark 3	
	played at Ibrox		

6th Round

Dec 15	Celtic 2	E Stirling 1	
Dec 15	Dumbarton 2	St Mirren 2	
Dec 15	Dumbarton A 1	Renton 2	
Dec 29	T Lanark 6	Campsie 1	

Replays

Dec 22	St Mirren 2	Dumbarton 2	
Dec 29	Dumbarton 3	St Mirren 1	
	played at Ibrox		

Semi-finals

Jan 12	Dumbarton 1	Celtic 4	
Jan 12	T Lanark 2	Renton 0	

Final

Feb 2	Celtic 0	T Lanark 3	
	played at Hampden Park		

Replay

After Protest

Feb 9	Celtic 1	T Lanark 2	
	played at Hampden Park		

Season 1889-90

SFA Cup

1st Round

	Aberdeen .....W	Portland 0	
Sep 7	Airdriehill 5	Motherwell 6	
Sep 7	Alloa 5	Denny 1	
Sep 7	Alva 3	King's Park 6	
Sep 7	Arbroath 3	Dundee H 5	
Sep 7	Armadale 2	Hibernian 3	
Sep 7	Arthurlie 2	St Mirren 4	
Sep 7	Ayr 16	Beith 0	
Sep 7	Bathgate 3	Champfleurie 3	
Sep 7	Bellstane 6	Norton Park 3	

Sep 7	Bowling 1	Renton 8
Sep 7	Broughty 1	Dundee East End .6
Sep 7	Bute R 1	Kilbarchan 2
Sep 7	Carfin S 4	Albion R 0
Sep 7	Carrington 0	Maryhill 3
Sep 7	Celtic *0*	Queen's Park ...0
	Abandoned	
Sep 7	Clydebank 3	Vale of Leven ...1
	Clydebank Scratched	
Sep 7	Clydesdale 1	Cambuslang 6
Sep 7	Cowdenbeath 8	Kirkcaldy W 0
Sep 7	Dalry 3	Kilbirnie 3
Sep 7	Dunblane 4	Caledonian R 1
Sep 7	Dundee OB 6	Strathmore 3
Sep 7	Dunipace 2	Laurieston 3
Sep 7	Duntocher H ...5	Smithston H 0
Sep 7	Fair City A 8	Coupar Angus ...0
Sep 7	Falkirk 11	Tillicoultry 1
Sep 7	Gairdoch 0	E Stirling 7
Sep 7	Glasgow H 1	Thistle 3
	Greenock A ...*W*	Renfrew *0*
Sep 7	Hamilton A 0	Wishaw S 5
Sep 7	Irvine 2	Lugar Boswell ...2
Sep 7	Jamestown 2	Methlan P 4
	Kelvinside A ..*W*	Southern A ...*0*
Sep 7	Kilmarnock 2	Annbank 3
Sep 7	Kilsyth W 5	Stenhousemuir ..1
Sep 7	Lassodie 3	Burntisland T ...2
Sep 7	Leith A 6	Adventurers 2
Sep 7	Lindertis 0	Dundee W 5
Sep 7	Linthouse 7	Fairfield 2
Sep 7	Lochee 4	Brechin 1
Apr 31	Lochwinnoch ...1	Abercorn 10
Sep 7	Mauchline 1	Newmilns 4
Sep 7	Maybole 6	Ayr A 6
Sep 7	Mid-Annandale .3	5th KRV 11
Sep 7	Moffat 8	Dumfries 0
Sep 7	Montrose 2	Forfar 4
Sep 7	Morton 8	Carlton 0
Sep 7	Mossend S 6	Bo'ness 0
Sep 7	Newton Stewart .3	Queen of South .4
Sep 7	Oban 5	Oban R 2
Sep 7	Old Kirkpatrick .1	Union 7
Sep 7	Orion 3	Victoria U 1
Sep 7	Perth OB 3	St Johnstone ...5
Sep 7	Pollokshaw 3	Dykebar 1
Sep 7	Pollokshaw H ..1	1st Rrv 7
Sep 7	Port Glasgow A .2	Neilston 1
Sep 7	Raith R 1	Dunfermline A ..2
Sep 7	Rangers 6	United Abstainer .2
Sep 7	Royal Albert ...12	Whifflet S 0
Sep 7	Rutherglen 2	Uddingston 8
Sep 7	Shettleston 1	Battlefield 7
Sep 7	Slamannan 0	Grangemouth ...8
Sep 7	St Bernard's ...0	Hearts 3
Sep 7	Stevenson T ...4	Kilmarnock A ...1
Sep 7	Stewarton C ...0	Hurlford 5
	Summerton A ..*W*	Temperance A ..*0*
	Thornliebank ...*W*	Johnstone H ...*0*
Sep 7	T Lanark 3	Partick T 2
	Vale of Atholl ..*W*	Crieff *0*
Sep 7	Vale of Bannock ..3	Campsie 6
Sep 7	Vale of Leven ..0	Dumbarton 0
Sep 7	Victoria 1	Cowlairs 21
Apr 31	West Calder ...2	Broxburn 9
Sep 7	Whitefield 0	Northern 5

Replays

	Champfleurie ..*W*	Bathgate *0*

Sep 14	Ayr 3	Maybole 1
Sep 14	Dumbarton 1	Vale of Leven 1
	Both Qualified	
Sep 14	Irvine 8	Lugar Boswell ..0
Sep 14	Kilbirnie 5	Dalry 2
Sep 14	Queen's Park ...2	Celtic 1

2nd Round

Sep 28	1st Rrv 2	Morton 10
Sep 28	Abercorn 10	Thornliebank 1
Sep 28	Aberdeen 2	Orion 1
Sep 28	Airdrie 5	Uddingston 2
Sep 28	Battlefield 0	Thistle 2
Sep 28	Bellstane 1	Hearts 4
Sep 28	Broxburn 2	Leith A 2
Sep 28	Camelon 4	Grangemouth ...4
Sep 28	Campsie 3	Alloa 7
Sep 28	Carfin S 6	Motherwell 2
Sep 28	Clyde 1	Northern 2
Sep 28	Cowlairs 1	Linthouse 1
Sep 28	Dundee H 5	Dundee OB 6
Sep 28	Dundee W 0	Dundee East End .2
	Dunfermline A ..*W*	Dunfermline ...*0*
Sep 28	Dumfries H 1	Queen of South .5
Sep 28	Duntocher H ...3	Vale of Leven ...4
Sep 28	Falkirk 5	King's Park 1
Sep 28	Hibernian 4	Mossend S 3
Sep 28	Kelvinside A ...0	Rangers 13
Sep 28	Kilbirnie 5	Newmilns 0
Sep 28	Lanemark 2	Hurlford 1
Sep 28	Lassodie 3	Cowdenbeath ...3
Sep 28	Laurieston 1	E Stirling 4
Sep 28	Lochee 1	Forfar A 7
Sep 28	Lugar Boswell ..0	Ayr 2
Sep 28	Moffat 4	5th Rrv 1
	Oban ....*W*	Lochgilphead ...*0*
Sep 28	Port Glasgow A ..8	Greenock A 0
Sep 28	Renton 1	Dumbarton 2
Sep 28	Royal Albert ...1	Cambuslang ...1
Sep 28	St Johnstone ...2	Fair City A 2
Sep 28	St Mirren 6	Kilbarchan 0
Sep 28	Stevenson T ...3	Annbank 2
Sep 28	Summerton A ...0	Queen's Park ..11
Sep 28	T Lanark 9	Maryhill 3
Sep 28	Union 5	Kirkintilloch A ..2
Sep 28	Vale of Atholl ..4	Dunblane 9
Sep 28	Vale of Leven ..4	Methlan Park ...1

Replays

Oct 5	Cambuslang 4	Royal Albert ...1
Oct 5	Fair City A 3	St Johnstone ...2
Oct 5	Grangemouth 7	Camelon 2
Oct 5	Leith A 2	Broxburn 1
Oct 5	Linthouse 3	Cowlairs 2
	Cowdenbeath	Lassodie ....

3rd Round

Oct 19	Abercorn 5	Stevenson T ...2
Oct 19	Aberdeen 5	Forfar A 3
Oct 19	Alloa 3	Oban 0
Oct 19	Champfleurie ...0	Hearts 5
Oct 19	Dumbarton 1	T Lanark 1
Oct 19	Dunblane 3	Fair City A 0
Oct 19	Dundee OB 2	Dundee East End .3
Oct 19	Dunfermline A ...4	Hibernian 4
Oct 19	Edinburgh Univ ..0	Leith A 9
Oct 19	Falkirk 1	E Stirling 6
Oct 19	Grangemouth ...2	Kilsyth W 2
Oct 19	Lanemark 4	Ayr A 3

Oct 19	Moffat 0	Queen of S'th W .0
Oct 19	Morton 1	Ayr 4
Oct 19	Northern 2	Carfin S 1
Oct 19	Port Glasgow A ..3	Kilbirnie 4
Oct 19	Queen's Park ...8	Vale of Leven W .0
Oct 19	Rangers 0	Vale of Leven ...0
Oct 19	St Mirren 5	Pollokshaw 1
Oct 19	Thistle 2	Airdrie 2
Oct 19	Union 1	Cambuslang ...3
Oct 19	Wishaw T 8	Linthouse 5

Replays

Oct 26	Airdrie 3	Thistle 1
Oct 26	Hibernian 11	Dunfermline A ..1
Oct 26	Kilsyth W 0	Grangemouth ...1
Oct 26	Queen of S'th W .5	Moffat 5
	Both Qualified	
Oct 26	T Lanark 1	Dumbarton 0
Oct 26	Vale of Leven ..3	Rangers 2
Nov 2	Cambuslang 6	Union 0
	After Protest	
Nov 2	Northern 3	Carfin S 4
	After Protest	

4th Round

Nov 9	Aberdeen 1	Queen's Park ...13
Nov 9	Airdrie 2	Abercorn 3
Nov 9	Ayr 1	Leith A 1
Nov 9	Dunblane 4	Cowdenbeath ...6
Nov 9	Dundee East End .3	Cambuslang ...2
Nov 9	Grangemouth ...1	Vale of Leven ...7
Nov 9	Hearts 9	Alloa 1
Nov 9	Kilbirnie 5	E Stirling 2
Nov 9	Lanemark 2	St Mirren 8
Nov 9	Moffat 4	Carfin S 2
Nov 9	Queen of S'th W .3	Hibernian 7
Nov 9	T Lanark 2	Linthouse 0

Replays

Nov 16	Leith A 4	Ayr 1
Nov 23	Dundee East End .3	Cambuslang ...2
	After Protest	

5th Round

Nov 30	Cowdenbeath 2	Abercorn 8
Nov 30	Moffat 2	Dundee East End .2
Nov 30	Queen's Park ...1	St Mirren 0
Nov 30	Vale of Leven ..3	Hearts 1

Replays

Dec 7	Dundee East End .5	Moffat 1

6th Round

Dec 21	Abercorn 6	Hibernian 2
Dec 21	Kilbirnie 1	T Lanark 4
Dec 21	Queen's Park ...1	Leith A 0
Dec 21	Vale of Leven ..4	Dundee East End .0

Semi-finals

Jan 27	Queen's Park ...2	Abercorn 0
Jan 27	Vale of Leven ..3	T Lanark 0

Final

Feb 15	Queen's Park ...1	Vale of Leven ...1
	played at Ibrox	

Replay

Feb 22	Queen's Park ...2	Vale of Leven ...1
	played at Ibrox	

SFA Cup
1st Round

Sep 6	Abercorn	..8	Irvine	..0
Sep 6	Annan	..2	Dumfries W	..8
Sep 6	Arthurlie	..2	St Mirren	..5
	Ayr	..W	Kilbarchan	..0
Sep 6	Ayr Parkhouse	..6	Kilbirnie	..1
Sep 6	Bathgate	..3	Dunfermline A	..1
Sep 6	Battlefield	..1	T Lanark	..4
	Boness	..W	Blair Adam	..0
Sep 6	Brechin	..3	Kirriemuir	..4
Sep 6	Bridge of Allan	..7	Southfield R	..2
	Broxburn	..W	West Calder	..0
Sep 6	Burnbank S	.11	United Abstainer	..0
Sep 6	Burntisland T	..4	Bonnyrigg R	..2
Sep 6	Caledonian	..2	Victoria U	..1
Sep 6	Cambuslang	..3	Glasgow W	..1
Sep 6	Camelon	..4	Alloa	..3
Sep 6	Campsie	..4	Laurieston	..1
Sep 6	Campsie H	..3	Clydebank A	..6
	Carfin S	..W	Cartha	..0
	Carlton	..W	Lugar Boswell	..0
Sep 6	Carrington	..1	Albion R	..2
Sep 6	Cathcart	..5	Pollokshaws H	..3
Sep 6	Celtic	..1	Rangers	..0
Sep 6	Clackmannan	..9	Milton	..0
Sep 6	Clyde	..7	Whitefield	..2
Sep 6	Cowdenbeath	.10	Linlithgow A	..1
Sep 6	Cowlairs	..1	Airdrie	..3
	Crieff	..W	Vale of Atholl	..0
Sep 6	Dalry	..5	Pollokshaws	..2
Sep 6	Denny	..1	Alloa	..4
Sep 6	Douglas R	..0	5th KRV	..5
Sep 6	Dumbarton	..8	Smithston H	..2
Sep 6	Dumfries	..9	Newton Stewart	..0
	Dundee H	..W	Lochee	..0
Sep 6	Dundee W	..3	Arbroath	..3
Sep 6	E Stirling	..8	Grangemouth	..2
Sep 6	Fair City A	..7	Dunblane	..3
	Falkirk	..W	Vale of Bannock	..0
Sep 6	Forfar A	..2	Dundee OB	..7
Sep 6	Greenock Abst	..0	Newmilns	.13
Sep 6	Hamilton A	..0	Linthouse	..8
Sep 6	Hearts	..7	Raith R	..2
Sep 6	Inveraray	..4	Lochgilphead	..1
Sep 6	Inverness T	..2	Inverness C	..4
Sep 6	Kelvinside A	..1	Glasgow H	..1
Sep 6	Kilmarnock	..4	Annbank	..4
Sep 6	Kilsyth W	..2	Renton	..1
Sep 6	Kirkcaldy W	..3	Hibernian	..4
Sep 6	Kirkintilloch A	..2	Clydebank	..2
	Lanemark	..W	Dykebar	..0
Sep 6	Leith A	..3	Armadale	..2
	Maryhill	..W	Southern A	..0
Sep 6	Mauchline	..1	Kilmarnock A	..3
Sep 6	Maybole	..3	Hurlford	..4
Sep 6	Methlan Park	..1	King's Park	..0
Sep 6	Mid-Annandale	.15	Rising T	..0
Sep 6	Montrose	..7	Broughty	..1
Sep 6	Morton	..7	Ayr A	..2
	Mossend S	..W	Lassodie	..0
Sep 6	Motherwell S	..3	Fairfield	..7
Sep 6	Neilston	..7	Bute R	..3
Sep 6	Northern	..5	Clydesdale	..0
Sep 6	Oban	..3	Oban R	..0
Sep 6	Old Kilpatrick	..1	Jamestown	..6
Sep 6	Orion	..1	Aberdeen	..5
Sep 6	Penicuik A	..5	Champfleurie	..3
Sep 6	Port Glasgow A	..0	Monkcastle	..2
Sep 6	Royal Albert	..5	Motherwell	..4
	Rutherglen	..W	St Brides	..0
Sep 6	Saltcoats V	..4	Lochwinnoch	..3
Sep 6	Slamannan	..6	Gairdoch	..2
Sep 6	St Bernard's	..7	Adventurers	..0

St Bernard's Disqualified

Sep 6	St Johnstone	..2	Coupar Angus	..2

Coupar A Disqualified

Sep 6	Stevenston T	..9	Stewarton C	..2
	Stranraer	..W	East End	..0
	Summerton A	..W	Whifflet S	..0
Sep 6	Thistle	..3	Queen's Park	..5
Sep 6	Tillicoultry	..1	Dalmuir T	..5
Sep 6	Uddingston	..6	Hamilton H	..0
Sep 6	Union	.12	Grasshoppers	..1
	Vale of Leven	..W	Stenhousemuir	..0
	Vale of Leven W	..W	Dunipace	..0
Sep 6	Wishaw T	..3	Partick T	..2

Replays

Sep 13	Annbank	..6	Kilmarnock	..2
Sep 13	Arbroath	..4	Dundee W	..1
Sep 13	Clydebank	..4	Kirkintilloch A	..3
Sep 13	Glasgow H	..5	Kelvinside A	..1
	Northern	..7	Clydesdale	..1

After Protest

2nd Round

Sep 27	5th KRV	..9	Mid-Annandale	..1
Sep 27	Abercorn	.12	Cathcart	..0
Sep 27	Aberdeen	..8	Caledonian	..0
	Adventurers	..W	Vale of Leven W	..0
Sep 27	Airdrie	..3	Annbank	..1
Sep 27	Ayr Parkhouse	..1	Summerton A	..2
Sep 27	Bathgate	..6	Union	..2
Sep 27	Beith	..2	Cambuslang	..4
Oct 11	Boness	..7	Bellstane	..0
Sep 27	Bridge of Allan	..1	Vale of Leven	..5
Sep 27	Broxburn	..5	Clackmannan	..2
Sep 27	Burnbank S	..2	Stevenston T	..1
Sep 27	Camelon	..2	Alva	..1
Sep 27	Campsie	..4	E Stirling	..4
Sep 27	Celtic	..2	Carfin S	..2
Sep 27	Clyde	..5	Hurlford	..3
Sep 27	Clydebank A	..3	Kilsyth W	..5
Sep 27	Crieff	..0	Fair City A	.11
Sep 27	Dalmuir T	..5	Cowdenbeath	..7
Sep 27	Dumfries W	..6	Dumfries	..5
Sep 27	East End	..4	St Johnstone	..2
Sep 27	Fairfield	..2	Royal Albert	..5
	Glengowan	..W	Carlton	..0
Sep 27	Harp	..1	Arbroath	..5
	Hearts	..W	Burntisland	..0
Sep 27	Hibernian	..1	Dumbarton	..9
Sep 27	Inveraray	..4	Oban	..2
	Inverness C	..W	Portland	..0
Sep 27	Jamestown	..2	Mossend S	..5
Sep 27	Kirriemuir	..1	Montrose	..3
Sep 27	Leith A	..7	Falkirk	..2
Sep 27	Linthouse	..7	Maryhill	..2
Sep 27	Monkcastle	..4	Dalry	..3
Sep 27	Morton	..3	Neilston	..2
Sep 27	Newmilns	..2	Uddingston	..2
Sep 27	Penicuik A	..3	Methlan P	..4
Sep 27	Queen's Park	..5	Northern	..1
Sep 27	Rutherglen	..1	Ayr	..3
Sep 27	Saltcoats V	..3	Lanemark	..2
Sep 27	Slamannan	..5	Clydebank	..2
Sep 27	St Mirren	..5	Albion R	..1
Sep 27	T Lanark	..8	Kilmarnock A	..1
Sep 27	Wishaw T	..4	Glasgow H	..1

Replays

Oct 4	Campsie	..1	E Stirling	..3
Oct 4	Carfin S	..1	Celtic	..3
Oct 4	Uddingston	..5	Newmilns	..1
Oct 11	Burnbank S	..3	Stevenston T	..0

After Protest

Oct 11	Slamannan	..3	Clydebank	..5

After Protest

3rd Round

Oct 18	Airdrie	..8	Glengowan	..0
Oct 18	Bathgate	..6	Broxburn	..0
Oct 18	Bo'ness	..1	Mossend S	..1
Oct 18	Cambuslang	..1	St Mirren	..2
Oct 18	Clyde	..3	Ayr	..4
Oct 18	Dumbarton	..6	Clydebank	..0
	Dumfries W	..W	Stranraer	..0
Oct 18	E Stirling	..3	Camelon	..3
Oct 18	Edinburgh Univ	..3	Cowdenbeath	..2
Oct 18	Inverness C	..6	Aberdeen	..2
Oct 18	Kilsyth W	..0	Vale of Leven	..8
Oct 18	Leith A	.12	Adventurers	..0
Oct 18	Linthouse	..3	Abercorn	..4
Oct 18	Methlan Park	..0	Hearts	..3
Oct 18	Monkcastle	..1	Burnbank S	..7
Oct 18	Montrose	..4	Fair City A	..1
Oct 18	Morton	.10	Inveraray	..0
Oct 18	Dundee OB	..4	Dundee East End	..0
Oct 18	Queen's Park	..6	Uddingston	..0
Oct 18	Royal Albert	..6	Saltcoats V	..2
Oct 18	T Lanark	..8	Summerton A	..1
Oct 18	Wilshaw T	..2	Celtic	..6

Replays

Oct 25	Camelon	..6	E Stirling	.10
Oct 25	Mossend S	..9	Bo'ness	..1

4th Round

Nov 8	5th KRV	..6	Arbroath	..2
Nov 8	Abercorn	..8	Bathgate	..0
Nov 8	Airdrie	..1	St Mirren	..2
Nov 8	Ayr	..3	Hearts	..4
Nov 8	Dumbarton	..7	Mossend S	..3
Nov 8	Dundee OB	..1	Celtic	..3
Nov 8	Edinburgh Univ	..0	Queen's Park	..7
Nov 8	E Stirling	..2	Inverness C	..0
Nov 8	Leith A	..3	Vale of Leven	..1
Nov 8	Montrose	..0	T Lanark	..3
Nov 8	Morton	..6	Dumfries W	..4
Nov 8	Royal Albert	..1	Burnbank S	..0

5th Round

Nov 29	Celtic	..2	Royal Albert	..2
Dec 6	Dumbarton	..8	5th KRV	..0
Nov 29	Hearts	..5	Morton	..1
Dec 6	St Mirren	..2	Queen's Park	..3

Replays

Dec 6	Royal Albert	..0	Celtic	..4

Abandoned

Dec 13	Celtic	..2	Royal Albert	..0

played at Ibrox

6th Round

Dec 20	Dumbarton	..3	Celtic	..0
Dec 20	Hearts	..3	E Stirling	..1
Dec 20	Leith A	..2	Abercorn	..3
Jan 10	Queen's Park	..1	T Lanark	..1

Replays

Jan 17	T Lanark	..2	Queen's Park	..2
Jan 24	Queen's Park	..1	T Lanark	..4

Semi-finals

Jan 17	Dumbarton	..3	Abercorn	..1
Jan 31	T Lanark	..1	Hearts	..4

Final

Feb 7	Dumbarton	..0	Hearts	..1

played at Hampden Park

DIVISION 1

	ABERCORN	CAMBUSLANG	CELTIC	COWLAIRS	DUMBARTON	HEARTS	RANGERS	ST MIRREN	T LANARK	VALE OF LEVEN	RENTON
ABERCORN		Dec06 2-5	Oct25 1-5	Mar21 1-0	Dec27 1-2	Apr25 1-0	Feb07 1-1	Jan24 5-1	Oct04 2-4	Mar07 6-0	Sep13 4-2
CAMBUSLANG	Apr11 4-5		Mar07 3-1	Jan17 4-0	Mar21 2-2	May02 2-6	Aug23 2-3	Sep13 3-2	Feb28 2-2	Aug16 8-2	
CELTIC	May12 2-0	Aug30 5-2		Mar14 2-0	Apr11 1-0	Feb28 1-0	Mar21 2-2	Feb07 3-2	Apr25 1-1	May05 2-0	Aug16 1-4
COWLAIRS	Feb28 7-5	Apr18 1-1	Apr29 0-5		Oct25 1-6	Mar07 1-2	Mar28 0-2	Apr25 4-2	Apr11 2-2	Aug23 3-2	
DUMBARTON	Oct11 5-1	Jan24 5-0	Feb21 2-2	Aug16 1-1		Aug30 3-1	Sep13 5-1	Mar07 5-1	Mar28 4-0	Feb28 4-0	
HEARTS	Mar28 1-1	Feb14 2-2	Aug23 0-5	Sep13 4-0	Apr20 0-4		Jan24 0-1	Feb21 4-1	Mar21 8-1	Oct25 8-1	
RANGERS	Mar14 2-0	Feb21 2-1	May02 1-2	Oct18 1-1	Apr25 4-2	Aug16 5-2		Oct04 8-2	May09 4-1	Apr04 4-0	Aug30 4-1
ST MIRREN	Sep20 4-2	Mar28 2-3	Apr04 1-0	Aug30 5-2	May02 2-4	Apr11 3-2	Feb28 3-7		Mar14 3-2	Oct11 1-1	
T LANARK	Apr28 2-1	Apr04 1-2	Sep13 2-1	May06 3-1	Aug23 4-0	Apr18 0-4	Mar07 5-3	Oct25 5-3		Feb21 4-1	
VALE OF LEVEN	Aug30 2-1	Apr25 2-1	Jan24 3-1	Feb07 2-1	Oct04 1-3	May09 2-4	Jan17 1-3	Mar21 5-2	May02 1-2		
RENTON								Aug23 2-2	Sep20 1-2		

DIVISION 1 FINAL TABLE

	P	W	D	L	F	A	Pts
Dumbarton†	18	13	3	2	61	21	29
Rangers†	18	13	3	2	58	25	29
Celtic*	18	11	3	4	48	21	21
Cambuslang	18	8	4	6	47	42	20
T Lanark*	18	8	3	7	38	39	15
Hearts	18	6	2	10	31	37	14
Abercorn	18	5	2	11	36	47	12
St Mirren	18	5	1	12	39	62	11
Vale of Leven	18	5	1	12	27	65	11
Cowlairs*	18	3	4	11	24	50	6

† Dumbarton and Rangers drew 2-2 in a play-off
and were declared joint Champions.
* Each had four points deducted for infringements.

Season 1891-92

SFA Cup
1st Round

Sep 5	Adventurers	0	St Bernard's	5
Sep 5	Alva	1	Stenhousemuir	0
Sep 5	Annbank	5	Ayr Parkhouse	0
Sep 5	Armadale	3	Bathgate	3
Sep 5	Ayr	12	Pollokshaw	0
Sep 5	Beith	2	Arthurlie	2

Arthurlie Awarded Tie

Sep 5	Blairgowrie OB	0	Dunblane	5
Sep 5	Bonnyrigg R	1	Penicuik A	6
Sep 5	Bridge of Allan	7	Dumbarton U	2
Sep 5	Broughty	3	Montrose	3
Sep 5	Broxburn	2	Raith R	1
Sep 5	Burnbank S	5	Hamilton H	1
Sep 5	Burntisland T	4	Linlithgow A	6
Sep 5	Bute R	3	Monkcastle	4
Sep 5	Camelon	1	Dalmuir T	3
Sep 5	Campsie	7	Kilsyth W	3
Sep 5	Cathcart	1	Ayr A	3
Sep 5	Clacknacuddin	0	Inverness C	5
Sep 5	Clydebank	7	Grasshoppers	1
Sep 5	Clydesdale	2	Whitefield	2
Sep 5	Cronberry	2	Hurlford	4
Sep 5	Douglas R	0	Queen of South	14
Sep 12	Dundee	2	Dundee OB	0
Sep 5	Dunfermline A	4	Bo'ness	0
Sep 5	E Stirling	8	Jamestown	2
Sep 5	Forfar A	1	Dundee East End	3
Sep 5	Gairsloch	2	Grangemouth	4
Sep 5	Glasgow W	1	Partick T	2
Sep 5	Hamilton A	1	21st RS Fusilier	4
Sep 5	Inveraray	3	Oban	2
Sep 5	Johnstone	20	Greenock Abst	1
Sep 5	Kilbarchan	10	1st ARV	0
Sep 5	Kilbirnie	2	Morton	2
Sep 5	Kilsyth S	3	Dunipace	4
Sep 5	King's Park	5	Clydebank A	3
Sep 5	Kirkcaldy W	2	Polton Vale	3
Sep 5	Lassosie	0	Cowdenbeath	3
Sep 5	Laurieston	2	Denny	4
Sep 5	Linthouse	12	Carfin H	0
Sep 5	Lochee U	3	Johnstone W	4
Sep 5	Methlan Park	1	Slamannan R	3
Sep 5	Mid Annandale	5	Dumfries	4
Sep 5	Motherwell	1	Cowlairs	4
Sep 5	Muirhouse R	1	Mossend S	7
Sep 5	Neilston	3	Kilmarnock A	6
Sep 5	Newmilns	1	Dykebar	7
Sep 5	Old Kilpatrick	0	Kirkintilloch A	3
Sep 5	Port Glasgow A	6	Lanemark	3
Sep 5	Saltcoats V	6	Lochwinnoch	3
Sep 5	Smithston H	6	Alloa	3
Sep 5	Southern A	1	Royal Albert	6
Sep 5	St Johnstone	2	Fair City A	3
Sep 5	Stevenston T	5	Galston	2
Sep 5	Stewarton	3	Irving	3
Sep 5	Stonehaven	0	Bon Accord	8
Sep 5	Stranraer	2	5th KRV	3
Sep 5	Strathmore	3	Kirriemuir	7
Sep 5	Thistle	6	Shettleston S	1
Sep 5	Vale of Bannoch	5	Slamannan	3
Sep 5	Vale of Gala	3	Selkirk	4
Sep 5	Vale of Leven	1	Coupar Angus	6
Sep 5	Wishaw T	7	Albion R	3

Replays

Sep 12	Bathgate	3	Armadale	0
Sep 12	Brechin	3	Arbroath	9
Sep 12	Dalry	5	Catrine T	0
Sep 12	Montrose	5	Broughty	1
Sep 12	Morton	8	Kilbirnie	1
Sep 12	Orion	5	Victoria U	1
Sep 12	Whitefield	7	Clydesdale	0
	Irving		Stewarton	

2nd Round

Sep 26	Alva	3	Mossend S	9
Sep 26	Annbank	4	Rutherglen	0
Sep 26	Arbroath	7	Fair City A	1
Sep 26	Ayr	3	21st RS Fusilier	3
Oct 3	Ayr A	1	Kilbarchan	4
Sep 26	Bathgate	8	Slamannan R	1
Sep 26	Battlefield	9	Whitefield	0
Sep 26	Bon Accord	2	Aberdeen	5
Sep 26	Bridge of Allan	3	Clackmannan	0
Sep 26	Broxburn S	6	Campsie	4
Sep 26	Carrington	2	Burnbank S	8
Sep 26	Coupar Angus	4	Montrose	0
Sep 26	Dalry	9	Stewarton	0
Sep 26	Denny	2	Dunfermline A	1
Sep 26	Dundee H	5	Johnstone W	2
Sep 26	Duntocher H	4	Broxburn	2
Sep 26	Dykebar	1	Mauchline	4
Sep 26	E Stirling	3	King's Park	0
Sep 26	Grangemouth	0	Falkirk	2
Sep 26	Inveraray	4	Oban R	2
Sep 26	Johnstone	4	Thistle	7
Sep 26	Kirkintilloch A	4	Polton Vale	2
Sep 26	Kirriemuir	1	Dunblane	8
Sep 26	Morton	3	Airdrie	1
Sep 26	Newton Stewart	1	Mid-Annandale	1
Sep 26	Partick T	0	Hurlford	3
Sep 26	Penicuik A	2	Dalmuir T	3
Sep 26	Port Glasgow A	4	Glengowan	1
Sep 26	Queen of South	6	Moffat	1
Sep 26	Royal Albert	6	Cowlairs	6
Sep 26	Smithston H	11	Linlithgow A	1
Sep 26	St Bernard's	7	Dunipace	1
Sep 26	Stevenston T	3	Kilmarnock A	3
Sep 26	Vale of Atholl	1	Dundee East End	7
Sep 26	Vale of Bannoch	0	Clydebank	7
Sep 26	Wishaw T	5	Arthurlie	2

Replays

Oct 3	Broxburn S	3	Campsie	1

After Protest

Oct 3	Cowlairs	4	Royal Albert	4

Both In Next Round

Oct 3	E Stirling	7	King's Park	2

After Protest

Oct 3	Kilmarnock A	2	Stevenston T	2

Both In Next Round

Oct 3	Mid-Allondale	W	Newton Stewart	0
Oct 3	21st Rs Fusilier	1	Ayr	3

3rd Round

Oct 17	Aberdeen	3	Orion	1
Oct 17	Annbank	2	Hurlford	0
Oct 17	Ayr	6	Inveraray	1
Oct 17	Bathgate	5	Falkirk	5
Oct 17	Battlefield	4	Stevenston T	2
Oct 17	Bridge of Allan	4	Duntocher H	2
Oct 17	Burnbank S	5	Mauchline	0
Oct 17	Coupar Angus	2	Dunblane	3
Oct 17	Cowdenbeath	0	Clydebank	3
Oct 17	Cowlairs	5	Dalry	0
Oct 17	Denny	6	Edinburgh U	1
Oct 17	Dundee East End	1	Dundee H	1
Oct 17	Inverness	2	Inverness C	1
Oct 17	Kilmarnock A	5	Port Glasgow A	4
Oct 17	Monkcastle	4	Morton	2
Oct 17	Mossend S	4	E Stirling	5
Oct 17	Queen of South	4	5th KRV	7
Oct 17	Saltcoats V	1	Linthouse	7
Oct 17	Smithston H	1	Broxburn S	2
Oct 17	St Bernard's	5	Kirkintilloch	1
Oct 17	Thistle	9	Kilbarchan	1
Oct 17	Wishaw T	3	Royal Albert	2

Replays

Oct 24 Dunblane ....W Coupar Angus ...0
After Protest
Oct 24 Dundee H ....0 Dundee East End ..2
Oct 24 Falkirk ....0 Bathgate 3

4th Round

Nov 7 Annbank .... Wishaw T ....
Nov 7 Arbroath ....10 Denny 0
Nov 7 Bathgate ....5 Clydebank 1
Nov 7 Cowlairs ....9 5th KRV 3
Nov 7 Dalmuir T ....1 Aberdeen 2
Nov 7 Dundee East End ..3 Monkcastle 6
Nov 7 Inverness T ....0 Battlefield 1
Nov 7 Thistle ....5 Burnbank S 2

5th Round

Nov 28 Abercorn ....2 Queen's Park ...3
Nov 28 Annbank ....2 Battlefield 1
Nov 28 Bathgate ....6 Linthouse 0
Nov 28 Broxburn S ......7 Northern 2
Dec 12 Cowlairs ....3 Cambuslang 1
Nov 28 Dumbarton ....4 Thistle 0
Nov 28 E Stirling ....1 Kilmarnock 6
Nov 28 Hearts ....3 Clyde 1
Abandoned
Nov 28 Kilmarnock A ....7 Bridge of Allan ...2
Nov 28 Leith A ....5 Dunblane 0
Dec 5 Mid-Annandale ..6 Aberdeen 2
Nov 28 Monkcastle .....3 Arbroath 4
Nov 28 Rangers ....5 St Bernard's 1
Nov 28 Renton ....7 Ayr 4
Nov 28 St Mirren ....2 Celtic 4
Nov 28 T Lanark ....3 Vale of Leven ...0

Replays

Dec 5 Hearts ....8 Clyde 0
Dec 12 Cowlairs ....3 Cambuslang 1
After Protest

6th Round

Dec 19 Annbank ....2 Leith A 1
Dec 19 Arbroath ....0 Renton 3
Dec 19 Broxburn S ......4 Hearts 5
Dec 19 Celtic ....3 Kilmarnock A 0
Dec 19 Cowlairs ....11 Mid-Annandale ...2
Dec 19 Queen's Park .....6 Bathgate 0
Dec 19 Rangers ....0 Kilmarnock 0
Dec 19 T Lanark ....1 Dumbarton 3

Replays

Dec 26 Kilmarnock ......1 Rangers 1
Jan 23 Kilmarnock ......2 Rangers 3
played at St Mirren

7th Round

Jan 23 Celtic ....4 Cowlairs 1
Jan 23 Dumbarton ....2 Queen's Park ...2
Jan 30 Rangers ....2 Annbank 0
Jan 23 Renton ....4 Hearts 4

Replays

Jan 30 Hearts ....2 Renton 2
Jan 30 Queen's Park ....4 Dumbarton 1
Feb 6 Hearts ....2 Renton 3
played at Hampden Park

Semi-finals

Feb 6 Celtic ....5 Rangers 3
Feb 13 Renton ....1 Queen's Park ...1

Replay

Feb 27 Queen's Park .....3 Renton 0

Final

Mar 12 Celtic ....1 Queen's Park ...0
played at Ibrox

Replay Crowd Trouble
Apr 9 Celtic ....5 Queen's Park 1
played at Ibrox

DIVISION 1 FINAL TABLE

	P	W	D	L	F	A	Pts
Dumbarton	22	18	1	3	78	27	37
Celtic	22	16	3	3	62	21	35
Hearts	22	15	4	3	65	35	34
Leith A	22	12	1	9	51	40	25
Rangers	22	11	2	9	59	46	24
T Lanark	22	8	5	9	44	47	21
Renton	22	8	5	9	37	43	21
Clyde	22	8	4	10	63	61	20
Abercorn	22	6	5	11	44	59	17
St Mirren	22	5	5	12	43	60	15
Cambuslang	22	2	6	14	21	53	10
Vale of Leven	22	0	5	17	24	99	5

DIVISION 1

	ABERCORN	CAMBUSLANG	CELTIC	CLYDE	DUMBARTON	HEARTS	LEITH A	RANGERS	RENTON	ST MIRREN	T LANARK	VALE OF LEVEN
ABERCORN		Feb06 3-1	Sep12 2-5	Dec26 3-3	May07 1-1	Mar12 1-3	Aug29 3-2	Mar26 0-1	Nov14 0-3	Sep19 1-1	Oct24 2-4	Oct10 6-3
CAMBUSLANG	Oct03 0-2		Jan30 0-4	Jan23 3-5	Aug15 0-2	Sep05 3-3	Sep26 1-3	Feb21 0-6	Apr30 1-1	Aug29 1-1	Apr09 1-1	Nov21 1-0
CELTIC	Apr30 3-1	Apr16 2-0		Mar19 0-0	Sep26 2-0	Oct17 3-0	May14 3-0	Aug22 2-1	Sep05 5-1	Dec26 6-1	Feb27	Oct24
CLYDE	Jan30 7-2	Dec19 2-0	Aug29 2-7		Apr30 4-1	Oct03 3-101-2	May07 1-1	May21 1-3	Apr04 4-1	Sep12 3-3	Apr23 10-3	Aug15
DUMBARTON	Aug22 8-1	Mar26 5-2	Apr23 1-0	Nov14 8-2		Sep19 5-1	Sep12 6-0	May04 6-0	Dec26 2-1	Oct24 4-2	Oct17 2-0	Dec12 8-0
HEARTS	Sep21 2-1	Dec26 1-0	Aug15 3-1	Apr16 2-1	Aug29 3-1		Oct24 3-1	Apr23 4-2	Sep12 2-2	Oct10 2-0	Sep26 3-1	Mar19 7-0
LEITH A	Oct17 3-2	May05 3-0	Apr18 2-1	Sep05 1-0	Oct31 1-3	Apr30 2-2		Oct03 3-1	Aug22 2-3	Sep21 4-2	Nov14 2-2	Sep19 10-0
RANGERS	Sep26 6-2	Oct17 2-1	May07 1-1	Oct24 1-5	Sep05 1-3	Nov21 0-1	Apr16 3-2		Mar19 5-2	May10 2-3	Aug29 2-3	Feb13 7-0
RENTON	Dec05 2-1	Oct24 1-1	May05 0-4	Sep26 2-1	Nov07 1-2	Apr09 0-3	Oct10 3-0	Aug15 1-4		Mar12 5-2	Nov21 1-0	Aug29 3-0
ST MIRREN	Feb27 0-3	Apr23 1-2	Oct03 1-4	Apr02 2-3	Mar19 2-5	Aug22 3-1	Nov07 3-4	Dec05 2-1	Oct17		Sep05 1-2	Sep26 6-4
T LANARK	Mar19 1-1	Sep12 3-1	May24 1-3	Feb13 3-2	Dec05 2-5	May07 3-2	Aug15 0-3	Oct10 2-2	Oct03 1-1	Jan23 2-3		Dec26 9-2
VALE OF LEVEN	Sep05 0-3	Aug22 0-1	Apr02 2-2	Oct17 2-2	Oct03 1-2	Oct31 2-2	Jan30 0-3	Sep12 1-6	May07 1-1	Nov14 2-2	Feb06 0-2	

SFA Cup

1st Round

Nov 26 5th KRV ....5 Camelon 3
Nov 26 Abercorn ....6 Renton 0
Nov 26 Aberdeen ....4 St Mirren 6
Nov 26 Airdrie ....3 T Lanark 6
Nov 26 Albion R ....1 Kilmarnock 2
Nov 26 Celtic ....3 Linthouse 1
Nov 26 Clyde ....4 Dumbarton 1
Nov 26 Cowlairs ....2 Queen's Park ...5
Nov 26 Dunblane ....0 Broxburn S 3
Nov 26 King's Park ......6 Monkcastle 2
Nov 26 Motherwell .....9 Campsie 2
Nov 26 Northern ....1 Leith A 3
Nov 26 Rangers ....7 Annbank 0
Nov 26 Royal Albert .....6 Cambuslang 1

Nov 26 St Bernard's ......5 Queen of S'th W ..1
Nov 26 Stenhousemuir ....1 Hearts 1

Replays

Dec 17 Dumbarton ....6 Clyde 1
After Protest
Dec 17 Hearts ....8 Stenhousemuir ...0
Dec 17 Motherwell .....6 Campsie 4
After Protest
Jan 21 Queen's Park ....4 Cowlairs 1
After Protest

2nd Round

Dec 17 Abercorn ....4 T Lanark 5
Dec 17 Broxburn S ......3 King's Park 0
Dec 17 Celtic ....7 5th KRV 0

Jan 28 Kilmarnock ......0 Queen's Park 8
Dec 17 Leith A ....0 St Mirren 2
Dec 24 Motherwell .....2 Hearts 4
Jan 21 Rangers ....1 Dumbarton 0
Dec 17 Royal Albert ......1 St Bernard's 1

Replay

Dec 24 St Bernard's ......5 Royal Albert 2

3rd Round

Jan 21 Broxburn S ......4 St Mirren 3
Jan 21 Celtic ....5 T Lanark 1
Feb 4 Hearts ....1 Queen's Park ...1
Jan 28 St Bernard's ......3 Rangers 2

Replay

Feb 11 Queen's Park ...5 Hearts 2

Semi-finals

Feb 4   Celtic ....5 St Bernard's 0
Feb 18 Queen's Park ...4 Broxburn S 2

Final

Feb 25 Celtic ....1 Queen's Park ..0
played at Ibrox

Replay Because of Pitch

Mar 11 Celtic ....1 Queen's Park ..2
played at Ibrox

DIVISION 1 FINAL TABLE

	P	W	D	L	F	A	Pts
Celtic	18	14	1	3	54	25	29
Rangers	18	12	4	2	41	27	28
St Mirren	18	9	2	7	40	39	20
T Lanark	18	9	1	8	53	39	19
Hearts	18	8	2	8	39	41	18
Leith A	18	8	1	9	35	31	17
Dumbarton	18	8	1	9	35	35	17
Renton	18	5	5	8	31	44	15
Abercorn	18	5	1	12	35	52	11
Clyde	18	2	2	14	25	55	6

DIVISION 1

	ABERCORN	CELTIC	CLYDE	DUMBARTON	HEARTS	LEITH A	RANGERS	RENTON	ST MIRREN	T LANARK
ABERCORN		Feb11 4-2	Nov05 5-1	Apr29 4-0	Sep03 3-4	Sep24 1-0	Aug20 0-4	Oct15 1-2	Mar04 1-2	May06 5-2
CELTIC	Sep10 3-2		Oct01 3-1	Mar18 5-1	Nov05 5-0	May09 3-1	Apr29 3-0	Aug20 4-3	May02 4-1	May18 2-5
CLYDE	Aug27 5-2	May06 1-2		Feb18 1-2	Oct15 2-3	Apr22 1-2	Mar11 0-3	Sep24 2-2	Feb11 1-2	Sep03 1-4
DUMBARTON	Oct22 5-1	Oct15 0-3	Apr15 3-1		Apr01 5-1	Sep10 2-1	Apr22 3-0	Mar04 1-1	Aug20 1-2	Sep24 1-2
HEARTS	Mar11 3-1	Aug27 3-1	Apr29 2-3	Oct08 1-3		Apr15 3-1	Mar18 1-2	Sep10 2-2	Apr04 4-0	May04 2-2
LEITH A	Mar25 1-1	Jan28 0-1	Aug20 0-3	Nov19 1-0	Sep17 1-3		Oct01 1-2	Apr01 6-2	Nov05 5-1	Oct15 2-1
RANGERS	Feb04 4-3	Sep24 2-2	Oct22 4-2	Sep03 3-2	May06 2-1	Aug27 3-2		Apr15 2-0	Oct15 0-0	Apr01 2-1
RENTON	Feb11 2-1	Mar25 0-2	Mar18 1-1	May20 0-4	Oct01 4-1	Feb04 2-3	Nov05 2-2		Sep03 3-2	Feb04 3-1
ST MIRREN	Sep17 4-0	Oct22 1-3	Sep10 8-1	Oct01 1-3	Feb18 3-1	Feb04 4-1	Mar25 2-2	Mar11 3-0		Aug27 1-4
T LANARK	Oct01 8-0	Apr22 0-6	Jan28 4-1	Nov05 3-0	Aug20 1-4	Mar18 1-2	Sep10 2-4	Oct22 6-2	Apr29 6-1	

Season 1893-94

SFA Cup

1st Round

Nov 25 Abercorn ....2 5th KRV 1
Nov 25 Albion R ....6 Black Watch ..0
Nov 25 Broxburn S ..3 Arbroath 8
Nov 25 Cambuslang .3 E Stirling 2
Nov 25 Celtic ......6 Hurlford 0
Nov 25 Clyde .....5 King's Park ..2
Nov 25 Grangemouth 1 Renton 7
Nov 25 Kilmarnock ..1 St Bernard's ..3
Nov 25 Leith A ....11 Orion 2
Nov 25 Linthouse ..1 Queen's Park .5
Nov 25 Port Glasgow A 7 Airdrie 5
Nov 25 Rangers ....8 Cowlairs 0
Nov 25 St Mirren ...1 Hearts 0
Nov 25 Thistle .....1 Battlefield ...3
Nov 25 T Lanark ....9 Inverness 3
Nov 25 Vale of Leven 1 Dumbarton ..2

2nd Round

Dec 16 Battlefield ...3 Abercorn ...3
Dec 16 Celtic ......7 Albion R 0
Dec 16 Clyde .....6 Cambuslang .0
Dec 16 Dumbarton ...1 St Bernard's ..3
Dec 16 Queen's Park .3 Arbroath 0
Dec 16 Rangers ....2 Leith A 0
Dec 16 Renton .....2 Port Glasgow A 2
Dec 16 T Lanark ....3 St Mirren 2

Replays

Dec 23 Abercorn ....3 Battlefield ...0
Dec 23 Renton .....1 Port Glasgow A 3

3rd Round

Jan 13 Abercorn ....3 Queen's Park .3
Jan 13 Celtic .....8 St Bernard's ..1
Jan 13 Clyde ......0 Rangers 5
Jan 13 T Lanark ....2 Port Glasgow A 1

Replays

Jan 20 Queen's Park 3 Abercorn ...3
Jan 27 Abercorn ...0 Queen's Park 2
played at Ibrox

Semi-finals

Feb 3 Rangers ....1 Queen's Park 1
Feb 3 T Lanark ...3 Celtic 5

Replay

Feb 10 Queen's Park 1 Rangers ...3

Final

Feb 17 Celtic ......1 Rangers ...3
played at Hampden Park

DIVISION 1 FINAL TABLE

	P	W	D	L	F	A	Pts
Celtic	18	14	1	3	53	32	29
Hearts	18	11	4	3	46	32	26
St Bernard's	18	11	1	6	53	39	23
Rangers	18	8	4	6	44	30	20
Dumbarton	18	7	5	6	32	35	19
St Mirren	18	7	3	8	49	47	17
T Lanark	18	7	3	8	38	44	17
Dundee	18	6	3	9	47	49	15
Leith A	18	4	2	12	36	46	10
Renton	18	1	2	15	23	57	4

DIVISION 2 FINAL TABLE

	P	W	D	L	F	A	Pts
Hibernian	18	13	3	2	83	29	29
Cowlairs	18	13	1	4	72	32	27
Clyde†	18	11	2	5	51	36	24
Motherwell	18	11	1	6	61	46	23
Partick T	18	10	0	8	56	58	20
Port Glasgow A*	18	9	2	7	52	52	13
Abercorn	18	5	2	11	42	60	12
Morton	18	4	1	13	36	62	9
Northern	18	3	3	12	29	66	9
Thistle	18	2	3	13	31	72	7

* Port Glasgow Athletic had 7 points deducted for fielding an ineligible player
† Clyde promoted to First Division

DIVISION 1

	CELTIC	DUMBARTON	DUNDEE	HEARTS	LEITH A	RANGERS	RENTON	ST BERNARD'S	ST MIRREN	T LANARK
CELTIC		Aug26 0-0	Nov04 3-1	Mar10 2-3	Aug23 4-1	Feb24 3-2	Dec02 3-2	Oct14 5-2	Feb10 5-1	Aug12 5-0
DUMBARTON	Dec23 4-5		Sep16 1-1	Sep30 2-2	Feb03 3-1	Jan20 2-0	Nov18 2-0	Oct21 1-5	Sep21 3-3	Mar17 2-1
DUNDEE	Aug19 1-4	Dec09 4-0		Oct21 2-5	Nov11 4-3	Aug12 3-3	Feb10 4-2	Sep30 1-3	Sep23 0-3	Feb24 1-1
HEARTS	Sep09 2-4	Apr28 2-1	Dec16 3-0		Aug19 0-2	Oct14 4-2	Mar03 5-1	Apr07 2-4	Nov18 1-1	Sep23 2-2
LEITH A	Mar17 5-0	Oct28 2-4	Sep09 3-5	Dec02 2-2		Sep30 2-2	Oct21 2-1	Apr14 4-2	Sep02 2-5	Apr14 2-3
RANGERS	Sep02 5-0	Sep23 2-4	Mar10 7-2	Apr14 1-2	Nov04 1-0		Aug19 5-3	May02 1-2	Apr21 4-2	Dec23 2-3
RENTON	Nov11 0-3	Oct07 1-1	Aug26 2-3	Nov04 1-3	Feb17 2-1	Sep09 1-2		Oct28 0-1	Dec09 0-4	Jan27 0-3
ST BERNARD'S	Jan20 1-2	Nov04 2-1	Jan27 3-5	Oct07 1-2	Mar10 3-2	Aug26 0-0	Sep23 4-2		Mar31 8-3	Oct21 6-2
ST MIRREN	Sep30 1-2	Nov11 1-2	Feb17 10-3	Aug26 2-3	Oct14 3-1	Jan27 2-1	Sep16 4-2	Sep09 1-3		Nov04 4-2
T LANARK	Dec30 1-3	Sep09 1-3	Oct14 4-3	Sep02 1-3	Aug26 2-1	Nov11 1-2	Sep30 3-3	Aug19 5-3	Jan20 3-1	

DIVISION 2

	ABERCORN	CLYDE	COWLAIRS	HIBERNIAN	MORTON	MOTHERWELL	NORTHERN	PARTICK T	PORT GLASGOW A	THISTLE
ABERCORN		Sep23 0-2	Dec02 0-4	Mar03 3-3	Feb03 2-1	Aug19 2-3	Oct21 4-2	Feb10 2-3	Mar31 0-3	Apr14 5-2
CLYDE	Nov11 5-4		Dec23 1-1	Sep09 0-4	Oct21 5-0	Apr21 3-2	Mar17 2-1	Sep30 3-2	Aug19 2-2	Oct07 6-1
COWLAIRS	Feb24 7-1	Mar31 2-1		Mar17 2-3	Apr14 7-3	May05 4-1	Sep09 7-0	Apr07 8-1	May12 5-1	Aug12 4-2
HIBERNIAN	Sep16 7-2	Mar10 4-3	Oct07 3-4		Aug26 9-2	Nov25 6-0	Apr07 6-0	Feb03 10-1	May19 4-0	Nov04 6-1
MORTON	Mar24 0-2	Apr07 1-3	Sep30 4-2	Dec02 0-1		Nov11 2-3	Feb17 7-1	Aug19 2-3	Sep16 1-0	Apr21 1-1
MOTHERWELL	Feb17 5-3	Apr12 4-1	Aug26 3-2	Apr14 2-1	May02 4-1		May19 2-0	Feb03 2-3	Sep30 7-2	Dec16 6-2
NORTHERN	Mar10 5-2	Aug26 1-3	Mar03 2-2	Sep30 2-7	Apr28 2-2	Dec02 1-8		Dec23 2-1	Apr21 0-1	Feb03 13-1
PARTICK T	Aug26 0-3	Feb24 5-4	Jan13 5-3	Mar31 1-7	Oct14 5-2	Oct07 4-2	Nov25 4-3		Mar24 0-1	Mar10 13-1
PORT GLASGOW A	Sep09 5-4	Feb03 1-4	Apr07 1-3	Oct21 3-3	May05 10-1	May12 5-3	Aug12 6-1	Jan20 4-1		Aug26 4-3
THISTLE	Sep30 3-3	Sep02 1-3	Feb10 1-3	Aug19 1-2	Sep09 2-1	Mar24 1-8	Oct14 3-0	Oct21 3-4	Dec02 1-2	

Season 1894-95

SFA Cup

1st Round
Nov 24 Abercorn ....1 Leith A 5
Nov 24 Annbank ....5 T Lanark ...4
Nov 24 Ayr Parkhouse 5 Polton Vale .3
Nov 24 Celtic .....4 Queen's Park 1
Nov 24 Clyde ......7 Stevenston T 2
Nov 24 Dumbarton ..2 Galston 1
Nov 24 Dundee .....5 Orion 1
   played at Aberdeen
Nov 24 Hibernian ...6 Forfar A 1
Nov 24 Kilmarnock ..5 E Stirling ...1
Nov 24 Lochee .....2 King's Park .5
Nov 24 Motherwell ..1 Mossend S .2
Nov 24 Raith R .....6 5th KRV 3
Nov 24 Rangers ....1 Hearts 2
Nov 24 Slamannan ..2 Renton 3
Nov 24 St Bernard's .4 Airdrie 2
Nov 24 St Mirren ..5 Battlefield .. 0

Replays
Dec 8 Abercorn ....4 Leith 1
   After Protest
Dec 8 Renton .....4 Slamannan .0
   After Protest
Dec 8 St Mirren ...8 Battlefield ..1
   After Protest

2nd Round
Dec 15 Abercorn ....1 Hearts 6
Dec 15 Ayr Parkhouse 3 Mossend S .1
Dec 15 Clyde ......4 Annbank ...2
Dec 15 Dundee .....2 St Mirren .. 0
Dec 15 Hibernian ...2 Celtic 0
Dec 15 King's Park ..2 Dumbarton .1
Dec 15 Renton .....6 5th KRV 0
Dec 15 St Bernard's ..3 Kilmarnock .1

Replay
Dec 29 Celtic ......2 Hibernian .. 0
   After Protest

3rd Round
Jan 19 Ayr Parkhouse 2 Renton ...3
Feb 2 Clyde ......2 St Bernard's .6
Jan 19 Dundee .....1 Celtic 0
Jan 12 Hearts ......4 King's Park .2

Replay
Feb 23 Clyde ......1 St Bernard's .2
   After Protest

Semi-finals
Feb 16 Dundee .....1 Renton 1
Mar 3 St Bernard's ..0 Hearts 0

Replays
Feb 23 Dundee .....3 Renton 3
   played at Hampden Park
Mar 9 Dundee .....0 Renton 3
   played at Celtic Park
Mar 16 Hearts ......0 St Bernard's .1
   played at Logie Green

Final
Apr 20 Renton ......1 St Bernard's .2
played at Ibrox

DIVISION 1

DIVISION 1	CELTIC	CLYDE	DUMBARTON	DUNDEE	HEARTS	LEITH A	RANGERS	ST BERNARD'S	ST MIRREN	T LANARK
CELTIC	—	Apr27 2-0	Oct20 6-0	May04 2-1	Nov03 0-2	Mar16 4-0	Sep22 5-3	Aug18 5-2	Dec22 2-2	Feb23 4-4
CLYDE	Oct13 2-4	—	Mar16 3-1	May18 3-2	Nov03 3-2	Aug25 6-2	Dec08 0-5	Sep08 1-4	May11 0-2	Sep29 4-3
DUMBARTON	Mar09 0-2	Nov03 2-3	—	Oct13 2-4	Sep29 1-4	Sep01 3-2	Dec01 1-0	Sep15 3-4	Mar30 4-1	Mar02 2-4
DUNDEE	Aug11 1-1	Aug18 4-1	Sep08 3-0	—	Dec22 0-2	Dec01 4-1	Jan26 2-1	Sep29 2-2	Mar16 0-1	Nov03 1-2
HEARTS	Feb16 4-0	Dec01 2-4	Oct27 3-1	Mar30 4-0	—		Sep15 3-1	Jan19 0-0	Oct06 4-3	Sep01 1-0
LEITH A	Mar30 5-6	Mar02 2-1	Apr06 3-2	Oct20 3-2	Nov17 1-4	—	Sep08 3-4	Oct13 0-2	Aug18 1-2	Sep22 3-2
RANGERS	Mar23 1-1	Feb22 4-1	Aug18 3-0	Sep01 1-0	Oct20 0-1	Nov03 5-1	—	Apr27 2-1	Sep29 4-3	Feb16 0-1
ST BERNARD'S	Nov10 0-2	Sep22 0-3	Dec22 5-0	Dec08 2-0	Sep17 0-3	Aug25 6-3		—	Nov03 2-0	Oct20 2-4
ST MIRREN	Sep08 0-3	Oct20 4-2	Sep22 4-3	Sep15 5-1	Oct13 1-2	Nov10 3-2	Mar09 4-2	Mar23 0-1	—	Dec01 2-0
T LANARK	Aug25 2-1	Apr06 4-2	Nov10 6-3	Apr27 1-3	Sep08 0-3	Dec22 7-1	Oct13 4-0	May11 4-0	Apr04 4-0	—

DIVISION 2

DIVISION 2	ABERCORN	AIRDRIE	COWLAIRS	DUNDEE W	HIBERNIAN	MORTON	MOTHERWELL	PARTICK T	PORT GLASGOW A	RENTON
ABERCORN	—	Apr27 3-1	Aug25 3-0	Apr13 9-2	Sep01 1-5	Mar23 5-3	May04 4-3	Jan19 3-3	Mar16 3-3	Nov10 3-2
AIRDRIE	Apr20 4-0	—	May11 4-3	Dec01 15-1	May25 2-4	Sep08 6-1	Dec29 2-2	Sep30 9-0	Aug25 4-2	Oct06 4-1
COWLAIRS	Mar30 3-3	Nov10 4-4	—	Apr27 2-1	Mar16 2-8	Feb23 2-4	Sep29 4-3	Dec15 3-3	Dec01 0-3	Apr13 3-1
DUNDEE W	Mar02 3-4	Oct20 1-2	Apr06 6-3	—	Nov10 0-6	Apr08 0-1	Aug25 2-2	Mar09 6-5	Sep15 9-1	Mar16 4-5
HIBERNIAN	Nov03 4-2	Sep15 6-1	Dec22 8-2	Sep08 8-2	—	Oct20 6-3	Feb02 5-0	Apr06 3-3	May04 9-1	
MORTON	Sep15 5-1	Apr06 3-1	Apr20 6-0	Dec15 7-3	Oct13 1-7	—	Mar16 3-5	Nov24 4-2	Feb02 4-3	Aug25 5-1
MOTHERWELL	Sep08 7-0	Aug11 4-2	May18 4-0	Mar30 5-0	Oct06 2-0	Mar09 6-4	—	Apr06 3-0	Apr20 2-0	Dec01 0-2
PARTICK T	Feb23 5-1	Dec22 3-2	Jan05 4-2	Apr13 5-2	Sep29 0-4	Apr13 4-4	Sep29 5-3	—	May25 5-0	Mar23 0-1
PORT GLASGOW A	Oct20 5-1	May04 5-4	Aug11 5-3	Mar23 6-2	Mar09 2-2	Nov10 9-1	Aug18 3-1	Sep08 1-3	—	Mar30 4-3
RENTON	Dec29 8-2	Aug18 2-1	Oct13 4-1	Aug29 3-2	Nov17 2-0	Dec22 3-4	Sep15 1-3	May18 4-2	May11	—

DIVISION 1 FINAL TABLE

	P	W	D	L	F	A	Pts
Hearts	18	15	1	2	50	18	31
Celtic	18	11	4	3	50	29	26
Rangers	18	10	2	6	41	26	22
T Lanark	18	10	1	7	51	39	21
St Mirren	18	9	1	8	34	34	19
St Bernard's	18	8	1	9	37	40	17
Clyde	18	8	0	10	38	47	16
Dundee	18	6	2	10	28	33	14
Leith A	18	3	1	14	32	64	7
Dumbarton	18	3	1	14	27	58	7

DIVISION 2 FINAL TABLE

	P	W	D	L	F	A	Pts
Hibernian†	18	14	2	2	92	28	30
Motherwell	18	10	2	6	56	39	22
Port Glasgow A	18	8	4	6	62	56	20
Renton*	17	10	0	7	46	44	20
Morton	18	9	1	8	59	63	19
Airdrie	18	8	2	8	68	45	18
Patrick	18	8	2	8	51	59	18
Abercorn	18	7	3	8	48	66	17
Dundee Wand*	17	3	1	13	44	86	9
Cowlairs	18	2	3	13	37	77	7

† Hibernian elected to First Division
* Dundee Wanderers and Renton played each other only once. Dundee were awarded two points when Renton failed to turn up for the return fixture.

Season 1895-96

1st Round
Jan 18 Annbank .....3 Kilmarnock 2
Jan 11 Arbroath ....5 King's Park 0
Jan 18 Ayr ....3 Abercorn 2
Jan 11 Blantyre ....1 Hearts 12
Jan 18 Celtic ....2 Queen's Park ...4
Jan 18 Dumbarton ....1 Rangers 1
Jan 11 E Stirling .....2 Hibernian 3
Jan 11 Lochgelly U ...2 Raith R 1
Jan 11 Morton ....2 Dundee 3
Jan 11 Polton Vale ...0 Clyde 3
Jan 18 Port Glasgow A .4 Arthurlie 2
Jan 11 Renton ....1 Cowdenbeath ...0
Jan 11 St Bernard's ....8 Clackmannan ...1
Jan 11 St Johnstone ...4 Dundee W 3
Jan 11 St Mirren .....7 Alloa 0
Jan 18 T Lanark ......6 Leith A 0

Season 1895-96 cont.

Replay
Jan 25 Rangers ....3 Dumbarton 1
Feb 1 Lochgelly U ....2 Raith R 5
After Protest

2nd Round
Jan 25 Arbroath ....3 St Johnstone ...1
Feb 1 Ayr ....1 Hearts 5
Feb 8 Hibernian ....6 Raith R 1
Jan 25 Queen's Park ...8 Port Glasgow A .1
Feb 1 Rangers ....5 St Mirren 0
Jan 25 Renton ....2 Clyde 1
Jan 25 St Bernard's ....2 Annbank 0
Jan 25 T Lanark ....4 Dundee 1

3rd Round
Feb 8 Arbroath ....0 Hearts 4
Feb 8 Queen's Park ...2 St Bernard's 3
Feb 15 Rangers ....2 Hibernian 3
Feb 8 T Lanark ....3 Renton 3

Replay
Feb 15 Renton ....2 T Lanark 0

Semi-finals
Feb 22 Hearts ....1 St Bernard's ...0
Feb 22 Hibernian ....2 Renton 1

Final
Mar 14 Hearts ....3 Hibernian 1
played at Logie Green

DIVISION 1 FINAL TABLE

	P	W	D	L	F	A	Pts
Celtic	18	15	0	3	64	25	30
Rangers	18	11	4	3	57	39	26
Hibernian	18	11	2	5	58	39	24
Hearts	18	11	0	7	68	36	22
Dundee	18	7	2	9	33	42	16
T Lanark	18	7	1	10	47	51	15
St Bernard's	18	7	1	10	36	53	15
St Mirren	18	5	3	10	31	51	13
Clyde	18	4	3	11	39	59	11
Dumbarton	18	4	0	14	36	74	8

DIVISION 2 FINAL TABLE

	P	W	D	L	F	A	Pts
Abercorn*	18	12	3	3	55	31	27
Leith A	18	11	1	6	55	37	23
Renton	18	9	3	6	40	28	21
Kilmarnock	18	10	1	7	50	45	21
Airdrieonians	18	7	4	7	48	44	18
Partick T	18	8	2	8	44	54	18
Port Glasgow A	18	6	4	8	40	41	16
Motherwell	18	5	3	10	31	52	13
Morton	18	4	4	10	32	40	12
Linthouse	18	5	1	12	25	48	11

* Abercorn elected to First Division

DIVISION 1

	CELTIC	CLYDE	DUMBARTON	DUNDEE	HEARTS	HIBERNIAN	RANGERS	ST BERNARD'S	ST MIRREN	T LANARK
CELTIC		Aug17 3-0	Dec21 11-0	Oct26 5-0	Sep14 0-5	Oct05 3-1	Dec14 6-2	Dec07 2-1	Aug31 4-0	Nov09 7-0
CLYDE	Oct12 1-5		Nov30 5-1	Sep07 0-1	Aug24 1-2	Feb01 0-3	Feb08 2-2	Sep28 5-0	Nov23 1-3	Feb22 2-7
DUMBARTON	Sep28 2-3	Aug31 5-4		1-2	Oct19 2-9	Nov09 1-3	Aug17 3-5	Oct26 4-3	4-2	Dec14 2-4
DUNDEE	Aug10 1-2	Dec14 1-2	Aug24 4-1		Oct12 5-0	Aug31 0-2	Nov30 1-3	Oct05 2-2	Sep21 1-3	Nov23 2-0
HEARTS	Nov23 1-4	Oct05 9-1	Feb15 7-0	Nov02 2-0		Sep28 4-3	Aug31 1-2	Dec14 6-0	Oct26 5-1	Sep07 3-0
HIBERNIAN	Aug24 4-2	Sep14 4-3	7-2	Jan18 3-1	Dec21 3-2		Oct12 1-1	Nov30 2-3	Oct12 5-1	Dec07 2-5
RANGERS	Sep07 2-4	Nov09 4-4	Jan04 3-1	Feb29 2-1	Dec07 3-2	Nov23 7-2		Oct12 4-0	Feb22 3-3	Aug24 0-4
ST BERNARD'S	Sep16 3-0	Feb15 1-4	Sep07 4-3	Aug17 4-2	Sep21 0-5	Oct19 2-5	Sep14 3-4		Nov09 4-3	Feb01 4-1
ST MIRREN	Nov30 1-3	Dec07 2-2	Nov02 1-2	Sep28 3-1	Sep21 2-1	Sep07 1-3	Oct05 1-7	Aug24 1-3		Mar07 3-2
T LANARK	Feb29 1-2	Oct26 6-2	Oct05 5-2	Sep14 3-4	Nov30 5-4	Aug17 2-7	Dec21 2-3	Aug31 0-0	Apr04 0-2	

DIVISION 2

	ABERCORN	AIRDRIE	KILMARNOCK	LEITH A	LINTHOUSE	MORTON	MOTHERWELL	PARTICK T	PORT GLASGOW A	RENTON
ABERCORN		Oct12 5-1	Apr18 3-2	Dec21 4-0	Apr11 2-1	Sep21 1-0	Feb15 4-2	Aug24 3-0		Mar21 4-2
AIRDRIE	Jan25 3-3		Nov09 5-3	Aug24 1-0	Jan18 3-2	Feb01 5-1	Oct19 0-0	Mar07 4-2	Oct05 4-1	Apr18 2-2
KILMARNOCK	May07 2-4	Feb22 6-4		Mar21 1-0	Feb01 3-2	Aug31 5-1	Aug24 7-1	Apr11 2-3	Mar14 2-1	Sep14 4-2
LEITH A	Oct05 3-1	Mar28 5-2	Aug17 3-1		Oct19 4-1	Nov23 2-1	Feb15 6-1	Dec14 7-0	Sep07 6-1	Aug31 0-4
LINTHOUSE	Feb29 1-6	Aug17 2-1	Dec21 1-2	Mar14 3-2		Nov30 1-0	Oct26 0-3	Oct05 1-3	Mar28 2-4	Dec14 1-3
MORTON	Sep07 2-3	Apr11 1-1	Oct26 2-3	Sep21 2-2	Aug24 1-2		Oct05 4-1	Apr14 7-1	Nov02 1-1	Nov09 2-1
MOTHERWELL	Mar28 1-4	Mar14 3-6	Nov16 2-4	Jan25 2-4	Jan25 1-3	Feb22 2-2		Jan11 3-3	Aug10 2-1	Aug17 1-0
PARTICK T	Feb01 4-2	Nov16 0-6	Sep07 2-2	Feb22 3-5	Feb08 5-1	Apr18 2-1	Nov30 1-2		Nov09 2-1	Nov23 1-2
PORT GLASGOW A	Feb22 2-2	Nov30 3-1	Sep28 6-1	Dec07 6-2	Feb15 2-2	Sep14 1-2	Dec21 3-4	Aug17 3-2		Oct12 2-1
RENTON	Nov30 1-1	Feb29 2-0	Oct19 3-0	Oct26 3-0	Nov02 4-0	Sep28 3-0	Jan18 3-2	Aug24 2-6	Sep21 2-2	

Season 1896-97

SFA Cup
1st Round
Jan 9 Abercorn ....4 Hurlford 0
Jan 9 Arthurlie ....4 Celtic 2
Jan 9 Blantyre ....5 Bathgate 0
Jan 9 Dumbarton ....2 Raith R 1
Jan 9 Duncrub Park ....1 Hibernian 10
Jan 9 Dundee ....7 Inverness T 1
Jan 9 Falkirk ....2 Orion 0
Jan 9 Hearts ....2 Clyde 0
Jan 9 Leith A ....5 Dunblane 1
Jan 9 Lochgelly ....1 King's Park 2
Jan 9 Morton ....3 Johnstone 1
Jan 9 Motherwell .....3 Kilmarnock 3
Jan 9 Partick T ....2 Rangers 4
Jan 9 St Bernard's ....2 Queen's Park 1
Jan 9 St Mirren ....5 Renton 1
Jan 9 T Lanark ....8 Newton Stewart ...1

Replay
Jan 16 Kilmarnock .....5 Motherwell 2

2nd Round
Jan 23 Abercorn ....4 Blantyre 1
Feb 13 Arthurlie ....1 Morton 5
Feb 6 Dumbarton ....4 Leith A 4
Jan 30 Dundee ....5 King's Park 0
Jan 23 Kilmarnock ......3 Falkirk 1
Jan 23 Rangers ....3 Hibernian 0
Jan 30 St Bernard's .....5 St Mirren 0
Feb 6 T Lanark ....5 Hearts 2

Replay
Feb 6 Kilmarnock ......7 Falkirk 3
After Protest
Feb 13 Leith A ....3 Dumbarton 3
Feb 20 Dumbarton ....3 Leith A 2
played at Motherwell

3rd Round
Feb 27 Dumbarton ....2 St Bernard's 0
Feb 13 Dundee ....0 Rangers 4
Feb 13 Kilmarnock ......3 T Lanark 1
Feb 20 Morton ....2 Abercorn 2

Replay
Feb 27 Abercorn ....2 Morton 3

Semi-finals
Mar 13 Dumbarton ....4 Kilmarnock 3
Mar 13 Morton ....2 Rangers 7

Final
Mar 20 Dumbarton ....1 Rangers 5
played at Hampden Park

DIVISION 1 FINAL TABLE

	P	W	D	L	F	A	Pts
Hearts	18	13	2	3	47	22	28
Hibernian	18	12	2	4	50	20	26
Rangers	18	11	3	4	64	30	25
Celtic	18	10	4	4	42	18	24
Dundee	18	10	2	6	38	30	22
St Mirren	18	9	1	8	38	29	19
St Barnard's	18	7	0	11	32	40	14
T Lanark	18	5	1	12	29	46	11
Clyde	18	4	0	14	27	65	8
Abercorn	18	1	1	16	21	88	3

DIVISION 2 FINAL TABLE

	P	W	D	L	F	A	Pts
Partick T†	18	14	3	1	61	28	31
Leith A	18	13	1	4	55	27	27
Kilmarnock	18	10	1	7	42	33	21
Airdrieonians	18	10	1	7	47	39	21
Morton	18	7	2	9	38	40	16
Linthouse*	18	8	2	8	44	53	14
Renton	18	6	2	10	34	41	14
Port Glasgow A	18	4	5	9	38	50	13
Motherwell	18	6	1	11	40	53	13
Dumbarton	18	2	2	14	27	64	6

* Four points deducted for fielding an ineligible player.
† Partick elected to First Division

Season 1896-97 cont.

DIVISION 1

(home \ away)	ABERCORN	CELTIC	CLYDE	DUNDEE	HEARTS	HIBERNIAN	RANGERS	ST BERNARD'S	ST MIRREN	T LANARK
ABERCORN		Aug29 0-6	Nov28 1-3	Jan16 1-7	Oct31 0-1	Sep12 2-2	Sep26 2-9	Oct10 2-3	Oct24 3-2	Nov14 1-2
CELTIC	Nov07 5-0		Dec12 4-1	Feb20	Sep05 2-1	Nov28 1-1	Oct10 2-0	Aug22 2-1	Sep26 2-0	Oct17
CLYDE	Oct03 6-2	Aug17 2-7		Oct24 0-2	Feb13 1-5	Aug29 0-7	Dec05 2-7	Aug15 1-2	Sep12 3-1	Dec19 3-2
DUNDEE	Oct17 3-0	Oct03 2-2	Nov07 1-0		Aug15 0-5	Aug22 3-0	Sep26 3-2	Dec12 3-2	Sep12 2-0	
HEARTS	Aug22 6-1	Oct24 1-1	Feb20 5-0	Sep19 1-0		Dec05 1-0	Sep21 2-1	Nov07 3-1	Aug29 2-1	Nov21 2-0
HIBERNIAN	Nov21 9-0	Aug15 3-1	Nov14 5-1	Oct31 3-1	Sep26 2-0		Sep05 4-3	Sep19 2-0	Jan16 3-0	Aug19 2-0
RANGERS	Dec12 6-1	Dec19 2-0	Oct17 2-1	Aug29 3-1	Sep12 5-0	Oct03 4-3		Feb20 3-2	Aug15 5-1	Oct24 6-1
ST BERNARD'S	Dec19 6-0	Sep12 1-2	Sep05 4-1	Nov14 2-5	Oct03 2-5	Oct17 0-1	Dec26 0-2		Oct31 0-2	Aug29 2-3
ST MIRREN	Sep19 4-2	Mar13 2-0	Aug22 5-0	Sep05 4-1	Oct17 0-2	Feb13 2-0	Nov07 2-2	Nov21 4-0		Oct03 2-0
T LANARK	Sep05 8-3	Dec05 0-3	Sep26 3-2	Oct10 3-1	Dec12 1-5	Nov07 1-3	Aug22 1-1	Nov28 2-3	Feb20 1-3	

DIVISION 2

(home \ away)	AIRDRIE	DUMBARTON	KILMARNOCK	LEITH A	LINTHOUSE	MORTON	MOTHERWELL	PARTICK T	PORT GLASGOW	RENTON
AIRDRIE		Oct03 3-2	Jan02 4-5	Oct31 2-1	Oct24 3-0	Sep19 4-1	Mar20 3-5	Nov28 1-2	Sep26 3-1	Nov14 3-0
DUMBARTON	Dec05 1-3		Apr10 0-6	Sep26 0-3	Mar06 3-1	Aug29 2-0	May15 2-1	Aug15 2-0	May08 4-2	Nov07 1-3
KILMARNOCK	Mar13 1-2	Sep05 5-1		Oct17 1-0	May08 0-3	May15 3-2	May06 2-0	Mar27 1-3	May11 3-0	Aug15 5-1
LEITH A	Jan16 3-1	Oct24 7-1	Aug22 4-1		Oct03 4-0	Sep12 4-2	Mar06 6-3	Oct03 3-1	May03 5-0	Apr10 4-1
LINTHOUSE	Nov07 1-4	Nov28 2-1	Apr27 1-4	Sep05 2-2		Dec26 2-5	Aug22 2-5	Feb27 2-2	Feb20 6-2	Feb06 6-2
MORTON	Nov21 3-1	Oct17 3-1	Oct10 3-2	Nov07 0-0	Dec05 4-0		May08 3-4	Apr24 3-4	Sep05 3-2	Sep26 0-1
MOTHERWELL	Sep05 2-3	May15 5-1	May01 1-2	Aug15 2-4	Apr15 4-5	Oct31 1-0		Feb13 0-6	Oct03 3-3	Feb27 4-2
PARTICK T	Oct10 4-3	Nov14 6-1	Apr17 2-0	Mar20 5-0	Nov21 2-2	Aug22 2-2	Feb20 6-2		Dec05 4-1	Sep05 2-1
PORT GLASGOW A	Aug15 4-4	Aug22 3-2	Mar20 5-2	Sep19 0-3	Dec12 6-3	May01 5-1	Apr03 0-2	Jan16 2-2		Oct31 1-1
RENTON	Aug22 3-2	Sep12 4-0	Mar06 1-2	Oct10 2-3	Feb13 2-3	Oct24 4-0	Sep19 2-0	Jan23 1-2	Nov28 3-3	

Season 1897-98

SFA Cup
1st Round
Jan 8 Abercorn ....1 Hibernian 1
Jan 8 Arthurlie ....0 Celtic 7
Jan 8 Ayr Parkhouse ....2 Kilmarnock A 1
Jan 8 Bo'ness ....0 Queen's Park 6
Jan 8 Cartvale ....4 Bathgate 2
Jan 15 Clyde ....1 T Lanark 3
Jan 8 Dundee ....2 Partick T 1
Jan 8 Dundee W ....3 Orion 1
Jan 8 Hearts ....8 Lochee U 0
Jan 8 Kilmarnock .....5 6th GRV 1
Jan 8 Leith A ....2 Port Glasgow A ..0
Jan 8 Morton ....7 Motherwell 1
Jan 8 Raith R ....2 E Stirling 4
Jan 8 Rangers ....8 Polton Vale 0
Jan 8 St Bernard's ...1 Dumbarton 1
Jan 8 St Mirren ......7 Dumfries 2

Replays
Jan 15 Dumbarton .....1 St Bernard's ...3
Jan 15 Hibernian .....7 Abercorn 1

2nd Round
Jan 22 Dundee ....2 St Mirren 0
Jan 22 Dundee W ......3 Ayr Parkhouse ...6
Jan 22 Hearts ....4 Morton 1
Jan 22 Hibernian .....3 E Stirling 1
Jan 22 Kilmarnock ....9 Leith A 2
Jan 22 Rangers ....12 Cartvale 0
Jan 22 St Bernard's ..0 Queen's Park ...5
Jan 22 T Lanark ......3 Celtic 2

3rd Round
Feb 5 Ayr Parkhouse ..2 Kilmarnock 7
Feb 5 Dundee ....3 Hearts 0
Feb 5 Queen's Park ...1 Rangers 3
Feb 5 T Lanark ......2 Hibernian 0

Semi-finals
Feb 19 Kilmarnock ....3 Dundee 2
Feb 19 Rangers ....1 T Lanark 1

Replay
Feb 26 T Lanark ......2 Rangers 2
Mar 12 Rangers ....2 T Lanark 0
played at Cathkin Park

Final
Mar 26 Kilmarnock ....0 Rangers 2
played at Hampden Park

DIVISION 1 FINAL TABLE

	P	W	D	L	F	A	Pts
Celtic	18	15	3	0	56	13	33
Rangers	18	13	3	2	71	15	29
Hibernian	18	10	2	6	47	29	22
Hearts	18	8	4	6	54	33	20
T Lanark	18	8	2	8	37	38	18
St Mirren	18	8	2	8	30	36	18
Dundee*	18	5	3	10	29	36	13
Partick T*	18	6	1	11	34	64	13
St Bernard's	18	4	1	13	35	67	9
Clyde	18	1	3	14	21	83	5

DIVISION 2 FINAL TABLE

	P	W	D	L	F	A	Pts
Kilmarnock	18	14	1	3	64	29	29
Port Glasgow A	18	12	1	5	66	36	25
Morton	18	9	4	5	47	38	22
Leith A	18	9	2	7	40	39	20
Linthouse	18	6	4	8	38	39	16
Ayr U	18	7	2	9	36	43	16
Abercorn	18	6	4	8	33	41	16
Airdrie	18	6	2	10	45	56	14
Hamilton A*	18	5	2	11	28	51	12
Motherwell	18	3	4	11	31	56	10

* Took the place of Renton, who resigned

DIVISION 1

(home \ away)	CELTIC	CLYDE	DUNDEE	HEARTS	HIBERNIAN	PARTICK T	RANGERS	ST BERNARD'S	ST MIRREN	T LANARK
CELTIC		Sep25 6-1	Jan15 2-1	Oct23 3-2	Sep04 4-1	Jan29 3-1	Apr11 0-0	Dec18 5-1	Feb12 3-0	Dec04 4-0
CLYDE	Dec25 1-9		Nov27 1-5	Nov06 2-2	Jan03 2-4	Nov13 2-3	Oct16 1-8	Oct02 4-2	Dec11 2-3	Jan01 1-1
DUNDEE	Nov06 1-2	Sep04 6-0		Oct16 0-1	Dec04 1-6	Oct23 5-0	Feb12 2-1	Sep11 0-0	Nov20 0-0	Oct02 4-2
HEARTS	Sep11 0-0	Dec04 8-1	Oct30 2-0		Dec18 4-1	Dec25 6-2	Sep20 2-2	Oct09 5-1	Sep25 2-4	Nov13 2-3
HIBERNIAN	Nov27 1-2	Oct09 5-0	Nov13 2-0	Sep18 1-1		Oct02 4-2	Dec11 0-5	Oct16 6-1	Dec25 3-1	Nov06 6-0
PARTICK T	Dec11 3-6	Oct30 1-1	Sep25 3-1	Sep04 2-0	Nov20		Oct09 1-5	Nov06 2-4	Oct16 1-0	Jan01
RANGERS	Sep27 0-4	Oct23 7-0	Dec25 5-0	Oct02 3-0	Sep11 1-0	Jan03 6-1		Mar19 8-1	Dec04 9-0	Apr09 0-0
ST BERNARD'S	Sep20 0-2	Jan01 3-1	Dec11 4-1	Nov20 1-5	Sep25 3-2	Sep04 9-1	2-4		Oct30 1-2	Oct23 1-3
ST MIRREN	Oct02 0-0	Feb05 4-0	Oct09 2-1	Nov27 3-1	Oct23 2-3	Sep11 1-1	Nov06 0-5	Sep18 7-2		Dec18 0-1
T LANARK	Oct09 0-1	Nov20 6-1	Jan29 3-0	Dec11 2-5	Sep27 1-3	Feb12 5-2		Dec25 6-0	Sep04 2-0	

DIVISION 2

(home \ away)	ABERCORN	AIRDRIE	AYR U	HAMILTON A	KILMARNOCK	LEITH A	LINTHOUSE	MORTON	MOTHERWELL	PORT GLASGOW A	RENTON
ABERCORN		Sep04 2-0	Feb12 4-1	Nov20 3-1	Oct30 3-3	Sep25 2-3	Dec04 2-3	Nov13 2-0	Feb19 0-1	Mar19 1-4	
AIRDRIE	Feb05 2-1		Oct30 5-1	Dec04 2-4	Feb12 2-1	Mar05 3-1	Jan08 5-2	Sep18 1-2	Apr30 7-2	Jan15 2-2	
AYR U	Nov27 2-3	Jan22 4-1		Jan15 3-0	Mar12 0-3	Nov06 5-3	Sep04 1-4	Mar26 6-1	Jan29 3-3	Sep25 3-0	
HAMILTON A	Dec18 1-2	Feb19 3-2	Jan08		Nov06 2-3		Nov27 2-7	Dec11		Jan29 5-1	
KILMARNOCK	Sep11 7-1	Nov27 5-2	Oct16 5-2	Mar05 5-0		Oct09 3-1	Nov13 5-0	Oct23 5-2	Dec18 6-2	Apr02 2-1	
LEITH A	Oct23 2-1	Apr23 6-3	Dec04 1-0		Nov20 2-2		Mar26 2-1	Apr23 3-3	Feb12 1-0	Apr25 3-1	Sep04 4-0
LINTHOUSE	Nov06 1-1	Oct23 1-3	Dec25 0-1	Feb12 2-1	Mar19 1-3	Dec11		Oct02 2-5	Mar05 4-2	Feb05 5-2	
MORTON	Oct09 1-1	Nov06 3-2	Dec18 4-0	Feb05 3-0	Sep25 3-4	Nov27 2-0	Oct30 0-0		Jan15 6-1	Sep04 3-4	
MOTHERWELL	Oct02 3-2	Apr09 2-2	Feb05 2-3	Dec25 3-3	Jan22 1-2	2-4	Nov20 1-1	Dec04 1-3		Apr16 0-4	
PORT GLASGOW A	Dec11 8-2	Mar26 8-1	Apr30 4-1		Apr09 4-2	Apr18 5-2	Mar12 4-1	Oct16 3-0	Jan22 4-3		Oct02 8-0
RENTON						Oct16 1-3			Sep18 1-4		

Season 1898-99

SFA Cup

1st Round

Jan 14	6th GRV	1	Celtic	8
Jan 14	Airdrie	3	Arbroath	3
Jan 14	Ayr Parkhouse	3	Dundee	1
Jan 14	Bo'ness	3	St Bernard's	3
Jan 14	Clyde	3	Wishaw T	0
Jan 14	E Stirling	4	Dumbarton	1
Jan 14	Forfar A	4	West Calder	5
Jan 14	Hibernian	2	Royal Albert	1
Jan 14	Morton	3	Annbank	1
Jan 14	Orion	0	Kilmarnock	2
Jan 14	Partick T	5	Irvine	0
Jan 14	Port Glasgow A	3	Renton	2
Jan 14	Queen's Park	4	Kilsyth W	0
Jan 14	Rangers	4	Hearts	1
Jan 14	St Mirren	7	Leith A	1
Jan 14	T Lanark	4	Arthurlie	1

Replays

Jan 21	Arbroath	3	Airdrie	2
Jan 21	St Bernard's	4	Bo'ness	2

2nd Round

Feb 11	Ayr Parkhouse	1	Rangers	4
Feb 4	Celtic	3	St Bernard's	0
Feb 4	Clyde	3	Arbroath	1
Feb 11	E Stirling	1	Kilmarnock	1
Feb 11	Partick T	2	Morton	2
Feb 4	Port Glasgow A	3	West Calder	1
Feb 11	Queen's Park	5	Hibernian	1
Feb 11	T Lanark	1	St Mirren	2

Replays

Feb 18	Kilmarnock	0	E Stirling	0
Feb 18	Morton	1	Partick T	2
Feb 25	E Stirling	2	Kilmarnock	4
	played at Cathkin Park			

3rd Round

Mar 11	Kilmarnock	1	St Mirren	2
Feb 25	Port Glasgow A	7	Partick T	3
Feb 25	Queen's Park	1	Celtic	2
Feb 18	Rangers	4	Clyde	0

Semi-finals

Mar 11	Celtic	4	Port Glasgow A	2
Apr 15	St Mirren	1	Rangers	2

Final

Apr 22	Celtic	2	Rangers	0
	played at Hampden Park			

DIVISION 1 FINAL TABLE

	P	W	D	L	F	A	Pts
Rangers	18	18	0	0	79	18	36
Hearts	18	12	2	4	56	30	26
Celtic	18	11	2	5	51	33	24
Hibernian	18	10	3	5	42	43	23
St Mirren	18	8	4	6	46	32	20
T Lanark	18	7	3	8	33	38	17
St Bernard's	18	4	4	10	30	37	12
Clyde	18	4	4	10	23	48	12
Partick T	18	2	2	14	19	58	6
Dundee	18	1	2	15	23	65	4

DIVISION 2 FINAL TABLE

	P	W	D	L	F	A	Pts
Kilmarnock*	18	14	4	0	73	24	32
Leith A	18	12	3	3	63	38	27
Port Glasgow A	18	12	1	5	75	51	25
Motherwell	18	7	6	5	41	40	20
Hamilton A	18	7	1	10	48	58	15
Airdrie	18	6	3	9	36	46	15
Morton	18	6	1	11	36	42	13
Ayr U	18	5	3	10	35	51	13
Linthouse	18	5	1	12	29	62	11
Abercorn	18	4	1	13	41	65	9

DIVISION 1

	CELTIC	CLYDE	DUNDEE	HEARTS	HIBERNIAN	PARTICK T	RANGERS	ST BERNARD'S	ST MIRREN	T LANARK
CELTIC		Nov05 9-2	Jan07 4-1	Dec17 3-2	Sep26 1-2	Nov26 4-0	Sep24 0-4	Oct08 1-0	Sep03 4-1	Aug20 2-1
CLYDE	Aug27 0-0		Sep10 1-0	Oct22 3-3	Oct01 2-2	Oct29 1-3	Jan07 2-4	Nov19 1-0	Dec03 4-1	Dec24 2-3
DUNDEE	Nov19 1-4	Nov12 1-3		Dec03 2-5	Sep17 2-4	Oct01 5-1	Oct08 1-2	Sep03 1-1	Nov05 1-7	Oct22 1-3
HEARTS	Sep19 2-2	Sep24 4-0	Nov26 6-3		Oct08 4-0	Oct15 5-1	Sep03 2-3	Nov05 3-4	Dec03 4-2	Nov12 2-1
HIBERNIAN	Sep10 2-1	Dec17 2-1	Oct15 5-0	Oct29 1-5		Dec10 1-1	Nov19 3-4	Sep24 4-3	Oct22 4-3	Dec03 1-1
PARTICK T	Dec03 3-8	Oct08 0-1	Dec31 2-0	Jan07 0-1	Sep03 1-4		Nov05 0-5	Sep10 0-3	Sep24 1-4	Dec17 1-3
RANGERS	Jan02 4-1	Nov26 8-0	Dec17 7-0	Oct01 3-1	Sep03 10-0	Nov12 6-2		Dec03 5-2	Dec03 3-2	Sep10 4-1
ST BERNARD'S	Oct29 2-3	Dec10 4-1	Dec24 1-2	Sep17 1-3	Nov12 2-3	Oct22 0-2	Sep19 0-2		Dec17 0-0	Oct01 4-2
ST MIRREN	Oct01 4-0	Aug20 2-2	Oct29 5-1	Sep10 2-3	Nov26 2-0	Nov12 2-2	Aug27 1-3	Oct15 2-1		Nov19 4-1
T LANARK	Dec31 2-4	Sep03 3-1	Sep24 3-1	Dec10 2-1	Nov05 1-4	Aug27 1-0	Sep26 2-3	Nov26 1-1	Oct08 2-2	

DIVISION 2

	ABERCORN	AIRDRIE	AYR U	HAMILTON A	KILMARNOCK	LEITH A	LINTHOUSE	MORTON	MOTHERWELL	PORT GLASGOW A
ABERCORN		Feb11 3-1	Apr08 2-3	Oct08 7-1	Sep03 2-1	Dec03 1-5	Dec24 2-1	Dec10 1-5	Dec31 1-1	Oct22 2-5
AIRDRIE	Aug20 3-2		Apr22 4-0	Nov19 2-0	Oct22 4-4	Oct29 0-2	Dec03 4-0	Sep03 1-2	Dec24 2-2	Sep24 6-2
AYR U	Oct15 7-3	Feb25 0-1		Nov26 3-0	Nov19 1-1	Dec03 2-2	Aug20 4-0	Dec31 1-0	Sep03 1-0	Oct22 2-3
HAMILTON A	Dec17 6-1	Sep17 7-1	Jan14 6-4		Dec03 1-7	Apr22 4-1	Oct01 5-2	Aug20 3-2	Jan21 4-1	Nov05 4-5
KILMARNOCK	Nov26 3-0	Aug27 5-0	Jan07 5-1	Dec10 7-1		Oct08 5-3	Nov05 8-0	Oct15 2-0	Apr22 5-0	Sep10 4-1
LEITH A	Nov12 8-1	Oct01 3-2	Nov05 4-1	Sep03 3-1	Apr15 3-3		Apr01 2-1	Nov26 3-2	Dec10 5-0	Dec10 5-1
LINTHOUSE	Aug27 4-2	Mar18 2-1	Apr15 6-2	Nov12 3-2	Apr08 3-4	Jan21 2-2		Oct29 0-1	Oct08 2-4	Feb11 2-4
MORTON	Nov19 4-2	Oct08 3-1	Aug27 4-0	Dec24 6-1	Sep24 1-2	Sep10 0-5	Oct22 1-2		Nov05 2-4	Dec03 2-4
MOTHERWELL	Oct29 3-2	Jan07 1-1	Dec03 3-1	Aug27 1-1	Mar18 3-3	Oct22 2-2	Dec10 6-1	Oct01 2-2		Nov19 4-3
PORT GLASGOW A	Oct01 4-3	Nov26 8-2	Apr01 6-2	Oct29 5-0	Dec17 4-5	Oct15 8-5	Sep03 5-0	Sep17 7-3	Aug20 2-0	

Season 1899-1900

SFA Cup

1st Round

Jan 13	Abercorn	5	Ayr Parkhouse	2
Jan 13	Airdrie	0	Clyde	1
Jan 13	Arbroath	0	St Bernard's	1
Jan 13	Celtic	7	Bo'ness	1
Jan 13	Dundee	8	Douglas W	0
Jan 13	Forfar A	3	Motherwell	4
Jan 13	Forres Mechanic	1	Orion	1
Jan 13	Galston	1	Partick T	2
Jan 13	Hearts	0	St Mirren	0
Jan 13	Hibernian	3	Hamilton A	2
Jan 13	Kilmarnock	2	E Stirling	0
Jan 13	Maybole	4	Wishaw T	2
Jan 13	Port Glasgow A	7	Falkirk	1
Jan 13	Queen's Park	3	Leith A	0
Jan 13	Rangers	4	Morton	2
Jan 13	T Lanark	5	Raith R	0

Replays

Jan 20	Orion	4	Forres Mechanic	1
Jan 20	St Mirren	0	Hearts	3

2nd Round

Jan 27	Celtic	5	Port Glasgow A	1
Jan 27	Dundee	3	Clyde	3
Jan 27	Hearts	1	Hibernian	1
Jan 27	Kilmarnock	10	Orion	0
Jan 27	Partick T	2	St Bernard's	1
Jan 27	Queen's Park	5	Abercorn	1
Jan 27	Rangers	12	Maybole	0
Jan 27	T Lanark	2	Motherwell	1

Replays

Feb 3	Hibernian	1	Hearts	2
Feb 17	Clyde	0	Dundee	3

3rd Round

Feb 17	Celtic	4	Kilmarnock	0
Feb 17	Partick T	1	Rangers	6
Feb 24	Queen's Park	1	Dundee	0
Feb 10	T Lanark	1	Hearts	2

Semi-finals

Mar 3	Queen's Park	2	Hearts	1
Feb 24	Rangers	2	Celtic	2

Replay

Mar 3	Celtic	4	Rangers	0

Final

Apr 14	Celtic	4	Queen's Park	3
	played at Ibrox			

DIVISION 1 FINAL TABLE

	P	W	D	L	F	A	Pts
Rangers	18	15	2	1	69	27	32
Celtic	18	9	7	2	46	27	25
Hibernian	18	9	6	3	43	24	24
Hearts	18	10	3	5	41	24	23
Kilmarnock	8	6	6	6	30	37	18
Dundee	18	4	7	7	36	39	15
T Lanark	18	5	5	8	31	38	15
St Mirren	18	3	6	9	30	46	12
St Bernard's	18	4	4	10	29	47	12
Clyde	18	2	0	16	24	70	4

DIVISION 2 FINAL TABLE

	P	W	D	L	F	A	Pts
Partick T*	18	14	1	3	55	26	29
Morton*	18	14	0	4	66	25	28
Port Glasgow A	18	10	0	8	50	41	20
Motherwell	18	9	1	8	38	36	19
Leith A	18	9	1	8	32	37	19
Abercorn	18	7	2	9	46	39	16
Hamilton A	18	7	1	10	33	45	15
Ayr	18	6	2	10	39	48	14
Airdrie	18	4	3	11	27	49	11
Linthouse	18	2	5	11	28	68	9

* Partick Thistle and Morton were elected to the First Division.

DIVISION 1

	CELTIC	CLYDE	DUNDEE	HEARTS	HIBERNIAN	KILMARNOCK	RANGERS	ST BERNARD'S	ST MIRREN	T LANARK
CELTIC		Aug19 3-2	Dec23 1-1	Sep30 0-2	Sep09 2-1	Dec16 3-3	Jan01 3-2	Oct28 5-0	Dec09 3-1	Sep02 5-2
CLYDE	Sep23 0-5		Dec02 0-7	Oct21 1-2	Nov04 3-4	Dec30 2-3	Aug26 2-6	Sep23 2-4	Nov25 3-1	Jan20 4-2
DUNDEE	Nov25 1-2	Sep02 3-1		Dec16 1-1	Sep16 2-2	Jan06 3-3	Jan20 2-3	Sep23 3-0	Oct14 5-2	Oct28 0-0
HEARTS	Nov04 3-2	Dec09 4-1	Nov11 4-1		Nov25 1-3	Sep23 1-0	Sep18 1-1	Oct14 5-0	Sep16 3-0	Oct07 2-0
HIBERNIAN	Sep18 1-1	Dec23 5-0	Nov18 3-3	Oct28 1-0		Sep02 3-1	Oct21 0-2	Jan06 1-1	Sep23 5-1	Dec16 3-2
KILMARNOCK	Aug26 2-2	Oct07 3-1	Oct21 2-1	Mar17 2-1	Oct14 0-3		Sep09 2-4	Sep16 1-2	Nov11 1-1	Sep30 1-1
RANGERS	Oct07 3-3	Oct14 7-0	Nov04 6-0	Sep02 4-3	Sep25 3-2	Dec09 6-1		Nov25 4-3	Dec16 4-1	Jan06 2-1
ST BERNARD'S	Dec02 1-1	Nov18 3-2	Oct07 2-0	Sep09 2-4	Nov11 0-4	Nov04 1-1	Feb03 1-4		Dec30 3-3	Dec09 4-0
ST MIRREN	Oct21 2-2	Sep30 3-0	Sep09 4-0	Nov18 2-2	Oct07 1-1	Aug19 0-1	1-3	Sep02 4-3		Nov04 1-1
T LANARK	Sep25 0-3	Sep09 5-0	Dec30 3-3	Dec23 3-2	Dec02 2-0	Nov25 2-1	Aug19 1-5	Oct21 2-0	Aug26 5-1	

DIVISION 2

	ABERCORN	AIRDRIE	AYR U	HAMILTON A	LEITH A	LINTHOUSE	MORTON	MOTHERWELL	PARTICK T	PORT GLASGOW A
ABERCORN		Jan20 4-1	Nov25 3-3	Dec23 5-0	Aug26 3-0	Oct28 3-4	Feb17 2-3	Mar17 1-2	Dec30 2-2	Sep16 2-0
AIRDRIE	Sep02 2-1		Aug26 5-2	Sep30 2-1	Jan27 2-2	Nov25 3-3	Feb17 0-5	Dec09 1-3	Nov04 0-2	Oct28 2-1
AYR U	Dec09 1-2	Dec30 5-0		Oct07 2-1	Oct14 0-1	Sep02 1-5	Dec23 1-4	Feb17 2-1	Oct21 2-1	Aug19 1-3
HAMILTON A	Jan06 5-3	Mar17 4-0	Dec16 0-4		Feb17 3-0	Aug26 1-1	Jan27 3-4	Mar03 4-2	Mar31 2-4	Mar10 2-0
LEITH A	Feb03 4-1	Sep16 3-2	Dec02 3-1	Aug19 3-1		Jan06 4-1	0-1	Mar24 0-1	Sep09 2-1	4-1
LINTHOUSE	Dec02 0-6	Aug19 1-1	Nov11 5-2	Dec30 0-1	Oct21 2-4		Nov04 0-5	Mar10 2-2	Sep30 0-4	Dec16
MORTON	Aug19 3-2	Dec02 2-0	Sep16 7-1	Sep02 7-0	Sep30 4-0	Jan20 5-0		Apr07 3-0	Oct28 2-3	Oct21 3-1
MOTHERWELL	Mar31 1-3	Jan06 4-2	Nov04 4-2	Jan20 1-2	Sep02 2-1	Dec02 4-0	Nov25 4-3		Aug19 1-3	Dec09 4-2
PARTICK T	Mar24 5-3	Oct07 4-1	Sep23 2-1	Dec02 2-1	Nov11 2-1	Dec09 2-1	Aug26 2-1	Feb03 2-1		Sep02 3-1
PORT GLASGOW A	Feb24 3-0	Dec23 3-2	Jan06 2-8	Dec09 3-0	Sep23 7-1	Mar03 6-3	Sep09 6-4	Aug26 3-1	Oct14 4-1	

Season 1900-01

SFA Cup

1st Round

Jan 12	Ayr	2	Orion	2	
Jan 12	Celtic	1	Rangers	0	
Jan 5	Clyde	6	E Stirling	0	
Jan 12	Dundee	3	Arthurlie	1	
Dec 31	Dundee W	0	Abercorn	3	
Jan 12	Forfar A	0	Leith A	4	
Jan 12	Hearts	7	Mossend S	0	
Jan 12	Hibernian	7	Dumbarton	0	
Jan 12	Kilmarnock	3	Airdrie	2	
Jan 12	Morton	10	Bo'ness	0	
Jan 12	Port Glasgow A	9	Newton Stewart	1	
Jan 12	Royal Albert	1	St Johnstone	1	
Jan 12	St Bernard's	5	Partick T	0	
Jan 12	St Mirren	10	Kilwinning	0	
Jan 12	Stenhousemuir	1	Queen's Park	3	
Jan 12	T Lanark	5	Douglas W	0	

Replay

Jan 19 Orion ....1 Ayr 3
Feb 9 St Johnstone ......0 Royal Albert 2

2nd Round

Jan 26 Ayr ....1 St Mirren 3
Feb 9 Celtic ....6 Kilmarnock 0
Feb 9 Clyde ....3 Dundee 5
Feb 9 Hearts ....2 Queen's Park 1
Feb 9 Leith A ....0 Port Glasgow A 3
Jan 26 Morton ....1 St Bernard's 1
Feb 16 Royal Albert ......1 Hibernian 1
Jan 26 T Lanark ....1 Abercorn 1

Replays

Feb 9 Abercorn ....0 T Lanark 1
Feb 9 Morton ....3 St Bernard's 1
Feb 23 Hibernian ....1 Royal Albert 0

3rd Round

Feb 16 Dundee ....0 Celtic 1
Mar 2 Hibernian ....2 Morton 0
Feb 16 Port Glasgow A ...1 Hearts 5
Feb 16 St Mirren ....0 T Lanark 1

Replay

Feb 23 T Lanark ....1 St Mirren 1
Mar 2 St Mirren ....3 T Lanark 3
played at Hampden Park

Mar 9 St Mirren ....1 T Lanark 0
played at Hampden Park

Semi-finals

Mar 23 Celtic ....1 St Mirren 0
Mar 9 Hearts ....1 Hibernian 1

Replay

Mar 23 Hearts ....2 Hibernian 1
played at Easter Road

Final

Apr 6 Celtic ....3 Hearts 4
played at Ibrox

DIVISION 1 FINAL TABLE

	P	W	D	L	F	A	Pts
Rangers	20	17	1	2	60	25	35
Celtic	20	13	3	4	49	28	29
Hibernian	20	9	7	4	29	22	25
Morton	20	9	3	8	40	40	21
Kilmarnock	20	7	4	9	35	47	18
T Lanark	20	6	6	8	20	29	18
Dundee	20	6	5	9	36	35	17
Queen's Park	20	7	3	10	33	37	17
St Mirren	20	5	6	9	33	43	16
Hearts	20	5	4	11	22	30	14
Partick T	20	4	2	14	28	49	10

DIVISION 2 FINAL TABLE

	P	W	D	L	F	A	Pts
St Bernard's	18	11	4	3	42	26	25
Airdrie	18	11	1	6	43	32	23
Abercorn	18	9	3	6	37	33	21
Clyde	18	9	2	7	43	35	20
Port Glasgow A	18	10	0	8	45	43	20
Ayr U	18	9	0	9	32	34	18
E Stirling	18	7	3	8	34	39	17
Hamilton	18	4	4	10	43	49	12
Leith A	18	5	2	11	22	32	12
Motherwell	18	4	3	11	26	42	11

DIVISION 1

	CELTIC	DUNDEE	HEARTS	HIBERNIAN	KILMARNOCK	MORTON	PARTICK T	QUEEN'S PARK	RANGERS	ST MIRREN	T LANARK
CELTIC		Dec22 1-2	Nov17 1-3	Aug25 3-1	Oct27 1-0	Oct13 4-2	Aug15 3-3	Oct06 2-0	Oct13 2-1	Dec15 3-0	Sep24 5-1
DUNDEE	Nov10 1-1		Sep29 1-2	Dec01 1-3	Sep15 3-0	Oct13 5-2	Dec29 4-0	Sep01 1-5	Dec15 1-1	Feb02 0-0	Nov24 0-0
HEARTS	Sep17 0-2	Sep08 0-4		Oct13 0-0	Dec08 7-0	Oct27 1-2	Oct06 1-3	Sep22 1-2	Aug25 0-1	Dec01 0-0	Nov03 0-0
HIBERNIAN	Sep29 2-2	Oct27 2-1	Sep01 3-0		Nov24 2-2	Dec22 1-1	Jan19 2-0	Oct06 0-1	Sep17 4-1	Sep15 1-0	Dec15 2-0
KILMARNOCK	Nov03 2-1	Aug25 2-0	Nov10 1-3	Sep08 2-0		Oct20 4-1	Sep22 2-1	Oct06 2-1	Dec01 1-2	Dec22 2-2	Jan01 2-1
MORTON	Aug18 2-3	Jan19 5-1	Sep15 2-2	Mar30 1-0	Dec29 3-2		Dec08 2-3	Jan05 6-2	Nov17 1-3	Sep01 1-0	Nov10 1-0
PARTICK T	Dec01 2-6	Nov17 1-1	Oct13 0-1	Sep24 0-1	Aug18 1-2	Jan05 1-2		Dec22 1-4		Feb09 5-3	Sep29 3-1
QUEEN'S PARK	Sep08 0-2	Jan05 1-0	Jan19 3-0	Apr27 1-1	Dec15 5-5	Nov03 3-0	Nov24 2-3		Sep29 2-3	Oct27 0-0	Nov17 0-2
RANGERS	Jan01 2-1	Oct20 4-2	Sep24 1-0	Jan26 6-0	Sep01 5-1	Feb16 3-2	Nov03 4-1	Dec29 3-2		Nov24 5-2	Aug18 4-0
ST MIRREN	Jan19 3-4	Mar30 3-3	Dec22 2-1	Nov17 1-0	Oct13 0-2	Dec01 3-1	Jan19 3-4	Aug25 5-2	Nov10 4-3		Sep08 2-1
T LANARK	Sep01 1-2	Oct06 2-1	Dec22 1-0	Sep22 0-0	Aug22 3-2	Aug25 2-2	Oct20 1-0	Dec08 1-0	Oct13 1-1	Dec29 2-2	

DIVISION 2

	ABERCORN	AIRDRIE	AYR U	CLYDE	E STIRLING	HAMILTON A	LEITH A	MOTHERWELL	PORT GLASGOW A	ST BERNARD'S
ABERCORN		Sep01 3-2	Mar16 2-1	Feb16 0-0	Mar09 3-0	Feb23 5-1	Dec22 5-1	Aug18 2-2	Dec01 3-0	Dec29 1-1
AIRDRIE	Nov24 5-1		Dec15 5-4	Aug25 2-3	Feb16 2-1	Dec29 1-1	Dec08 2-0	Oct20 2-0	Nov17 6-2	Oct13 3-1
AYR U	Sep15 1-0	Nov10 5-1		Jan01 3-2	Apr06 3-2	Aug25 4-2	Oct13 1-0	Dec01 3-1	Oct13 1-0	Nov17 1-0
CLYDE	Dec08 3-4	Sep22 2-2	Apr13		Apr22 3-3	Nov24 4-2	Sep01 4-1	Dec29 0-0	Sep29 0-1	Oct27 1-2
E STIRLING	Sep29 2-0	Aug18 2-3	Sep01 2-1	Feb23 2-1		May04 5-2	Dec29 1-1	Dec22 3-4	Sep15 1-1	Dec01 1-1
HAMILTON A	Jan05 5-0	Oct27 1-2	May11 3-1	Nov17 2-4	Jan12 5-0		Nov10 1-1	Sep01 2-4	Aug18 2-3	Nov24 2-3
LEITH A	Oct13 1-0	Sep08 1-2	Jan05 1-3	Oct20 1-1	Apr27 1-3	Dec01 1-3		Nov17 1-2	Nov24 2-4	Oct06 1-2
MOTHERWELL	Jan12 1-2	Dec01 0-2	Mar09 2-1	Nov03 2-3	Aug25 0-3	Oct13 4-2	Sep29 0-2		Nov10 5-1	Dec15 2-2
PORT GLASGOW A	Aug25 2-3	Nov03 1-2	Jan19 5-0	Jan19 3-2	Mar23 3-2	Dec15 6-3	Sep22 3-2	Oct27 5-0		Oct20 3-2
ST BERNARD'S	Nov10 2-0	Dec22 4-3	Apr27 1-0	Sep08 3-1	Jan19 5-0	Nov03 3-3	Sep15 2-0	Nov24 4-3	Sep01 4-1	

SFA Cup

1st Round

Dec 28	Arbroath	3	Kilwinning	2
Jan 11	Arthurlie	1	Port Glasgow A	1
Jan 11	Ayr	0	Dundee	0
Jan 11	Celtic	3	Thornliebank	0
Jan 11	Cowdenbeath	0	Hearts	0
Jan 11	Forfar A	3	Abercorn	2
Jan 11	Hibernian	2	Clyde	0
Jan 11	Inverness C	6	Stranraer	1
Jan 11	Kilmarnock	4	Partick T	0
Jan 11	Lochgelly U	0	Falkirk	2
Jan 11	Queen's Park	7	Maxwelltown V	0
Jan 11	Rangers	6	Johnstone	1
Jan 11	St Bernard's	1	Motherwell	0
Jan 11	St Mirren	1	Airdrie	0
Jan 11	Stenhousemuir	6	Stanley	1
Jan 11	T Lanark	0	Morton	0

Replays

Jan 18	Dundee	2	Ayr	0
Jan 18	Hearts	3	Cowdenbeath	0
Jan 18	Morton	2	T Lanark	3
Jan 18	Port Glasgow A	3	Arthurlie	1

2nd Round

Jan 25	Arbroath	2	Celtic	3
Jan 25	Falkirk	2	St Bernard's	0
Jan 25	Forfar A	1	Queen's Park	4
Jan 25	Hearts	4	T Lanark	1
Jan 25	Kilmarnock	2	Dundee	0
Jan 25	Port Glasgow A	1	Hibernian	5
Jan 25	Rangers	5	Inverness C	1
Jan 25	St Mirren	6	Stenhousemuir	0

3rd Round

Feb 8	Falkirk	0	St Mirren	2
Feb 15	Hearts	1	Celtic	1
Feb 22	Queen's Park	1	Hibernian	7
Feb 22	Rangers	2	Kilmarnock	0

Replay

Feb 22	Celtic	2	Hearts	1

Semi-finals

Mar 22	St Mirren	2	Celtic	3
Mar 22	Rangers	0	Hibernian	2

Final

Apr 26	Celtic	0	Hibernian	1

played at Celtic Park

DIVISION 1 FINAL TABLE

	P	W	D	L	F	A	Pts
Rangers	18	13	2	3	43	29	28
Celtic	18	11	4	3	38	28	26
Hearts	18	10	2	6	32	21	22
T Lanark	18	7	5	6	30	26	19
St Mirren	18	8	3	7	29	28	19
Hibernian	18	6	4	8	36	23	16
Kilmarnock	18	5	6	7	22	27	16
Queen's Park	18	5	4	9	21	32	14
Dundee	18	4	5	9	15	31	13
Morton	18	1	5	12	20	41	7

DIVISION 2 FINAL TABLE

	P	W	D	L	F	A	Pts
Port Glasgow A*	22	14	4	4	75	31	32
Partick T*	22	13	4	5	50	29	30
Motherwell	22	12	2	8	50	44	26
Airdrie	22	10	5	7	41	32	25
Hamilton A	22	11	3	8	45	40	25
St Bernard's	22	10	2	10	30	31	22
Leith A	22	9	3	10	34	38	21
Ayr U	22	8	5	9	27	33	21
E Stirling	22	8	3	11	38	46	19
Arthurlie	22	6	5	11	32	42	17
Clyde	22	5	3	14	21	45	13
Abercorn	22	4	5	13	27	59	13

* Elected to First Division

DIVISION 1

	CELTIC	DUNDEE	HEARTS	HIBERNIAN	KILMARNOCK	MORTON	QUEEN'S PARK	RANGERS	ST MIRREN	T LANARK
CELTIC		Aug17 1-1	Nov30 1-2	Dec14 2-2	Dec28 4-2	Sep21 2-1	Oct19 1-0	Jan01 2-4	Nov09 3-1	Aug31 3-2
DUNDEE	Nov16 2-3		Dec07 2-0	Sep21 0-0	Aug24 0-0	Nov02 2-0	Mar01 0-3	Aug31 1-2	Sep14 1-1	Oct19 1-1
HEARTS	Nov02 2-2	Oct12 4-0		Aug17 2-1	Sep21 3-0	Aug31 3-1	Sep28 1-1	Sep16 0-2	Nov23 2-0	Oct05 4-1
HIBERNIAN	Sep16 1-2	Nov30 5-0	Sep14 1-2		Nov16 5-0	Oct26 1-2	Sep07 8-1	Oct19 2-3	Aug24 1-2	Oct05 2-2
KILMARNOCK	Sep28 0-1	Nov09 4-0	Oct19 1-0	Aug31		Sep14 3-2	Jan18 1-1	Aug17 4-2	Oct12 1-2	Dec07 1-2
MORTON	Aug24 1-2	Sep07 1-4	Nov16 1-3	Oct12 0-2	Oct05 1-1		Nov30 2-2	Nov09 2-3	Sep28 1-3	Nov23 1-4
QUEEN'S PARK	Dec07 3-2	Oct05 1-0	Oct26 2-1	Nov09 2-0	Mar15 0-1	Mar08 1-1		Jan04 0-1	Aug31 3-0	Dec21 0-1
RANGERS	Oct05 2-2	Mar29 3-1	Aug24 2-3	Sep23 0-2	Sep07 3-2	Dec07 2-1	Nov02 2-1		Jan18 3-2	Nov16 1-4
ST MIRREN	Sep07 2-3	Oct26 3-0	Oct05 1-2	Nov02 1-1	Dec21 1-1	Oct19 1-1	Dec28 4-0	Sep21 1-5		Jan04 2-0
T LANARK	Sep23 0-2	Dec28 0-0	Sep07 2-0	Mar01 1-2	Nov02 0-0	Dec14 4-1	Aug24 4-3	Sep28 2-2	Nov30 0-1	

DIVISION 2

	ABERCORN	AIRDRIE	ARTHURLIE	AYR U	CLYDE	E STIRLING	HAMILTON A	LEITH A	MOTHERWELL	PARTICK T	PORT GLASGOW A	ST BERNARD'S
ABERCORN		Mar08 0-3	Oct12 1-1	Aug17 5-2	Nov09 2-3	Feb22 5-4	Sep14 2-3	Nov30 3-1	Aug31 0-3	Aug24 2-2	Sep28 1-1	Jan18 1-0
AIRDRIE	Sep07 4-0		Jan04 3-0	Mar29 3-2	Oct19 3-2	Sep28 3-0	Oct26 1-3	Jan25 3-0	Nov09 0-3	Aug17 2-1	Oct05 0-2	Mar01 3-1
ARTHURLIE	Dec07 2-0	Apr12 3-3		Nov02 0-1	Oct26 3-1	Oct19 3-3	Nov30 1-4	Oct05 2-0	Mar01 2-1	Feb22 1-5	Aug24 3-1	Apr05 0-1
AYR U	Mar15 3-0	Nov16 1-1	Sep14 1-0		Nov30 0-1	Mar01 1-2	Aug24 2-3	Jan04 1-1	Apr19 1-2	Nov09 2-3	Feb22 1-2	Jan02 2-1
CLYDE	Oct05 3-1	Dec07 1-1	Sep28 1-0	Jan25 1-0		Jan18 0-2	Nov02 0-0	Feb08 0-1	Jan04 0-4	Nov16 1-0	Sep07 1-2	Aug24 0-1
E STIRLING	Nov16 4-1	Nov30 3-1	Dec21 1-1	Mar22 0-1	Aug17 2-4		Oct05 4-1	Jan11 2-1	Aug24 1-3	Nov02 1-4	Sep14 0-0
HAMILTON A	Jan04 3-0	Apr19 1-1	Aug31 1-3	Dec07 4-1	Mar01 2-1	Nov09 2-3		Oct19 5-2	Apr12 2-0	Apr05 2-3	Aug17 3-1	Sep28 4-1
LEITH A	Dec21 5-0	Nov02 0-0	Nov16 2-1	Oct12 1-1	Nov23 3-1	Sep21 1-0	Dec14 4-1		Sep28 3-0	Jan18 0-1	Nov09 3-3	Feb01 2-1
MOTHERWELL	Oct26 3-1	Sep14 1-2	Aug17 2-2	Apr05 2-2	Nov16 6-2	Mar15 2-3	Jan25 3-0	Oct12 4-2		Nov30 3-2	Mar29 4-2	Mar22 2-1
PARTICK T	Oct19 5-0	Sep21 2-1	Jan25 2-1	Mar08 3-2	Dec28 2-0	Aug31 3-1	Nov23 1-0	Dec07 4-1	Dec21		Jan04 1-6	Sep07 5-1
PORT GLASGOW A	Nov02 4-1	Aug31 4-2	Feb15 3-1	Feb01 3-0	Sep21 6-0	Nov23 6-2	Dec28 5-2	Sep14 6-1	Dec07 8-1	Oct26 1-1		Oct19 5-0
ST BERNARD'S	Sep21 1-1	Oct12 2-1	Mar08 2-1	Aug31 4-1	Dec21 4-0	Dec07 2-1	Nov16 0-1	Oct26 0-1	Nov02 4-0	Oct05 2-0	Nov30 2-1	

35

SFA Cup

1st Round

Jan 24	Abercorn	2	Douglas W	2
Jan 17	Arbroath	1	Kilmarnock	3
Jan 10	Ayr U	2	Camelon	0
Jan 24	Celtic	0	St Mirren	0
Jan 10	Clyde	1	Hearts	2
	Dundee	W	Barholm R	O
Jan 24	Hamilton A	5	Airdrie	0
Jan 10	Hibernian	7	Morton	0
Jan 17	Leith A	4	Broxburn U	1
Jan 24	Nithsdale W	1	Orion	0
Jan 24	Queen's Park	1	Motherwell	2
Jan 10	Rangers	7	Auchterarder T	0
Jan 17	St Bernard's	1	Port Glasgow A	2
Jan 24	St Johnstone	1	T Lanark	10
Jan 2	Stenhousemuir	2	Inverness C	1
Jan 24	Vale of Leven	0	Partick T	4

Replays

Jan 31	Douglas W	3	Abercorn	1
Jan 31	St Mirren	1	Celtic	1
Feb 14	Celtic	4	St Mirren	0
	played at Ibrox			

2nd Round

Jan 24	Ayr U	2	Hearts	4
Feb 21	Celtic	2	Port Glasgow A	0
Jan 31	Dundee	7	Nithsdale W	1
Jan 31	Hamilton A	2	T Lanark	2
Jan 24	Hibernian	4	Leith A	1
Jan 31	Motherwell	0	Partick T	2
Jan 24	Rangers	4	Kilmarnock	0
Feb 14	Stenhousemuir	6	Douglas W	1

Replay

Feb 14	T Lanark	3	Hamilton A	1

3rd Round

Feb 28	Celtic	0	Rangers	3
Feb 7	Dundee	0	Hibernian	0
Feb 21	Hearts	2	T Lanark	1
Feb 21	Stenhousemuir	3	Partick T	0

Replay

Feb 14	Hibernian	0	Dundee	0
Feb 21	Dundee	1	Hibernian	0
	played at Ibrox			

Semi-finals

Feb 28	Dundee	0	Hearts	0
Mar 7	Stenhousemuir	1	Rangers	4

Replay

Mar 7	Hearts	1	Dundee	0

Final

Apr 11	Hearts	1	Rangers	1
	played at Celtic Park			

Replay

Apr 18	Hearts	0	Rangers	0
	played at Celtic Park			
Apr 25	Hearts	0	Rangers	2
	played at Celtic Park			

DIVISION 1

	CELTIC	DUNDEE	HEARTS	HIBERNIAN	KILMARNOCK	MORTON	PARTICK T	PORT GLASGOW A	QUEEN'S PARK	RANGERS	ST MIRREN	T LANARK
CELTIC		Nov29 2-2	Sep29 2-2	Jan02 0-4	Nov01 3-1	Dec20 1-1	Nov15 4-1	Nov22 3-0	Sep06 1-1	Oct18 1-1	Aug23 2-2	Sep27 1-0
DUNDEE	Mar21 2-0		Oct18 0-1	Oct25 0-3	Aug30 2-0	Nov15 3-0	Dec27 3-0	Sep13 2-1	Aug16 2-0	Sep06 3-1	Oct04 2-1	Oct04 0-0
HEARTS	Sep15 1-2	Aug23 0-2		Oct11 1-1	Dec06 1-1	Dec27 3-0	Nov29 4-2	Oct25 3-1	Sep20 4-0	Sep06 2-1	Nov08 1-3	Jan03 2-1
HIBERNIAN	Aug16 1-1	Sep27 1-0	Sep13 0-0		Nov15 2-1	Oct18 3-1	Nov01 2-2	Jan31 5-1	Aug30 3-2	Sep15 1-0	Oct04 4-3	Nov22 1-0
KILMARNOCK	Sep20 1-3	Dec13 0-2	Nov22 1-3	Sep06 1-4		Aug23 4-2	Oct25 2-0	Oct04 1-0	Oct11 1-1	Dec20 0-0	Dec27 2-3	Nov08 2-2
MORTON	Mar14 0-2	Nov22 0-2	Aug16 3-2	Dec06 0-1	Sep13 0-1		Oct04 3-3	Nov08 1-2	Feb14 0-4	Oct11 2-3	Sep06 0-3	Dec13 0-3
PARTICK T	Dec06 0-0	Sep06 0-2	Sep27 2-2	Dec20 0-2	Aug16 2-1	Aug30 1-1		Jan03 4-2	Nov22 4-2	Nov08 2-4	Oct18 2-2	Feb28 1-0
PORT GLASGOW A	Mar07 1-1	Nov01 0-0	Dec20 0-3	Aug23 0-1	Feb14 0-1	Sep27 3-0	Sep20 0-3		Oct18 4-0	Aug30 0-3	Nov15 3-2	Nov29 0-0
QUEEN'S PARK	Oct04 2-1	Dec20 0-5	Nov01 1-3	Nov08 2-3	Jan31 4-0	Nov29 4-1	Dec13 2-2	Feb28		Sep27 0-2	Feb21 1-1	Aug23 2-0
RANGERS	Jan01 3-3	Jan17 1-1	Oct04 2-1	Sep29 2-5	Nov29 5-0	Sep20 4-1	Aug23 9-0	Dec13 4-2	Nov15 3-2		Jan03 2-2	Nov01 2-0
ST MIRREN	Dec13 3-1	Oct11 1-0	Aug30 1-1	Nov29 1-1	Sep27 4-0	Nov01 1-1	Jan01 0-3	Aug16 2-2	Dec27 3-1	Nov22 0-1		Dec20 1-2
T LANARK	Aug30 1-2	Apr04 0-1	Nov15 0-3	Sep20 1-0	Oct18 2-0	Mar28 2-2	Sep29 1-1	Sep06 5-1	Dec27 3-2	Aug16 4-2	Dec06 6-0	

DIVISION 2

	ABERCORN	AIRDRIE	ARTHURLIE	AYR U	CLYDE	E STIRLING	FALKIRK	HAMILTON A	LEITH A	MOTHERWELL	RAITH R	ST BERNARD'S
ABERCORN		Sep13 2-4	Feb14 0-1	May11 1-2	May06 0-6	Nov15 3-2	Apr04 2-1	Dec27 0-2	Feb21 1-1	Aug23 0-1	Oct04 3-1	Nov08 3-5
AIRDRIE	Feb28 3-1		Jan03 3-1	Nov22 2-0	Nov29 1-1	Nov01 2-0	Oct11 0-0	Aug30 4-0	Aug16 3-0	Sep27 4-2	Dec20 4-3	Sep06 1-0
ARTHURLIE	Nov01 3-3	Aug23 0-3		Sep13 1-1	Dec13 2-2	Oct18 2-1	Nov22 2-3	Apr25 2-1	Nov29 3-1	Feb21 0-2	Nov08 3-3	Dec20 1-2
AYR U	Oct11 1-0	Dec27 2-1	Aug16 2-0		Sep27 2-0	Dec13 1-0	Mar07 2-0	Dec06 3-0	Nov15 3-0	Feb28 1-0	Aug30 5-0	Jan03 1-2
CLYDE	Aug30 1-5	Nov08 1-2	Oct25 1-1	Dec20 1-1		Oct04 0-1	Aug16 0-2	Nov22 1-1	Dec06 0-2	Jan03 1-2	Jan24 2-1	Sep20 0-1
E STIRLING	Dec20 6-4	Dec06 0-0	Sep27 5-2	Oct25 3-2	Dec27		Aug30 0-2	Nov08 2-5	Jan03 5-1	Oct11 2-1	Aug16 4-1	Nov22 4-1
FALKIRK	Nov29 4-1	Nov15 0-0	Dec27 0-0	Jan31 2-0	Nov01 1-1	Feb28 2-2		Apr18 4-2	Sep13 2-3	Apr11 4-2	Feb21 4-2	Aug23 0-1
HAMILTON A	Sep27 2-3	Dec13 4-0	Apr11 2-3	Aug23 4-1	Nov15 3-1	Nov29 3-1	Dec06 1-0		Nov01 5-1	Sep13 0-1	Jan03 2-0	Oct11 3-2
LEITH A	Dec13 4-1	Sep20 1-1	Oct11 4-2	Nov08 1-1	Sep06 4-1	Aug23 1-4	Dec06 4-1	Mar21 2-1		Dec20 4-3	Nov22 4-1	Sep27 1-0
MOTHERWELL	Nov22 1-0	Mar14 1-3	Aug30 2-2	Mar28 2-0	Feb14 3-0	Apr18 2-2	Nov08 2-2	Aug16 1-0	Oct04 3-3		Mar07 2-1	Oct25 4-3
RAITH R	Mar14 3-1	Oct18 0-1	Sep20 7-1	Nov29 0-3	Aug23 1-1	Jan31 1-0	Jan01 2-2	Oct25 1-3	Dec27 2-2	Mar21 2-5		Dec13 1-2
ST BERNARD'S	Aug16 4-1	Oct04 0-1	Nov15 2-2	Feb14 2-0	Dec06 3-0	Sep13 3-1	Oct18 8-3	Apr04 2-1	Aug30 0-1	Nov29 1-2	Nov01 1-1	

DIVISION 1 FINAL TABLE

	P	W	D	L	F	A	Pts
Hibernian	22	16	5	1	48	18	37
Dundee	22	13	5	4	31	12	31
Rangers	22	12	5	5	56	30	29
Hearts	22	11	6	5	46	27	28
Celtic	22	8	10	4	36	30	26
St Mirren	22	7	8	7	39	40	22
T Lanark	22	8	5	9	34	27	21
Partick T	22	6	7	9	34	50	19
Kilmarnock	22	6	4	12	24	43	16
Queen's Park	22	5	5	12	33	48	15
Port Glasgow A	22	3	5	14	26	49	11
Morton	22	2	5	15	22	55	9

DIVISION 2 FINAL TABLE

	P	W	D	L	F	A	Pts
Airdrie*	22	15	5	2	43	19	35
Motherwell*	22	12	4	6	44	35	28
Ayr U	22	12	3	7	34	24	27
Leith A	22	11	5	6	43	42	27
St Bernard's	22	12	2	8	45	32	26
Hamilton A	22	11	1	10	45	35	23
Falkirk	22	8	7	7	39	37	23
E Stirling	22	9	3	10	46	41	21
Arthurlie	22	6	8	8	34	46	20
Abercorn	22	5	2	15	35	58	12
Raith R	22	3	5	14	34	55	11
Clyde	22	2	7	13	22	40	11

Elected to First Division

Season 1903-04

SFA Cup

1st Round

Jan 23	Abercorn	2	Maxwelltown V	2
Jan 23	Albion R	2	Kilwinning	1
Jan 23	Alloa	2	Aberdeen	1
Jan 23	Ayr U	0	St Mirren	2
	Celtic	W	Stanley	0
Jan 23	Clyde	2	Arbroath	2
Jan 23	Dundee	3	Queen's Park	0
Jan 23	Hibernian	2	Airdrie	1
Jan 16	Morton	8	6th GRV	1
Jan 23	Motherwell	2	Partick T	1
Jan 23	Nithsdale	2	Kilmarnock	2
Jan 23	Port Glasgow A	1	Leith A	2
Jan 23	Rangers	3	Hearts	2
Jan 23	St Bernard's	1	West Calder S	1
Jan 23	St Johnstone	2	Hearts of Beath	0
	T Lanark	W	Newton Stewart	0

Replays

Jan 30	Arbroath	4	Clyde	0
Jan 30	Kilmarnock	1	Nithsdale W	1
Jan 30	Maxwelltown V	1	Abercorn	1
Jan 30	West Calder S	3	St Bernard's	3
Feb 6	Abercorn	2	Maxwelltown V	1
	played at Ayr			
Feb 6	Kilmarnock	2	Nithsdale W	1
	played at Kilmarnock			
Feb 6	St Bernard's	2	West Calder S	0
	played at Bathgate			

2nd Round

Feb 13	Dundee	4	Abercorn	0
Feb 6	Hibernian	1	Rangers	2
Feb 13	Kilmarnock	2	Albion R	2
Feb 6	Leith A	3	Motherwell	1
Feb 6	Morton	2	Arbroath	0
Feb 13	St Bernard's	0	Celtic	4
Feb 6	St Mirren	4	St Johnstone	0
Feb 6	T Lanark	3	Alloa	1

Replay

Feb 20	Albion R	0	Kilmarnock	1

3rd Round

Feb 20	Celtic	1	Dundee	1
Feb 20	Leith A	1	Morton	3
Feb 20	St Mirren	0	Rangers	1
Feb 27	T Lanark	3	Kilmarnock	0

Replays

Feb 27	Dundee	0	Celtic	0
Mar 5	Celtic	5	Dundee	0
	played at Celtic Park			

Semi-finals

Mar 19	Celtic	2	T Lanark	1
Mar 5	Rangers	3	Morton	0

Final

Apr 16	Celtic	3	Rangers	2
	played at Hampden Park			

DIVISION 1

	AIRDRIE	CELTIC	DUNDEE	HEARTS	HIBERNIAN	KILMARNOCK	MORTON	MOTHERWELL	PARTICK T	PORT GLASGOW A	QUEEN'S PARK	RANGERS	ST MIRREN	T LANARK
AIRDRIE		Jan09 4-3	Dec19 2-1	Dec26 1-2	Aug29 0-2	Oct10 1-2	Nov07 1-3	Sep26 2-1	Feb20 2-2	Dec05 1-0	Oct24 0-1	Aug22 1-3	Sep12 3-1	Mar05 0-4
CELTIC	Dec12 3-0		Oct10 4-2	Oct24 4-0	Sep26 2-0	Apr23 6-1	Jan23 5-1	Jan16 6-0	Aug15 2-1	Dec26 4-1	Oct03 2-0	Jan01 3-0	Mar12 2-1	Aug29 3-0
DUNDEE	Nov14 4-3	Jan30 2-1		Oct17 2-1	Dec12 1-2	Sep05 4-0	Aug15 6-0	Dec05 7-1	Jan16 3-0	Sep12 3-1	Aug22 2-2	Nov21 3-1	Oct24 1-1	Oct03 0-1
HEARTS	Feb27 5-0	Apr02 2-1	Aug29 4-2		Oct10 2-0	Sep26 2-1	Dec19 1-0	Sep12 5-0	Oct31 4-1	Nov14 2-0	Jan02 3-1	Jan23 2-1	Aug15 5-1	Feb13 4-1
HIBERNIAN	Oct03 4-0	Sep05 0-2	Nov28 0-1	Feb20 1-2		Mar12 2-2	Nov21 2-0	Aug22 2-1	Feb27 2-2	Oct24 1-1	Dec19 1-2	Dec26 2-1	Sep19 0-2	Oct17 0-2
KILMARNOCK	Nov28 0-2	Nov14 1-6	Nov07 1-2	Mar05 2-3	Sep12 0-0		Sep19 1-1	Jan09 2-1	Aug29 1-3	Oct03 0-4	Aug15 2-1	Dec05 2-2	Oct17 2-0	Oct31 1-2
MORTON	Sep05 3-1	Dec05 0-1	Jan02 1-1	Jan09 1-2	Oct31 3-1	Aug22 4-2		Dec26 2-3	Sep12 1-3	Oct03 0-1	Nov14 2-1	Nov28 0-5	Dec03 1-0	Jan30 1-2
MOTHERWELL	Aug15 1-2	Mar26 1-4	Sep19 2-1	Nov28 1-3	Jan30 0-4	Oct24 4-2	Oct17 0-0		Oct03 2-0	Oct31 1-0	Aug29 2-4	Sep05 2-5	Nov14 1-0	Dec19 0-2
PARTICK T	Mar12 3-0	Dec19 0-4	Feb06 6-1	Sep05 1-1	Jan09 3-1	Nov21 4-0	Oct10 2-1	Mar05 2-2		Aug22 1-0	Dec05 2-0	Sep28 1-4	Jan01 1-1	Oct22 2-2
PORT GLASGOW A	Oct17 2-2	Feb06 2-3	Mar26 1-0	Nov21 1-1	Aug15 3-1	Dec12 4-1	Aug29 2-0	Oct10 4-3	Sep19 1-2		Jan16 2-1	Dec19 1-1	Jan09 0-1	Feb20 0-1
QUEEN'S PARK	Jan30 1-1	Oct31 1-0	Jan09 2-1	Feb06 1-1	Feb13 2-1	Dec26 1-1	Mar19 1-1	Nov21 1-1	Oct17 1-1	Nov28 1-0		Nov07 2-3	Feb27 0-0	Dec12 2-8
RANGERS	Mar26 5-0	Oct17 0-0	Oct31 6-1	Sep19 5-1	Nov14 1-1	Jan16 3-0	Oct24 3-1	Dec12 2-0	Jan02 2-0	Feb13 8-1	Sep26 5-0		Aug29 2-2	Aug15 4-3
ST MIRREN	Oct31 5-2	Aug22 0-1	Sep26 2-0	Jan16 3-0	Nov07 3-0	Dec19 3-1	Dec26 3-2	Jan02 0-0	Nov28 1-1	Sep05 5-1	Oct10 3-1	Jan09 5-4		Jan04 1-2
T LANARK	Sep19 1-1	Sep28 3-1	Apr23 4-1	Aug22 2-1	Apr30 1-1	Mar26 3-2	Jan16 1-2	Mar12 3-0	Nov14 1-0	Jan02 3-0	Sep05 0-0	Oct10 1-0	Dec05 4-2	

DIVISION 2

	ABERCORN	ALBION	ARTHURLIE	AYR PARKHOUSE	AYR U	CLYDE	E STIRLING	FALKIRK	HAMILTON A	LEITH A	RAITH R	ST BERNARD'S
ABERCORN		Dec05 2-1	Mar12 1-3	Nov21 4-1	May07 1-1	Sep12 2-2	Nov14 3-2	May03 2-5	Mar26 2-2	Aug29 1-1	Oct24 7-3	Mar05 0-2
ALBION	Jan02 3-0		Jan16 3-3	Mar12 5-1	Mar26 2-3	Dec12 1-2	Apr23 2-0	Oct17 1-1	Jan30 1-1	Aug15 2-2	Feb06 3-2	Sep26 4-0
ARTHURLIE	Oct10 2-1	Apr16 1-3		Nov14 5-2	Aug22 0-1	Jan02 2-2	Oct24 2-2	Dec26 1-3	Aug29 3-2	Sep19 3-2	Jan09 3-1	Dec12 1-3
AYR PARKHOUSE	Dec19 1-3	Aug22 2-5	Feb06 1-1		Feb13 1-3	Oct31 0-3	Nov07 2-1	Sep19 2-2	Nov28 0-3	Oct17 1-0	Jan16 0-0	Oct03 1-2
AYR U	Feb27 0-1	Apr09 2-1	Mar07 2-1	Jan09 2-2		Aug29 2-2	Sep26 2-1	Jan30 1-0	Jan02 0-2	Jan02 1-0	Feb27 2-1	Aug15 2-0
CLYDE	Feb20 5-2	Dec26 2-1	Dec19 4-1	Aug15 3-1	Mar19 2-0		Nov28 5-1	Mar05 1-1	Feb06 0-3	Feb27 3-1	Aug22 1-0	Jan09 1-1
E STIRLING	Oct31 2-0	Apr30 4-2	Sep12 3-3	Jan30 1-0	Feb06 1-1	Mar26 1-3		Jan09 2-1	Oct17 0-0	Mar19 3-2	Dec26 3-0	Aug22 3-1
FALKIRK	Nov07 4-2	Dec19 0-1	Dec05 2-1	Oct10 6-1	Nov14 4-1	Nov14 3-4	Aug29 2-1		Aug15 1-5	Sep26 5-1	Oct02 2-0	Jan02 3-1
HAMILTON A	Aug22 3-1	Jan09 1-1	Nov07 5-0	Oct24 3-1	Jan16 3-1	Nov21 3-0	Jan23 3-1	Dec12		Dec19 2-1	Nov14 1-4	Sep12 1-3
LEITH A	Jan09 4-3	Sep12 3-2	Jan30 4-1	Dec26 4-0	Nov07 3-4	Jan16 2-2	Oct10 4-0	Aug22 2-0	Oct31 0-1		Mar05 0-2	Nov21 3-2
RAITH R	Dec12 4-0	Nov07 2-2	Jan23 2-1	Aug29 2-3	Dec19 2-2	Feb13 5-1	Aug15 1-2	Oct31 3-1	Dec05 1-1	Nov21 1-1		Oct10 1-2
ST BERNARD'S	Dec26 4-2	Aug29 2-1	Oct31 2-1	Jan02 2-1	Sep19 1-1	Mar12 1-4	Dec19 1-1	Nov21 1-3	Jan01 0-1	Sep05 2-1	Oct17 1-2	

DIVISION 1 FINAL TABLE

	P	W	D	L	F	A	Pts
T Lanark	26	20	3	3	61	26	43
Hearts	26	18	3	5	63	35	39
Celtic	26	18	2	6	69	28	38
Rangers	26	16	6	4	80	33	38
Dundee	26	13	2	11	55	46	28
St Mirren	26	11	5	10	45	38	27
Partick T	26	10	7	9	46	48	27
Queen's Park	26	6	9	11	28	47	21
Port Glasgow A	26	8	4	14	33	49	20
Hibernian	26	7	5	14	31	42	19
Morton	26	7	4	15	31	51	18
Airdrie	26	7	4	15	32	62	18
Motherwell	26	6	3	17	26	61	15
Kilmarnock	26	4	5	17	27	66	13

DIVISION 2 FINAL TABLE

	P	W	D	L	F	A	Pts
Hamilton A	22	16	5	1	56	19	37
Clyde	22	12	5	5	51	36	29
Ayr U	22	11	6	5	34	31	28
Falkirk	22	11	4	7	50	36	26
Raith	22	8	5	9	40	38	21
E Stirling	22	8	4	10	35	40	20
Leith A	22	8	4	10	42	40	20
St Bernard's	22	9	2	11	31	43	20
Albion *	22	8	5	9	47	37	19
Abercorn	22	6	4	12	40	55	16
Arthurlie	22	5	5	12	37	50	15
Ayr Parkhouse	22	3	4	15	24	62	10

* Albion had 2pts deducted

Season 1904-05

DIVISION 1 FINAL TABLE

	P	W	D	L	F	A	Pts
Celtic*	26	18	5	3	68	31	41
Rangers	26	19	3	4	83	28	41
T Lanark	26	14	7	5	60	28	35
Airdrie	26	11	5	10	38	45	27
Hibernian	26	9	8	9	39	39	26
Partick T	26	12	2	12	36	56	26
Dundee	26	10	5	11	38	32	25
Hearts	26	11	3	12	43	44	25
Kilmarnock	26	9	5	12	29	45	23
St Mirren	26	9	4	13	33	36	22
Port Glasgow A	26	8	5	13	30	48	21
Queen's Park	26	6	8	12	28	45	20
Morton	26	7	4	15	27	50	18
Motherwell	26	6	2	18	28	53	14

Celtic won a deciding match against Rangers

DIVISION 2 FINAL TABLE

	P	W	D	L	F	A	Pts
Clyde	22	13	6	3	38	22	32
Falkirk*	22	12	4	6	32	25	28
Hamilton A	22	12	3	7	40	24	27
Leith A	22	10	4	8	36	26	24
Ayr U	22	11	1	10	46	37	23
Arthurlie	22	9	5	8	37	41	23
Aberdeen*	22	7	7	8	36	26	21
Albion	22	8	4	10	38	53	20
E Stirling	22	7	5	10	37	38	19
Raith R	22	9	1	12	30	34	19
Abercorn	22	8	1	13	31	45	17
St Bernard's	22	3	5	14	23	53	11

Aberdeen and Falkirk were elected to the First Division

DIVISION 1

	AIRDRIE	CELTIC	DUNDEE	HEARTS	HIBERNIAN	KILMARNOCK	MORTON	MOTHERWELL	PARTICK T	PORT GLASGOW A	QUEEN'S PARK	RANGERS	ST MIRREN	T LANARK
AIRDRIE		Nov26 1-3	Nov05 2-0	Sep24 3-2	Sep10 1-1	Oct22 1-1	Aug27 3-2	Aug20 3-2	Dec24 3-0	Oct01 2-0	Jan21 0-1	Dec31 2-2	Nov19 1-3	Feb04 1-1
CELTIC	Jan03 2-3		Nov19 3-0	Sep03 1-1	Jan21 2-0	Dec31 3-1	Feb04 5-2	Oct15 4-2	Dec17 2-2	Dec24 3-0	Apr01 1-1	Sep10 2-2	Aug20 1-0	Dec10 2-1
DUNDEE	Sep03 0-1	Jan14 2-0		Nov12 4-1	Dec03 3-0	Sep24 6-1	Oct15 0-0	Jan07 0-1	Oct22 4-0	Dec31 3-0	Apr01 0-0	Sep10 2-0	Aug20 2-0	Dec10 0-0
HEARTS	Dec03 6-0	Sep19 2-0	Feb25 3-1		Jan02 1-0	Jan07 1-3	Mar04 2-0	Dec31 4-1	Oct01 0-1	Nov19 2-0	Mar11 2-0	Nov05 0-5	Oct22 3-1	Aug27 4-1
HIBERNIAN	Dec10 3-2	Nov12 2-2	Sep17 1-1	Oct29 3-0			Nov26 2-1	Jan14 4-0	Mar18 2-0	Feb18 4-0	Mar11 1-1	Sep19 1-2	Sep03 2-0	Dec24 1-1
KILMARNOCK	Jan14 1-0	Nov05 0-3	Feb11 2-1	Aug20 3-2	Oct01 2-1			Dec24 1-0	Aug27 0-2	Jan02 3-2	Sep03 1-1	Oct08 2-1	Dec03 0-3	Oct29 2-1
MORTON	Nov12 2-0	Dec10 0-1	Dec17 5-1	Feb18 1-0	Nov19 2-2	Sep10 2-1			Sep03 1-0	Oct29 0-1	Aug20 1-0	Dec31 1-1	Apr29 0-2	Jan07 1-3
MOTHERWELL	Oct29 1-0	Mar04 2-6	Dec17 0-2	Sep17 2-4	Oct01 1-2	Nov19 2-1	Oct08 0-3		Apr08 1-0	Jan21 0-2		Oct01 1-1	Mar25 3-2	Mar18 0-1
PARTICK T	Oct08 0-3	Aug20 0-5	Jan21 2-1	Oct15 0-2	Sep26 3-1	Dec10 1-0	Sep17 3-1	Nov05 1-0		Nov12 3-0	Jan07 3-1	Jan03 1-4	Dec31 0-1	Dec03 3-2
PORT GLASGOW A	Sep17 1-3	Aug27 1-4	Mar25 1-0	Dec24 3-0	Oct22 1-1	Oct15 1-1	Nov05 2-1	Sep24 2-1	Jan14 1-4		Mar04 4-2	Feb04 0-3	Oct08 0-2	Oct08 1-1
QUEEN'S PARK	Oct15 1-1	Oct01 2-3	Aug27 0-1	Feb04 2-0	Sep24 4-2	Dec17 1-1	Dec03 2-0	Jan14 2-0	Nov19 1-4	Dec10 2-0		Sep17 0-4	Jan14 2-1	Nov05 0-1
RANGERS	Dec17 4-1	Feb18 1-4	Oct29 2-0	Sep26 3-2	Aug27 3-1	Jan21 4-0	Apr01 5-0	Jan14 2-0	Sep03 1-4	Mar18 5-1	Oct22 5-0		Oct01 2-3	Nov19 3-1
ST MIRREN	Mar11 0-1	Sep17 2-3	Oct08 1-1	Dec10 1-1	Nov05 2-0	Feb18 1-0	Sep24 1-0	Jan02 1-2	Aug27 2-2	Sep10 1-2	Mar18 1-1	Nov12 3-0		Oct15 1-2
T LANARK	Jan07 6-0	Oct22 1-2	Dec26 2-2	Nov26 7-1	Dec31 4-1	Nov12 3-1	Jan21 5-0	Sep10 4-3	Feb18 6-1	Oct29 3-0	Sep03 2-0	Aug20 2-1	Apr01 3-0	

DIVISION 2

	ABERCORN	ABERDEEN	ALBION R	ARTHURLIE	AYR U	CLYDE	E STIRLING	FALKIRK	HAMILTON A	LEITH A	RAITH R	ST BERNARD'S
ABERCORN		Feb04 3-1	Nov19 3-0	Dec03 1-2	Dec31 2-1	Jan07 2-1	Oct22 1-0	Dec24 0-2	Oct01 1-0	Oct29 1-4	Aug20 3-1	Dec17 3-2
ABERDEEN	Sep24 3-1		Mar04 7-2	Apr08 0-0	Mar25 2-0	Aug27 0-1	Dec31 3-0	Aug20 1-2	Dec10 1-2	Apr15 0-0	Oct22 3-1	Jan21 1-1
ALBION R	Sep10 5-1	Jan14 1-0		Oct15 1-2	Oct29 3-2	Dec03 2-1	Nov12 4-4	Jan07 2-2	Oct08 0-1	Dec10 5-3	Sep17 1-1	Oct22 3-2
ARTHURLIE	Aug27 1-2	Mar11 2-0	Dec24 2-2		Sep10 5-2	Feb25 1-1	Jan21 3-1	Nov19 0-2	Oct29 3-1	Feb18 0-3	Dec31 1-1	Sep03 1-1
AYR U	Nov12 3-1	Nov19 3-3	Aug27 0-1	Aug20 4-0		Feb18 5-1	Jan14 1-0	Oct01 5-3	Jan21 1-0	Dec24 4-1	Nov05 4-0	Jan07 5-1
CLYDE	Jan21 2-1	Dec17 1-0	Aug20 2-1	Oct01 4-4	Feb11 4-1		Sep24 1-0	Dec31 1-0	Mar04 2-0	Dec10 1-0	Jan14 5-0	
E STIRLING	Jan28 3-1	Nov05 1-4	Dec17 5-2	Jan07 2-0	Oct15 2-2	Mar11 2-2		Sep10 2-0	Dec03 0-1	Aug20 1-3	Dec24 4-0	Nov19 4-0
FALKIRK	Dec10 2-1	Apr01 0-0	Sep24 3-1	Jan14 2-0	Nov26 2-1	Oct08 0-0	Oct29 3-1		Oct22 1-3	Nov12 1-0	Feb04 1-0	Aug27 2-1
HAMILTON A	Nov05 5-1	Sep10 3-3	Dec31 3-0	Nov12 4-1	Sep24 1-2	Oct15 0-1	Feb04 1-1	Dec17 3-1		Jan07 2-0	Nov19 1-0	Aug20 4-0
LEITH A	Jan14 2-1	Mar18 1-1	Jan21 7-0	Nov05 2-0	Oct22 2-0	Nov19 0-1	Feb11 0-2	Dec03 1-3	Aug27		Sep24 4-1	Dec31 4-1
RAITH R	Nov26 2-1	Jan07 1-0	Oct01 1-0	Dec17 4-1	Dec03 3-0	Jan02 1-0	Aug20 4-1	Oct15 1-3	Jan14 0-2	Oct08 0-1		Oct29 1-2
ST BERNARD'S	Oct15 2-0	Dec24 0-3	Nov05 1-2	Dec10 2-3	Oct08 2-1	Feb04 1-1	Feb18 1-1	Jan28 1-2	Feb25 1-1	Nov26 0-1	Nov12 1-5	

SFA Cup

1st Round

Jan 28	Aberdeen	2	Queen's Park	1
Jan 28	Airdrie	7	St Johnstone	0
Jan 28	Arthurlie	0	Motherwell	0
Jan 28	Bathgate	2	Arbroath	1
Jan 21	Cowdenbeath	2	6th GRV	0
Jan 28	Dumfries	1	Celtic	2
Jan 28	Dundee	1	Hearts	3
Jan 28	Hibernian	1	Partick T	1
Jan 28	Kilmarnock	2	Beith	2
Jan 21	Kirkcaldy U	3	Crieff	1
Jan 28	Lochgelly U	5	Inverness C	1
Jan 28	Morton	2	Renton	0
Jan 28	Port Glasgow A	3	Stranraer	0
Jan 28	Rangers	2	Ayr Parkhouse	1
Jan 28	St Mirren	1	Clyde	0
Jan 28	T Lanark	4	Leith A	1

Replays

Feb 4	Beith	3	Kilmarnock	1
Feb 4	Motherwell	1	Arthurlie	0
Feb 4	Partick T	4	Hibernian	2

2nd Round

Feb 18	Aberdeen	6	Bathgate	1
Feb 11	Airdrie	3	Port Glasgow A	0
Feb 11	Beith	4	Cowdenbeath	0
Feb 11	Celtic	3	Lochgelly U	0
Feb 11	Kirkcaldy U	0	Partick T	1
Feb 11	Morton	0	Rangers	6
Feb 11	Motherwell	0	T Lanark	1
Feb 11	St Mirren	2	Hearts	1

3rd Round

Feb 25	Celtic	3	Partick T	0
Feb 25	Rangers	5	Beith	1
Feb 25	St Mirren	0	Airdrie	0
Feb 25	T Lanark	4	Aberdeen	1

Replay

Mar 4	Airdrie	3	St Mirren	1

Semi-finals

Mar 25	Celtic	0	Rangers	2
Mar 25	T Lanark	2	Airdrie	1

Final

Apr 8	Rangers	0	T Lanark	0

played at Hampden Park

Replay

Apr 15	Rangers	1	T Lanark	3

played at Hampden Park

Season 1905-06

SFA Cup

1st Round

Jan 27	Aberdeen	3	Dunfermline A	0
Jan 27	Airdrie	9	Maxwelltown V	0
Jan 27	Arbroath	1	Bo'ness U	4
Jan 27	Arthurlie	1	Rangers	7
Jan 27	Beith	2	Inverness T	0
Jan 27	Dundee	1	Celtic	2
Jan 27	Falkirk	1	Hibernian	2
Jan 27	Forfar A	0	Queen's Park	4
Jan 27	Hearts	4	Nithsdale W	1
Jan 27	Kilmarnock	2	Clyde	1
Jan 27	Leith A	1	Partick T	2
Jan 27	Morton	4	Lochgelly U	3
Jan 27	Motherwell	2	Hamilton A	3
Jan 27	Port Glasgow A	6	Dunblane	1
Jan 27	St Mirren	7	Black Watch	2
Jan 27	T Lanark	5	Galston	0

2nd Round

Feb 10	Aberdeen	2	Rangers	3
Feb 10	Beith	0	Hearts	3
Feb 10	Celtic	3	Bo'ness U	0
Feb 10	Hibernian	1	Partick T	1
Feb 10	Kilmarnock	2	Port Glasgow A	2
Feb 10	Queen's Park	1	Airdrie	2
Feb 10	St Mirren	3	Morton	1
Feb 10	T Lanark	2	Hamilton A	2

Replays

Feb 17	Hamilton A	1	T Lanark	3
Feb 17	Partick T	1	Hibernian	1
Feb 17	Port Glasgow A	0	Kilmarnock	0
Feb 24	Hibernian	2	Partick T	1
	played at Ibrox			
Feb 24	Kilmarnock	0	Port Glasgow A	0
	played at Cathkin Park			
Mar 3	Kilmarnock	0	Port Glasgow A	1
	played at Celtic Park			

3rd Round

Feb 24	Airdrie	0	St Mirren	0
Feb 24	Celtic	1	Hearts	2
Mar 10	Hibernian	2	T Lanark	3
Mar 10	Port Glasgow A	1	Rangers	0

Replay

Mar 3	St Mirren	2	Airdrie	0

Semi-finals

Mar 31	Port Glasgow A	0	Hearts	2
Mar 31	St Mirren	1	T Lanark	1

Replays

Apr 14	T Lanark	0	St Mirren	0
	played at Ibrox			
Apr 21	St Mirren	0	T Lanark	1
	played at Ibrox			

Final

Apr 28	Hearts	1	T Lanark	0
	played at Ibrox			

DIVISION 1

	ABERDEEN	AIRDRIE	CELTIC	DUNDEE	FALKIRK	HEARTS	HIBERNIAN	KILMARNOCK	MORTON	MOTHERWELL	PARTICK T	PORT GLASGOW A	QUEEN'S PARK	RANGERS	ST MIRREN	T LANARK
ABERDEEN		Feb17 1-2	Mar03 1-0	Jan06 1-2	Dec23 2-0	Dec02 2-1	Sep16 2-1	Sep02 2-0	Nov04 3-0	Feb24 2-2	Aug19 0-1	Oct21 2-2	Sep25 2-2	Dec16 1-1	Oct07 1-0	Nov25 1-2
AIRDRIE	Sep23 2-0		Jan13 2-5	Nov25 1-2	Oct07 4-1	Jan06 1-1	Aug19 2-0	Oct28 1-1	Dec09 4-2	Mar17 2-1	Sep16 3-2	Oct14 4-1	Sep02 5-1	Dec16 0-0		
CELTIC	Dec09 1-0	Sep30 2-1		Oct28 3-1	Jan06 7-0	Apr21 1-0	Sep02 4-0	Jan02 3-1	Dec23 4-0	Aug19 3-1	Jan20 4-1	Nov11 0-1	Oct14 5-1	Jan01 1-0	Nov25 2-1	May07 0-1
DUNDEE	Nov18 6-0	Mar10 0-0	Feb03 1-0		Dec09 3-0	Oct21 1-1	Dec23 1-1	Oct07 0-0	Sep02 2-1	Jan20 2-0	Sep09 1-1	Dec30 1-1	Sep23 1-0	Feb17 1-1	Aug19 1-2	Nov04 2-0
FALKIRK	Sep09 1-1	Jan01 0-0	Sep16 0-5	Nov11 2-0		Jan20 2-2	Mar17 2-1	Apr13 4-0	Sep30 2-0	Feb03 2-0	Aug26 0-1				Apr07 2-0	Feb24 2-0
HEARTS	Oct28 1-1	Nov11 2-1	Sep11 1-1	Jan13 0-1	Nov25 1-0		Nov04 1-0	Sep16 3-0	Mar10 4-0	Sep02 4-0	Oct14 4-0	Dec09 6-1	Feb17 4-1	Apr07 2-2	Dec23 1-0	Aug19 3-0
HIBERNIAN	Jan02 1-0	Jan20 0-4	Dec30 0-1	Aug26 2-1	Dec16 4-1	Sep18 0-3		Mar31 2-1	Sep30 1-2	Feb03 2-3	Dec02 1-1	Mar24 3-1	Nov18 4-0	Sep11 1-2	Jan06 0-1	Oct21 2-1
KILMARNOCK	Dec30 1-0	Feb03 0-0	Aug26 2-4	Dec16 2-2	Nov04 2-1	Nov18 1-1	Dec09 0-2		Sep09 3-1		Oct21 1-2	Apr28 3-2	Jan06 7-0	Oct14 1-3	Jan20 2-0	
MORTON	Feb03 2-2	Aug26 0-4	Nov18 0-4	Feb24 2-2	Oct21 2-1	Dec16 1-1	Nov11 0-3	Apr07 1-0		Oct14 1-1	Mar31 1-0	Sep23 3-2	Dec30 7-0	Dec09 1-3	Jan20 5-3	Sep16 2-0
MOTHERWELL	Jan13 3-3	Nov04 2-1	Dec16 0-4	Sep16 4-1	Sep23 2-3	Dec30 2-1	Nov25 0-2	Mar10 5-1	Feb17 1-1		Jan01 2-3	Aug26 2-0	Oct07 4-2	Nov18 3-3	Oct21 1-1	Mar03 2-1
PARTICK T	Mar10 1-2	Dec09 1-0	Nov04 0-3	Mar10 1-0	Sep02 2-0	Feb03 4-1	Sep25 1-0	Jan13 2-1	Oct07 2-2	Oct28 2-2		Apr14 3-0	Dec16 2-1	Mar17 1-1	Mar24 1-1	Jan06 2-5
PORT GLASGOW A	Mar17 3-1	Apr21 2-2	Dec02 0-1	Sep30 2-1	Aug19 2-2	Sep09 2-5	Oct28 0-0	Nov25 3-2	Jan06 1-3	Apr07 1-3	Dec23 1-4		Jan13 1-2	Oct07 3-2	Nov04 0-4	Sep02 2-5
QUEEN'S PARK	Jan20 3-0	Oct21 1-3	Mar10 0-6	Mar31 0-0	Mar03 0-5	Sep30 0-3	Mar17 2-2	Dec23 4-1	Aug19 2-3	Jan06 2-1	Nov25 1-2	Sep16 2-2		Nov04 1-2	Sep02 3-1	Dec09 0-5
RANGERS	Aug26 1-0	Dec30 1-3	Oct21 3-2	Jan13 1-1	Mar24 3-1	Sep25 0-5	Mar03 1-1	Aug19 3-2	Dec25 2-1	Jan02 1-0	Jan20 4-0	Dec02 3-1			Sep16 1-0	Nov11 2-4
ST MIRREN	Sep30 4-2	Sep09 0-1	Feb17 1-3	Dec02 1-1	Mar10 2-0	Aug26 2-1	Sep23 3-1	May12 2-1	Oct28 3-1	Dec09 1-1	Apr28 1-2	May05 3-0	Feb03 3-1	Jan13 3-2		Mar17 2-0
T LANARK	Oct14 1-0	May10 1-2	Sep25 0-1	Dec25 1-2	Apr09 2-0	Jan02 1-3	Jan13 3-1	Dec02 5-0	Mar24 0-1	Sep09 6-1	Aug26 2-1	Dec16 3-0	Oct28 6-3	Feb03 3-0	Dec30 1-0	

DIVISION 2

	ABERCORN	ALBION R	ARTHURLIE	AYR U	CLYDE	COWDENBEATH	E STIRLING	HAMILTON A	LEITH A	RAITH R	ST BERNARD'S	VALE OF LEVEN
ABERCORN		Nov25 2-2	Dec23 4-2	Dec30 2-0	Jan01 1-0	Jan20 4-0	Jan06 1-1	Aug26 0-1	Oct21 0-3	Aug19 2-2	Jan27 2-1	Nov04 1-1
ALBION R	Dec16 1-0		Nov04 2-0	Aug26 2-4	Dec09 0-2	Sep09 5-1	Jan27 3-1	Dec30 3-1	Mar10 0-1	Oct21 3-1	Oct28 4-0	Nov11 0-3
ARTHURLIE	Oct28 5-2	Jan13 3-0		Nov25 2-4	Mar10 0-3	Nov11 3-2	Dec30 4-0	Apr07 1-3	Aug26 6-2	Jan06 2-0	Dec16 4-0	Feb03 1-1
AYR U	Sep09 4-1	Jan06 1-1	Aug19 3-0		Dec02 1-1	Dec16 3-0	Nov11 2-4	Nov04 1-2	Jan13 1-5	Feb03 2-1	Jan06 0-0	Oct14 5-1
CLYDE	Nov11 3-1	Oct07 1-4	Feb17 2-0	Jan20 3-1		Dec30 2-0	Jan13 2-0	Dec16 2-0	Mar03 1-0	Feb03 1-1	Jan06 2-0	Sep30 2-0
COWDENBEATH	Sep23 1-1	Feb03 2-1	Dec09 2-3	Nov18 3-5	Nov04 0-1		Aug26 2-1	Oct07 1-3	Aug19 1-0	Jan27 2-1	Sep16 2-2	Jan06 2-0
E STIRLING	Nov18 1-3	Oct14 1-4	Mar03 1-2	Oct07 1-2	Oct21 4-4	Dec23 2-2		Sep23 0-1	Dec09 1-1	Dec16 1-1	Nov04 1-1	Aug19 1-1
HAMILTON A	Mar03 3-0	Feb24 0-2	Dec02 6-4	Feb03 1-2	Aug19 1-0	Mar24 4-0	Mar10 1-0		Apr14 0-1	Dec09 3-0	Sep09 0-4	Dec23 5-3
LEITH A	Jan13 5-2	Mar31 3-1	Mar24 4-1	Feb17 4-1	Dec23 0-0	Nov25 3-1	Feb03 0-0	Jan06 2-1		Nov18 1-0	Mar17 1-0	Dec16 3-1
RAITH R	Dec02 5-1	Sep02 0-3	Feb24 1-1	Oct28 5-2	Aug26 2-2	Oct14 0-1	Sep09 2-2	Jan01 1-1	Dec30 2-1		Dec23 4-3	Nov25 3-2
ST BERNARD'S	Feb03 1-0	Aug19 1-2	Feb10 4-1	Dec09 1-0	Nov25 3-2	Jan13 1-3	Dec02 3-2	Nov11 0-1	Feb24 2-3	Jan20 5-2		Dec30 3-0
VALE OF LEVEN	Dec09 4-1	Dec02 2-2	Sep09 0-1	Jan27 2-1	Feb10 1-3	Oct21 3-2	Oct28 1-0	Jan13 2-1	Oct07 1-3	Sep23 1-2	Aug26 3-2	

DIVISION 1 FINAL TABLE

	P	W	D	L	F	A	Pts
Celtic	30	24	1	5	76	19	49
Hearts	30	18	7	5	64	27	43
Airdrie	30	15	8	7	53	31	38
Rangers	30	15	7	8	58	48	37
Partick T	30	15	6	9	44	40	36
T Lanark	30	16	2	12	62	38	34
Dundee	30	11	12	7	40	33	34
St Mirren	30	13	5	12	41	37	31
Motherwell	30	9	8	13	50	54	26
Morton	30	10	6	14	35	54	26
Hibernian	30	10	5	15	35	40	25
Aberdeen	30	8	8	14	36	48	24
Falkirk	30	9	5	16	52	68	23
Kilmarnock	30	8	4	18	46	68	20
Port Glasgow A	30	6	8	16	38	68	20
Queen's Park	30	5	4	21	41	88	14

DIVISION 2 FINAL TABLE

	P	W	D	L	F	A	Pts
Leith A	22	15	4	3	46	22	34
Clyde*	22	11	9	2	37	21	31
Albion	22	12	3	7	48	31	27
Hamilton A*	22	12	2	8	45	33	26
St Bernard's	22	9	4	9	42	34	22
Arthurlie	22	10	2	10	46	46	22
Ayr U	22	9	3	10	44	51	21
Raith R	22	6	7	9	36	42	19
Cowdenbeath	22	7	3	12	28	40	17
Abercorn	22	6	5	11	31	46	17
Vale of Leven	22	6	4	12	33	49	16
E Stirling	22	1	10	11	26	47	12

Elected to First Division

SFA Cup

1st Round

Jan 26	Aberdeen	0	Johnstone	0
Jan 26	Arbroath	1	Queen's Park	1
Feb 2	Arthurlie	1	St Mirren	2
Jan 26	Ayr U	2	Cowdenbeath	0
Feb 2	Celtic	2	Clyde	1
Jan 26	Dumfries	2	P Glasgow A	2
Jan 26	Falkirk	1	Rangers	2
Feb 9	Galston	2	Motherwell	1
Jan 26	Hearts	0	Airdrie	0
Jan 23	Hibernian	5	Forfar	0
Feb 2	Kilmarnock	4	Clacknacuddin	0
Jan 26	Maxwelltown V	1	Morton	3
Feb 9	Partick T	2	Dundee	2
Jan 26	Raith R	5	Aberdeen Univ	1
Jan 26	Renton	0	St Bernard's	0
Jan 26	T Lanark	4	St Johnstone	1

Replays

Feb 2	Port Glasgow A	2	Dumfries	0
Feb 2	Queen's Park	4	Arbroath	0
Feb 2	St Bernard's	1	Renton	1
Feb 9	Airdrie	0	Hearts	2
Feb 9	Johnstone	2	Aberdeen	1
Feb 9	Renton	2	St Bernard's	0
	played at Celtic Park			
Feb 16	Dundee	5	Partick T	1

2nd Round

Feb 16	Galston	0	Rangers	4
Feb 16	Hibernian	1	Johnstone	1
Feb 16	Kilmarnock	0	Hearts	0
Feb 9	Morton	0	Celtic	0
Feb 9	Queen's Park	3	T Lanark	1
Feb 9	Raith R	4	Ayr U	0
Feb 23	Renton	1	Dundee	0
Feb 9	St Mirren	4	Port Glasgow A	0

Replays

Feb 16	Celtic	1	Morton	1
Feb 23	Celtic	2	Morton	1
	played at Celtic Park			
Feb 23	Hearts	2	Kilmarnock	1
Feb 23	Johnstone	0	Hibernian	5

3rd Round

Mar 9	Hearts	2	Raith	2
Mar 2	Hibernian	1	St Mirren	1
Mar 9	Queen's Park	4	Renton	1
Mar 9	Rangers	0	Celtic	3

Replays

Mar 9	St Mirren	1	Hibernian	1
Mar 23	Hibernian	2	St Mirren	0
	played at Tynecastle			
Mar 23	Raith	0	Hearts	1

Semi-finals

Mar 30	Celtic	0	Hibernian	0
Mar 30	Hearts	1	Queen's Park	0

Replays

Apr 6	Hibernian	0	Celtic	0
Apr 13	Celtic	3	Hibernian	0
	played at Celtic Park			

Final

Apr 20	Celtic	3	Hearts	0
	played at Hampden Park			

DIVISION 1

	ABERDEEN	AIRDRIE	CELTIC	CLYDE	DUNDEE	FALKIRK	HAMILTON A	HEARTS	HIBERNIAN	KILMARNOCK	MORTON	MOTHERWELL	PARTICK T	PORT GLASGOW A	QUEEN'S PARK	RANGERS	ST MIRREN	T LANARK
ABERDEEN		Sep22 0-0	Mar02 3-0	Apr13 0-0	Dec08 0-3	Oct06 1-1	Feb16 2-1	Nov03 1-3	May06 2-0	Jan19 3-0	Mar09 2-0	Feb23 2-2	Oct20 0-0	Nov24 1-0	Sep24 2-1	Dec22 0-3	Sep08 4-2	Aug25 0-2
AIRDRIE	Mar03 0-2		Sep29 0-2	Aug25 4-0	Nov24 1-2	Nov03 4-2	Feb23 1-0	Oct20 3-2	Mar16 3-2	Dec22 1-0	Apr13 3-2	Jan05 0-0	Mar02 1-0	Sep15 5-0	Nov10 3-2	Jan19 2-3	Oct06 1-0	Sep08 4-1
CELTIC	Oct13 2-1	Dec31 2-1		Nov24 3-3	Mar23 0-0	Nov03 3-2	Jan02 2-0	Sep15 3-0	Nov10 2-1	Aug25 5-0	Jan19 2-1	Mar15 1-1	Dec22 4-1	Apr01 4-0	Oct27 2-1	Apr27 2-1	Nov11 1-1	Sep24 2-0
CLYDE	Nov17 1-3	Apr06 0-2	Jan12 0-2		Sep24 1-1	Oct20 2-0	Aug15 3-2	Aug18 1-0	Oct06 1-3	Feb09 2-1	Nov03 0-0	Mar30 1-0	Dec29 3-1	Dec15 3-1	Mar16 2-2	Dec08 1-5	Apr24 3-1	Mar09 1-2
DUNDEE	Nov10 0-0	Mar30 1-1	Oct20 0-0	Jan01 0-2		Sep01 3-2	Mar16 1-0	Apr08 2-0	Apr20 0-0	Nov03 4-2	Oct06 1-0	Jan19 1-0	Dec15 5-0	Aug18 0-1	Apr13 0-0	Sep22 2-0	Dec29 2-1	Mar02 2-1
FALKIRK	Jan01 3-2	Dec29 3-0	Nov17 2-3	Mar02 3-0	Apr06 4-2		Oct27 5-2	Sep29 2-1	Apr13 2-1	Jan12 2-2	Sep08 2-1	Oct13 2-2	Apr20 6-1	Mar16 2-1	Feb16 1-1	Dec01 3-2
HAMILTON A	Dec01 4-2	Dec08 1-2	Nov03 2-5	Sep03 1-3	Aug25 3-1	Jan19		May06 5-1	Dec15 2-4	Mar30 0-2	Sep08 0-2	Oct06 0-3	Mar23 0-1	Mar02 3-1	Jan05 0-3	Feb09 2-3	Oct20 0-1	Jan01 3-1
HEARTS	Apr15 1-1	Jan12 0-1	May11 3-3	May04 0-1	Sep08 0-0	May01 2-1	Oct13 3-1		Sep22 4-1	Mar16 1-0	Dec01 1-0	Apr06 1-1	Apr27 5-1	Nov10 2-0	Oct27 2-2	Apr13 1-1	Aug25 1-1	Dec15 1-1
HIBERNIAN	Aug18 2-1	Nov17 4-0	Mar09 0-1	Dec22 2-0	Sep29 0-4	Feb09 1-2	May04 0-1	Jan01 0-0		Sep15 1-0	Dec08 2-1	Jan20 1-1	Apr15 2-2	Jan05 1-0	Sep01 2-1	Nov24 1-3	Jan19 2-2	Nov03 1-1
KILMARNOCK	Oct27 1-3	Aug18 0-1	Dec29 1-2	Sep08 1-3	Mar09 1-1	Nov24 1-4	Sep22 0-1	Nov17 2-2	Dec01 1-3		Apr06 3-0	Mar23 3-2	Sep01 3-1	Apr27 3-1	Mar02 1-1	Oct13 1-3	Jan01 1-0	Jan12 3-3
MORTON	Sep15 2-1	Oct27 1-1	Sep01 0-2	Apr27 0-1	Dec22 1-2	Nov10 3-1	Feb02 3-0	Mar02 0-0	Oct13 2-1	Dec15 2-2		Mar16 1-1	Mar30 0-2	Jan03 3-0	Aug18 3-0	Nov24 2-1	Sep24 2-0	Sep29 0-1
MOTHERWELL	Sep29 3-2	Sep01 1-1	Aug25 0-6	Oct13 0-1	Oct13 0-3	Mar09 4-0	Dec22 0-2	Dec08 2-0	Dec29 0-0	Nov10 3-0	Nov17 4-1		Jan12 2-2	Apr13 4-1	Feb16 0-5	Sep22 1-0	Sep22 1-3	Nov24 3-2
PARTICK T	Apr06 2-0	Oct13 1-1	Apr24 0-2	Sep19 0-0	Oct27 0-0	Dec08 0-3	Nov10 1-0	Nov24 3-0	Sep24 5-0	Jan05 3-2	Aug25 2-2	Sep15		Mar16 0-1	Dec22 0-1	Jan02 1-4	Apr13 1-0	Feb23 1-1
PORT GLASGOW A	Jan12 2-2	Mar09 0-3	May04 1-1	Feb16 3-3	Dec01 1-1	Feb23 2-3	Nov17 0-0	Jan19 0-0	Sep08 1-2	Oct20 3-2	Sep22 2-1	Nov03 0-1	Oct13 1-0		Dec08 3-1	Aug25 0-2	Apr06 0-2	Dec29 1-3
QUEEN'S PARK	May04 2-0	Apr27 1-3	Dec15 0-4	Sep01 0-3	Jan12 1-2	Mar23 3-1	Apr24 3-1	Apr09 1-2	Oct06 3-0	Dec29 1-1	Sep22 2-3	Nov03 2-1	Sep29 3-2			Apr06 1-2	May11 0-3	Oct20 0-1
RANGERS	Sep01 6-2	Dec01 2-1	Jan01 2-1	Mar23 4-0	Apr01 2-2	Aug18 2-2	Dec29 1-1	Sep24 1-1	Jan12 3-0	Apr20 1-0	Oct20 3-0	Dec15 0-1	Sep29 5-0	Mar30 3-2	Nov17		Nov03 1-1	Feb02 0-0
ST MIRREN	Mar16 2-2	May04 4-2	Dec08 0-3	Nov10 1-0	Nov17 1-1	Mar30 1-1	Jan12 1-1	Dec22 0-2	Oct27 1-1	Sep29 3-0	Apr20 2-1	Dec01 1-0	Aug18 1-1	Sep01 4-1	Oct13 1-1	Feb23 0-0		Sep15 0-2
T LANARK	Mar30 2-0	Feb16 2-2	Mar16 2-1	Oct13 4-2	Dec25 2-0	Dec22 2-3	Aug18 2-2	Sep01 2-2	Jan02 0-0	Dec08 2-1	Mar23 2-3	Dec31 3-1	Aug15 3-1	Oct27 3-1	Jan19 2-2	Nov10 0-2	Jan05 2-3	

DIVISION 2

	ABERCORN	ALBION R	ARTHURLIE	AYR PARKHOUSE	AYR U	COWDENBEATH	DUMBARTON	E STIRLING	LEITH A	RAITH R	ST BERNARD'S	VALE OF LEVEN
ABERCORN		Nov24 2-3	Dec29 2-2	Feb23 1-1	Feb16 1-1	Apr13 2-0	Oct20 0-5	Aug25 4-3	Jan19 3-1	Nov03 2-1	Mar02 0-0	Sep08 1-2
ALBION R	Oct27 4-0		Aug18 3-0	Sep22 2-1	Mar09 1-2	Dec08 4-1	Nov17 2-2	Feb16 7-3	Dec29 6-2	Jan12 4-1	Mar30 0-0	Dec01 3-1
ARTHURLIE	Jan12 3-4	Mar16 1-1		Jan19 3-1	Mar23 3-1	Nov17 2-2	Oct13 3-0	Oct27 1-0	Nov24 3-2	Feb23 3-2	May11 5-1	Sep15 5-4
AYR PARKHOUSE	Aug18 2-1	Dec22 1-0	Feb09 1-3		Nov24 3-3	Mar23 2-3	Dec08 2-0	Sep29 1-4	Oct27 0-4	Oct13 0-3	Jan12 0-3	Nov10 3-1
AYR U	Nov17 1-2	Feb02 1-0	Dec01 3-1	Nov03 2-1		Dec15 0-0	Jan05 5-0	Dec29 4-2	Feb23 1-1	Jan19 3-1	Aug25 0-3	Sep22 1-2
COWDENBEATH	Mar30 3-1	Feb23 4-0	Mar09 2-5	Dec01 3-1	Jan12 2-2		Oct27 3-2	Aug18 2-1	Aug18 1-1	Apr06 3-0	Feb16 3-2	Dec22 1-2
DUMBARTON	Dec01 1-1	Nov03 3-2	Nov10 6-0	Aug25 6-1	Dec22 4-0	Dec29		Jan12 0-2	Sep01 1-2	Feb02 3-0	Feb23 2-3	Sep29 2-1
E STIRLING	Dec22 1-1	Nov10 2-0	Dec08 1-0	Mar09 6-2	Aug18 1-1	Nov24 0-1	Oct06 3-4		Feb09 2-1	Mar02 3-3	Sep15 1-3	Oct20 2-1
LEITH A	Nov10 3-1	Aug25 2-1	Feb16 1-2	Nov17 2-0	Oct13 1-0	Sep22 0-0	Dec01 4-0			Jan05 4-1	Dec15 1-0	Jan12 2-3
RAITH R	Mar16 4-0	Sep08 0-1	Mar30 1-3	Feb16 4-3	Dec08 3-1	Aug25 1-2	Dec15 0-4	Nov17 3-3	Dec22		Apr01 1-1	Dec29 1-1
ST BERNARD'S	Dec08 2-0	Jan19 3-1	Dec22 3-2	Apr06 3-5	Oct06 2-1	Apr20 2-0	Aug18 3-0	Mar23 1-1	Oct20 2-1	Apr13 3-2		Nov03 1-0
VALE OF LEVEN	Oct13 4-1	Jan05 6-0	Sep15 2-0	Oct06 5-2	Oct27 3-1	Jan19 6-0	Nov24 2-2	Dec15 3-1	Dec08 4-1	Aug18 2-0	Mar16 0-1	

DIVISION 1 FINAL TABLE 0

	P	W	D	L	F	A	Pts
Celtic	34	23	9	2	80	30	55
Dundee	34	18	12	4	53	26	48
Rangers	34	19	7	8	69	33	45
Airdrie	34	18	6	10	59	44	42
Falkirk	34	17	7	10	73	58	41
T Lanark	34	15	9	10	57	48	39
St Mirren	34	12	13	9	50	44	37
Clyde	34	15	6	13	47	52	36
Hearts	34	11	13	10	46	43	35
Motherwell	34	12	9	13	45	48	33
Aberdeen	34	10	10	14	48	55	30
Hibernian	34	10	10	14	40	49	30
Morton	34	11	6	17	41	50	28
Partick T	34	9	8	17	40	60	26
Queen's Park	34	9	6	19	51	66	24
Hamilton A	34	8	5	21	40	64	21
Kilmarnock	34	8	5	21	40	72	21
Port Glasgow A	34	7	7	20	30	67	21

DIVISION 2 FINAL TABLE

	P	W	D	L	F	A	Pts
St Bernard's	22	14	4	4	41	24	32
Vale of Leven	22	13	1	8	54	35	27
Arthurlie	22	12	3	7	51	40	27
Dumbarton	22	11	3	8	52	35	25
Leith A	22	10	4	8	40	35	24
Albion R	22	10	3	9	43	36	23
Cowdenbeath*	22	10	5	7	36	40	23
Ayr U	22	7	6	9	35	39	20
Abercorn	22	5	7	10	29	47	17
Raith R	22	6	4	12	40	48	16
E Stirling	22	6	4	12	36	40	16
Ayr Parkhouse	22	5	2	15	34	64	12

two points deducted for an irregularity

SFA Cup

1st Round
Jan 25	Aberdeen	3	Albion R	0
Jan 25	Airdrie	0	Dundee	1
Jan 25	Celtic	4	Peebles R	0
Jan 25	Dumfries	0	Motherwell	4
Jan 25	Dunblane	8	Elgin C	3
Jan 25	Falkirk	2	Rangers	2
Jan 18	Galston	6	Uphall	0
Jan 25	Hearts	4	St Johnstone	1
Jan 25	Hibernian	5	Abercorn	0
Jan 25	Kilmarnock	2	Hamilton A	1
Jan 25	Morton	7	Vale of Atholl	0
Jan 25	Partick T	4	Bo'ness	0
Jan 25	Port Glasgow A	7	Ayr Parkhouse	2
Jan 25	Raith R	2	Inverness T	0
Jan 25	St Bernard's	1	Queen's Park	1
Jan 25	St Mirren	3	T Lanark	1

Replays
Feb 1	Queen's Park	1	St Bernard's	1
Feb 1	Rangers	4	Falkirk	1
Feb 5	Queen's Park	1	St Bernard's	0

played at Cathkin Park

2nd Round
Feb 8	Aberdeen	0	Dundee	0
Feb 8	Hearts	4	Port Glasgow A	0
Feb 8	Hibernian	3	Morton	0
Feb 8	Kilmarnock	3	Dunblane	0
Feb 8	Motherwell	2	St Mirren	2
Feb 8	Partick T	1	Raith R	1
Feb 8	Queen's Park	6	Galston	2
Feb 8	Rangers	1	Celtic	2

Replays
Feb 15	Dundee	2	Aberdeen	2
Feb 15	Raith R	2	Partick T	1
Feb 15	St Mirren	2	Motherwell	0

Feb 19	Aberdeen	3	Dundee	1

played at Hampden Park

3rd Round
Feb 22	Aberdeen	3	Queen's Park	1
Feb 22	Hibernian	0	Kilmarnock	1
Feb 22	Raith R	0	Celtic	3
Mar 21	St Mirren	3	Hearts	1

Semi-finals
Mar 21	Aberdeen	0	Celtic	1
Mar 28	Kilmarnock	0	St Mirren	0

Replay
Apr 11	St Mirren	2	Kilmarnock	0

played at

Final
Apr 18	Celtic	5	St Mirren	1

played at Hampden Park

DIVISION 1

	ABERDEEN	AIRDRIE	CELTIC	CLYDE	DUNDEE	FALKIRK	HAMILTON A	HEARTS	HIBERNIAN	KILMARNOCK	MORTON	MOTHERWELL	PARTICK T	PORT GLASGOW A	QUEEN'S PARK	RANGERS	ST MIRREN	T LANARK
ABERDEEN		Mar28 0-1	Sep23 2-1	Aug17 3-1	Dec07 0-0	Jan11 1-1	Nov02 3-0	Dec21 1-0	Apr18 1-1	Oct05 1-0	Aug31 2-1	Sep28 2-1	Nov23 1-0	Apr20 3-0	Jan18 0-0	Sep14 1-3	Oct19 1-1	
AIRDRIE	Jan01 0-1		Dec28 0-0	Aug31 2-0	Jan11 0-2	Sep28 2-2	Jan18 5-2	Nov09 2-3	Sep14 0-2	Mar14 1-0	Dec07 3-0	Oct26 1-1	Dec14 7-2	Feb22 3-1	Aug17 2-0	Jan04 3-0	Nov23 3-0	Oct05 3-0
CELTIC	Jan02 3-0	Sep21 1-1		Jan11 5-1	Aug31 3-2	Sep07 3-2	Aug15 3-0	Apr20 6-0	Mar07 4-0	Apr04 4-1	Aug17 2-0	Feb01 3-0	Nov02 4-1	Nov16 5-0	Jan01 2-1	Dec07 4-0	Feb29 1-1	
CLYDE	Apr25 2-2	Feb08 0-3	Nov09 0-2		Dec28 2-3	Feb15 1-2	Aug21 3-2	Aug24 1-1	Oct26 0-0	Nov30 1-0	Jan18 0-4	Mar28 2-2	Sep30 0-0	Oct19 5-4	Dec14 0-2	Mar14 1-6	Feb01 2-1	Nov23 1-1
DUNDEE	Sep21 1-0	Sep07 3-1	Mar28 2-0	Oct12 6-1		Feb29 2-2	Nov30 3-0	Jan04 1-0	Jan02 0-0	Nov02 4-0	Nov23 5-2	Sep24 0-0	Feb01 0-0	Aug24 1-0	Jan01 3-1	Oct19 5-0	Feb21 1-2	Oct26 6-0
FALKIRK	Oct12 4-0	Mar07 1-2	Apr27 1-1	Nov16 2-0	Aug17 1-2		Feb08 5-1	Oct19 3-0	Mar14 3-1	Jan02 5-0	Apr01 4-1	Dec07 2-1	Oct05 3-1	Nov30 9-0	Mar21 5-1	Apr11 4-4	Dec21 5-2	Nov02 1-0
HAMILTON A	Feb01 3-0	Feb29 1-1	Feb14 2-4	Apr20 0-1	Mar07 0-3	Nov23 1-3		Mar28 2-1	Aug17 1-1	Apr04 3-3	Nov09 1-0	Oct26 2-3	Apr11 4-1	Feb15 2-2	Aug31 2-2	Apr25 1-1	Dec21 2-2	Jan01 0-1
HEARTS	Oct26 3-1	Apr11 2-0	Nov23 1-0	Apr18 1-0	Sep14 1-0	Dec14 2-3	Sep28 4-3		Apr04 1-2	Aug17 6-0	Feb15 1-2	Mar14 0-3	Dec28 1-3	Jan02 5-0	Aug31 5-7	Dec07 1-2	Jan11 0-1	Mar07 1-2
HIBERNIAN	Sep07 1-0	Feb01 4-0	Oct05 1-2	Mar21 2-1	Nov02 0-1	Aug24 0-4	Apr29 2-5	Nov16 2-3		Oct19 3-1	Nov30 3-0	Sep21 1-1	Nov09 6-0	Feb29 2-1	Jan18 4-1	Mar28 0-3	Apr27 2-1	Jan04 2-0
KILMARNOCK	Feb29 1-0	Sep14 0-1	Sep14 0-0	Sep28 2-2	Jan11 1-1	Oct26 1-6	Feb01 2-0	Dec07 2-0	Dec14 3-0		Oct12 1-2	Jan11 2-0	Mar07 0-1	Feb15 1-1	Mar07 2-2	Oct12 0-2	Aug24 2-2	Aug12 2-2
MORTON	Dec28 2-0	Nov02 0-2	Aug24 0-0	Mar07 2-0	Dec14 0-3	Nov09 1-1	Mar14 3-2	Sep07 1-1	Jan11 0-3	Apr22 2-2		Oct19 0-1	Dec31 2-0	Oct05 3-2	Apr18 2-3	Sep21 2-1	Feb29 1-1	Mar28 0-2
MOTHERWELL	Nov16 2-3	Jan02 2-0	Jan18 2-2	Jan01 3-0	Oct05 0-1	Sep14 1-5	Jan11 2-1	Nov30 3-0	Sep28 0-0	Nov02 1-2	Nov23 4-0		Feb29 3-4	Aug24 6-0	Sep07 6-1	Apr04 1-2	Aug15 2-3	Dec21 2-1
PARTICK T	Apr04 0-6	Oct19 1-4	Apr25 0-3	Dec21 3-1	Feb01 1-3	Nov02 1-1	Apr11 1-1	Apr17 1-1	Mar20 1-1	Aug31 2-2	Apr22 2-2	Apr18 2-0		Mar07 1-1	Mar28 0-3	Nov16 1-2	Sep25 1-2	Dec07 2-0
PORT GLASGOW A	Mar14 1-1	Nov30 1-3	Feb15 0-3	Dec07 0-0	Nov16 0-1	Mar28 1-3	Sep14 1-0	Jan18 1-1	Aug31 1-4	Jan04 1-2	Dec21 2-0	Mar21 0-5	Oct12 1-1		Oct26 2-0	Aug17 1-2	Sep28 2-3	Feb01 1-1
QUEEN'S PARK	Nov09 2-2	Dec21 3-2	Apr11 0-2	Feb29 4-1	Mar14 1-3	Apr08 2-4	Aug24 0-3	Apr29 6-3	Dec07 1-2	Sep21 5-1	Sep14 1-1	Apr25 1-2	Nov23 0-0	Jan11 1-1		Nov02 3-1	Mar07 2-0	Mar21 0-1
RANGERS	Aug24 4-0	Dec21 1-2	Oct25 0-1	Apr11 1-1	Apr20 2-0	Dec28 2-2	Mar21 1-0	Nov23 2-1	Nov09 1-1	Sep14 1-0	Aug15 3-0	Dec14 4-2	Jan02 3-2	Apr18 5-1	Sep30 1-1		Nov09 2-2	Jan11 2-0
ST MIRREN	Nov30 0-3	Aug24 3-1	Apr30 0-2	Nov02 1-1	Apr28 0-3	Apr04 2-2	Oct19 3-1	Sep21 2-1	Sep28 2-0	Jan18 0-0	Nov16 2-1	Oct12 0-0	Sep07 2-1	Dec14 2-2	Oct05 1-3	Apr13 2-0		Mar14 1-2
T LANARK	Dec14 1-1	Feb15 3-0	Sep30 0-1	Jan02 1-1	Dec25 1-1	Jan18 0-1	Nov16 2-0	Oct05 2-1	Apr11 0-6	Apr25 3-0	Oct26 2-0	Aug31 1-3	Apr20 2-1	Sep07 3-2	Dec28 3-5	Nov30 1-2	Aug17 1-2	

DIVISION 1 FINAL TABLE

	P	W	D	L	F	A	Pts
Celtic	34	24	7	3	86	27	55
Falkirk	34	22	7	5	103	42	51
Rangers	34	21	8	5	74	40	50
Dundee	34	20	8	6	71	28	48
Hibernian	34	17	8	9	55	42	42
Airdrie	34	18	5	11	58	41	41
St Mirren	34	13	10	11	50	59	36
Aberdeen	34	13	9	12	45	44	35
T Lanark	34	13	7	14	45	50	33
Motherwell	34	12	7	15	61	53	31
Hamilton A	34	10	8	16	55	65	28
Hearts	34	11	6	17	50	62	28
Morton	34	9	9	16	43	66	27
Partick T	34	8	9	17	43	69	25
Kilmarnock	34	6	13	15	38	61	25
Queen's Park	34	7	8	19	54	84	22
Clyde	34	5	8	21	36	75	18
Port Glasgow A	34	5	7	22	39	98	17

DIVISION 2

	ABERCORN	ALBION R	ARTHURLIE	AYR PARKHOUSE	AYR U	COWDENBEATH	DUMBARTON	E STIRLING	LEITH A	RAITH R	ST BERNARD'S	VALE OF LEVEN
ABERCORN		Oct26 1-2	Nov09 3-3	Aug17 2-0	Sep14 2-1	Feb08 1-1	Feb01 2-4	Dec21 2-1	Dec07 2-2	Sep28 2-0	Aug31 2-1	Feb29 0-0
ALBION R	Mar07 2-3		Feb08 5-2	Jan18 3-2	Aug24 1-1	Mar28 3-1	Oct05 1-2	Mar21 0-1	Nov16 1-3	Feb01 1-1	Feb22 0-2	Feb15 1-1
ARTHURLIE	Nov30 0-1	Aug17 0-1		Aug31 2-1	Feb15 1-3	Mar21 3-2	Oct26 0-0	Mar14 2-1	Nov02 3-1	Dec14 1-4	Sep28 2-1	Oct12 2-1
AYR PARKHOUSE	Nov02 2-0	Oct12 0-3	Dec28 2-1		Jan02 2-1	Feb15 4-3	Dec14 3-1	Aug24 5-1	Jan11 3-2	Jan04 2-1	Sep14 1-2	
AYR U	Nov23 2-1	Nov09 4-1	Oct19 3-0	Nov16 1-0		Jan18 3-0	Dec21 2-1	Apr04 2-0	Oct26 3-2	Aug31 2-2	Aug17 2-1	Nov30 1-2
COWDENBEATH	Dec14 1-2	Aug31 5-0	Oct05 1-0	Dec21 3-1	Nov02 1-3		Dec07 3-1	Apr25 0-1	Feb28 1-0	Aug17 0-1	Nov23 0-1	Nov16 0-0
DUMBARTON	Nov16 2-1	Dec28 1-1	Aug24 6-2	Nov30 1-0	Sep28 2-3	Sep14 3-1		Oct19 2-2	Aug17 4-0	Mar14 3-1	Nov02 4-1	
E STIRLING	Aug24 0-3	Sep14 1-1	Apr11 2-1	Feb01 2-0	Dec14 1-2	Oct26 3-1	Nov23 2-1		Feb29 3-0	Apr30 0-1	Nov09 2-3	Sep28 2-1
LEITH A	Jan04 1-0	Dec14 5-3	Feb01 2-1	Nov23 2-3	Oct12 5-1	Nov30 3-3	Nov09 2-4	Aug31 2-1		Apr11 0-1	Oct05 1-1	Dec21 5-2
RAITH R	Jan18 1-0	Dec07 1-2	Nov23 4-2	Dec04 2-0	Jan04 2-0	Apr06 2-0	Mar28 2-2				Dec21 2-0	Aug31 3-0
ST BERNARD'S	Feb15 2-2	Jan11 5-2	Mar07 1-0	Feb08 1-1	Dec07 1-1	Aug24 1-1	Jan18 1-1	Dec28 1-1	Sep14 2-3	Feb29 2-1		Oct26 2-1
VALE OF LEVEN	Dec28 2-1	Nov23 4-1	Dec07 1-1	Nov09 0-1	Oct05 2-1	Feb01 0-0	Aug31 0-1	Aug17 4-0	Oct19 2-2	Mar21 1-1	Dec14 0-0	

DIVISION 2 FINAL TABLE

	P	W	D	L	F	A	Pts
Raith R	22	14	2	6	37	23	30
Dumbarton*	22	12	5	5	49	32	27
Ayr U	22	11	5	6	40	33	27
Abercorn	22	9	5	8	33	30	23
E Stirling	22	9	5	8	30	32	23
Ayr Parkhouse	22	11	0	11	38	38	22
Leith A	22	8	5	9	41	40	21
St Bernard's	22	8	5	9	31	32	21
Albion R	22	7	5	10	36	48	19
Vale of Leven	22	5	8	9	25	31	18
Arthurlie	22	6	5	11	33	45	17
Cowdenbeath	22	5	4	13	26	35	14

* Two points deducted for a registration irregularity

SFA Cup

1st Round

Jan 23	Alloa 2	St Mirren 2
Jan 23	Broxburn 1	Beith 1
Jan 23	Clyde 4	Dykehead 0
Jan 23	Dundee 9	Ayr Parkhouse ...0
Jan 23	Falkirk 2	E Stirling 1
Jan 23	Hamilton A 0	Queen's Park 0
Jan 23	Hearts 2	Kilmarnock 1
Jan 23	Hibernian 2	Ayr 1
Jan 23	Leith A 2	Celtic 4
Jan 23	Morton 0	Aberdeen 4
Jan 23	Motherwell 6	Elgin C 1
Jan 23	Port Glasgow A ...5	Dunblane 0
Jan 23	St Johnstone 0	Rangers 3
Jan 23	T Lanark 5	Brechin C 1
Jan 23	Vale of Leven 0	Airdrie 0
Jan 23	West Calder 0	Partick T 0

Replays

	Partick T ....W	West Calder 0
Jan 30	Airdrie 1	Vale of Leven 0

Jan 30	Beith 0	Broxburn 0
Jan 30	Queen's Park 2	Hamilton A 0
Jan 30	St Mirren 5	Alloa 0
Feb 3	Beith 1	Broxburn 1
	played at Ibrox	
Feb 4	Beith 1	Broxburn 1
	played at Ibrox	
Feb 5	Beith 4	Broxburn 2
	played at Love Street	

2nd Round

Feb 6	Airdrie 2	Hearts 0
Feb 6	Celtic 4	Port Glasgow A ..0
Feb 6	Clyde 1	Hibernian 0
Feb 6	Dundee 0	Rangers 0
Feb 6	Motherwell 1	Falkirk 3
Feb 6	Queen's Park 3	Partick T 0
Feb 6	St Mirren 3	Beith 0
Feb 6	T Lanark 4	Aberdeen 1

Replays

Feb 13	Rangers 1	Dundee 0

3rd Round

Feb 20	Celtic 3	Airdrie 1
Feb 20	Clyde 3	St Mirren 1
Feb 20	Rangers 1	Queen's Park 0
Feb 20	T Lanark 1	Falkirk 2

Semi-finals

Mar 20	Celtic 0	Clyde 0
Mar 20	Falkirk 0	Rangers 1

Replay

Mar 27	Celtic 2	Clyde 0

Final

Apr 10	Celtic 2	Rangers 2
	played at Hampden Park	

Replay

Apr 17	Celtic 1	Rangers 1
	played at Hampden Park	
	Cup Withheld	

DIVISION 1 FINAL TABLE

	P	W	D	L	F	A	Pts
Celtic	34	23	5	6	71	24	51
Dundee	34	22	6	6	70	32	50
Clyde	34	21	6	7	61	37	48
Rangers	34	19	7	8	91	38	45
Airdrie	34	16	9	9	67	46	41
Hibernian	34	16	7	11	40	32	39
St Mirren	34	15	6	13	53	45	36
Aberdeen	34	15	6	13	61	53	36
Falkirk	34	13	7	14	58	56	33
Kilmarnock	34	13	7	14	47	61	33
T Lanark	34	11	10	13	56	49	32
Hearts	34	12	8	14	54	49	32
Port Glasgow A	34	10	8	16	39	52	28
Motherwell	34	11	6	17	47	73	28
Queen's Park	34	6	13	15	42	65	25
Hamilton A	34	6	12	16	42	72	24
Morton	34	8	7	19	39	90	23
Partick T	34	2	4	28	38	102	8

DIVISION 2 FINAL TABLE

	P	W	D	L	F	A	Pts
Abercorn	22	13	5	4	39	17	31
Raith R	22	11	6	5	46	22	28
Vale of Leven	22	12	4	6	38	25	28
Dumbarton	22	10	5	7	34	34	25
Ayr U	22	10	3	9	43	36	23
Leith A	22	10	3	9	37	33	23
Ayr Parkhouse	22	8	5	9	29	31	21
St Bernard's	22	9	3	10	34	37	21
E Stirling	22	9	3	10	27	33	21
Albion R	22	9	2	11	37	47	20
Cowdenbeath	22	4	4	14	19	42	12
Arthurlie	22	5	1	16	29	55	11

DIVISION 1

	ABERDEEN	AIRDRIE	CELTIC	CLYDE	DUNDEE	FALKIRK	HAMILTON A	HEARTS	HIBERNIAN	KILMARNOCK	MORTON	MOTHERWELL	PARTICK T	PORT GLASGOW A	QUEEN'S PARK	RANGERS	ST MIRREN	T LANARK
ABERDEEN		Sep12 2-0	Dec19 0-2	Jan01 2-4	Oct24 1-1	Nov07 3-1	Oct17 4-2	Feb13 1-0	Apr03 4-0	Sep26 2-0	Aug22 2-0	Nov28 1-3	Oct10 3-2	Jan02 3-1	Sep28 1-1	Sep05 0-2	Aug15 4-2	Jan30 6-1
AIRDRIE	Dec05 4-2		Nov21 1-2	Jan09 1-2	Sep19 2-5	Apr10 1-1	Jan02 0-1	Mar20 2-1	Apr21 2-1	Jan09 1-1	Dec12 1-1	Aug22 4-1	Apr22 3-0	Apr26 4-0	Nov07 1-1	Nov14 3-3	Mar13 4-3	Sep05 3-2
CELTIC	Feb24 2-0	Apr24 0-1		Dec26 2-0	Oct10 0-1	Jan30 1-1	Apr21 1-1	Jan09 1-1	Dec12 1-1	Aug22 2-1	Apr22 5-1	Apr26 4-0	Nov07 3-0	Nov14 2-1	Apr22 4-0	Mar13 2-0	Sep05 0-1	Sep28 1-0
CLYDE	Aug29 2-1	Oct17 0-0	Oct31 0-2		Mar06 0-2	Jan02 6-3	Aug15 1-0	Mar13 1-0	Apr17 2-0	Aug19 5-2	Apr03 4-1	Feb13 4-0	Apr24 3-0	Aug25 2-1	Dec19 4-0	Nov21 4-0	Apr21 2-1	Jan20 2-0
DUNDEE	Dec12 2-2	Nov28 1-0	Aug29 2-1	Jan30 1-0		Sep12 1-1	Apr03 3-0	Aug15 2-1	Oct17 3-0	Nov14 5-0	Feb27 1-2	Oct31 3-1	Jan16 3-2	Jan01 1-0	Sep26 7-1	Jan09 4-0	Dec19 4-1	Mar27 1-0
FALKIRK	Oct03 0-1	Dec19 0-2	Mar06 1-1	Feb27 0-0	Nov21 3-3		Oct10 5-3	Apr03 4-1	Sep05 0-0	Apr03 3-1	Feb13 7-0	Aug22 4-1	Jan01 3-1	Mar27 2-0	Dec12 1-3	Dec05 1-0	Oct24 1-1	Nov14 1-0
HAMILTON A	Sep19 1-2	Oct31 2-2	Apr30 1-2	Apr10 1-3	Oct03 0-1	Nov28 3-4		Nov14 1-1	Aug22 1-1	Sep26 0-0	Dec19 3-1	Mar06 2-0	Mar13 4-2	Feb20 1-1	Jan09 1-1	Dec12 0-7	Feb13 1-0	Feb27 1-1
HEARTS	Oct31 1-1	Sep26 2-6	Apr19 1-2	Aug22 1-1	Apr22 1-0	Apr17 1-0	Dec26 1-1		Sep19 1-1	Oct10 0-0	Dec05 5-0	Jan16 3-2	Apr28 1-0	Jan01 3-0	Sep05 3-0	Apr03 0-1	Nov21 1-2	Jan02 1-2
HIBERNIAN	Nov14 1-1	Aug15 0-1	Apr29 0-2	Sep12 0-1	Feb20 0-1	Mar13 2-0	Apr24 2-0	Nov07 0-1		Jan30 2-1	Nov28 4-1	Jan30 3-0	Nov28 1-1	Jan30 1-1	Apr19 1-0	Apr27 1-0	Mar27 2-1	Aug29 3-0
KILMARNOCK	Mar13 3-2	Aug29 0-1	Jan02 1-2	Nov07 2-1	Dec26 2-0	Oct17 3-1	Mar20 2-5	Feb20 0-1	Nov21		Dec12 2-1	Sep19 4-1	Feb27 1-1	Oct31 0-5	Oct24 1-1	Sep12 1-1	Jan01 4-2	Nov28 1-1
MORTON	Feb20 2-3	Mar27 3-1	Aug15 0-5	Nov14 2-4	Oct31 0-0	Sep26 1-1	Jan30 3-3	Jan02 4-1	Feb06 1-0	Feb06 1-1		Mar13 1-1	Aug29 1-0	Nov28 1-2	Oct17 0-2	Apr28 1-7	Apr17 2-0	Dec26 1-1
MOTHERWELL	Feb27 3-2	Jan01 2-4	Dec26 1-2	Oct24 0-1	Jan02 1-4	Dec26 3-1	Nov07 2-2	Sep12 1-6	Sep26 3-0	Oct10 2-1	Feb20 3-3		Aug29 0-3	Nov03 0-3	Jan30 2-5	Mar20 1-0	Aug15 1-0	
PARTICK T	Jan09 0-1	Nov14 0-6	Mar29 0-1	Sep28 1-1	Sep05 1-2	Sep26 2-4	Mar27 3-2	Oct24 1-5	Apr10 1-4	Aug15 5-1	Nov21 4-2	Dec12		Mar20 1-2	Apr08 0-6	Jan02 2-3	Dec05 1-7	Feb13
PORT GLASGOW A	Nov21 1-1	Jan16 0-1	Feb13 1-4	Apr29 0-1	Nov07 2-3	Jan09 2-1	Oct24 0-0	Dec12 1-0	Apr17 1-2	Sep12 2-0	Apr03 0-2	Dec19 0-0		Aug22 2-2	Feb27 2-0	Apr24 3-0	Apr05 1-1	
QUEEN'S PARK	Dec26 2-2	Apr15 0-3	Sep28 0-5	Apr22 0-3	Apr24 0-2	Aug29 0-2	Mar27 1-1	Sep26 2-2	Dec12 0-1	Mar06 0-2	Jan30 4-0	Oct31 0-1	Mar13 1-2		Nov14 1-1	Jan02 1-1	Apr03 1-1	
RANGERS	Mar27 3-1	Oct24 2-0	Jan01 1-3	Apr12 2-0	Sep28 4-1	Aug29 4-0	Mar30 4-3	Nov21 0-1	Mar06 1-1	Dec19 8-0	Nov07 3-1	Oct17 2-0	Aug22 7-0	Aug15 2-3	Apr26		Sep19 1-1	Oct31 2-2
ST MIRREN	Mar06 1-0	Dec12 1-1	Apr03 0-1	Nov28 4-1	Mar13 1-2	Apr10 2-1	Sep12 5-0	Aug29 2-0	Oct31 1-0	Oct03 3-0	Jan09 1-2	Nov14 3-1	Sep26 4-2	Oct10 4-1	Dec26 1-1	Oct26 1-3		Apr19 1-0
T LANARK	Mar20 2-0	Mar31 1-2	Apr12 1-1	Dec12 2-1	Dec25 2-1	Apr29 3-1	Nov21 6-1	Dec19 1-3	Apr27 0-0	Jan04 1-1	Sep05 3-1	Jan09 7-0	Oct03 0-4	Mar06 2-2	Nov07 1-0	Apr24 0-1	Aug22	

DIVISION 2

	ABERCORN	ALBION R	ARTHURLIE	AYR PARKHOUSE	AYR U	COWDENBEATH	DUMBARTON	E STIRLING	LEITH A	RAITH R	ST BERNARD'S	VALE OF LEVEN
ABERCORN		Aug22 3-1	Oct31 5-2	Mar20 4-0	Feb13 1-0	Dec19 6-0	Oct24 1-0	Nov21 1-1	Nov07 3-1	Oct03 1-0	Jan02 2-1	Feb06 1-1
ALBION R	Nov28 1-2		Aug15 3-3	Dec19 1-2	Dec12 2-0	Oct31 3-1	Sep26 2-4	Nov14 0-1	Aug29 1-0	Sep12 2-0	Oct17 1-0	Apr24 5-0
ARTHURLIE	Jan16 1-2	Jan30 1-2		Dec26 1-0	Nov21 3-5	Nov14 2-0	Jan23 2-0	Oct10 3-2	Sep26 4-0	Oct24 1-3	Oct03 0-4	Aug22 0-1
AYR PARKHOUSE	Oct10 1-1	Oct24 4-0	Aug29 2-1		Apr30 0-0	Feb13 1-0	Mar27 2-2	Apr03 3-0	Mar13 4-2	Nov28 2-2	Dec12 1-0	Sep19 1-2
AYR U	Nov14 2-1	Dec05 5-1	Sep12 3-0	Jan02 2-1		Feb06 3-0	Oct31 1-0	Dec19 2-0	Dec26 1-1	Jan09 2-1	Aug22 1-2	Mar20 2-1
COWDENBEATH	Dec26 0-2	Oct03 1-4	Jan09 2-0	Mar06 2-1	Nov07 2-2		Jan02 2-2	Nov28 0-1	Jan30 0-1	Aug22 0-0	Oct24 2-1	Dec12 0-2
DUMBARTON	Dec12 1-0	Nov07 1-3	Oct17 2-0	Jan30 3-2	Apr03 4-3	Nov21 0-0		Apr24 4-1	Aug15 1-1	Dec26 2-1	Nov28 1-0	Sep19 3-1
E STIRLING	Aug29 0-0	Feb06 4-1	Dec12 3-1	Sep12 3-0	Mar27 3-1	Sep26 2-1	Feb20 1-1		Aug15 1-3	Nov07 1-4	Jan09 1-0	Apr10 2-1
LEITH A	Jan09 1-2	Jan02 6-2	Feb06 5-1	Aug22 1-0	Apr03 2-0	Feb20 2-0	Dec19 2-0	Feb27 1-0		Dec12 0-3	Sep12 3-0	Mar06 2-2
RAITH R	Oct17 0-0	Oct10 3-1	Dec19 6-2	Apr10 3-0	Aug29 4-0	Dec05 4-1	Aug15 1-1	Jan02 2-0	Feb13 0-0		Oct31 4-1	Sep26 4-2
ST BERNARD'S	Sep26 2-1	Nov21 1-0	Nov07 1-0	Jan30 3-0	Oct10 2-5	Aug15 4-2	Aug29 0-0	Feb13 1-0	Dec05 3-2	Nov14 3-3		Dec26 0-2
VALE OF LEVEN	Feb27 1-0	Jan09 5-0	Jan02 4-1	Apr17 4-1	Aug15 3-0	Oct10 1-0	Aug29 1-1	Feb13 1-1	Mar27 2-1	Feb20 4-0	Dec19	

Season 1909-10

SFA Cup
1st Round
Feb 5	Aberdeen	3	Bo'ness	0
Jan 22	Ayr	3	Alloa	2
Jan 22	Bathgate	0	Hearts	4
Jan 22	Douglas W	0	Airdrie	6
Jan 22	Dumbarton	1	Celtic	2
Jan 22	Dundee	1	Beith	1
Jan 15	East Fife	4	Hurlford	1
Jan 22	Falkirk	3	Port Glasgow A	0
Jan 22	Hamilton A	0	Hibernian	0
Jan 22	Kilmarnock	0	T Lanark	0
Jan 22	Leith A	0	Clyde	1
Jan 22	Morton	4	Partick T	3
Jan 22	Motherwell	1	Forfar A	0
Jan 22	Queen's Park	0	Kircaldy U	0
Jan 22	Rangers	3	Inverness T	1
Jan 22	St Mirren	8	Elgin C	0

Replays
Jan 29	Dundee	1	Beith	0

Jan 29	Hibernian	2	Hamilton A	0
Feb 5	Queen's Park	6	Kircaldy U	1
Feb 5	T Lanark	2	Kilmarnock	0

2nd Round
Feb 12	Aberdeen	3	Airdrie	0
Feb 5	Ayr U	0	Hibernian	1
Feb 12	Celtic	3	T Lanark	1
Feb 5	Clyde	2	Rangers	0
Feb 5	Dundee	3	Falkirk	0
Feb 12	East Fife	2	Queen's Park	3
Feb 5	Motherwell	3	Morton	0
Feb 5	St Mirren	2	Hearts	2

Replays
Feb 12	Hearts	0	St Mirren	0
Feb 16	Hearts	4	St Mirren	0
	played at Ibrox			

3rd Round
Feb 19	Celtic	2	Aberdeen	1

Feb 19	Queen's Park	2	Clyde	2
Feb 26	Hearts	0	Hibernian	1
Feb 26	Motherwell	1	Dundee	3

Replays
Feb 26	Clyde	2	Queen's Park	2
Mar 2	Clyde	2	Queen's Park	1
	played at Celtic Park			

Semi-finals
Mar 12	Clyde	3	Celtic	1
Mar 12	Hibernian	0	Dundee	0

Replays
Mar 19	Dundee	0	Hibernian	0
Mar 23	Dundee	1	Hibernian	0
	played at Celtic Park			

Final
Apr 9	Clyde	2	Dundee	2
	played at Ibrox			

Replays
Apr 16
	Clyde	0	Dundee	0
	played at Ibrox			

Apr 20
	Clyde	1	Dundee	2
	played at Ibrox			

DIVISION 1

	ABERDEEN	AIRDRIE	CELTIC	CLYDE	DUNDEE	FALKIRK	HAMILTON A	HEARTS	HIBERNIAN	KILMARNOCK	MORTON	MOTHERWELL	PARTICK T	PORT GLASGOW A	QUEEN'S PARK	RANGERS	ST MIRREN	T LANARK
ABERDEEN		Oct09 1-0	Nov27 0-1	Jan15 1-1	Apr23 3-1	Dec04 0-1	Apr20 1-0	Mar12 3-0	Sep25 1-0	Mar26 0-1	Apr02 1-0	Oct23 2-2	Jan03 1-1	Nov06 3-0	Sep27 3-1	Mar05 1-1	Oct02 2-0	Aug28 2-1
AIRDRIE	Dec25 1-3		Jan08 0-2	Dec11 2-0	Apr19 3-0	Sep04 2-1	Jan03 2-1	Apr27 3-1	Nov27 0-2	Nov13 2-2	Mar12 2-2	Oct16 1-3	Sep25 1-1	Oct02 3-4	Aug21 2-1	Oct30 0-0	Feb19 1-1	
CELTIC	Apr09 2-0	Nov20 3-1		Mar28 2-1	Oct02 1-0	Aug21 0-0	Aug17 3-1	Nov06 0-0	Apr25 2-1	Dec04 3-0	Apr06 2-2	Sep04 3-1	Mar26 4-6	Jan15 1-1	Oct23 0-1	Jan01 1-1	Dec11 2-0	Mar16
CLYDE	Oct16 2-1	Sep18 1-1	Jan03 0-1		Apr27 2-0	Dec18 0-0	Dec25 1-0	Apr13 2-2	Oct30 2-1	Apr02 0-0	Apr21 1-0	Aug16 3-1	Sep27 5-0	Aug28 0-1	Oct09 0-1	Nov13 1-0	Apr30 2-1	Mar19 2-1
DUNDEE	Jan01 0-0	Dec18 3-0	Apr30 0-0	Dec04 1-1		Jan15 1-0	Mar05 2-1	Nov13 4-1	Apr13 4-2	Oct16 2-2	Feb12 2-1	Apr06 2-0	Sep02 1-1	Apr02 4-0	Sep04 3-0	Sep18 2-1	Oct30 2-0	
FALKIRK	Oct30 1-0	Jan01 4-1	Apr23 2-0	Mar26 6-1	Dec11 6-1		Aug28 2-1	Jan29 2-1	Nov27 2-0	Nov13 4-0	Oct02 2-0	Sep25 3-1	Apr02 2-0	Sep11 0-0	Apr20 1-1	Dec25 3-1	Apr09 3-1	Oct16 1-1
HAMILTON A	Nov13 1-0	Feb26 1-1	Sep18 1-5	Oct23 2-1	Jan08 3-3	Mar12 1-3		Apr23 2-1	Dec11 1-1	Feb12 1-7	Aug21 2-2	Oct30 3-1	Mar19 1-0	Oct09 3-1	Sep04 4-2	Jan15 2-3	Mar26 3-1	Nov27 4-2
HEARTS	Sep04 0-0	Jan15 0-1	Dec11 1-2	Aug21 2-0	Jan03 1-0	Apr16 4-2	Nov20 1-2		Jan01 1-0	Oct02 3-0	Oct16 5-1	Dec11 5-1	Oct30 2-2	Mar19 6-0	Dec25 3-2	Apr18 1-3	Nov27 0-1	Apr02 2-2
HIBERNIAN	Apr18 1-2	Dec04 3-0	Aug28 1-0	Feb12 0-1	Nov06 0-0	Mar05 1-1	Apr30 1-0	Oct23 1-4		Sep18 2-1	Jan03 2-1	Apr23 1-1	Apr09 1-0	Dec18 1-0	Jan08 0-0	Sep20 0-0	Nov13 0-1	Oct09 1-0
KILMARNOCK	Feb26 0-2	Aug28 3-3	Dec25 0-1	Nov06 6-3	Apr26 2-1	Mar26 0-2	Sep25 1-0	Apr30 1-1	Nov20 4-0		Dec11 2-0	Oct09 2-1	Feb19 2-1	Mar12 4-0	Sep11 6-1	Oct23 0-2	Jan01 2-1	Jan15 0-0
MORTON	Nov20 0-1	Oct23 0-1	Sep11 2-1	Dec25 2-1	Sep04 1-0	Nov06 0-1	Dec18 3-3	Jan15 2-0	Mar05 4-0			Mar19 0-1	Aug16 2-1	Jan29 2-0	Dec04 0-2	Mar12 1-4	Dec04 1-0	Apr09 0-2
MOTHERWELL	Jan08 2-1	Sep11 0-1	Dec18 1-3	Nov20 0-0	Apr25 1-1	Nov06 2-2	Jan01 0-1	Apr09 3-1	Oct02 3-1	Jan03 5-0	Dec25		Aug28 2-2	Mar05 6-3	Dec04 3-0	Jan29 2-3	Oct16 5-2	Sep18 2-1
PARTICK T	Dec11 1-1	Feb05 1-1	Nov13 1-3	Oct02 1-1	Mar28 1-0	Oct23 2-2	Jan05 2-3	Mar05 1-3	Dec25 3-1	Jan08 3-0	Aug25 0-1	Feb12 2-1		Feb26 3-1	Apr16 0-2	Nov06 0-0	Jan15 3-2	Mar12 0-0
PORT GLASGOW A	Aug21 0-3	Apr02 1-2	Oct18 2-3	Jan08 0-5	Mar26 0-3	Feb05 0-1	Feb05 2-1	Sep18 0-2	Oct30 0-1	Jan01 1-1	Nov27 0-1	Nov27 2-4		Dec11 3-0	Oct02 1-1	Feb19 0-2	Apr23 2-4	
QUEEN'S PARK	Apr30 2-2	Apr13 2-4	Mar19 0-1	Mar05 0-1	Nov27 3-0	Sep18 1-4	Dec18 2-0	Aug28 2-2	Oct16 1-1	Apr09 5-2	Oct30 2-0	Jan15 1-1	Jan01 4-0	Apr26 6-1		Mar12 3-2	Apr23 4-3	Nov13
RANGERS	Sep18 2-1	Mar19 3-0	Oct30 0-0	Apr23 1-0	Sep27 2-1	Apr30 0-1	Oct16 5-1	Jan08 1-0	Mar26 1-0	Aug16 3-0	Feb19 2-1	Nov27 4-1	Dec18 2-1	Jan03 4-0	Nov20 7-1		Aug28 1-1	Mar28 1-0
ST MIRREN	Mar19 1-2	Mar05 2-1	Jan29 2-1	Sep04 0-2	Oct23 3-2	Sep11 1-5	Oct09 2-0	Sep11 2-0	Oct09 1-3	Apr02 0-2	Aug21 2-1	Jan08 1-2	Sep25 3-2	Feb26 4-1	Apr16 2-0	Feb26 1-6		Dec18 3-1
T LANARK	Apr16 2-0	Nov06 3-0	Sep27 0-1	Jan01 1-3	Dec25 0-2	Jan08 1-1	Oct02 2-1	Apr20 3-1	Aug21 0-1	Sep04 7-0	Feb26 6-2	Mar26 0-2	Nov20 3-1	Oct23 5-0	Apr06 4-0	Dec11 2-1	Jan03 5-2	

DIVISION 1 FINAL TABLE
	P	W	D	L	F	A	Pts
Celtic	34	24	6	4	63	22	54
Falkirk	34	22	8	4	71	28	52
Rangers	34	20	6	8	70	35	46
Aberdeen	34	16	8	10	44	29	40
Clyde	34	14	9	11	47	40	37
Dundee	34	14	8	12	52	44	36
T Lanark	34	13	8	13	62	44	34
Hibernian	34	14	6	14	33	40	34
Airdrie	34	12	9	13	46	57	33
Motherwell	34	12	8	14	59	60	32
Kilmarnock	34	12	8	14	53	59	32
Hearts	34	12	7	15	59	50	31
St Mirren	34	13	5	16	48	58	31
Queen's Park	34	12	6	16	54	74	30
Hamilton A	34	11	6	17	50	67	28
Partick T	34	8	10	16	45	59	26
Morton	34	11	3	20	38	60	25
Port Glasgow A	34	3	5	26	25	93	11

DIVISION 2

	ABERCORN	ALBION R	ARTHURLIE	AYR PARKHOUSE	AYR U	COWDENBEATH	DUMBARTON	E STIRLING	LEITH A	RAITH R	ST BERNARD'S	VALE OF LEVEN
ABERCORN		Nov13 3-2	Sep18 2-3	Sep11 2-1	Oct16 2-0	Oct30 1-0	Feb12 5-2	Oct02 2-1	Jan01 3-1	Dec11 1-1	Nov27 3-3	Oct09 2-2
ALBION R	Feb05 5-2		Nov20 4-1	Oct09 1-3	Dec18 2-0	Aug28 1-1	Nov06 3-1	Jan01 2-1	Feb26 1-2	Sep11 0-0	Oct30 3-2	Mar05 2-1
ARTHURLIE	Aug28 1-1	Sep25 2-2		Oct02 1-0	Apr30 2-1	Oct16 1-2	Dec04 1-2	Nov13 1-2	Feb19 3-1	Dec18 1-2	Oct30 1-2	Oct23 2-1
AYR PARKHOUSE	Dec18 2-2	Nov27 2-2	Apr27 1-3		Jan01 1-3	Mar26 4-0	Feb26 4-2	Sep25 1-2	Aug28 1-1	Nov06 0-2	Nov20 2-3	Oct30 0-2
AYR U	Dec25 2-1	Aug21 4-3	Apr02 2-2	Nov13 2-0		Feb19 1-1	Mar19 3-1	Dec11 2-1	Dec04 1-3	Oct09 2-3	Sep09 3-0	Jan15 4-3
COWDENBEATH	Sep25 2-1	Oct02 1-0	Dec11 1-2	Aug21 1-0	Nov06 1-0		Dec25 1-3	Nov27 2-1	Feb12 2-1	Oct23 2-0	Sep11 1-0	Sep18 2-1
DUMBARTON	Oct23 1-1	Dec11 0-0	Sep11 3-2	Feb05 5-0	Nov27 3-1	Apr02 1-0		Apr23 5-2	Jan15 1-1	Jan01 4-1	Feb19 1-0	Aug21 1-1
E STIRLING	Nov06 3-1	Apr09 1-0	Oct09 2-2	Oct23 3-0	Nov20 2-5	Feb18 3-0			Apr30 2-2	Apr16 1-2	Aug21 3-1	Nov27 2-0
LEITH A	Nov20 3-0	Dec25 1-0	Aug21 3-0	Dec04 4-0	Jan08 4-0	Apr09 2-1	Mar12 3-1	Mar26		Feb05 1-0	Dec18 2-1	Sep11 3-0
RAITH R	Aug21 2-0	Oct30 3-0	Apr09 4-2	Mar12 1-2	Feb26 2-0	Nov20 3-2	Aug28 2-1	Oct16 1-0	Mar05 2-2		Dec25 2-1	Nov27 0-0
ST BERNARD'S	Jan15 1-1	Feb12 4-0	Jan01 2-1	Jan29 3-0	Nov13 3-0	Sep25 6-2	Oct16 1-1	Apr02 2-1		Dec25	Oct02 6-1	
VALE OF LEVEN	Feb26 2-2	Oct16 4-1	Nov06 3-0	Dec11 2-1	Sep25 1-0	Dec18 3-0	Nov20 3-3	Aug28 3-1	Mar19 1-3	Nov13 2-1	Dec04 1-2	

DIVISION 2 FINAL TABLE
	P	W	D	L	F	A	Pts
Leith A	22	13	7	2	44	19	33
Raith R*	22	14	5	3	36	21	33
St Bernard's	22	12	3	7	43	31	27
Dumbarton	22	9	5	8	44	38	23
Abercorn	22	7	8	7	38	40	22
Vale of Leven	22	8	5	9	36	38	21
Ayr U	22	9	3	10	37	40	21
E Stirling	22	9	2	11	38	43	20
Albion R	22	7	5	10	34	39	19
Arthurlie	22	6	5	11	34	47	17
Cowdenbeath	22	7	3	12	22	34	17
Ayr Parkhouse	22	4	3	15	27	43	11

* Elected to First Division

SFA Cup

1st Round
Jan 28 Aberdeen .... 3 Brechin C 0
Jan 28 Airdrie .... 2 Bo'ness 0
Jan 28 Annbank .... 0 Motherwell 5
Jan 28 Celtic .... 2 St Mirren 0
Jan 28 Dundee .... 2 Hibernian 1
Jan 28 E Stirling .... 1 Morton 4
Jan 28 Forfar A .... 3 5th Ksob 0
Jan 28 Galston .... 8 Lochgelly 0
Jan 28 Hearts .... 1 Clyde 1
Jan 28 Inverness T ...... 0 Johnstone 1
Jan 28 Leith A .... 2 Falkirk 2
Jan 28 Nithsdale W ...... 3 Inverness C 1
Jan 28 Partick T .... 7 St Bernard's 2
Jan 28 Rangers .... 2 Kilmarnock 1
Jan 28 Stanley .... 1 Queen's Park 6
Jan 28 T Lanark .... 0 Hamilton A 1

Replays
Feb 4 Clyde .... 1 Hearts 0
Feb 4 Falkirk .... 4 Leith A 1

2nd Round
Feb 11 Aberdeen .... 1 Airdrie 0
Feb 11 Celtic .... 1 Galston 0
Feb 11 Clyde .... 4 Queen's Park 1
Feb 11 Forfar A .... 2 Falkirk 0
Feb 11 Hamilton A ...... 1 Johnstone 1
Feb 11 Motherwell ......0 Nithsdale W ... 0
Feb 11 Partick T .... 0 Dundee 3
Feb 11 Rangers .... 3 Morton 0

Replays
Feb 18 Motherwell ...... 1 Nithsdale W 0
Feb 25 Johnstone .... 1 Hamilton A 3

3rd Round
Feb 25 Aberdeen .... 6 Forfar A 0
Feb 25 Celtic .... 1 Clyde 0
Feb 25 Dundee .... 2 Rangers 1
Mar 4 Hamilton A ...... 2 Motherwell 1

Semi-finals
Mar 11 Celtic .... 1 Aberdeen 0
Mar 11 Hamilton A ...... 3 Dundee 2

Final
Apr 8 Celtic ....0 Hamilton A 0
played at Ibrox

Replay
Apr 15 Celtic .... 2 Hamilton A 0
played at Ibrox

DIVISION 1 FINAL TABLE

	P	W	D	L	F	A	Pts
Rangers	34	23	6	5	90	34	52
Aberdeen	34	19	10	5	53	28	48
Falkirk	34	17	10	7	65	42	44
Partick T	34	17	8	9	50	41	42
Celtic	34	15	11	8	48	18	41
Dundee	34	18	5	11	54	42	41
Clyde	34	14	11	9	45	36	39
T Lanark	34	16	7	11	59	53	39
Hibernian	34	15	6	13	44	48	36
Kilmarnock	34	12	10	12	42	45	34
Airdrie	34	12	9	13	49	53	33
St Mirren	34	12	7	15	46	57	31
Morton	34	9	11	14	49	51	29
Hearts	34	8	8	18	42	59	24
Raith R	34	7	10	17	36	55	24
Hamilton A	34	8	5	21	31	60	21
Motherwell	34	8	4	22	37	66	20
Queen's Park	34	5	4	25	28	80	14

DIVISION 2 FINAL TABLE

	P	W	D	L	F	A	Pts
Dumbarton	22	15	1	6	52	30	31
Ayr U	22	12	3	7	54	36	27
Albion R	22	10	5	7	26	21	25
Leith A	22	9	6	7	42	43	24
Cowdenbeath	22	9	5	8	31	27	23
St Bernard's	22	10	2	10	36	41	22
E Stirling	22	7	6	9	28	34	20
Port Glasgow A	22	8	3	11	27	32	19
Dundee Hibs	22	7	5	10	29	36	19
Arthurlie	22	7	5	10	26	33	19
Abercorn	22	9	1	12	39	50	19
Vale of Leven	22	4	8	10	21	28	16

DIVISION 1

	ABERDEEN	AIRDRIE	CELTIC	CLYDE	DUNDEE	FALKIRK	HAMILTON A	HEARTS	HIBERNIAN	KILMARNOCK	MORTON	MOTHERWELL	PARTICK T	QUEEN'S PARK	RAITH R	RANGERS	ST MIRREN	T LANARK
ABERDEEN		Oct22 1-0	Jan14 1-0	Jan02 1-0	Dec24 0-0	Sep24 1-0	Sep03 2-2	Nov05 3-2	Apr08 1-1	Feb18 1-1	Mar04 3-1	Oct08 3-0	Apr01 1-1	Sep26 5-1	Aug20 2-0	Dec03 1-0	Nov19 2-1	Feb04 3-1
AIRDRIE	Mar18 1-3		Nov12 0-0	Aug27 2-2	Oct15 3-1	Nov26 3-1	Feb04 0-1	Mar11 4-1	Oct29 3-0	Jan07 3-1	Apr08 2-1	Dec10 1-1	Mar04 2-0	Jan21 5-2	Oct01 3-3	Dec17 1-4	Jan21 3-2	Dec17 0-1
CELTIC	Apr29 0-0	Aug17 3-0		Jan03 2-0	Sep17 0-0	Jan21 3-0	Apr26 2-1	Oct15 0-0	Mar25 2-0	Dec17 0-1	Aug27 3-0	Dec03 2-0	Jan07 0-1	Feb18 3-0	Dec31 0-0	Oct29 5-0	Nov05 5-0	Nov19 0-0
CLYDE	Oct01 0-0	Apr15 2-0	Dec10 0-2		Sep26 1-1	Oct22 2-1	Dec24 1-0	Aug20 4-0	Oct08 2-0	Aug15 0-0	Apr01 0-0	Jan14 2-0	Nov12 1-2	Nov26 3-0	Apr17 0-0	Apr22 0-1	Mar11 1-1	Sep03 2-0
DUNDEE	Nov12 2-0	Apr10 1-0	Nov26 1-0	Dec17 1-0		Jan02 1-1	Dec31 2-0	Dec10 4-1	Oct08 1-1	Aug27 1-2	Apr29 3-1	Apr15 5-0	Nov05 2-1	Sep24 5-0	Jan21 3-1	Apr08 0-2	Jan14 5-1	Oct22 2-1
FALKIRK	Jan07 1-1	Dec31 2-1	Aug20 4-1	Feb18 0-1	Oct01 1-1		Apr01 4-0	Mar04 3-1	Mar18 2-1	Oct29 1-2	Oct15 2-0	Dec17 3-1	Sep03 2-0	Sep17 1-0	Nov19 1-1	Apr15 0-0	Dec03 2-2	Feb25 3-2
HAMILTON A	Mar25 1-0	Sep24 1-1	Oct22 0-1	Jan21 1-1	Apr19 1-2	Aug27 3-2		Nov12 1-1	Dec03 0-2	Apr10 2-1	Nov26 1-0	Apr22 0-1	Apr24 2-1	Jan07 3-1	Dec17 2-4	Sep10 2-0	Oct29 1-4	Oct08 1-4
HEARTS	Dec17 0-3	Nov19 2-2	Apr01 1-1	Dec03 1-1	Oct29 2-3	Mar25 1-1	Mar18 2-0		Oct22 2-0	Feb11 5-0	Sep24 2-0	Jan14 4-1	Jan07 0-0	Sep19 1-4	Jan21 0-0	Dec31 0-1		
HIBERNIAN	Dec10 2-1	Dec24 0-4	Sep19 1-1	Mar04 4-1	Feb18 1-1	Nov05 4-2	Oct01 0-0	Jan02 1-1		Nov26 0-1	Nov12 3-3	Feb25 1-0	Sep17 2-0	Oct15 0-1	Apr22 3-0	Mar11 1-3	Sep03 2-0	Aug20 1-0
KILMARNOCK	Oct15 0-1	Aug20 0-1	Sep03 1-0	Nov19 5-2	Dec03 2-0	Apr08 2-2	Nov05 3-0	Sep17 3-1	Jan14 3-1		Feb04 2-3	Oct22 1-0	Mar04 1-1	Dec24 2-1	Mar25 0-0	Dec31 1-5	Jan02 0-2	Oct01 1-5
MORTON	Apr15 1-1	Dec03 0-1	Dec24 1-1	Nov19 0-2	Nov19 1-1	Apr22 0-1	Jan02 2-1	Feb25 2-2	Apr08 2-2	Sep10		Oct29 3-0	Aug20 0-1	Oct08 4-1	Aug17 1-0	Mar25 2-2	Jan14 2-3	
MOTHERWELL	Jan21 1-1	Jan02 2-1	Feb04 1-2	Oct15 0-2	Aug20 3-0	Mar11 0-3	Sep17 2-2	Sep03 2-2	Nov19 2-2	Apr01 2-2	Dec31		Dec24 2-3	Dec10 3-3	Mar18 0-1	Oct01 1-2	Apr08 2-0	Nov05 2-3
PARTICK T	Oct29 1-0	Oct08 1-1	Sep26 1-1	Mar25 0-0	Feb04 3-2	Apr29 3-1	Nov19 1-0	Oct01 2-1	Dec31 2-1	Sep24 1-0	Dec17 2-1	Aug27 1-0		Jan21 3-0	Dec03 3-0	Jan03 2-2	Oct15 2-2	Jan02 1-0
QUEEN'S PARK	Apr22 2-4	Sep03 0-1	Oct01 0-1	Dec31 1-3	Apr01 1-2	Jan14 0-2	Aug20 2-1	Apr29 0-1	Dec17 1-1	Feb25 0-0	Mar11 1-0	Mar25 0-3	Oct22		Nov05 2-1	Nov19 0-4	Dec03 2-0	Jan02 1-4
RAITH R	Nov26 0-1	Feb25 1-2	Oct03 1-3	Oct29 2-0	Jan07 0-2	Dec24 3-2	Oct15 0-3	Feb18 1-1	Sep24 2-4	Dec10 3-0	Aug31 1-5	Nov12 7-1	Mar11 2-0	Apr08 4-0		Aug27 0-2	Mar04 4-1	Feb11 2-2
RANGERS	Sep17 2-4	Nov05 1-1	Jan02 1-1	Jan07 6-1	Sep03 1-2	Dec10 1-1	Jan14 4-0	Dec24 2-0	Sep26 4-0	Nov12 3-0	Oct22 1-5	Nov26 7-1	Feb18 2-0	Mar18 4-0	Feb04 4-1		Aug20 1-0	Apr20 3-1
ST MIRREN	Dec31 2-0	Feb18 3-1	Mar18 1-1	Sep17 0-2	Mar25 1-0	Oct08 1-3	Apr29 0-0	Nov26 4-0	Feb11 2-0	Dec10 1-1	Sep24 1-2	Feb25 4-1	Nov12 2-1	Oct22 3-1	Dec17 2-1			Sep10 1-2
T LANARK	Aug27 2-2	Sep17 0-0	Apr17 1-1	Mar18 2-4	Dec26 2-0	Nov12 3-1	Dec10 3-1	Sep26 1-0	Jan07 0-3	Jan21 3-2	Feb18 2-4	Aug15 4-3	Nov26 2-1	Oct29 2-1	Apr15 1-1	Oct15 2-2	Dec24	

DIVISION 2

	ABERCORN	ALBION R	ARTHURLIE	AYR U	COWDENBEATH	DUMBARTON	DUNDEE H	E STIRLING	LEITH A	PORT GLASGOW A	ST BERNARD'S	VALE OF LEVEN
ABERCORN		Apr08 1-0	Nov19 2-0	Oct15 3-3	Apr15 1-3	Dec03 3-2	Nov05 1-2	Oct29 3-2	Mar11 1-4	Sep10 3-0	Apr01 1-0	Jan07 1-2
ALBION R	Aug20 2-1		Dec03 3-2	Feb11 1-2	Aug27 1-0	Oct22 3-0	Sep24 0-0	Dec31 1-0	Nov05 2-2	Oct08 0-1	Feb25 5-0	Nov19 1-1
ARTHURLIE	Aug27 2-1	Oct01 1-1		Apr08 1-4	Feb11 2-0	Nov12 1-3	Dec17 3-1	Feb25 0-0	Oct22 5-1	Jan07 3-0	Nov26 1-0	Nov05 2-0
AYR U	Nov26 3-4	Oct29 1-2	Oct08 2-0		Oct22 3-0	Apr01 5-1	Nov12 3-0	Dec17 4-0	Dec31 3-1	Aug20 2-0	Dec10 5-1	Sep10 2-2
COWDENBEATH	Sep24 2-1	Dec24 0-0	Aug20 1-0	Nov19 5-1		Feb04 2-3	Dec31 3-1	Jan07 1-0	Apr22 2-0	Nov05 4-0	Dec17 3-1	Jan02 1-2
DUMBARTON	Dec17 4-1	Dec10 2-0	Dec31 4-1	Nov05 3-2	Mar25 2-0		Apr15 3-1	Apr29 4-0	Jan07 2-0	Oct29 2-1	Feb11 8-2	Sep24 1-0
DUNDEE H	Sep17 4-1	Jan07 1-0	Oct29 2-0	Dec03 1-1	Oct01 2-0	Nov19 0-3		Apr01 0-0	Aug20 2-3	Mar18 4-1	Dec24 1-2	Oct08 1-1
E STIRLING	Mar18 5-1	Mar11 0-1	Mar25 1-1	Sep24 1-2	Dec10 0-1	Apr20 2-3	Jan02 2-1		Jan14 3-3	Dec24 2-1	Apr22 1-2	Jan21 1-1
LEITH A	Mar25 4-2	Mar04 0-1	Dec24 1-1	Aug27 4-6	Nov26 1-1	Feb25 2-3	Dec10 2-1	Feb11 3-1		Dec17 1-0	Jan21 1-1	Mar18 3-2
PORT GLASGOW A	Dec12 2-3	Nov26 3-1	Oct15 3-0	Oct01 1-0	Sep17 5-1	Aug27 2-0	Oct22 1-2	Feb04 4-0	Feb18 1-1		Sep24 0-0	Dec10 1-1
ST BERNARD'S	Oct08 3-2	Nov12 0-3	Feb18 3-1	Jan07 1-0	Mar11 0-0	Sep17 2-1	Sep10 4-3	Aug20 5-1	Dec03 1-3	Nov19 0-1		Dec31 2-0
VALE OF LEVEN	Oct22 1-2	Oct15 1-2	Mar11 0-0	Dec24 0-1	Nov12 1-1	Aug20 1-1	Nov26 2-0	Oct01 1-1	Apr08 1-2	Dec03 1-0	Aug27 1-2	

Season 1911-12

SFA Cup

1st Round

Feb 3	Armadale	2	Peterhead	1
Jan 27	Broxburn	6	Beith	0
Jan 27	Celtic	1	Dunfermline A	... 0
Jan 27	Clyde	2	Abercorn	0
Jan 20	E Stirling	3	Dumbarton	1
	played at Falkirk			
Jan 27	Falkirk	2	King's Park	2
Jan 27	Hearts	0	Hibernian	0
Jan 27	Kilmarnock	1	Hamilton A	0
Jan 27	Leith A	3	Ayr U	0
Jan 27	Morton	2	Clacknacuddin	0
Jan 27	Partick T	2	Dundee	2
Jan 27	Raith R	0	Airdrie	0
Jan 27	Rangers	3	Stenhousemuir	...1
Jan 27	St Johnstone	0	Motherwell	2
Jan 27	St Mirren	3	Aberdeen	3
Jan 27	T Lanark	5	Renton	0

Replays

Feb 3	Dundee	3	Partick T	0
Feb 3	Airdrie	3	Raith R	1
Feb 3	Falkirk	6	King's Park	1
Feb 10	Aberdeen	4	St Mirren	0
Feb 10	Hibernian	1	Hearts	1
Feb 14	Hearts	3	Hibernian	1
	played at Ibrox			

2nd Round

Feb 17	Aberdeen	3	Armadale	0
Feb 10	Celtic	3	E Stirling	0
Feb 10	Clyde	3	Rangers	1
	Abandoned - Rangers stratched			
Feb 10	Falkirk	0	Morton	0
Feb 24	Hearts	1	Dundee	0
Feb 10	Leith A	0	Kilmarnock	2
Feb 10	Motherwell	5	Airdrie	1
Feb 10	T Lanark	6	Broxburn	1

Replay

Feb 17	Morton	3	Falkirk	1

3rd Round

Feb 24	Aberdeen	2	Celtic	2
Feb 24	Kilmarnock	1	Clyde	6
Mar 9	Morton	0	Hearts	1
Feb 24	T Lanark	3	Motherwell	1

Replay

Mar 9	Celtic	2	Aberdeen	0

Semi-finals

Mar 30	Celtic	3	Hearts	0
	played at Ibrox			
Mar 9	Clyde	3	T Lanark	1
	played at Hampden Park			

Final

Apr 6	Celtic	2	Clyde	0
	played at Ibrox			

DIVISION 1

	ABERDEEN	AIRDRIE	CELTIC	CLYDE	DUNDEE	FALKIRK	HAMILTON A	HEARTS	HIBERNIAN	KILMARNOCK	MORTON	MOTHERWELL	PARTICK T	QUEEN'S PARK	RAITH R	RANGERS	ST MIRREN	T LANARK
ABERDEEN		Nov04 3-0	Mar23 1-1	Mar30 0-0	Dec16 2-1	Apr17 1-0	Jan06 2-0	Mar16 1-0	Mar02 1-1	Sep30 1-2	Apr06 1-1	Dec02 0-1	Oct21 3-1	Sep25 3-0	Aug19 3-1	Sep16 1-2	Dec30 2-1	Aug26 1-2
AIRDRIE	Apr20 3-0		Dec30 0-0	Sep09 0-1	Nov11 0-0	Oct28 2-1	Sep23 1-1	Apr06 2-0	Jan13 1-0	Aug19 1-0	Nov25 0-1	Jan01 1-0	Jan20 1-2	Feb17 4-2	Mar02 5-1	Oct14 2-2	Feb17 1-2	Oct07 1-1
CELTIC	Oct14 1-0	Aug15 3-0		Sep02 3-2	Mar02 2-0	Aug19 3-1	Nov11 2-1	Jan06 1-1	Oct28 3-1	Apr13 2-0	Dec23 1-1	Jan13 2-0	Sep25 3-0	Feb17 2-1	Apr20 1-1	Jan01 3-0	Dec02 3-1	Feb03 3-1
CLYDE	Oct07 0-1	Mar16 2-1	Jan02 1-1		Dec30 3-0	Sep16 1-2	Dec09 3-0	Apr13 1-2	Nov25 1-0	Aug16 3-1	Nov04 1-0	Nov18 1-2	Dec16 2-1	Apr27 0-1	Oct21 2-0	Aug26 0-2	Apr08 3-0	Jan20 1-0
DUNDEE	Jan13 4-0	Sep30 1-1	Sep16 3-1	Dec02 2-0		Dec09 1-1	Dec23 2-0	Oct07 1-1	Nov04 3-2	Mar23 5-2	Mar09 0-3	Jan09 3-1	Mar09 0-2	Feb10 4-0	Mar16 2-2	Feb10 2-1	Nov18 4-0	Mar30 3-1
FALKIRK	Sep23 3-0	Apr27 2-1	Nov04 1-1	Mar23 2-1	Jan01 0-0		Aug26 1-0	Dec02 2-2	Apr20 1-0	Apr06 2-0	Nov18 2-1	Oct21 2-1	Feb24 0-1	Jan13 3-1	Apr13 0-3	Dec23 0-2	Oct07 3-1	Mar02 7-0
HAMILTON A	Sep02 1-1	Nov18 1-2	Oct07 1-0	Jan01 0-0	Apr20 0-1	Mar30 1-3		Mar02 1-1	Sep30 3-0	Jan13 4-0	Mar23 3-1	Nov04 0-3	Dec30 2-1	Aug19 0-1	Sep16 1-1	Feb03 1-0	Oct21 1-1	Dec02 1-1
HEARTS	Nov25 1-2	Sep02 2-1	Sep30 1-1	Aug19 1-0	Oct28 1-4	Dec16 0-2	Apr24 2-0		Jan01 3-0	Sep16 1-1	Jan20 2-0	Apr22 2-1	Apr27 2-1	Nov04 0-0	Apr15 2-0	Jan13 2-1	Dec30 4-0	
HIBERNIAN	Dec23 1-1	Oct21 1-1	Nov18 1-2	Feb17 2-1	Aug26 1-1	Nov11 0-4	Mar09 0-1	Dec09 1-2		Dec02 1-0	Dec16 1-0	Oct07 4-0	Apr06 3-0	Mar16 5-0	Sep23 0-0	Jan06 3-2	Mar30 0-1	Sep18 3-2
KILMARNOCK	Apr27 3-0	Jan06 2-1	Sep23 0-2	Dec23 1-3	Nov25 1-0	Dec16 2-3	Sep09 1-3	Nov18 1-2	Jan20		Mar16 1-0	Mar09 1-1	Nov04 0-1	Oct21 1-2	Oct07 3-1	Mar30 3-2	Jan01 1-1	Dec09 0-0
MORTON	Jan01 2-1	Apr13 1-0	Aug26 0-1	Mar02 4-2	Apr27 4-2	Jan06 2-1	Oct28 3-1	Sep16 2-2	Feb24 2-1	Oct14		Feb03 0-2	Jan13 2-0	Dec07 2-2	Dec09 0-1	Dec02 2-1	Sep09 1-0	Nov11 0-1
MOTHERWELL	Apr13 2-0	Dec09 0-0	Nov25 3-2	Oct14 2-3	Jan06 0-0	Jan20 2-0	Feb17 0-2	Dec23 0-3	Mar23 0-1	Oct28 0-1	Dec30 0-1		Aug26 1-2	Aug23 1-0	Mar16 2-1	Nov11 0-3	Sep23 1-0	Sep09 0-2
PARTICK T	Dec09 3-1	Dec02 1-2	Mar16 1-1	Sep30 1-0	Feb17 2-0	Sep02 0-0	Oct14 2-2	Nov11 3-0	Sep16 3-1	Mar02 1-1	Aug15 2-0	Apr20 1-0		Dec23 2-1	Mar30 2-2	Oct28 0-1	Aug19 0-0	Jan01 2-2
QUEEN'S PARK	Nov11 2-5	Mar30 2-1	Nov04 1-4	Oct28 2-2	Jan20 1-0	Dec30 0-2	Aug06 0-3	Feb24 2-0	Apr20 1-0	Feb03 1-1	Apr20 0-1	Aug16 1-1	Feb10 0-1		Dec02 2-1	Mar02 0-0	Apr13 2-0	Jan06 1-1
RAITH R	Nov18 1-1	Aug26 0-1	Oct02 1-2	Jan06 0-5	Oct14 1-0	Sep30 1-2	Jan20 3-1	Feb17 2-2	Dec30 1-1	Nov11 3-2	Sep02 1-1	Dec16 3-2	Nov25 0-0	Mar09		Mar23 0-1	Feb24 1-1	Oct28 4-0
RANGERS	Jan20 2-0	Feb24 4-1	Oct21 3-1	Jan13 1-2	Sep02 2-1	Mar09 4-0	Nov25 7-0	Dec16 2-1	Sep25 2-0	Dec30 6-1	Aug19 6-1	Apr27 3-1	Jan02 4-1	Nov18 1-0	Aug16 5-0		Nov04 4-0	Sep30 4-0
ST MIRREN	Oct28 1-3	Sep16 1-1	Jan20 1-1	Nov11 0-2	Apr06 1-1	Mar16 1-1	Dec16 0-1	Apr20 2-0	Sep02 2-0	Aug26 2-4	Sep30 1-1	Mar02 1-0	Jan06 0-3	Nov06 2-0	Dec23 2-0	Dec09 1-5		Oct14 1-1
T LANARK	Apr08 0-2	Dec23 0-1	Dec16 1-0	Sep25 1-5	Dec25 1-0	Nov25 1-2	Mar16 3-0	Oct21 2-0	Aug19 3-1	Sep02 1-1	Sep16 1-2	Apr06 2-0	Nov18 2-0	Nov04 2-0	Jan13 1-3	Feb17 4-2	Apr27	

DIVISION 1 FINAL TABLE

	P	W	D	L	F	A	Pts
Rangers	34	24	3	7	86	34	51
Celtic	34	17	11	6	58	33	45
Clyde	34	19	4	11	56	32	42
Hearts	34	16	8	10	54	40	40
Partick T	34	16	8	10	47	40	40
Morton	34	14	9	11	44	44	37
Falkirk	34	15	6	13	46	43	36
Dundee	34	13	9	12	52	41	35
Aberdeen	34	14	7	13	44	44	35
Airdrie	34	12	8	14	40	41	32
T Lanark	34	12	7	15	40	57	31
Hamilton A	34	11	8	15	32	44	30
Hibernian	34	12	5	17	44	47	29
Motherwell	34	11	5	18	34	44	27
Raith R	34	9	9	16	39	59	27
Kilmarnock	34	11	4	19	38	60	26
Queen's Park	34	8	9	17	29	53	25
St Mirren	34	7	10	17	32	59	24

DIVISION 2

	ABERCORN	ALBION R	ARTHURLIE	AYR U	COWDENBEATH	DUMBARTON	DUNDEE H	E STIRLING	LEITH A	ST BERNARD'S	ST JOHNSTONE	VALE OF LEVEN
ABERCORN		Sep09 3-1	Dec30 1-1	Jan13 0-1	Nov04 2-2	Oct21 2-1	Feb10 3-1	Feb24 3-0	Dec02 3-0	Mar23 3-0	Oct07 2-1	Nov18 3-2
ALBION R	Dec23 1-4		Oct21 0-1	Nov04 0-2	Dec02 2-5	Mar02 2-1	Sep16 1-0	Nov18 4-1	Jan06 1-0	Dec09 2-3	Sep23 0-1	Aug26 1-0
ARTHURLIE	Aug26 0-1	Nov11 5-0		Feb03 0-1	Dec23 1-0	Sep23 4-2	Sep30 1-1	Dec02 0-1	Oct07 3-4	Oct28 2-2	Feb10 4-1	Sep16 4-2
AYR U	Aug19 4-2	Feb17 4-0	Jan06 3-0		Apr13 4-0	Dec02 2-1	Oct21 6-0	Oct07 2-0	Dec23 4-2	Jan01 3-2	Jan20 1-1	Dec09 4-0
COWDENBEATH	Nov25 2-0	Oct28 2-1	Oct14 0-1	Aug26 1-2		Jan06 0-3	Nov18 2-0	Mar30 1-0	Sep23 3-1	Nov11 5-0	Dec16 3-1	Aug19 1-3
DUMBARTON	Sep30 1-5	Dec30 2-0	Dec09 1-0	Feb10 6-1	Sep09 2-0		Jan02 1-0	Jan27 2-1	Jan13 5-2	Aug19 3-0	Feb24 4-1	Dec16 2-0
DUNDEE H	Oct28 1-1	Oct07 0-1	Nov25 0-0	Dec16 2-2	Apr08 5-2	Feb17 4-2		Jan06 1-0	Aug26 1-0	Oct14 2-2	Nov11 1-0	Dec30 0-1
E STIRLING	Dec16 0-0	Sep23 4-0	Sep09 2-0	Mar16 1-0	Oct28 0-1	Mar09 3-1	Aug19		Sep16 0-1	Dec30 2-4	Feb17 2-2	Mar02 2-0
LEITH A	Nov11 2-1	Aug19 0-1	Feb17 2-2	Nov25 2-2	Dec30 2-2	Oct14 1-1	Dec09 2-1	Mar23		Sep30 2-0	Mar09 0-0	Sep09 2-0
ST BERNARD'S	Jan06 0-1	Dec16 1-0	Jan27 1-1	Mar30 2-2	Oct21 0-1	Dec23 2-1	Nov04 7-1	Aug26 1-3	Nov18 2-1		Dec02 2-0	Oct07 5-0
ST JOHNSTONE	Dec09 1-0	Nov25 3-1	Aug19 4-1	Dec30 1-0	Mar23 0-3	Nov04 0-1	Sep23 1-0	Jan13 3-1	Jan01 2-0	Sep09 0-0		Oct28 2-0
VALE OF LEVEN	Jan20 0-3	Oct14 2-1	Nov04 2-1	Sep23 2-3	Feb17 1-3	Aug26 2-4	Dec02 2-0	Dec23 3-1	Oct21 2-4	Nov25 1-2	Jan06 1-4	

DIVISION 2 FINAL TABLE

	P	W	D	L	F	A	Pts
Ayr U	22	16	3	3	54	24	35
Abercorn	22	13	4	5	43	22	30
Dumbarton	22	13	1	8	47	31	27
Cowdenbeath	22	12	2	8	39	31	26
St Johnstone	22	10	4	8	29	27	24
St Bernard's	22	9	5	8	38	36	23
Leith A	22	9	4	9	31	34	22
Arthurlie	22	7	5	10	30	30	19
E Stirling	22	7	3	12	21	31	17
Dundee Hibs	22	5	5	12	21	41	15
Vale of Leven	22	6	1	15	26	50	13
Albion R	22	6	1	15	19	41	13

Season 1912-13

SFA Cup

1st Round
Jan 25 Hamilton A .....0 St Bernard's 0
Jan 25 Kilmarnock ....3 Nithsdale W 0

Replay
Feb 1 St Bernard's ....0 Hamilton A 3

2nd Round
Feb 8 Aberdeen Univ ..0 Peebles R 3
Feb 8 Ayr U ....0 Airdrie 2
Feb 8 Celtic ....4 Arbroath 0
Feb 8 Clyde ....0 E Stirling 0
Feb 8 Dumbarton ....2 Aberdeen 1
Feb 8 Dundee ....5 Thornehill 0
Feb 8 Hamilton A ....1 Rangers 1
Feb 8 Hearts ....3 Dunfermline A ...1
Feb 8 Kilmarnock ....5 Abercorn 1
Feb 8 Morton ....2 Falkirk 2
Feb 8 Motherwell ....1 Hibernian 1
Feb 8 Partick T .....4 Inverness C 1
Feb 8 Queen's Park ...4 Dundee H 2
Feb 8 Raith R ....5 Broxburn 0
Feb 8 St Johnstone ..3 East Fife 0
Feb 8 St Mirren .....0 T Lanark 0

Replays
Feb 15 E Stirling .....1 Clyde 1
Feb 15 Falkirk ....3 Morton 1
Feb 15 Hibernian .....0 Motherwell 0
Feb 15 Rangers ....2 Hamilton A 0
Feb 15 T Lanark ......0 St Mirren 2
Feb 18 Clyde ....1 E Stirling 0
played at Shawfields
Feb 19 Hibernian .....2 Motherwell 1
played at Celtic Park

3rd Round
Feb 22 Celtic ....3 Peebles R 0
Feb 22 Clyde ....1 Queen's Park ..0
Feb 22 Dumbarton ....1 St Johnstone ...0
Feb 22 Kilmarnock ....0 Hearts 2
Feb 22 Partick T .....0 Dundee 1
Feb 22 Raith R ....2 Hibernian 2
Feb 22 Rangers ......1 Falkirk 3
Feb 22 St Mirren ....1 Airdrie 0

Replay
Mar 1 Hibernian .....0 Raith R 1

4th Round
Mar 8 Celtic ....0 Hearts 1
Mar 8 Dundee ....0 Clyde 0
Mar 8 Falkirk ....1 Dumbarton 0
Mar 8 Raith R ....2 St Mirren 1

Replay
Mar 15 Clyde ....1 Dundee 1
Mar 19 Clyde ....2 Dundee 1
played at Hampden Park

Semi-finals
Mar 29 Clyde ....1 Raith R 1
played at Tynecastle
Mar 29 Falkirk ....1 Hearts 0
played at Ibrox

Replay
Apr 5 Clyde ....0 Raith R 1
played at Tynecastle

Final
Apr 12 Falkirk ....2 Raith R 0
played at Celtic Park

DIVISION 1 FINAL TABLE

	P	W	D	L	F	A	Pts
Rangers	34	24	5	5	76	41	53
Celtic	34	22	5	7	53	28	49
Hearts	34	17	7	10	71	43	41
Airdrie	34	15	11	8	64	46	41
Falkirk	34	14	12	8	56	38	40
Motherwell	34	12	13	9	47	39	37
Aberdeen	34	14	9	11	47	40	37
Hibernian	34	16	5	13	63	54	37
Clyde	34	13	9	12	41	44	35
Hamilton A	34	12	8	14	44	47	32
Kilmarnock	34	10	11	13	37	54	31
St Mirren	34	10	10	14	50	60	30
Morton	34	11	7	16	50	59	29
Dundee	34	8	13	13	33	46	29
T Lanark	34	8	12	14	31	41	28
Raith R	34	8	10	16	46	60	26
Partick T	34	10	4	20	40	55	24
Queen's Park	34	5	3	26	34	88	13

DIVISION 2 FINAL TABLE

	P	W	D	L	F	A	Pts
Ayr U*	26	13	8	5	45	19	34
Dunfermline	26	13	7	6	45	27	33
E Stirling	26	12	8	6	43	27	32
Abercorn	26	12	7	7	33	31	31
Cowdenbeath	26	12	6	8	36	28	30
Dumbarton*	26	12	5	9	38	30	29
St Bernard's	26	12	3	11	36	34	27
Johnstone	26	9	6	11	31	43	24
Albion R	26	10	3	13	38	40	23
Dundee Hibs	26	6	10	10	34	43	22
St Johnstone	26	7	7	12	29	38	21
Vale of Leven	26	8	5	13	28	44	21
Arthurlie	26	7	5	14	37	49	19
Leith A	26	5	8	13	26	47	18

Ayr United and Dumbarton were elected to the First Division. Nevertheless, no clubs were demoted from the First Division.

DIVISION 1

	ABERDEEN	AIRDRIE	CELTIC	CLYDE	DUNDEE	FALKIRK	HAMILTON A	HEARTS	HIBERNIAN	KILMARNOCK	MORTON	MOTHERWELL	PARTICK T	QUEEN'S PARK	RAITH R	RANGERS	ST MIRREN	T LANARK
ABERDEEN		Jan18 4-1	Feb15 3-0	Sep23 0-1	Jan01 1-0	Oct26 2-2	Sep21 2-0	Oct19 0-1	Dec21 1-3	Nov09 0-0	Dec07 0-0	Mar29 2-2	Nov16 3-1	Sep30 4-0	Oct05 2-0	Mar01 1-3	4-0	Feb22 2-0
AIRDRIE	Oct12 1-1		Sep14 1-4	Aug24 2-3	Nov02 1-1	Mar15 5-1	Mar22 4-0	Nov23 1-0	Apr26 3-2	Dec07 5-1	Mar08 1-1	Sep28 2-0	Sep21 4-3	Jan04 0-1	Nov16 3-0	Dec21 2-2	Mar29 3-2	Mar01 3-2
CELTIC	Sep07 2-0	Jan25 1-1		Jan02 3-0	Dec21 2-0	Mar22 1-2	Dec07 2-1	Nov09 1-0	Aug24 1-1	Mar29 4-1	Oct05 1-2	Nov23 1-0	Jan04 1-0	Jan11 1-0	Mar24 4-1	Oct26 3-2	Apr05 2-1	Feb01 2-0
CLYDE	Nov02 0-1	Dec14 0-0	Nov30 1-1		Apr12 2-2	Dec31 0-0	Nov16 2-1	Aug17 0-0	Apr29 2-0	Oct12 0-1	Sep21 3-2	Dec07 0-1	Apr22 3-0	Oct19 1-0	Aug31 0-1	Apr15 1-2	Mar24 1-1	Sep30 1-1
DUNDEE	Aug24 1-3	Jan11 1-1	Sep21 3-1	Sep07 1-3		Oct12 2-2	Apr05 3-1	Dec14 2-2	Nov30 0-1	Feb01 0-0	Nov16 0-1	Mar01 0-0	Dec28 1-0	Sep28 0-0	Nov09 1-0	Apr19 2-0	Apr07 1-0	Oct26 1-0
FALKIRK	Dec14 3-1	Aug31 2-3	Aug17 0-0	Jan25 0-2	Jan04 2-0		Apr19 6-0	Oct05 2-0	Apr05 0-2	Nov23 0-0	Oct19 2-1	Apr16 1-1	Jan11 1-0	Mar01 3-1	Apr28 0-1	Nov30 2-0	Nov02 2-0	Dec28 2-2
HAMILTON A	Mar15 3-0	Oct26 1-3	0-1	Mar01 0-1	Jan25 1-0	Sep28 0-0		Jan11 4-2	Oct12 3-1	Sep07 3-1	Feb22 3-1	Jan01 0-0	Dec14 2-0	Mar29 2-1	Dec28 4-0	Aug24 0-3	Nov30 3-1	Nov09 0-0
HEARTS	Feb01 4-1	Sep07 1-1	Apr21 0-0	Jan04 3-2	Mar22 4-3	Apr23 0-2	Dec21 1-0		Sep28 1-0	Oct26 5-0	Apr12 4-2	Apr26 0-1	Nov02 4-0	Aug24 10-3	Nov30 2-0	Mar15 1-1	Nov16 2-0	Oct12 1-2
HIBERNIAN	Nov23 3-1	Dec28 2-2	Jan18 1-0	Dec07 3-1	Jan25 4-0	Nov09 3-3	Apr21 3-1	Apr16 0-3		Apr19 4-0	Jan11 3-1	Mar08 1-2	Aug31 1-0	Oct05 3-0	Dec14 1-2	Oct19 0-1	Sep21 1-1	Aug17 1-4
KILMARNOCK	Mar08 3-1	Oct19 0-1	Oct19 0-2	Jan11 3-2	Oct05 2-0	Apr30 1-1	1-1	Dec28 2-2	Nov16 0-1		Sep14 1-1	Oct14 0-1	Aug17 2-1	Nov02 0-2	Mar15 4-3	Jan01 2-3	Jan01 2-1	Sep21 2-0
MORTON	Sep28 0-1	Jan01 2-0	Dec14 1-2	Mar22 3-0	Mar29 1-1	Jan18 1-1	Aug31 1-1	Mar01 1-3	Oct26 0-1	Jan04 2-0		Nov09 2-2	Oct12 3-1	Sep07 2-1	Apr19 1-0	Jan25 0-4	Aug17 0-3	Nov30 2-0
MOTHERWELL	Nov30 1-1	Apr05 2-1	Mar15 1-0	Oct05 0-1	Aug17 0-0	Nov16 1-4	Oct19 0-0	Aug31 1-2	Nov02 5-1	Apr12 0-1	Dec21 2-0		Jan25 4-1	Dec07 6-3	Sep21 1-1	Sep14 1-2	Jan04 3-1	Jan18 0-0
PARTICK T	Apr19 0-1	Feb15 1-1	Sep30 2-3	Nov09 2-2	Oct19 2-0	Sep07 0-1	Oct05 2-1	Dec07 1-3	Mar29 1-2	Nov30 4-1	Mar15 5-3	Aug24 1-1		Dec21 1-0	Oct26 2-0	Apr22 2-3	Jan18 2-1	Jan01 3-1
QUEEN'S PARK	Jan25 0-1	Nov30 0-4	Nov16 0-1	Apr26 0-3	Jan18 1-3	Sep21 2-1	Aug17 0-5	Feb15 1-6	Apr12 3-5	Apr22 1-3	Dec28 3-0	Oct26 1-1	Feb01 3-0		Apr30 1-0	Nov09 2-3	Aug31 0-2	Dec14 1-3
RAITH R	Jan04 0-0	Apr23 2-4	Oct19 2-1	Dec21 5-1	Feb15 0-0	Aug24 0-1	Nov02 3-5	Jan18 3-3	Sep07 4-2	Sep28 0-0	Nov23 2-2	Mar22 2-0	Apr07 0-2	Oct12 5-0		Dec07 2-2	Oct05 2-2	Jan25 1-3
RANGERS	Dec28 3-1	Aug17 4-2	Jan01 0-1	Nov23 3-0	Aug31 3-3	Apr26 2-1	Apr26 3-2	Sep21 2-4	Jan04 5-3	Sep30 3-0	Nov02 1-1	Jan11 3-1	Mar22 2-0	Apr07 4-0	Feb01 4-0		Dec14 2-1	Nov16 6-1
ST MIRREN	Jan11 2-2	Nov09 1-0	Dec28 1-3	Oct26 2-0	Dec07 2-0	Dec21 1-4	Sep14 0-0	Jan25 2-1	Mar22 0-1	Aug24 0-3	Feb01 4-2	Oct12 2-1	Nov23 5-0	Mar15 4-4	Apr26 0-3	Sep07		Sep28 2-2
T LANARK	Aug31 0-0	Oct05 0-0	Nov02 0-2	Apr19 0-3	Dec25 4-1	Dec07 1-1	Jan04 0-0	Apr05 1-0	Mar15 3-0	Dec21 0-0	Apr26 1-5	Sep07 0-1	Mar08 0-1	Oct19 1-0	Jan11 0-0	Mar24 0-1	Oct19	

DIVISION 2

	ABERCORN	ALBION R	ARTHURLIE	AYR U	COWDENBEATH	DUMBARTON	DUNDEE H	DUNFERMLINE A	E STIRLING	JOHNSTONE	LEITH A	ST BERNARD'S	ST JOHNSTONE	VALE OF LEVEN
ABERCORN		Jan04 1-0	Nov02 0-0	Dec14 3-1	Mar08 1-2	Feb15 2-0	Mar29 0-1	Apr21 2-2	Mar01 1-1	Jan18 3-0	Aug31 2-1	Apr26 3-2	Apr08 2-1	Oct05 2-0
ALBION R	Apr19 0-0		Feb15 4-2	Oct19 0-1	Aug31 0-3	Dec28 1-0	Oct26 5-1	Jan18 2-1	Jan25 0-0	Aug17 3-1	Dec14 3-0	Feb08 3-2	Jan11 2-1	Feb22 5-0
ARTHURLIE	Aug24 2-3	Feb01 3-1		Nov09 1-2	Oct12 0-2	Mar22 0-2	Sep28 4-1	Apr12 2-2	Dec28 1-1	Oct26 2-0	Jan11 4-1	Dec07 2-1	Nov30 3-0	Jan18 1-0
AYR U	Aug17 0-2	Nov02 3-0	Jan25 1-1		Nov23 1-0	Feb01 1-1	Nov16 5-0	Mar29 3-1	Jan11 3-0	Dec28 5-0	Dec07 6-0	Jan01 3-1	Mar08 2-1	Aug31 6-0
COWDENBEATH	Apr12 0-1	Mar01 2-0	Dec14 1-1	Aug24 1-1		Apr19 2-1	Feb15 1-1	Aug17 2-2	Nov02 1-2	Jan04 2-0	Oct26 3-1	Jan11 2-0	Sep14 2-2	Nov30 1-0
DUMBARTON	Apr16 3-0	Dec21 3-2	Jan04 4-0	Apr12 1-0	Mar29 0-1		2-0	Nov23 2-1	Nov09 0-1	Nov16 1-1	Mar15 2-1	Apr05 0-2	Jan25 1-0	Oct05 1-1
DUNDEE H	Feb22 2-1	Mar15 3-1	Aug31 1-0	Jan18 1-1	Dec21 3-0	Jan01 1-1		Mar22 1-1	Aug17 2-3	Jan25 7-1	Nov23 2-1	Jan02 3-0	Dec07 2-0	Sep14 1-1
DUNFERMLINE A	Apr30 3-0	Sep14 5-2	Mar08 5-1	Nov30 0-0	Jan04 1-0	Jan11 3-0	Mar01 0-0		Apr05 1-0	Apr19 2-1	Feb15 1-1	Aug24 2-1	Apr26 1-0	Jan04 4-0
E STIRLING	Apr28 5-1	Jan18 0-1	Jan18 4-2	Dec21 1-1	Oct12 0-1	Mar22 3-1	Mar08 1-1	Mar15 4-2		1-1	Nov09 1-1	Nov16 2-0	Aug24 2-0	Oct12 1-2
JOHNSTONE	Sep14 1-1	Dec07 0-1	Nov16 1-1	Mar15 1-1	Feb08 1-2	Aug24 2-2	Jan11 4-1	Dec14 1-1	Oct05 1-1		Oct19 1-0	Oct12 1-0	Nov23 2-0	Dec21 2-1
LEITH A	Mar15 1-1	Oct12 0-1	Oct05 4-1	Feb22 1-4	Nov16 0-3	Jan18 2-2	Aug24 2-0	Jan25 0-2	Jan04 0-3	Nov30 1-0		Sep14 3-0	Dec21 0-1	Feb08 1-1
ST BERNARD'S	Apr05 3-0	Nov23 3-2	Mar01 0-0	Apr12 3-0	Sep28 2-1	Dec28 1-3	Sep21 3-0	Dec14 4-1	Feb22 2-1	Aug31 1-1	Apr19 1-2		Jan18 1-0	Nov02 2-0
ST JOHNSTONE	Jan01 1-1	Nov16 2-3	Aug17 1-2	Jan04 2-2	Nov09 2-2	Apr05 2-1	Oct12 2-2	Dec28 2-2	Feb01 2-0	Aug31 3-1	Sep28 2-1	Mar01 1-0		Oct26 1-1
VALE OF LEVEN	Mar22 1-3	Aug24 1-0	Oct19 2-1	Mar01 1-3	Jan18 3-0	Nov16 0-2	Feb01 2-2	Dec07 2-1	Dec14 0-2	Nov02 2-1	Dec28 5-0	Mar08 0-2	Feb15 0-1	

Season 1913-14

SFA Cup

1st Round
Jan 24 Falkirk ....1 Queen's Park 3
Jan 24 St Mirren ......5 Inverness C 1

2nd Round
Feb 7 Aberdeen ......4 Albion R 1
Feb 7 Airdrie ....5 Dundee H 0
Feb 7 Broxburn U .....5 Dumfries 1
Feb 7 Celtic ....0 Clyde 0
Feb 7 E Stirling ......1 Forfar A 1
Feb 7 Forres Mechanic ..0 Peebles R 4
Feb 7 Kilmarnock ....3 Hamilton A 1
Jan 31 Kirkcaldy U ......0 Stevenston U 4
Feb 7 Leith A ....1 Motherwell 1
Feb 7 Morton ....1 Hibernian 1
Feb 7 Partick T ....1 Nithsdale W 0
Feb 7 Queen's Park .....1 Arthurlie 0
Feb 7 Raith R ....2 Hearts 0
Feb 7 Rangers ....5 Alloa 0
Feb 7 St Mirren ....2 Dundee 1

Feb 7 T Lanark ....2 Dumbarton 0

Replays
Feb 10 Clyde ....0 Celtic 2
Feb 11 Hibernian ....2 Morton 1
Feb 14 Forfar A ....2 E Stirling 0
Feb 14 Motherwell ......5 Leith A 2

3rd Round
Feb 21 Aberdeen ....1 St Mirren 2
Feb 21 Airdrie ....1 Queen's Park 1
Feb 21 Broxburn ....0 Motherwell 2
Feb 21 Forfar A ....0 Celtic 5
Feb 21 Hibernian ....2 Rangers 1
Feb 21 Kilmarnock ......1 Partick T 4
Feb 21 Stevenston U ....3 Peebles R 2
Feb 21 T Lanark ....4 Raith R 1

Replay
Feb 24 Queen's Park .....2 Airdrie 1

4th Round
Mar 7 Motherwell ......1 Celtic 3
Mar 7 Queen's Park ....1 Hibernian 3
Mar 7 St Mirren ....1 Partick T 0
Mar 7 T Lanark ....0 Stevenston U 0

Replays
Mar 21 Stevenston U .....1 T Lanark 1
Mar 24 Stevenston U .....0 T Lanark 1
played at Cathkin Park

Semi-finals
Mar 28 Celtic ....2 T Lanark 0
played at Ibrox
Mar 28 Hibernian ....3 St Mirren 1
played at Tynecastle

Final
Apr 11 Celtic ....0 Hibernian 0
played at Ibrox

Replay
Apr 16
Celtic ......4 Hibernian 1
played at Ibrox

DIVISION 1

	ABERDEEN	AIRDRIE	AYR U	CELTIC	CLYDE	DUMBARTON	DUNDEE	FALKIRK	HAMILTON A	HEARTS	HIBERNIAN	KILMARNOCK	MORTON	MOTHERWELL	PARTICK T	QUEEN'S PARK	RAITH R	RANGERS	ST MIRREN	T LANARK
ABERDEEN		Aug30 0-0	Oct25 2-2	Oct11 0-1	Aug16 1-2	Dec20 2-3	Mar28 2-2	Sep13 0-0	Jan24 5-0	Jan10 0-1	Mar21 1-2	Dec06 1-2	Mar07 2-1	Apr11 0-0	Nov15 0-0	Nov22 2-1	Jan03 1-0	Sep22 0-0	Sep27 2-1	Mar18 0-0
AIRDRIE	Apr04 4-1		Mar07 1-1	Nov29 0-1	Apr19 1-1	Oct18 4-1	Dec13 3-0	Oct04 0-0	Nov08 3-2	Dec27 2-2	Apr25 4-3	Sep20 3-1	Jan31 7-1	Jan03 3-1	Sep06 0-0	Nov01 0-3	Aug23 5-2	Feb14 0-3	Jan10 3-1	Jan17 0-0
AYR U	Apr18 2-1	Dec06 0-2		Dec27 0-6	Nov22 0-2	Sep17 1-3	Feb14 3-2	Nov01 1-1	Apr04 0-4	Aug23 1-2	Dec20 0-0	Mar14 0-2	Jan05 4-0	Oct18 0-2	Nov08 2-2	Oct11 2-0	Mar21 2-1	Jan10 1-0	Nov29 2-0	Jan24 0-0
CELTIC	Oct04 2-1	Jan24 1-0	Aug16 5-1		Sep29 2-0	Jan10 4-0	Oct18 1-0	Aug30 4-0	Nov22 1-0	Mar24 0-0	Apr18 3-0	Nov01 4-0	Feb14 3-0	Dec20 0-0	Apr25 1-1	Apr13 5-0	Apr29 2-1	Jan01 4-0	Sep13 0-2	Dec06 3-0
CLYDE	Dec13 1-0	Oct25 0-0	Mar17 1-2	Jan05 0-1		Dec27 0-0	Aug23 2-1	Mar03 1-1	Jan31 0-2	Sep20 2-2	Feb28 4-0	Jan24 0-0	Apr25 3-0	Jan17 5-0	Mar21 2-1	Sep06 0-1	Nov29 0-1	Oct11 0-1	Nov08 3-1
DUMBARTON	Jan31 0-1	Apr18 1-0	Sep01 2-1	Nov15 1-3	Feb21 2-3		Mar07 2-3	Jan03 0-4	Nov29 3-1	Jan17 2-6	Oct11 1-1	Aug23 1-1	Mar28 2-6	Sep27 1-4	Oct25 2-1	Aug16 0-2	Apr06 2-1	Mar14 1-0	Dec13 0-1	Apr23 3-1
DUNDEE	Jan01 0-1	Sep13 2-0	Aug30 2-0	Jan17 0-1	Mar14 2-0	Dec06 5-1		Oct06 4-1	Oct11 1-0	Nov22 2-2	Jan03 2-2	Apr11 3-1	Nov15 0-0	Apr04 2-1	Jan31 4-1	Sep27 5-2	Oct25 2-1	Dec20 0-0	Aug16 1-0	Apr29 3-1
FALKIRK	Mar14 2-0	Mar28 1-1	Sep08 1-3	Feb28 1-0	Jan01 1-0	Nov22 3-1	Nov08 4-0		Jan10 2-1	Sep06 0-0	Apr04 3-2	Jan31 4-1	Oct11 1-1	Apr22 2-0	Aug23 4-3	Dec20 3-2	Dec06 4-0	Apr01 4-1	Oct25 3-1	Sep20 1-1
HAMILTON A	Nov01 3-0	Mar25 2-4	Sep27 4-0	Apr24 1-2	Oct04 1-1	Apr11 2-1	Feb21 2-1	Aug16 1-3		Oct18 0-1	Sep13 6-0	Dec20 1-1	Jan03 6-0	Apr15 1-1	Dec06 2-1	Feb14 2-3	Jan17 1-0	Aug30 1-0	Apr18 1-1	Nov15 0-1
HEARTS	Nov29 4-0	Aug16 3-1	Jan03 2-1	Sep15 2-0	Dec20 1-0	Apr04 5-1	Jan24 3-0	Mar21 1-0	Feb28 1-0		Feb14 3-1	Mar07 0-1	Sep27 4-0	Dec06 2-1	Oct11 1-0	Aug30 1-0	Apr18 2-0	Sep13 1-2	Nov15 6-0	Oct25 0-0
HIBERNIAN	Aug23 1-0	Nov22 1-4	Jan31 0-5	Sep06 1-2	Nov01 1-1	Oct04 1-1	Oct18 4-1	Dec13 0-3	Nov08 6-0	Jan17 0-1		Mar25 1-2	Apr28 2-0	Sep20 0-2	Mar14 2-3	Jan10 0-3	Sep15 0-3	Mar18 5-3	Dec27 1-0	
KILMARNOCK	Apr22 1-2	Feb28 0-3	Sep13 2-1	Apr08 2-2	Aug30 6-0	Jan24 0-0	Nov29 2-3	Nov15 5-2	Oct25 0-3	Dec13 0-3	Sep27 0-1		Apr18 0-1	Apr25 2-0	Dec27 2-0	Mar28 3-0	Oct11 1-3	Aug16 1-6	Jan01 3-1	Jan10 1-1
MORTON	Nov08 3-1	Jan01 0-2	Jan17 2-1	Sep20 0-4	Apr04 0-4	Mar21 3-1	Jan10 3-0	Dec27 6-0	Sep06 4-2	Feb21 3-0	Nov29 2-1	Oct18 2-0		Nov01 3-1	Dec13 1-0	Apr11 2-1	Feb28 2-1	Oct04 4-1	Mar14 4-0	Aug23 3-1
MOTHERWELL	Sep20 3-2	Oct11 0-1	Mar28 2-0	Aug23 1-1	Jan10 2-1	Jan10 4-3	Apr01 0-6	Nov29 0-1	Apr01 0-2	Oct25 2-3	Aug30 4-0	Jan24 2-3		Mar21 1-1	Dec13 1-3	Mar14 3-2	Nov22 1-0	Dec27 3-0	Jan31 1-2	
PARTICK T	Feb28 0-1	Sep27 0-1	Apr11 0-3	Jan03 0-0	Oct18 1-1	Feb14 2-1	Nov01 2-1	Apr18 1-2	Mar14 0-2	Mar28 4-2	Jan24 1-3	Aug30 4-2	Aug16 1-2		Oct04 1-1	Dec20 2-1	Apr13 1-1	Jan10 2-1	Jan01 1-0
QUEEN'S PARK	Dec27 2-2	Jan10 0-2	Apr15 3-3	Nov08 0-2	Dec06 0-2	Mar31 3-0	Apr18 0-4	Jan17 3-1	Aug23 0-0	Jan31 4-2	Nov15 3-1	Sep06 4-2	Oct25 1-0	Mar23 0-0	Apr28		Sep20 2-0	Feb28 0-6	Apr22 0-0	Nov29 2-2
RAITH R	Oct18 4-1	Oct16 1-1	Nov15 5-1	Dec13 1-2	Jan24 2-0	Dec27 1-2	Sep27 4-1	Mar07 5-2	Oct04 0-0	Apr30 2-1	Feb14 1-1	Aug16 1-2	Jan17 0-3	Nov22 3-0	Apr25 1-0		Nov01 0-3	Apr04 5-1	Mar25 3-0	
RANGERS	Sep06 5-1	Nov15 2-0	Mar25 4-1	Oct25 2-0	Mar07 1-2	Nov08 3-2	Sep20 3-2	Dec13 0-1	Dec27 3-2	Apr25 3-3	Apr07 1-1	Mar21 1-0	Dec06 0-0	Jan17 2-0	Jan05 4-0	Sep29 0-0	Jan31		Aug23 2-1	Apr18 2-0
ST MIRREN	Jan17 0-2	Dec20 1-4	Apr25 1-1	Jan31 0-3	Feb14 3-2	Aug30 1-1	Feb28 0-3	Apr11 1-1	Sep20 1-1	Nov01 0-0	Dec06 1-0	Jan06 0-2	Nov22 4-0	Oct04 1-0	Mar31 3-1	Oct18 0-1	Nov08 0-1	Jan03		Sep06 1-2
T LANARK	Apr25 0-0	Mar14 1-1	Dec13 4-2	Apr01 1-3	Apr13 0-0	Nov01 2-1	Dec25 2-1	Feb14 1-2	Apr21 2-1	Aug16 1-1		Oct04 2-1	Dec20 0-1	Aug30 0-1	Sep29 2-0	Jan03 5-0	Apr08 0-2	Oct18 2-4	Apr08 1-0	

DIVISION 1 FINAL TABLE

	P	W	D	L	F	A	Pts
Celtic	38	30	5	3	81	14	65
Rangers	38	27	5	6	79	31	59
Hearts	38	23	8	7	70	29	54
Morton	38	26	2	10	76	51	54
Falkirk	38	20	9	9	69	51	49
Airdrie	38	18	12	8	72	43	48
Dundee	38	19	5	14	64	53	43
T Lanark	38	13	10	15	42	51	36
Clyde	38	11	11	16	44	44	33
Ayr U	38	13	7	18	56	72	33
Raith R	38	13	6	19	56	57	32
Kilmarnock	38	11	9	18	48	68	31
Hibernian	38	12	6	20	58	75	30
Aberdeen	38	10	10	18	38	55	30
Partick T	38	10	9	19	37	51	29
Queen's Park	38	10	9	19	52	84	29
Hamilton A	38	11	6	21	49	66	28
Motherwell	38	11	6	21	46	65	28
Dumbarton	38	10	7	21	45	87	27
St Mirren	38	8	6	24	38	73	22

DIVISION 2 FINAL TABLE

	P	W	D	L	F	A	Pts
Cowdenbeath	22	13	5	4	34	17	31
Albion R	22	10	7	5	38	33	27
Dunfermline A	22	11	4	7	46	28	26
Dundee Hibs	22	11	4	7	36	31	26
St Johnstone	22	9	5	8	48	38	23
Abercorn	22	10	3	9	32	32	23
St Bernard's	22	8	6	8	39	31	22
E Stirling	22	7	8	7	40	36	22
Arthurlie	22	8	4	10	35	38	20
Leith A	22	5	9	8	37	37	19
Vale of Leven	22	5	3	14	23	47	13
Johnstone	22	4	4	14	21	55	12

DIVISION 2

	ABERCORN	ALBION R	ARTHURLIE	COWDENBEATH	DUNDEE H	DUNFERMLINE A	E STIRLING	JOHNSTONE	LEITH A	ST BERNARD'S	ST JOHNSTONE	VALE OF LEVEN
ABERCORN		Feb21 1-0	Dec27 2-1	Dec13 0-0	Sep13 2-0	Feb07 1-6	Mar21 2-1	Aug16 3-1	Mar28 1-1	Oct11 3-3	Nov15 0-1	Sep27 4-0
ALBION R	Nov22 4-1		Aug16 1-1	Jan03 3-1	Oct11 2-1	Feb28 1-0	Jan10 1-1	Sep13 5-1	Mar14 6-4	Aug30 2-1	Dec06 2-2	Oct25 2-1
ARTHURLIE	Jan31 0-2	Jan17 3-0		Aug30 1-0	Nov22 3-2	Oct04 3-2	Mar14 2-2	Mar07 4-1	Mar21 5-0	Dec06 3-3	Jan03 2-0	Dec13 3-1
COWDENBEATH	Oct04 2-1	Nov08 0-0	Feb21 1-0		Mar14 7-0	Aug16 0-0	Dec20 2-1	Aug23 2-0	Jan31 3-0	Oct25 2-0	Sep13 3-0	Nov15 3-1
DUNDEE H	Jan24 2-1	Feb14 2-2	Aug23 1-0	Mar07 3-0		Feb21 2-1	Nov08 3-1	Jan03 5-0	Jan03 1-1	Jan10 1-3	Apr27 3-2	Sep27 2-0
DUNFERMLINE A	Nov01 2-0	Nov29 3-2	Dec20 6-1	Jan01 0-0	Nov15 1-0		Jan31 1-1	Jan30 7-1	Aug23 1-0	Dec13 1-0	Aug30 4-3	Oct11 2-0
E STIRLING	Aug30 2-1	Mar07 2-0	Apr11 3-2	Nov29 3-0	Jan17 1-3	Dec27 4-1		Nov01 5-0	Feb21 1-1	Nov15 1-1	Dec13 2-2	Aug16 1-1
JOHNSTONE	Nov08 1-3	Aug23 0-0	Sep27 2-0	Oct11 1-0	Jan03 2-2	Dec06 1-0			Dec13 0-1	Jan24 1-1	Sep27 3-1	Feb07 4-0
LEITH A	Dec06 3-0	Jan24 1-1	Feb28 2-0	Sep27 1-1	Aug30 1-1	Oct25 1-1	Dec20 1-1	Nov15		Aug16 1-1	Oct11 1-1	Nov29 3-1
ST BERNARD'S	Aug23 0-1	Mar28 0-1	Apr04 1-0	Sep20 1-2	Feb08 1-2	Nov08 1-0	Apr28 5-2	Oct18 3-0	Nov22 4-0		Nov01 1-1	Dec27 4-2
ST JOHNSTONE	Dec20 2-1	Jan31 5-0	Nov08 6-0	Nov22 0-0	Oct18 0-3	Jan24 5-3	Nov29 4-2	Nov29 4-3	Sep27 1-3			Aug23 4-0
VALE OF LEVEN	Oct18 0-2	Apr11 2-3	Jan24 1-1	Nov01 1-3	Apr04 0-3	Dec06 1-2	Nov22 2-1	Aug30 2-0	Nov08 3-3	Dec20 2-1	Oct04 0-2	

Season 1914-15

DIVISION 1 FINAL TABLE

	P	W	D	L	F	A	Pts
Celtic	38	30	5	3	91	25	65
Hearts	38	27	7	4	83	32	61
Rangers	38	23	4	11	74	47	50
Morton	38	18	12	8	74	48	48
Ayr U	38	20	8	10	55	40	48
Falkirk	38	16	7	15	48	48	39
Hamilton A	38	16	6	16	60	55	38
Partick T	38	15	8	15	56	58	38
St Mirren	38	14	8	16	56	65	36
Airdrie	38	14	7	17	54	60	35
Hibernian	38	12	11	15	59	66	35
Kilmarnock	38	15	4	19	55	59	34
Dumbarton	38	13	8	17	51	66	34
Aberdeen	38	11	11	16	39	52	33
Dundee	38	12	9	17	43	61	33
T Lanark	38	10	12	16	51	57	32
Clyde	38	12	6	20	44	59	30
Motherwell	38	10	10	18	49	66	30
Raith R	38	9	10	19	53	68	28
Queen's Park	38	4	5	29	27	90	13

DIVISION 2 FINAL TABLE

	P	W	D	L	F	A	Pts
Cowdenbeath	26	16	5	5	49	17	37
St Bernard's	26	18	1	7	66	34	37
Leith A	26	15	7	4	54	31	37
E Stirling	26	13	5	8	53	44	31
Clydebank	26	13	4	9	67	37	30
Dunfermline A	26	13	2	11	49	39	28
Johnstone	26	11	5	10	41	52	27
St Johnstone	26	10	6	10	56	53	26
Albion R	26	9	7	10	37	42	25
Lochgelly U	26	9	3	14	43	60	21
Dundee Hibs	26	8	3	15	48	61	19
Abercorn	26	5	7	14	35	65	17
Arthurlie	26	6	4	16	36	66	16
Vale of Leven	26	4	5	17	33	66	13

DIVISION 1 — Results grid

	ABERDEEN	AIRDRIE	AYR U	CELTIC	CLYDE	DUMBARTON	DUNDEE	FALKIRK	HAMILTON A	HEARTS	HIBERNIAN	KILMARNOCK	MORTON	MOTHERWELL	PARTICK T	QUEEN'S PARK	RAITH R	RANGERS	ST MIRREN	T LANARK
ABERDEEN		Mar20 3-0	Jan09 1-1	Dec05 0-1	Sep05 2-0	Nov21 0-0	Jan01 2-1	Jan23 1-2	Apr17 1-0	Apr03 0-0	Feb20 0-0	Dec19 3-0	Feb06 2-0	Sep19 3-1	Mar06 0-1	Sep28 1-1	Nov07 1-3	Aug22 0-2	Oct03 0-5	Oct17 0-1
AIRDRIE	Oct10 3-0		Apr17 1-2	Dec19 0-1	Feb20 2-1	Feb06 4-1	Oct24 3-4	Dec05 3-2	Sep12 3-2	Mar13 2-2	Jan09 1-3	Sep26 0-2	Jan01 0-0	Nov07 4-1	Mar27 0-0	Aug22 2-1	Apr10 3-3	Nov21 1-2	Jan23 2-1	Aug15 1-0
AYR U	Sep12 1-0	Aug29 0-0		Oct10 1-0	Apr24 3-1	Dec19 2-1	Apr06 0-0	Mar06 1-2	Mar27 2-0	Apr13 0-2	Oct31 2-1	Jan04 2-0	Feb06 2-0	Nov14 2-1	Mar13 1-1	Aug15 4-0	Oct31 2-1	Dec05 3-0	Sep26 2-0	Jan02 1-0
CELTIC	Apr10 1-0	Apr03 0-1	Nov21 4-0		Sep28 3-0	Feb20 6-0	Oct03 1-0	Oct17 2-0	Dec26 1-0	Jan30 2-0	Mar06 3-0	Jan04 4-0	Sep05 0-0	Aug22 3-0	Jan09 6-1	Dec12 5-1	Mar27 3-1	Oct31 2-1	Feb06 1-0	Nov14 3-1
CLYDE	Jan16 3-0	Sep19 0-0	Mar20 3-1	Jan02 0-2		Oct24 2-1	Feb13 1-1	Jan01 4-2	Feb27 2-2	Nov07 1-2	Apr15 1-0	Jan23 1-0	Dec05 2-3	Apr03 0-0	Dec19 1-3	Apr17 2-1	Aug29 1-0	Mar13 1-2	Nov28 1-2	Apr05 1-2
DUMBARTON	Jan30 3-2	Oct17 1-4	Sep05 1-2	Jan04 1-4	Dec26 2-1		Sep19 1-1	Apr24 0-1	Feb13 0-1	Nov07 0-3	Apr15 3-2	Jan23 1-0	Mar20 1-0	Apr03 3-2	Apr10 1-1	Dec05 0-2	Jan09 3-0	Jan01 3-1	Nov14 1-1	Aug22 2-4
DUNDEE	Aug15 1-3	Feb27 2-0	Dec12 2-3	Sep26 1-3	Apr12 3-0	Oct05 1-0		Jan09 2-4	Aug29 1-0	Oct17 2-4	Dec26 0-1	Oct31 1-2	Jan23 2-4	Nov14 0-1	Feb06 0-2	Apr03 2-0	Apr17 1-2	Sep12 2-0	Feb20 0-0	Dec05 1-2
FALKIRK	Oct24 1-1	Jan30 2-1	Nov07 1-1	Jan16 0-1	Nov21 3-1	Aug15 1-3	Oct10 0-1		Sep26 2-0	Jan02 1-1	Mar27 0-0	Apr10 3-2	Dec19 2-0	Nov28 5-1	Aug29 2-1	Feb13 1-0	Feb27 3-1	Sep05 1-3	Apr03 2-0	Mar13 1-1
HAMILTON A	Nov14 3-0	Mar06 0-1	Aug22 2-1	Oct24 0-1	Oct03 3-2	Dec19 4-1	Mar20 2-0	Feb20 2-0		Nov28 1-3	Feb06 2-2	Mar13 0-0	Jan01 1-1	Jan23 0-3	Jan09 2-2	Sep05 3-0	Apr03 1-1	Apr10 4-3	Jan09 5-2	Feb20 4-2
HEARTS	Sep26 2-0	Dec12 3-1	Sep21 2-1	Aug15 0-1	Mar27 3-1	Mar06 3-0	Jan16 4-0	Nov14 2-1	Jan04 1-3		Dec05 3-1	Feb06 2-1	Jan09 1-0	Oct10 2-0	Mar20 3-1	Oct24 2-2	Dec26 4-0	Feb20 2-1	Sep12 6-1	Aug29 2-0
HIBERNIAN	Oct31 1-2	Sep05 1-0	Oct03 0-4	Sep19 1-1	Sep21 3-1	Nov07 2-2	Nov21 1-0	Aug22 2-1	Oct17 0-2	Feb27 2-2		Jan02 3-1	Mar13 1-1	Jan23 4-1	Nov28 4-0	Apr10 2-1	Feb13 1-2	Jan30 3-2	Dec19 4-2	Apr03 4-2
KILMARNOCK	Nov28 5-2	Dec26 2-1	Sep19 1-2	Nov07 1-3	Aug22 0-3	Jan16 4-0	Oct03 3-2	Jan30 1-0	Sep05 0-2	Oct24 5-1	Apr24 2-2		Mar06 2-2	Mar20 2-0	Oct24 2-2	Dec26 0-1	Feb06 1-1	Apr17 0-1	Feb13 2-1	Jan30 2-1
MORTON	Aug29 1-1	Nov28 2-1	Dec26 1-2	Feb13 0-3	Dec12 2-1	Sep12 1-0	Nov07 4-0	Jan04 2-0	Jan02 1-1	Apr10 1-0	Sep26 2-0	Aug15 2-2		Mar20 2-0	Oct24 2-2	Oct10 0-1	Nov21 3-1	Jan16 3-3	Mar06 4-2	Jan30 3-1
MOTHERWELL	Dec26 1-1	Jan02 4-2	Jan16 1-0	Apr24 0-2	Oct31 1-0	Sep26 2-3	Jan30 1-1	Dec12 4-1	Dec05 2-4	Feb13 0-1	Aug29 3-0	Sep12 3-2	Oct17 1-1		Apr17 1-0	Nov21 1-0	Aug15 1-2	Feb27 2-4	Mar27 2-2	Oct03 3-2
PARTICK T	Dec12 3-0	Oct31 4-0	Jan30 2-0	Feb27 0-2	Nov14 1-3	Mar13 1-2	Feb20 4-1	Apr10 2-4	Feb20 1-4	Oct02 0-2	Nov21 3-1	Jan16 0-1	Oct17 1-1	Apr03 0-1		Sep05 1-0	Dec26 5-0	Jan05 2-1	Apr24 0-1	Jan01 1-1
QUEEN'S PARK	Mar13 0-3	Jan16 1-1	Nov28 0-1	Apr05 1-2	Oct17 0-3	Aug29 1-2	Jan02 3-1	Sep12 0-2	Oct31 1-3	Dec19 0-4	Nov07 1-0	Dec05 0-1	Mar27 0-0	Feb20 0-3	Oct03 0-2		Jan30 1-3	Apr24 0-4	Aug15 1-1	Mar06 0-2
RAITH R	Jan02 5-1	Oct03 3-0	Apr03 0-0	Oct05 0-2	Mar06 2-2	Dec12 2-0	Nov28 1-2	Oct31 1-1	Jan16 1-3	Aug22 1-3	Sep12 1-3	Nov14 1-1	Feb20 3-0	Feb06 1-1	Jan23 2-2	Sep19 1-2		Oct10 1-2	Oct17 2-2	Dec19 1-1
RANGERS	Mar27 1-1	Jan04 0-5	Feb13 1-3	Jan01 2-1	Jan09 1-2	Jan23 1-2	Mar06 2-0	Feb06 3-0	Dec19 1-0	Sep28 1-2	Apr24 4-2	Aug29 2-1	Oct03 0-2	Dec19 5-0	Apr05 0-1	Nov07 4-1	Oct24 1-2		Dec05 5-0	Nov28 3-0
ST MIRREN	Feb13 0-2	Nov14 0-1	Feb27 1-2	Aug29 3-3	Jan30 3-1	Jan02 1-1	Sep05 1-0	Dec26 1-2	Dec12 1-0	Apr17 1-2	Oct10 0-1	Nov21 4-2	Oct31 2-3	Oct24 1-0	Sep19 3-1	Mar20 4-0	Mar13 1-1	Apr10 1-1		Jan16 2-0
T LANARK	Feb27 0-1	Feb13 0-2	Oct24 2-1	Apr17 0-4	Feb06 1-1	Apr13 1-0	Dec25 7-0	Sep19 0-0	Apr27 1-2	Jan23 2-2	Dec12 2-2	Oct10 3-2	Aug22 3-3	Jan09 1-0	Sep28 4-0	Sep05 1-1	Sep26 3-0	Dec26 1-1	Nov07 0-0	

DIVISION 2 — Results grid

	ABERCORN	ALBION R	ARTHURLIE	CLYDEBANK	COWDENBEATH	DUNDEE H	DUNFERMLINE A	E STIRLING	JOHNSTONE	LEITH A	LOCHGELLY U	ST BERNARD'S	ST JOHNSTONE	VALE OF LEVEN
ABERCORN		Sep12 1-0	Feb20 1-2	Oct03 4-2	Sep26 2-2	Oct17 4-2	Feb06 1-2	Nov07 3-3	Aug22 1-1	Mar06 0-1	Dec05 1-1	Aug15 0-3	Jan09 0-1	Nov28 3-1
ALBION R	Nov14 0-0		Oct17 2-0	Nov28 2-2	Dec12 0-1	Oct31 3-0	Sep19 3-0	Jan02 4-2	Aug29 2-2	Oct03 0-4	Jan16 2-1	Dec26 1-1	Feb27 4-1	Mar06 4-1
ARTHURLIE	Aug29 1-1	Feb06 0-3		Dec26 0-3	Feb13 0-2	Jan09 2-1	Dec05 2-0	Sep19 0-1	Jan23 1-3	Feb20 0-2	Apr03 5-3	Oct24 1-2	Oct10 2-2	Feb27 5-1
CLYDEBANK	Oct31 6-1	Sep26 3-1	Jan16 6-0		Jan01 1-0	Nov14 5-1	Nov21 5-1	Aug15 5-1	Oct10 1-4	Dec05 9-2	Mar06 2-2	Feb06 2-2	Dec19 2-2	Aug22 3-1
COWDENBEATH	Nov21 5-0	Oct24 2-0	Nov07 5-1	Feb20 2-1		Sep12 3-0	Aug22 3-1	Dec19 2-1	Jan02 3-0	Jan30 0-1	Feb06 2-0	Sep05 2-0	Oct17 1-0	Dec05 3-0
DUNDEE H	Jan16 2-1	Dec19 6-1	Aug22 3-3	Sep19 1-3	Nov28 2-2		Nov07 0-2	Oct24 1-3	Jan30 3-0	Nov21 1-3	Oct03 4-3	Oct10 1-0	Jan02 3-1	Feb13 4-1
DUNFERMLINE A	Oct10 3-0	Jan09 4-0	Jan02 3-2	Dec12 1-0	Jan23 3-1	Aug15 3-1		Aug29 2-2	Nov28 2-3	Oct31 1-3	Jan01 2-1	Sep26 2-1	Oct24 2-2	Nov14 7-2
E STIRLING	Dec12 3-2	Aug22 0-0	Apr17 3-0	Mar27 3-1	Jan09 0-4	Feb06 3-2	Mar06 2-0		Dec26 4-1	Oct17 3-0	Jan23 3-2	Sep12 3-0	Feb20 2-1	Oct31 3-2
JOHNSTONE	Jan30 4-1	Nov07 2-2	Oct03 2-1	Jan23 1-0	Oct31 2-1	Dec05 2-1	Oct17 1-0	Jan16 3-1		Jan09 0-0	Mar20 3-1	Feb20 2-1	Aug15 3-4	Feb06 2-0
LEITH A	Oct24 3-3	Feb20 3-0	Aug15 3-2	Aug29 0-2	Oct10 0-0	Sep26 4-2	Sep12 1-0	Apr03 1-0	Nov14 3-0		Jan02 5-0	Nov28 3-0	Feb06 4-1	Dec26 4-1
LOCHGELLY U	Mar20 4-0	Oct10 1-0	Mar13 2-2	Jan30 1-3	Aug15 0-4	Dec26 2-1	Mar27 1-4	Feb27 6-1	Apr17 6-0	Dec12 0-0		Aug29 1-3	Sep26 1-1	Jan09 1-0
ST BERNARD'S	Feb27 4-0	Nov21 3-1	Jan30 6-0	Oct17 2-1	Jan23 1-0	Mar20 5-1	Dec19 2-1	Feb13 3-2	Mar06 4-2	Aug22 2-0	Apr10 6-0		Mar27 3-1	Sep19 2-1
ST JOHNSTONE	Dec26 4-0	Jan23 2-3	Apr24 4-3	Nov07 2-1	Mar20 3-1	Aug29 2-2	Oct03 2-2	Jan30 5-1	Feb13 2-1	Jan01 5-1	Aug22 2-2	Nov14 3-1		Mar13 2-0
VALE OF LEVEN	Jan23 5-1	Aug15 0-1	Dec19 4-1	Jan02 0-0	Aug29 2-2	Dec12 1-1	Jan16 0-3	Oct10 1-1	Apr24 2-1	Nov07 1-1	Apr24 1-2	Feb20 1-7	Sep12 4-2	

There were no Scottish FA Cup matches in 1914-15

Season 1915-16

DIVISION 1

	ABERDEEN	AIRDRIE	AYR U	CELTIC	CLYDE	DUMBARTON	DUNDEE	FALKIRK	HAMILTON A	HEARTS	HIBERNIAN	KILMARNOCK	MORTON	MOTHERWELL	PARTICK T	QUEEN'S PARK	RAITH R	RANGERS	ST MIRREN	T LANARK
ABERDEEN		Dec11 2-1	Sep25 1-1	Feb05 0-4	Oct09 1-1	Aug28 2-2	Nov20 2-0	Feb26 2-0	Oct30 1-3	Mar11 1-1	Oct23 1-1	Jan08 2-0	Apr08 0-1	Apr01 5-0	Jan22 1-1	Sep27 5-1	Nov13 2-1	Apr30 0-0	Dec25 2-1	Sep11 1-1
AIRDRIE	Sep18 1-1		Nov13 3-1	Aug28 0-5	Dec04 4-1	Jan29 2-1	Sep11 1-2	Jan08 2-3	Jan15 1-1	Feb26 0-0	Dec18 1-0	Oct16 0-0	Nov20 0-0	Feb12 4-0	Apr22 0-2	Oct30 3-0	Mar11 2-1	Oct02 0-1	Apr15 0-0	Apr01 1-0
AYR U	Feb12 2-1	Apr08 2-0		Dec11 0-4	Jan04 2-0	Jan03 3-1	Mar11 1-2	Apr30 4-1	Sep11 1-0	Jan08 3-1	Aug28 2-3	Dec25 2-0	Nov06 1-1	Oct16 3-2	Nov27 0-0	Jan22 4-1	Oct02 1-1	Feb26 1-0	Feb05 1-1	Mar25 6-0
CELTIC	Nov06 3-1	Dec25 6-0	Jan29 3-1		Sep27 5-0	Feb12 6-0	Feb26 3-0	Sep04 2-1	Mar11 5-1	Apr22 0-0	Jan15 3-1	Nov20 2-0	Apr01 0-0	Aug21 3-1	Apr30 5-0	Dec04 6-2	Apr15 6-0	Jan01 2-2	Oct23 0-2	Apr24 4-1
CLYDE	Mar04 3-2	Feb05 1-2	Mar18 1-3	Jan03 1-3		Apr15 3-1	Oct16 2-0	Nov27 3-2	Dec11 1-2	Sep18 1-4	Feb19 2-1	Apr18 1-1	Jan08 2-3	Jan22 1-2	Apr08 1-2	Nov13 0-1	Aug28 1-0	Dec18 0-2	Oct30 4-1	Oct02 2-2
DUMBARTON	Apr25 2-1	Oct23 3-1	Sep04 0-3	Jan08 1-2	Nov06 2-1		Oct02 1-1	Sep18 3-1	Feb26 7-0	Feb05 1-1	Apr08 2-1	Apr30 1-1	Jan22 1-1	Dec25 0-0	Dec11 2-0	Oct09 2-4	Dec04 1-0	Aug21 1-3	Mar04 2-0	Nov20 1-1
DUNDEE	Jan01 1-1	Jan03 4-0	Aug21 2-0	Sep18 0-2	Jan29 1-0	Mar18 0-1		Mar04 3-3	Nov27 3-1	Nov06 1-0	Feb12 2-1	Apr08 2-0	Apr22 0-1	Sep04 1-3	Feb19 3-0	Sep25 7-1	Dec18 3-0	Jan15 2-0	Oct09 1-0	Oct23 1-0
FALKIRK	Dec18 0-3	Mar25 3-2	Dec04 1-0	Apr08 0-2	Jan01 1-2	Feb19 1-2	Oct30 2-0		Sep25 2-1	Oct02 1-1	Sep11 1-1	Aug28 0-0	Jan03 0-0	Dec31 0-1	Mar11 1-0	Feb12 3-2	Oct16 0-0	Nov20 2-0	Jan29 2-1	Jan15 1-1
HAMILTON A	Mar18 2-0	Apr30 2-1	Mar04 2-3	Oct16 2-3	Aug21 3-1	Dec18 1-1	Feb05 4-4	Apr15 0-1		Jan22 3-2	Dec04 3-2	Oct02 5-2	Sep04 5-2	Nov20 3-1	Jan08 1-0	Dec25 5-2	Sep18 2-0	Apr01 0-1	Feb19 4-1	Nov06 2-1
HEARTS	Dec04 1-2	Sep25 1-1	Oct09 0-5	Nov13 2-0	Apr01 3-1	Nov27 3-1	Apr30 1-0	Mar18 0-2	Aug28 3-0		Apr17 1-3	Sep11 0-1	Oct23 2-0	Dec18 4-0	Mar04 1-0	Apr08 5-3	Jan29 2-1	Feb12 1-2	Jan15 3-1	Feb19 2-0
HIBERNIAN	Apr15 0-0	Jan22 3-0	Apr22 3-1	Oct02 0-4	Sep04 0-1	Oct30 1-1	Dec25 0-2	Feb05 2-1	Apr26 1-3	Sep20 1-2		Feb26 1-0	Sep18 0-2	Nov06 1-2	Oct16 0-4	Aug21 3-0	Jan08 1-0	Mar11 2-3	Nov20 2-1	Dec11 0-1
KILMARNOCK	Aug21 5-0	Feb19 4-0	Oct23 0-1	Mar04 0-3	Jan15 0-1	Sep25 5-1	Nov13 2-0	Apr01 1-3	Jan29 3-0	Apr15 3-1	Oct09 0-0		Mar18 1-1	Sep18 1-0	Oct30 1-1	Nov27 4-0	Jan03 2-0	Sep04 0-3	Jan01 1-1	Dec18 1-1
MORTON	Oct16 3-0	Jan01 8-2	Jan15 0-1	Sep11 0-1	Sep25 3-0	Nov13 3-1	Aug28 3-1	Oct09 6-0	Feb12 8-1		Jan29 5-1	Dec11 2-0		Apr30 1-0	Dec25 0-1	Feb26 5-0	Oct30 4-0	Dec04 2-0	Mar11 3-0	Apr15 2-0
MOTHERWELL	Nov27 2-2	Oct09 3-2	Apr15 0-3	Apr15 1-3	Oct23 2-2	Sep11 4-2	Dec11 3-0	Nov13 1-1	Jan01 0-3	Oct30 1-3	Mar04 1-1	Mar11 1-1	Feb19 2-3		Aug28 2-2	Apr22 2-1	Jan15 1-4	Jan29 2-2	Sep25 3-1	Feb05 3-4
PARTICK T	Oct02 3-0	Nov06 4-1	Apr01 1-1	Dec18 0-4	Apr24 2-3	Jan15 0-0	Dec04 2-0	Oct23 5-2	Oct09 0-1	Sep04 0-2	Mar18 4-1	Feb12 4-0	Aug21 3-2	Feb26 3-1		Jan29 5-0	Nov20 2-0	Apr15 5-2	Apr19 4-0	Jan01 1-0
QUEEN'S PARK	Jan15 0-1	Mar18 3-0	Jan01 2-2	Feb19 0-1	Mar11 2-2	Apr01 0-2	Apr15 2-0	Dec11 2-1	Oct23 2-1	Nov20 0-3	Jan03 4-2	Feb05 1-2	Dec18 4-4	Oct02 1-4	Sep18 1-1		Apr30 4-1	Nov06 0-6	Aug28 2-1	Mar04 0-0
RAITH R	Apr22 3-1	Aug21 1-1	Feb19 0-4	Nov27 0-2	Dec25 2-0	Jan01 1-0	Apr01 0-2	Jan22 3-1	Jan04 2-0	Dec11 1-2	Sep25 1-1	Nov06 1-1	Mar04 2-1	Mar18 1-0	Feb05 2-0	Sep04 0-3		Oct23 1-3	Sep11 0-1	Oct09 0-1
RANGERS	Feb19 4-0	Mar04 3-0	Sep18 5-2	Oct30 3-0	Apr22 2-2	Apr20 2-2	Apr10 3-2	Dec25 1-0	Nov13 3-0	Oct16 0-4	Nov27 4-2	Jan22 3-1	Feb05 1-0	Jan08 4-1	Jan03 0-1	Apr24 6-0	Apr08 3-0		Dec11 4-0	Aug28 4-0
ST MIRREN	Sep04 3-2	Nov27 2-4	Dec18 1-0	Mar18 0-5	Feb12 1-0	Oct16 1-2	Jan22 1-2	Nov06 2-1	Apr22 5-0	Aug21 4-1	Apr01 3-1	Dec04 3-0	Oct02 1-3	Apr08 5-0	Nov13 0-2	Jan08 1-2	Feb26 2-0	Apr17 1-1		Sep18 1-0
T LANARK	Jan29 6-2	Sep04 0-1	Oct30 1-1	Jan22 0-4	Feb26 1-1	Mar11 4-0	Jan08 2-1	Aug21 0-0	Apr08 0-1	Dec25 1-3	Nov13 3-0	Apr22 1-2	Nov27 1-3	Dec04 1-3	Sep27 0-0	Oct16 0-0	Feb12 2-0	Mar18 0-1	Apr30 3-0	

There were no Scottish FA Cup matches in 1915-16

DIVISION 1 FINAL TABLE

	P	W	D	L	F	A	Pts
Celtic	38	32	3	3	116	23	67
Rangers	38	25	6	7	87	39	56
Morton*	37	22	7	8	86	35	51
Ayr U	38	20	8	10	72	45	48
Partick T	38	19	8	11	65	41	46
Hearts*	37	20	6	11	66	45	46
Hamilton A	38	19	3	16	68	76	41
Dundee	38	18	4	16	56	49	40
Dumbarton	38	13	11	14	54	64	37
Kilmarnock	38	12	11	15	46	49	35
Aberdeen	38	11	12	15	51	64	34
Falkirk	38	12	9	17	45	61	33
St Mirren	38	13	4	21	50	67	30
Motherwell	38	11	8	19	55	82	30
Airdrie	38	11	8	19	44	74	30
T Lanark	38	9	11	18	40	56	29
Clyde	38	11	7	20	49	71	29
Queen's Park	38	11	6	21	53	100	28
Hibernian	38	9	7	22	44	71	25
Raith R	38	9	5	24	30	65	23

** Morton and Hearts only played each other once.*

Season 1916-17

DIVISION 1

	ABERDEEN	AIRDRIE	AYR U	CELTIC	CLYDE	DUMBARTON	DUNDEE	FALKIRK	HAMILTON A	HEARTS	HIBERNIAN	KILMARNOCK	MORTON	MOTHERWELL	PARTICK T	QUEEN'S PARK	RAITH R	RANGERS	ST MIRREN	T LANARK
ABERDEEN		Oct07 1-2	Jan06 1-0	Mar24 0-0	Jan20 0-1	Mar10 2-4	Jan01 5-1	Dec16 0-1	Nov04 0-1	Nov18 2-0	Apr21 2-1	Oct21 1-1	Sep23 1-1	Dec02 0-1	Aug19 2-0	Sep16 2-4	Feb17 1-2	Feb03 3-1	Sep02 1-1	Dec23 0-1
AIRDRIE	Feb24 3-1		Apr14 1-0	Mar17 1-2	Feb03 3-0	Sep16 2-1	Dec23 2-3	Apr28 1-0	Nov25 2-2	Sep02 3-2	Mar31 3-1	Feb17 3-2	Jan01 2-1	Aug26 3-1	Mar03 3-1	Jan06 3-0	Nov11 2-0	Dec09 2-0	Oct14 7-0	Oct28 1-0
AYR U	Sep30 1-0	Oct21 1-1		Sep02 0-1	Feb17 1-1	Nov04 3-1	Feb03 1-2	Jan02 2-2	Dec30 1-1	Sep16 2-0	Nov25 2-1	Dec16 0-2	Mar03 0-3	Jan13 1-2	Dec02 0-0	Apr07 1-1	Apr21 2-1	Oct07 1-3	Mar17 2-1	Aug19 0-1
CELTIC	Nov25 1-0	Sep09 3-1	Dec09 5-0		Jan02 0-0	Jan20 1-1	Feb17 2-0	Dec30 2-0	Mar10 6-1	Sep30 1-0	Aug26 3-1	Apr21 0-2	Oct21 0-0	Jan06 1-0	Nov18 0-0	Mar03 3-2	Feb03 5-0	Oct28 0-0	Mar31 3-0	Apr09 2-0
CLYDE	Oct14 2-0	Dec02 1-1	Nov11 1-4	Apr28 0-5		Dec23 2-2	Mar24 2-0	Jan01 1-1	Aug19 1-1	Mar17 0-1	Feb10 1-2	Sep02 1-1	Dec16 1-0	Apr07 0-1	Jan27 2-1	Nov04 1-1	Sep16 2-0	Jan13 0-1	Apr14 2-1	Feb24 1-1
DUMBARTON	Oct28 1-1	Apr21 1-1	Feb24 3-1	Apr07 1-3	Jan06 5-1		Nov11 4-3	Mar31 1-1	Mar03 0-0	Feb03 4-1	Sep09 2-1	Nov25 1-1	Oct07 1-4	Sep23 3-1	Dec16 2-1	Dec30 0-2	Jan01 2-2	Feb17 0-3	Aug26 2-1	Dec09 2-3
DUNDEE	Sep09 1-1	Sep23 2-2	Jan20 2-1	Nov04 1-2	Aug26 0-1	Mar17 4-1		Oct07 1-2	Oct21 3-1	Jan27 2-3	Jan02 3-1	Dec30 0-2	Feb24 3-1	Apr14 0-2	Feb10 5-1	Mar31 2-1	Dec09 6-2	Apr28 2-1	Nov18 0-2	Dec02 0-1
FALKIRK	Apr07 4-2	Nov04 0-0	Mar10 1-2	Oct14 1-1	Dec09 3-3	Sep30 2-3	Jan06 2-0		Jan20 4-0	Mar24 2-1	Oct21 0-1	Aug19 2-0	Feb17 2-1	Nov18 3-1	Sep16 0-1	Jan27 1-2	Feb24 1-1	Mar17 0-2	Dec23 0-2	Sep02 1-1
HAMILTON A	Mar17 4-1	Jan13 1-0	Mar24 2-1	Dec16 0-4	Mar31 2-1	Nov18 3-1	Apr07 2-4	Sep09 1-1		Oct28 1-0	Feb24 4-1	Feb03 3-0	Jan06 0-1	Jan01 2-4	Sep23 0-1	Aug26 2-0	Apr28 3-1	Apr21 3-1	Dec02 1-1	Feb17 1-1
HEARTS	Feb10 2-0	Mar10 1-4	Dec23 1-2	Jan13 0-1	Oct21 0-3	Dec02 0-1	Dec16 1-0	Sep23 1-6	Jan02 3-1		Sep18 2-1	Apr07 0-0	Mar31 4-1	Feb24 1-3	Nov04 1-0	Nov25 2-0	Oct07 2-1	Aug26 1-3	Mar03 1-2	Sep09 2-1
HIBERNIAN	Dec09 3-3	Aug19 1-1	Oct14 1-4	Apr14 0-1	Oct28 1-1	Jan27 3-1	Sep16 1-2	Feb03 1-2	Sep02 4-3	Apr16 0-2		Jan20 2-1	Dec30 2-4	Feb17 2-3	Mar24 1-0	Mar17 5-1	Nov18 3-3	Nov11 0-0	Jan06 2-1	Sep30 1-1
KILMARNOCK	Jan27 7-0	Nov18 1-3	Sep09 1-2	Feb24 2-2	Mar03 2-0	Mar24 0-0	Oct28 3-0	Apr14 4-1	Dec09 4-0	Oct14 3-0	Sep23 1-3		Aug26 3-2	Mar10 3-0	Jan06 0-1	Feb10 4-2	Dec23 3-0	Mar31 4-1	Jan01 1-4	Nov11 2-1
MORTON	Apr28 2-0	Jan27 2-1	Nov18 2-0	Feb10 0-1	Sep30 3-1	Apr14 3-1	Oct14 1-0	Nov11 2-0	Dec23 3-0	Aug19 3-2	Dec02 1-1	Jan02 2-1		Oct28 2-1	Sep02 3-2	Jan20 4-2	Mar17 7-0	Mar10 1-0	Sep16 0-3	Jan13 3-0
MOTHERWELL	Nov11 1-2	Jan02 1-0	Jan27 2-1	Sep16 0-4	Nov25 3-3	Feb10 3-0	Sep02 4-2	Mar03 1-0	Oct07 2-2	Dec09 2-0	Nov04 1-1	Sep30 0-1	Apr21 0-2		Dec30 2-3	Oct21 4-1	Aug19 2-2	Dec23 2-1	Jan20 2-1	Mar24 0-2
PARTICK T	Mar31 4-0	Sep30 0-0	Aug26 3-0	Dec23 0-2	Apr09 1-0	Oct21 6-0	Nov25 3-0	Jan13 1-0	Oct14 5-0	Feb17 0-0	Mar10 0-3	Oct07 1-1	Feb03 0-0	Mar17 1-1		Apr21 0-2	Oct28 2-0	Jan02 0-1	Dec09 0-1	Jan01 1-0
QUEEN'S PARK	Jan13 2-1	Mar24 0-5	Jan01 3-2	Nov11 1-3	Mar10 2-2	Aug19 1-0	Sep30 2-2	Oct28 1-1	Apr14 4-2	Apr28 1-1	Dec23 4-1	Dec02 0-1	Dec09 3-4	Feb03 0-0	Feb24 2-1		Sep02 3-1	Apr09 1-4	Feb17 1-2	Oct14 3-4
RAITH R	Jan02 3-0	Feb10 0-2	Sep23 1-3	Dec02 1-4	Dec30 1-1	Oct14 0-3	Mar03 3-2	Aug26 0-6	Sep30 0-1	Jan20 1-4	Jan13 2-1	Nov04 0-4	Sep09 1-2	Mar31 2-1	Apr14 3-1	Dec16 2-0		Nov25 1-4	Jan27 1-1	Mar10 0-1
RANGERS	Mar03 1-0	Dec30 3-0	Feb10 1-0	Jan01 0-0	Nov18 1-0	Sep02 6-0	Aug19 3-0	Dec02 3-1	Jan27 2-0	Jan06 1-0	Dec16 5-1	Sep16 3-0	Nov04 0-1	Oct14 2-1	Jan20 3-0	Apr21 1-0	Mar24 4-3		Sep30 1-0	Apr07 0-2
ST MIRREN	Dec30 1-0	Dec16 1-0	Oct28 0-0	Aug19 1-5	Apr21 0-1	Apr28 0-0	Mar10 2-0	Nov25 5-0	Feb10 2-2	Nov11 0-1	Oct07 1-1	Jan13 2-1	Mar24 0-0	Sep09 3-1	Apr07 1-2	Sep23 3-0	Oct21 0-0	Feb24 1-1		Feb03 2-0
T LANARK	Aug26 2-0	Jan20 1-0	Mar31 4-3	Jan27 0-0	Apr14 1-0	Jan02 1-1	Apr21 0-0	Feb10 5-4	Sep16 3-1	Dec30 1-1	Mar03 1-1	Mar17 3-0	Nov25 0-0	Dec16 2-1	Apr28 2-0	Oct07 4-1	Jan06 0-1	Oct21 1-1	Nov04 1-0	

There were no Scottish FA Cup matches in 1916-17

DIVISION 1 FINAL TABLE

	P	W	D	L	F	A	Pts
Celtic	38	27	10	1	79	17	64
Morton	38	24	6	8	72	39	54
Rangers	38	24	5	9	68	32	53
Airdrie	38	21	8	9	71	38	50
T Lanark	38	19	11	8	53	37	49
Kilmarnock	38	18	7	13	69	46	43
St Mirren	38	15	10	13	49	43	40
Motherwell	38	16	6	16	57	59	38
Partick T	38	14	7	17	44	43	35
Dumbarton	38	12	11	15	56	73	35
Hamilton A	38	13	9	16	53	72	35
Falkirk	38	12	10	16	58	57	34
Clyde	38	10	14	14	40	52	34
Hearts	38	14	4	20	44	59	32
Ayr U	38	12	7	19	47	59	31
Dundee	38	13	4	21	58	71	30
Hibernian	38	10	10	18	57	72	30
Queen's Park	38	11	7	20	56	81	29
Raith R	38	8	7	23	42	91	23
Aberdeen	38	7	7	24	36	68	21

Season 1917-18

DIVISION 1

DIVISION 1 FINAL TABLE

	P	W	D	L	F	A	Pts
Rangers	34	25	6	3	66	24	56
Celtic	34	24	7	3	66	26	55
Kilmarnock	34	19	5	10	69	41	43
Morton	34	17	9	8	53	42	43
Motherwell	34	16	9	9	70	51	41
Partick T	34	14	12	8	51	37	40
Queen's Park	34	14	6	14	64	63	34
Dumbarton	34	13	8	13	48	49	34
Clydebank	34	14	5	15	55	56	33
Hearts	34	14	4	16	41	58	32
St Mirren	34	11	7	16	42	50	29
Hamilton A	34	11	6	17	52	63	28
T Lanark	34	10	7	17	56	62	27
Falkirk	34	9	9	16	38	58	27
Airdrie	34	10	6	18	46	58	26
Hibernian	34	8	9	17	42	57	25
Clyde	34	9	2	23	37	72	20
Ayr U	34	5	9	20	32	61	19

Results grid

	AIRDRIE	AYR U	CELTIC	CLYDE	CLYDEBANK	DUMBARTON	FALKIRK	HAMILTON A	HEARTS	HIBERNIAN	KILMARNOCK	MORTON	MOTHERWELL	PARTICK T	QUEEN'S PARK	RANGERS	ST MIRREN	T LANARK
AIRDRIE		Dec22 4-1	Nov03 2-0	Dec08 3-0	Jan12 1-2	Mar16 0-0	Sep15 3-1	Oct13 2-1	Mar09 0-1	Feb16 3-0	Nov10 0-1	Oct20 1-1	Sep29 3-1	Feb02 0-1	Aug18 2-4	1-2	Sep01 1-0	Nov24 0-3
AYR U	Sep08 1-2		Dec29 1-2	Sep22 1-3	Mar09 1-2	Nov10 0-1	Oct13 1-4	Aug25 2-1	Mar23 1-2	Oct27 0-3	Nov24 0-1	Dec08 1-3	Mar02 0-0	Dec15 2-3	Feb16 0-2	Jan26 2-1	Jan12 1-0	Feb02 2-2
CELTIC	Jan26 3-3	Aug18 4-0		Sep01 3-2	Dec08 3-0	Dec22 3-0	Jan12 0-0	Nov10 1-0	Feb09 3-0	Nov24 2-0	Oct13 2-3	Apr13 2-0	Sep15 1-1	Oct27 2-1	Sep29 1-1	Feb23 2-1	Mar16 1-0	Mar23 1-3
CLYDE	Aug25 3-1	Mar30 4-0	Jan02 1-4		Dec29 0-3	Nov03 0-4	Mar09 1-0	Mar09 1-3	Dec01 3-0	Oct20 2-5	Dec15 1-2	Jan05 0-2	Feb02 0-2	Sep29 0-0	Feb16 1-2	Apr20 2-0	Sep22 2-4	Feb16 5-2
CLYDEBANK	Oct06 3-3	Sep29 1-2	Mar02 1-2	Aug18 0-4		Dec31	Sep01 1-1	Feb09 2-1	Mar23 3-1	Apr13 1-0	Sep15 1-2	Oct20 1-2	Dec01 3-1	Jan05 1-1	Dec15 2-1	Nov17 2-2		
DUMBARTON	Dec15 2-0	Feb23 1-0	Nov17 0-2	Jan26 2-3	Oct13 2-3		Aug18 4-1	Mar23 1-2	Dec29 1-1	Dec08 1-0	Oct27 1-4	Sep01 0-3	Nov24 4-3	Apr06 1-1	Sep15 2-1	Sep29 2-4	Mar02 5-2	Feb09 0-1
FALKIRK	Dec01 4-3	Nov17 3-0	Aug25 1-3	Apr20 4-0	Feb02 0-4	Apr20 1-1		Feb23 2-1	Sep22 4-0	Feb23 2-2	Sep08 1-0	Nov03 0-3	Jan05 1-1	Apr06 1-1	Mar09 2-0	Oct20 1-0	Oct06 1-1	
HAMILTON A	Dec29 1-1	Jan05 0-3	Feb16 1-2	Sep15 3-0	Nov24 2-0	Oct20 1-1	Sep29		Nov17 3-0	Aug18 1-0	Apr06 4-1	Dec22 2-1	Sep01 3-3	Apr13 2-2	Mar02 1-2	Dec08 1-2	Feb02 2-1	Nov03 4-0
HEARTS	Oct27 1-0	Oct20 2-0	Sep29 0-1	Mar16 3-0	Feb16 1-0	Apr13 1-2	Nov24 0-2	Jan26 3-2		Sep01 1-0	Nov17 3-0	Sep15 1-0	Dec22 0-1	Mar30 1-1	Jan05 2-1	Nov10 0-3	Aug18 2-1	Feb23 3-1
HIBERNIAN	Sep22 3-1	Apr20 1-1	Apr06 0-2	Jan12 2-0	Sep08 0-1	Oct06 0-3	Mar23 2-1	Dec15 1-1	Feb02 1-3		Aug25 0-3	Nov17 2-2	Nov03 2-2	Feb23 2-1	Oct13 4-2	Feb09 0-1	Dec01 3-1	Mar09 4-1
KILMARNOCK	Apr13 3-0	Sep01 2-0	Mar30 1-3	Feb23 4-0	Dec22 4-2	Feb02 2-0	Feb09 2-3	Dec01 4-3	Oct06 3-1	Jan05		Sep29 4-0	Nov17 0-0	Nov03 3-1	Mar16 0-1	Aug18 5-1	Sep15 3-1	Oct20 3-1
MORTON	Jan01 0-3	Apr06 1-0	Dec01 1-1	Oct27 2-0	Aug25 2-1	Feb16 2-2	Dec29 1-0	Sep22 3-0	Dec15 1-1	Jan26 1-1	Jan12 2-2		Mar09 2-0	Mar02 1-3	Nov10 2-1	Oct13 1-1	Feb09 2-0	Sep08 2-0
MOTHERWELL	Feb09 2-0	Dec01 5-1	Dec15 3-4	Nov10 1-3	Jan26 4-1	Aug25 0-0	Oct27 2-1	Jan01 3-0	Sep08 4-0	Mar02 2-1	Sep22 1-1	Oct06 1-3		Mar16 4-1	Jan12 6-3	Feb23 2-0	Oct13 2-1	Dec29 3-1
PARTICK T	Jan05 2-1	Feb09 1-3	Mar09 0-0	Nov24 0-0	Feb23 1-2	Sep08 3-1	Nov10 5-0	Oct27 4-1	Oct13 2-2	Sep29 2-0	Jan26 1-1	Aug18 1-0	Dec08		Dec22 5-1	Sep01 2-0	Mar23 1-1	Jan01 3-5
QUEEN'S PARK	Mar30 3-0	Jan01 0-0	Feb02 0-2	Feb09 4-2	Sep22 3-1	Mar09 2-0	Dec08 5-0	Oct06 2-1	Aug25 4-0	Feb23 2-0	Feb23 3-0	Mar23 3-0	Oct20 2-2	Nov17 2-0		Nov24 2-3	Nov03 1-1	Dec15 3-3
RANGERS	Nov17 4-0	Nov03 0-0	Oct20 1-2	Apr13 2-1	Mar30 1-0	Dec01 2-1	Oct13 4-1	Mar16 4-2	Jan12 2-0	Sep15 3-0	Sep22 3-0	Feb02 4-2	Apr06 2-1	Jan01 1-0	Sep24 3-0		Dec29 2-0	Aug25 4-2
ST MIRREN	Feb02 2-0	Oct06 1-1	Jan05 0-0	Dec22 2-0	Nov10 1-0	Sep22 1-0	Mar30 5-1	Sep08 3-2	Apr20 1-1	Apr13 2-0	Jan01 0-1	Nov24 1-1	Feb16 0-1	Aug25 1-0	Jan26 3-1	Oct27 0-0		Dec08 3-1
T LANARK	Mar02 2-2	Sep15 1-1	Sep24 0-2	Oct13 3-0	Oct27 0-1	Jan05 4-1	Jan26 4-0	Jan12 2-1	Apr06 2-3	Nov10 1-0	Feb16 1-1	Mar16 1-2	Aug18 2-4	Dec01 0-1	Sep01 5-0	Dec22 0-1	Sep29 1-2	

> There were no Scottish FA Cup matches in 1917-18

Season 1918-19

DIVISION 1

DIVISION 1 FINAL TABLE

	P	W	D	L	F	A	Pts
Celtic	34	26	6	2	71	22	58
Rangers	34	26	5	3	86	16	57
Morton	34	18	11	5	76	40	47
Partick T	34	17	7	10	62	43	41
Motherwell	34	14	10	10	51	40	38
Ayr U	34	15	8	11	62	53	38
Hearts	34	14	9	11	59	52	37
Queen's Park	34	15	5	14	59	57	35
Kilmarnock	34	14	7	13	61	59	35
Clydebank	34	12	8	14	54	65	32
St Mirren	34	10	12	12	43	55	32
T Lanark	34	11	9	14	60	62	31
Airdrie	34	9	11	14	45	54	29
Hamilton A	34	11	5	18	49	75	27
Dumbarton	34	7	8	19	31	58	22
Falkirk	34	6	8	20	46	73	20
Clyde	34	7	6	21	45	75	20
Hibernian	34	5	3	26	30	91	13

Results grid

	AIRDRIE	AYR U	CELTIC	CLYDE	CLYDEBANK	DUMBARTON	FALKIRK	HAMILTON A	HEARTS	HIBERNIAN	KILMARNOCK	MORTON	MOTHERWELL	PARTICK T	QUEEN'S PARK	RANGERS	ST MIRREN	T LANARK
AIRDRIE		Dec21 0-1	Feb08 1-2	Oct05 1-2	Apr26 2-1	Oct19 1-1	Dec07 1-1	Sep14 0-2	Aug31 1-0	May10 3-3	Jan18 2-2	Jan01 2-1	Nov02 1-1	Aug17 1-1	Apr05 1-2	Nov16 0-0	Nov23 3-1	Jan11 1-6
AYR U	Nov09 1-4		May10 0-2	Feb15 4-1	Feb01 2-0	Dec28 5-0	Feb22 4-1	Nov23 1-2	Jan04 5-0	Nov02 3-1	Dec14 1-5	Sep21 0-1	Oct05 2-0	Aug31 1-1	Oct19 2-0	Mar22 1-1	Jan25 2-0	Aug17 0-2
CELTIC	Apr21 3-0	Sep07 1-0		Jan02 2-0	Jan11 3-1	Dec14 2-0	Apr19 4-0	Feb15 4-1	Nov09 1-1	Dec28 2-0	Feb01 2-1	Aug24 1-1	Jan25 0-0	Feb22 2-1	Mar22 2-0	Oct19 0-3	Nov02 1-0	Sep30 3-1
CLYDE	Mar08 3-5	Sep14 3-1	Aug31 0-3		Mar29 0-2	Aug17 4-1	Jan01 2-4	Jan18 0-1	Oct26 4-2	Oct12 2-1	Nov23 1-1	Apr12 0-2	Feb08 1-2	Jan04 0-1	Dec21 0-4	May10 1-1	Dec07 1-1	Sep28 1-1
CLYDEBANK	Oct12 2-2	Nov30 1-3	Apr12 0-2	Nov02 3-1		Sep14 3-1	Oct19 3-3	Sep28 3-3	Feb08 1-3	Apr05 2-1	Aug31 2-1	Jan04 2-1	Feb15 1-3	Mar08 3-2	Dec28 0-5	Dec14 1-1	Aug17 1-1	Oct05 1-1
DUMBARTON	Feb15 0-0	Dec07 0-0	Oct26 0-5	Feb22 1-0	Dec31		Nov02 1-2	Nov09 1-2	Sep21 4-0	Nov23 0-1	Mar08 0-1	Jan18 0-1	Aug24 2-0	Dec21 1-1	Oct05 0-0	Jan11 0-2	Apr05 0-0	
FALKIRK	Sep07 1-0	Oct26 4-4	Sep28 1-2	Aug24 1-3	Jan18 0-0	Jan04 5-1		Oct12 3-1	Dec21 0-0	Feb01 1-1	Nov09 0-1	Nov30 1-2	Mar22 2-3	Apr05 2-2	Mar29 0-4	Feb08 1-2	Apr12 4-5	Sep14
HAMILTON A	Jan25 3-1	Feb08 2-2	Dec21 1-2	Apr19 4-2	Mar22 1-3	Mar29 0-3	Jan11 1-2		Oct05 1-4	Aug24 1-0	Apr05 2-0	Nov02 1-1	Jan01 3-1	Sep21 1-2	Apr12 0-1	Sep07 0-3	Oct26 2-1	Nov16 4-5
HEARTS	Dec28 0-0	Oct12 2-3	Apr28 2-3	Mar22 3-0	Dec07 2-0	May03 5-0	Nov16 4-1	Feb01		Jan11 3-1	Nov02 1-4	Apr05 1-1	Sep07 0-0	Sep28 1-0	Feb15 2-2	Aug24 1-4	Sep14 0-0	Nov23 2-0
HIBERNIAN	Oct26 2-1	Mar08 0-1	Aug17 0-3	Nov30 3-1	Sep21 1-2	Feb08 1-0	Dec14 2-1	Feb22 1-2	Oct19 1-3		Jan04 1-4	Oct05 0-3	Dec21 0-3	Jan18 0-2	Apr26 1-0	Jan25 1-2	Nov09 1-2	Apr05 1-5
KILMARNOCK	Sep21 2-1	Nov16 2-3	Oct12 1-1	Jan25 5-3	Mar15 2-3	Sep28 0-0	Dec28 0-0	Feb22 5-0	Sep07 7-1			Mar22 0-1	Nov30 0-3	Oct26 1-0	Aug24 1-3	Jan11 0-3	Apr05 1-0	Feb08 1-1
MORTON	Sep28 3-2	Mar29 1-1	Mar08 0-3	Dec28 0-0	Oct26 3-2	Aug31 3-1	Jan25 2-4	Dec14 3-3	Aug17 2-0	Feb15 9-2	Sep14 2-2		Jan11 6-2	Dec07 3-0	Nov09 3-3	Nov23 1-0	Jan02 3-1	Oct12 1-1
MOTHERWELL	Feb01 1-3	Jan18 4-0	Dec07 3-1	Dec14 3-2	Nov09 1-1	Apr26 3-0	Aug31 2-1	Jan11 1-1	Mar08 1-2	May10 0-0	Aug17 1-2	Oct19 2-0		Oct12 1-1	Jan25 3-1	Dec21 0-1	Sep28 1-2	Apr05 1-1
PARTICK T	Mar22 0-1	Jan11 1-3	Nov23 0-1	Sep30 2-0	Aug24 1-0	Jan25 2-1	Oct05 1-1	Oct19 6-3	Dec14 3-1	Apr21 2-0	Feb15 4-0	Feb01 2-1	Apr12		Nov02 2-1	Jan02 0-0	Dec28 5-1	Jan01 1-2
QUEEN'S PARK	Dec14 1-0	Jan01 2-2	Sep14 0-3	Jan11 3-1	Nov23 3-4	Apr19 1-0	Aug31 3-2	Aug17 4-0	Jan25 3-2	Sep28 3-0	Mar29 4-0	Feb22 2-1	Apr21 4-2	Feb08 1-3		Sep30 0-2	Oct12 4-1	Oct26 3-4
RANGERS	Jan04 2-1	Sep28 6-2	Jan01 1-1	Nov09 3-0	Feb22 3-0	Oct12 3-0	Aug17 1-0	Mar08 3-2	Mar01 5-1	Dec21 8-0	Dec07 1-0	Feb08 0-0	Oct26 5-0	Sep14 2-0	Jan18 4-0		Aug31 2-0	Apr21 4-0
ST MIRREN	Feb22 1-2	Aug24 0-4	Jan18 1-1	Oct19 0-1	Dec21 2-1	Mar22 1-0	Sep21 2-1	Jan04 1-1	May10 1-5	May03 2-2	Oct05 0-1	Sep07 1-1	Apr05 1-1	Apr19 1-1	Feb01 1-1	Feb15 2-2		Dec14 0-0
T LANARK	Aug24 1-1	Mar01 1-1	Jan04 2-3	Feb01 1-4	Jan02 2-0	Apr12 2-4	Feb15 2-2	Dec28 3-1	Jan18 3-1	Mar22 4-2	Nov02 3-4	Oct19 0-1	Dec21 1-1	Sep21 1-2	Nov09 1-3	Dec07 1-2	Nov02 1-0	

> There were no Scottish FA Cup matches in 1918-19

Season 1919-20

SFA Cup

1st Round
Jan 24 Albion R ....0 Dykehead 0
Jan 24 Armadale ......1 Clyde 0
Jan 24 Cowdenbeath .....0 Aberdeen 1
Jan 24 Dumbarton Harp ...0 Alloa 0
Jan 24 Dundee ....1 Airdrie 0
Jan 24 East Fife ......4 Arthurlie 0
Jan 24 E Stirling ......6 Thornhill ...0
played at Falkirk
Jan 24 Galston ....0 Hibernian 0
Jan 24 Hearts ....5 Nithsdale W 1
Jan 24 Lochgelly U ....2 Clacknacuddin ...0
Jan 24 Morton ....4 Forfar A 0
Jan 24 Partick T ......3 Motherwell 1
Jan 24 Queen's Park ....2 Hamilton A 0
Jan 24 Rangers ......0 Dumbarton 0
Jan 24 Royal Albert ....7 Forres Mechanic ..0
Jan 24 Stevenston U ....1 St Mirren 2
Jan 24 T Lanark ......4 Inverness C 1

Replays
Jan 27 Rangers ....1 Dumbarton 0
Jan 31 Alloa ....1 Dumbarton H 0
Jan 31 Dykehead ......1 Albion R 2
Jan 31 Hibernian ......2 Galston 1

2nd Round
Feb 7 Aberdeen ......2 Gala Fairydean ...0
      Albion ....W Huntingtower 0
Feb 7 Alloa ....0 Kilmarnock 2
Feb 7 Armadale ......1 Hibernian 0
Feb 7 Ayr U ....2 St Mirren 1
Feb 7 Broxburn U ....1 Queen of South ...0
Feb 7 Dundee ....1 Celtic 3
Feb 7 E Stirling ......0 Raith R 0
Feb 7 Hearts ....2 Falkirk 0
Feb 7 Lochgelly U ....2 Royal Albert 1
Feb 7 Partick T ......5 East Fife 0
Feb 7 Queen's Park ....3 Vale of Leithen ...0
Feb 7 Rangers ......5 Arbroath 0
Jan 24 St Bernard's ....2 Bathgate 0
Feb 7 St Johnstone ....1 Morton 1
Feb 7 T Lanark ......2 Vale of Leven 1

Replays
Feb 11 Morton ....5 St Johnstone 3
Feb 11 Raith R ....1 E Stirling 1
Feb 18 E Stirling ....0 Raith R 0
played at Tynecastle
Feb 19 E Stirling ....0 Raith R 4
played at Tynecastle

3rd Round
Feb 21 Aberdeen ....1 Hearts 0
Feb 21 Ayr U ....1 Armadale 1
Feb 21 Celtic ....2 Partick T 0
Feb 21 Kilmarnock ....4 Queen of South ...1
Feb 21 Lochgelly U .....0 T Lanark 3
Feb 21 Raith R ....2 Morton 2
Feb 21 Rangers ......3 Broxburn U 0
Feb 21 St Bernard's .....1 Albion R 1

Replays
Feb 25 Albion R ......4 St Bernard's 1
Feb 25 Morton ....3 Raith R 0
Feb 28 Armadale ......1 Ayr U 0

4th Round
Mar 6 Albion R ....2 Aberdeen 1
Mar 6 Armadale ......1 Kilmarnock 2
Mar 6 Morton ....3 T Lanark 0
Mar 6 Rangers ......1 Celtic 0

Semi-finals
Mar 27 Albion R ....1 Rangers 1
played at Celtic Park
Mar 27 Kilmarnock ......3 Morton 2
played at Hampden Park

Replays
Mar 31 Albion R ....0 Rangers 0
played at Celtic Park
Apr 7 Albion R ....2 Rangers 0
played at Celtic Park

Final
Apr 17 Albion R ....2 Kilmarnock 3
played at Hampden Park

DIVISION 1 FINAL TABLE

	P	W	D	L	F	A	Pts
Rangers	42	31	9	2	106	25	71
Celtic	42	29	10	3	89	31	68
Motherwell	42	23	11	8	74	53	57
Dundee	42	22	6	14	79	65	50
Clydebank	42	20	8	14	78	54	48
Morton	42	16	13	13	71	48	45
Airdrie	42	17	10	15	57	43	44
T Lanark	42	16	11	15	56	62	43
Kilmarnock	42	20	3	19	59	74	43
Ayr U	42	15	10	17	72	69	40
Dumbarton	42	13	13	16	55	65	39
Queen's Park	42	14	10	18	67	73	38
Partick T	42	13	12	17	51	62	38
St Mirren	42	15	8	19	63	81	38
Clyde	42	14	9	19	64	71	37
Hearts	42	14	9	19	57	72	37
Aberdeen	42	11	13	18	46	64	35
Hibernian	42	13	7	22	60	79	33
Raith R	42	11	10	21	61	83	32
Falkirk	42	10	11	21	45	74	31
Hamilton A	42	11	7	24	56	86	29
Albion R	42	10	8	24	43	65	28

DIVISION 1 — Results Grid

	ABERDEEN	AIRDRIE	ALBION R	AYR U	CELTIC	CLYDE	CLYDEBANK	DUMBARTON	DUNDEE	FALKIRK	HAMILTON A	HEARTS	HIBERNIAN	KILMARNOCK	MORTON	MOTHERWELL	PARTICK T	QUEEN'S PARK	RAITH R	RANGERS	ST MIRREN	T LANARK
ABERDEEN		Nov01 2-1	Aug16 2-0	Sep13 2-1	Nov29 0-1	Aug30 1-0	Apr17 0-2	Apr24 3-4	Sep22 2-0	Dec06 1-1	Jan03 2-0	Jan17 1-1	Dec20 1-1	Nov15 1-0	Sep27 0-0	May01 1-1	Apr19 0-0	Jan11 1-1	Mar13 3-1	Mar20 0-2	Oct18 0-1	Mar27 0-1
AIRDRIE	Dec27 2-0		Jan01 2-1	Aug30 0-0	Dec13 0-0	Sep20 1-1	Feb14 1-2	Nov22 1-0	Sep03 4-1	Jan17 2-0	Oct25 0-0	Apr21 0-1	Sep13 2-0	Nov08 0-0	Mar20 0-1	Jan05 2-0	Feb28 3-1	Oct11 1-1	Apr10 3-1	Aug16 0-1	Dec06 1-1	Mar13 1-2
ALBION R	Apr05 1-1	Apr24 0-2		Nov01 2-1	Apr14 0-5	Jan10 0-2	Sep06 2-1	Feb07 1-2	Jan03 1-2	Dec20 2-1	Apr28 1-1	Apr03 6-2	Sep29 1-2	May01 0-2	Apr19 2-4	Oct18 1-1	Aug23 2-0	Nov15 2-0	Apr26 0-0	Dec25 0-4	— 0-2	May05 3-2
AYR U	Apr03 0-0	Mar06 1-1	Sep17 4-0		Nov15 1-1	Dec06 3-1	Jan31 1-1	Apr10 5-3	Sep06 5-1	Nov08 4-0	Aug23 1-2	Oct25 1-0	Sep13 5-0	Jan10 2-0	Dec06 0-0	Mar20 3-0	Sep03 2-2	Mar27 1-1	Dec20 2-5	Mar27 0-3	— 1-2	Oct04 2-0
CELTIC	Apr10 5-0	Apr28 1-0	Feb14 3-0	Apr24 4-0		Sep27 3-1	Aug16 3-1	Aug18 1-1	Apr26 1-1	Nov08 1-1	Feb28 5-0	May01 0-0	Oct11 3-1	Aug27 3-0	Jan10 1-1	Dec06 5-0	Nov22 0-3	Oct25 1-1	Aug30 3-0	Jan01 1-1	Apr22 2-2	Dec27 2-1
CLYDE	Jan31 2-0	Dec20 0-2	Apr10 2-2	Apr17 4-0	Jan05 0-2		Mar23 0-3	Nov01 1-2	Jan17 3-2	Mar02 4-0	Sep03 2-2	Oct18 0-1	Feb17 2-0	Apr03 2-1	Aug19 4-2	Aug23 4-1	Sep29 3-2	Dec13 4-2	Nov29 4-3	Sep13 0-0	Mar06 3-3	Apr05 0-1
CLYDEBANK	Nov08 3-0	Aug23 1-2	Oct04 5-2	Nov22 4-3	Aug16 2-0	Jan24 2-3		Dec31 1-1	Nov01 3-3	Mar06 3-1	Apr24 3-0	Mar20 0-1	Apr01 3-3	Sep13 1-0	Feb21 5-1	Dec27 2-1	Jan17 1-1	Dec27 4-1	Dec13 0-0	Sep29 3-1	Oct18 0-0	—
DUMBARTON	Jan10 4-0	Sep10 1-1	Dec06 2-1	Aug16 1-0	Dec20 0-0	Feb21 1-0	Aug30 1-0		Oct11 0-3	Apr03 1-2	Sep27 2-0	Nov29 2-0	Feb14 2-2	Sep01 2-0	Apr12 2-3	Jan31 1-1	May01 1-5	Feb28 1-1	Oct25 0-0	Apr28 3-1	Mar13 1-1	Sep06 1-0
DUNDEE	Jan01 1-3	Oct04 1-1	Nov22 3-2	Nov29 7-1	Jan31 2-1	Nov08 3-0	Apr12 1-0	Mar20 3-1		Feb21 1-0	Apr03 2-1	Sep20 1-0	Dec27 3-1	Jan10 3-2	Apr21 2-0	Oct06 3-0	Apr17 2-1	Mar27 1-1	Dec13 5-4	Oct25 0-2	Sep06 1-2	Aug23 3-1
FALKIRK	Feb28 3-1	Oct25 0-2	Oct25 1-1	Sep08 1-2	Dec27 1-2	Oct04 1-1	Oct11 1-0	Dec27 3-2	Sep13 2-1		Feb14 3-2	Dec13 3-3	Jan10 3-0	Jan05 1-0	Aug27 1-1	Aug30 2-2	Aug16 2-0	— 4-1	Nov15 3-1	Nov29 1-3	—	—
HAMILTON A	Sep20 2-1	Feb07 1-0	Dec13 0-2	May01 2-1	Aug23 2-0	Dec27 2-0	Dec06 1-3	Mar27 0-1	Oct18 3-1	Nov01 1-1		Mar13 2-2	Feb21 0-3	Sep06 3-2	Jan31 0-2	Sep10 0-3	Mar06 5-5	Apr14 1-2	Oct04 2-1	Jan10 0-0	Apr16 2-1	Jan05 1-0
HEARTS	Oct25 1-1	Nov15 3-1	Oct11 0-0	Jan05 0-1	Sep13 0-1	Mar20 0-3	Sep27 4-2	Apr17 1-2	Feb14 2-1	Apr19 3-0	Aug30 2-0		Jan01 1-3	Apr28 0-1	Dec27 3-6	Nov01 2-0	Dec06 3-1	Aug16 3-1	Feb28 1-1	Apr10 0-0	Oct20 1-2	Jan10 1-1
HIBERNIAN	Sep06 2-1	Mar27 1-4	Mar13 0-1	Jan17 1-2	Apr19 1-2	Feb17 1-0	Apr01 2-0	Jan03 3-3	Dec27 0-0	Oct01 2-0	Sep20 2-4	Sep15 1-3		Dec13 4-1	Nov29 1-0	Mar06 6-2	Oct18 3-2	Apr24 2-0	Nov08 2-1	Aug23 2-1	Apr03 1-2	—
KILMARNOCK	Apr21 0-3	Jan31 3-2	Aug30 1-0	Jan03 2-1	Jan17 2-3	Aug16 2-4	Nov29 3-1	Sep13 2-1	Mar13 2-1	Oct18 4-1	Mar20 3-0	Nov22 2-1	Feb28 4-1		Oct11 0-1	Apr19 2-0	Dec20 1-0	Apr07 2-0	Jan24 1-0	Sep15 2-0	Nov01 1-0	Feb14 2-0
MORTON	Sep08 3-1	Sep06 0-2	Jan17 1-1	Mar13 3-1	Nov01 1-2	Aug19 2-0	Apr14 1-0	Apr12 4-0	Oct18 0-0	Dec06 3-4	Aug23 0-0	Nov22 2-0	Oct04 1-1	Apr10 4-0		Apr26 0-1	Sep20 0-0	Jan03 0-1	Nov08 0-0	Apr24 0-2	Feb14 3-1	Dec20 5-1
MOTHERWELL	Oct04 3-3	Nov29 2-1	Feb28 2-0	Oct11 1-1	Feb14 0-0	Dec20 5-1	Dec06 3-2	Nov08 1-1	Nov22 3-1	Jan03 4-0	Aug30 1-0	Nov01 4-1	Mar16 3-2	Jan05 1-1	Apr03 4-3		Jan17 1-0	Apr10 4-1	Sep13 4-1	Apr24 3-0	Mar20 3-3	—
PARTICK T	Oct11 0-1	Jan10 3-1	Dec27 2-2	Feb14 1-2	Apr05 0-0	Mar27 3-2	Oct25 1-1	Apr10 0-0	Apr30 1-1	Apr24 1-1	Sep13 1-0	Jan31 1-0	Apr14 1-1	Sep09 1-0	Aug16 1-1	Dec13 2-1		Sep27 2-0	Aug26 2-0	Nov08 1-1	Nov29 0-2	Jan01 2-0
QUEEN'S PARK	Feb14 3-0	May01 1-0	Apr21 2-1	Oct18 6-3	Mar13 1-2	Apr26 4-1	Aug19 3-2	Aug23 2-1	Dec20 3-2	Sep29 2-1	Nov01 3-2	Mar06 2-2	Nov01 1-3	Dec27 4-3	Apr05 1-1	Sep06 0-1	Apr03 0-1		Jan10 1-2	Nov22 0-0	Oct04 1-1	Jan31 2-0
RAITH R	Nov22 2-2	Oct18 3-2	Apr26 3-0	Dec20 2-1	Aug30 0-3	Nov29 3-1	Dec13 0-0	Oct25 2-0	Apr03 1-3	Nov15 2-0	Apr17 1-0	Feb28 0-1	Nov08 5-1	Jan24 1-1	Nov08 0-2	Sep13 2-5	Aug26 2-0	Jan10 2-5		Oct11 1-2	Sep20 3-0	May01 0-2
RANGERS	Aug23 3-2	Apr03 3-2	Aug26 2-0	Apr13 2-1	Oct18 3-0	Feb28 3-0	Apr05 7-0	Sep20 3-0	Apr24 6-1	Jan03 3-0	Dec20 7-0	Dec29 3-2	Dec06 3-0	Oct04 2-0	May01 2-0	Mar16 0-0	Jan05 2-2	Apr17 3-1	Sep09 3-0		Jan17 3-1	Nov01 6-1
ST MIRREN	Apr12 3-1	Feb21 4-2	Sep13 1-2	Sep27 1-4	Apr03 0-2	Oct11 0-0	Jan10 0-3	Dec13 1-5	Feb28 1-3	May01 1-0	Aug16 2-0	Nov08 4-1	Sep22 2-1	Jan01 1-3	Oct25 2-1	Dec27 2-0	Mar20 3-1	Sep02 1-1	Jan31 1-1	Aug30 0-4		Nov22 2-2
T LANARK	Dec13 2-2	Jan03 1-1	Nov08 1-0	Apr08 0-4	Sep29 1-4	Oct25 4-1	Feb28 1-2	Jan17 1-0	Dec25 2-0	Sep02 0-1	Oct11 1-3	Apr24 2-1	Aug16 2-0	Dec06 0-1	Aug30 0-4	Apr14 2-0	Aug19 0-0	Sep13 1-1	Sep27 4-3	Apr27 0-2	Apr10 4-1	

SFA Cup
1st Round
Jan 22 Alloa ....0 Falkirk 0
Jan 22 Arbroath ....2 Kilmarnock 4
Jan 22 Ayr U ....1 Queen's Park ... 0
Jan 22 Boness ....1 Galston 0
Jan 22 Clyde ....1 Airdrie 1
Jan 22 Dundee ....8 Inverness C ...1
Jan 22 Hamilton A .....3 Raith R 1
Jan 29 Johnstone ......0 Stevenston U 2
Jan 22 Peterhead ......0 Dykehead 3
Jan 22 Queen of South .8 Blairgowrie 0
Jan 22 St Mirren ......2 Armadale 3
Jan 22 T Lanark ....1 Hibernian 1

Replays
Jan 26 Airdrie ....0 Clyde 1
Jan 26 Hibernian ....1 T Lanark 1
Jan 29 Falkirk ....1 Alloa 1
Feb 1 Hibernian ....1 T Lanark 0
played at Ibrox
Feb 2 Falkirk ....1 Alloa 1
played at Firhill Park
Feb 3 Alloa ....1 Falkirk 0
played at Firhill Park

2nd Round
Feb 5 Albion R ....3 Mid Annandale ...1
Feb 5 Alloa ....1 Clydebank 1
Feb 5 Ayr U ....4 Dykehead 0
Feb 5 Boness ....0 Armadale 0
Feb 5 Broxburn U .....1 Hamilton A 2
Feb 5 Clyde ....1 Hearts 1
Feb 5 Dumbarton .....3 Elgin C 0
Feb 5 Dundee ....1 Stenhousemuir ...0
Feb 5 Hibernian ....0 Partick T 0
Feb 5 Kilmarnock ......1 Aberdeen 2
Feb 5 Motherwell ......3 Renton 0
Feb 5 Queen of South ..1 Nithsdale W 3
Feb 5 Rangers ....2 Morton 0
Feb 5 Solway Star .....1 E Stirling 5
Feb 5 Stevenston U ....0 East Fife 0
Feb 5 Vale of Leven ....0 Celtic 3

Replays
Feb 8 Partick T ....0 Hibernian 0
Feb 9 Hearts ....0 Clyde 0
Feb 12 Armadale ......2 Boness 0
Feb 12 Clydebank ....0 Alloa A 0
Feb 12 East Fife ....2 Stevenston U 1
Feb 15 Hibernian ....0 Partick T 1
played at Celtic Park
Feb 16 Alloa ....1 Clydebank 0
played at Ibrox
Feb 16 Clyde ....2 Hearts 3
played at Shawfield

3rd Round
Feb 19 Armadale ....2 Albion R 2
Feb 19 Ayr U ....1 Motherwell 1
Feb 19 Dumbarton ......5 Nithsdale W 0
Feb 19 Dundee ....0 Aberdeen 0
Feb 19 East Fife ....1 Celtic 3
Feb 19 E Stirling ....1 Partick T 2
Feb 19 Hamilton A ......0 Hearts 1
Feb 19 Rangers ....0 Alloa 0

Replays
Feb 23 Aberdeen ....1 Dundee 1
Feb 23 Motherwell .....1 Ayr U 1
Feb 26 Albion R ....0 Armadale 0
Feb 26 Alloa ....1 Rangers 4
played at Ibrox
Mar 1 Aberdeen ....0 Dundee 2
played at Ibrox
Mar 2 Albion R ....0 Armadale 0
played at Hampden Park
Mar 2 Ayr U ....1 Motherwell 3
played at Celtic Park
Mar 3 Albion R ....2 Armadale 0
played at Hampden Park

4th Round
Mar 5 Celtic ....1 Hearts 2
Mar 5 Dumbarton ......0 Rangers 3
Mar 5 Dundee ....0 Albion R 2
Mar 5 Motherwell ......2 Partick T 2

Replays
Mar 8 Partick T ....0 Motherwell 0
Mar 15 Motherwell ......1 Partick T 2
played at Firhill Park

Semi-finals
Mar 26 Albion R ....1 Rangers 4
played at Celtic Park
Mar 26 Hearts ....0 Partick T 0
played at Ibrox

Replays
Mar 30 Hearts ....0 Partick T 0
played at Ibrox
Apr 5 Hearts ....0 Partick T 2
played at Ibrox

Final
Apr 16 Partick T ....1 Rangers 0
played at Celtic Park

DIVISION 1 FINAL TABLE

	P	W	D	L	F	A	Pts
Rangers	42	35	6	1	91	24	76
Celtic	42	30	6	6	86	35	66
Hearts	42	20	10	12	74	49	50
Dundee	42	19	11	12	54	48	49
Motherwell	42	19	10	13	75	51	48
Partick T	42	17	12	13	53	39	46
Clyde	42	21	3	18	63	62	45
T Lanark	42	19	6	17	74	61	44
Morton	42	15	14	13	66	58	44
Airdrie	42	17	9	16	71	64	43
Aberdeen	42	14	14	14	53	54	42
Kilmarnock	42	17	8	17	62	68	42
Hibernian	42	16	9	17	58	57	41
Ayr U	42	14	12	16	62	69	40
Hamilton A	42	14	12	16	44	57	40
Raith R	42	16	5	21	54	58	37
Albion R	42	11	12	19	57	68	34
Falkirk	42	11	12	19	54	72	34
Queen's Park	42	11	11	20	45	80	33
Clydebank	42	7	14	21	47	72	28
Dumbarton	42	10	4	28	41	89	24
St Mirren	42	7	4	31	43	92	18

DIVISION 1

	ABERDEEN	AIRDRIE	ALBION R	AYR U	CELTIC	CLYDE	CLYDEBANK	DUMBARTON	DUNDEE	FALKIRK	HAMILTON A	HEARTS	HIBERNIAN	KILMARNOCK	MORTON	MOTHERWELL	PARTICK T	QUEEN'S PARK	RAITH R	RANGERS	ST MIRREN	T LANARK
ABERDEEN		Dec04 1-0	Apr30 1-0	Sep11 0-0	Aug28 1-2	Sep07 3-0	Jan22 4-0	Mar26 2-0	Jan01 0-1	Jan15 3-1	Sep15 5-2	Apr09 0-1	Oct09 1-1	Mar12 0-3	Feb26 2-2	Dec18 1-0	Dec25 1-1	Sep27 0-3	Oct23 1-0	Sep25 1-1	Nov20 0-3	Nov06 1-3
AIRDRIE	Feb19 5-2		Aug28 5-1	Feb09 1-2	Apr30 2-3	Sep11 5-1	Apr02 2-1	Oct30 1-1	Apr16 1-1	Sep08 1-1	Mar26 1-3	Nov06 0-1	Sep25 5-1	Jan03 3-0	Dec25 3-2	Dec11 1-1	Nov20 1-2	Sep22 4-1	Jan29 3-1	Jan08 0-3	Jan08 1-1	Mar05 1-3
ALBION R	Sep04 0-2	Jan01 1-1		Oct23 1-2	Sep21 0-1	Dec18 5-2	Jan15 1-1	Mar26 3-0	Apr02 2-3	Sep18 3-1	Aug23 3-4	Feb12 1-1	Oct16 0-2	Oct02 2-0	Oct02 3-2	Mar12 1-1	Aug16 0-0	Nov13 2-1	Aug16 0-1	Nov13 1-2	Nov13 1-2	Sep20 1-2
AYR U	Jan03 2-2	Sep04 1-2	Apr16 3-0		Mar12 3-1	Jan29 1-3	Feb26 5-1	Sep16 3-0	Dec04 1-1	Apr30 2-2	Oct30 1-1	Sep18 0-0	Nov13 2-1	Oct02 0-0	Aug18 0-2	Nov27 0-0	Aug21 2-1	Jan08 3-1	Feb12 1-0	Dec18 1-1	Oct16 4-2	Apr27 5-1
CELTIC	Jan29 3-1	Dec18 2-1	Oct26 0-2	Sep25 3-1		Jan03 1-0	Apr20 1-1	Apr02 1-1	Mar09 2-0	Oct12 4-1	Sep11 2-1	Mar19 3-2	Apr23 3-0	Nov13 2-0	Sep01 1-1	Sep07 1-0	Dec11 1-0	Oct09 5-1	Oct23 5-0	Feb12 1-2	Feb06 6-0	Sep27 3-0
CLYDE	Oct30 2-0	Feb22 3-0	Apr04 2-0	Nov06 3-1	Nov20 2-1			Nov06 4-0	Apr30 2-1	Oct16 5-2	Aug21 1-1	Jan08 2-1	Dec04 1-2	Apr11 0-0	Feb05 1-2	Apr23 2-1	Dec25 1-3	Mar12 3-1	Mar28 2-2			
CLYDEBANK	Oct02 1-1	Sep18 1-2	Oct30 4-1	Nov20 2-0	Jan08 0-2	Sep04 1-0		Jan05 1-2	Feb09 0-1	Feb19 1-0	Jan29 2-2	Sep14 1-2	Dec25 2-4	Sep01 3-4	Mar12 3-0	Apr23	Aug24	Apr02	Dec11	Nov13	Mar26	Oct16
DUMBARTON	Nov27 0-1	Feb12 1-2	Sep11 0-4	Jan01 0-1	Nov06 1-3	Sep25 0-2	Aug21 1-0		Aug28 1-1	Mar07 4-1	Apr16 3-0	Apr11 0-3	Mar12 1-0	Dec18 1-0	Aug25 1-2	Feb26 2-0	Dec04 0-1	Oct23 4-0	Jan15 2-0	Oct09 2-5	Apr08 1-0	Mar19 0-1
DUNDEE	Aug21 1-1	Nov13 0-1	Dec11 3-0	Mar26 2-0	Oct16 1-2	Nov27 2-1	Apr11 0-2	Jan29 2-1		Sep04 2-0	Oct04 4-0	Oct04 3-0	Jan03 1-1	Jan03 3-1	Jan08 0-0	Apr09 2-1	Mar12 1-0	Feb26 1-1	Feb05 0-0	Apr23 1-2	Apr23 2-0	Sep18 2-1
FALKIRK	Apr23 0-0	Oct02 2-3	Apr09 0-2	Oct09 2-2	Dec04 1-3	Feb12 2-2	Aug28 3-5	Jan08 1-2	Aug16 2-1			Nov06 1-2	Nov20 2-2	Sep11 0-3	Feb09 1-2	Oct23 2-0	Mar12 1-2	Apr26 4-0	Mar26 1-1	Jan01 0-4	Mar02 1-3	Sep13 4-0
HAMILTON A	Oct16 0-2	Oct23 0-0	Mar19 0-0	Aug25 3-0	Aug18 1-1	Dec11 0-0	Nov27 1-1	Sep04 1-0	Sep08 1-1	Feb26 2-0		Oct02 3-1	Dec18 1-1	Feb12 2-0	Apr23 4-2	Jan01 1-4	Apr08 1-0	Nov13 0-1	Mar12 0-0	Jan15 0-1	Sep18 3-0	Aug21 1-1
HEARTS	Nov13 0-0	Mar12 2-1	Oct09 1-1	Sep25 4-1	Sep08 0-1	Oct30 6-0	Apr02 6-2	Sep11 3-1	Jan03 0-2	Apr30 3-0			Aug28 5-1	Apr01 4-1	Jan29 0-1	Feb12 1-0	Apr23 4-0	Sep25 2-0	Oct04 0-4	Sep20 1-0	Dec18 1-0	Feb26 3-0
HIBERNIAN	Mar05 2-3	Sep01 0-2	Nov06 5-2	Jan15 3-2	Sep20 0-3	Mar19 0-1	Dec04 2-0	Sep18 0-0	Nov20 0-0	Aug25 0-0	Feb23 1-0	Jan01 3-0		Oct02 2-1	Sep04 0-0	Mar26 2-1	Oct16 1-1	Apr27 1-1	Dec11 1-1	Apr16 1-1	Apr09 1-0	Aug21 2-1
KILMARNOCK	Dec11 1-0	Apr23 2-0	Feb09 3-1	Mar05 2-1	Mar26 3-2	Apr09 0-1	Sep25 2-2	Feb23 4-1	Mar19 5-0	Dec25 2-0	Oct09 5-0	Jan15 1-2	Apr02 1-3		Sep22 3-1	Oct23 0-3	Nov06 0-1	Sep11 1-1	Oct30 1-0	Aug28 1-2	Jan01 3-2	Nov20 3-2
MORTON	Sep18 6-1	Nov13 0-0	Dec11 1-3	Dec25 0-0	Jan08 1-1	Dec18 2-1	Oct02 4-1	Apr04 1-0	Mar05 0-0	Sep04 0-1	Nov27 1-1	Nov27 1-1	Sep04 9-2	Aug21 4-1		Oct30 4-0	Apr09 4-3	Sep15 1-3	Oct16 0-0	Feb19 1-0	Apr21 1-1	1-1
MOTHERWELL	Apr16 4-0	Jan05 1-1	Jan08 1-1	Dec25 6-1	Jan22 1-3	Mar23 0-0	Nov06 2-0	Nov20 8-2	Oct09 1-2	Sep25 4-2	Aug28 2-2	Dec04 4-2	Aug16 2-2	Apr30 2-2	Jan03 1-0		Sep11 0-4	Apr20 2-0	Mar26 3-2	Sep01	Oct30 4-0	Jan29
PARTICK T	Apr02 2-2	Jan15 0-0	Jan29 0-0	Apr23 0-0	Apr28 0-1	Sep27 2-2	Oct09 1-2	Aug21 1-0	Dec18 2-1	Nov13 2-1	Sep25 1-1	Jan22 1-0	Oct23 3-2	Feb26 1-1	Feb12 4-0	Mar19 0-0		Nov27 5-0	Aug28 3-1	Jan03 0-2	Sep04 5-1	Jan01 1-0
QUEEN'S PARK	Mar19 1-0	Aug21 2-1	Nov20 1-1	Sep04 3-0	Sep02 0-2	Apr02 2-6	Jan01 3-0	Apr30 3-0	Nov13 0-0	Oct30 0-3	Jan29 0-1	Feb23 1-1	Oct30 1-0	Feb09	Nov06 1-1				Dec18 3-2	Mar28 1-1	Aug17 2-2	Feb12 2-1
RAITH R	Jan08 1-0	Mar19 3-2	Dec25 2-1	Apr02 0-0	Apr09 1-2	Nov13 0-1	Mar05	Oct16	Oct02 1-1	Aug21	Dec04	Feb23 2-1	Oct30	Sep18	Nov20	Sep04	Sep08	Oct04		Apr30	Jan29	Jan03
RANGERS	Aug24 2-1	Aug17 4-1	Sep07 2-1	Mar09 7-2	Jan01 0-2	Apr19 3-1	Mar19 1-0	Jan22 2-0	Nov06 5-0	Dec11 2-0	Nov20 4-0	Apr27 0-0	Sep27 1-0	Jan08 2-0	Sep11 2-1	Aug21 3-0	Oct16 3-1	Dec04 1-0	Feb09		Oct02 2-0	Oct30 2-1
ST MIRREN	Feb08 1-1	Feb05 0-1	Feb22 1-2	Dec25 1-4	Mar19 0-3	Oct23 3-2	Dec11 4-1	Sep11 1-1	Nov27 2-3	Apr15 1-0	Feb26 0-4	Sep25 1-2	Sep21 2-2	Sep04 1-2	Jan04 0-2	Apr21 0-1						Jan15 1-3
T LANARK	Aug30 3-1	Nov27 7-3	Sep25 2-2	Aug28 3-1	Feb23 1-2	Oct23 3-0	Apr30 1-3	Nov13 4-0	Aug25 1-3	Feb05 4-0	Jan08 0-1	Dec11 5-0	Feb19 1-1	Aug18 3-0	Oct09 0-2	Apr02 4-4	Apr19 1-2	Dec25 0-1	Sep11 1-0	Apr23 3-0	Dec04 0-1	

SFA Cup

1st Round

Jan 28	Aberdeen	1	Dumbarton	0
Jan 28	Airdrie	1	Dykehead	0
Jan 28	Albion R	6	Johnstone	0
Jan 28	Alloa	3	St Bernard's	1
Jan 28	Bathgate	3	Helensburgh	2
Jan 28	Blairgowrie Am	1	Queen of South	5
Jan 28	Bo'ness	6	Stranraer	0
Jan 28	Buckie T	1	Royal Albert	2
Jan 28	Celtic	4	Montrose	0
Feb 4	Clackmannan	3	Inver Citadel	5
Jan 28	Clacknacuddin	0	Rangers	5
Jan 28	Clydebank	1	Arbroath	1
Jan 28	Cowdenbeath	9	Vale of Atholl	1
Jan 28	Dundee H	0	Broxburn U	2
Jan 28	Dunfermline A	3	Stevenston U	1
Jan 28	East Fife	0	Motherwell	3
Jan 28	E Stirling	3	Douglas W	1
Jan 28	Forfar A	0	Falkirk	3
Jan 28	Hamilton A	9	Gala Fairydean	0
Jan 28	Hearts	2	Arthurlie	1
Jan 28	Hibernian	3	Armadale	0
Jan 28	Kilmarnock	5	Inverness Cal	1
Feb 4	King's Park	1	St Johnstone	1
	played at Falkirk			
Feb 1	Lochgelly U	1	Ayr U	5
Jan 28	Morton	4	Vale of Leithen	0
Jan 28	Partick T	7	Dumbarton H	0
Jan 28	Queen's Park	3	Nithsdale W	1
Jan 28	Raith R	2	Clyde	2
Jan 28	St Mirren	7	Solway Star	2
Jan 28	Stenhousemuir	0	Dundee	2
Jan 28	T Lanark	6	Leith A	0
Jan 28	Vale of Leven	1	Fraserburgh	0

Replays

Feb 1	Arbroath	0	Clydebank	1
Feb 1	Clyde	1	Raith R	0
Feb 8	St Johnstone	1	King's Park	1
Feb 15	King's Park	1	St Johnstone	0
	played at Dunfermline			

2nd Round

Feb 11	Aberdeen	1	Queen's Park	1
Feb 11	Albion R	1	Rangers	1
Feb 11	Ayr U	0	Partick T	1
Feb 11	Bathgate	1	Falkirk	0
Feb 11	Clyde	5	Bo'ness	1
Feb 11	Cowdenbeath	0	Airdrie	0
Feb 11	E Stirling	2	Dunfermline A	1
Feb 18	Hamilton A	4	King's Park	1
Feb 11	Hearts	2	Broxburn U	2
Feb 11	Inver Citadel	2	Queen of South	2
Feb 11	Kilmarnock	1	St Mirren	4
Feb 11	Morton	1	Clydebank	1
Feb 11	Motherwell	3	Hibernian	2
Feb 11	Royal Albert	0	Dundee	1
Feb 11	T Lanark	0	Celtic	1
Feb 11	Vale of Leven	0	Alloa	0

Replays

Feb 14	Alloa	1	Vale of Leven	0
Feb 14	Clydebank	1	Morton	3
Feb 14	Queen's Park	1	Aberdeen	2
Feb 15	Airdrie	4	Cowdenbeath	1
Feb 15	Broxburn U	2	Hearts	2
Feb 15	Rangers	4	Albion R	0
Feb 18	Queen of South	2	Inver Citadel	1
Feb 20	Broxburn U	1	Hearts	3
	played at Tynecastle			

3rd Round

Feb 25	Aberdeen	3	Dundee	0
Feb 25	Celtic	1	Hamilton A	3
Feb 25	Hearts	0	Rangers	4
Feb 25	Morton	4	Clyde	1
Feb 25	Motherwell	1	Alloa	0
Feb 25	Partick T	3	Bathgate	0
Feb 25	Queen of South	2	E Stirling	0
Feb 25	St Mirren	3	Airdrie	0

4th Round

Mar 11	Hamilton A	0	Aberdeen	0
Mar 11	Motherwell	1	Morton	2
Mar 11	Partick T	1	Queen of South	0
Mar 11	Rangers	1	St Mirren	1

Replays

Mar 14	St Mirren	0	Rangers	2
Mar 15	Aberdeen	2	Hamilton A	0

Semi-finals

Apr 1	Aberdeen	1	Morton	3
	played at Dens Park			
Mar 25	Partick T	0	Rangers	2
	played at Ibrox			

Final

Apr 15	Morton	1	Rangers	0
	played at Hampden Park			

DIVISION 1

	ABERDEEN	AIRDRIE	ALBION R	AYR U	CELTIC	CLYDE	CLYDEBANK	DUMBARTON	DUNDEE	FALKIRK	HAMILTON A	HEARTS	HIBERNIAN	KILMARNOCK	MORTON	MOTHERWELL	PARTICK T	QUEEN'S PARK	RAITH R	RANGERS	ST MIRREN	T LANARK
ABERDEEN		Nov12 3-0	Mar22 2-0	Aug30 1-0	Sep10 1-1	Oct15 4-2	Dec31 2-0	Jan14 3-0	Sep03 1-2	Sep14 1-1	Feb04 0-0	Apr29 0-1	Oct01 1-2	Apr08 0-1	Feb18 2-2	Dec17 2-0	Nov26 2-1	Sep26 2-1	Jan03 1-2	Apr05 0-0	Dec10 0-1	Oct29 3-0
AIRDRIE	Jan07 4-0		Jan02 1-1	Mar11 2-1	Aug24 0-2	Aug20 1-1	Nov19 2-3	Feb04 3-1	Oct01 0-2	Oct29 3-0	Sep17 1-1	Feb18 3-0	Sep03 2-1	Nov26 0-2	Dec31 3-2	Apr08 2-0	Dec10 1-1	Apr29 0-2	Sep19 1-2	Oct15 4-1	Jan14 0-1	Mar25 0-1
ALBION R	Nov05 0-2	Sep10 2-0		Dec03 2-3	Apr15 0-2	Jan21 1-1	Aug27 2-0	Dec24 1-0	Mar04 1-0	Mar11 4-0	Nov12 1-0	Mar01 2-0	Feb22 2-1	Aug15 4-0	Jan03 1-2	Sep24 0-0	Oct08 0-1	Oct22 1-1	Sep05 2-0	Dec17 0-5	Apr22 0-0	Mar18 1-0
AYR U	Mar25 1-1	Sep24 1-2	Feb04 2-1		Dec10 0-0	Dec24 3-2	Sep14 1-0	Apr29 2-0	Apr29 0-2	Jan14 1-1	Oct22 2-0	Apr18 2-1	Feb18 2-2	Nov26 4-2	Oct08 0-0	Aug27 2-1	Nov05 2-1	Jan07 0-1	Mar18 2-3	Aug24 2-0		
CELTIC	Jan21 2-0	Dec03 1-0	Oct15 3-1	Oct29 1-0		Feb18 6-0	Dec17 4-0	Sep06 4-0	Apr08 0-0	Dec24 4-0	Mar01 3-1	Nov05 1-0	Aug20 2-0	Mar11 1-0	Sep26 2-0	Mar15 3-1	Apr17 0-0	Nov19 2-0	Aug15 1-0	Jan02 1-0	Oct04 2-0	Jan07 1-0
CLYDE	Feb21 2-0	Mar04 1-1	Nov26 1-1	Sep20 2-1	Jan03 1-1		Oct22 2-1	Apr01 5-0	Dec31 3-1	Nov12 1-2	Dec10 1-1	Aug23 3-2	Jan14 2-0	Apr27 3-0	Sep24 1-0	Sep13 1-0	Apr15 4-0	Oct08 0-2	Mar25 1-1	Apr29 0-0	Sep10 1-1	Feb04 0-0
CLYDEBANK	Sep21 1-1	Mar18 2-0	Feb18 0-3	Sep03 2-0	Jan14 0-2	Mar01 1-2		Apr26 0-1	Oct29 0-3	Aug24 0-0	Oct01 1-1	Nov26 0-2	Dec03 2-1	Jan14 2-1	Nov12 2-0	Apr15 1-3	Feb04 0-0	Aug20 0-3	Apr08 1-7	Apr01 3-2		0-4
DUMBARTON	Aug27 1-1	Oct08 1-0	Mar25 1-2	Feb13 3-1	Sep24 0-5	Nov19 4-1	Sep17 2-0		Dec17 2-0	Dec10 0-0	Aug31 3-0	Apr22 2-1	Mar04 5-3	Oct22 2-1	Apr19 3-2	Dec31 1-4	Oct01 2-3	Nov05 1-2	Apr08 2-3	Feb27 0-4	Sep10 2-3	
DUNDEE	Jan02 1-0	Aug17 1-1	Nov19 2-0	Sep17 1-0	Oct08 0-0	Dec03 2-1	Apr22 1-1	Feb18 2-0		Apr15 3-0	Sep24 2-0	Mar18 2-0	Jan03 0-0	Oct22 5-0	Jan14 1-1	Oct03 0-1	Sep24 1-0	Apr19 0-0	Nov05 3-1	Feb04 0-0	Oct22 2-2	Aug27 2-0
FALKIRK	Nov19 2-1	Sep07 2-0	Sep17 0-1	Sep17 1-1	Mar18 1-1	Apr08 0-0	Oct08 3-1	Aug20 1-0		Feb22 0-0	Feb04 1-0	Apr04 3-1	Jan14 2-1	Dec17 7-0	Mar04 3-0	Nov05 2-0	Mar29 1-1	Sep03 1-0	Dec03 2-3	Oct22 3-1	Dec31 1-2	
HAMILTON A	Oct22 2-2	Mar08 0-0	Jan07 5-3	Dec17 1-1	Dec31 1-2	Mar22 1-1	Mar04 1-1	Jan03 2-1	Mar25 1-2	Aug27 1-1		Aug17 1-2	Nov19 7-1	Oct08 1-1	Nov05 3-1	Sep10 2-3	Sep07 0-1	Apr08 1-2	Dec03 0-2	Jan21 2-3	Sep24 0-1	Apr22 1-1
HEARTS	Dec03 2-1	Dec17 4-0	Aug20 2-2	Mar04 6-2	Mar25 1-2	Sep17 0-1	Mar11 3-0	Oct29 2-0	Oct15 0-0	Oct01 4-1	Sep03 0-0		Jan02 2-0	Dec26 0-2	Apr08 1-0	Mar29 0-0	Apr01 0-0	Jan14 1-3	Nov19 0-1	Sep19 1-2	Jan03 3-2	Jan21 3-1
HIBERNIAN	Apr22 0-1	Apr15 0-0	Dec10 0-1	Dec31 1-1	Sep19 2-1	Nov05 2-1	Sep24 6-0	Nov26 1-1	Nov12 1-1	Sep24 1-0	Mar18 2-1	Sep10 2-1		Feb04 3-0	Oct08 2-1	Jan07 2-0	Oct22 2-0	Mar29 3-0	Dec24 2-1	Apr08 1-1	Mar01 0-1	
KILMARNOCK	Sep17 2-3	Jan03 2-1	Sep03 4-3	Oct01 1-3	Nov12 0-4	Mar18 3-2	Jan21 1-1	Aug20 5-3	Feb15 1-1	Feb25 3-1	Apr01 1-1	Dec31 0-1	Oct29 3-0		Aug23 1-1	Nov19 2-1	Mar04 2-0	Dec03 4-0	Dec17 2-1	Apr24 2-2	Sep21 1-1	Oct15 3-0
MORTON	Dec24 2-1	Mar01 3-0	Oct29 2-0	Jan21 2-1	Apr29 1-1	Jan02 0-3	Mar25 3-0	Mar18 1-0	Sep10 2-1	Jan07 2-0	Apr19 1-0	Apr27 1-1	Apr05 2-2	Dec10 5-1		Aug17 0-0	Feb22 4-0	Sep17 1-0	Oct15 2-1	Nov19 0-1	Nov12 1-1	Oct01 1-1
MOTHERWELL	Apr12 3-0	Dec24 1-2	Apr29 1-1	Apr15 2-1	Nov01 1-1	Oct01 2-0	Feb18 5-2	Oct15 5-0	Sep21 2-1	Jan07 0-1	Aug02 2-1	Nov12 2-1	Apr27 4-1	Mar03 3-0	Sep03 2-0		Jan14 2-0	Mar18 5-1	Aug20 2-1	Feb04 2-0	Oct29 1-1	Feb18 1-3
PARTICK T	Aug30 2-0	Apr04 1-1	Apr08 0-1	Apr22 1-1	Feb04 4-1	Dec17 1-0	Aug16 2-1	Sep03 0-0	Jan07 4-1	Oct15 0-0	Oct29 2-0	Sep24 3-2	Mar15 2-0	Nov05 0-2	Aug20 0-0	Dec03 0-0		Dec24 1-0	Oct01 0-1	Feb18 0-3	Nov19 1-3	Jan03 2-2
QUEEN'S PARK	Mar01 3-1	Aug27 1-1	Sep20 0-4	Aug17 1-6	Apr01 1-3	Apr22 0-1	Jan07 2-2	Feb25 1-0	Jan21 0-4	Nov26 2-1	Oct15 1-5	Dec10 1-1	Dec17 1-3	Mar25 1-1	Feb04 1-3	Dec31 2-1	Sep10 0-1		Aug31 1-3	Oct29 2-4	Feb18 1-0	Nov12 0-0
RAITH R	Oct08 2-1	Oct22 1-0	Dec31 3-0	Jan07 5-0	Oct29 1-1	Sep10 5-0	Feb11 1-1	Oct22 0-0	Apr29 2-1	Jan07 3-1	Jan24 4-0	Apr22 1-1	Apr04 4-1	Mar18 2-0	Feb22 1-1		Apr03 0-3	Dec24 2-3	Nov26 2-2			
RANGERS	Sep24 1-0	Apr22 3-0	Aug23 1-0	Apr01 3-0	Oct22 1-0	Sep26 3-0	Feb21 2-1	Nov12 5-0	Dec26 3-0	Feb27 2-1	Nov26 2-1	Oct08 2-0	Mar28 0-0	Sep10 1-0	Mar04 2-2	Apr27 2-1	Jan03 2-0	Apr17 3-3	Jan14 4-1		Dec31 2-1	Dec10 1-1
ST MIRREN	Mar04 2-1	Apr01 1-0	Oct01 2-1	Oct15 1-1	Feb14 0-2	Jan07 6-3	Nov05 4-1	Dec03 4-2	Nov26 2-0	Jan21 0-0	Aug23 5-0	Apr15 2-1	Sep13 1-1	Jan02 1-1	Mar21 1-1	Apr29 2-1	Aug20 1-2	Sep17 5-0	Sep03 1-1	Feb22 1-2		Dec17 1-2
T LANARK	Apr19 2-0	Nov05 2-2	Jan14 2-2	Nov19 1-0	Mar04 0-0	Apr17 1-1	Sep24 4-1	Oct04 1-1	Mar11 1-0	Feb16 2-2	Aug20 2-2	Dec24 2-2	Apr29 3-1	Dec26 3-1	Oct22 0-1	Apr05 4-3	Jan03 1-1	Jan03 0-0	Aug16 1-0	Oct08 0-1		

DIVISION 1 FINAL TABLE

	P	W	D	L	F	A	Pts
Celtic	42	27	13	2	83	20	67
Rangers	42	28	10	4	83	26	66
Raith R	42	19	13	10	66	43	51
Dundee	42	19	11	12	57	40	49
Falkirk	42	16	17	9	48	38	49
Partick T	42	20	8	14	57	53	48
Hibernian	42	16	14	12	55	44	46
St Mirren	42	17	12	13	71	61	46
T Lanark	42	17	12	13	58	52	46
Clyde	42	16	12	14	60	51	44
Albion R	42	17	10	15	55	51	44
Morton	42	16	10	16	58	57	42
Motherwell	42	16	7	19	63	58	39
Ayr U	42	13	12	17	55	63	38
Aberdeen	42	13	9	20	48	54	35
Airdrie	42	12	11	19	46	56	35
Kilmarnock	42	13	9	20	56	83	35
Hamilton A	42	9	16	17	51	62	34
Hearts	42	11	10	21	50	60	32
Dumbarton*	42	10	10	22	46	81	30
Queen's Park*	42	9	10	23	38	82	28
Clydebank*	42	6	8	28	34	103	20

* Three clubs relegated to Second Division

DIVISION 2 FINAL TABLE

	P	W	D	L	F	A	Pts
Alloa*	38	26	8	4	81	32	60
Cowdenbeath	38	19	9	10	57	30	47
Armadale	38	20	5	13	64	48	45
Vale of Leven	38	17	10	11	54	43	44
Bathgate	38	16	11	11	56	41	43
Bo'ness	38	16	7	15	56	49	39
Broxburn U	38	14	11	13	43	43	39
Dunfermline A	38	14	10	14	56	42	38
St Bernard's	38	15	8	15	50	49	38
East Fife	38	15	8	15	54	54	38
Stenhousemuir	38	14	10	14	50	51	38
Johnstone	38	14	10	14	46	59	38
St Johnstone	38	12	11	15	41	52	35
Forfar A	38	11	12	15	43	51	34
E Stirling	38	12	10	16	43	60	34
Arbroath	38	11	11	16	45	56	33
King's Park	38	10	12	16	47	65	32
Lochgelly U	38	11	9	18	46	54	31
Dundee Hibs	38	10	8	20	47	65	28
Clackmannan	38	9	8	21	40	75	26

* Only Alloa promoted

DIVISION 2 (results grid)

	ALLOA	ARBROATH	ARMADALE	BATHGATE	BO'NESS	BROXBURN U	CLACKMANNAN	COWDENBEATH	DUNDEE H	DUNFERMLINE A	EAST FIFE	E STIRLING	FORFAR A	JOHNSTONE	KING'S PARK	LOCHGELLY U	ST BERNARD'S	ST JOHNSTONE	STENHOUSEMUIR	VALE OF LEVEN
ALLOA		Nov26 2-1	Oct29 2-2	Sep03 3-2	Feb21 5-1	Oct15 3-0	Jan02 2-0	Apr01 2-0	Mar18 3-0	Feb18 2-0	Nov12 1-1	Dec17 3-1	Oct01 3-1	Sep17 1-1	Apr15 1-1	Mar04 2-0	Apr29 2-1	Jan07 1-0	Aug20 1-0	Jan21 4-0
ARBROATH	Dec24 0-1		Jan14 3-1	Mar04 2-0	Sep03 1-0	Sep24 0-0	Feb18 2-0	Dec03 0-1	Jan03 2-0	Feb04 0-0	Apr22 2-1	Oct01 2-1	Mar18 2-2	Aug20 3-1	Oct15 2-5	Jan07 1-0	Apr08 2-2	Nov05 3-1	Oct01 0-1	Jan02 1-1
ARMADALE	Dec03 2-0	Mar25 1-0		Sep21 1-0	Jan21 2-1	Mar04 1-0	Apr04 2-2	Oct22 0-1	Sep17 2-0	Oct01 1-2	Nov19 0-1	Feb18 1-0	Sep03 2-2	Oct15 3-1	Jan07 3-0	Apr15 4-0	Aug20 2-2	Dec24 3-1	Nov05 0-1	Feb22 1-1
BATHGATE	Jan03 0-0	Sep10 2-0	Aug27 0-0		Nov12 2-0	Dec17 1-1	Mar18 1-0	Apr22 0-0	Sep24 4-2	Nov26 3-1	Mar11 2-3	Jan14 2-2	Feb04 2-1	Apr08 4-0	Mar01 3-1	Dec10 1-2	Oct29 2-2	Apr29 0-0	Dec31 4-0	Oct08 0-0
BO'NESS	Sep24 1-1	Apr29 3-1	Oct08 1-0	Feb18 2-0		Aug27 3-1	Apr15 2-0	Nov19 0-2	Jan14 1-0	Sep17 2-1	Mar04 5-0	Feb04 4-2	Nov05 1-1	Mar25 2-0	Nov26 3-4	Dec17 0-1	Oct22 5-1	Jan03 2-1	Apr01 2-1	
BROXBURN U	Mar11 0-1	Jan21 0-0	Dec10 2-1	Nov05 1-0	Jan02 0-3		Jan07 1-0	Oct08 1-0	Oct22 2-1	Aug20 3-2	Mar01 0-0	Dec03 4-1	Mar18 2-1	Dec24 2-0	Apr29 0-1	Oct01 3-4	Sep17 0-1	Feb25 5-1	Sep03 2-1	Nov19 0-2
CLACKMANNAN	Aug27 1-2	Oct08 2-2	Sep24 0-1	Nov19 1-3	Dec03 2-1	Apr08 2-2		Dec24 0-1	Apr22 1-1	Nov05 2-0	Sep10 0-4	Dec31 3-1	Feb25 2-0	Dec10 2-1	Jan14 1-0	Mar25 1-3	Mar11 2-3	Apr05 0-0	Oct22 0-0	
COWDENBEATH	Nov05 1-2	Apr15 2-2	Feb04 2-0	Sep17 0-0	Mar22 0-1	Feb18 4-0	Nov26 2-0		Dec31 1-0	Mar04 1-0	Apr17 0-0	Oct15 0-1	Aug20 4-3	Jan03 3-0	Apr08 2-0	Oct01 4-1	Dec10 2-0	Jan20 1-0	Oct08 4-1	Dec10 1-0
DUNDEE H	Dec10 0-4	Nov12 1-2	Apr29 2-0	Feb15 2-2	Aug20 1-0	Mar25 2-2	Oct01 1-0	Jan07 2-6		Apr08 1-0	Apr10 2-0	Sep03 0-1	Oct15 0-1	Feb11 0-1	Oct29 0-1	Nov26 0-4	Mar04 2-0	Sep10 3-1	Dec17 1-1	Dec31 0-2
DUNFERMLINE A	Sep10 0-1	Apr17 5-1	Mar11 4-0	Mar25 1-1	Dec24 4-1	Apr01 0-0	Jan21 2-0	Jan02 2-2	Oct08 4-1		Sep24 2-0	Mar04 4-0	Apr15 1-0	Nov12 2-0	Aug27 3-1	Dec03 3-1	Feb22 1-2	Nov19 0-0	Apr29 1-1	Jan07 1-1
EAST FIFE	Jan14 0-2	Jan03 0-2	Jan20 1-2	Dec31 2-1	Jan21 2-1	Feb25 2-0	Nov05 2-2	Dec17 0-0	Oct02 0-2			Sep17 4-2	Mar04 0-1	Apr15 2-2	Oct15 5-4	Jan02 1-0	Oct29 4-2	Mar25 2-2	Apr08 4-0	Apr08 1-2
E STIRLING	Mar25 1-2	Mar01 0-2	Nov26 2-2	Dec24 2-1	Sep10 1-1	Nov12 0-2	Oct15 1-0	Jan21 0-1	Apr01 3-2	Oct29 2-1	Jan07 2-2		Apr19 1-0	Feb15 1-2	Jan02 2-0	Apr08 1-0	Mar11 1-0	Sep24 1-0	Dec10 0-0	Aug27 0-3
FORFAR A	Apr22 2-1	Feb11 1-1	Apr08 1-2	Jan07 2-1	Mar11 1-0	Sep10 1-1	Sep17 2-2	Aug27 1-1	Feb25 0-0	Dec10 2-3	Oct08 0-2	Oct22 0-0		Nov26 1-1	Nov12 2-0	Dec17 1-0	Jan02 3-2	Apr13 1-0	Mar25 3-1	Jan03 0-0
JOHNSTONE	Dec31 2-5	Apr17 4-0	Apr22 1-0	Oct22 0-3	Feb04 1-1	Mar04 1-1	Aug27 0-0	Mar18 1-0	Nov19 3-1	Jan14 1-3	Sep10 4-1	Nov05 2-0	Dec03 1-0		Oct08 1-1	Dec24 2-1	Sep17 1-0	Jan14 0-0	Oct08 1-1	Feb18 2-1
KING'S PARK	Nov19 1-8	Dec17 3-2	Jan04 1-0	Oct01 0-3	Apr08 1-1	Jan03 2-1	Sep03 0-2	Feb22 0-2	Dec03 3-1	Apr22 2-3	Oct22 1-2	Aug20 2-3	Apr01 1-1	Mar11 3-0		Sep17 1-0	Jan14 0-0	Oct08 0-0	Mar04 0-0	Nov05 2-1
LOCHGELLY U	Oct22 1-3	Mar11 0-0	Sep10 1-0	Apr01 0-1	Jan07 0-3	Apr22 1-1	Feb10 4-0	Mar25 2-1	Dec24 1-1	Feb25 1-1	Jan02 3-1	Oct08 4-1	Nov19 4-1	Apr29 0-1	Jan21 0-0		Nov12 0-0	Aug27 2-1	Feb18 4-0	Sep24 2-0
ST BERNARD'S	Oct08 2-0	Aug27 1-0	Feb11 1-0	Apr15 1-2	Feb18 1-2	Nov26 4-0	Sep10 0-0	Nov19 0-2	Dec31 1-0	Jan21 2-0	Nov05 0-1	Sep24 1-5	Jan07 6-0	Dec24 1-1	Feb04 1-1	Dec10 1-0		Oct22 3-1	Dec10 1-0	Apr22 2-1
ST JOHNSTONE	Mar01 4-3	Dec31 1-0	Dec17 3-0	Oct15 1-1	Apr22 1-2	Oct29 1-3	Aug20 1-1	Nov12 1-3	Jan02 1-0	Jan14 3-1	Apr01 2-0	Mar18 2-0	Dec03 2-1	Sep03 1-0	Mar08 2-2	Jan03 1-1	Oct01 1-3		Sep17 1-0	Mar04 0-0
STENHOUSEMUIR	Feb04 1-1	Jan07 2-1	Feb25 2-1	Apr19 2-1	Oct15 1-0	Nov26 1-0	Nov12 1-2	Apr12 2-0	Mar11 3-0	Mar22 5-2	Aug27 2-0	Apr15 1-1	Jan02 4-0	Jan22 2-2	Sep24 1-1	Oct29 1-0	Apr01 4-1	Feb11 3-1		Sep10 0-1
VALE OF LEVEN	Mar07 1-1	Sep17 2-1	Nov12 0-2	Dec03 4-1	Oct01 3-0	Apr15 3-0	Dec17 4-2	Mar11 0-0	Feb04 2-2	Oct15 1-1	Dec24 1-0	Apr29 3-1	Aug20 3-0	Oct29 3-2	Feb25 3-2	Mar18 2-0	Sep03 2-1	Nov26 2-1	Jan14 1-0	

Season 1922-23

SFA Cup

1st Round

Jan 13	Aberdeen	1	Forfar A	0
Jan 13	Airdrie	2	Mid-Annandale	1
Jan 13	Alloa	0	Queen's Park	1
Jan 13	Arbroath A	0	Ayr U	3
Jan 13	Bo'ness	6	Clacknacuddin	0
Jan 13	Clyde	0	Rangers	4
Jan 13	Clydebank	0	Royal Albert	0
Jan 10	Cowdenbeath	10	St Andrew's Univ	1
Jan 13	Dumbarton	0	Dunfermline A	1
Jan 13	Dundee	6	Vale of Atholl	0
Jan 13	Dundee H	3	Beith	1
Jan 13	East Fife	7	Berwick R	1
Jan 13	E Stirling	1	Bathgate	1
Jan 13	Elgin C	0	St Mirren	3
Jan 13	Falkirk	10	Breadalbane	0
Jan 13	Galston	1	Stenhousemuir	0
Jan 13	Hamilton A	1	Albion R	0
Jan 13	Hearts	6	Thornhill	0
Jan 13	Hibernian	4	Clackmannan	0
Jan 13	Hurlford	2	Fraserburgh	1
Jan 13	Johnstone	2	Armadale	0
Jan 13	Kilmarnock	5	Broxburn U	0
Jan 13	Lochgelly U	2	Celtic	3
Jan 13	Moor Park	0	Peebles R	4
Jan 13	Nithsdale W	4	Arbroath	0
Jan 13	Partick T	1	T Lanark	1
Jan 13	Peterhead	3	Vale of Leithen	0
Jan 13	Queen of South	0	King's Park	1
Jan 13	Raith R	1	Morton	0
Jan 13	St Bernard's	8	Dalbeattie Star	1
Jan 13	St Johnstone	1	Motherwell	2
Jan 13	Vale of Leven	6	Inverness T	1

Replays

Jan 16	T Lanark	3	Partick T	2
Jan 17	Bathgate	3	E Stirling	2
Jan 17	Royal Albert	0	Clydebank	0
Jan 23	Clydebank	2	Royal Albert	0

played at Firhill Park

2nd Round

Jan 27	Airdrie	1	Aberdeen	1
Jan 27	Ayr U	2	Rangers	0
Jan 27	Bo'ness	3	Hearts	2
Jan 27	Celtic	4	Hurlford	0
Jan 27	Dundee	0	St Bernard's	0
Jan 27	Dunfermline A	1	Clydebank	0
Jan 27	Hamilton A	1	King's Park	0
Jan 27	Hibernian	0	Peebles R	0
Jan 27	Johnstone	0	Falkirk	1
Jan 27	Kilmarnock	1	East Fife	1
Jan 27	Motherwell	2	St Mirren	1
Jan 24	Nithsdale W	1	Dundee H	0
Jan 27	Peterhead	1	Galston	0
Jan 27	Queen's Park	1	Bathgate	1
Jan 27	Raith R	2	Cowdenbeath	0
Jan 27	Vale of Leven	2	T Lanark	2

Replays

Jan 30	Hibernian	3	Peebles R	0
Jan 30	T Lanark	2	Vale of Leven	1
Jan 31	Aberdeen	2	Airdrie	0
Jan 31	Bathgate	0	Queen's Park	2
Jan 31	East Fife	1	Kilmarnock	0
Jan 31	St Bernard's	2	Dundee	3

3rd Round

Feb 10	Aberdeen	13	Peterhead	0
Feb 10	Bo'ness	2	Nithsdale W	0
Feb 10	Celtic	2	East Fife	1
Feb 10	Dundee	0	Hamilton A	0
Feb 10	Dunfermline A	0	Raith R	3
Feb 10	Hibernian	2	Queen's Park	0
Feb 10	Motherwell	3	Falkirk	0
Feb 10	T Lanark	2	Ayr U	0

Replay

Feb 14	Hamilton A	0	Dundee	1

4th Round

Feb 24	Celtic	1	Raith R	0
Feb 24	Hibernian	2	Aberdeen	0
Feb 24	Motherwell	4	Bo'ness	2
Feb 24	T Lanark	1	Dundee	1

Replay

Feb 28	Dundee	0	T Lanark	0
Mar 6	Dundee	0	T Lanark	1

played at Ibrox

Season 1922-23 cont.

Semi-finals

Mar 10 Celtic . . . . 2 Motherwell 0
         played at Ibrox

Mar 10 Hibernian . . . . . . .1 T Lanark 0
         played at Tynecastle

Final

Mar 31 Celtic . . . . 1 Hibernian 0
         played at Hampden Park

DIVISION 1

	ABERDEEN	AIRDRIE	ALBION R	ALLOA	AYR U	CELTIC	CLYDE	DUNDEE	FALKIRK	HAMILTON A	HEARTS	HIBERNIAN	KILMARNOCK	MORTON	MOTHERWELL	PARTICK T	RAITH R	RANGERS	ST MIRREN	T LANARK
ABERDEEN		Dec23 0-1	Apr14 1-2	Dec02 1-0	Feb03 4-1	Sep25 3-1	Dec09 1-0	Jan01 0-0	Feb28 1-1	Oct28 1-0	Nov11 0-1	Sep09 2-0	Nov18 5-0	Jan20 1-1	Apr28 2-1	Feb17 0-0	Aug26 1-0	Oct14 0-0	Sep30 4-2	Mar24 1-1
AIRDRIE	Oct07 2-0		Aug26 2-0	Sep23 0-2	Dec30 2-1	Nov18 1-0	Oct28 1-1	Feb17 5-1	Apr21 3-1	Jan02 2-2	Nov25 2-1	Mar24 4-1	Mar03 1-0	Sep09 4-1	Mar17 3-3	Feb07 4-0	Aug30 1-0	Feb10 2-1	Oct21 1-0	Dec13 1-0
ALBION R	Sep02 0-2	Jan01 1-2		Nov04 2-1	Feb24 2-1	Dec02 2-3	Jan06 3-0	Sep30 0-0	Sep16 1-2	Aug23 2-0	Dec23 1-2	Mar14 1-1	Aug19 1-1	Feb03 3-0	Nov11 1-1	Apr28 0-1	Dec16 1-2	Mar31 2-1	Jan20 2-0	Oct14 0-1
ALLOA	Oct02 0-2	Mar31 0-3	Jan27 2-0		Nov25 4-1	Aug19 2-3	Nov04 1-0	Oct14 1-3	Jan02 1-2	Nov30 0-2	Sep30 0-3	Sep21 2-1	Dec27 3-1	Apr14 1-1	Sep16 0-3	Feb10 2-0	Feb27 1-1	Dec23 2-1	Feb24 1-1	Mar13 1-1
AYR U	Mar10 2-1	Sep02 1-2	Nov18 1-0	Apr07 1-1		Apr25 0-1	Dec23 4-1	Mar03 1-0	Oct14 0-0	Mar24 4-1	Sep16 1-1	Dec02 1-1	Jan02 2-1	Oct28 2-0	Jan31 2-1	Mar31 2-0	Feb14 2-0	Dec16 1-1	Aug19 1-1	Sep30 1-2
CELTIC	Jan06 1-2	Apr28 1-1	Feb14 1-1	Mar03 1-0	Nov11 1-4			Jan02 0-0	Mar17 2-1	Dec09 1-1	Apr26 2-1	Apr07 2-1	Jan31 0-0	Dec23 1-2	Mar24 3-1	Oct14 1-0	Oct07 4-3	Sep09 3-0	Oct28 1-3	Feb27 1-0	Nov25 3-0
CLYDE	Apr21 0-1	Feb03 2-0	Sep23 0-3	Jan01 1-0	Oct21 1-0	Nov04 0-1		Aug29 4-3	Sep22 0-1	Dec16 4-1	Aug19 1-0	Nov18 1-0	Mar10 2-0	Feb17 0-0	Mar31 3-0	Dec30 2-0	Jan20 0-0	Sep25 2-1	Dec02 2-1	Apr20 1-0
DUNDEE	Aug19 1-1	Nov04 1-0	Dec30 3-0	Dec16 2-1	Oct07 1-0	Sep23 0-1	Apr07 1-0		Apr09 3-0	Oct21 0-0	Jan20 1-0	Jan02 2-0	Sep02 0-1	Mar10 3-1	Apr14 0-0	Sep16 1-0	Dec02 1-2	Mar24 0-1	Nov18 2-0	Oct02 2-0
FALKIRK	Sep23 2-2	Dec16 1-1	Apr07 1-0	Aug26 0-0	Jan06 1-0	Feb17 0-0	Mar24 1-1	Dec23 1-0		Jan20 3-1	Mar03 1-0	Nov04 5-0	Apr28 0-0	Oct07 3-0	Dec02 1-0	Oct21 1-1	Jan20 1-1	Sep09 2-0	Feb03 1-1	Apr14 4-0
HAMILTON A	Apr07 0-0	Aug19 0-1	Jan31 1-1	Apr28 2-0	Nov04 0-1	Mar14 1-1	Apr13 1-2	Mar31 0-0	Sep30		Sep02 3-1	Feb28 2-1	Sep16 3-3	Dec02 1-1	Jan01 1-1	Jan06 3-0	Mar17 6-1	Nov11 1-1	Oct14 0-3	Dec23 2-1
HEARTS	Mar31 0-0	Feb24 1-1	Sep09 1-0	Mar24 1-1	Apr21 0-3	Dec16 2-1	Feb07 1-1	Aug26 1-0	Oct28 1-2	Dec30		Sep23 2-2	Feb10 5-0	Nov18 3-1	Mar14 1-2	Dec02 3-0	Oct07 0-0	Sep18 0-0	Nov04 2-2	Jan06 2-0
HIBERNIAN	Mar03 2-0	Oct14 3-0	Nov25 0-2	Feb17 2-1	Jan20 3-0	Sep18 1-0	Mar17 1-2	Nov11 3-3	Aug16 1-0	Dec09 2-0	Jan01 2-1		Sep30 1-1	Dec23 0-1	Sep02 2-1	Aug19 2-0	Oct21 1-0	Apr07 0-3	Sep16 0-3	Feb03 2-0
KILMARNOCK	Aug16 1-0	Nov11 0-1	Mar17 7-0	Feb17 2-2	Aug26 0-0	Sep08 4-3	Sep09 4-1	Jan06 2-0	Nov25 2-0	Feb17 3-0	Oct21 1-2	Dec30 1-0		Mar31 3-2	Nov04 0-6	Dec16 1-3	Sep23 1-2	Jan20 1-2	Jan01 1-2	Mar21 2-0
MORTON	Sep16 2-1	Jan06 3-1	Dec09 0-0	Dec30 0-0	Jan01 0-1	Oct21 1-0	Oct11 2-3	Nov25 1-1	Jan31 3-1	Mar03 0-1	Mar17 1-0	Feb14 1-0	Oct14 1-4		Aug19 2-0	Apr07 1-2	Nov04 4-0	Feb24 2-1	Apr21 0-1	Sep02 2-3
MOTHERWELL	Oct21 3-1	Jan20 0-0	Mar03 1-0	Feb03 2-0	Sep23 4-0	Apr21 0-0	Nov25 5-3	Sep09 3-4	Dec30 3-2	Oct07 0-0	Dec16 4-1	Apr07 0-2	Jan02 4-1	Nov18 4-3		Nov18 1-1	Mar24 2-0	Aug26 0-4	Feb17 1-1	Oct28 1-1
PARTICK T	Nov25 2-1	Sep30 0-0	Oct28 2-0	Jan20 3-0	Sep09 2-0	Apr02 0-2	Aug26 0-0	Feb03 1-0	Mar10 1-0	Sep23 5-3	Oct14 2-2	Apr21 1-0	Mar24 1-1	Nov11 1-0	Feb28		Dec23 3-0	Jan02 0-1	Dec12 1-1	Jan01 4-1
RAITH R	Jan02 1-1	Sep16 0-0	Feb17 1-1	Jan06 1-0	Dec09 0-3	Dec30 0-0	Oct14 1-0	Oct28 0-3	Jan01 0-1	Nov25 2-1	Feb03 1-1	Apr02 1-0	Feb07 1-1	Apr28 1-1	Sep30 1-0	Apr14		Mar10 2-0	Sep02 2-1	Nov11 1-0
RANGERS	Dec30 1-1	Dec02 4-1	Oct21 2-2	Aug15 2-2	Mar14 2-1	Jan01 2-0	Mar03 2-1	Dec09 4-1	Mar26 2-0	Feb03 3-0	Apr28 3-0	Oct07 0-7	Apr21 0-0	Oct21 2-1	Jan06 4-1	Nov04 1-0	Nov18		Apr02 1-1	Aug19 5-1
ST MIRREN	Dec16 0-1	Mar10 4-0	Oct07 1-1	Sep09 0-1	Apr28 0-1	Feb13 1-0	Feb06 2-0	Nov11 4-0	Aug15 2-2	Jan02 2-1	Jan06 2-1	Oct28 2-1	Apr26 1-1	Mar03 3-3	Apr07 1-0	Nov25 1-1	Sep23 3-1			Sep23 3-1
T LANARK	Nov04 2-1	Apr07 1-3	Jan02 2-2	Oct21 0-1	Mar17 3-0	Jan20 1-0	Oct07 2-0	Dec25 1-1	Nov18 1-1	Sep09 3-1	Feb17 0-1	Apr26 1-2	Dec02 1-1	Dec16 1-2	Feb13 1-1	Sep25 2-1	Mar03 2-2	Nov06 1-3	Dec30	

DIVISION 2

	ARBROATH	ARMADALE	BATHGATE	BO'NESS	BROXBURN U	CLYDEBANK	COWDENBEATH	DUMBARTON	DUNFERMLINE A	EAST FIFE	E STIRLING	FORFAR A	JOHNSTONE	KING'S PARK	LOCHGELLY U	QUEEN'S PARK	ST BERNARD'S	ST JOHNSTONE	STENHOUSEMUIR	VALE OF LEVEN
ARBROATH		Jan06 1-2	Aug26 0-0	Apr07 0-0	Sep16 0-3	Feb24 0-0	Oct07 1-3	Jan27 1-1	Feb03 3-1	Feb07 4-1	Dec16 1-2	Mar17 2-0	Nov25 0-1	Dec23 3-2	Oct21 1-1	Sep25 1-1	Nov18 3-2	Oct28 1-1	Apr28 1-1	Jan01 1-0
ARMADALE	Sep23 3-0		Sep09 2-2	Apr21 3-0	Feb10 2-1	Oct21 2-0	Mar31 1-1	Mar03 1-0	Nov18 1-0	Jan02 0-0	Jan02 2-2	Apr07 5-0	Oct07 7-2	Dec23 2-3	Dec13 5-1	Jan20 2-0	Nov04 3-0	Mar10 2-0	Feb17 3-2	Apr18 2-2
BATHGATE	Mar24 2-1	Jan01 4-2		Nov25 3-3	Aug19 2-2	Jan06 1-0	Feb24 0-1	Feb03 4-1	Sep20 1-1	Sep02 3-2	Nov04 5-3	Apr07 3-0	Mar17 5-0	Dec02 5-0	Dec30 2-0	Apr28 0-1	Oct14 4-0	Dec16 0-1	Mar10 4-1	
BO'NESS	Nov11 1-0	Aug19 0-0	Feb14 2-1		Jan01 2-0	Sep16 1-1	Jan06 2-0	Oct21 0-2	Dec02 0-0	Mar24 2-1	Apr28 0-0	Dec30 1-4	Sep02 2-2	Feb28 2-1	Oct14 0-0	Mar31 1-1	Apr09 1-0	Mar17 0-1	Oct07 1-1	Dec16 2-1
BROXBURN U	Jan20 1-1	Oct21 2-0	Apr21 2-0	Sep23 1-2		Mar10 1-0	Aug26 0-0	Feb17 1-1	Nov04 0-2	Nov25 1-0	Mar03 3-2	Nov18 2-0	Mar24 3-0	Jan29 4-1	Apr14 0-0	Oct06 1-0	Sep09 0-0	Dec09 0-2	Feb03 1-1	Dec23 1-1
CLYDEBANK	Nov04 3-1	Dec30 1-0	Jan20 5-0	Mar20 4-0	Sep23 3-0		Mar17 2-0	Sep09 1-1	Feb28 3-0	Apr28 3-2	Feb03 5-0	Jan02 1-0	Oct21 3-1	Aug26 1-2	Nov25 1-1	Sep23 3-1	Apr14 2-0	Feb03 1-1		Dec02 2-0
COWDENBEATH	Apr14 7-4	Sep16 0-1	Oct21 3-1	Nov18 1-1	Dec30 1-1	Dec09 1-1		Jan20 1-0	Sep02 0-1	Oct14 1-2	Feb17 1-2	Jan02 3-2	Apr28 3-3	Feb03 1-2	Mar03 0-0	Dec02 2-4	Mar24 1-1	Sep30 4-0	Nov04 1-1	Aug19 0-0
DUMBARTON	Aug19 3-0	Sep02 3-0	Nov18 2-0	Dec23 3-0	Sep30 1-1	Jan01 1-1	Dec16 1-0		Sep25 2-0	Mar10 1-2	Jan06 3-0	Jan06 1-1	Feb24 2-0	Jan29 6-1	Oct14 2-0	Apr28 5-0	Apr09 0-2	Oct28 2-1	Mar24 1-0	Sep16 3-0
DUNFERMLINE A	Apr21 1-2	Feb24 2-2	Apr09 0-2	Apr14 2-1	Dec16 1-1	Feb24 2-2	Jan01 2-0	Aug26 3-0		Nov11 0-1	Sep09 5-1	Mar10 0-1	Oct07 1-1	Nov25 2-0	Sep23 2-1	Mar17 4-1	Jan06 3-1	Apr07 4-1	Apr07 3-1	Oct28 3-0
EAST FIFE	Dec02 2-1	Dec16 3-1	Feb17 4-1	Nov04 0-0	Mar31 0-2	Nov18 2-1	Mar15 1-0	Oct07 2-1	Mar03		Sep23 2-0	Jan20 4-1	Apr14 3-2	Apr21 1-2	Jan01 0-2	Oct21 0-0	Apr26 1-3	Dec23 4-0	Sep09 2-2	Jan06 2-0
E STIRLING	Oct14 3-0	Apr14 5-2	Jan02 1-2	Oct28 1-0	Sep02 0-1	Sep30 1-2	Nov11 3-1	Dec20 2-0	Mar24 1-1	Dec30 0-3		Mar31 2-0	Feb24 3-2	Jan01 2-2	Nov18 1-1	Feb07 3-3	Dec16 2-0	Sep16 1-1	Mar10 1-1	Apr21 1-0
FORFAR A	Sep30 2-1	Oct14 1-1	Mar31 3-1	Sep09 1-1	Jan27 2-0	Sep02 0-1	Oct28 0-1	Dec09 0-3	Aug19 2-0	2-0	Dec02		Mar15 5-2	Apr24 4-2	Jan06 3-1	Sep23 2-2	Apr21 2-2	Jan01 4-3	Apr14 3-3	
JOHNSTONE	Feb17 2-2	Mar17 2-1	Dec09 1-1	Feb03 1-0	Jan06 0-2	Oct14 1-0	Sep23 4-1	Nov04 0-0	Sep30 0-0	Apr21 0-0	Oct21 1-1	Dec02		Mar31 1-1	Dec30 0-1	Sep09 1-0	Apr21 1-0	Aug19 1-0	Jan01 4-2	Nov11 0-3
KING'S PARK	Mar10 2-0	Apr28 3-1	Oct07 2-1	Jan20 0-0	Dec02 3-2	Feb10 2-3	Apr07 3-2	Dec30 2-2	Oct28 2-1	Aug26 2-0	Nov11 1-0		Feb17 0-1		Dec16 0-1	Sep23 1-0	Jan31 1-3	Mar03 3-1	Mar24 0-0	
LOCHGELLY U	Feb10 1-0	Nov11 0-2	Oct23 1-1	Mar10 1-1	Oct28 0-5	Nov22 3-2	Nov25 3-2	Feb10 2-0	Sep16 3-0	Jan27 2-1	Aug26 0-1	Sep02		Apr21 2-4		Feb24 1-0	Apr07 0-1	Jan06 3-1	Sep30 2-1	
QUEEN'S PARK	Mar03 6-1	Feb03 2-1	Oct28 0-2	Sep30 5-0	Feb24 2-0	Mar24 1-1	Apr02 4-1	Nov11 2-1	Aug19 4-1	Apr07 2-1	Nov25 2-1	Apr28 4-0	Mar10 1-0	Sep20 0-3	Dec09		Jan06 1-1	Sep12 0-0	Dec23 3-1	Oct14 1-2
ST BERNARD'S	Jan02 2-2	Sep30 0-0	Nov11 1-1	Dec09 0-0	Apr07 0-2	Aug19 1-2	Dec23 0-1	Mar17 2-1	Oct14 2-2	Feb03 0-1	Jan20 2-1	Oct21 3-0	Sep16 1-0	Apr14 3-0	Nov04 1-0	Feb17		Mar03 4-4	Nov25 1-0	Sep02 3-1
ST JOHNSTONE	Dec30 6-3	Dec02 2-1	Mar31 2-1	Aug26 0-0	Sep23 1-1	Apr14 1-4	Mar10 0-1	Oct21 3-0	Feb24 1-0	Feb07 0-2	Nov04 2-2	Nov25 6-1	Apr28 3-1	Sep09 0-0	Jan02 1-1	Oct07 1-1			Jan20 3-0	Feb10 4-2
STENHOUSEMUIR	Dec13 3-0	Jan27 1-1	Apr14 2-1	Jan02 0-1	Oct14 5-0	Mar31 1-1	Jan31 4-2	Apr21 4-1	Sep16 1-1	Mar17 2-1	Feb10 1-1	Nov11 0-1	Oct28 2-1	Sep30 0-2	Aug19 0-1	Nov18 0-0	Dec30 2-2	Sep02		Feb24 2-1
VALE OF LEVEN	Sep09 0-0	Nov25 2-2	Sep23 4-1	Feb17 3-1	Mar17 3-0	Aug23 2-1	Apr07 1-2	Dec30 0-3	Jan02 5-4	Dec09 0-1	Aug26 4-3	Oct07 2-0	Mar03 2-0	Nov04 5-1	Feb03 0-x	Jan20 1-2	Mar31 2-0	Nov11 0-1	Oct21 1-0	

SFA Cup

1st Round
Jan 26	Aberdeen 2	Dumbarton 1	
Jan 26	Airdrie 2	Morton 1	
Jan 26	Alloa 2	Buckie T 2	
Jan 26	Ayr U 3	Albion R 1	
Jan 26	Bathgate 1	Bo'ness 1	
Jan 26	Clydebank 8	Blairgowrie 2	
Jan 26	Coldstream 0	Armadale 1	
Jan 26	Dundee 2	Dykehead 0	
Jan 26	Dunfermline A 0	Arbroath 1	
Jan 26	Falkirk 3	Brechin C 0	
Jan 19	Galston 6	Gala Fairydean 2	
Jan 26	Hibernian 1	Dundee U 0	
Jan 26	Inverness Cal 0	Cowdenbeath 5	
Jan 26	Inverness T 1	Forfar A 3	
Jan 26	Johnstone 1	East Fife 3	
Jan 26	Kilmarnock 2	Celtic 0	
Jan 26	King's Park 0	Hamilton A 0	
Jan 26	Mid-Annandale 3	Forres Mechanic 1	
Jan 26	Motherwell 5	Breadalbane 0	
Jan 26	Newton Stewart 1	E Stirling 8	
Jan 12	Partick T 11	Dunkeld 0	
Jan 26	Queen of South 8	Stranraer 0	
Jan 26	Queen's Park 1	Dumbarton H 1	
Jan 26	Raith R 3	Broxburn U 0	
Jan 26	Rangers 4	Lochgelly U 1	
Jan 26	St Bernard's 3	Fraserburgh 0	
Jan 26	St Johnstone 3	Moor Park 0	
Jan 26	St Mirren 3	Beith 2	
Jan 26	Stenhousemuir 2	Clackmannan 1	
Jan 26	Thornhill 0	Clyde 0	
Jan 26	T Lanark 0	Hearts 0	
Jan 26	Vale of Leven 0	Leith A 0	

Replays
Jan 29	Clyde 4	Thornhill 0	
Jan 29	Leith A 1	Vale of Leven 2	
Jan 30	Alloa 3	Buckie T 0	played at Aberdeen
Jan 30	Bo'ness 1	Bathgate 0	
Jan 30	Dumbarton H 1	Queen's Park 4	played at Hampden Park
Jan 30	Hamilton A 1	King's Park 0	
Jan 30	Hearts 3	T Lanark 0	

2nd Round
Feb 9	Airdrie 4	St Johnstone 0	
Feb 9	Ayr U 1	Kilmarnock 0	
Feb 9	Clyde 2	Vale of Leven 0	
Feb 9	Clydebank 4	Arbroath 0	
Feb 9	Cowdenbeath 0	Aberdeen 2	
Feb 9	Dundee 0	Raith R 0	
Feb 9	E Stirling 1	Mid-Annandale 0	
Feb 9	Falkirk 2	East Fife 0	
Feb 9	Forfar A 1	Motherwell 3	
Feb 9	Hamilton A 2	Queen of South 1	
Feb 9	Hearts 6	Galston 0	
Feb 9	Hibernian 1	Alloa 1	
Feb 9	Partick T 3	Bo'ness 0	
Feb 9	Queen's Park 3	Armadale 1	
Feb 9	St Bernard's 0	Stenhousemuir 0	
Feb 9	St Mirren 0	Rangers 1	

Replays
Feb 12	Alloa 0	Hibernian 5	
Feb 13	Raith R 1	Dundee 0	
Feb 13	Stenhousemuir 0	St Bernard's 0	
Feb 20	St Bernard's 2	Stenhousemuir 0	played at Tynecastle

3rd Round
Feb 23	Aberdeen 2	E Stirling 0	
Feb 23	Clydebank 2	Ayr U 3	
Feb 23	Falkirk 0	Queen's Park 0	
Feb 23	Hearts 3	Clyde 1	
Feb 23	Motherwell 0	Airdrie 5	
Feb 23	Partick T 1	Hamilton A 1	
Feb 23	Raith R 0	St Bernard's 1	
Feb 23	Rangers 1	Hibernian 2	

Replays
Feb 27	Hamilton A 1	Partick T 2	
Feb 27	Queen's Park 0	Falkirk 2	

4th Round
Mar 8	Aberdeen 3	St Bernard's 0	
Mar 8	Airdrie 1	Ayr U 1	
Mar 8	Hearts 1	Falkirk 2	
Mar 8	Hibernian 2	Partick T 2	

Replays
Mar 12	Ayr U 0	Airdrie 0	
Mar 12	Partick T 1	Hibernian 1	
Mar 18	Hibernian 2	Partick T 1	played at Celtic Park
Mar 19	Airdrie 1	Ayr U 1	played at Ibrox
Mar 20	Airdrie 1	Ayr U 0	played at Ibrox

Semi-finals
Mar 22	Aberdeen 0	Hibernian 0	played at Dens Park
Mar 22	Airdrie 2	Falkirk 1	played at Celtic Park

Replays
Mar 26	Aberdeen 0	Hibernian 0	played at Dens Park
Apr 9	Aberdeen 0	Hibernian 1	played at Dens Park

Final
Apr 19	Airdrie 2	Hibernian 0	played at Ibrox

DIVISION 1

Home \ Away	ABE	AIR	AYR	CEL	CLY	CLB	DUN	FAL	HAM	HEA	HIB	KIL	MOR	MOT	PAR	QPK	RAI	RAN	STM	TLA
ABERDEEN	—	Mar01 1-2	Jan12 1-0	Sep29 0-2	Dec29 3-0	Aug18 3-1	Sep01 0-0	Dec15 0-0	Oct13 2-0	Jan05 2-1	Jan02 1-1	Apr19 2-0	Sep15 0-2	Oct27 3-1	Nov10 2-1	Sep24 1-1	Dec01 1-0	Mar19 1-0	Feb02 2-0	Feb13 2-2
AIRDRIE	Dec22 2-1	—	Sep01 4-0	Mar29 2-0	Oct27 6-1	Feb27 3-2	Jan01 4-2	Aug18 4-1	Nov17 3-2	Sep15 3-0	Dec01 1-1	Oct13 2-2	Nov10 1-1	Mar26 2-0	Dec29 1-1	Apr26 2-2	Jan12 1-0	Feb02 0-0	Jan12 4-0	Feb02 3-1
AYR U	Sep08 1-1	Jan19 2-3	—	Sep22 4-2	Feb27 3-1	Mar15 2-1	Dec15 2-0	Apr05 0-0	Dec01 1-0	Mar22 0-0	Nov10 2-1	Aug25 2-2	Jan01 3-0	Oct06 1-0	Feb16 0-0	Nov24 2-1	Apr12 2-2	Jan05 1-0	Oct20 2-2	Mar29 3-0
CELTIC	Jan19 4-0	Nov03 2-2	Apr05 3-0	—	Oct06 4-0	Mar04 1-2	Nov17 0-0	Aug18 2-1	Jan05 1-0	Feb26 4-1	Apr21 1-1	Mar08 2-1	Sep24 3-0	Dec15 2-1	Sep01 1-2	Feb16 1-0	Oct20 0-0	Jan01 2-2	Apr12 0-1	Dec01 3-1
CLYDE	Nov24 1-0	Aug15 1-1	Dec08 1-0	Jan02 0-0	—	Oct13 2-0	Feb02 0-2	Mar29 2-1	Feb02 2-1	Apr21 2-2	Mar01 2-0	Sep08 1-1	Nov10 3-0	Jan12 2-3	Mar08 4-4	Aug25 0-1	Nov03 2-1	Jan02 3-1	Dec01 0-3	Oct27 0-1
CLYDEBANK	Apr12 2-1	Feb16 0-1	Dec22 1-0	Aug25 0-0	Jan05 2-1	—	Apr19 0-0	Sep08 0-1	Oct20 1-2	Jan19 2-2	Feb20 2-4	Sep22 1-2	Mar22 0-2	Apr05 2-0	Nov24 2-1	Nov03 2-1	Jan02 2-2	Dec01 1-1	Oct06 1-1	Mar01 1-5
DUNDEE	Jan01 1-1	Oct20 3-1	Feb20 2-1	Dec22 2-1	Apr05 3-1	Nov10 4-1	—	Dec01 4-2	Mar15 1-1	Aug25 5-1	Oct27 7-2	Jan19 4-2	Mar01 1-1	Mar08 4-1	Dec08 0-0	Sep22 3-0	Jan05 1-1	Oct06 1-4	Mar29 1-1	Sep08 1-0
FALKIRK	Oct06 0-0	Aug25 0-3	Mar15 2-0	Nov03 1-0	Feb02 2-0	Jan02 4-1	Mar26 1-2	—	Oct20 2-0	Dec08 0-0	Dec22 1-1	Nov24 2-1	Apr19 2-0	Feb20 2-0	Mar01 0-1	Dec01 1-3	Apr19 3-0	Mar01 0-1	Dec15 0-0	Apr19 4-1
HAMILTON A	Mar12 3-0	Jan02 5-1	Dec29 0-0	Nov10 0-2	Dec15 1-2	Apr26 3-2	Nov24 0-0	Sep22 1-2	—	Feb16 1-3	Apr23 2-1	Mar29 2-3	Oct27 2-0	Aug25 2-3	Mar05 2-1	Oct06 2-0	Sep08 2-3	Jan19 2-0	Dec08 2-3	Apr05 2-0
HEARTS	Dec08 0-1	Feb13 4-2	Sep29 2-3	Oct13 0-0	Aug18 6-0	Sep15 2-0	Dec29 1-0	Apr05 3-1	Sep01 4-0	—	Jan01 1-1	Nov10 4-1	Dec01 3-1	Mar29 2-1	Oct27 2-1	Jan12 5-2	Mar01 1-2	Sep17 0-0	Jan02 2-0	Mar15 3-1
HIBERNIAN	Aug25 0-1	Apr12 2-0	Feb02 3-0	Sep17 2-1	Nov17 1-1	Feb16 3-2	Jan05 2-0	Nov03 1-3	Sep08 1-1	Dec29 1-1	—	Feb27 3-1	Nov24 2-1	Sep22 2-4	Apr16 3-1	Oct06 4-0	Oct20 4-0	Apr02 1-1	Apr12 1-1	Jan19 5-2
KILMARNOCK	Nov03 2-1	Apr02 1-2	Jan02 1-1	Dec08 0-0	Mar15 3-0	Jan12 2-3	Sep29 1-3	Oct13 2-1	Sep15 1-0	Dec22 2-1	Sep01 2-1	—	Feb13 1-3	Apr26 1-4	Feb02 1-2	Aug18 2-0	Nov17 1-1	Mar05 3-4	Oct27 2-0	Dec29 0-0
MORTON	Feb27 1-1	Apr05 2-1	Nov17 4-0	Feb02 1-0	Mar08 1-2	Dec08 1-0	Nov03 2-1	Feb16 2-0	Jan12 0-0	Sep22 1-0	Dec29 0-2	Oct06 1-0	—	Jan02 3-2	Aug25 1-2	Oct20 3-1	Apr19 2-0	Sep08 0-1	Mar15 4-0	Dec15 2-2
MOTHERWELL	Apr05 1-1	Jan05 1-0	Mar01 1-0	Jan01 0-1	Sep15 1-1	Sep29 3-2	Oct13 4-2	Jan19 3-1	Nov01 3-1	Nov03 3-2	Mar15 2-1	Oct20 4-0	Sep01 3-1	—	Apr12 1-1	Nov17 2-1	Dec22 1-3	Apr18 0-3	Dec01 0-2	Apr19 2-2
PARTICK T	Mar29 1-0	Oct06 2-1	Aug18 3-0	Mar01 1-1	Oct20 6-1	Aug16 1-1	Mar22 5-2	Dec29 0-1	Nov17 0-1	Apr19 1-0	Dec01 1-0	Dec15 2-2	Jan05 0-2	Sep08 1-0	—	Apr21 3-0	Jan19 0-2	Nov03 2-1	Feb12 1-2	Dec31 2-2
QUEEN'S PARK	Apr05 1-0	Dec15 0-2	Apr26 0-0	Sep08 0-2	Dec01 1-1	Mar29 1-1	Apr12 1-1	Oct27 4-2	Mar01 2-1	Feb02 1-1	Sep29 1-1	Jan05 3-1	Jan19 3-1	Dec29 2-2	Oct13 0-2	—	Sep15 2-1	Feb12 0-2	Nov10 0-1	Aug25 1-0
RAITH R	Feb16 1-0	Dec08 2-0	Oct27 4-1	Apr12 1-0	Jan01 2-1	Sep01 1-0	Aug18 3-0	Nov10 3-0	Nov24 1-1	Jan12 0-2	Apr05 4-1	Sep22 4-0	Feb27 1-1	Apr05 4-1	Nov24 2-0	Feb02 2-0	—	Dec15 0-1	Apr26 1-1	Oct13 6-1
RANGERS	Sep22 2-0	Nov24 5-0	Oct13 0-0	Oct27 2-1	Sep24 3-0	Feb26 0-1	Jan12 1-4	Aug21 1-2	Dec22 4-0	Mar11 2-1	Apr05 2-1	Feb19 2-1	Apr12 3-0	Feb02 1-0	Jan02 0-1	Dec08 2-1	Mar29 1-1	—	Aug25 5-0	Nov10 1-0
ST MIRREN	Nov17 2-0	Sep08 0-1	Apr19 4-0	Nov24 0-1	Jan19 3-1	Mar08 6-2	Sep15 2-2	Sep01 1-0	Sep29 4-1	Dec15 0-0	Oct13 1-1	Jan01 0-1	Aug18 3-1	Feb16 4-0	Apr05 1-2	Mar04 2-0	Nov03 1-1	Dec29 0-0	—	Jan05 3-1
T LANARK	Oct20 2-1	Sep22 0-0	Nov03 3-0	Jan12 1-3	Feb16 0-0	Nov17 2-1	Dec25 3-5	Mar04 2-1	Apr21 3-2	Oct06 1-4	Aug18 2-1	Nov24 0-2	Aug22 2-1	Dec08 2-4	Sep24 2-3	Jan02 1-1	Mar08 1-3	Mar22 3-0	Dec22 3-0	—

DIVISION 2

	ALBION R	ALLOA	ARBROATH	ARMADALE	BATHGATE	BO'NESS	BROXBURN U	COWDENBEATH	DUMBARTON	DUNDEE U	DUNFERMLINE A	EAST FIFE	FORFAR A	JOHNSTONE	KING'S PARK	LOCHGELLY U	ST BERNARD'S	ST JOHNSTONE	STENHOUSEMUIR	VALE OF LEVEN
ALBION R		Mar22 2-0	Dec08 7-1	Oct06 4-0	Dec15 2-2	Nov03 4-0	Apr26 1-3	Nov24 2-1	Jan02 1-0	Apr05 1-2	Sep08 1-2	Mar01 1-1	Apr19 3-1	Jan19 3-1	Jan05 3-0	Oct20 5-1	Sep22 2-1	Aug25 0-0	Feb25 2-2	Mar08 5-0
ALLOA	Sep29 0-1		Oct13 3-2	Dec29 1-0	Apr05 0-0	Feb16 1-0	Jan12 1-0	Nov10 0-2	Sep08 0-1	Aug25 1-1	Jan01 2-1	Aug28 1-1	Sep22 3-3	Mar29 1-1	Mar01 3-1	Dec01 3-1	Dec04 4-2	Oct27 1-0	Mar15 2-1	Feb02 4-0
ARBROATH	Feb02 1-1	Apr19 1-0		Sep08 2-1	Mar15 2-1	Nov24 0-0	Oct20 0-0	Feb16 0-0	Apr05 3-0	Sep22 2-1	Nov17 0-1	Dec15 3-0	Oct06 0-1	Aug18 1-2	Apr26 5-1	Mar22 3-0	Jan02 0-3	Jan12 0-0	Nov03 0-1	Jan01 3-0
ARMADALE	Apr12 3-1	Sep01 2-1	Jan19 2-2		Jan01 4-4	Mar01 1-0	Mar15 3-1	Mar15 1-4	Mar15 4-1	Jan05 3-1	Aug18 2-1	Dec05 0-0	Oct13 2-4	Mar22 1-0	Mar22 3-2	Apr26 1-3	Feb16 1-0	Oct20 3-0	Sep15 1-0	Sep15 2-0
BATHGATE	Jan12 2-0	Dec22 2-1	Oct27 2-1	Aug25 0-0		Mar29 2-0	Sep08 2-1	Oct06 1-1	Sep22 1-1	Dec08 4-2	Mar08 3-0	Feb23 0-0	Jan02 4-2	Nov24 3-0	Apr19 2-0	Dec29 4-1	Feb02 0-1	Feb16 0-1	Oct20 2-0	Nov10 1-1
BO'NESS	Dec29 1-1	Oct20 2-1	Apr12 3-0	Sep22 3-1	Nov17 2-3		Aug25 3-0	Oct27 1-1	Mar22 0-2	Mar15 1-1	Feb23 2-1	Dec08 2-1	Sep08 2-0	Feb13 2-1	Nov10 1-1	Nov08 0-2	Jan12 2-0	Oct06 1-2	Jan02 2-0	Apr26 1-1
BROXBURN U	Oct13 4-2	Nov03 1-2	Mar01 0-0	Oct06 3-1	Jan19 0-0	Jan01 1-3		Feb02 0-1	Jan05 1-2	Nov24 1-1	Mar29 1-0	Sep29 3-0	Mar15 0-3	Aug18 3-2	Dec15 3-1	Dec01 2-2	Sep15 0-0	Sep01 1-3		
COWDENBEATH	Feb02 4-0	Mar08 1-0	Dec29 2-1	Oct20 0-1	Feb13 2-1	Aug15 3-1	Sep22 3-0		Apr12 4-1	Dec31 4-4	Mar22 3-2	Jan12 3-0	Nov03 4-1	Sep29 2-0	Dec01 5-0	Mar29 2-1	Aug25 1-1	Sep08 1-1	Nov17 2-0	Dec15 2-0
DUMBARTON	Aug18 0-1	Feb23 5-0	Sep15 1-0	Mar29 0-2	Apr26 6-2	Sep29 1-1	Nov17 2-0	Sep01 2-2		Oct27 3-0	Dec29 1-0	Feb02 1-1	Apr19 5-1	Jan01 2-1	Dec15 0-5	Mar12 3-0	Nov03 1-0	Dec08 1-4	Apr16 0-1	Oct13 1-0
DUNDEE U	Sep01 2-0	Jan02 0-1	Feb23 2-1	Jan12 4-0	Apr12 2-0	Dec15 0-0	Aug22 0-0	Aug18 0-0	Feb16 0-1		Apr19 2-2	Oct13 0-0	Apr26 2-0	Nov24 1-1	Feb06 0-0	Nov17 1-0	Nov03 3-2	Feb02 1-1	Apr16 0-1	Sep29 3-1
DUNFERMLINE A	Feb16 1-1	Aug18 1-2	Dec22 2-2	Oct27 1-0	Oct13 1-1	Sep01 1-0	Nov10 2-1	Sep15 1-3	Nov24 1-2	Oct06 2-0		Apr05 2-0	Feb02 2-0	Mar01 0-1	Jan19 3-2	Jan02 6-1	Aug22 1-1	Mar15 0-1	Apr26 4-2	Dec08 2-2
EAST FIFE	Nov17 1-2	Sep15 1-0	Mar29 2-0	Jan02 2-1	Dec01 0-1	Jan05 2-1	Feb20 2-0	Dec22 3-2	Oct06 2-0	Jan19 0-0	Oct20 1-2		Mar22 7-0	Nov03 2-1	Mar08 2-2	Aug25 1-0	Sep08 2-0	Apr19 1-1	Apr12 6-0	Dec29 0-1
FORFAR A	Sep15 3-1	Feb28 2-1	Jan05 0-5	Mar08 1-5	Sep01 2-2	Jan19 2-2	Dec01 0-1	Mar01 1-0	Dec01 2-1	Nov10 0-0	Aug25 1-0	Oct27 0-1		Oct13 3-2	Sep29 0-0	Mar01 3-1	Jan01 1-2	Mar29 1-2	Dec22 2-4	Feb23 1-0
JOHNSTONE	Nov10 3-3	Dec08 2-1	Mar08 1-3	Feb02 3-2	Mar22 3-0	Dec01 4-1	Oct06 2-0	Jan02 2-0	Oct20 2-1	Dec22 0-1	Jan17 1-0	Feb16 3-1	Apr05 4-2		Oct27 1-0	Feb23 2-0	Apr26 3-1	Sep22 1-1	Aug25 2-1	Apr12 4-1
KING'S PARK	Dec22 1-1	Oct06 1-0	Feb13 2-2	Aug15 1-2	Nov03 3-0	Feb02 4-0	Jan02 1-2	Apr05 0-3	Aug25 2-3	Oct20 1-0	Sep22 2-2	Nov24 1-0	Mar15 2-1	Dec15 3-1		Sep08 4-0	Feb27 1-0	Apr12 1-0	Jan12 2-1	Nov17 1-1
LOCHGELLY U	Mar15 1-0	Apr26 0-2	Nov10 0-2	Oct06 1-0	Aug18 1-0	Sep15 1-2	Oct13 1-1	Mar01 0-2	Jan05 0-0	Sep29 1-1	Jan01 0-4	Nov24 0-2	Mar15 0-1	Feb16 3-8			Apr05 1-1	Dec22 0-3	Feb02 0-1	Feb20 1-2
ST BERNARD'S	Mar29 1-1	Jan19 2-1	Sep01 2-0	Nov10 0-0	Sep29 0-2	Oct13 2-3	Apr12 1-2	Dec08 0-3	Dec22 0-0	Mar05 2-2	Dec01 2-3	Mar15 2-2	Aug18 4-3	Jan05 2-2	Sep15 1-1	Oct06 1-0		Mar01 0-1	Nov24 1-1	Oct27 3-1
ST JOHNSTONE	Jan01 6-1	Dec15 2-1	Sep29 2-1	Sep15 5-0	Apr05 0-0	Feb23 3-0	Jan05 3-1	Feb13 0-4	Aug25 4-4	Nov03 4-1	Sep01 1-0	Nov17 3-0	Dec29 2-0	Dec08 2-1	Jan19 5-1	Oct20 6-0	Apr12 4-1		Mar22 1-1	Aug18 2-1
STENHOUSEMUIR	Oct27 1-1	Jan05 3-1	Dec01 2-0	Feb23 2-0	Mar01 5-1	Aug18 1-1	Nov24 4-3	Apr19 1-2	Jan19 1-2	Sep08 3-0	Dec15 1-0	Nov10 3-0	Feb16 1-0	Jan01 2-1	Sep01 3-5	Sep01 3-0	Dec29 3-0	Oct13 0-0		Mar29 0-1
VALE OF LEVEN	Dec01 0-0	Nov24 3-1	Aug25 3-2	Apr19 3-2	Jan05 1-2	Dec22 2-2	Apr05 1-1	Jan19 3-0	Mar15 0-3	Mar01 2-2	Feb13 1-1	Sep22 1-2	Oct20 1-0	Sep08 0-4	Mar22 2-0	Nov03 2-0	Feb16 0-4	Jan02 2-2	Oct06 1-0	

DIVISION 3

	ARTHURLIE	BEITH	BRECHIN C	CLACKMANNAN	DUMBARTON H	DYKEHEAD	E STIRLING	GALSTON	HELENSBURGH	MID ANNANDALE	MONTROSE	NITHSDALE W	PEEBLES	QUEEN OF SOUTH	ROYAL ALBERT	SOLWAY STAR
ARTHURLIE		Feb09 0-1	Sep22 4-0	Dec01 2-0	Jan12 3-0	Mar08 3-0	Aug25 2-3	Feb16 3-2	Jan02 5-0	Nov10 3-2	Feb02 3-0	Dec08 2-1	Jan26 1-1	Dec22 3-2	Oct20 2-0	Oct06 3-2
BEITH	Nov24 0-1		Apr12 2-1	Mar29 3-2	Mar08 6-2	Feb16 0-3	Jan02 2-0	Sep22 4-1	Dec15 3-4	Oct06 1-1	Feb02 3-0	Apr05 2-0	Dec08 4-0	Aug25 1-0	Mar01 1-0	Apr21 4-0
BRECHIN C	Nov17 2-0	Mar22 1-0		Sep08 0-1	Apr05 1-3	Apr19 1-2	Mar01 1-0	Nov10 2-3	Mar08 1-1	Jan05 3-0	Aug18 0-0	Jan01 0-1	Dec01 3-2	Feb02 0-1	Jan12 0-0	Dec08 0-2
CLACKMANNAN	Nov03 0-1	Jan05 2-2	Feb09 2-1		Dec31 1-1	Jan19 3-0	Sep15 5-1	Nov24 1-1	Sep22 3-0	Feb23 1-2	Dec15 1-3	Aug18 0-0	Oct06 0-1	Oct20 3-2	Dec08 2-1	Apr19 2-1
DUMBARTON H	Mar15 0-2	Sep08 0-0	Feb23 0-2	Aug25 2-3		Nov24 1-0	Oct20 0-0	Nov03 4-1	Feb16 1-1	Oct06 4-3	Dec22 1-0	Feb02 1-0	Jan02 0-5	Mar22 2-0	Jan02 2-0	Sep22 3-1
DYKEHEAD	Feb23 1-2	Apr28 5-1	Mar29 4-0	Jan12 3-0	Dec15 3-2		Nov03 4-0	Aug25 3-1	Oct20 3-1	Feb02 3-2	Apr05 2-0	Mar15 4-1	Sep22 2-1	Jan02 4-2	Apr26 2-2	Mar01 0-1
E STIRLING	Jan01 1-1	Aug18 2-1	Jan19 4-1	Sep01 5-0	Dec01 4-1	Jan05 1-0		Mar29 3-1	Apr26 2-0	Sep08 2-0	Sep22 3-0	Nov10 4-0	Apr05 2-1	Oct27 1-1	Feb16 1-1	
GALSTON	Mar22 0-3	Feb23 3-0	Mar15 2-0	Feb02 1-1	Nov17 3-1	Jan01 2-3	Mar08 1-4		Jan05 1-0	Apr23 1-4	Sep08 3-1	Sep22 2-3	Oct20 5-3	Dec15 2-0	Feb16 2-0	Aug18 2-0
HELENSBURGH	Aug18 0-2	Nov10 3-2	Nov24 1-2	Dec22 2-2	Feb09 1-3	Sep08 2-4	Dec08 3-3	Oct13 2-1		Jan01 3-3	Mar01 4-0	Oct27 0-0	Feb23 2-4	Apr19 2-2	Mar29 6-1	Feb02 1-1
MID ANNANDALE	Mar01 2-2	Mar15 2-3	Apr26 6-1	Nov17 6-1	Dec08 2-1	Apr12 1-0	Dec01 0-1	Aug25 4-3	Apr19 1-1		Nov24 2-0	Jan02 3-2	Nov03 1-3	Sep22 4-1	Mar29 0-1	
MONTROSE	Mar29 1-1	Dec22 2-1	Jan02 4-2	Sep29 1-0	Nov01 1-1	Dec08 6-2	Mar22 2-1	Feb16 5-0	Apr12 4-1	Oct27 2-0		Oct13 2-1	Jan01 1-0	Nov10 1-1	Nov24 2-1	Apr12 5-1
NITHSDALE W	Jan19 0-1	Apr19 2-0	Aug25 5-0	Mar01 1-0	Mar22 0-4	Feb09 3-0	Jan12 1-0	Apr05 4-0	Dec15 2-0	Mar08 3-2	Dec01 2-2		Nov03 3-2	Sep22 3-2	Oct06 0-2	Oct20 2-0
PEEBLES	Oct13 1-3	Mar01 0-0	Feb16 2-0	Nov10 4-0	Dec29 0-0	Dec22 2-1	Sep29 2-6	Oct27 1-3	Jan19 5-2	Aug18 1-2	Sep08 3-1	Jan05 0-0		Nov17 1-1	Feb09 3-0	Jan01 2-2
QUEEN OF SOUTH	Sep08 0-0	Apr26 2-0	Dec15 7-2	Mar08 5-0	Mar29 5-2	Aug18 2-0	Nov24 1-0	Nov15 6-1	Dec29 4-0	Mar20 3-0	Aug25 3-3	Feb16 0-0	Mar22 4-0		Mar01 0-1	Jan05 1-1
ROYAL ALBERT	Jan05 0-1	Dec01 2-1	Nov03 0-3	Feb16 3-0	Aug18 2-1	Oct13 1-3	Feb02 2-1	Dec22 2-4	Nov17 2-1	Mar22 1-1	Feb23 2-4	Sep29 2-0	Nov24 2-0	Mar15 2-0		Mar08 3-3
SOLWAY STAR	Dec15 2-0	Oct13 1-0	Dec29 1-1	Oct27 0-0	Nov10 0-0	Mar22 3-0	Nov17 3-3	Jan02 4-1	Dec01 2-1	Jan12 1-3	Feb23 3-1	Aug25 2-1	Apr12 0-2	Sep08 2-3		

DIVISION 1 FINAL TABLE

	P	W	D	L	F	A	Pts
Rangers	38	25	9	4	72	22	59
Airdrie	38	20	10	8	72	46	50
Celtic	38	17	12	9	56	33	46
Raith R	38	18	7	13	56	38	43
Dundee	38	15	13	10	70	57	43
St Mirren	38	15	12	11	53	45	42
Hibernian	38	15	11	12	66	52	41
Partick T	38	15	9	14	58	55	39
Hearts	38	14	10	14	61	50	38
Motherwell	38	15	7	16	58	63	37
Morton	38	16	5	17	48	54	37
Hamilton A	38	15	6	17	52	57	36
Aberdeen	38	13	10	15	37	41	36
Ayr U	38	12	10	16	38	60	34
Falkirk	38	13	6	19	46	53	32
Kilmarnock	38	12	8	18	48	65	32
Queen's Park	38	11	9	18	43	60	31
T Lanark	38	11	8	19	54	78	30
Clyde	38	10	9	19	40	70	29
Clydebank	38	10	5	23	42	71	25

DIVISION 2 FINAL TABLE

	P	W	D	L	F	A	Pts
St Johnstone	38	22	12	4	79	33	56
Cowdenbeath	38	23	9	6	78	33	55
Bathgate	38	16	12	10	58	49	44
Stenhousemuir	38	16	11	11	58	45	43
Albion R	38	15	12	11	67	53	42
King's Park	38	16	10	12	67	57	42
Dunfermline A	38	14	11	13	52	45	39
Johnstone	38	16	7	15	60	56	39
Dundee U	38	12	15	11	41	41	39
Dumbarton	38	17	5	16	55	56	39
Armadale	38	16	6	16	56	63	38
East Fife	38	14	9	15	54	47	37
Bo'ness	38	13	11	14	45	53	37
Forfar A	38	14	7	17	42	67	35
Alloa	38	14	6	18	44	53	34
Vale of Leven	38	12	9	17	43	65	33
Arbroath	38	12	8	18	49	51	32
St Bernard's	38	11	10	17	49	54	32
Broxburn U	38	12	8	18	48	58	32
Lochgelly U	38	4	4	30	21	86	12

DIVISION 3 FINAL TABLE

	P	W	D	L	F	A	Pts
Arthurlie	30	21	5	4	59	24	47
E Stirling	30	17	8	5	63	36	42
Queen of South	30	14	10	6	64	31	38
Montrose	30	15	6	9	60	48	36
Dykehead	30	16	1	13	55	41	33
Nithsdale W	30	13	7	10	42	35	33
Beith	30	14	4	12	49	41	32
Mid Annandale	30	13	5	12	59	48	31
Royal Albert	30	12	4	14	44	53	28
Dumbarton H	30	10	8	12	40	51	28
Solway Star	30	9	9	12	42	48	27
Clackmannan	30	10	7	13	37	54	27
Galston	30	11	3	16	53	70	25
Peebles	30	7	8	15	43	56	22
Helensburgh	30	5	7	18	46	72	17
Brechin C	30	4	6	20	28	76	14

Season 1924-25

SFA Cup

1st Round

Jan 24	Albion R 1	Clyde 1
Jan 24	Armadale 3	Civil Service 1
Jan 24	Arthurlie 3	Cowdenbeath 1
Jan 24	Ayr U 3	St Johnstone 1
Jan 24	Bathgate 0	Partick T 4
Jan 24	Bo'ness 1	Helensburgh 1
Jan 24	Broxburn U 3	Nithsdale W 2
Jan 24	Celtic 5	T Lanark 1
Jan 24	Clydebank 0	Queen's Park 1
Jan 24	Dundee 5	Johnstone 0
Jan 24	Dundee U 5	Aberdeen Univ .1
Jan 24	Dunfermline A 1	Arbroath 1
Jan 24	Dykehead 1	Forfar A 0
Jan 24	East Fife 1	Rangers 3
Jan 24	E Stirling 4	Clacknacuddin ...0
Jan 24	Falkirk 1	Morton 1
Jan 24	Hamilton A 5	St Bernard's 2
Jan 24	Hearts 4	Leith A 1
Jan 24	Hibernian 0	Aberdeen 2
Jan 24	Kilmarnock 3	Arbroath A 0
Jan 24	King's Park 0	Airdrie 4
Jan 24	Lochgelly U 4	Bredalban 0
Jan 24	Montrose 6	Inver Citadel 2
Jan 24	Motherwell 6	Galston 3
Jan 24	Newton Stewart ..0	Dumbarton 2
Jan 24	Queen of South ...1	Alloa 1
Jan 24	Raith R 3	Clackmannan 0
Jan 24	Royal Albert 9	Stranraer 1
Jan 24	Solway Star 4	Stenhousemuir ...2
Jan 24	St Cuthbert's 0	Peebles R 0
Jan 24	St Mirren 3	Peterhead 1
Jan 24	Vale of Leven 2	Inverness Cal 0

Replays

Jan 27	Alloa 2	Queen of South ..0
Jan 28	Arbroath 1	Dunfermline A ...0
Jan 28	Clyde 3	Albion R 1
Jan 28	Helensburgh 0	Bo'ness 0
Jan 28	Morton 0	Falkirk 3
Jan 28	Peebles R 5	St Cuthbert's 0
Feb 3	Bo'ness 2	Helensburgh 0

played at Firhill Park

2nd Round

Feb 7	Airdrie 4	Queen's Park 0
Feb 7	Arbroath 3	Clyde 0
Feb 7	Armadale 1	Aberdeen 1
Feb 7	Celtic 2	Alloa 1
Feb 7	Dundee 2	Lochgelly U 1
Feb 7	Dykehead 3	Peebles R 1
Feb 7	Falkirk 2	Dumbarton 0
Feb 7	Hamilton A 4	E Stirling 0
Feb 7	Kilmarnock 2	Hearts 1
Feb 7	Montrose 0	Rangers 2
Feb 7	Motherwell 2	Arthurlie 0
Feb 7	Partick T 5	Dundee U 1
Feb 7	Raith R 0	Bo'ness 0
Feb 7	Royal Albert 1	Broxburn U 3
Feb 7	St Mirren 1	Ayr U 0
Feb 7	Vale of Leven 2	Solway Star 2

Replays

Feb 11	Aberdeen 2	Armadale 0
Feb 11	Bo'ness 1	Raith R 3
Feb 12	Solway Star 3	Vale of Leven 3
Feb 16	Solway Star 2	Vale of Leven 1

played at Cathkin Park

3rd Round

Feb 21	Aberdeen 0	Motherwell 0
Feb 21	Broxburn U 2	Falkirk 1
Feb 21	Celtic 2	Solway Star 0
Feb 21	Dundee 3	Airdrie 1
Feb 21	Hamilton A 1	Raith R 0
Feb 21	Kilmarnock 5	Dykehead 0
Feb 21	Rangers 5	Arbroath 3
Feb 21	St Mirren 2	Partick T 0

Replay

Feb 25	Motherwell 1	Aberdeen 2

4th Round

Mar 7	Aberdeen 0	Hamilton A 2
Mar 7	Dundee 1	Broxburn U 0
Mar 7	Kilmarnock 1	Rangers 2
Mar 7	St Mirren 0	Celtic 0

Replays

Mar 10	Celtic 1	St Mirren 1
Mar 16	Celtic 1	St Mirren 0

played at Ibrox

Semi-finals

Mar 21	Celtic 5	Rangers 0

played at Hampden Park

Mar 21	Dundee 1	Hamilton A 1

played at Tynecastle

Replays

Mar 25	Dundee 2	Hamilton A 0

played at Easter Road

Final

Apr 11	Celtic 2	Dundee 1

played at Hampden Park

DIVISION 1

	ABERDEEN	AIRDRIE	AYR U	CELTIC	COWDENBEATH	DUNDEE	FALKIRK	HAMILTON A	HEARTS	HIBERNIAN	KILMARNOCK	MORTON	MOTHERWELL	PARTICK T	QUEEN'S PARK	RAITH R	RANGERS	ST JOHNSTONE	ST MIRREN	T LANARK
ABERDEEN		Oct04 1-2	Mar18 0-1	Sep06 0-4	Sep20 3-0	Oct18 0-0	Jan03 1-1	Apr01 2-0	Apr04 0-0	Jan05 0-1	Nov29 0-0	Sep22 0-1	Apr25 2-0	Jan17 2-0	Sep29 3-1	Feb28 2-3	Aug23 0-1	Nov01 2-1	Nov15 2-3	Dec20 3-1
AIRDRIE	Feb14 0-0		Nov01 3-0	Jan03 3-1	Dec27 2-0	Apr22 1-1	Nov15 1-1	Jan05 4-2	Mar07 2-2	Apr18 2-0	Feb11 4-1	Jan17 6-2	Mar28 5-0	Dec13 4-3	Nov22 1-0	Oct11 1-0	Sep27 6-0	Sep13 2-0	Aug16 3-0	Aug30 3-0
AYR U	Aug30 3-3	Aug20 0-1		Feb11 1-2	Jan17 1-2	Nov08 1-0	Apr04 0-0	Nov29 3-1	Jan03 2-1	Feb28 2-2	Oct18 0-1	Jan05 4-0	Apr11 1-0	Nov15 0-1	Oct25 1-1	Mar14 3-2	Sep13 0-4	Sep27 5-3	Dec13 1-1	Aug16 0-0
CELTIC	Jan10 3-1	Aug23 1-1	Dec06 2-0		Sep29 3-1	Feb28 4-0	Apr01 6-1	Dec20 0-2	Oct11 1-0	Jan31 1-1	Nov08 6-0	Mar24 2-1	Sep27 4-0	Oct11 1-2	Apr18 1-1	Mar28 2-0	Oct25 1-1	Feb14 2-1	Sep13 5-0	Jan05 7-0
COWDENBEATH	Mar28 2-1	Nov08 2-1	Dec20 4-0	Mar14 3-0		Jan31 2-0	Feb11 1-2	Apr04 2-0	Aug16 1-2	Nov29 1-1	Oct25 5-2	Sep13 4-0	Mar04 2-1	Apr25 1-2	Dec13 2-2	Jan01 1-1	Oct11 2-2	Aug30 1-2	Sep27 5-4	Jan10 3-4
DUNDEE	Jan01 2-0	Dec20 3-2	Feb25 1-0	Aug16 0-0	Nov15 1-1		Jan17 1-0	Feb14 2-0	Aug30 6-0	Apr04 3-0	Sep13 3-1	Oct11 0-0	Mar14 1-0	Jan03 0-2	Sep27 2-4	Nov29 2-0	Dec06 0-0	Mar28 2-0	Apr15 0-2	Nov01 1-2
FALKIRK	Aug16 2-0	Jan01 0-2	Nov22 0-3	Aug30 1-2	Dec06 5-1	Dec13 1-2		Oct11 2-1	Sep13 2-1	Jan10 0-0	Sep27 0-1	Aug20 3-0	Oct25 2-1	Apr11 1-0	Nov08 7-0	Jan31 1-1	Feb18 1-1	Apr25 2-0	Mar28 2-1	Dec27 1-2
HAMILTON A	Sep13 2-1	Oct25 1-2	Dec27 1-0	Feb24 4-5	Oct04 1-4	Nov22 1-2	Apr25 1-2		Sep27 0-2	Nov08 0-2	Mar11 1-1	Apr11 1-1	Jan05 1-1	Mar28 3-1	Mar14 1-0	Aug30 3-2	Jan31 1-3	Aug16 1-3	Jan10 1-2	Dec06 1-2
HEARTS	Nov08 1-1	Sep20 2-0	Aug23 2-3	Dec13 3-1	Aug20 3-3	Apr18 1-0	Nov29 3-2	Feb28 3-2		Oct18 2-0	Mar14 1-1	Sep06 5-1	Oct04 2-2	Feb11 2-1	Mar28 3-1	Jan10 2-2	Sep15 1-2	Jan31 1-1	Dec27 5-2	Nov15 2-3
HIBERNIAN	Nov22 4-1	Dec06 1-1	Oct11 7-0	Sep15 2-3	Feb21 4-1	Oct25 4-2	Nov01 1-2	Jan17 2-1	Jan01 2-1		Jan03 2-0	Sep27 3-2	Aug29 1-0	Feb25 3-2	Mar11 3-0	Apr11 4-1	Feb14 5-0	Mar24 2-0	Apr01 1-2	Feb07 5-1
KILMARNOCK	Jan31 0-1	Sep06 2-3	Jan01 4-1	Apr15 2-1	Mar21 0-0	Jan10 2-0	Feb28 1-0	Sep20 1-1	Nov22 0-0	Aug23 0-0		Feb25 1-1	Dec06 3-1	Dec27 2-1	Oct11 1-1	Dec20 3-0	Mar28 0-0	Apr22 0-4	Nov01 3-2	Oct04 2-2
MORTON	Dec13 1-1	Oct18 0-1	Sep20 3-1	Nov01 1-0	Mar07 1-3	Dec27 1-1	Oct04 2-0	Nov15 2-0	Feb14 2-0	Mar28 2-2	Aug16 2-2		Jan31 0-0	Aug30 1-6	Feb21 4-0	Apr18 2-3	Jan10 1-1	Apr04 1-1	Jan01 2-1	Nov29 1-0
MOTHERWELL	Oct11 1-2	Nov29 1-5	Sep06 1-1	Jan17 1-0	Nov20 0-3	Sep20 4-1	Jan05 4-1	Apr04 3-3	Oct04 0-0	Feb11 1-1	Apr04 2-1	Aug23 3-0		Aug28 1-3		Dec13 4-1	Apr18 2-1	Nov15 4-1	Apr01 1-2	Aug01 8-0
PARTICK T	Sep27 1-4	Jan10 2-1	Jan31 2-2	Aug19 6-1	Nov22 1-4	Aug23 1-3	Dec20 3-0	Sep06 3-3	Oct25 3-3	Mar14 3-1	Feb14 1-4	Dec06 3-1	Nov08 0-3		Feb24 3-1	Sep13 3-1	Jan05 0-1	Oct11 1-1	Apr18 0-1	Jan01 2-0
QUEEN'S PARK	Apr13 4-1	Jan31 1-2	Jan10 4-1	Nov15 3-1	Feb14 1-1	Mar10 0-1	Mar25 0-2	Nov01 1-3	Dec06 2-0	Dec27 1-0	Aug20 1-2	Dec20 0-2	Aug16 2-1	Oct04 0-0		Apr25 2-0	Aug26 1-3	Nov29 2-2	Apr03 2-1	Oct18 1-1
RAITH R	Dec06 2-2	Apr11 0-2	Oct04 2-1	Dec27 2-2	Oct18 3-1	Nov05 4-3	Sep20 2-0	Jan03 0-1	Apr11 0-1	Dec13 1-3	Oct25 3-1	Nov22 2-0	Feb11 1-0	Aug30 0-4			Nov15 5-1	Feb18 1-1		
RANGERS	Mar07 2-0	Feb25 1-1	Apr25 2-1	Jan01 1-0	Apr01 2-0	Feb10 1-0	Oct18 0-1	Dec13 5-1	Sep29 3-1	Nov15 1-0	Aug30 1-0	Jan03 1-1	Dec27 3-1	Nov01 2-0	Jan17 1-0	Aug16 3-0		Aug20 3-1	Nov29 3-1	Apr11 5-2
ST JOHNSTONE	Dec27 1-1	Apr25 1-0	Mar21 2-2	Oct18 0-0	Sep03 2-2	Oct04 1-2	Aug23 0-0	Feb11 4-1	Apr11 4-3	Sep06 2-3	Dec13 4-2	Nov08 1-3	Jan10 2-1	Mar07 1-1	Dec25 2-1	Oct25 4-2	Nov22 1-3		Feb28 2-2	Sep24 4-0
ST MIRREN	Mar03 1-3	Mar07 1-0	Feb14 1-0	Apr25 2-1	Jan31 2-2	Sep06 2-1	Sep20 0-3	Aug23 1-0	Jan17 1-3	Oct04 2-2	Nov22 3-0	Oct25 3-1	Nov22 4-1	Nov08 1-3	Dec20 3-0	Dec06 1-4	Apr18 0-1			Jan31 3-1
T LANARK	Oct25 4-0	Mar11 1-7	Mar28 0-1	Nov22 1-1	Aug23 1-1	Dec25 3-0	Apr18 4-0	Aug19 2-1	Feb21 2-2	Dec13 1-2	Jan17 2-0	Feb28 2-3	Sep13 1-2	Sep29 1-2	Feb11 1-3	Sep27 2-4	Nov08 1-1	Jan03 0-2	Oct11 0-1	

DIVISION 2

	ALBION R	ALLOA	ARBROATH	ARMADALE	ARTHURLIE	BATHGATE	BO'NESS	BROXBURN U	CLYDE	CLYDEBANK	DUMBARTON	DUNDEE U	DUNFERMLINE A	EAST FIFE	E STIRLING	FORFAR A	JOHNSTONE	KING'S PARK	ST BERNARD'S	STENHOUSEMUIR
ALBION R		Mar14 3-6	Jan01 1-1	Dec06 3-1	Feb14 3-1	Sep20 3-2	Jan31 2-1	Oct18 1-1	Jan10 1-1	Apr03 0-0	Apr11 3-1	Nov29 1-0	Dec20 2-1	Oct04 5-2	Oct25 3-0	Apr25 1-3	Feb21 4-1	Sep06 1-1	Aug23 2-1	Nov08 4-1
ALLOA	Dec13 1-0		Feb14 1-1	Apr18 1-0	Sep06 0-0	Aug23 2-2	Feb28 1-1	Nov22 3-0	Mar21 1-0	Sep20 2-3	Mar28 2-1	Mar07 2-0	Jan01 1-1	Apr11 1-1	Nov08 2-0	Oct04 1-0	Oct18 4-1	Dec06 2-0	Jan10 2-0	Jan31 1-0
ARBROATH	Nov01 1-4	Aug16 2-2		Jan05 1-3	Dec06 2-1	Dec20 2-0	Nov08 2-0	Mar11 3-0	Jan03 2-1	Feb25 0-0	Nov29 2-2	Dec20 1-2	Nov08 0-1	Apr25 1-1	Dec06 2-1	Apr11 1-1	Oct04 2-0	Sep06 3-1	Oct25 2-1	
ARMADALE	Mar07 0-1	Nov29 3-2	Oct04 1-3		Jan10 1-0	Nov08 1-2	Sep20 2-2	Mar14 3-0	Oct25 2-1	Apr25 4-1	Dec13 2-1	Mar28 3-0	Oct11 0-1	Sep06 2-1	Dec27 1-0	Aug23 3-2	Jan03 1-0	Apr11 5-1	Jan31 1-1	Feb21 2-0
ARTHURLIE	Sep27 3-0	Jan03 0-0	Apr11 2-2	Sep13 4-2		Oct25 2-0	Feb21 3-0	Oct11 3-0	Mar28 3-1	Aug16 1-1	Jan05 2-1	Jan17 1-2	Apr30 2-1	Nov22 3-1	Mar14 2-2	Dec13 1-0	Nov08 4-5	Feb10 1-2	Sep22 5-2	Dec27 3-0
BATHGATE	Feb28 3-1	Jan17 2-1	Apr24 0-0	Jan01 0-1	Mar21 1-1		Nov15 4-1	Aug30 2-2	Jan05 3-2	Mar18 0-3	Nov01 2-0	Sep27 2-2	Feb07 1-4	Apr11 4-1	Dec06 2-0	Mar27 1-0	Dec13 4-3	Nov22 5-2	Oct18 6-0	Sep13 0-0
BO'NESS	Sep13 3-1	Sep27 2-1	Feb18 1-1	Jan17 3-1	Dec20 2-0	Sep03 0-0		Nov01 3-0	Oct11 4-1	Aug30 4-1	Mar07 1-1	Aug16 2-2	Apr25 2-3	Dec27 3-0	Feb14 2-4	Jan05 1-3	Nov22 2-1	Jan03 6-1	Oct18 3-1	Mar28 6-0
BROXBURN U	Mar27 2-1	Apr03 2-1	Sep20 2-1	Nov15 0-1	Jan31 1-1	Jan10 3-0	Jan01 3-1		Feb28 0-0	Feb25 2-2	Nov29 1-2	Dec20 0-1	Nov08 1-1	Apr25 2-1	Dec06 1-1	Apr11 2-0	Sep20 3-0	Oct04 1-0	Sep06 0-1	Oct25 2-1
CLYDE	Aug16 1-0	Aug30 2-1	Dec27 2-0	Apr04 1-0	Nov01 5-0	Oct04 2-0	Apr10 2-1	Dec13 6-0		Sep16 1-1	Nov15 3-0	Mar14 1-1	Feb21 1-2	Sep20 4-0	Jan17 3-2	Oct18 1-0	Apr10 1-1	Jan07 0-0	Dec27 2-2	Nov22 0-0
CLYDEBANK	Nov15 3-0	Dec27 2-1	Aug23 2-0	Nov01 1-0	Feb28 3-0	Oct11 4-1	Apr18 1-0	Sep27 1-0	Jan31 1-0		Jan01 1-0	Dec13 5-0	Nov29 2-1	Feb07 3-3	Sep13 2-1	Oct18 3-4	Apr11 4-0	Mar14 4-3	Mar28 3-2	Jan10 3-2
DUMBARTON	Nov22 2-0	Dec20 1-1	Apr04 0-0	Mar21 1-0	Sep20 2-0	Feb21 1-0	Dec06 1-0	Jan17 1-0	Apr25 0-4	Nov08 1-0		Aug30 3-3	Oct25 2-0	Jan03 2-1	Sep01 1-1	Sep06 2-0	Oct04 4-1	Aug16 2-0	Feb11 0-1	Mar14 3-2
DUNDEE U	Feb11 3-2	Oct25 1-2	Mar14 1-1	Nov22 5-2	Oct18 4-1	Feb21 2-1	Dec06 1-0	Jan10 0-0	Apr18 2-2	Jan05 1-0	Jan31 0-0		Mar21 2-3	Sep20 1-0	Apr11 2-1	Nov08 2-1	Sep06 3-1	Feb20 2-0	Oct04 3-0	Dec25 3-0
DUNFERMLINE A	Apr18 3-0	Nov01 4-1	Oct18 2-1	Feb28 1-2	Mar07 1-4	Sep06 1-0	Oct04 1-1	Mar28 0-0	Dec06 1-1	Jan17 1-0	Feb14 0-2	Nov15 0-4		Aug23 0-4	Nov22 5-2	Jan03 1-0	Dec27 5-2	Sep20 2-0	Oct06 1-2	Apr11 3-1
EAST FIFE	Mar28 5-0	Oct11 2-1	Nov29 0-1	Apr04 4-1	Apr18 3-0	Jan31 4-1	Oct25 2-1	Aug16 2-1	Nov08 0-3	Dec20 1-1	Sep13 2-1	Feb14 1-1	Jan10 1-1		Sep27 4-1	Feb21 3-2	Dec13 2-1	Aug30 3-0	Mar14 3-0	Jan01 5-1
E STIRLING	Jan17 1-0	Jan05 1-2	Sep06 0-1	Apr04 4-1	Apr18 1-1	Oct04 3-0	Jan03 2-4	Dec13 0-1	Feb21 2-4	Mar07 2-2	Aug23 2-3	Nov01 2-0	Apr04 5-2	Feb28 1-2		Mar28 1-2	Sep20 1-1	Nov15 2-1	Apr18 2-0	Mar21 1-1
FORFAR A	Aug30 2-2	Feb12 3-2	Jan10 1-0	Feb14 1-1	Apr04 3-1	Mar14 1-1	Nov29 5-0	Sep13 1-1	Apr18 1-3	Mar21 2-1	Dec27 1-0	Jan01 3-1	Aug16 2-0	Nov15 1-0	Oct11 1-0		Oct25 1-1	Dec20 0-2	Feb28 0-1	Sep27 4-0
JOHNSTONE	Oct11 1-2	Apr25 2-2	Nov15 1-0	Aug30 2-1	Jan13 3-1	Nov29 3-1	Mar14 3-1	Sep27 1-3	Dec06 4-0	Apr03 0-2	Sep13 2-1	Jan05 1-2	Apr11 3-0	Mar07 1-1	Jan31 3-2	Jan14 3-2		Nov01 1-1	Dec20 0-3	Aug16 0-3
KING'S PARK	Jan05 2-1	Feb21 2-0	Oct25 3-0	Sep27 2-1	Nov29 2-3	Aug23 1-1	Dec27 2-0	Feb14 2-1	Nov22 2-2	Sep13 3-1	Jan31 1-1	Jan31 0-0	Mar21 1-1	Jan14 2-1	Mar07 1-0	Aug20 5-1	Nov01 1-1		Nov08 2-0	Oct11 2-0
ST BERNARD'S	Dec27 2-0	Sep13 1-1	Apr25 2-0	Aug16 5-0	Nov15 0-1	Apr11 2-2	Mar21 1-2	Jan03 2-2	Oct25 2-2	Oct11 3-0	Feb21 1-2	Sep27 2-0	Dec06 2-1	Aug30 3-4	Nov01 2-1	Mar07 3-0	Apr25 5-1	Mar07 1-0		Feb18 1-1
STENHOUSEMUIR	Jan03 1-0	Nov15 0-0	Feb28 2-0	Dec20 4-1	Aug23 2-0	Mar07 5-2	Sep06 1-0	Jan05 2-1	Apr04 0-0	Oct04 2-1	Oct18 3-0	Apr25 1-3	Dec13 1-4	Nov01 2-1	Nov29 0-2	Jan17 5-2	Feb07 3-0	Apr18 2-1	Sep20 1-1	

DIVISION 3

	BEITH	BRECHIN C	CLACKMANNAN	DYKEHEAD	GALSTON	HELENSBURGH	LEITH A	LOCHGELLY U	MID ANNANDALE	MONTROSE	NITHSDALE W	PEEBLES	QUEEN OF SOUTH	ROYAL ALBERT	SOLWAY STAR	VALE OF LEVEN	DUMBARTON H
BEITH		Jan10 7-1	Dec27 3-0	Nov01 1-1	Jan01 4-2	Sep27 3-2	Apr25 2-1	Oct18 1-2	Oct04 8-3	Apr29 3-2	Apr11 0-1	Sep13 1-1	Dec13 2-1	Nov22 2-3	Aug23 2-0	Mar21 2-0	
BRECHIN C	Feb28 5-0		Dec13 3-0	Mar14 3-1	Dec27 0-0	Aug23 3-2	Jan03 2-1	Apr04 0-1	Nov22 5-0	Oct11 0-1	Sep13 1-1	Feb21 4-1	Sep27 1-3	Mar28 2-2	Sep20 0-2	Nov08 4-2	Oct25 4-2
CLACKMANNAN	Aug16 1-0	Nov15 2-1		Apr21 1-1	Oct11 3-2	Feb07 0-0	Feb21 2-1	Mar14 2-0	Jan10 3-1	Sep04 1-0	Apr01 0-1	Feb14 3-2	Oct25 2-2	Sep27 2-0	Mar28 3-0	Dec20 4-1	
DYKEHEAD	Mar07 2-2		Nov22 2-1		Feb28 2-1	Mar21 0-0	Dec06 2-2	Apr25 2-3	Jan17 1-2	Apr28 0-1	Dec27 3-1	Aug16 1-1	Apr04 4-1	Sep27 3-1	Oct25 1-0	Aug30 5-0	Jan05 5-0
GALSTON	Mar14 1-0	Aug30 3-0	Apr24 2-1	Dec20 0-2		Nov29 4-2	Oct25 1-1	Sep13 3-2	Feb21 1-1	Jan03 1-1	Apr11 1-1	Oct18 2-1	Nov08 1-0	Dec06 1-0	Jan17 1-0	Aug16 5-0	
HELENSBURGH	Dec06 8-4	Dec20 2-1	Sep20 3-1	Apr08 1-0	Apr18 5-0		Apr04 3-2	Feb21 2-1	Jan01 1-1	Feb28 5-0	Mar07 4-0	Mar07 3-1	Sep13 3-4	Jan10 1-1	Jan10 0-0	Aug16 1-4	
LEITH A	Nov08 3-1	Mar07 1-2	Aug23 1-2	Apr15 5-0	Jan31 2-1	Mar14 1-1		Jan10 0-0	Apr11 2-0	Nov15 0-3	Nov29 2-1	Dec13 0-2	Mar28 2-3	Dec27 4-0	Feb28 2-0	Apr18 1-0	
LOCHGELLY U	Sep20 4-1	Nov01 3-1	Dec06 3-1	Aug23 5-1	Mar07 6-0	Apr15 3-2	Nov22 0-1		Mar21 2-0	Dec27 4-1	Nov15 0-2	Feb28 3-3	Apr11 4-0	Feb14 2-1	Sep06 1-3	Oct04 6-0	
MID ANNANDALE	Mar28 2-1	Jan31 3-1	Nov08 1-1	Oct11 1-1	Feb07 2-2	Sep13 4-4	Dec20 1-0	Sep27 1-2		Aug23 2-2	Dec06 4-2	Jan03 3-2	Mar14 1-2	Apr16 4-1	Apr04 0-2	Jan17 2-3	Oct25 2-3
MONTROSE	Aug30 3-0	Jan01 3-1	Apr11 2-0	Mar28 2-0	Jan10 0-2	Dec13 2-3	Feb14 1-2	Nov08 5-0	Mar07 3-1		Oct25 0-2	Nov22 2-0	Mar14 4-1	Aug16 2-0	Jan17 0-3	Oct04 1-2	
NITHSDALE W	Dec27 3-1	Jan17 5-3	Jan01 3-1	Sep20 4-0	Nov22 4-2	Oct11 4-3	Aug16 3-2	Aug30 2-1	Feb28 8-0	Apr18 3-1		Jan10 7-1	Feb07 2-0	Jan31 6-2	Nov08 3-0	Feb21 6-1	Sep27 0-0
PEEBLES	Apr18 7-1	Dec06 3-1	Sep06 4-3	Nov29 2-0	Apr29 4-0	Jan17 5-0	Apr20 1-1	Oct25 1-1	Aug30 4-0	Apr03 4-3	Mar21 3-2		Jan10 5-1	Dec20 0-1	Sep20 0-1	Aug16 1-0	
QUEEN OF SOUTH	Oct25 0-0	Oct04 3-1	Mar07 0-2	Nov15 2-0	Mar21 2-0	Apr11 2-0	Feb21 3-1	Aug16 0-0	Nov01 1-1	Dec06 2-1	Oct02 1-6	Jan31 0-0		Jan10 5-1	Dec20 4-0	Sep20 0-1	Aug30 1-0
ROYAL ALBERT	Jan17 3-2	Feb14 1-5	Feb28 0-0	Dec13 7-0	Apr27 1-1	Jan03 3-1	Mar21 4-2	Dec20 2-0	Apr18 2-3	Apr04 2-1	Mar07 1-4	Oct11 2-2	Aug23 1-1		Nov29 2-0	Apr25 3-0	
SOLWAY STAR	Jan03 5-0	Aug16 4-1	Mar21 0-0	Apr11 1-1	Nov01 3-2	Oct18 2-1	Aug30 1-0	Nov08 2-1	Dec13 1-1	Dec27 0-0	Feb28 1-1	Oct18 1-0	Apr13 1-0			Mar07 0-0	Nov22 7-1
VALE OF LEVEN	Oct11 5-2	Apr11 1-1	Nov01 1-1	Jan10 4-0	Aug23 3-0	Dec27 2-1	Sep13 2-1	Nov29 3-1	Dec13 4-1	Sep27 6-2	Mar14 2-2	Nov15 2-1	Feb28 2-1	Oct18 3-1	Jan31 0-0		
DUMBARTON H	Nov15 2-2	Nov29 1-0		Sep13 0-3	Dec13 3-2			Oct11 1-1	Oct18 3-1		Aug23 1-4		Dec27 6-3		Dec31 3-1		

DIVISION 1 FINAL TABLE

	P	W	D	L	F	A	Pts
Rangers	38	25	10	3	76	26	60
Airdrie	38	25	7	6	85	31	57
Hibernian	38	22	8	8	78	43	52
Celtic	38	18	8	12	77	44	44
Cowdenbeath	38	16	10	12	76	65	42
St Mirren	38	18	4	16	65	63	40
Partick T	38	14	10	14	60	61	38
Dundee	38	14	8	16	47	54	36
Raith R	38	14	8	16	53	61	36
Hearts	38	12	11	15	64	68	35
St Johnstone	38	12	11	15	57	72	35
Kilmarnock	38	12	9	17	53	64	33
Hamilton A	38	15	3	20	50	63	33
Morton	38	12	9	17	46	69	33
Aberdeen	38	11	10	17	46	56	32
Falkirk	38	12	8	18	44	54	32
Queen's Park	38	12	8	18	50	71	32
Motherwell	38	10	10	18	54	63	30
Ayr U	38	11	8	19	43	65	30
T Lanark	38	11	8	19	53	84	30

DIVISION 2 FINAL TABLE

	P	W	D	L	F	A	Pts
Dundee U	38	20	10	8	58	44	50
Clydebank	38	20	8	10	65	42	48
Clyde	38	20	7	11	72	39	47
Alloa	38	17	11	10	57	41	45
Arbroath	38	16	10	12	47	46	42
Bo'ness	38	16	9	13	71	48	41
Broxburn U	38	16	9	13	48	54	41
Dumbarton	38	15	10	13	45	44	40
East Fife	38	17	5	16	66	58	39
King's Park	38	15	8	15	54	46	38
Stenhousemuir	38	15	7	16	51	58	37
Arthurlie	38	14	8	16	56	60	36
Dunfermline A	38	14	7	17	62	57	35
Albion R	38	15	5	18	58	64	35
Armadale	38	15	5	18	55	62	35
Bathgate	38	12	10	16	58	74	34
St Bernard's	38	14	4	20	52	71	32
E Stirling	38	11	8	19	58	72	30
Johnstone	38	12	4	22	53	85	28
Forfar A	38	10	7	21	46	67	27

DIVISION 3 FINAL TABLE

	P	W	D	L	F	A	Pts
Nithsdale W	30	18	7	5	81	40	43
Queen of South	30	17	6	7	67	32	40
Solway Star	30	15	10	5	41	28	40
Vale of Leven	30	17	4	9	61	43	38
Lochgelly U	30	15	4	11	59	41	34
Leith A	30	13	5	12	48	42	31
Helensburgh	30	12	7	11	68	60	31
Peebles	30	12	7	11	64	57	31
Royal Albert	30	9	8	13	48	61	26
Clackmannan	30	10	6	14	35	48	26
Galston	30	10	6	14	39	70	26
Dykehead	30	7	11	11	30	47	25
Beith	30	9	6	15	62	74	24
Brechin C	30	9	4	16	51	61	24
Mid Annandale	30	7	7	16	47	70	21
Montrose	30	8	4	18	39	66	20
Dumbarton H	17	5	3	9	25	47	13

Season 1925-26

SFA Cup

1st Round

Jan 23	Aberdeen	8	St Bernard's	1
Jan 23	Albion R	6	Nithsdale W	1
Jan 23	Arbroath	8	Berwick R	0
Jan 23	Arthurlie	5	Armadale	4
Jan 23	Bathgate	5	E Stirling	4
Jan 23	Bo'ness	2	East Fife	1
Jan 23	Brechin C	12	Thornhill	1
Jan 23	Clyde	3	Dunfermline A	0
Jan 23	Cowdenbeath	1	Hamilton A	2
Jan 23	Douglas W	1	Forfar A	4
Jan 23	Dumbarton	1	Buckie T	1
Jan 20	Dundee	2	Inverness Cal	0
Jan 23	Dundee U	1	Hearts	1
Jan 23	Dykehead	1	Morton	1
Jan 23	Falkirk	10	Breadalbane	0
Jan 23	Hibernian	1	Broxburn U	1
Jan 23	Kilmarnock	0	Celtic	5
Jan 23	King's Park	5	Peterhead	2
Jan 23	Leith A	2	Civil Service	0
Jan 23	Montrose	4	Clacknacuddin	0
Jan 23	Partick T	3	Motherwell	0
Jan 23	Peebles R	7	Keith	3
Jan 23	Queen of South	0	Airdrie	0
Jan 23	Queen's Park	4	Clydebank	2
Jan 23	Raith R	3	Ayr U	1
Jan 23	Rangers	3	Lochgelly U	0
Jan 23	Royal Albert	0	Alloa	1
Jan 23	Solway Star	2	Johnstone	2
Jan 23	St Johnstone	6	Nairn Co	1
Jan 23	St Mirren	4	Mid-Annandale	0
Jan 23	Stenhousemuir	1	Vale of Leven	1
Jan 23	T Lanark	7	Moor Park	0

Replays

Jan 26	Hibernian	1	Broxburn U	0
Jan 26	Johnstone	0	Solway Star	3
Jan 27	Airdrie	7	Queen of South	0
Jan 27	Buckie T	1	Dumbarton	2
Jan 27	Hearts	1	Dundee U	1
Jan 27	Morton	4	Dykehead	1
Jan 27	Vale of Leven	1	Stenhousemuir	2
Feb 1	Dundee U	6	Hearts	0

played at Tynecastle

2nd Round

Feb 6	Aberdeen	0	Dundee	0
Feb 6	Albion R	1	Peebles R	1
Feb 6	Alloa	2	Hearts	5
Feb 6	Arbroath	0	St Mirren	0
Feb 6	Arthurlie	2	Clyde	2
Feb 6	Bo'ness	1	Bathgate	1
Feb 6	Celtic	4	Hamilton A	0
Feb 6	Falkirk	5	Montrose	1
Feb 6	Forfar A	2	Dumbarton	2
Feb 6	Hibernian	2	Airdrie	3
Feb 6	Morton	3	Raith R	1
Feb 6	Partick T	4	King's Park	1
Feb 6	Rangers	1	Stenhousemuir	0
Feb 6	Solway Star	0	Brechin C	3
Feb 6	St Johnstone	7	Queen's Park	2
Feb 6	T Lanark	6	Leith A	1

Replays

Feb 9	Clyde	1	Arthurlie	0
Feb 9	St Mirren	3	Arbroath	0
Feb 10	Bathgate	3	Bo'ness	1
Feb 10	Dumbarton	4	Forfar A	1
Feb 10	Dundee	0	Aberdeen	3
Feb 10	Peebles R	0	Albion R	4

3rd Round

Feb 20	Aberdeen	2	St Johnstone	2
Feb 20	Bathgate	2	Airdrie	5
Feb 20	Dumbarton	3	Clyde	0
Feb 20	Falkirk	0	Rangers	2
Feb 20	Hearts	0	Celtic	4
Feb 20	Morton	1	Albion R	0
Feb 20	St Mirren	2	Partick T	1
Feb 20	T Lanark	4	Brechin C	0

Replay

Feb 24	St Johnstone	0	Aberdeen	0
Mar 1	Aberdeen	1	St Johnstone	0

played at Aberdeen

4th Round

Mar 6	Celtic	6	Dumbarton	1
Mar 6	Morton	0	Rangers	4
Mar 6	St Mirren	2	Airdrie	0
Mar 6	T Lanark	1	Aberdeen	1

Replays

Mar 10	Aberdeen	3	T Lanark	0

Semi-finals

Mar 20	Aberdeen	1	Celtic	2

played at Tynecastle

Mar 20	Rangers	0	St Mirren	1

played at Celtic Park

Final

Apr 10	Celtic	0	St Mirren	2

played at Hampden Park

DIVISION 1

	ABERDEEN	AIRDRIE	CELTIC	CLYDEBANK	COWDENBEATH	DUNDEE	DUNDEE U	FALKIRK	HAMILTON A	HEARTS	HIBERNIAN	KILMARNOCK	MORTON	MOTHERWELL	PARTICK T	QUEEN'S PARK	RAITH R	RANGERS	ST JOHNSTONE	ST MIRREN
ABERDEEN	—	Feb27 3-1	Nov07 2-4	Dec19 4-1	Aug29 2-1	Jan01 2-1	Apr03 1-0	Jan16 0-0	Aug15 3-3	Dec05 0-2	Oct10 5-0	Oct31 3-2	Sep26 1-2	Mar13 1-0	Feb17 0-0	Jan04 3-1	Apr17 1-1	Sep12 3-1	Nov21 0-1	Sep28 1-2
AIRDRIE	Aug22 4-1	—	Oct03 5-1	Nov07 2-0	Jan04 3-2	Nov14 4-1	Dec26 0-1	Jan01 2-1	Oct24 2-2	Feb13 5-1	Mar27 2-2	Apr17 2-0	Dec05 3-2	Mar10 2-0	Jan16 1-3	Mar13 6-0	Feb24 2-1	Sep05 2-1	Sep19 7-1	Nov28 2-1
CELTIC	Mar30 4-1	Dec19 3-2	—	Dec05 1-1	Sep12 6-1	Oct31 0-0	Apr24 6-2	Sep26 3-1	Aug29 2-0	Nov25 3-0	Aug15 5-0	Apr03 0-0	Apr14 3-1	Jan30 3-1	Jan04 3-0	Oct13 4-1	Jan09 1-0	Jan09 2-2	Mar23 4-1	Mar09 6-1
CLYDEBANK	Sep19 0-0	Dec12 0-1	Aug22 1-2	—	Oct31 4-3	Jan30 1-2	Oct03 6-1	Nov14 2-3	Apr17 1-5	Mar13 0-1	Feb20 5-1	Feb13 2-1	Apr10 1-1	Oct17 3-2	Nov28 3-0	Dec05 2-3	Apr10 2-2	Jan02 2-2	Jan02 2-0	Sep05 1-0
COWDENBEATH	Jan09 2-1	Apr10 1-0	Dec26 1-1	Feb06 5-2	—	Sep19 5-0	Aug22 3-1	Dec05 4-2	Feb27 1-2	Jan02 4-2	Nov07 3-1	Mar13 5-0	Nov21 2-2	Oct03 3-1	Apr17 7-3	Dec23 2-3	Oct17 2-3	Jan30 1-0	Sep05 1-1	Oct24 1-0
DUNDEE	Oct17 3-2	Apr03 0-1	Mar17 1-2	Sep26 3-1	Apr24 4-3	—	Nov21 0-0	Feb17 1-0	Sep12 2-2	Oct03 1-0	Dec26 1-4	Dec12 1-0	Aug15 3-0	Oct05 1-2	Nov07 3-1	Apr10 2-1	Jan02 1-1	Feb27 1-5	Aug22 0-1	Jan09 1-1
DUNDEE U	Nov14 2-0	Mar20 1-2	Sep19 1-0	Mar27 5-0	Jan16 1-2	Jan04 0-1	—	Aug29 1-2	Oct10 2-5	Feb24 2-3	Feb13 2-2	Oct24 3-1	Oct31 2-2	Sep09 1-1	Dec05 1-0	Mar06 1-2	Sep19 2-1	Apr17 0-0	Feb13 1-2	Dec05 1-2
FALKIRK	Oct03 2-1	Oct17 2-1	Feb13 1-1	Apr24 2-2	Mar20 1-0	Mar06 1-0	Jan09 1-0	—	Nov21 1-0	Jan30 1-1	Apr17 1-0	Sep05 2-3	Nov07 2-0	Jan02 3-3	Dec26 2-2	Dec12 1-4	Sep19 2-1	Feb24 0-0	Oct24 2-0	Aug22 1-1
HAMILTON A	Jan30 1-1	Jan02 3-4	Apr17 1-3	Apr03 2-0	Nov28 2-1	Feb13 0-0	Dec12 3-1	Mar13 1-1	—	Aug22 3-0	Nov14 1-0	Sep19 2-2	Feb24 2-5	Oct17 0-2	Mar06 2-1	Oct31 1-0	Sep05 3-1	Jan09 3-3	Oct03 7-2	Dec19 3-2
HEARTS	Sep21 1-0	Aug29 0-2	Sep12 1-2	Sep12 7-0	Oct10 4-3	Mar27 2-2	Nov07 1-0	Apr15 1-1	Feb10 4-0	—	Jan01 1-4	Nov28 1-0	Mar13 6-1	Oct24 3-1	Jan09 4-2	Apr03 5-1	Sep30 3-0	Dec12 4-2	Dec26 1-0	
HIBERNIAN	Jan02 0-0	Jan30 1-4	Jan16 4-4	Nov21 5-1	Mar06 1-2	Sep05 3-5	Apr10 3-1	Oct31 5-1	Dec05 3-1	Oct17 0-1	—	Aug22 8-0	Jan13 3-4	Feb13 1-2	Sep19 3-3	Feb20 0-0	Mar20 0-2	Sep21 0-3	Jan04 2-0	Oct03 1-1
KILMARNOCK	Mar17 3-0	Oct10 3-2	Feb10 2-1	Aug29 2-2	Sep26 1-1	Jan16 5-2	Jan02 2-3	Dec19 2-3	Jan04 4-1	Mar20 5-1	Apr24 2-1	—	Sep12 2-0	Apr10 1-2	Feb13 3-3	Aug15 2-1	Nov21 3-0	Dec05 2-2	Nov07 3-2	Oct17 2-3
MORTON	Dec30 2-0	Apr24 3-2	Oct24 0-5	Mar10 2-2	Dec12 3-4	Jan30 3-0	Dec26 3-1	Apr17 3-1	Aug22 3-0	Sep05 1-1	Jan09 2-5	Sep12 1-2	—	Nov14 1-1	Oct03 1-1	Apr03 2-1	Oct17 1-3	Apr03 1-3	Oct17 1-2	Jan02 3-3
MOTHERWELL	Oct24 1-1	Sep26 2-1	Mar27 2-1	Aug15 2-1	Feb20 2-1	Mar20 4-0	Feb06 3-0	Oct10 3-1	Jan01 4-1	Dec19 3-1	Sep12 2-5	Feb27 1-2	Jan04 1-2	—	Apr03 1-0	Aug29 4-1	Nov07 1-0	Nov25 1-3	Jan16 3-1	Dec05 1-0
PARTICK T	Dec12 2-2	Oct31 2-3	Apr05 0-0	Jan01 2-2	Aug15 3-1	Feb23 0-1	Feb27 2-0	Sep12 2-2	Sep26 2-3	Apr24 3-3	Jan09 1-4	Nov14 2-1	Mar27 2-4	Nov28 3-3	—	Jan30 3-3	Dec19 2-1	Oct10 2-0	Mar20 3-1	Apr13 3-2
QUEEN'S PARK	Sep05 0-1	Nov24 1-5	Feb13 1-4	Mar20 4-1	Dec05 3-4	Oct17 1-3	Apr03 3-1	Sep12 6-2	Sep19 3-4	Sep26 2-0	Mar27 2-2	Apr17 2-0	Feb27 0-3	Oct03 2-1		—	Aug22 4-0	Nov07 3-6	Feb27 2-0	Feb16 1-0
RAITH R	Nov28 0-1	Sep12 2-1	Nov14 1-0	Feb27 1-3	Jan01 3-0	Oct10 1-2	Aug15 4-2	Mar27 1-0	Apr10 1-0	Jan04 1-0	Sep26 1-3	Dec26 1-0	Jan16 1-3	Dec12 0-3	Aug29 2-1	Apr24 4-0	—	Oct31 1-0	Feb10 1-0	Mar13 1-3
RANGERS	Mar27 0-1	Feb10 1-2	Oct17 1-0	Jan04 3-1	Nov14 3-0	Oct24 1-2	Apr05 2-1	Nov28 2-3	Apr24 2-0	Jan16 2-2	Dec12 3-1	Oct03 3-0	Aug29 4-1	Aug22 1-0	Jan02 2-1	Mar10 1-2	Feb13 4-2	—	Dec26 0-1	Sep19 4-1
ST JOHNSTONE	Feb13 1-1	Jan09 3-7	Nov28 0-3	Oct10 3-1	Nov14 1-1	Dec19 0-0	Sep12 2-1	Apr17 2-1	Mar06 1-1	Mar06 1-1	Aug30 0-0	Jan01 3-1	Feb26 2-2	Jan01 2-2	Mar13 1-4	Sep26 2-1	Dec05 3-1	Aug15 0-3	—	Nov14 1-0
ST MIRREN	Apr24 3-0	Aug15 1-1	Dec12 0-2	Jan16 3-0	Mar27 2-1	Aug29 2-2	Sep26 2-0	Jan04 2-0	Nov07 1-0	Oct31 1-4	Feb27 2-1	Jan01 2-1	Oct10 3-0	Feb23 2-2	Nov21 2-1	Sep12 3-1	Jan30 0-3	Mar23 3-2	Apr03 3-1	—

DIVISION 2

	ALBION R	ALLOA	ARBROATH	ARMADALE	ARTHURLIE	AYR U	BATHGATE	BO'NESS	BROXBURN U	CLYDE	DUMBARTON	DUNFERMLINE A	EAST FIFE	E STIRLING	KING'S PARK	NITHSDALE W	QUEEN OF SOUTH	ST BERNARD'S	STENHOUSEMUIR	T LANARK
ALBION R		Mar27 1-2	Aug15 2-0	Jan25 0-1	Feb27 3-2	Aug29 0-0	Mar13 3-2	Dec19 2-0	Dec12 5-2	Jan09 1-3	Jan30 11-1	Jan02 1-0	Sep12 2-0	Apr10 3-1	Oct10 4-1	Feb17 3-0	Oct31 3-4	Sep26 2-4	Oct17 4-4	Apr14 0-0
ALLOA	Nov07 1-2		Sep26 2-2	Feb27 4-0	Aug29 1-2	Feb09 0-1	Feb13 4-2	Jan30 6-0	Oct05 0-3	Oct13 0-0	Dec12 0-2	Oct17 1-1	Dec26 2-1	Mar20 1-0	Jan02 0-1	Sep12 2-4	Jan09 2-3	Apr10 3-3	Mar06 1-2	Nov21 2-1
ARBROATH	Feb24 4-2	Apr17 2-3		Mar27 2-2	Nov21 4-3	Jan02 1-3	Dec05 4-0	Mar13 4-1	Mar06 5-1	Apr10 0-1	Sep19 6-0	Oct03 5-0	Aug29 2-4	Nov07 2-1	Jan09 0-1	Dec23 1-5	Sep12 2-4	Nov14 4-1	Jan30 3-0	Oct24 2-1
ARMADALE	Apr03 3-1	Dec05 1-2	Dec12 3-0		Aug15 2-2	Mar13 1-0	Jan01 5-1	Sep26 1-3	Nov07 4-3	Jan30 1-3	Oct31 6-2	Dec19 0-5	Oct10 4-5	Feb19 2-2	Sep12 4-1	Aug29 2-4	Oct17 4-3	Jan09 5-1	Apr17 3-1	Feb13 3-0
ARTHURLIE	Sep05 4-2	Mar13 3-1	Apr03 3-1	Dec26 7-4		Dec05 2-2	Oct17 2-1	Nov14 3-0	Dec19 4-0	Jan02 1-2	Nov03 2-6	Nov28 5-0	Oct03 4-1	Apr17 1-0	Feb13 6-6	Jan30 2-0	Nov07 2-3	Oct24 1-2	Apr17 1-2	
AYR U	Jan01 2-2	Aug15 2-1	Aug22 5-0	Sep05 2-0	Mar06 1-0		Apr17 4-1	Feb20 4-1	Oct03 5-0	Feb24 2-0	Dec26 1-1	Nov14 1-2	Oct31 2-2	Jan09 5-0	Oct24 0-0	Nov28 6-1	Mar27 3-0	Jan30 2-0	Dec12 1-1	Sep19 0-0
BATHGATE	Sep19 3-1	Sep05 3-1	Mar03 4-0	Aug22 3-1	Jan04 1-3	Nov21 2-1		Feb24 0-4	Jan16 2-2	Mar20 3-7	Mar27 5-0	Apr10 2-4	Apr05 1-1	Jan13 1-1	Nov28 1-2	Oct24 1-1	Nov14 1-2	Mar06 1-3	Jan02 1-4	Oct03 2-1
BO'NESS	Oct24 4-1	Oct03 0-0	Sep05 1-3	Mar20 2-1	Apr10 1-0	Jan04 1-3	Nov07 4-0		Jan01 2-0	Nov21 4-3	Feb27 2-0	Aug22 3-1	Dec12 1-2	Apr17 0-4	Mar27 3-1	Jan16 4-1	Apr17 5-0	Dec26 6-3	Sep19 5-1	Feb17 1-1
BROXBURN U	Feb13 4-3	Feb20 0-5	Oct31 1-2	Apr24 3-4	Mar20 1-2	Feb27 3-4	Sep26 2-3	Aug29 3-2		Sep12 1-1	Nov14 1-1	Jan30 3-4	Mar27 2-7	Oct17 1-5	Aug15 0-1	Oct10 0-2	Apr17 2-2	Jan02 4-7	Jan09 1-2	Dec05 0-1
CLYDE	Aug22 1-0	Jan16 1-0	Nov28 2-1	Oct03 4-1	Mar27 2-1	Oct17 0-2	Dec12 3-1	Jan02 4-0	Feb17 3-2		Apr17 6-0	Feb27 0-1	Mar13 1-3	Sep19 7-1	Nov14 3-1	Nov07 2-0	Dec26 5-0	Oct24 4-2	Feb13 2-1	Dec25 1-0
DUMBARTON	Dec05 0-1	Apr24 0-0	Jan01 1-0	Feb17 2-0	Sep12 0-0	Sep26 1-1	Oct10 4-1	Aug15 3-0	Feb24 5-1	Aug29 1-1		Mar10 1-3	Jan16 2-1	Oct24 3-0	Jan04 4-1	Apr03 2-2	Mar20 1-1	Nov21 1-0	Nov07 1-1	Nov07 1-1
DUNFERMLINE A	Apr17 1-1	Jan01 1-0	Dec26 3-0	Oct24 7-1	Oct10 0-0	Mar20 2-1	Sep12 4-0	Apr03 4-1	Nov21 6-1	Sep26 5-5	Nov28 4-0		Sep17 5-3	Feb13 6-2	Feb20 4-1	Aug15 4-0	Dec12 3-0	Aug29 1-1	Nov07 1-1	Jan16 1-1
EAST FIFE	Mar06 1-3	Oct24 1-0	Mar20 4-0	Apr10 7-1	Feb20 2-2	Feb13 7-3	Dec19 4-1	Sep05 2-1	Dec05 6-1	Oct17 3-3	Sep19 5-1	Jan30 2-1		Jan30 3-1	Nov07 4-3	Apr24 4-2	Oct03 1-0	Nov21 0-1	Aug22 1-1	Jan02 3-1
E STIRLING	Nov28 0-1	Oct31 1-1	Jan16 2-1	Nov14 1-1	Feb17 3-1	Oct10 2-4	Aug15 2-2	Sep12 0-2	Apr03 8-2	Jan04 1-3	Mar13 3-1	Dec05 1-5	Sep26 2-1		Aug29 0-0	Mar06 3-2	Jan02 4-2	Apr24 2-0	Dec19 0-3	Mar27 2-1
KING'S PARK	Dec26 1-2	Sep19 2-0	Oct17 2-2	Feb06 1-3	Oct31 0-0	Jan16 0-0	Apr03 4-2	Feb13 1-3	Jan04 7-1	Apr24 4-3	Aug22 2-0	Sep05 5-0	Feb27 7-3	Jan01 0-0		Nov21 2-0	Dec05 2-0	Dec12 0-0	Oct03 0-0	Mar20 3-3
NITHSDALE W	Oct03 3-0	Feb20 0-3	Feb27 2-3	Jan02 4-2	Dec12 3-1	Feb06 1-1	Jan09 2-1	Oct31 0-0	Dec26 4-0	Apr03 0-2	Sep05 5-1	Mar13 0-1	Nov14 3-1	Aug22 3-3	Jan30 2-5		Sep19 3-2	Dec05 2-1	Mar20 5-1	Oct17 1-0
QUEEN OF SOUTH	Mar20 3-3	Aug22 4-0	Jan04 2-2	Jan16 2-2	Nov07 2-0	Feb27 1-3	Mar06 4-2	Oct24 1-1	Aug15 2-1	Feb13 3-4	Feb06 3-0	Apr17 2-2	Feb06 3-4	Mar10 3-0	Apr10 4-1	Jan01 0-3		Oct10 2-0	Sep05 2-2	Dec19 0-2
ST BERNARD'S	Jan04 3-1	Nov28 2-1	Feb13 0-0	Jan09 6-2	Jan16 5-3	Oct31 1-2	Oct17 4-0	Aug22 1-1	Jan01 8-0	Oct03 1-2	Feb06 3-2	Apr17 1-4	Sep05 2-2	Mar13 4-0	Feb10 1-0	Mar27 1-2	Feb20 4-1		Apr03 3-2	Feb27 3-2
STENHOUSEMUIR	Jan16 3-0	Nov14 1-1	Oct10 3-1	Jan04 3-1	Apr24 2-3	Sep12 5-0	Aug29 1-0	Dec05 2-1	Oct31 6-2	Oct31 1-0	Apr10 4-0	Mar27 1-3	Jan01 1-1	Feb27 2-0	Feb10 1-2	Sep26 3-0	Mar13 3-2	Aug15 2-1		Dec26 1-0
T LANARK	Nov14 3-2	Jan04 4-1	Apr24 4-2	Nov28 3-0	Jan01 3-0	Apr03 1-1	Jan30 4-3	Oct10 2-0	Mar13 2-0	Mar17 4-1	Jan09 1-2	Aug15 3-2	Dec12 4-0	Sep26 1-1	Apr09 4-1	Aug29 3-2	Sep12 1-0	Feb24 4-2	3-0	

DIVISION 3

	BEITH	BRECHIN C	CLACKMANNAN	DYKEHEAD	FORFAR A	GALSTON	HELENSBURGH	JOHNSTONE	LEITH A	LOCHGELLY U	MID ANNANDALE	MONTROSE	PEEBLES	ROYAL ALBERT	SOLWAY STAR	VALE OF LEVEN
BEITH		Jan01 7-3	Jan09 2-0	Feb27 2-2	Nov07 2-2		Jan30 2-2	Apr21 3-1	Apr19 2-4	Nov21 5-1	Mar27 2-0	Mar13 4-1	Aug15 1-2	Oct17 2-1	Sep12 2-5	Feb20 3-1
BRECHIN C	Apr03 3-0			Aug29 3-1	Jan16 2-3	Jan02 9-2	Mar06 2-2	Dec05 0-4	Apr19 0-1	Nov07 4-4	Aug15 5-3	Apr26 4-1		Mar27 4-2	Apr17 4-2	Sep26 4-5
CLACKMANNAN	Nov14 7-3	Mar13 1-1		Oct03 2-2			Jan23 2-2	Mar27 1-1	Apr24 3-3	Aug22 3-0	Nov28 3-2	Dec05 2-2	Sep12 2-4	Jan01 4-3	Oct24 1-7	
DYKEHEAD	Sep26 3-1	Nov28 3-0	Jan30 5-1		Jan02 2-3		Dec19 2-0	Aug15 2-1	Sep12 2-0	Jan09 2-1	Aug29 2-1	Nov07 4-1	Feb13 8-2	Apr10 2-2	Mar20 1-1	
FORFAR A		Oct31 3-1	Sep26 5-0	Aug22 2-1		Nov14 1-1	Aug15 3-1	Sep19 3-5	Mar13 5-3	Oct17 1-0	Oct10 5-2	Mar06 3-2	Jan30 2-0	Dec12 2-1	Jan09 1-0	Jan01 6-2
GALSTON	Oct24 3-3	Sep12 6-1		Jan01 2-2				Dec12 2-0			Nov28 1-2	Aug22 1-5				
HELENSBURGH	Oct10 2-1	Nov14 4-3	Nov07 2-0	Feb20 0-1	Feb27 3-0	Dec05 6-0		Sep12 4-1	Mar20 3-2	Mar13 1-1	Feb13 1-1	Apr17 5-1	Jan09 1-0	Sep26 5-1	Jan16 1-1	Jan16 1-5
JOHNSTONE	Oct03 3-0	Apr10 2-3	Oct17 2-2	Dec12 1-3	Sep05 4-0		Nov28 2-4		Aug22 2-2	Jan02 2-2	Oct24 6-2	Mar20 3-1	Mar13 2-1	Jan30 3-0	Feb20 3-4	Oct10 3-4
LEITH A	Mar06 4-0	Dec12 0-2	Oct10 4-0	Apr14 3-0	Oct24 2-1	Aug29 3-5	Nov21 5-3	Apr17 4-1			Jan30 2-2	Apr10 4-0	Aug15 6-1	Jan09 2-0	Sep26 2-0	Feb13 2-1
LOCHGELLY U	Jan16 5-2	Jan09 7-2	Dec12 5-0	Feb06 4-4	Mar20 1-0	Aug15 5-2	Sep26 1-2	Apr03 2-2			Mar06 0-1	Mar27 3-3	Feb20 5-3	Apr24 1-1	Nov07 1-0	
MID ANNANDALE	Oct31 4-1	Mar20 0-3	Feb06 5-2	Oct17 4-1	Dec19 2-1	Jan01 1-0	Jan16 3-2	Feb27 2-1	Sep12 0-3			Nov14 1-0	Dec26 2-0	Mar13 1-3	Aug22 1-0	Dec05 3-1
MONTROSE	Dec12 4-3	Aug22 5-2	Feb13 2-1	Apr24 4-1	Sep12 0-2		Jan02 1-2	Feb27 4-1	Feb20 1-0	Jan01 2-1	Jan30 4-0		Sep26 5-3	Apr03 4-0	Nov21 4-2	
PEEBLES	Jan02 0-4	Oct24 3-0		Mar27 3-1	Apr10 2-1		Apr03 2-3	Feb13 2-1	Jan01 0-6	Oct31 5-0	Nov21 2-4			Apr17 1-4	Oct17 5-0	Aug29 2-4
ROYAL ALBERT		Feb27 6-1	Aug15 7-1	Oct10 2-1	Nov21 5-2	Nov07 5-4	Feb06 2-0	Jan01 1-0	Jan04 0-6	Dec05 0-0	Aug29 3-0	Apr16 5-3	Mar20 0-5		Jan16 4-1	Sep12 2-4
SOLWAY STAR	Mar20 2-1	Jan30 0-3	Dec26 0-0	Mar13 2-1	Aug29 2-1	Oct10 2-1	Dec12 0-2	Apr03 2-3	Nov28 0-0	Feb13 1-1	Jan02 0-1	Sep05 1-2	Mar06 7-1	Oct24 5-2		Aug15 1-6
VALE OF LEVEN	Aug22 3-1		Oct31 2-3	Nov21 2-1	Mar27 0-1		Oct17 3-0	Feb06 6-3	Sep19 2-4	Dec19 8-2	Apr03 2-2	Jan09 5-3	Dec12 4-2	Nov14 2-0	Feb27 1-2	

DIVISION 1 FINAL TABLE

	P	W	D	L	F	A	Pts
Celtic	38	25	8	5	97	40	58
Airdrie	38	23	4	11	95	54	50
Hearts	38	21	8	9	87	56	50
St Mirren	38	20	7	11	62	52	47
Motherwell	38	19	8	11	67	46	46
Rangers	38	19	6	13	79	55	44
Cowdenbeath	38	18	6	14	87	68	42
Falkirk	38	14	14	10	61	57	42
Kilmarnock	38	17	7	14	79	77	41
Dundee	38	14	9	15	47	59	37
Aberdeen	38	13	10	15	49	54	36
Hamilton A	38	13	9	16	68	79	35
Queen's Park	38	15	4	19	70	81	34
Partick T	38	10	13	15	64	73	33
Morton	38	12	7	19	57	84	31
Hibernian	38	12	6	20	72	77	30
Dundee U	38	11	6	21	52	74	28
St Johnstone	38	9	10	19	43	78	28
Raith R	38	11	4	23	46	81	26
Clydebank	38	7	8	23	55	92	22

DIVISION 2 FINAL TABLE

	P	W	D	L	F	A	Pts
Dunfermline A	38	26	7	5	109	43	59
Clyde	38	24	5	9	87	50	53
Ayr U	38	20	12	6	77	39	52
East Fife	38	20	9	9	98	73	49
Stenhousemuir	38	19	10	9	74	52	48
T Lanark	38	19	8	11	72	46	46
Arthurlie	38	17	5	16	81	75	39
Bo'ness	38	17	5	16	66	70	39
Albion R	38	16	6	16	78	71	38
Arbroath	38	17	4	17	80	73	38
Dumbarton	38	14	10	14	54	78	38
Nithsdale W	38	15	7	16	78	82	37
King's Park	38	14	9	15	67	73	37
St Bernard's	38	15	5	18	86	82	35
Armadale	38	14	5	19	82	101	33
Alloa	38	11	8	19	54	63	30
Queen of South	38	10	8	20	64	88	28
E Stirling	38	10	7	21	59	89	27
Bathgate	38	7	6	25	60	105	20
Broxburn U	38	4	6	28	55	127	14

DIVISION 3 FINAL TABLE

	P	W	D	L	F	A	Pts
Helensburgh	30	16	6	8	66	47	38
Leith A	29	16	5	8	73	41	37
Forfar A	28	16	3	9	61	42	35
Dykehead	28	14	5	9	62	47	33
Royal Albert	28	16	1	11	75	61	33
Mid Annandale	29	14	3	12	50	54	31
Vale of Leven	26	14	2	10	78	55	30
Montrose	26	12	3	11	56	58	27
Lochgelly U	29	9	9	11	58	63	27
Brechin C	28	12	3	13	67	73	27
Solway Star	29	9	6	14	50	62	24
Beith	27	9	4	14	58	68	22
Johnstone	29	7	6	16	55	74	20
Peebles	26	6	9	17	52	76	18
Clackmannan	25	5	8	12	42	74	18
Galston	15	4	4	7	38	46	12

Season 1926-27

SFA Cup

1st Round

Jan 22	Aberdeen 4	Helensburgh 2
Jan 22	Alloa 3	Morton 0
Jan 22	Ayr U 2	Airdrie 2
Jan 22	Bathgate 2	Dunfermline A ...2
Jan 22	Beith 7	Huntly 1
Jan 22	Bo'ness 3	Lochgelly U 0
Jan 22	Brechin C 8	Vale of Leithen ...3
Jan 22	Broxburn U 2	Armadale 1
Jan 15	Buckie T 2	Fraserburgh 1
Jan 22	Clyde 3	Hearts 2
Jan 22	Clydebank 6	Douglas W 0
Jan 22	Cowdenbeath 3	Hibernian 0
Jan 22	Dundee 3	Motherwell 0
Jan 19	Dundee U 7	Arbroath A 0
Feb 5	Dykehead 3	Montrose 3
Jan 22	East Fife 8	Thornhill 1
Jan 22	E Stirling 0	Dumbarton 1
Jan 22	Elgin C 1	Albion R 0
Jan 22	Falkirk 1	St Johnstone 0
Jan 22	Forfar A 4	Raith R 2
Jan 22	Forres Mechanic ...0	Mid-Annandale ...2
Jan 22	Hamilton A 6	Stranraer 0
Jan 22	Kilmarnock 3	Peebles R 1
Jan 22	King's Park 1	T Lanark 0
Jan 22	Leith A 1	Rangers 4
Jan 25	Nithsdale W 0	Arthurlie 2
Jan 22	Partick T 3	Stenhousemuir ...0
Jan 22	Queen of South ...0	Celtic 0
Jan 22	Queen's Park 2	Inverness Cal ...0
Jan 22	St Bernard's 3	Vale of Atholl 0
Jan 22	St Mirren 2	Arbroath 0
Jan 22	Vale of Leven ...6	Johnstone 2

Replays

Jan 26	Airdrie 2	Ayr U 1
Jan 26	Celtic 4	Queen of South ...1
Jan 26	Dunfermline A 5	Bathgate 2
Feb 7	Montrose 3	Dykehead 1

2nd Round

Feb 5	Alloa 1	Dumbarton 1
Feb 5	Bo'ness 2	Cowdenbeath 1
Feb 5	Brechin C 3	Celtic 6
Feb 12	Broxburn U 2	Montrose 2
Feb 5	Buckie T 2	Beith 0
Feb 5	Dundee U 4	Vale of Leven ...1
Feb 5	Dunfermline A 2	Airdrie 1
Feb 5	East Fife 1	Aberdeen 1
Feb 5	Elgin C 2	Clyde 4
Feb 5	Falkirk 6	Queen's Park 3
Feb 5	Hamilton A 5	Clydebank 1
Feb 5	Kilmarnock 1	Dundee 1
Feb 5	King's Park 2	Partick T 4
Feb 5	Mid-Annandale ...3	Forfar A 0
Feb 5	Rangers 6	St Mirren 0
Feb 5	St Bernard's 0	Arthurlie 3

Replays

Feb 9	Aberdeen 1	East Fife 2
Feb 9	Dumbarton 0	Alloa 4
Feb 9	Dundee 5	Kilmarnock 1
Feb 16	Montrose 1	Broxburn U 0

3rd Round

Feb 19	Alloa 0	Arthurlie 0
Feb 19	Buckie T 0	Bo'ness 3
Feb 19	Clyde 0	Partick T 1
Feb 19	Dundee 2	Celtic 4
Feb 23	Dundee U 2	Montrose 2
Feb 19	East Fife 2	Dunfermline A ...0
Feb 19	Falkirk 3	Mid-Annandale ...0
Feb 19	Rangers 4	Hamilton A 0

Replay

Feb 22	Arthurlie 3	Alloa 0
Feb 24	Montrose 1	Dundee U 3

4th Round

Mar 5	Arthurlie 0	East Fife 3
Mar 5	Bo'ness 2	Celtic 5
Mar 5	Falkirk 2	Rangers 2
Mar 5	Partick T 5	Dundee U 0

Replay

Mar 9	Rangers 0	Falkirk 1

Semi-finals

Mar 26	Celtic 1	Falkirk 0
	played at Ibrox	
Mar 26	East Fife 2	Partick T 1
	played at Tynecastle	

Final

Apr 16	Celtic 3	East Fife 1
	played at Hampden Park	

Newcomers to the First Division, Dunfermline's promotion-winning side that held its place on goal-average; Back row (left to right): T.Burns, R.Wylie, E.Miller, G.Turner. Middle row: E.Dowie, Bain, Mitchell, Herd, Gibb, Wilson, Clark, Masterton. Front row: Paterson (manager), Ritchie, Sutton, Skinner, Dickson, Stein, J.Fraser, J.Farrell (linesman).

DIVISION 1

	ABERDEEN	AIRDRIE	CELTIC	CLYDE	COWDENBEATH	DUNDEE	DUNDEE U	DUNFERMLINE A	FALKIRK	HAMILTON A	HEARTS	HIBERNIAN	KILMARNOCK	MORTON	MOTHERWELL	PARTICK T	QUEEN'S PARK	RANGERS	ST JOHNSTONE	ST MIRREN
ABERDEEN		Apr16 1-1	Mar09 0-0	Aug21 5-2	Dec25 0-0	Oct30 2-1	Mar26 2-2	Dec11 3-1	Jan15 3-0	Oct02 3-3	Nov20 6-5	Jan03 2-5	Sep27 5-1	Sep18 6-1	Apr30 2-0	Nov06 1-4	Sep04 2-0	Feb16 2-2	Oct16 3-1	Nov27 1-0
AIRDRIE	Dec04 2-1		Nov06 2-2	Dec25 1-1	Sep18 5-2	Jan15 3-1	Mar09 7-2	Apr09 6-2	Oct30 2-1	Jan03 7-1	Apr23 0-0	Sep04 3-0	Oct02 2-0	Feb09 4-0	Oct16 1-3	Mar30 3-1	Feb19 5-0	Aug21 3-3	Dec18 6-1	Nov20 2-2
CELTIC	Oct23 6-2	Mar16 2-1		Jan15 7-0	Aug21 2-0	Oct02 0-0	Nov27 7-2	Apr02 2-1	Feb23 3-1	Sep18 2-2	Nov13 1-0	Feb02 2-3	Dec25 4-0	Sep04 3-0	Apr20 3-2	Apr30 2-1	Jan03 2-3	Apr18 0-1	Dec11 4-0	Feb26 6-2
CLYDE	Mar12 5-1	Aug14 2-1	Sep11 2-2		Mar26 0-2	Dec04 2-2	Jan29 1-0	Feb12 1-1	Oct16 2-1	Apr23 0-0	Oct09 2-3	Mar05 2-0	Nov20 1-1	Dec18 6-0	Jan08 1-4	Jan01 0-5	Nov06 5-0	Apr09 0-0	Aug28 1-1	Sep25 1-2
COWDENBEATH	Aug14 0-0	Jan29 6-0	Mar12 2-1	Nov13 1-0		Feb26 0-1	Sep11 4-1	Jan01 1-2	Dec04 3-2	Oct23 5-1	Aug28 2-1	Apr30 2-0	Dec11 3-1	Apr02 3-2	Sep25 1-1	Oct09 1-2	Apr09 1-1	Mar23 1-0	Feb12 0-1	Jan08 5-1
DUNDEE	Jan01 1-1	Sep11 1-0	Feb12 1-2	Apr16 1-2	Oct16 1-2		Aug28 5-0	Sep25 1-1	Mar16 2-3	Apr02 1-0	Aug14 4-1	Nov06 3-0	Mar26 1-2	Nov27 6-1	Jan29 3-1	Jan08 4-2	Apr30 3-0	Dec11 1-1	Mar12 4-1	Oct09 2-1
DUNDEE U	Nov13 2-2	Oct23 2-4	Apr09 3-3	Sep18 3-1	Jan15 0-2	Jan03 1-0		Feb26 4-4	Feb09 0-2	Mar02 1-2	Dec04 5-3	Aug21 0-2	Sep04 1-2	Oct30 0-0	Nov20 0-1	Apr23 2-1	Oct02 2-2	Dec25 2-0	Mar19 1-2	Dec18 2-1
DUNFERMLINE A	Apr23 1-0	Nov27 0-2	Nov20 0-6	Oct02 3-1	Oct30 0-3	Feb16 4-3	Oct16 2-0		Sep04 0-1	Aug21 0-1	Dec18 0-2	Sep18 4-2	Jan03 2-3	Dec25 1-1	Nov06 0-4	Mar09 1-1	Jan15 3-3	Feb23 1-3	Apr16 4-0	Mar26 3-1
FALKIRK	Sep11 1-1	Jan01 2-1	Apr06 4-1	Feb26 3-3	Apr16 2-2	Oct23 3-1	Sep25 5-3	Oct09 2-0		Dec18 8-2	Feb12 2-1	Nov27 2-0	Mar19 0-1	Nov13 6-1	Aug28 1-1	Aug14 1-1	Dec11 6-0	Apr02 3-3	Jan29 4-0	Mar12 1-1
HAMILTON A	Feb12 2-0	Aug28 4-2	Feb16 3-3	Dec11 4-2	Mar05 4-2	Nov20 1-4	Oct09 1-1	Mar12 2-2	Apr30 3-1		Jan08 2-1	Oct16 0-1	Apr09 2-0	Nov06 1-1	Jan01 0-3	Sep11 0-2	Mar26 1-5	Apr16 1-1	Sep25 1-4	Aug14 2-3
HEARTS	Apr02 2-2	Dec11 1-3	Mar30 3-0	Feb23 5-0	Jan03 4-3	Dec25 0-0	Apr16 1-2	Apr30 1-2	Oct02 0-0	Sep04 1-1		Oct30 2-2	Feb19 1-1	Jan15 3-0	Feb05 1-3	Oct16 1-0	Aug21 4-1	Sep18 0-2	Nov27 0-0	Nov06 4-3
HIBERNIAN	Aug28 2-3	Jan08 2-1	Sep25 3-2	Oct23 3-0	Dec18 2-0	Mar19 0-1	Mar12 3-2	Jan29 2-2	Apr09 1-0	Feb26 3-1	Jan01 2-2		Dec04 5-1	Apr23 1-1	Oct09 1-1	Feb12 3-2	Nov20 2-0	Nov13 2-2	Aug14 1-5	Sep11 2-1
KILMARNOCK	Oct09 0-0	Feb12 4-2	Aug14 2-3	Apr02 4-1	Apr23 1-4	Nov13 3-2	Jan08 3-0	Aug28 2-3	Nov06 1-1	Nov27 0-1	Sep25 1-4	Apr20 4-0		Oct16 2-0	Mar12 1-4	Jan29 2-0	Mar05 2-2	Dec18 0-0	Sep11 2-0	Jan01 2-2
MORTON	Jan29 3-4	Sep25 2-1	Jan08 2-6	Apr30 0-2	Nov20 3-2	Apr09 3-1	Jan01 3-1	Aug14 3-0	Mar30 4-1	Mar19 3-0	Sep11 1-3	Dec11 3-0	Feb26 3-2		Feb12 0-3	Mar12 3-0	Dec04 2-0	Oct23 2-8	Oct09 0-2	Aug28 0-2
MOTHERWELL	Dec18 1-0	Feb26 1-5	Dec04 0-1	Sep04 2-0	Feb09 0-0	Sep18 2-5	Apr02 6-0	Mar19 2-1	Jan03 3-3	Oct30 3-1	Oct23 5-1	Feb19 2-1	Aug21 1-0	Oct02 6-0		Nov27 3-1	Dec25 2-1	Jan15 1-4	Nov13 5-2	Apr23 1-0
PARTICK T	Mar19 4-0	Nov13 5-1	Dec18 0-3	Oct30 3-0	Feb23 5-3	Sep04 3-3	Dec11 2-2	Oct23 5-1	Dec25 0-1	Jan15 2-3	Feb26 2-2	Oct02 5-1	Sep18 5-0	Aug21 4-5	Apr09 3-0		Feb08 1-7	Jan03 1-4	Apr02 3-1	Dec04 5-2
QUEEN'S PARK	Jan08 1-1	Oct13 3-3	Aug28 1-6	Mar19 4-0	Nov27 3-1	Apr18 1-4	Feb12 5-3	Sep11 4-1	Apr23 1-2	Nov13 4-0	Mar12 2-0	Apr05 3-4	Oct23 1-0	Apr20 2-1	Aug14 1-2	Sep25 4-3		Mar01 1-2	Jan01 5-2	Jan29 1-0
RANGERS	Sep25 3-2	Mar12 1-1	Jan01 2-1	Nov27 6-0	Nov06 4-1	Apr23 0-0	Aug14 2-0	Aug17 2-0	Nov20 2-1	Dec04 1-4	Jan29 1-0	Mar29 2-0	Apr30 1-0	Mar16 2-1	Sep11 2-0	Aug28 2-1	Oct16 0-1		Jan08 4-2	Feb12 4-0
ST JOHNSTONE	Feb26 1-1	Apr30 1-1	Apr23 1-0	Jan03 1-3	Oct02 1-3	Aug21 0-1	Nov06 4-1	Dec04 1-0	Sep18 4-0	Feb09 3-2	Apr09 1-1	Dec25 0-0	Jan15 3-3	Feb19 4-0	Mar26 0-1	Nov20 1-1	Oct30 1-0	Sep04 2-1		Oct23 0-0
ST MIRREN	Apr09 6-3	Apr02 1-3	Oct16 3-1	Feb08 3-2	Sep04 5-1	Feb22 2-2	Apr30 4-3	Nov13 4-0	Aug21 3-0	Dec25 0-1	Mar19 0-1	Jan15 3-1	Oct30 1-0	Jan03 3-1	Dec11 5-1	Apr16 1-3	Sep18 5-1	Oct02 3-7	Mar05 2-1	

DIVISION 2

	ALBION R	ALLOA	ARBROATH	ARMADALE	ARTHURLIE	AYR U	BATHGATE	BO'NESS	CLYDEBANK	DUMBARTON	EAST FIFE	E STIRLING	FORFAR A	KING'S PARK	NITHSDALE W	QUEEN OF SOUTH	RAITH R	ST BERNARD'S	STENHOUSEMUIR	T LANARK
ALBION R		Jan08 1-1	Mar19 2-2	Sep11 1-3	Oct23 3-0	Jan01 5-1	Dec11 1-0	Mar12 1-0	Nov13 2-3	Aug14 4-0	Nov27 4-2	Oct09 2-2	Aug28 1-1	Apr30 6-1	Apr02 2-2	Jan29 3-2	Feb26 1-1	Apr16 2-1	Sep25 1-3	Feb12 0-1
ALLOA	Sep04 4-3		Jan15 3-1	Nov13 2-0	Sep18 1-2	Nov27 1-3	Feb15 2-3	Mar01 0-1	Oct02 0-2	Dec04 1-1	Dec25 1-0	Oct23 1-1	Apr23 2-0	Jan03 2-2	Oct16 5-2	Nov06 3-2	Dec18 3-2	Aug21 2-3	Apr02 1-0	Mar12 2-2
ARBROATH	Nov06 1-2	Sep11 1-1		Jan08 4-3	Mar12 3-0	Jan29 1-1	Mar26 3-1	Dec18 0-0	Oct23 2-3	Oct09 1-3	Nov20 2-0	Aug14 5-0	Jan01 0-3	Apr16 3-0	Dec11 2-0	Feb12 1-0	Aug28 1-3	Apr09 1-2	Feb26 2-1	Sep25 1-0
ARMADALE	Jan15 1-1	Mar26 2-6	Sep04 3-1		Mar02 2-2	Nov20 4-1	Aug21 2-0	Dec25 1-2	Sep18 3-3	Nov06 3-4	Oct16 5-1	Mar12 1-1	Apr09 1-1	Oct02 4-0	Jan03 5-1	Apr30 2-1	Oct23 2-0	Feb09 2-2	Dec11 3-1	Apr16 2-1
ARTHURLIE	Mar08 1-4	Jan29 4-0	Oct30 4-1	Oct09 2-0		Jan08 0-0	Apr30 4-0	Apr02 1-1	Nov27 3-1	Sep11 2-1	Apr19 4-0	Sep25 0-1	Aug14 3-1	Mar19 4-3	Nov13 7-1	Feb26 2-4	Feb12 3-2	Dec11 3-2	Aug28 7-2	Jan01 2-3
AYR U	Aug21 3-0	Apr09 3-2	Sep18 3-1	Apr02 1-1	Sep04 1-1		Dec25 2-2	Oct02 2-1	Jan15 0-0	Apr30 0-5	Jan03 1-1	Nov13 3-2	Nov06 2-0	Feb09 5-2	Feb19 4-0	Dec04 1-2	Dec11 2-1	Oct16 1-1	Mar12 0-2	Oct23 1-1
BATHGATE	Apr23 1-0	Sep25 3-3	Nov13 5-5	Jan01 2-1	Dec18 5-2	Aug14 4-2		Mar19 2-3	Apr02 2-2	Aug28 2-1	Mar09 5-3	Feb12 0-2	Feb26 4-3	Nov27 2-1	Apr16 3-0	Jan08 8-3	Sep11 1-3	Oct30 2-1	Oct09 2-2	Jan29 0-5
BO'NESS	Oct30 5-3	Oct09 1-1	Apr30 1-1	Aug14 4-2	Nov20 2-1	Feb12 1-1	Nov06 7-0		Apr16 3-2	Jan29 3-1	Dec11 3-2	Feb26 3-1	Jan08 6-0	Mar09 1-1	Nov27 3-0	Aug28 3-0	Sep25 2-0	Mar26 2-1	Jan01 1-1	Sep11 2-0
CLYDEBANK	Mar26 3-1	Feb12 5-1	Mar05 6-1	Jan29 4-1	Apr09 5-2	Sep11 1-1	Nov20 5-1	Dec04 0-2		Dec31 6-2	Oct30 2-4	Aug28 1-4	Sep25 2-2	Apr23 2-1	Dec18 4-1	Aug14 1-1	Oct09 2-0	Nov06 4-1	Jan08 4-1	Feb26 2-2
DUMBARTON	Dec25 3-0	Apr16 3-1	Feb19 1-0	Mar19 2-0	Jan15 4-1	Dec18 3-5	Jan03 1-1	Sep18 1-0	Aug21 1-1		Sep04 1-3	Nov27 3-2	Mar12 1-3	Oct16 0-1	Feb16 6-2	Apr23 0-3	Apr02 1-3	Oct02 3-0	Oct23 2-1	Nov13 1-1
EAST FIFE	Apr09 8-2	Aug14 4-1	Apr02 4-1	Feb26 3-2	Dec04 7-1	Aug28 4-3	Oct23 5-4	Apr23 2-1	Mar12 3-2	Jan08 5-3		Sep11 3-3	Jan29 4-2	Nov13 5-2	Mar19 5-3	Sep25 2-0	Jan01 0-1	Dec18 3-2	Feb12 6-0	Oct09 3-0
E STIRLING	Feb19 4-4	Mar05 5-2	Dec25 3-1	Oct30 1-1	Feb09 4-5	Mar26 2-0	Oct02 1-0	Oct16 2-3	Jan03 4-1	Apr09 3-2	Jan15 4-2		Apr30 5-2	Aug21 2-2	Sep04 7-2	Nov20 2-1	Dec04 3-0	Sep18 5-2	Nov06 3-0	Apr23 1-1
FORFAR A	Jan03 1-0	Dec11 3-2	Aug21 2-0	Nov27 4-3	Dec25 1-3	Mar19 2-2	Oct16 1-2	Sep04 1-3	Apr07 5-4	Oct30 4-2	Sep18 3-1	Dec18 3-2		Jan15 3-2	Oct02 2-0	Mar05 2-0	Nov13 2-2	Feb19 1-0	Apr16 1-1	Apr02 0-1
KING'S PARK	Dec18 4-1	Aug28 3-2	Dec04 2-1	Feb12 1-1	Nov06 2-4	Sep25 1-1	Apr09 4-1	Oct23 1-3	Dec11 4-1	Feb26 2-0	Mar30 5-0	Jan01 3-0	Sep11 2-2		Mar12 2-2	Oct09 2-2	Aug14 3-2	Nov20 5-0	Jan29 5-0	Jan08 2-0
NITHSDALE W	Nov20 2-2	Feb26 0-3	Apr23 2-3	Aug28 2-2	Mar26 3-1	Oct09 2-2	Dec04 2-0	Apr09 1-1	Apr30 3-4	Sep25 3-0	Nov06 3-1	Jan08 1-2	Feb12 2-0	Oct30 3-3		Aug21 1-1	Jan29 2-4	Mar05 2-3	Sep11 2-2	Aug14 2-1
QUEEN OF SOUTH	Sep18 5-3	Mar19 1-0	Oct02 7-4	Dec18 6-0	Oct16 4-1	Feb05 1-2	Sep04 2-1	Jan03 0-2	Dec25 2-3	Dec11 3-2	Mar17 3-0	Apr02 1-4	Oct23 2-1	Feb19 3-2	Jan01 2-1		Mar12 1-1	Jan15 1-0	Nov13 2-0	Nov27 1-2
RAITH R	Oct16 7-1	Apr30 2-3	Jan03 4-2	Mar05 3-0	Oct02 1-2	Apr23 3-1	Jan15 1-0	Apr04 3-3	Feb19 0-0	Nov20 4-2	Aug21 4-2	Apr16 6-3	Mar26 5-0	Dec25 2-0	Sep18 1-0	Oct30 7-2		Sep04 5-1	Nov27 4-0	Nov06 3-0
ST BERNARD'S	Dec04 4-1	Jan01 3-3	Nov27 1-2	Sep25 1-2	Apr23 3-2	Feb26 2-4	Mar12 6-3	Nov13 2-5	Mar19 4-1	Feb12 1-1	Apr30 2-1	Jan29 2-0	Oct09 3-0	Apr02 3-0	Oct23 1-0	Sep11 4-1	Jan08 1-2		Aug14 3-3	Aug28 2-0
STENHOUSEMUIR	Feb05 1-1	Nov20 2-2	Oct16 1-3	Apr23 4-0	Jan03 3-3	Oct30 1-1	Feb19 5-2	Aug21 2-1	Sep04 4-0	Mar05 7-0	Oct02 3-3	Mar19 3-1	Dec04 2-1	Sep18 1-0	Jan15 3-4	Mar26 3-0	Apr09 0-0	Dec25 0-0		Dec18 3-1
T LANARK	Oct02 3-3	Nov02 1-0	Feb05 6-0	Dec04 2-0	Aug21 2-1	Mar05 5-1	Sep18 2-2	Jan15 1-1	Oct16 1-2	Mar26 2-2	Feb22 3-1	Dec11 3-1	Nov20 2-3	Sep04 1-0	Dec25 1-0	Apr09 4-0	Mar19 0-0	Jan03 2-0	Apr30 4-1	

DIVISION 1 FINAL TABLE

	P	W	D	L	F	A	Pts
Rangers	38	23	10	5	85	41	56
Motherwell	38	23	5	10	81	52	51
Celtic	38	21	7	10	101	55	49
Airdrie	38	18	9	11	97	64	45
Dundee	38	17	9	12	77	51	43
Falkirk	38	16	10	12	77	60	42
Cowdenbeath	38	18	6	14	74	60	42
Aberdeen	38	13	14	11	73	72	40
Hibernian	38	16	7	15	62	71	39
St Mirren	38	16	5	17	78	76	37
Partick T	38	15	6	17	89	74	36
Queen's Park	38	15	6	17	74	84	36
Hearts	38	12	11	15	65	64	35
St Johnstone	38	13	9	16	55	69	35
Hamilton A	38	13	9	16	60	85	35
Kilmarnock	38	12	8	18	54	71	32
Clyde	38	10	9	19	54	85	29
Dunfermline A	38	10	8	20	53	85	28
Morton	38	12	4	22	56	101	28
Dundee U	38	7	8	23	56	101	22

DIVISION 2 FINAL TABLE

	P	W	D	L	F	A	Pts
Bo'ness	38	23	10	5	86	41	56
Raith R	38	21	7	10	92	52	49
Clydebank	38	18	9	11	94	75	45
T Lanark	38	17	10	11	67	48	44
E Stirling	38	18	8	12	93	75	44
East Fife	38	19	3	16	103	91	41
Arthurlie	38	18	5	15	90	83	41
Ayr U	38	13	15	10	67	68	41
Forfar A	38	15	7	16	66	79	37
Stenhousemuir	38	12	12	14	69	76	36
Queen of South	38	16	4	18	72	80	36
King's Park	38	13	9	16	76	75	35
St Bernard's	38	14	6	18	70	77	34
Alloa	38	12	10	16	70	77	34
Armadale	38	12	10	16	70	78	34
Albion R	38	11	11	16	74	87	33
Bathgate	38	13	7	18	76	98	33
Dumbarton	38	13	6	19	69	84	32
Arbroath	38	13	6	19	64	83	32
Nithsdale	38	7	9	22	59	100	23

Season 1927-28

SFA Cup
1st Round
Jan 21	Albion R	5	Glasgow Univ	1
Jan 21	Alloa	2	Fraserburgh	0
Jan 21	Arbroath	2	Nithsdale W	3
Jan 21	Armadale	3	Berwick R	1
Jan 21	Ayr U	2	Bo'ness	0
Jan 21	Beith	1	Airdrie	4
Jan 21	Brechin C	3	Lochgelly U	1
Jan 21	Celtic	3	Bathgate	1
Jan 21	Civil Service	0	King's Park	3
Jan 21	Clydebank	0	Dunfermline A	3
Jan 21	Cowdenbeath	12	Johnstone	0
Jan 25	Dumbarton	2	Hamilton A	3
Jan 21	East Fife	1	Dundee U	1
Jan 21	E Stirling	0	Rangers	6
Jan 21	Falkirk	3	St Bernard's	1
Jan 21	Forfar A	2	Queen of South	1
Jan 21	Forres Mechanic	2	Elgin C	1
Jan 21	Hearts	2	St Johnstone	2
	Hibernian	W	Dykehead	0
Jan 21	Huntly	0	Motherwell	3
Jan 21	Keith	5	Dalbeattie Star	2
Jan 21	Leith A	2	Kilmarnock	3
Jan 21	Montrose	0	Stenhousemuir	5
Jan 21	Morton	7	Mid-Annandale	3
Jan 21	Partick T	9	Inverness Cal	1
Jan 21	Queen's Park	2	Arthurlie	0
Jan 21	Raith R	4	Aberdeen	3
Jan 21	St Mirren	6	Clyde	1
Jan 21	Stranraer	2	Dundee	4
Jan 21	T Lanark	10	Clackmannan	0
Jan 21	Vale of Atholl	2	Newton Stewart	1
Jan 21	Vale of Leven	1	Leith Amat	2

Replays
Jan 25	Dundee U	2	East Fife	1
Jan 25	St Johnstone	0	Hearts	1

2nd Round
Feb 4	Airdrie	2	Hamilton A	1
Feb 4	Armadale	2	King's Park	4
Feb 4	Ayr U	2	Falkirk	4
Feb 4	Brechin C	1	Albion R	4
Feb 4	Dundee U	3	Dundee	3
Feb 4	Dunfermline A	3	Leith Amat	1
Feb 4	Forfar A	1	Kilmarnock	2
Feb 4	Hearts	7	Forres Mechanic	0
Feb 4	Keith	1	Celtic	6
Feb 4	Motherwell	2	Raith R	2
Feb 4	Partick T	4	Nithsdale W	0
Feb 4	Queen's Park	4	Morton	1
Feb 4	Rangers	4	Cowdenbeath	2
Feb 4	St Mirren	5	Vale of Atholl	1
Feb 4	Stenhousemuir	1	Alloa	2
Feb 4	T Lanark	0	Hibernian	2

Replays
Feb 8	Dundee	1	Dundee U	0
Feb 8	Raith R	1	Motherwell	2

3rd Round
Feb 18	Albion R	3	Airdrie	1
Feb 18	Celtic	2	Alloa	0
Feb 18	Dundee	1	Dunfermline A	2
Feb 18	Hearts	1	Motherwell	2
Feb 18	Hibernian	0	Falkirk	0
Feb 18	Kilmarnock	4	Queen's Park	4
Feb 18	Rangers	3	King's Park	1
Feb 18	St Mirren	0	Partick T	5

Replay
Feb 22	Falkirk	0	Hibernian	1
Feb 22	Queen's Park	1	Kilmarnock	0

4th Round
Mar 3	Albion R	0	Rangers	1
Mar 3	Dunfermline A	0	Hibernian	4
Mar 3	Motherwell	0	Celtic	2
Mar 3	Queen's Park	1	Partick T	0

Semi-finals
Mar 24	Celtic	2	Queen's Park	1
	played at Ibrox			
Mar 24	Hibernian	0	Rangers	3
	played at Tynecastle			

Final
Apr 14	Celtic	0	Rangers	4
	played at Hampden Park			

Five Aberdeen stars of the mid-1920s: Bob McDermid, Jimmy Smith, Willie Jackson, Tommy McLeod and Alec Reid.

DIVISION 1

	ABERDEEN	AIRDRIE	BO'NESS	CELTIC	CLYDE	COWDENBEATH	DUNDEE	DUNFERMLINE A	FALKIRK	HAMILTON A	HEARTS	HIBERNIAN	KILMARNOCK	MOTHERWELL	PARTICK T	QUEEN'S PARK	RAITH R	RANGERS	ST JOHNSTONE	ST MIRREN
ABERDEEN		Dec03 0-0	Nov12 0-1	Oct22 3-1	Jan14 6-0	Apr14 3-0	Jan02 3-1	Oct08 2-1	Sep24 2-1	Feb08 2-0	Mar24 2-0	Sep10 4-2	Aug27 1-2	Dec17 2-0	Mar10 3-0	Dec31 2-1	Mar03 3-0	Aug13 2-3	Sep26 4-0	Mar31 3-2
AIRDRIE	Apr07 2-1		Oct22 4-2	Apr09 3-1	Oct08 1-2	Nov26 1-2	Sep24 1-1	Mar07 3-1	Jan02 0-1	Sep10 2-0	Dec10 2-0	Dec31 2-2	Feb08 0-2	Feb22 0-2	Nov12 2-0	Aug27 0-0	Aug13 2-4	Jan14 2-7	Apr21 2-0	Mar24 2-3
BO'NESS	Mar17 0-0	Feb25 2-2		Nov26 0-1	Mar03 0-0	Oct29 0-3	Sep10 2-0	Sep24 4-2	Aug13 2-1	Aug27 2-2	Apr07 2-2	Jan14 2-1	Oct08 2-1	Mar24 1-1	Dec10 1-4	Feb08 2-0	Jan02 1-1	Apr28 1-1	Nov05 1-2	Apr21 2-3
CELTIC	Feb25 1-1	Nov05 3-2	Mar31 4-1		Sep24 3-0	Nov19 1-1	Feb14 3-1	Jan14 9-0	Aug27 3-0	Mar06 4-0	Mar17 2-1	Aug13 3-0	Aug16 6-1	Dec03 1-2	Dec17 0-0	Sep10 3-0	Apr23 0-3	Jan02 1-0	Apr18 3-0	Oct29 6-0
CLYDE	Sep17 3-2	Jan28 2-2	Aug20 3-0	Feb11 0-1		Oct01 2-3	Apr07 0-0	Nov12 4-0	Feb29 1-1	Dec10 3-1	Jan07 2-2	Oct22 0-2	Mar24 1-1	Sep03 1-2	Oct15 0-2	Mar10 2-1	Apr21 1-1	Nov26 1-4	Jan03 1-0	Dec24 1-0
COWDENBEATH	Dec10 2-2	Mar31 2-1	Feb18 2-3	Mar26 0-2	Feb08 1-1		Aug13 1-0	Jan02 1-1	Dec31 0-2	Jan14 3-1	Apr21 0-1	Mar07 3-1	Sep10 1-1	Mar21 3-4	Oct22 2-1	Sep24 1-0	Oct08 3-1	Aug27 1-4	Dec03 4-2	Nov12 2-4
DUNDEE	Oct15 3-2	Feb11 3-0	Jan03 3-2	Oct01 1-4	Dec03 4-3	Dec24 3-1		Feb22 3-2	Oct22 1-0	Nov19 3-1	Jan28 2-7	Mar10 4-1	Nov12 7-0	Aug20 0-3	Sep03 4-2	Dec17 1-3	Mar31 1-2	Apr18 0-1	Sep17 1-2	Jan07 2-1
DUNFERMLINE A	Jan28 2-3	Aug20 1-4	Feb11 1-2	Sep17 1-1	Mar17 2-3	Oct15 3-2	Oct29 3-1		Apr07 1-0	Feb25 1-2	Jan03 0-2	Dec17 0-2	Apr14 0-4	Dec24 0-5	Jan07 1-7	Nov26 3-1	Nov19 0-4	Nov05 0-5	Oct01 2-3	Sep03 1-2
FALKIRK	Feb11 5-1	Oct15 3-1	Dec24 3-2	Jan07 1-3	Nov29 4-2	Sep03 1-3	Feb25 5-1	Dec03 5-1		Apr21 1-2	Oct01 1-3	Mar31 2-2	Nov05 6-0	Jan03 2-1	Jan28 2-1	Apr14 1-2	Mar17 4-1	Nov19 1-2	Aug20 5-1	Sep17 3-0
HAMILTON A	Oct01 2-3	Jan03 0-2	Jan07 7-0	Aug20 0-0	Apr13 1-1	Sep17 5-1	Mar24 3-3	Oct22 6-3	Dec17 3-0		Sep03 1-6	Feb29 4-1	Nov26 3-1	Oct15 1-3	Feb11 0-2	Nov12 2-1	Mar10 4-1	Dec03 1-1	Dec24 2-1	Jan28 1-2
HEARTS	Nov19 3-0	Apr14 1-1	Dec03 5-0	Nov12 2-2	Aug27 5-0	Dec17 2-3	Oct08 1-0	Sep10 6-0	Feb08 9-3	Dec31 2-1		Jan02 2-2	Aug13 0-1	Oct22 0-0	Feb22 1-2	Jan14 4-2	Sep24 2-0	Mar07 0-0	Mar31 0-2	Mar10 2-1
HIBERNIAN	Jan03 0-0	Sep03 2-3	Sep17 3-0	Dec24 2-2	Feb25 0-1	Aug20 3-0	Nov05 4-0	Apr21 3-3	Nov26 3-1	Oct29 5-1	Oct15 2-1		Apr07 3-1	Jan07 2-2	Oct01 4-1	Mar26 6-2	Dec10 3-2	Mar17 2-1	Jan28 2-2	Feb11 1-1
KILMARNOCK	Jan07 2-1	Oct01 2-2	Sep03 3-1	Jan28 2-2	Nov19 3-0	Jan03 2-1	Mar17 1-2	Dec10 2-1	Mar10 1-1	Mar31 3-1	Dec24 5-0	Dec03 2-1		Sep17 1-3	Aug20 2-3	Oct22 1-1	Feb29 1-0	Dec17 1-1	Feb11 1-7	Oct15 6-2
MOTHERWELL	Apr16 2-1	Oct29 1-1	Nov19 3-2	Apr07 3-1	Dec31 5-0	Nov05 2-1	Mar07 2-2	Aug13 4-0	Sep10 2-3	Jan02 5-1	Feb25 0-3	Aug27 2-1	Jan14 3-3		Mar31 1-3	Oct08 4-1	Feb15 6-0	Sep24 1-1	Mar17 1-0	Dec10 4-0
PARTICK T	Nov05 7-0	Mar17 0-2	Apr14 2-1	Apr21 3-3	Jan02 2-1	Apr09 2-4	Dec31 2-2	Aug27 2-1	Oct08 1-1	Sep24 5-2	Oct29 1-3	Feb08 3-0	Mar07 2-0	Nov26 1-1		Aug13 2-0	Jan14 5-0	Sep10 0-6	Nov19 2-2	Dec03 6-2
QUEEN'S PARK	Sep03 4-3	Jan07 1-1	Oct01 1-0	Jan03 1-3	Nov05 2-2	Feb11 1-1	Apr21 1-2	Mar31 4-0	Dec10 0-1	Mar17 4-1	Sep17 0-2	Nov19 6-2	Feb25 5-3	Jan28 3-1	Dec24 4-2		Dec03 8-1	Oct29 3-1	Oct15 1-1	Aug20 3-4
RAITH R	Aug20 2-3	Dec24 5-0	Oct15 3-2	Sep03 0-3	Dec17 2-0	Jan28 0-1	Nov26 1-1	Mar24 5-1	Nov12 2-2	Nov05 3-3	Feb11 0-5	Apr14 3-0	Oct29 1-3	Oct01 2-4	Sep17 4-2	Apr07 1-0		Apr02 0-0	Jan07 0-0	Jan03 1-2
RANGERS	Dec24 5-0	Sep17 2-1	Jan28 3-1	Oct15 1-0	Mar31 3-1	Jan07 2-2	Dec10 5-1	Apr09 4-0	Mar26 4-0	Apr07 3-1	Aug20 4-1	Nov12 4-1	Apr21 5-1	Feb11 0-2	Jan03 2-1	Feb28 4-0	Oct22 7-0		Sep03 5-1	Oct01 4-2
ST JOHNSTONE	Oct29 1-0	Dec17 6-1	Mar10 4-1	Dec10 3-5	Sep10 0-0	Apr07 0-3	Jan14 5-1	Feb08 1-1	Mar03 2-1	Aug13 2-1	Nov26 2-3	Oct08 2-0	Sep24 1-1	Nov12 1-4	Mar24 1-2	Jan02 5-1	Aug27 2-1	Dec31 0-1		Feb25 0-0
ST MIRREN	Nov26 0-1	Nov19 2-2	Dec17 5-0	Feb21 0-2	Aug13 3-1	Mar17 3-2	Aug27 0-0	Dec31 5-1	Jan14 3-2	Oct08 1-0	Nov05 2-0	Sep24 3-2	Jan02 1-1	Apr14 1-1	Apr07 2-2	Mar06 5-1	Sep10 4-3	Feb14 3-3	Oct22 3-2	

DIVISION 2

	ALBION R	ALLOA	ARBROATH	ARMADALE	ARTHURLIE	AYR U	BATHGATE	CLYDEBANK	DUMBARTON	DUNDEE U	EAST FIFE	E STIRLING	FORFAR A	KING'S PARK	LEITH A	MORTON	QUEEN OF SOUTH	ST BERNARD'S	STENHOUSEMUIR	T LANARK
ALBION R		Nov05 3-1	Jan07 3-1	Sep03 3-0	Feb25 0-1	Jan03 1-1	Apr14 2-1	Mar17 4-2	Sep17 2-3	Feb11 2-0	Dec24 3-0	Oct01 2-3	Dec17 1-2	Oct29 0-1	Aug20 0-0	Nov19 0-0	Dec03 3-1	Mar31 6-2	Oct15 4-0	Jan28 0-3
ALLOA	Mar10 4-3		Sep03 4-0	Aug20 3-3	Nov26 2-2	Jan07 1-3	Mar24 4-0	Dec10 0-1	Oct01 3-3	Oct15 0-0	Jan03 1-1	Jan28 6-3	Feb21 3-2	Nov12 2-1	Feb11 1-1	Apr07 3-3	Apr21 4-0	Oct22 3-0	Dec24 3-3	Sep17 1-0
ARBROATH	Aug27 4-2	Dec31 4-1		Feb18 5-0	Sep24 2-3	Oct22 0-2	Oct08 5-0	Jan14 1-3	Apr14 3-0	Dec03 3-2	Nov12 2-1	Mar31 2-2	Jan02 1-2	Feb08 2-1	Nov05 5-3	Aug13 1-1	Sep10 4-1	Mar03 3-2	Nov19 3-0	Apr21 4-0
ARMADALE	Dec31 2-3	Mar03 1-0	Oct29 4-5		Feb08 2-0	Mar31 3-1	Jan02 0-0	Oct08 1-3	Dec03 2-0	Dec17 4-2	Feb25 1-5	Apr14 0-0	Aug27 1-3	Jan14 1-1	Mar17 1-0	Sep24 2-1	Aug13 1-4	Sep10 2-1	Nov05 2-2	Nov19 2-2
ARTHURLIE	Oct22 6-4	Mar31 1-0	Feb11 4-1	Oct01 10-0		Sep03 4-1	Dec17 1-1	Nov05 5-1	Dec24 0-1	Sep17 1-3	Aug20 2-1	Jan07 4-3	Nov19 3-0	Apr07 1-1	Jan28 1-1	Dec10 4-2	Mar17 4-1	Feb18 3-4	Jan03 4-1	Oct15 2-0
AYR U	Sep10 5-3	Aug27 3-0	Feb25 7-3	Nov26 5-0	Dec31 6-1		Jan14 7-2	Feb08 3-1	Mar24 0-1	Apr14 7-1	Oct29 3-0	Apr07 2-1	Sep24 7-0	Mar03 2-2	Dec17 3-1	Jan02 4-1	Oct08 3-1	Aug13 4-4	Mar17 2-2	Nov05 6-2
BATHGATE	Dec10 3-1	Nov19 2-0	Jan28 3-3	Oct15 1-1	Apr21 2-3	Sep17 1-1		Feb18 5-0	Sep03 2-3	Dec24 1-2	Feb11 2-3	Aug20 3-1	Oct22 3-3	Nov26 0-0	Jan03 3-2	Mar17 1-1	Nov05 2-1	Dec03 1-1	Jan07 1-0	Oct01 3-2
CLYDEBANK	Nov12 0-2	Apr13 4-1	Sep17 1-2	Jan28 1-0	Mar21 2-0	Oct01 1-4	Oct29 2-3		Oct15 1-2	Aug20 2-1	Jan07 2-3	Jan03 4-1	Dec03 5-1	Mar24 5-0	Sep03 2-2	Feb25 2-1	Nov26 6-3	Dec17 7-1	Feb11 3-1	Dec24 1-1
DUMBARTON	Jan14 0-1	Feb08 2-1	Dec10 2-0	Apr07 6-2	Aug13 0-1	Nov19 2-0	Dec31 2-1	Jan02 0-2		Mar31 3-0	Nov05 1-3	Mar17 6-1	Oct08 2-0	Sep24 4-5	Oct29 2-2	Sep10 5-0	Mar03 1-0	Aug27 3-3	Apr21 4-1	Feb25 0-0
DUNDEE U	Sep24 3-2	Jan02 2-1	Apr07 1-0	Apr21 1-1	Jan14 9-2	Dec10 1-3	Aug13 4-2	Mar03 2-2	Nov26 3-1		Mar24 2-3	Nov05 3-1	Dec31 4-0	Sep10 1-1	Feb25 3-1	Feb15 3-2	Aug27 1-1	Oct08 5-3	Oct29 5-3	Mar17 4-3
EAST FIFE	Aug13 2-0	Sep10 2-4	Mar17 2-1	Oct22 4-1	Mar03 6-1	Feb18 2-0	Sep24 2-3	Aug27 2-1	Mar10 4-1	Nov19 2-1		Apr21 2-2	Jan14 4-3	Dec31 1-1	Dec10 3-4	Oct08 5-0	Jan02 5-1	Feb04 2-2	Mar31 1-3	Dec03 2-2
E STIRLING	Feb08 3-1	Oct08 2-3	Nov26 3-0	Dec10 4-1	Aug27 8-0	Dec03 2-3	Mar03 1-0	Sep10 2-1	Nov12 5-0	Mar10 3-1	Dec17 4-1		Aug13 4-0	Jan02 2-2	Mar24 1-1	Jan14 2-2	Dec31 2-2	Sep24 1-2	Feb25 0-1	Oct29 0-0
FORFAR A	Apr21 4-1	Oct29 4-0	Oct15 2-2	Jan07 3-0	Mar24 4-1	Feb11 1-2	Feb25 2-0	Apr07 2-1	Jan28 3-2	Sep03 0-0	Sep17 4-0	Dec24 1-1		Mar10 3-1	Oct01 2-2	Nov26 5-2	Dec10 4-1	Nov12 9-2	Aug20 3-1	Jan03 3-2
KING'S PARK	Dec22 0-4	Mar17 2-2	Oct01 5-1	Sep17 5-2	Dec03 5-1	Aug20 2-1	Mar31 1-0	Nov19 5-1	Feb11 4-0	Jan03 0-1	Sep03 1-1	Oct15 2-2	Nov05 1-1		Dec24 1-0	Dec17 3-1	Oct26 4-3	Apr14 8-1	Jan28 4-2	Jan07 4-2
LEITH A	Mar06 4-1	Sep24 2-1	Mar10 4-2	Nov12 5-0	Oct08 3-4	Apr21 2-1	Sep10 2-2	Dec31 4-0	Feb04 2-1	Oct22 0-2	Apr14 2-3	Nov19 2-3	Feb08 3-1	Aug13 4-1		Aug27 2-3	Jan14 3-1	Oct15 2-1	Dec03 1-2	Mar31 2-3
MORTON	Mar24 0-2	Dec03 2-1	Dec24 1-0	Feb11 2-1	Apr14 3-1	Oct15 0-2	Nov12 2-2	Oct22 5-6	Jan03 2-0	Oct01 1-1	Jan28 1-1	Sep17 3-1	Mar31 2-1	Apr21 2-3	Jan07 3-1		Feb18 2-0	Mar10 3-1	Sep03 1-0	Aug20 1-2
QUEEN OF SOUTH	Apr07 2-4	Dec17 2-2	Jan03 3-2	Dec24 8-5	Nov12 1-0	Jan28 2-4	Mar10 4-3	Feb04 3-2	Aug20 6-2	Jan07 2-2	Oct15 2-4	Sep03 5-3	Apr14 2-1	Feb25 2-2	Sep17 5-2	Oct29 4-1		Nov19 6-3	Oct01 4-3	Feb11 2-2
ST BERNARD'S	Nov26 3-1	Feb25 2-2	Aug20 1-2	Jan03 2-1	Oct29 3-2	Dec24 0-4	Apr07 2-0	Apr21 1-0	Jan07 2-0	Jan28 3-2	Oct01 2-1	Feb11 1-2	Mar17 3-0	Dec10 2-1	Jan02 1-0	Nov05 2-5	Mar24 8-2		Sep17 3-1	Sep03 0-1
STENHOUSEMUIR	Jan02 0-3	Aug13 2-4	Mar24 6-2	Mar10 1-0	Sep10 4-1	Nov12 6-2	Aug27 4-2	Sep24 2-0	Dec17 1-0	Feb18 2-2	Nov26 4-1	Oct22 2-5	Mar03 2-3	Oct08 3-2	Apr07 0-0	Dec31 5-2	Feb08 1-2	Jan14 2-0		Dec10 1-0
T LANARK	Oct05 2-2	Jan14 5-0	Dec17 4-3	Mar24 10-3	Jan02 2-1	Apr09 3-3	Feb07 6-1	Aug13 4-0	Oct22 4-1	Nov12 5-1	Apr07 3-2	Feb18 5-0	Sep10 1-1	Aug27 5-1	Nov26 2-4	Mar03 3-1	Sep24 1-2	Dec31 6-1	Apr17 3-1	

DIVISION 1 FINAL TABLE

	P	W	D	L	F	A	Pts
Rangers	38	26	8	4	109	36	60
Celtic	38	23	9	6	93	39	55
Motherwell	38	23	9	6	92	46	55
Hearts	38	20	7	11	89	50	47
St Mirren	38	18	8	12	77	76	44
Partick T	38	18	7	13	85	67	43
Aberdeen	38	19	5	14	71	61	43
Kilmarnock	38	15	10	13	68	78	40
Cowdenbeath	38	16	7	15	66	68	39
Falkirk	38	16	5	17	76	69	37
St Johnstone	38	14	8	16	66	67	36
Hibernian	38	13	9	16	73	75	35
Airdrie	38	12	11	15	59	69	35
Dundee	38	14	7	17	65	80	35
Clyde	38	10	11	17	46	72	31
Queen's Park	38	12	6	20	69	80	30
Raith R	38	11	7	20	60	89	29
Hamilton A	38	11	6	21	67	86	28
Bo'ness	38	9	8	21	48	86	26
Dunfermline A	38	4	4	30	41	126	12

DIVISION 2 FINAL TABLE

	P	W	D	L	F	A	Pts
Ayr U	38	24	6	8	117	60	54
T Lanark	38	18	9	11	101	66	45
King's Park	38	16	12	10	84	68	44
East Fife	38	18	7	13	87	73	43
Forfar A	38	18	7	13	83	73	43
Dundee U	38	17	9	12	81	73	43
Arthurlie	38	18	4	16	85	90	40
Albion R	38	17	4	17	79	69	38
E Stirling	38	14	10	14	84	76	38
Arbroath	38	16	4	18	84	86	36
Dumbarton	38	16	4	18	66	72	36
Queen of South	38	15	6	17	92	106	36
Leith A	38	13	9	16	76	71	35
Clydebank	38	16	3	19	78	80	35
Alloa	38	12	11	15	72	76	35
Stenhousemuir	38	15	5	18	75	82	35
St Bernard's	38	15	5	18	75	103	35
Morton	38	13	8	17	65	82	34
Bathgate	38	10	11	17	62	81	31
Armadale	38	8	8	22	53	112	24

The Aberdeen squad of 1928-29. Back row (left to right): Merrie, Cooper, Donald, McHale, McLaren, McKenzie, Legge. Middle row: Ritchie (assistant trainer), Black, Smith, Jackson, Blackwell, Yuill, Love, McLeod, Livingstone, Russell (trainer). Front row: Robertson (secretary), Polland, Wilson, Falloon, McDermid, Muir, Yorston, Cheyne, Hill, Travers (manager).

SFA Cup
1st Round
Jan 19	Aberdeen	5	Solway Star	0
Jan 19	Albion R	7	Galston	1
Jan 19	Alloa	3	E Stirling	3
Jan 19	Arbroath	2	Inverness T	0
Jan 19	Armadale	9	Moor Park	2
Jan 19	Beith	2	Raith R	2
Jan 19	Berwick R	3	Ayr U	9
Jan 19	Bo'ness	7	Newton Stewart	1
Jan 26	Breadalbane	0	Brechin C	6
Jan 19	Buckie T	0	Queen's Park	3
Jan 19	Celtic	5	Arthurlie	1
Jan 12	Civil Service	1	Fraserburgh	1
	Clackmannan	W	Dunkeld	0
Jan 19	Clyde	4	Montrose	1
Jan 19	Dumbarton	6	Inver Citadel	1
Jan 19	Dundee	1	King's Park	1
Jan 19	Dundee U	3	Morton	1
Jan 19	Dunfermline A	1	Cowdenbeath	3
Jan 19	East Fife	1	Partick T	2
Jan 19	Hamilton A	2	Forfar A	1
Jan 19	Hearts	0	Airdrie	2
Jan 19	Hibernian	1	St Johnstone	2
Jan 19	Huntly	1	Stenhousemuir	3
Jan 19	Kilmarnock	8	Glasgow Univ	1
Jan 19	Motherwell	4	Leith A	1
Jan 19	Nithsdale W	0	St Mirren	4
Jan 19	Queen of South	2	Inverness Cal	2
Jan 19	Rangers	11	Edinburgh C	1
Jan 19	St Andrew's Univ	0	Bathgate	3
Jan 19	St Bernard's	1	Falkirk	2
Jan 12	Thornhill	0	Murrayfield A	4
Jan 19	T Lanark	6	Clydebank	2

Replays
Jan 19	Fraserburgh	4	Civil Service	3
Jan 23	E Stirling	2	Alloa	1
Jan 23	King's Park	1	Dundee	5
Jan 24	Inverness Cal	0	Queen of South	3
Jan 26	Raith R	4	Beith	1

2nd Round
Feb 2	Aberdeen	4	Queen's Park	0
Feb 2	Albion R	8	Clackmannan	1
Feb 2	Ayr U	5	Armadale	1
Feb 2	Bathgate	1	Raith R	1
Feb 2	Celtic	3	E Stirling	0
Feb 2	Clyde	1	Hamilton A	1
Feb 2	Cowdenbeath	0	Airdrie	0
Feb 2	Dundee	6	Brechin C	1
Feb 2	Fraserburgh	0	Dumbarton	3
Feb 2	Kilmarnock	3	Bo'ness	2
Feb 2	Murrayfield A	1	Arbroath	1
Feb 2	Queen of South	1	Falkirk	2
Feb 2	Rangers	5	Partick T	1
Feb 2	St Johnstone	2	Motherwell	3
Feb 2	Stenhousemuir	1	Dundee U	1
Feb 2	T Lanark	0	St Mirren	1

Replays
Feb 6	Airdrie	3	Cowdenbeath	2
Feb 6	Arbroath	5	Murrayfield A	2
Feb 6	Dundee U	2	Stenhousemuir	0
Feb 6	Hamilton A	1	Clyde	2
Feb 6	Raith R	5	Bathgate	2

3rd Round
Feb 16	Airdrie	1	Motherwell	1
Feb 16	Albion R	0	Kilmarnock	1
Feb 16	Ayr U	0	St Mirren	2
Feb 16	Celtic	4	Arbroath	1
Feb 16	Clyde	0	Rangers	2
Feb 16	Dundee	1	Dundee U	1
Feb 16	Falkirk	3	Aberdeen	5
Feb 16	Raith R	3	Dumbarton	2

Replays
Feb 20	Dundee U	1	Dundee	0
Feb 20	Motherwell	3	Airdrie	1

4th Round
Mar 6	Celtic	0	Motherwell	0
Mar 2	Raith R	2	Kilmarnock	3
Mar 2	Rangers	3	Dundee U	1
Mar 5	St Mirren	4	Aberdeen	3

Replay
Mar 13	Motherwell	1	Celtic	2

Semi-finals
Mar 23	Celtic	0	Kilmarnock	1
	played at Ibrox			
Mar 23	Rangers	3	St Mirren	2
	played at Hampden Park			

Final
Apr 6	Kilmarnock	2	Rangers	0
	played at Hampden Park			

Season 1928-29

DIVISION 1

	ABERDEEN	AIRDRIE	AYR U	CELTIC	CLYDE	COWDENBEATH	DUNDEE	FALKIRK	HAMILTON A	HEARTS	HIBERNIAN	KILMARNOCK	MOTHERWELL	PARTICK T	QUEEN'S PARK	RAITH R	RANGERS	ST JOHNSTONE	ST MIRREN	T LANARK
ABERDEEN		Oct13 2-1	Mar09 2-1	Nov10 2-2	Sep22 3-1	Aug11 4-2	Mar23 4-0	Dec15 5-3	Dec01 4-1	Oct27 1-3	Jan05 0-1	Sep24 2-1	Feb23 1-1	Mar30 5-0	Aug18 3-0	Sep29 3-1	Apr20 2-2	Sep08 2-0	Jan12 6-0	Jan01 4-0
AIRDRIE	Mar12 5-0		Feb27 3-0	Dec22 0-1	Apr20 2-2	Sep08 3-2	Nov03 1-1	Oct20 2-3	Mar02 1-0	Sep22 1-1	Oct06 0-2	Aug25 2-1	Aug11 0-1	Nov17 1-0	Dec25 2-2	Mar16 3-1	Dec15 2-5	Mar30 5-1	Feb11 3-0	Jan12 2-1
AYR U	Nov03 3-3	Sep29 2-0		Aug25 0-2	Mar02 3-1	Oct06 3-1	Jan02 0-3	Apr13 2-0	Feb09 1-1	Jan12 2-4	Mar30 4-1	Nov17 2-4	Sep08 2-0	Mar16 1-3	Oct20 4-2	Dec15 0-1	Dec01 1-3	Apr20 1-2	Aug11 2-2	Dec22 3-0
CELTIC	Mar16 2-2	Aug18 4-1	Jan05 3-0		Nov17 4-0	Feb12 1-0	Dec29 2-1	Apr20 3-0	Feb19 3-0	Dec15 1-0	Apr13 1-4	Sep08 3-0	Mar19 2-0	Apr01 1-0	Apr17 1-2	Nov03 3-1	Oct20 1-2	Dec01 0-0	Sep22 0-3	Mar30 3-1
CLYDE	Feb09 2-1	Dec08 3-1	Oct13 1-0	Mar26 0-1		Dec22 2-3	Nov10 2-1	Aug11 2-1	Apr27 2-3	Aug25 1-1	Sep15 0-1	Sep29 1-1	Jan12 1-1	Jan01 0-4	Dec25 2-2	Apr06 2-0	Nov24 2-3	Oct27 2-1	Feb23 4-0	Mar09 3-2
COWDENBEATH	Dec29 1-1	Apr27 2-1	Feb23 3-1	Sep15 0-1	Aug18 1-2		Nov24 4-2	Nov03 3-1	Dec08 2-0	Mar02 1-2	Sep01 2-0	Jan02 2-0	Apr06 1-3	Jan26 2-0	Sep22 0-1	Oct20 2-0	Jan05 0-2	Mar16 1-0	Sep29 0-0	Nov17 1-1
DUNDEE	Nov17 1-1	Mar09 2-2	Oct27 2-3	Aug11 0-1	Mar16 1-2	Mar30 4-0		Feb09 1-2	Sep15 0-1	Sep29 5-3	Jan26 1-0	Jan12 1-3	Dec08 3-0	Dec22 0-0	Apr06 0-0	Feb23 0-3	Sep08 2-3	Jan01 0-2	Aug25 2-3	Oct13 2-2
FALKIRK	Jan26 2-0	Jan01 2-1	Sep15 5-2	Dec08 3-0	Dec29 2-1	Mar09 2-2	Sep22 1-3		Sep01 4-2	Feb23 3-3	Apr27 2-1	Dec01 2-2	Oct27 0-7	Aug25 0-0	Mar23 1-0	Nov24 4-1	Nov10 1-4	Dec22 2-0	Oct13 2-2	Feb20 3-1
HAMILTON A	Apr06 3-2	Oct27 1-3	Sep22 2-0	Sep29 1-1	Sep08 2-0	Apr20 0-0	Apr12 3-3	Jan12 2-2		Dec22 3-2	Nov10 2-1	Dec15 0-2	Jan01 0-3	Feb23 2-2	Nov24 3-3	Mar05 5-1	Mar27 3-1	Aug25 2-1	Mar09 3-0	Aug11 1-4
HEARTS	Jan02 3-2	Feb09 3-0	Sep01 7-3	Jan26 2-1	Jan05 4-0	Oct13 4-1	Mar06 1-1	Oct06 6-2	Aug18 5-0		Oct20 1-1	Mar30 3-3	Nov10 5-1	Dec08 2-1	Dec29 4-1	Apr27 1-1	Sep15 0-1	Mar09 0-3	Dec25 1-0	Dec01 4-1
HIBERNIAN	Aug25 4-1	Apr06 1-1	Nov24 2-2	Feb23 2-1	Feb20 3-0	Jan12 1-2	Dec15 2-0	Sep08 3-2	Mar16 0-1	Jan01 1-0		Dec22 1-1	Sep22 1-1	Sep29 3-1	Mar02 1-2	Nov17 2-0	Nov03 1-2	Aug11 2-2	Apr20 3-5	Oct27 6-1
KILMARNOCK	Sep15 0-1	Jan05 0-2	Apr24 1-2	Apr27 2-3	Apr01 3-1	Oct27 4-2	Sep01 3-1	Apr09 1-1	Jan26 0-0	Nov24 3-2	Aug18 1-0		Mar09 4-2	Oct13 2-2	Nov10 7-4	Dec08 7-1	Dec29 1-3	Feb23 1-1	Jan01 2-4	Sep22 3-0
MOTHERWELL	Oct06 1-0	Dec29 4-2	Apr27 5-0	Oct13 3-3	Sep01 1-0	Dec01 5-1	Apr20 1-1	Jan02 2-1	Oct20 4-3	Mar16 3-2	Feb09 3-1	Nov03 2-3		Sep15 5-4	Jan05 0-5	Aug18 3-1	Apr17 2-4	Nov17 1-1	Mar30 1-1	Dec15 3-2
PARTICK T	Nov24 3-2	Mar23 1-1	Nov10 4-8	Jan12 3-0	Oct20 2-0	Dec15 2-1	Aug18 4-2	Mar02 5-2	Oct06 8-0	Apr20 2-0	Feb16 3-0	Mar12 2-1	Feb06 1-3		Nov03 2-2	Dec29 6-1	Apr24 1-1	Sep22 6-2	Dec01 2-4	Sep08 3-4
QUEEN'S PARK	Dec22 6-2	Feb23 2-0	Jan01 3-0	Oct27 4-4	Dec15 2-1	Feb09 6-1	Dec01 2-4	Nov17 1-3	Mar30 5-0	Aug11 1-3	Oct13 6-1	Mar20 2-0	Aug25 2-3	Mar09 3-2		Sep15 5-0	Jan12 0-4	Feb16 6-0	Sep08 5-0	Apr20 8-3
RAITH R	Feb20 2-2	Nov10 3-2	Oct01 4-2	Mar09 1-4	Dec01 3-0	Jan01 0-2	Oct06 0-3	Mar30 2-0	Oct13 3-1	Sep08 0-2	Mar23 1-0	Apr20 5-3	Dec22 2-2	Aug11 2-4	Apr24 1-1		Feb09 1-3	Jan12 3-3	Oct27 1-5	Aug25 0-0
RANGERS	Dec08 2-0	Jan26 2-0	Apr09 0-0	Jan01 3-0	Mar30 0-0	Aug25 3-1	Apr27 3-0	Mar16 1-1	Nov17 4-0	Mar12 2-0	Mar09 3-0	Aug11 4-2	Sep29 0-0	Jan02 1-0	Apr01 2-1	Sep22 7-1		Oct13 8-0	Dec22 1-1	Feb26 5-1
ST JOHNSTONE	Apr27 2-1	Nov24 1-0	Dec08 0-0	Apr06 1-1	Jan02 5-0	Nov10 3-1	Oct20 2-2	Aug18 3-1	Jan05 2-2	Nov03 0-3	Dec29 4-0	Oct06 1-0	Mar23 2-3	Feb09 1-3	Sep29 1-0	Sep01 3-1	Mar06 1-3		Dec15 1-0	Mar02 2-1
ST MIRREN	Sep01 5-2	Sep15 2-0	Dec29 2-3	Feb09 0-1	Oct06 1-0	Feb19 1-4	Apr22 2-2	Mar12 5-0	Nov03 1-3	Nov17 2-2	Dec08 1-0	Oct20 5-4	Nov24 2-3	Apr06 3-0	Apr27 1-2	Apr09 5-2	Aug18 1-5	Jan26 2-2		Mar16 5-0
T LANARK	Oct20 1-3	Sep01 4-0	Aug18 2-2	Nov24 0-2	Nov03 2-4	Mar23 3-1	Dec25 1-2	Sep29 5-2	Dec29 3-2	Apr01 2-2	Jan02 2-1	Feb09 2-3	Jan26 2-2	Apr27 2-5	Dec08 3-1	Jan05 5-1	Oct06 2-5	Sep15 4-1	Nov10 1-2	

DIVISION 1 FINAL TABLE

	P	W	D	L	F	A	Pts
Rangers	38	30	7	1	107	32	67
Celtic	38	22	7	9	67	44	51
Motherwell	38	20	10	8	85	66	50
Hearts	38	19	9	10	91	57	47
Queen's Park	38	18	7	13	100	69	43
Partick T	38	17	7	14	91	70	41
Aberdeen	38	16	8	14	81	68	40
St Mirren	38	16	8	14	78	75	40
St Johnstone	38	14	10	14	57	70	38
Kilmarnock	38	14	8	16	79	74	36
Falkirk	38	14	8	16	68	86	36
Hamilton A	38	13	9	16	58	83	35
Cowdenbeath	38	14	5	19	55	69	33
Hibernian	38	13	6	19	54	62	32
Airdrie	38	12	7	19	56	65	31
Ayr U	38	12	7	19	65	84	31
Clyde	38	12	6	20	47	71	30
Dundee	38	9	11	18	59	69	29
T Lanark	38	10	6	22	71	102	26
Raith R	38	9	6	23	52	105	24

DIVISION 2

	ALBION R	ALLOA	ARBROATH	ARMADALE	ARTHURLIE	BATHGATE	BO'NESS	CLYDEBANK	DUMBARTON	DUNDEE U	DUNFERMLINE A	EAST FIFE	E STIRLING	FORFAR A	KING'S PARK	LEITH A	MORTON	QUEEN OF SOUTH	ST BERNARD'S	STENHOUSEMUIR
ALBION R		Jan05 3-1	Feb09 2-1	Mar09 9-1	Sep01 4-1	Dec08 2-1	Oct27 4-0	Sep15 3-0	Mar23 6-4	Oct13 2-0	Dec29 3-4	Dec01 4-1	Feb23 3-1	Apr27 6-2	Mar20 0-0	Sep29 6-2	Nov10 2-2	Nov24 2-0	Aug18 3-2	Jan01 2-0
ALLOA	Aug25 0-0		Mar09 1-2	Nov10 5-2	Jan26 3-0	Sep01 1-2	Sep29 2-2	Apr06 3-1	Dec22 0-2	Apr13 3-0	Nov24 1-1	Oct27 2-4	Sep22 5-0	Feb02 2-4	Apr27 1-0	Aug11 2-4	Mar23 1-3	Dec08 0-4	Oct13 0-3	Feb23 7-1
ARBROATH	Sep22 5-3	Nov03 6-3		Mar02 6-1	Dec29 4-1	Dec01 3-1	Jan26 3-0	Aug18 4-2	Feb20 7-1	Mar30 1-2	Apr27 2-1	Mar23 1-0	Nov10 5-2	Oct20 1-0	Apr20 0-0	Apr13 3-2	Jan05 1-1	Jan02 1-0	Oct06 1-1	Sep01 5-2
ARMADALE	Nov03 0-0	Mar16 1-1	Oct13 1-1		Feb23 1-1	Oct20 2-1	Sep15 0-1	Sep01 2-2	Mar30 1-1	Sep29 0-2	Jan09 3-1	Feb09 4-2	Dec08 2-1	Jan26 3-1	Dec01 2-0	Dec15 1-0	Aug18 1-3	Nov17 2-3	Apr12 0-3	Dec29 3-2
ARTHURLIE	Jan12 2-1	Sep08 1-2	Aug11 1-1	Oct06 3-1		Nov03 4-3		Mar16 1-0	Sep22 3-3	Nov17 3-1	Oct20 1-0		Dec01 2-3		Dec22 1-4	Mar02 2-2	Feb02 1-2	Aug25 4-0	Mar30 1-1	
BATHGATE		Jan12 3-1					Nov24 3-5	Dec15 0-2	Oct06 2-3	Aug11 0-4	Sep22 1-1	Aug25 4-1			Feb16 1-3	Oct27 0-5	Sep08 1-3	Dec22 1-3	Nov10 0-0	
BO'NESS	Jan02 2-2	Feb16 2-3	Sep08 2-3	Feb06 2-0	Dec08 0-2			Nov03 2-0	Mar02 6-0	Dec22 1-0	Mar16 2-1	Aug11 4-1	Aug25 2-0	Oct06 4-3	Nov17 1-3	Sep22 3-0	Oct20 2-2	Jan12 5-1	Apr27 1-0	Dec01 5-1
CLYDEBANK	Feb06 2-4	Dec01 1-3	Dec22 4-3	Jan12 4-0	Nov10 5-1		Mar09 3-0		Dec31 1-6	Aug25 4-1	Dec08 5-2	Mar30 0-3	Oct27 1-3	Mar23 1-1	Mar02 5-1	Sep08 3-1	Feb13 3-3	Oct06 3-1	Feb16 1-3	Sep22 2-0
DUMBARTON	Nov17 1-0	Aug18 4-1	Sep29 0-2	Nov24 5-2	Feb09 2-0	Feb23 3-0	Oct13 0-3	Oct20 1-1		Apr06 1-1	Sep15 3-1	Apr27 2-2	Apr08 3-2	Jan05 0-0	Sep01 3-3	Mar16 1-4	Jan02 1-0	Nov03 4-2	Dec08 2-1	Jan26 0-1
DUNDEE U	Mar06 8-1	Oct20 5-0	Nov24 4-3	Feb27 5-0	Mar23 4-3	Dec29 6-1	Aug18 4-1	Jan05 2-1	Dec01 3-1		Sep01 1-0	Apr08 4-3	Apr27 3-1	Apr20 0-1	Jan02 4-0	Nov03 5-3	Oct06 3-0	Sep22 3-2	Oct01 3-1	Nov10 8-0
DUNFERMLINE A	Aug11 1-5	Mar30 0-1	Dec15 3-3	Aug25 3-2	Jan01 5-1	Feb09 8-0	Nov10 1-0	Apr20 2-1	Apr01 3-2	Jan12 1-1		Oct13 2-3	Mar09 3-1	Dec01 4-0	Oct06 2-2	Dec22 3-1	Feb16 0-0	Sep08 2-1	Mar23 3-1	Oct27 4-3
EAST FIFE	Apr06 3-4	Jan02 1-1	Nov17 2-3	Sep22 1-1	Sep29 2-2	Jan05 6-2	Dec29 4-2	Nov24 4-0	Dec15 6-3	Sep15 4-5	Mar02 5-1		Jan26 3-1	Aug18 4-2	Mar16 1-2	Feb23 3-1	Nov03 2-1	Oct20 6-1	Sep01 2-1	Dec08 2-1
E STIRLING	Oct06 5-3	Feb09 1-1	Mar16 3-0	Apr20 0-1	Apr06 2-1	Nov17 5-0	Jan05 1-2	Jan02 4-2	Aug11 1-0	Dec15 2-3	Nov03 3-1	Sep08 4-2		Sep29 2-2	Oct20 5-2	Jan12 0-2	Mar30 0-2	Mar02 4-5	Sep15 2-1	Aug18 0-1
FORFAR A	Dec15 3-3	Sep15 4-1	Jan01 2-2	Sep08 3-1	Oct27 1-1	Oct13 8-2	Feb23 5-1	Nov17 3-2	Aug25 1-1	Dec08 2-1	Apr06 2-0	Dec22 3-1	Mar14 3-1		Aug11 2-1	Nov24 1-0	Jan12 0-2	Mar16 4-4	Feb09 3-1	Mar09 4-1
KING'S PARK	Sep08 1-1	Dec15 1-1	Dec08 2-2	Apr06 4-0	Aug18 2-1	Sep29 3-1	Mar23 0-0	Oct13 4-3	Jan12 1-1	Oct27 0-2	Feb23 5-1	Nov10 2-2	Jan01 3-5	Apr13 1-1		Aug25 1-3	Sep22 4-3	Feb06 2-3	Mar09 2-4	Nov24 3-3
LEITH A	Apr15 3-1	Dec29 4-2	Sep15 4-2	Apr27 5-1	Oct13 6-1	Jan02 1-2	Feb09 2-0	Jan26 0-0	Nov10 3-0	Mar09 3-2	Aug18 1-1	Oct06 5-2	Sep01 1-1	Mar30 5-0	Jan05 4-0		Dec08 1-0	Apr06 2-0	Oct20 0-0	Mar23 1-0
MORTON	Mar16 3-1	Nov17 3-4	Aug25 3-0	Dec22 4-2	Sep15 2-0	Jan26 2-0	Jan01 4-0	Aug11 3-2	Oct27 3-1	Feb23 2-0	Sep29 1-1	Mar09 3-2	Nov24 2-2	Sep01 4-0	Feb09 5-0	Apr20 4-1		Dec15 0-0	Apr06 4-1	Oct13 3-0
QUEEN OF SOUTH	Mar30 2-0	Apr20 2-1	Oct27 0-3	Mar23 7-3	Jan05 3-6	Aug18 3-4	Sep01 2-0	Feb23 7-2	Mar09 3-0	Feb09 2-3	Jan26 2-1	Jan01 1-1	Oct13 1-4	Nov10 9-2	Sep15 6-1	Dec01 4-1	Apr27 2-3		Dec29 3-1	Sep29 1-0
ST BERNARD'S	Dec22 1-1	Mar02 2-0	Feb23 3-2	Oct27 5-1	Nov24 5-1		Dec15 2-2	Sep29 1-2	Apr20 3-0	Sep08 2-2	Nov17 3-0	Jan12 2-1	Feb06 2-0	Sep22 2-1	Nov03 4-1	Jan01 1-1	Dec01 7-3	Aug11 1-1		Aug25 2-2
STENHOUSEMUIR	Oct20 3-1	Oct06 3-0	Jan12 1-1	Aug11 3-1	Dec15 1-2	Sep15 4-1	Apr06 3-2	Feb09 3-1	Sep08 1-0	Mar16 1-4	Jan02 1-7	Apr20 2-3	Dec22 0-4	Nov03 3-3	Mar30 2-2	Nov17 0-0	Mar02 1-2	Feb16 2-1	Jan05 3-4	

DIVISION 2 FINAL TABLE

	P	W	D	L	F	A	Pts
Dundee U	36	24	3	9	99	55	51
Morton	36	21	8	7	85	49	50
Arbroath	36	19	9	8	90	60	47
Albion R	36	18	8	10	95	67	44
Leith A	36	18	7	11	78	56	43
St Bernard's	36	16	9	11	77	55	41
Forfar A	35	14	10	11	69	75	38
East Fife	35	15	6	14	88	77	36
Queen of South	36	16	4	16	86	79	36
Bo'ness	35	15	5	15	62	62	35
Dunfermline A	36	13	7	16	66	72	33
E Stirling	36	14	4	18	71	75	32
Alloa	36	12	7	17	64	77	31
Dumbarton	36	11	9	16	59	78	31
King's Park	36	8	13	15	60	84	29
Clydebank	36	11	5	20	70	85	27
Arthurlie*	32	9	7	16	51	73	25
Stenhousemuir	35	9	6	20	51	90	24
Armadale	36	8	7	21	47	99	23
Bathgate**	28	5	2	21	37	92	12

**Arthurlie resigned towards the end of the season - but their record was allowed to stand.*
***Bathgate resigned, record shown but not recognised by League*

Season 1929-30

SFA Cup
1st Round

Jan 18	Airdrie 3	Dunfermline A 1
Jan 18	Albion R 4	Alloa 2
Jan 18	Arbroath 6	Galston 1
Jan 18	Ayr U 5	Mid-Annandale ...0
Jan 18	Beith 4	Royal Albert 1
Jan 18	Bo'ness 0	St Johnstone 0
Jan 18	Buckie T 0	Falkirk 2
Jan 18	Clacknacuddin ...2	Civil Service 0
Jan 18	Clyde 7	Keith 0
Jan 18	Dalbeattie Star ...1	Partick T 6
Jan 18	Dumbarton 1	Cowdenbeath 4
Jan 18	Dundee 2	Morton 0
Jan 18	Falkirk A 0	Leith A 3
Jan 18	Forfar A 7	Brechin C 2
Jan 18	Hamilton A 6	Stenhousemuir ...0
Jan 18	Hearts 1	Clydebank 0
Jan 18	Hibernian 2	Leith Amat 0
Jan 15	Inver Citadel 1	Armadale 0
Jan 18	Inverness Cal ...0	Celtic 6
Jan 18	Kilmarnock 11	Paisley A 1
Jan 18	King's Park 6	Bathgate 2
Jan 18	Montrose 8	Solway Star 0
Jan 18	Motherwell 6	E Stirling 0
Jan 11	Murrayfield A 2	Burntisland 2
Jan 18	Nithsdale W 6	St Andrew's Univ ..1
Jan 18	Peterhead 3	Vale of Leithen ...3
Jan 18	Queen of South ...2	East Fife 1
Jan 18	Queen's Park 0	Rangers 1
Jan 18	Raith R 3	Aberdeen 3
Jan 18	St Bernard's 5	T Lanark 3
Jan 18	St Cuthbert's W ...1	St Mirren 5
Jan 18	Stranraer 0	Dundee U 2

Replays

Jan 18	Burntisland 0	Murrayfield A 3

Jan 22	Aberdeen 7	Raith R 0
Jan 22	St Johnstone 3	Bo'ness 1
Jan 25	Vale of Leithen ...2	Peterhead 1

2nd Round

Feb 1	Aberdeen 5	Nithsdale W 1
Feb 1	Airdrie 8	Murrayfield A 3
Feb 1	Albion R 2	Beith 1
Feb 1	Ayr U 1	Hibernian 3
Feb 1	Celtic 5	Arbroath 0
Feb 1	Dundee 4	St Johnstone ...1
Feb 1	Dundee U 0	Partick T 3
Feb 1	Falkirk 1	Queen of South ..1
Feb 1	Forfar A 0	St Mirren 0
Feb 1	Hamilton A 4	Kilmarnock 2
Feb 1	Hearts 0	St Bernard's 0
Feb 1	Leith A 2	Clacknacuddin ...0
Feb 1	Montrose 3	Inver Citadel 1
Feb 1	Motherwell 3	Clyde 0
Feb 1	Rangers 2	Cowdenbeath 2
Feb 1	Vale of Leithen ...2	King's Park 7

Replays

Feb 4	St Mirren 3	Forfar A 0
Feb 5	Cowdenbeath 0	Rangers 3
Feb 5	St Bernard's 1	Hearts 5
Feb 6	Queen of South ...3	Falkirk 4

3rd Round

Feb 15	Albion R 2	Montrose 2
Feb 15	Celtic 1	St Mirren 3
Feb 15	Dundee 0	Airdrie 0
Feb 15	Falkirk 0	Leith A 0
Feb 15	Hamilton A 4	King's Park 0
Feb 15	Hibernian 1	Hearts 3
Feb 15	Motherwell 2	Rangers 5
Feb 15	Partick T 3	Aberdeen 2

Replays

Feb 19	Airdrie 0	Dundee 0
Feb 19	Leith A 1	Falkirk 1
Feb 19	Montrose 3	Albion R 1
Feb 24	Airdrie 1	Dundee 2
	played at Ibrox	
Feb 24	Falkirk 1	Leith A 1
	played at Tynecastle	
Feb 25	Falkirk 1	Leith A 0
	played at Tynecastle	

4th Round

Mar 1	Dundee 2	Hearts 2
Mar 1	Partick T 3	Falkirk 1
Mar 1	Rangers 3	Montrose 0
Mar 1	St Mirren 3	Hamilton A 4

Replay

Mar 5	Hearts 4	Dundee 0

Semi-finals

Mar 22	Hamilton A 1	Partick T 3
	played at Celtic Park	
Mar 22	Hearts 1	Rangers 4
	played at Hampden Park	

Final

Apr 12	Partick T 0	Rangers 0
	played at Hampden Park	

Replay

Apr 16	Partick T 1	Rangers 2
	played at Hampden Park	

Three famous Celtic players of the 1920s: Paddy Connolly, Alec Thomson and probably the game's greatest-ever scorer Jimmy McGrory.

DIVISION 1

(home) \ (away)	ABERDEEN	AIRDRIE	AYR U	CELTIC	CLYDE	COWDENBEATH	DUNDEE	DUNDEE U	FALKIRK	HAMILTON A	HEARTS	HIBERNIAN	KILMARNOCK	MORTON	MOTHERWELL	PARTICK T	QUEEN'S PARK	RANGERS	ST JOHNSTONE	ST MIRREN
ABERDEEN	—	Jan11 3-1	Oct12 4-1	Jan04 3-1	Sep23 5-2	Nov09 2-0	Oct26 1-0	Mar29 2-2	Dec21 1-0	Nov30 4-2	Jan02 2-2	Dec07 2-0	Mar08 4-3	Sep21 5-3	Aug17 2-2	Sep28 2-1	Apr19 3-0	Sep07 1-1	Feb22 1-0	Mar22 3-3
AIRDRIE	Aug31 0-2	—	Nov02 2-0	Sep14 0-1	Oct05 2-4	Mar12 4-1	Mar22 3-2	Jan25 3-4	Jan01 4-1	Oct19 1-0	Apr12 3-2	Dec21 3-0	Nov09 2-2	Nov23 2-2	Feb08 2-0	Apr26 2-0	Nov30 1-2	Apr19 1-0	Aug17 5-1	Mar05 2-2
AYR U	Mar01 5-1	Mar08 3-1	—	Sep28 1-3	Mar22 2-2	Oct05 3-1	Nov30 2-2	Oct19 6-1	Feb08 0-0	Mar29 3-3	3-1	3-2	1-1	2-0	3-2	2-4	2-5	0-3	4-0	1-0
CELTIC	Aug24 3-4	Feb05 1-2	Feb18 4-0	—	Apr21 0-2	Nov16 7-0	Sep21 3-0	Mar01 2-1	Oct05 4-0	Apr15 3-0	Aug10 2-1	Nov02 4-0	Apr19 0-4	Dec28 2-0	Mar15 1-2	Apr05 1-2	Oct19 6-2	Jan01 1-2	Mar29 6-2	Dec07 3-0
CLYDE	Sep14 1-3	Feb22 2-0	Dec14 3-1	Jan25 2-3	—	Apr11 4-1	Mar08 1-1	Dec21 3-2	Sep28 1-2	Mar26 3-1	Nov03 3-3	Feb08 0-2	Jan04 1-1	Oct12 2-1	Aug10 1-2	Oct26 2-3	Nov09 2-1	Nov23 3-3	Jan02 2-0	Aug17 3-2
COWDENBEATH	Mar15 0-1	Feb08 2-0	Feb22 7-1	Mar22 1-2	Dec07 4-0	—	Nov23 2-1	Jan01 4-1	Apr05 3-0	Apr19 3-0	Aug24 0-1	Jan25 0-0	Oct19 2-3	Oct12 2-0	Sep14 0-0	Dec21 0-2	Apr26 1-1	Aug31 3-2	Feb08 2-1	Feb08 2-3
DUNDEE	Jan01 0-3	Nov16 3-0	Apr05 0-2	Feb08 2-0	Nov02 3-0	Mar29 3-0	—	Aug31 1-0	Aug17 0-0	Mar12 3-2	Dec14 1-0	Oct19 3-2	Sep28 2-2	Mar15 3-1	Jan04 1-1	Dec21 3-2	Oct05 1-3	Apr23 1-3	Sep14 0-1	Jan25 2-1
DUNDEE U	Nov23 2-4	Sep07 0-3	Jan02 1-2	Oct23 2-2	Aug10 3-3	Oct26 2-1	Jan11 0-1	—	Dec07 2-2	Dec28 1-2	Apr02 2-3	Apr19 2-2	Mar22 6-4	Aug24 3-1	Aug08 1-1	Nov09 3-2	Sep21 2-1	Feb19 0-1	Nov30 1-1	Feb22 0-2
FALKIRK	Aug10 3-2	Oct26 3-2	Sep21 1-1	Feb22 2-1	Nov30 2-2	May05 5-2	Dec28 5-2	Apr12 5-2	—	Apr26 1-0	Oct12 2-3	Nov16 1-1	Mar29 1-0	Sep07 3-0	Jan02 4-1	Mar08 0-0	Aug24 1-2	Apr30 2-1	Dec14 4-0	Mar15 1-0
HAMILTON A	Apr05 4-2	Jan02 0-1	Nov23 6-2	Aug31 1-3	Nov16 5-1	Dec14 2-0	Oct12 5-2	Aug17 0-2	Sep14 0-2	—	Mar08 2-1	Jan04 1-1	Dec21 4-0	Feb22 2-3	Oct26 2-1	Jan25 4-2	Apr11 1-1	Feb08 3-0	Sep28 2-0	—
HEARTS	Oct19 2-2	Dec07 1-0	Mar15 2-1	Dec21 1-3	Apr05 0-1	Jan04 2-2	Apr19 1-0	Sep14 3-1	Mar12 0-2	Nov02 6-4	—	Jan01 1-1	Aug17 4-0	Nov16 3-2	Jan25 0-0	Feb08 0-3	Mar29 2-0	Oct05 2-2	Sep28 2-2	Aug31 5-0
HIBERNIAN	Apr12 0-1	Aug10 3-1	Jan11 1-0	Mar08 0-2	Sep07 1-1	Sep07 1-1	Jan02 0-1	Dec14 3-0	Mar22 1-0	Aug24 1-2	Oct26 1-1	—	Nov30 0-0	Apr26 0-1	Feb22 1-1	Oct12 3-0	Mar01 6-3	Dec28 0-0	Nov09 3-1	Nov23 2-2
KILMARNOCK	Nov02 4-2	Mar15 2-1	Sep07 2-0	Dec14 1-1	Aug24 2-1	Jan02 3-2	Apr21 0-2	Nov16 0-2	Aug10 3-2	Dec28 3-0	Apr05 2-1	Feb15 7-2	—	Apr12 2-3	Feb22 1-1	Jan11 1-5	Sep21 1-0	Oct12 3-1	Oct26 2-3	—
MORTON	Feb08 1-2	Mar29 1-1	Apr12 3-4	Aug17 1-2	Mar01 1-2	Dec21 3-4	Nov09 2-1	Jan04 6-1	Jan25 1-4	Oct05 4-4	Mar26 3-2	Sep28 3-2	Sep14 4-2	—	Dec14 1-3	Aug31 2-2	Feb01 2-4	Nov30 2-2	Oct26 4-1	Jan02 2-0
MOTHERWELL	Dec28 4-1	Sep21 2-0	Apr21 4-1	Nov09 2-1	Jan11 2-1	Mar01 7-2	Aug24 3-0	Nov02 6-1	Oct19 4-3	Jan01 5-1	Sep07 0-2	Oct05 2-0	Dec07 2-0	Apr19 3-0	—	Mar29 4-0	Apr26 9-0	Aug10 2-5	Mar22 5-0	Nov30 3-0
PARTICK T	Feb19 2-1	Aug28 4-0	Dec28 2-3	Nov30 1-1	Jan01 3-1	Apr30 3-1	Aug10 1-0	Mar15 5-0	Nov02 5-0	Sep07 2-2	Sep21 2-1	Mar05 0-0	Oct05 3-2	Jan11 4-1	Nov23 6-1	—	Dec25 1-0	Oct19 0-1	Apr23 2-1	Apr19 3-2
QUEEN'S PARK	Dec14 2-2	Apr05 1-3	Oct26 2-3	Jan02 2-1	Feb15 1-1	Aug17 1-2	Feb22 2-1	Feb11 1-0	Jan04 2-0	Dec07 2-0	Nov03 6-2	Sep14 2-0	Aug31 1-4	Nov02 2-4	Sep28 0-3	Nov16 4-1	—	Mar04 1-3	Jan25 3-0	Dec21 1-6
RANGERS	Jan25 3-1	Dec14 2-0	Nov16 9-0	Oct26 1-0	Mar29 3-0	Mar08 5-0	Dec07 4-1	Sep28 3-1	Aug31 4-0	Nov09 5-2	Feb22 1-3	Feb08 3-0	Feb08 4-0	Apr21 3-0	Jan02 4-2	Jan02 2-1	Sep03 1-0	—	Jan04 6-1	Sep14 2-1
ST JOHNSTONE	Oct05 0-1	Dec28 2-1	Aug10 3-1	Nov23 0-1	Oct19 1-3	Jan11 2-0	Dec25 3-2	Apr05 1-1	Apr19 3-4	Sep21 2-2	Feb19 0-3	Mar01 4-3	Jan01 1-3	Jan01 1-1	Nov16 1-1	Dec07 4-0	Sep07 4-0	Apr12 0-1	—	Nov02 1-3
ST MIRREN	Nov16 1-0	Oct12 0-1	Aug24 3-0	Apr12 0-0	Dec28 3-0	Sep21 2-0	Sep07 3-0	Oct05 6-1	Nov09 2-3	Feb18 2-0	Jan11 6-2	Mar29 1-2	Jan01 3-1	Oct19 5-0	Apr05 0-2	Dec14 0-3	Aug10 1-1	Feb11 0-1	Mar08 3-2	—

DIVISION 2

(home) \ (away)	ALBION R	ALLOA	ARBROATH	ARMADALE	BO'NESS	BRECHIN C	CLYDEBANK	DUMBARTON	DUNFERMLINE A	EAST FIFE	E STIRLING	FORFAR A	KING'S PARK	LEITH A	MONTROSE	QUEEN OF SOUTH	RAITH R	ST BERNARD'S	STENHOUSEMUIR	T LANARK
ALBION R	—	Aug24 4-2	Feb22 3-2	Nov16 2-1	Jan02 6-1	Oct12 7-1	Mar08 3-0	Apr05 2-0	Mar15 3-5	Jan11 3-0	Sep21 2-1	Aug10 6-1	Sep07 3-1	Dec28 7-0	Apr30 5-1	Mar29 7-0	Dec14 2-1	Dec07 5-2	Oct26 5-2	Sep28 4-2
ALLOA	Jan04 0-0	—	Aug31 2-4	Sep14 0-1	Jan01 2-1	Dec21 0-2	Nov16 1-0	Jan25 2-1	Feb08 1-3	Jan02 3-4	Feb22 1-1	Nov30 2-6	Aug17 1-2	Oct12 1-3	Apr19 1-3	Dec07 0-0	Mar15 2-3	Sep28 0-1	Mar29 1-2	Nov02 2-4
ARBROATH	Oct05 3-3	Jan11 3-0	—	Mar01 3-2	Mar29 4-0	Aug10 4-2	Apr12 6-1	Apr24 4-3	Feb15 2-2	Apr21 1-4	Oct26 5-2	Mar15 2-1	Nov30 2-2	Sep21 1-1	Apr19 1-1	Nov02 0-2	Nov16 1-0	Dec28 2-1	Jan11 2-1	Jan04 1-4
ARMADALE	Mar22 1-3	Feb01 2-3	Oct12 0-1	—	Sep21 3-3	Nov02 0-4	Feb15 3-1	Nov23 1-1	Jan01 2-3	Dec14 3-2	Dec28 4-2	Mar15 4-2	Apr02 2-2	Aug24 2-2	Sep07 6-0	Nov09 3-0	Apr12 1-0	Oct19 1-1	Aug10 2-1	Feb22 1-0
BO'NESS	Oct19 1-1	Oct26 2-0	Jan25 2-1	Feb08 4-3	—	Sep14 4-2	Nov09 1-0	Feb22 3-1	Mar22 4-2	Mar01 1-4	Nov30 0-1	Dec14 1-1	Dec21 2-2	Mar08 3-3	Dec28 5-1	Sep28 2-1	Aug31 2-1	Aug17 1-0	Apr12 2-0	Jan04 1-3
BRECHIN C	Mar01 1-0	Jan11 2-2	Sep28 2-3	Mar08 3-1	Feb01 1-2	—	Jan04 2-0	Aug24 3-2	Mar15 1-0	Apr19 2-3	Sep07 3-4	Jan11 1-1	Sep21 3-6	Nov16 1-1	Jan02 2-0	Oct26 2-0	Oct05 0-3	Dec14 0-3	Apr05 0-1	Feb15 0-1
CLYDEBANK	Nov02 1-3	Mar22 2-2	Dec21 2-3	Sep28 1-3	Mar15 1-2	Jan04 —	—	Oct26 4-0	Aug31 1-2	Aug17 1-1	Jan02 4-1	Nov23 5-5	Dec14 2-1	Feb22 0-0	Dec07 1-0	Feb08 0-3	Jan25 1-3	Sep14 0-1	Oct12 5-2	Apr26 0-2
DUMBARTON	Nov30 1-2	Sep07 1-2	Dec07 1-4	Mar29 6-0	Oct05 2-5	Nov09 4-1	Jan01 1-3	—	Dec28 1-3	Feb01 6-3	Feb15 5-3	Sep21 1-2	Aug10 4-2	Jan11 2-3	Mar01 3-1	Oct19 4-0	Apr19 2-3	Nov16 3-0	Mar08 5-1	Nov16 4-3
DUNFERMLINE A	Nov09 2-3	Apr14 4-1	Jan11 6-4	Oct26 7-1	Nov16 5-0	Dec14 10-1	Jan11 4-2	Aug17 2-3	—	Oct05 0-6	Aug31 3-1	Mar29 3-0	Mar01 2-5	Sep07 0-1	Mar12 3-2	Aug08 0-2	Nov30 2-2	Dec21 1-2	Jan02 5-1	Mar15 3-5
EAST FIFE	Aug31 0-1	Oct19 3-1	Sep28 3-0	Apr19 5-0	Oct12 3-2	Jan25 7-2	Dec28 4-2	Sep14 4-1	Feb22 3-3	—	Aug24 2-1	Apr12 5-2	Nov02 5-4	Nov23 1-3	Aug10 2-0	Mar22 4-1	Jan01 0-2	Feb08 3-1	Nov30 7-0	Mar15 2-0
E STIRLING	Feb08 2-6	Oct05 2-4	Sep14 3-1	Aug17 6-0	Apr05 4-1	Aug31 7-0	Oct19 3-1	Sep28 1-0	Nov23 4-1	Jan04 3-3	—	Mar01 4-2	Jan01 3-2	Apr16 2-3	Dec21 2-0	Mar22 0-2	Nov02 3-1	Mar15 4-0	Jan25 5-0	Jan25 2-1
FORFAR A	Dec21 4-0	Apr05 5-4	Feb08 4-3	Nov09 1-1	Apr19 5-2	Feb08 2-0	Mar29 5-2	Sep14 1-2	Jan04 1-4	Sep14 1-0	Dec07 1-4	—	Oct12 2-3	Nov02 5-2	Aug17 2-1	Dec21 2-0	Jan25 3-2	Feb22 4-1	Aug31 1-1	—
KING'S PARK	Jan25 4-0	Dec28 9-0	Nov09 3-4	Aug31 3-0	Aug10 5-3	Mar22 1-1	Apr19 3-3	Feb08 3-3	Dec07 3-2	Mar08 4-2	Oct26 1-0	Jan02 12-1	—	Mar12 2-2	May05 3-0	Sep14 2-2	Nov23 5-1	Oct05 3-2	Aug24 7-3	Apr05 2-1
LEITH A	Aug17 2-1	Mar01 7-1	Apr05 1-2	Jan04 2-0	Nov02 5-1	Oct19 4-0	Oct05 5-0	Dec21 6-2	Jan25 1-1	Mar29 0-0	Dec07 2-0	Nov16 3-2	Sep28 4-0	—	Mar15 2-2	Aug31 3-1	Feb08 4-1	Jan01 0-0	Apr19 5-1	Sep14 2-0
MONTROSE	Sep14 2-1	Dec14 5-1	Feb08 2-2	Jan25 2-1	Mar29 4-2	Jan01 1-1	Nov30 2-1	Sep28 6-0	Dec21 1-1	Apr26 2-2	Oct12 3-2	Sep14 1-2	—	Oct19 4-1	—	Jan04 1-2	Jun20 4-1	Nov16 5-3	Nov16 6-6	Aug17 1-0
QUEEN OF SOUTH	Nov23 1-1	Apr12 1-2	Dec14 2-2	Apr05 1-3	Feb15 1-3	Feb22 2-1	Sep21 2-5	Oct12 1-0	Nov02 2-4	Nov16 4-2	Aug10 2-2	Dec28 3-1	Apr26 1-0	Jan11 —	Jan02 1-3	—	Aug24 1-3	Mar15 2-1	Sep07 3-1	Oct26 0-4
RAITH R	Apr19 6-2	Nov09 7-2	Mar08 3-1	Dec07 8-0	Jan11 4-2	Aug17 6-1	Sep07 6-0	Jan02 1-2	Apr05 3-1	Oct26 0-2	Nov16 4-1	Feb15 1-4	Mar29 1-3	Sep21 1-2	Oct05 1-1	Jan04 0-1	—	Mar01 2-1	Feb01 6-2	Dec21 1-1
ST BERNARD'S	Apr12 1-1	Feb15 5-2	Mar22 5-2	Jan02 5-1	Dec28 4-2	Nov30 3-1	Apr14 3-2	Sep21 5-0	Aug10 1-0	Sep21 1-2	Mar08 4-2	Feb22 1-2	Oct12 0-0	Aug24 0-1	Nov09 0-1	Oct12 1-2	Mar15 2-2	—	Jan11 3-3	Mar15 3-2
STENHOUSEMUIR	Jan01 0-3	Nov23 2-3	Aug17 0-1	Dec21 1-2	Dec07 5-0	Sep28 4-3	Mar01 3-2	Nov02 5-0	Oct19 3-2	Apr05 5-3	Nov09 1-3	Oct05 3-2	Jan04 0-1	Dec14 1-1	Mar22 6-1	Jan25 0-1	Sep14 2-2	Aug31 —	—	Feb08 0-2
T LANARK	Apr21 4-0	Mar08 1-1	Oct19 4-2	Oct05 2-0	Dec21 2-0	Apr12 6-3	Dec25 2-2	Mar22 2-2	Oct12 3-1	Nov09 1-1	Sep07 1-0	Jan11 5-0	Nov30 5-1	Apr23 2-1	Jan01 3-2	Aug10 6-2	Dec07 4-2	Aug10 1-4	Mar29 1-0	—

Dundee United's Second Division promotion side. Back row (left to right): Taylor, Penson, Milne, McCallum, Gardner, Quiskley. Front row: Logie, Bain, Bennett, Kay, Cuthill.

SFA Cup
1st Round

Jan 17	Aberdeen	6	Dumbarton	1
Jan 17	Albion R	6	Vale of Atholl	0
Jan 17	Alloa	2	Dalbeattie Star	0
Jan 17	Arbroath	7	Moor Park	1
Jan 17	Armadale	1	Rangers	7
Jan 17	Ayr U	11	Clackmannan	2
Jan 17	Bo'ness	3	Peterhead	0
Jan 17	Brechin C	1	Edinburgh C	3
Jan 17	Civil Service	2	Tarff R	0
Jan 17	Clyde	7	Leith A	0
Jan 17	Dundee	10	Fraserburgh	1
Jan 17	Dundee U	14	Nithsdale W	0
Jan 17	Dunfermline A	2	Airdrie	2
Jan 17	East Fife	1	Celtic	2
Jan 17	E Stirling	0	Hamilton A	2
Jan 17	Glasgow Univ	0	Inverness Cal	1
Jan 17	Hearts	9	Stenhousemuir	1
Jan 17	Hibernian	3	St Cuthbert's	1
Jan 17	Inver Citadel	0	Kilmarnock	7
Jan 17	King's Park	7	Falkirk A	0
Jan 17	Montrose	2	Mid-Annandale	0
Jan 17	Morton	1	Raith R	1
Jan 17	Motherwell	6	Bathgate	0
Jan 17	Murrayfield A	3	Beith	2
Jan 17	Partick T	16	Royal Albert	0
Jan 17	Peebles R	0	Falkirk	4
Jan 17	Queen of South	2	Cowdenbeath	3
Jan 17	Queen's Park	5	Elgin C	0
Jan 17	St Bernard's	6	Stranraer	2
Jan 17	St Johnstone	3	Forfar A	2
Jan 17	St Mirren	3	Clydebank	1
Jan 17	T Lanark	6	Buckie T	2

Replays

Jan 21	Airdrie	6	Dunfermline A	1
Jan 21	Raith R	1	Morton	1
Jan 26	Morton	2	Raith R	0
	played at Firhill Park			

2nd Round

Jan 31	Aberdeen	1	Partick T	1
Feb 7	Arbroath	2	Edinburgh C	0
Feb 4	Bo'ness	4	Alloa	2
Feb 3	Clyde	1	St Mirren	1
Feb 4	Cowdenbeath	1	St Johnstone	1
Feb 4	Dundee U	2	Celtic	3
Jan 31	Hamilton A	2	Hibernian	2
Jan 31	Inverness Cal	2	Falkirk	7
Jan 31	Kilmarnock	3	Hearts	2
Feb 4	King's Park	1	St Bernard's	1
Feb 7	Montrose	1	Civil Service	0
Jan 31	Motherwell	4	Albion R	1
Jan 31	Murrayfield A	0	Ayr U	1
Jan 31	Queen's Park	0	Morton	1
Jan 31	Rangers	1	Dundee	2
Jan 31	T Lanark	1	Airdrie	0

Replays

Feb 4	Hibernian	5	Hamilton A	2
Feb 4	Partick T	0	Aberdeen	3
Feb 10	St Mirren	3	Clyde	1
Feb 11	St Bernard's	1	King's Park	0
Feb 11	St Johnstone	0	Cowdenbeath	4

3rd Round

Feb 14	Bo'ness	1	Ayr U	0
Feb 14	Cowdenbeath	3	St Bernard's	0
Feb 14	Dundee	1	Aberdeen	1
Feb 14	Hibernian	0	Motherwell	3
Feb 14	Montrose	0	Kilmarnock	3
Feb 14	Morton	1	Celtic	4
Feb 14	St Mirren	2	Falkirk	0
Feb 14	T Lanark	4	Arbroath	2

Replay

Feb 18	Aberdeen	2	Dundee	0

4th Round

Feb 28	Bo'ness	1	Kilmarnock	1
Feb 28	Celtic	4	Aberdeen	0
Feb 28	Cowdenbeath	0	Motherwell	1
Feb 28	T Lanark	1	St Mirren	1

Replays

Mar 3	St Mirren	3	T Lanark	0
Mar 4	Kilmarnock	5	Bo'ness	0

Semi-finals

Mar 14	Celtic	3	Kilmarnock	0
	played at Hampden Park			
Mar 14	Motherwell	1	St Mirren	0
	played at Ibrox			

Final

Apr 11	Celtic	2	Motherwell	2
	played at Hampden Park			

Replay

Apr 15	Celtic	4	Motherwell	2
	played at Hampden Park			

Season 1930-31

DIVISION 1

	ABERDEEN	AIRDRIE	AYR U	CELTIC	CLYDE	COWDENBEATH	DUNDEE	EAST FIFE	FALKIRK	HAMILTON A	HEARTS	HIBERNIAN	KILMARNOCK	LEITH A	MORTON	MOTHERWELL	PARTICK T	QUEEN'S PARK	RANGERS	ST MIRREN
ABERDEEN		Aug30 2-0	Feb07 3-1	Jan24 1-1	Apr18 8-1	Jan03 1-1	Jan01 6-1	Feb21 4-1	Apr04 2-1	Sep22 0-2	Sep27 2-1	Nov15 7-0	Nov08 2-0	Aug16 2-1	Nov29 4-0	Sep13 2-4	Dec20 3-1	Oct25 3-1	Mar07 1-3	Oct11 0-0
AIRDRIE	Jan10 2-0		Nov01 2-1	Dec06 1-2	Sep06 2-1	Nov29 2-1	Nov15 2-0	Apr06 0-3	Sep20 1-3	Feb14 3-1	Apr25 2-2	Feb18 4-1	Aug23 4-3	Feb28 4-1	Dec27 2-0	Oct18 0-5	Mar14 0-2	Aug09 1-3	Oct04 3-3	Apr04 3-0
AYR U	Oct04 2-1	Mar07 0-0		Nov22 2-6	Oct11 0-2	Apr25 5-1	Nov08 2-6	Jan05 3-1	Aug23 2-5	Jan10 4-2	Oct25 1-1	Sep06 1-3	Apr29 1-0	Mar21 2-0	Aug09 2-2	Nov29 2-3	Feb21 1-1	Mar28 3-1	Feb18 2-2	Apr18 2-0
CELTIC	Sep06 1-0	Apr18 3-1	Apr04 4-1		Feb18 0-1	Mar21 6-0	Mar25 2-2	Jan10 9-1	Dec27 3-0	Feb24 2-1	Nov08 2-1	Aug23 6-0	Aug09 3-1	Dec13 4-0	Oct04 4-1	Mar04 4-1	Nov01 5-1	Apr28 1-1	Sep20 2-0	Oct18 3-1
CLYDE	Dec06 2-5	Jan24 2-1	Aug16 1-1	Apr06 0-2		Aug30 5-2	Dec20 2-2	Mar07 3-0	Nov15 0-1	Feb21 3-1	Sep13 1-2	Mar14 3-2	Apr25 0-3	Sep27 2-2	Oct25 1-0	Feb07 0-6	Jan01 1-2	Nov22 2-4	Feb14 0-8	Jan03 3-0
COWDENBEATH	Aug23 2-0	Apr11 2-1	Dec13 1-1	Nov15 1-1	Jan10 0-1		Feb21 3-0	Sep20 2-1	Sep06 3-0	Apr01 3-1	Mar07 2-2	Oct04 2-1	Jan05 3-1	Nov22 7-1	Mar28 3-0	Apr18 1-0	Oct25 0-3	Dec27 1-3	Aug09 1-3	Mar18 3-1
DUNDEE	Sep20 4-2	Mar21 0-1	Mar18 5-2	Apr22 0-0	Aug09 2-1	Oct18 2-0		Dec27 2-0	Oct04 3-1	Sep06 4-2	Nov22 1-3	Jan05 1-0	Mar28 0-2	Dec06 6-0	Jan10 3-0	Nov01 2-1	Dec13 0-0	Feb28 3-0	Aug23 0-1	Mar09 2-0
EAST FIFE	Oct18 1-3	Sep13 1-5	Sep27 4-1	Aug30 2-6	Nov01 1-4	Jan01 0-0	Aug16 1-2		Nov29 4-4	Apr04 2-0	Jan03 1-0	Feb28 1-0	Mar21 4-1	Oct11 0-0	Nov08 2-3	Dec20 1-1	Jan24 0-2	Apr18 3-2	Apr25 0-4	Feb07 3-2
FALKIRK	Nov22 5-3	Jan01 1-3	Jan03 2-0	Aug16 3-2	Mar21 4-0	Jan24 4-0	Feb07 4-1	Apr11 1-0		Dec06 1-4	Oct11 0-3	Apr25 2-2	Oct25 4-2	Dec20 2-3	Mar07 3-1	Sep27 0-1	Aug30 2-4	Feb21 3-0	Nov08 1-3	Sep13 1-3
HAMILTON A	Dec13 3-0	Sep27 1-1	Aug30 3-1	Sep13 0-0	Oct18 4-0	Oct11 0-1	Jan24 1-0	Nov22 4-1	Apr18 5-1		Dec20 3-2	Nov29 1-0	Mar07 0-0	Jan03 2-3	Mar21 1-1	Jan01 1-0	Feb07 2-0	Nov08 3-1	Feb28 0-3	Aug16 1-0
HEARTS	Jan05 3-2	Dec13 6-3	Feb28 9-0	Mar18 1-1	Mar28 0-3	Nov01 1-1	Apr04 2-0	Aug23 6-1	Feb18 4-2	Aug09 0-4		Sep20 4-1	Jan10 1-4	Oct18 5-2	Sep06 2-4	Nov15 5-1	Apr18 1-2	Oct04 2-1	Dec27 3-0	Nov29 3-1
HIBERNIAN	Mar21 1-2	Oct11 2-0	Jan24 2-0	Jan03 2-0	Nov08 1-2	Feb07 1-0	Sep27 2-3	Oct25 2-1	Dec13 5-2	Apr11 1-0	Jan01 2-2		Nov22 3-2	Aug30 0-1	Feb21 1-1	Aug16 2-2	Sep13 0-3	Mar11 4-2	Dec06 1-2	Dec20 2-3
KILMARNOCK	Mar18 1-1	Jan03 1-0	Sep13 2-1	Dec20 0-3	Dec13 2-1	Sep27 0-1	Oct11 1-2	Nov15 5-1	Mar11 1-1	Nov01 3-1	Aug30 0-1	Apr04 4-0		Feb07 2-1	Apr18 3-0	Jan24 1-4	Aug16 2-0	Nov29 2-1	Oct18 1-0	Jan01 2-3
LEITH A	Dec27 0-0	Oct25 0-1	Nov15 1-1	Apr25 0-3	Jan05 2-4	Apr04 2-2	Apr18 3-1	Jan31 6-1	Aug09 2-2	Aug23 1-2	Feb21 2-1	Jan10 1-1	Oct04 0-1		Sep20 2-3	Mar17 2-5	Nov29 2-1	Sep06 2-0	Mar14 1-3	Nov01 1-1
MORTON	Apr11 1-2	Aug16 3-0	Dec20 1-1	Feb07 0-1	Feb28 0-1	Sep13 1-2	Aug30 2-1	Mar14 3-0	Nov01 5-3	Nov15 1-0	Jan24 2-4	Oct18 5-4	Dec06 2-2	Jan01 1-1		Oct11 0-3	Jan03 3-1	Dec13 1-3	Apr04 1-2	Dec25 4-2
MOTHERWELL	Feb09 5-0	Feb21 4-0	Apr22 1-1	Oct25 3-3	Oct04 4-4	Dec06 3-1	Mar07 2-0	Aug09 4-1	Mar30 6-1	Sep20 3-0	Mar21 2-0	Dec27 6-0	Sep06 1-1	Nov08 4-1	Feb18 3-0		Apr04 0-0	Aug23 2-1	Jan10 1-0	Apr25 3-1
PARTICK T	Aug09 2-1	Nov08 2-0	Oct18 5-1	Mar07 1-0	Sep20 2-0	Mar10 4-1	Apr25 4-1	Sep06 8-0	Jan10 3-2	Oct04 1-1	Dec06 2-1	Feb10 1-0	Dec27 3-1	Apr11 2-0	Aug23 2-1	Dec25 0-3		Oct11 5-1	Apr22 1-1	Nov15 2-1
QUEEN'S PARK	Mar03 2-2	Dec20 0-0	Dec25 4-1	Sep27 3-3	Apr04 4-1	Aug16 0-3	Sep13 2-2	Dec06 5-1	Oct18 2-0	Mar17 5-0	Feb11 1-2	Nov01 2-2	Apr21 2-0	Jan24 1-1	Apr25 5-2	Jan03 1-3	Feb14 2-1		Nov15 0-2	Aug30 4-1
RANGERS	Nov01 4-0	Feb07 0-1	Apr06 5-1	Jan01 1-0	Nov29 5-1	Dec20 7-0	Jan03 3-0	Dec13 4-0	Mar18 1-0	Sep02 1-0	Aug16 4-1	Apr18 1-0	Feb21 1-0	Sep13 4-1	Nov22 7-1	Aug30 1-1	Sep27 3-1	Apr01 2-0		Jan24 1-1
ST MIRREN	Feb23 2-2	Nov22 2-3	Dec06 0-0	Feb21 1-3	Aug23 2-1	Nov08 0-1	Oct25 3-1	Oct04 2-0	Apr14 0-5	Dec27 4-2	Apr11 0-3	Aug09 1-0	Sep20 4-2	Mar07 2-2	Apr20 0-0	Dec13 2-1	Mar21 0-1	Jan10 2-1	Sep06 1-1	

DIVISION 1 FINAL TABLE

	P	W	D	L	F	A	Pts
Rangers	38	27	6	5	96	29	60
Celtic	38	24	10	4	101	34	58
Motherwell	38	24	8	6	102	42	56
Partick T	38	24	5	9	76	43	53
Hearts	38	19	6	13	90	63	44
Aberdeen	38	17	7	14	79	63	41
Cowdenbeath	38	17	7	14	58	65	41
Dundee	38	17	5	16	65	63	39
Airdrie	38	17	5	16	59	66	39
Hamilton A	38	16	5	17	59	57	37
Kilmarnock	38	15	5	18	59	60	35
Clyde	38	15	4	19	60	87	34
Queen's Park	38	13	7	18	71	72	33
Falkirk	38	14	4	20	77	87	32
St Mirren	38	11	8	19	49	72	30
Morton	38	11	7	20	58	83	29
Leith A	38	8	11	19	51	85	27
Ayr U	38	8	11	19	53	92	27
Hibernian	38	9	7	22	49	81	25
East Fife	38	8	4	26	45	113	20

DIVISION 2

	ALBION R	ALLOA	ARBROATH	ARMADALE	BO'NESS	BRECHIN C	CLYDEBANK	DUMBARTON	DUNDEE U	DUNFERMLINE A	E STIRLING	FORFAR A	KING'S PARK	MONTROSE	QUEEN OF SOUTH	RAITH R	ST BERNARD'S	ST JOHNSTONE	STENHOUSEMUIR	T LANARK
ALBION R		Sep27 0-0	Apr29 3-1	Feb07 5-2	Dec13 4-0	Oct25 3-0	Oct11 5-2	Apr11 1-1	Mar18 0-5	Mar07 3-0	Aug30 3-1	Aug16 4-2	Apr18 2-4	Jan03 4-0	Nov08 4-2	Dec20 2-0	Feb21 4-4	Sep13 1-3	Jan01 2-2	Jan24 0-0
ALLOA	Jan02 3-3		Oct04 5-2	Oct25 2-0	Sep20 3-1	Sep06 3-0	Apr11 0-2	Feb14 2-0	Dec27 1-4	Mar28 2-1	Mar07 1-3	Apr21 3-0	Jan10 0-4	Apr25 8-1	Aug09 2-1	Mar21 3-2	Aug23 2-0	Nov08 2-2	Feb21 3-2	Dec06 2-1
ARBROATH	Mar28 3-2	Feb11 5-3		Aug16 5-1	Nov22 5-0	Apr11 3-0	Jan24 2-1	Oct25 3-1	Apr13 1-2	Feb21 2-0	Sep13 2-2	Jan01 5-3	Nov15 5-2	Oct11 4-2	Mar07 1-4	Jan03 0-1	Dec13 4-4	Dec20 4-0	Aug30 1-0	Sep27 1-2
ARMADALE	Oct04 4-0	Feb28 5-1	Dec27 2-1		Aug23 4-0	Feb14 0-0	Oct18 3-3	Sep06 3-4	Aug09 1-4	Sep20 0-2	Apr11 5-2	Nov01 3-0	Mar28 2-1	Mar18 5-1	Jan10 2-1	Apr04 4-3	Jan05 2-1	Apr25 3-0	Dec06 3-5	Nov15 1-2
BO'NESS	Nov15 1-4	Jan01 2-1	Apr04 3-1	Jan03 1-2		Apr22 4-0	Aug30 6-3	Feb21 4-4	Dec06 1-3	Oct25 1-2	Jan24 0-6	Sep13 3-2	Mar18 2-4	Dec20 3-3	Apr11 4-0	Sep27 3-2	Nov01 0-1	Feb07 2-0	Aug16 1-1	Oct11 0-3
BRECHIN C	Feb28 1-2	Jan24 1-0	Nov29 1-0	Oct11 3-0	Mar28 4-1		Jan03 4-2	Apr04 2-2	Oct18 2-4	Nov15 1-4	Aug16 2-3	Apr29 1-1	Nov01 1-1	Jan01 2-1	Dec13 2-1	Sep13 2-2	Mar18 1-4	Sep27 3-5	Dec20 4-1	Aug30 2-2
CLYDEBANK	Feb14 4-1	Nov29 3-0	Sep06 0-2	Feb21 5-2	Jan10 1-0	Aug23 1-2		Sep20 1-4	Apr06 1-2	Oct04 1-2	Oct25 1-4	Apr18 3-2	Aug09 1-2	Mar07 1-0	Jan31 0-1	Apr25 1-5	Dec27 2-1	Nov15 1-3	Nov08 1-3	Apr04 3-3
DUMBARTON	Nov29 1-0	Oct11 1-0	Feb28 3-1	Jan24 6-2	Oct18 3-1	Apr13 0-1	Jan01 0-2		Nov01 4-1	Jan31 0-0	Sep27 5-0	Dec20 2-2	Dec13 3-2	Sep13 4-1	Mar21 1-2	Aug16 3-1	Apr18 0-3	Aug30 3-2	Feb07 4-1	Jan03 2-4
DUNDEE U	Apr04 4-0	Aug16 1-1	Nov08 4-0	Dec20 4-0	Apr18 0-1	Feb21 6-0	Sep27 5-2	Mar07 1-1		Apr25 2-1	Feb07 1-1	Jan24 4-3	Nov29 2-0	Aug30 4-1	Oct25 5-2	Oct11 1-2	Nov15 5-3	Jan01 1-1	Jan03 5-2	Sep13 1-2
DUNFERMLINE A	Nov01 6-0	Sep13 4-0	Oct18 1-1	Jan01 1-0	Mar25 3-0	Mar21 8-0	Feb07 2-1	Nov08 2-1	Dec13 4-4		Dec20 2-1	Jan03 3-0	Apr04 0-2	Jan24 3-3	Apr18 1-2	Aug30 3-1	Nov29 1-2	Oct11 1-0	Sep27 11-2	Aug16 1-3
E STIRLING	Jan10 3-0	Nov01 3-2	Apr22 0-3	Nov29 5-0	Sep06 2-1	Dec27 1-1	Feb28 6-1	Jan05 7-1	Oct04 3-1	Aug09 0-2		Mar14 3-3	Sep20 1-5	Nov15 3-2	Aug23 1-1	Apr18 1-1	Mar28 0-1	Apr04 1-2	Dec13 3-2	Oct18 2-1
FORFAR A	Dec27 4-4	Apr04 1-3	Sep20 5-3	Mar26 4-3	Apr16 2-1	Oct04 6-1	Dec06 3-1	Aug09 3-0	Sep06 2-2	Aug23 1-4	Nov08 4-1		Jan05 5-1	Oct25 0-1	Feb14 1-1	Nov29 1-0	Jan10 1-0	Feb21 2-1	Mar21 3-2	Apr25 4-1
KING'S PARK	Dec06 5-3	Aug30 1-1	Mar21 5-1	Sep13 3-2	Nov08 5-1	Mar07 0-1	Dec20 1-2	Apr25 0-2	Apr11 1-2	Apr15 0-1	Jan01 2-3	Sep27 0-1		Aug16 2-3	Feb21 3-0	Jan24 5-1	Oct25 3-1	Jan03 1-1	Oct11 0-1	Feb07 1-3
MONTROSE	Aug23 3-2	Dec13 3-2	Feb18 1-0	Nov08 5-3	Aug09 2-1	Sep20 1-0	Nov01 1-0	Mar28 2-1	Jan10 2-1	Sep06 3-0	Mar21 4-3	Feb28 4-2	Dec27 2-1		Jan05 3-1	Oct18 2-1	Oct04 1-3	Apr18 4-1	Nov22 2-2	Apr11 1-2
QUEEN OF SOUTH	Mar14 3-3	Dec20 7-0	Nov01 4-2	Aug30 3-2	Nov29 5-0	Apr25 4-1	Sep13 5-0	Nov15 3-0	Feb28 0-0	Dec06 5-1	Jan03 1-3	Oct11 3-0	Oct18 1-1	Sep27 1-6		Feb07 4-1	Apr04 0-4	Aug16 3-2	Jan24 4-1	Jan01 1-3
RAITH R	Aug09 3-3	Nov15 7-0	Aug23 3-2	Nov22 4-0	Jan02 2-0	Jan31 2-1	Dec13 5-0	Dec27 2-0	Feb14 0-0	Jan10 1-1	Dec06 2-1	Apr11 4-3	Sep06 5-6	Feb21 2-1	Oct04 2-0		Sep20 4-2	Mar07 4-2	Oct25 5-2	Mar14 3-1
ST BERNARD'S	Oct18 2-4	Jan03 5-0	Apr25 8-0	Sep27 3-1	Mar07 2-2	Nov08 2-3	Aug16 6-1	Dec06 2-2	Mar21 2-1	Apr11 2-2	Oct11 1-1	Aug30 0-2	Feb28 3-0	Feb25 7-2	Nov22 1-2	Jan01 1-1		Jan24 1-1	Sep13 2-2	Dec20 0-1
ST JOHNSTONE	Apr06 3-0	Mar14 2-1	Aug09 6-1	Dec13 3-0	Oct04 2-0	Dec25 1-0	Mar21 3-2	Jan10 4-1	Sep20 2-0	Feb14 1-0	Nov22 3-1	Oct18 1-0	Aug23 1-1	Dec06 4-0	Dec27 1-1	Nov01 2-3	Sep06 5-1		Apr11 4-1	Mar18 0-3
STENHOUSEMUIR	Sep20 0-0	Oct18 2-3	Jan10 7-3	Apr18 3-1	Dec27 6-2	Aug09 1-2	Mar14 3-2	Oct04 3-3	Aug23 0-1	Jan05 0-1	Jan31 1-2	Nov15 3-2	Feb14 3-2	Apr04 1-0	Sep06 0-3	Feb28 3-6	Apr15 1-0	Nov29 6-2		Nov01 0-6
T LANARK	Sep06 2-2	Apr18 5-0	Jan02 3-3	Sep17 3-1	Mar21 3-1	Jan10 2-0	Nov22 9-3	Aug23 1-0	Feb10 4-0	Dec27 2-2	Feb21 4-2	Dec13 5-0	Oct04 1-1	Apr06 6-1	Sep20 2-1	Nov08 6-0	Aug09 2-0	Oct25 2-0	Mar07 2-0	

DIVISION 2 FINAL TABLE

	P	W	D	L	F	A	Pts
T Lanark	38	27	7	4	107	42	61
Dundee U	38	21	8	9	93	54	50
Dunfermline A	38	20	7	11	83	50	47
Raith R	38	20	6	12	93	72	46
St Johnstone	38	19	6	13	76	61	44
Queen of South	38	18	6	14	83	66	42
E Stirling	38	17	7	14	85	74	41
Montrose	38	19	3	16	75	90	41
Albion R	38	14	11	13	83	84	39
Dumbarton	38	15	8	15	73	72	38
St Bernard's	38	14	9	15	85	66	37
Forfar A	38	15	6	17	80	84	36
Alloa	38	15	5	18	65	87	35
King's Park	38	14	6	18	78	70	34
Arbroath	38	15	4	19	83	94	34
Brechin C	38	13	7	18	52	84	33
Stenhousemuir	38	12	6	20	75	101	30
Armadale	38	13	2	23	74	99	28
Clydebank	38	10	2	26	61	108	22
Bo'ness	38	9	4	25	54	100	22

Season 1931-32

SFA Cup

1st Round

Jan 16	Arbroath	2 Aberdeen	1
Jan 16	Armadale	3 Montrose	1
Jan 16	Ayr U	3 St Johnstone	3
Jan 16	Celtic	3 Falkirk	2
Jan 16	Clyde	4 T Lanark	0
Jan 16	Cowdenbeath	5 Alloa	1
Jan 16	Dalbeattie Star	2 Bo'ness	3
Jan 16	Dundee	4 Morton	1
Jan 16	Dunfermline A	5 E Stirling	2
Jan 13	Edinburgh C	3 Murrayfield A	0
	played at Tynecastle		
Jan 16	Forfar A	1 Airdrie	3
Jan 16	Hamilton A	2 Dumbarton	0
Jan 16	Hearts	13 Lochgelly U	3
Jan 16	Hibernian	2 Dundee U	3
Jan 16	Inver Citadel	0 Partick T	3
Jan 16	Kilmarnock	4 East Fife	1
Jan 16	King's Park	7 Thornhill	1
Jan 16	Leith A	1 Albion R	1
Jan 16	Motherwell	7 Stenhousemuir	2
Jan 16	Queen of South	11 Stranraer	1
Jan 16	Queen's Park	4 St Mirren	1
Jan 16	Raith R	8 Inverness T	1
Jan 16	Rangers	8 Brechin C	2
Jan 16	St Bernard's	4 Beith	3

Replays

Jan 20	Albion R	4 Leith A	2
Jan 20	St Johnstone	2 Ayr U	0

2nd Round

Jan 30	Airdrie	2 King's Park	2
Jan 30	Bo'ness	2 Partick T	2
Jan 30	Clyde	1 Arbroath	0
Jan 30	Dunfermline A	1 Dundee	0
Jan 30	Edinburgh C	2 St Bernard's	3
Jan 30	Hamilton A	5 Armadale	2
Jan 30	Hearts	4 Cowdenbeath	1
Jan 30	Kilmarnock	2 Albion R	0
Jan 30	Queen of South	2 Dundee U	2
Jan 30	Queen's Park	0 Motherwell	2
Jan 30	Raith R	0 Rangers	5
Jan 30	St Johnstone	2 Celtic	4

Replays

Feb 3	Dundee U	1 Queen of South	1
Feb 3	King's Park	1 Airdrie	3
Feb 3	Partick T	5 Bo'ness	1
Feb 8	Dundee U	2 Queen of South	1
	played at Ibrox		

3rd Round

Feb 13	Clyde	2 St Bernard's	0
Feb 13	Dundee U	1 Kilmarnock	1
Feb 13	Hearts	0 Rangers	1
Feb 13	Motherwell	2 Celtic	0

Replay

Feb 17	Kilmarnock	3 Dundee U	0

4th Round

Mar 5	Airdrie	4 Partick T	1
Mar 5	Clyde	0 Hamilton A	2
Mar 5	Dunfermline A	1 Kilmarnock	3
Mar 5	Rangers	2 Motherwell	0

Semi-finals

Mar 26	Airdrie	2 Kilmarnock	3
	played at Firhill Park		
Mar 26	Hamilton A	2 Rangers	5
	played at Celtic Park		

Final

Apr 16	Kilmarnock	1 Rangers	1
	played at Hampden Park		

Replay

Apr 20	Kilmarnock	0 Rangers	3
	played at Hampden Park		

A tragic day for football as Celtic's goalkeeper John Thomson is stretchered off by ambulancemen after a collision with Rangers' player Sam English. The injury was diagnosed as a depressed fracture of the skull and Thomson died later that night without regaining consciousness.

DIVISION 1

	ABERDEEN	AIRDRIE	AYR U	CELTIC	CLYDE	COWDENBEATH	DUNDEE	DUNDEE U	FALKIRK	HAMILTON A	HEARTS	KILMARNOCK	LEITH A	MORTON	MOTHERWELL	PARTICK T	QUEEN'S PARK	RANGERS	ST MIRREN	T LANARK
ABERDEEN		Dec26 2-2	Sep19 5-1	Aug22 1-1	Aug26 1-0	Aug08 2-0	Sep05 1-1	Oct17 5-2	Sep28 3-1	Mar19 5-0	Jan02 1-2	Nov14 1-1	Sep02 1-0	Oct31 1-0	Jan23 0-1	Oct03 2-0	Mar05 1-1	Dec12 0-0	Feb20 0-2	Feb06 1-0
AIRDRIE	Aug15 2-4		Feb27 2-2	Apr09 1-1	Jan09 3-0	Nov14 2-1	Nov07 2-2	Aug29 4-2	Jan01 2-1	Sep12 2-0	Dec05 3-1	Dec19 0-2	Oct10 8-2	Sep26 5-1	Aug26 2-2	Aug19 0-3	Feb13 2-0	Apr25 3-0	Oct24 0-2	Mar12 2-2
AYR U	Jan30 3-2	Oct17 5-1		Mar05 2-3	Apr02 5-0	Mar19 5-0	Dec05 1-0	Sep26 2-0	Dec19 2-0	Aug15 1-3	Nov14 1-2	Sep12 1-1	Jan09 6-1	Oct10 2-1	Aug19 1-3	Oct31 0-2	Jan01 0-1	Aug29 1-3	Sep09 2-5	Nov28 3-4
CELTIC	Jan09 2-0	Dec12 6-1	Oct24 4-2		Oct10 1-1	Aug26 7-0	Feb27 0-2	Aug15 3-2	Sep26 4-1	Aug29 6-1	Aug19 3-0	Apr23 4-1	Dec19 6-0	Apr02 6-3	Mar12 2-4	Nov14 1-2	Sep12 2-2	Jan01 1-2	Mar28 1-0	Dec05 5-0
CLYDE	Nov28 0-1	Aug22 3-2	Oct03 3-3	Feb20 2-1		Dec26 1-1	Feb06 0-1	Aug31 4-1	Sep14 1-0	Oct31 1-1	Jan23 6-2	Oct17 0-0	Nov21 3-2	Apr19 3-0	Sep19 2-3	Sep05 2-1	Apr27 1-0	Apr23 1-1	Aug08 2-0	Jan02 2-4
COWDENBEATH	Dec19 3-1	Apr23 1-0	Nov07 1-1	Nov28 1-2	Aug15 3-0		Mar12 2-1	Jan01 1-1	Jan09 2-1	Oct10 1-0	Sep09 2-1	Apr09 7-1	Sep12 3-0	Aug29 2-2	Oct24 1-5	Dec05 2-0	Sep26 2-2	Apr02 1-7	Nov21 1-3	Feb27 2-0
DUNDEE	Jan01 0-0	Mar19 4-1	Sep02 2-2	Oct17 2-0	Sep26 1-1	Oct31 0-4		Sep12 1-1	Feb13 2-0	Jan09 0-3	Mar05 1-0	Oct10 1-1	Apr02 2-2	Aug15 2-1	Nov14 2-2	Dec12 3-1	Aug29 4-0	Dec19 4-2	Aug26 1-2	Sep28 6-3
DUNDEE U	Feb27 0-4	Jan23 2-7	Feb06 1-2	Dec26 1-0	Dec05 1-1	Sep05 0-0	Jan02 0-3		Nov07 2-2	Apr16 0-5	Aug08 0-2	Sep09 0-0	Oct24 0-0	Nov28 3-4	Feb20 1-6	Aug22 3-1	Nov21 0-5	Mar12 0-5	Sep19 1-0	Oct03 3-2
FALKIRK	Nov21 3-0	Sep05 3-0	Aug08 2-2	Feb06 2-0	Dec12 4-3	Aug22 2-2	Oct03 5-2	Mar19 4-0		Nov28 2-1	Feb20 0-2	Apr02 4-1	Mar26 9-1	Oct17 2-2	Jan02 2-3	Dec26 1-2	Oct31 4-1	Sep02 1-2	Jan23 1-4	Sep19 1-3
HAMILTON A	Nov07 4-1	Jan02 3-1	Dec26 1-3	Jan23 1-0	Mar12 6-1	Feb20 1-1	Aug22 6-2	Nov14 4-2	Aug26 2-2		Oct03 1-4	Aug19 1-3	Feb27 7-0	Dec12 5-0	Sep05 2-2	Sep19 3-1	Apr02 2-1	Oct24 1-2	Feb06 2-0	Aug08 2-3
HEARTS	Sep12 0-0	Sep01 0-2	Mar26 1-1	Nov21 2-1	Aug29 2-0	Dec12 3-2	Oct24 3-1	Dec19 5-0	Oct10 2-0	Apr09 4-2		Aug15 3-0	Jan01 4-2	Jan09 0-0	Feb27 0-1	Aug25 0-1	Apr16 2-0	Sep26 0-0	Mar12 2-2	Nov07 2-3
KILMARNOCK	Apr06 0-2	Aug08 4-2	Jan02 5-1	Oct03 2-3	Feb27 1-0	Sep19 3-2	Feb20 0-0	Dec12 8-0	Oct24 2-1	Nov21 1-1	Dec26 2-1		Mar12 6-3	Sep02 1-0	Aug22 1-0	Feb06 3-4	Aug26 4-1	Apr30 2-4	Sep05 3-0	Jan23 2-1
LEITH A	Dec05 1-2	Feb20 0-3	Aug22 4-1	Aug08 0-3	Apr16 1-4	Jan02 1-2	Sep19 1-0	Mar05 1-5	Nov14 2-1	Oct17 1-4	Sep05 2-0	Oct31 3-1		Mar19 0-2	Feb06 0-5	Jan23 1-3	Sep09 1-3	Nov28 2-5	Oct03 0-4	Dec26 2-1
MORTON	Mar12 1-1	Feb06 2-1	Feb13 4-2	Sep19 3-3	Oct24 0-1	Jan23 1-3	Dec26 4-1	Aug26 4-2	Feb27 4-3	Sep09 1-0	Aug22 1-2	Dec05 3-1	Nov07 9-1		Oct03 2-2	Aug08 1-2	Mar26 6-2	Nov21 1-2	Jan02 2-2	Sep05 5-0
MOTHERWELL	Aug29 3-0	Nov28 3-0	Nov21 6-0	Oct31 2-2	Apr30 3-0	Apr16 3-0	Mar26 4-0	Oct10 5-0	Sep12 4-1	Jan01 3-1	Oct17 2-0	Jan09 4-0	Sep26 7-1	Feb17 4-2		Mar19 1-0	Dec19 4-1	Aug15 4-2	Dec05 4-1	Sep16 6-0
PARTICK T	Feb13 1-0	Nov21 3-1	Mar12 2-1	Apr30 0-2	Jan01 3-1	Sep02 5-1	Sep16 1-3	Jan09 3-0	Aug15 1-2	Apr23 1-6	Nov28 1-0	Sep26 4-2	Aug29 2-2	Dec19 1-0	Apr02 0-0		Mar28 2-1	Sep12 1-3	Feb27 2-1	Oct24 0-0
QUEEN'S PARK	Oct24 1-3	Oct03 3-1	Sep05 3-2	Jan02 0-3	Nov07 2-3	Feb06 2-1	Jan23 0-1	Aug18 1-2	Mar12 2-1	Sep01 1-1	Sep19 5-2	Nov28 2-0	Dec12 3-3	Nov14 4-1	Aug08 1-5	Feb20 2-0		Feb27 1-6	Dec26 2-0	Aug22 1-3
RANGERS	Sep15 4-1	Aug11 2-1	Jan23 6-1	Sep05 0-0	Nov14 2-2	Oct03 6-1	Aug08 4-1	Oct31 5-0	Dec05 4-0	Apr27 1-0	Feb06 4-2	Mar19 3-0	Aug25 4-0	Aug18 7-3	Dec26 1-0	Jan02 4-0	Oct17 0-1		Aug22 4-0	Feb20 6-1
ST MIRREN	Oct10 4-2	Apr02 2-1	Dec12 4-0	Mar19 1-2	Dec19 3-1	Aug18 1-4	Nov28 6-1	Apr09 5-1	Aug29 3-1	Sep26 1-0	Oct31 5-1	Jan01 2-0	Feb13 6-3	Sep12 2-0	Sep01 0-1	Oct17 1-1	Aug15 2-0	Jan09 0-2		Nov14 1-1
T LANARK	Sep26 2-0	Oct31 5-2	Aug25 2-0	Sep02 3-3	Sep12 4-2	Oct17 5-3	Nov21 6-1	Apr02 4-1	Jan30 1-0	Dec19 4-1	Mar19 3-4	Aug29 1-3	Aug15 2-0	Jan01 6-2	Dec12 0-2	Apr09 3-1	Jan09 2-1	Mar28 4-3	Mar26 4-0	

DIVISION 1 FINAL TABLE

	P	W	D	L	F	A	Pts
Motherwell	38	30	6	2	119	31	66
Rangers	38	28	5	5	118	42	61
Celtic	38	20	8	10	94	50	48
T Lanark	38	21	4	13	92	81	46
St Mirren	38	20	4	14	77	56	44
Partick T	38	19	4	15	58	59	42
Aberdeen	38	16	9	13	57	49	41
Hearts	38	17	5	16	63	61	39
Kilmarnock	38	16	7	15	68	70	39
Hamilton A	38	16	6	16	84	65	38
Dundee	38	14	10	14	61	72	38
Cowdenbeath	38	15	8	15	66	78	38
Clyde	38	13	9	16	58	70	35
Airdrie	38	13	6	19	74	81	32
Morton	38	12	7	19	78	87	31
Queen's Park	38	13	5	20	59	79	31
Ayr U	38	11	7	20	70	90	29
Falkirk	38	11	5	22	70	76	27
Dundee U	38	6	7	25	40	118	19
Leith A	38	6	4	28	46	137	16

DIVISION 2

	ALBION R	ALLOA	ARBROATH	ARMADALE	BO'NESS	BRECHIN C	DUMBARTON	DUNFERMLINE A	EAST FIFE	E STIRLING	EDINBURGH C	FORFAR A	HIBERNIAN	KING'S PARK	MONTROSE	QUEEN OF SOUTH	RAITH R	ST BERNARD'S	ST JOHNSTONE	STENHOUSEMUIR
ALBION R		Jan02 6-2	Nov28 2-2	Sep19 5-3	Oct17 1-3	Mar05 4-1	Oct31 5-0	Dec12 1-2	Nov21 2-1	Dec26 3-2	Feb06 5-2	Feb20 1-4	Mar26 1-0	Sep02 0-3	Aug08 0-1	Mar19 4-0	Oct03 1-3	Aug22 2-1	Jan23 3-4	Sep05 1-3
ALLOA	Sep12 4-2		Apr16 2-0	Oct24 3-2	Aug29 1-1	Jan09 2-0	Sep26 1-1	Jan01 1-4	Oct10 0-2	Dec12 1-2	Nov07 8-2	Nov21 6-1	Dec19 1-2	Aug15 2-2	Feb27 1-4	Feb13 3-4	Mar12 0-0	Aug18 1-3	Mar26 1-0	Nov28 2-1
ARBROATH	Apr09 6-4	Sep19 2-3		Feb20 1-0	Oct31 3-1	Mar26 0-2	Oct17 5-0	Nov21 1-0	Mar19 2-0	Jan23 3-1	Aug22 6-2	Sep05 2-0	Dec05 3-3	Dec12 6-3	Feb06 3-2	Mar05 4-0	Aug08 3-1	Jan02 3-0	Oct03 2-3	Dec26 4-1
ARMADALE	Apr16 3-2	Mar05 1-1	Oct10 0-1		Jan01 7-1	Sep26 3-1	Jan09 0-0	Dec19 1-4	Feb13 5-4	Mar19 1-0	Mar26 3-3	Oct17 0-0	Sep12 1-1	Aug29 0-1	Apr02 5-1	Aug15 1-3	Dec05 1-2	Nov28 2-0	Aug27 1-3	Oct31 1-4
BO'NESS	Feb27 4-3	Jan23 3-3	Mar12 1-4	Sep05 2-1		Nov21 3-0	Apr09 1-3	Mar26 1-3	Aug19 1-0	Aug22 2-5	Dec26 3-2	Aug08 3-1	Oct24 2-2	Nov07 3-2	Oct03 2-0	Dec12 1-1	Jan02 4-3	Feb06 1-2	Sep19 1-0	Feb20 3-1
BRECHIN C	Oct24 1-1	Aug22 2-5	Nov14 2-0	Feb06 3-4	Apr02 4-2		Dec12 1-1	Nov07 3-0	Nov28 2-5	Feb20 0-1	Aug08 4-3	Sep19 1-1	Mar12 3-3	Feb27 0-5	Sep05 1-0	Aug19 0-2	Jan23 0-1	Dec26 2-2	Jan02 0-1	Oct03 1-7
DUMBARTON	Mar12 3-1	Feb06 3-1	Feb27 2-2	Aug22 3-1	Nov28 6-2	Aug25 2-2		Oct24 2-1	Apr16 3-2	Jan02 2-3	Sep05 1-1	Oct03 1-3	Nov07 0-2	Mar26 3-2	Jan23 5-1	Apr02 5-0	Feb20 6-1	Aug08 1-1	Dec26 3-0	Sep19 4-0
DUNFERMLINE A	Aug26 2-0	Sep05 1-2	Apr02 6-0	Aug08 3-0	Nov14 3-1	Mar19 0-1	Apr04 2-0		Oct31 4-3	Feb06 2-1	Sep19 0-0	Jan23 4-2	Apr16 1-1	Nov28 8-3	Aug22 2-2	Oct17 5-2	Dec26 0-3	Oct03 1-1	Feb20 2-2	Jan02 0-0
EAST FIFE	Apr02 6-2	Feb20 2-1	Nov07 4-1	Oct03 4-1	Dec05 4-0	Apr09 5-1	Sep03 4-1	Mar12 5-2		Sep19 2-0	Jan02 6-0	Aug22 3-3	Feb27 1-1	Oct24 7-1	Dec26 4-1	Nov14 3-1	Sep05 1-4	Jan23 0-2	Feb06 2-4	Aug08 3-3
E STIRLING	Aug15 5-1	Aug26 2-1	Aug29 1-0	Nov07 6-1	Jan09 5-2	Oct10 2-0	Sep12 3-0	Sep26 4-1	Jan30 5-1		Feb27 6-4	Nov14 5-0	Feb13 4-1	Jan01 3-1	Oct24 4-1	Dec19 5-0	Apr09 5-1	Apr02 5-1	Mar12 0-1	Apr16 1-1
EDINBURGH C	Sep26 1-4	Mar19 2-4	Jan09 4-2	Nov14 4-6	Aug15 2-3	Dec19 1-1	Dec25 4-2	Apr30 4-1	Sep12 0-7	Oct17 0-2		Oct31 2-2	Oct10 2-1	Feb13 3-4	Apr23 4-4	Aug29 4-8	Dec12 2-4	Mar05 1-6	Apr09 1-7	Nov21 2-5
FORFAR A	Oct10 4-3	Apr02 1-1	Jan01 3-2	Feb27 1-3	Dec19 4-2	Jan30 2-1	Feb13 3-0	Aug29 3-2	Jan09 6-1	Mar26 6-3	Mar12 2-2		Aug15 1-0	Sep12 4-2	Nov28 7-0	Sep26 2-1	Nov07 2-1	Dec12 5-3	Oct24 3-1	Apr23 2-3
HIBERNIAN	Nov14 4-1	Aug08 1-0	Aug18 3-1	Jan02 1-0	Mar05 2-1	Oct31 4-0	Mar19 0-1	Sep02 6-2	Oct17 3-2	Oct03 1-1	Feb20 3-1	Dec26 5-1		Apr02 2-1	Sep19 0-0	Nov28 1-4	Feb06 0-1	Sep05 2-4	Aug22 6-0	Jan23 0-2
KING'S PARK	Dec05 1-2	Dec26 1-0	Aug26 5-2	Jan23 9-0	Mar19 5-0	Oct17 5-1	Nov14 2-2	Apr09 3-1	Mar05 2-2	Sep05 2-3	Oct03 3-2	Jan02 3-2	Nov21 1-4		Feb20 9-2	Oct31 2-3	Aug22 1-1	Sep19 2-2	Aug08 0-2	Feb06 7-1
MONTROSE	Dec19 0-3	Oct17 4-1	Sep26 1-1	Nov21 4-3	Feb13 5-1	Jan01 1-2	Aug29 1-0	Jan09 0-1	Aug15 3-2	Mar05 0-3	Dec05 0-1	Apr09 2-2	Jan30 0-1	Oct10 2-0		Sep12 4-2	Nov14 3-4	Oct31 1-2	Sep02 2-3	Mar19 3-2
QUEEN OF SOUTH	Nov07 4-0	Oct03 0-3	Oct24 2-2	Dec26 4-2	Aug27 3-4	Dec05 7-2	Nov21 2-1	Feb27 2-4	Mar26 3-3	Aug08 5-1	Jan23 5-4	Feb06 2-1	Apr09 2-3	Mar12 4-2	Jan02 5-1		Sep19 3-1	Feb20 2-2	Sep05 4-1	Aug22 2-4
RAITH R	Feb13 4-0	Oct31 2-1	Dec19 5-1	Aug19 5-1	Sep12 3-1	Aug29 1-3	Oct10 4-2	Aug15 0-2	Jan01 2-1	Nov28 4-2	Aug26 7-2	Mar19 0-2	Sep26 1-2	Jan09 2-0	Mar26 2-2	Apr16 2-0		Oct17 4-3	Nov21 1-1	Mar05 0-0
ST BERNARD'S	Jan09 3-2	Dec05 3-0	Sep12 3-1	Apr09 3-1	Sep26 1-3	Aug15 5-1	Dec19 0-0	Apr23 4-0	Aug29 2-3	Nov21 0-4	Oct24 4-2	Aug26 1-2	Jan01 1-0	Apr16 4-0	Mar12 1-2	Oct10 1-0	Feb27 2-0		Nov07 2-2	Mar26 3-1
ST JOHNSTONE	Aug29 7-0	Nov14 4-1	Feb13 4-1	Dec12 6-1	Apr23 6-1	Sep12 3-1	Aug15 3-0	Oct10 3-1	Sep26 3-0	Oct31 2-2	Nov28 4-1	Mar05 3-0	Jan09 2-1	Dec19 5-0	Apr16 4-0	Jan01 2-2	Apr02 2-0	Mar19 0-2		Oct17 2-2
STENHOUSEMUIR	Jan01 5-3	Apr09 1-3	Aug15 2-0	Mar12 3-2	Oct10 2-0	Feb13 3-2	Jan30 1-1	Sep12 5-1	Dec19 0-2	Sep08 1-4	Apr02 3-1	Dec05 4-2	Aug29 2-1	Sep26 3-2	Nov07 3-0	Jan09 1-5	Oct24 3-3	Nov14 3-1	Feb27 2-2	

DIVISION 2 FINAL TABLE

	P	W	D	L	F	A	Pts
E Stirling	38	26	3	9	111	55	55
St Johnstone	38	24	7	7	102	52	55
Raith R	38	20	6	12	83	65	46
Stenhousemuir	38	19	8	11	88	76	46
St Bernard's	38	19	7	12	81	62	45
Forfar A	38	19	7	12	90	79	45
Hibernian	38	18	8	12	73	52	44
East Fife	38	18	5	15	107	77	41
Queen of South	38	18	5	15	99	91	41
Dunfermline A	38	17	6	15	78	73	40
Arbroath	38	17	5	16	82	78	39
Dumbarton	38	14	10	14	70	68	38
Alloa	38	14	7	17	73	74	35
Bo'ness	38	15	4	19	70	103	34
King's Park	38	14	5	19	97	93	33
Albion R	38	13	2	23	81	104	28
Montrose	38	11	6	21	60	96	28
Armadale	38	10	5	23	68	102	25
Brechin C	38	9	7	22	52	97	25
Edinburgh C	38	5	7	26	78	146	17

Celtic in September 1932. They went on to win the SFA Cup that season, beating Motherwell in the Final. Back row (left to right): McGonagle, Geatens, Kennaway, Hughes, Cameron, Quiskley (trainer). Front row: McGrory, Cook, R.Thomson, McStay, Wilson, A.Thomson, Napier.

SFA Cup

1st Round

Jan 21	Aberdeen	1	Penicuik A	0	
Jan 21	Airdrie	2	Alloa	1	
Jan 21	Albion R	2	Inverness T	0	
Jan 21	Armadale	0	Dundee U	2	
Jan 21	Clyde	3	Fraserburgh	2	
Jan 21	Cowdenbeath	1	Dundee	1	
Jan 21	Dumbarton	3	Beith	1	
Jan 21	Dunfermline A	1	Celtic	7	
Jan 21	E Stirling	0	Montrose	2	
Jan 18	Edinburgh C	1	Ayr U	3	
	played at Tynecastle				
Jan 21	Hamilton A	0	Motherwell	2	
Jan 21	Hearts	3	Solway Star	0	
Jan 21	Hibernian	2	Forfar A	2	
Jan 21	Kilmarnock	3	Lochgelly U	1	
Jan 21	King's Park	0	St Mirren	0	
Jan 21	Leith A	5	Brechin C	1	
Jan 21	Queen of South	0	T Lanark	1	
Jan 21	Queen's Park	4	Falkirk A	0	
Jan 21	Raith R	1	Falkirk	2	
Jan 23	Rangers	3	Arbroath	1	
Jan 21	St Bernard's	2	Partick T	2	
Jan 21	St Johnstone	2	East Fife	2	
Jan 21	Stenhousemuir	1	Morton	0	
Jan 21	Stranraer	1	Bo'ness	1	

Replays

Jan 24	St Mirren	5	King's Park	1	
Jan 25	Dundee	3	Cowdenbeath	0	
Jan 25	East Fife	1	St Johnstone	2	
Jan 25	Partick T	3	St Bernard's	0	
Jan 26	Forfar A	3	Hibernian	7	
Jan 28	Bo'ness	3	Stranraer	0	

2nd Round

Feb 4	Aberdeen	1	Hibernian	1	
Feb 4	Ayr U	1	Partick T	1	
Feb 4	Celtic	2	Falkirk	0	
Feb 4	Dumbarton	1	Albion R	2	
Feb 1	Dundee	4	Bo'ness	0	
Feb 4	Dundee U	3	St Johnstone	4	
Feb 4	Hearts	6	Airdrie	1	
Feb 4	Leith A	1	Clyde	1	
Feb 4	Motherwell	7	Montrose	1	
Feb 4	Rangers	1	Queen's Park	1	
Feb 4	St Mirren	0	Kilmarnock	1	
Feb 4	Stenhousemuir	2	T Lanark	0	

Replays

Feb 7	Clyde	5	Leith A	0	
Feb 7	Partick T	2	Ayr U	0	
Feb 8	Hibernian	1	Aberdeen	0	
Feb 8	Queen's Park	1	Rangers	1	
Feb 13	Queen's Park	1	Rangers	3	
	played at Hampden Park				

3rd Round

Feb 18	Celtic	2	Partick T	1	
Feb 18	Hearts	2	St Johnstone	0	
Feb 18	Kilmarnock	1	Rangers	0	
Feb 18	Motherwell	5	Dundee	0	

4th Round

Mar 4	Albion R	1	Celtic	1	
Mar 4	Clyde	3	Stenhousemuir	2	
Mar 4	Hibernian	0	Hearts	0	
Mar 4	Kilmarnock	3	Motherwell	3	

Replays

Mar 8	Celtic	3	Albion R	1	
Mar 8	Hearts	2	Hibernian	0	
Mar 8	Motherwell	8	Kilmarnock	3	

Semi-finals

Mar 18	Celtic	0	Hearts	0	
	played at Hampden Park				
Mar 18	Clyde	0	Motherwell	2	
	played at Ibrox				

Replay

Mar 22	Celtic	2	Hearts	1	
	played at Hampden Park				

Final

Apr 15	Celtic	1	Motherwell	0	
	played at Hampden Park				

Season 1932-33

DIVISION 1

	ABERDEEN	AIRDRIE	AYR U	CELTIC	CLYDE	COWDENBEATH	DUNDEE	E STIRLING	FALKIRK	HAMILTON A	HEARTS	KILMARNOCK	MORTON	MOTHERWELL	PARTICK T	QUEEN'S PARK	RANGERS	ST JOHNSTONE	ST MIRREN	T LANARK
ABERDEEN		Sep03 2-0	Jan07 5-0	Dec24 1-0	Nov19 8-1	Feb25 6-2	Jan02 3-2	Sep17 1-3	Sep14 8-2	Oct29 2-1	Sep26 3-0	Aug24 7-1	Mar11 6-0	Aug20 1-1	Jan28 0-0	Dec17 3-4	Apr15 1-1	Nov26 0-0	Oct15 5-1	Oct01 1-0
AIRDRIE	Jan14 2-0		Dec10 3-2	Dec03 0-3	Aug13 5-2	Aug24 1-2	Mar18 3-0	Apr08 8-1	Sep10 1-0	Jan03 2-1	Dec31 2-7	Oct08 2-1	Mar04 2-1	Nov19 1-4	Nov12 0-1	Sep24 1-1	Aug27 1-2	Feb11 1-1	Apr29 1-3	Oct22 1-2
AYR U	Aug27 3-1	Apr22 4-2		Dec17 0-1	Sep24 3-1	Oct29 3-2	Apr08 6-0	Aug24 4-2	Oct08 0-1	Feb11 0-1	Jan14 1-1	Jan03 2-3	Sep10 0-1	Nov12 2-6	Mar11 2-0	Aug13 4-3	Dec31 3-3	Mar04 2-0	Dec03 1-0	Mar25 1-0
CELTIC	Aug13 3-0	Apr18 2-1	Aug30 4-1		Apr10 2-1	Nov19 3-0	Dec10 3-2	Nov12 3-0	Jan14 0-1	Dec31 0-3	Feb11 3-2	Sep24 0-0	Aug27 7-1	Oct22 4-1	Aug24 1-2	Dec26 2-0	Sep10 1-1	Oct08 5-0	Apr03 0-0	Aug16 4-2
CLYDE	Mar25 2-0	Dec24 6-0	Jan28 2-0	Oct15 0-2		Oct01 2-1	Sep03 0-3	Aug20 4-3	Dec03 3-1	Mar11 7-2	Nov26 0-1	Apr22 0-1	Dec17 2-1	Jan07 2-3	Jan02 1-0	Oct29 6-2	Nov05 0-5	Sep12 2-3	Feb25 2-1	Sep17 1-0
COWDENBEATH	Oct08 0-3	Nov05 6-1	Mar18 6-2	Mar25 1-5	Feb11 5-2		Oct22 4-1	Dec03 4-3	Aug13 4-3	Mar04 1-2	Sep10 0-0	Aug27 4-1	Dec31 0-0	Apr29 1-4	Apr08 0-0	Jan14 0-2	Sep24 2-3	Jan03 3-2	Sep14 1-3	Dec10 2-1
DUNDEE	Sep10 0-2	Oct29 4-2	Nov26 1-1	Apr22 3-0	Jan14 2-1	Mar11 4-2		Dec17 3-0	Sep24 3-0	Aug13 1-5	Jan03 2-2	Mar29 3-0	Feb11 2-2	Aug24 0-3	Apr15 1-0	Dec31 2-1	Oct08 0-3	Aug27 0-0	Nov19 1-1	Nov12 2-2
E STIRLING	Jan03 2-1	Nov26 1-0	Nov05 4-0	Sep14 1-3	Dec31 2-2	Apr15 1-1	Apr29 3-2		Mar04 1-2	Sep24 1-5	Oct08 1-3	Feb11 2-3	Aug13 0-3	Dec10 1-4	Apr01 2-7	Aug27 1-1	Jan14 2-3	Sep10 1-3	Oct22 2-1	Mar18 2-0
FALKIRK	Nov12 2-0	Jan02 3-1	Feb25 1-2	Sep03 1-1	Feb18 2-1	Dec24 6-0	Jan28 0-0	Oct15 3-0		Mar25 5-0	Oct29 3-1	Dec17 2-2	Apr22 2-1	Sep17 2-2	Oct01 1-2	Mar11 2-3	Nov26 1-4	Aug24 1-1	Aug20 2-3	Jan07 7-1
HAMILTON A	Mar18 1-0	Sep17 7-0	Oct01 3-0	Aug20 1-1	Oct22 1-1	Oct15 10-2	Dec24 1-2	Jan28 4-3	Nov19 2-0		Aug24 3-2	Nov12 0-0	Apr14 2-2	Jan02 2-3	Jan07 4-3	Nov26 3-2	Apr29 2-4	Dec10 1-1	Sep03 4-3	Feb25 3-2
HEARTS	Dec10 3-1	Aug20 4-0	Sep03 4-2	Oct01 1-1	Apr08 1-1	Jan02 3-1	Sep17 1-0	Feb25 3-1	Apr01 3-2	Nov05 6-1		Dec03 1-0	Mar25 5-2	Oct15 2-0	Dec24 1-2	Sep13 5-0	Oct22 1-0	Apr29 2-1	Jan07 0-0	Jan28 3-1
KILMARNOCK	Nov05 4-3	Feb25 2-4	Sep17 3-5	Jan28 2-2	Dec10 1-2	Jan07 4-1	Oct15 2-2	Oct01 2-1	Apr29 1-1	Sep14 3-2	Apr12 0-0		Nov26 1-1	Dec24 1-3	Sep03 3-0	Nov19 3-1	Mar18 2-6	Oct22 5-4	Jan02 0-1	Aug20 6-0
MORTON	Oct22 0-1	Oct15 4-2	Feb18 1-1	Jan07 0-1	Apr29 0-0	Aug20 2-2	Oct01 1-4	Dec24 3-1	Dec10 3-4	Dec03 2-5	Nov19 1-5	Apr08 5-2		Jan28 1-2	Feb25 2-3	Nov05 0-2	Aug17 1-3	Mar18 2-0	Sep17 0-1	Sep03 1-3
MOTHERWELL	Dec31 2-3	Mar25 4-1	Sep14 3-1	Mar11 4-2	Aug27 1-0	Dec17 2-0	Nov05 6-1	Apr22 4-1	Jan03 2-0	Sep10 4-1	Mar29 5-1	Aug13 3-3	Sep24 7-0		Oct29 1-2	Oct08 7-2	Feb11 1-3	Jan14 1-0	Apr08 3-0	Dec03 6-3
PARTICK T	Sep24 1-2	Dec26 3-0	Oct22 7-0	Nov05 3-0	Sep10 2-3	Nov26 4-1	Dec03 4-0	Mar25 6-3	Feb11 2-1	Aug27 1-2	Aug13 1-2	Jan14 1-3	Oct08 2-1	Apr03 0-1		Mar04 3-4	Jan03 0-0	Dec31 2-2	Dec10 3-1	Apr29 2-2
QUEEN'S PARK	Apr29 4-0	Feb18 0-0	Dec24 4-1	Sep17 4-1	Apr19 1-4	Sep03 5-0	Aug20 2-0	Jan07 6-2	Oct22 1-3	Apr10 1-0	Nov12 2-1	Apr26 1-2	Aug23 1-1	Feb25 4-2	Mar15 2-1		Dec10 0-0	Apr03 3-3	Oct01 4-2	Jan02 1-1
RANGERS	Dec03 3-1	Jan07 5-1	Aug20 4-1	Jan02 0-0	Aug23 2-2	Jan28 4-1	Feb25 6-4	Sep03 4-0	Apr08 5-1	Dec17 4-4	Mar11 4-4	Oct29 2-0	Nov12 6-1	Oct01 2-2	Sep17 3-0	Apr22 1-0		Nov19 3-0	Dec24 4-0	Aug31 5-0
ST JOHNSTONE	Apr08 2-2	Oct01 1-0	Oct15 4-0	Feb25 1-0	Nov12 2-1	Sep17 3-1	Jan07 2-1	Jan02 2-0	Nov05 1-0	Apr22 2-0	Dec17 2-1	Mar11 6-1	Oct29 7-1	Sep03 0-1	Aug20 2-1	Dec03 5-2	Mar25 0-2		Jan28 3-1	Dec24 2-2
ST MIRREN	Mar04 2-2	Dec17 7-1	Apr15 3-1	Oct29 3-1	Oct08 2-1	Nov12 7-1	Mar25 2-1	Mar11 3-0	Dec31 1-2	Jan14 3-0	Aug27 0-1	Sep10 3-2	Jan03 1-1	Nov26 2-5	Apr22 1-1	Feb11 1-2	Aug13 2-0	Sep24 2-0		Aug23 3-1
T LANARK	Feb11 3-0	Mar11 3-2	Nov19 5-1	Nov26 0-4	Jan03 4-1	Apr22 3-1	Dec26 1-1	Oct29 4-1	Aug27 4-0	Oct08 2-1	Sep24 2-1	Dec31 3-2	Jan14 2-0	Apr25 1-1	Dec17 0-3	Sep10 6-0	Mar04 1-3	Aug13 2-2	Nov05 1-3	

DIVISION 1 FINAL TABLE

	P	W	D	L	F	A	Pts
Rangers	38	26	10	2	113	43	62
Motherwell	38	27	5	6	114	53	59
Hearts	38	21	8	9	84	51	50
Celtic	38	20	8	10	75	44	48
St Johnstone	38	17	10	11	70	55	44
Aberdeen	38	18	6	14	85	58	42
St Mirren	38	18	6	14	73	60	42
Hamilton A	38	18	6	14	90	78	42
Queen's Park	38	17	7	14	78	79	41
Partick T	38	17	6	15	75	55	40
Falkirk	38	15	6	17	70	70	36
Clyde	38	15	5	18	69	75	35
T Lanark	38	14	7	17	70	80	35
Kilmarnock	38	13	9	16	72	86	35
Dundee	38	12	9	17	60	77	33
Ayr U	38	13	4	21	62	95	30
Cowdenbeath	38	10	5	23	65	111	25
Airdrie	38	10	3	25	55	102	23
Morton	38	6	9	23	49	97	21
E Stirling	38	7	3	28	55	115	17

DIVISION 2

	ALBION R	ALLOA	ARBROATH	BRECHIN C	DUMBARTON	DUNDEE U	DUNFERMLINE A	EAST FIFE	EDINBURGH C	FORFAR A	HIBERNIAN	KING'S PARK	LEITH A	MONTROSE	QUEEN OF SOUTH	RAITH R	ST BERNARD'S	STENHOUSEMUIR	ARMADALE	BO'NESS
ALBION R		Sep17 5-2	Nov05 4-0	Nov26 5-1	Jan02 3-1	Dec17 4-2	Sep07 5-0	Sep14 3-2	Oct29 0-1	Sep03 4-1	Aug20 2-0	Apr22 3-4	Mar11 5-1	Feb25 5-1	Oct15 0-3	Oct01 1-2	Dec24 3-1	Jan28 0-1		
ALLOA	Jan03 0-2		Aug27 2-0	Aug13 1-3	Nov26 4-1	Jan14 1-0	Sep10 2-1	Oct08 1-2	Sep24 4-1	Mar18 9-2	Oct22 0-3	Dec31 4-3	Feb11 4-1	Mar25 1-0	Apr15 3-2	Dec10 4-1	Apr29 2-1	Nov12 0-0	Aug23 6-0	
ARBROATH	Aug24 1-2	Jan07 0-0		Dec03 2-0	Dec24 3-1	Nov12 0-0	Mar18 1-4	Apr29 3-2	Apr08 4-0	Jan02 5-1	Oct01 0-3	Nov19 4-1	Apr22 3-1	Sep03 3-2	Aug20 4-0	Oct15 1-3	Sep17 1-2	Feb25 2-1		Oct22 3-3
BRECHIN C	Apr08 1-4	Dec24 3-1	Apr15 3-1		Apr01 2-1	Apr22 1-3	Apr04 2-2	Oct22 2-3	Dec17 2-1	Jan07 0-1	Sep17 2-4	Nov05 2-2	Nov19 8-2	Jan02 5-2	Jan28 2-2	Aug20 2-4	Oct15 3-1	Oct01 1-2	Sep03 3-2	
DUMBARTON	Sep10 3-0	Apr08 3-1	Sep24 2-1	Oct08 2-0		Jan03 2-0	Mar04 1-2	Feb11 2-1	Aug27 6-2	Nov19 2-2	Dec03 3-2	Jan14 2-0	Dec31 3-0	Apr22 6-2	Nov12 1-1	Feb18 3-2	Mar18 6-0	Aug24 2-0	Oct22 3-1	Aug13 5-1
DUNDEE U	Dec03 2-0	Sep03 1-1	Sep14 2-1	Dec10 3-1	Sep17 5-2		Oct22 2-4	Nov05 3-3	Mar25 5-0	Feb25 4-1	Dec24 0-2	Mar18 7-3	Apr08 4-3	Oct15 3-1	Jan02 1-2	Jan07 2-1	Oct01 1-0	Aug20 2-1		
DUNFERMLINE A	Apr01 3-1	Jan02 3-0	Oct29 2-2	Nov12 4-2	Oct15 3-0	Mar11 5-1		Feb18 7-3	Aug24 4-0	Aug20 6-1	Sep03 2-2	Dec17 4-1	Dec03 6-0	Dec24 4-1	Jan07 4-1	Jan28 1-0	Apr22 4-0	Sep17 1-1	Oct01 9-1	
EAST FIFE	Nov12 6-1	Apr01 5-0	Dec17 4-2	Mar11 3-4	Oct01 1-1	Aug24 1-0	Nov19 0-1		Dec03 3-1	Dec24 3-0	Jan07 0-5	Apr08 4-2	Oct29 6-1	Jan28 2-0	Sep17 3-3	Jan02 2-1	Aug20 4-0	Sep03 6-2	Oct15 8-1	
EDINBURGH C	Mar18 0-7	Jan28 0-2	Nov26 0-7	Apr29 4-3	Jan07 1-1	Nov19 1-1	Nov05 1-3	Apr15 2-4		Oct01 4-3	Oct15 0-4	Oct22 4-4	Sep06 1-0	Aug20 2-4	Sep03 1-2	Feb25 2-5	Dec26 2-8	Dec24 0-3	Sep17 4-3	Sep13 1-2
FORFAR A	Jan14 1-1	Oct29 2-1	Sep10 2-4	Aug27 3-0	Mar25 8-3	Oct08 1-4	Dec31 0-3	Aug13 3-0	Feb11 4-1		Apr29 3-3	Jan03 1-1	Mar04 5-0	Nov12 3-2	Mar11 1-3	Aug25 4-1	Apr15 4-0	Dec10 1-2		Sep24 3-2
HIBERNIAN	Dec31 2-1	Mar11 1-0	Feb11 2-0	Jan03 3-1	Apr15 1-0	Aug13 2-0	Jan14 3-1	Aug27 2-1	Feb18 7-1	Dec17 2-0		Sep24 0-1	Sep10 3-0	Aug24 4-1	Apr22 1-2	Oct29 2-1	Mar25 4-1	Nov26 4-1	Nov12 8-2	Oct08 7-0
KING'S PARK	Dec10 2-3	Oct15 2-1	Mar25 1-1	Aug24 2-3	Sep03 3-3	Oct29 7-2	Apr29 2-1	Nov26 2-1	Mar11 7-1	Sep17 3-0	Jan28 0-0		Nov12 4-0	Oct01 3-1	Feb25 4-0	Dec24 6-0	Jan07 2-4	Jan02 3-1	Aug20 1-1	
LEITH A	Oct22 1-2	Oct01 1-0	Dec10 1-2	Mar25 4-0	Aug20 3-1	Nov26 2-1	Apr15 0-0	Mar18 1-1	Apr01 3-0	Oct15 2-1	Jan02 0-1	Sep14 4-2		Sep17 1-1	Dec24 2-2	Sep03 1-0	Jan28 1-1	Jan07 2-1		
MONTROSE	Oct08 2-3	Nov19 1-3	Jan14 2-4	Sep10 0-1	Dec10 3-1	Mar04 3-0	Aug13 1-1	Sep24 4-3	Dec31 2-2	Sep14 2-3	Nov05 1-3	Feb11 3-3	Jan03 3-1		Oct29 3-1	Mar11 4-2	Nov26 1-1	Apr29 1-2		Aug27 3-1
QUEEN OF SOUTH	Feb18 4-1	Dec03 1-1	Dec31 3-1	Sep24 9-1	Sep29 2-0	Sep10 1-0	Aug27 3-1	Jan03 5-3	Jan14 4-1	Oct22 5-1	Dec10 0-0	Oct08 4-2	Aug13 5-2	Mar18 4-3		Apr08 2-2	Nov05 2-2	Nov19 5-3		Oct01 10-0
RAITH R	Feb11 2-1	Apr22 4-3	Mar04 4-0	Dec31 5-3	Apr29 2-2	Aug27 4-1	Sep24 1-1	Sep10 3-1	Oct08 5-0	Nov05 2-1	Mar18 1-2	Aug13 9-1	Jan14 3-0	Oct22 4-2	Nov26 1-3		Sep14 4-2	Apr15 1-1		
ST BERNARD'S	Aug13 4-1	Dec17 2-2	Jan03 0-0	Mar04 8-0	Oct29 4-0	Feb11 3-2	Oct08 2-0	Dec31 2-1	Sep10 8-1	Dec03 0-1	Nov19 0-1	Aug27 1-0	Sep24 0-1	Apr08 1-3	Aug23 2-2	Nov12 3-2		Mar11 3-2		
STENHOUSEMUIR	Sep24 0-0	Sep13 1-0	Oct08 5-2	Feb11 1-1	Nov05 3-2	Dec31 3-1	Jan03 2-1	Jan14 2-1	Aug13 4-1	Apr22 5-3	Apr08 3-2	Sep10 2-2	Aug27 2-1	Dec17 4-1	Mar25 2-5	Dec03 3-1	Oct22 1-0			
ARMADALE	Aug27 2-3	Nov05 0-2	Aug13 1-4			Sep24 5-3					Sep15 2-4		Oct08 2-2			Nov19 1-5		Oct29 2-4		Sep10 1-3
BO'NESS		Aug20 2-2		Oct29 4-3									Aug24 2-1			Sep17 1-2	Sep03 3-6	Oct15 2-3		

DIVISION 2 FINAL TABLE

	P	W	D	L	F	A	Pts
Hibernian	34	25	4	5	80	29	54
Queen of South	34	20	9	5	93	59	49
Dunfermline A	34	20	7	7	89	44	47
Stenhousemuir	34	18	6	10	67	58	42
Albion R	34	19	2	13	82	57	40
Raith R	34	16	4	14	83	67	36
East Fife	34	15	4	15	85	71	34
King's Park	34	13	8	13	85	80	34
Dumbarton	34	14	6	14	69	67	34
Arbroath	34	14	5	15	65	62	33
Alloa	34	14	5	15	60	58	33
St Bernard's	34	13	6	15	67	64	32
Dundee U	34	14	4	16	65	67	32
Forfar A	34	12	4	18	68	87	28
Brechin C	34	11	4	19	65	95	26
Leith A	34	10	5	19	43	81	25
Montrose	34	8	5	21	63	89	21
Edinburgh C	34	4	4	26	39	133	12

Season 1933-34

SFA Cup

1st Round

Jan 20	Aberdeen	1	Raith R	0
Jan 20	Airdrie	1	Kilmarnock	1
Jan 20	Albion R	4	Vale Ocoba	1
Jan 20	Alloa	4	Dundee U	2
Jan 20	Arbroath	2	Dumbarton	1
Jan 20	Ayr U	2	Dunfermline A	0
Jan 20	Beith	1	Brechin C	2
Jan 20	Dalbeattie Star	0	Celtic	6
Jan 20	Falkirk	3	Leith Amat	0
Jan 20	Galston	8	Keith	2
Jan 20	Hearts	5	Montrose	1
Jan 20	Hibernian	5	Clyde	4
Jan 20	King's Park	0	Dundee	1
Jan 17	Leith A	0	Cowdenbeath	1
Jan 20	Motherwell	4	Gala Fairydean	0
Jan 20	Nithsdale W	0	E Stirling	2
Jan 20	Partick T	1	Morton	0
Jan 20	Penicuik A	2	St Mirren	2
Jan 20	Peterhead	0	Hamilton A	2
Jan 20	Queen of South	5	Edinburgh C	2
Jan 20	Queen's Park	1	Forfar A	0
Jan 20	Rangers	14	Blairgowrie	2
Jan 20	Ross Co	3	Burntisland	2
Jan 20	St Bernard's	3	Wick A	0
Jan 20	St Johnstone	3	East Fife	1
Jan 20	Stenhousemuir	1	T Lanark	1
Jan 20	Vale of Leithen	3	Rosyth Dockyard	0

Replays

Jan 23	St Mirren	4	Penicuik A	1
Jan 24	Kilmarnock	3	Airdrie	2
Jan 24	T Lanark	1	Stenhousemuir	0

2nd Round

Feb 3	Aberdeen	2	Dundee	0
Feb 3	Albion R	2	Kilmarnock	1
Feb 3	Ayr U	2	Celtic	3
Feb 3	Brechin C	0	St Mirren	4
Feb 3	Cowdenbeath	2	St Bernard's	1
Feb 3	East Stirling	1	Arbroath	1
Feb 3	Hamilton A	2	Falkirk	4
Feb 3	Hibernian	6	Alloa	0
Feb 3	Partick T	3	Motherwell	3
Feb 3	Queen's Park	1	Hearts	2
Feb 3	Ross Co	3	Galston	1
Feb 3	T Lanark	0	Rangers	3
Feb 3	Vale of Leithen	1	St Johnstone	3

Replays

Feb 7	Arbroath	0	E Stirling	3
Feb 7	Motherwell	2	Partick T	1

3rd Round

Feb 17	Albion R	6	Ross Co	1
Feb 17	Celtic	3	Falkirk	1
Feb 17	Hibernian	0	Aberdeen	1
Feb 17	Motherwell	5	E Stirling	0
Feb 17	Queen of South	3	Cowdenbeath	0
Feb 17	Rangers	0	Hearts	0

Replay

Feb 21	Hearts	1	Rangers	2

4th Round

Mar 3	Albion R	1	Motherwell	1
Mar 3	Rangers	1	Aberdeen	0
Mar 3	St Johnstone	2	Queen of South	0
Mar 3	St Mirren	2	Celtic	0

Replay

Mar 7	Motherwell	6	Albion R	0

Semi-finals

Mar 31	Motherwell	1	St Mirren	3
	played at Tynecastle			
Mar 31	Rangers	1	St Johnstone	0
	played at Hampden Park			

Final

Apr 21	Rangers	5	St Mirren	0
	played at Hampden Park			

Runners-up in Division Two, Dunfermline were promoted along with Albion Rovers. Back row (left to right): J.Low, E.Dowie. Middle row: Laidlaw, R.Driver, Currie, Rarity, Steele, Rodgers, R.Wylie, J.Anderson, W.Knight. Front row: Reid, Dobson, Paterson, McKendrick, Watson, Weir, Garland.

DIVISION 1

	ABERDEEN	AIRDRIE	AYR U	CELTIC	CLYDE	COWDENBEATH	DUNDEE	FALKIRK	HAMILTON A	HEARTS	HIBERNIAN	KILMARNOCK	MOTHERWELL	PARTICK T	QUEEN OF SOUTH	QUEEN'S PARK	RANGERS	ST JOHNSTONE	ST MIRREN	T LANARK
ABERDEEN		Dec30 4-0	Aug12 8-0	Oct07 3-0	Mar24 4-0	Jan02 5-0	Sep09 1-3	Nov11 5-0	Feb10 5-1	Apr21 0-1	Sep23 2-1	Nov04 2-0	Sep25 1-1	Aug26 3-0	Oct21 5-0	Apr28 2-2	Dec02 1-2	Nov25 1-1	Apr14 0-0	Jan13 3-0
AIRDRIE	Aug19 0-1		Apr28 2-4	Apr07 1-0	Feb24 2-0	Dec09 2-1	Oct28 2-2	Jan01 3-4	Sep30 0-3	Apr14 3-2	Nov25 2-3	Jan27 3-1	Mar24 3-6	Sep13 2-1	Jan06 2-5	Oct14 3-4	Dec23 2-7	Sep02 1-1	Nov04 4-1	Mar10 1-2
AYR U	Dec23 1-2	Dec16 1-1		Nov18 3-1	Jan06 4-2	Mar17 6-2	Nov25 3-3	Jan27 1-0	Sep02 3-1	Aug19 4-3	Apr07 4-1	Sep30 1-1	Apr21 2-3	Oct21 3-1	Jan01 0-3	Feb24 2-6	Sep16 0-2	Oct14 3-2	Sep13 2-2	Nov04 5-1
CELTIC	Feb24 2-2	Dec02 4-2	Mar24 0-3		Apr02 2-1	Sep19 7-0	Apr21 3-2	Aug19 2-2	Apr23 5-1	Sep02 0-0	Oct28 2-1	Jan06 4-1	Mar10 3-0	Nov04 2-0	Dec23 0-1	Sep30 3-1	Jan01 2-2	Jan27 0-0	Apr11 3-0	Nov25 3-1
CLYDE	Nov18 2-2	Oct07 4-2	Aug26 5-2	Apr18 1-1		Jan13 2-3	Mar03 3-0	Dec30 2-0	Oct21 0-2	Apr14 1-2	Dec09 1-0	Apr26 0-1	Sep23 0-1	Apr28 3-3	Mar17 1-1	Aug12 1-6	Nov11 3-0	Sep23 0-0	Jan20 4-2	Apr02 4-2
COWDENBEATH	Sep30 2-4	Apr21 1-3	Oct28 2-2	Nov11 0-1	Sep02 1-1		Mar10 1-1	Feb24 0-3	Oct14 4-0	Jan27 1-5	Aug23 2-4	Dec23 0-1	Dec16 0-4	Nov25 1-3	Sep16 1-3	Aug19 0-2	Jan06 3-4	Jan01 1-5	Apr30 1-5	Nov18 0-1
DUNDEE	Jan01 1-1	Mar17 4-0	Mar31 2-1	Dec09 3-2	Aug19 1-1	Oct21 4-2		Jan06 1-3	Feb24 0-1	Sep30 0-1	Apr28 1-0	Oct14 0-2	Nov04 2-3	Dec02 1-2	Sep02 8-0	Sep16 1-0	Jan27 0-6	Dec23 3-0	Mar24 3-0	Sep13 3-0
FALKIRK	Sep13 6-5	Aug09 0-2	Sep23 2-3	Dec30 2-6	Dec02 2-2	Oct07 4-3	Aug26 2-1		Nov18 2-0	Mar17 2-1	Apr28 3-1	Jan02 2-2	Jan13 1-3	Dec09 3-0	Oct21 1-3	Apr25 1-3	Nov04 4-0	Apr17 2-1	Aug12 2-1	Mar23 3-3
HAMILTON A	Oct28 2-1	Jan02 4-2	Jan13 1-1	Apr14 1-0	Mar10 3-2	Mar03 1-0	Oct07 2-1	Mar24 2-1		Nov04 1-1	Aug25 4-1	Sep13 2-2	Sep09 1-2	Aug12 3-7	Dec02 0-2	Mar31 2-1	Mar14 1-2	Apr21 4-1	Dec30 1-2	Sep23 4-2
HEARTS	Dec09 0-0	Dec25 8-1	Dec30 1-1	Jan13 2-1	Nov25 1-1	Sep23 5-4	Jan02 6-1	Oct28 3-1	Aug22 4-2		Sep09 0-0	Apr07 1-1	Apr16 1-3	Nov18 1-0	Nov11 1-3	Mar10 4-0	Nov11 1-2	Apr28 2-1	Aug12 6-0	Aug26 5-1
HIBERNIAN	Jan27 3-2	Mar31 0-2	Dec02 0-0	Mar17 1-2	Sep16 3-0	Nov04 6-1	Dec16 1-3	Jan06 1-4	Jan01 1-2	Sep09 4-1		Sep13 4-1	Apr02 0-2	Feb24 0-2	Dec23 2-1	Mar24 0-0	Sep30 2-6	Oct21 2-1	Apr21 3-1	—
KILMARNOCK	Aug23 2-0	Sep23 7-1	Jan02 4-3	Aug26 4-3	Feb17 4-2	Aug12 1-3	Mar03 1-1	Dec16 1-1	Nov11 1-1	Dec02 2-5	Jan13 2-0		Oct07 1-3	Dec30 2-6	Mar31 3-1	Apr18 1-3	Oct28 1-0	Mar10 3-0	Sep09 1-0	Aug16 2-2
MOTHERWELL	Sep16 4-1	Nov18 3-1	Dec09 5-2	Oct21 1-1	Dec23 1-2	Apr11 6-1	Aug23 1-0	Sep30 2-1	Jan01 2-1	Oct14 2-1	Nov11 2-1	Feb24 2-0		Mar17 2-3	Jan06 1-2	Jan27 3-0	Sep02 2-1	Aug19 1-0	Nov25 1-0	Apr07 2-2
PARTICK T	Jan06 4-0	Nov11 1-0	Mar10 5-1	Aug23 0-3	Feb17 2-0	Mar31 5-3	Sep02 0-3	Dec23 1-2	Mar24 7-2	Oct07 3-2	Nov25 2-3	Aug19 1-4	Oct28 1-1		Jan27 1-1	Apr18 5-2	Dec02 3-4	Sep16 0-3	Apr24 2-3	Apr14 3-0
QUEEN OF SOUTH	Mar10 4-1	Apr26 1-2	Sep09 2-4	Aug12 3-2	Dec16 2-2	Feb10 4-0	Jan13 3-1	Apr21 3-1	Apr07 1-0	Mar24 4-1	Oct07 0-5	Nov25 4-3	Aug26 0-5	Sep23 2-3		Aug23 1-4	Nov11 0-4	Oct28 2-3	Jan02 3-0	Dec30 2-0
QUEEN'S PARK	Mar28 1-5	Aug26 2-1	Oct07 4-5	Dec25 2-3	Oct28 1-2	Dec30 1-0	Feb17 2-4	Apr14 1-0	Nov25 2-4	Sep12 1-1	Aug12 2-1	Nov18 2-1	Sep23 3-4	Mar03 1-5	Nov04 0-1		Apr30 1-1	Apr07 1-0	Jan13 0-0	Jan01 1-0
RANGERS	Apr07 2-1	Aug12 5-1	Aug15 9-1	Sep09 2-2	Nov04 3-1	Aug26 3-1	Sep23 1-0	Apr25 3-1	Oct21 4-2	Dec30 6-0	Mar31 2-2	Jan13 4-2	Jan02 2-2	Sep13 5-1	Aug23 4-0	Mar24 3-0		Mar24 3-0	Oct07 3-0	Mar21 1-0
ST JOHNSTONE	Apr11 5-1	Jan13 4-0	Feb17 0-2	Sep23 1-1	Sep13 1-0	Sep09 3-0	Aug12 0-1	Aug23 5-1	Dec09 3-1	Dec16 2-1	Jan02 0-3	Oct21 1-2	Dec30 4-0	Feb10 1-2	Mar17 4-0	Dec02 1-0	Nov18 3-1		Aug26 1-1	Oct07 1-4
ST MIRREN	Oct14 2-3	Aug22 1-1	Nov11 1-1	Apr27 1-2	Jan27 2-0	Dec02 0-0	Nov18 0-3	Sep16 3-1	Aug19 2-3	Dec23 1-1	Mar10 0-3	Jan01 3-1	Nov20 1-3	Dec09 2-0	Sep30 0-3	Sep02 1-2	Feb24 1-2	Jan06 1-4		Oct28 7-2
T LANARK	Sep02 2-3	Oct21 3-1	Aug22 3-7	Mar31 1-1	Sep30 3-3	Mar24 5-1	Nov11 4-1	Dec23 3-1	Jan27 1-1	Jan06 1-1	Dec09 1-0	Sep16 1-1	Dec02 2-2	Apr28 3-1	Aug19 1-2	Sep08 2-5	Apr02 0-1	Feb24 3-0	Mar17 1-5	

DIVISION 2

	ALBION R	ALLOA	ARBROATH	BRECHIN C	DUMBARTON	DUNDEE U	DUNFERMLINE A	EAST FIFE	E STIRLING	EDINBURGH C	FORFAR A	KING'S PARK	LEITH A	MONTROSE	MORTON	RAITH R	ST BERNARD'S	STENHOUSEMUIR
ALBION R		Jan03 2-1	Mar10 4-0	Apr14 3-0	Sep09 2-0	Nov04 4-3	Jan13 3-2	Oct07 1-1	Aug26 3-1	Oct14 8-1	Dec02 3-2	Mar31 4-2	Oct21 2-0	Aug12 6-2	Dec30 3-1	Feb10 2-2	Sep23 1-1	Jan06 4-0
ALLOA	Sep02 1-1		Mar31 2-2	Mar03 3-1	Nov11 2-0	Aug19 1-2	Jan01 1-2	Feb10 2-2	Dec02 4-1	Apr14 4-0	Sep30 2-1	Dec09 1-2	Oct14 3-1	Mar17 1-1	Apr03 3-1	Jan06 1-3	Jan27 1-3	Oct28 3-6
ARBROATH	Oct28 4-1	Aug12 5-0		Mar17 2-3	Aug26 4-1	Jan27 4-2	Dec23 3-5	Sep23 6-1	Oct07 2-0	Apr07 4-1	Sep09 2-1	Dec02 2-0	Oct14 2-1	Mar03 2-0	Jan06 1-4	Nov11 1-0	Dec09 5-2	Feb10 3-0
BRECHIN C	Nov25 3-1	Oct07 1-2	Dec30 2-0		Sep23 4-0	Oct21 4-2	Feb24 0-4	Apr07 2-1	Feb10 0-0	Nov04 1-4	Aug12 4-4	Nov18 5-0	Dec16 1-1	Sep09 0-0	Aug26 2-1	Jan06 0-0	Dec09 3-1	Mar31 3-1
DUMBARTON	Jan01 2-0	Feb24 3-2	Nov18 2-0	Dec23 3-1		Sep02 4-2	Sep30 1-3	Oct14 3-4	Mar17 2-0	Apr21 4-1	Nov04 3-0	Aug19 2-1	Jan13 1-2	Mar31 2-0	Sep16 2-1	Apr21 3-1	Mar03 2-0	Dec02 2-0
DUNDEE U	Apr28 2-3	Nov25 0-4	Dec16 2-9	Jan13 0-1	Dec30 4-4		Oct28 4-2	Aug12 1-3	Sep23 2-2	Nov18 9-3	Aug26 0-3	Mar03 8-1	Mar10 5-2	Sep09 1-2	Apr21 5-2	Oct06 4-1	Apr21 5-2	Nov11 2-4
DUNFERMLINE A	Mar17 1-2	Sep09 1-1	Oct21 3-0	Dec02 2-1	Feb10 3-0	Mar24 1-0		Aug26 4-0	Dec30 10-3	Mar10 7-0	Nov04 2-1	Nov18 3-2	Jan06 3-2	Aug12 4-2	Mar31 3-3	Oct07 1-3	Dec09 3-0	—
EAST FIFE	Dec09 0-2	Oct21 1-1	Nov04 2-4	Sep30 6-3	Jan06 3-3	Dec23 5-1	Jan27 1-2		Mar31 0-2	Sep02 3-0	Mar03 4-3	Sep16 2-3	Apr19 2-1	Feb24 1-1	Nov25 3-0	Jan01 2-6	Apr14 3-2	Nov11 4-1
E STIRLING	Mar24 1-3	Apr27 3-0	Dec09 3-1	Sep16 3-1	Nov25 3-3	Apr07 1-1	Sep02 1-4	Oct28 4-3		Sep30 2-2	Apr14 5-1	Jan01 2-1	Dec23 3-4	Feb24 4-1	Aug19 5-1	Nov11 2-0	Oct14 1-2	—
EDINBURGH C	Mar28 0-1	Aug26 1-2	Nov25 1-3	Jan27 3-2	Aug12 2-1	Feb10 2-1	Nov11 1-6	Dec25 2-2	Jan06 1-2		Apr21 2-2	Dec09 1-0	Mar31 0-2	Oct07 1-2	Oct21 0-5	Sep09 2-2	Sep23 0-5	Dec23 6-0
FORFAR A	Aug19 3-1	Aug26 4-1	Jan01 0-3	Oct14 1-1	Mar24 4-0	Mar31 4-1	Nov25 3-3	Nov18 1-3	Nov18 4-1	Sep16 5-2		Sep02 3-3	Sep30 4-0	Dec16 2-2	Nov11 2-2	Mar10 3-0	Oct28 2-1	Dec23 6-0
KING'S PARK	Nov11 2-0	Jan06 1-1	Apr14 3-3	Mar10 7-1	Oct28 5-2	Oct14 0-0	Apr07 2-0	Dec16 4-4	Sep09 4-2	Mar24 4-2	Jan06 6-1		Feb10 1-1	Sep23 1-5	Oct07 2-2	Nov25 3-1	Aug12 3-2	Aug26 5-1
LEITH A	Jan27 0-1	Dec30 0-1	Feb24 1-1	Nov11 2-2	Oct07 0-1	Dec09 1-5	Mar03 4-1	Apr21 4-4	Aug12 1-2	Oct28 3-1	Jan06 3-0	Mar17 5-0		Nov25 5-0	Sep23 3-1	Nov04 2-0	Aug26 4-1	Sep09 1-2
MONTROSE	Apr07 2-1	Apr21 4-1	Aug19 2-1	Jan01 1-2	Oct28 2-4	Sep30 0-2	Sep16 1-4	Apr14 2-0	Nov02 1-2	Dec23 3-1	Feb10 3-0	Jan13 2-4	Sep02 1-3		Mar10 4-2	Dec09 2-1	Mar17 4-2	Dec30 0-0
MORTON	Sep16 1-0	Nov18 3-3	Sep30 2-9	Mar24 4-3	Dec09 4-3	Jan01 1-4	Apr14 0-2	Jan13 2-4	Oct21 1-5	Aug19 4-0	Feb24 2-4	Dec23 1-0	Apr07 2-2	Oct28 4-1		Sep02 2-1	Feb10 0-2	Mar03 3-1
RAITH R	Nov18 2-0	Sep23 2-2	Jan13 0-1	Oct28 5-1	Apr07 1-1	Dec02 4-1	Oct14 1-1	Sep09 0-1	Mar03 3-0	Oct07 6-0	Jan27 3-4	Mar24 2-1	Aug26 3-1	Dec16 1-1		Dec30 3-1	Aug12 1-3	—
ST BERNARD'S	Dec23 2-0	Nov04 5-1	Jan13 1-0	Aug19 2-1	Mar10 7-2	Dec02 3-0	Oct14 4-1	Nov18 2-2	Jan13 1-1	Jan01 5-0	Feb24 1-1	Oct21 2-0	Dec02 0-1	Mar24 2-0	Oct14 10-1	Sep30 3-1		Apr07
STENHOUSEMUIR	Sep30 2-2	Mar24 3-0	Sep16 1-4	Sep02 2-0	Jan27 6-4	Mar17 3-0	Aug19 3-1	Mar10 3-1	Apr21 0-2	Jan13 5-2	Oct21 4-2	Feb24 2-1	Jan01 1-1	Nov18 4-3	Nov04 1-0	Apr14 5-4	Nov25 3-0	

DIVISION 1 FINAL TABLE

	P	W	D	L	F	A	Pts
Rangers	38	30	6	2	118	41	66
Motherwell	38	29	4	5	97	45	62
Celtic	38	18	11	9	78	53	47
Queen of South	38	21	3	14	75	78	45
Aberdeen	38	18	8	12	90	57	44
Hearts	38	17	10	11	86	59	44
Kilmarnock	38	17	9	12	73	64	43
Ayr U	38	16	10	12	87	92	42
St Johnstone	38	17	6	15	74	53	40
Falkirk	38	16	6	16	73	68	38
Hamilton A	38	15	8	15	65	79	38
Dundee	38	15	6	17	68	64	36
Partick T	38	14	5	19	73	78	33
Clyde	38	10	11	17	56	70	31
Queen's Park	38	13	5	20	65	85	31
Hibernian	38	12	3	23	51	69	27
St Mirren	38	9	9	20	46	75	27
Airdrie	38	10	6	22	59	103	26
T Lanark	38	8	9	21	62	103	25
Cowdenbeath	38	5	5	28	58	118	15

DIVISION 2 FINAL TABLE

	P	W	D	L	F	A	Pts
Albion R	34	20	5	9	74	47	45
Dunfermline A	34	20	4	10	90	52	44
Arbroath	34	20	4	10	83	53	44
Stenhousemuir	34	18	4	12	70	73	40
Morton	34	17	5	12	67	64	39
Dumbarton	34	17	3	14	67	68	37
King's Park	34	14	8	12	78	70	36
Raith R	34	15	5	14	71	55	35
E Stirling	34	14	7	13	65	74	35
St Bernard's	34	15	4	15	75	56	34
Forfar A	34	13	7	14	77	71	33
Leith A	34	12	8	14	63	60	32
East Fife	34	12	8	14	71	76	32
Brechin C	34	13	5	16	60	70	31
Alloa	34	11	9	14	55	68	31
Montrose	34	11	4	19	53	81	26
Dundee U	34	10	4	20	81	88	24
Edinburgh C	34	4	6	24	37	111	14

Season 1934-35

SFA Cup
1st Round
Jan 26	Albion R	7	Paisley A	0
Jan 26	Ayr U	3	Queen of South	1
Jan 26	Berwick R	1	Rosyth Dockyard	3
Jan 26	Brechin C	3	Leith A	2
Jan 26	Buckie T	1	Beith	0
Jan 26	Celtic	4	Montrose	1
Jan 26	Dundee	1	Motherwell	2
Jan 26	Dunfermline A	1	Hamilton A	2
Jan 26	East Fife	1	Clyde	2
Jan 23	E Stirling	1	Raith R	2
Jan 26	Falkirk	2	Aberdeen	3
Jan 26	Forfar A	7	Chirnside U	1
Jan 26	Fraserburgh	2	Dundee U	6
Jan 26	Galston	0	Kilmarnock	1
Jan 26	Hearts	7	Solway Star	0
Jan 23	Hibernian	5	Vale of Atholl	0
Jan 26	Inver Citadel	1	Clacknacuddin	3
Jan 26	King's Park	3	Edinburgh	1
Jan 26	Morton	9	Bo'ness	0
Jan 26	Partick T	3	Stenhousemuir	0
Jan 26	Queen's Park	2	Alloa	1
Jan 26	Rangers	3	Cowdenbeath	1
Jan 26	St Bernard's	1	Airdrie	3
Jan 26	St Johnstone	1	Arbroath	0
Jan 26	St Mirren	3	Peebles R	1
Jan 26	T Lanark	6	Creetown	2
Jan 26	Vale Ocoba	1	Dumbarton	6

2nd Round
Feb 9	Aberdeen	4	Albion R	0
Feb 9	Airdrie	1	Rosyth Dockyard	0
Feb 9	Ayr U	1	King's Park	1
Feb 9	Brechin C	1	Raith R	1
Feb 9	Celtic	1	Partick T	1
Feb 9	Clyde	3	Hamilton A	3
Feb 9	Dundee U	6	Queen's Park	3
Feb 9	Hearts	2	Kilmarnock	0
Feb 9	Hibernian	7	Clacknacuddin	1
Feb 9	Motherwell	7	Morton	1
Feb 9	Rangers	2	T Lanark	0
Feb 9	St Johnstone	4	Dumbarton	0
Feb 9	St Mirren	3	Forfar A	0

Replays
Feb 13	Hamilton A	6	Clyde	3
Feb 13	Kings' Park	2	Ayr U	2
Feb 13	Partick T	1	Celtic	3
Feb 13	Raith R	2	Brechin C	4
Feb 18	Ayr U	4	King's Park	4

played at Firhill Park

Feb 19	Ayr U	1	King's Park	2

played at Hampden Park

3rd Round
Feb 23	Aberdeen	0	Hibernian	0
Feb 23	Airdrie	6	King's Park	2
Feb 23	Brechin C	2	Hamilton A	4
Feb 23	Buckie T	0	St Johnstone	1
Feb 23	Hearts	2	Dundee U	2
Feb 23	Rangers	1	St Mirren	0

Replays
Feb 27	Dundee U	2	Hearts	4
Feb 27	Hibernian	1	Aberdeen	1
Mar 4	Aberdeen	3	Hibernian	2

played at Easter Road

4th Round
Mar 9	Aberdeen	3	Celtic	1
Mar 9	Airdrie	2	Hearts	3
Mar 9	Hamilton A	3	St Johnstone	0
Mar 9	Motherwell	1	Rangers	4

Semi-finals
Mar 30	Aberdeen	1	Hamilton A	2

played at Celtic Park

Mar 30	Hearts	1	Rangers	1

played at Hampden Park

Replay
Apr 10	Hearts	0	Rangers	2

played at Hampden Park

Final
Apr 20	Hamilton A	1	Rangers	2

played at Hampden Park

Fashion 1930s style as Rangers embark on a Transatlantic trip, with manager Bill Struth, extreme right.

DIVISION 1

	ABERDEEN	AIRDRIE	ALBION R	AYR U	CELTIC	CLYDE	DUNDEE	DUNFERMLINE A	FALKIRK	HAMILTON A	HEARTS	HIBERNIAN	KILMARNOCK	MOTHERWELL	PARTICK T	QUEEN OF SOUTH	QUEEN'S PARK	RANGERS	ST JOHNSTONE	ST MIRREN
ABERDEEN		Sep29 1-3	Mar16 1-1	Feb16 7-1	Jan19 2-1	Nov03 3-0	Jan01 3-0	Sep01 3-0	Aug18 1-0	Dec15 3-3	Nov24 1-0	Jan05 2-0	Sep24 1-3	Sep15 2-2	Dec22 2-0	Aug22 1-0	Dec01 5-0	Apr13 1-3	Nov10 2-0	Oct13 1-0
AIRDRIE	Feb02 4-1		Sep08 3-0	Apr27 3-2	Nov17 0-2	Sep22 0-0	Sep12 0-3	Apr20 2-3	Dec08 2-1	Jan02 2-2	Jan12 4-7	Mar29 7-0	Aug25 3-2	Nov03 2-0	Mar16 0-2	Mar02 3-1	Aug11 4-2	Oct06 1-2	Dec29 1-1	Oct20 1-0
ALBION R	Oct27 1-1	Jan01 0-3		Jan05 8-0	Sep29 2-1	Apr13 4-1	Dec22 1-2	Jan19 1-2	Feb16 0-0	Mar23 4-1	Dec15 2-2	Oct13 2-0	Dec01 1-0	Sep01 2-3	Aug18 2-0	Nov24 3-2	Apr20 0-0	Nov10 1-5	Mar13 2-4	Sep15 2-3
AYR U	Oct06 0-3	Dec01 2-1	Aug25 0-1		Mar23 1-0	Aug11 2-3	Mar30 3-2	Dec15 1-2	Apr10 1-2	Dec29 0-3	Feb02 1-1	Nov17 1-1	Jan02 1-0	Nov24 3-2	Aug22 1-1	Sep08 2-4	Sep22 3-0	Jan12 2-4	Mar02 3-0	Oct27 1-0
CELTIC	Sep22 4-1	Apr13 2-0	Feb02 5-1	Nov03 7-0		Mar02 0-2	Nov24 4-0	Oct27 3-0	Apr17 7-3	Jan12 3-1	Dec29 4-2	Sep11 4-0	Aug11 4-1	Dec08 3-2	Feb23 3-1	Oct06 1-2	Dec25 4-1	Sep08 1-1	Aug25 0-0	Apr27 2-1
CLYDE	Mar23 1-1	Jan19 3-0	Nov17 1-1	Dec22 5-1	Oct13 0-3		Sep29 2-2	Aug18 2-1	Sep01 3-0	Apr21 3-3	Nov10 0-1	Sep15 3-2	Mar09 1-1	Feb16 3-3	Jan01 3-4	Dec15 1-2	Dec15 3-0	Oct20 2-1	Mar16 4-1	Jan05 5-2
DUNDEE	Sep08 0-0	Dec15 2-0	Aug11 3-2	Nov10 5-4	Oct01 0-0	Feb02 2-2		Aug22 1-1	Oct27 1-1	Sep22 1-5	Jan02 0-2	Dec01 0-2	Mar02 3-1	Feb23 2-0	Mar09 5-0	Dec29 4-1	Jan12 3-2	Aug25 1-2	Oct06 0-2	Mar23 3-2
DUNFERMLINE A	Jan02 1-1	Nov24 1-1	Sep22 1-3	Sep12 1-2	Mar16 1-3	Dec29 4-2	Dec08 2-5		Mar23 2-1	Mar02 4-1	Aug25 1-2	Oct20 2-1	Oct06 2-2	Apr27 1-0	Mar30 2-1	Jan12 3-1	Feb02 2-2	Aug11 1-7	Sep08 1-2	Nov17 3-2
FALKIRK	Dec29 3-2	Aug22 2-4	Oct06 3-0	8-1	Nov10 1-2	Jan02 2-4	Mar16 1-1	Nov03 2-0		Aug25 1-2	Aug11 1-2	Apr20 0-2	Jan12 5-2	Apr13 5-2	Dec01 0-3	Feb02 1-2	Sep08 3-1	Mar02 1-1	Oct13 0-3	Dec15 1-1
HAMILTON A	Sep12 6-1	Aug31 4-2	Nov03 3-2	Aug18 4-2	Sep15 4-3	Dec08 1-1	Jan19 3-0	Oct13 1-2	Jan05 3-0		Apr05 2-0	Dec22 2-1	Oct27 1-1	Jan01 2-2	Mar20 2-1	Apr13 2-2	Nov10 2-1	Apr27 2-2	Nov24 3-0	Sep29 2-2
HEARTS	Apr20 2-1	Sep15 1-0	Sep12 4-0	Sep29 5-0	Aug18 0-0	Apr15 2-0	Sep01 1-1	Jan05 0-1	Dec22 4-1	Oct24 1-1		Jan01 5-2	Nov17 2-2	Oct13 2-1	Jan19 4-2	Mar23 2-1	Mar16 4-1	Dec08 2-2	Dec01 0-1	Feb16 0-1
HIBERNIAN	Aug25 2-3	Nov10 2-2	Mar02 3-3	Apr13 1-1	Dec15 3-2	Jan12 4-0	Apr21 2-1	Mar09 3-1	Nov24 2-0	Aug11 3-1	Sep08 1-0		Dec29 1-0	Oct27 1-1	Nov03 2-0	Sep08 0-6	Oct06 5-1	Feb02 1-2	Jan02 1-1	Aug22 0-0
KILMARNOCK	Oct20 1-3	Jan05 0-0	Apr27 2-1	Sep01 6-3	Dec22 2-3	Nov24 2-0	Oct13 1-3	Feb16 1-3	Sep15 4-1	Mar16 4-1	Apr13 0-1	Aug18 3-3		Jan19 3-3	Sep29 2-0	Nov10 3-1	Nov03 5-0	Sep04 1-3	Dec08 1-0	Jan01 1-4
MOTHERWELL	Jan12 1-2	Mar23 3-2	Jan02 5-2	Apr20 2-3	Aug22 1-0	Oct06 1-1	Oct20 5-3	Dec01 9-3	Nov17 5-2	Sep08 0-0	Mar02 2-2	Mar16 4-1	Sep22 3-2		Dec15 4-1	Aug11 4-0	Aug25 3-0	Dec29 2-2	Feb02 0-1	Mar30 3-0
PARTICK T	Aug11 2-1	Oct27 4-1	Dec29 1-0	Oct20 1-1	Sep08 0-0	Nov17 1-4	Mar09 7-1	Nov10 2-0	Apr27 2-2	Oct06 0-1	Sep22 1-3	Mar23 3-1	Feb02 4-2	Sep12 1-1		Aug25 2-1	Mar02 2-2	Jan02 1-0	Jan12 3-0	Nov24 2-1
QUEEN OF SOUTH	Dec08 1-1	Oct13 1-1	Apr20 2-0	Jan01 1-1	Feb16 3-4	Aug18 1-0	Sep15 2-1	Sep29 2-0	Nov17 1-1	Nov03 4-1	Jan19 3-3	Mar30 0-2	Dec22 2-4	Jan05 2-1			Oct20 1-0	Oct27 2-3	Sep12 0-2	Sep01 2-0
QUEEN'S PARK	Apr27 1-1	Dec22 4-2	Dec08 1-1	Jan19 5-4	Sep11 1-0	Sep15 0-1	Sep29 4-0	Jan01 1-0	Apr08 4-3	Oct27 3-3	Apr15 3-1	Feb23 1-4	Jan05 1-1	Apr22 3-1	Mar09 2-1			Nov24 0-4	Apr13 2-1	Aug18 4-1
RANGERS	Nov17 2-2	Feb16 3-1	Apr24 2-2	Sep15 2-0	Jan04 2-1	Mar20 4-2	Jan05 3-1	Dec25 8-1	Oct06 1-1	Aug22 2-1	Sep29 4-2	Apr15 1-0	Sep01 4-0	Sep01 5-0	Mar16 0-1		Apr30		Nov03 3-1	Jan19 1-0
ST JOHNSTONE	Apr03 1-1	Aug18 2-0	Oct20 4-0	Oct13 1-0	Jan05 1-2	Oct27 0-1	Feb16 5-2	Jan01 0-1	Jan19 5-1	Apr10 4-0	Apr27 3-1	Sep01 2-1	Aug22 1-1	Sep29 2-1	Sep15 1-1	Dec15 1-1	Nov17 2-0	Mar23 2-0		Dec22 4-0
ST MIRREN	Mar02 3-0	Mar12 1-0	Jan12 5-4	Mar16 3-3	Dec01 2-4	Aug25 1-2	Nov03 0-1	Apr13 3-0	Sep11 2-1	Feb02 1-2	Oct06 2-4	Dec08 1-2	Sep08 0-2	Nov10 1-0	Apr20 2-1	Jan02 1-1	Dec29 2-3	Sep22 0-2	Aug11 1-1	

DIVISION 2

	ALLOA	ARBROATH	BRECHIN C	COWDENBEATH	DUMBARTON	DUNDEE U	EAST FIFE	E STIRLING	EDINBURGH C	FORFAR A	KING'S PARK	LEITH A	MONTROSE	MORTON	RAITH R	ST BERNARD'S	STENHOUSEMUIR	T LANARK
ALLOA		Apr06 0-0	Mar02 5-1	Sep22 5-2	Mar16 4-1	Dec29 3-3	Aug25 5-2	Sep08 1-2	Aug11 5-0	Oct27 5-2	Jan19 4-0	Oct06 1-2	Dec01 3-0	Dec15 2-1	Feb16 5-2	Nov03 2-1	Nov17 1-1	Jan05 0-2
ARBROATH	Sep15 1-0		Jan12 2-0	Dec29 1-0	Mar30 4-0	Feb02 2-2	Apr13 5-0	Mar16 1-0	Jan05 1-0	Jan01 0-3	Mar02 3-1	Nov24 3-1	Sep29 6-0	Sep01 6-2	Dec15 2-0	Aug18 2-5	Oct27 3-1	Oct20 2-1
BRECHIN C	Sep01 3-0	Nov17 0-1		Jan19 1-2	Oct20 1-4	Oct27 0-8	Nov03 2-1	Nov24 1-0	Dec29 7-1	Sep15 1-1	Aug18 3-2	Feb02 3-2	Jan01 3-2	Mar23 0-0	Mar09 2-3	Apr20 3-5	Dec15 3-5	Sep29 1-1
COWDENBEATH	Apr13 2-2	Mar09 1-3	Oct13 2-2		Jan01 8-1	Nov24 1-0	Feb16 1-1	Nov17 0-0	Oct27 7-0	Aug18 1-2	Dec15 7-2	Nov10 3-2	Apr06 5-2	Jan05 4-0	Apr13 3-3	Sep01 1-10	Feb09 5-3	Sep15 1-3
DUMBARTON	Oct13 0-0	Aug11 2-1	Aug25 2-0	Oct06 4-2		Jan12 5-1	Nov24 4-2	Sep22 2-2	Dec22 2-0	Mar23 2-3	Oct27 1-1	Nov10 4-2	Apr13 2-1	Sep01 2-5	Feb16 3-4	Apr13 1-4	2-1	Apr05 0-1
DUNDEE U	Sep29 2-0	Nov03 3-2	Dec22 9-2	Oct20 0-2	Aug18 4-0		Jan05 4-0	Mar30 9-6	Nov28 5-3	Jan19 2-1	Dec08 4-3	Nov17 4-1	Sep15 4-0	Jan01 2-1	Sep01 3-1	Feb16 8-0	Mar16 0-2	Oct13 1-3
EAST FIFE	Mar30 0-1	Oct13 1-2	Apr06 1-2	Dec22 3-2	Sep29 9-1	Nov10 1-1		Oct27 2-0	Jan19 3-1	Feb02 5-0	Sep01 2-1	Dec29 5-2	Dec15 4-2	Oct06 1-0	Apr12 4-2	Sep15 1-1	6-1	Mar02 1-3
E STIRLING	Nov07 0-0	Dec01 1-2	Jan05 0-1	Dec08 2-1	Jan19 6-2	Mar09 1-2	Mar23 3-2		Apr06 2-4	Sep01 5-1	Jan01 0-3	Jan12 1-1	Oct20 3-1	Dec22 3-1	Sep15 2-1	Feb16 0-0	Aug18 1-3	Aug18 2-2
EDINBURGH C	Oct31 2-2	Nov10 0-4	Jan05 1-1	Mar23 1-6	Sep08 2-8	Dec15 0-5	Nov17 1-3	Sep10 0-5		Apr13 0-5	Feb02 1-4	Oct13 2-6	Sep01 1-3	Sep17 1-3	Jan12 2-6	Dec25 1-3	Dec05 0-4	Feb23 0-2
FORFAR A	Mar30 1-1	Oct06 1-3	Dec08 5-1	Mar02 2-2	Jan05 4-1	Aug11 0-2	Sep22 1-3	Dec15 5-2	Aug25 4-1		Oct13 0-3	Sep08 4-2	Jan12 5-1	Dec01 1-1	Dec22 3-1	Mar16 4-4	Mar30 6-4	Nov10 3-1
KING'S PARK	Mar30 4-1	Aug25 2-1	Feb16 8-1	Aug11 1-0	Nov03 3-2	Sep08 3-1	Oct06 5-1	Sep29 2-1	Sep15 9-4	Mar09 1-2		Sep22 2-1	Apr13 5-1	Nov17 2-1	Oct20 4-2	Jan12 2-3	Dec22 2-4	
LEITH A	Jan01 4-4	Dec08 0-4	Dec01 2-1	Mar16 5-3	Sep15 2-1	Apr20 4-0	Oct20 1-1	Mar02 1-5	Mar30 6-0	Feb16 2-1	Jan05 5-4		Aug18 5-4	Sep29 2-2	Jan19 3-0	Dec22 2-1	Nov03 3-1	Sep01 1-2
MONTROSE	Dec22 2-2	Jan19 0-5	Oct06 1-5	Aug25 5-3	Feb16 5-0	Mar23 2-1	Sep08 1-4	Aug11 2-3	Mar09 3-2	Nov03 2-1	Nov24 3-3	Apr13 0-0		Nov17 2-1	Oct13 3-2	Jan05 0-4	Sep22 1-1	Dec08 2-4
MORTON	Nov24 4-1	Feb16 0-1	Sep22 7-0	Sep08 2-1	Mar09 3-2	Oct06 3-3	Jan12 8-1	Aug25 9-2	Sep15 3-1	Dec29 3-1	Nov10 4-2	Apr06 5-1	Mar30 4-1		Oct27 5-1	Oct13 3-4	Aug11 0-1	Jan19 1-0
RAITH R	Dec08 3-0	Sep22 3-4	Aug11 7-0	Nov03 2-3	Dec01 4-2	Mar02 0-3	Jan01 3-0	Feb02 2-1	Aug18 2-2	Oct20 2-2	Apr06 2-0	Aug25 6-0	Dec29 1-0	Mar16 6-0		Mar30 3-0	Sep08 1-0	Nov24 0-1
ST BERNARD'S	Jan12 2-1	Mar23 0-0	Sep08 5-1	Feb02 2-0	Dec08 5-0	Sep22 1-0	Nov24 6-1	Apr13 7-0	Oct06 6-2	Nov17 0-0	Dec29 4-1	Aug11 0-1	Oct27 1-1	Mar02 0-1	Nov10 6-2		Aug25 4-1	Mar09 3-2
STENHOUSEMUIR	Aug18 2-0	Dec22 6-0	Nov10 3-0	Sep11 2-3	Apr12 6-1	Sep01 3-2	Dec08 2-1	Oct13 3-2	Nov24 2-1	Sep29 4-2	Sep15 2-2	Mar09 1-4	Feb02 9-4	Oct20 3-1	Jan05 2-1	Jan19 1-2		Jan01 2-2
T LANARK	Feb02 6-1	Sep08 5-2	Mar16 4-0	Jan12 3-2	Nov17 4-2	Aug25 5-0	Aug11 3-0	Dec29 3-3	Sep22 3-0	Apr27 3-1	Oct27 1-2	Dec15 5-0	Mar02 4-0	Nov03 2-2	Jan02 5-3	Dec01 2-1	Oct06 3-3	

DIVISION 1 FINAL TABLE

	P	W	D	L	F	A	Pts
Rangers	38	25	5	8	96	46	55
Celtic	38	24	4	10	92	45	52
Hearts	38	20	10	8	87	51	50
Hamilton A	38	19	10	9	87	67	48
St Johnstone	38	18	10	10	66	46	46
Aberdeen	38	17	10	11	68	54	44
Motherwell	38	15	10	13	83	64	40
Dundee	38	16	8	14	63	63	40
Kilmarnock	38	16	6	16	76	68	38
Clyde	38	14	10	14	71	69	38
Hibernian	38	14	8	16	59	70	36
Queen's Park	38	13	10	15	61	80	36
Partick T	38	15	5	18	61	68	35
Airdrie	38	13	7	18	64	72	33
Dunfermline A	38	13	5	20	56	96	31
Albion R	38	10	9	19	62	77	29
Queen of South	38	11	7	20	52	72	29
Ayr U	38	12	5	21	61	112	29
St Mirren	38	11	5	22	49	70	27
Falkirk	38	9	6	23	58	82	24

DIVISION 2 FINAL TABLE

	P	W	D	L	F	A	Pts
T Lanark	34	23	6	5	94	43	52
Arbroath	34	23	4	7	78	42	50
St Bernard's	34	20	7	7	103	47	47
Dundee U	34	18	6	10	105	65	42
Stenhousemuir	34	17	5	12	86	80	39
Morton	34	17	4	13	88	64	38
King's Park	34	18	2	14	86	71	38
Leith A	34	16	5	13	69	71	37
East Fife	34	16	3	15	79	73	35
Alloa	34	12	10	12	67	60	34
Forfar A	34	13	8	13	77	73	34
Cowdenbeath	34	13	6	15	84	75	32
Raith R	34	13	3	18	68	73	29
E Stirling	34	11	7	16	57	76	29
Brechin C	34	10	6	18	51	98	26
Dumbarton	34	9	4	21	60	105	22
Montrose	34	7	6	21	58	105	20
Edinburgh C	34	3	2	29	44	133	8

Celtic's League championship winning team pictured before a Charity Cup-tie with Partick Thistle. Back row (left to right): Geatons, Hogg, Kennaway, Morrison, Buchan, Paterson. Front row: J.McMenemy (trainer), Delaney, McGrory, Lyon, Crum, Murphy, W.Maley (manager).

SFA Cup
1st Round

Jan 29	Aberdeen	4	Hamilton A	1
Jan 25	Albion R	7	Wigtown	1
Jan 29	Arbroath	1	Motherwell	3
Jan 25	Ayr U	2	St Mirren	3
Feb 1	Bo'ness	1	Airdrie	3
Jan 25	Burntisland	2	Dumbarton	2
	Celtic	W	Berwick R	0
Jan 25	Clyde	2	Forfar A	1
Jan 25	Dundee	6	Babcock & W	0
Jan 25	Dundee U	2	Alloa	2
Jan 29	Dunfermline A	6	Brechin C	2
Jan 29	E Stirling	2	Kilmarnock	5
Jan 25	Edinburgh C	2	Cowdenbeath	3
Feb 1	Elgin C	2	Chirnside U	2
Feb 1	Galston	5	Stranraer	3
Feb 1	King's Park	6	Wick A	1
Jan 25	Leith A	3	Buckie T	3
Jan 25	Montrose	0	Falkirk	2
Feb 1	Morton	11	Blairgowrie	1
Jan 25	Peebles R	3	Dalbeattie Star	3
Jan 25	Queen of South	2	Partick T	0
Jan 25	Raith R	2	St Johnstone	4
Jan 29	Rangers	3	East Fife	1
Feb 1	Ross Co	0	St Bernard's	5
Jan 29	Stenhousemuir	1	Queen's Park	0
Jan 29	T Lanark	2	Hearts	0
Feb 1	Vale Ocoba	1	Hibernian	3

Replays

Jan 29	Alloa	1	Dundee U	1
Jan 29	Buckie T	1	Leith A	2
Feb 1	Dalbeattie Star	1	Peebles R	0
Feb 1	Dumbarton	4	Burntisland	2
Feb 3	Alloa	1	Dundee U	2
	played at Tynecastle			
Feb 5	Chirnside U	3	Elgin C	4

2nd Round

Feb 8	Aberdeen	6	King's Park	0
Feb 8	Albion R	1	Rangers	3
Feb 8	Celtic	1	St Johnstone	2
Feb 8	Clyde	4	Hibernian	1
Feb 8	Cowdenbeath	5	Dundee U	3
Feb 8	Dalbeattie Star	0	St Mirren	1
Feb 8	Dundee	2	Airdrie	1
Feb 8	Dunfermline A	5	Galston	2
Feb 8	Elgin C	0	Queen of South	3
Feb 8	Falkirk	1	Kilmarnock	1
Feb 8	Morton	3	Stenhousemuir	0
Feb 8	Motherwell	3	St Bernard's	0
Feb 8	T Lanark	2	Leith A	0

Replay

Feb 12	Kilmarnock	1	Falkirk	3

3rd Round

Feb 22	Aberdeen	1	St Johnstone	1
Feb 22	Clyde	1	Dundee	1
Feb 22	Cowdenbeath	1	Motherwell	3
Feb 22	Morton	2	Queen of South	0
Feb 22	St Mirren	1	Rangers	2
Feb 22	T Lanark	8	Dumbarton	0

Replays

Feb 26	Dundee	0	Clyde	3
Feb 26	St Johnstone	0	Aberdeen	1

4th Round

Mar 7	Aberdeen	0	Rangers	1
Mar 7	Clyde	3	Motherwell	2
Mar 7	Falkirk	5	Dunfermline A	0
Mar 7	Morton	3	T Lanark	5

Semi-finals

Mar 28	Clyde	0	Rangers	3
	played at Hampden Park			
Mar 28	Falkirk	1	T Lanark	3
	played at Tynecastle			

Final

Apr 18	Rangers	1	T Lanark	0
	played at Hampden Park			

Season 1935-36

DIVISION 1

(home \ away)	ABERDEEN	AIRDRIE	ALBION R	ARBROATH	AYR U	CELTIC	CLYDE	DUNDEE	DUNFERMLINE A	HAMILTON A	HEARTS	HIBERNIAN	KILMARNOCK	MOTHERWELL	PARTICK T	QUEEN OF SOUTH	QUEEN'S PARK	RANGERS	ST JOHNSTONE	T LANARK
ABERDEEN	—	Jan18 2-2	Apr11 6-1	Feb29 1-2	Sep07 3-0	Aug10 3-1	Aug28 3-0	Sep21 3-0	Jan02 3-3	Sep23 2-1	Nov30 3-0	Aug24 2-1	Mar14 1-1	Dec28 4-0	Oct05 4-3	Nov02 2-1	Oct19 1-0	Nov23 3-0	Mar28 3-0	Feb01 2-0
AIRDRIE	Sep14 3-4	—	Jan01 1-2	Nov30 3-3	Nov09 2-3	Apr04 5-3	Aug28 2-0	Feb02 6-2	Aug17 2-4	Dec14 3-1	Jan04 3-2	Apr11 1-4	Apr18 1-1	Oct12 3-0	Feb01 1-0	Oct19 1-1	Jan11 1-1	Aug14 0-2	Sep28 3-3	Oct26 1-2
ALBION R	Nov16 1-3	Sep21 4-1	—	Dec28 5-2	Aug24 5-1	Jan18 0-3	Apr08 4-4	Oct05 1-1	Dec07 4-0	Jan01 0-1	Feb29 0-1	Nov02 2-3	Oct19 2-1	Aug31 2-1	Sep28 1-2	Feb01 5-2	Dec21 0-0	Feb15 2-2	Mar11 1-3	Sep07 2-0
ARBROATH	Oct12 0-1	Apr25 1-1	Aug17 1-2	—	Sep11 3-1	Apr11 0-2	Jan04 2-1	Nov23 1-0	Oct26 2-1	Sep14 0-1	Jan11 1-3	Dec07 2-3	Jan01 0-0	Mar28 1-1	Nov02 1-3	Aug31 1-0	Sep28 0-0	Dec21 2-2	Feb15 1-3	Mar11 3-1
AYR U	Jan11 1-1	Mar28 3-1	Jan04 4-1	Dec14 0-2	—	Nov23 0-2	Feb15 4-3	Mar14 1-2	Apr11 1-2	Sep28 1-0	Sep14 1-3	Nov02 3-0	Aug31 1-3	Oct19 1-0	Jan01 3-1	Dec21 1-0	Aug17 2-2	Oct12 1-2	Nov30 1-3	Aug28 6-0
CELTIC	Dec21 5-3	Oct19 4-0	Sep14 4-0	Nov16 5-0	Apr18 6-0	—	Apr13 2-1	Nov02 4-2	Sep16 5-3	Aug17 1-0	Mar28 4-1	Feb15 4-0	Mar14 5-0	Nov30 1-1	Aug31 5-0	Jan01 3-0	Jan01 3-4	Apr11 2-0	Jan04 2-0	Aug28 6-0
CLYDE	Dec07 0-3	Aug10 1-1	Nov09 5-2	Aug24 1-3	Oct05 2-0	Feb29 0-4	—	Jan18 2-1	Feb01 4-2	Mar21 1-2	Apr11 1-0	Dec28 7-4	Nov09 1-1	Sep07 1-4	Apr25 1-3	Dec14 1-4	Oct26 3-1	Mar17 1-4	Jan02 0-1	
DUNDEE	Jan01 2-2	Dec07 1-0	Feb15 2-0	Apr18 3-0	Oct26 6-1	Mar21 0-2	Sep14 4-3	—	Nov09 2-3	Dec21 3-0	Aug31 2-5	Apr25 2-1	Jan11 0-0	Aug28 2-2	Aug17 3-3	Nov16 6-4	Sep28 0-3	Jan04 0-2	Oct12 0-2	Nov23 3-2
DUNFERMLINE A	Aug31 2-3	Nov02 3-1	Dec21 7-2	Mar14 2-2	Nov16 4-2	Dec14 0-2	Sep28 1-0	Feb01 1-1	—	Oct12 2-2	Aug24 2-0	Apr25 0-1	Jan11 0-1	Oct19 1-3	Aug28 1-1	Aug17 4-1	Feb15 2-2	Apr11 2-6	Apr04 2-6	Nov23 1-0
HAMILTON A	Dec14 2-3	Jan02 3-1	Aug28 7-2	Feb08 2-2	Feb01 4-2	Dec28 0-2	Nov02 2-0	Aug10 0-2	Feb29 6-1	—	Nov23 3-4	Oct05 2-3	Oct19 3-2	Apr25 0-1	Jan11 0-1	Sep21 1-3	Mar14 1-1	Mar28 4-1	Apr04 1-0	Aug24 5-1
HEARTS	Apr25 1-2	Dec28 3-0	Aug28 4-2	Sep07 2-1	Jan18 3-0	Feb01 1-0	Nov16 3-3	Jan02 3-0	Aug24 1-1	Feb22 4-1	—	Sep21 8-3	Apr01 4-2	Feb29 2-2	Aug10 2-0	Dec14 2-0	Apr22 4-1	Nov02 1-1	Oct05 6-1	Feb15 2-0
HIBERNIAN	Jan04 1-4	Sep18 3-2	Oct12 3-0	Aug28 0-0	Mar21 0-1	Nov09 0-5	Aug17 1-1	Oct19 1-0	Nov30 2-3	Feb15 3-2	Jan01 1-1	—	Sep28 3-1	Apr01 2-3	Feb29 2-0	Aug10 2-0	Dec14 2-0	Dec21 4-1	Sep14 1-1	Apr11 3-0
KILMARNOCK	Oct26 2-5	Aug24 2-2	Mar21 2-2	Sep21 5-0	Jan02 7-2	Oct05 1-1	Apr29 2-0	Feb29 4-1	Sep07 1-2	Mar07 4-3	Nov09 2-0	Apr08 0-1	—	Aug10 2-3	Dec07 2-0	Jun22 4-3	Nov16 4-1	Apr25 0-3	Sep18 6-1	Dec28 2-0
MOTHERWELL	Aug17 2-2	Nov16 6-2	Aug31 2-0	Nov09 4-0	Dec07 4-1	Oct26 1-2	Jan11 1-1	Apr25 3-0	Apr22 2-3	Jan01 2-1	Oct12 4-2	Apr18 1-1	Apr04 3-2	—	Dec14 5-3	Feb15 0-2	Jan04 1-0	Sep28 0-2	Sep14 3-0	Mar21 2-1
PARTICK T	Feb15 3-3	Nov23 3-1	Sep28 5-3	Mar07 1-1	Mar07 2-2	Dec21 1-3	Apr11 4-1	Dec07 1-0	Jan11 2-0	Feb08 3-0	Oct05 1-0	Sep14 2-1	Sep17 2-0	Apr11 4-1	—	Jan04 1-1	Oct12 7-0	Aug31 1-3	Apr11 3-1	Nov02 0-0
QUEEN OF SOUTH	Mar21 1-1	Feb29 3-3	Mar07 1-2	Jan02 3-2	Sep21 2-1	Sep07 1-3	Nov30 2-0	Feb01 1-2	Dec28 2-0	Oct26 2-0	Sep18 1-2	Aug10 2-1	Aug28 1-1	Oct05 2-1	Aug24 0-0	—	Apr18 4-0	Nov09 1-1	Apr11 2-1	Jan18 0-1
QUEEN'S PARK	Apr04 0-1	Oct05 3-2	Nov30 0-1	Feb01 0-0	Aug10 1-2	Feb22 2-3	Sep17 4-1	Dec28 3-2	Jan18 2-1	Nov09 1-1	Aug27 2-2	Sep07 6-1	Apr11 1-0	Aug24 2-2	Feb29 1-1	Nov23 1-1	—	Mar21 1-3	Oct26 5-1	Jan01 1-0
RANGERS	Apr29 2-3	Sep07 5-3	Dec14 5-1	Oct28 6-0	Dec28 6-1	Sep21 1-2	Mar14 4-1	Apr11 4-3	Oct05 6-2	Nov16 3-1	Oct19 1-1	Nov30 3-0	Jan02 2-1	Apr08 0-0	Apr08 3-1	Jan20 3-1	Nov02 3-3	—	Aug28 7-0	Feb29 4-2
ST JOHNSTONE	Nov09 0-0	Apr13 4-1	Apr18 2-3	Oct05 2-1	Feb29 2-3	Aug24 2-3	Oct19 1-2	Sep07 2-0	Sep21 4-2	Apr25 1-1	Mar21 3-1	Jan02 2-2	Dec14 0-0	Jan18 2-3	Dec28 3-0	Nov16 3-1	Mar07 5-2	Dec07 1-2	—	Aug10 3-1
T LANARK	Sep28 5-1	Mar14 2-0	Jan11 0-1	Oct19 1-1	Apr24 6-4	Dec07 1-3	Aug31 3-0	Apr27 2-1	Jan04 3-1	Feb15 0-1	Nov16 1-5	Aug17 3-2	Nov02 2-1	Apr01 0-4	Sep14 2-2	Apr11 3-0	Apr13 1-3	Dec21 3-1	Sep21 3-1	—

DIVISION 2

(home \ away)	ALLOA	BRECHIN C	COWDENBEATH	DUMBARTON	DUNDEE U	EAST FIFE	E STIRLING	EDINBURGH C	FALKIRK	FORFAR A	KING'S PARK	LEITH A	MONTROSE	MORTON	RAITH R	ST BERNARD'S	ST MIRREN	STENHOUSEMUIR
ALLOA	—	Oct19 3-1	Mar21 5-1	Nov16 5-0	Aug17 2-3	Nov23 2-1	Dec21 0-0	Apr04 2-0	Jan04 2-2	Aug31 1-1	Dec07 4-0	Jan01 2-1	Sep14 1-2	Jan18 1-5	Feb15 1-0	Nov02 4-3	Feb29 1-1	Sep28 4-2
BRECHIN C	Mar28 3-1	—	Jan11 1-2	Mar07 6-1	Aug31 2-1	Feb08 1-1	Sep14 3-2	Oct12 0-4	Apr22 2-2	Nov23 2-2	Sep28 0-2	Jan04 1-2	Mar14 1-4	Dec07 2-1	Feb01 2-8	Nov02 2-3	Dec21 1-2	
COWDENBEATH	Aug10 1-2	Sep07 3-0	—	Oct05 6-2	Oct26 7-0	Feb29 1-4	Apr04 1-1	Nov30 2-1	Feb01 2-7	Mar07 1-0	Sep21 8-0	Jan04 5-1	Dec07 3-1	Aug24 1-3	Dec28 4-2	Jan18 2-6	Apr18 2-3	Nov09 2-1
DUMBARTON	Jan11 0-3	Nov30 1-5	Jan01 3-3	—	Sep28 3-5	Aug17 4-2	Feb15 3-3	Feb08 1-2	Dec14 2-7	Oct19 1-2	Oct12 6-1	Aug31 1-1	Nov23 4-4	Nov09 1-3	Apr11 3-4	Apr25 2-0	Mar14 1-2	Sep14 2-0
DUNDEE U	Feb01 4-0	Dec14 2-2	Mar14 6-1	Dec28 8-0	—	Oct19 4-2	Apr13 12-1	Sep07 4-1	Apr11 3-1	Sep21 4-1	Aug24 8-2	Apr04 2-3	Oct05 1-1	Jan18 4-3	Sep21 2-2	Sep21 1-2	Sep21 1-2	Mar28 6-1
EAST FIFE	Sep07 0-2	Aug24 4-3	Dec21 2-2	Jan18 6-1	Jan04 4-3	—	Oct26 4-2	Feb22 5-1	Sep21 0-0	Feb15 1-4	Mar14 9-2	Nov09 6-2	Oct12 3-1	Dec07 3-1	Oct05 5-2	Dec28 1-3	Aug10 1-6	Nov30 4-1
E STIRLING	Aug24 1-2	Sep21 5-1	Nov02 2-0	Aug10 1-1	Dec07 2-3	Feb01 4-2	—	Oct12 2-0	Jan11 0-5	Mar28 1-2	Oct05 4-0	Nov23 1-1	Apr11 4-1	Sep07 2-1	Jan04 2-1	Dec14 4-2	Nov16 2-2	Dec28 3-0
EDINBURGH C	Sep21 3-1	Dec28 4-0	Mar28 2-3	Aug31 3-3	Apr04 0-0	Mar07 3-6	Nov16 2-2	—	Jan18 1-1	Aug10 1-3	Nov02 2-2	Feb01 5-0	Jan11 2-3	Feb29 5-3	Oct05 1-4	Dec07 2-3	Oct05 3-2	Apr18 1-1
FALKIRK	Oct26 3-0	Apr04 4-0	Aug31 1-0	Apr18 3-0	Nov09 4-2	Mar21 8-0	Sep28 3-3	Oct19 2-2	—	Dec21 1-2	Jan18 10-2	Sep14 3-1	Aug17 5-0	Feb15 7-1	Mar14 1-5	Feb29 2-3	Nov30 1-1	Jan01 5-1
FORFAR A	Dec28 1-2	Jan04 1-1	Oct12 0-0	Sep21 3-1	Apr11 3-4	Dec14 1-2	Nov09 0-4	Mar21 2-2	Sep28 1-4	—	Sep07 3-0	Nov30 1-2	Feb08 7-3	Aug10 3-2	Nov16 2-2	Oct05 2-5	Oct26 2-3	
KING'S PARK	Apr11 1-1	Nov09 5-4	Oct19 1-4	Sep21 5-2	Feb15 2-1	Sep14 2-1	Jan01 0-1	Aug17 2-0	Dec28 3-5	Jan01 3-1	—	Dec21 1-0	Oct26 1-0	Oct12 2-2	Nov30 3-0	Mar28 2-4	Aug31 1-1	Aug31 1-5
LEITH A	Oct05 1-2	Jan18 5-4	Feb15 1-2	Oct26 5-2	Nov16 2-1	Mar07 2-1	Apr18 4-2	Dec14 1-2	Dec07 2-5	Apr25 4-0	Aug10 0-1	—	Nov02 1-1	Dec28 2-1	Sep07 2-6	Sep21 0-5	Aug24 0-2	Feb29 1-3
MONTROSE	Mar14 0-2	Oct05 4-1	Nov16 1-1	Sep07 3-0	Nov30 3-2	Mar28 1-3	Oct19 3-1	Nov09 4-2	Apr25 0-4	Feb01 1-2	Dec14 3-0	Jan11 1-3	—	Aug10 1-3	Sep21 1-3	Apr25 1-3	Dec28 1-0	Feb15 2-1
MORTON	Mar11 2-2	Nov16 3-1	Dec14 8-4	Apr04 5-1	Jan01 4-1	Sep28 4-1	Jan11 4-2	Nov02 2-2	Sep14 3-0	Mar21 5-3	Aug17 2-0	Jan04 4-0	Nov30 3-0	—	Aug10 1-3	Sep21 6-2	Oct19 1-0	Apr06 9-2
RAITH R	Oct12 1-3	Feb01 2-4	Aug17 0-1	Nov02 1-1	Sep14 1-2	Jan01 1-6	Aug31 4-6	Sep28 2-3	Nov16 4-0	Nov23 1-4	Apr04 2-3	Oct19 2-2	Mar21 2-2	Mar28 2-2	—	Mar07 4-1	Dec14 1-6	Jan11 2-3
ST BERNARD'S	Nov30 1-2	Feb15 2-3	Sep14 2-3	Mar21 7-0	Jan11 3-1	Aug31 2-4	Aug17 2-0	Jan01 2-0	Nov23 3-0	Sep28 5-3	Jan04 5-2	Mar14 2-1	Dec21 3-2	Oct12 6-2	Nov09 6-2	—	Apr04 2-0	Oct19 1-2
ST MIRREN	Nov09 4-0	Mar21 7-0	Sep28 1-0	Jan04 8-0	Dec21 6-2	Jan11 3-1	Sep14 4-1	Feb15 5-0	Apr11 0-2	Jan01 6-0	Aug17 8-1	Oct12 6-0	Nov23 1-0	Oct26 5-4	Oct26 6-0	Dec07 4-2	—	Aug17 2-0
STENHOUSEMUIR	Dec14 2-0	Aug10 2-1	Nov23 1-2	Dec07 3-0	Oct12 5-0	Nov02 1-1	Mar07 3-0	Jan04 2-2	Oct05 1-0	Mar14 3-1	Nov16 2-0	Mar21 1-4	Apr04 1-4	Sep21 1-2	Aug24 3-6	Sep07 2-0	Jan18 1-3	—

DIVISION 1 FINAL TABLE

	P	W	D	L	F	A	Pts
Celtic	38	32	2	4	115	33	66
Rangers	38	27	7	4	110	43	61
Aberdeen	38	26	9	3	96	50	61
Motherwell	38	18	12	8	77	58	48
Hearts	38	20	7	11	88	55	47
Hamilton A	38	15	7	16	77	74	37
St Johnstone	38	15	7	16	70	81	37
Kilmarnock	38	14	7	17	69	64	35
T Lanark	38	15	5	18	63	65	35
Partick T	38	12	10	16	64	72	34
Arbroath	38	11	11	16	46	69	33
Dundee	38	11	10	17	67	80	32
Queen's Park	38	11	10	17	58	75	32
Dunfermline A	38	12	8	18	67	92	32
Queen of South	38	11	9	18	54	72	31
Albion R	38	13	4	21	69	92	30
Hibernian	38	11	7	20	56	82	29
Clyde	38	10	8	20	63	84	28
Airdrie	38	9	9	20	68	91	27
Ayr U	38	11	3	24	53	98	25

DIVISION 2 FINAL TABLE

	P	W	D	L	F	A	Pts
Falkirk	34	28	3	3	132	34	59
St Mirren	34	25	2	7	114	41	52
Morton	34	21	6	7	117	60	48
Alloa	34	19	6	9	65	51	44
St Bernard's	34	18	4	12	106	78	40
East Fife	34	16	6	12	86	79	38
Dundee U	34	16	5	13	108	81	37
E Stirling	34	13	8	13	70	75	34
Leith A	34	15	3	16	67	77	33
Cowdenbeath	34	13	5	16	76	77	31
Stenhousemuir	34	13	3	18	59	78	29
Montrose	34	13	3	18	58	82	29
Forfar A	34	10	7	17	60	81	27
King's Park	34	11	5	18	55	109	27
Edinburgh C	34	8	9	17	57	83	25
Brechin C	34	8	6	20	57	96	22
Raith R	34	9	3	22	60	96	21
Dumbarton	34	5	6	23	52	121	16

Season 1936-37

SFA Cup

1st Round

Jan 30	Aberdeen	6	Inverness T	0
Jan 30	Airdrie	3	Dundee U	1
Feb 2	Alloa	2	Hibernian	5
Jan 30	Ayr U	0	Partick T	2
Jan 30	Babcock & W	0	Inverness Cal	1
Jan 30	Bo'ness	0	Cowdenbeath	6
Jan 30	Clyde	8	Vale Ocoba	0
Jan 30	Dalbeattie Star	1	Queen's Park	2
Jan 30	Dumbarton	3	Keith	1
Feb 3	Dundee	4	E Stirling	1
Feb 3	Dunfermline A	0	Arbroath	0
Feb 6	Edinburgh C	2	Duns	5
Jan 30	Falkirk	6	Peebles R	0
Feb 4	Forfar A	0	East Fife	3
Jan 30	Hearts	3	St Bernard's	1
Jan 30	Kilmarnock	1	Brechin C	2
Feb 6	King's Park	1	Elgin C	1
Jan 23	Larbert A	1	Solway Star	3
Feb 3	Leith A	4	Albion R	4
Jan 30	Montrose	1	T Lanark	1
Jan 27	Moor Park	1	Hamilton A	7
Jan 30	Motherwell	3	Galston	1
Jan 27	Murrayfield A	3	Morton	3
Jan 30	Queen of South	1	Rangers	0
Feb 3	Raith R	0	St Johnstone	5
Jan 30	St Mirren	4	Beith	0
Jan 30	Stenhousemuir	1	Celtic	1

Replays

Jan 30	Morton	6	Murrayfield A	1
Feb 3	Celtic	2	Stenhousemuir	0
Feb 3	T Lanark	5	Montrose	0
Feb 10	Albion R	5	Leith A	3
Feb 10	Arbroath	1	Dunfermline A	0
Feb 10	Elgin C	3	King's Park	4

2nd Round

Feb 13	Aberdeen	4	T Lanark	2
Feb 13	Albion R	2	Celtic	5
Feb 13	Clyde	3	St Johnstone	1
Feb 13	Cowdenbeath	9	Solway Star	1
Feb 13	Dundee	2	Queen's Park	0
Feb 13	Duns	2	Dumbarton	1
Feb 13	Falkirk	0	Motherwell	3
Feb 13	Hamilton A	2	Hibernian	1
Feb 13	Hearts	15	King's Park	0
Feb 13	Inverness Cal	1	East Fife	6
Feb 13	Partick T	4	Arbroath	1
Feb 13	Queen of South	2	Airdrie	0
Feb 13	St Mirren	1	Brechin C	0

3rd Round

Feb 27	Clyde	0	Dundee	0
Mar 10	Duns	2	Motherwell	5
	played at Tynecastle			
Feb 27	East Fife	0	Celtic	3
Mar 3	Hamilton A	2	Hearts	1
Feb 27	Morton	1	Partick T	1
Feb 27	St Mirren	1	Cowdenbeath	0

Replays

Mar 3	Dundee	0	Clyde	1
Mar 3	Partick T	1	Morton	2

4th Round

Mar 17	Hamilton A	1	Aberdeen	2
Mar 13	Morton	4	Queen of South	1
Mar 17	Motherwell	4	Celtic	4
Mar 13	St Mirren	0	Clyde	3

Replay

Mar 24	Celtic	2	Motherwell	1

Semi-finals

Apr 3	Aberdeen	2	Morton	0
	played at Easter Road			
Apr 3	Celtic	2	Clyde	0
	played at Ibrox			

Final

Apr 24	Aberdeen	1	Celtic	2
	played at Hampden Park			

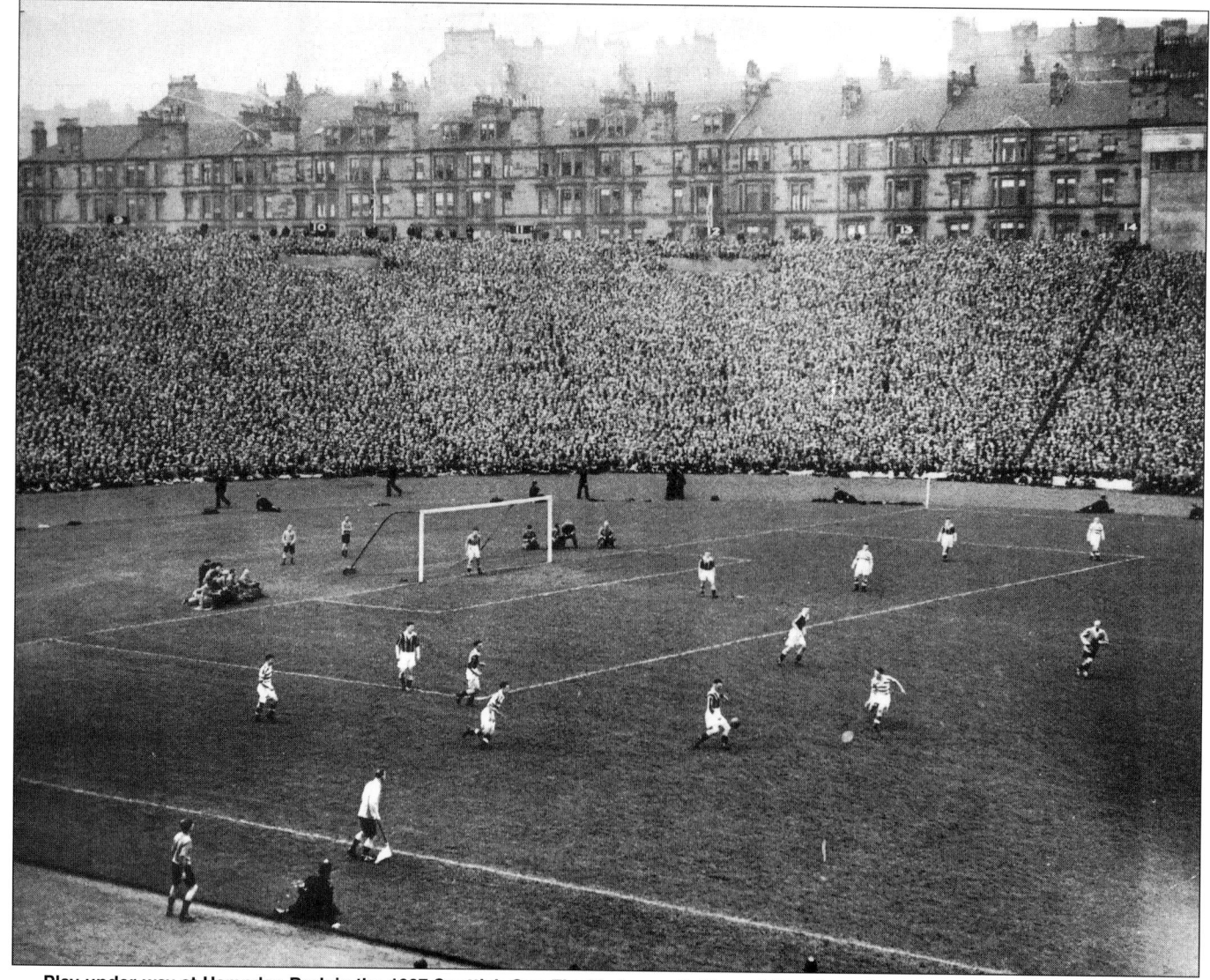

Play under way at Hampden Park in the 1937 Scottish Cup Final between Celtic and Aberdeen. The attendance of 146,433 is still a record for a club match in Europe.

DIVISION 1

Results grid (home team = row, away team = column; cell shows match date and score):

Home \ Away	ABERDEEN	ALBION R	ARBROATH	CELTIC	CLYDE	DUNDEE	DUNFERMLINE A	FALKIRK	HAMILTON A	HEARTS	HIBERNIAN	KILMARNOCK	MOTHERWELL	PARTICK T	QUEEN OF SOUTH	QUEEN'S PARK	RANGERS	ST JOHNSTONE	ST MIRREN	T LANARK
ABERDEEN	—	Oct31 4-1	Aug15 4-0	Jan23 1-0	Nov21 3-0	Jan01 3-1	Oct10 3-1	Aug29 4-0	Nov28 3-0	Mar27 4-0	Aug19 1-1	Dec12 2-0	Sep26 2-0	Jan09 4-2	Feb20 1-1	Sep28 2-1	Mar20 1-1	Oct24 4-1	Dec19 5-4	Sep12 2-2
ALBION R	Mar24 1-5	—	Sep12 2-0	Aug29 1-3	Oct24 1-1	Jan09 4-0	Jan23 1-4	Jan01 2-3	Apr03 1-3	Dec12 1-4	Aug15 1-3	Feb20 0-3	Oct10 1-4	Sep26 2-4	Jan04 4-0	Nov14 2-3	Nov28 2-3	Mar20 0-4	Aug19 2-6	Dec19 0-4
ARBROATH	Sep09 1-4	Jan16 4-2	—	Oct31 2-3	Aug08 2-1	Mar20 3-0	Apr24 1-1	Nov14 1-2	Dec26 1-2	Aug22 0-3	Apr03 1-0	Feb06 0-0	Oct24 0-0	Feb20 2-1	Jan02 4-0	Oct03 2-0	Sep05 0-0	Sep19 3-1	Nov28 2-2	Dec05 4-1
CELTIC	Oct03 3-2	Dec26 4-0	Apr16 5-1	—	Sep09 3-1	Feb20 1-2	Nov28 3-1	Mar29 1-0	Jan16 3-3	Feb06 3-2	Oct24 5-1	Sep05 2-4	Dec12 3-2	Aug22 1-1		Sep12 4-0	Sep19 1-1		Aug08 3-0	Nov21 6-3
CLYDE	Apr07 0-0	Mar06 4-1	Aug18 4-2	Aug15 1-1	—	Aug29 1-2	Sep12 2-1	Jan23 2-1	Oct17 3-1	Mar23 1-0	Sep26 0-3	Mar20 2-0	Dec19 1-2	Jan01 1-0	Nov14 2-1	Apr10 0-2	Apr23 1-2	Dec05 2-0	Jan09 1-2	Oct10 2-4
DUNDEE	Sep19 2-2	Sep05 1-0	Nov07 6-1	Oct17 0-0	Dec26 2-2	—	Mar06 2-2	Apr03 1-1	Oct03 1-2	Jan02 1-0	Dec05 3-1	Sep09 2-2	Mar27 0-0	Apr12 2-2	Jan16 1-3	Feb06 2-2	Aug08 0-0	Aug22 3-1	Apr24 4-0	Mar20 0-3
DUNFERMLINE A	Jan02 2-2	Oct03 3-3	Dec12 1-4	Apr10 3-4	Jan16 1-3	Oct24 3-4	—	Feb20 0-2	Sep09 4-2	Aug08 2-5	Aug22 2-3	Nov21 0-5	Jan04 2-2	Nov21 1-1	Sep10 5-0	Dec26 2-2	Feb06 2-3	Sep05 0-0	Mar17 1-0	Mar20 0-0
FALKIRK	Dec26 1-2	Sep19 3-2	Mar27 0-1	Dec05 0-3	Oct03 5-0	Nov21 6-4		—	Aug08 3-2							Sep05 3-0				Feb27 5-2
HAMILTON A	Apr10 3-2	Nov21 2-3	Aug29 1-4	Sep12 1-2	Feb20 2-1	Jan23 5-1	Aug15 4-2	Aug19 3-2	—	Mar20 5-1	Jan09 4-1	Apr16 2-2	Jan01 2-3	Dec19 3-2	Dec12 1-1	Oct24 5-2	Apr07 1-5	Oct10 5-2	Oct10 2-1	Sep26 3-1
HEARTS	Nov14 2-0	Apr24 5-0	Dec19 4-1	Sep26 0-1	Apr19 1-0	Oct10 4-0	Aug19 3-2	Sep12 3-1	Nov07 6-0	—	Jan01 3-2	Oct24 5-0	Apr10 3-4	Apr03 5-1	Dec05 4-2	Feb20 3-1				Jan09 5-2
HIBERNIAN	Aug08 1-1	Sep09 4-2	Nov21 1-0	Mar06 0-1	Feb06 4-0	Apr19 3-0	Mar27 2-2	Nov28 0-0	Sep05 2-2	Sep19 3-3	—	Jan16 0-0	Mar20 2-2	Dec12 2-2	Oct03 3-3	Aug22 1-0	Dec26 0-1	Jan02 3-3	Oct17 0-0	Oct31 0-1
KILMARNOCK	Apr29 1-2	Oct17 3-1	Sep26 2-0	Jan09 3-3	Nov07 3-1	Aug15 1-1	Dec19 3-3	Oct10 3-2	Dec05 2-2	Mar06 3-2	Sep12 3-2	—	Jan23 0-1	Aug29 1-0	Apr03 0-0	Apr23 0-0	Nov14 1-2	Nov28 4-2	Jan01 2-1	Jan09 0-3
MOTHERWELL	Feb06 1-0	Jan02 9-1	Mar31 3-1	Apr30 8-0	Apr30 4-1	Apr30 2-1	Sep19 6-0	Apr19 4-2	Sep09 5-2	Nov07 1-3	Oct03 3-4	Nov28 2-1	—	Apr10 4-2	Sep05 4-1	Jan16 3-1	Dec26 1-4	Apr03 2-2	Apr10 4-1	Oct17 1-2
PARTICK T	Sep05 0-2	Feb06 6-1	Oct17 1-1	Nov14 6-0	Sep19 1-1	Oct31 0-4	Apr03 2-2	Mar20 2-2	Aug22 3-1	Oct03 3-4	Apr21 2-1	Dec26 1-0	Nov28 1-0	—	Aug08 4-1	Sep08 3-1	Jan02 1-4	Jan16 1-1	Dec25 1-1	Mar06 1-3
QUEEN OF SOUTH	Oct17 2-3	Dec05 5-2	Oct10 2-3	Dec19 1-0	Sep12 1-2	Jan01 2-3	Aug15 2-1	Apr24 1-4	Nov28 3-3	Jan23 0-4	Nov21 1-0	Jan09 0-2	Aug19 3-3		—	Nov07 1-1	Mar06 0-1	Oct31 0-1	Sep26 2-2	Aug29 2-3
QUEEN'S PARK	Dec26 1-1	Apr07 3-3	Dec05 2-1	Oct10 0-2	Nov28 1-3	Aug29 0-2	Aug29 3-6	Nov21 0-1	Oct24 0-2	Nov21 2-0	Oct31 2-1	Mar20 0-0	Aug18 4-5	Mar20 2-3		—	Oct17 1-1	Feb27 2-2	Sep12 2-2	Jan01 2-1
RANGERS	Nov07 2-1	Apr10 1-0	Jan09 4-0	Jan01 1-0	Dec12 3-0	Aug19 5-3	Sep26 3-0	Dec19 4-0	Mar24 4-1	Jan04 4-0	Apr29 4-1	Feb27 5-2	Sep12 3-2	Mar29 1-1	Oct24 1-1	Feb20 2-2	—	Nov21 0-0	Jan23 2-3	Aug15 3-1
ST JOHNSTONE	Mar29 2-1	Nov07 4-0	Jan01 6-1	Aug19 2-1	Jan04 2-1	Dec19 3-3	Jan09 1-0	Sep26 1-0	Nov14 6-1	Oct17 3-0	Oct10 1-3	Apr10 1-3	Aug29 0-2	Sep12 4-0	Mar24 0-1	Dec12 1-2	Apr03 1-2	—	Aug15 4-2	Jan23 2-3
ST MIRREN	Aug22 1-4	Aug08 3-0	Apr10 5-0	Mar20 1-2	Sep05 1-3	Oct31 4-0	Oct31 2-1	Jan02 3-3	Dec26 1-2	Feb06 2-2	Sep19 1-3	Nov21 3-2	Oct24 1-3	Dec26 6-2	Sep19 1-2	Oct03 1-4	Jan16 2-1	Oct03 2-1	—	Mar27 2-1
T LANARK	Jan16 2-0	Aug22 0-0	Jan04 3-2	Apr06 4-2	Jan02 0-2	Apr10 4-0	Nov07 6-3	Dec12 2-3	Feb06 3-2	Sep05 3-0	Mar29 1-1	Aug08 2-1	Feb20 1-0	Oct24 4-1	Dec26 1-2	Sep19 0-0	Sep09 2-0	Oct03 0-0	Nov14 3-0	—

DIVISION 2

Results grid (home team = row, away team = column):

Home \ Away	AIRDRIE	ALLOA	AYR U	BRECHIN C	COWDENBEATH	DUMBARTON	DUNDEE U	EAST FIFE	E STIRLING	EDINBURGH C	FORFAR A	KING'S PARK	LEITH A	MONTROSE	MORTON	RAITH R	ST BERNARD'S	STENHOUSEMUIR
AIRDRIE	—	Nov07 3-1	Oct17 1-1	Feb06 7-5	Dec26 2-5	Mar27 4-0	Aug22 2-2	Sep19 4-1	Jan16 4-0	Oct03 2-3	Aug08 5-2	Oct31 2-1	Nov21 8-2	Jan02 1-1	Mar06 3-2	Apr10 3-2	Apr23 4-2	Sep05 2-1
ALLOA	Apr03 3-0	—	Mar06 1-4	Mar13 2-2	Oct03 2-0	Oct31 2-0	Dec26 2-0	Aug22 0-2	Sep19 0-2	Aug29 3-2	Nov28 2-1	Nov14 2-3	Sep05 2-0	Jan16 3-1	Dec12 4-3	Feb06 1-3	Oct10 0-0	Jan02 3-3
AYR U	Feb20 5-2	Oct24 4-0	—	Oct31 8-1	Feb06 2-0	Dec12 4-1	Sep19 4-1	Oct03 4-1	Jan02 7-2	Sep05 3-2	Sep05 6-1	Oct17 5-0	Apr03 2-1	Dec26 8-1	Mar20 1-1	Feb13 5-2	Nov21 8-3	
BRECHIN C	Nov14 0-0	Dec05 4-3	Jan23 2-3	—	Aug22 1-1	Jan16 4-3	Jan02 4-3	Aug08 2-5	Sep19 0-1	Mar20 1-2	Feb20 6-1	Oct17 3-1	Apr03 1-3	Sep05 1-1	Dec26 1-1	Nov28 1-1	Nov07 1-1	Oct03 2-0
COWDENBEATH	Aug15 4-0	Jan23 1-1	Sep12 2-1	Jan09 1-1	—	Jan01 1-0	Oct17 5-3	Oct10 3-1	Nov06 3-1	Dec19 2-2	Dec05 7-1	Nov28 4-0	Oct31 0-2	Apr03 3-3	Nov21 0-0	Sep26 4-1	Aug29 2-0	Mar27 1-0
DUMBARTON	Dec19 2-3	Jan23 1-1	Nov07 1-3	Oct10 2-1	Sep05 3-2	—	Nov28 4-5	Jan02 2-1	Oct03 2-1	Sep19 2-0		Aug29 6-3	Mar06 1-1		Nov14 3-1		Feb27 3-4	
DUNDEE U	Oct10 2-1	Sep26 1-2	Dec19 2-3	Aug15 1-1	Feb20 1-1	Sep12 1-1	—	Dec12 0-0	Oct31 4-6	Nov21 2-2	Nov14 5-0	Jan09 2-2	Mar20 5-1	Oct24 4-1	Jan01 2-3	Apr10 0-2	Apr03 0-3	Jan23 1-2
EAST FIFE	Jan09 3-0	Oct17 2-0	Apr16 4-1	Dec19 7-0	Mar20 0-4	Sep26 1-2	Feb06 4-4	—	Dec05 5-1	Nov28 3-0	Mar27 3-0	Aug29 2-1	Nov14 1-0		Oct31 1-2	Sep12 3-4	Aug15 6-1	Apr03 1-2
E STIRLING	Sep12 1-3	Dec19 2-2	Aug29 2-0	Dec12 5-4	Oct24 3-1	Apr03 4-1	Jan23 2-1	Feb06 0-2	—	Apr17 4-1	Mar20 4-2	Feb06 2-0	Nov28 3-0	Nov14 5-2	Sep26 5-3	Oct03 0-3	Nov11 1-1	Mar13 7-2
EDINBURGH C	Jan23 3-2	Jan09 2-8	Nov14 1-4	Aug29 2-2	Nov07 2-3	Feb20 2-3	Mar27 2-3	Apr03 0-2	Oct17 1-3	—	Apr10 0-1	Sep26 2-3	Dec26 1-3	Dec05 2-4	Aug15 0-3	Sep12 1-3	Jan01 0-3	Feb13 1-3
FORFAR A	Oct24 2-2	Aug15 4-3	Jan01 0-5	Sep26 3-1	Apr24 4-2	Apr03 3-4	Jan16 3-3	Nov21 3-3	Nov07 1-2	Dec12 4-1	—	Feb27 5-0	Feb06 3-0	Oct10 4-1	Aug29 2-2	Jan09 1-1	Sep12 1-8	Dec26 8-1
KING'S PARK	Mar13 1-3	Mar20 1-4	Dec05 2-6	Apr10 2-1	Sep19 3-8	Nov21 1-1	Jan16 2-4	Dec26 3-2	Sep05 3-1	Jan02 4-1	Aug22 1-1	—	Oct03 6-4	Nov07 2-4	Apr24 2-1	Oct10 5-1	Oct24 3-2	Jan16 1-3
LEITH A	Aug29 1-1	Jan01 4-2	Jan09 3-2	Sep12 2-5	Apr10 3-0	Aug15 2-1	Dec05 2-2	Oct24 2-1	Mar27 2-2	Oct10 2-1	Dec19 3-0	Feb20 2-1	—	Apr24 2-2	Sep26 2-1	Nov14 2-4	Jan23 2-0	Nov07 2-1
MONTROSE	Sep26 0-5	Aug29 1-1	Aug15 2-3	Jan01 4-3	Dec12 2-1	Feb06 2-1	Mar06 5-0	Apr10 0-1	Nov21 2-1	Oct31 4-2	Jan23 4-0	Sep12 3-0	Oct17 2-1	—	Jan09 1-3	Mar27 0-2	Dec19 1-3	Mar20 1-2
MORTON	Nov28 0-1	Feb20 2-0	Oct10 3-2	Mar27 6-0	Aug08 6-1	Apr21 5-0	Sep05 4-1	Nov07 2-1	Aug22 3-0	Jan16 7-2	Oct31 4-2	Dec19 6-0	Sep19 5-3	Oct03 8-3	—	Feb13 5-1	Apr14 4-1	Sep19 6-1
RAITH R	Dec12 0-0	Nov21 4-3	Apr03 3-2	Oct24 1-3	Jan02 2-3	Oct17 2-2	Nov07 4-1	Sep05 2-2	Dec26 3-1	Mar06 3-0	Oct03 1-0	Apr17 3-0	Aug22 0-2	Sep19 0-2	Jan23 0-2	—	Feb20 0-1	Aug08 2-1
ST BERNARD'S	Mar20 6-1	Mar27 3-0	Nov28 2-5	Nov21 6-0	Jan16 2-2	Dec26 4-0	Oct03 3-0	Mar06 4-3	Sep05 4-1	Jan02 3-1	Dec12 6-1	Sep19 2-0	Aug08 7-1	Oct17 2-1	Oct31 3-0		—	Aug22 3-2
STENHOUSEMUIR	Jan01 1-2	Sep12 1-2	Sep26 1-1	Mar06 7-1	Nov14 5-2	Aug29 4-1	Apr16 9-2	Feb20 2-0	Oct10 1-2	Oct24 4-2	Oct17 4-0	Aug15 0-1	Dec12 1-1	Nov28 4-4	Apr10 1-4	Dec19 2-7	Jan09 2-1	—

DIVISION 1 FINAL TABLE

	P	W	D	L	F	A	Pts
Rangers	38	26	9	3	88	32	61
Aberdeen	38	23	8	7	89	44	54
Celtic	38	22	8	8	89	58	52
Motherwell	38	22	7	9	96	54	51
Hearts	38	24	3	11	99	60	51
T Lanark	38	20	6	12	79	61	46
Falkirk	38	19	6	13	98	66	44
Hamilton A	38	18	5	15	91	96	41
Dundee	38	12	15	11	58	69	39
Clyde	38	16	6	16	59	70	38
Kilmarnock	38	14	9	15	60	70	37
St Johnstone	38	14	8	16	74	68	36
Partick T	38	11	12	15	73	68	34
Arbroath	38	13	5	20	57	84	31
Queen's Park	38	9	12	17	51	77	30
St Mirren	38	11	7	20	68	81	29
Hibernian	38	6	13	19	54	83	25
Queen of South	38	8	8	22	49	95	24
Dunfermline A	38	5	11	22	66	99	21
Albion R	38	5	6	27	53	116	16

DIVISION 2 FINAL TABLE

	P	W	D	L	F	A	Pts
Ayr U	34	25	4	5	122	49	54
Morton	34	23	5	6	110	42	51
St Bernard's	34	22	4	8	100	51	48
Airdrie	34	18	8	8	85	60	44
East fife	34	15	8	11	76	51	38
Cowdenbeath	34	14	10	10	75	59	38
E Stirling	34	18	2	14	81	78	38
Raith R	34	16	4	14	72	66	36
Alloa	34	13	7	14	64	65	33
Stenhousemuir	34	14	4	16	82	86	32
Leith A	34	13	5	16	62	65	31
Forfar A	34	11	8	15	73	89	30
Montrose	34	11	6	17	65	98	28
Dundee U	34	9	9	16	72	97	27
Dumbarton	34	11	5	18	57	83	27
Brechin C	34	8	9	17	64	98	25
King's Park	34	11	3	20	61	106	25
Edinburgh C	34	2	3	29	42	120	7

Season 1937-38

SFA Cup
1st Round
Jan 22 Airdrie ....1 East Fife 2
Jan 22 Albion R ....4 Dundee 2
Jan 22 Alloa ....1 Rangers 6
Jan 22 Ayr U ....4 E Stirling 1
Jan 22 Bo'ness ....0 Hamilton A 4
Jan 22 Chirnside U ....2 Ross Co 3
Jan 22 Clyde ....1 Motherwell 4
Jan 22 Cowdenbeath ....4 Brechin C 1
Jan 22 Dundee U ....3 Hearts 1
Jan 22 Dunfermline A ....0 St Mirren 1
Jan 22 Elgin C ....1 Aberdeen 6
Jan 22 Falkirk ....6 Dalbeattie Star 0
Jan 22 Forfar A ....7 Blairgowrie 4
Jan 22 Hibernian ....2 Edinburgh C 3
Jan 22 Huntly ....0 Nithsdale W 1
Jan 22 Kilmarnock ....6 Dumbarton 0
Jan 22 Moor Park A ....2 Larbert A 5
Jan 22 Morton ....4 Peterhead 0
Jan 22 Penicuik A ....1 King's Park 3
Jan 22 Queen of South ....4 Leith A 2
Jan 22 Queen's Park ....2 Galston 0
Jan 22 Raith R ....1 Montrose 0
Jan 22 St Bernard's ....1 Vale of Leithen 0
Jan 22 St Johnstone ....1 Arbroath 1
Jan 22 Stenhousemuir ....3 Babcock & W 1
Jan 22 Stranraer ....2 Partick T 2
Jan 22 T Lanark ....1 Celtic 2

Replays
Jan 26 Arbroath ....1 St Johnstone 3
Jan 26 Partick T ....8 Stranraer 0

2nd Round
Feb 12 Aberdeen ....5 St Johnstone 1
Feb 12 Celtic ....5 Nithsdale W 0
Feb 12 East Fife ....5 Dundee U 0
Feb 12 Falkirk ....3 St Mirren 2
Feb 12 Hamilton A ....5 Forfar A 1
Feb 12 Larbert A ....2 Morton 3
Feb 12 Partick T ....1 Cowdenbeath 0
Feb 12 Queen's Park ....1 Ayr U 1
Feb 12 Raith R ....9 Edinburgh C 2
Feb 12 Rangers ....3 Queen of South 1
Feb 12 Ross Co ....2 Albion R 5
Feb 12 St Bernard's ....1 King's Park 1
Feb 12 Stenhousemuir ....1 Motherwell 1

Replays
Feb 16 Ayr U ....2 Queen's Park 1
Feb 16 King's Park ....3 St Bernard's 4
Feb 16 Motherwell ....6 Stenhousemuir 1

3rd Round
Mar 5 Celtic ....1 Kilmarnock 2
Mar 5 East Fife ....1 Aberdeen 1
Mar 5 Falkirk ....4 Albion R 0
Mar 5 Morton ....1 Ayr U 1
Mar 5 Motherwell ....2 Hamilton A 0
Mar 5 Partick T ....1 Raith R 2

Replays
Mar 9 Aberdeen ....1 East Fife 2
Mar 9 Ayr U ....4 Morton 1

4th Round
Mar 19 East Fife ....2 Raith R 2
Mar 19 Falkirk ....1 Rangers 2
Mar 19 Kilmarnock ....1 Ayr U 1
Mar 19 St Bernard's ....3 Motherwell 1

Replay
Mar 23 Ayr U ....0 Kilmarnock 5
Mar 23 Raith R ....2 East Fife 3

Semi-finals
Apr 2 East Fife ....1 St Bernard's 1
 played at Tynecastle
Apr 2 Kilmarnock ....4 Rangers 3
 played at Hampden Park

Replays
Apr 6 East Fife ....1 St Bernard's 1
 played at Tynecastle
Apr 13 East Fife ....2 St Bernard's 1
 played at Tynecastle

Final
Apr 23 East Fife ....1 Kilmarnock 1
 played at Hampden Park

Replay
Apr 27 East Fife ....4 Kilmarnock 2
 played at Hampden Park

Another championship title for Celtic, pictured in 1938. Back row (left to right): Geatons, Hogg, Kennaway, Morrison, Crum, Paterson. Front row: Delaney, McDonald, Lyon, Divers, Murphy.

DIVISION 1

(home \ away)	ABERDEEN	ARBROATH	AYR U	CELTIC	CLYDE	DUNDEE	FALKIRK	HAMILTON A	HEARTS	HIBERNIAN	KILMARNOCK	MORTON	MOTHERWELL	PARTICK T	QUEEN OF SOUTH	QUEEN'S PARK	RANGERS	ST JOHNSTONE	ST MIRREN	T LANARK
ABERDEEN	—	Sep27 3-0	Jan03 4-0	Sep25 1-1	Sep01 5-2	Sep11 2-3	Sep15 1-2	Mar26 1-0	Nov06 0-0	Oct09 5-0	Apr09 2-1	Feb19 4-1	Jan08 4-0	Aug28 3-1	Dec11 2-3	Nov27 1-1	Apr13 0-3	Jan29 4-0	Aug14 4-0	Sep08 1-0
ARBROATH	Dec18 3-3	—	Aug28 4-0	Oct09 1-2	Nov27 0-3	Aug14 2-0	Jan08 3-5	Mar12 2-1	Apr16 2-2	Jan03 1-1	Nov20 2-2	Feb26 1-1	Sep15 2-2	Jan05 2-1	Oct23 2-2	Mar05 2-1	Nov13 0-1	Sep11 2-0	Jan29 2-1	Sep08 3-2
AYR U	Oct16 4-1	Dec25 0-1	—	Nov20 1-1	Sep04 3-3	Apr30 0-0	Dec11 2-3	Oct02 2-3	Feb05 2-4	Mar12 1-1	Aug25 4-2	Jan15 6-2	Nov27 3-3	Apr27 1-1	Jan01 1-0	Aug21 6-2	Sep18 1-1	Apr09 3-1	Oct23 1-1	Oct30 1-1
CELTIC	Jan15 5-2	Feb05 4-0	Mar26 1-1	—	Oct02 3-1	Apr18 3-0	Nov27 2-0	Sep04 4-2	Sep18 2-1	Apr30 3-0	Dec25 8-0	Aug21 4-0	Apr09 4-1	Nov06 6-0	Oct16 2-2	Oct23 4-3	Dec04 3-0	Oct09 6-0	Aug28 5-1	Jan03 1-1
CLYDE	Nov13 2-1	Apr02 6-1	Dec31 0-0	Jan29 1-6	—	Sep14 3-2	Sep25 2-4	Apr16 2-0	Feb19 1-3	Jan08 1-2	Oct30 2-2	Mar16 4-3	Aug14 2-2	Sep11 1-1	Apr12 0-0	Nov20 5-0	Dec04 1-1	Oct09 5-1	Aug28 1-1	Jan03 2-1
DUNDEE	Jan01 0-1	Aug25 1-0	Apr11 5-1	Apr16 2-3	Aug21 4-1	—	Nov13 1-4	Jan15 3-0	Oct16 0-2	Apr02 1-2	Oct02 1-2	Dec25 2-2	Nov06 2-2	Oct23 5-3	Sep04 4-1	Sep18 2-0	Feb05 6-1	Feb26 6-1	Mar05 0-0	Oct04 2-1
FALKIRK	Aug21 4-1	Sep18 2-2	Apr16 1-1	Apr02 3-0	Jan15 1-2	Feb05 5-0	—	Feb05 4-5	Sep04 4-2	Nov20 0-0	Oct16 2-2	Feb19 6-1	Dec02 2-2	Dec25 0-1	Aug21 2-1	Nov06 3-1	Mar23 2-1	Oct23 3-1	Apr23 3-1	Mar23 3-1
HAMILTON A	Nov20 0-1	Nov06 2-2	Jan29 0-3	Aug18 1-2	Apr23 4-1	Sep25 5-0	Oct09 2-3	—	Oct30 2-3	Aug27 4-2	Nov27 0-0	Mar19 2-2	Sep11 6-1	Aug14 0-1	Apr09 2-1	Apr30 3-1	Feb19 3-1	Sep15 1-2	Jan03 8-3	Jan08 3-1
HEARTS	Mar12 2-1	Dec11 4-1	Oct09 7-0	Jan08 2-4	Oct23 0-0	Jan03 2-1	Jan04 1-0	Feb26 2-1	—	Sep11 3-2	Apr30 5-1	Dec04 2-1	Jan29 3-0	Sep25 0-0	Nov20 0-0	Nov13 3-2	Apr23 2-1	Aug14 4-0	Sep15 2-1	Aug28 2-1
HIBERNIAN	Feb05 1-1	Oct16 5-0	Nov06 3-0	Oct18 0-3	Sep18 6-3	Mar27 2-1	Mar26 2-4	Dec25 1-1	Jan01 2-2	—	Sep04 1-1	Oct30 4-2	Oct02 1-1	Apr09 2-1	Jan15 2-0	Aug25 0-2	Apr30 0-0	Mar19 2-2	Apr16 2-1	Feb19 2-2
KILMARNOCK	Dec04 3-3	Mar26 2-1	Aug14 2-1	Aug28 3-1	Feb26 2-1	Jan29 3-1	Jan03 2-2	Apr13 2-2	Feb12 3-1	Dec29 0-3	—	Apr29 3-0	Sep25 0-1	Sep15 1-1	Nov13 1-3	Oct23 2-1	Mar12 1-2	Jan08 2-3	Sep11 3-1	Oct09 1-3
MORTON	Oct23 3-5	Oct30 4-5	Sep25 7-3	Sep15 2-3	Apr30 1-3	Aug28 0-2	Sep11 1-1	Nov11 2-6	Apr13 1-2	Jan29 2-4	Dec11 4-2	—	Jan03 4-1	Jan08 1-2	Apr02 2-5	Apr20 1-2	Mar26 2-3	Dec31 3-2	Oct09 3-1	Aug14 1-3
MOTHERWELL	Sep18 2-1	Aug21 5-1	Apr03 4-3	Oct04 1-2	Aug25 1-0	Oct23 1-1	Jan01 3-2	Oct02 0-1	Feb26 3-3	Jan15 1-0	Oct16 4-1	Oct16 4-1	—	Nov20 1-1	Dec25 5-1	Feb05 3-0	Sep04 1-1	Mar23 3-1	Nov13 3-2	Apr12 4-4
PARTICK T	Dec25 3-1	Sep04 0-0	Nov13 6-2	Mar12 1-6	Oct16 4-1	Feb19 1-0	Oct30 3-0	Aug24 2-4	Jan15 2-3	Dec04 3-1	Aug21 0-0	Sep18 3-0	Mar26 3-0	—	Feb05 1-2	Oct02 3-1	Apr18 1-2	Apr16 6-1	Apr02 3-2	Apr12 4-4
QUEEN OF SOUTH	Mar19 1-0	Feb19 0-1	Sep11 0-1	Aug14 2-2	Nov06 1-1	Sep30 2-2	Jan29 2-3	Dec04 3-1	Mar26 2-3	Sep25 2-3	Apr16 3-2	Nov27 1-0	Aug28 0-3	Oct09 0-0	—	Feb26 1-3	Mar05 0-2	Jan03 2-3	Jan08 1-0	Sep15 2-4
QUEEN'S PARK	Apr05 1-1	Dec04 1-1	Sep14 1-1	Jan29 0-3	Mar26 1-1	Jan08 3-1	Aug26 1-5	Mar30 1-4	Apr19 1-1	Feb19 1-1	Oct09 5-1	Jan29 1-3	Oct30 3-3	—	Apr16 0-3	—	Sep25 2-0	Sep27 4-0	—	Apr16 4-1
RANGERS	Feb26 2-2	Mar23 1-1	Jan08 1-1	Sep11 3-1	Apr09 1-0	Oct09 6-0	Aug14 0-0	Oct23 2-2	Nov27 0-3	Sep15 2-0	Nov06 4-1	Nov20 1-3	Aug18 2-3	Jan03 2-1	Apr30 2-1	Dec11 2-1	—	Aug28 2-2	Sep25 4-0	Jan29 3-0
ST JOHNSTONE	Oct02 1-1	Jan01 2-2	Apr20 4-1	Feb19 1-2	Feb05 2-1	Oct30 4-2	Mar12 0-0	Aug21 6-3	Jan15 1-2	Sep18 2-0	Sep04 6-2	Apr30 3-2	Apr23 2-2	Oct16 3-1	Jan15 3-1	Dec25 1-5	—	—	Nov20 3-0	Apr02 2-1
ST MIRREN	Aug24 2-1	Oct02 4-1	Feb19 2-3	Mar23 1-3	Dec25 6-1	Mar19 3-1	Apr30 0-3	Oct16 3-1	Apr21 1-1	Jan01 0-2	Apr12 7-0	Nov27 3-0	Apr09 4-2	Jan15 4-1	Apr16 1-1	Sep04 0-1	Aug28 0-1	Jan15 0-1	—	Nov06 1-4
T LANARK	Sep04 2-0	Jan15 1-1	Feb26 2-2	Nov13 1-1	Mar05 2-3	Nov20 4-3	Apr09 2-2	Sep18 1-1	Dec25 3-0	Feb05 2-4	Aug25 3-0	Dec11 5-3	Apr30 1-1	Aug21 1-1	Sep11 1-1	Oct02 1-2	Oct27 0-5	Mar12 1-0	—	—

DIVISION 2

(home \ away)	AIRDRIE	ALBION R	ALLOA	BRECHIN C	COWDENBEATH	DUMBARTON	DUNDEE U	DUNFERMLINE A	EAST FIFE	E STIRLING	EDINBURGH C	FORFAR A	KING'S PARK	LEITH A	MONTROSE	RAITH R	ST BERNARD'S	STENHOUSEMUIR
AIRDRIE	—	Sep11 2-1	Aug28 4-1	Feb12 10-0	Oct30 4-4	Sep25 1-3	Nov06 4-3	Aug14 5-3	Nov20 1-1	Apr02 4-2	Dec25 4-2	Mar12 7-2	Jan29 2-0	Apr16 1-0	Oct09 1-1	Jan03 2-3	Jan08 3-0	Feb05 3-0
ALBION R	Jan01 0-2	—	Dec04 7-1	Jan15 10-0	Sep04 4-3	Mar19 3-0	Sep18 4-1	Oct16 2-2	Feb19 2-2	Apr20 7-0	Nov13 5-3	Aug21 3-0	Apr09 3-3	Feb26 2-1	Apr30 1-1	Nov27 1-5	Oct23 5-0	Oct02 1-1
ALLOA	Jan15 4-3	Feb05 1-2	—	Aug21 3-2	Sep18 2-4	Nov13 2-1	Feb26 2-4	Nov06 2-4	Mar12 2-1	Oct02 3-0	Apr30 6-0	Nov27 3-3	Jan01 3-2	Oct23 5-2	Apr02 1-2	Dec25 0-1	Sep04 2-5	Mar19 0-4
BRECHIN C	Feb19 0-4	Feb05 1-4	Mar19 5-6	—	Apr16 1-1	Aug14 3-4	May05 3-0	Dec25 0-4	Nov13 1-2	Oct16 3-3	Jan08 2-7	Apr02 2-1	Mar03 3-4	Apr23 0-3	Sep11 2-3	Feb26 2-8	Oct09 2-3	Nov06 3-4
COWDENBEATH	Mar05 1-1	Dec25 2-3	Jan08 5-3	Nov20 10-0	—	Jan03 1-1	Feb05 3-1	Sep11 5-2	Dec04 6-0	Mar19 3-1	Sep25 8-1	Nov06 2-6	Aug28 6-1	Oct16 4-3	Aug14 4-3	Mar12 5-0	Apr12 4-2	Apr02 5-0
DUMBARTON	Apr09 2-0	Nov06 3-2	Apr16 2-2	Dec04 7-0	Oct02 4-4	—	Sep04 4-1	Mar12 3-2	Dec18 2-1	Jan15 3-1	Jan01 8-1	Feb26 2-6	Sep18 5-0	Nov20 3-0	Oct16 4-0	Mar26 2-2	Apr26 2-1	Aug21 5-1
DUNDEE U	Apr30 5-5	Apr23 1-4	Sep25 2-2	Mar12 1-6	Feb19 2-3	Jan29 1-4	—	Oct09 4-2	Oct30 0-2	Sep04 6-1	Nov27 5-2	Feb05 2-0	Aug28 3-4	Feb19 2-1	Apr30 4-4	Aug14 1-7	Mar19 0-4	
DUNFERMLINE A	Feb26 0-4	Jan08 3-3	Jan29 0-3	Oct02 1-1	Jan01 3-1	Oct23 4-1	Apr16 2-0	—	Apr09 1-1	Sep04 3-1	Oct30 4-4	Sep18 4-4	Mar26 3-0	Aug21 6-1	Apr30 0-3	Nov13 1-3	Feb19 1-1	
EAST FIFE	Oct16 2-0	Aug28 1-2	Aug14 3-1	Feb05 4-2	Mar26 1-2	Oct09 4-1	Apr29 7-0	Sep25 5-4	—	Nov06 4-1	Dec11 13-2	Apr28 3-0	Dec25 4-0	Nov27 3-1	Jan03 6-2	Sep11 3-5	Jan15 3-3	Feb26 5-1
E STIRLING	Nov27 0-3	Aug14 1-4	Mar24 3-1	Feb26 2-1	Oct23 2-3	Aug28 2-2	Apr25 1-1	Apr23 4-2	Apr25 2-1	—	Oct09 3-2	Nov13 2-0	Sep11 6-0	Jan29 1-2	Apr11 4-1	Jan08 1-8	Sep11 1-1	Oct30 0-0
EDINBURGH C	Aug21 0-4	Mar26 0-2	Nov20 3-2	Sep18 4-5	Oct23 2-4	Apr02 2-0	Jan01 3-5	Dec18 3-3	Sep04 3-3	Feb19 3-4	—	Jan29 2-8	Apr16 5-4	Jan08 5-4	Nov06 1-6	Dec04 0-4	Oct16 5-2	
FORFAR A	Apr23 1-5	Jan03 2-2	Oct09 4-2	Oct30 3-4	Feb26 0-5	Sep11 4-3	Jan15 4-3	Feb05 1-3	Oct23 3-5	Dec25 5-0	Aug28 4-4	—	Aug14 3-1	Mar05 2-2	Sep25 3-3	Mar26 2-3	Apr16 1-2	Nov20 1-1
KING'S PARK	Sep18 2-3	Nov20 0-2	Oct16 4-2	Sep04 2-1	Nov13 0-4	Oct30 1-0	Oct02 4-4	Jan01 1-3	Dec25 0-2	Feb05 2-1	Apr02 5-4	Apr02 1-0	—	Feb05 2-0	Mar12 4-3	Apr13 1-4	Feb19 0-1	Mar05 1-4
LEITH A	Nov13 0-2	Oct09 1-0	Sep11 0-1	Oct23 3-1	Apr23 2-0	Jan08 1-1	Mar26 1-1	Nov20 1-1	Jan29 3-1	Dec04 1-1	Mar12 1-1	Feb19 3-1	Sep25 1-1	—	Dec25 3-2	Aug14 3-4	Apr28 1-1	Jan15 5-2
MONTROSE	Mar19 3-1	Oct30 0-1	Feb19 1-1	Jan01 2-0	Jan15 3-3	Feb12 0-0	Dec04 1-3	Apr02 0-1	Oct02 3-0	Aug21 2-2	Feb26 4-1	Oct16 2-4	Nov06 4-2	Sep04 1-3	—	Feb05 2-2	Apr23 1-2	Sep18 2-3
RAITH R	Sep04 2-0	Aug12 4-1	Dec18 6-3	Apr23 3-0	Jan29 6-2	Feb19 7-0	Feb19 4-2	Apr16 4-1	Jan13 1-3	Sep18 1-1	Jan15 3-1	Apr09 3-0	Oct23 5-1	Oct30 3-1	Nov13 6-0	—	Nov20 4-2	Dec04 6-2
ST BERNARD'S	Oct02 3-2	Jan29 2-3	Oct30 6-1	Apr09 6-1	Aug21 4-3	Nov27 0-3	Oct16 1-0	Apr20 4-3	Sep18 3-0	Feb05 3-1	Jan03 2-1	Sep04 3-0	Apr30 2-1	Nov06 0-2	Mar05 1-0	Feb26 0-3	—	Jan01 2-1
STENHOUSEMUIR	Oct23 2-3	Apr16 2-3	Jan03 5-1	Jan29 5-0	Nov27 1-1	Dec25 4-2	Nov13 3-1	Aug28 2-5	Mar12 3-2	Aug14 5-2	Apr09 3-1	Oct09 1-0	Apr30 6-0	Mar26 2-2	Sep25 2-1	Sep11 2-1	—	

DIVISION 1 FINAL TABLE

	P	W	D	L	F	A	Pts
Celtic	38	27	7	4	114	42	61
Hearts	38	26	6	6	90	50	58
Rangers	38	18	13	7	75	49	49
Falkirk	38	19	9	10	82	52	47
Motherwell	38	17	10	11	78	69	44
Aberdeen	38	15	9	14	74	59	39
Partick T	38	15	9	14	68	70	39
St Johnstone	38	16	7	15	78	81	39
T Lanark	38	11	13	14	68	73	35
Hibernian	38	11	13	14	57	65	35
Arbroath	38	11	13	14	58	79	35
Queen's Park	38	11	12	15	59	74	34
Hamilton A	38	13	7	18	81	76	33
St Mirren	38	14	5	19	58	66	33
Clyde	38	10	13	15	68	78	33
Queen of South	38	11	11	16	58	71	33
Ayr U	38	9	15	14	66	85	33
Kilmarnock	38	13	7	18	65	91	33
Dundee	38	13	6	19	70	74	32
Morton	38	6	3	29	64	127	15

DIVISION 2 FINAL TABLE

	P	W	D	L	F	A	Pts
Raith R	34	27	5	2	142	54	59
Albion R	34	20	8	6	97	50	48
Airdrie	34	21	5	8	100	53	47
St Bernard's	34	20	5	9	75	49	45
East Fife	34	19	5	10	104	61	43
Cowdenbeath	34	17	9	8	115	71	43
Dumbarton	34	17	5	12	85	66	39
Stenhousemuir	34	17	5	12	87	78	39
Dunfermline A	34	17	5	12	82	76	39
Leith A	34	16	5	13	71	56	37
Alloa	34	11	4	19	78	106	26
King's Park	34	11	4	19	64	96	26
E Stirling	34	9	7	18	55	95	25
Dundee U	34	9	5	20	69	104	23
Forfar A	34	8	6	20	67	100	22
Montrose	34	7	8	19	56	88	22
Edinburgh C	34	7	3	24	77	135	17
Brechin C	34	5	2	27	53	139	12

Pre-season training for these Rangers players as they parade the very latest in track suit fashion, back in 1938.

SFA Cup
1st Round

Jan 21	Aberdeen 1	Albion R	0
Jan 21	Alloa 2	Ayr U	1
Jan 21	Blairgowrie 3	Dumbarton	2
Jan 21	Bo'ness 1	Hamilton A	4
Jan 21	Burntisland 3	Celtic	8
Jan 21	Clyde 2	St Johnstone ...	0
Jan 21	Cowdenbeath 3	Partick T	3
Jan 21	Dundee 2	St Bernard's	0
Jan 21	Dundee U 2	Stenhousemuir ...	0
Jan 21	Dunfermline A 5	Morton	2
Jan 21	Duns 4	Girvan	1
Jan 21	East Fife 1	Montrose	2
Jan 21	Edinburgh C 3	Stranraer	3
Jan 21	Falkirk 5	Brechin C	0
Jan 21	Falkirk A 2	Elgin C	4
Jan 21	Forfar A 0	Hibernian	3
Jan 21	Hearts 14	Penicuik A	2
Jan 21	Huntly 1	Motherwell	8
Jan 21	Kilmarnock 6	Berwick R	1
Jan 21	King's Park 5	Babcock & W ...5	
Jan 21	Leith A 0	Airdrie	2
Jan 21	Nithsdale W 5	Buckie T	5
Jan 21	Queen of South ...5	Arbroath	4
Jan 21	Queen's Park 4	St Cuthbert's 1	
Jan 21	Raith R 0	Rangers	1
Jan 21	St Mirren 7	E Stirling	0
Jan 21	T Lanark 8	Clacknacuddin ...2	

Replays

Jan 25	Babcock & W ...3	King's Park	2
Jan 25	Partick T 1	Cowdenbeath 2	
Jan 25	Stranraer 1	Edinburgh C 2	
Jan 28	Buckie T 5	Nithsdale W 2	

2nd Round

Feb 4	Aberdeen 5	Queen's Park 1	
Feb 4	Blairgowrie 3	Buckie T 3	
Feb 4	Dundee 0	Clyde	0
Feb 4	Dundee U 1	Motherwell 5	
Feb 4	Dunfermline A 2	Duns 0	
Feb 1	Edinburgh C 1	St Mirren 3	
Feb 4	Falkirk 7	Airdrie	0
Feb 4	Hearts 14	Elgin C 1	
Feb 4	Hibernian 3	Kilmarnock 1	
Feb 4	Montrose 1	Celtic 7	
Feb 4	Queen of South ...5	Babcock & W ...	*0*
Feb 4	Rangers 2	Hamilton A	0
Feb 4	T Lanark 3	Cowdenbeath 0	

Replays

Feb 8	Buckie T 4	Blairgowrie 1	
Feb 8	Clyde 1	Dundee 0	

3rd Round

Feb 18	Buckie T 0	T Lanark	6
Feb 18	Dunfermline A 1	Alloa 1	
Feb 18	Falkirk 2	Aberdeen	3

Feb 18	Hearts 2	Celtic	2
Feb 18	Motherwell 4	St Mirren	2
Feb 18	Rangers 1	Clyde	4

Replays

Feb 22	Alloa 3	Dunfermline A ...2	
Feb 22	Celtic 2	Hearts 1	

4th Round

Mar 4	Aberdeen 2	Queen of South ...0	
Mar 4	Clyde 1	T Lanark 0	
Mar 4	Hibernian 3	Alloa 1	
Mar 4	Motherwell 3	Celtic 1	

Semi-finals

Mar 25	Aberdeen 1	Motherwell 1	
	played at Ibrox		
Mar 25	Clyde 1	Hibernian	0
	played at Tynecastle		

Replay

Mar 29	Aberdeen 1	Motherwell 3	
	played at Ibrox		

Final

Apr 22	Clyde 4	Motherwell 0	
	played at Hampden Park		

Season 1938-39

DIVISION 1

	ABERDEEN	ALBION R	ARBROATH	AYR U	CELTIC	CLYDE	FALKIRK	HAMILTON A	HEARTS	HIBERNIAN	KILMARNOCK	MOTHERWELL	PARTICK T	QUEEN OF SOUTH	QUEEN'S PARK	RAITH R	RANGERS	ST JOHNSTONE	ST MIRREN	T LANARK
ABERDEEN	—	Dec10 2-1	Jan02 4-0	Oct15 5-2	Dec24 1-2	Oct29 4-1	Oct01 5-0	Nov05 6-1	Feb25 1-2	Jan07 6-1	Nov19 1-2	Sep03 3-0	Aug24 4-3	Apr01 2-0	Mar18 6-3	Dec03 2-0	Apr29 3-0	Sep17 3-2	Jan28 3-2	Aug20 6-1
ALBION R	Apr22 1-0	—	Aug24 3-2	Dec28 3-3	Oct01 1-8	Dec03 3-0	Sep30 0-3	Mar04 5-0	Nov19 0-1	Sep17 0-1	Apr01 6-1	Oct15 5-3	Sep03 3-1	Nov12 2-1	Oct22 1-3	Apr29 2-1	Nov05 2-7	Aug20 2-3	Jan11 2-1	Jan28 2-4
ARBROATH	Sep10 0-2	Aug13 3-2	—	Apr08 3-0	Nov06 0-2	Jan14 3-0	Mar04 1-2	Apr27 4-1	Jan03 1-1	Nov12 2-4	Feb25 4-1	Apr22 2-0	Feb18 4-0	Dec31 1-1	Oct08 0-4	Mar24 3-3	Sep17 3-1	Mar25 2-1		Nov05 0-5
AYR U	Jan03 3-3	Aug27 4-1	Dec03 4-1	—	Mar11 1-4	Sep14 2-4	Apr01 3-0	Feb11 2-1	Sep24 3-1	Oct22 2-2	Oct08 6-1	Mar18 3-0	Oct29 2-3	Sep10 2-1	Jan25 3-4	Aug13 2-0	Dec31 0-0	Nov19 2-3	Apr22 2-3	Apr29 3-3
CELTIC	Aug27 1-2	Jan25 4-1	Apr01 2-0	Nov05 3-3	—	Feb11 3-1	Mar18 1-2	Sep14 2-2	Dec31 2-2	Dec03 5-4	Aug13 9-1	Nov19 1-3	Feb25 3-1	Oct08 5-1	Jan03 0-1	Sep24 6-1	Apr22 6-2	Dec17 1-1	Oct29 3-2	Oct22 6-1
CLYDE	Mar07 1-1	Apr08 0-0	Oct01 2-0	Aug20 3-1	Nov05 1-4	—	Dec26 4-3	Nov26 2-6	Dec10 3-0	Sep03 5-1	Apr29 5-1	Jan02 4-0	Oct22 4-1	Nov12 1-1	Jan10 3-1	Apr23 0-2	Aug23 2-0	Oct01 4-1	Aug23 2-0	Apr10 4-1
FALKIRK	Jan14 1-3	Sep10 4-3	Oct29 2-0	Nov26 3-1	Nov12 1-1	Aug27 0-2	—	Sep24 4-0	Sep13 0-1	Mar11 1-1	Jan03 4-0	Dec10 2-1	Dec17 2-5	Feb11 2-1	Aug13 1-0	Dec31 6-1	Oct08 2-2	Feb25 1-1	Apr08 2-1	Mar25 3-1
HAMILTON A	Mar11 1-0	Oct29 2-1	Dec29 1-1	Sep17 2-0	Aug20 0-1	Apr01 1-2	Jan11 1-3	—	Apr29 4-1	Aug24 4-1	Mar18 3-1	Jan02 2-1	Jan28 4-0	Nov19 1-0	Dec10 3-1	Oct01 2-1	Oct15 1-2	Sep03 4-3		
HEARTS	Oct22 5-2	Mar29 4-2	Oct15 1-1	Jan11 2-0	Apr08 1-5	Sep26 2-0	Apr26 6-2	Aug20 2-3	—	Dec17 2-3	Jan02 2-0	Dec03 4-0	Sep24 5-0	Mar11 4-0	Mar04 8-3	Apr11 2-1	Feb18 1-3	Jan28 8-2	Oct01 5-2	Aug24 4-2
HIBERNIAN	Sep24 5-0	Feb11 1-2	Mar18 1-1	Feb25 2-3	Apr08 1-0	Dec31 1-1	Nov05 3-0	Aug13 2-2	Sep10 1-0	—	Sep14 0-1	Apr29 2-1	Nov19 1-2	Aug27 1-2	Oct08 2-3	Jan03 2-1	Jan14 1-1	Oct29 5-2	Nov26 6-1	Dec10 1-1
KILMARNOCK	Apr05 0-3	Nov26 4-2	Sep17 1-1	Jan28 2-2	Aug20 0-0	Dec17 1-4	Oct15 1-1	Nov12 2-2	Apr08 4-1	Aug20 0-1	—	Dec28 1-3	Oct01 4-2	Mar08 1-1	Apr22 3-0	Nov05 4-2	Oct22 3-1	Sep03 1-0	Jan02 3-2	Jan07 5-2
MOTHERWELL	Dec31 2-2	Jan30 3-1	Sep24 4-0	Nov12 1-2	Oct08 2-3	Jan02 2-3	Apr14 1-3	Sep10 2-1	Feb11 0-4	Dec17 3-2	Aug27 5-2	—	Mar11 4-3	Aug20 8-5	Jan14 2-4	Apr22 0-5	Mar08 3-1	Mar08 2-1	Mar08 2-1	Nov05 5-1
PARTICK T	Aug13 2-1	Dec31 1-3	Dec10 2-0	Mar04 2-3	Oct22 0-0	Sep10 2-0	Apr29 2-0	Oct08 3-1	Aug27 3-4	Feb18 4-3	Nov05 1-0	Sep24 1-2	—	Feb11 2-2	Sep13 2-1	Jan03 2-1	Nov26 1-4	Nov12 3-0	Apr08 4-1	
QUEEN OF SOUTH	Nov26 1-1	Mar18 3-3	Aug20 2-0	Jan02 6-1	Jan28 1-1	Feb25 3-2	Sep17 2-0	Feb18 3-0	Nov05 0-1	Dec24 2-1	Oct22 2-0	Aug24 4-3	Jan11 0-0	—	Sep24 1-2	Dec17 3-2	Dec10 4-2	Apr08 1-1	Oct15 1-1	Oct01 1-2
QUEEN'S PARK	Nov12 2-1	Feb25 5-2	Sep03 2-0	Oct01 1-3	Apr08 1-0	Nov05 4-2	Aug23 1-1	Apr08 1-2	Jan28 2-3	Dec10 1-5	Jan11 0-0	Sep17 1-1	Apr29 2-0		—	Mar25 3-0	Nov26 2-3	Oct22 2-3	Aug20 0-0	Jan14 1-4
RAITH R	Apr08 3-2	Dec17 1-4	Jan28 3-1	Aug24 4-0	Jan07 0-2	Mar18 0-1	Sep03 0-1	Oct22 1-2	Nov26 1-2	Oct15 1-2	Mar11 2-3	Oct01 2-4	Aug20 1-3	Apr22 0-4	Nov19 4-5	—	Mar04 0-2	Jan02 5-6	Sep17 1-3	Dec24 2-2
RANGERS	Dec17 5-2	Mar11 5-0	Jan11 4-0	Sep03 4-1	Jan02 2-1	Nov19 2-0	Jan28 2-1	Apr21 3-2	Mar18 1-1	Oct01 5-2	Feb25 2-2	Aug20 2-2	Oct15 4-1	Dec03 4-1	Apr01 1-0	Oct29 4-0	—	Aug24 4-2	Dec26 3-0	Sep17 5-1
ST JOHNSTONE	Feb11 1-0	Sep14 4-0	Apr06 4-3	Mar25 0-1	Dec10 1-4	Feb04 3-2	Aug22 1-4	Jan14 0-2	Mar08 0-1	Dec31 1-7	Apr01 0-1	Jan25 1-3	Aug27 2-1	Apr11 7-0	Sep10 0-1			—	Mar11 6-2	Apr04 4-0
ST MIRREN	Oct08 3-1	Sep24 1-2	Nov19 1-2	Dec10 1-2	Apr29 1-2	Aug13 2-4	Dec03 1-2	Jan03 0-0	Jan24 0-1	Apr01 2-2	Sep10 1-2	Oct29 1-5	Mar18 4-0	Dec31 1-2	Sep13 2-1	Feb11 1-2	Aug27 1-5	Nov05 4-0	—	Feb25 3-2
T LANARK	Sep14 1-1	Oct08 4-0	Mar11 3-0	Dec17 3-2	Mar08 0-2	Jan03 3-1	Nov19 2-2	Dec31 1-4	Aug13 2-0	Apr21 3-3	Sep10 3-1	Apr06 1-4	Dec03 2-4	Jan14 0-1	Sep10 5-1	Aug27 5-0	Feb11 1-2	Mar18 1-3	Oct22 3-3	—

DIVISION 1 FINAL TABLE

	P	W	D	L	F	A	Pts
Rangers	38	25	9	4	112	55	59
Celtic	38	20	8	10	99	53	48
Aberdeen	38	20	6	12	91	61	46
Hearts	38	20	5	13	98	70	45
Falkirk	38	19	7	12	73	63	45
Queen of South	38	17	9	12	69	64	43
Hamilton A	38	18	5	15	67	71	41
St Johnstone	38	17	6	15	85	82	40
Clyde	38	17	5	16	78	70	39
Kilmarnock	38	15	9	14	73	86	39
Partick T	38	17	4	17	74	87	38
Motherwell	38	16	5	17	82	86	37
Hibernian	38	14	7	17	68	69	35
Ayr U	38	13	9	16	76	83	35
T Lanark	38	12	8	18	80	96	32
Albion R	38	12	6	20	65	90	30
Arbroath	38	11	8	19	54	75	30
St Mirren	38	11	7	20	57	80	29
Queen's Park	38	11	5	22	57	83	27
Raith R	38	10	2	26	65	99	22

DIVISION 2

	AIRDRIE	ALLOA	BRECHIN C	COWDENBEATH	DUMBARTON	DUNFERMLINE A	DUNDEE	DUNDEE U	EAST FIFE	E STIRLING	EDINBURGH C	FORFAR A	KING'S PARK	LEITH A	MONTROSE	MORTON	ST BERNARD'S	STENHOUSEMUIR
AIRDRIE	—	Oct29 2-1	Apr08 6-1	Mar25 3-1	Feb11 6-1	Dec31 4-3	Jan14 1-2	Aug27 8-1	Nov26 3-0	Dec10 4-0	Oct08 2-1	Mar18 6-3	Feb25 2-1	Sep24 3-1	Mar11 4-3	Sep10 3-2	Dec17 4-3	Aug13 1-5
ALLOA	Jan07 3-1	—	Apr29 1-1	Oct15 2-1	Apr08 2-1	Aug13 4-1	Nov19 3-0	Jan28 1-4	Apr15 5-0	Mar11 1-3	Aug27 3-1	Feb11 2-6	Nov05 0-4	Sep10 2-3	Dec10 1-2	Oct08 1-4	Dec24 2-0	Sep24 0-2
BRECHIN C	Sep03 1-1	Sep17 3-3	—	Mar11 2-5	Aug20 0-3	Oct17 2-2	Feb11 2-1	Nov26 2-2	Oct01 2-2	Jan14 4-4	Apr43 4-3	Dec31 6-0	Mar25 5-2	Sep30 3-2	Jan24 1-4	Apr22 4-2	Oct22 4-1	Nov12 4-2
COWDENBEATH	Dec03 7-2	Nov26 4-2	Oct08 3-3	—	Jan14 3-1	Sep10 2-0	Oct22 2-1	Dec31 3-1	Apr08 2-0	Feb11 4-0	Dec17 2-2	Aug13 3-6	Apr22 6-2	Aug27 3-2	Nov12 5-3	Sep24 3-1	Mar18 7-1	Feb25 7-1
DUMBARTON	Nov12 0-0	Dec03 2-3	Feb04 1-3	Nov19 1-4	—	Feb25 2-2	Oct29 4-4	Sep24 1-0	Jan28 2-0	Aug13 4-0	Apr22 5-1	Sep10 2-0	Oct15 2-1	Dec31 1-1	Dec17 2-2	Aug27 2-9	Apr01 1-2	Oct08 2-2
DUNFERMLINE A	Aug20 0-0	Oct22 1-4	Nov19 8-3	Jan02 1-4	Feb25 2-2	—	Sep03 4-1	Oct15 3-0	Sep10 1-1	Oct29 7-1	Feb18 2-1	Feb25 4-1	Nov26 7-1	Dec31 5-0	Dec03 3-1	Dec17 7-1	Apr01 4-1	Dec10 7-1
DUNDEE	Nov05 1-2	Dec17 1-4	Aug13 5-0	Jan28 5-0	Apr15 1-1	Apr01 7-1	—	Mar18 2-0	Oct15 1-5	Oct08 6-2	Sep10 3-0	Sep24 7-0	Feb18 3-0	Feb25 7-0	Nov26 5-0	Dec31 2-3	Dec03 3-1	Mar11 3-1
DUNDEE U	Nov19 1-2	Sep03 1-0	Dec24 1-0	Aug20 1-4	Dec10 4-2	Jan14 1-0	Sep17 2-5	—	Jan02 2-5	Mar25 10-1	Feb11 1-3	Mar04 6-0	Oct01 2-1	Nov11 6-1	Apr22 3-5	Oct22 1-9	Nov12 2-0	Oct29 3-1
EAST FIFE	Apr01 3-1	Nov12 3-1	Feb25 6-0	Oct29 0-1	Feb11 5-1	Mar11 3-7	Mar11 0-2	Sep10 3-2	—	Aug27 7-5	Sep24 7-1	Jan02 2-1	Dec03 2-0	Oct22 3-1	Dec31 4-0	Aug13 6-5	Mar25 3-4	Dec17 2-4
E STIRLING	Oct01 1-1	Aug20 1-3	Oct15 3-2	Sep17 2-2	Feb18 6-4	Dec03 3-5	Mar04 3-3	Nov05 1-2	Mar18 1-8	—	Apr29 2-3	Nov19 5-2	Jan02 1-2	Apr15 3-1	Apr01 5-2	Sep02 0-2	Apr01 5-2	Sep02 0-2
EDINBURGH C	Mar04 1-2	Mar18 3-1	Dec10 1-5	Sep03 0-4	Sep17 2-2	Nov26 2-3	Jan03 1-4	Feb25 3-2	Nov05 2-5	Nov12 2-7	—	Apr15 2-3	Oct22 2-5	Mar25 0-2	Aug20 4-2	Jan28 4-1	Oct01 0-4	Feb18 3-3
FORFAR A	Sep17 2-3	Oct01 2-6	Apr01 4-4	Apr01 1-8	Jan02 6-6	Nov12 4-2	Dec10 2-1	Feb25 2-1	Dec17 1-4	Feb25 5-3	Oct29 5-3	—	Apr08 5-6	Nov26 1-0	Oct22 4-3	Mar11 6-5	Aug20 2-2	Dec17 1-0
KING'S PARK	Jan28 2-5	Dec31 0-4	Sep24 6-0	Dec10 1-6	Sep26 2-3	Aug27 1-2	Nov12 1-2	Apr01 3-1	Jan14 3-4	Sep10 2-2	Aug13 13-3	Feb11 1-3	—	Oct29 7-1	Feb04 6-5	Mar04 5-0	Apr04 1-0	
LEITH A	Oct22 1-7	Jan02 2-3	Apr01 3-1	Apr29 2-3	Sep03 1-2	Mar18 1-2	Oct01 2-3	Dec03 0-2	Mar04 1-1	Dec17 6-3	Oct15 3-0	Apr22 4-0	Aug20 2-2	—	Sep17 5-2	Nov12 4-5	Apr19 1-1	Jan28 1-4
MONTROSE	Feb18 0-1	Mar25 1-2	Sep10 2-5	Jan07 0-1	Nov05 2-2	Apr29 2-3	Apr29 5-5	Mar04 3-2	Sep24 4-5	Apr01 4-0	Dec03 7-3	Mar18 1-0	Jan14 2-0		—	Feb25 5-1	Oct15 2-2	Apr08 4-3
MORTON	Jan02 1-1	Jan14 0-0	Nov05 3-2	Mar04 0-1	Mar18 2-2	Apr14 2-3	Aug20 4-0	Apr08 6-4	Dec24 6-4	Nov26 4-1	Nov19 3-1	Sep03 5-0	Dec10 2-2	Oct01 4-1		—	Sep17 2-2	Feb04 5-3
ST BERNARD'S	Apr15 0-1	Feb25 2-0	Aug27 7-1	Nov05 1-2	Nov26 2-4	Sep24 3-1	Apr08 1-1	Oct08 5-3	Dec10 0-1	Dec31 3-2	Mar11 4-3	Feb18 6-2	Aug13 5-4	Aug13 2-1	Feb11 2-1	Oct29 5-0	—	Sep10 1-0
STENHOUSEMUIR	Oct15 3-2	Feb04 0-2	Mar18 7-2	Oct01 1-0	Mar04 2-0	Mar11 4-0	Dec24 1-1	Apr29 3-0	Aug20 2-2	Oct22 5-1	Apr01 2-1	Nov05 2-0	Sep17 1-3	Nov19 3-2	Sep03 2-0	Dec03 2-0	Jan02 2-2	—

DIVISION 2 FINAL TABLE

	P	W	D	L	F	A	Pts
Cowdenbeath	34	28	4	2	120	45	60
Alloa	34	22	4	8	91	46	48
East Fife	34	21	6	7	99	61	48
Airdrie	34	21	5	8	85	57	47
Dunfermline A	34	18	5	11	99	78	41
Dundee	34	15	7	12	99	63	37
St Bernard's	34	15	6	13	79	79	36
Stenhousemuir	34	15	5	14	74	69	35
Dundee U	34	15	3	16	78	69	33
Brechin C	34	11	9	14	82	106	31
Dumbarton	34	9	12	13	68	76	30
Morton	34	11	6	17	74	88	28
King's Park	34	12	2	20	87	92	26
Montrose	34	10	5	19	82	99	25
Forfar A	34	11	3	20	74	138	25
Leith A	34	10	4	20	57	83	24
E Stirling	34	9	4	21	89	130	22
Edinburgh C	34	6	4	24	58	119	16

DIVISION A FINAL TABLE

	P	W	D	L	F	A	Pts
Rangers	5	4	1	0	14	3	9
Falkirk	5	4	0	1	20	10	8
Aberdeen	5	3	0	2	9	9	6
Celtic	5	3	0	2	7	7	6
Hearts	5	2	2	1	13	9	6
Partick T	5	2	2	1	7	7	6
Motherwell	5	2	1	2	14	12	5
Hamilton A	5	2	1	1	7	11	5
T Lanark	5	2	1	2	9	8	5
Queen of South	5	2	1	2	10	9	5
Albion R	5	2	1	2	12	7	5
St Mirren	5	1	3	1	8	8	5
Kilmarnock	5	2	1	2	10	9	5
Hibernian	5	2	0	3	11	13	4
Alloa	5	2	0	3	8	13	4
Arbroath	5	2	0	3	9	9	4
St Johnstone	5	2	0	3	7	8	4
Ayr U	5	2	0	3	10	17	4
Clyde	5	1	0	4	10	14	2
Cowdenbeath	5	1	0	4	6	14	2

DIVISION B FINAL TABLE

	P	W	D	L	F	A	Pts
Dundee	4	3	1	0	13	5	7
Dunfermline A	4	2	2	0	10	5	6
King's Park	4	2	2	0	11	7	6
East Fife	4	2	1	1	12	6	5
Queen's Park	4	1	3	0	7	5	5
Stenhousemuir	4	2	1	1	6	5	5
Dundee U	4	2	1	1	8	7	5
Dumbarton	4	2	1	1	9	9	5
E Stirling	4	1	2	1	7	7	4
St Bernard's	4	1	2	1	7	7	4
Airdrie	4	2	0	2	7	8	4
Edinburgh C	4	1	1	2	9	8	3
Montrose	4	1	1	2	7	8	3
Raith R	4	1	1	2	8	12	3
Morton	4	1	1	2	4	7	3
Leith A	4	1	0	3	4	7	2
Brechin C	4	0	2	2	3	8	2
Forfar A	4	0	0	4	7	18	0

DIVISION A

Saturday, 12 August 1939

Aberdeen	3	Celtic	1
Albion R	5	Ayr U	0
Alloa	3	St Johnstone	0
Clyde	4	Falkirk	6
Cowdenbeath	2	T Lanark	1
Hamilton A	2	Arbroath	0
Hearts	1	Partick T	1
Kilmarnock	3	Motherwell	3
Queen of South	2	Hibernian	1
Rangers	5	St Mirren	1

Saturday, 19 August 1939

Arbroath	5	Alloa	2
Ayr U	0	Rangers	4
Celtic	2	Hearts	0
Falkirk	7	Cowdenbeath	1
Hibernian	3	Clyde	2
Motherwell	3	Aberdeen	0
Partick T	2	Albion R	1
St Johnstone	0	Kilmarnock	3
St Mirren	3	Queen of South	3
T Lanark	2	Hamilton A	2

Tuesday, 22 August 1959

Partick T	2	Hearts	2
St Mirren	0	Rangers	0
T Lanark	4	Cowdenbeath	2

Wednesday, 23 August 1939

Arbroath	2	Hamilton A	0
Ayr U	2	Albion R	1
Celtic	1	Aberdeen	3
Falkirk	4	Clyde	2
Hibernian	3	Queen of South	1
Motherwell	4	Kilmarnock	2
St Johnstone	4	Alloa	0

Saturday, 26 August 1939

Aberdeen	3	Hibernian	1
Albion R	0	St Mirren	0
Alloa	3	Motherwell	2
Clyde	2	St Johnstone	0
Cowdenbeath	1	Celtic	2
Hamilton A	2	Falkirk	1
Hearts	6	Ayr U	2
Kilmarnock	0	T Lanark	1
Queen of South	3	Partick T	0
Rangers	3	Arbroath	1

Saturday, 2 September 1939

Arbroath	1	Kilmarnock	2
Ayr U	6	Hamilton A	1
Celtic	1	Clyde	0
Falkirk	2	Queen of South	1
Hibernian	3	Albion R	5
Motherwell	2	Hearts	4
Partick T	2	Alloa	0
St Johnstone	3	Aberdeen	0
St Mirren	4	Cowdenbeath	0
T Lanark	1	Rangers	2

DIVISION B

Saturday, 12 August 1939

Brechin C	0	St Bernard's	0
Dundee	5	Raith R	1
East Fife	3	Morton	0
E Stirling	4	Montrose	1
Edinburgh C	2	Dundee U	3
Forfar A	3	King's Park	5
Leith A	1	Dumbarton	2
Queen's Park	2	Airdrie	0
Stenhousemuir	0	Dunfermline A	0

Saturday, 19 August 1939

Airdrie	2	Dundee	4
Dumbarton	3	East Fife	3
Dundee U	4	Stenhousemuir	2
Dunfermline A	3	Queen's Park	3
King's Park	3	Leith A	1
Montrose	2	Edinburgh C	2
Morton	3	E Stirling	0
Raith R	2	Brechin C	0
St Bernard's	6	Forfar A	2

Saturday, 26 August 1939

Brechin C	1	King's Park	1
Dundee	3	Dumbarton	1
East Fife	5	St Bernard's	1
E Stirling	1	Dundee U	1
Edinburgh C	3	Morton	0
Forfar A	1	Airdrie	3
Leith A	0	Dunfermline A	2
Queen's Park	2	Raith R	1
Stenhousemuir	1	Montrose	0

Saturday, 2 September 1939

Airdrie	2	East Fife	1
Dumbarton	3	Edinburgh C	2
Dundee U	0	Leith A	2
Dunfermline A	5	Brechin C	2
King's Park	2	E Stirling	2
Montrose	4	Forfar A	1
Morton	1	Dundee	1
Raith R	1	Stenhousemuir	3
St Bernard's	0	Queen's Park	0

Curtailment of Season 1939-40 due to war.

There were no Scottish FA Cup matches in 1939-40

DIVISION A

	ABE	CEL	CLY	FAL	HAM	HEA	HIB	KIL	MOR	MOT	PAR	QOS	QPK	RAN	STM	TLA
ABERDEEN		Dec15 1-1	Oct20 1-2	Sep08 2-0	Nov17 4-0	Feb09 2-1	Dec22 2-1	Dec01 2-0	Nov03 3-1	Sep22 4-1	Jan03 3-0	Jan05 7-1	Jan12 5-0	Aug25 4-1	Aug11 6-1	Aug11 3-0
CELTIC	Sep01 1-1		Aug18 2-2	Oct27 2-1	Sep15 5-0	Dec29 3-5	Feb02 0-1	Feb16 1-1	Nov24 2-1	Nov10 3-0	Oct06 4-1	Sep29 2-0	Dec08 3-3	Jan01 0-1	Oct20 2-2	Jan12 3-2
CLYDE	Jan19 0-0	Dec01 3-3		Feb13 6-2	Jan26 3-2	Nov03 3-1	Sep22 2-0	Dec22 4-3	Feb09 2-0	Jan02 0-2	Sep08 2-2	Nov17 4-4	Aug25 0-1	Jan05 2-3	Aug11 1-2	Sep05 1-2
FALKIRK	Jan01 3-1	Jan26 4-2	Sep01 4-1		Aug18 7-0	Nov24 3-5	Oct06 2-1	Oct20 3-4	Sep15 3-2	Jan12 3-3	Nov17 2-1	Dec08 3-2	Sep29 1-1	Dec29 0-3	Dec09 1-3	Nov03 3-1
HAMILTON A	Feb16 3-3	Dec22 0-1	Oct27 2-4	Dec01 3-1		Jan12 2-0	Aug25 1-1	Sep22 4-4	Oct20 2-2	Sep08 3-6	Aug11 0-1	Oct06 2-2	Nov10 3-4	Feb02 1-4	Dec15 0-3	Jan02 0-1
HEARTS	Nov10 1-2	Sep22 2-2	Feb02 1-1	Aug11 4-1	Oct13 4-1		Sep08 0-2	Jan02 1-4	Oct06 6-0	Aug25 0-0	Dec01 4-1	Apr15 1-1	Oct27 2-1	Feb16 1-1	Dec22 2-2	Dec15 1-2
HIBERNIAN	Sep15 1-1	Nov03 1-1	Dec29 3-2	Jan05 4-1	Dec08 1-2	Jan01 1-0		Jan12 4-1	Sep29 5-0	Oct20 0-0	Feb09 3-1	Nov24 6-1	Sep01 4-0	Aug18 2-1	Nov17 3-2	Jan26 4-0
KILMARNOCK	Aug18 1-4	Nov17 2-1	Sep15 0-0	Apr06 6-2	Dec29 0-2	Sep29 2-2	Oct13 3-4		Dec08 1-1	Oct06 2-5	Jan26 2-1	Jan01 1-1	Nov24 2-2	Sep01 0-7	Nov17 6-4	Feb09 1-3
MORTON	Feb02 3-2	Aug11 1-1	Nov10 1-1	Dec22 3-3	Jan19 3-1	Jan05 4-2	Jan02 0-2	Aug25 6-1		Dec01 3-3	Dec15 1-1	Oct13 7-1	Feb16 1-1	Oct27 2-2	Sep08 0-1	Sep22 4-4
MOTHERWELL	Dec29 1-3	Feb09 1-3	Sep29 3-2	Oct13 1-1	Jan01 0-0	Dec08 5-4	Jan19 0-0	Jan05 2-2	Aug18 2-1		Nov03 2-1	Sep01 2-1	Sep15 1-2	Nov24 1-2	Jan26 5-1	Nov17 1-3
PARTICK T	Sep29 1-1	Jan05 0-3	2-1	Feb16 4-3	Nov24 5-1	Aug25 1-3	Nov10 0-2	Oct27 5-3	Sep01 2-2	Feb02 3-0		Sep15 2-1	Dec29 1-3	Dec08 1-5	Jan12 1-0	Oct20 6-2
QUEEN OF SOUTH	Oct27 3-2	Jan02 0-0	Feb16 1-2	Aug25 0-2	Jan05 5-1	Oct20 3-3	Aug11 0-3	Sep08 2-1	Jan12 1-3	Dec15 5-3	Dec22		Feb02 3-3	Nov10 1-1	Sep22 2-2	Dec01 2-1
QUEEN'S PARK	Dec25 3-1	Aug16 2-0	Jan12 1-2	Jan02 2-0	Feb09 3-2	Jan26 0-1	Apr23 2-4	Aug11 2-3	Nov17 3-4	Dec22 4-0	Sep22 1-1	Nov03 2-3		Oct20 0-2	Dec01 3-0	Jan01 1-1
RANGERS	Oct13 3-1	Sep08 5-3	Dec25 3-1	Sep01 1-0	Nov03 5-1	Nov17 1-1	Dec01 3-2	Dec15 5-1	Jan26 4-4	Aug16 0-3	Aug16 4-2	Sep22 5-2	Jan19 2-1		Jan02 3-1	Dec22 1-0
ST MIRREN	Dec08 4-1	Jan19 1-2	Nov24 2-0	Nov10 0-0	Sep01 2-3	Sep15 3-1	Feb16 0-3	Feb02 4-1	Jan01 2-4	Oct27 0-0	Oct13 0-2	Dec29 4-1	Aug18 2-3	Sep29 2-2		Oct06 3-4
T LANARK	Nov24 3-1	Oct13 0-2	Dec08 1-6	Feb02 2-3	Sep29 7-2	Sep01 1-2	Oct27 4-1	Nov10 2-1	Dec29 0-2	Feb16 2-1	Jan19 4-2	Aug18 5-1	Sep08 1-0	Sep15 1-5	Jan05 3-1	

DIVISION B

	AIR	ALB	ALL	ARB	AYR	COW	DUM	DUN	DUU	DFA	EAF	RAI	STJ	STE
AIRDRIE		Jan01 2-5	Jan12 3-0	Nov03 5-0	Nov17 3-2	Oct13 5-2	Jan19 3-2	Sep01 3-3	Dec22 1-1	Sep15 1-1	Dec29 2-0	Nov24 4-2	Sep22 5-5	Aug18 6-0
ALBION R	Sep08 3-2		Aug11 6-2	Dec15 1-1	Dec08 3-2	Dec01 0-0	Nov10 3-0	Oct20 0-2	Aug25 1-0	Jan05 2-0	Sep29 3-2	Jan02 3-0	Oct27 1-6	Oct06 0-0
ALLOA	Oct20 2-3	Nov17 0-2		Oct06 4-4	Aug18 1-3	Oct27 2-0	Sep29 2-1	Sep15 0-1	Dec08 1-5	Sep01 1-1	Nov03 6-0	Jan05 3-1	Nov24 2-1	Jan01 4-0
ARBROATH	Jan02 0-5	Sep15 1-0	Dec29 1-2		Jan19 2-4	Sep29 4-1	Dec08 0-3	Aug18 1-4	Oct13 4-1	Nov24 3-1	Jan12 2-6	Nov17 2-1	Jan01 0-1	Sep01 0-3
AYR U	Aug11 0-3	Sep22 3-1	Nov10 2-6	Oct27 4-1		Aug25 3-1	Dec29 8-1	Dec01 2-3	Dec22 2-1	Dec15 1-1	Oct20 1-1	Jan02 1-0	Jan05 10-1	
COWDENBEATH	Jan05 2-3	Sep01 1-0	Jan19 1-1	Dec22 4-2	Nov24 1-1		Oct20 1-5	Jan02 2-6	Oct06 4-2	Jan01 1-0	Sep22 1-3	Aug18 2-1	Sep15 5-1	Nov17 5-1
DUMBARTON	Oct27 1-2	Aug18 4-0	Dec22 4-1	Sep22 2-0	Jan01 1-3	Jan12 3-1		Nov24 0-1	Nov03 2-1	Oct06 2-1	Oct13 3-0	Sep01 6-3	Nov17 3-5	Sep15 1-1
DUNDEE	Dec01 4-1	Jan12 2-0	Dec15 5-1	Nov10 8-0	Oct06 1-4	Nov03 5-0	Aug25 5-2		Sep08 1-0	Aug11 3-1	Nov17 2-1	Oct13 7-0	Sep15 5-1	Dec08 6-1
DUNDEE U	Sep29 4-2	Nov24 2-3	Sep22 2-5	Jan05 4-1	Sep01 3-2	Dec29 0-2	Jan02 4-1	Jan01 2-3		Nov17 1-2	Oct27 5-2	Sep15 0-7	Aug18 3-4	Oct20 7-0
DUNFERMLINE A	Dec15 5-2	Oct13 5-2	Dec01 2-3	Aug25 6-1	Sep29 2-3	Dec08 4-1	Dec29 1-1	Oct27 0-6	Aug11 7-0		Nov10 0-4	Dec08 8-1	Jan12 0-1	Nov03 5-1
EAST FIFE	Oct06 2-1	Dec22 0-0	Jan02 1-1	Oct20 8-0	Sep15 2-0	Dec08 6-2	Jan05 1-4	Nov17 2-0	Jan19 0-0	Aug18		Jan01 4-0	Sep01 2-1	Nov24 7-2
RAITH R	Aug25 4-0	Nov03 0-1	Oct13 1-2	Aug11 3-2	Jan12 2-3	Nov10 3-2	Dec01 1-1	Sep29 3-5	Dec15 5-0	Sep22 3-2	Sep08 0-2		Dec29 4-5	Oct27 1-2
ST JOHNSTONE	Dec08 0-0	Jan19 3-0	Dec01 0-4	Sep08 4-6	Nov03 3-2	Dec15 1-1	Aug11 3-3	Jan05 4-1	Nov10 3-0	Oct20 1-1	Dec01 1-4	Oct06 5-3		Sep29 4-1
STENHOUSEMUIR	Nov10 0-2	Dec29 0-1	Sep08 3-2	Dec01 3-2	Oct13 0-6	Aug11 4-3	Dec15 2-2	Sep22 1-5	Jan12 2-2	Jan02 1-3	Aug25 1-2	Jan19 2-2	Dec22 4-1	

DIVISION A FINAL TABLE

	P	W	D	L	F	A	Pts
Rangers	30	22	4	4	85	41	48
Hibernian	30	17	6	7	67	37	40
Aberdeen	30	16	6	8	73	41	38
Celtic	30	12	11	7	55	44	35
Clyde	30	11	9	10	64	54	31
Motherwell	30	11	9	10	54	55	31
Hearts	30	11	8	11	63	57	30
Queen's Park	30	11	8	11	60	60	30
T Lanark	30	14	2	14	63	68	30
Morton	30	9	11	10	72	69	29
Falkirk	30	11	5	14	62	70	27
Partick T	30	11	4	15	54	65	26
Queen of South	30	9	6	15	62	82	24
St Mirren	30	9	5	16	54	70	23
Kilmarnock	30	7	8	15	56	87	22
Hamilton A	30	5	6	19	44	88	16

DIVISION B FINAL TABLE

	P	W	D	L	F	A	Pts
Dundee	26	21	2	3	92	28	44
East Fife	26	15	4	7	64	34	34
Ayr U	26	15	4	7	69	43	34
Airdrie	26	14	5	7	69	50	33
St Johnstone	26	12	6	8	66	60	30
Albion R	26	14	2	10	45	41	30
Alloa	26	12	4	10	59	53	28
Dumbarton	26	11	4	11	59	54	26
Dunfermline A	26	10	4	12	63	47	24
Cowdenbeath	26	8	5	13	43	62	21
Stenhousemuir	26	6	5	15	36	89	17
Dundee U	26	6	3	17	46	70	15
Raith R	26	6	2	18	48	80	14
Arbroath	26	6	2	18	40	88	14

There were no Scottish FA Cup matches in 1945-46

SFA Cup

1st Round

Jan 25	Aberdeen	2	Partick T	1
Jan 25	Albion R	3	Airdrie	0
Jan 25	Alloa	0	Hibernian	8
Jan 25	Arbroath	2	Stenhousemuir	2
Feb 1	Clacknacuddin	1	E Stirling	1
Jan 25	Dundee	2	Celtic	1
Jan 25	East Fife	6	Dunfermline A	2
Jan 25	Falkirk	2	Kilmarnock	0
Jan 25	Hamilton A	1	T Lanark	1
Jan 25	Hearts	3	St Johnstone	0
Jan 25	Morton	4	Edinburgh C	0
Jan 25	Motherwell	3	Forfar A	0
Jan 25	Peterhead	1	Ayr U	5
Jan 25	Queen of South	3	Raith R	4
Jan 25	Queen's Park	3	Dundee U	0
Jan 25	Rangers	2	Clyde	1
Jan 25	St Mirren	2	Dumbarton	3
Jan 25	Stranraer	0	Cowdenbeath	5

Replays

Feb 8	E Stirling	5	Clacknacuddin	1
Feb 8	Stenhousemuir	0	Arbroath	2
Feb 8	T Lanark	2	Hamilton A	1

2nd Round

Feb 8	Aberdeen	8	Ayr U	0
Feb 15	East Fife	5	E Stirling	1

3rd Round

Feb 22	Aberdeen	1	Morton	1
Feb 22	Arbroath	5	Raith R	4
Feb 22	Dumbarton	2	T Lanark	0
Feb 22	Dundee	3	Albion R	0
Feb 22	East Fife	3	Queen's Park	1
Feb 22	Falkirk	0	Motherwell	0
Mar 8	Hearts	2	Cowdenbeath	1
Feb 22	Rangers	0	Hibernian	0

Replays

Mar 8	Hibernian	2	Rangers	0
Mar 8	Morton	1	Aberdeen	2
Mar 8	Motherwell	1	Falkirk	0

4th Round

Mar 15	Arbroath	2	Hearts	1
Mar 29	Dundee	1	Aberdeen	2
Mar 15	East Fife	0	Motherwell	2
Mar 15	Hibernian	2	Dumbarton	0

Semi-finals

Apr 12	Aberdeen	2	Arbroath	0
	played at Dens Park			
Mar 29	Hibernian	2	Motherwell	1
	played at Hampden Park			

Final

Apr 19	Aberdeen	2	Hibernian	1
	played at Hampden Park			

League Cup results for 1946-47 are detailed on page 180.

DIVISION A

	ABERDEEN	CELTIC	CLYDE	FALKIRK	HAMILTON A	HEARTS	HIBERNIAN	KILMARNOCK	MORTON	MOTHERWELL	PARTICK T	QUEEN OF SOUTH	QUEEN'S PARK	RANGERS	ST MIRREN	T LANARK
ABERDEEN		Aug17 6-2	Feb01 2-1	Jan01 0-4	May14 3-0	Nov23 2-1	Aug28 2-1	Aug14 1-0	May05 2-2	Dec21 3-1	Sep14 2-2	Nov02 0-0	Nov16 3-1	Sep04 1-0	May03 4-2	Dec07 1-0
CELTIC	Jan02 1-5		Dec14 3-3	Apr26 0-0	Dec28 2-1	Aug21 2-3	Nov30 4-1	Aug30 4-2	Nov30 1-2	May03 3-2	Mar22 2-0	Jan04 2-0	Dec25 1-0	Sep07 2-3	Feb22 2-1	Sep04 1-4
CLYDE	Aug31 0-2	Aug14 4-0		Aug17 2-1	Nov02 0-2	Feb08 3-3	Dec21 2-1	Aug28 4-2	Nov23 1-2	Sep14 3-3	Jan01 2-4	Mar08 1-1	Jan18 2-5	Nov16 2-4	Dec07 2-2	Jan11 0-3
FALKIRK	Sep07 2-0	Nov02 1-4	Jan02 1-2		Dec14 6-0	Aug10 3-3	May17 2-3	Feb01 3-3	Dec28 1-1	Sep04 5-2	Apr19 6-1	Aug24 2-3	Apr24 3-1	Aug21 0-5	Nov23 2-3	Mar29 2-2
HAMILTON A	Nov30 2-5	Aug28 2-2	Feb15 1-2	Aug14 1-4		Sep04 3-1	Jan11 0-0	Dec21 2-2	Feb01 2-2	Jan01 2-2	Dec07 1-3	Mar22 2-3	Apr19 1-2	Nov09 0-6	Aug17 1-4	Sep14 2-2
HEARTS	May17 4-0	Dec21 2-1	Nov09 1-1	Dec07 1-1	Jan18 4-3		Jan01 2-3	Sep14 2-0	Apr05 2-0	Jan11 2-0	Aug14 2-1	Aug31 1-4	Mar29 1-1	Nov30 3-2	Aug28 2-1	Aug17 4-1
HIBERNIAN	Dec28 1-1	Apr12 2-0	Aug21 1-0	Nov16 2-2	Aug24 3-2	Sep07 0-1		Sep04 6-0	Jan04 1-1	Feb01 1-2	Nov23 5-1	Aug10 9-1	Jan02 3-1	Dec14 1-1	Apr26 1-0	Nov02 4-1
KILMARNOCK	Dec14 2-1	Mar29 1-2	Dec28 2-2	Aug31 2-1	Apr12 1-1	Jan04 0-0	Jan18 3-5		Aug24 2-3	Mar22 2-0	Sep02 3-1	Sep07 1-3	Aug10 2-2	Jan02 0-2	Apr05 1-5	Nov23 0-2
MORTON	Nov09 0-0	Dec07 2-1	Mar15 2-2	Aug28 3-3	Aug31 2-1	Nov16 1-1	Sep14 0-2	Feb08 0-0		Aug14 3-1	Aug17 3-4	Jan18 4-1	Nov30 5-4	Feb15 0-1	Jan01 4-0	Dec21 2-0
MOTHERWELL	Aug21 2-2	Nov23 1-2	Jan04 3-3	Jan18 2-0	Sep07 4-0	Aug24 0-2	Aug31 2-1	Nov16 2-1	Dec14 0-1		Apr26 3-3	Jan02 5-1	Dec28 1-0	Aug10 2-4	Nov02 4-2	Apr19 2-1
PARTICK T	Jan04 4-0	Nov16 4-1	Sep07 1-3	Nov30 4-1	Apr12 4-1	Dec14 1-2	May03 0-2	Apr12 5-2	Jan02 3-1	Nov02 0-2		Dec28 1-2	Apr12 4-0	Sep21 3-2	Sep04 3-0	Mar08 3-1
QUEEN OF SOUTH	Apr28 1-5	Sep14 3-1	Nov30 1-3	Jan11 2-2	Nov16 2-3	Feb01 1-3	Dec07 1-1	Jan01 1-1	Sep04 2-2	Aug17 1-6	Aug28 0-0		Nov09 1-4	Feb08 0-2	Dec21 3-2	Aug14 4-1
QUEEN'S PARK	Apr26 0-0	Jan11 1-3	Sep04 1-3	Sep14 0-1	Nov23 2-1	Nov02 2-2	Apr12 0-1	Dec07 0-1	May03 2-3	Aug28 1-1	Apr12 2-6	Apr12 4-1		Feb01 4-1	Aug14 3-2	Jan01 0-0
RANGERS	Jan18 1-0	Aug17 1-1	Mar29 5-0	Dec21 2-1	Apr07 4-1	Aug14 1-2	Jan11 1-2	Nov02 3-2	Dec07 2-1	Jan11 4-0	Nov23 2-1	Aug31 2-0			Sep14 4-0	Aug31 8-1
ST MIRREN	Aug24 4-2	Aug31 0-1	Aug10 1-3	Apr12 1-1	Jan02 1-0	Dec28 0-1	Nov30 1-3	Nov09 1-1	Sep07 1-1	Apr21 1-2	Aug18 1-4	Aug20 1-2	Dec14 3-2	Jan04 1-0		Mar22 2-4
T LANARK	Aug10 0-3	Jan18 0-0	Dec25 5-3	Nov09 4-2	Apr07 2-1	Jan02 4-1	May10 0-2	Mar15 1-4	Aug21 1-4	Nov30 2-1	Dec14 4-1	Sep07 3-4	Dec28 3-4	Nov16 5-1		

DIVISION B

	AIRDRIE	ALBION R	ALLOA	ARBROATH	AYR U	COWDENBEATH	DUMBARTON	DUNDEE	DUNDEE U	DUNFERMLINE A	EAST FIFE	RAITH R	ST JOHNSTONE	STENHOUSEMUIR
AIRDRIE		Aug24 1-2	Nov30 3-2	Jan04 3-1	Aug10 2-1	Jan18 7-2	Mar22 5-4	Dec28 2-1	Apr19 5-0	Mar08 6-4	Apr26 2-2	Sep07 1-1	Nov09 2-1	Jan02 3-1
ALBION R	Jan01 0-1		Dec21 1-6	Sep14 3-1	Jan11 2-1	Aug31 1-1	Aug31 3-0	Feb01 2-2	May03 5-1	Dec07 5-1	Nov09 1-4	Aug31 2-1	Nov23 1-1	Dec14 1-1
ALLOA	Apr05 1-0	Aug10 2-2		Dec14 1-1	Jan02 3-2	Nov23 0-2	Nov02 0-10	Mar08 4-1	Nov09 1-1	Dec28 4-1	Jan04 1-1	Dec07 4-1	Sep07 1-0	Aug24 2-0
ARBROATH	Nov16 2-5	Mar08 3-3	Apr19 1-1		Mar22 2-5	Nov02 1-0	Apr26 2-3	Jan02 1-4	Jan18 5-4	Sep07 1-2	Nov30 3-2	Aug10 2-3	Aug24 2-1	Dec28 3-3
AYR U	Dec21 2-5	Nov09 1-3	Aug31 4-1	Nov23 4-0		Apr26 6-1	Jan01 2-1	Dec14 2-6	Aug17 3-3	Feb15 3-1	Sep14 2-1	Jan04 0-1	Jan04 2-0	Dec07 4-2
COWDENBEATH	Dec07 2-1	Dec28 2-4	Apr23 2-0	Apr05 3-3	Sep07		Apr12 2-1	Nov16 2-8	Mar29 1-3	Aug24 2-3	Nov09 3-3	Jan02 3-4	Apr19 2-2	Aug10 1-2
DUMBARTON	Nov23 2-3	Jan02 1-1	Feb15 2-2	Nov09 0-1	Aug24 2-2	Nov30 5-1		Sep07 2-1	Jan04 0-2	Dec14 1-2	Jan18 1-0	Dec28 1-1	Aug10 2-3	Mar08 4-1
DUNDEE	Aug17 1-1	Nov30 6-2	Sep14 6-2	Aug31 5-0	May03 6-2	Jan04 6-2	Apr05 4-0		Jan01 2-0	Mar22 10-0	Dec14 2-0	Apr23 5-2	Jan18 2-0	Nov09 4-1
DUNDEE U	Nov02 1-2	Sep07 1-3	Jan11 6-2	Dec07 1-3	Dec28 5-1	Dec14 3-2	Nov16 2-1	Aug24		Aug10 3-0	Nov23 2-1	Apr14 4-1	Jan02 2-4	Apr12 2-2
DUNFERMLINE A	Sep14 0-5	Jan18 5-1	Aug17 0-3	Mar29 3-1	Nov02 4-0	Jan01 2-2	Apr19 3-2	Nov23 2-5	Dec21 4-3		Aug31 0-2	Jan11 4-1	Nov30 0-4	Jan04 2-2
EAST FIFE	Dec14 2-2	Apr19 2-1	Nov16 3-1	May03 2-1	Jan08 6-2	Dec07 5-0	Apr10 1-0	Feb01 1-2	Jan02 2-1			Aug24 4-4	Dec28 1-0	Nov02 7-1
RAITH R	Apr07 1-2	Jan04 2-0	Jan18 3-2	Dec21 1-0	Nov30 4-1	Aug31 3-0	Aug17 5-1	Nov02 1-4	Sep14 5-1	Nov09 0-0	Jan01		Mar29 2-1	Nov23 1-1
ST JOHNSTONE	Jan11 2-4	Mar22 3-0	Apr07 0-3	Jan01 1-1	Nov16 7-2	Sep14 0-2	Dec21 5-2	Dec07 1-5	Apr31 3-1	Apr12 2-1	Aug17 1-4	Dec14 2-0		Nov02 1-1
STENHOUSEMUIR	Aug31 0-5	Apr23 4-1	Jan01 3-0	Aug17 1-2	Jan18 3-1	Dec21 4-2	Sep14 0-1	Jan11 0-0	Nov30 3-2	Nov16 1-2	Mar29 0-1	Mar22 4-1	Apr26 2-0	

DIVISION A FINAL TABLE

	P	W	D	L	F	A	Pts
Rangers	30	21	4	5	76	26	46
Hibernian	30	19	6	5	69	33	44
Aberdeen	30	16	7	7	58	41	39
Hearts	30	16	6	8	52	43	38
Partick T	30	16	3	11	74	59	35
Morton	30	12	10	8	58	45	34
Celtic	30	13	6	11	53	55	32
Motherwell	30	12	5	13	58	54	29
T Lanark	30	11	6	13	56	64	28
Clyde	30	9	9	12	55	65	27
Falkirk	30	8	10	12	62	61	26
Queen of South	30	9	8	13	44	69	26
Queen's Park	30	8	6	16	47	60	22
St Mirren	30	9	4	17	47	65	22
Kilmarnock	30	6	9	15	44	66	21
Hamilton A	30	2	7	21	38	85	11

DIVISION B FINAL TABLE

	P	W	D	L	F	A	Pts
Dundee	26	21	3	2	113	30	45
Airdrie	26	19	4	3	78	38	42
East Fife	26	12	7	7	58	39	31
Albion R	26	10	7	9	50	54	27
Alloa	26	11	5	10	51	57	27
Raith R	26	10	6	10	45	52	26
Stenhousemuir	26	8	7	11	43	53	23
Dunfermline A	26	10	3	13	50	72	23
St Johnstone	26	9	4	13	45	47	22
Dundee U	26	9	4	13	53	60	22
Ayr U	26	9	2	15	56	73	20
Arbroath	26	7	6	13	42	63	20
Dumbarton	26	7	4	15	41	54	18
Cowdenbeath	26	6	6	14	44	77	18

Season 1947-48

SFA Cup

1st Round

Jan 24	Albion R	0	Hibernian	2
Jan 24	Arbroath	9	Babcock & W	1
Jan 24	Ayr U	1	Morton	2
Jan 24	Berwick R	2	Cowdenbeath	4
Jan 17	Clacknacuddin	0	St Johnstone	2
Jan 24	Dundee	2	Hearts	4
Jan 24	East Fife	2	Kilmarnock	0
Jan 24	Inverness C	1	Falkirk	6
Jan 24	Motherwell	2	Hamilton A	2
Jan 24	Queen of South	1	Stenhousemuir	0
Jan 24	St Mirren	8	Shawfield	0
Jan 24	Stranraer	0	Rangers	1

Replays

Jan 31	Hamilton A	0	Motherwell	2

2nd Round

Feb 7	Airdrie	2	Hearts	1
Feb 7	Alloa	0	Queen of South	1
Feb 7	Celtic	3	Cowdenbeath	0
Feb 7	Clyde	2	Dunfermline A	1
Feb 7	East Fife	5	St Johnstone	1
Feb 7	Hibernian	4	Arbroath	0
Feb 7	Montrose	2	Duns	0
Feb 7	Morton	3	Falkirk	2
Feb 7	Motherwell	1	T Lanark	0
Feb 7	Nithsdale W	0	Aberdeen	5
Feb 7	Partick T	4	Dundee U	3
Feb 7	Peterhead	1	Dumbarton	2
Feb 7	Queen's Park	8	Deveronvale	2
Feb 7	Rangers	4	Leith A	0
Feb 7	St Mirren	2	E Stirling	0
Feb 7	Stirling A	2	Raith R	4

3rd Round

Feb 21	Airdrie	3	Raith R	0
Feb 21	Celtic	1	Motherwell	0
Feb 21	Dumbarton	0	East Fife	1
Feb 21	Hibernian	4	Aberdeen	2
Feb 21	Montrose	2	Queen of South	1
Feb 21	Morton	3	Queen's Park	0
Feb 21	Rangers	3	Partick T	0
Feb 21	St Mirren	2	Clyde	0

4th Round

Mar 6	Airdrie	0	Morton	3
Mar 6	Celtic	4	Montrose	0
Mar 6	Hibernian	3	St Mirren	1
Mar 6	Rangers	1	East Fife	0

Semi-finals

Mar 27	Celtic	0	Morton	1
	played at Ibrox			
Mar 27	Hibernian	0	Rangers	1
	played at Hampden Park			

Final

Apr 17	Morton	1	Rangers	1
	played at Hampden Park			

Replay

Apr 21	Morton	0	Rangers	1
	played at Hampden Park			

League Cup results for 1947-48 are detailed on pages 180-181.

DIVISION A

	ABERDEEN	AIRDRIE	CELTIC	CLYDE	DUNDEE	FALKIRK	HEARTS	HIBERNIAN	MORTON	MOTHERWELL	PARTICK T	QUEEN OF SOUTH	QUEEN'S PARK	RANGERS	ST MIRREN	T LANARK
ABERDEEN		Feb28 3-0	Oct04 3-1	Dec06 3-2	Sep20 3-2	Oct18 1-2	Nov15 1-1	Aug13 0-2	Mar20 2-1	Jan03 2-1	Feb14 0-1	Nov01 2-2	Nov22 6-0	Apr03 1-1	Dec27 5-0	Jan17 2-3
AIRDRIE	Nov08 2-1		Aug13 3-2	Mar13 1-3	Oct18 2-0	Jan03 3-1	Nov29 1-1	Dec27 0-3	Dec06 0-3	Sep20 1-5	Jan17 0-1	Apr03 6-1	Nov15 2-5	May01 1-2	Oct04 1-4	Feb14 2-1
CELTIC	Jan10 1-0	Dec20 0-0		Jan31 0-0	Dec06 1-1	Nov08 0-3	Dec25 4-2	Apr03 2-4	Oct11 3-2	Sep27 0-1	Jan24 1-2	Oct25 4-3	Aug27 4-0	Jan02 0-4	Nov15 0-0	Apr10 1-3
CLYDE	Mar26 1-3	Nov22 5-1	Oct18 2-0		Oct04 1-4	Aug13 1-1	Dec13 2-2	Jan30 2-2	Nov01 3-2	Feb14 3-2	Sep20 2-4	Mar20 5-2	Oct25 2-0	Nov15 1-2	Jan17 3-2	Dec27 1-1
DUNDEE	Jan01 0-0	Sep27 6-0	Apr17 2-3	Jan10 7-0		Feb21 4-0	Oct06 2-1	May01 3-1	Dec20 0-4	Mar13 2-0	Dec13 2-2	Aug27 1-0	Oct25 2-1	Dec25 1-3	Nov08 6-1	Nov29 5-2
FALKIRK	Jan31 3-1	Jan05 0-0	Feb28 0-1	Dec20 1-1	Mar06 3-2		Apr17 0-2	Nov22 3-1	Aug27 4-1	Apr03 2-2	Mar20 1-2	Jan01 1-1	Apr10 3-0	Jan10 1-5	Apr24 1-1	Dec06 8-1
HEARTS	Mar06 1-1	Mar20 2-2	Jan03 1-1	Apr03 3-2	Jan17 0-1	Feb14 1-3		Sep20 2-1	Feb28 3-0	Dec27 0-1	Oct18 1-2	Nov22 1-0	Nov01 1-0	Dec06 1-2	Aug13 3-2	Oct04 1-3
HIBERNIAN	Dec20 4-0	Aug27 7-1	Dec13 3-1	Sep27 2-1	Nov15 2-1	Mar13 2-1	Jan01 3-1		Oct25 1-1	Apr19 6-0	Apr17 4-0	Oct11 1-0	Jan10 6-1	Jan31 5-0	Nov29 5-0	Nov08 8-0
MORTON	Nov29 0-1	May05 1-1	Jan17 4-0	May03 0-1	Aug13 3-0	Dec27 2-1	Nov08 1-1	Feb14 1-2		Oct18 2-3	Oct04 0-2	Apr24 0-1	Dec13 0-1	Mar13 0-1	Sep20 2-2	Jan03 2-2
MOTHERWELL	Apr17 2-1	Jan01 2-0	Mar20 0-1	Oct25 4-1	Nov22 0-2	Dec13 4-1	Aug27 4-1	Apr09 0-2		Feb28 2-0	Jan10 3-1	Dec20 0-2	Apr24 0-1	Mar27 0-1	Oct11 2-1	
PARTICK T	Oct25 2-1	Oct11 8-2	Nov15 3-5	Jan01 1-2	Apr03 6-2	Nov29 0-2	Jan31 1-1	Dec06 1-1	Jan10 1-2	Nov08 2-1		Dec20 4-0	Sep27 5-1	Aug27 2-0	Apr09 3-1	Mar13 2-2
QUEEN OF SOUTH	Apr09 0-0	Dec13 3-3	Feb14 2-0	Nov29 3-0	Dec27 5-2	Sep20 6-6	Mar13 0-1	Jan17 0-3	Nov15 4-3	Oct04 3-0	Aug13 0-1		Mar27 3-1	Nov08 0-3	Jan03 2-3	Oct18 2-1
QUEEN'S PARK	Mar13 3-1	Apr20 2-1	Dec27 3-2	Nov08 2-4	Feb14 0-1	Jan17 1-4	Apr24 0-0	Apr03 2-3	Aug13 0-3	Aug13 2-5	Dec06 1-2		Nov29 1-4	Oct18 3-0	Jan01 2-2	
RANGERS	Dec13 4-0	Nov01 3-0	Sep20 2-0	Apr26 2-1	Jan03 2-1	Mar29 1-1	May03 1-2	Oct18 2-1	Nov22 1-1	Jan17 2-0	Dec27 2-3	Feb28 1-2	Mar20 0-2		Feb14 3-2	Aug13 5-2
ST MIRREN	Aug26 3-0	Jan10 2-1	Nov22 1-2	Oct11 1-1	Feb28 4-1	Nov15 1-1	Dec20 1-0	Mar20 2-4	Jan01 0-4	Dec06 4-2	Nov01 3-1	Sep27 0-1	Jan31 6-1	Oct25 2-1		Apr03 1-0
T LANARK	Dec25 3-2	Jan24 2-2	Mar29 5-1	Aug27 2-1	Mar20 1-4	Mar26 2-0	Jan10 4-1	Feb28 1-4	Sep27 2-1	Nov15 0-3	Nov22 1-2	Jan31 5-1	Sep20 4-2	D20 0-1	Dec13 1-4	

DIVISION A

	ALBION R	ALLOA	ARBROATH	AYR U	COWDENBEATH	DUMBARTON	DUNDEE U	DUNFERMLINE A	EAST FIFE	HAMILTON A	KILMARNOCK	LEITH A	RAITH R	ST JOHNSTONE	STENHOUSEMUIR	STIRLING A
ALBION R		Dec13 3-1	Nov01 2-0	Dec20 3-1	Mar27 5-3	Feb28 1-0	Aug27 2-1	Sep27 1-4	Apr24 1-2	Jan01 2-2	Nov22 2-0	Jan10 1-1	Oct11 1-3	Oct25 2-2	Jan31 2-2	Mar20 2-0
ALLOA	Apr03 1-3		Feb28 3-1	Jan10 4-4	Nov15 1-2	Nov01 4-1	Dec20 3-1	Aug27 3-1	Dec06 3-3	Dec25 4-1	Mar20 2-2	Oct25 5-2	Jan31 0-7	Oct11 4-2	Apr10 3-1	Nov22 3-1
ARBROATH	Feb21 1-3	Nov08 1-1		Sep27 2-2	Apr03 3-1	Jan10 2-3	Dec06 6-0	Nov29 2-1	Aug27 1-4	Nov22 2-4	Mar06 5-1	Jan05 3-2	Dec06 1-6	Nov22 2-0	Oct11 1-0	Dec06 1-2
AYR U	Aug13 0-2	Oct04 2-0	Oct18 1-0		Jan17 2-1	Feb14 1-1	Dec13 3-3	Nov01 0-0	Jan03 2-3	Feb28 5-1	Sep20 2-4	Mar06 2-1	Nov22 6-0	Mar06 2-0	Feb07 0-0	Dec27 2-0
COWDENBEATH	Dec06 1-3	Sep27 0-0	Nov22 2-1	Oct11 0-0		Mar20 2-1	Oct25 6-2	Jan01 3-0	Apr03 0-3	Dec20 0-1	Nov01 1-0	Aug27 1-2	Jan10 1-1	Jan31 3-1	Dec25 0-3	Feb28 5-2
DUMBARTON	Nov08 1-1	Apr24 3-1	Dec13 3-3	Oct25 3-1	Nov29 1-1		Jan31 3-2	Mar13 4-2	Jan10 2-4	Nov22 0-4	Jan24 1-2	Nov15 5-1	Mar20 4-2	Dec06 2-4	Aug27 2-2	Nov15 5-1
DUNDEE U	Dec27 3-0	Aug13 5-3	Oct04 0-4	Apr03 2-0	Feb14 0-1	Oct18 0-1		Feb28 0-4	Jan17 3-2	Nov22 2-3	Jan03 2-1	Nov15 3-0	Mar20 3-3	Dec06 4-2	Nov01 2-3	Sep20 2-3
DUNFERMLINE A	Jan03 4-0	Dec27 0-2	Aug13 4-3	Apr17 2-1	Sep20 3-4	Jan17 5-1	Nov08 5-3		Oct04 1-1	Mar27 2-1	Feb14 3-1	Nov29 6-1	Dec13 2-4	Mar13 4-3	Mar06 5-2	Oct18 3-5
EAST FIFE	Nov15 3-0	Mar27 6-0	Mar20 3-0	Dec24 3-2	Sep20 3-0	Nov22 6-3	Apr14 5-1	Jan10 4-2		Apr17 5-0	Feb28 1-3	Dec20 5-1	Jan01 3-2	Apr07 2-0	Apr07 4-0	Jan01 6-4
HAMILTON A	Sep20 3-0	Jan03 3-2	Dec27 3-0	Nov08 5-0	Aug13 1-1	Oct04 6-5	Mar13 6-0	Dec06 1-0	Oct18 2-2		Jan17 3-1	Feb21 3-0	Nov15 1-2	Nov29 1-3	Apr03 5-2	Feb14 2-0
KILMARNOCK	Mar13 1-4	Nov29 5-1	Nov15 2-1	Jan01 4-4	Feb21 1-3	Dec06 2-2	Sep27 5-2	Oct25 3-0	Nov08 0-2	Oct11 3-0		Jan31 6-2	Aug27 7-1	Dec20 1-0	Jan10 7-2	Apr03 2-2
LEITH A	Oct04 1-3	Jan03 3-0	Jan03 2-4	Dec06 1-1	Dec27 2-2	Sep20 4-2	Mar06 1-0	Aug13 3-1	Nov01 0-1	Nov01 0-4	Oct18 3-1		Feb28 1-1	Apr03 1-1	Nov22 4-4	Apr03 2-3
RAITH R	Jan17 2-3	Oct18 7-1	Feb14 2-0	Mar13 1-3	Oct04 0-0	Aug13 5-1	Nov29 1-3	Apr03 0-4	Sep20 3-3	Mar06 4-3	Dec27 5-1	Nov08		Apr24 6-1	Dec06 1-6	Jan03 2-2
ST JOHNSTONE	Feb14 0-1	Jan24 5-2	Sep20 1-0	Nov15 4-1	Oct18 3-4	Jan03 4-0	Apr24 0-1	Nov22 2-2	Dec27 0-2	Mar20 2-3	Aug13 2-2	Dec13 2-0	Nov01 2-5		Feb28 2-2	Oct04 3-2
STENHOUSEMUIR	Oct18 3-3	Jan03 0-0	Jan17 0-3	Nov29 0-3	Dec27 2-1	Apr24 4-2	Nov22 3-0	Dec06 3-3	Feb14 1-5	Dec13 1-1	Jan10 1-0	Mar13 2-2	Oct04 1-1	Nov08 2-6		Aug13 0-0
STIRLING A	Nov29 7-0	Mar13 0-1	Mar27 0-2	Aug27 4-1	Nov08 2-2	Mar06 3-1	Jan24 2-0	Jan31 3-4	Apr21 0-2	Oct25 2-1	Dec13 7-1	Oct11 3-3	Sep27 4-4	Jan10 1-5	Dec20	

DIVISION A FINAL TABLE

	P	W	D	L	F	A	Pts
Hibernian	30	22	4	4	86	27	48
Rangers	30	21	4	5	64	28	46
Partick T	30	16	4	10	61	42	36
Dundee	30	15	3	12	67	51	33
St Mirren	30	13	5	12	54	58	31
Clyde	30	12	7	11	52	57	31
Falkirk	30	10	10	10	55	48	30
Motherwell	30	13	3	14	45	47	29
Hearts	30	10	8	12	37	42	28
Aberdeen	30	10	7	13	45	45	27
T Lanark	30	10	6	14	56	73	26
Celtic	30	10	5	15	41	56	25
Queen of South	30	10	5	15	49	74	25
Morton	30	9	6	15	47	43	24
Airdrie	30	7	7	16	40	78	21
Queen's Park	30	9	2	19	45	75	20

DIVISION B FINAL TABLE

	P	W	D	L	F	A	Pts
East Fife	30	25	3	2	103	36	53
Albion R	30	19	4	7	58	49	42
Hamilton A	30	17	6	7	75	45	40
Raith R	30	14	6	10	83	66	34
Cowdenbeath	30	12	8	10	56	53	32
Kilmarnock	30	13	4	13	72	62	30
Dunfermline A	30	13	3	14	72	71	29
Stirling A	30	11	6	13	65	66	28
St Johnstone	30	11	5	14	69	63	27
Ayr U	30	9	9	12	59	61	27
Dumbarton	30	9	7	14	66	79	25
Alloa*	30	10	6	14	56	77	24
Arbroath	30	10	3	17	55	62	23
Stenhousemuir	30	6	11	13	53	83	23
Dundee U	30	10	2	18	58	88	22
Leith A	30	6	7	17	45	84	19

* Two points deducted for fielding unregistered players.

Season 1948-49

SFA Cup
1st Round
Jan 22	Alloa	8	Montrose	3
Jan 22	Arbroath	3	Partick T	4
Jan 22	Ayr U	2	Queen's Park	1
Jan 22	Clyde	2	Fraserburgh	0
Jan 22	Cowdenbeath	6	Keith	2
Jan 22	Dumbarton	5	Kilmarnock	2
Jan 22	Dundee	5	St Johnstone	1
Jan 22	Dundee U	4	Celtic	3
Jan 22	East Fife	2	Falkirk	1
Jan 22	Forfar A	0	Hibernian	4
Jan 22	Hamilton A	1	Albion R	2
Jan 22	Hearts	4	Airdrie	1
Jan 22	Inverness Cal	2	Morton	2
Jan 22	Leith A	0	Raith R	1
Jan 22	Motherwell	3	Stranraer	0
Jan 22	Queen of South	2	E Stirling	0
Jan 22	Rangers	6	Elgin C	1
Jan 22	St Mirren	2	Stirling A	0
Jan 22	Stenhousemuir	2	Dunfermline A	0
Jan 22	T Lanark	2	Aberdeen	1

Replays
Jan 26	Morton	2	Inverness Cal	0

2nd Round
Feb 5	Ayr U	0	Morton	2
Feb 9	Clyde	3	Alloa	1
Feb 5	Cowdenbeath	1	East Fife	2
Feb 5	Dumbarton	1	Dundee U	1
Feb 5	Dundee	0	St Mirren	0
Feb 5	Hearts	3	T Lanark	1
Feb 5	Hibernian	1	Raith R	1
Feb 5	Motherwell	0	Rangers	3
Feb 5	Partick T	3	Queen of South	0
Feb 9	Stenhousemuir	5	Albion R	1

Replays
Feb 9	Dundee U	1	Dumbarton	3
Feb 9	Raith R	3	Hibernian	4
Feb 9	St Mirren	1	Dundee	2

3rd Round
Feb 19	Clyde	2	Morton	0
	played at Ibrox			
Feb 19	Hearts	3	Dumbarton	0

4th Round
Mar 5	Hearts	2	Dundee	4
Mar 5	Hibernian	0	East Fife	2
Mar 5	Rangers	4	Partick T	0
Mar 5	Stenhousemuir	0	Clyde	1

Semi-finals
Mar 26	Clyde	2	Dundee	2
	played at Easter Road			
Mar 26	East Fife	0	Rangers	3
	played at Hampden Park			

Replay
Apr 4	Clyde	2	Dundee	1
	played at Hampden Park			

Final
Apr 23	Clyde	1	Rangers	4
	played at Hampden Park			

League Cup results for 1948-49 are detailed on pages 181-182.

DIVISION A

	ABERDEEN	ALBION R	CELTIC	CLYDE	DUNDEE	EAST FIFE	FALKIRK	HEARTS	HIBERNIAN	MORTON	MOTHERWELL	PARTICK T	QUEEN OF SOUTH	RANGERS	ST MIRREN	T LANARK
ABERDEEN		Mar12 4-0	Aug18 1-0	Oct23 4-4	Jan01 1-3	Nov20 1-4	Nov06 2-2	Dec04 1-2	Sep04 0-0	Apr02 2-0	Aug28 4-2	Feb26 1-2	Dec11 1-2	Feb12 0-2	Jan29 2-2	Jan08 2-0
ALBION R	Mar05 2-1		Sep04 3-3	Apr15 1-2	Nov06 0-6	Feb12 0-3	Aug28 2-0	Dec18 1-5	Jan29 0-3	Oct23 2-1	Jan01 1-3	Jan08 2-3	Dec04 1-3	Apr30 1-4	Aug18 1-2	Feb26 1-5
CELTIC	Dec25 3-0	Jan15 3-0		Apr18 2-1	Oct23 0-1	Nov13 0-1	Nov07 4-4	Mar05 2-0	Feb12 1-2	Aug14 0-0	Dec18 3-2	Mar19 3-0	Sep01 2-2	Jan01 0-1	Mar26 2-1	Apr16 1-0
CLYDE	Apr09 0-0	Dec11 1-0	Nov06 0-4		Aug18 3-3	Apr02 2-4	Sep04 3-3	Oct30 3-5	Aug28 0-3	Nov20 1-0	Feb26 0-1	Jan01 4-0	Mar12 1-3	Dec04 4-1	Jan08 2-0	Jan29 1-1
DUNDEE	Aug21 3-0	Feb19 5-0	Apr11 3-2	Dec25 3-1		Sep01 2-5	Apr20 3-1	Aug14 2-1	Mar19 4-3	Jan15 3-1	Apr27 2-1	Apr23 4-2	Nov13 2-1	Jan03 3-1	Nov27 1-0	Dec18 1-1
EAST FIFE	Apr20 1-4	Apr23 5-1	Feb26 3-2	Dec18 1-2	Jan29 3-0		Jan01 1-1	Apr29 5-1	Jan08 2-3	Dec04 3-1	Apr18 0-1	Sep04 2-0	Apr16 4-0	Nov20 1-2	Aug28 3-1	Nov06 4-0
FALKIRK	Feb19 1-2	Jan03 3-1	Mar12 4-2	Jan15 1-0	Apr30 0-2	Aug21 1-2		Nov13 5-3	Dec11 1-1	Sep01 3-0	Feb12 1-3	Apr02 3-2	Aug14 2-2	Dec25 2-5	Mar19 2-3	Oct23 5-1
HEARTS	Mar19 1-1	Apr02 7-1	Aug28 1-2	Feb12 3-0	Jan08 0-1	Dec11 4-0	Feb26 3-1		Jan01 3-2	Mar12 2-4	Jan29 5-1	Nov06 1-1	Nov20 2-0	Oct23 1-3	Sep04 2-2	Aug18 3-2
HIBERNIAN	Jan15 4-1	Sep01 4-4	Oct30 1-2	Dec04 3-0	Aug14 2-1	Apr23 5-2	Mar05 2-0	Aug21 3-1		Nov13 3-4	Apr16 5-1	Apr09 2-1	Dec25 1-1	Feb19 0-1	Dec18 1-1	Nov27 1-0
MORTON	Dec18 1-1	Apr09 3-0	Jun08 0-0	Apr13 2-2	Aug16 2-2	Mar19 2-0	Mar05 0-1	Nov27 0-2	Feb26 2-3		Nov06 1-1	Aug18 2-1	Oct30 1-1	Apr25 0-1	Jan01 1-1	Aug28 3-3
MOTHERWELL	Apr30 1-1	Aug21 5-1	Apr02 0-1	Nov13 2-3	Dec11 0-2	Dec25 1-2	Oct30 0-3	Sep01 3-0	Nov20 5-1	Apr23 1-0		Mar12 3-1	Jan15 2-3	Aug14 1-1	Apr09 4-1	Mar19 1-0
PARTICK T	Nov13 0-0	Aug14 3-0	Dec04 1-2	Apr13 3-2	Feb12 4-4	Jan15 0-0	Dec18 3-3	Apr20 1-1	Oct23 2-6	Dec25 1-1	Nov27 1-1		Jan03 1-1	Sep01 1-1	Apr13 3-0	Oct30 1-3
QUEEN OF SOUTH	Mar26 0-0	Mar19 4-0	Jan29 1-0	Nov27 4-1	Feb26 0-1	Oct23 0-3	Jan08 0-0	Apr23 1-4	Aug18 1-1	Feb12 2-1	Sep04 8-2	Aug28		Dec18 0-2	Nov06 3-2	Jan01 2-1
RANGERS	Apr16 1-1	Apr18 3-1	Jan01 4-0	Mar19 4-1	Aug28 1-1	Apr13 3-0	Apr05 4-3	Nov06 2-1	Dec11 2-4	Jan08 4-1	Jan29 2-0	Apr02 3-0			Feb26 2-1	Sep04 2-1
ST MIRREN	Aug31 3-1	Dec25 3-2	Dec11 1-1	Apr18 2-1	Mar12 6-1	Jan03 2-0	Dec04 2-0	Jan15 1-2	Apr02 2-0	Aug18 2-1	Oct23 0-0	Nov20 4-2	Feb19 1-1	Nov13 0-2		Feb12 1-2
T LANARK	Aug14 1-0	Nov13 4-1	Nov20 3-2	Sep01 0-1	Apr02 2-3	Feb19 2-2	Apr09 3-2	Dec25 1-1	Apr19 3-2	Jan03 1-0	Dec04 1-3	Dec11 1-2	Aug21 6-1	Jan15 2-1	Apr22 3-1	

DIVISION B

	AIRDRIE	ALLOA	ARBROATH	AYR U	COWDENBEATH	DUMBARTON	DUNDEE U	DUNFERMLINE A	E STIRLING	HAMILTON A	KILMARNOCK	QUEEN'S PARK	RAITH R	ST JOHNSTONE	STENHOUSEMUIR	STIRLING A
AIRDRIE		Apr23 3-0	Nov13 4-1	Sep01 2-2	Aug14 3-1	Mar19 3-1	Jan03 1-1	Apr02 2-2	Dec25 3-0	Aug21 2-1	Nov20 5-0	Jan15 2-2	Apr16 0-3	Dec11 7-1	Feb19 3-0	Mar12 4-1
ALLOA	Oct23 4-5		Aug14 1-1	Jan15 1-2	Nov13 4-2	Feb12 2-4	Mar19 3-3	Jan03 0-6	Apr02 1-0	Dec11 2-1	Apr30 1-0	Dec25 2-6	Apr02 1-5	Feb19 2-1	Dec04 1-0	Mar12 1-0
ARBROATH	Feb26 3-3	Jan08 2-1		Oct30 1-0	Mar19 2-2	Jan29 3-0	Apr09 1-0	Nov07 1-1	Apr02 5-1	Dec11 5-1	Aug28 1-1	Mar12 1-2	Dec04 1-2	Aug18 3-2	Nov20 4-1	Jan01 2-1
AYR U	Jan29 1-1	Sep04 1-4	Feb12 0-1		Oct23 2-1	Aug18 3-2	Mar19 8-0	Aug28 1-3	Dec11 1-1	Apr02 1-1	Jan01 1-1	Nov20 3-2	Feb26 2-3	Jan08 0-2	Mar12 3-1	Nov06 1-2
COWDENBEATH	Jan08 5-1	Feb26 3-0	Dec04 0-3	Apr09 9-2		Sep04 1-2	Oct30 3-4	Jan01 4-2	Mar12 0-0	Apr16 1-0	Nov06 1-0	Apr02 2-1	Aug18 0-3	Aug28 1-1	Dec11 0-2	Jan29 1-0
DUMBARTON	Dec04 0-4	Apr16 5-3	Sep01 1-1	Dec25 0-0	Jan15 1-3		Aug14 3-2	Nov20 3-3	Oct30 2-2	Nov13 5-3	Mar12 2-2	Aug21 5-2	Apr09 0-1	Apr02 1-0	Jan03 2-2	Dec11 1-5
DUNDEE U	Aug28 1-3	Mar19 5-1	Oct23 5-5	Sep04 1-2	Feb12 2-1	Jan08 4-0		Aug18 0-1	Nov20 1-1	Mar12 2-2	Apr13 4-1	Dec11 5-2	Nov06 1-4	Jan01 4-3	Apr02 2-0	Feb26 0-1
DUNFERMLINE A	Dec18 2-4	Mar26 4-2	Feb19 5-0	Jan03 6-4	Aug21 3-2	Mar05 2-0	Dec25		Nov13 5-2	Jan15 3-4	Feb12 5-2	Sep01 2-0	Nov27 0-1	Oct23 1-1	Aug14 3-3	Mar19 3-3
E STIRLING	Aug17 1-1	Aug28 1-2	Dec18 2-1	Apr23 0-4	Nov27 2-0	Nov06 2-3	Mar05 3-0	Feb26 2-2		Apr23 1-0	Jan08 3-0	Apr09 0-1	Jan01 1-5	Jan29 3-1	Dec04 2-4	Sep01 1-2
HAMILTON A	Jan01 2-0	Aug18 1-2	Mar26 3-2	Dec18 2-2	Apr15 4-0	Feb26 4-0	Nov27 2-4	Jan15 2-4	Feb12 2-1		Jan29 3-1	Dec04 1-1	Nov06 1-4	Oct23 0-3	Apr02 2-0	Feb26 3-1
KILMARNOCK	Mar05 3-3	Dec18 6-0	Jan03 8-0	Aug21 1-2	Feb19 2-2	Nov27 4-2	Jan15 3-3	Oct30 1-2	Aug14 3-2	Sep01 3-1		Dec25 1-1	Mar26 3-1	Dec04 3-1	Nov13 1-0	Feb05 0-2
QUEEN'S PARK	Sep04 1-0	Nov06 3-0	Nov27 3-1	Mar05 4-1	Dec18 2-1	Jan01 2-0	Apr20 0-0	Jan29 4-4	Oct23 3-0	Mar19 4-0	Aug18 0-3		Jan08 1-1	Feb26 5-0	Feb12 1-0	Apr02 2-3
RAITH R	Feb12 0-3	Jan15 5-0	Nov13 3-1	Dec25 6-0	Oct23 3-2	Feb19 4-3	Jan08 1-3	Apr30 4-0	Aug21 5-1	Dec11 3-0	Apr23 3-2	Aug14 4-1		Apr23 1-0	Sep01 3-0	Apr02 0-0
ST JOHNSTONE	Mar26 1-1	Nov27 5-0	Dec25 2-2	Aug14 2-4	Nov20 3-0	Dec18 3-1	Aug21 3-0	Feb05 1-2	Sep01 3-2	Feb19 4-1	Mar19 3-2	Nov13 5-3	Mar05		Jan15 1-1	Oct23 2-1
STENHOUSEMUIR	Nov06 1-3	Jan01 2-0	Apr16 1-0	Nov27 7-1	Mar26 2-2	Aug28 5-0	Dec18 3-2	Jan08 3-3	Mar19 0-0	Apr09 1-1	Feb26 6-2	Oct30 1-3	Jan29 3-1	Sep04 2-3		Aug18 2-5
STIRLING A	Nov27 1-0	Mar05 5-1	Aug21 1-6	Feb19 4-1	Aug31 2-1	Mar26 3-1	Nov13 5-2	Dec04 2-3	Jan15 3-1	Aug14 3-0	Oct23 3-1	Jan03 2-5	Dec18 5-2	Feb12 2-1	Dec25 1-0	

DIVISION A FINAL TABLE

	P	W	D	L	F	A	Pts
Rangers	30	20	6	4	63	32	46
Dundee	30	20	5	5	71	48	45
Hibernian	30	17	5	8	75	52	39
East Fife	30	16	3	11	64	46	35
Falkirk	30	12	8	10	70	54	32
Celtic	30	12	7	11	48	40	31
T Lanark	30	13	5	12	56	52	31
Hearts	30	12	6	12	64	54	30
St Mirren	30	13	4	13	51	47	30
Queen of South	30	11	8	11	47	53	30
Partick T	30	9	9	12	50	63	27
Motherwell	30	10	5	15	44	49	25
Aberdeen	30	7	11	12	39	48	25
Clyde	30	9	6	15	50	67	24
Morton	30	7	8	15	39	51	22
Albion R	30	3	2	25	30	105	8

DIVISION B FINAL TABLE

	P	W	D	L	F	A	Pts
Raith R	30	20	2	8	80	44	42
Stirling A	30	20	2	8	71	47	42
Airdrie	30	16	9	5	76	42	41
Dunfermline A	40	16	9	5	80	58	41
Queen's Park	30	14	7	9	66	49	35
St Johnstone	30	14	4	12	58	51	32
Arbroath	30	12	8	10	62	56	32
Dundee U	30	10	7	13	60	67	27
Ayr U	30	10	7	13	51	70	27
Hamilton A	30	9	7	14	58	61	25
Kilmarnock	30	9	7	14	58	61	25
Stenhousemuir	30	8	8	14	50	54	24
Cowdenbeath	30	9	5	16	53	58	23
Alloa	30	10	3	17	48	75	23
Dumbarton	30	8	6	16	52	79	22
E Stirling	30	6	6	18	38	67	18

92

SFA Cup 1st Round

Jan 28	Alloa	0	Albion R	1
Jan 28	Brechin C	0	Celtic	3
Jan 28	Clacknacuddin	2	Stenhousemuir	3
Jan 28	Clyde	4	Newton Stewart	3
Feb 1	Cowdenbeath	1	Hamilton A	0
Jan 28	Dumbarton	1	Queen's Park	0
Jan 28	Dundee U	4	Ayr U	0
Jan 28	Dunfermline A	5	Forfar A	3
Jan 28	East Fife	4	Fraserburgh	0
Jan 28	Hearts	1	Dundee	1
Jan 28	Hibernian	0	Partick T	1
Jan 28	Inverness C	0	Queen of South	1
Jan 28	Kilmarnock	1	Stirling A	1
Jan 28	Motherwell	2	Rangers	4
Jan 28	Raith R	3	Airdrie	0
Jan 28	Ross Co	0	Morton	3
Jan 28	St Johnstone	7	Leith A	3
Jan 28	St Mirren	1	Aberdeen	2
Jan 28	Stranraer	1	Falkirk	3
Jan 28	T Lanark	2	Arbroath	1

Replays

Feb 1	Stirling A	3	Kilmarnock	1
Feb 6	Dundee	1	Hearts	2

2nd Round

Feb 11	Aberdeen	3	Hearts	1
Feb 15	Albion R	1	Dunfermline A	2
Feb 11	Falkirk	2	East Fife	3
Feb 14	Partick T	5	Dundee U	0
Feb 11	Queen of South	1	Morton	1
Feb 11	Raith R	3	Clyde	2
Feb 11	Rangers	8	Cowdenbeath	0
Feb 11	Stenhousemuir	2	St Johnstone	2
Feb 11	Stirling A	2	Dumbarton	2
Feb 15	T Lanark	1	Celtic	1

Replays

Feb 15	Dumbarton	1	Stirling A	1
Feb 15	Morton	0	Queen of South	3
Feb 15	St Johnstone	2	Stenhousemuir	4
Feb 20	Celtic	4	T Lanark	1
Feb 22	Dumbarton	2	Stirling A	6
	played at Ibrox			

3rd Round

Feb 25	Celtic	0	Aberdeen	1
Feb 25	Dunfermline A	1	Stenhousemuir	4

4th Round

Mar 11	Partick T	5	Stirling A	1
Mar 11	Queen of South	3	Aberdeen	3
Mar 11	Rangers	1	Raith R	1
Mar 11	Stenhousemuir	0	East Fife	3

Replay

Mar 15	Aberdeen	1	Queen of South	2
Mar 15	Raith R	1	Rangers	1
Mar 27	Raith R	0	Rangers	2
	played at Ibrox			

Semi-finals

Apr 1	East Fife	2	Partick T	1
	played at Ibrox			
Apr 1	Queen of South	1	Rangers	1
	played at Hampden Park			

Replay

Apr 5	Queen of South	0	Rangers	3
	played at Hampden Park			

Final

Apr 22	East Fife	0	Rangers	3
	played at Hampden Park			

League Cup results for 1949-50 are detailed on page 182.

DIVISION A

	ABERDEEN	CELTIC	CLYDE	DUNDEE	EAST FIFE	FALKIRK	HEARTS	HIBERNIAN	MOTHERWELL	PARTICK T	QUEEN OF SOUTH	RAITH R	RANGERS	ST MIRREN	STIRLING A	T LANARK
ABERDEEN		Jan14 4-0	Sep17 1-1	Sep24 2-2	Dec31 1-2	Apr01 1-2	Apr08 0-5	Jan03 0-3	Dec17 5-0	Nov12 3-1	Mar18 2-0	Nov26 3-0	Oct29 1-3	Sep10 2-3	Apr22 6-2	Oct08 2-1
CELTIC	Oct15 4-2		Nov05 4-1	Jan21 2-0	Mar25 4-1	Mar04 4-3	Sep17 2-2	Oct29 3-2	Jan07 3-1	Dec03 2-1	Dec24 0-0	Oct01 2-2	Jan02 1-1	Dec10 1-1	Feb18 0-0	Nov19 2-1
CLYDE	Oct22 0-1	Apr15 2-2		Jan14 1-0	Nov12 0-1	Jan03 2-2	Feb04 3-4	Dec31 0-1	Feb25 1-0	Sep24 4-1	Nov26 3-2	Mar18 1-1	Apr10 1-2	Oct08 2-0	Dec17 6-0	Sep10 0-2
DUNDEE	Jan02 1-1	Oct22 3-0	Oct15 2-3		Dec10 1-0	Nov19 2-0	Jan07 3-1	Dec03 1-2	Oct01 3-1	Jan21 1-0	Sep17 3-0	Nov05 2-1	Apr17 0-1	Mar04 2-0	Dec24 4-1	Mar18 1-4
EAST FIFE	Apr15 3-1	Dec17 5-1	Feb18 4-1	Mar18 1-0		Feb04 1-2	Dec24 0-1	Feb25 2-1	Nov05 1-1	Nov26 4-1	Oct01 3-0	Jan02 0-2	Jan07 3-3	Oct22 0-2	Oct15 3-1	Dec03 4-1
FALKIRK	Nov05 1-0	Nov26 1-1	Oct01 7-4	Feb25 2-2	May01 0-2		Feb18 1-1	Mar18 1-2	Dec24 2-4	Dec17 0-3	Jan07 3-3	Sep17 1-1	Oct15 0-2	Dec03 2-2	Jan02 1-1	Jan21 2-1
HEARTS	Dec03 4-1	Dec31 4-2	Oct29 6-2	Apr22 6-2	Sep10 0-1	Nov12 9-0		Sep24 5-2	Nov26 2-0	Dec17 3-3	Jan07 3-0	Sep17 2-0	Oct15 0-1	Jan03 5-0	Mar18 5-2	Jan14 1-0
HIBERNIAN	Oct01 2-0	Feb04 4-1	Apr08 6-3	Mar11 4-2	Nov19 4-1	Dec10 5-1	Jan02 1-2		Feb18 6-1	Oct22 2-0	Oct15 4-2	Dec24 1-0	Nov05 5-0	Mar25 4-1	Jan07 0-1	Mar04 —
MOTHERWELL	Mar25 5-1	Oct08 1-2	Nov19 5-2	Jan03 0-2	Apr17 3-4	Sep10 2-2	Mar04 2-3	Nov12 1-3		Jan14 0-2	Feb04 1-0	Oct22 1-1	Dec10 4-0	Dec03 2-2	Dec31 4-0	—
PARTICK T	Feb18 0-2	Apr10 1-0	Jan02 1-0	Oct29 2-3	Mar04 1-2	Mar25 3-1	Nov05 0-1	Jan21 2-2	Oct15 0-2		Apr08 5-2	Jan07 1-0	Dec24 1-3	Nov19 4-0	Oct01 4-1	Dec10 5-1
QUEEN OF SOUTH	Dec10 1-0	Sep10 0-2	Mar04 2-3	Nov12 1-1	Jan03 0-5	Oct08 2-2	Nov19 0-4	Jan14 2-2	Oct29 2-0	Dec31 3-1		Dec03 0-0	Mar25 1-2	Apr17 1-1	Jan21 3-1	Sep24 0-1
RAITH R	Mar04 1-2	Jan03 1-1	Dec10 7-1	Apr08 4-1	Dec31 4-4	Mar25 6-4	Sep10 2-0	Jan21 0-6	Oct08 0-2	Apr22 1-3	Nov19 2-0		Jan14 1-3	Oct29 2-1	Nov12 2-0	—
RANGERS	Feb04 2-2	Mar18 4-0	Dec03 5-4	Dec31 2-2	Apr08 2-2	Jan14 3-0	Oct22 1-0	Apr29 0-0	Mar18 2-0	Sep10 2-0	Dec17 1-0	Feb25 2-0		Nov12 1-0	Nov26 2-1	Jan03 3-1
ST MIRREN	Dec24 4-0	Mar18 0-1	Jan07 2-0	Nov26 1-1	Jan21 0-0	Mar11 0-1	Oct01 3-3	Dec17 1-1	Jan02 0-2	Feb25 3-3	Nov05 1-0	Oct15 3-0	Feb18 1-2		Sep17 2-0	Oct29 6-1
STIRLING A	Nov19 0-1	Nov12 2-1	Mar25 1-2	Sep10 2-2	Jan14 1-1	Sep24 3-2	Dec10 2-4	Apr01 3-5	Apr08 1-4	Apr29 2-1	Oct22 1-0	Feb04 1-2	Mar04 0-2	Dec31 1-3		Apr15 0-2
T LANARK	Jan07 3-1	Mar11 1-0	Dec24 1-3	Dec17 1-0	Apr29 4-1	Oct22 0-2	Oct15 3-0	Nov26 0-2	Sep17 2-7	Mar18 2-1	Jan02 0-1	Feb18 2-2	May01 2-1	Feb04 2-4	Nov05 —	

DIVISION B

	AIRDRIE	ALBION R	ALLOA	ARBROATH	AYR U	COWDENBEATH	DUMBARTON	DUNDEE U	DUNFERMLINE A	FORFAR A	HAMILTON A	KILMARNOCK	MORTON	QUEEN'S PARK	ST JOHNSTONE	STENHOUSEMUIR
AIRDRIE		Jan02 4-1	Oct22 3-2	Feb18 8-3	Dec24 5-1	Jan07 7-1	Dec03 5-2	Apr08 2-0	Dec17 4-2	Nov26 0-1	Feb04 3-2	Feb25 2-0	Oct15 0-1	Oct01 2-0	Mar18 3-0	Nov05 3-1
ALBION R	Sep24 2-2		Jan14 3-2	Dec10 0-1	Mar25 3-5	Nov19 3-1	Nov12 2-1	Mar04 2-0	Jan03 1-3	Oct08 6-1	Dec31 1-3	Sep10 3-1	Oct29 0-0	Mar11 3-3	Apr01 3-0	Jan21 1-1
ALLOA	Jan21 2-4	Oct15 0-0		Jan07 2-2	Oct01 2-0	Feb18 4-2	Oct29 1-0	Dec24 3-3	Mar18 4-1	Feb25 1-2	Dec03 2-3	Dec17 1-5	Sep17 3-7	Nov05 0-2	Nov26 1-3	Jan02 —
ARBROATH	Nov12 2-2	Mar18 1-3	Oct08 1-2		Feb04 0-0	Dec03 2-1	Sep10 1-1	Oct22 3-3	Apr01 2-1	Jan03 2-3	Mar25 2-3	Dec31 1-2	Nov26 1-1	Jan14 1-2	Apr22 3-1	—
AYR U	Sep10 2-3	Dec17 0-0	Jan03 4-1	Oct29 3-2		Jan21 1-2	Jan14 4-2	Dec03 0-4	Dec31 1-1	Feb11 5-0	Nov12 3-3	Sep24 2-1	Feb25 2-2	Oct08 3-2	Dec31 4-0	Mar18 3-3
COWDENBEATH	Oct08 1-2	Feb25 3-0	Nov12 4-1	Mar11 2-2	Oct22 4-2		Jan03 3-2	Feb04 2-1	Sep24 2-0	Sep10 4-2	Jan14 3-2	Apr01 2-1	Nov26 0-1	Apr15 1-1	Dec31 5-1	Mar18 6-1
DUMBARTON	Mar11 0-1	Feb18 0-3	Feb04 4-0	Dec24 4-2	Oct15 2-0	Oct01 1-0		Jan07 3-0	Apr08 2-4	Mar18 1-1	Oct22 0-1	Nov26 0-1	Nov05 3-4	Jan02 1-3	Dec17 0-2	Sep17 3-0
DUNDEE U	Dec31 0-1	Nov26 2-5	Sep10 6-1	Jan21 3-4	Mar11 4-1	Oct29 2-2	Oct08 5-0		Jan14 1-1	Nov12 0-2	Oct03 4-1	Jan03 3-0	Apr22 2-2	Sep24 7-1	Dec31 3-1	—
DUNFERMLINE A	Mar25 2-5	Oct01 4-1	Dec10 6-2	Nov05 4-0	Apr22 3-0	Jan02 1-0	Nov19 5-0	Oct15 1-3		Dec03 —	Mar04 2-1	Apr29 2-0	Feb18 2-2	Dec24 1-6	Jan21 4-1	Jan07 0-2
FORFAR A	Mar04 4-4	Jan07 6-1	Nov19 6-2	Jan02 3-1	Nov05 5-1	Dec24 2-2	Dec10 2-1	Feb18 0-3	Mar11 1-2		Mar25 0-2	Jan21 1-0	Oct01 1-3	Apr01 3-0	Oct29 2-1	Oct15 1-1
HAMILTON A	Oct29 2-2	Sep17 1-1	Mar11 4-0	Oct01 2-1	Feb18 2-1	Oct15 2-0	Jan21 1-1	Nov05 4-1	Nov26 1-1	Dec17 2-0		Mar18 1-0	Jan02 0-2	Jan07 3-0	Feb25 2-2	Oct08 5-1
KILMARNOCK	Nov19 1-1	Dec24 2-1	Mar25 3-0	Sep17 2-2	Jan02 4-0	Nov05 2-0	Mar04 1-1	Oct01 2-3	Feb04 1-2	Oct22 3-1	Dec10 —		Jan07 2-0	Oct15 3-3	Mar11 1-1	Feb18 3-2
MORTON	Jan14 1-0	Feb04 2-0	Dec31 3-1	Mar25 3-1	Dec10 7-0	Mar04 5-3	Apr01 1-0	Nov19 5-2	Nov12 2-2	Jan03 1-1	Jan21 2-0	Sep24 3-1	Oct08 —	Oct22 4-2	Sep10 5-0	Dec03 4-0
QUEEN'S PARK	Jan03 2-0	Dec03 1-0	Apr19 4-2	Apr08 2-2	Nov19 4-1	Mar25 1-2	Sep24 4-1	Apr29 0-1	Sep10 2-0	Dec31 0-0	Apr10 3-2	Jan14 1-3	Jan21 2-4		Nov12 2-2	Apr24 2-0
ST JOHNSTONE	Dec10 1-0	Nov05 5-0	Mar04 5-2	Oct15 2-1	Jan07 4-2	Apr08 2-1	Mar25 5-0	Jan02 3-4	Oct22 2-1	Feb04 2-0	Nov19 2-1	Dec03 2-0	Dec24 1-1	Sep17 1-1		Oct01 2-2
STENHOUSEMUIR	Apr01 1-1	Oct22 6-0	Sep24 4-1	Nov19 1-1	Mar04 4-2	Dec10 0-1	Dec31 1-2	Apr15 1-5	Jan14 7-6	Sep10 1-1	Nov12 3-2	Apr08 0-2	Oct08 2-1	Jan03 2-2	Oct01 2-5	

DIVISION A FINAL TABLE

	P	W	D	L	F	A	Pts
Rangers	30	22	6	2	58	26	50
Hibernian	30	22	5	3	86	34	49
Hearts	30	20	3	7	86	40	43
East Fife	30	15	7	8	58	43	37
Celtic	30	14	7	9	51	50	35
Dundee	30	12	7	11	49	46	31
Partick T	30	13	3	14	55	45	29
Aberdeen	30	11	4	15	48	56	26
Raith R	30	9	8	13	45	54	26
Motherwell	30	10	5	15	53	58	25
St Mirren	30	8	9	13	42	49	25
T Lanark	30	11	3	16	44	62	25
Clyde	30	10	4	16	56	73	24
Falkirk	30	7	10	13	48	72	24
Queen of South	30	5	6	19	31	63	16
Stirling A	30	6	3	21	38	77	15

DIVISION B FINAL TABLE

	P	W	D	L	F	A	Pts
Morton	30	20	7	3	77	33	47
Airdrie	30	19	6	5	79	40	44
Dunfermline A	30	16	4	10	71	57	36
St Johnstone	30	15	6	9	64	56	36
Cowdenbeath	30	16	3	11	63	56	35
Hamilton A	30	14	6	10	57	44	34
Dundee U	30	14	5	11	74	56	33
Kilmarnock	30	14	5	11	50	43	33
Queen's Park	30	12	7	11	63	59	31
Forfar A	30	11	8	11	53	56	30
Albion R	30	10	7	13	49	61	27
Stenhousemuir	30	8	8	14	54	72	24
Ayr U	30	8	6	16	53	80	22
Arbroath	30	5	9	16	47	69	19
Dumbarton	30	6	4	20	39	62	16
Alloa	30	5	3	22	47	96	13

SFA Cup

1st Round
Jan 27	Aberdeen	6	Inverness Cal	1
Jan 27	Albion R	1	Stenhousemuir	1
Jan 27	Alloa	2	Hearts	3
Jan 27	Brechin C	3	Berwick R	2
Jan 27	Dumbarton	0	St Johnstone	2
Jan 27	Dundee	2	Dundee U	2
Jan 27	Dunfermline A	0	Clyde	3
Jan 27	Duns	3	Forres Mechanic	1
Jan 27	East Fife	2	Celtic	2
Jan 27	E Stirling	2	Kilmarnock	1
Jan 27	Falkirk	0	Airdrie	2
Jan 27	Hamilton A	2	Elgin C	2
Jan 27	Morton	2	Cowdenbeath	2
Jan 27	Partick T	1	Raith R	1
Jan 27	Peterhead	0	Motherwell	4
Jan 27	Queen's Park	3	Arbroath	1
Jan 27	Rangers	2	Queen of South	0
Jan 27	St Mirren	1	Hibernian	1
Jan 27	Stirling A	1	Ayr U	2
Jan 27	T Lanark	5	Forfar A	2

Replays
Jan 31	Celtic	4	East Fife	2
Jan 31	Cowdenbeath	1	Morton	2
Jan 31	Dundee U	0	Dundee	1
Jan 31	Elgin C	0	Hamilton A	3
Jan 31	Hibernian	5	St Mirren	0
Jan 31	Raith R	1	Partick T	0
Jan 31	Stenhousemuir	1	Albion R	2

2nd Round
Feb 10	Aberdeen	4	T Lanark	0
Feb 10	Albion R	0	Clyde	2
Feb 10	Celtic	4	Duns	0
Feb 10	E Stirling	1	Hearts	5
Feb 10	Morton	3	Airdrie	3
Feb 10	Motherwell	4	Hamilton A	1
Feb 10	Queen's Park	1	Ayr U	3
Feb 10	Raith R	5	Brechin C	2
Feb 10	Rangers	2	Hibernian	3
Feb 10	St Johnstone	1	Dundee	3

Replays
Feb 14	Airdrie	2	Morton	1

3rd Round
Feb 24	Airdrie	4	Clyde	0
Feb 24	Hearts	1	Celtic	2

4th Round
Mar 10	Airdrie	0	Hibernian	3
Mar 10	Ayr U	2	Motherwell	2
Mar 10	Celtic	3	Aberdeen	0
Mar 10	Dundee	1	Raith R	2

Replay
Mar 14	Motherwell	2	Ayr U	1

Semi-finals
Mar 31	Celtic	3	Raith R	2
	played at Hampden Park			
Mar 31	Hibernian	2	Motherwell	3
	played at Tynecastle			

Final
Apr 21	Celtic	1	Motherwell	0
	played at Hampden Park			

League Cup results for 1950-51 are detailed on page 183.

DIVISION A

	ABERDEEN	AIRDRIE	CELTIC	CLYDE	DUNDEE	EAST FIFE	FALKIRK	HEARTS	HIBERNIAN	MORTON	MOTHERWELL	PARTICK T	RAITH R	RANGERS	ST MIRREN	T LANARK
ABERDEEN		Dec23 1-1	Oct14 2-1	Oct21 5-3	Jan01 1-0	Mar07 1-2	Nov18 5-1	Dec02 2-0	Sep30 2-1	Mar24 3-0	4-2	4-1	Mar03 1-2	2-4	1-1	Nov04 1-2
AIRDRIE	Sep09 2-5		Nov18 2-4	Oct07 2-0	Mar24 2-2	Dec02 2-2	Apr28 1-1	Apr14 2-3	Mar03 2-1	Dec30 2-0	Sep23 2-3	Dec09 1-2	Nov11 2-5	Mar31 2-1	Oct28 2-0	Jan20 2-1
CELTIC	Jan13 3-4	Apr11 0-1		Apr28 1-0	Oct21 0-0	Dec16 6-2	Nov11 3-0	Dec30 2-2	Feb03 0-1	Sep09 3-4	Apr25 3-1	Apr16 0-3	Oct07 2-3	Sep23 3-2	Mar17 2-1	Nov25 1-1
CLYDE	Jan20 0-2	Jan06 2-2	Nov04 1-3		Oct14 2-1	Feb17 1-1	Mar24 3-1	Oct28 0-4	Apr11 1-1	Nov18 1-1	Mar03 1-2	Jan01 1-0	Dec09 1-0	Dec02 2-2	Jan20 2-1	Sep30 0-2
DUNDEE	Sep23 2-0	Dec16 3-0	Jan20 3-1	Mar31 1-1		Mar17 2-4	Oct07 2-2	Sep09 2-1	Mar07 2-1	Jan02 0-0	Nov11 3-2	Oct28 2-0	Apr02 2-0	Dec30 2-0	Nov25 5-0	Feb24 2-1
EAST FIFE	Dec30 0-0	Apr21 4-1	Mar24 3-0	Nov11 2-1	Dec09 1-3		Feb10 2-1	Oct07 1-4	Nov18 1-2	Apr14 3-3	May08 3-2	Mar03 1-1	Sep23 3-1	Sep09 0-3	Jan20 1-1	Oct28 3-1
FALKIRK	Feb24 1-1	Apr21 4-1	Feb17 0-2	Dec16 1-0	Jan06 2-1	Oct14 1-1		Mar17 5-4	Dec23 1-5	Dec02 0-1	Nov18 2-4	Sep30 2-1	Oct28 2-3	Sep16 1-1	Nov25 0-2	Jan01 2-0
HEARTS	Apr18 4-1	Oct14 3-1	Mar07 2-0	Feb03 4-0	Dec23 1-1	Sep16 5-1	Dec09 4-2		Jan01 2-1	Mar03 3-3	Nov18 4-5	Nov04 3-1	Mar24 0-1	Apr21 1-0	Sep30 4-0	Feb17 1-0
HIBERNIAN	Jan02 6-2	Nov25 5-0	Sep30 3-1	Dec30 1-0	Dec02 2-0	Feb24 2-0	Sep09 6-0	Sep23 0-1		Nov11 2-0	Jan13 3-1	Apr25 1-1	Apr28 3-0	Dec16 4-1	3-1	Mar17 3-1
MORTON	Dec16 1-2	Sep16 4-1	Mar28 0-2	Apr21 1-4	Sep30 2-3	Nov04 4-2	Mar10 0-1	Nov25 0-1	Feb17 2-4		Apr28 5-0	Oct14 3-2	Jan20 2-0	Mar17 0-2	5-2	Jan06 1-3
MOTHERWELL	Mar17 1-1	Jan01 2-0	Jan06 2-1	Nov25 1-1	Feb17 0-2	Sep30 4-2	Oct21 2-4	May05 2-4	Oct14 2-6	Feb24 1-1		Apr11 3-2	May02 2-3	Mar07 2-4	Nov04 2-3	Dec23 4-1
PARTICK T	Nov11 1-4	Mar17 2-0	Dec02 0-1	Sep23 2-1	Apr28 1-1	Mar10 4-0	Mar31 4-1	Oct21 5-2	Mar07 0-0	Apr14 1-1			Sep09 5-2	Oct07 2-1	Feb24 1-1	Dec16 1-0
RAITH R	Nov25 1-0	Feb17 0-1	Sep28 1-2	Mar17 4-1	Nov04 0-1	Jan01 3-0	Feb03 3-0	Dec16 2-0	Nov25 1-3	Oct21 1-1	Dec02 3-4	Dec23 2-2		Feb24 3-1	Oct14 2-0	Sep16 4-0
RANGERS	Oct28 1-2	Sep30 4-1	Jan01 1-0	Mar10 4-0	Sep16 0-0	Dec23 5-2	Mar03 2-1	Jan20 1-1	Nov04 2-0	Dec09 3-0	Mar24 3-0	Jan06 4-1	Nov18 2-0		Feb17 2-0	Oct14 1-4
ST MIRREN	Oct07 4-2	Mar07 3-2	0-0	Sep09 3-1	Mar03 2-2	Oct21 1-2	Dec30 0-0	Jan02 1-0	0-1	Sep23 2-3	Apr17 3-0	Nov18 2-1	Apr28 2-0	Nov11 0-2		Dec02 0-4
T LANARK	Apr28 2-0	Oct21 1-0	Mar03 0-3	Jan02 2-0	Nov18 0-2	Mar30 1-1	Sep23 2-1	Nov11 1-2	Dec09 1-2	Oct07 0-2	Sep09 2-0	Mar24 0-2	Dec30 0-2	Apr25 1-5	Mar10 1-1	

DIVISION B

	ALBION R	ALLOA	ARBROATH	AYR U	COWDENBEATH	DUMBARTON	DUNDEE U	DUNFERMLINE A	FORFAR A	HAMILTON A	KILMARNOCK	QUEEN OF SOUTH	QUEEN'S PARK	ST JOHNSTONE	STENHOUSEMUIR	STIRLING A
ALBION R		Mar10 4-2	Mar17 4-0	Apr21 2-1	Feb24 1-3	Feb17 0-4	Nov25 1-2	Sep30 3-1	Dec23 0-4	Jan01 1-3	Apr07 4-2	Apr18 1-4	Oct21 3-2	Nov04 4-4	Oct14 2-0	Sep16 1-3
ALLOA	Dec02 3-3		Feb24 2-0	Nov25 3-5	Mar17 7-4	Mar31 3-4	Dec16 1-2	Apr25 2-0	Oct14 3-2	Nov04 2-4	Feb17 1-4	Oct21 0-2	Oct28 1-0	Sep30 1-0	Jan01 3-3	Jan06 1-4
ARBROATH	Dec09 0-3	Nov18 3-4		Oct28 0-2	Jan06 2-1	Jan20 1-3	Nov04 1-1	Jan01 2-1	Feb17 0-0	Sep16 0-2	Mar24 1-3	Mar03 2-2	Dec23 1-6	Sep30 5-1	Feb24 6-1	Sep30 3-3
AYR U	Mar24 0-0	Mar03 4-1	Feb03 1-1		Oct21 0-0	Oct14 3-1	Apr28 2-2	Apr07 8-0	Nov04 4-1	Jan06 0-0	Jan01 2-1	Dec09 0-0	Nov18 2-2	Dec23 3-1	Sep30 4-1	Feb17 2-0
COWDENBEATH	Nov18 1-0	Dec09 6-3	Dec02 3-2	Jan20 1-4		Sep30 1-1	Oct28 6-0	Jan01 3-0	Apr07 8-2	Nov04 4-3	Feb10 3-0	Mar03 1-3	Sep23 3-0	Apr28 0-0	Feb17 2-0	Oct14 1-2
DUMBARTON	Nov11 1-5	Dec09 2-2	Oct07 0-2	Jan13 2-1	Jan02 1-0		Sep30 1-1	Nov18 1-2	Mar10 4-1	Feb10 2-1	2-1	Sep23 0-1	Oct21 2-1	Apr28 3-3	Oct28 3-4	Jan20 4-0
DUNDEE U	Mar03 2-1	Mar24 4-1	Oct21 2-1	Dec02 3-1	Feb03 1-5	Dec23 3-2		Oct14 5-1	Feb17 2-1	Oct02 1-3	Sep30 5-3	Nov18 5-0	Dec09 3-2	Jan01 2-0	Jan06 6-0	Nov04 1-3
DUNFERMLINE A	Apr02 0-1	Sep09 4-0	Feb10 5-1	Dec30 3-1	Sep23 3-1	Feb24 2-2	Mar31 1-0		Mar10 2-4	Dec16 1-3	Feb03 4-2	Nov11 3-1	Oct07 4-3	Oct21 2-7	5-2	Nov25 2-4
FORFAR A	Sep09 1-0	Dec09 2-4	Sep23 2-1	Mar31 3-2	Sep30 2-0	Oct17 1-4	Nov11 1-3	Dec02 4-2		Nov25 2-2		Apr28 0-2	Dec30 3-2	Feb03 1-3	Feb24 3-1	Dec16 1-0
HAMILTON A	Sep23 5-1	Apr21 5-1	Nov11 8-2	Apr14 2-3	Sep09 3-2	Dec02 1-2	Dec30 2-0	Mar24 2-0	Mar03 3-0		Nov18 2-3	Apr25 0-0	Jan02 0-0	Dec09 2-0	Jan20 2-4	Oct28 4-0
KILMARNOCK	Oct07 3-2	Nov11 2-2	Dec30 1-1	Sep23 0-1	Feb10 4-0	Nov25 1-3	Jan02 2-0	Oct28 1-1	Jan20 1-1	Feb24 1-1		Sep09 0-1	Jan13 3-4	Dec02 2-2	Dec16 1-2	Mar17 1-1
QUEEN OF SOUTH	Oct28 2-0	Dec16 5-1	Dec16 3-1	Mar17 2-1	Mar03 3-0	Nov04 1-2	Feb24 3-3	Sep30 3-0	Nov25 2-2	Oct14 4-1	Feb24 0-1		Mar10 2-1	Jan06 2-1	Apr20 5-2	Apr21 1-0
QUEEN'S PARK	Jan20 1-1	Apr14 2-1	Nov25 4-3	Feb24 2-0	Dec16 2-0	Jan06 1-0	Mar17 1-2	Jan06 4-2	Sep16 3-3	Sep30 0-1	Oct14 0-2	Dec02 0-0		Feb17 4-3	Nov04 0-3	Dec23 0-2
ST JOHNSTONE	Mar31 0-3	Apr28 3-1	Apr21 1-3	Sep09 2-1	Dec30 2-1	Dec16 3-0	Sep23 2-2	Jan20 2-1	Oct28 3-0	Oct07 1-0	Mar10 1-0	Apr07 0-6	Nov11 6-1		Nov25 7-1	Feb24 4-2
STENHOUSEMUIR	Apr28 0-1	Mar31 3-1	Sep09 2-3	Jan02 3-2	Nov04 4-0	Apr07 3-1	Oct07 3-1	Nov18 4-1	Oct21 1-2	Jan20 4-1	Apr14 1-3	Apr20 0-3	Mar03 0-2			Mar10 0-1
STIRLING A	Dec30 3-2	Oct07 4-2	Jan02 4-0	Nov11 1-1	Jan13 2-4	Oct21 3-2	Feb10 3-1	Mar03 1-3	Mar24 4-0	Mar31 5-1	Dec09 1-0	Sep23 5-2	Sep09 3-1	Nov18 4-1	Dec02 4-2	

DIVISION A FINAL TABLE

	P	W	D	L	F	A	Pts
Hibernian	30	22	4	4	78	26	48
Rangers	30	17	4	9	64	37	38
Dundee	30	15	8	7	47	30	38
Hearts	30	16	5	9	72	45	37
Aberdeen	30	15	5	10	61	50	35
Partick T	30	13	7	10	57	48	33
Celtic	30	12	5	13	48	46	29
Raith R	30	13	2	15	52	52	28
Motherwell	30	11	6	13	58	65	28
East Fife	30	10	8	12	48	66	28
St Mirren	30	9	7	14	35	51	25
Morton	30	10	4	16	47	59	24
T Lanark	30	11	2	17	40	51	24
Airdrie	30	10	4	16	52	67	24
Clyde	30	8	7	15	37	57	23
Falkirk	30	7	4	19	35	81	18

DIVISION B FINAL TABLE

	P	W	D	L	F	A	Pts
Queen of South	30	21	3	6	69	35	45
Stirling A	30	21	3	6	78	44	45
Ayr U	30	15	6	9	64	40	36
Dundee U	30	16	4	10	78	58	36
St Johnstone	30	14	5	11	68	53	33
Queen's Park	30	13	7	10	56	53	33
Hamilton A	30	12	8	10	65	49	32
Albion R	30	14	4	12	56	51	32
Dumbarton	30	12	5	13	52	53	29
Dunfermline A	30	12	4	14	58	73	28
Cowdenbeath	30	12	3	15	61	57	27
Kilmarnock	30	8	8	14	44	49	24
Arbroath	30	8	5	17	46	78	21
Forfar A	30	9	3	18	43	76	21
Stenhousemuir	30	9	2	19	51	80	20
Alloa	30	7	4	19	58	98	18

SFA Cup 1st Round

Jan 26	Berwick R	7	Peebles R	0
Jan 26	Brechin C	0	Queen of South	6
Jan 30	Celtic	0	T Lanark	0
Jan 30	Deveronvale	1	Clyde	3
Jan 26	Dundee	4	Ayr U	0
Jan 26	Duns	1	Alloa	2
Jan 26	Eyemouth U	0	East Fife	4
Jan 26	Forfar A	2	Motherwell	4
Jan 26	Inverness Cal	3	Dundee U	3
Jan 26	Kilmarnock	2	Stenhousemuir	0
Jan 26	Montrose	1	Wigtown & Blad	2
Jan 26	Morton	2	E Stirling	0
Jan 26	Partick T	0	Hamilton A	1
Jan 26	Raith R	0	Hibernian	0

Replays

Jan 30	Dundee U	4	Inverness Cal	0
Jan 30	Hibernian	0	Raith R	0
Feb 4	Hibernian	1	Raith R	4
	played at Tynecastle			
Feb 4	T Lanark	2	Celtic	1

2nd Round

Feb 9	Aberdeen	2	Kilmarnock	1
Feb 9	Airdrie	2	East Fife	1
Feb 9	Albion R	1	Stranraer	1
Feb 9	Alloa	0	Berwick R	0
Feb 9	Clacknacuddin	1	Morton	2
Feb 9	Clyde	3	Dunfermline A	4
Feb 9	Cowdenbeath	1	Arbroath	4
Feb 9	Dumbarton	1	Queen's Park	0
Feb 9	Falkirk	3	Stirling A	3
Feb 9	Hamilton A	1	T Lanark	1
Feb 9	Hearts	5	Raith R	0
Feb 9	Leith A	1	Dundee U	4
Feb 9	Rangers	6	Elgin C	1
Feb 9	St Johnstone	2	Queen of South	2
Feb 9	St Mirren	2	Motherwell	3
Feb 9	Wigtown & Blad	1	Dundee	7

Replays

Feb 13	Queen of South	3	St Johnstone	1
Feb 13	Stirling A	1	Falkirk	2
Feb 13	Stranraer	3	Albion R	4
Feb 13	T Lanark	4	Hamilton A	0
Feb 14	Berwick R	4	Alloa	1

3rd Round

Feb 23	Airdrie	4	Morton	0
Feb 23	Albion R	1	T Lanark	3
Feb 23	Arbroath	0	Rangers	2
Feb 23	Dumbarton	1	Falkirk	3
Feb 23	Dundee	1	Berwick R	0
Feb 23	Dundee U	2	Aberdeen	2
Feb 23	Dunfermline A	1	Motherwell	1
Feb 23	Queen of South	1	Hearts	3

Replays

Feb 27	Aberdeen	3	Dundee U	2
Feb 27	Motherwell	4	Dunfermline A	0

4th Round

Mar 8	Airdrie	2	Hearts	2
Mar 8	Dundee	4	Aberdeen	0
Mar 8	Rangers	1	Motherwell	1
Mar 8	T Lanark	1	Falkirk	0

Replays

Mar 12	Hearts	6	Airdrie	4
Mar 12	Motherwell	2	Rangers	1

Semi-finals

Mar 29	Dundee	2	T Lanark	0
	played at Easter Road			
Mar 29	Hearts	1	Motherwell	1
	played at Hampden Park			

Replays

Apr 7	Hearts	1	Motherwell	1
	played at Hampden Park			
Apr 9	Hearts	1	Motherwell	3
	played at Hampden Park			

Final

Apr 19	Dundee	0	Motherwell	4
	played at Hampden Park			

League Cup results for 1951-52 are detailed on pages 183-184.

DIVISION A

	ABERDEEN	AIRDRIE	CELTIC	DUNDEE	EAST FIFE	HEARTS	HIBERNIAN	MORTON	MOTHERWELL	PARTICK T	QUEEN OF SOUTH	RAITH R	RANGERS	ST MIRREN	STIRLING A	T LANARK
ABERDEEN		Oct06 1-4	Dec29 3-4	Sep22 3-1	Jan02 2-1	Jan26 3-0	Jan12 1-2	Dec15 3-1	Mar15 2-2	Nov10 4-2	Nov03 1-1	Nov24 2-2	Apr19 1-1	Sep08 3-0	Mar12 6-0	Jan19 2-3
AIRDRIE	Jan05 3-0		Feb27 2-1	Dec15 4-3	Apr19 3-1	Sep15 2-0	Nov24 0-2	Sep29 3-5	Apr23 1-2	Mar15 2-2	Oct20 3-0	Oct13 2-1	Feb16 0-1	Feb02 2-2	Nov03 2-2	Dec22 2-4
CELTIC	Mar29 2-0	Nov17 3-1		Jan19 1-1	Mar22 2-1	Sep29 1-3	Oct27 1-1	Mar05 2-2	Dec22 2-2	Dec08 2-1	Mar01 6-1	Feb23 0-1	Jan01 1-4	Dec08 2-1	Feb16 3-1	Nov03 2-2
DUNDEE	Jan01 3-2	Mar22 0-1	Oct20 2-1		Dec08 3-4	Jan05 1-3	Dec01 1-4	Apr02 2-2	Feb16 1-2	Apr12 0-2	Nov17 0-0	Nov03 2-0	Sep29 1-0	Mar01 3-0	Dec22 4-1	Apr26 6-0
EAST FIFE	Sep29 2-1	Dec01 3-1	Dec15 3-1	Mar15 3-1		Dec22 2-4	Feb23 3-1	Nov03 4-1	Apr26 6-1	Nov24 1-1	Feb02 5-0	Jan01 0-1	Jan05 2-1	Oct20 3-3	Sep15 4-0	Oct13 3-2
HEARTS	Dec01 2-2	Dec29 6-1	Jan02 2-1	Oct06 4-2	Sep08 3-1		Sep22 1-1	Nov24 4-1	Apr30 2-1	Feb13 1-2	Nov10 4-3	Dec15 4-2	Jan19 2-2	Jan12 2-1	Mar15 5-2	Oct27 2-2
HIBERNIAN	Sep15 4-4	Mar01 3-1	Feb02 2-1	Apr09 4-2	Nov17 2-3	Jan01 1-1		Oct13 1-0	Apr21 3-1	Oct20 5-0	Dec08 5-0	Dec22 5-0	Nov03 1-1	Feb16 1-1	Jan05 8-0	Sep29 5-2
MORTON	Mar22 3-2	Feb13 2-3	Oct10 0-1	Jan12 3-0	Oct06 0-2	Mar01 3-1	Nov10 2-1		Apr12 0-2	Dec29 1-2	Sep08 2-2	Oct20 1-4	Dec08 0-1	Sep22 3-0	Dec01 7-1	Nov17 3-1
MOTHERWELL	Dec08 3-3	Sep22 4-1	Sep08 2-2	Nov10 2-1	Jan12 2-1	Nov17 0-5	Dec29 3-1	Oct27 1-2		Jan02 1-1	Oct06 4-0	Dec01 1-3	Apr03 2-1	Feb13 2-0	Jan19 5-2	Mar01 1-1
PARTICK T	Feb16 1-4	Dec08 5-2	Mar08 2-4	Dec25 1-3	Mar01 2-0	Nov03 2-0	Jan19 1-2	Sep15 2-1	Sep29		Mar22 3-0	Jan09 1-1	Dec22 1-3	Nov17 0-0	Oct13 2-1	Jan01 4-2
QUEEN OF SOUTH	Oct13 1-2	Jan19 4-2	Nov24 4-0	Feb27 1-0	Oct27 2-3	Feb16 1-1	Mar15 5-2	Dec22 4-1	Jan09 4-1	Dec15 2-1		Sep29 2-2	Mar29 2-2	Dec01 3-1	Jan01 2-0	Sep15 1-0
RAITH R	Mar01 2-1	Nov10 1-1	Jan12 1-0	Jan16 1-2	Sep22 2-3	Mar22 2-1	Sep08 0-2	Jan19 2-0	Apr28 2-0	Oct06 1-2	Jan02 0-0		Nov17 3-1	Dec29 2-1	Oct27 3-0	Dec01 1-0
RANGERS	Feb02 3-2	Jan12 1-0	Sep22 1-1	Jan02 2-0	Oct10 1-1	Oct20 2-0	Feb13 1-2	Mar15 2-2	Dec15 3-0	Sep08 4-1	Dec29 3-2	Feb27 1-0		Nov10 5-1	Nov24 3-0	Dec01 4-1
ST MIRREN	Dec22 3-1	Oct27 2-0	Mar15 3-1	Nov24 1-1	Jan19 0-2	Oct13 1-0	Dec15 0-4	Jan01 1-1	Nov03 3-0	Feb23 1-2	Mar08 3-1	Sep15 3-0	Jan26 0-5		Sep29 4-1	Jan15 3-0
STIRLING A	Nov17 0-4	Jan26 3-6	Nov10 2-1	Sep08 2-2	Oct06 3-2	Dec08 0-4	Mar08 1-4	Oct06 1-1	Oct20 2-1	Jan12 2-1	Sep22 1-1	Feb02 1-2	Mar01 1-5	Jan23 0-3		Mar22 3-3
T LANARK	Oct20 2-0	Sep08 4-0	Apr12 3-3	Dec29 0-2	Nov10 1-3	Apr14 4-0	Jan02 0-5	Feb27 3-1	Nov24 0-1	Sep22 0-0	Jan12 2-1	Mar15 3-1	Apr16 1-1	Oct06 4-2	Dec15 1-3	

DIVISION B

	ALBION R	ALLOA	ARBROATH	AYR U	CLYDE	COWDENBEATH	DUMBARTON	DUNDEE U	DUNFERMLINE A	FALKIRK	FORFAR A	HAMILTON A	KILMARNOCK	QUEEN'S PARK	ST JOHNSTONE	STENHOUSEMUIR
ALBION R		Mar05 1-1	Nov17 3-1	Mar01 2-0	Mar22 0-3	Jan12 0-0	Oct27 1-1	Dec08 1-3	Dec01 1-1	Oct06 1-5	Dec29 2-0	Sep22 0-0	Jan09 1-1	Sep08 1-1	Nov10 1-0	Apr12 2-6
ALLOA	Nov03 2-1		Oct13 2-2	Sep15 1-2	Feb16 3-3	Jan19 1-0	Jan01 4-1	Dec22 2-3	Apr26 5-4	Mar12 0-1	Dec15 4-2	Oct27 3-2	Feb23 1-2	Apr23 2-0	Nov24 2-0	Sep29 2-0
ARBROATH	Jan26 2-2	Jan12 2-1		Oct27 0-2	Jan19 1-3	Sep08 3-3	Nov24 1-2	Dec15 1-3	Nov10 5-3	Sep22 2-4	Dec29 1-2	Feb13 3-1	Jan02 2-1	Oct06 0-2	Oct06 4-3	Mar15 0-2
AYR U	Nov24 3-2	Oct06 2-0	Feb02 4-1		Dec01 1-1	Nov10 2-1	Feb27 4-1	Oct20 2-0	Mar15 3-1	Jan12 3-1	Jan09 4-0	Sep08 2-1	Sep22 1-0	Feb13 3-3	Dec29 2-1	Dec15 2-1
CLYDE	Sep15 5-1	Nov10 4-3	Oct20 2-1	Mar08 1-1		Oct06 11-1	Mar15 3-3	Mar11 3-0	Mar04 4-0	Dec29 1-1	Feb12 5-1	Jan12 0-2	Sep08 1-3	Sep22 5-2	Jan02 6-0	Nov24 3-1
COWDENBEATH	Oct13 3-1	Dec22 2-2	Dec22 8-1	Feb16 2-0	Jan05 3-2		Nov03 2-2	Sep29 2-2	Jan01 1-0	Apr12 5-0	Feb23 6-2	Dec01 3-1	Nov24 3-1	Dec15 2-3	Mar15 2-2	Sep15 1-0
DUMBARTON	Apr21 1-4	Sep22 1-2	Mar01 2-1	Nov17 2-2	Dec08 2-5	Jan26 1-5		Mar22 2-1	Oct20 0-0	Sep08 0-1	Nov10 3-1	Jan02 2-2	Dec29 4-2	Oct06 1-0	Jan12 3-1	Dec01 4-1
DUNDEE U	Mar15 0-0	Sep08 4-1	Mar08 3-1	Jan19 2-2	Oct27 3-5	Jan02 5-1	Dec15 4-1		Nov24 2-1	Apr14 2-3	Jan12 8-1	Oct06 3-2	Nov10 1-0	Dec29 5-0	Sep22 4-3	Mar05 3-0
DUNFERMLINE A	Mar08 5-1	Dec22 1-0	Mar22 5-0	Dec08 2-0	Nov17 3-7	Sep22 3-0	Jan19 3-2	Mar01 1-2		Jan02 0-6	Sep08 7-2	Nov10 3-6	Oct06 5-2	Jan12 2-1	Jan26 4-1	Dec01 2-2
FALKIRK	Jan16 3-1	Dec01 1-1	Feb16 5-1	Oct13 5-1	Apr05 2-1	Oct27 0-1	Dec22 1-1	Nov03 6-0	Sep29 5-1		Mar15 6-0	Jan19 0-1	Dec15 3-3	Nov24 6-0	Feb27 3-0	Jan01 1-2
FORFAR A	Apr19 2-0	Mar22 4-1	Jan01 4-1	Sep29 2-1	Nov03 1-2	Nov17 4-2	Feb16 1-3	Oct13 3-3	Dec22 3-2	Dec08 2-2		Mar01 1-6	Oct20 1-0	Feb20 2-1	Mar08 4-5	Jan05 4-1
HAMILTON A	Jan01 0-0	Feb02 0-1	Sep15 1-0	Dec01 1-1	Jan01 10-5	Mar08 3-2	Sep22 3-2	Jan05 1-1	Jan05 0-3	Feb12 0-1	Nov02 3-3		Mar15 2-1	Feb23 1-0	Dec15 4-2	Nov03 3-1
KILMARNOCK	Sep29 3-1	Nov17 1-0	Nov03 4-0	Jan01 4-0	Dec22 4-2	Mar01 5-1	Sep15 2-1	Feb16 5-1	Jan05 2-1	Mar22 6-3	Jan19 5-3	Dec08 2-1		Mar08 3-0	Oct27 0-1	Oct13 1-1
QUEEN'S PARK	Dec22 2-1	Dec08 0-2	Sep29 3-1	Nov03 0-1	Jan01 5-1	Mar22 2-2	Jan05 0-1	Sep15 1-2	Dec25 2-0	Jan26 0-3	Apr26 1-1	Nov17 1-3	Dec01 1-0		Jan19 4-5	Feb16 4-2
ST JOHNSTONE	Feb16 3-0	Mar01 2-2	Jan05 2-0	Feb23 2-0	Sep29 0-1	Dec08 6-0	Oct13 1-3	Jan01 4-1	Nov03 2-3	Jan01 1-3	Nov03 6-2	Feb20 1-1	Mar22 0-2	Oct20 1-1		Dec22 4-1
STENHOUSEMUIR	Oct20 3-3	Jan02 1-4	Dec08 3-0	Mar22 2-3	Mar01 0-8	Dec29 2-2	Mar08 1-1	Nov17 6-2	Apr19 3-2	Sep22 1-1	Oct06 5-2	Feb20 3-0	Jan12 1-2	Nov10 3-4	Sep08 1-1	

DIVISION A FINAL TABLE

	P	W	D	L	F	A	Pts
Hibernian	30	20	5	5	92	36	45
Rangers	30	16	9	5	61	31	41
East Fife	30	17	3	10	71	49	37
Hearts	30	14	7	9	69	53	35
Raith R	30	14	5	11	43	42	33
Partick T	30	12	7	11	48	51	31
Motherwell	30	12	7	11	51	57	31
Dundee	30	11	6	13	53	52	28
Celtic	30	10	8	12	52	55	28
Queen of South	30	10	8	12	50	60	28
Aberdeen	30	10	7	13	65	58	27
T Lanark	30	9	8	13	51	62	26
Airdrie	30	11	4	15	54	69	26
St Mirren	30	10	5	15	43	58	25
Morton	30	9	6	15	49	56	24
Stirling A	30	5	5	20	36	99	15

DIVISION B FINAL TABLE

	P	W	D	L	F	A	Pts
Clyde	30	19	6	5	100	45	44
Falkirk	30	18	7	5	80	34	43
Ayr U	30	17	5	8	55	45	39
Dundee U	30	16	5	9	75	60	37
Kilmarnock	30	16	2	12	62	48	34
Dunfermline A	30	15	2	13	74	65	32
Alloa	30	13	6	11	55	49	32
Cowdenbeath	30	12	8	10	66	67	32
Hamilton A	30	12	6	12	47	51	30
Dumbarton	30	10	8	12	51	57	28
St Johnstone	30	9	7	14	62	68	25
Forfar A	30	10	4	16	59	97	24
Stenhousemuir	30	8	6	16	57	74	22
Albion R	30	6	10	14	39	57	22
Queen's Park	30	8	4	18	40	62	20
Arbroath	30	6	4	20	40	83	16

SFA Cup

1st Round

Jan 24	Berwick R	3	Dundee U	3
Jan 24	Dumbarton	1	Cowdenbeath	3
Jan 24	East Fife	7	Vale of Leithen	1
Jan 24	Elgin C	2	T Lanark	3
Jan 24	Eyemouth U	0	Celtic	4
Jan 24	Hibernian	8	Stenhousemuir	1
Jan 24	Leith A	1	Airdrie	8
Jan 24	Morton	3	Dunfermline A	1
Jan 24	Newton Stewart	2	Falkirk	2
Jan 24	Queen of South	2	Huntly	1
Jan 24	Raith R	5	Clacknacuddin	0
Jan 24	Rangers	4	Arbroath	0
Jan 24	St Mirren	1	Brechin C	1
Jan 24	Stranraer	0	Kilmarnock	4

Replays

Jan 28	Brechin C	0	St Mirren	1
Jan 28	Dundee U	2	Berwick R	3
Jan 28	Falkirk	4	Newton Stewart	0

2nd Round

Feb 7	Aberdeen	2	St Mirren	0
Feb 7	Airdrie	3	East Fife	0
Feb 7	Albion R	2	E Stirling	0
Feb 7	Alloa	0	Motherwell	2
Feb 7	Berwick R	2	Queen of South	3
Feb 7	Buckie T	1	Ayr U	5
Feb 7	Cowdenbeath	0	Morton	2
Feb 7	Dundee	0	Rangers	2
Feb 7	Forfar A	2	Falkirk	4
Feb 7	Hamilton A	2	Kilmarnock	2
Feb 7	Hibernian	4	Queen's Park	2
Feb 7	Partick T	0	Clyde	2
Feb 7	Raith R	0	Hearts	1
Feb 7	St Johnstone	1	Montrose	1
Feb 7	Stirling A	1	Celtic	1
Feb 7	Wigtown & Blad	1	T Lanark	3

Replays

Feb 11	Celtic	3	Stirling A	0
Feb 11	Kilmarnock	0	Hamilton A	2

3rd Round

Feb 21	Aberdeen	5	Motherwell	5
Feb 21	Airdrie	0	Hibernian	4
Feb 21	Clyde	8	Ayr U	3
Feb 21	Falkirk	2	Celtic	3
Feb 21	Hearts	3	Montrose	1
Feb 21	Morton	1	Rangers	4

Feb 21	Queen of South	2	Albion R	0
Feb 21	T Lanark	1	Hamilton A	0

Replay

Feb 25	Motherwell	1	Aberdeen	6

4th Round

Mar 14	Clyde	1	T Lanark	2
Mar 14	Hearts	2	Queen of South	1
Mar 14	Hibernian	1	Aberdeen	1
Mar 14	Rangers	2	Celtic	0

Replay

Mar 18	Aberdeen	2	Hibernian	0

Semi-finals

Apr 4	Aberdeen	1	T Lanark	0

played at Ibrox

Apr 4	Hearts	1	Rangers	2

played at Hampden Park

Replay

Apr 8	Aberdeen	2	T Lanark	1

played at Ibrox

Final

Apr 25	Aberdeen	1	Rangers	1

played at Hampden Park

Replay

Apr 29	Aberdeen	0	Rangers	1

played at Hampden Park

League Cup results for 1952-53 are detailed on page 184.

DIVISION A

	ABERDEEN	AIRDRIE	CELTIC	CLYDE	DUNDEE	EAST FIFE	FALKIRK	HEARTS	HIBERNIAN	MOTHERWELL	PARTICK T	QUEEN OF SOUTH	RAITH R	RANGERS	ST MIRREN	T LANARK
ABERDEEN		Sep13 1-2	Sep27 2-2	Dec13 3-2	Jan01 2-2	Oct25 6-3	Nov22 7-2	Nov15 3-0	Apr11 1-1	Nov01 5-1	Dec20 4-2	Mar21 4-0	Feb28 0-2	Mar28 2-2	Jan10 1-2	Oct11 4-3
AIRDRIE	Oct18 4-7		Nov22 0-0	Oct04 4-4	Mar21 2-1	Nov15 3-1	Jan17 1-1	Jan03 1-2	Feb28 3-7	Sep20 2-0	Nov01 1-0	Apr11 1-2	Sep06 3-1	Dec27 2-2	Dec06 3-1	Apr27 4-2
CELTIC	Apr15 1-3	Mar18 0-1		Jan17 2-4	Dec13 5-0	Apr18 1-1	Sep06 5-3	Feb14 1-1	Mar28 1-3	Oct04 3-0	Mar07 3-1	Oct18 1-1	Dec27 0-1	Sep20 2-1	Apr11 3-2	Nov08 5-4
CLYDE	Jan24 3-0	Jan10 6-1	Oct11 1-2		Sep27 1-1	Dec20 1-2	Mar15 1-4	Oct18 3-2	Mar07 2-3	Sep06 3-2	Dec06 2-2	Jan01 5-0	Nov22 3-2	Nov01 4-6	Nov15 3-1	Jan31 1-0	Apr22 5-2
DUNDEE	Sep20 3-1	Nov29 0-2	Apr04 4-0	Jan03 4-1		Feb21 1-1	Mar15 2-1	Oct18 2-1	Mar07 0-0	Sep06 6-0	Dec06 0-0	Jan17 2-3	Feb14 1-1	Mar18 0-0	Mar18 3-0	
EAST FIFE	Feb14 4-1	Mar07 3-1	Mar21 4-1	Sep06 7-1	Nov01 3-2		Jan03 3-1	Oct04 3-1	Nov22 3-5	Dec27 2-2	Feb28 2-3	Jan17 0-0	Sep20 2-0	Oct18 0-3	Apr04 3-2	Dec06 7-0	3-1
FALKIRK	Apr20 4-1	Oct11 2-2	Dec20 2-3	Nov29 2-1	Jan10 2-1	Sep27 0-1		Apr18 2-4	Jan31 1-3	Apr04 2-1	Sep13 0-4	Nov15 2-0	Dec06 3-2	Nov08 1-2	Oct25 1-2	Jan01 5-1
HEARTS	Mar07 3-1	Sep27 4-0	Oct25 1-0	Mar28 7-0	Jan31 1-1	Apr28 4-2	Nov01 0-1		Jan01 1-2	Nov22 3-1	Oct11 2-1	Feb28 3-0	Mar21 1-2	Dec13 2-2	Sep13 1-2	Dec20 3-0
HIBERNIAN	Dec27 3-0	Nov08 3-1	Dec06 1-1	Feb14 5-1	Nov15 3-0	Apr20 2-1	Oct18 4-2	Sep20 3-1		Jan03 7-2	Apr04 1-1	Sep06 1-3	Apr29 4-1	Jan17 1-1	Nov29 0-2	Apr25 7-1
MOTHERWELL	Apr18 4-1	Jan01 4-1	Jan10 4-2	Nov08 3-6	Dec20 2-1	Sep13 3-3	Dec13 2-1	Jan24 1-3	Sep27 3-7		Oct25 1-2	Mar07 3-2	Apr20 2-1	Oct11 0-3	Jan31 1-1	1-5
PARTICK T	Sep06 1-1	Apr25 3-2	Nov15 3-0	Sep20 1-5	Mar28 0-3	Nov08 1-3	Dec27 0-3	Feb14 2-2	Dec13 5-4	Feb14 4-2		Apr06 2-2	Oct18 4-1	Apr11 1-2	Feb21 5-3	0-0
QUEEN OF SOUTH	Nov29 4-0	Oct25 1-2	Jan31 2-1	Sep13 3-1	Apr18 1-0	Oct11 0-1	Mar07 2-2	Nov08 4-2	Dec20 2-7	Dec06 3-1	Sep27 0-1		Apr04 1-1	May07 1-1	Jan01 1-4	Jan10 3-1
RAITH R	Nov08 2-1	Mar15 3-0	Sep13 1-1	Apr11 3-2	Oct11 1-1	Jan01 0-0	Jan01 0-2	Mar28 1-1	Nov29 4-2	Nov15 1-1	Mar31 2-2	Dec13 1-1		Mar18 3-1	Sep27 0-1	Oct25 3-4
RANGERS	Dec06 4-0	Apr15 8-2	Jan01 1-0	Mar07 1-2	May02 3-1	Mar31 4-0	Feb28 3-0	Apr06 1-2	Oct11 4-1	Mar21 1-0	Jan10 2-1	Nov01 3-2	Nov22		Dec20 4-0	Sep27 4-1
ST MIRREN	Oct04 2-1	Apr28 2-2	Nov01 1-2	Oct18 2-2	Feb28 0-0	Dec13 1-1	Feb14 3-0	Dec27 1-0	Mar21 2-2	Jan17 2-5	Nov22 1-1	Sep20 6-0	Apr25 3-2	Sep06 2-3		Nov15 1-0
T LANARK	Jan17 0-1	Dec13 2-1	Feb28 1-3	Dec27 1-3	Nov22 0-0	Mar28 0-3	Sep20 1-1	Sep06 2-3	Nov01 2-0	Oct18 1-2	Oct18 3-1	Oct04 5-0	Feb14 2-1	Jan03 0-2	Mar07 4-3	

DIVISION B

	ALBION R	ALLOA	ARBROATH	AYR U	COWDENBEATH	DUMBARTON	DUNDEE U	DUNFERMLINE A	FORFAR A	HAMILTON A	KILMARNOCK	MORTON	QUEEN'S PARK	ST JOHNSTONE	STENHOUSEMUIR	STIRLING A
ALBION R		Mar07 1-2	Jan31 1-2	Jan24 5-6	Sep13 2-2	Dec20 3-1	Nov08 2-4	Mar14 2-2	Apr18 1-1	Jan01 0-6	Jan10 2-1	Mar28 4-1	Dec13 1-1	Oct11 3-0	Sep27 0-1	Oct25 0-1
ALLOA	Nov15 4-2		Sep27 2-0	Nov08 3-6	Jan31 2-2	Oct25 4-1	Nov29 6-2	Feb21 3-3	Mar14 4-1	Oct11 0-5	Dec20 1-2	Dec13 3-0	Mar28 1-1	Jan24 2-0	Jan01 2-2	Apr11 1-3
ARBROATH	Oct18 3-0	Jan03 2-0		Jan17 1-1	Nov15 2-2	Feb21 2-1	Sep06 2-1	Dec13 4-1	Dec27 0-0	Sep20 3-2	Nov08 2-2	Dec27 1-0	Oct25 0-2	Dec28 1-3	Mar14 6-2	Nov29 3-1
AYR U	Mar21 4-3	Feb28 2-4	Oct11 7-2		Oct25 1-0	Sep27 5-0	Mar07 2-1	Dec13 8-1	Mar28 0-2	Jan10 2-1	Jan01 4-0	Nov01 4-0	Nov22 5-2	Jan31 2-4	Sep13 5-2	Dec20 2-4
COWDENBEATH	Dec27 3-2	Oct18 1-4	Mar07 3-0	Apr18 0-1		Mar14 2-2	Jan03 0-0	Sep20 4-3	Jan17 3-2	Nov29 2-0	Mar28 2-3	Sep06 1-2	Oct04 1-4	Dec13 3-3	Feb21 2-0	Nov08 0-3
DUMBARTON	Sep06 1-0	Feb14 4-2	Nov01 5-5	Jan03 2-2	Nov22 4-0		Oct18 1-3	Dec27 1-1	Oct04 2-1	Mar07 1-2	Feb28 4-2	Jan17 4-2	Sep20 2-1	Dec27 2-2	Dec06 1-0	Apr04 4-1
DUNDEE U	Feb28 2-1	Sep13 4-2	Dec20 1-2	Nov15 0-4	Sep27 0-0	Jan31 2-3		Mar28 1-1	Dec13 4-1	Oct25 2-3	Apr18 5-4	Nov22 0-4	Nov01 2-1	Jan01 1-0	Jan10 2-1	Oct11 1-3
DUNFERMLINE A	Nov22 2-1	Nov01 2-2	Jan10 0-0	Apr04 0-1	Jan01 2-1	Sep13 2-2	Dec06 1-1		Nov15 5-0	Jan31 2-1	Oct11 2-1	Feb28 0-1	Apr11 1-2	Oct25 2-0	Dec20 3-5	Sep27 5-1
FORFAR A	Nov01 4-2	Nov22 5-2	Jan01 4-0	Dec06 1-2	Oct11 2-0	Jan10 5-2	Jan10 1-3	Mar07 2-1		Apr07 1-3	Mar22 6-0	Feb28 5-1	Sep27 3-6	Apr11 1-3	Sep27 5-0	Jan24 1-3
HAMILTON A	Sep20 3-2	Jan17 2-0	Feb28 2-1	Oct04 4-0	Mar21 0-1	Nov01 3-1	Feb14 3-1	Oct18 7-1	Sep06 2-0		Nov22 2-2	Jan03 3-3	Dec27 4-2	Nov01 1-0	Apr04 2-1	Dec06 4-1
KILMARNOCK	Apr11 4-0	Sep06 1-2	Apr04 4-0	Sep20 0-1	Dec06 2-0	Nov08 2-0	Dec27 1-0	Jan17 2-3	Apr25 4-0	Mar14 6-1		Oct18 3-2	Jan03 0-1	Nov15 2-3	Nov29 4-1	Feb21 6-0
MORTON	Dec06 5-0	Apr04 4-1	Apr18 4-0	Jan10 6-1	Dec27 1-0	Nov08 6-0	Jan10 1-2	Sep27 7-1	Feb21 5-3	Jan10 1-4		Apr25 2-2	Jan10 1-1	Sep06 4-1	Oct11 1-2	Jan01 2-2
QUEEN'S PARK	Apr22 4-0	Dec06 1-2	Apr06 5-1	Mar14 2-0	Jan10 4-0	Jan01 1-3	Feb21 3-0	Apr14 6-2	Nov08 1-1	Sep13 1-1	Sep27 2-7	Nov15		Dec20 4-1	Oct11 1-2	Jan31 3-4
ST JOHNSTONE	Jan17 1-3	Dec27 3-0	Dec06 0-4	Oct18 1-4	Apr04 1-2	Nov29 3-2	Sep20 1-1	Feb14 1-0	Jan03 0-2	Apr11 1-2	Mar07 2-1	Sep06 0-2		Nov08 2-2	Mar14 4-2
STENHOUSEMUIR	Jan03 3-1	Sep20 4-1	Nov22 1-2	Apr12 2-0	Nov01 3-0	Mar28 1-2	Oct04 0-4	Sep18 5-0	Oct11 4-1	Jan17 0-4	Feb14 2-5	Jan17 2-2	Feb28 3-0		Mar07 0-0
STIRLING A	Apr25 3-0	Oct04 2-1	Mar21 4-1	Sep06 1-0	Feb28 2-0	Dec13 2-1	Jan17 2-0	Jan03 3-0	Dec27 7-2	Mar28 0-0	Nov01 3-1	Sep20 3-1	Oct18 3-2	Nov22 3-0	Nov15 2-1	

DIVISION A FINAL TABLE

	P	W	D	L	F	A	Pts
Rangers	30	18	7	5	80	39	43
Hibernian	30	19	5	6	93	51	43
East Fife	30	16	7	7	72	48	39
Hearts	30	12	6	12	59	50	30
Clyde	30	13	4	13	78	78	30
St Mirren	30	11	8	11	52	58	30
Dundee	30	9	11	8	44	37	29
Celtic	30	11	7	12	51	54	29
Partick T	30	10	9	11	55	63	29
Queen of South	30	10	8	12	43	61	28
Aberdeen	30	11	5	14	64	68	27
Raith R	30	9	8	13	47	53	26
Falkirk	30	11	4	15	53	63	26
Airdrie	30	10	6	14	53	75	26
Motherwell	30	10	5	15	57	80	25
T Lanark	30	8	4	18	52	75	20

DIVISION B FINAL TABLE

	P	W	D	L	F	A	Pts
Stirling A	30	20	4	6	64	43	44
Hamilton A	30	20	3	7	72	40	43
Queen's Park	30	15	7	8	70	46	37
Kilmarnock	30	17	2	11	74	48	36
Ayr U	30	17	2	11	76	56	36
Morton	30	15	3	12	79	57	33
Arbroath	3	13	7	10	52	57	33
Dundee U	30	12	5	13	52	56	29
Alloa	30	12	5	13	63	68	29
Dumbarton	30	11	6	13	58	67	28
Dunfermline A	30	9	9	12	51	58	27
Stenhousemuir	30	10	6	14	56	65	26
Cowdenbeath	30	8	7	15	37	54	23
St Johnstone	30	8	6	16	41	63	22
Forfar A	30	8	4	18	54	88	20
Albion R	30	5	4	21	44	77	14

SFA Cup

1st Round

Jan 30	Alloa	1	Clyde	3
Jan 30	Berwick R	7	E Stirling	0
Jan 30	East Fife	0	Queen of South	3
Jan 30	Fraserburgh	5	Leith A	4
Jan 30	Inverness T	3	Hamilton A	3
Jan 30	Montrose	0	Peebles R	1
Jan 30	Morton	3	Dundee U	2
Jan 30	Partick T	1	Airdrie	0
Jan 30	Rangers	2	Queen's Park	0
Jan 30	St Johnstone	1	Hibernian	2
Jan 30	St Mirren	1	Motherwell	2
Jan 30	Stirling A	2	Dumbarton	1
Jan 30	Stranraer	1	Dunfermline A	4
Jan 30	T Lanark	2	Stenhousemuir	2

Replays

Feb 3	Hamilton A	3	Inverness T	1
Feb 3	Stenhousemuir	0	T Lanark	0
Feb 8	Stenhousemuir	0	T Lanark	1
	played at Ibrox			

2nd Round

Feb 13	Albion R	1	Dundee	1
Feb 13	Berwick R	5	Ayr U	1
Feb 13	Brechin C	2	Hamilton A	3
Feb 13	Coldstream	1	Raith R	10
Feb 13	Duns	0	Aberdeen	8
Feb 17	Falkirk	1	Celtic	2
Feb 13	Fraserburgh	0	Hearts	3
Feb 13	Hibernian	7	Clyde	0
Feb 13	Morton	4	Cowdenbeath	0
Feb 13	Motherwell	5	Dunfermline A	2
Feb 13	Peebles R	1	Buckie T	1
Feb 13	Queen of South	3	Forfar A	0
Feb 13	Rangers	2	Kilmarnock	2
Feb 17	Stirling A	0	Arbroath	0
Feb 13	Tarff R	1	Partick T	9
Feb 13	T Lanark	7	Deveronvale	2

Replays

Feb 17	Dundee	4	Albion R	0
Feb 17	Kilmarnock	1	Rangers	3
Feb 20	Buckie T	7	Peebles R	2
Feb 22	Arbroath	1	Stirling A	3

3rd Round

Feb 27	Berwick R	3	Dundee	0
Feb 27	Hamilton A	2	Morton	0
Feb 27	Hibernian	1	Aberdeen	3
Feb 27	Motherwell	4	Raith R	1
Feb 27	Partick T	5	Buckie T	3
Feb 27	Queen of South	1	Hearts	2
Feb 27	Stirling A	3	Celtic	4
Feb 27	T Lanark	0	Rangers	0

Replays

Mar 3	Rangers	4	T Lanark	4
Mar 8	Rangers	3	T Lanark	2
	played at Ibrox			

4th Round

Mar 13	Aberdeen	3	Hearts	0
Mar 13	Hamilton A	1	Celtic	2
Mar 13	Partick T	1	Motherwell	1
Mar 13	Rangers	4	Berwick R	0

Replay

Mar 17	Motherwell	2	Partick T	1

Semi-finals

Apr 10	Aberdeen	6	Rangers	0
	played at Hampden Park			
Mar 27	Celtic	2	Motherwell	2
	played at Hampden Park			

Replay

Apr 5	Celtic	3	Motherwell	1
	played at Hampden Park			

Final

Apr 24	Aberdeen	1	Celtic	2
	played at Hampden Park			

> League Cup results for 1953-54 are detailed on page 185.

DIVISION A

	ABERDEEN	AIRDRIE	CELTIC	CLYDE	DUNDEE	EAST FIFE	FALKIRK	HAMILTON A	HEARTS	HIBERNIAN	PARTICK T	QUEEN OF SOUTH	RAITH R	RANGERS	ST MIRREN	STIRLING A
ABERDEEN		Oct17 5-0	Jan02 2-0	Feb20 5-3	Sep19 1-1	Feb06 1-0	Mar17 0-1	Oct10 5-1	Mar20 1-0	Jan16 1-3	Oct03 2-1	Nov14 2-0	Dec05 2-0	Nov07 1-1	Sep05 0-3	Dec26 8-0
AIRDRIE	Jan23 1-3		Mar17 0-6	Dec19 3-4	Nov14 2-2	Mar20 3-2	Sep12 2-2	Jan01 5-0	Sep26 2-1	Dec05 2-2	Mar31 3-6	Oct24 1-1	Jan09 1-2	Apr24 2-0	Feb27 1-3	Oct31 1-1
CELTIC	Sep26 3-0	Nov21 4-1		Sep12 1-0	Feb20 5-1	Mar06 4-1	Jan09 1-0	Apr26 2-0	Oct24 2-2	Nov07 2-1	Nov28 3-1	Jan23 3-0	Oct10 1-0	Jan01 4-0	Dec12 4-0	Mar29 4-0
CLYDE	Oct31 2-4	Sep05 4-1	Dec26 1-7		Jan02 2-0	Oct03 3-1	Nov14 4-1	Apr14 4-1	Apr17 0-1	Feb06 3-6	Sep19 0-4	Mar13 2-0	Apr03 4-2	Mar20 2-5	Oct17 4-2	Jan16 1-1
DUNDEE	Jan01 4-2	Mar10 1-0	Oct31 1-1	Sep26 2-0		Dec12 1-1	Dec19 1-0	Jan09 3-2	Jan23 2-4	Mar28 1-0	Apr17 6-0	Oct10 4-1	Sep12 0-0	Oct24 1-0	Mar27 2-0	Nov21 2-1
EAST FIFE	Apr14 2-0	Nov28 1-0	Nov14 3-1	Jan09 3-1	Apr03 1-1		Sep26 4-1	Apr21 4-1	Dec19 1-3	Mar13 4-1	Dec05 4-0	Apr24 1-1	Jan01 2-1	Jan23 2-0	Oct31 2-0	Apr10 2-1
FALKIRK	Nov21 2-2	Dec26 4-1	Apr14 0-3	Feb27 1-1	Sep05 4-0	Jan02 3-3		Oct31 2-2	Dec12 1-3	Oct17 2-4	Jan16 2-2	Apr10 0-4	Mar27 0-3	Feb06 4-3	Dec26 4-0	Sep19 2-0
HAMILTON A	Dec12 3-2	Sep19 0-1	Sep05 2-0	Mar27 1-3	Oct03 2-3	Jan16 0-1	Feb20 2-1		Nov21 1-5	Jan02 2-6	Feb06 1-3	Nov07 0-5	Dec19 2-1	Mar06 1-1	Dec26 0-2	Oct17 0-1
HEARTS	Nov28 3-2	Jan02 4-3	Feb06 3-2	Nov07 1-2	Oct17 2-1	Sep05 2-0	Jan30 0-0	Mar17 3-0		Sep19 4-0	Dec26 0-2	Sep12 2-3	Nov14 5-1	Feb20 3-3	Jan16 5-1	Oct03 6-1
HIBERNIAN	Apr19 3-0	Mar27 8-1	Apr17 0-3	Oct24 4-0	Mar20 2-0	Nov21 2-1	Jan23 2-3	Sep26 4-1	Jan01 1-2		Oct31 1-2	Jan09 1-0	Dec19 5-0	Apr26 2-2	Mar06 2-1	Dec12 1-2
PARTICK T	Jan09 6-3	9-0	Nov20 1-3	Jan01 3-4	Nov07 1-0	0-1	Mar27 5-1	Apr24 4-0	Apr10 2-1	Feb20 0-2		Sep26 1-2	Jan23 5-3	Dec19 0-1	Nov21 2-0	Mar06 3-1
QUEEN OF SOUTH	Mar06 2-4	Apr10 6-2	Oct17 2-1	Nov21 1-2	Jan16 5-1	Dec26 5-0	Nov28 5-3	Apr17 2-2	Dec05 2-2	Oct03 2-6	Jan02 5-1		Oct31 2-1	Dec12 5-5	Sep19 2-1	Sep05 4-1
RAITH R	Mar27 3-1	Oct03 5-1	Jan16 2-0	Dec12 3-4	Dec26 1-2	Sep19 2-2	Nov07 0-2	Mar06 5-0	Sep05 4-2	Oct17 4-0	Feb20 1-1		Nov21 1-2	Jan02 1-2	Feb06 1-1
RANGERS	Apr17 1-3	Jan16 3-0	Apr19 1-1	Nov28 1-1	Feb06 2-0	Oct17 3-0	Apr21 0-1	Nov14 8-1	Oct31 0-1	Dec26 3-0	Sep05 3-0	Apr03 2-0	Mar17 2-2		Apr14 1-1	Jan02 3-1
ST MIRREN	Dec19 1-4	Nov07 1-0	Apr07 3-3	Jan23 0-1	Apr10 3-0	Feb13 1-1	Oct24 3-1	Sep12 1-3	Oct10 5-3	Nov14 5-1	Mar24 3-3	Jan01 5-1	Sep26 0-1	Jan09		Mar20 3-0
STIRLING A	Sep12 1-0	Feb20 2-1	Dec05 2-1	Oct10 2-2	Mar13 2-3	Nov07 3-2	Jan01 0-1	Jan23 6-0	Jan09 0-3	Apr07 2-1	Nov14 1-2	Dec19 3-0	Oct24 1-3	Sep26 2-0	Nov28 0-2	

DIVISION A FINAL TABLE

	P	W	D	L	F	A	Pts
Celtic	30	20	3	7	72	29	43
Hearts	30	16	6	8	70	45	38
Partick T	30	17	1	12	76	54	35
Rangers	30	13	8	9	56	35	34
Hibernian	30	15	4	11	72	51	34
East Fife	30	13	8	9	55	45	34
Dundee	30	14	6	10	46	47	34
Clyde	30	15	4	11	64	67	34
Aberdeen	30	15	3	12	66	51	33
Queen of South	30	14	4	12	72	58	32
St Mirren	30	12	4	14	44	54	28
Raith R	30	10	6	14	56	60	26
Falkirk	30	9	7	14	47	61	25
Stirling A	30	10	4	16	39	62	24
Airdrie	30	5	5	20	41	92	15
Hamilton A	30	4	3	23	29	94	11

DIVISION B FINAL TABLE

	P	W	D	L	F	A	Pts
Motherwell	30	21	3	6	109	43	45
Kilmarnock	30	19	4	7	71	39	42
T Lanark	30	13	10	7	78	48	36
Stenhousemuir	30	14	8	8	66	58	36
Morton	30	15	3	12	85	65	33
St Johnstone	30	14	3	13	80	71	31
Albion R	30	12	7	11	55	63	31
Dunfermline A	30	11	9	10	48	57	31
Ayr U	30	11	8	11	50	56	30
Queen's Park	30	9	9	12	56	51	27
Alloa	30	7	10	13	50	72	24
Forfar A	30	10	4	16	38	69	24
Cowdenbeath	30	9	5	16	67	81	23
Arbroath	30	8	7	15	53	67	23
Dundee U	30	8	6	16	54	79	22
Dumbarton	30	7	8	15	51	92	22

DIVISION B

	ALBION R	ALLOA	ARBROATH	AYR U	COWDENBEATH	DUMBARTON	DUNDEE U	DUNFERMLINE A	FORFAR A	KILMARNOCK	MORTON	MOTHERWELL	QUEEN'S PARK	ST JOHNSTONE	STENHOUSEMUIR	T LANARK
ALBION R		Feb20 1-3	Feb06 1-1	Nov21 4-2	Jan16 3-2	Dec26 4-1	Dec12 3-3	Nov28 3-1	Jan30 1-2	Jan02 1-1	Nov07 3-2	Sep19 2-3	Apr21 2-0	Oct03 3-2	Oct17 1-0	Sep05 1-0
ALLOA	Oct31 2-2		Jan16 3-3	Dec12 4-1	Jan02 2-2	Feb06 2-2	Nov21 1-3	Feb27 4-5	Mar06 4-3	Oct17 1-0	Mar20 1-2	Dec26 2-3	Apr28 5-1	Sep05 2-3	Sep19 1-1	Oct03 2-0
ARBROATH	Oct24 3-1	Oct10 1-1		Jan30 1-0	Mar27 2-1	Nov21 2-3	Jan09 4-3	Jan23 5-0	Jan01 2-3	Feb20 1-0	Sep26 2-3	Dec12 1-4	Dec19 3-2	Nov07 3-4	Mar06 1-1	Mar20 2-2
AYR U	Mar13 2-2	Apr03 2-4	Dec26 3-0		Sep05 4-0	Jan16 0-0	Nov28 2-1	Nov07 1-2	Sep19 3-1	Dec05 1-0	Jan02 2-1	Feb20 0-3	Oct17 0-0	Oct03 3-4	Feb27 1-2	Feb06 0-6
COWDENBEATH	Oct31 4-3	Sep26 6-1	Dec05 2-1	Dec19 5-2		Oct31 6-1	Oct24 4-2	Jan01 1-1	Jan30 2-3	Sep12 6-0	Nov28 1-2	Jan23 1-1	Apr24 3-3	Feb27 1-3	Nov14 1-3
DUMBARTON	Sep12 5-1	Oct24 0-0	Mar13 1-0	Oct10 3-1	Feb20 2-2		Dec19 4-4	Sep26 0-1	Jan23 2-5	Nov14 2-4	Jan01 1-4	Nov07 1-1	Jan09 3-2	Apr17 1-2	Apr28 3-2
DUNDEE U	Mar31 6-2	Mar13 0-1	Oct03 2-2	Mar20 4-0	Feb06 3-3	Sep05 2-1		Dec05 1-0	Feb20 0-1	Oct31 0-2	Nov14 1-5	Oct17 1-0	Nov07 1-2	Sep19 1-1	Jan04 1-1
DUNFERMLINE A	Mar20 2-0	Nov07 2-1	Oct17 2-0	Mar10 0-0	Sep19 5-3	Jan02 6-1	Mar27 0-1		Dec12 1-1	Sep05 1-0	Feb20 1-3	Oct03 4-3	Nov21 3-1	Dec26 0-4	Feb06 3-2	Jan16 0-3
FORFAR A	Dec05 1-2	Nov14 2-2	Sep19 0-3	Feb27 0-1	Oct03 1-0	Oct17 1-2	Oct31 3-2	Apr24 0-1		Feb06 2-3	Mar13 3-2	Sep05 0-5	Nov28 0-3	Jan02 1-0	Jan16 1-1	Dec26 2-3
KILMARNOCK	Sep26 0-3	Jan23 2-0	Oct31 4-0	Jan01 0-3	Nov21 1-0	Mar06 7-2	Oct10 3-2	Dec19 2-2	Oct24 6-0		Jan09 2-0	Mar31 4-2	Apr24 2-0	Mar20 5-0	Dec12 6-2	Apr17 1-1
MORTON	Apr10 0-1	Apr17 3-0	Jan23 5-2	Mar27 2-2	Dec26 5-2	Sep19 8-0	Mar06 4-1	Oct31 3-3	Apr03 4-0	Apr06 4-6		Feb06 2-5	Dec12 0-3	Jan16 4-3	Sep05 3-3	Oct17 0-3
MOTHERWELL	Jan01 6-0	Sep12 6-0	Apr07 2-1	Sep26 3-4	Mar20 5-2	Apr10 6-6	Jan23 12-1	Jan09 3-0	Dec19 5-1	Dec05 0-2	Oct24 3-2		Oct10 4-0	Nov14 0-3	Oct31 4-0	Mar24 1-1
QUEEN'S PARK	Nov14 2-2	Apr14 4-1	Sep05 3-4	Oct31 2-4	Oct17 7-1	Feb27 6-0	Mar13 3-1	Mar20 4-0	Feb06 2-1	Apr17 1-1	Jan16 4-2		Feb06 2-4	Jan02 4-0	Jan01 1-1
ST JOHNSTONE	Jan09 3-3	Jan16 7-0	Feb27 3-1	Jan23 1-2	Nov28 6-1	Jan01 3-1	Apr10 5-1	Sep26 5-2	Nov28 1-4	Oct19 1-2	Mar06 2-6	Oct24 0-0		Nov21 5-1	Oct31 1-1
STENHOUSEMUIR	Jan23 3-0	Jan01 2-2	Nov14 5-1	Jan09 2-2	Nov07 2-4	Oct28 6-0	Sep12 4-3	Oct24 2-2	Oct10 2-1	Apr03 0-1	Dec19 4-1	Feb20 2-1	Sep26 2-1	Mar13 3-0		Dec05 5-3
T LANARK	Dec19 1-0	Sep19 0-3	Nov28 2-2	Apr21 4-2	Mar06 2-1	Dec12 9-1	Sep26 1-1	Apr19 1-1	Apr12 3-7	Nov07 1-9	Jan23 2-4	Nov21 4-0	Sep19 0-1	Feb20 9-2	Mar30 1-1	

SFA Cup

1st Round
Sep 11	Aberdeen Univ	3	Girvan A	3
Sep 11	Babcock	3	Shawfield A	1
Sep 11	Burntisland	1	Forres Mechanic	7
Sep 11	Chirnside U	1	Peterhead	4
Sep 11	Civil Service S	2	Vale of Leithen	3
Sep 11	Deveronvale	0	Inverness T	4
Sep 11	Eyemouth	2	Buckie T	3
Sep 11	Fraserburgh	9	Edinburgh Univ	0
Sep 11	Gala Fairydean	5	Keith	3
Sep 11	Glasgow Univ	1	Huntly	5
Sep 11	Inverness C	7	Rothes	3
	Leith	W	Selkirk	0
Sep 11	Lossiemouth	6	Murrayfield A	0
Sep 11	Newton Stewart	3	Elgin C	5
Sep 11	Ross Co	2	Peebles R	2
Sep 11	St Cuthbert's	5	Vale of Atholl	1
Sep 11	Tarff R	1	Duns	1
Sep 11	Wick A	2	Coldstream	4

Replays
Sep 18	Duns	3	Tarff R	0
Sep 18	Girvan A	2	Aberdeen Univ	0
Sep 18	Peebles R	5	Ross Co	1

2nd Round
Sep 25	Brora R	2	Coldstream	0
Sep 25	Duns	1	Buckie T	1
Sep 25	Elgin C	1	Clacknacuddin	1
Sep 25	Forres Mechanic	5	Huntly	1
Sep 25	Inverness C	5	Wigtown	0
Sep 25	Inverness T	7	Selkirk	1
Sep 25	Lossiemouth	1	Gala Fairydean	0
Sep 25	Peebles R	4	Girvan A	3
Sep 25	Peterhead	7	Babcock	0
Sep 25	St Cuthbert's	4	Whithorn	2
Sep 25	Vale of Leithen	0	Fraserburgh	4

Replays
Sep 25	Clacknacuddin	7	Elgin C	1

3nd Round
Oct 9	Berwick R	3	Clacknacuddin	3
Oct 9	Brora R	3	Inverness C	3
Oct 9	Fraserburgh	4	E Stirling	2
Oct 9	Inverness T	2	Stranraer	1
Oct 9	Lossiemouth	3	Dumbarton	1
Oct 9	Peebles R	5	St Cuthbert's	2
Oct 9	Peterhead	0	Buckie T	4

Replays
Oct 16	Clacknacuddin	2	Berwick R	1
Oct 16	Forres Mechanic	5	Lossiemouth	3
Oct 16	Inverness C	8	Brora R	2

4th Round
Oct 23	Alloa	4	Fraserburgh	2
Oct 23	Arbroath	2	Brechin C	0
Oct 23	Buckie T	1	Queen's Park	1
Oct 23	Clacknacuddin	1	Inverness T	2
Oct 23	Cowdenbeath	2	Ayr U	2
Oct 23	Dundee U	1	Forfar A	3

League Cup results for 1954-55 are detailed on page 186.

DIVISION A FINAL TABLE

	P	W	D	L	F	A	Pts
Aberdeen	30	24	1	5	73	26	49
Celtic	30	19	8	3	76	37	46
Rangers	30	19	3	8	67	33	41
Hearts	30	16	7	7	74	45	39
Hibernian	30	15	4	11	64	54	34
St Mirren	30	12	8	10	55	54	32
Clyde	30	11	9	10	59	50	31
Dundee	30	13	4	13	48	48	30
Partick T	30	11	7	12	49	61	29
Kilmarnock	30	10	6	14	46	58	26
East Fife	30	9	6	15	51	62	24
Falkirk	30	8	8	14	42	54	24
Queen of South	30	9	6	15	38	56	24
Raith R	30	10	3	17	49	57	23
Motherwell	30	9	4	17	42	62	22
Stirling A	30	2	2	26	29	105	6

DIVISION B FINAL TABLE

	P	W	D	L	F	A	Pts
Airdrie	30	18	10	2	103	61	46
Dunfermline A	30	19	4	7	72	40	42
Hamilton A	30	17	5	8	74	51	39
Queen's Park	30	15	5	10	65	36	35
T Lanark	30	13	7	10	63	49	33
Stenhousemuir	30	12	8	10	70	51	32
St Johnstone	30	15	2	13	60	51	32
Ayr U	30	14	4	12	61	73	32
Morton	30	12	5	13	58	69	29
Forfar A	30	11	6	13	63	80	28
Albion R	30	8	10	12	50	69	26
Arbroath	30	8	8	14	55	72	24
Dundee U	30	8	6	16	55	70	22
Cowdenbeath	30	8	5	17	55	72	21
Alloa	30	7	6	17	51	75	20
Brechin C	30	8	3	19	53	89	19

DIVISION A (results grid — home team in rows, date over score)

	ABERDEEN	CELTIC	CLYDE	DUNDEE	EAST FIFE	FALKIRK	HEARTS	HIBERNIAN	KILMARNOCK	MOTHERWELL	PARTICK T	QUEEN OF SOUTH	RAITH R	RANGERS	ST MIRREN	STIRLING A
ABERDEEN		Oct09 0-2	Dec18 3-0	Jan01 1-0	Oct23 4-1	Nov27 1-0	Nov20 1-0	Sep25 3-1	Mar30 4-1	Jan08 4-1	Feb12 4-0	Nov06 2-0	Apr23 3-2	Apr02 4-0	Jan22 2-1	Sep11 5-0
CELTIC	Apr16 2-1		Dec25 2-2	Dec18 4-1	Dec04 2-2	Mar30 3-1	Jan29 2-0	Apr02 1-2	Oct02 6-3	Mar19 1-0	Oct16 0-0	Sep18 1-1	Apr23 4-1	Feb26 2-0	Sep18 5-2	Nov13 7-0
CLYDE	Apr09 0-1	Sep11 2-2		Oct09 2-0	Feb12 0-3	Mar30 6-3	Dec11 1-1	Oct23 2-2	Nov27 2-2	Jan22 2-2	Jan01 3-0	Mar09 1-1	Nov06 3-2	Nov20 1-2	Jan08 3-3	Sep25 5-1
DUNDEE	Sep18 0-2	Apr09 0-1	Apr11 2-1		Mar09 1-1	Oct16 2-0	Oct02 3-2	Mar12 2-2	Jan03 2-5	Dec04 4-1	Dec11 3-1	Oct30 3-1	Dec25 4-1	Jan29 2-1	Nov13 0-1	Mar19 4-1
EAST FIFE	Jan29 1-1	Mar30 3-4	Oct30 0-3	Nov06 4-1		Apr16 2-0	Oct16 0-2	Nov27 1-5	Dec25 1-5	Mar12 4-2	Jan03 0-2	Sep18 0-1	Jan03 3-1	Oct02 2-7	Apr09 6-1	Dec11 5-0
FALKIRK	Mar19 1-2	Feb12 1-1	Dec04 2-1	Apr30 2-2	Apr23 2-2		Feb26 2-2	Jan08 3-1	Nov20 5-3	Sep11 1-1	Sep25 3-1	Apr09 2-1	Dec11 2-1	Nov13 0-3	Oct23 0-3	Jan01 4-1
HEARTS	Mar12 2-0	Apr30 0-3	Apr02 3-0	Jan08 2-1	Apr13 1-3	Nov06 5-3		Jan01 5-1	Apr06 2-2	Apr18 3-2	Sep11 5-4	Nov27 3-1	Mar26 2-0	Dec18 3-4	Apr22 1-1	Feb12 3-0
HIBERNIAN	Jan03 0-1	Dec11 0-5	Nov20 2-3	Mar19 3-1	0-0	Oct02 0-1	Sep18 2-3		Oct30 3-2	Nov13 4-1	Apr09 3-1	Apr16 1-1	Oct16 2-1	Dec25 2-1	Dec04 2-1	Mar23 4-1
KILMARNOCK	Dec04 0-4	Jan08 1-2	Mar19 1-2	Sep25 0-2	Sep11 0-0	Mar12 2-3	Nov24 0-3	Feb12 1-2		Apr13 1-2	Oct09 4-1	Dec11 2-2	Apr09 1-0	Feb26 1-5	Jan01 3-0	Apr30 3-1
MOTHERWELL	Oct02 1-3	Nov27 2-2	Oct16 2-0	Mar26 0-2	Nov20 3-5	Dec25 0-3	Apr16 1-1	Mar09 1-5	Jan29 0-1		Nov06 1-2	Sep18 2-1	Oct30 3-2	Jan03 2-0	Dec11 2-3	Apr09 3-1
PARTICK T	Oct30 1-0	Nov20 4-2	Sep18 2-3	Apr02 2-1	Nov13 1-0	Jan03 2-2	Dec25 4-4	Dec18 0-3	Apr16 0-3	Feb26 0-1		Jan29 1-0	Oct02 1-1	Oct16 2-5	Mar19 1-1	Dec04 3-3
QUEEN OF SOUTH	Feb26 2-6	Jan22 0-2	Nov13 2-1	Feb12 1-1	Apr30 1-0	Dec18 3-2	Mar19 1-1	Oct09 0-2	Mar05 1-0	Jan01 1-0	Oct23 0-2		Mar12 2-0	Dec04 1-2	Jan08 0-3	
RAITH R	Nov13 1-2	Sep25 1-3	Feb26 2-3	Sep11 3-0	Jan01 4-1	Apr02 3-0	Dec04 0-6	Apr30 2-1	Dec18 0-0	Feb12 3-2	Jan08 2-3	Nov20 3-1		Mar19 1-0	Oct09 4-0	Oct23 5-1
RANGERS	Dec11 3-1	Jan01 4-1	Jan22 1-0	Oct23 3-0	Jan08 2-0	Mar09 4-1	Apr09 2-1	Sep11 1-1	Nov06 6-0	Apr30 2-0	Apr11 3-1	Mar26 1-0	Nov27 1-0		Feb12 1-1	Oct09 6-1
ST MIRREN	Oct16 0-4	Nov06 1-1	Oct02 4-4	Mar05 0-2	Dec18 2-7	Jan29 2-0	Jan03 0-1	Mar26 2-0	Sep18 2-0	Mar29 3-2	Dec25 3-2	Apr16 0-2	Oct30 2-1			Nov20 7-1
STIRLING A	Dec25 3-4	Mar09 2-3	Jan03 1-4	Nov27 0-2	Apr02 0-4	Sep18 1-1	Oct30 0-5	Nov06 2-4	Oct16 1-2	Dec18 1-3	Mar26 0-1	Oct02 0-3	Jan29 2-1	Mar05 0-2	Mar12 2-1	

DIVISION B (results grid — home team in rows, date over score)

	AIRDRIE	ALBION R	ALLOA	ARBROATH	AYR U	BRECHIN C	COWDENBEATH	DUNDEE U	DUNFERMLINE A	FORFAR A	HAMILTON A	MORTON	QUEEN'S PARK	ST JOHNSTONE	STENHOUSEMUIR	T LANARK
AIRDRIE		Sep18 3-3	Dec25 5-1	Nov06 3-1	Dec11 5-4	Nov27 6-1	Nov20 3-1	Oct02 2-1	Oct30 6-2	Oct16 6-2	Jan29 6-3	Jan03 6-2	Apr23 4-2	Mar30 4-1	Apr09 2-1	Apr16 1-1
ALBION R	Jan01 2-2		Apr20 0-2	Oct09 4-4	Sep11 4-5	Apr27 2-0	Apr30 2-3	May02 3-2	Mar12 2-1	Apr11 1-1	Dec04 3-2	Mar19 3-3	Feb12 1-3	Jan08 4-2	Feb12 2-3	Oct23 1-1
ALLOA	Sep11 2-2	Apr09 1-2		Sep25 3-3	Apr16 4-6	Feb12 4-1	Oct09 0-0	Mar19 2-3	Dec11 0-2	Dec04 2-2	Nov20 2-3	Nov13 0-0	May04 2-4	Jan22 1-1	Jan01 2-1	Jan08 1-3
ARBROATH	Feb26 3-3	Apr23 1-0	Jan03 0-2		Mar19 5-1	Mar12 1-1	Nov13 2-2	Jan29 3-1	Oct02 2-3	Sep18 4-3	Oct30 0-3	Oct16 2-4	Dec25 1-4	Apr02 1-2	Dec04 1-0	Dec18 2-0
AYR U	Apr02 3-2	Dec25 2-2	Jan29 3-0	Nov27 2-0		Nov06 4-0	Oct16 2-0	Apr23 5-1	Oct02 1-1	Apr20 3-3	Jan03 2-0	Sep18 3-1	Mar30 1-0	Nov20 0-4	Dec11 2-0	Mar26 2-0
BRECHIN C	Mar19 1-1	Oct16 1-1	Oct30 2-4	Nov20 4-5	Apr13 0-3		3-6	Dec04 2-3	Feb05 1-5	Jan03 2-4	Dec25 3-1	Oct02 2-3	Sep18 1-2	Jan29 1-0	Dec18 0-0	Nov13 1-0
COWDENBEATH	Mar12 1-1	Jan03 4-2	Feb19 2-5	Mar05 3-5	Apr09 1-2	Mar26 1-1		Apr23 3-1	Sep18 3-1	Jan29 2-3	Dec25 2-5	Oct02 0-2	Oct16 0-4	Nov06 2-3	Dec11 3-2	Nov27 2-4
DUNDEE U	Jan08 3-4	Nov06 1-1	Nov13 5-4	Jan22 6-1	Feb12 3-0	Oct09 2-3	Feb12 0-0		Mar05 1-4	Mar23 3-4	Apr02 1-2	Nov20 5-0	Jan01 1-3	Sep11 1-5	Nov27 1-1	Sep25 2-0
DUNFERMLINE A	Feb12 2-2	Nov20 7-0	Apr02 5-2	Jan08 2-1	Oct09 3-0	Sep25 2-3	Jan01 3-1	Nov13		Apr27 5-1	Dec18 2-1	Mar19 3-2	Dec04 2-1	Sep11 2-1	Oct23 2-1	Apr30 4-3
FORFAR A	Jan22 2-4	Apr13 4-1	Apr26 3-1	Jan01 1-1	Jan08 6-1	Sep11 2-4	Apr16 3-1	Nov09 1-4	Nov06 2-1		Nov27 0-3	Nov20 5-3	Dec11 1-0	Oct09 0-2	Sep25 2-2	Feb12 3-3
HAMILTON A	Oct23 3-3	Dec11 5-0	Mar12 2-1	Feb19 3-2	Jan08 5-1	Dec25 3-1	Nov06 2-1	Apr02 1-1		Mar19 3-0		Feb26 1-0	Nov13 0-5	Apr23 4-2	Apr30 1-1	Oct09 5-1
MORTON	Apr30 3-1	Mar26 1-1	Mar05 2-4	Feb19 1-0	Feb12 2-3	Jan01 3-2	Jan08 0-2	Dec11 2-1	Nov27 2-3	Mar12 3-1	Nov06 1-1		Apr13 2-3	Oct23 1-1	Oct09 3-1	Sep11 1-1
QUEEN'S PARK	Apr11 1-1	Nov27 2-0	Nov06 6-0	Sep11 2-0	Apr30 2-2	Apr16 5-2	Apr26 0-1	Mar12 1-1	Mar30 0-1	Apr02 4-0	Mar23 1-2	Dec18 1-2		Jan08 4-1	May02 1-1	Jan01 3-1
ST JOHNSTONE	Dec04 2-2	Oct30 0-1	Oct16 0-1	Mar05 3-0	Nov13 2-1	Apr09 0-4	Nov06 2-3	Sep18 0-4	Feb26 1-2	Dec25 2-0	Apr23 3-1	Jan29 6-1	Oct02 1-4		Mar19 3-1	Mar12 1-3
STENHOUSEMUIR	Dec18 3-6	Oct02 1-1	Sep18 1-1	Mar26 2-2	Mar12 2-5	Mar05 5-0	Apr02 2-2	Dec25 5-2	Jan29 2-2	Jan03 1-2	Oct16 4-2	Apr16 3-1	Apr20 1-1	Nov27 1-2		Nov06 0-2
T LANARK	Nov13 3-4	Jan29 1-2	Oct02 2-0	Apr09 3-2	Dec04 9-0	Mar19 4-2	Jan03 2-0	Oct16 4-1	Oct30 1-1	Apr20 4-1	Dec25 1-1	Sep18 3-1	Nov20 1-2	Feb26 0-2		

Oct 23 Montrose ....1 Inverness C 3
Oct 23 Peebles R ....0 Forres Mechanic ..2

Replays
Oct 30 Ayr U ....3 Cowdenbeath ...3
Oct 30 Queen's Park .....1 Buckie T 2
Nov 10 Ayr U ....3 Cowdenbeath 1
　　　　played at Firhill Park

5th Round
Feb 5 Airdrie ....4 Forfar A 3
Feb 5 Alloa ....2 Celtic 4
Feb 5 Arbroath ....0 St Johnstone 4
Feb 5 Buckie T ....2 Inverness T 0
Feb 5 Clyde ....3 Albion R 0
Feb 5 Dunfermline A ....4 Partick T 2
Feb 5 East Fife ....1 Kilmarnock 2
Feb 5 Falkirk ....4 Stenhousemuir ...0
Feb 5 Forres Mechanic ..3 Motherwell 4
Feb 5 Hamilton A ......2 St Mirren 1
Feb 5 Hearts ....5 Hibernian 0
Feb 5 Inverness C .....1 Ayr U 1
Feb 5 Morton ....1 Raith R 3
Feb 5 Rangers ....0 Dundee 0
Feb 5 Stirling A ......0 Aberdeen 6
Feb 5 T Lanark ....2 Queen's Park 1

Replays
Feb 9 Ayr U ....2 Inverness C 4
Feb 9 Dundee ....0 Rangers 1

6th Round
Feb 19 Aberdeen ....2 Rangers 1
Feb 19 Airdrie ....7 Dunfermline A 0
Feb 19 Buckie T ....0 Hearts 6
Feb 19 Clyde ....3 Raith R 1
Feb 19 Inverness C ......0 Falkirk 7
Feb 19 Kilmarnock ......1 Celtic 1
Feb 19 St Johnstone .....0 Hamilton A 1
Feb 19 T Lanark ....1 Motherwell 3

Replays
Feb 23 Celtic ....1 Kilmarnock 0

7th Round
Mar 5 Airdrie ....4 Motherwell 1
Mar 5 Celtic ....2 Hamilton A 1
Mar 5 Clyde ....5 Falkirk 0
Mar 5 Hearts ....1 Aberdeen 1

Replays
Mar 9 Aberdeen ....2 Hearts 0

Semi-finals
Mar 26 Aberdeen ....2 Clyde 2
　　　　played at Easter Road
Mar 26 Airdrie ....2 Celtic 2
　　　　played at Hampden Park

Replay
Apr 4 Aberdeen ....0 Clyde 1
　　　　played at Easter Road
Apr 4 Airdrie ....0 Celtic 2
　　　　played at Hampden Park

Final
Apr 23 Celtic ....1 Clyde 1
　　　　played at Hampden Park

Replay
Apr 27 Celtic ....0 Clyde 1
　　　　played at Hampden Park

Aberdeen, Division 'A' champions in 1954-55. Back row (left to right): Shaw (trainer), Mitchell, Caldwell, Martin, Allister, Young, Glen. Front row: Leggat, Yorston, Buckley, Wishart, O'Neill, Hather. Inset: David Halliday (manager) and Smith.

Brown of Kilmarnock rushes out to intercept the ball from the oncoming South African-born Johnny Hubbard of Rangers.

Although he has five Partick defenders to deal with, Conn of Hearts manages to squeeze the ball home between defender Collins and goalkeeper Ledgerwood.

Season 1955-56

SFA Cup

1st Round

Sep 10	Babcock 2	Clacknacuddin 5	
Sep 10	Buckie T 2	Rothes 1	
Sep 10	Chirnside U 1	Elgin C 9	
Sep 10	Duns 3	Deveronvale 0	
Sep 10	Edinburgh Univ ...0	Inverness T 7	
Sep 10	Eyemouth 5	Brora R 1	
Sep 10	Forres Mechanic ..3	Glasgow Univ 2	
Sep 10	Fraserburgh 3	Aberdeen Univ 1	
Sep 10	Gala Fairydean ...2	Peterhead 1	
Sep 10	Huntly 4	Civil Service S 2	
Sep 10	Lossiemouth 7	Wick A 0	
Sep 10	Murrayfield A 2	Shawfield A 2	
Sep 10	Nairn Co 1	Inverness C 4	
Sep 10	Newton Stewart ...3	Peebles R 5	
Sep 10	Ross Co 4	Coldstream 2	
Sep 10	St Cuthbert's 3	Vale of Atholl 1	
Sep 10	Selkirk 3	Burntisland 2	
Sep 10	Tarff R 2	Girvan A 2	
Sep 17	Whithorn 7	Vale of Leithen ... 0	
Sep 10	Wigtown 0	Keith 7	

Replays

Sep 17	Girvan A 0	Tarff R 1	
Sep 17	Shawfield A 2	Murrayfield A 1	

2nd Round

Sep 24	Clacknacuddin ...3	St Cuthbert's 0	
Sep 24	Gala Fairydean ...6	Shawfield A 2	
Sep 24	Huntly 2	Forres Mechanic ..4	
Sep 24	Inverness T 5	Buckie T 2	
Sep 24	Keith 2	Elgin C 0	
Sep 24	Lossiemouth 3	Duns 1	
Oct 1	Peebles R 4	Eyemouth 3	
Sep 24	Ross Co 3	Tarff R 2	
Sep 24	Whithorn 2	Selkirk 3	

3nd Round

Oct 8	Berwick R 3	Fraserburgh 0	
Oct 8	Dumbarton 5	Inverness C 3	
Oct 8	Forres Mechanic ..2	Clacknacuddin 4	
Oct 8	Gala Fairydean ...4	Montrose 5	
Oct 8	Inverness T 1	Peebles R 1	
Oct 8	Keith 2	E Stirling 4	
Oct 8	Lossiemouth 1	Selkirk 0	
Oct 8	Ross Co 2	Stranraer 3	

Replay

Oct 15	Peebles R 2	Inverness T 1	

4th Round

Oct 22	Albion R 1	Alloa 1	
Oct 22	Berwick R 5	Lossiemouth 1	
Oct 22	Brechin C 1	Peebles 1	
Oct 22	Cowdenbeath 6	Montrose 0	
Oct 22	Dundee U 4	Dumbarton 1	
Oct 22	E Stirling 0	Arbroath 2	
Oct 22	Forfar A 5	Stranraer 2	
Oct 22	Morton 5	Clacknacuddin 2	

Replays

Oct 29	Alloa 4	Albion R 0	
Oct 29	Peebles 4	Brechin C 4	
Nov 2	Brechin C 0	Peebles 0	
	played at Easter Road		
Nov 16	Brechin C 6	Peebles 2	
	played at Tannadice		

5th Round

Feb 4	Airdrie 7	Hamilton A 1	
Feb 4	Ayr U 5	Berwick R 2	
Feb 4	Brechin C 1	Arbroath 1	
Feb 8	Clyde 5	Dunfermline A 0	
Feb 4	Dundee U 2	Dundee 2	
Feb 8	East Fife 1	Stenhousemuir ...3	
Feb 4	Falkirk 0	Kilmarnock 3	
Feb 4	Hearts 3	Forfar A 0	
Feb 8	Hibernian 1	Raith R 1	
Feb 4	Morton 0	Celtic 2	
Feb 8	Motherwell 0	Queen's Park 2	
Feb 4	Partick T 2	Alloa 0	
Feb 4	Queen of South ..3	Cowdenbeath 1	
Feb 4	Rangers 2	Aberdeen 1	
Feb 4	St Mirren 6	T Lanark 0	
Feb 4	Stirling A 2	St Johnstone 1	

Replays

Feb 8	Arbroath 2	Brechin C 3	
Feb 8	Dundee 3	Dundee U 0	
Feb 13	Raith R 3	Hibernian 1	

6th Round

Feb 18	Airdrie 4	St Mirren 4	
Feb 18	Ayr U 0	Celtic 3	
Feb 18	Dundee 0	Rangers 1	
Feb 18	Hearts 5	Stirling A 0	
Feb 18	Kilmarnock 2	Queen of South ..2	
Feb 18	Partick T 3	Brechin C 1	
Feb 18	Raith R 2	Queen's Park 2	
Feb 18	Stenhousemuir ...0	Clyde 1	

Hearts go into the lead after only one minute against Celtic at Parkhead during this League game in January. Goldie, Peacock and Stein are helpless as Young scores. The game ended 1-1. Hearts later met Celtic again in the Scottish Cup, winning 3-1 in the Final.

Replays

Feb 21 St Mirren ....1 Airdrie 3
Feb 22 Queen of South ..2 Kilmarnock 0
Feb 22 Queen's Park ....1 Raith R 2

Mar 24 Hearts ....0 Raith R 0
played at Easter Road

7th Round

Mar 3 Celtic ....2 Airdrie 1
Mar 3 Hearts ....4 Rangers 0
Mar 3 Queen of South ..2 Clyde 4
Mar 3 Raith R ....2 Partick T 1

Replay

Mar 28 Hearts ....3 Raith R 0
played at Easter Road

Final

Apr 21 Celtic ....1 Hearts 3
played at Hampden Park

Semi-finals

Mar 24 Celtic ....2 Clyde 1
played at Hampden Park

DIVISION A FINAL TABLE

	P	W	D	L	F	A	Pts
Rangers	34	22	8	4	85	27	52
Aberdeen	34	18	10	6	87	50	46
Hearts	34	19	7	8	99	47	45
Hibernian	34	19	7	8	86	50	45
Celtic	34	16	9	9	55	39	41
Queen of South	34	16	5	13	69	73	37
Airdrie	34	14	8	12	85	96	36
Kilmarnock	34	12	10	12	52	45	34
Partick T	34	13	7	14	62	60	33
Motherwell	34	11	11	12	53	59	33
Raith R	34	12	9	13	58	75	33
East Fife	34	13	5	16	61	69	31
Dundee	34	12	6	16	56	65	30
Falkirk	34	11	6	17	58	75	28
St Mirren	34	10	7	17	57	70	27
Dunfermline A	34	10	6	18	42	82	26
Clyde	34	8	6	20	50	74	22
Stirling A	34	4	5	25	23	82	13

DIVISION B FINAL TABLE

	P	W	D	L	F	A	Pts
Queen's Park	36	23	8	5	78	28	54
Ayr U	36	24	3	9	103	55	51
St Johnstone	36	21	7	8	86	45	49
Dumbarton	36	21	5	10	83	62	47
Stenhousemuir	36	20	4	12	82	54	44
Brechin C	36	18	6	12	60	56	42
Cowdenbeath	36	16	7	13	80	85	39
Dundee U	36	12	14	10	78	65	38
Morton	36	15	6	15	71	69	36
T Lanark	36	16	3	17	80	64	35
Hamilton A	36	13	7	16	86	84	33
Stranraer	36	14	5	17	77	92	33
Alloa	36	12	7	17	67	73	31
Berwick R	36	11	9	16	52	77	31
Forfar A	36	10	9	17	62	75	29
E Stirling	36	9	10	17	66	94	28
Albion R	36	8	11	17	58	82	27
Arbroath	36	10	6	20	47	67	26
Montrose	36	4	3	29	44	133	11

League Cup results for 1955-56 are detailed on pages 186-187.

DIVISION A

Results grid (row = home team, column = opponent). Column abbreviations: AB=Aberdeen, AI=Airdrie, CE=Celtic, CL=Clyde, DU=Dundee, DF=Dunfermline A, EF=East Fife, FA=Falkirk, HE=Hearts, HI=Hibernian, KI=Kilmarnock, MO=Motherwell, PT=Partick T, QS=Queen of South, RR=Raith R, RA=Rangers, SM=St Mirren, ST=Stirling A.

	AB	AI	CE	CL	DU	DF	EF	FA	HE	HI	KI	MO	PT	QS	RR	RA	SM	ST
ABERDEEN		Dec24 7-2	Jan07 1-0	Nov05 1-4	Sep24 2-0	Mar17 1-0	Feb03 7-3	Feb18 2-2	Apr07 4-1	Sep07 6-2	Apr21 3-2	Nov19 1-1	Apr28 0-4	Oct08 3-2	Mar31 3-5	Dec08 0-0	Feb11 4-1	Jan03 7-0
AIRDRIE	Apr25 2-2		Nov26 1-2	Mar17 1-8	Nov05 3-3	Oct15 1-2	Apr07 1-4	Sep17 0-1	Oct01 3-1	Mar07 3-2	Jan14 3-0	Jan02 3-3	Apr18 4-3	Dec17 0-4	Feb25 4-2	Jan28 2-4	Apr28 4-0	Nov19 4-0
CELTIC	Apr10 1-1	Mar31 3-1		Feb25 4-1	Mar17 1-0	Oct29 4-2	Nov05 0-0	Apr30 1-0	Jan28 1-1	Apr25 0-3	Dec10 0-2	Oct15 2-2	Dec17 5-1	Apr28 1-3	Oct01 2-0	Jan02 0-1	Nov19 3-0	Sep17 3-0
CLYDE	Mar10 0-5	Nov12 2-3	Oct22 1-3		Jan21 4-1	Dec03 1-2	Feb11 0-1	Dec24 1-2	Apr11 2-2	Nov26 2-2	Apr18 1-3	Sep10 1-1	Apr21 1-3	Sep10 0-4	Apr02 1-1	Mar17 2-1		
DUNDEE	Jan02 2-4	Mar10 4-1	Nov12 1-2	Oct01 2-1		Sep17 3-0	Nov26 1-0	Oct29 0-0	Jan14 0-2	Apr23 3-2	Feb25 1-1	Dec31 2-1	Mar24 3-0	Dec03 6-3	Oct15 0-3	Apr02 5-1	Dec17 2-1	Apr13 2-1
DUNFERMLINE A	Nov12 2-2	Feb11 3-7	Mar07 1-1	Apr07 4-1	Oct08 2-1		Mar24 2-3	Dec17 1-5	Nov26 1-5	Oct22 2-1	Dec31 0-3	Nov05 1-0	Sep10 1-1	Sep24 0-1	Apr18 3-2	Apr25 1-0	Jan07 2-3	Jan21 0-0
EAST FIFE	Oct29 1-1	Dec03 8-1	Mar10 3-0	Oct15 1-1	Mar31 5-4	Nov19 3-1		Jan28 6-1	Feb25 1-4	Mar17 1-2	Sep17 2-1	Jan14 0-2	Oct01 1-0	Apr18 3-1	Jan02 3-0	Apr09 2-1	Apr25 1-1	Apr20 2-0
FALKIRK	Dec31 3-6	Jan07 1-4	Sep10 3-1	Apr25 2-1	Mar03 0-1	Apr21 0-1	Oct08 6-3		Dec10 1-1	Feb11 2-0	Apr07 0-0	Mar17 3-3	Oct22 4-3	Jan21 1-0	Nov19 3-1	Nov05 5-2	Nov26 5-1	Sep24 2-0
HEARTS	Dec03 3-0	Jan21 4-1	Oct08 2-1	Nov19 5-1	Sep10 4-0	Mar31 5-0	Oct22 3-1	Apr16 8-3		Sep24 0-1	Apr25 0-2	Dec17 7-1	Jan07 5-0	Feb11 2-2	Apr28 7-2	Mar17 1-1	Mar07 4-1	Nov05 5-0
HIBERNIAN	Jan14 1-3	Oct29 3-3	Dec24 2-3	Mar31 1-0	Dec10 6-3	Feb25 7-1	Nov12 3-1	Oct15 1-0	Jan02 2-2		Oct01 2-1	Jan28 7-0	Mar21 5-1	Feb11 4-1	Mar10 2-2	Apr21 2-2	Apr07 2-0	Dec31 6-1
KILMARNOCK	Dec17 1-0	Sep10 2-1	Apr13 0-0	Mar31 1-0	Oct22 2-0	Apr28 3-0	Jan07 4-4	Dec03 2-4	Dec24 0-0	Jan21 2-2		Mar03 2-1	Oct08 0-1	Nov05 2-2	Mar17 1-1	Nov19 1-1	Sep24 1-1	Feb11 3-2
MOTHERWELL	Mar24 1-1	Sep24 0-2	Feb11 2-2	Dec10 2-2	Apr28 1-2	Nov19 2-1	Sep10 5-2	Apr23 0-0	Apr16 1-0	Oct29 2-1			Dec03 3-1	Oct22 1-2	Dec24 5-1	Mar31 1-2	Jan21 1-1	Jan07 2-0
PARTICK T	Apr30 0-2	Dec10 1-3	Apr23 2-0	Dec17 1-0	Nov19 1-2	Apr11 1-1	Feb25 2-2	Apr02 3-2	Jan28 2-0	Apr07 1-1	Apr25 2-1			Oct29	Oct15 1-3	Nov05 2-0	Mar17 6-1	
QUEEN OF SOUTH	Jan28 2-2	Apr21 2-5	Dec31 1-3	Jan14 5-2	Apr07 2-1	Jan02 5-2	Dec10 2-1	Oct01 6-0	Oct15 4-3	Nov19 1-3	Mar10 2-0	Feb25 0-0	Dec24 0-0		Sep17 0-1	Oct29 2-1	Mar17 4-1	Nov26 4-0
RAITH R	Nov26 1-1	Oct22 3-3	Jan21 1-1	Dec17 1-3	Dec10 1-1	Sep24 1-1	Apr02 4-0	Dec31 2-0	Nov05 1-1	Mar10 0-4	Apr26 2-1	Mar07 4-3	Jan07 2-3	3-1		Apr07 0-5	Sep10 2-2	Oct08 2-0
RANGERS	Apr18 1-0	Oct08 4-4	Sep24 0-0	Apr28 0-1	Jan07 3-1	Jan02 6-0	Jan28 3-0	Mar10 4-0	Nov12 1-1	Nov05 4-1	Mar24 3-2	Nov26 2-2	Feb11 1-0	Mar07 8-0	Dec03 4-0		Mar21 4-1	Dec10 0-0
ST MIRREN	Oct15 0-3	Dec31 7-2	Mar28 0-2	Jan28 3-1	Apr21 4-2	Mar03 0-3	Apr25 2-0	Mar31 3-1	Oct29 0-1	Dec03 2-2	Jan02 1-1	Apr09 1-1	Mar10 4-1	Nov12 0-1	Apr13 4-1	Feb25 0-1		Dec10 5-2
STIRLING A	Feb25 0-2	Mar24 1-1	Dec03 0-3	Oct29 1-2	Dec24 0-0	Oct01 1-2	Dec17 2-1	Jan02 1-0	Mar10 0-2	Apr28 0-3	Oct15 1-2	Apr11 0-1	Nov12 2-4	Mar31 2-0	Apr30 0-1	Oct22 2-2	Apr18 2-1	

DIVISION B

Results grid (row = home team, column = opponent). Column abbreviations: AL=Albion R, ALO=Alloa, AR=Arbroath, AY=Ayr U, BE=Berwick R, BR=Brechin C, CO=Cowdenbeath, DM=Dumbarton, DU=Dundee U, ES=E Stirling, FO=Forfar A, HA=Hamilton A, MT=Montrose, MO=Morton, QP=Queen's Park, SJ=St Johnstone, SN=Stenhousemuir, SR=Stranraer, TL=T Lanark.

	AL	ALO	AR	AY	BE	BR	CO	DM	DU	ES	FO	HA	MT	MO	QP	SJ	SN	SR	TL
ALBION R		Nov12 1-1	Mar31 1-0	Oct08 4-2	Dec10 1-2	Mar24 1-3	Aug24 5-1	Mar10 0-1	Dec03 1-1	Sep14 2-2	Sep21 4-0	Sep24 3-2	Dec24 4-0	Apr23 0-2	Jan07 0-6	Feb11 2-2	Jan21 3-1	Jan28 2-3	Apr02 2-1
ALLOA	Mar17 5-1		Oct08 3-1	Sep10 1-0	Nov19 5-2	Feb11 3-3	Jan07 1-0	Aug24 3-3	Feb25 1-0	Apr21 3-0	Dec31 4-3	Jan21 3-3	Nov26 6-0	Feb18 5-1	Sep28 0-4	Mar03 2-0	Sep24 2-1	Apr07 2-1	Dec10 2-4
ARBROATH	Nov26 2-2	Jan28 2-1		Dec03 2-0	Oct15 4-0	Mar10 2-2	Nov12 0-2	Oct29 0-1	Oct01 2-4	Jan02 0-0	Sep21 2-3	Jan14 2-1	Aug24 2-1	Apr18 0-1	Apr16 1-0	Dec31 0-1	Sep17 2-2	Dec17 1-0	
AYR U	Jan28 3-2	Jan14 5-0	Apr07 5-0		Sep14 4-1	Apr30 2-0	Dec31 4-1	Nov12 5-1	Mar24 1-0	Nov26 8-1	Apr21 3-1	Sep17 7-0	Jan02 3-1	Oct22 4-3	Apr25 1-0	Oct15 3-0	Oct01 1-0		
BERWICK R	Apr18 1-1	Mar24 0-0	Feb11 3-0	Sep28 3-1		Jan21 2-0	Sep24 2-2	Feb25 2-2	Dec17 3-2	Sep10 0-6	Nov12 0-1	Apr28 1-2	Apr07 3-1	Dec31 1-2	Nov05 2-0	Nov05 5-3	Jan07 0-4	Jan28 3-0	Oct29 1-1
BRECHIN C	Nov19 1-0	Oct15 4-1	Nov05 1-2	Mar03 1-0	Oct01 2-1		Oct08 5-4	Jan28 0-2	Aug24 2-2	Jan14 2-2	Dec24 1-1	Jan02 3-1	Sep17 3-1	Dec31 0-0	Mar17 2-0	Nov26 2-1	Apr21 1-3	Feb25 2-5	3-1
COWDENBEATH	Apr28 3-1	Sep17 3-1	Mar17 2-1	Sep07 4-0	Jan02 1-1	Dec03 2-1		Jan14 2-6	Apr10 3-2	Oct15 1-1	Sep14 4-0	Dec10 0-0	Sep14 3-1	Feb18 1-1	Nov19 4-3	Oct29 4-3	Mar31 1-4		
DUMBARTON	Nov05 3-2	Apr28 4-2	Mar03 1-3	Mar17 3-2	Sep28 1-4	Apr13 3-1	Sep10 3-1		Dec31 2-0	Sep24 5-1	Feb18 5-1	Jan03 2-1	Dec10 2-0	Nov26 2-2	Oct15 2-1	Jan07 5-2	Apr21 5-2	Nov19 2-0	Apr07
DUNDEE U	Apr07 2-0	Sep21 6-2	Jan21 2-1	Nov19 3-3	Apr21 8-1	Dec26 3-1	Nov05 4-4	Apr25 1-1		Jan07 4-0	Sep14 2-2	Feb11 3-3	Mar17 6-3	Dec10 4-2	Sep10 2-2	Sep24 1-1	Mar03 2-2	Mar31 0-2	Oct08 1-0
E STIRLING	Sep28 4-1	Dec17 2-1	Sep24 3-2	Nov19 0-4	Jan14 0-0	Apr18 0-2	Sep21 2-3	Jan02 3-1	Apr25 4-4		Oct29 3-3	Jan28 2-1	Nov12 3-0	Dec03 3-3	Sep07 1-1	Jan03 2-4	Oct01 2-3	Feb11 1-4	Nov26 1-5
FORFAR A	Feb25 2-2	Sep07 2-1	Sep24 1-0	Apr28 4-1	Mar17 3-0	Sep10 0-1	Feb11 1-5	Dec24 1-1	Sep28 1-5	Mar03 3-3		Mar31 3-3	Nov05 4-3	Apr07 2-4	Apr21 4-3	Apr11 1-1	Oct08 0-1	Dec10 0-1	Nov19 3-1
HAMILTON A	Jan02 2-2	Oct01 3-0	Feb25 2-0	Dec17 1-2	Aug24 3-3	Apr25 4-1	Apr18 3-3	Sep28 3-0	Oct15 4-2	Nov05 5-0	Nov26		Nov19 8-1	Jan28 5-1	Mar03 0-1	Apr07 2-2	Mar17 1-0	Jan14 6-1	Oct22 1-3
MONTROSE	Apr25 2-2	Mar31 2-4	Jan07 1-6	Apr28 2-4	Jan07 0-1	Jan02 1-2	Dec03 2-4	Sep24 1-4	Apr18 2-2	Nov12 5-1	Feb18 1-2	Mar24 2-1		Oct29 1-2	Jan12 1-2	Feb11 0-6	Nov05 1-5	Sep17 4-1	Feb10 2-0
MORTON	Dec17 2-2	Dec24 2-1	Apr28 2-0	Sep24 4-0	Apr25 2-4	Jan07 1-2	Sep28 3-0	Mar31 1-2	Apr18	Apr17	Dec03	Oct08	Mar03		Jan21 2-5	Nov19 2-3	Sep10 3-0	Feb25 3-2	Nov05 6-1
QUEEN'S PARK	Sep17 2-0	Sep14 2-0	Nov19 2-0	Nov05 4-2	Mar31 1-2	Feb11 1-1	Jan14 3-0	Apr07 7-0	Dec17 0-0	Oct29 1-0	Feb25 3-2	Apr02 3-0				Oct08 0-2	Dec10 2-0	Mar17 0-1	Jan02 3-1
ST JOHNSTONE	Oct15 7-2	Jan02 4-1	Sep28 3-0	Apr18 0-0	Nov05 3-1	Mar31 2-1	Sep17 4-2	Jan07 2-1	Apr02 2-1	Jan14	Dec31	Apr17	Apr02		Oct22 5-2		Mar17 3-2		Jan14 2-0
STENHOUSEMUIR	Oct01 1-1	Jan02 1-1	Sep06 2-0	Oct24 1-2	Sep17 2-1	Mar31 2-4	Mar24 1-5	Dec17 0-1	Oct29 2-3	Aug24 1-0	Jan28 2-1	Nov12 1-0	Oct15 1-3	Jan14 1-0	Apr28 2-1	Feb25 2-1		Mar10 4-1	Sep13 1-1
STRANRAER	Sep07 3-1	Dec03 2-1	Jan07 3-3	Feb11 3-6	Feb18 1-2	Dec17 1-2	Mar03 2-4	Mar24 2-0	Nov26 6-5	Jan21 2-2	Jan03 4-2	Sep10 6-1	Sep28 6-1	Sep21 1-1	Nov12 0-2	Dec24 1-3	Nov05 4-2		Apr28 4-2
T LANARK	Mar03 7-0	Apr24 2-0	Feb18 2-1	Jan21 3-2	Dec24 3-3	Sep21 1-2	Nov26 2-2	Dec03 1-0	Jan28 0-1	Oct15 1-3	Mar24 0-0	Jan07 6-1	Dec31 9-0	Mar10 4-0	Sep10 0-2	Sep28 5-2	Aug24 6-2		

After drawing the sixth-round tie 4-4 at Parkhead, Celtic went on to win the replay 2-0 with this headed goal from Mochan with Higgins getting the second. Celtic were themselves knocked out of the competition by finalists Kilmarnock.

SFA Cup
1st Round
Sep 8	Arbroath	10	Rothes	2
Sep 8	Babcock	6	Selkirk	3
Sep 8	Buckie T	4	Lossiemouth	0
Sep 8	Chirnside	1	Montrose	9
Sep 8	Civil Service S	0	Clacknacuddin	7
Sep 8	Coldstream	6	Whithorn	0
Sep 8	Edinburgh Univ	1	Duns	11
Sep 8	Elgin C	5	Shawfield A	1
Sep 8	Eyemouth	3	Burntisland	2
Sep 8	Forres Mechanic	6	Keith	1
Sep 8	Fraserburgh	5	Deveronvale	2
Sep 8	Peebles R	4	Murrayfield A	2
Sep 8	Peterhead	4	Huntly	2
Sep 8	Ross Co	6	Aberdeen Univ	3
Sep 8	Tarff R	1	Inverness C	7
Sep 8	Vale of Leithen	6	Glasgow Univ	1
Sep 8	Wick A	3	Girvan A	1
Sep 8	Wigtown	1	Brora R	4

2nd Round
Sep 22	Arbroath	6	Brora	1
Sep 22	Babcock	0	Inverness C	2
Sep 22	Elgin C	2	Clacknacuddin	2
Sep 22	Eyemouth	3	Duns	1
Sep 22	Fraserburgh	9	Gala Fairydean	0
Sep 22	Montrose	2	Buckie T	4
Sep 22	Peebles R	2	Albion R	2
Sep 22	Peterhead	2	Forres Mechanic	3
Sep 22	Ross Co	6	Coldstream	0
Sep 22	Vale of Leithen	7	Wick A	2

Replay
Sep 29	Albion R	6	Peebles R	0
Sep 29	Clacknacuddin	3	Elgin C	2

3rd Round
Oct 6	Buckie T	9	Newton S	2
Oct 6	Clacknacuddin	1	E Stirling	4
Oct 6	Eyemouth	0	Nairn Co	3
Oct 6	Forfar A	3	Arbroath	1
Oct 6	Fraserburgh	0	Forres Mechanic	2
Oct 6	Inverness T	0	Ross Co	2
Oct 6	St Cuthbert's	2	Inverness C	7
Oct 6	Vale of Leithen	0	Albion R	2

4th Round
Oct 20	Alloa	4	Forfar A	0
Oct 20	Buckie T	2	Hamilton A	3
Oct 20	Cowdenbeath	3	Inverness C	5
Oct 20	Dundee U	5	T Lanark	2
Oct 20	E Stirling	1	Morton	1
Oct 20	Forres Mechanic	3	Albion R	0
Oct 20	Nairn Co	5	Berwick R	5
Oct 20	Stranraer	3	Ross Co	0

Replays
Oct 27	Berwick R	3	Nairn Co	0
Oct 27	Morton	4	E Stirling	1

5th Round
Feb 2	Berwick R	1	Falkirk	2
Feb 2	Dundee	0	Clyde	0
Feb 2	Dunfermline A	3	Morton	0
Feb 2	East Fife	4	St Johnstone	0
Feb 2	Forres Mechanic	0	Celtic	5
Feb 2	Hamilton A	2	Alloa	2
Feb 2	Hearts	0	Rangers	4
Feb 2	Hibernian	3	Aberdeen	4
Feb 2	Inverness C	2	Raith R	3
Feb 2	Kilmarnock	1	Ayr U	0
Feb 2	Queen of South	2	Dumbarton	2

Feb 2	Queen's Park	3	Brechin C	0
Feb 2	St Mirren	1	Partick T	1
Feb 2	Stenhousemuir	1	Dundee U	1
Feb 2	Stirling A	1	Motherwell	2
Feb 2	Stranraer	1	Airdrie	2

Replays
Feb 6	Alloa	3	Hamilton A	5
Feb 6	Clyde	2	Dundee	1
Feb 6	Dumbarton	4	Queen of South	2
Feb 6	Dundee U	4	Stenhousemuir	0
Feb 6	Partick T	2	St Mirren	2
Feb 11	Partick T	1	St Mirren	5
	played at Hampden Park			

6th Round
Feb 16	Celtic	4	Rangers	4
Feb 16	East Fife	0	Kilmarnock	0
Feb 16	Falkirk	3	Aberdeen	1
Feb 16	Hamilton A	1	Airdrie	2
Feb 16	Motherwell	1	Dumbarton	3
Feb 16	Queen's Park	1	Clyde	1
Feb 16	Raith R	7	Dundee U	0
Feb 16	St Mirren	1	Dunfermline A	0

Replays
Feb 20	Clyde	2	Queen's Park	1
Feb 20	Kilmarnock	2	East Fife	0
Feb 20	Rangers	0	Celtic	2

7th Round
Mar 2	Celtic	2	St Mirren	1
Mar 2	Dumbarton	0	Raith R	4
Mar 2	Falkirk	2	Clyde	1
Mar 2	Kilmarnock	3	Airdrie	1

Semi-finals
Mar 23 Celtic ....1 Kilmarnock 1
  played at Hampden Park
Mar 23 Falkirk ....2 Raith R 2
  played at Tynecastle

Replay
Mar 27 Celtic ....1 Kilmarnock 3
  played at Hampden Park
Mar 27 Falkirk ....2 Raith R 0
  played at Tynecastle

Final
Apr 20 Falkirk ....1 Kilmarnock 1
  played at Hampden Park

Replay
Apr 24 Falkirk ....2 Kilmarnock 1
  played at Hampden Park

DIVISION 1 FINAL TABLE

	P	W	D	L	F	A	Pts
Rangers	34	26	3	5	96	48	55
Hearts	34	24	5	5	81	48	53
Kilmarnock	34	16	10	8	57	39	42
Raith R	34	16	7	11	84	58	39
Celtic	34	15	8	11	58	43	38
Aberdeen	34	18	2	14	79	59	38
Motherwell	34	16	5	13	72	66	37
Partick T	34	13	8	13	53	51	34
Hibernian	34	12	9	13	69	56	33
Dundee	34	13	6	15	55	61	32
Airdrie	34	13	4	17	77	89	30
St Mirren	34	12	6	16	58	72	30
Queen's Park	34	11	7	16	55	59	29
Falkirk	34	10	8	16	51	70	28
East Fife	34	10	6	18	59	82	26
Queen of South	34	10	5	19	54	96	25
Dunfermline A	34	9	6	19	54	74	24
Ayr U	34	7	5	22	48	89	19

DIVISION 2 FINAL TABLE

	P	W	D	L	F	A	Pts
Clyde	36	29	6	1	122	39	64
T Lanark	36	24	3	9	105	51	51
Cowdenbeath	36	20	5	11	87	65	45
Morton	36	18	7	11	81	70	43
Albion R	36	18	6	12	98	80	42
Brechin C	36	15	10	11	72	68	40
Stranraer	36	15	10	11	79	77	40
Stirling A	36	17	5	14	81	64	39
Dumbarton	36	17	4	15	101	70	38
Arbroath	36	17	4	15	79	57	38
Hamilton A	36	14	8	14	69	68	36
St Johnstone	36	14	6	16	79	80	34
Dundee U	36	14	6	16	75	80	34
Stenhousemuir	36	13	6	17	71	81	32
Alloa	36	11	5	20	66	99	27
Forfar A	36	9	5	22	75	100	23
Montrose	36	7	7	22	54	124	21
Berwick R	36	7	6	23	58	114	20
E Stirling	36	5	7	24	56	121	17

DIVISION 1

	ABERDEEN	AIRDRIE	AYR U	CELTIC	DUNDEE	DUNFERMLINE A	EAST FIFE	FALKIRK	HEARTS	HIBERNIAN	KILMARNOCK	MOTHERWELL	PARTICK T	QUEEN OF SOUTH	QUEEN'S PARK	RAITH R	RANGERS	ST MIRREN
ABERDEEN		Oct13 2-3	Feb09 2-2	Apr22 0-1	Jan01 2-1	Nov17 3-2	Jan19 1-0	Apr13 3-1	Dec29 2-3	Sep29 3-1	Nov10 1-3	Dec22 2-3	Apr24 2-0	Dec01 5-1	Sep15 2-1	Mar06 1-0	Mar23 1-2	Jan05 4-0
AIRDRIE	Jan26 1-5		Mar27 4-1	Dec22 3-7	Mar23 3-2	Apr27 3-1	Mar16 5-2	Oct06 2-3	Oct20 3-4	Dec08 5-3	Apr13 0-1	Sep22 1-4	Nov01 0-1	Mar06 4-0	Jan12 2-0	Jan02 2-2	Sep08 3-3	Dec01 4-1
AYR U	Oct20 1-6	Oct27 4-1		Nov17 1-3	Feb16 0-1	Mar23 2-1	Dec08 2-2	Jan02 6-1	Oct06 0-2	Mar30 2-3	Jan26 0-2	Mar02 2-1	Dec29 0-1	Sep22 4-4	Apr19 0-3	Sep08 1-0	Jan12 1-0	Nov10 1-2
CELTIC	Feb23 2-1	Apr20 3-0	Mar16 4-0		Mar06 1-1	Dec15 3-1	Nov10 4-0	Jan26 4-0	Dec01 1-1	Apr27 2-1	Jan02 1-1	Jan12 2-1	Nov24 1-1	Apr29 0-0	Sep08 2-0	Oct20 1-1	Sep22 0-2	Apr17 2-3
DUNDEE	Sep22 4-2	Nov24 2-1	Dec15 5-0	Nov03 2-1		Dec08 2-0	Apr20 0-1	Mar30 1-2	Jan12 0-3	Mar09 0-3	Sep08 1-1	Apr08 3-1	Feb23 5-1	Jan26 5-2	Oct20 3-1	Apr27 3-0	Jan02 1-3	Mar16 1-1
DUNFERMLINE A	Mar16 3-3	Dec29 1-3	Nov24 0-1	Apr13 1-1	Mar02 1-1		Feb23 1-4	Sep22 2-1	Sep08 2-3	Dec22 3-1	Oct06 3-1	Jan26 2-1	Dec01 4-3	Nov10 3-0	Jan02 2-2	Jan12 3-4	Apr29 0-2	Nov03 0-2
EAST FIFE	Oct06 4-3	Nov17 4-2	Apr06 2-2	Mar09 2-0	Dec22 2-0	Oct27 3-4		Oct20 1-3	Jan26 1-6	Nov24 0-0	Jan12 1-2	Jan02 2-1	Dec15 3-1	Sep08 0-1	Mar02 2-3	Sep22 0-3	Mar30 0-3	Apr27 5-2
FALKIRK	Dec15 2-5	Jan19 4-1	Sep15 2-3	Dec13 0-1	Dec01 1-1	Jan01 4-3	Feb09		Oct27 0-2	Jan05 0-1	Mar06 2-0	Apr27 1-2	Apr29 4-1	Apr10 3-2	Nov10 1-1	Dec22 0-4	Nov17 0-2	Sep29 4-5
HEARTS	Apr27 3-0	Feb09 2-2	Jan19 2-3	Mar30 3-1	Sep29 2-1	Jan05 2-1	Oct13 5-5	Feb23 1-1		Jan01 0-2	Nov17 3-2	Dec08 4-1	Nov03 3-1	Dec22 6-1	Nov24 2-1	Mar09 1-1	Apr13 0-1	Sep15 2-2
HIBERNIAN	Jan12 4-1	Apr06 6-0	Dec01 3-0	Dec29 3-3	Nov10 1-1	Mar23 0-0	Apr30 4-0	Sep08 6-1	Sep22 2-3		Oct27 0-0	Oct20 1-1	Mar16 2-0	Jan02 1-1	Oct06 1-1	Jan26 1-4	Mar02 2-3	Dec15 1-1
KILMARNOCK	Mar09 2-1	Dec15 3-4	Oct13 4-1	Apr26 0-0	Jan05 4-0	Jan19 0-0	Sep29 1-1	Nov03 1-1	Mar16 4-1	Feb23 2-1		Dec01 2-2	Feb09 1-1	Apr03 1-3	Apr27 1-0	Nov24 3-0	Dec22 3-2	Jan01 1-3
MOTHERWELL	Apr20 2-5	Jan01 2-0	Nov03 4-2	Sep29 1-0	Jan19 3-2	Oct13 2-2	Sep15 1-3	Dec29 1-3	Apr06 3-0	Feb09 0-2	Mar30		Jan05 2-2	Oct27 7-0	Dec15 4-2	Nov17 0-2	Mar09 2-5	Nov24 3-0
PARTICK T	Jan02 1-2	Mar09 2-1	Apr27 5-1	Apr10 3-1	Apr22 5-0	Mar30 3-0	Apr13 2-1	Dec08 2-2	Mar02 3-0	Nov17 2-1	Oct20 2-3	Sep08 2-3		Jan12 2-1	Sep22 0-0	Dec25 1-1	Jan26 0-3	Dec22 2-0
QUEEN OF SOUTH	Mar30 2-2	Nov03 3-3	Jan01 5-1	Jan19 4-3	Oct13 3-1	Mar09 3-2	Apr16 4-2	Nov24 1-2	Apr20 0-2	Sep15 2-0	Dec08 0-3	Apr24 2-2	Sep29 3-0		Mar16 1-6	Oct06 1-5	Apr27 0-3	Feb09 2-0
QUEEN'S PARK	Dec08 0-2	Sep29 2-0	Dec25 2-0	Jan05 2-0	Feb09 1-3	Apr16 0-3	Nov03 1-1	Mar09 0-1	Mar25 2-1	Jan19 1-2	Dec29 1-0	Apr13 1-1	Jan01 7-0	Nov17		Apr30 1-0	Apr22 4-6	Oct13 5-0
RAITH R	Nov03 3-2	Sep15 4-6	Jan05 5-2	Feb09 3-1	Dec29 1-2	Sep29 2-2	Jan01 4-1	Apr26 2-3	Nov10 2-3	Oct13 1-1	Apr15 4-2	Mar16 3-2	Jan19 0-3	Apr13 3-1	Dec01 3-0		Dec08 5-1	Feb23 7-0
RANGERS	Nov24 3-1	Apr17 3-2	Sep29 3-1	Jan01 2-0	Mar20 4-0	Feb09 2-1	Dec01 6-1	Mar16 1-1	Dec15 5-3	Nov03 5-3	Sep15 0-1	Nov10 2-3	Oct13 4-1	Dec29 4-0	Feb23 3-3	Apr02 3-1		Jan19 1-0
ST MIRREN	Sep08 0-2	Mar30 2-3	Mar09 1-0	Dec08 0-2	Nov17 3-2	Mar06 3-2	Dec29 3-1	Jan12 0-0	Jan02 0-2	Apr13 4-2	Sep22 2-0	Mar23 4-0	Apr20 1-1	Oct20 7-1	Jan26 4-1	Oct27 3-3	Oct06 1-2	

DIVISION 2

	ALBION R	ALLOA	ARBROATH	BERWICK R	BRECHIN C	CLYDE	COWDENBEATH	DUMBARTON	DUNDEE U	E STIRLING	FORFAR A	HAMILTON A	MONTROSE	MORTON	ST JOHNSTONE	STENHOUSEMUIR	STIRLING A	STRANRAER	T LANARK
ALBION R		Mar09 1-2	Jan19 6-3	Dec15 2-3	Oct27 1-1	Nov24 5-1	Dec29 5-1	Apr20 7-1	Mar30 3-1	Jan05 3-1	Mar02 4-1	Jan01 6-1	Sep19 1-1	Apr29 3-2	Oct13 4-1	Nov17 6-1	Sep05 1-1	Sep15 4-0	Feb09 5-0
ALLOA	Nov10 2-1		Apr27 0-6	Feb16 2-2	Mar02 2-3	Dec01 1-2	Apr06 3-2	Dec15 2-3	Aug22 2-2	Sep29 2-2	Mar23 5-3	Nov17 3-0	Sep12 7-0	Feb09 2-4	Jan19 1-4	Jan01 0-4	Jan05 2-3	Oct13 2-1	Sep15 1-1
ARBROATH	Feb16 5-3	Dec29 2-0		Jan02 5-1	Dec01 1-1	Jan12 0-1	Jan26 3-0	Oct27 3-2	Apr08 2-2	Nov17 5-0	Feb02 5-1	Apr06 6-1	Sep19 3-2	Oct20 2-1	Dec29 1-0	Mar02 1-1	Mar23 4-2	Apr15 2-3	Dec08 2-0
BERWICK R	Apr13 1-2	Feb23 4-2	Sep15 2-1		Apr24 1-2	Apr17 0-6	Mar16 0-2	Jan12 4-3	Dec25 6-2	Mar23 1-2	Nov10 6-2	Nov03 1-4	Oct13 0-3	Dec08 1-5	Dec29 1-4	Dec22 7-2	Dec01 4-2	Jan05 3-4	Aug22 2-5
BRECHIN C	Jan12 1-1	Nov03 2-4	Mar30 2-1	Feb09 2-2		Sep08 1-1	Oct06 0-2	Mar09 4-1	Feb16 0-0	Apr13 4-1	Sep19 2-2	Apr29 3-1	Dec29 2-0	Mar23 0-2	Oct20 2-1	Nov17 2-0	Nov17 6-0	Dec22 1-3	Dec08 1-3
CLYDE	Mar13 5-0	Mar30 4-0	Sep29 2-1	Feb09 6-0	Jan05 2-2		Nov03 4-0	Dec29 5-3	Mar09 7-1	Apr03 6-1	Dec22 3-1	Feb16 4-1	Nov17 9-0	Oct27 4-1	Oct13 3-2	Oct13 5-2	Apr13 3-1	Jan01 2-1	Jan01 2-1
COWDENBEATH	Apr27 5-2	Dec08 5-2	Oct13 2-0	Nov17 3-1	Jan19 3-3	Apr01		Aug22 2-1	Dec15 4-1	Jan01 4-0	Feb09 6-0	Jan05 1-2	Oct27 3-2	Mar09 3-2	Apr20 2-2	Sep29 4-1	Apr17 1-3	Mar30 5-1	Feb16 3-4
DUMBARTON	Dec22 8-1	Apr13 5-0	Mar06 3-1	Sep29 4-0	Nov10 2-2	Oct20 2-3	Sep19 2-3		Dec08 3-2	Sep15 3-2	Apr10 5-1	Sep05 2-0	Nov01 7-0	Mar23 2-2	Feb09 4-1	Jan05 6-2	Jan01 1-3	Jan19 4-1	Oct13 0-1
DUNDEE U	Dec01 7-0	Sep19 4-3	Jan05 1-0	Oct01 6-1	Apr22 2-1	Nov10 2-4	Apr13 4-1	Apr17 3-1		Dec22 3-1	Nov17 2-1	Oct13 2-1	Mar23 2-2	Jan01 0-7	Jan01 1-2	Nov17 2-0	Feb09 2-0	Sep29 2-2	Oct13 0-1
E STIRLING	Sep08 1-5	Jan12 4-3	Apr24 1-1	Nov24 2-2	Feb23 5-2	Sep05 2-6	Sep22 2-3	Jan02 2-3	Apr30 2-0		Jan26 2-0	Dec29 0-9	Feb02 1-1	Mar30 0-6	Apr13 1-0	Dec08 1-2	Sep19 3-3	Mar09 4-2	Nov03 1-4
FORFAR A	Dec08 3-3	Nov24 3-0	Jan01 2-1	Mar09 6-1	Dec15 2-3	Apr20 4-1	Apr24 4-0	Nov03 0-2	Mar16 3-1	Oct13 3-4		Jan19 2-4	Mar30 6-1	Sep12 3-2	Jan05 3-3	Apr27 1-1	Feb23 0-4	Aug22 1-2	Sep29 2-1
HAMILTON A	Apr22 2-1	Nov24 5-0	Dec08 2-1	Apr02 4-0	Aug22 4-1	Apr27 0-0	Sep12 1-4	Sep21 1-1	Feb09 4-1	Apr27 4-0	Sep22 3-2		Jan12 4-1	Jan02 1-1	Dec01 4-0	Oct20 1-2	Nov17 1-2	Feb23 1-1	Mar16 1-1
MONTROSE	Aug22 3-0	Sep05 3-4	Dec15 2-1	Jan26 1-2	Jan01 2-4	Apr22 1-6	Feb23 2-2	Mar16 5-4	Nov24 5-3	Jan19 1-1	Dec01 3-3	Sep29 1-1		Feb16 1-2	Sep15 0-2	Mar02 3-2	Nov10 2-2	Apr27 4-4	Jan05 1-1
MORTON	Apr08 2-5	Apr24 3-1	Aug22 4-3	Apr06 2-2	Apr27 6-3	Mar16 0-0	Nov10 0-1	Nov24 1-1	Nov03 4-1	Dec01 4-3	Sep05 5-1	Sep15 3-1	Dec22 1-0		Sep29 2-3	Oct13 1-0	Jan19 0-0	Jan01 5-3	Apr13 1-5
ST JOHNSTONE	Jan26 1-1	Oct06 1-2	Mar16 2-2	Apr27 2-1	Nov24 1-2	Apr29 0-4	Apr24 1-0	Sep22 0-6	Dec01 3-2	Mar09 5-0	Oct27 4-2	Apr29 4-1	Nov10 5-1		Aug22 5-2	Feb16 1-3	Apr23 1-3	Nov03 3-6
STENHOUSEMUIR	Mar16 4-3	Sep22 1-3	Nov24 0-3	Apr19 2-1	Sep05 5-1	Jan02 1-1	Jan12 3-1	Sep08 3-1	Oct06 3-1	Apr17 4-0	Dec29 4-1	Mar09 7-2	Nov03 1-2	Jan26 4-2	Sep19		Dec15 4-3	Apr23 0-0	Mar30 0-3
STIRLING A	Sep12 1-1	Sep08 5-1	Nov03 1-3	Mar30 7-1	Mar16 2-1	Jan02 2-4	Nov24 0-4	Sep22 3-1	Apr24 2-1	Aug22 3-1	Oct27 4-1	Apr19 1-2	Oct06 3-0	Dec08 6-0	Sep15 1-1		Nov24 3-3	Dec29 3-0
STRANRAER	Jan02 3-5	Jan26 3-0	Sep12 0-6	Dec22 5-3	Apr19 3-1	Dec15 2-2	Oct06 5-4	Jan12 1-0	Nov03 1-1	Sep19 4-2	Oct27 0-2	Sep22 0-2	Mar02 1-2	Feb09 4-3	Mar23 3-1	Apr23 4-2		Nov17 2-0
T LANARK	Apr23 4-0	Jan02 4-3	Apr29 3-0	Sep19 2-0	Apr06 5-1	Sep22 1-3	Jan26 3-2	Apr15 7-0	Mar02 2-3	Jan12 5-2	Nov24 6-1	Oct06 3-0	Dec15 6-1	Nov10 5-1	Dec01 1-2	Apr27 7-0	Mar16 3-0	

League Cup results for 1956-57 are detailed on page 188.

SFA Cup
1st Round
Feb 1	Airdrie	3	Celtic	4
Feb 1	Albion R	3	Berwick R	1
Feb 1	Alloa	0	Dunfermline A	2
Feb 1	Ayr U	1	St Mirren	1
Feb 1	Brechin C	1	Montrose	1
Feb 1	Chirnside	0	T Lanark	4
Feb 1	Cowdenbeath	1	Rangers	3
Feb 1	Dumbarton	0	Clyde	5
Feb 1	East Fife	1	Hearts	2
Feb 1	E Stirling	3	Motherwell	7
Feb 1	Falkirk	2	Hamilton A	0
Feb 1	Raith R	4	Peebles R	0
Feb 1	Stranraer	6	Eyemouth U	2

Replays
Feb 5	Montrose	3	Brechin C	1
Feb 5	St Mirren	2	Ayr U	1

2nd Round
Feb 15	Celtic	7	Stirling A	2
Feb 15	Clyde	4	Arbroath	0
Feb 15	Dundee U	0	Hibernian	0
Feb 15	Falkirk	6	St Johnstone	3
Feb 15	Forfar A	1	Rangers	9
Feb 15	Hearts	4	Albion R	1
Feb 15	Inverness C	5	Stenhousemuir	2
Feb 15	Kilmarnock	7	Vale of Leithen	0
Feb 15	Montrose	2	Buckie T	2
Feb 15	Morton	0	Aberdeen	1
Feb 15	Motherwell	2	Partick T	2
Feb 15	Queen of South	7	Stranraer	0
Feb 15	Queen's Park	7	Fraserburgh	2
Feb 15	Raith R	0	Dundee	1
Feb 15	St Mirren	1	Dunfermline A	4
Feb 15	T Lanark	6	Lossiemouth	1

Replays
Feb 19	Buckie T	4	Montrose	1
Feb 19	Hibernian	2	Dundee U	0
Feb 19	Partick T	0	Motherwell	4

3rd Round
Mar 1	Buckie T	1	Falkirk	2
Mar 1	Celtic	0	Clyde	2
Mar 1	Dundee	1	Aberdeen	3
Mar 1	Dunfermline A	1	Rangers	2
Mar 1	Hearts	3	Hibernian	4
Mar 1	Inverness C	0	Motherwell	7
Mar 1	Kilmarnock	2	Queen of South	2
Mar 1	T Lanark	5	Queen's Park	3

Replay
Mar 5	Queen of South	3	Kilmarnock	0

4th Round
Mar 15	Clyde	2	Falkirk	1
Mar 15	Hibernian	3	T Lanark	2
Mar 15	Motherwell	2	Aberdeen	1
Mar 15	Queen of South	3	Rangers	4

Semi-finals
Apr 5	Clyde	3	Motherwell	2
	played at Celtic Park			
Apr 5	Hibernian	2	Rangers	2
	played at Hampden Park			

Replay
Apr 9	Hibernian	2	Rangers	1
	played at Hampden Park			

Final
Apr 26	Clyde	1	Hibernian	0
	played at Hampden Park			

Coates of Queen's Park beats Third Lanark's goalkeeper Robertson in this third-round tie. But Queen's Park were the losers in this eight-goal thriller.

Kilmarnock's goalkeeper is in a spot of bother in this Cup-tie against Queen of the South.

DIVISION 1

Results grid (home team = row, away team = column; each cell shows date and score):

(home \ away)	ABERDEEN	AIRDRIE	CELTIC	CLYDE	DUNDEE	EAST FIFE	FALKIRK	HEARTS	HIBERNIAN	KILMARNOCK	MOTHERWELL	PARTICK T	QUEEN OF SOUTH	QUEEN'S PARK	RAITH R	RANGERS	ST MIRREN	T LANARK
ABERDEEN	—	Oct05 5-1	Apr05 0-1	Dec07 2-1	Sep21 3-0	Jan02 6-2	Feb22 1-2	Apr16 0-4	Sep07 0-1	Nov23 1-2	Apr09 4-3	Oct26 1-3	Apr12 3-4	Nov09 5-2	Mar22 3-2	Dec28 1-2	Jan11 3-1	Mar08 2-4
AIRDRIE	Oct12 2-6	—	Nov30 2-5	Apr21 7-1	Dec28 2-1	Nov02 6-2	Apr05 2-7	Sep14 1-4	Nov16 2-1	Jan04 4-1	Jan01 4-1	Mar15 4-1	Apr02 2-1	Dec21 2-2	Jan18 2-1	Mar01 3-4	Mar01 2-3	Oct19 2-3
CELTIC	Jan18 1-1	Mar22 4-2	—	Apr09 6-2	Dec07 0-0	Mar05 4-0	Jan04 2-2	Dec28 0-2	Mar19 4-0	Nov02 4-0	Apr21 2-2	Dec21 2-3	Dec25 1-2	Apr07 5-1	Oct12 1-1	Jan01 0-1	Nov16 2-2	Apr30 4-1
CLYDE	Mar29 5-1	Jan11 3-1	Dec14 3-6	—	Jan18 2-0	Oct05 3-1	Sep07 2-1	Nov09 5-0	Nov23 2-1	May03 2-1	Apr16 3-2	Nov30 4-1	Apr16 6-1	Feb22 2-3	Mar08 6-2	Oct26 1-3	May10 1-1	Apr30 2-0
DUNDEE	Jan01 1-2	Apr26 5-3	Mar29 5-3	Jan18 2-0	—	Apr30 2-0	Dec21 0-4	Jan04 0-5	Oct19 3-0	Oct12 3-0	Nov16 1-0	Nov30 1-0	Sep14 1-2	Nov02 1-0	Sep14 0-2	Mar14 1-2	Mar15 0-0	Mar20 2-0
EAST FIFE	Apr21 3-2	Feb22 0-6	Nov09 0-3	Jan04 1-3	Oct26 3-1	—	Apr16 2-1	Jan18 2-3	Dec14 1-2	Oct12 2-1	Dec21 2-2	Sep14 2-1	Mar08 4-0	Sep28 2-2	Jan01 2-0	Mar22 0-1	Jan11 1-2	Nov23 0-6
FALKIRK	Nov02 4-4	Dec14 3-0	Sep07 0-1	Mar05 1-1	Apr12 0-2	Oct19 4-1	—	Mar22 0-4	Oct05 1-3	Dec07 1-1	Apr30 1-1	Mar31 1-2	Sep21 1-1	Dec28 3-2	Mar08 3-2	Nov23 0-4	Jan02 3-1	Jan11 4-2
HEARTS	Oct19 4-0	Jan02 4-0	Mar14 5-3	Apr19 2-2	Sep07 6-0	Oct05 9-0	Nov30 9-1	—	Sep21 3-1	Dec14 2-2	Nov02 2-2	Jan11 4-1	Mar10 3-1	Nov16 8-0	Apr19 4-1	Dec21 2-1	Jan25 5-1	Jan25 7-2
HIBERNIAN	Jan04 0-1	Sep28 3-1	Nov23 1-1	Dec28 0-1	Apr16 1-3	Apr18 0-1	Jan18 0-3	Jan01 0-2	—	Apr12 1-2	Sep14 2-1	Nov09 5-1	Mar22 1-2	Oct12 2-0	Oct26 2-2	Apr21 3-1	Feb22 5-5	Dec07 4-0
KILMARNOCK	Mar19 2-0	Sep07 3-1	Feb22 1-1	Oct19 3-2	Jan11 1-1	Mar15 4-0	Mar29 1-1	Apr05 1-1	Dec21 1-4	—	Nov16 0-1	Jan30 4-1	Jan02 2-0	Oct26 3-1	Apr26 1-1	Mar10 3-3	Sep21 4-2	Oct05 2-4
MOTHERWELL	Dec14 4-0	Sep21 1-2	Jan11 1-3	Mar22 1-1	Apr28 1-0	Apr12 0-2	Oct26 2-5	Feb22 0-4	Jan02 2-2	Mar08 2-2	—	Oct05 4-1	Apr16 4-2	Nov09 0-2	Dec07 2-2	Sep07 4-2	Apr26 1-2	—
PARTICK T	Feb01 1-0	Nov23 2-2	Apr12 0-1	Jan01 2-2	Mar08 2-0	Dec28 5-1	Oct12 3-0	Nov11 1-3	Mar05 2-0	Mar22 3-2	Jan18 2-3	—	Dec07 4-3	Jan04 1-4	Dec14 3-2	May05 1-2	Oct19 3-2	Nov02 2-3
QUEEN OF SOUTH	Dec21 1-2	Oct26 3-2	Apr16 4-3	Oct12 0-3	Feb22 4-0	Nov09 0-3	Jan01 2-2	Nov09 1-4	Nov30 3-0	Feb01 1-1	Mar19 1-2	Mar29 1-3	—	Sep14 2-1	Sep28 1-1	Jan04 1-1	Apr26 2-2	Apr05 6-1
QUEEN'S PARK	Mar05 2-5	Dec07 1-3	Jan02 0-3	Dec21 1-4	Mar22 2-7	Jan11 1-4	Mar08 0-2	Apr16 1-1	Jan25 1-2	Apr30 1-2	Apr23 0-7	Sep07 0-6	Oct05 3-0	—	Nov23 2-3	Oct26 2-4	Apr14 0-1	Jan01 1-3
RAITH R	Nov30 0-1	Apr12 4-0	Jan25 1-2	Nov02 5-0	Jan02 4-0	Sep21 0-2	Nov16 4-1	Dec07 0-3	Apr30 2-0	Dec28 1-1	Mar05 1-1	Apr05 3-2	Oct19 3-1	Mar15 3-1	—	Apr23 1-3	Oct05 1-0	Sep07 4-2
RANGERS	Apr26 5-0	May03 1-2	Nov16 2-3	Nov16 2-0	May10 0-1	Mar19 3-3	Oct26 3-2	Jan11 2-3	Mar29 3-1	Mar29 3-4	Apr16 2-2	Jan18 2-0	Sep07 4-2	Feb22 5-1	Apr16 4-1	—	Apr28 1-0	Dec21 5-1
ST MIRREN	Sep28 3-1	Nov09 0-1	Mar08 1-1	Apr30 1-0	Nov23 1-1	Dec07 3-0	Sep14 2-1	Apr12 1-2	Nov02 2-3	Jan04 2-1	Apr18 1-1	Dec14 1-2	Jan18 1-1	Oct12 0-4	1-3		—	Mar22 2-2
T LANARK	Nov16 3-1	Apr16 3-1	Oct26 0-2	Jan02 2-5	Nov09 5-1	Mar19 1-2	Sep28 3-5	Oct12 0-0	Mar29 1-1	Jan18 2-1	Dec28 4-2	Feb22 1-4	Dec14 2-3	Sep21 1-3	Jan04 2-0	Apr12 1-5	Nov30 1-3	—

DIVISION 1 FINAL TABLE

	P	W	D	L	F	A	Pts
Hearts	34	29	4	1	132	29	62
Rangers	34	22	5	7	89	49	49
Celtic	34	19	8	7	84	47	46
Clyde	34	18	6	10	84	61	42
Kilmarnock	34	14	9	11	60	55	37
Partick T	34	17	3	14	69	71	37
Raith R	34	14	7	13	66	56	35
Motherwell	34	12	8	14	68	67	32
Hibernian	34	13	5	16	59	60	31
Falkirk	34	11	9	14	64	82	31
Dundee	34	13	5	16	49	65	31
Aberdeen	34	14	2	18	68	76	30
St Mirren	34	11	8	15	59	66	30
T Lanark	34	13	4	17	69	88	30
Queen of South	34	12	5	17	61	72	29
Airdrie	34	13	2	19	71	92	28
East Fife	34	10	3	21	45	88	23
Queen's Park	34	4	1	29	41	114	9

DIVISION 2

Results grid (home team = row, away team = column; each cell shows date and score):

(home \ away)	ALBION R	ALLOA	ARBROATH	AYR U	BERWICK R	BRECHIN C	COWDENBEATH	DUMBARTON	DUNDEE U	DUNFERMLINE A	E STIRLING	FORFAR A	HAMILTON A	MONTROSE	MORTON	ST JOHNSTONE	STENHOUSEMUIR	STIRLING A	STRANRAER
ALBION R	—	Nov09 2-3	Apr26 2-4	Sep18 2-1	Oct26 1-0	Sep07 2-2	Apr28 1-3	Aug21 3-1	Dec14 3-1	Nov23 1-0	Oct05 3-1	Apr12 1-1	Sep21 1-1	Feb22 0-3	Mar08 2-2	Mar22 2-1	Jan11 6-1	Jan02 0-2	Dec07 3-0
ALLOA	Mar01 4-1	—	Sep07 2-3	Feb22 2-2	Nov02 5-3	Jan02 5-3	Dec07 4-2	Sep18 2-4	Oct19 2-3	Mar08 2-2	Feb15 4-2	Apr30 4-1	Jan11 2-1	Dec28 1-2	Mar22 2-1	Oct05 1-1	Sep21 0-2	Aug21 0-2	Nov03 2-1
ARBROATH	Dec28 1-3	Jan04 2-2	—	Nov16 4-3	Jan18 4-0	Dec14 1-2	Oct19 4-2	Feb22 3-5	Sep04 3-1	Sep14 0-5	Dec07 4-1	Jan01 2-1	Apr12 2-3	Sep11 2-2	Nov23 2-3	Nov09 2-0	Feb01 2-0	Mar22 3-2	Sep28 3-2
AYR U	Sep04 4-0	Oct12 4-3	Mar08 3-3	—	Apr16 0-0	Feb15 4-0	Nov09 5-3	Sep21 3-0	Jan04 1-1	Sep10 0-3	Sep28 3-2	Mar22 7-4	Apr12 2-3	Sep14 2-1	Dec28 4-1	Nov23 4-3	Dec14 2-1	Jan01 0-0	Apr18 2-3
BERWICK R	Apr23 2-1	Sep14 2-2	Oct05 1-2	Oct19 0-6	—	Jan11 1-3	Sep07 0-2	Jan25 2-2	Nov16 1-9	Nov09 2-2	Dec28 4-5	Mar22 3-1	Dec26 2-6	Dec07 1-1	Mar01 0-4	Nov23 2-0	Aug21 0-1	Sep21 0-3	Dec14 2-1
BRECHIN C	Jan04 2-1	Apr21 2-2	Apr05 2-1	Mar01 3-5	Apr30 4-1	—	Feb15 3-2	Oct19 5-2	Oct12 1-1	Nov23 1-4	Apr23 3-2	Feb22 3-0	Jan01 0-2	Jan18 4-2	Apr12 0-2	Dec28 2-1	Dec07 1-1	Mar22 2-1	Mar22 2-1
COWDENBEATH	Oct12 3-2	Mar29 2-4	Apr16 3-2	Mar15 6-5	Jan04 3-2	Oct26 2-2	—	Apr26 3-2	Sep11 1-1	Jan01 0-4	Mar22 6-0	Sep14 5-2	Nov23 1-1	Apr23 4-2	Feb22 6-0	Mar08 3-4	Nov09 2-2	Dec07 3-0	Nov30 8-1
DUMBARTON	Sep11 6-0	Sep04 4-0	Nov02 4-4	Oct26 5-1	Oct12 1-1	Apr18 5-1	Dec28 6-1	—	Sep28 2-0	Dec14 1-3	Mar01 1-1	Nov23 4-0	Mar08 6-0	Jan18 1-0	Jan01 3-1	Dec07 4-0	Mar22 6-0	Apr12 2-2	Sep14 1-0
DUNDEE U	Apr05 2-1	Apr16 1-7	Sep18 5-5	Sep07 3-4	May03 7-0	Apr28 1-2	Aug21 0-4	Jan11 1-2	—	Feb22 3-3	Jan02 7-0	Nov09 5-2	Mar22 3-0	Apr12 2-1	Dec07 4-1	Oct05 2-1	Nov23 1-2	Dec28 1-2	Dec28 0-0
DUNFERMLINE A	Mar15 8-1	Nov16 8-1	Jan02 0-1	Oct05 5-2	Apr18 4-0	Sep18 1-2	Sep21 5-5	Apr05 3-0	Nov02 6-1	—	Jan11 1-2	Oct19 4-2	Apr30 5-0	Apr30 5-1	Aug21 2-1	Dec07 7-1	Sep07 5-2	Sep07 5-2	Apr12 9-1
E STIRLING	Jan18 2-1	Dec21 0-2	Mar29 1-2	Aug21 5-0	Apr26 1-1	Mar15 4-0	Nov30 0-2	Nov09 1-2	Sep14 0-0	Sep28 2-1	—	Oct12 2-1	Apr16 3-1	Nov16 2-0	Jan04 1-1	Oct26 0-5	Apr05 4-2	Sep18 1-4	Feb22 2-2
FORFAR A	Dec21 0-1	Oct26 1-1	Sep21 2-3	Jan11 1-1	Nov30 3-1	Aug21 3-0	Jan02 1-2	May03 2-0	Mar01 1-1	Apr16 0-1	Apr28 3-1	—	Apr26 2-0	Apr05 3-0	Nov02 2-1	Sep18 1-3	Sep07 4-2	Oct05 4-1	Mar08 2-1
HAMILTON A	Jan01 1-4	Sep28 2-0	Apr21 2-2	Mar29 4-5	Apr21 3-1	Nov02 4-2	Mar15 3-2	Nov16 0-3	Sep14 1-2	Oct19 3-1	Apr16 4-2	Dec28 3-1	—	Jan04 2-2	Apr18 5-1	Mar01 1-2	Mar01 7-2	Apr30 3-5	Apr23 3-3
MONTROSE	Nov02 0-0	Apr26 3-2	Aug21 1-3	Nov30 2-3	Mar29 3-2	Sep21 1-3	Sep18 2-1	Oct05 2-1	Dec21 2-1	Oct26 2-1	Mar08 2-1	Dec14 2-1	Sep07 1-2	—	Apr16 1-2	Apr28 1-0	Jan02 2-1	Jan11 3-1	Nov09 0-0
MORTON	Nov16 4-0	Nov30 4-3	Mar15 1-3	Jan02 1-2	Dec21 8-0	Oct05 5-6	Apr05 2-2	Sep21 0-0	Mar29 3-2	Feb22 0-0	Sep07 3-0	Feb22 2-2	Aug21 1-1	Oct19 3-1	—	Jan11 6-1	Sep18 0-4	Apr23 2-2	Oct26 2-1
ST JOHNSTONE	Nov30 1-1	Jan18 2-2	Oct26 0-4	Mar15 4-2	Dec21 4-0	Nov02 3-3	Mar29 3-3	Jan01 2-3	Sep21 3-3	Apr30 2-2	Jan04 3-1	Dec14 1-0	Oct12 3-3	Feb01 1-3	Oct19 1-5	—	Oct19 2-2	Mar08 2-2	Apr28 2-1
STENHOUSEMUIR	Sep28 2-1	Jan01 1-5	Oct26 2-3	Mar15 0-1	Sep10 1-3	Apr26 2-2	Nov16 2-4	Nov30 1-6	Jan18 3-2	Mar29 2-3	Dec14 3-2	Jan04 4-1	Nov09 1-2	Sep14 3-0	Sep04 2-1	Apr23 —	—	Feb22 2-4	Oct12 3-0
STIRLING A	Sep14 4-0	Sep11 1-0	Nov30 2-1	Apr05 4-0	Jan01 5-0	Mar29 3-2	Mar01 7-1	Dec21 4-1	Mar15 5-3	Jan04 2-1	Jan18 4-1	Oct26 3-3	Sep28 3-0	Oct12 7-0	Nov16 2-1	Apr30 4-1	Nov02 4-0	—	Apr16 2-1
STRANRAER	Mar29 4-0	Mar15 2-1	Jan11 2-3	Sep21 3-2	Apr05 3-0	Nov30 1-1	Oct05 2-3	Jan02 2-1	Apr26 1-4	Dec21 0-3	Nov02 1-1	Nov16 1-0	Sep18 2-2	Mar01 3-0	Apr30 3-1	Sep07 1-4	Apr28 6-5	Oct19 1-4	—

DIVISION 2 FINAL TABLE

	P	W	D	L	F	A	Pts
Stirling A	36	25	5	6	105	48	55
Dunfermline A	36	24	5	7	120	42	53
Arbroath	36	21	5	10	89	72	47
Dumbarton	36	20	4	12	92	57	44
Ayr U	36	18	6	12	98	81	42
Cowdenbeath	36	17	8	11	100	85	42
Brechin C	36	16	8	12	80	81	40
Alloa	36	15	9	12	88	78	39
Dundee U	36	12	9	15	81	77	33
Hamilton A	36	12	9	15	70	79	33
St Johnstone	36	12	9	15	67	85	33
Forfar A	36	13	6	17	70	71	32
Morton	36	12	8	16	77	83	32
Montrose	36	13	6	17	55	72	32
E Stirling	36	12	5	19	55	79	29
Stenhousemuir	36	12	5	19	68	98	29
Albion R	36	12	5	19	53	79	29
Stranraer	36	9	7	20	54	83	25
Berwick R	36	5	5	26	37	109	15

League Cup results for 1957-58 are detailed on page 189.

Aberdeen's Jack Hather greets the Duke of Gloucester at Tynecastle in December 1958.

SFA Cup

1st Round

Jan 31	Aberdeen 2	East Fife 1
Jan 31	Babcock & Wilcox .4	Forres Mechanic . . 0
Jan 31	Celtic 4	Albion R 0
Jan 31	Cowdenbeath 2	Dunfermline A 2
Jan 31	Dumbarton 4	Buckie T 0
Feb 9	E Stirling 1	Dundee U 1
Jan 31	Forfar A 1	Rangers 3
Jan 31	Fraserburgh 1	Dundee 0
Jan 31	Peebles R 2	Ross Co 0
Feb 4	Queen of South . .1	Hearts 3
Jan 31	Raith R 1	Hibernian 1
Jan 31	Stenhousemuir . . .5	Eyemouth U 2
Jan 31	Stranraer 3	Berwick R 2

Replays

Feb 9	Dunfermline A . .4	Cowdenbeath 1
Feb 9	Hibernian 2	Raith R 1

Feb 10	Dundee U 0	E Stirling 0
Feb 11	Dundee U 4	E Stirling 0
	played at Tynecastle	

2nd Round

Feb 14	Aberdeen 3	Arbroath 0
Feb 14	Airdrie 2	Motherwell 7
Feb 14	Ayr U 3	Stranraer 0
Feb 14	Babcock & Wilcox . .0	Morton 5
Feb 14	Brechin C 3	Alloa 3
Feb 18	Celtic 1	Clyde 1
Feb 14	Coldstream 0	Hamilton A 4
Feb 14	Dumbarton 2	Kilmarnock 8
Feb 14	Dundee U 0	T Lanark 4
Feb 14	Fraserburgh 3	Stirling A 4
Feb 14	Hibernian 3	Falkirk 1
Feb 14	Montrose 0	Dunfermline A 1
Feb 14	Rangers 3	Hearts 2
Feb 14	St Johnstone 3	Queen's Park 1
Feb 13	St Mirren 10	Peebles R 0

Feb 14	Stenhousemuir . . . 1	Partick T 3

Replays

Feb 18	Alloa 3	Brechin C 1
Feb 23	Clyde 3	Celtic 4

3rd Round

Feb 28	Celtic 2	Rangers 1
Feb 28	Dunfermline A . . . 2	Ayr U 1
Feb 28	Hamilton A 0	Kilmarnock 5
Feb 28	Hibernian 4	Partick T 1
Feb 28	St Johnstone 1	Aberdeen 2
Feb 28	St Mirren 3	Motherwell 2
Feb 28	Stirling A 3	Morton 1
Feb 28	T Lanark 3	Alloa 2

4th Round

Mar 14	Aberdeen 3	Kilmarnock 1
Mar 14	St Mirren 2	Dunfermline A 1
Mar 14	Stirling A 1	Celtic 3

Season 1958-59

Mar 14 T Lanark ....2 Hibernian 1

Semi-finals

Apr 4 Aberdeen ....1 T Lanark 1
played at Ibrox

Apr 4 Celtic ....0 St Mirren 4
played at Hampden Park

Replay

Apr 8 Aberdeen ....1 T Lanark 0
played at Ibrox

Final

Apr 25 Aberdeen ....1 St Mirren 3
played at Hampden Park

DIVISION 1 FINAL TABLE

	P	W	D	L	F	A	Pts
Rangers	34	21	8	5	92	51	50
Hearts	34	21	6	7	92	51	48
Motherwell	34	18	8	8	83	50	44
Dundee	34	16	9	9	61	51	41
Airdrie	34	15	7	12	64	62	37
Celtic	34	14	8	12	70	53	36
St Mirren	34	14	7	13	71	74	35
Kilmarnock	34	13	8	13	58	51	34
Partick T	34	14	6	14	59	66	34
Hibernian	34	13	6	15	68	70	32
T Lanark	34	11	10	13	74	83	32
Stirling A	34	11	8	15	54	64	30
Aberdeen	34	12	5	17	63	66	29
Raith R	34	10	9	15	60	70	29
Clyde	34	12	4	18	62	66	28
Dunfermline A	34	10	8	16	68	87	28
Falkirk	34	10	7	17	58	79	27
Queen of South	34	6	6	22	38	101	18

DIVISION 2 FINAL TABLE

	P	W	D	L	F	A	Pts
Ayr U	36	28	4	4	115	48	60
Arbroath	38	23	5	8	86	59	51
Stenhousemuir	36	20	6	10	87	68	46
Dumbarton	36	19	7	10	94	61	45
Brechin C	36	16	10	10	79	65	42
St Johnstone	36	15	10	11	54	44	40
Hamilton A	36	15	8	13	76	62	38
East Fife	36	15	8	13	83	81	38
Berwick R	38	16	6	14	63	66	38
Albion R	36	14	7	15	84	79	35
Morton	36	13	8	15	68	85	34
Forfar A	36	12	9	15	73	87	33
Alloa	36	12	7	17	76	81	31
Cowdenbeath	36	13	5	18	67	79	31
E Stirling	36	10	8	18	50	79	28
Stranraer	36	8	11	17	63	76	27
Dundee U	36	9	7	20	62	86	25
Queen's Park	36	9	6	21	53	80	24
Montrose	36	6	6	24	49	96	18

League Cup results for 1958-59 are detailed on page 190.

DIVISION 1

Home team (row) vs away team (column); date and score.

Home \ Away	ABERDEEN	AIRDRIE	CELTIC	CLYDE	DUNDEE	DUNFERMLINE A	FALKIRK	HEARTS	HIBERNIAN	KILMARNOCK	MOTHERWELL	PARTICK T	QUEEN OF SOUTH	RAITH R	RANGERS	ST MIRREN	STIRLING A	T LANARK
ABERDEEN		Aug20 0-1	Sep27 3-1	Mar21 1-0	Jan01 4-0	Sep13 5-0	Oct25 2-4	Apr15 4-0	Oct18 2-2	Mar04 3-4	Dec13 3-4	Jan24 5-0	Nov29 2-2	Nov15 1-3	Dec20 2-1	Mar07 1-3	Feb07 2-1	Mar11 4-1
AIRDRIE	Dec27 2-1		Oct18 1-4	Jan17 2-1	Apr18 1-1	Nov22 2-1	Mar28 2-2	Jan03 2-3	Feb21 4-3	Oct04 3-0	Sep06 1-5	Mar07 1-2	Feb07 0-1	Dec06 4-0	Sep20 5-4	Dec13 4-2	Nov01 0-1	Mar18 1-1
CELTIC	Mar25 4-0	Mar10 1-2		Dec27 3-1	Mar04 1-1	Mar07 3-1	Oct11 3-4	Apr18 2-1	Mar28 3-0	Jan02 2-0	Mar21 3-3	Sep20 2-0	Sep06 3-1	Nov15 2-2	Dec13 3-3	7-3		Oct25 3-1
CLYDE	Nov22 4-0	Sep27 0-2	Aug20 2-1		Oct18 3-2	Nov01 1-1	Apr04 2-2	Mar14 2-1	Feb07 4-1	Dec20 2-4	Feb21 2-0	Jan01 0-3	Mar31 3-0	Nov29 4-1	Nov08 1-1	Jan24 4-2	Jan10 2-2	Sep13 1-2
DUNDEE	Sep06 2-1	Dec20 1-1	Nov01 1-1	Feb28 2-1		Apr13 2-2	Dec27 3-2	Oct11 3-3	Dec06 2-1	Sep20 1-0	Oct04 1-1	Mar28 3-2	Mar14 2-1	Jan03 2-0	Jan28 4-6	Feb21 3-0	Nov08 3-0	Nov22
DUNFERMLINE A	Jan03 1-1	Mar21 2-1	Nov08 1-0	Mar04 2-4	Dec13 2-1		Jan17 4-1	Dec27 3-3	Nov15 1-2	Sep20 0-3	Dec20 0-4	Sep29 10-14-2	Apr18 3-3	Sep29 1-7	Oct04 2-3	Dec06 3-2	Dec06 2-3	Dec03 2-3
FALKIRK	Feb21 5-1	Nov29 1-2	Feb07 3-2	Dec06 1-4	Aug20 2-5	Sep27 0-2		Mar21 0-2	Jan24 1-0	Nov08 0-0	Oct18 1-1	Jan10 0-2	Nov01 4-0	Apr18 2-2	Mar14 5-5	Sep13 3-4	Jan05 2-1	Dec13 2-0
HEARTS	Dec06 5-1	Sep13 4-3	Dec20 1-1	Nov15 2-2	Feb07 1-0	Aug20 6-2	Nov22 5-1		Jan01 1-3	Mar28 3-1	Nov01 0-2	Oct18 2-1	Apr07 2-1	Feb21 2-1	Apr11 2-0	Mar09 4-0	Jan24 1-4	Sep27 8-3
HIBERNIAN	Feb18 1-0	Oct25 2-3	Nov29 3-2	Oct11 2-1	Apr04 1-2	Mar18 3-1	Oct04 2-3	Sep06 0-4		Dec27 4-3	Jan03 2-2	Dec13 4-0	Sep20 4-0	Jan21 4-2	Mar04 2-2	Apr18 0-1	0-1	Nov08 4-4
KILMARNOCK	Nov01 2-0	Jan24 1-3	Sep13 4-1	Apr18 1-1	Jan10 1-1	Oct11 4-1	Mar07 1-1	Nov29 1-1	Aug20 1-1		Mar18 1-3	Feb21 5-0	Oct18 2-0	Dec13 0-3	Nov22 1-0	Jan01 0-3	Sep27 1-1	Apr21 1-2
MOTHERWELL	Apr11 2-0	Jan01 5-2	Apr08 2-0	Oct25 1-0	Jan24 2-0	Jan21 1-0	Jan31 1-0	Mar04 0-1	Sep13 2-5	Nov15 1-1		Aug20 3-1	Nov08 6-1	Nov29 3-3	Sep27 2-2	Mar21 2-2	3-0	Oct11 8-1
PARTICK T	Oct04 2-3	Nov08 1-3	Nov22 2-0	Sep06 1-0	Nov29 3-0	Dec20 3-3	Sep20 3-1	Feb18 2-1	Apr11 2-2	Oct29 1-1	Dec27 4-0		Jan20 2-3	Feb07 1-3	Jan03 2-0	Dec06 3-1	Mar14 1-5	Mar04 1-1
QUEEN OF SOUTH	Mar28 2-1	Oct11 0-2	Jan24 2-2	Dec13 2-1	Nov15 1-3	Oct25 2-3	Feb28 2-1	Nov08 0-5	Jan10 1-4	Feb18 0-5	Apr18 1-0	Sep27		Mar21 1-1	Dec06 3-6	Aug20 2-2	Sep13 1-1	Jan01 2-5
RAITH R	Mar18 0-1	Feb28 3-0	Apr06 3-1	Mar28 1-0	Sep13 4-1	Jan01 2-2	Dec20 1-2	Oct29 0-5	Sep27 5-2	Oct25 1-0	Oct11 3-0	Nov22 2-2			Feb18 1-0	Nov01 2-1	Aug20 0-1	Jan24 2-4
RANGERS	Apr18 1-2	Jan01 2-1	Jan01 2-1	Mar07 3-1	Sep27 1-2	Jan24 1-0	Jan21 3-0	Jan03 5-0	Nov01 4-0	Sep13 2-1	Apr06 3-1	Oct18 4-4				Oct11 1-1	Feb21 3-0	Aug20 2-2
ST MIRREN	Nov08 1-5	Mar25 2-1	Mar18 1-3	Oct04 2-2	Oct25 6-2	Feb18 1-2	Jan03 1-1	Sep20 2-1	Nov22 0-2	Sep06 4-1	Feb23 4-3	Apr08 1-1	Dec27 3-1	Mar04 3-1	Feb07 1-3		Nov29 3-2	Apr18 4-1
STIRLING A	Oct11 3-2	Mar04 0-0	Apr11 0-1	Sep20 2-1	Mar07 0-1	Apr04 1-1	Sep10 1-1	Oct04 1-2	Dec20 0-3	Jan17 3-1	Nov26 2-5	Nov15 1-1	Jan03 4-0	Dec27 2-1	Oct25 2-2	Mar28 3-0		Jan31 2-3
T LANARK	Sep20 0-2	Nov15 1-1	Feb21 1-1	Jan20 2-2	Mar21 0-3	Mar28 7-1	Apr11 3-3	Feb25 3-3	Mar07 0-4	Mar24 2-0	Feb07 5-2	Nov01 0-1	Sep06 7-1	Oct04 3-2	Dec27 2-3	Dec20 2-3	Oct18 3-0	

DIVISION 2

Home team (row) vs away team (column); date and score.

Home \ Away	ALBION R	ALLOA	ARBROATH	AYR U	BERWICK R	BRECHIN C	COWDENBEATH	DUMBARTON	DUNDEE U	EAST FIFE	E STIRLING	FORFAR A	HAMILTON A	MONTROSE	MORTON	QUEEN'S PARK	ST JOHNSTONE	STENHOUSEMUIR	STRANRAER
ALBION R		Apr04 2-0	Jan24 3-4	Oct11 1-4	Apr22 2-2	Oct25 4-3	Feb28 1-3	Nov29 1-2	Apr11 3-1	Aug20 8-0	Nov08 3-0	Apr25 2-0	Apr27 3-0	Nov15 2-5	Mar21 5-2	Dec20 5-2	Sep13 6-2	Jan10	Apr29 4-0
ALLOA	Dec06 5-2		Sep13 2-3	Feb21 1-2	Dec20 2-2	Nov08 2-0	Feb07 2-0	Aug20 3-5	Nov01 3-1	Apr25 3-0	Mar14 4-2	Oct18 5-1	Nov29 2-4	Sep17 4-1	Mar21 2-3	Sep27 3-1	Apr15 2-1	Apr11 2-3	1-0
ARBROATH	Oct04 1-1	Jan03 3-3		Mar14 1-3	Sep20 2-0	Feb28 2-0	Jan17 2-0	Nov08 5-4	Mar28 2-0	Sep20 3-2	Feb07 3-0	Sep06 6-1	Apr25 6-0	Apr27 3-0	Apr11 4-1	Oct29 2-1	Apr29 3-1	Oct18 4-1	Nov22 2-0
AYR U	Feb07 6-2	Oct25 6-2	Nov15 5-2		Jan03 2-0	Jan31 1-4	Sep20 1-2	Apr27 3-1	Nov08 6-2	Mar28 2-4	Dec06 3-0	Apr11 4-1	Mar21 8-2	Jan17 3-2	Sep06 2-2	Oct04 2-2	Dec20 2-2	Apr29 4-4	Dec27
BERWICK R	Oct18 3-2	Apr18 2-1	Jan10 1-1	Sep13 0-4		Jan24 3-1	Mar21 2-0	Sep27 0-3	Feb21 8-2	Sep17 1-0	Jan01 2-0	Feb07 4-2	Dec13 2-3	Dec06 2-1	Apr25 2-1	Aug20 1-1	Mar14 1-4	Nov01 3-0	
BRECHIN C	Feb21 3-2	Mar07 3-2	Nov01 3-0	Oct18 0-4	Oct04 3-2		Apr18 4-7	Sep16 2-1	Sep10 1-0	Apr04 2-2	Dec13 4-0	Dec27 3-3	Nov06 0-0	Jan17 2-3	Sep06 3-0	Jan03 5-0	Nov29 0-0	Oct03 0-3	Sep22 2-2
COWDENBEATH	Nov01 4-0	Oct11 1-2	Sep27 3-1	Jan10 1-5	Feb14 2-3	Dec20 1-2		Apr20 2-2	Mar14 6-0	Jan01 4-2	Apr29 2-5	Oct25 1-2	Aug20 0-6	Apr04 1-1	Mar28 2-2	Apr11 4-2	Jan24 1-0	Apr25 1-2	Mar07 4-2
DUMBARTON	Mar28 2-0	Dec27 1-1	Mar07 2-0	Nov15 1-2	Apr29 0-2	Sep03 2-3	Oct18 4-2		Sep20 4-3	Feb28 5-0	Apr25 2-1	Dec06 1-1	Dec20 6-3	Jan03 3-1	Oct04 6-1	Sep06 1-0	Feb07 5-1	Mar21 5-1	Feb21 4-1
DUNDEE U	Dec13 3-4	Apr22 1-1	Nov22 2-3	Mar07 2-3	Oct25 4-1	Apr25 1-2	Nov15 2-0	Jan10 1-1		Jan24 1-1	Aug20 2-5	Sep03 3-2	Mar21 3-1	Apr18 3-0	Jan01 4-1	Sep27 1-1	Apr04 2-3	5-2	1-0
EAST FIFE	Dec27 5-1	Sep10 3-1	Feb21 2-0	Nov29 1-3	Sep03 4-0	Dec06 2-6	Sep06 5-1	Dec13 2-6	Oct04 1-1		Mar21 6-2	Jan17 4-3	Apr08 2-2	Apr18 1-2	Sep20 3-2	Oct18 1-2	Nov15 6-2	Feb07 2-1	Jan03 5-2
E STIRLING	Mar07 1-0	Nov15 2-2	Oct11 0-1	Apr04 1-0	Sep06 3-2	Apr11 0-0	Sep03 5-2	Sep10 3-2	Dec27 1-1	Nov22 0-0		Sep27 1-3	Apr20 4-2	Oct04 3-1	Apr22 1-1	Feb28 1-2	Oct25 1-0	Dec20 2-2	Mar28 1-1
FORFAR A	Sep10 4-1	Sep20 4-1	Jan01 1-4	Apr22 1-2	Oct11 2-1	Aug20 2-2	Dec06 2-3	Apr18 3-1	Sep17 2-2	Apr04 4-4			Jan24 0-5	Nov01 2-1	Nov15 5-1	Nov29 4-2	Sep13 2-3	Apr15 2-1	
HAMILTON A	Sep06 2-2	Sep20 1-0	Apr22 4-0	Nov22 0-0	Mar07 1-3	Mar14 3-4	Dec27 0-0	Apr18 4-1	Jan03 1-0	Nov01 5-1	Oct18 5-0	Oct04 7-1		Feb21 5-2	Feb07 1-2	Mar28 2-2	Dec13 4-2	Dec06 0-3	Apr15 1-1
MONTROSE	Mar14 1-1	Apr28 3-3	Aug20 1-4	Sep27 2-4	Apr11 1-2	Jan01 2-4	Dec06 2-0	Sep13 1-6	Nov22 1-2	Jan24 1-0	Feb28 0-4	Oct25 4-0	Jan31		Sep03 4-0	Apr25 0-1	Nov08 0-5	Oct11 1-1	
MORTON	Nov22 4-3	Sep03 4-1	Dec31 3-4	Mar25 3-3	Apr04 2-3	Sep27 2-4	Dec13 1-1	Oct04 2-0	Apr29 0-1	Sep13 2-1	Mar14 4-1	Oct11 0-1	Oct18 5-2			Nov01 1-1	Mar07 1-3	Feb21 2-2	
QUEEN'S PARK	Apr18 1-2	Nov22 1-2	Mar30 1-1	Jan24 0-4	Sep10 1-2	Sep13 4-2	Dec13 2-3	Jan01 1-1	Oct11 2-0	Apr22 2-2	Sep27 1-3	Nov08 2-3	Nov29 2-2	Sep17 1-3	Apr27		Apr15 1-2	Aug20 1-3	Mar14 1-1
ST JOHNSTONE	Jan03 1-1	Apr20 3-0	Apr04 1-1	Apr18 1-0	Dec27 2-0	Nov22 1-0	Oct04 1-0	Oct11 3-4	Sep06 6-1	Mar14 3-0	Feb21 2-1	Mar28 1-1	Jan31 0-1	Sep10 0-1	Nov08 0-0	Sep20 0-0		Nov01 3-0	Apr22 0-0
STENHOUSEMUIR	Sep20 2-6	Sep06 5-4	Apr20 7-0	Sep03 1-2	Nov15 2-8	Mar28 0-0	Nov22 2-0	Jan27 3-1	Nov20 1-0	Jan03 3-2	Apr04 2-2	Mar07 2-0	Oct25 5-1	Dec27 3-2	Apr11 1-0				Oct04 4-1
STRANRAER	Sep17 0-0	Dec13 2-2	Mar21 1-3	Aug20 2-3	Feb28 3-1	Jan10 1-3	Nov08 4-0	Oct25 2-3	Dec06 4-1	Sep13 2-2	Nov29 2-1	Apr18 1-1	Sep27 1-3	Feb07 5-3	Apr25 5-1	Nov15 2-1	Oct18 2-3	Jan24 4-1	

Hearts, who won the Scottish League for the second time in three years. They also won the League Cup. Back row (left to right): McLeod (assistant trainer), Kirk, Marshall, Brown, Blackwood, Cumming, McFadzean, Higgins, Bauld, Harvey (trainer). Front row: Smith, Young, Milne, Crawford, Hamilton, Murray, Thomson, Bowman.

SFA Cup

1st Round

Jan 30	Aberdeen 0	Brechin C	0
Jan 30	Albion R 2	Tarff R	1
Jan 30	Berwick R 1	Rangers	3
Jan 30	Clyde 2	T Lanark	0
Jan 30	Dunfermline A ...1	St Johnstone ...	1
Jan 30	East Fife 0	Partick T	2
Jan 30	Keith 3	Hamilton A	0
Jan 30	Kilmarnock 5	Stranraer	0
Jan 30	Morton 0	E Stirling	1
Jan 30	Queen of South ..2	Dumbarton	1
Jan 30	Queen's Park 2	Raith R	0
Jan 30	St Mirren 15	Glasgow Univ ...	0
Jan 30	Stenhousemuir ...2	Rothes	0

Replays

Feb 3	Brechin C 3	Aberdeen	6
Feb 3	St Johnstone 1	Dunfermline A ...	4

2nd Round

Feb 13	Aberdeen 0	Clyde	2
Feb 13	Alloa 1	Airdrie	5
Feb 13	Cowdenbeath 1	Falkirk	0
Feb 13	Dundee U 2	Partick T	2
Feb 13	Dunfermline A ...2	Stenhousemuir ..3	
Feb 13	E Stirling 2	Inverness C	2

Feb 13	Elgin C 5	Forfar A	1
Feb 13	Eyemouth U 1	Albion R	0
Feb 22	Hearts 1	Kilmarnock 1	
Feb 29	Hibernian 3	Dundee	0
Feb 13	Montrose 2	Queen's Park ...2	
Feb 13	Motherwell 6	Keith	0
Feb 22	Peebles R 1	Ayr U 6	
Feb 13	Rangers 2	Arbroath	0
Feb 13	St Mirren 1	Celtic	1
Feb 13	Stirling A 3	Queen of South ..3	

Replays

Feb 17	Partick T 4	Dundee U	1
Feb 17	Queen of South ..5	Stirling A	1
Feb 24	Celtic 4	St Mirren	4
Feb 24	Kilmarnock 2	Hearts	1
Feb 27	Inverness C 1	E Stirling	4
Feb 29	Celtic 5	St Mirren	2
	played at Celtic Park		
Feb 29	Queen's Park 1	Montrose	1
Mar 1	Montrose 1	Queen's Park ...2	
	played at Tynecastle		

3rd Round

Feb 27	Ayr U 4	Airdrie	2
Mar 5	Clyde 6	Queen's Park ...	0
Mar 5	E Stirling 0	Hibernian 3	

Mar 5	Elgin C 1	Celtic	2
Feb 27	Eyemouth U 3	Cowdenbeath ...	0
Feb 27	Kilmarnock 2	Motherwell	0
Feb 27	Partick T 3	Queen of South ..2	
Feb 27	Stenhousemuir ...0	Rangers 3	

4th Round

Mar 12	Ayr U 0	Clyde	2
Mar 12	Celtic 2	Partick T	0
Mar 12	Eyemouth U 1	Kilmarnock	2
Mar 12	Rangers 3	Hibernian	2

Semi-finals

Apr 2	Celtic 1	Rangers	1
	played at Hampden Park		
Apr 2	Clyde 0	Kilmarnock	2
	played at Ibrox		

Replay

Apr 6	Celtic 1	Rangers	4
	played at Hampden Park		

Final

Apr 23	Kilmarnock 0	Rangers 2	
	played at Hampden Park		

Season 1959-60

DIVISION 1

	ABERDEEN	AIRDRIE	ARBROATH	AYR U	CELTIC	CLYDE	DUNDEE	DUNFERMLINE A	HEARTS	HIBERNIAN	KILMARNOCK	MOTHERWELL	PARTICK T	RAITH R	RANGERS	ST MIRREN	STIRLING A	T LANARK
ABERDEEN		Jan16 2-2	Dec12 0-0	Apr30 2-0	Feb06 3-2	Mar08 0-2	Sep05 0-3	Jan02 1-1	Nov21 1-3	Dec26 6-4	Mar22 0-1	Mar12 2-2	Sep19 5-2	Apr02 4-2	Oct24 0-5	Oct03 3-1	Dec05 3-1	Nov14 3-1
AIRDRIE	Sep26 1-0		Jan09 2-1	Oct31 1-2	Apr18 2-5	Feb20 2-4	Apr02 3-3	Dec05 6-3	Oct10 2-5	Oct24 1-11	Sep12 1-3	Jan01 0-1	Nov21 3-0	Aug19 1-2	Dec05 0-5	Mar19 1-3	Mar12 2-4	Jan23 3-2
ARBROATH	Apr23 1-3	Sep19 1-1		Jan16 1-1	Oct03 0-5	Mar26 2-3	Mar05 1-1	Feb06 2-2	Oct17 0-3	Dec05 3-1	Oct24 2-2	Dec19 0-3	Dec26 2-2	Mar12 0-4	Nov14 6-2	Jan02 4-3	Sep05 2-1	Nov28 2-1
AYR U	Dec19 2-1	Mar05 1-0	Sep26 1-0		Mar16 1-1	Aug19 1-2	Mar09 1-0	Oct24 3-3	Jan23 1-1	Apr22 2-1	Sep12 1-3	Dec05 5-2	Oct10 4-1	Jan09 4-0	Oct10 2-4	Nov14 4-3	Jan01 1-1	2-3
CELTIC	Oct10 1-1	Dec12 0-0	Jan23 4-0	Nov07 2-3		Sep26 1-1	Dec05 2-3	Nov14 4-2	Sep12 3-4	Mar07 1-0	Apr19 2-0	Oct24 5-1	Apr12 2-4	Jan09 1-0	Apr30 0-1	Jan30 3-3	Mar28 4-0	
CLYDE	Oct31 7-2	Oct17 2-1	Nov21 3-0	Dec26 3-3	Jan16 4-3		Sep19 1-1	Apr23 1-3	Nov28 2-2	Oct03 2-1	Dec19 1-2	Mar19 5-0	Sep05 1-0	Feb27 6-1	Apr25 4-1	Mar22 2-2	Jan02 2-2	Apr16 2-1
DUNDEE	Jan01 4-1	Nov28 1-2	Oct31 5-0	Oct17 3-1	Apr16 2-0	Jan09 2-0		Nov07 3-2	Aug19 1-3	Mar26 6-3	Jan23 0-4	Sep26 1-1	Mar19 3-0	Sep12 0-2	Oct10 1-3	Feb27 3-1	Apr23 4-1	Dec19 2-1
DUNFERMLINE A	Sep12 1-3	Dec12 1-0	Oct10 5-1	Mar01 3-4	Nov07 3-2	Dec12 4-5	Mar12 2-2		Jan09 2-2	Feb27 2-2	Apr04 1-0	Oct31 6-0	Jan23 3-3	Nov21 0-2	Dec19 0-5	Sep26 2-1	1-1	3-1
HEARTS	Mar26 3-0	Feb06 4-1	Mar09 5-3	Oct03 1-3	Jan02 2-0	Apr05 2-1	Dec26 2-3	Sep19 2-2		Sep05 2-2	Nov14 3-1	Jan30 1-1	Nov07 3-0	Dec19 0-2	Mar05 0-2	Dec05 4-0	Jan16 4-0	Oct28 6-2
HIBERNIAN	Aug19 2-1	Mar30 3-3	Apr16 5-0	Dec12 5-1	Oct31 3-3	Jan23 5-5	Nov21 4-2	Oct17 7-4	Jan01 1-5		Sep26 4-2	Oct10 1-3	Apr30 2-2	Mar19 0-3	Sep12 0-1	Aug16 1-3	Sep05 3-1	Jan09 6-0
KILMARNOCK	Oct17 2-0	Jan02 1-0	Mar01 3-2	Nov21 2-0	Dec26 2-1	Apr30 0-2	Oct03 2-2	Nov09 3-2	Mar19 2-1	Jan16 3-1		Oct31 2-0	Feb06 5-1	Dec12 1-0	Apr16 1-1	Sep05 0-5	Feb20 2-0	Nov07 3-2
MOTHERWELL	Nov07 3-1	Sep05 6-0	Apr30 2-1	Jan02 3-2	Mar21 0-0	Nov14 3-2	Jan16 2-0	Dec26 0-0	Feb06 1-1	Mar05 0-1			Oct03 4-0	Apr16 2-1	Nov28 1-4	Sep19 1-4	Oct17	Mar26
PARTICK T	Jan09 1-0	Mar26 0-3	Aug19 2-0	Apr16 3-1	Nov28 3-1	Jan01 0-1	Nov14 0-5	Mar05 2-0	Mar15 1-2	Dec19 2-10	Oct10 3-2	Jan23 1-2		Feb20 1-0	Sep26 0-3	Dec12 4-2	Oct24 1-0	Sep12 2-0
RAITH R	Nov28 5-1	Dec26 2-3	Nov07 5-0	Feb20 2-0	Sep19 0-3	Oct24 3-1	Jan02 1-1	Apr30 2-2	Nov14 4-2	Apr27 0-2	Dec05 1-1	Oct17 1-2			Mar26 1-2	Jan06 6-1	Mar05 0-1	2-3
RANGERS	Mar01 2-2	Apr30 0-0	Mar19 1-1	Sep19 3-1	Sep05 6-0	Nov07 0-0	Feb09 4-1	Oct03 0-2	Oct31 1-1	Jan02 5-0	Dec05 0-2	Apr18 1-1	Jan16 3-0	Nov21 0-2		Oct17 1-3	Dec26 3-0	May07 1-2
ST MIRREN	Jan23 3-0	Nov14 1-2	Sep12 8-1	Nov28 4-3	Dec19 0-3	Oct10 2-2	Oct24 2-3	Apr16 0-2	Nov07 4-4	Jan01 2-3	Jan09 0-3	Apr23 5-1	Sep26 2-4	Apr25 3-2	1-1		Mar05 0-7	Aug19 1-3
STIRLING A	Apr16 0-2	Nov07 1-2	Jan01 5-0	Mar19 3-4	Sep12 2-2	Dec12 1-1	Apr30 0-1	Apr02 1-4	Apr20 2-2	Feb20 2-3	Mar02 2-1	Jan23 4-2	Aug19 2-3	Oct31 3-2				Oct10 0-3
T LANARK	Mar19 2-1	Oct03 4-2	Apr05 7-1	Sep05 5-0	Oct17 4-2	Dec05 2-3	Apr30 2-2	Jan16 2-0	Feb27 1-4	Sep19 5-3	Mar14 3-4	Nov21 1-4	Jan02 1-2	Oct31 1-3	Dec12 0-2	Jan06 2-2	Feb09 3-3	

DIVISION 2

	ALBION R	ALLOA	BERWICK R	BRECHIN C	COWDENBEATH	DUMBARTON	DUNDEE U	EAST FIFE	E STIRLING	FALKIRK	FORFAR A	HAMILTON A	MONTROSE	MORTON	QUEEN OF SOUTH	QUEEN'S PARK	ST JOHNSTONE	STENHOUSEMUIR	STRANRAER
ALBION R		Dec12 2-2	Oct03 1-3	Sep16 6-3	Apr16 1-1	Nov28 0-0	Feb27 1-4	Sep19 1-1	Jan16 2-1	Oct17 2-2	Jan02 7-1	Sep05 0-3	Sep23 5-1	Nov14 3-2	Mar26 0-3	Apr30 4-1	Mar05 2-1	Dec26 2-0	Apr27 3-1
ALLOA	Apr23 2-3		Mar05 0-3	Dec19 1-7	Apr13 4-2	Sep16 1-1	Mar26 3-2	Nov14 4-0	Jan02 5-1	Nov28 2-1	Sep19 5-1	Dec26 3-1	Oct24 1-2	Sep23 2-1	Oct03 1-2	Jan16 1-2	Sep05 0-1	Mar12 4-2	
BERWICK R	Jan23 4-1	Oct31 1-1		Oct10 4-0	Jan09 1-0	Dec19 0-0	Feb13 1-2	Sep23 2-0	Aug19 5-3	Sep12 2-1	Jan01 1-1	Sep02 0-1	Mar12 4-3	Apr27 2-2	Oct24 3-1	Apr02 0-2	3-0	2-1	
BRECHIN C	Sep02 2-2	Apr30 3-0	Feb06 5-2		Apr02 1-2	Sep26 3-1	Jan23 1-1	Mar05 1-1	Jan09 1-0	Oct17 1-3	Sep23 1-3	Jan01 1-0	Dec12 4-0	Nov21 1-1	Dec05 2-1	Jan16 1-1	Dec05 2-1	Oct24 0-3	
COWDENBEATH	Dec05 2-6	Oct17 1-1	Jan16 2-0	Nov28 3-1		Apr23 0-4	Nov07 0-2	Sep05 2-3	Oct24 0-3	Apr25 2-4	Oct03 3-2	Sep19 1-3	Mar05 1-3	Mar26 2-5	Apr30 1-9	Feb06 0-4	Dec26 1-6	Nov14 0-1	Jan02 4-1
DUMBARTON	Mar12 6-0	Sep02 2-1	Sep19 0-4	Jan16 2-0	Dec12 6-0		Sep09 3-2	Apr13 4-2	Dec05 4-2	Mar19 1-0	Oct24 4-1	Apr30 2-1	Nov21 0-1	Feb13 1-1	Oct17 1-3	Sep05 3-2	Jan02 1-0	Oct03 0-1	Dec26 4-1
DUNDEE U	Oct24 0-0	Sep02 2-1	Apr30 1-0	Oct03 3-1	Jan30 2-3	Sep23 2-1		Dec26 6-0	Feb06 6-1	Dec12 1-0	Apr02 4-0	Nov14 5-1	Dec05 3-3	Jan02 4-3	Jan16 3-1	Mar05 0-1	Dec19 1-2	Nov14 1-2	Sep19 2-1
EAST FIFE	Jan09 4-1	Mar19 4-7	Nov21 4-3	Oct31 1-0	Jan01 1-0	Oct10 1-3	Aug19 1-3		Apr06 1-3	Feb27 6-1	Sep23	Apr16	Apr02	Sep26	Sep12	Dec12	Mar12	Feb20	Dec19
E STIRLING	Sep26 3-0	Sep12 6-3	Sep08 0-0	Nov07 0-1	Apr20 4-1	Apr16 2-2	Oct10 1-0	Sep02 2-2		Jan01 1-5	Mar26 1-4	Oct17 2-3	Jan09 2-3	Aug19 3-1	Jan23 4-3	Mar19 2-0	Dec26 3-5	Nov28 0-1	Oct31 2-3
FALKIRK	Apr13 2-1	Sep02 5-0	Dec26 4-0	Sep19 1-3	Apr06 8-1	Apr23 0-0	Oct24 1-2	Sep05 5-0	2-3		Dec19 7-2	Jan16 4-2	Mar12 2-0	Mar04 4-1	Dec16 3-2	Jan02 0-1	Oct03 1-1	4-1	3-1
FORFAR A	Sep12 1-0	Jan09 2-2	Apr16 3-0	Feb20 1-0	Jan23 2-0	Feb27 2-2	Nov28 1-3	Apr20 2-1	Nov21 1-2	Apr30 1-6		Nov07 1-6	Aug19	Dec12	Sep26 2-5	Oct31 1-1	Sep16 1-4	Oct10 1-4	Mar05
HAMILTON A	Jan01 0-3	Aug19 2-2	Mar19 3-0	Sep08 4-1	Jan09 2-0	Dec19 5-0	Oct31 2-0	Dec05 2-0	Apr27 2-2	Sep26 2-0	Mar12 3-2		Sep02 0-0	Jan23 7-3	Oct10 0-3	Apr02 2-1	Oct24 4-3	Apr23 5-1	Nov01 5-2
MONTROSE	Sep09 4-1	Jan30 2-2	Jan02 2-1	Sep05 3-1	Oct31 2-0	Mar26 1-2	Mar19 1-3	Sep19 2-0	Nov07 5-0	Dec26 2-2	Sep05 2-1	1-1		Oct13 1-0	Apr27 1-2	Jan16 3-1	Oct03 3-0	Dec03 0-3	Apr23 1-0
MORTON	Mar19 1-3	Feb27 3-0	Sep05 1-2	Jan02 3-0	Nov21 2-0	Nov07 1-2	Oct17 1-3	Jan16 2-0	Dec26 5-0	Apr20 2-2	Apr23 2-1	Oct03 1-1	Apr16 1-1		Nov28 3-1	Sep19 1-2	Apr30 3-2	Mar05 2-0	Sep16
QUEEN OF SOUTH	Nov21 4-1	Sep09 2-1	Sep16 2-1	Apr23 5-0	Dec19 1-0	Apr06 4-4	Apr16 5-1	Jan02 2-2	Oct03 1-1	Oct31 0-0	Jan16 3-3	Feb06 3-1	Oct24 2-0	Apr02		Dec26 7-1	Sep19 1-2	Mar12 2-0	Sep05 4-2
QUEEN'S PARK	Dec19 0-2	Jan23 2-0	Nov07 3-1	Apr27 2-1	Oct10 4-2	Jan01 2-3	Sep12 1-8	Apr23 1-0	Nov14 1-0	Apr16 0-3	Sep26 2-2	Feb27 2-1	Jan23 2-1	Dec19 2-0	Aug19 3-4		Sep23 3-0	Sep15 3-2	Apr20 0-1
ST JOHNSTONE	Oct31 4-1	Sep26 5-0	Oct17 2-0	Feb13 6-2	Aug19 7-3	Sep12 7-2	Jan01 1-1	Nov07 2-3	Apr23 2-0	Oct10 2-0	Sep02 2-5	Feb27 3-0	Jan23 2-0	Dec19 4-1	Jan09 3-1	Sep09 3-4		Mar26 3-2	Dec05 3-2
STENHOUSEMUIR	Aug19 3-3	Jan01 5-3	Apr12 2-1	Apr16 3-2	Mar19 4-4	Jan23 1-2	Sep26 0-3	Oct17 4-0	Apr02 2-1	Sep12 1-3	Feb06 3-1	Dec12 4-5	Apr30 2-1	Oct31 4-2	Nov07 2-1	Sep02 6-0	Nov21 3-2		Sep07 0-0
STRANRAER	Oct10 6-1	Nov07 1-2	Nov28 0-3	Feb27 3-2	Sep12 3-1	Aug19 0-1	Jan09 3-3	Mar26 2-1	Apr08 2-1	Jan23 1-1	Nov14 4-0	Feb13 1-2	Dec12 0-1	Sep02 2-3	Jan01 0-3	Oct17 2-3	Apr16 0-2	Sep23 4-7	

DIVISION 1 FINAL TABLE

	P	W	D	L	F	A	Pts
Hearts	34	23	8	3	102	51	54
Kilmarnock	34	24	2	8	67	45	50
Rangers	34	17	8	9	72	38	42
Dundee	34	16	10	8	70	49	42
Motherwell	34	16	8	10	71	61	40
Clyde	34	15	9	10	77	69	39
Hibernian	34	14	7	13	106	85	35
Ayr U	34	14	6	14	65	73	34
Celtic	34	12	9	13	73	59	33
Partick T	34	14	4	16	54	78	32
Raith R	34	14	3	17	64	62	31
T Lanark	34	13	4	17	75	83	30
Dunfermline A	34	10	9	15	72	80	29
St Mirren	34	11	6	17	78	86	28
Aberdeen	34	11	6	17	54	72	28
Airdrie	34	11	6	17	56	80	28
Stirling A	34	7	8	19	55	72	22
Arbroath	34	4	7	23	38	106	15

DIVISION 2 FINAL TABLE

	P	W	D	L	F	A	Pts
St Johnstone	36	24	5	7	87	47	53
Dundee U	36	22	6	8	90	45	50
Queen of South	36	21	7	8	94	52	49
Hamilton A	36	21	6	9	91	62	48
Stenhousemuir	36	20	4	12	86	67	44
Dumbarton	36	18	7	11	67	53	43
Montrose	36	19	5	12	60	52	43
Falkirk	36	15	9	12	77	43	39
Berwick R	36	16	5	15	62	55	37
Albion R	36	14	8	14	71	78	36
Queen's Park	36	17	2	17	65	79	36
Brechin C	36	14	6	16	66	66	34
Alloa	36	13	5	18	70	85	31
Morton	36	10	8	18	67	79	28
E Stirling	36	10	8	18	68	82	28
Forfar A	36	10	8	18	53	84	28
Stranraer	36	10	3	23	53	79	23
East Fife	36	7	6	23	50	87	20
Cowdenbeath	36	6	2	28	42	124	14

League Cup results for 1959-60 are detailed on pages 190-191.

Season 1960-61

SFA Cup

1st Round
Jan 28	Alloa	5	E Stirling	4
Jan 28	Berwick R	1	Dunfermline A	4
Jan 28	Clyde	0	Hibernian	2
Jan 28	Deveronvale	1	Stirling A	0
Jan 28	Elgin C	2	Airdrie	2
Jan 28	Falkirk	1	Celtic	3
Jan 28	Hearts	9	Tarff R	0
Jan 28	Keith	1	East Fife	2
Jan 28	Montrose	3	Albion R	1
Jan 28	Peebles	4	Gala Fairydean	2
Jan 28	Queen of South	1	St Johnstone	1
Jan 28	Queen's Park	2	Arbroath	3
Jan 28	T Lanark	2	Stenhousemuir	0

Replays
Feb 1	Airdrie	2	Elgin C	0
Feb 1	St Johnstone	1	Queen of South	2

2nd Round
Feb 11	Aberdeen	4	Deveronvale	2
Feb 11	Alloa	2	Dumbarton	0
Feb 11	Ayr U	0	Airdrie	0
Feb 11	Brechin C	5	Duns	3
Feb 11	Buckie T	0	Raith R	2
Feb 11	Celtic	6	Montrose	0
Feb 11	Cowdenbeath	1	Motherwell	4
Feb 11	Dundee	1	Rangers	5
Feb 11	Dundee U	0	St Mirren	1
Feb 11	East Fife	1	Partick T	3
Feb 11	Forfar A	2	Morton	0
Feb 11	Hibernian	15	Peebles	1
Feb 11	Kilmarnock	1	Hearts	2
Feb 11	Queen of South	0	Hamilton A	2
Feb 11	Stranraer	1	Dunfermline A	3
Feb 11	T Lanark	5	Arbroath	2

Replays
Feb 15	Airdrie	3	Ayr U	1

3rd Round
Feb 25	Aberdeen	3	Dunfermline A	6
Feb 25	Alloa	2	Forfar A	1
Feb 25	Brechin C	0	Airdrie	3
Feb 25	Hamilton A	0	Hibernian	4
Feb 25	Motherwell	2	Rangers	2
Feb 25	Partick T	1	Hearts	2
Feb 25	Raith R	1	Celtic	4
Feb 25	St Mirren	3	T Lanark	3

Replay
Feb 28	T Lanark	0	St Mirren	8
Mar 1	Rangers	2	Motherwell	5

4th Round
Mar 11	Celtic	1	Hibernian	1
Mar 11	Dunfermline A	4	Alloa	0
Mar 11	Hearts	0	St Mirren	1
Mar 11	Motherwell	0	Airdrie	1

Replay
Mar 15	Hibernian	0	Celtic	1

Semi-finals
Apr 1	Airdrie	0	Celtic	4

played at Hampden Park

Apr 1	Dunfermline A	0	St Mirren	0

played at Tynecastle

Replay
Apr 5	Dunfermline A	1	St Mirren	0

played at Tynecastle

Final
Apr 22	Celtic	0	Dunfermline A	0

played at Hampden Park

Replay
Apr 26	Celtic	0	Dunfermline A	2

played at Hampden Park

Dunfermline Athletic, winners of the Scottish Cup in 1961. Back row (left to right): Dickson, Sweeney, Fraser, Connachan, Smith, Miller, J.Stevenson (trainer). Front row: Peebles, Thomson, Mailer, Cunningham, Melrose.

DIVISION 1

(home \ away)	ABERDEEN	AIRDRIE	AYR U	CELTIC	CLYDE	DUNDEE	DUNDEE U	DUNFERMLINE A	HEARTS	HIBERNIAN	KILMARNOCK	MOTHERWELL	PARTICK T	RAITH R	RANGERS	ST JOHNSTONE	ST MIRREN	T LANARK
ABERDEEN		Oct29 1-1	Jan21 3-1	Jan14 1-3	Feb18 4-2	Jan02 2-1	Nov26 1-3	Aug24 1-4	Mar14 0-2	Mar25 1-4	Dec10 3-2	Nov12 3-3	Dec17 2-1	Mar01 0-1	Apr08 6-1	Sep17 4-2	Apr29 1-0	Oct08 5-3
AIRDRIE	Mar04 3-1		Dec03 4-2	Oct01 2-0	Dec24 0-2	Apr12 2-4	Feb04 4-4	Apr10 0-1	Sep24 2-2	Oct22 4-3	Nov05 1-1	Sep10 4-2	Mar25 2-3	Apr22 1-0	Jan07 1-1	Feb18 3-0	Nov12 2-1	Dec31 4-1
AYR U	Oct01 1-1	Apr08 2-2		Mar04 1-3	Jan07 2-4	Nov19 3-0	Apr22 4-1	Feb04 1-0	Oct15 0-1	Mar18 2-2	Sep24 2-2	Dec31 2-0	Mar01 1-1	Dec10 1-1	Dec24 1-0	Nov05 0-5	Nov26 2-3	Sep10 2-3
CELTIC	Sep24 0-0	Jan21 4-0	Oct29 2-0		Feb27 6-1	Dec26 2-1	Dec10 1-1	Mar25 2-1	May02 1-3	Feb18 2-0	Dec31 3-2	Dec24 1-0	Nov12 0-1	Mar20 1-1	Sep10 1-5	Apr05 1-1	Oct08 4-2	Jan07 2-3
CLYDE	Oct15 1-1	Apr29 3-1	Sep17 2-2	Oct22 0-3		Jan14 0-0	Mar04 3-1	Apr12 6-0	Nov19 1-1	Dec17 3-3	Feb04 1-3	Oct01 1-0	Jan02 3-3	Mar18 0-2	Sep10 1-3	Feb11 0-0	Aug24 4-2	Nov12 2-4
DUNDEE	Sep10 3-3	Dec10 2-1	Mar25 6-1	Apr08 0-1	Sep24 4-1		Jan07 3-0	Mar04 4-0	Dec24 3-0	Nov05 4-0	Oct15 1-0	Apr22 2-2	Nov26 1-2	Dec31 2-3	Feb08 4-2	Oct01 2-1	Mar08 2-0	Nov12 0-2
DUNDEE U	Apr01 3-3	Oct08 1-2	Dec17 2-1	Apr10 1-1	Oct29 2-1	Sep17 3-1		Apr29 5-0	Jan21 3-0	Aug24 3-1	Nov19 2-4	Oct22 0-1	Jan14 3-0	Feb18 4-1	Mar18 1-1	Jan02 0-2	Dec03 2-0	Mar11 1-2
DUNFERMLINE A	Dec31 2-6	Nov26 6-4	Oct08 2-2	Nov19 2-2	Dec10 2-2	Dec24 4-2	Dec24 3-2		Jan07 2-1	Apr08 4-2	May01 2-4	Sep24 1-6	Mar13 2-1	Sep10 3-2	Feb18 0-0	Mar18 5-1	Jan21 1-2	Mar06 2-3
HEARTS	Nov05 3-4	Jan14 3-1	Feb18 2-1	Dec17 3-1	Mar25 4-2	Apr29 2-1	Oct01 1-1	Sep17 1-2		Jan02 1-2	Mar18 0-1	Mar04 1-5	Oct08 0-1	Nov26 1-3	Oct26 3-1	Aug24 0-0	Apr15 1-0	Apr08 1-0
HIBERNIAN	Nov19 2-2	Feb27 3-3	Nov12 3-1	Oct15 0-6	Apr22 4-0	Mar20 1-0	Dec31 2-0	Dec03 2-1	Sep10 1-4		Jan07 4-0	Apr01 2-1	Jan21 1-1	Sep24 0-1	Dec10 1-2	Feb08 3-1	Oct29 4-3	Dec24 8-4
KILMARNOCK	Mar11 4-1	Mar15 1-0	Jan14 5-1	Aug24 2-2	Oct08 1-0	Feb18 1-1	Mar25 1-1	Dec17 2-1	Nov12 3-2	Sep17 3-2		Dec03 5-3	Apr29 4-1	Jan21 6-0	Oct22 2-0	Oct22 2-2	Jan02 1-2	Nov02 3-1
MOTHERWELL	Mar18 1-0	Jan02 2-0	Aug24 2-2	Apr29 2-1	Jan21 2-1	Dec17 2-0	Mar07 4-3	Jan14 2-4	Oct29 1-1	Nov26 4-0	Apr08 1-3		Sep17 2-0	Oct08 2-2	Dec26 0-3	Dec10 3-0	Mar15 3-2	Oct15 2-1
PARTICK T	Apr22 3-4	Nov19 2-2	Oct22 3-3	Mar18 1-2	Sep10 3-1	Apr01 2-2	Nov05 1-0	Feb04 1-0	Oct01 4-1	Dec24 3-1	Jan07 2-3	Jan07 1-3		Apr08 2-2	Dec31 0-3	Mar04 3-0	Feb18 3-2	Dec10 2-1
RAITH R	Oct22 0-3	Dec17 2-0	Apr12 3-1	Nov05 2-2	Nov12 1-0	Apr15 0-1	Jan02 1-1	Jan14 0-2	Oct01 1-1	Feb04 1-3	Dec03 1-3				Mar04 2-3	Apr29 1-3	Sep17 5-2	Mar25 3-6
RANGERS	Dec03 4-0	Sep17 3-0	Apr29 7-3	Jan02 2-1	Mar11 2-1	Oct08 5-1	Nov12 5-0	Oct15 3-1	Mar08 3-0	Apr11 1-0	Nov26 0-2	Mar25 6-3	Aug24 3-0	Nov02 3-0		Jan14 1-0	Dec17 5-1	Jan21 4-3
ST JOHNSTONE	Jan07 2-1	Oct15 2-2	Mar11 4-1	Nov26 2-1	Dec03 2-2	Jan21 1-1	Sep10 0-2	Dec31 2-1	Oct08 2-3	Feb25 2-0	Apr19 1-1	Dec24 2-1	Sep24 2-1		Dec24 0-2		Mar25 1-1	Apr22 3-4
ST MIRREN	Dec24 1-3	Mar18 1-1	Apr17 2-2	Feb04 2-1	Dec31 1-2	Oct22 0-3	Apr08 0-2	Oct01 2-0	Dec10 2-0	Mar04 2-1	Sep10 0-1	Oct15 5-0	Jan09 3-0	Jan28 1-1	Nov19 0-0			Sep24 1-0
T LANARK	Feb04 5-1	Aug24 5-2	Jan02 3-3	Sep17 2-0	Apr03 7-4	Mar18 2-1	Nov05 6-1	Oct22 4-2	Dec03 0-3	Apr29 6-1	Mar04 0-1	Feb18 1-1	Apr12 3-2	Nov19 4-3	Oct01 2-4	Dec17 4-2	Jan14 1-2	

DIVISION 2

(home \ away)	ALBION R	ALLOA	ARBROATH	BERWICK R	BRECHIN C	COWDENBEATH	DUMBARTON	EAST FIFE	E STIRLING	FALKIRK	FORFAR A	HAMILTON A	MONTROSE	MORTON	QUEEN OF SOUTH	QUEEN'S PARK	STENHOUSEMUIR	STIRLING A	STRANRAER
ALBION R		Apr26 3-1	Sep17 0-1	Feb11 1-2	Jan14 0-2	Jan21 4-2	Nov26 5-0	Sep07 2-0	Oct15 2-4	Dec17 0-0	Apr19 1-1	Jan02 5-3	Oct08 0-3	Oct29 3-3	Apr05 1-4	Aug24 1-0	Apr08 2-5	Nov19 2-4	Mar18 2-2
ALLOA	Nov05 4-1		Nov19 4-0	Apr01 5-0	Oct15 2-2	Apr19 5-3	Dec10 1-2	Aug24 4-1	Sep21 4-1	Sep07 1-1	Apr08 4-0	Mar18 2-3	Apr22 4-2	Apr22 2-0	Jan14 4-1	Jan02 2-3	Apr05 2-4	Apr29 1-0	Oct01 1-0
ARBROATH	Jan07 1-0	Mar25 3-3		Oct15 2-0	Sep19 2-2	Apr22 1-3	Dec24 1-2	Mar04 0-0	Apr08 0-1	Nov12 1-3	Sep10 2-1	Apr19 2-2	Dec31 2-1	Nov26 1-2	Sep24 2-1	Oct01 0-3	Sep07 1-1	Nov05 0-3	Feb04 4-5
BERWICK R	Dec24 1-1	Nov26 1-1	Feb18 2-2		Apr22 2-1	Mar18 0-4	Oct29 2-2	Jan14 4-0	Aug24 3-2	Mar11 0-1	Dec10 5-2	Sep28 0-1	Nov19 1-0	Oct22 4-0	Apr19 1-1	Feb04 3-1	Sep17 1-2	Oct01 2-0	Apr08 2-2
BRECHIN C	Sep24 2-6	Feb18 2-0	Sep28 2-1	Dec17 1-1		Nov26 1-1	Apr08 3-2	Apr29 1-2	Sep14 3-2	Jan21 0-2	Dec31 3-4	Sep10 1-2	Jan07 2-3	Oct22 1-5	Nov05 2-0	Mar18 0-2	Dec10 6-2	Mar04 0-2	
COWDENBEATH	Oct01 2-1	Oct22 2-1	Dec17 3-1	Nov12 1-3	Apr01 3-3		Apr04 3-2	Jan03 1-2	Apr26 4-2	Apr15 3-2	Mar04 2-4	Jan28 2-1	Apr29 5-1	Dec03 1-0	Mar25 2-1	Sep17 3-1	Aug24 2-1	Oct15 0-3	Nov05 4-5
DUMBARTON	Apr01 2-0	Apr10 3-1	Apr29 4-2	Mar04 4-3	Dec03 2-0	Sep28 0-2		Sep17 1-0	Nov19 3-3	Oct22 1-2	Oct01 7-2	Aug24 5-1	Nov05 2-4	Oct12 2-4	Feb18 3-1	Jan02 3-2	Jan14 2-4	Mar18 2-4	Dec17 1-2
EAST FIFE	Sep14 4-2	Dec31 3-1	Sep24 1-2	Sep24 4-0	Dec24 3-3	Jan07 1-4	Dec10 8-1		Oct08 3-1	Apr22 4-2	Apr22 4-0	Nov26 2-4	Feb18 3-1	Sep28 0-2	Feb25 1-2	Apr08 0-1	Nov05 1-1		
E STIRLING	Feb18 0-4	Oct29 1-1	Apr12 1-3	Dec31 2-1	Sep07 1-2	Oct08 2-4	Mar25 2-3	Apr15 1-4		Sep10 0-0	Nov12 1-2	Dec17 1-1	Jan21 4-1	Sep24 4-1	Jan07 1-1	Oct22 2-2	Apr04 1-4	Apr29 1-4	Nov26 1-4
FALKIRK	Apr22 8-2	Sep28 4-3	Mar18 3-0	Nov05 4-0	Oct01 0-0	Dec10 3-3	Feb25 7-1	Feb15 3-0	Jan02 6-0		Apr08 2-1	Oct15 4-4	Sep14 2-1	Dec24 3-0	Apr01 2-1	Nov19 8-0	Mar04 1-2	Jan14 2-1	Sep17 1-2
FORFAR A	Oct22 2-2	Sep14 1-1	Jan02 1-3	Apr15 4-1	Aug24 5-2	Sep28 0-0	Jan21 1-0	Mar18 4-1	Dec03 1-6			Sep17 5-3	Sep28 1-3	Mar11 0-3	Oct29 2-4	Nov19 1-4	Apr01 0-3		Jan14 4-5
HAMILTON A	Sep10 4-3	Dec03 0-3	Oct22 2-2	Apr26 2-6	Feb04 2-2	Apr12 4-3	Dec31 1-3	Oct01 5-2	Apr22 1-1	Feb18 3-0	Jan07 1-2		Sep24 5-1	Mar25 3-0	Nov12 3-2	Apr01 6-1	Nov05 0-1	Mar04 0-3	Apr15 2-1
MONTROSE	Feb04 2-1	Nov12 3-2	Aug24 4-0	Mar25 2-2	Jan02 0-1	Dec24 0-2	Mar11 4-1	Apr01 1-2	Oct01 6-0	Sep07 2-3	Sep21 2-1	Jan14 4-1		Apr15 3-2	Oct29 3-1	Dec03 2-1	Oct15 4-0	Sep17 1-0	Feb25 0-2
MORTON	Mar04 4-0	Dec17 3-1	Apr01 2-2	Feb25 1-2	Sep17 3-3	Apr08 0-0	Aug28 2-3	Oct15 1-1	Jan14 2-2	Nov05 1-5	Nov05 1-4	Dec10 1-0			Sep28 1-1	Apr17 1-4	Feb04 2-3	Apr22 2-2	Aug24 2-2
QUEEN OF SOUTH	Apr15 1-2	Apr29 2-1	Feb25 4-1	Sep07 0-1	Apr12 3-1	Nov19 1-3	Oct15 0-2	Nov05 5-1	Sep17 5-1	Nov26 4-1	Feb04 1-0	Mar18 4-1	Mar04 0-4	Apr26		Dec17 4-2	Oct01 1-2	Aug24 2-4	Jan02 5-0
QUEEN'S PARK	Dec31 2-1	Sep24 0-2	Jan21 1-2	Oct08 1-2	Mar11 2-2	Jan07 2-3	Sep10 1-1	Sep21 2-1	Feb25 4-4	Mar25 2-1	Dec24 0-2	Nov26 1-4	Apr08 2-1	Nov12 3-1	Apr24 3-2		Dec10 4-2	Sep07 1-1	Oct15 2-4
STENHOUSEMUIR	Dec03 3-0	Sep10 6-1	Apr26 0-2	Jan07 7-2	Nov12 4-1	Dec31 3-0	Oct22 4-4	Sep24 3-2	Oct29 2-3	Mar25 5-0	Feb18 1-2	Oct08 0-3	Nov05 3-2	Apr15 3-2		Dec17 3-3			Apr29 4-1
STIRLING A	Feb25 6-0	Oct08 2-0	Mar11 7-0	Jan21 1-0	Mar25 3-0	Feb18 5-0	Nov12 5-0	Dec03 1-0	Dec24 5-0	Sep24 1-0	Nov26 5-1	Oct29 1-2	Jan07 2-2	Sep10 4-0	Dec31 2-1	Sep14 2-1	Apr22 6-2		Sep21 1-0
STRANRAER	Nov12 4-0	Jan21 2-2	Oct08 5-1	Dec03 2-1	Oct29 2-1	Mar11 2-0	Apr22 4-2	Mar25 6-2	Apr01 2-3	Jan07 2-3	Sep24 4-1	Dec10 5-0	Oct22 6-0	Dec31 2-0	Sep10 0-1	Apr19 4-2	Dec24 1-3	Sep28 0-1	

DIVISION 1 FINAL TABLE

	P	W	D	L	F	A	Pts
Rangers	34	23	5	6	88	46	51
Kilmarnock	34	21	8	5	77	45	50
T Lanark	34	20	2	12	100	80	42
Celtic	34	15	9	10	64	46	39
Motherwell	34	15	8	11	70	57	38
Aberdeen	34	14	8	12	72	72	36
Hearts	34	13	8	13	51	53	34
Hibernian	34	15	4	15	66	69	34
Dundee U	34	13	7	14	60	58	33
Dundee	34	13	6	15	61	53	32
Partick T	34	13	6	15	59	69	32
Dunfermline A	34	12	7	15	65	81	31
Airdrie	34	10	10	14	61	71	30
St Mirren	34	11	7	16	53	58	29
St Johnstone	34	10	9	15	47	63	29
Raith R	34	10	7	17	46	67	27
Clyde	34	6	11	17	55	77	23
Ayr U	34	5	12	17	51	81	22

DIVISION 2 FINAL TABLE

	P	W	D	L	F	A	Pts
Stirling A	36	24	7	5	89	37	55
Falkirk	36	24	6	6	100	40	54
Stenhousemuir	36	24	2	10	99	69	50
Stranraer	36	19	6	11	83	55	44
Queen of South	36	20	3	13	77	52	43
Hamilton A	36	17	7	12	84	80	41
Montrose	36	19	2	15	75	65	40
Cowdenbeath	36	17	6	13	71	65	40
Berwick R	36	14	9	13	62	69	37
Dumbarton	36	15	5	16	78	82	35
Alloa	36	13	7	16	78	68	33
Arbroath	36	13	7	16	56	76	33
East Fife	36	14	4	18	70	80	32
Brechin C	36	9	9	18	60	78	27
Queen's Park	36	10	6	20	61	87	26
E Stirling	36	9	7	20	59	100	25
Albion R	36	9	6	21	60	89	24
Forfar A	36	10	4	22	65	98	24
Morton	36	5	11	20	56	93	21

League Cup results for 1960-61 are detailed on pages 191-192.

Happy times as Dundee lift the 1961-62 League championship. Back row (left to right): Liney, Smith, Gilzean, Wishart, Ure, S.Keen (trainer), Seith. Front row: Penman, Cox, Hamilton, Cousin, Robertson.

SFA Cup
1st Round
Dec 9	Aberdeen	5	Airdrie	2
Dec 9	Arbroath	2	Peterhead	1
Dec 9	Ayr U	3	Clyde	4
Dec 9	Berwick R	2	T Lanark	6
Dec 13	Celtic	5	Cowdenbeath	1
Dec 13	Dunfermline A	5	Forfar A	1
Dec 13	East Fife	3	Gala Fairydean	...1
Dec 9	Eyemouth	1	Montrose	3
Dec 13	Falkirk	1	Rangers	2
Dec 13	Motherwell	4	Dundee U	0
Dec 13	Partick T	2	Hibernian	2
Dec 9	Raith R	1	Queen's Park	1

Replays
Dec 13	Queen's Park	1	Raith R	4
Jan 10	Hibernian	2	Partick T	3

2nd Round
Jan 27	Alloa	1	Raith R	2
Jan 27	Brechin C	1	Kilmarnock	6
Jan 27	Clyde	2	Aberdeen	2
Jan 27	Dumbarton	2	Ross Co	3
Jan 27	Dundee	0	St Mirren	1
Jan 27	Dunfermline A	...9	Wigtown	... 0
Jan 27	East Fife	1	Albion R	0
Jan 27	Hamilton A	0	T Lanark	2
Jan 27	Inverness C	3	E Stirling	0
Jan 27	Morton	1	Celtic	3
Jan 27	Motherwell	4	St Johnstone	 0
Jan 27	Queen of South	...0	Stenhousemuir	2
Jan 27	Rangers	6	Arbroath	0
Jan 27	Stirling A	3	Partick T	1
Jan 27	Stranraer	0	Montrose	... 0
Jan 27	Vale of Leithen	0	Hearts	5

Replays
Jan 31	Aberdeen	10	Clyde	3
Jan 31	Montrose	0	Stranraer	1

3rd Round
Feb 17	Aberdeen	2	Rangers	2
Feb 17	Dunfermline A	...0	Stenhousemuir	...0
Feb 17	Hearts	3	Celtic	4
Feb 17	Kilmarnock	7	Ross Co	0
Feb 17	Raith R	1	St Mirren	1
Feb 17	Stirling A	4	East Fife	1
Feb 17	Stranraer	1	Motherwell	3
Feb 17	T Lanark	6	Inverness C	1

Replay
Feb 19	St Mirren	4	Raith R	0
Feb 21	Rangers	5	Aberdeen	1
Feb 26	Stenhousemuir	...0	Dunfermline A	...3

Season 1961-62

4th Round
Mar 10 Celtic .... 4 T Lanark 4
Mar 10 Kilmarnock ...... 2 Rangers 4
Mar 10 St Mirren ...... 1 Dunfermline A ... 0
Mar 10 Stirling A .... 0 Motherwell 6

Replay
Mar 14 T Lanark .... 0 Celtic 4
played at Hampden Park

Semi-finals
Mar 31 Celtic .... 1 St Mirren 3
played at Ibrox
Mar 31 Motherwell ......1 Rangers 3
played at Hampden Park

Final
Apr 21 Rangers .... 2 St Mirren 0
played at Hampden Park

DIVISION 1 FINAL TABLE

	P	W	D	L	F	A	Pts
Dundee	34	25	4	5	80	46	54
Rangers	34	22	7	5	84	31	51
Celtic	34	19	8	7	81	37	46
Dunfermline A	34	19	5	10	77	46	43
Kilmarnock	34	16	10	8	74	58	42
Hearts	34	16	6	12	54	49	38
Partick T	34	16	3	15	60	55	35
Hibernian	34	14	5	15	58	72	33
Motherwell	34	13	6	15	65	62	32
Dundee U	34	13	6	15	70	71	32
T Lanark	34	13	5	16	59	60	31
Aberdeen	34	10	9	15	60	73	29
Raith R	34	10	7	17	51	73	27
Falkirk	34	11	4	19	45	68	26
Airdrie	34	9	7	18	57	78	25
St Mirren	34	10	5	19	52	80	25
St Johnstone	34	9	7	18	35	61	25
Stirling A	34	6	6	22	34	76	18

DIVISION 2 FINAL TABLE

	P	W	D	L	F	A	Pts
Clyde	36	25	4	7	108	47	54
Queen of South	36	24	5	7	78	33	53
Morton	36	19	6	11	78	64	44
Alloa	36	17	8	11	92	78	42
Montrose	36	15	11	10	63	50	41
Arbroath	36	17	7	12	66	59	41
Stranraer	36	14	11	11	61	62	39
Berwick R	36	16	6	14	83	70	38
Ayr U	36	15	8	13	71	63	38
East Fife	36	15	7	14	60	59	37
E Stirling	36	15	4	17	70	81	34
Queen's Park	36	12	9	15	64	62	33
Hamilton A	36	14	5	17	78	79	33
Cowdenbeath	36	11	9	16	65	77	31
Stenhousemuir	36	13	5	18	69	86	31
Forfar A	36	11	8	17	68	76	30
Dumbarton	36	9	10	17	49	66	28
Albion R	36	10	5	21	42	74	25
Brechin C	36	5	2	29	44	123	12

DIVISION 1

Home \ Away	ABERDEEN	AIRDRIE	CELTIC	DUNDEE	DUNDEE U	DUNFERMLINE A	FALKIRK	HEARTS	HIBERNIAN	KILMARNOCK	MOTHERWELL	PARTICK T	RAITH R	RANGERS	ST JOHNSTONE	ST MIRREN	STIRLING A	T LANARK
ABERDEEN	—	Jan13 1-1	Nov25 0-0	Sep16 3-1	Dec16 1-3	Mar17 1-4	Mar28 2-2	Oct14 0-2	Mar03 1-2	Mar31 3-3	Oct28 3-0	Sep30 1-3	Jan23 3-3	Apr25 1-0	Jan10 1-1	Feb03 3-1	Aug23 7-0	Nov11 2-1
AIRDRIE	Sep23 7-1	—	Mar17 1-0	Apr07 1-2	Nov04 3-3	Mar14 3-1	Nov25 2-3	Feb10 2-3	Sep09 4-2	Feb10 2-1	Apr28 1-0	Jan31 2-5	Oct28 2-2	Mar19 3-1	Dec27 0-1	Jan06 0-2		
CELTIC	Mar24 2-0	Nov18 3-0	—	Mar03 2-1	Sep23 3-1	Oct28 2-1	Jan20 3-0	Feb21 2-1	Dec16 4-3	Jan06 2-2	Jan22 5-1	Dec02 0-1	Apr21 1-1	Apr09 1-1	Feb03 7-1	Nov15 5-0	Oct14 3-0	Sep09 1-0
DUNDEE	Jan17 2-1	Dec16 5-1	Nov04 2-1	—	Sep09 4-1	Mar06 1-2	Jan06 2-1	Sep23 2-0	Mar24 1-0	Oct07 5-3	Feb10 1-3	Oct28 3-2	Nov18 5-4	Mar14 0-0	Jan24 2-1	Apr25 2-0	Dec02 2-2	Jan20 2-1
DUNDEE U	Apr07 2-2	Mar03 3-3	Jan13 4-5	Apr09 1-2	—	Aug23 3-2	Mar31 4-1	Sep30 0-1	Sep30 4-0	Oct21 1-2	Mar17 1-1	Dec23 3-5	Feb03 4-2	Jan15 2-3	Dec16 3-0	Oct14 1-0	Nov11 2-0	Dec02 3-0
DUNFERMLINE A	Nov18 4-0	Nov11 0-3	Feb24 2-0	Oct21 0-3	Jan06 1-2	—	Sep23 2-1	Sep09 2-1	Mar19 4-0	Mar24 2-0	Jan20 2-1	Feb03 4-2	Jan15 3-0	Dec16 1-0	Oct14 7-0	Dec30 3-0	Mar03 1-1	Dec02 1-1
FALKIRK	Oct21 0-1	Mar24 1-0	Sep30 3-1	Aug23 1-3	Dec02 1-2	Jan13 1-2	—	Dec23 0-2	Feb03 1-4	Feb24 0-1	Apr07 4-2	Oct14 0-2	Mar03 3-0	Mar17 1-7	Nov11 0-1	Jan10 3-3	Sep16 1-0	Apr28 2-0
HEARTS	Feb10 1-1	Sep30 4-1	Oct21 2-1	Jan13 0-2	Jan24 2-1	Jan31 3-2	Apr21 2-3	—	Sep16 4-2	Dec16 3-3	Dec02 2-6	Nov11 2-0	Feb24 0-1	Mar03 1-1	Aug23 2-2	Feb03 0-0	Feb07 2-1	
HIBERNIAN	Nov04 1-1	Oct14 2-2	Apr07 1-0	Nov25 0-3	Jan20 3-2	Dec23 1-2	Oct07 2-2	Jan17 2-3	—	Sep23 3-2	Mar14 1-2	Feb12 3-2	Sep09 2-0	Jan06 0-3	Mar17 2-1	Apr04 0-2	Apr28 2-1	Oct28 1-3
KILMARNOCK	Dec02 4-2	Jan10 4-2	Aug23 3-2	Feb03 1-1	Feb21 5-3	Nov25 2-2	Oct28 2-0	Apr07 2-0	Jan13 4-2	—	Dec23 1-2	Mar03 1-1	Nov11 2-3	Dec30 0-1	Sep30 2-0	Sep16 4-3	Mar17 2-1	Oct14 2-2
MOTHERWELL	Feb24 1-3	Apr20 5-2	Apr23 0-4	Oct14 2-4	Nov18 2-1	Sep30 1-1	Dec16 3-0	Apr02 1-2	Nov11 5-1	Apr21 0-2	—	Aug23 1-3	Feb03 3-0	Jan13 2-2	Mar03 2-1	Jan13 5-3		Mar24 0-3
PARTICK T	Jan20 4-2	Dec30 2-2	Apr04 1-0	Feb24 2-4	Apr23 2-1	Oct07 1-0	Feb10 1-2	Mar10 3-1	Oct21 4-1	Nov04 2-4	Jan06 1-0	—	Sep23 3-2	Sep09 3-0	Dec16 0-1	Mar17 2-0	Nov25 2-0	Jan01 2-2
RAITH R	Apr28 3-1	Mar31 1-1	Dec23 2-3	Mar17 2-3	Oct28 0-0	Sep16 2-2	Nov04 1-2	Nov25 0-1	Jan02 0-2	Mar14 2-2	Oct07 0-3	Jan13 1-0	—	Feb10 1-3	Aug23 1-1	Sep30 4-0	Apr07 2-1	Feb28 4-3
RANGERS	Dec23 2-4	Feb03 4-0	Sep16 2-2	Nov11 1-5	Oct21 0-1	Apr07 1-0	Nov18 4-0	Apr07 2-1	Aug23 3-0	Sep23 1-1	Jan24 2-1	Feb28 6-0	Oct14	—	Dec02 2-0	Apr20 4-0	Jan13 4-1	Mar03 3-1
ST JOHNSTONE	Sep09 4-1	Oct07 0-3	Oct18 0-3	Apr28 0-3	Jan17 0-3	Feb10 1-2	Mar10 2-5	Nov04 2-1	Nov18 1-1	Jan20 1-0	Sep23 0-0	Apr07 0-4	Jan06	Apr04 0-4	—	Nov25 0-3	Oct21 2-0	Dec23 2-3
ST MIRREN	Oct07 3-2	Oct21 0-2	Mar26 0-5	Dec23 1-1	Feb10 1-1	Apr28 4-1	Sep09 2-0	Jan06 0-1	Dec02 2-3	Jan17 2-1	Apr20 1-3	Nov18 5-1	Jan20 1-3	Sep23 1-1	Mar24 1-3	—	Feb24 3-1	Apr07 1-2
STIRLING A	Jan06 3-0	Apr20 2-2	Feb10 1-0	Mar31 2-3	Oct07 0-1	Apr13 2-3	Feb13 3-0	Mar17 3-1	Feb24 0-1	Feb10 0-1	Nov25 2-4	Sep16 0-0	Oct21 0-3	Nov04 0-6	Apr20 0-3	Dec16 0-3	—	Sep23 2-0
T LANARK	Mar20 3-5	Aug23 3-0	Jan10 1-1	Sep30 1-3	Oct07 7-2	Apr13 1-1	Feb13 1-4	Mar17 1-0	Feb24 3-1	Feb10 2-1	Nov25 4-2	Sep16 2-1	Oct21 0-3	Nov04 2-1	Apr20 0-3	Dec16 5-2	Jan13 1-1	—

DIVISION 2

Home \ Away	ALBION R	ALLOA	ARBROATH	AYR U	BERWICK R	BRECHIN C	CLYDE	COWDENBEATH	DUMBARTON	EAST FIFE	E STIRLING	FORFAR A	HAMILTON A	MONTROSE	MORTON	QUEEN OF SOUTH	QUEEN'S PARK	STENHOUSEMUIR	STRANRAER
ALBION R	—	Mar31 1-2	Feb03 2-3	Aug23 1-1	Oct21 0-4	Oct14 0-2	Nov11 2-3	Mar03 0-4	Dec16 2-1	Jan13 1-0	Mar24 1-2	Apr20 1-0	Sep16 2-1	Sep27 4-1	Apr13 1-0	Nov18 0-3	Apr04 1-1	Feb24 3-2	Sep30 2-2
ALLOA	Dec02 2-1	—	Sep06 4-1	Mar17 7-2	Nov04 5-4	Mar03 4-1	Feb03 2-7	Oct14 3-0	Apr28 1-1	Apr13 4-3	Aug23 2-3	Apr07 2-2	Sep09 3-2	Jan20 2-0	Nov11 2-1	Sep23 0-0	Nov04 7-5	Sep16 6-1	Oct21 1-1
ARBROATH	Oct07 3-1	Sep13 2-0	—	Nov25 2-2	Dec02 3-4	Mar17 4-1	Jan06 0-2	Dec30 2-1	Feb10 4-0	Sep27 1-0	Oct21 1-2	Jan01 4-3	Apr21 4-2	Sep09 1-2	Jan20 0-1	Sep23 4-1	Nov04 4-2	Apr07 1-1	Feb24 1-2
AYR U	Jan06 1-3	Sep23 2-3	Mar24 3-5	—	Nov04 5-1	Dec16 5-1	Nov18 1-2	Oct21 5-1	Oct07 3-0	Mar31 1-1	Feb24 0-0	Jan20 6-3	Sep06 1-0	Apr28 1-2	Jan01 4-1	Sep09 1-0	Feb10 1-0	Nov11 1-0	Apr25 4-1
BERWICK R	Feb17 1-1	Nov18 4-2	Mar31 0-1	Mar03 4-2	—	Sep06 2-5	Oct28 2-2	Jan06 1-0	Sep30 2-1	Jan27 3-1	Feb24 4-0	Apr11 4-4	Jan27 0-0	Apr07 2-3	Oct14 0-2	Dec16 2-0	Feb03 5-1	Sep20 5-1	Feb03 6-0
BRECHIN C	Feb10 1-2	Nov04 0-3	Nov18 0-3	Apr07 2-0	Sep13 1-3	—	Sep23 1-5	Feb24 1-4	Jan20 2-0	Oct07 0-7	Apr25 1-4	Sep09 1-1	Sep25 0-1	Apr18 0-4	Jan06 0-3	Oct21 0-3	Dec23 0-4	Mar10 0-3	Mar10 1-3
CLYDE	Mar10 2-1	Oct07 5-1	Aug23 3-0	Mar17 5-0	Feb24 7-1	Jan13 5-0	—	Sep06 4-1	Sep20 2-2	Nov25 4-1	Dec23 4-1	Nov04 0-0	Apr11 6-2	Oct21 2-3	Feb10 3-1	Apr25 1-0		Sep30 4-1	Mar31 4-1
COWDENBEATH	Nov04 3-0	Feb10 4-2	Apr28 3-3	Feb03 1-0	Aug23 0-3	Oct28 3-1	Sep13 1-0	—	Mar10 1-0	Sep16 0-1	Mar17 4-4	Sep27 2-5	Feb24 2-0	Sep27 7-1	Mar31 1-2	Apr07 0-3	Apr25 2-0	Apr13 2-2	Dec23 1-1
DUMBARTON	Apr07 2-1	Apr25 2-2	Oct14 2-2	Feb03 1-3	Apr13 1-0	Sep30 2-0	Sep27 1-5	Nov11 3-0	—	Mar17 3-0	Sep16 2-1	Oct21 2-2	Mar24 0-2	Dec02 2-2	Feb24 0-2	Mar03 0-0	Apr20 2-0	Aug23 2-3	Sep06 3-0
EAST FIFE	Sep23 3-0	Sep09 3-2	Apr18 2-4	Dec02 0-0	Jan20 2-0	Feb03 2-1	Mar24 1-0	Jan01 1-0	Nov18 5-3	—	Nov11 4-1	Apr04 1-2	Mar03 0-2	Feb24 2-0	Oct21 0-3	Apr21 1-0	Apr09 2-1	Oct14 2-1	Dec16 0-1
E STIRLING	Nov25 1-2	Apr04 1-2	Feb17 1-1	Oct28 1-3	Jan13 1-5	Mar31 8-2	Jan06 1-4	Feb24 3-5	Apr09 1-0	Mar10 1-4	—	Feb10 2-1	Dec16 0-2	Jan20 4-2	Oct07 1-3	Sep13 5-1	Sep20 2-3	Apr27 2-2	Nov04 1-2
FORFAR A	Dec23 5-1	Dec16 2-3	Sep16 3-2	Sep30 1-3	Nov11 0-3	Jan02 5-1			Sep20 2-0	Feb17 4-4	Apr28 2-5	—	Feb10 2-5	Nov18 1-2	Mar24 1-0	Oct28 1-3	Aug23 1-3	Sep06 5-1	Jan13 5-1
HAMILTON A	Apr23 5-1	Oct28 2-2	Dec23 5-0	Apr18 1-3	Apr28 3-5	Feb17 5-2	Sep09 1-3	Sep23 3-3	Nov25 2-1	Nov04 3-4	Apr07 3-0	Feb10 0-2	—	Jan06 4-0	Jan20 2-2	Mar10 2-4	Dec02 3-0	Mar17 5-1	
MONTROSE	Sep20 3-0	Apr25 2-2	Jan02 2-0	Nov25 1-1	Dec02 2-1	Feb20 6-0	Feb21 1-1	Apr07 4-0	Oct28 1-2	Jan01 3-4			Dec16 1-3	—	Nov11 2-3	Oct07 1-0	Apr03 0-2	Aug23 2-1	
MORTON	Sep13 2-0	Mar10 6-5	Sep30 1-1	Sep16 1-0	Dec23 2-0	Dec30 2-5	Oct14 0-1	Dec02 1-0	Oct28 2-5	Apr25 2-1	Feb03 1-3	Nov25 5-2	Aug23 2-2	Apr07 2-1	—	Sep27	Apr16 2-2	Jan13 1-3	Jan02 2-1
QUEEN OF SOUTH	Dec09 2-1	Nov25 2-1	Jan13 2-0	Jan02 0-2	Feb10 3-2	Aug23 5-0	Apr28 2-3	Dec16 7-1	Nov04 4-1	Dec23 3-1	Sep06 2-1	Feb24 0-3	Sep30 0-1	Mar10 2-2	Mar31 3-1	—	Oct21 4-1	Sep16 3-1	
QUEEN'S PARK	Nov18 1-1	Sep20 2-1	Mar07 1-1	Oct14 1-1	Apr07 2-1	Jan27 3-0		Mar31 3-0	Feb10 2-2	Dec30 1-2	Sep11 2-3	Mar31 4-1	Nov04 2-3	Sep23 1-0	Mar17 2-5	Dec01	—	Feb03 2-3	Apr28 2-2
STENHOUSEMUIR	Oct28 2-1	Jan01 3-2	Dec16 1-2	Mar10 2-1	Sep27 5-1	Apr21 1-4	Jan20 2-2	Sep09 1-6	Jan06 2-5	Feb10 2-1	Dec30 3-0	Sep11 3-1	Mar31 1-1	Nov04 4-1	Sep23 3-2	Mar17 1-0	Oct07	—	Nov25 0-1
STRANRAER	Jan20 2-1	Apr18 1-1	Oct28 0-2	Sep27 4-1	Oct21 4-0	Nov11 4-0	Dec02 2-1	Apr21 1-1	Sep13 2-2	Apr07 2-2	Mar03 4-1	Nov18 3-0	Jan06 1-1	Sep09 4-2	Jan01 0-3	Dec30 2-1	Mar24 4-0		—

League Cup results for 1961-62 are detailed on pages 192-193.

In the 1962 Scottish Cup Final replay Ralph Brand puts Rangers ahead after only six minutes as he turns in a Henderson cross.
Rangers went on to complete the double that season.

SFA Cup

1st Round

Date	Home	Score	Away	Score
Mar 11	Airdrie	3	Stranraer	0
Jan 12	Arbroath	2	Dumbarton	0
Jan 26	Dundee U	3	Albion R	0
Jan 12	East Fife	5	Edinburgh Univ	0
Jan 26	E Stirling	2	Stirling A	0
Jan 28	Falkirk	0	Celtic	2
Jan 12	Forfar A	1	Hearts	3
Jan 19	Gala Fairydean	4	Keith	0
Jan 12	Inverness C	1	Dundee	5
Jan 12	Inverness T	0	Queen of South	2
Feb 4	Partick T	3	Morton	2
Jan 12	Raith R	2	Eyemouth	0
Mar 7	St Johnstone	1	Stenhousemuir	0

2nd Round

Date	Home	Score	Away	Score
Mar 13	Airdrie	0	Rangers	6
Feb 2	Ayr U	1	Dundee U	2
Jan 26	Berwick R	1	St Mirren	3
Jan 26	Brechin C	0	Hibernian	2
Mar 6	Celtic	3	Hearts	1
Mar 11	Cowdenbeath	2	Dunfermline A	3
Feb 4	Dundee	8	Montrose	0
Feb 4	East Fife	1	T Lanark	1
Mar 6	E Stirling	1	Motherwell	0
Jan 26	Gala Fairydean	1	Duns	1
Jan 26	Hamilton A	1	Nairn Co	1

Date	Home	Score	Away	Score
Jan 26	Kilmarnock	0	Queen of South	0
Mar 4	Partick T	1	Arbroath	1
Jan 26	Queen's Park	5	Alloa	1
Jan 26	Raith R	3	Clyde	2
Mar 13	St Johnstone	1	Aberdeen	2

Replays

Date	Home	Score	Away	Score
Jan 30	Nairn Co	1	Hamilton A	2
Mar 6	T Lanark	2	East Fife	0
Mar 11	Duns	1	Gala Fairydean	2
Mar 11	Queen of South	1	Kilmarnock	0
Mar 13	Arbroath	2	Partick T	2
Mar 14	Arbroath	2	Partick T	3
	played at Gayfield			

3rd Round

Date	Home	Score	Away	Score
Mar 20	Aberdeen	4	Dunfermline A	0
Mar 13	Celtic	6	Gala Fairydean	0
Mar 18	Dundee	1	Hibernian	0
Mar 20	Queen of South	3	Hamilton A	0
Mar 11	Queen's Park	1	Dundee U	1
Mar 20	Rangers	7	E Stirling	2
Mar 19	St Mirren	1	Partick T	1
Mar 13	T Lanark	0	Raith R	1

Replay

Date	Home	Score	Away	Score
Mar 20	Dundee U	3	Queen's Park	1
Mar 22	Partick T	0	St Mirren	1

4th Round

Date	Home	Score	Away	Score
Mar 30	Dundee	1	Rangers	1
Mar 29	Dundee U	1	Queen of South	1
Mar 30	Raith R	2	Aberdeen	1
Mar 30	St Mirren	0	Celtic	1

Replay

Date	Home	Score	Away	Score
Apr 3	Rangers	3	Dundee	2
Apr 3	Queen of South	1	Dundee U	1
Apr 8	Dundee U	4	Queen of South	0
	played at Ibrox			

Semi-finals

Date	Home	Score	Away	Score
Apr 13	Celtic	5	Raith R	2
	played at Ibrox			
Apr 13	Dundee U	2	Rangers	5
	played at Hampden Park			

Final

Date	Home	Score	Away	Score
Mar 4	Celtic	1	Rangers	1
	played at Hampden Park			

Replay

Date	Home	Score	Away	Score
Mar 15	Celtic	0	Rangers	3
	played at Hampden Park			

DIVISION 1

Home \ Away	ABE	AIR	CEL	CLY	DUN	DUU	DUF	FAL	HEA	HIB	KIL	MOT	PAR	QOS	RAI	RAN	STM	TLA
ABERDEEN		Aug22 2-1	Jan05 1-5	Apr06 0-2	Jan01 1-0	May07 1-2	Sep15 4-0	Nov24 1-0	Mar09 2-1	Nov10 3-0	Dec22 1-1	Mar23 1-1	Dec15 4-1	Mar26 1-1	Oct13 10-0	Oct27 2-3	Feb16 0-1	Sep29 4-1
AIRDRIE	Apr10 2-0		Oct27 1-6	Oct06 3-1	Mar09 1-0	Apr27 4-2	Dec08 0-1	Oct20 2-1	May13 4-2	Nov24 2-1	Apr24 0-3	Sep08 1-4	Apr06 2-0	Dec15 1-3	Sep22 8-1	May06 0-2	Mar23 4-2	Nov10 1-4
CELTIC	Sep22 1-2	Mar02 3-1		May06 2-0	Apr23 4-1	Oct20 1-0	Dec26 2-1	Sep29 2-1	Dec08 2-2	Apr06 0-1	Oct06 1-1	May13 6-0	Nov24 0-2	Oct01 0-1	Mar19 4-1	Sep08 0-1	Oct13 1-1	Apr20 2-1
CLYDE	Dec01 1-3	Mar20 2-0	Sep15 1-3		Jan05 3-2	Nov17 1-3	Sep29 0-1	Apr13 0-6	Mar16 3-1	Aug22 0-5	Nov03 2-3	Apr27 1-1	Jan01 2-3	Oct13 0-1	Mar27 3-0	May22 2-6	Dec15 3-2	Oct27 3-2
DUNDEE	Sep08 2-2	Nov03 2-1	Nov17 0-0	Sep22 2-0		Apr17 1-2	May15 1-0	Oct06 2-1	May06 2-2	Apr08 1-3	Dec15 1-0	Mar16 2-2	Dec01 2-1	Apr27 10-2	May25 1-1	Apr13 0-0	5-1	May13 5-2
DUNDEE U	Dec08 3-3	Dec22 2-1	May11 3-0	Mar23 4-1	Sep15 1-1		Aug22 0-4	Apr06 1-0	Apr20 0-0	Sep29 5-0	Nov24 3-3	Mar09 2-1	2-2	Oct27 8-1	Nov10 0-1	Oct13 1-1	Apr29 1-0	
DUNFERMLINE A	Apr17 3-0	Apr13 2-0	Apr27 1-1	Apr24 2-2	Oct27 2-0	Mar25 1-2		Sep22 2-1	Oct06 2-2	Dec15 3-2	Apr06 1-1	Nov24 4-3	May11 1-1	Mar23 3-2	Sep08 6-0	Mar09 1-2	Nov10 1-3	Oct13 3-0
FALKIRK	Apr03 2-1	May11 0-1	Aug22 1-3	Dec08 7-3	May18 0-2	Dec01 4-1	Apr10 2-0		Oct30 2-0	Mar27 3-1	Apr20 0-5	Nov10 3-2	Oct13 0-2	Sep15 2-2	Mar09 2-3	Mar23 0-2	Sep29 4-2	Jan01 3-5
HEARTS	Nov03 1-1	Sep15 6-1	Apr29 4-3	Nov10 1-1	Aug22 1-3	Dec15 2-2	May18 2-0	Mar13 5-0		May04 3-3	Mar18 2-3	Oct20 2-1	Apr20 2-4	Sep29 3-0	Apr06 0-5	Mar27 0-5	Oct13 2-0	Mar23 2-0
HIBERNIAN	Mar16 2-3	Mar30 0-2	Dec01 1-1	Dec29 1-2	Oct13 2-2	Apr24 1-1	Apr20 0-3	Apr27 0-4	Sep08		Nov17 0-2	Apr17 0-2	Dec08 3-0	Oct27 1-0	Oct06 3-0	Sep22 1-1	May11 1-1	Mar09 1-1
KILMARNOCK	Apr27 2-2	Sep22 8-0	Mar27 6-0	Mar09 3-2	May11 1-0	May01 2-2	Dec15 5-1	Oct13 3-1	Mar23 2-0			Oct31 7-1	Aug22 1-2	Jan05 7-0	Nov10 3-1	May13 1-0	Jan01 5-2	Sep15 2-2
MOTHERWELL	Nov21 0-2	Jan01 1-0	Oct13 3-0	Dec22 6-2	Apr20 2-1	Nov03 0-0	Mar30 0-0	Nov10 4-1	Apr24 1-3	May11 1-3	Sep15 2-1		Sep22 2-1	Aug22 2-2	May15 5-1	Dec01 1-1	Jan05 1-1	Mar20 3-3
PARTICK T	Apr20 2-3	Dec01 3-0	Apr02 1-5	Sep08 5-1	Nov10 1-0	Oct06 3-0	Oct20 2-1	May01 2-0	Sep22 2-4	Apr13 2-2	Dec29 4-2	Apr24 2-0		Mar09 0-1	Mar23 4-1	Apr17 2-0	Oct27 2-1	Mar30 3-1
QUEEN OF SOUTH	Oct20 2-1	Apr20 1-1	Mar16 2-5	May04 2-2	Apr05 1-0	Sep08 1-0	Nov17 1-0	Jan02 0-1	Apr24 0-3	May15 0-4	Sep22 1-1	Dec29 0-2	Nov03 0-1		Nov24 5-1	Oct06 0-4	Dec22 2-3	Dec08 2-1
RAITH R	May04 0-4	Jan05 0-1	Sep29 0-2	Oct20 1-1	Dec22 2-4	Mar02 2-7	Apr01 1-2	May01 1-3	Sep08 0-3	Oct13 0-4	May18 1-4	Dec01 1-4	Mar16 2-5	Nov17 2-3		May11 1-1	Apr20 2-0	Aug22 1-1
RANGERS	May27 2-2	Oct13 5-2	Jan01 1-0	Nov24 3-0	Sep29 3-1	Mar16 1-1	Nov03 5-0	Nov17 1-1	Apr27 4-0	Apr10 1-1	Dec08 6-1	Apr29 1-1	Sep15 3-1	May18 4-2	Dec15 3-0		Aug22 3-0	May11 1-0
ST MIRREN	Oct06 2-1	Nov17 1-1	Nov03 0-7	Apr20 1-2	Dec08 0-3	May03 2-1	Mar16 3-1	Mar06 2-2	Apr02 7-3	Oct20 2-2	Sep08 2-4	Sep22 2-0	Mar02 1-1	Apr27 4-0	Jan02 1-2	Dec29 0-2		Dec01 2-4
T LANARK	Apr24 1-2	Mar16 2-3	Dec15 2-0	Mar02 2-1	Nov24 4-3	Sep22 1-1	May03 4-0	Sep08 3-3	Nov17 1-2	Nov03 1-4	Jan02 0-1	Oct06 2-2	Apr27 0-1	Apr13 1-0	Dec29 2-1	Oct23 1-4	Apr05 1-1	

DIVISION 2

Home \ Away	ALB	ALL	ARB	AYR	BER	BRE	COW	DUM	EFI	EST	FOR	HAM	MON	MOR	QPK	STJ	STE	STI	STR
ALBION R		May15 0-2	Sep15 2-0	Sep29 0-3	Nov03 3-3	Apr20 5-2	Apr13 3-3	Jan05 1-4	Aug22 2-0	May01 4-2	May11 2-0	Jan01 0-2	Dec22 2-1	Mar16 3-0	Apr03 4-2	Apr29 1-0	Dec01 4-1	Oct13 3-2	Sep26 1-0
ALLOA	Oct27 4-2		Sep29 1-3	Sep15 1-1	Nov17 3-2	Apr17 3-0	Oct13 0-1	Aug22 2-0	Mar30 2-1	May11 0-0	Nov10 6-1	Dec01 1-3	May18 1-2	Apr20 0-2	Sep19 2-1	Dec08 0-0	Apr03 1-0	Apr10 3-0	Sep05 4-0
ARBROATH	Apr17 3-0	Apr24 2-0		Oct27 4-1	Sep22 4-0	Mar30 2-0	Sep03 1-1	Apr24 4-2	Nov17 3-0	Sep19 5-2	Nov24 1-2	Feb23 3-1	Apr03 0-0	Dec01 1-2	Dec15 2-1	Oct06 1-2	Nov09 4-4	Mar09 4-4	Apr06 6-1
AYR U	Apr24 5-0	May04 2-2	Mar02 3-5		May06 4-1	Sep05 0-1	Sep22 2-2	Apr06 2-0	Oct20 1-1	Mar30 1-4	Apr27 4-2	Mar16 4-3	Nov17 2-1	Sep08 0-3	Oct06 3-1	Apr17 2-3	Apr20 0-1	Sep19 0-1	Dec08 0-2
BERWICK R	Mar09 1-5	Mar23 1-0	Jan05 0-2	Oct13 1-1		Dec08 3-2	Nov10 0-0	Sep29 1-0	Dec01 2-4	Apr03 1-1	Sep19 5-1	Feb02 3-6	Mar30 0-0	Apr10 2-3	Feb23 4-4	Apr13 1-3	Sep15 4-0	Sep15 2-0	May01 1-1
BRECHIN C	Dec15 2-3	Oct06 1-2	Nov24 0-1	Feb23 2-1	Apr13 1-2		Apr24 0-4	Oct13 0-3	Sep26 1-3	Dec27 1-3	Dec22 1-1	Sep08 0-0	Mar30 0-3	Jan02 3-5	Oct27 3-0	Dec01 1-2	Apr06 0-0	Mar16 3-6	Apr20 1-3
COWDENBEATH	Dec08 4-1	May01 1-0	Sep12 2-2	Apr29 1-2	Mar16 5-4	Sep29 5-2		Apr10 5-2	Apr01 2-1	Dec01 3-2	Apr15 1-2	Aug22 3-1	Sep26 2-0	Oct20 6-2	Nov03 1-2	May15 0-1	Mar30 5-0	Apr20 0-1	May18 1-1
DUMBARTON	Sep22 1-3	Dec29 1-0	Apr13 3-1	Dec01 3-1	Apr24 3-0	Apr03 4-3	Apr27 1-0		Nov03 5-2	Jan26 2-2	Nov17 1-0	Apr17 0-1	Oct06 3-0	Sep08 0-3	Mar16 1-2	Apr20 2-3	Mar30 2-1	Oct27 3-0	May01 5-1
EAST FIFE	Mar27 2-0	Nov24 1-1	Mar23 1-3	Feb23 0-1	Sep19 2-1	Sep08 3-0	Mar09 3-0			Nov10 2-2	Sep05 2-1	Apr13 4-0	Apr20 1-0	Sep22 0-0	Apr27 2-1	Dec13 2-2	Oct13 2-0	Oct27 1-4	Apr17 1-0
E STIRLING	Oct06 4-2	Oct20 2-3	Sep26 1-0	Nov24 5-0	Sep08 3-3	Apr29 3-1	Apr06 2-1	Mar13 1-1	Mar16 2-1		Sep22 4-1	Nov03 2-0	Apr13 5-1	May04 0-0	Apr24 2-2	May06 5-1	Nov17 0-2	Apr27 2-0	Dec15 6-0
FORFAR A	Oct20 4-1	Mar16 1-1	Jan01 2-1	Dec22 2-6	Sep26 6-0	Aug22 7-2	Mar23 2-1	Apr20 3-4	Sep12 4-2	Apr10 3-1		Sep15 2-2	Nov24 2-4	May15 2-3	Apr13 0-4	Nov03 3-3	Sep29 4-1	Apr29 0-2	Oct13 0-3
HAMILTON A	Sep08 4-3	Jan12 1-2	Oct20 1-0	Nov10 2-2	Oct06 4-1	Apr27 1-0	Apr29 1-0	Mar23 4-2	Dec08 2-1	Mar09 1-3	Jan02 2-2		Dec15 5-1	Jan19 0-1	Sep22 2-2	Apr01 2-0	Oct27 1-0	Sep05 2-3	Mar23 3-3
MONTROSE	Apr27 2-0	Nov03 4-2	Aug22 3-2	Mar23 0-1	Mar02 1-2	Jan12 2-4	Sep19 0-2	Sep15 2-4	Sep29 0-2	Dec08 3-0	Mar30 4-2	Apr20 0-0		Sep04 2-1	May08 1-3	Oct20 0-1	Feb02 2-6	Dec01 1-2	Nov10 3-3
MORTON	Nov10 5-2	Mar27 5-3	Dec22 3-2	Apr03 6-1	Nov24 2-1	Mar23 7-0	May11 6-1	Feb02 0-0	Apr10 5-0	Oct13 2-3	Oct27 8-2	Sep29 1-0	Mar13 6-0		Apr15 4-1	Sep26 0-1	Sep15 4-0	Aug22 3-2	Mar09 3-1
QUEEN'S PARK	Mar23 1-3	Sep26 3-1	Apr20 1-1	Sep12 4-1	Sep15 2-4	Mar09 6-1	Jan01 1-3	Apr29 2-1	Dec08 3-2	Jan05 0-1	Oct13 2-0	Dec01 1-2		Mar30 1-0		Aug22 0-3	Nov10 5-2	Apr13 1-0	
ST JOHNSTONE	Sep05 7-1	Apr13 4-0	May18 1-0	Aug22 1-0	Dec22 7-0	Dec01 1-0	Oct27 1-0	Nov10 1-0	Apr20 1-0	Sep15 0-6	Mar09 5-2	Oct13 2-1	May11 1-0	Apr24 2-0	May04 1-2		Apr10 1-3	Apr03 0-1	Mar23 2-0
STENHOUSEMUIR	Apr06 3-0	Sep08 2-1	Mar16 3-2	Dec15 2-0	Oct20 2-2	Nov03 3-1	Nov24 1-2	Aug28 1-0	Feb16 1-2	Mar23 1-2	Apr24 1-0	Apr29 2-5	Oct06 1-2	Apr17 0-5	Dec29 3-0	Sep22 5-5		Dec08 3-1	Apr27 1-3
STIRLING A	Mar13 3-3	Dec15 1-2	Nov02 2-0	Sep26 2-2	Jan02 0-3	Oct20 7-2	Dec15 2-1	Nov24 3-1	May13 3-2	Mar30 2-1	Sep12 4-3	Apr06 0-2	Dec22 4-2	May06 0-2	Sep08 1-4	Apr13 4-1			Apr24 1-3
STRANRAER	Sep19 2-1	Sep12 6-2	Dec01 2-0	Apr13 7-2	Aug22 3-1	Jan05 2-0	Oct06 3-3	Mar02 5-5	Sep15 6-1	Apr20 2-2	May04 5-4	Mar30 1-0	Mar16 2-2	Nov03 3-1	Oct20 2-1	Nov17 1-3	Dec22 2-2	Sep29 2-0	

DIVISION 1 FINAL TABLE

	P	W	D	L	F	A	Pts
Rangers	34	25	7	2	94	28	57
Kilmarnock	34	20	8	6	92	40	48
Partick T	34	20	8	6	66	44	46
Celtic	34	19	6	9	76	44	44
Hearts	34	17	9	8	85	59	43
Aberdeen	34	17	7	10	70	47	41
Dundee U	34	15	11	8	67	52	41
Dunfermline A	34	13	8	13	50	47	34
Dundee	34	12	9	13	60	49	33
Motherwell	34	10	11	13	60	63	31
Airdrie	34	14	2	18	52	76	30
St Mirren	34	10	8	16	52	72	28
Falkirk	34	12	3	19	54	69	27
T Lanark	34	9	8	17	56	68	26
Queen of South	34	10	6	18	36	75	26
Hibernian	34	8	9	17	47	67	25
Clyde	34	9	5	20	49	83	23
Raith R	34	2	5	27	35	118	9

DIVISION 2 FINAL TABLE

	P	W	D	L	F	A	Pts
St Johnstone	36	25	5	6	83	37	55
E Stirling	36	20	9	7	80	50	49
Morton	36	23	2	11	100	49	48
Hamilton A	36	18	8	10	69	56	44
Stranraer	36	16	10	10	81	70	42
Arbroath	36	18	4	14	74	51	40
Albion R	36	18	2	16	72	79	38
Cowdenbeath	36	15	7	14	72	61	37
Alloa	36	15	6	15	57	56	36
Stirling A	36	16	4	16	74	75	36
East Fife	36	15	6	15	60	69	36
Dumbarton	36	15	4	17	64	64	34
Ayr U	36	13	8	15	68	77	34
Queen's Park	36	13	6	17	66	72	32
Montrose	36	13	5	18	57	70	31
Stenhousemuir	36	13	5	18	54	75	31
Berwick R	36	11	7	18	57	77	29
Forfar A	36	9	5	22	73	99	23
Brechin C	36	3	3	30	39	113	9

League Cup results for 1962-63 are detailed on pages 193-194.

Season 1963-64

SFA Cup

1st Round

Jan 11	Aberdeen	5	Hibernian	2
Jan 11	Ayr U	3	Inverness T	2
Jan 11	Berwick R	5	St Cuthbert's W	2
Jan 11	Celtic	3	Eyemouth U	0
Jan 11	Dumbarton	4	Raith R	0
Jan 11	Dundee U	0	St Mirren	0
Jan 11	Forres Mechanic	3	Dundee	6
Jan 11	Kilmarnock	2	Gala Fairydean	1
Jan 11	Montrose	1	Alloa	1
Jan 11	Morton	0	Cowdenbeath	0
Jan 11	Stenhousemuir	1	Rangers	5
Jan 11	Stirling A	1	Brechin C	1
Jan 11	Stranraer	2	T Lanark	1

Replays

Jan 14	Alloa	3	Montrose	2
Jan 15	Brechin C	5	Stirling A	1
Jan 15	Cowdenbeath	1	Morton	4
Jan 15	St Mirren	1	Dundee U	2

2nd Round

Jan 25	Aberdeen	1	Queen's Park	1
Jan 25	Albion R	4	Arbroath	3
Jan 25	Alloa	1	Airdrie	3
Jan 25	Brechin C	2	Dundee	9
Jan 25	Buckie T	1	Ayr U	3
Jan 25	Clyde	2	Forfar A	2
Jan 25	Dunfermline A	7	Fraserburgh	0
Jan 25	East Fife	0	E Stirling	1
Jan 25	Falkirk	2	Berwick R	2
Jan 25	Hamilton A	1	Kilmarnock	3
Jan 25	Morton	1	Celtic	3
Jan 25	Motherwell	4	Dumbarton	1
Jan 25	Partick T	2	St Johnstone	0
Jan 25	Queen of South	0	Hearts	3
Jan 25	Rangers	9	Duns	0
Jan 25	St Mirren	2	Stranraer	0

Replays

Jan 29	Berwick R	1	Falkirk	5
Jan 29	Forfar A	3	Clyde	2
Jan 29	Queen's Park	1	Aberdeen	2

3rd Round

Feb 15	Aberdeen	1	Ayr U	2
Feb 15	Celtic	4	Airdrie	1
Feb 15	Dundee	6	Forfar A	1
Feb 15	E Stirling	1	Dunfermline A	6
Feb 15	Kilmarnock	2	Albion R	0
Feb 15	Motherwell	3	Hearts	3
Feb 15	Rangers	3	Partick T	0
Feb 15	St Mirren	0	Falkirk	1

Replay

Feb 19	Hearts	1	Motherwell	2

4th Round

Mar 7	Dundee	1	Motherwell	1
Mar 7	Dunfermline A	7	Ayr U	0
Mar 7	Falkirk	1	Kilmarnock	2
Mar 7	Rangers	2	Celtic	0

Replay

Mar 11	Motherwell	2	Dundee	4

Semi-finals

Mar 28	Dundee	4	Kilmarnock	0
	played at Ibrox			
Mar 28	Dunfermline A	0	Rangers	1
	played at Hampden Park			

Final

Apr 25	Dundee	1	Rangers	3
	played at Hampden Park			

> League Cup results for 1963-64 are detailed on page 194.

DIVISION 1 FINAL TABLE

	P	W	D	L	F	A	Pts
Rangers	34	25	5	4	85	31	55
Kilmarnock	34	22	5	7	77	40	49
Celtic	34	19	9	6	89	34	47
Hearts	34	19	9	6	74	40	47
Dunfermline A	34	18	9	7	64	33	45
Dundee	34	20	5	9	94	50	45
Partick T	34	15	5	14	55	54	35
Dundee U	34	13	8	13	65	49	34
Aberdeen	34	12	8	14	53	53	32
Hibernian	34	12	6	16	59	66	30
Motherwell	34	9	11	14	51	62	29
St Mirren	34	12	5	17	44	74	29
St Johnstone	34	11	6	17	54	70	28
Falkirk	34	11	6	17	54	84	28
Airdrie	34	11	4	19	52	97	26
T Lanark	34	9	7	18	47	74	25
Queen of South	34	5	6	23	40	92	16
E Stirling	34	5	2	27	37	91	12

DIVISION 1

	ABERDEEN	AIRDRIE	CELTIC	DUNDEE	DUNDEE U	DUNFERMLINE A	E STIRLING	FALKIRK	HEARTS	HIBERNIAN	KILMARNOCK	MOTHERWELL	PARTICK T	QUEEN OF SOUTH	RANGERS	ST JOHNSTONE	ST MIRREN	T LANARK
ABERDEEN		Jan18 2-2	Feb08 0-3	Sep07 2-4	Apr18 0-0	Apr08 0-1	Dec07 4-1	Oct26 3-0	Feb29 1-2	Mar28 3-1	Feb19 0-0	Nov16 6-2	Dec28 0-5	Mar21 3-0	Mar11 1-1	Jan02 0-1	Sep21 0-2	Oct05 1-1
AIRDRIE	Sep28 1-7		Feb22 0-2	Mar18 3-1	Feb01 3-1	Nov30 0-0	Mar21 5-2	Nov16 2-5	Aug21 0-2	Dec07 5-3	Sep14 4-5	Jan01 1-1	Dec21 2-0	Apr10 2-1	Nov02 0-4	Oct19 3-3	Apr18 2-4	Oct12 1-0
CELTIC	Oct12 3-0	Oct26 9-0		Apr01 2-1	Feb19 1-0	Oct05 2-2	Feb29 5-2	Jan04 7-0	Apr18 1-1	Mar14 5-0	Nov23 5-0	Dec21 2-1	Nov09 5-3	Sep21 4-0	Jan01 0-1	Dec07 3-1	Jan18 3-0	Sep14 4-4
DUNDEE	Jan01 1-4	Nov09 4-0	Nov30 1-1		Sep14 1-1	Oct26 2-1	Sep28 3-1	Dec21 4-3	Mar21 2-4	Feb19 3-0	Apr04 2-1	Oct12 1-3	Feb01 5-2	Feb01 6-2	Apr18 1-1	Sep07 2-1	Feb29 9-2	Jan04 6-0
DUNDEE U	Dec14 1-2	Oct05 9-1	Oct19 0-3	Jan02 2-1		Jan18 1-2	Sep21 2-0	Nov02 3-1	Nov16 0-0	Apr24 1-1	Mar11 2-1	Feb22 4-1	Feb08 1-2	Mar28 2-3	Dec07 3-1	Sep07 6-2	Dec28 4-1	Nov23 4-1
DUNFERMLINE A	Apr24 3-1	Mar30 5-1	Feb01 1-0	Feb22 1-2	Sep28 4-2		Mar14 4-1	Nov09 1-0	Sep14 2-2	Oct12 3-0	Jan04 2-3	Aug21 2-0	Oct19 0-0	Jan01 0-0	Nov23 1-4	Nov02 4-0	Dec07 5-0	Dec14 3-0
E STIRLING	Apr04 2-1	Nov26 1-2	Nov02 1-5	Jan18 1-5	Jan04 1-1	Nov16 0-2		Jan01 1-2	Dec21 2-3	Dec14 1-3	Aug21 0-2	Mar17 0-0	Sep14 1-0	Feb19 4-0	Feb19 0-5	Oct05 0-1	Oct05 2-1	Dec14 2-3
FALKIRK	Feb22 2-3	Mar14 2-1	Sep21 1-0	Apr29 0-2	Feb29 2-1	Nov09 2-2	Sep07 1-0		Sep28 1-2	Jan02 1-4	Oct12 1-1	Mar21 0-4	Nov30 3-0	Apr18 3-2	Feb01 0-1	Dec28 1-1	Oct19 2-0	Dec07 2-2
HEARTS	Nov02 0-0	Dec28 4-0	Dec14 1-1	Nov23 1-3	Mar14 0-4	Jan02 2-1	Jan11 4-0	Jan17 4-1		Sep07 4-2	Feb22 1-1	Dec07 1-1	Sep21 4-1	Oct12 0-1	Apr01 1-2	Oct05 3-3	Nov09 5-1	Mar04 4-1
HIBERNIAN	Nov30 2-0	Jan02 2-1	Mar21 1-1	Dec07 0-4	Nov09 2-3	Sep21 0-0	Feb08 5-2	Apr18 2-2	Sep14 1-1		Sep28 0-2	Feb22 3-1	Dec07 2-1	Mar07 5-2	Jan04 0-1	Jan04 4-1	Mar21 1-0	Apr25 3-0
KILMARNOCK	Oct19 2-0	Jan02 4-1	Mar21 0-4	Dec07 1-1	Nov09 4-1	Sep21 9-2	Dec28 3-1	Feb08 2-1	Oct26 1-1	Jan18 1-1		Nov30 5-2	Oct05 3-0	Feb29 2-1	Nov16 1-1	Apr18 4-1	Sep07 2-0	2-0
MOTHERWELL	Mar14 0-1	Sep07 3-0	Mar28 0-4	Feb08 2-2	Oct26 0-3	Dec28 1-1	Nov09 4-1	Nov23 3-0	Apr04 0-1	Oct05 4-3	Apr01 2-0		Jan18 2-1	Jan11 0-0	Dec14 3-3	Apr21 1-3	Jan02 3-0	Feb29 1-1
PARTICK T	Aug21 1-1	Apr24 1-0	Mar11 2-2	Dec14 2-0	Sep21 1-0	Feb19 0-1	Feb19 3-2	Apr18 4-1	Jan04 2-1	Dec07 2-1	Sep28 2-0	Dec07 6-1		Oct05 0-3	Aug21 0-3	Apr13 2-1	Nov16 2-1	Jan04 0-1
QUEEN OF SOUTH	Nov23 2-3	Sep21 0-2	Dec28 0-5	Oct05 5-1	Nov30 1-1	Sep07 1-2	Jan02 2-1	Dec14 3-6	Feb08 1-4	Nov09 3-2	Nov02 4-2	Oct19 2-2	Apr04 1-2		Feb22 1-4	Jan18 0-3	Apr25 1-1	Mar14 2-1
RANGERS	Nov09 0-0	Feb29 4-1	Sep07 2-1	Dec28 2-1	Apr04 2-0	Mar21 3-1	Oct19 4-0	Oct05 0-3	Nov30 5-0	Sep21 2-0	Mar14 5-1	Apr18 4-3	Jan02 2-0	Oct30		Dec21 2-3	Feb08 2-3	Jan18 2-1
ST JOHNSTONE	Sep14 3-1	Apr04 0-1	Mar11 1-1	Dec14 1-6	Nov16 2-2	Jan01 3-2	Apr12 3-0	Aug21 5-0	Feb01 1-4	Feb01 0-4	Dec14 0-2	Jan04 1-1	Sep28 2-3	Apr29 1-0			Nov30 2-1	Oct24 0-1
ST MIRREN	Jan04 3-1	Dec14 2-4	Sep28 2-1	Nov02 3-0	Aug21 2-2	Apr04 2-1	Feb01 3-0	Feb19 1-0	Mar07 4-2	Nov23 1-3	Jan01 1-2	Sep14 2-3	Mar14 2-3	Dec21 1-0	Oct12 2-3	Mar28		1-0
T LANARK	Feb01 1-2	Feb08 1-2	Jan02 1-1	Sep21 1-2	Mar21 2-2	Apr18 0-1	Nov30 1-2	Apr04 3-7	Oct19 0-2	Dec28 1-0	Dec21 1-2	Nov02 3-1	Sep07 3-2	Nov16 1-1	Sep28 0-5	Mar07 4-2	Feb25 4-2	

Ralph Brand drenches his Rangers teammates after their hat-trick of Scottish Cup Final wins in 1964. Shearer has the trophy.

DIVISION 2

	ALBION R	ALLOA	ARBROATH	AYR U	BERWICK R	BRECHIN C	CLYDE	COWDENBEATH	DUMBARTON	EAST FIFE	FORFAR A	HAMILTON A	MONTROSE	MORTON	QUEEN'S PARK	RAITH R	STENHOUSEMUIR	STIRLING A	STRANRAER
ALBION R		Nov23 4-3	Oct05 1-1	Oct26 3-1	Mar28 1-2	Sep21 3-1	Apr29 2-2	Mar14 1-1	Sep25 3-3	Feb08 1-1	Apr24 1-1	Sep07 3-3	Dec14 1-0	Apr04 0-0	Dec28 1-0	Sep11 1-0	Nov09 1-3	Feb29 2-2	Jan02 4-1
ALLOA	Mar21 2-2		Dec28 0-2	Jan02 5-1	Sep28 1-2	Mar14 3-1	Oct12 1-4	Apr24 0-0	Apr18 2-1	Feb29 2-3	Dec07 6-1	Nov09 2-0	Oct19 2-4	Nov30 0-3	Sep18 1-2	Feb22 0-6	Sep07 1-2	Feb01 4-2	Sep21 4-0
ARBROATH	Feb01 4-0	Aug21 3-0		Feb29 0-1	Mar07 2-2	Mar28 3-1	Jan04 0-0	Oct12 2-0	Nov16 4-0	Apr18 2-3	Jan01 5-1	Apr25 2-0	Sep14 2-4	Nov23 1-2	Sep11 2-1	Sep24 8-1	Dec07 2-6	Sep28 3-0	Oct26 2-0
AYR U	Feb22 4-3	Sep14 0-2	Nov02 1-2		Aug21 5-1	Oct12 1-4	Mar14 0-2	Apr29 0-1	Apr29 1-0	Dec21 1-1	Apr04 1-4	Sep23 2-5	Jan01 1-3	Sep28 1-3	Feb01 1-1	Jan18 3-2	Nov30 4-1	Apr22 4-1	Apr06 0-2
BERWICK R	Nov30 2-2	Jan18 4-0	Nov09 1-3	Dec28 6-1		Apr25 2-2	Feb29 2-3	Sep23 1-2	Dec07 2-3	Mar21 4-0	Oct26 1-1	Jan02 1-2	Apr01 3-1	Feb15 4-2	Apr18 1-1	Apr08 2-2	Sep21 6-0	Oct12 1-3	Sep07 0-3
BRECHIN C	Jan04 2-4	Nov16 5-1	Nov30 1-1	Feb08 3-4	Apr29 5-2		Oct05 2-2	Nov02 2-1	Mar07 2-1	Jan18 0-6	Sep14 3-0	Dec14 0-2	Jan01 1-2	Sep25 3-7	Apr04 2-2	Aug21 2-1	Oct19 3-2	Feb22 4-2	Sep11 2-2
CLYDE	Oct19 3-2	Feb08 0-1	Sep21 2-0	Nov16 6-0	Nov02 3-1	Feb01 5-0			Mar21 2-1	Apr23 4-2	Nov30 1-3	Sep14 5-2	Dec28 1-0	Apr04 2-0	Sep28 1-2	Sep07 1-0	Mar07 3-3	Jan02 0-0	Dec14 1-1
COWDENBEATH	Nov16 2-2	Dec21 8-2	Feb08 0-2	Sep21 2-1	Apr22 1-1	Feb29 2-3	Oct26 2-3			Nov30 0-1	Jan02 0-0	Apr29 0-0	Jan18 2-2	Nov09 1-1	Apr18 0-3	Apr20 2-1	Sep04 2-3	Dec28 2-2	Oct05 2-2
DUMBARTON	Sep18 0-2	Dec14 2-1	Mar14 1-0	Nov09 3-2	Apr04 1-1	Nov23 1-1	Dec21 0-1	Mar28 8-0			Sep21 1-3	Feb29 3-1	Feb22 2-0	Apr13 2-1	Jan02 0-2	Oct19 1-4	Feb01 4-0	Sep07 3-2	Oct12 4-1
EAST FIFE	Oct12 2-0	Nov02 8-0	Dec14 2-0	Apr25 3-3	Sep23 6-0	Sep28 0-0	Mar28 1-1	Sep14 2-2			Sep24 2-2	Jan11 2-1	Aug21 1-1	Mar07 3-1	Jan01 3-0	Oct19 3-4	Apr25 5-1	Dec21 6-0	
FORFAR A	Dec21 3-0	Apr04 3-3	Sep07 1-2	Apr15 3-3	Feb22 3-3	Jan02 2-4	Sep04 0-5	Oct19 2-1	Jan18 0-2	Apr22 5-4		Oct05 3-3	Nov30 2-8	Nov02 2-2	Sep21 2-1	Dec14 2-3	Dec28 6-2	Apr08 2-0	Nov09 0-1
HAMILTON A	Jan01 5-2	Mar07 3-4	Dec21 2-2	Dec07 2-4	Sep14 2-0	Apr18 3-3	Apr25 2-3	Sep07 3-2	Nov02 1-3	Sep04 2-2	Feb01 1-0		Jan04 3-4	Feb22 1-3	Oct19 1-2	Oct12 1-5	Mar21 3-0	Apr15 6-1	Nov30 3-3
MONTROSE	Apr18 3-4	Feb15 2-2	Jan02 1-2	Sep18 2-0	Apr15 7-1	Sep07 4-0	Dec07 1-2	Oct26 2-1	Dec28 3-0	Mar28 5-0	Sep21 2-0			Oct12 0-2	Feb01 2-1	Nov09 1-0	Feb22 2-2	Mar14 4-1	Apr25 2-1
MORTON	Dec07 3-1	Mar28 2-2	Mar21 2-2	Sep07 2-0	Oct19 7-1	Oct01 3-0	Jan18 2-0	Dec14 2-0	Sep04 4-2	Oct05 2-0	Feb29 8-0	Nov04 2-0	Feb08 2-0		Nov16 4-0	Apr24 2-0	Jan02 2-0	Nov09 2-0	Dec28 3-1
QUEEN'S PARK	Aug21 4-2	Sep24 1-0	Sep04 3-2	Jan18 3-2	Dec18 1-2	Dec04 3-0	Jan01 2-4	Nov23 0-1	Sep14 2-1	Nov09 2-0	Jan04 2-0	Feb15 0-0	Oct05 0-3	Mar14 0-3		Apr01 2-3	Oct12 2-0	Apr29 2-1	Apr15 2-0
RAITH R	Sep04 3-0	Oct26 4-1	Sep18 5-3	Oct05 2-1	Nov16 2-0	Dec28 2-0	Nov09 1-2	Feb15 2-0	Sep07 1-1	Apr18 1-4	Feb08 4-0	Jan18 6-1	Dec21 0-3	Nov30 2-3			Feb29 2-2	Sep21 7-0	Mar21 2-1
STENHOUSEMUIR	Mar07 1-2	Jan01 2-1	Apr04 0-4	Apr18 1-2	Jan04 8-2	Feb15 4-0	Sep24 1-3	Sep09 5-1	Oct05 3-3	Oct26 4-2	Aug20 3-3	Nov23 4-2	Nov16 1-1	Sep14 0-5	Apr10 1-0	Nov02 1-0		Dec14 3-1	Jan18 4-0
STIRLING A	Nov02 2-1	Oct05 2-2	Jan18 0-1	Sep04 4-2	Feb08 1-2	Sep07 5-1	Oct26 1-1	Sep14 2-1	Aug21 1-1	Jan01 2-5	Nov16 2-1	Sep23 2-3	Mar21 1-1	Nov07 1-2	Dec21 2-1	Jan04 3-0	Apr18 0-2		Apr04 0-2
STRANRAER	Sep14 1-5	Jan04 3-2	Feb22 3-2	Oct19 1-0	Jan01 3-2	Sep04 4-0	Apr18 3-1	Feb01 3-2	Feb08 2-2	Nov16 3-3	Mar07 5-2	Dec21 1-2	Aug21 4-0	Nov02 1-3	Nov23 2-0	Sep28 2-3	Apr18 5-2	Dec07 5-0	

DIVISION 2 FINAL TABLE

	P	W	D	L	F	A	Pts
Morton	36	32	3	1	135	37	67
Clyde	36	22	9	5	81	44	53
Arbroath	36	20	6	10	79	46	46
East Fife	36	16	13	7	92	57	45
Montrose	36	19	6	11	79	57	44
Dumbarton	36	16	6	14	67	59	38
Queen's Park	36	17	4	15	57	54	38
Stranraer	36	16	6	14	71	73	38
Albion R	36	12	12	12	67	71	36
Raith R	36	15	5	16	70	61	35
Stenhousemuir	36	15	5	16	83	75	35
Berwick R	36	10	10	16	68	84	30
Hamilton A	36	12	6	18	65	81	30
Ayr U	36	12	5	19	58	83	29
Brechin C	36	10	8	18	61	98	28
Alloa	36	11	5	20	64	92	27
Cowdenbeath	36	7	11	18	46	72	25
Forfar A	36	6	8	22	57	104	20
Stirling A	36	6	8	22	47	99	20

Season 1964-65

FA Cup

1st Preliminary
Jan 9	Berwick R 2	Stenhousemuir	...2
Jan 9	Brechin C 3	Albion R	4
Jan 9	Coldstream 2	Stranraer	4
Jan 9	Hamilton A 5	Clacknacuddin	3
Jan 9	Peebles 1	Stirling A	4

Replays
Jan 13	Stenhousemuir ...1	Berwick R	0

2nd Preliminary
Jan 23	Cowdenbeath 2	Alloa	1
Jan 27	Edinburgh Univ ..1	Forfar A	4
Jan 23	Hamilton A 3	Stranraer	0
Jan 23	Inverness C 2	Raith R	1
Jan 23	Keith 1	Ayr U	1
Jan 23	Queen's Park 0	Albion R	0
Feb 6	Stenhousemuir ...4	Elgin C	1
Jan 23	Vale of Leithen ..0	Stirling A	5

Replay
Jan 27	Ayr U 4	Keith	2
Feb 3	Albion R 1	Queen's Park	1
Feb 4	Albion R 0	Queen's Park	1
	played at Firhill Park		

1st Round
Feb 6	Aberdeen 0	East Fife	0
Feb 10	Airdrie 7	Montrose	3
Feb 6	Ayr U 1	Partick T	1
Feb 6	Clyde 0	Morton	4
Feb 6	Dumbarton 0	Queen's Park	0
Feb 6	Falkirk 0	Hearts	3
Feb 6	Forfar A 0	Dundee U	3
Feb 6	Hibernian 1	Clydebank	1
Feb 6	Inverness C 1	T Lanark	5
Feb 6	Kilmarnock 5	Cowdenbeath	0
Feb 13	Motherwell 3	Stenhousemuir	...2
Feb 6	Queen of South ...0	Dunfermline A	2
Feb 6	Rangers 3	Hamilton A	0
Feb 6	St Johnstone 1	Dundee	0
Feb 6	St Mirren 0	Celtic	3
Feb 6	Stirling A 2	Arbroath	1

Replays
Feb 10	Clydebank 0	Hibernian	2
Feb 10	East Fife 1	Aberdeen	0
Feb 10	Partick T 7	Ayr U	1
Feb 10	Queen's Park 2	Dumbarton	1

2nd Round
Feb 20	Dundee U 0	Rangers	2
Feb 20	East Fife 0	Kilmarnock	0
Feb 20	Hibernian 5	Partick T	1
Feb 20	Morton 3	Hearts	3
Feb 20	Motherwell 1	St Johnstone	0
Feb 20	Queen's Park 0	Celtic	1
Feb 20	Stirling A 1	Airdrie	1
Feb 20	T Lanark 1	Dunfermline A	1

Replays
Feb 24	Airdrie 0	Stirling A	2
Feb 24	Dunfermline A ...2	T Lanark	2
Feb 24	Hearts 2	Morton	0
Feb 24	Kilmarnock 3	East Fife	0
Feb 26	Dunfermline A ...4	T Lanark	2
	played at Tynecastle		

3rd Round
Mar 6	Celtic 3	Kilmarnock	2
Mar 6	Dunfermline A ...2	Stirling A	0
Mar 6	Hibernian 2	Rangers	1
Mar 6	Motherwell 1	Hearts	0

Semi-finals
Mar 27	Celtic 2	Motherwell	2
	played at Hampden Park		
Mar 27	Dunfermline A ...2	Hibernian	0
	played at Tynecastle		

Replays
Mar 31	Celtic 3	Motherwell	0
	played at Hampden Park		

Final
Apr 24	Celtic 3	Dunfermline A	2
	played at Hampden Park		

> League Cup results for 1964-65 are detailed on page 195.

DIVISION 1 FINAL TABLE

	P	W	D	L	F	A	Pts
Kilmarnock	34	22	6	6	62	33	50
Hearts	34	22	6	6	90	49	50
Dunfermline A	34	22	5	7	83	36	49
Hibernian	34	21	4	9	75	47	46
Rangers	34	18	8	8	78	35	44
Dundee	34	15	10	9	86	63	40
Clyde	34	17	6	11	64	58	40
Celtic	34	16	5	13	76	57	37
Dundee U	34	15	6	13	59	51	36
Morton	34	13	7	14	54	54	33
Partick T	34	11	10	13	57	58	32
Aberdeen	34	12	8	14	59	75	32
St Johnstone	34	9	11	14	57	62	29
Motherwell	34	10	8	16	45	54	28
St Mirren	34	9	6	19	38	70	24
Falkirk	34	7	7	20	43	85	21
Airdrie	34	5	4	25	48	110	14
T Lanark	34	3	1	30	22	99	7

DIVISION 1

	ABERDEEN	AIRDRIE	CELTIC	CLYDE	DUNDEE	DUNDEE U	DUNFERMLINE A	FALKIRK	HEARTS	HIBERNIAN	KILMARNOCK	MORTON	MOTHERWELL	PARTICK T	RANGERS	ST JOHNSTONE	ST MIRREN	T LANARK
ABERDEEN		Mar24 5-2	Oct10 1-3	Dec19 0-3	Jan01 1-1	Apr03 1-0	Feb27 2-2	Oct31 2-1	Apr17 0-3	Jan09 1-1	Nov21 1-1	Nov14 2-1	Oct17 0-1	Sep26 5-1	Mar13 2-0	Sep12 5-5	Aug19 2-1	Jan30 3-1
AIRDRIE	Apr10 2-4		Mar10 0-6	Feb17 3-5	Apr24 2-2	Oct24 3-3	Oct17 3-4	Oct03 2-2	Dec26 1-2	Dec12 0-1	Jan02 2-1	Sep19 0-2	Sep05 0-3	Apr03 0-5	Jan16 0-4	Nov21 1-2	Mar20 5-1	Nov07 2-1
CELTIC	Jan30 8-0	Oct31 2-1		Jan02 4-0	Nov14 4-1	Sep19 1-1	Dec19 1-2	Nov01 3-0	Jan16 1-2	Mar22 2-4	Feb27 2-0	Oct12 1-0	Dec26 4-1	Apr17 0-1	Sep05 1-1	Mar13 0-1	Oct17 4-1	Apr03 1-0
CLYDE	Apr24 4-0	Oct10 1-1	Sep12 1-0		Feb20 1-0	Nov07 2-0	Jan09 1-0	Mar20 6-1	Mar27 2-5	Aug19 1-3	Nov28 1-2	Feb13 1-0	Apr07 1-1	Jan01 4-1	Mar10 0-3	Oct24 4-1	Dec12 1-1	Sep26 1-0
DUNDEE	Sep05 3-1	Dec19 4-0	Mar20 3-3	Oct03 1-2		Mar24 2-4	Nov07 3-1	Feb10 3-2	Oct24 1-2	Apr03 2-1	Oct17 1-3	Dec26 1-1	Nov21 4-2	Jan16 3-3	Apr14 4-1	Dec05 4-4	Mar06 2-1	Apr17 6-1
DUNDEE U	Nov28 0-3	Feb27 3-2	Jan09 3-1	Oct03 6-0	Sep12 1-4		Nov14 2-0	Feb13 4-1	Apr10 1-1	Sep26 0-1	Oct31 0-1	Mar27 3-2	Apr24 3-1	Aug19 1-2	Dec12 4-1	Jan01 2-0	Jan23 2-1	Oct10 6-1
DUNFERMLINE A	Oct24 2-0	Feb13 3-1	Apr28 5-1	Sep19 7-2	Mar13 3-3	Mar20 0-3		Sep05 5-1	Jan02 3-2	Nov21 1-0	Jan16 6-0	Feb10 3-0	Oct03 2-0	Apr14 3-1	Apr17 1-1	Apr03 2-1		Mar22 8-0
FALKIRK	Mar06 0-1	Mar01 4-1	Apr14 6-2	Nov14 0-0	Oct10 4-2	Oct17 0-0	Jan01 0-4		Nov07 2-2	Sep12 0-1	Apr07 0-1	Dec19 0-2	Dec12 1-1	Jan09 2-2	Nov28 0-5	Sep26 3-2	Aug19 2-0	Mar20 3-0
HEARTS	Dec12 6-3	Aug19 8-1	Sep26 4-2	Nov21 3-0	Feb27 1-7	Dec05 3-1	Sep12 1-1	Mar13 5-2		Jan01 0-1	Apr24 2-1	Oct31 2-0	Mar20 0-1	Jan23 1-0	Oct17 1-1	Apr03 4-0	Oct10 2-1	Jan09 3-1
HIBERNIAN	Sep19 4-2	Apr17 5-1	Apr07 0-1	Dec26 4-3	Nov28 2-2	Jan16 3-4	Mar31 1-0	Jan02 6-0	Sep05 3-5		Oct03 1-2	Oct24 2-1	Mar10 2-0	Dec19 2-1	Jan30 1-0	Feb13 1-0	Nov07 1-1	Nov14 5-0
KILMARNOCK	Mar27 2-1	Sep12 2-0	Oct28 5-2	Apr03 2-1	Feb13 1-4	Mar10 4-2	Sep26 2-0	Dec05 2-0	Dec19 3-1	Feb16 4-3		Apr17 3-0	Nov07 1-1	Apr07 0-0	Sep26 1-1	Jan01 4-0	Aug19 3-1	
MORTON	Mar20 1-1	Jan09 5-0	Jan23 3-3	Oct17 0-0	Apr19 3-2	Nov21 2-0	Oct10 2-0	Apr24 4-0	Mar10 2-3	Feb27 3-2	Dec12 5-1		Apr03 0-2	Nov07 1-3	Apr07 1-3	Sep26 2-0	Sep12 2-0	Jan01 1-1
MOTHERWELL	Apr14 2-2	Jan01 1-0	Aug19 1-0	Mar22 2-0	Sep26 2-1	Dec19 1-1	Jan23 2-2	Apr17 3-1	Nov14 1-3	Oct31 0-2	Mar13 4-1	Nov28 2-1		Feb27 0-2	Apr21 1-3	Oct10 2-2	Jan09 4-0	Sep12 3-3
PARTICK T	Jan16 2-1	Nov28 3-1	Dec12 2-4	Sep05 0-3	Mar27 4-4	Apr19 0-0	Mar08 1-2	Sep19 4-1	Oct03 4-2	Apr23 1-0	Jan30 1-1	Mar13 1-2	Oct24		Jan02 1-1	Nov14 2-2	Apr07 1-2	Oct31 0-1
RANGERS	Nov07 2-2	Aug19 9-2	Jan02 1-0	Sep26 6-1	Apr19 4-0	Apr03 0-1	Feb13 0-1	Oct10 4-1	Dec19 1-2	Apr23 1-4	Oct03 1-1	Mar30 1-0	Nov21 5-0	Sep12 1-1		Mar24 1-1	Feb27 2-2	Dec19 7-1
ST JOHNSTONE	Feb17 2-4	Mar27 1-3	Nov07 0-1	Feb27 3-0	Apr07 0-3	Sep05 1-3	Dec12 0-2	Mar10 2-1	Nov21 0-3	Oct17 2-5	Sep19 0-1	Jan16 3-0	Feb10 1-1	Mar20 0-2	Oct07 0-1		Apr24 5-1	Mar06 5-0
ST MIRREN	Dec26 4-0	Nov14 3-0	Feb13 1-5	Apr17 2-3	Oct31 0-2	Oct03 2-1	Nov28 1-4	Jan16 3-0	Jan30 2-1	Mar13 0-0	Sep05 0-2	Jan02 1-1	Sep19 1-4	Dec05 4-1	Apr23 0-3	Dec19 0-7		Mar27 2-1
T LANARK	Oct03 4-1	Mar13 0-4	Nov28 0-3	Jan16 0-4	Dec12 0-1	Feb17 1-2	Apr10 1-2	Feb27 1-2	Sep19 1-5	Mar20 0-2	Dec26 0-4	Sep05 1-2	Apr28 0-2	Feb13 0-3	Apr23 0-1	Oct31 0-2	Nov21 2-1	

118

Aberdeen in 1964. Back row (left to right): Bennett, Shewan, Ogston, Cooke, Smith, Kerr. Front row: Kerrigan, Morrison, Coutts, Winchester, McIntosh.

DIVISION 2

	ALBION R	ALLOA	ARBROATH	AYR U	BERWICK R	BRECHIN C	COWDENBEATH	DUMBARTON	EAST FIFE	E STIRLING	FORFAR A	HAMILTON A	MONTROSE	QUEEN OF SOUTH	QUEEN'S PARK	RAITH R	STENHOUSEMUIR	STIRLING A	STRANRAER
ALBION R		Apr28 2-3	Feb20 0-0	Aug19 2-0	Sep26 2-1	Oct31 4-2	Apr17 0-3	Nov28 0-3	Feb27 2-2	Sep12 3-1	Mar13 3-1	Jan01 3-1	Dec19 3-0	Mar27 1-2	Sep16 1-2	Feb13 3-0	Nov14 1-1	Sep09 3-1	Oct10 5-0
ALLOA	Apr07 3-2		Sep09 0-1	Jan09 2-1	Feb06 4-3	Nov28 6-0	Apr23 0-1	Oct17 2-2	Sep26 2-7	Aug19 1-4	Mar27 3-2	Nov14 2-2	Sep30 4-4	Nov07 1-1	Dec12 0-3	Sep16 4-2	Jan01 3-2	Apr21 0-0	Oct24 2-1
ARBROATH	Oct03 2-1	Sep19 2-1		Sep23 1-1	Nov14 4-0	Feb13 2-1	Dec26 3-2	Apr24 1-1	Apr10 4-1	Oct24 0-1	Sep05 1-1	Mar13 1-1	Jan02 2-2	Jan16 2-0	Jan16 1-2	Jan16 0-1	Mar27 0-0	Nov28 1-1	Dec12 2-1
AYR U	Dec26 1-3	Oct03 1-2	Sep30 1-4		Feb27 0-1	Mar13 5-1	Jan30 2-1	Sep19 3-0	Nov28 0-4	Mar20 4-1	Jan16 4-1	Apr14 0-1	Nov21 2-0	Jan02 2-1	Sep05 2-1	Oct31 4-3	Dec12 3-0	Apr07 1-2	Apr24 2-0
BERWICK R	Jan16 3-0	Oct10 2-4	Mar20 4-1	Oct24 3-0		Sep09 5-1	Oct03 4-1	Jan23 3-2	Apr24 2-2	Mar06 2-1	Apr19 1-2	Dec19 1-4	Sep05 2-2	Sep26 1-1	Nov21 1-1	Dec26 2-3	Sep12 2-1	Nov07 0-3	Apr03 0-1
BRECHIN C	Apr21 0-1	Apr03 2-3	Oct17 4-3	Nov07 2-2	Sep19 2-3		Mar20 1-1	Sep16 1-1	Jan23 4-1	Oct10 0-1	Apr19 2-3	Dec19 3-6	Sep05 2-2	Sep26 3-3	Nov21 1-4	Dec26 3-3	Sep28 1-0	Feb27 1-3	Feb06 0-7
COWDENBEATH	Dec12 3-1	Dec19 2-0	Aug19 2-0	Oct10 0-2	Feb20 4-1	Nov14 1-0		Mar27 1-0	Sep12 1-1	Sep26 4-1	Nov28 2-3	Apr21 0-3	Feb27 5-2	Sep02 4-2	Apr10 0-0	Sep23 2-1	Mar06 1-1	Jan01 1-1	Oct17 1-2
DUMBARTON	Apr03 2-1	Feb13 3-1	Dec19 1-1	Sep09 2-1	Dec05 4-4	Sep01 1-3	Nov21 3-0		Nov07 5-0	Jan01 3-0	Oct24 1-3	Sep12 0-4	Oct10 6-2	Sep23 1-3	Jan09 0-0	Apr17 2-1	Aug19 0-1	Apr10 0-1	Feb20 4-1
EAST FIFE	Oct24 2-0	Jan16 3-4	Dec05 4-0	Apr03 1-0	Dec19 4-2	Oct03 3-1	Jan02 0-0	Mar13 3-1		Apr17	Apr28 5-2	Feb13 3-0	Dec26 2-5	Sep23 2-3	Oct31 2-1	Sep05 2-1	Mar23 3-3		Sep23 5-2
E STIRLING	Jan02 2-1	Apr26 2-2	Feb27 3-1	Nov14 0-0	Oct31 2-1	Feb20 6-1	Jan16 3-3	Sep05 3-0	Dec12 1-2		Apr23 3-2	Nov28 5-0	Sep16 1-1	Oct03 2-2	Sep19 1-2	Mar13 0-1	Oct17 1-3	Mar27 1-2	Sep30 3-1
FORFAR A	Nov07 4-0	Nov21 1-3	Jan01 2-2	Sep16 4-2	Sep12 3-3	Apr03 2-3	Feb27 2-2	Oct10 0-2		Dec19 2-2		Feb20 0-1	Oct17 3-2	Apr17 0-3	Sep30 1-2	Dec05 2-3	Sep09 1-3	Aug19 0-4	Mar06 1-4
HAMILTON A	Sep05 2-2	Mar20 3-4	Nov07 0-3	Apr14 1-0	Sep30 1-1	Apr24 1-1	Sep19 1-1	Oct17 4-3	Apr03 5-0	Oct03 3-0		Mar06 5-1	Jan30 3-3	Dec26 0-2	Oct24 2-4	Apr10 1-0	Dec12 1-4	Nov21 2-2	
MONTROSE	Apr24 0-0	Sep23 5-3	Sep12 2-2	Mar27 4-2	Apr17 2-3	Jan01 3-1	Oct24 4-3	Apr27 5-0	Aug19 1-4	Sep02 2-1	Feb13 0-0	Oct31 3-7		Dec05 3-3	Mar13 0-2	Oct03 4-0	Nov28 1-4	Nov14 0-2	Jan16 2-2
QUEEN OF SOUTH	Apr24 2-1	Sep12 2-1	Mar13 2-3	Apr14 4-3	Sep12 1-1	Jan16 5-1	Sep30 1-1	Apr16 4-0	Sep30 3-2	Jan23 1-0	Dec12 2-2	Oct10 1-2	Feb20 6-1		Apr24 4-0	Nov14 1-1	Oct24 7-1	Feb13 1-1	Jan01 5-1
QUEEN'S PARK	Sep02 1-0	Apr17 5-6	Sep26 2-1	Jan01 1-2	Oct17 1-1	Apr14 4-1	Dec05 0-0	Sep16 3-0	Nov06 3-0	Mar06 0-0	Sep09 2-1	Aug19 2-3	Nov07 2-0	Dec19 1-0		Apr20 0-1	Apr10 1-1	Oct10 0-1	Sep12 2-0
RAITH R	Oct17 1-2	Sep02 0-0	Oct10 1-1	Apr28 1-1	Mar27 3-0	Aug19 2-2	Sep30 0-3	Dec12 1-1	Jan01 1-1	Nov07 3-0	Apr07 5-2	Feb27 0-1	Jan09 3-0	Mar20 2-8	Nov28 7-1		Sep26 1-2	Sep12 0-1	Sep09 0-4
STENHOUSEMUIR	Mar20 2-3	Sep05 2-1	Nov21 1-3	Feb20 2-1	Jan02 2-2	Sep23 3-0	Oct31 3-4	Apr13 4-0	Apr20 1-1	Apr27 2-1	Sep19 2-3	Dec05 2-5	Apr03 0-2	Feb27 2-1	Oct03 2-2	Jan16 0-0		Apr24 0-1	Mar13 3-2
STIRLING A	Sep19 3-0	Oct31 2-3	Apr03 2-1	Dec05 3-1	Mar13 1-0	Oct24 5-2	Sep05 2-2	Jan16 1-6	Sep30 4-0	Nov21 1-4	Apr14 4-0	Apr17 2-3	Mar20 2-1	Sep26 2-1	Jan30 2-0	Jan02 1-2	Dec19 5-1		Sep16 1-1
STRANRAER	Jan30 4-0	Feb27 4-0	Apr17 2-0	Dec19 2-0	Nov28 1-3	Dec05 2-1	Feb13 1-0	Oct03 0-4	Mar20 3-2	Sep23 1-3	Oct31 4-4	Mar27 2-0	Sep26 1-1	Sep05 1-1	Jan02 3-1	Sep19 3-3	Nov07 4-0	Sep02 0-6	

DIVISION 2 FINAL TABLE

	P	W	D	L	F	A	Pts
Stirling A	36	26	7	3	84	31	59
Hamilton A	36	21	8	7	86	53	50
Queen of South	36	16	13	7	84	50	45
Queen's Park	36	17	9	10	57	41	43
E Stirling	36	15	10	11	64	50	40
Stranraer	36	17	6	13	74	64	40
Arbroath	36	13	13	10	56	51	39
Berwick R	36	15	9	12	73	70	39
East Fife	36	15	7	14	78	77	37
Alloa	36	14	8	14	71	81	36
Albion R	36	14	5	17	56	60	33
Cowdenbeath	36	11	10	15	55	62	32
Raith R	36	9	14	13	54	61	32
Dumbarton	36	13	6	17	55	67	32
Stenhousemuir	36	11	8	17	49	74	30
Montrose	36	10	9	17	80	91	29
Forfar A	36	9	7	20	63	89	25
Ayr U	36	9	6	21	49	67	24
Brechin C	36	6	7	23	53	102	19

Season 1965-66

FA Cup
1st Preliminary
Jan 8 Berwick R ......1 Stenhousemuir ... 0
Jan 8 Dumbarton ......2 Peebles 2
Jan 8 Forfar A ....1 Brechin C 1
Jan 8 Gala Fairydean .. 6 Selkirk 1
Jan 8 Raith R ....1 Inverness C 0

Replays
Jan 12 Brechin C ......1 Forfar A 3
Jan 12 Peebles ....2 Dumbarton 3

2nd Preliminary
Jan 22 Arbroath ....2 Cowdenbeath 2
Jan 22 Ayr U ....1 Fraserburgh 0
Jan 22 Berwick R ......0 Albion R 0
Jan 22 East Fife ....1 Elgin C 0
Jan 22 Gala Fairydean ... 4 Montrose 5
Jan 22 Glasgow Univ ... 1 Dumbarton 2
Jan 22 Raith R ....0 Alloa 1
Jan 22 Ross Co ....4 Forfar A 3

Replays
Jan 26 Albion R ....3 Berwick R 0
Jan 26 Cowdenbeath ....1 Arbroath 1
Jan 31 Arbroath ....2 Cowdenbeath 3
        played at Tannadice

1st Round
Feb 10 Alloa ....3 Ross Co 5
Feb 5 Ayr U ....1 St Johnstone 1
Feb 5 Celtic ....4 Stranraer 0
Feb 9 Cowdenbeath ....1 St Mirren 0
Feb 9 Dumbarton ......2 Montrose 1
Feb 9 Dundee ....9 East Fife 1
Feb 7 Dundee U ....0 Falkirk 0
Feb 5 Dunfermline A ...3 Partick T 1
Feb 9 E Stirling ....0 Motherwell.......0
Feb 5 Hamilton A .....1 Aberdeen 3
Feb 9 Hearts ....2 Clyde 1
Feb 5 Hibernian ......4 T Lanark 3
Feb 5 Morton ....1 Kilmarnock 1
Feb 5 Queen of South ..3 Albion R 0
Feb 5 Rangers ....5 Airdrie 1
Feb 5 Stirling A ....3 Queen's Park ...1

Replays
Feb 9 Kilmarnock .....3 Morton 0
Feb 14 Motherwell .....4 E Stirling 1
Feb 14 St Johnstone ....1 Ayr U 0
Feb 16 Falkirk ....1 Dundee U 2

2nd Round
Feb 23 Aberdeen ....5 Dundee U 0
Feb 28 Cowdenbeath ....3 St Johnstone 3
Feb 23 Dumbarton ......1 Queen of South ...0
Feb 23 Dundee ....0 Celtic 2
Feb 21 Hearts ....2 Hibernian 1
Feb 21 Kilmarnock .....5 Motherwell 0
Feb 28 Ross Co ....0 Rangers 2
Feb 23 Stirling A ....0 Dunfermline A ... 0

Replays
Feb 28 Dunfermline A ...4 Stirling A 1
Mar 1 St Johnstone ...3 Cowdenbeath 0

3rd Round
Mar 5 Dumbarton ......0 Aberdeen 3
Mar 5 Dunfermline A ...2 Kilmarnock 1
Mar 5 Hearts ....3 Celtic 3
Mar 5 Rangers ....1 St Johnstone 0

Replay
Mar 9 Celtic ....3 Hearts 1

Semi-finals
Mar 26 Aberdeen ....0 Rangers 0
        played at Hampden Park
Mar 26 Celtic ....2 Dunfermline A ... 0
        played at Ibrox

Replays
Mar 29 Aberdeen ....1 Rangers 2
        played at Hampden Park

Final
Apr 23 Celtic ....0 Rangers 0
        played at Hampden Park

Replay
Apr 27 Celtic ....0 Rangers 1
        played at Hampden Park

Billy McNeill and Tommy Gemmell join the attack as Celtic go on to gain two vital points in their quest for the championship with a 2-0 win at Morton in April 1966.

DIVISION 1

Home \ Away	ABERDEEN	CELTIC	CLYDE	DUNDEE	DUNDEE U	DUNFERMLINE	FALKIRK	HAMILTON A	HEARTS	HIBERNIAN	KILMARNOCK	MORTON	MOTHERWELL	PARTICK T	RANGERS	ST JOHNSTONE	ST MIRREN	STIRLING A
ABERDEEN	—	Jan15 3-1	Mar02 2-0	Sep18 2-3	Dec11 0-0	Oct16 2-2	Nov20 2-0	Jan29 5-2	Feb26 0-1	Dec25 1-3	Nov06 1-0	Apr04 5-3	Apr23 1-2	Mar12 2-1	Apr13 1-2	Jan03 2-3	Oct02 4-1	Aug25 2-2
CELTIC	Sep25 7-1	—	Sep11 2-1	Feb28 5-0	Jan08 4-0	May04 2-1	Feb12 6-0	Nov20 5-0	Oct09 5-2	Sep05 2-0	Nov27 2-1	Dec25 8-1	Jan22 1-0	Nov06 1-1	Jan03 5-1	Mar12 3-2	Apr09 5-0	Oct30 6-1
CLYDE	Oct23 2-2	Jan01 1-3	—	Aug25 0-2	Mar26 4-1	Mar19 6-1	Apr06 3-2	Apr30 4-1	Sep16 0-1	Oct02 1-2	Feb26 1-4	Nov13 2-0	Mar05 1-3	Sep18 2-2	Dec18 3-2	Jan29 0-1	Oct16 0-1	Jan15 0-1
DUNDEE	Apr20 1-2	Oct27 1-2	Jan08 1-4	—	Sep11 0-5	Apr27 0-2	Oct09 2-0	Mar09 2-1	Apr13 1-0	Nov13 4-3	Feb12 0-2	Mar05 5-1	Dec25 4-0	Apr23 1-1	Sep25 1-1	Nov20 3-1	Feb26 3-2	Mar26 6-2
DUNDEE U	Apr16 3-0	Aug25 0-4	Nov27 0-2	Jan03 2-1	—	Jan29 0-4	Feb23 2-3	Oct16 7-0	Nov06 2-2	Sep05 5-4	Dec18 0-0	Oct30 4-2	Apr02 5-1	Mar21 5-2	Jan15 1-0	Nov27 5-1	Dec11 3-1	Apr30 1-1
DUNFERMLINE A	Mar21 2-3	Dec18 0-2	Nov20 6-4	Apr09 2-2	Oct09 2-4	—	Apr13 6-1	Mar12 1-0	Sep11 1-1	Apr06 3-0	Sep25 2-1	Jan01 6-1	Jan08 4-3	Oct23 3-2	Apr30 1-2	Feb26 5-1	Nov06 5-1	Dec11 5-1
FALKIRK	Mar19 3-0	Oct16 3-4	Apr09 0-1	Jan29 3-1	Nov13 1-4	Oct02 0-3	—	Jan03 0-0	Nov27 0-1	Jan15 3-2	Dec11 3-2	Apr23 3-2	Oct30 2-0	Dec25 2-0	Mar09 3-2	Aug25 2-1	Apr23 2-3	Sep18 2-0
HAMILTON A	Oct30 0-4	Mar19 1-7	Dec25 1-4	Apr16 1-4	Feb12 2-5	Nov13 1-6	Sep11 1-4	—	Jan08 0-4	Mar05 1-2	Apr30 1-4	Sep25 2-5	Jan01 1-2	Mar26 1-4	Oct30 1-7	Apr23 1-1	Apr23 1-0	Oct23 3-1
HEARTS	Oct30 1-1	Jan29 3-2	Dec11 4-1	Oct02 0-0	Mar16 0-1	Jan03 0-0	Mar26 1-2	Aug25 2-0	—	Sep18 0-4	Apr09 2-3	Nov20 2-1	Oct23 5-2	Feb12 3-1	Nov13 0-2	Jan15 0-0	Dec25 4-1	Apr23 1-1
HIBERNIAN	Apr30 0-1	Apr16 4-0	Mar23 3-1	Mar12 1-1	Apr20 3-3	Nov27 1-1	Sep25 5-1	Nov06 11-1	Jan01 2-3	—	Sep11 3-3	Jan08 4-1	Oct09 2-2	Feb26 2-0	Oct16 1-2	Dec18 3-0	Mar02 3-2	Mar19 1-0
KILMARNOCK	Mar09 1-3	Mar29 0-2	Oct30 1-1	Nov06 2-2	Apr23 5-3	Jan15 1-0	Apr16 1-0	Oct02 3-1	Apr04 2-2	Jan03 1-0	—	Feb28 4-0	Nov13 5-0	Aug25 2-1	Mar19 1-1	Dec25 3-1	Sep18 3-1	Jan29 2-1
MORTON	Nov27 1-3	Apr30 0-2	Mar15 1-1	Nov06 2-2	Feb26 2-0	Sep18 1-1	Dec18 0-1	Jan15 3-0	Mar19 0-3	Aug25 1-5	Oct23 1-4	—	Mar09 3-1	Jan29 0-0	Apr16 0-5	Oct02 1-2	Jan03 0-0	Feb12 2-1
MOTHERWELL	Dec18 1-0	May07 0-1	Nov06 0-1	Apr30 2-0	Nov20 0-3	Aug25 1-3	Feb26 3-0	Sep18 4-2	Mar23 4-2	Jan29 4-0	Mar12 0-3	Apr09 3-0	—	Jan15 0-3	Nov27 0-3	Oct16 5-3	Dec11 4-1	Jan03 0-1
PARTICK T	Nov13 0-3	Mar21 2-2	Apr11 2-2	Dec18 4-1	Jan22 2-6	Apr20 3-0	Apr28 1-0	Oct16 3-3	Oct30 3-2	Jan08 1-0	Oct09 1-2	Sep25 1-1		—	Sep11 1-1	Apr16 3-1	Mar05 4-1	Mar05 1-1
RANGERS	Apr09 1-0	Sep18 2-1	May04 4-0	Apr06 2-0	Oct27 2-0	Dec25 2-3	Nov06 3-0	Feb26 4-1	Mar12 2-0	Feb12 5-1	Nov20 2-0	Dec11 5-1	Apr19 2-1	Jan01 1-4	—	Aug25 3-2	Jan29 4-1	Oct02 6-0
ST JOHNSTONE	Sep11 2-2	Nov13 1-4	Oct09 3-3	Mar19 1-0	Mar30 1-2	Oct23 1-5	Apr09 2-1	Sep25 5-0	Apr23 3-2	Apr30 1-3	Apr13 1-1	Feb12 4-2	Apr06 3-3	Jan08 2-2		—	Nov27 3-2	Mar09 1-1
ST MIRREN	Jan22 1-0	Apr05 0-3	Feb12 1-0	Oct30 2-5	Sep30 1-2	Mar09 4-3	Aug25 6-0	Oct30 1-0	Dec18 0-1	Apr30 1-1	Jan01 0-2	Sep11 4-7	Nov20 0-1	Nov20 0-0	Oct09 1-6	Mar26 2-3	—	Nov13 0-0
STIRLING A	Jan08 2-1	Feb26 1-0	Sep25 3-2	Nov27 1-4	Dec25 2-4	Apr16 2-1	Mar30 0-1	Mar24 3-0	Dec18 2-2	Nov20 1-2	Oct09 2-3	Oct16 2-4	Sep11 1-0	Apr09 2-2	Jan22 0-2	Nov06 1-0	Mar12 0-1	—

DIVISION 2

Home \ Away	AIRDRIE	ALBION R	ALLOA	ARBROATH	AYR U	BERWICK R	BRECHIN C	COWDENBEATH	DUMBARTON	EAST FIFE	E STIRLING	FORFAR A	MONTROSE	QUEEN OF SOUTH	QUEEN'S PARK	RAITH R	STENHOUSEMUIR	STRANRAER	T LANARK
AIRDRIE	—	Jan01 7-2	Mar26 4-2	Mar31 5-1	Nov13 3-0	Mar28 3-0	Apr25 7-3	Sep25 4-1	Mar23 1-3	Apr16 1-0	May05 1-0	Oct23 6-1	Feb12 2-0	Apr23 0-1	Oct09 1-2	Sep11 0-1	Oct30 7-1	Sep08 5-2	Dec25 3-3
ALBION R	Sep18 2-1	—	Feb26 0-4	Apr13 1-1	Jan15 0-2	Nov06 0-0	Oct16 4-0	Mar12 2-1	Apr27 0-0	Jan03 0-1	Oct02 4-1	Sep29 2-3	Apr09 3-0	Sep14 1-0	Apr30 1-0	Dec11 1-0	Apr20 2-2	Dec18 2-0	Jan29 1-1
ALLOA	Nov27 3-0	Oct30 1-3	—	Aug25 2-2	Mar19 2-1	Apr27 3-3	Apr09 0-2	Apr23 1-0	Mar22 0-2	Nov13 1-0	Mar05 4-0	Sep08 2-3	Mar16 2-1	Apr16 1-0	Dec25 1-2	Sep18 1-1	Oct02 3-3	Mar29 3-0	
ARBROATH	Sep29 2-2	Oct23 2-2	Jan08 2-2	—	Apr23 1-1	Sep25 2-1	Apr16 3-1	Apr27 1-0	Feb26 2-1	Mar05 3-1	Dec25 5-0	Jan01 3-1	Sep11 6-2	Feb12 3-3	Sep15 4-1	Oct09 3-1	Nov13 4-2	Apr20 5-2	
AYR U	Mar12 1-1	Sep25 2-0	Nov20 2-2	Dec18 2-1	—	Oct09 4-2	Sep29 1-0	Jan01 1-0	Nov06 2-0	Apr27 5-2	Dec11 4-1	Apr11 4-1	Jan08 2-2	Sep11 1-2	Feb12 1-3	Oct23 2-0	Apr09 2-2	Apr20 2-0	Feb26 2-0
BERWICK R	Oct02 3-0	Mar05 4-1	Sep27 6-3	Feb05 2-1	Jan29 2-2	—	Oct30 1-3	Dec11 2-0	Sep15 0-1	Apr23 2-1	Sep18 2-2	Dec25 8-1	Nov27 3-1	Mar19 0-1	Apr09 2-2	Jan03 0-2	Apr13 0-2	Nov06 4-0	
BRECHIN C	Apr09 2-2	Mar30 1-4	Oct23 1-2	Dec11 1-1	Apr06 2-2	Feb26 1-2	—	Apr20 1-4	Sep25 3-1	Mar19 2-1	Nov27 3-1	Sep11 1-1	Jan01 0-9	Oct09 2-2	Apr27 0-4	Feb05 1-8	Sep08 3-1	Nov06 1-3	
COWDENBEATH	Jan15 3-0	Nov13 1-2	Apr06 0-3	Oct02 2-1	Sep18 3-1	Apr25 3-1	Aug25 2-1	—	Dec25 1-2	Apr13 3-3	Jan29 2-2	Apr23 3-1	Sep22 2-1	Nov27 0-0	Oct30 2-0	Sep08 0-0	Mar19 4-1	Jan03 3-3	Oct16 3-3
DUMBARTON	Aug25 1-3	Mar19 2-0	Dec18 3-0	Oct30 1-2	Mar30 1-3	Sep08 1-1	Jan15 7-1	Apr30 2-4	—	Oct02 1-0	Oct16 3-1	Apr23 1-3	Sep25 0-0	Nov13 4-1	Apr16 2-3	Mar09 0-2	Dec25 5-2	Feb26 2-0	Jan03 3-1
EAST FIFE	Dec11 6-3	Sep11 1-2	Mar31 3-1	Nov06 1-0	Mar09 2-3	Mar02 3-1	Nov20 2-4	Oct23 1-3	Apr20 6-1	—	Apr09 2-1	Oct09 2-0	Apr23 3-0	Sep25 3-3	Sep22 3-1	Nov13 1-1	Dec25 3-1	Feb26 2-1	Jan03 1-0
E STIRLING	Nov06 2-3	Mar31 2-4	Sep11 2-3	Apr30 4-2	Apr16 0-1	Apr20 1-1	Mar26 1-5	Oct09 5-4	Feb12 3-1	Jan08 1-1	—	Apr06 4-3	Feb26 3-2	Oct23 1-3	Dec18 0-0	Apr27 2-1	Sep22 0-2	Mar12 2-0	Nov20 2-3
FORFAR A	Apr27 2-3	Sep22 1-2	Mar12 2-3	Sep18 2-3	Oct02 1-4	Apr30 3-2	Jan03 1-2	Dec18 2-3	Apr29 2-2	Jan15 4-2		—	Mar30 3-0	Mar19 1-2	Nov27 3-3	Nov06 1-1	Aug25 0-2	Oct16 2-4	Apr13 1-2
MONTROSE	Oct16 0-6	Dec04 4-0	Apr20 1-1	Jan03 0-0	Aug25 0-3	Mar26 3-2	Sep18 3-0	Sep29 3-1	Mar12 2-4	Dec18 4-1	Apr16 5-2	Dec25 1-1	—	Mar05 3-1	Apr13 1-2	Jan29 4-2	Oct02 3-0		
QUEEN OF SOUTH	Dec18 2-1	Sep08 1-0	Nov06 2-0	Oct16 2-2	Jan03 2-2	Mar12 2-1	Jan29 4-2	Mar26 4-4	Dec11 3-3	Jan15 4-3	Mar30 6-0	Nov20 4-1	Apr30 1-1	—	Apr09 3-0	Feb26 1-2	Oct02 5-1	Sep18 4-1	Aug25 4-1
QUEEN'S PARK	Jan29 2-2	Dec25 3-4	Jan12 1-3	Sep07 1-2	Oct16 0-3	Nov20 0-0	Oct02 5-0	Apr23 4-2	Apr05 2-3	Sep29 2-0	Apr12 1-0	Apr19 4-1	Nov06 1-0	Mar02 1-2	—	Mar15 1-1	Jan15 3-2	Aug25 2-2	Sep18 0-2
RAITH R	Jan03 0-8	Apr16 1-1	Apr30 2-1	Jan29 0-1	Apr13 1-0	Mar09 1-1	Dec18 4-0	Mar31 1-3	Nov27 4-0	Sep18 1-3	Aug25 3-1	Mar05 6-0	Mar19 3-0	Mar19 0-1	Nov13 5-1	—	Oct16 2-0	Jan15 5-0	Sep29 6-1
STENHOUSEMUIR	Feb26 0-3	Mar26 0-1	Jan01 2-3	Mar12 1-0	Apr25 0-4	Sep11 2-2	Sep13 0-1	Nov20 2-3	Oct09 1-1	Apr30 1-2	Sep28 3-2	Feb05 5-7	Oct23 1-4	Jan22 1-1	Sep25 1-4	Feb12 2-0	—	Nov06 4-1	Apr16 4-1
STRANRAER	Apr06 2-5	Apr23 2-3	Apr25 1-1	Mar19 0-0	Jan29 1-5	Oct23 3-3	Dec25 5-1	Sep29 4-1	Apr30 2-1	Nov13 4-1	Feb12 5-0	Oct09 2-2	Jan01 1-3	Jan08 1-1	Sep25 2-1	Mar05 2-2	Nov06 4-1	—	Dec04 2-1
T LANARK	Apr30 0-2	Oct09 2-1	Sep25 7-1	Apr20 1-0	Oct30 1-1	Dec18 1-1	Mar05 1-1	Feb12 0-0	Sep11 1-0	Nov13 0-2	Mar19 4-1	Sep15 0-2	Apr28 9-1	Jan08 1-2	Jan01 1-1	Apr06 1-0	Dec11 1-1	Apr09 2-1	—

DIVISION 1 FINAL TABLE

	P	W	D	L	F	A	Pts
Celtic	34	27	3	4	106	30	57
Rangers	34	25	5	4	91	29	55
Kilmarnock	34	20	5	9	73	46	45
Dunfermline A	34	19	6	9	94	55	44
Dundee U	34	19	5	10	79	51	43
Hibernian	34	16	6	12	81	55	38
Hearts	34	13	12	9	56	48	38
Aberdeen	34	15	6	13	61	54	36
Dundee	34	14	6	14	61	61	34
Falkirk	34	15	1	18	48	72	31
Clyde	34	13	4	17	62	64	30
Partick T	34	10	10	14	55	64	30
Motherwell	34	12	4	18	52	69	28
St Johnstone	34	9	8	17	58	81	26
Stirling A	34	8	8	17	40	68	26
St Mirren	34	9	4	21	44	82	22
Morton	34	8	5	21	42	84	21
Hamilton A	34	3	2	29	27	117	8

DIVISION 2 FINAL TABLE

	P	W	D	L	F	A	Pts
Ayr U	36	22	9	5	78	37	53
Airdrie	36	22	6	8	107	56	50
Queen of South	36	18	11	7	83	53	47
East Fife	36	20	4	12	72	55	44
Raith R	36	16	11	9	71	43	43
Arbroath	36	15	13	8	72	52	43
Albion R	36	18	7	11	58	54	43
Alloa	36	14	10	12	65	65	38
Montrose	36	15	7	14	67	63	37
Cowdenbeath	36	15	7	14	69	68	37
Berwick R	36	12	11	13	69	58	35
Dumbarton	36	14	7	15	63	61	35
Queen's Park	36	13	7	16	62	65	33
T Lanark	36	12	8	16	55	65	32
Stranraer	36	9	10	17	64	83	28
Brechin C	36	10	7	19	52	92	27
E Stirling	36	9	5	22	59	91	23
Stenhousemuir	36	6	7	23	47	93	19
Forfar A	36	7	3	26	61	120	17

League Cup results for 1965-66 are detailed on pages 195-196.

Alex Willoughby ends up in Motherwell's net after scoring his fourth and Rangers' fifth in the Glasgow side's 5-1 League win at Fir Park as they chased rivals Celtic for the title.

SFA Cup

1st Preliminary

Dec 17	Chirnside	1	Elgin C	7
Dec 17	Forfar A	1	E Stirling	0
Dec 17	Hawick	4	Gala Fairydean	1
Dec 17	Nairn Co	0	Stenhousemuir	3
Dec 17	Rothes	1	Clydebank	2
Dec 17	Vale of Leithen	1	Berwick R	8

2nd Preliminary

Jan 7	Albion R	0	Cowdenbeath	1
Jan 7	Alloa	2	Montrose	1
Jan 7	Berwick R	2	Forfar A	0
Jan 7	Brechin C	1	T Lanark	0
Jan 7	Dumbarton	2	Clydebank	0
Jan 14	Hawick	1	Elgin C	1
Jan 7	Inverness C	0	Stranraer	0
Jan 16	Queen's Park	3	Stenhousemuir	0

Replay

Jan 11	Stranraer	1	Inverness C	2
Jan 23	Elgin C	2	Hawick	0

1st Round

Jan 28	Aberdeen	5	Dundee	0
Jan 28	Berwick R	1	Rangers	0
Jan 28	Celtic	4	Arbroath	0
Feb 1	Elgin C	2	Ayr U	0

Jan 28	Falkirk	3	Alloa	1
Jan 28	Hearts	0	Dundee U	3
Jan 28	Hibernian	2	Brechin C	0
Jan 28	Inverness C	1	Hamilton A	3
Jan 28	Kilmarnock	2	Dunfermline A	2
Jan 28	Morton	0	Clyde	1
Jan 28	Motherwell	0	East Fife	1
Jan 28	Partick T	3	Dumbarton	0
Jan 28	Queen's Park	3	Raith R	2
Jan 28	St Johnstone	4	Queen of South	0
Jan 28	St Mirren	1	Cowdenbeath	1
Jan 28	Stirling A	1	Airdrie	2

Replays

Feb 1	Cowdenbeath	0	St Mirren	2
Feb 1	Dunfermline A	1	Kilmarnock	0

2nd Round

Feb 18	Aberdeen	5	St Johnstone	0
Feb 18	Celtic	7	Elgin C	0
Feb 18	Clyde	4	East Fife	1
Feb 18	Dundee U	1	Falkirk	0
Feb 18	Hibernian	1	Berwick R	0
Feb 18	Partick T	1	Dunfermline A	1
Feb 18	Queen's Park	1	Airdrie	1
Feb 18	St Mirren	0	Hamilton A	1

Replays

Feb 20	Airdrie	1	Queen's Park	2
Feb 22	Dunfermline A	5	Partick T	1

3rd Round

Mar 11	Celtic	5	Queen's Park	3
Mar 11	Clyde	0	Hamilton A	0
Mar 11	Dundee U	1	Dunfermline A	0
Mar 11	Hibernian	1	Aberdeen	1

Replay

Mar 22	Aberdeen	3	Hibernian	0
Mar 22	Hamilton A	1	Clyde	5

Semi-finals

Apr 1	Aberdeen	1	Dundee U	0
	played at Dens Park			
Apr 1	Celtic	0	Clyde	0
	played at Hampden Park			

Replays

Apr 5	Celtic	2	Clyde	0
	played at Hampden Park			

Final

Apr 29	Aberdeen	0	Celtic	2
	played at Hampden Park			

Season 1966-67

DIVISION 1

Home \ Away	ABE	AIR	AYR	CEL	CLY	DUN	DUU	DFA	FAL	HEA	HIB	KIL	MOT	PAR	RAN	STJ	STM	STA
ABERDEEN		Feb11 7-0	Oct15 2-0	Dec24 1-1	Oct01 1-1	Jan02 5-2	Mar25 0-1	Jan21 1-2	Apr08 6-1	Nov05 3-1	Oct29 2-1	Dec31 4-0	Dec03 2-1	Nov19 5-2	Jan18 1-2	Sep17 3-2	Mar27 0-0	Apr15 1-0
AIRDRIE	Oct22 1-2		Mar25 3-1	Feb04 0-3	Mar18 2-3	Apr22 1-4	Sep24 2-2	Jan14 0-3	Sep24 1-0	Apr26 1-2	Dec31 0-1	Feb25 1-4	Feb25 2-0	Dec10 3-1	Apr01 0-1	Oct08 2-0	Oct08 1-0	Nov12 7-0
AYR U	Feb04 2-5	Nov26 0-1		Feb11 0-5	Apr19 1-1	Nov12 0-7	Sep24 0-1	Sep10 0-1	Jan14 0-1	Oct08 0-2	Dec17 2-3	Jan03 3-3	Mar01 1-2	Dec31 1-4	Mar18 1-0	Apr08 0-0	Apr22 0-0	Mar04 0-1
CELTIC	Apr19 0-0	Oct15 3-0	Oct24 5-1		Jan11 5-1	Jan07 5-1	May03 2-3	Mar18 3-2	Feb04 5-0	Nov26 3-0	Jan21 2-0	May15 4-2	Dec10 6-2	Dec17 2-0	Sep17 6-1	Oct01 1-1	Nov05 1-1	Nov02 7-3
CLYDE	Jan14 0-0	Nov19 1-0	Dec03 0-0	Sep10 0-3		Apr08 1-3	Feb04 2-0	Mar04 1-0	Oct22 4-0	Feb25 2-1	Nov12 5-1	Sep10 1-3	Apr26 4-1	Feb08 1-5	Apr11 2-0	Mar25 2-1	Apr04 0-1	
DUNDEE	Sep10 2-1	Dec24 3-1	Mar10 1-2	Sep24 3-4	Dec10 1-2		Jan03 2-3	Apr12 4-1	Feb04 4-1	Jan14 2-1	Nov19 1-1	Oct08 1-3	Oct22 0-0	Feb25 1-1	Apr29 0-3	Nov05 2-0	Dec03 2-0	Mar25 2-0
DUNDEE U	Nov26 1-3	Mar04 3-1	Jan07 4-0	Dec31 3-2	Oct15 4-3	Sep17 1-4		Oct29 2-4	Apr05 4-4	Apr08 2-0	Feb11 1-3	Nov12 1-1	Mar18 1-1	Apr22 2-2	Oct01 2-3	Jan02 1-0	Dec17 2-3	Jan21 2-0
DUNFERMLINE A	Oct08 1-1	Oct01 0-1	Nov19 6-0	Nov05 4-5	Nov05 4-0	Dec17 0-1	Feb25 3-3		Apr29 4-0	Mar22 1-0	Sep17 5-6	Apr08 1-1	Oct22 2-1	Dec03 3-2	Mar25 4-1	Feb04 2-0	Feb04 3-3	Apr22 3-3
FALKIRK	Dec10 1-0	Apr19 2-1	Oct01 5-3	Nov12 0-3	Feb11 3-2	Oct15 0-3	Dec03 3-1	Dec31 1-0		Apr12 2-1	Mar04 1-0	Mar18 3-0	Apr22 1-0	Mar25 2-0	Jan21 0-3	Oct29 2-0	Sep17 1-1	Jan02 1-1
HEARTS	Mar04 0-3	Sep17 1-1	Jan21 1-0	Mar25 0-3	Oct29 0-1	Oct01 3-1	Dec10 2-1	Nov12 1-1	Dec17 1-1		Jan02 0-0	Apr22 1-0	Dec31 1-2	Apr01 0-0	Oct15 1-1	Feb11 1-0	Nov19 4-0	Apr19 5-1
HIBERNIAN	Feb25 1-0	Apr29 0-2	Apr15 4-1	Oct08 3-5	Mar28 1-1	Mar28 2-1	Oct22 2-2	Jan03 2-0	Nov05 3-1	Sep10 1-0		Feb04 3-1	Apr29 2-1	Sep24 7-0	Nov26 2-5	Dec24 1-1	Apr08 1-1	Dec03 6-0
KILMARNOCK	May01 1-1	Oct29 1-0	Sep17 1-0	Dec03 0-3	Jan07 1-3	Jan21 4-4	Mar20 4-0	Dec10 1-1	Nov19 3-0	Dec24 1-2	Oct15 2-1		Apr12 3-0	Nov05 0-1	Feb11 1-2	Mar25 5-3	Jan02 3-0	Oct01 2-1
MOTHERWELL	Apr04 3-2	Jan02 2-2	Oct29 0-0	Apr08 0-2	Jan21 1-1	Feb11 5-3	Nov19 1-1	Nov26 6-2	Apr01 1-2	Apr29 1-0	Oct01 1-2	Dec17 2-0		Mar11 5-0	Mar04 1-5	Oct15 3-3	Apr19 4-0	Sep17 1-1
PARTICK T	Mar18 1-1	Apr08 2-2	Mar27 4-1	Sep17 1-4	Oct29 0-1	May06 3-0	Feb11 0-0	Oct22 1-0	Nov26 1-1	Jan07 1-4	Apr29 1-2	Oct01 2-2		Jan02 1-1	Jan21 1-3	Oct01 2-2	Oct15	
RANGERS	Sep24 3-0	Dec17 3-0	Nov19 4-0	May06 2-2	Apr22 1-1	Dec31 2-3	Jan14 3-1	Apr01 0-1	Oct08 5-0	Feb04 6-1	Mar25 3-1	Nov09 6-1	Nov05 5-1	Sep10		Mar29 4-3	Feb25 3-0	Dec10
ST JOHNSTONE	Jan03 1-0	Apr01 1-0	Apr26 3-0	Jan14 0-4	Dec17 2-4	Mar04 0-3	Sep10 2-0	Sep24 3-3	Feb25 2-1	Oct22 3-2	Apr22 1-2	Nov26 1-3	Feb04 1-1	Oct08 3-5	Nov12 1-1		Dec31 3-0	Mar18 4-1
ST MIRREN	Nov12 1-3	Jan21 0-3	Dec24 3-1	Mar04 0-5	Nov26 1-3	Apr01 0-5	Apr01 0-1	Oct15 0-5	Mar11 1-2	Dec10 3-0	Sep10 1-3	Sep10 3-2	Jan14 0-3	Nov02 1-6	Apr27 0-0			Feb11 4-0
STIRLING A	Dec17 2-6	Mar11 0-0	Nov05 1-1	Feb25 1-1	Apr29 2-5	Nov26 2-3	Oct08 1-4	Mar29 1-1	Sep10 1-1	Sep24 0-3	Apr01 1-0	Jan14 1-4	Jan03 0-0	Feb04 1-3	Apr08 0-1	Apr08 2-1	Nov19 2-0	

DIVISION 2

Home \ Away	ALB	ALL	ARB	BER	BRE	CLY	COW	DUM	EFI	ESt	FOR	HAM	MON	MOR	QoS	QPk	RAI	STE	STR	TLA
ALBION R		Mar11 0-2	Feb18 0-4	Nov26 2-3	Oct15 4-2	Jan21 0-2	Apr29 0-0	Apr01 2-2	Dec24 5-1	Oct01 5-1	Nov19 1-0	Jan02 1-0	Feb11 4-1	Sep14 2-0	Aug24 1-0	Oct29 1-1	Sep17 4-1	Dec17 1-1		Jan28 1-0
ALLOA	Nov12 1-4		Oct01 3-3	Sep07 2-1	Apr26 4-1	Mar04 3-0	Sep21 2-1	Apr22 3-2	Apr12 2-2	Dec31 4-3	Mar25 1-3	Sep17 3-2	Dec03 0-1	Oct29 1-1	Mar18 0-2	Dec10 2-3	Feb11 2-0	Jan02 0-1	Feb18 2-3	Oct15 2-1
ARBROATH	Sep24 1-1	Jan14 3-0		Oct22 1-0	Apr29 4-1	Sep21 3-0	Nov05 2-1	Mar11 1-1	Feb04 2-0	Apr12 3-0	Nov19 9-2	Jan03 3-2	Dec24 3-0	Oct08 0-0	Feb25 2-1	Dec10 2-1	Mar25 5-1	Apr01 1-0	Apr01 1-0	Sep07 2-1
BERWICK R	Mar25 2-1	Sep14 2-1	Feb11 3-1		Oct29 3-0	Oct15 1-5	Sep17 2-0	Dec01 0-1	Apr19 4-1	Apr11 2-1	Apr11 6-0	Oct01 0-1	Nov04 1-1	Aug24 1-1	Dec03 0-2	Feb03 2-0	Dec31 6-0	Jan02 3-1	Jan21 2-0	
BRECHIN C	Feb04 2-3	Oct08 4-1	Dec31 1-2	Feb25 2-1		Mar18 1-2	Dec17 0-0	Sep24 2-3	Aug24 1-1	Mar04 2-1	Jan03 1-2	Apr08 4-2	Sep10 2-4	Apr17 1-5	Jan14 3-3	Oct22 2-2	Nov12 2-4	Dec03 4-5	Nov26 5-1	Apr22 3-3
CLYDEBANK	Oct08 3-5	Nov05 0-2	Aug24 0-3	Feb04 2-4	Nov19 4-2		Mar25 2-3	Sep10 1-3	Sep14 2-3	Dec10 3-1	Mar11 3-0	Apr01 0-4	Jan14 0-4	Oct22 0-1	Dec31 3-3	Jan03 4-2	Apr29 3-2	Feb25 2-3	Feb25 4-0	Feb18 0-2
COWDENBEATH	Dec31 0-2	Aug24 1-2	Mar04 0-2	Apr08 0-1	Apr15 2-2	Nov26 4-0		Jan14 6-1	Jan21 2-2	Dec24 2-3	Dec24 3-1	Feb11 3-3	Sep10 4-2	Dec10 0-1	Sep07 3-0	Apr01 1-2	Oct29 0-1	Apr01 7-0	Oct15 2-1	Mar18 2-1
DUMBARTON	Dec03 3-0	Dec24 2-1	Nov12 1-3	Apr08 0-2	Feb18 2-2	Jan02 2-2	Oct01		Sep17 0-3	Oct15 4-1	Sep21 1-2	Jan21 1-3	Mar18 2-0	Nov26 0-1	Oct29 1-1	Apr11 4-0	Sep07 2-3	Mar04 3-1	Feb11 1-0	Apr28 5-1
EAST FIFE	Apr22 1-2	Dec17 1-0	Oct15 0-1	Sep24 2-1	Sep21 4-0	Sep07 3-1	Oct08 2-1	Jan03 2-1		Mar18 0-0	Dec10 2-4	Oct29 2-1	Nov12 3-1	Apr01 0-1	Mar04 1-2	Jan14 1-1	Sep10 1-2	Feb11 4-3	Dec31 2-2	Nov26 3-1
E STIRLING	Jan14 2-0	Apr29 2-1	Apr17 1-0	Sep17 1-1	Nov05 3-1	Apr08 1-5	Mar11 2-3	Feb04 4-0	Nov19 0-4		Oct22 2-4	Nov26 1-4	Feb25 0-0	Jan03 1-2	Dec24 2-2	Oct08 0-0	Sep24 1-2	Sep07 1-3	Apr07 0-5	Apr01 1-0
FORFAR A	Mar18 4-2	Nov26 2-3	Jan02 0-2	Apr26 4-1	Sep17 0-3	Nov12 4-1	Apr22 0-3	Aug24 0-2	Apr08 1-2	Feb11 2-2		Apr19 3-3	Dec31 5-2	Mar04 1-2	Dec03 3-4	Sep14 1-2	Oct15 2-2	Oct01 3-4	Jan21 2-2	Oct29 2-3
HAMILTON A	Sep10 2-1	Jan03 4-3	Mar18 0-2	Jan14 1-1	Dec10 0-0	Dec03 0-0	Oct22 1-0	Oct08 4-2	Feb25 3-0	Mar25 3-1	Sep24 3-0		Feb04 2-1	Dec31 1-2	Apr15 1-0	Nov05 3-3	Apr22 1-3	Nov12 0-0	Sep07 0-2	Sep21 1-1
MONTROSE	Dec10 1-2	Apr01 3-0	Sep17 2-1	Jan02 1-0	Jan28 2-0	Sep07 1-1	Nov19 5-1	Mar11 3-1	Oct29 1-2	Apr29 2-2	Oct15 1-3	Oct15 0-2		Apr15 2-0	Mar25 2-0	Apr26 1-1	Jan21 1-0		Feb11 0-0	Feb11 4-1
MORTON	Oct22 2-1	Feb25 6-0	Apr22 2-0	Mar11 1-0	Sep28 4-1	Oct01 6-0	Jan02 2-0	Mar25 2-0	Dec03 4-0	Sep17 3-0	Nov05 6-1	Apr29 7-0	Dec17		Feb04 3-1	Nov22 5-0	Oct08 1-0	Oct04 9-1	Apr08 5-0	Dec26 6-0
QUEEN OF SOUTH	Sep07 7-4	Nov19 2-1	Jan21 2-3	Sep21 1-1	Oct01 6-0	Feb11 2-0	Apr08 0-1	Feb25 2-3	Nov05 2-3	Apr22 0-2	Apr01 2-1	Oct17 4-2	Nov26 6-2	Oct15 2-5		Apr19 1-2	Dec31 2-0	Feb18 2-2	Jan02 1-0	Dec03 3-2
QUEEN'S PARK	Sep21 5-1	Apr08 4-1	Mar28 0-0	Feb18 2-1	Feb11 2-1	Mar22 4-2	Apr22 2-2	Dec17 1-1	Oct01 4-1	Jan21 1-1	Sep07 7-2	Mar04 1-3	Apr22 2-3	Apr24 1-2	Nov12 3-4		Nov26 1-2	Oct15 4-1	Sep17 4-0	Jan02 3-1
RAITH R	Feb25 2-1	Oct22 3-1	Apr08 0-2	Nov19 1-3	Mar11 0-1	Sep17 6-1	Dec03 2-0	Sep14 1-0	Jan02 6-1	Feb18 3-1	Feb04 1-1	Dec24 5-1	Aug24 0-7	Jan21 2-4	Apr29 0-1	Mar25 7-2		Apr12 1-1	Nov05 2-1	Oct01 4-1
STENHOUSEMUIR	Jan03 0-0	Sep10 1-2	Nov26 3-0	Apr29 2-1	Apr01 3-0	Dec24 4-4	Feb25 1-1	Nov05 1-1	Oct22 2-3	Sep12 6-3	Jan14 0-5	Apr25 5-3	Oct08 1-3	Aug24 1-4	Sep24 2-6	Feb04 1-2	Apr18 0-4		Nov19 3-2	Apr08 0-2
STRANRAER	Apr15 0-2	Sep24 2-1	Dec03 2-1	Apr29 2-4	Feb25 2-1	Oct29 2-2	Feb04 2-3	Oct22 2-1	Apr29 0-3	Aug24 3-0	Oct08 3-1	Sep14 0-4	Jan14 4-1	Dec10 1-3	Oct10 1-1	Sep10 2-1	Jan03 1-1	Mar04 1-2		Nov12 2-2
T LANARK	Nov05 2-0	Feb04 3-0	Sep14 2-0	Oct08 3-0	Dec24 1-1	Apr15 1-0	Nov19 1-1	Dec31 0-1	Mar25 3-2	Dec03 0-0	Feb25 6-2	Aug24 3-2	Oct22 7-4	Sep24 1-1	Apr25 3-3	Sep10 4-3	Jan14 1-6	Dec10 3-1	Mar11 1-3	

League Cup results for 1966-67 are detailed on pages 197-198.

Season 1967-68

SFA Cup

1st Preliminary
Dec 16	Dumbarton 0	Berwick R	0
Dec 16	Elgin C 3	Albion R	1
Dec 16	Fraserburgh 1	E Stirling	4
Dec 16	Hawick RA. 4	Vale of Leithen	..0
Dec 16	Stranraer 2	Stenhousemuir	...2

Replay
Dec 23	Berwick R 2	Dumbarton	1
Dec 23	Stenhousemuir ...5	Stranraer	0

2nd Preliminary
Jan 6	Berwick R 2	Nairn Co	.0
Jan 6	Brechin C 2	Montrose	1
Jan 17	Forfar A 3	Queen's Park	2
Jan 13	Keith 1	E Stirling	3
Jan 6	Queen of South ...2	Clydebank	2
Jan 6	St Cuthbert's 2	Hawick RA.	6
Jan 6	Stenhousemuir ...1	Alloa	3
Jan 6	Tarff R 2	Elgin C	3

Replay
Jan 17	Clydebank 2	Queen of South	..2
Jan 18	Clydebank 0	Queen of South	...1
	played at Firhill Park		

1st Round
Jan 27	Aberdeen 1	Raith R	.1
Jan 27	Ayr U 0	Arbroath	.2

(continued)
Jan 27	Celtic 0	Dunfermline A 2
Jan 27	Clyde 2	Berwick R 0
Jan 27	Cowdenbeath 0	Dundee 1
Jan 27	Dundee U 3	St Mirren 1
Jan 27	East Fife 3	Alloa 0
Jan 27	E Stirling 3	Hibernian 5
Jan 27	Elgin C 3	Forfar A 1
Jan 27	Hearts 4	Brechin C 1
Jan 27	Morton 4	Falkirk 0
Jan 27	Motherwell 1	Airdrie 1
Jan 27	Partick T 0	Kilmarnock 0
Jan 27	Queen of South ...1	Stirling A 1
Jan 27	Rangers 3	Hamilton A 1
Jan 27	St Johnstone 3	Hawick RA. 0

Replays
Jan 31	Airdrie 1	Motherwell 0
Jan 31	Kilmarnock 1	Partick T 2
Jan 31	Raith R 0	Aberdeen 1
Jan 31	Stirling A 1	Queen of South ...3

2nd Round
Feb 17	Airdrie 1	Hibernian 0
Feb 17	Dundee 1	Rangers 1
Feb 17	Dundee U 5	Hearts 6
Feb 19	Dunfermline A 2	Aberdeen 1
Feb 17	East Fife 0	Morton 0
Feb 17	Elgin C 2	Arbroath 0
Feb 23	Partick T 3	Clyde 2
Feb 17	St Johnstone 5	Queen of South ...2

Replays
Feb 21	Morton 5	East Fife 2
Mar 4	Rangers 4	Dundee 1

3rd Round
Mar 9	Dunfermline A 1	Partick T 0
Mar 9	Morton 2	Elgin C 1
Mar 9	Rangers 1	Hearts 1
Mar 9	St Johnstone 2	Airdrie 1

Replay
Mar 13	Hearts 1	Rangers 0

Semi-finals
Mar 30	Dunfermline A 1	St Johnstone 1
	played at Tynecastle		
Mar 30	Hearts 1	Morton 1
	played at Hampden Park		

Replays
Apr 2	Dunfermline A 2	St Johnstone 1
	played at Tynecastle		
Apr 2	Hearts 2	Morton 1
	played at Hampden Park		

Final
Apr 27	Dunfermline A 3	Hearts 1
	played at Hampden Park		

A stretcher is called for as Dunfermline's Jim Fraser lies injured, while Celtic's Bertie Auld is booked for the foul. Dunfermline won this Scottish Cup-tie 2-0 and went on to collect the trophy by beating Hearts in the Final.

DIVISION 1

(home ↓ / away →)	ABERDEEN	AIRDRIE	CELTIC	CLYDE	DUNDEE	DUNDEE U	DUNFERMLINE A	FALKIRK	HEARTS	HIBERNIAN	KILMARNOCK	MORTON	MOTHERWELL	PARTICK T	RAITH R	RANGERS	ST JOHNSTONE	STIRLING A
ABERDEEN		Apr20 3-2	Apr10 0-1	Sep23 1-2	Sep09 6-2	Oct14 0-0	Oct07 2-0	Mar30 2-0	Feb10 2-0	Mar16 0-5	Apr06 1-1	Feb12 1-0	Nov25 0-1	Mar02 6-2	Nov11 1-0	Dec30 1-4	Apr17 1-0	Dec16 1-0
AIRDRIE	Dec23 1-0		Nov11 0-2	Oct21 1-2	Nov04 0-0	Sep30 2-0	Mar20 1-2	Sep16 1-1	Apr13 2-2	Mar06 1-2	Feb21 3-2	Feb03 2-0	Jan01 2-2	Apr27 0-0	Jan20 4-1	Mar30 1-2	Mar16 2-1	Nov25 3-1
CELTIC	Mar06 4-1	Mar13 4-0		Sep09 3-0	Apr13 5-2	Dec02 1-1	Dec30 3-2	Nov18 3-0	Dec09 3-1	Oct07 4-0	Nov15 3-0	Apr20 2-1	Oct24 4-2	Feb03 4-1	Mar23 5-0	Jan02 2-2	Sep23 1-1	Feb14 2-0
CLYDE	Mar27 1-0	Feb10 0-0	Jan01 2-3		Nov25 1-0	Dec16 5-0	Mar02 0-2	Sep23 6-3	Jan20 2-2	Apr06 2-2	Oct28 2-1	Mar16 4-2	Dec23 5-0	Sep16 4-2	Apr30 1-3	Oct14 0-1	Apr10 2-0	Nov11 2-0
DUNDEE	Jan01 0-2	Mar02 6-2	Dec16 4-5	Mar23 3-0		Sep16 2-2	Nov18 4-0	Apr27 1-1	Apr17 1-0	Nov11 1-4	Jan20 6-5	Apr24 0-3	Sep30 2-1	Dec02 3-4	Dec23 4-0	Feb10 2-4	Oct14 1-4	Nov08 4-2
DUNDEE U	Feb03 2-3	Mar25 1-0	Mar30 0-5	Apr13 2-1	Jan02 0-0		Apr20 1-4	Mar06 3-2	Sep23 2-1	Nov25 2-2	Oct07 3-2	Nov04 1-1	Oct21 2-2	Apr16 3-3	Apr02 0-0	Sep09 2-2		Dec30 9-0
DUNFERMLINE A	Jan20 2-0	Apr06 0-2	Apr30 1-2	Nov04 1-0	Mar16 2-0	Dec23 2-2		Oct21 1-2	Sep16 1-3	Feb03 0-1	Sep30 1-2	Mar23 4-0	Jan06 6-0	Dec16 1-2	Jan01 1-0	Mar06 6-0	Nov11 1-0	Dec02 6-0
FALKIRK	Dec02 2-2	Jan02 3-1	Mar16 0-3	Jan13 0-1	Dec30 0-2	Oct28 1-2	Feb10 1-1		Mar02 4-1	Apr20 2-3	Oct14 1-1	Dec16 1-1	Nov11 1-0	Nov25 2-3	Apr06 0-2	Sep23 0-1	Oct07 1-1	Sep09 0-0
HEARTS	Oct21 2-1	Dec16 3-1	Apr06 0-2	Oct14 2-3	Sep23 1-0	Nov01 1-0	Jan02 1-2	Nov04 1-0		Sep09 1-4	Apr10 1-0	Oct30 3-0	Feb28 3-2	Mar16 1-1	Mar04 0-1	Jan13 2-3	Nov25 1-1	Apr01 2-1
HIBERNIAN	Nov18 1-0	Oct28 5-0	Jan20 0-2	Apr24 2-1	Mar09 2-0	Jan06 3-0	Oct14 2-0	Dec23 1-1	Jan01 1-0		Apr27 3-3	Dec02 0-1	Apr13 2-1	Sep30 5-1	Sep16 3-0	Mar23 1-3	Feb10 4-2	Mar02 5-2
KILMARNOCK	Dec09 3-0	Sep23 2-2	Mar02 0-6	Feb28 5-1	Oct07 0-0	Apr17 4-0	Feb06 1-1	Feb03 3-0	Dec02 3-2	Dec30 1-0		Sep09 3-1	Mar16 1-1	Nov11 0-3	Oct21 1-2	Apr13 1-2	Jan02 1-0	5-2
MORTON	Sep30 3-3	Oct14 4-0	Dec23 0-4	Nov18 3-1	Dec09 0-0	Nov20 5-2	Nov25 0-3	Apr13 2-1	Apr29 1-0	Jan01 3-2			Sep16 2-1	Jan06 2-0	Nov04 3-3	Apr17 3-3	Oct28 0-2	Feb10 2-0
MOTHERWELL	Mar23 0-3	Sep09 1-2	Feb10 0-1	Apr20 0-1	Nov13 2-4	Mar02 1-3	Sep23 1-1	Mar09 1-1	Oct28 2-5	Dec16 0-1	Nov18 1-2	Jan02 2-1		Apr06 2-1	Dec02 2-2	Oct07 0-2	Dec30 2-1	Oct14 3-1
PARTICK T	Nov04 2-2	Dec30 3-1	Oct14 1-5	Jan02 2-0	Mar30 1-1	Feb10 1-0	Apr13 1-2	Mar23 2-2	Nov18 3-3	Jan13 1-2	Mar13 1-0	Sep23 0-1	Dec09 2-2		Feb28 3-0	Sep09 0-2	Apr20 0-4	Oct07 2-1
RAITH R	Mar09 3-1	Oct07 1-1	Nov25 0-3	Dec30 1-1	Apr20 0-2	Nov18 0-1	Sep09 1-2	Dec09 1-1	Feb10 2-4	Apr02 2-2	Feb10 1-2	Mar02 3-1	Mar30 3-1	Oct28 2-3		Apr13 2-3	Mar23 3-2	Sep23 7-1
RANGERS	Apr27 2-3	Dec02 2-1	Sep16 1-0	Feb03 1-0	Oct23 2-0	Apr06 4-1	Oct28 0-0	Jan06 2-0	Sep30 1-1	Nov25 2-0	Dec23 4-1	Nov11 1-0	Jan20 2-0	Jan01 5-2	Dec16 10-2		Mar02 6-2	Mar16 5-0
ST JOHNSTONE	Sep16 1-1	Nov18 0-0	Mar25 1-6	Dec02 0-2	Feb03 0-2	Apr24 2-1	Mar13 0-1	Jan20 0-1	Mar23 3-2	Oct21 2-3	Dec16 0-1	Nov06 1-2	Apr27 1-0	Dec23 2-1	Sep30 1-0	Nov04 2-3		Apr06 3-0
STIRLING A	Apr13 0-3	Mar23 0-4	Sep30 0-4	Mar09 3-0	Mar06 0-3	Apr27 2-2	Apr10 2-1	Mar13 1-2	Dec23 1-4	Nov04 4-1	Sep16 0-0	Oct21 0-6	Feb03 1-2	Jan20 2-1	Feb17 0-7	Nov18 2-4	Dec09 0-0	

DIVISION 2

(home ↓ / away →)	ALBION R	ALLOA	ARBROATH	AYR U	BERWICK R	BRECHIN C	CLYDEBANK	COWDENBEATH	DUMBARTON	EAST FIFE	E STIRLING	FORFAR A	HAMILTON A	MONTROSE	QUEEN OF SOUTH	QUEEN'S PARK	ST MIRREN	STENHOUSEMUIR	STRANRAER
ALBION R		Sep25 2-0	Mar09 1-1	Oct07 0-2	Nov18 5-2	Dec30 3-1	Jan13 0-0	Dec02 0-2	Apr10 3-1	Sep23 1-2	Mar02 3-2	Oct14 4-1	Sep09 2-0	Oct28 2-0	Sep13 3-0	Feb10 3-5	Apr24 0-5	Apr20 6-0	Apr06 3-0
ALLOA	Sep20 1-1		Dec30 0-2	Dec02 1-3	Aug23 1-5	Mar16 3-1	Feb03 0-1	Nov01 1-1	Oct07 2-0	Jan02 3-1	Apr20 2-0	Feb10 3-2	Oct28 0-2	Oct14 2-1	Sep09 2-1	Apr17 0-1	4-3	0-1	4-1
ARBROATH	Nov11 1-0	Apr27 3-2		Apr20 2-0	Apr10 1-0	Sep27 8-1	Feb10 4-0	Dec16 6-3	Apr06 5-0	Oct28 0-4	Mar27 1-1	Jan01 1-0	Oct14 2-1	Sep16 1-0	Jan20 2-1	Dec02 1-1	Sep30 0-1	Nov25 8-0	Mar16 1-0
AYR U	Jan20 5-2	Feb17 2-1	Dec23 3-1		Apr27 1-0	Apr06 0-0	Aug23 3-1	Nov04 1-0	Feb17 3-0	Nov25 2-0	Sep30 4-0	Dec16 1-2	Apr17 1-0	Sep16 4-0	Mar09 2-3	Jan01 1-3	Oct14 0-3	3-0	Sep20 5-2
BERWICK R	Mar16 0-1	Sep13 0-1	Sep23 0-2	Dec30 1-0		Dec02 1-0	Oct28 1-1	Apr06 2-0	Nov04 2-1	Jan13 0-1	Sep09 2-1	Apr24 2-1	Oct14 1-1	Feb10 0-2	Apr01 0-3	Nov25 1-3	Jan02 2-0	1-2	Nov11 2-1
BRECHIN C	Apr27 2-0	Nov18 1-1	Sep20 1-2	Apr10 5-1	Mar30 0-1		Nov11 1-1	Mar23 2-4	Jan20 1-3	Apr20 0-1	Oct14 4-1	Sep16 2-1	Oct28 2-1	Jan01 0-0	Mar02 1-1	Sep30 1-0	Dec16 0-4	Feb10 1-0	Apr24 2-0
CLYDEBANK	Sep30 2-2	Nov04 4-1	Oct21 2-3	Feb23 2-2	Feb17 1-0	Mar09 2-2		Sep16 2-0	Jan01 2-1	Sep27 3-1	5-5	Apr20 2-3	Apr06 3-2	Apr02 0-2	Jan20 2-4	Oct14 2-0	Oct14 0-2	Jan27 2-0	Dec02 5-1
COWDENBEATH	Mar30 2-3	Mar09 1-0	Sep20 0-3	Jan24 2-0	Dec09 2-2	Nov25 0-2	Jan02 0-2		Sep27 6-2	Sep09 1-2	Apr17 4-3	Oct28 2-0	Sep23 2-1	Apr20 4-2	Oct14 0-0	Feb10 1-3	1-2	Oct07 3-0	Feb10 2-0
DUMBARTON	Nov25 1-0	Apr13 3-0	Dec09 3-4	Apr29 1-0	Apr17 1-0	Oct07 2-0	Sep09 5-4	Sep20 2-0		Jan02 1-1	Oct28 2-0	Feb10 1-0	Jan13 1-3	Nov11 1-1	Mar30 0-4	Dec30 0-2	Aug23 0-4	Mar02 1-1	Sep23 4-0
EAST FIFE	Jan06 1-0	Jan20 4-0	Apr02 2-0	Oct21 1-0	Sep30 2-1	Dec23 3-0	Apr10 6-0	Jan01 3-3	Sep16 3-3		Apr06 6-0	Aug23 3-1	Dec02 0-0	Mar23 2-2	Apr27 2-1	Dec16 2-2	Nov04 2-1	Nov11 3-0	2-1
E STIRLING	Nov04 2-2	Sep16 3-0	Apr13 1-2	Apr22 2-0	Jan01 4-0	Feb03 0-0	Mar09 0-2	Sep30 1-1	Feb17 2-2	Dec09 1-2		Apr10 2-1	Nov18 1-4	Mar30 4-0	Jan20 2-2	Apr27 2-3	1-1	Aug23 5-0	Oct21 2-2
FORFAR A	Feb03 2-1	Mar23 1-1	Sep09 1-1	Mar30 1-1	Apr13 1-1	Jan02 2-2	Dec16 2-0	Feb17 3-3	Oct21 1-1	Apr17 2-1	Sep23 3-2		Mar09 3-2	Sep13 1-1	Nov18 0-5	Nov04 0-1	Dec23 0-1	Dec30	Oct07 1-1
HAMILTON A	Jan01 1-2	Dec23 0-0	Feb03 1-0	Apr13 0-4	Nov04 1-2	Feb17 1-3	Nov25 1-0	Jan06 2-1	Sep30 3-3	Mar30 0-1	Mar16 1-0	Nov11 2-1		Apr27 2-2	Dec09 2-1	Sep16 1-1	Jan20 1-3	Sep20 1-0	Aug23 3-0
MONTROSE	Feb17 3-0	Oct21 1-2	Jan02 2-2	Sep23 2-2	Feb03 3-0	Sep07 1-0	Dec23 3-2	Nov09 2-1	Dec02 1-3	Nov04 2-0	Apr13 1-1	Jan27 1-2	Apr10 3-5		Apr20 1-1	Sep20 2-3	Apr02 0-0	4-1	Sep09 1-2
QUEEN OF SOUTH	Aug23 1-0	Mar27 4-1	Oct07 1-0	Jan02 4-1	Oct21 0-3	Nov04 5-0	Sep23 5-2	Feb03 2-1	Dec30 4-4	Nov11	Mar16	Apr06	Dec16				Apr20 1-3	Sep20 1-1	Apr02 4-0
QUEEN'S PARK	Oct21 2-2	Dec09 3-1	Mar20 2-1	Nov11 1-1	Sep20 4-0	Feb28 1-1	Feb03 4-0	Mar12 4-1	Jan24 2-3	Apr13 3-0	Oct07 4-5	Apr29 0-0	Jan02 2-1	Aug23 1-2	Dec23 3-0		Feb17 1-4	Sep23 2-0	Nov25 2-1
ST MIRREN	Apr13 2-2	Feb03 6-1	Apr17 1-1	Sep09 3-3	Apr29 3-0	Sep23 3-2	Mar16 2-2	Oct21 4-0	Sep13 2-0	Dec30 7-0	Apr20 3-1	Oct07 2-0	Dec09 2-1	Apr27 1-0	Nov18	Sep30		Dec02 7-1	Jan02 2-0
STENHOUSEMUIR	Apr16 1-1	Jan01 1-1	Mar23 0-3	Feb03 1-1	Sep16 1-4	Oct21 2-1	Apr13 1-3	Jan20 1-1	Nov04 2-3	Mar09 0-3	Sep11 2-1	Apr27 3-1	Sep27 1-1	Nov18 0-3	Sep30 2-1	Apr24 0-2	Mar30 2-4		Feb17 3-1
STRANRAER	Dec09 2-2	Sep30 3-0	Nov18 1-5	Apr02 2-0	Mar09 0-3	Apr13 1-0	Mar30 1-1	Apr27 2-1	Jan06 1-3	Oct14 1-3	Feb10 1-2	Jan20 1-2	Sep13 1-2	Mar02 3-1	Jan01 2-4	Mar23 2-3	Sep16 0-1	Oct28 2-0	

DIVISION 1 FINAL TABLE

	P	W	D	L	F	A	Pts
Celtic	34	30	3	1	106	24	63
Rangers	34	28	5	1	93	34	61
Hibernian	34	20	5	9	67	49	45
Dunfermline A	34	17	5	12	64	41	39
Aberdeen	34	16	5	13	63	48	37
Morton	34	15	6	13	57	53	36
Kilmarnock	34	13	8	13	59	57	34
Clyde	34	15	4	15	55	55	34
Dundee	34	13	7	14	62	59	33
Partick T	34	12	7	15	51	67	31
Dundee U	34	10	11	13	53	72	31
Hearts	34	13	4	17	56	61	30
Airdrie	34	10	9	15	45	58	29
St Johnstone	34	10	7	17	43	52	27
Falkirk	34	7	12	15	36	50	26
Raith R	34	9	7	18	58	86	25
Motherwell	34	6	7	21	40	66	19
Stirling A	34	4	4	26	29	105	12

DIVISION 2 FINAL TABLE

	P	W	D	L	F	A	Pts
St Mirren	36	27	8	1	100	23	62
Arbroath	36	24	5	7	87	34	53
East Fife	36	21	7	8	71	47	49
Queen's Park	36	20	8	8	76	47	48
Ayr U	36	18	6	12	69	48	42
Queen of South	36	16	6	14	73	57	38
Forfar A	36	14	10	12	57	63	38
Albion R	36	14	9	13	62	55	37
Clydebank	36	13	8	15	62	73	34
Dumbarton	36	11	11	14	63	74	33
Hamilton A	36	13	7	16	49	58	33
Cowdenbeath	36	12	8	16	57	62	32
Montrose	36	10	11	15	54	64	31
Berwick R	36	13	4	19	34	54	30
E Stirling	36	9	10	17	61	74	28
Brechin C	36	8	12	16	45	62	28
Alloa	36	11	6	19	42	69	28
Stranraer	36	8	4	24	41	80	20
Stenhousemuir	36	7	6	23	34	93	20

League Cup results for 1967-68 are detailed on page 199.

SFA Cup

1st Preliminary

Dec 14	Alloa	6	Ross Co	1
Dec 14	Brechin C	1	Montrose	1
Dec 14	Cowdenbeath	1	Clydebank	0
Dec 14	Forfar A	1	Nairn Co	2
Dec 14	St Cuthbert's	1	Civil Service	0

Replay

Dec 18	Montrose	3	Brechin C	2

2nd Preliminary

Jan 4	Alloa	0	E Stirling	0
Jan 4	Dumbarton	3	Vale of Leithen	2
Jan 4	Glasgow Univ	5	St Cuthbert's	2
Jan 4	Hamilton A	0	Cowdenbeath	2
Jan 4	Montrose	6	Fraserburgh	1
Jan 4	Nairn Co	0	Berwick R	2
Jan 4	Stenhousemuir	1	Albion R	0
Jan 4	Stranraer	2	Elgin C	0

Replay

Jan 8	E Stirling	2	Alloa	1

1st Round

Jan 25	Aberdeen	3	Berwick R	0
Jan 25	Ayr U	1	Queen of South	0
Jan 25	Dumbarton	0	St Mirren	1
Jan 25	Dundee	1	Hearts	2
Jan 25	Dundee U	2	Queen's Park	1
Jan 25	E Stirling	2	Stirling A	0
Jan 25	Falkirk	1	Morton	2
Jan 25	Kilmarnock	6	Glasgow Univ	0
Jan 25	Montrose	1	Cowdenbeath	0
Jan 25	Motherwell	1	Clyde	1
Jan 25	Partick T	3	Celtic	3
Jan 25	Raith R	0	Dunfermline A	2
Jan 25	Rangers	1	Hibernian	0
Jan 25	St Johnstone	3	Arbroath	2
Jan 25	Stenhousemuir	0	Airdrie	3
Jan 25	Stranraer	3	East Fife	1

Replays

Jan 28	Clyde	2	Motherwell	1
Jan 29	Celtic	8	Partick T	1

2nd Round

Feb 25	Aberdeen	2	Dunfermline A	2
Feb 12	Airdrie	1	St Mirren	1
Feb 12	Clyde	0	Celtic	0
Feb 8	Dundee U	6	Ayr U	2
Feb 8	E Stirling	1	St Johnstone	1
Feb 8	Montrose	1	Kilmarnock	1
Feb 24	Rangers	2	Hearts	0
Feb 8	Stranraer	1	Morton	3

Replays

Feb 12	Kilmarnock	4	Montrose	1
Feb 24	Celtic	3	Clyde	0
Feb 24	St Johnstone	3	E Stirling	0
Feb 24	St Mirren	1	Airdrie	3
Feb 26	Dunfermline A	0	Aberdeen	2

3rd Round

Mar 1	Aberdeen	0	Kilmarnock	0
Mar 1	Celtic	3	St Johnstone	2
Mar 1	Dundee U	2	Morton	3
Mar 1	Rangers	1	Airdrie	0

Replay

Mar 5	Kilmarnock	0	Aberdeen	3

Semi-finals

Mar 22	Aberdeen	1	Rangers	6
	played at Celtic Park			
Mar 22	Celtic	4	Morton	1
	played at Hampden Park			

Final

Apr 26	Celtic	4	Rangers	0
	played at Hampden Park			

League Cup results for 1968-69 are detailed on pages 199-200.

League Cup results for 1968-69 are detailed on pages 199-200.

DIVISION 1 FINAL TABLE

	P	W	D	L	F	A	Pts
Celtic	34	23	8	3	89	32	54
Rangers	34	21	7	6	81	32	49
Dunfermline A	34	19	7	8	63	45	45
Kilmarnock	34	15	14	5	50	32	44
Dundee U	34	17	9	8	61	49	43
St Johnstone	34	16	5	13	66	59	37
Airdrie	34	13	11	10	46	44	37
Hearts	34	14	8	12	52	54	36
Dundee	34	10	12	12	47	48	32
Morton	34	12	8	14	58	68	32
St Mirren	34	11	10	13	40	54	32
Hibernian	34	12	7	15	60	59	31
Clyde	34	9	13	12	35	50	31
Partick T	34	9	10	15	39	53	28
Aberdeen	34	9	8	17	50	59	26
Raith R	34	8	5	21	45	67	21
Falkirk	34	5	8	21	33	69	18
Arbroath	34	5	6	23	41	82	16

DIVISION 1

	ABERDEEN	AIRDRIE	ARBROATH	CELTIC	CLYDE	DUNDEE	DUNDEE U	DUNFERMLINE A	FALKIRK	HEARTS	HIBERNIAN	KILMARNOCK	MORTON	PARTICK T	RAITH R	RANGERS	ST JOHNSTONE	ST MIRREN
ABERDEEN		Apr05 3-1	Nov16 2-2	Jan11 1-3	Oct19 0-1	Jan01 0-0	Sep21 0-1	Mar24 2-2	Dec21 2-0	Oct05 1-2	Dec07 2-6	Apr19 0-1	Apr02 6-3	Feb01 1-1	Nov02 2-1	Apr09 0-0	Sep14 2-0	Nov23 2-0
AIRDRIE	Dec14 2-0		Sep07 2-0	Dec28 0-0	Mar05 1-0	Sep28 0-3	Apr23 1-0	Nov23 2-2	Jan02 1-1	Sep21 2-1	Dec07 3-1	Oct12 0-2	Mar10 2-2	Apr12 2-1	Mar24 2-0	Nov16 3-0	Oct26 1-1	
ARBROATH	Mar08 2-1	Apr30 0-2		Nov09 0-5	Apr19 1-1	Oct19 1-2	Jan11 3-1	Feb15 0-1	Mar22 3-0	Dec21 2-3	Nov23 3-4	Oct05 1-2	Jan04 3-3	Dec14 2-2	Feb01 2-0	Nov02 3-1	Mar29 2-0	Sep14 1-1
CELTIC	Sep28 2-1	Apr19 2-2	Mar05 7-1			Jan01 5-0	Nov02 3-1	Oct05 2-0	Jan04 3-1	Apr09 5-2	Feb01 5-0	Mar24 1-1	Dec21 1-1	Apr28 2-4	Mar15 1-0	Nov16 2-0	Sep14 2-4	Oct19 2-1
CLYDE	Apr23 1-1	Nov09 3-1	Mar18 0-3	Sep07 0-3		Jan18 0-0	Mar11 0-2	Mar08 3-0	Oct26 2-0	Mar29 0-1	Oct12 1-1	Nov30 2-1	Dec14 0-0	Jan02 1-2	Sep21 3-2	Nov23 1-1	Jan11 0-3	Apr12 0-0
DUNDEE	Sep07 4-4	Jan11 1-1	Feb08 3-0	May01 1-2	Oct05 2-3		Jan02 1-2	Nov09 1-0	Mar08 0-0	Oct26 2-0	Dec14 0-1	Mar15 1-1	Mar29 0-1	Nov30 1-2	Mar26 2-2	Apr22 3-2	Sep21 2-3	Oct12 2-0
DUNDEE U	Jan04 1-4	Oct19 2-1	Sep28 4-2	Jan18 1-3	Nov02 1-0	Sep14 3-1		Apr19 2-2	Dec07 2-1	Nov16 4-2	Mar31 3-0	Feb01 2-2	Nov23 2-0	Dec21 2-1	Mar05 3-1	Apr05 2-1	Jan01 4-2	Mar22 2-2
DUNFERMLINE A	Nov30 5-1	Mar15 1-0	Oct26 2-0	Sep21 1-1	Nov16 2-1	Mar05 2-0	Dec28		Feb01 2-0	Jan02 4-2	Apr28 1-1	Jan11 1-1	Sep07 5-3	Mar29 2-0	Sep07 3-2	May01 0-3	Oct05 3-1	Dec14 6-2
FALKIRK	Apr12 1-0	Sep14 2-1	Nov30 2-2	Dec14 0-0	Feb15 3-3	Nov16 0-1	Mar29 2-2	Oct12 0-1		Oct19 1-3	Jan04 0-1	Apr12 1-1	Jan01 4-1	Apr19 2-2	Mar15 1-3	Jan18 0-3	Nov02 2-1	Sep28 0-0
HEARTS	Jan18 3-2	Jan04 1-1	Apr12 2-2	Oct12 0-1	Dec07 2-3	Mar12 2-2	Mar08 1-0	Sep14 3-1	Apr02 2-1		Jan01 0-0	Nov02 0-1	Mar24 2-2	Nov09 2-0	Dec14 1-0	Sep28 1-1	Nov23 2-2	Apr19 2-1
HIBERNIAN	Mar29 1-1	Sep14 5-1	Mar15 1-2	Nov30 2-5	Apr01 2-1	Apr08 1-3	Oct26 1-1	Sep21 3-1	Sep07 1-3		Oct19 1-0	Oct12 5-0	Jan02 1-2	Nov09 3-0	Jan02 4-0	Mar01 3-0		
KILMARNOCK	Dec28 2-1	Mar29 5-1	Jan18 1-2	Apr21 2-2	Mar22 0-0	Nov23 1-0	Oct12 3-0	Sep28 5-1	Nov09 1-0	Feb22 1-1	Feb19		Sep14 4-4	Mar08 3-3	Oct26 2-0	Jan04 0-0	Dec14	Jan01
MORTON	Nov09 1-0	Feb01 1-1	Sep21 5-1	Oct26 1-1	Apr05 1-1	Dec07 2-1	Mar15 1-2	Feb22 0-2	Sep07 2-0	Nov30 0-2	Mar08 4-3	Jan02 3-2		Oct05 3-3	Jan11 3-2	Apr12 0-2	Apr12 4-4	Mar18 3-0
PARTICK T	Oct12 1-0	Nov02 1-1	Apr05 2-1	Nov23 0-4	Sep14 4-0	Mar22 4-0	Apr12 1-2	Dec07 1-2	Mar04 5-1	Mar01 2-1	Oct28 4-2	Sep28 0-2		Feb11 2-1	Jan01 0-2	Apr12 1-1	Jan04 0-2	
RAITH R	Mar19 3-2	Dec21 1-2	Oct12 3-1	Mar08 1-3	Jan04 1-1	Apr19 4-0	Nov09 1-2	Jan01 0-3	Nov23 4-0	Apr05 3-2	Sep14 3-0	Mar04 0-3	Sep28	Oct19		Dec07 0-3	Mar22 1-5	Jan18 0-2
RANGERS	Oct26 2-3	Nov30 1-1	Mar11 2-0	Jan02 1-0	Mar15 6-0	Apr28 1-1	Dec14 2-1	Oct19 3-0	Oct05 2-1	Jan11 2-0	Nov09 6-1	Sep21 3-3	Apr19 3-0	Sep07 2-0	Mar29 2-1		Feb01 3-0	Mar08 6-0
ST JOHNSTONE	Jan02 3-1	Mar08 3-1	Dec07 5-1	Apr01 2-3	Sep28 0-0	Jan04 3-1	Sep07 1-4	Dec14 2-1	Apr23 4-0	Mar15 2-1	Apr05 2-1	Dec21 1-0	Oct26 2-3	Nov30 2-2	Oct12 3-0			Nov09 2-3
ST MIRREN	Mar15 1-2	Feb15 1-2	Jan02 2-1	Mar29 0-3	Dec21 1-0	Feb01 2-3	Nov30 1-1	Apr05 1-2	Jan11 3-0	Dec28 1-1	Nov02 3-0	Sep07 1-0	Oct19 2-1	Sep21 1-0	Oct05 2-2	Nov16 1-0	Mar05 1-2	

Action from the 1969 Scottish Cup Final. Although Celtic's Chalmers went on to score from this challenge on Rangers' Martin, his effort was disallowed. However, Celtic did manage to put four past Rangers that day and complete the treble of League title and both Cups.

DIVISION 2

	ALBION R	ALLOA	AYR U	BERWICK R	BRECHIN C	CLYDEBANK	COWDENBEATH	DUMBARTON	EAST FIFE	E STIRLING	FORFAR A	HAMILTON A	MONTROSE	MOTHERWELL	QUEEN OF SOUTH	QUEEN'S PARK	STENHOUSEMUIR	STIRLING A	STRANRAER
ALBION R		Mar08 2-0	Apr19 0-1	Apr05 2-1	Jan25 2-1	Nov30 3-1	Jan11 1-0	Feb01 1-2	Dec21 4-1	Nov02 2-1	Sep14 2-1	Jan01 5-0	Sep18 5-4	Apr29 0-1	Nov09 1-0	Oct05 0-0	Apr26 4-2	Mar15 2-1	Oct19 1-1
ALLOA	Nov16 1-2		Sep04 1-2	Sep11 1-0	Sep28 2-0	Jan18 3-3	Nov30 0-1	Mar29 1-2	Apr19 2-0	Mar15 0-3	Jan25 3-1	Apr26 2-0	Mar01 0-1	Oct12 1-2	Apr12 2-2	Apr15 4-4	Jan01 1-2	Nov02 0-2	Sep14
AYR U	Dec28 3-0	Aug21 3-0		Jan11 2-0	Dec21 6-1	Apr05 0-0	Feb01 4-0	Mar01 4-0	Feb15 2-1	Nov30 6-1	Nov02 4-1	Dec07 1-0	Jan02 4-0	Apr23 1-1	Oct05 2-2	Sep21 1-5	Oct19 7-1	Nov16 1-2	Mar15 3-0
BERWICK R	Dec14 0-0	Sep18 3-2	Sep28 1-1		Jan18 0-0	Mar26 5-0	Mar29 0-4	Oct19 2-0	Sep14 2-0	Jan01 3-0	Apr19 0-0	Nov02 0-0	Mar01 3-1	Sep04 1-3	Apr12 0-2	Mar15 1-1	Oct12 2-4	Feb15 0-1	Feb15 1-5
BRECHIN C	Sep21 1-4	Jan11 1-3	Apr12 0-3	Oct05 2-1		Aug21 3-1	Nov02 5-1	Apr09 5-1	Apr05 0-3	Nov16 1-2	Nov23 0-2	Sep18 2-1	Sep07 0-0	Mar22 1-1	Apr23 4-4	Dec07 4-4	Mar01 0-1	Oct19 1-2	Feb01 0-1
CLYDEBANK	Mar22 2-0	Oct05 0-2	Apr28 0-1	Sep21 1-1	Sep04 0-0		Sep18 1-1	Sep07 0-1	Nov23 1-4	Oct19 0-4	Jan04 3-0	Mar04 5-0	Feb15 5-0	Nov16 0-4	Jan11 3-3	Jan02 1-3	Mar29 2-2	Apr19 2-2	Nov02 2-2
COWDENBEATH	Sep28 0-2	Mar22 2-3	Oct12 1-1	Dec07 1-1	Apr14 3-0	Sep11 3-3		Nov23 3-1	Sep14 0-4	Oct19 1-3	Dec21 1-3	Jan18 1-2	Mar08 2-3	Oct19 0-5	Apr19 1-2	Sep18 6-0	Nov16 0-1		Apr26 4-1
DUMBARTON	Oct12 3-1	Dec07 4-1	Nov09 0-3	Feb08 3-1	Oct26 2-1	Jan01 3-3	Mar15 0-3		Dec14 1-1	Apr25 4-1	Mar08 2-3	Nov30 2-4	Aug21 0-2	Apr12 2-4	Feb22 0-2	Dec28 5-1	Jan18 1-3	Sep14 3-2	Sep28 2-1
EAST FIFE	Apr12 2-0	Dec28 5-0	Oct26 1-0	Jan02 4-1	Mar26 6-1	Mar15 1-1	Sep07 1-0	Sep18 1-1		Mar29 3-2	Oct05 1-2	Jan11 5-0	Nov02 6-1	Feb08 3-1	Sep21 1-1	Aug21 0-0	Nov30 5-0	Mar01 3-2	Nov16 2-1
E STIRLING	Apr23 1-0	Nov23 5-1	Mar22 2-1	Sep07 7-3	Mar08 0-1	Apr14 1-0	Jan02 1-0	Sep21 4-1	Dec07 3-0		Nov09 2-4	Apr05 1-0	Dec28 5-1	Oct26 0-4	Feb01 2-1	Sep11 6-0	Jan01 0-1		Aug21 2-2
FORFAR A	Jan02 4-1	Sep21 1-1	May01 0-1	Apr23 0-1	Apr28 3-3	Apr12 1-0	Feb08 1-3	Nov16 2-0	Apr26 3-2	Mar01 3-0		Aug21 1-1	Nov30 1-0	Sep07 1-0	Apr05 1-0	Oct26 2-1	Oct12 9-1	Sep28 3-2	Dec07 2-1
HAMILTON A	Sep07 3-5	Oct26 3-2	Mar29 2-2	Apr09 2-0	May01 2-1	Oct12 1-2	Apr12 2-2	Mar22 0-0	Sep28 0-1	Dec14 0-0	Sep04 1-3		Sep21 4-4	Jan02 0-1	Feb08 0-3	Nov23 0-2	Nov16 2-1	Jan18 1-1	Mar01 1-3
MONTROSE	Sep11 1-3	Nov09 2-1	Sep14 0-2	Mar08 1-0	Apr02 6-1	Oct26 5-3	May01 3-0	Sep04 2-0	Feb22 3-1	Jan18 2-2	Mar22 0-0	Apr16 1-2		Nov23 0-2	Oct12 1-0	Apr23 3-1	Sep28 3-0	Apr19 0-2	Apr19 2-0
MOTHERWELL	Aug21 7-0	Feb01 4-0	Sep18 4-1	Nov09 7-1	Nov30 2-0	Mar08 2-1	Oct05 4-1	Dec21 1-1	Oct19 4-0	Apr19 3-1	Jan01 2-1	Sep14 4-1	Mar15		Dec07 2-2	Jan11 5-1	Apr14 7-1	Apr26 3-0	Apr05
QUEEN OF SOUTH	Mar01 3-0	Dec21 3-0	Apr26 3-2	Aug21 1-0	Apr19 1-2	Sep28 1-1	Nov16 4-0	Nov02 4-1	Jan04 4-2	Apr02 3-3	Apr14 5-0	Oct19 1-2	Feb01 1-0	Mar29 1-2		Sep11 3-1	Sep14 5-1	Nov30 0-1	Jan01 0-2
QUEEN'S PARK	Jan18 1-1	Feb08 4-0	Jan04 0-3	Dec21 3-1	Mar12 2-1	Sep14 2-4	Apr19 0-1	Apr19 2-0	Sep04 0-2	Oct12 3-2	Feb15 2-2	Mar05 1-0	Oct19 1-0	Sep28 1-2	Sep18 0-4		Nov02 2-0	Jan01 0-2	Nov30 1-1
STENHOUSEMUIR	Oct26 2-3	Sep07 4-4	Apr08 0-3	Nov23 1-3	Nov09 2-1	Dec07 0-0	Dec28 1-3	Oct05 3-2	Mar22 1-4	Sep18 0-2	Feb01 1-2	Mar08 3-1	Jan11 2-2	Sep21 1-6	Jan02 3-4	Apr21 2-1		Apr05 2-0	Dec21 1-1
STIRLING A	Nov23 1-1	Feb22 1-1	Mar08 0-0	Feb01 3-1	Feb08 3-0	Dec28 2-0	Aug21 2-1	Jan02 3-0	Nov09 1-2	Apr12 1-1	Jan11 2-1	Oct05 7-1	Dec07 2-0	Oct26 0-4	Mar22 2-3	Sep07 3-0	Dec14 5-1		Sep18 3-2
STRANRAER	Apr14 3-0	Jan02 1-1	Nov23 0-2	Oct26 2-0	Oct12 3-1	Feb22 1-1	Sep21 0-1	Jan11 1-2	Mar08 1-2	Apr29 1-1	Mar29 3-0	Nov09 1-0	Dec28 0-1	Dec14 0-2	Sep07 2-0	Mar22 2-0	Apr12 5-2	Apr21 2-1	

DIVISION 2 FINAL TABLE

	P	W	D	L	F	A	Pts
Motherwell	36	30	4	2	112	23	64
Ayr U	36	23	7	6	82	31	53
East Fife	36	21	6	9	82	45	48
Stirling A	36	21	6	9	67	40	48
Queen of South	36	20	7	9	75	41	47
Forfar A	36	18	7	11	71	56	43
Albion R	36	19	5	12	60	56	43
Stranraer	36	17	7	12	57	45	41
E Stirling	36	17	5	14	70	62	39
Montrose	36	15	4	17	59	71	34
Queen's Park	36	13	7	16	50	59	33
Cowdenbeath	36	12	5	19	54	67	29
Clydebank	36	6	15	15	52	67	27
Dumbarton	36	11	5	20	46	69	27
Hamilton A	36	8	8	20	37	72	24
Berwick R	36	7	9	20	42	70	23
Brechin C	36	8	6	22	40	78	22
Alloa	36	7	7	22	45	79	21
Stenhousemuir	36	6	6	24	55	125	18

After their entry into the Scottish League in 1923 Dundee United wore black and white, but in 1969 the 'Tannadice Terriors' became the 'Tannadice Tangerines' when they changed to their now familiar strip. Players in this group are, back row (left to right): Rolland, Briggs, Gillespie, Mackay, Reid, Smith, Stuart. Front row: J.Cameron, Hogg, Gordon, K.Cameron, Mitchell, Scott, Markland.

SFA Cup

1st Preliminary

Dec 6	Alloa	3	Peterhead	1
Dec 6	Berwick R	1	Brechin C	0
Dec 6	Forres Mechanic	0	Clydebank	2
Dec 6	Stenhousemuir	0	Gala Fairydean	1
Dec 6	Stranraer	3	E Stirling	1

2nd Preliminary

Dec 24	Albion R	1	Berwick R	0
Dec 24	Clydebank	1	Queen's Park	0
Dec 27	Gala Fairydean	1	Dumbarton	4
Dec 20	Inverness C	5	Ross Co	0
Dec 20	Montrose	2	Cowdenbeath	1
Dec 20	Stranraer	1	St Cuthbert's	1
Dec 27	Tarff R	1	Alloa	0
Dec 20	Vale of Leithen	1	Hamilton A	2

Replay

Dec 25	St Cuthbert's	0	Stranraer	5

1st Round

Jan 24	Aberdeen	4	Clyde	0
Jan 24	Airdrie	5	Hamilton A	0
Jan 24	Albion R	1	Dundee	2
Jan 24	Arbroath	1	Clydebank	2
Jan 24	Celtic	2	Dunfermline A	1
Jan 24	Dumbarton	1	Forfar A	2
Jan 24	Dundee U	1	Ayr U	0
Jan 24	East Fife	3	Raith R	0
Jan 24	Falkirk	3	Tarff R	0
Jan 24	Kilmarnock	3	Partick T	0
Jan 24	Montrose	1	Hearts	1
Jan 24	Morton	2	Queen of South	0
Jan 24	Motherwell	2	St Johnstone	1
Jan 24	Rangers	3	Hibernian	1
Jan 24	St Mirren	2	Stirling A	0
Jan 24	Stranraer	2	Inverness C	5

Replays

Jan 27	Hearts	1	Montrose	0

2nd Round

Feb 11	Aberdeen	2	Clydebank	1
Feb 7	Celtic	4	Dundee U	0
Feb 7	Dundee	3	Airdrie	0
Feb 7	East Fife	1	Morton	0
Feb 7	Falkirk	2	St Mirren	1
Feb 7	Forfar A	0	Rangers	7
Feb 7	Kilmarnock	2	Hearts	0
Feb 7	Motherwell	3	Inverness C	1

3rd Round

Feb 21	Celtic	3	Rangers	1
Feb 21	East Fife	0	Dundee	1
Feb 21	Falkirk	0	Aberdeen	1
Feb 21	Motherwell	0	Kilmarnock	1

Semi-finals

Mar 14	Aberdeen	1	Kilmarnock	0
	played at Muirton Park			
Mar 14	Celtic	2	Dundee	1
	played at Hampden Park			

Final

Apr 11	Aberdeen	3	Celtic	1
	played at Hampden Park			

Season 1969-70

DIVISION 1

(home \ away)	ABERDEEN	AIRDRIE	AYR U	CELTIC	CLYDE	DUNDEE	DUNDEE U	DUNFERMLINE A	HEARTS	HIBERNIAN	KILMARNOCK	MORTON	MOTHERWELL	PARTICK T	RAITH R	RANGERS	ST JOHNSTONE	ST MIRREN
ABERDEEN	—	Jan31 0-1	Feb25 1-0	Oct29 2-3	Aug30 6-0	Sep27 1-1	Nov08 0-0	Mar21 0-0	Apr04 0-1	Mar09 0-2	Apr06 2-2	Sep13 2-2	Nov22 4-1	Oct11 2-1	Jan10 5-1	Dec20 2-3	Mar02 0-0	Mar18 1-1
AIRDRIE	Sep06 3-4	—	Apr08 0-0	Oct11 0-2	Nov24 4-4	Feb25 0-1	Jan17 6-3	Apr04 3-0	Sep03 1-2	Mar07 3-2	Apr01 1-0	Mar21 1-1	Mar11 1-0	Nov29 2-3	Mar04 3-0	Nov08 1-3	Oct29 3-1	Mar20 1-0
AYR U	Oct04 1-2	Dec06 1-3	—	Nov01 2-4	Mar14 1-0	Jan31 3-2	Feb28 2-3	Dec01 1-0	Oct18 0-0	Aug30 3-0	Jan03 3-2	Sep27 1-0	Oct27 1-0	Apr18 2-1	Nov15 2-1	Sep13 2-1	Feb14 0-0	Mar28 1-1
CELTIC	Mar25 1-2	Feb28 4-2	Mar21 3-0	—	Sep27 2-1	Dec06 7-2	Jan31 1-1	Nov08 4-0	Sep13 6-1	Dec20 2-0	Mar10 1-0	Apr04 2-1	Dec27 2-0	Oct04 1-0	Jan03 0-0	Aug30 3-0	Dec01 2-1	
CLYDE	Dec13 2-1	Apr18 0-1	Oct25 0-1	Jan01 0-2	—	Mar07 1-1	Sep03 2-2	Feb21 2-1	Dec16 2-1	Mar28 1-0	Nov01 2-3	Nov15 0-2	Sep06 0-2	Sep20 2-1	Feb07 1-1	Mar31 1-0	Oct11 3-0	Jan17 1-0
DUNDEE	Jan01 2-0	Oct04 4-2	Sep06 1-0	Apr06 1-2	Oct18 3-0	—	Sep20 1-2	Nov08 1-1	Nov22 2-0	Feb20 1-0	Dec27 3-0	Feb28 2-1	Mar25 1-3	Apr01 4-1	Apr17 0-0	Apr04 2-1	Apr04 0-2	Nov29 2-1
DUNDEE U	Mar28 2-0	Sep13 5-2	Oct11 3-1	Mar07 0-2	Mar11 3-1	Jan03 4-1	—	Apr22 1-3	Jan10 2-3	Nov15 0-1	Dec06 2-2	Jan31 5-4	Feb21 0-0	Nov01 1-0	Apr18 4-2	Aug30 0-0	Sep27 0-1	Oct25 3-1
DUNFERMLINE A	Nov01 2-1	Nov15 4-2	Sep03 0-1	Sep06 0-2	Oct04 0-3	Mar28 2-3	Dec10 1-0	—	Sep20 1-0	Apr18 1-2	Oct18 2-1	Feb28 1-2	Mar25 2-1	Jan17 1-1	Jan01 0-1	Mar14 2-1	Apr10 3-0	Dec13 2-0
HEARTS	Nov15 2-2	Dec20 5-0	Mar07 3-0	Mar28 0-0	Apr11 1-3	Dec27 2-2	Jan03 2-0	Sep20 0-2	—	Jan01 4-1	Aug30 0-1	Oct11 2-2	Nov01 1-1	Jan31 3-2	Feb21 1-2	Mar25 0-0	Dec06 1-0	Feb21 2-0
HIBERNIAN	Apr13 1-2	Nov11 3-1	Dec13 4-3	Jan17 1-2	Nov08 1-0	Feb16 4-1	Apr04 3-1	Nov22 3-0	Jan01 0-0	—	Mar25 2-1	Oct04 1-1	Nov29 1-1	Sep06 5-1	Sep20 3-1	Feb28 2-2	Mar21 3-1	Sep03 2-0
KILMARNOCK	Nov29 0-2	Apr11 1-0	Sep20 4-1	Sep03 2-4	Mar21 2-1	Oct11 3-0	Feb11 3-1	Mar07 0-0	Jan17 2-2	Oct25 0-0	—	Nov08 5-2	Dec13 2-2	Feb25 4-2	Sep06 1-0	Apr04 2-2	Dec02 4-1	Jan01 1-1
MORTON	Jan17 3-2	Nov01 3-3	Jan01 1-0	Nov29 0-3	Apr04 1-0	Oct25 0-1	Sep06 6-0	Oct11 3-1	Dec13 2-3	Feb21 1-1	Mar28 1-1	—	Sep20 1-0	Apr14 4-1	Sep03 2-1	Nov22 2-2	Mar07 1-1	Jan10 2-1
MOTHERWELL	Apr18 0-2	Sep27 2-2	Apr13 3-0	Nov15 1-2	Jan31 1-0	Dec20 0-1	Oct04 0-2	Feb28 0-0	Apr01 0-1	Aug30 0-0	Mar02 1-0	Mar28 3-1	—	Mar14 1-2	Oct29 2-2	Sep13 2-2	Nov01 1-1	Nov01 3-0
PARTICK T	Feb28 0-3	Feb14 1-3	Nov22 1-3	Feb16 1-5	Mar03 1-0	Aug30 1-2	Mar21 1-2	Sep13 1-0	Mar14 3-1	Jan31 1-0	Oct04 2-2	Apr08 1-2	Nov08 2-2	—	Oct18 1-1	Sep27 1-2	Feb07 4-3	Apr04 0-0
RAITH R	Dec27 0-1	Aug30 1-0	Apr04 1-1	Feb25 0-2	Dec06 1-1	Sep13 0-0	Nov22 0-1	Sep27 1-1	Mar21 0-3	Jan03 0-3	Jan31 2-3	Dec20 2-1	Oct25 2-2	Mar07 1-1	—	Mar11 2-1	Nov08 1-0	Oct11 1-3
RANGERS	Sep03 2-0	Mar28 1-1	Jan17 3-0	Sep20 0-1	Dec27 3-0	Nov01 3-1	Feb21 2-1	Oct25 2-0	Mar25 3-2	Oct11 1-5	Nov15 3-0	Apr18 2-2	Mar07 2-1	Jan01 3-1	Nov29 3-0	—	Feb25 3-1	Sep06 2-0
ST JOHNSTONE	Sep20 3-1	Mar25 2-0	Dec10 1-4	Dec13 3-2	Feb28 1-4	Nov15 1-0	Jan01 0-0	Dec27 3-3	Sep06 1-0	Nov01 1-1	Apr18 4-0	Oct18 4-3	Jan17 5-2	Sep03 1-1	Mar28 1-3	Oct04 0-4	—	Apr13 2-3
ST MIRREN	Nov05 2-0	Jan03 1-1	Nov08 2-1	Apr18 2-3	Sep13 4-0	Mar10 2-1	Mar14 3-1	Aug30 0-0	Oct04 3-3	Mar03 0-2	Sep27 1-1	Dec27 2-3	Mar21 1-0	Nov15 2-3	Feb28 1-0	Jan31 3-3	Dec06 0-4	—

DIVISION 2

(home \ away)	ALBION R	ALLOA	ARBROATH	BERWICK R	BRECHIN C	CLYDEBANK	COWDENBEATH	DUMBARTON	EAST FIFE	E STIRLING	FALKIRK	FORFAR A	HAMILTON A	MONTROSE	QUEEN OF SOUTH	QUEEN'S PARK	STENHOUSEMUIR	STIRLING A	STRANRAER
ALBION R	—	Feb28 1-0	Apr18 2-2	Sep13 1-3	Apr14 3-2	Sep24 1-4	Mar14 0-2	Nov01 0-0	Aug30 1-0	Apr07 2-0	Oct04 0-4	Dec06 3-2	Sep27 0-0	Nov15 1-3	Apr27 3-1	Mar28 4-1	Jan31 2-0	Sep09 1-1	Mar31 2-1
ALLOA	Oct11 1-0	—	Nov15 1-0	Jan24 3-1	Aug30 0-1	Sep13 2-0	Nov01 1-3	Feb21 0-1	Jan03 2-1	Feb14 1-1	Apr28 5-2	Sep10 3-0	Jan31 1-0	Mar28 2-1	Mar07 0-3	Oct25 5-0	Sep27 0-2	Sep24 0-1	Apr11 1-1
ARBROATH	Nov22 3-1	Apr04 1-0	—	Apr22 4-0	Jan03 3-0	Jan31 2-0	Jan10 2-1	Mar07 5-0	Dec06 1-1	Sep24 3-1	Nov08 3-1	Sep10 1-0	Aug30 2-1	Oct25 4-0	Feb21 3-1	Oct11 1-2	Sep10 6-0	Dec20 0-1	Sep13 3-1
BERWICK R	Jan17 0-2	Sep03 3-0	Sep17 2-1	—	Dec27 2-0	Apr18 0-2	Dec13 1-3	Oct01 0-1	Oct25 4-0	Nov29 4-1	Feb21 1-3	Apr11 4-1	Feb07 5-1	Sep20 3-0	Mar03 3-0	Oct11 6-1	Mar07 3-0	Dec20 0-1	Nov15 1-0
BRECHIN C	Oct01 5-0	Dec13 1-2	Sep20 1-5	Apr28 2-0	—	Nov15 0-0	Sep06 2-2	Jan17 1-1	Apr01 1-4	Mar07 2-2	Apr11 0-2	Oct11 2-3	Apr18 3-0	Jan01 0-2	Feb07 1-5	Nov29 1-0	Mar28 1-3	Oct25 1-3	Nov01 3-1
CLYDEBANK	Nov29 3-0	Jan17 3-4	Sep06 0-2	Nov22 1-1	Apr04 1-1	—	Sep03 1-3	Jan01 0-0	Oct11 4-1	Oct25 2-0	Sep20 0-7	Mar07 0-1	Nov01 2-1	Dec13 1-3	Sep17 1-1	Oct01 1-3	Feb21 0-0	Apr27 0-2	Mar28 2-1
COWDENBEATH	Oct25 1-1	Mar21 0-2	Dec27 2-2	Aug30 3-0	Jan31 1-0	Apr22 3-2	—	Oct11 1-0	Sep27 2-1	Sep10 0-3	Mar31 2-1	Feb21 5-1	Mar25 3-1	Apr04 0-1	Jan03 4-0	Apr04 7-2	Dec06 0-0	Sep24 3-1	
DUMBARTON	Mar21 2-0	Oct04 1-3	Oct18 0-3	Apr13 2-1	Sep13 1-2	Sep27 1-5	Feb28 1-2	—	Feb14 2-0	Apr21 0-2	Mar14 1-2	Jan31 2-1	Oct29 2-1	Apr18 0-2	Nov08 2-0	Nov15 0-0	Nov12 5-1	Jan03 1-0	Aug30 1-0
EAST FIFE	Dec13 2-4	Sep20 4-0	Oct01 2-0	Mar14 2-1	Oct04 6-3	Feb28 1-1	Jan01 0-1	Sep17 2-1	—	Mar28 2-1	Sep06 1-2	Jan10 4-1	Nov15 4-0	Nov29 1-0	Apr15 0-2	Sep03 1-2	Apr18 4-2	Nov01 3-1	Oct18 1-1
E STIRLING	Sep20 2-1	Sep17 0-0	Apr01 3-2	Oct18 2-0	Mar14 3-3	Feb07 2-1	Apr28 0-6	Apr21 2-1	Nov08 3-1	—	Dec13 1-6	Apr04 1-0	Oct01 2-2	Oct11 4-2	Jan17 1-3	Jan01 1-1	Dec27 4-2	Nov22 1-0	Feb28 4-0
FALKIRK	Mar03 4-1	Apr07 1-0	Mar28 1-0	Mar24 5-0	Mar17 1-2	Jan03 2-0	Apr18 0-0	Oct25 1-1	Jan31 1-1	Aug30 3-3	—	Sep13 6-1	Mar10 5-0	Mar07 7-5	Oct11 3-1	Nov01 2-1	Dec20 0-3	Sep27 0-0	Apr21 1-0
FORFAR A	Sep03 3-2	Apr21 1-2	Jan01 2-1	Oct04 0-3	Feb28 2-0	Oct18 3-1	Sep17 1-2	Sep06 1-4	Dec27 4-1	Nov15 2-4	Apr14 0-3	—	Mar14 3-1	Sep20 5-2	Nov29 1-2	Dec13 2-1	Nov01 3-3	Mar28 0-1	Apr18 2-3
HAMILTON A	Jan01 2-6	Sep06 2-4	Dec13 2-4	Nov22 2-1	Nov22 2-0	Feb21 2-3	Feb07 1-3	Apr04 3-2	Feb21 3-0	Sep27 1-4	Sep10 2-3	Sep03 1-1	—	Oct01 0-1	Sep20 1-0	Mar07 3-2	Oct11 1-1	Oct11 3-2	Dec20 3-2
MONTROSE	Apr04 1-0	Nov08 1-4	Mar14 2-0	Sep10 2-4	Sep27 1-0	Aug30 4-1	Oct04 0-1	Nov22 0-2	Sep24 1-2	Apr11 1-2	Oct18 1-2	Jan03 2-6	Apr22 0-0	—	Mar21 2-1	Dec27 2-1	Feb14 0-1	Sep13 1-1	Jan31 3-2
QUEEN OF SOUTH	Dec27 1-0	Oct18 3-3	Oct04 2-1	Jan03 4-2	Apr22 1-0	Feb14 1-1	Nov15 2-2	Mar28 3-4	Sep10 2-1	Sep13 0-2	Feb28 1-0	Sep24 3-0	Dec06 4-1	Nov01 4-1	—	Apr18 3-0	Aug30 2-0	Jan31 1-0	Sep27 1-1
QUEEN'S PARK	Nov08 2-1	Mar11 3-2	Jan31 1-2	Jan31 1-2	Sep24 1-2	Oct18 0-0	Oct18 2-2	Apr04 0-2	Apr18 0-2	Sep27 3-3	Dec06 0-3	Aug30 3-0	Apr28 3-0	Nov22 0-3	Apr20 0-3	—	Sep13 1-0	Feb25 0-3	Sep10 0-1
STENHOUSEMUIR	Sep06 0-3	Jan01 2-1	Feb07 1-0	Feb28 4-2	Nov08 1-1	Oct04 1-6	Sep20 1-2	Nov29 2-0	Nov22 2-2	Jan24 3-3	Sep30 0-3	Mar21 3-0	Oct18 1-6	Sep16 1-2	Dec13 1-1	Jan17 1-0	—	Apr04 2-2	Mar14 1-1
STIRLING A	Apr10 6-0	Nov29 0-2	Sep03 1-1	Oct18 3-3	Mar14 1-1	Dec27 5-2	Oct01 3-1	Sep20 2-2	Mar21 3-1	Apr18 1-2	Jan01 0-3	Nov08 6-0	Feb28 3-1	Jan17 2-1	Sep06 0-2	Sep17 1-1	Nov15 2-0	—	Oct04 5-1
STRANRAER	Sep17 0-4	Oct01 0-4	Jan17 0-3	Apr04 3-3	Mar21 6-1	Nov08 1-2	Nov29 0-2	Dec13 6-1	Mar07 4-2	Oct11 4-1	Sep03 3-1	Nov22 1-3	Jan10 4-1	Sep06 1-3	Jan01 4-5	Feb07 0-4	Oct25 2-0	Feb21 2-4	—

DIVISION 1 FINAL TABLE

	P	W	D	L	F	A	Pts
Celtic	34	27	3	4	96	33	57
Rangers	34	19	7	8	67	40	45
Hibernian	34	19	6	9	65	40	44
Hearts	34	13	12	9	50	36	38
Dundee U	34	16	6	12	62	64	38
Dundee	34	15	6	13	49	44	36
Kilmarnock	34	13	10	11	62	57	36
Aberdeen	34	14	7	13	55	45	35
Dunfermline A	34	15	5	14	45	45	35
Morton	34	13	9	12	52	52	35
Motherwell	34	11	10	13	49	51	32
Airdrie	34	12	8	14	59	64	32
St Johnstone	34	11	9	14	50	62	31
Ayr U	34	12	6	16	37	52	30
St Mirren	34	8	9	17	39	54	25
Clyde	34	9	7	18	34	56	25
Raith R	34	5	11	18	32	67	21
Partick T	34	5	7	22	41	82	17

DIVISION 2 FINAL TABLE

	P	W	D	L	F	A	Pts
Falkirk	36	25	6	5	94	34	56
Cowdenbeath	36	24	7	5	81	35	55
Queen of South	36	22	6	8	72	49	50
Stirling A	36	18	10	8	70	40	46
Arbroath	36	20	4	12	76	39	44
Alloa	36	19	5	12	62	41	43
Dumbarton	36	17	6	13	55	46	40
Montrose	36	15	7	14	57	55	37
Berwick R	36	15	5	16	67	55	35
East Fife	36	15	4	17	59	63	34
Albion R	36	14	5	17	53	64	33
E Stirling	36	14	5	17	58	75	33
Clydebank	36	10	10	16	47	65	30
Brechin C	36	11	6	19	47	74	28
Queen's Park	36	10	6	20	38	62	26
Stenhousemuir	36	10	6	20	47	89	26
Stranraer	36	9	7	18	56	75	25
Forfar A	36	11	1	24	55	83	23
Hamilton A	36	8	4	24	42	92	20

League Cup results for 1969-70 are detailed on pages 200-201.

Season 1970-71

SFA Cup

1st Round

Dec 5	Brechin C	3	Nairn Co	1
Dec 5	E Stirling	0	Clydebank	2
Dec 5	Forfar A	2	Albion R	0
Dec 5	St Cuthbert's	1	Stranraer	3
Dec 5	Stenhousemuir	0	Elgin C	1

2nd Round

Dec 19	Brechin C	4	Glasgow Trans	1
Dec 19	Clacknacuddin	2	Glasgow Univ	1
Dec 19	Clydebank	2	Hamilton A	1
Dec 19	Elgin C	2	Berwick R	0
Dec 19	Forfar A	1	Gala Fairydean	0
Dec 19	Queen's Park	2	Montrose	1
Dec 19	Ross Co	1	East Fife	4
Dec 19	Stranraer	3	Dumbarton	2

3rd Round

Jan 25	Aberdeen	5	Elgin C	0
Jan 23	Airdrie	1	Alloa	1
Jan 23	Celtic	5	Queen of South	1
Jan 23	Clacknacuddin	0	Cowdenbeath	3
Jan 23	Clyde	2	Brechin C	0
Jan 23	Clydebank	0	Dundee U	0
Jan 23	Dundee	1	Partick T	0
Jan 23	Dunfermline A	3	Arbroath	1
Jan 23	East Fife	1	St Mirren	1
Jan 23	Hearts	3	Stranraer	0
Jan 23	Hibernian	8	Forfar A	1
Jan 23	Morton	2	Ayr U	0
Jan 23	Queen's Park	0	Kilmarnock	1
Jan 23	Rangers	3	Falkirk	0
Jan 23	St Johnstone	2	Raith R	2
Jan 23	Stirling A	3	Motherwell	1

Replays

Jan 26	Alloa	0	Airdrie	2
Jan 26	Raith R	4	St Johnstone	3
Jan 26	St Mirren	1	East Fife	1
Jan 27	Dundee U	5	Clydebank	1
Feb 1	St Mirren	3	East Fife	1

4th Round

Feb 13	Celtic	1	Dunfermline A	1
Feb 13	Cowdenbeath	0	Airdrie	4
Feb 13	Dundee	2	Stirling A	0
Feb 13	Dundee U	1	Aberdeen	1
Feb 13	Hearts	1	Hibernian	2
Feb 13	Morton	1	Kilmarnock	2
Feb 13	Raith R	1	Clyde	1
Feb 13	St Mirren	1	Rangers	3

Replay

Feb 17	Aberdeen	2	Dundee U	0
Feb 17	Clyde	0	Raith R	2
Feb 17	Dunfermline A	0	Celtic	1

5th Round

Mar 6	Celtic	7	Raith R	1
Mar 6	Hibernian	1	Dundee	0
Mar 6	Kilmarnock	2	Airdrie	3
Mar 6	Rangers	1	Aberdeen	0

Semi-finals

Apr 3	Airdrie	3	Celtic	3
	played at Hampden Park			
Mar 31	Hibernian	0	Rangers	0
	played at Hampden Park			

Replay

Apr 5	Hibernian	1	Rangers	2
	played at Hampden Park			
Apr 7	Airdrie	0	Celtic	2
	played at Hampden Park			

Final

May 8	Celtic	1	Rangers	1
	played at Hampden Park			

Replay

May 12	Celtic	2	Rangers	1
	played at Hampden Park			

Celtic pictured in 1970. Continuing their domination of League championships, this was fifth successive title; they also collected the Scottish Cup and reached the Final of the League Cup, where Rangers had their revenge with a 1-0 victory.

Beaten 1970-71 Finalists of the Scottish Cup and winners of the League Cup, Glasgow Rangers' squad of 70-71: Back row (left to right): Conn, Stein, Donaldson, Neef, McCloy, Jackson, R.Watson, D.Stevenson, N.Stevenson, Fyfe, I.MacDonald. Middle row: J.Wallace (coach), T.Craig (physio), K.Watson, Mathieson, Renton, McKinnon, Miller, Jardine, Johnstone, Smith, McCallum, Craven (assistant trainer), S.Anderson (trainer). Front row: W.Waddell (manager), Henderson, Semple, A.MacDonald, Alexander, Greig, Parlane, Penman, Morrison, Johnston, W.Thornton (assistant manager).

DIVISION 1

(home ↓ / away →)	ABERDEEN	AIRDRIE	AYR U	CELTIC	CLYDE	COWDENBEATH	DUNDEE	DUNDEE U	DUNFERMLINE A	FALKIRK	HEARTS	HIBERNIAN	KILMARNOCK	MORTON	MOTHERWELL	RANGERS	ST JOHNSTONE	ST MIRREN
ABERDEEN	—	Aug29 1-1	Mar24 4-1	Apr17 1-1	Nov07 3-0	Dec05 7-0	Jan01 3-0	Oct31 4-0	Oct10 3-2	Dec19 3-2	Oct10 1-0	Nov21 1-0	Sep26 3-0	Jan09 3-0	Mar30 3-1	Apr03 0-0	Feb20 0-0	Sep12 0-0
AIRDRIE	Dec26 0-4	—	Sep19 2-0	Oct17 1-3	Oct23 1-2	Oct03 2-1	Mar20 2-6	Feb06 1-2	Apr24 1-0	Apr26 7-1	Jan16 0-0	Dec05 2-0	Apr14 1-1	Nov07 0-2	Sep05 3-0	Mar10 4-3	Nov21 5-0	Apr17 1-1
AYR U	Nov14 0-1	Jan09 0-0	—	Dec19 1-2	Sep26 4-0	Apr17 1-2	Oct10 0-1	Mar13 1-0	Aug29 4-1	Feb27 1-1	Apr03 1-0	Feb20 2-0	Sep12 1-1	Jan01 2-1	Dec05 0-0	Nov21 2-1	Jan30 1-3	Oct31 1-1
CELTIC	Dec12 0-1	Feb20 4-1	Apr29 2-0	—	May01 6-1	Nov07 3-0	Sep26 3-0	Apr10 1-1	Jan30 1-0	Oct28 4-0	Oct28 3-2	Jan09 2-1	Nov14 3-0	Aug29 2-0	Apr12 3-0	Sep12 2-0	Oct10 1-0	Nov28 3-0
CLYDE	Mar13 1-2	Feb27 1-1	Jan16 0-0	Sep05 0-5	—	Oct17 1-3	Apr03 0-3	Oct03 3-1	Oct31 3-2	Dec26 1-2	Sep19 0-0	Dec19 0-1	Apr17 1-0	Nov21 1-0	Apr21 1-2	Mar20 2-2	Dec05 3-0	Feb06 0-1
COWDENBEATH	Apr10 1-2	Jan30 1-3	Dec12 1-3	Mar13 1-5	Feb20 1-1	—	Aug29 0-1	Nov28 0-2	Jan01 2-1	Nov14 0-1	Apr24 0-4	Sep12 1-4	Sep26 1-2	Oct10 0-2	Oct23 0-1	Apr14 1-3	Nov02 2-2	Mar27 1-2
DUNDEE	Sep05 1-2	Nov14 3-0	Feb06 2-1	Jan16 1-8	Nov28 1-3	Dec26 5-1	—		Apr05 2-3	Mar27 0-0	Oct03 1-2	Oct17 1-0	Mar13 1-0	Oct31 3-0	Feb24 4-0	Apr24 1-0	Feb27 0-1	Sep19 2-2
DUNDEE U	Mar10 0-2	Oct10 4-2	Nov07 1-2	Dec05 4-2	Apr14 0-4	Apr03 3-2	Sep12 3-2	—	Oct23 2-2	Apr17 4-1	Mar20 1-1	Aug29 3-2	Feb20 2-3	Jan09 2-2	Nov21 2-0	Sep26 0-2	Jan01 0-1	Dec19 2-1
DUNFERMLINE A	Feb06 1-0	Dec19 4-1	Dec26 5-0	Oct03 0-2	Mar06 0-0	Sep05 1-2	Nov21 0-0	Feb27 3-1	—	Sep19 2-4	Apr24 1-2	Apr17 3-3	Feb20 0-1	Mar20 3-0	Oct17 0-1	Nov07 1-1	Apr03 1-1	Jan16 1-0
FALKIRK	Apr24 1-0	Sep12 0-2	Oct23 2-0	Nov21 0-0	Aug29 1-1	Mar20 1-2	Dec12 2-2	Jan09 1-1	Jan30 3-2	—	Mar06 2-4	Nov28 0-0	Oct10 3-0	Feb20 2-1	Nov07 1-0	Apr03 3-1	Jan16 0-3	Apr10 2-1
HEARTS	Mar27 1-3	Sep26 5-2	Nov28 2-1	Feb27 1-1	Jan09 1-3	Dec19 1-0	Feb20 0-0	Nov14 2-2	Sep12 1-1	Nov11 3-0	—	Jan01 0-0	Jan30 2-2	Dec05 2-2	Apr17 0-1	Oct10 3-1	Aug29 1-3	Mar13 1-0
HIBERNIAN	Jan16 2-1	Apr10 3-1	Oct17 4-0	Sep19 2-0	Apr24 5-1	Jan02 2-2	Nov07 1-2	Dec26 0-1	Dec12 2-2	Apr03 1-3	Sep05 0-0	—	Nov21 1-0	Mar10 2-4	Feb06 5-3	Apr24 3-2	Mar20 1-2	Oct03 3-3
KILMARNOCK	Sep19 0-4	Nov28 2-3	Jan02 1-1	Mar20 1-4	Dec12 1-1	Jan16 2-1	Mar09 1-1	Feb20 2-1	Apr10 0-0	Oct03 3-2	Oct03 3-0	Apr17 4-1	—	Oct23 2-2	Dec26 4-1	Apr24 2-4	Nov07 2-4	Sep05 1-2
MORTON	Oct03 2-0	Mar13 1-4	Sep05 3-2	Dec26 0-3	Mar27 0-0	Feb06 1-0	Apr17 1-0	Sep19 5-4	Nov14 1-0	Oct17 0-3	Apr10 0-2	Nov18 2-1	Feb27 3-0	—	Jan16 0-2	Nov28 3-1	Dec19 2-1	Jan02 1-1
MOTHERWELL	Nov28 0-2	Jan01 1-1	Apr10 1-0	Oct31 0-5	Sep12 2-1	Feb27 1-3	Dec19 1-1	Mar27 1-2	Feb20 4-3	Mar13 1-1	Dec12 1-2	Oct10 4-0	Aug29 4-1	Sep26 2-0	—	Jan30 1-2	Jan09 4-1	Nov14 2-1
RANGERS	Oct17 0-2	Oct31 5-0	Mar27 2-0	Jan02 1-1	Nov14 5-0	Sep19 5-0	Dec05 0-0	Jan16 1-1	Mar13 5-0	Sep05 2-0	Feb06 0-0	Feb27 1-1	Feb27 4-2	Apr03 0-0	Oct03 3-1	—	Apr17 0-2	Dec26 1-0
ST JOHNSTONE	Jan02 0-1	Mar27 4-1	Oct03 4-1	Feb06 3-2	Apr10 2-1	Mar06 0-1	Oct23 3-3	Sep05 5-2	Nov28 1-0	Feb13 2-1	Dec26 2-1	Nov14 0-1	Mar13 2-3	Apr24 0-0	Sep19 2-1	Dec12 2-1	—	Oct17 2-0
ST MIRREN	Oct23 1-3	Dec12 2-4	Mar06 0-2	Apr27 2-2	Oct10 0-1	Nov21 1-0	Jan09 2-4	Apr24 2-1	Sep26 1-1	Dec05 2-3	Nov07 0-1	Jan30 3-1	Jan01 2-3	Sep12 2-1	Mar20 0-2	Aug29 0-0	Feb20 0-1	—

DIVISION 2

(home ↓ / away →)	ALBION R	ALLOA	ARBROATH	BERWICK R	BRECHIN C	CLYDEBANK	DUMBARTON	EAST FIFE	E STIRLING	FORFAR A	HAMILTON A	MONTROSE	PARTICK T	QUEEN OF SOUTH	QUEEN'S PARK	RAITH R	STENHOUSEMUIR	STIRLING A	STRANRAER
ALBION R	—	Dec19 1-0	Nov28 1-2	Apr21 1-0	Oct10 4-1	Feb10 0-1	Apr27 2-6	Aug29 1-3	Jan30 4-2	Mar27 1-1	Jan01 3-0	Apr10 0-1	Nov14 1-0	Sep09 4-0	Mar13 2-1	Feb27 2-0	Jan09 0-2	Sep26 1-1	Sep12 2-1
ALLOA	Apr24 1-1	—	Oct24 3-6	Nov28 1-1	Apr14 2-2	Dec12 1-3	Oct10 3-1	Sep12 2-2	Apr29 2-2	Nov07 2-1	Jan09 5-4	Mar20 2-5	Mar27 1-4	Apr10 2-1	Sep23 2-1	Apr21 2-1	Jan01 1-1	Aug29 2-1	Sep26 2-1
ARBROATH	Apr03 2-0	Feb27 6-2	—	Sep12 4-0	Sep09 2-2	Jan30 0-1	Feb13 1-0	Jan09 1-1	Sep26 5-1	Jan01 5-0	Mar27 7-3	Mar06 3-1	Dec05 0-2	Nov14 2-0	Apr17 1-0	Sep23 4-0	Nov07 2-0	Oct10 0-3	Oct17 3-1
BERWICK R	Oct17 1-2	Apr03 1-1	Jan02 2-0	—	Mar13 0-0	Nov14 1-1	Apr24 2-1	Oct24 2-2	Aug29 2-4	Dec12 2-1	Sep19 4-3	Oct03 1-1	Mar27 1-1	Dec05 6-2	Mar06 0-0	Feb06 1-2			
BRECHIN C	Feb06 0-2	Oct03 3-2	Sep16 1-4	Nov07 0-2	—	Apr28 2-0	Jan02 0-2	Nov28 1-1	Apr24 3-1	Mar06 1-1	Apr10 2-0	Sep05 0-1	Oct17 1-1	Oct24 0-7	Dec26 1-4	Jan16 1-2	Mar20 0-2	Dec12 2-0	Feb13 2-0
CLYDEBANK	Mar06 2-0	Apr17 1-1	Oct03 1-2	Mar20 1-2	Mar27 2-0	—	Sep05 2-1	Feb20 3-0	Feb24 0-0	Apr14 3-0	Sep23 1-4	Sep19 3-0	Dec26 3-1	Sep09 0-0	Oct10 7-1	Oct24 3-0	Oct24 6-5	Nov07 1-3	
DUMBARTON	Sep02 1-1	Feb06 5-1	Apr24 3-0	Sep26 6-2	Sep12 3-1	Jan01 3-1	—	Sep16 1-1	Apr10 3-0	Jan30 5-1	Nov21 4-1	Nov21 4-0	Feb27 2-2	Mar13 2-1	Apr29 4-1	Oct17 3-2	Dec12 3-2	Apr21 7-0	Aug29 2-0
EAST FIFE	Dec26 3-0	Jan02 3-1	Sep19 4-0	Feb10 1-0	Apr03 2-0	Oct17 3-2	Dec05 3-2	—	Mar20 6-2	Sep23 5-0	Feb27 3-1	Jan16 1-0	Oct03 0-3	Apr17 5-1	Feb17 5-1	Sep05 3-1	Mar06 1-1	Nov07 5-1	Nov21 0-1
E STIRLING	Oct03 1-2	Oct17 1-1	Jan16 2-1	Feb27 0-1	Apr21 2-1	Apr27 0-1	Jan23 3-1	Nov14 3-5	—	Apr17 3-1	Mar13 2-1	Dec26 1-1	Jan02 0-2	Sep19 0-3	Feb06 1-2	Sep23 4-2	Sep09 2-2	Sep09 2-5	Apr27 4-0
FORFAR A	Nov21 1-0	Mar13 8-1	Sep05 2-2	Nov21 1-1	Oct31 2-0	Apr24 1-1	Sep02 3-3	Dec12 1-1		—	Nov28 5-6	Feb20 1-1	Jan16 1-2	Sep19 3-3	Oct24 6-1	Apr10 1-3			Nov01 1-0
HAMILTON A	Sep05 1-3	Sep19 0-4	Nov21 4-1	Apr17 1-0	Apr26 2-0	Apr21 0-3	Mar06 1-1	Oct24 0-3	Nov07 0-3	Apr03 3-1	—	Feb06 2-3	Jan16 1-3	Jan02 3-0	Oct03 0-1	Dec26 2-2	Feb20 0-2	Mar20 0-2	Sep16 0-0
MONTROSE	Jan23 1-1	Nov14 4-2	Oct31 3-3	Jan09 4-0	Jan01 1-0	Sep12 0-1	Mar27 3-1	Sep26 2-0	Aug29 3-4	Sep09 4-1	Oct10 4-1	—	Apr17 2-2	Sep23 4-1	Dec05 2-1	Apr03 6-2	Jan30 2-2	Feb20 2-5	Feb20 4-0
PARTICK T	Mar20 3-0	Nov21 3-0	Apr10 1-1	Apr05 4-1	Feb20 5-0	Jan09 1-0	Jan30 1-1	Oct24 4-0	Sep12 5-0	Sep26 6-2	Oct10 5-2	Dec12 3-2	—	Nov28 3-1	Apr19 2-1	Nov07 1-0	Aug29 4-0	Jan01 2-0	Apr24 3-0
QUEEN OF SOUTH	Sep16 1-1	Dec05 3-2	Mar20 1-4	Jan30 2-1	Feb27 2-1	Aug29 3-1	Nov07 0-2	Dec12 2-3	Jan09 4-5	Oct17 2-2	Sep12 4-2	Sep02 2-0	Apr03 1-4	—	Oct31 3-2	Nov21 0-1	Sep26 1-2	Apr24 1-1	Jan01 2-1
QUEEN'S PARK	Nov07 2-3	Sep02 3-0	Dec12 2-4	Nov21 1-0	Aug29 1-0	Nov28 1-1	Oct10 2-1	Apr13 1-3	Sep26 2-1	Mar30 0-0	Apr21 1-0	Sep15 0-4	Mar06 1-1	Mar06 1-2	—	Mar20 0-1	Apr26 0-2	Sep12 0-6	Jan09 4-2
RAITH R	Oct24 2-2	Oct31 4-1	Sep02 2-1	Apr10 2-1	Sep26 5-0	Sep16 2-0	Feb13 1-0	Jan01 2-1	Oct10 1-1	Sep12 3-2	Apr24 0-0	Nov28 2-2	Mar27 0-2	Nov14 1-1	Nov14 6-4	—	Sep12 1-1	Jan30 4-1	Dec12 0-1
STENHOUSEMUIR	Sep19 3-3	Sep05 1-4	Mar13 1-0	Sep16 1-0	Nov14 2-0	Feb06 2-0	Apr17 2-3	Oct31 4-3	Sep02 2-2	Feb27 2-3	Jan23 4-4	Oct03 5-0	Dec26 0-0	Jan16 3-3	Oct17 2-1	Jan02 3-3	—	Mar27 5-1	Apr20
STIRLING A	Jan16 1-1	Dec26 5-0	Feb06 1-1	Apr29 0-1	Apr17 1-2	Feb27 2-0	Sep19 2-2	Mar13 1-1	Sep16 1-3	Apr26 3-1	Nov14 2-0	Oct17 0-1	Sep05 2-2	Dec19 1-0	Jan02 0-2	Oct03 0-1	Nov21 1-2	—	Apr03 0-1
STRANRAER	Jan02 4-1	Jan16 1-1	Feb20 1-1	Oct10 3-0	Sep23 1-0	Mar13 3-0	Dec26 2-2	Mar27 1-2	Mar06 5-2	Nov14 1-1	Sep09 2-0	Oct24 3-2	Apr14 1-2	Sep05 1-1	Sep19 4-0	Apr17 3-5	Apr10 1-2	Nov28 3-0	—

DIVISION 1 FINAL TABLE

	P	W	D	L	F	A	Pts
Celtic	34	25	6	3	89	23	56
Aberdeen	34	24	6	4	68	18	54
St Johnstone	34	19	6	9	59	44	44
Rangers	34	16	9	9	58	34	41
Dundee	34	14	10	10	53	45	38
Dundee U	34	14	8	12	53	54	36
Falkirk	34	13	9	12	46	53	35
Morton	34	13	8	13	44	44	34
Airdrie	34	13	8	13	60	65	34
Motherwell	34	13	8	13	43	47	34
Hearts	34	13	7	14	41	40	33
Hibernian	34	10	10	14	47	53	30
Kilmarnock	34	10	8	16	43	67	28
Ayr U	34	9	8	17	37	54	26
Clyde	34	8	10	16	33	59	26
Dunfermline A	34	6	11	17	44	56	23
St Mirren	34	7	9	18	38	56	23
Cowdenbeath	34	7	3	24	33	77	17

DIVISION 2 FINAL TABLE

	P	W	D	L	F	A	Pts
Partick T	36	23	10	3	78	26	56
East Fife	36	22	7	7	86	44	51
Arbroath	36	19	8	9	80	52	46
Dumbarton	36	19	6	11	87	46	44
Clydebank	36	17	8	11	57	43	42
Montrose	36	17	7	12	78	64	41
Albion R	36	15	9	12	53	52	39
Raith R	36	15	9	12	62	62	39
Stranraer	36	14	8	14	54	52	36
Stenhousemuir	36	14	8	14	64	70	36
Queen of South	36	13	9	14	50	56	35
Stirling A	36	12	8	16	61	61	32
Queen's Park	36	13	4	19	51	72	30
Berwick R	36	10	10	16	42	60	30
Forfar A	36	9	11	16	63	75	29
Alloa	36	9	11	16	56	86	29
E Stirling	36	9	9	18	57	86	27
Hamilton A	36	8	7	21	50	79	23
Brechin C	36	6	7	23	30	73	19

League Cup results for 1970-71 are detailed on page 201.

SFA Cup

1st Round

Dec 18	Burntisland	2	Coldstream	0
Dec 18	Elgin C	2	Stenhousemuir	0
Dec 18	Gala Fairydean	1	Queen of South	5
Dec 18	Queen's Park	2	E Stirling	1
Dec 18	St Cuthbert's	0	Brechin C	3

2nd Round

Jan 15	Albion R	3	Queen's Park	2
Jan 15	Burntisland	1	Elgin C	4
Jan 15	Forfar A	2	Stranraer	2
Jan 15	Huntly	0	Hamilton A	2
Jan 15	Inverness T	3	Inverness C	4
Jan 15	Queen of South	0	Berwick R	0
Jan 15	Raith R	2	Brechin C	1
Jan 15	Stirling A	1	Alloa	2

Replays

Jan 19	Berwick R	0	Queen of South	1
Jan 22	Stranraer	1	Forfar A	2

3rd Round

Feb 5	Arbroath	1	Airdrie	3
Feb 5	Celtic	5	Albion R	0
Feb 5	Clyde	0	Ayr U	1
Feb 5	Clydebank	1	East Fife	1
Feb 5	Dumbarton	3	Hamilton A	1
Feb 8	Dundee	3	Queen of South	0
Feb 5	Dundee U	0	Aberdeen	4
Feb 5	Elgin C	3	Inverness C	1
Feb 5	Falkirk	2	Rangers	2
Feb 5	Forfar A	0	St Mirren	1
Feb 5	Hearts	2	St Johnstone	0
Feb 5	Kilmarnock	5	Alloa	1
Feb 5	Morton	1	Cowdenbeath	0
Feb 5	Motherwell	2	Montrose	0
Feb 5	Partick T	0	Hibernian	2
Feb 5	Raith R	2	Dunfermline A	0

Replays

Feb 9	East Fife	0	Clydebank	1
Feb 9	Rangers	2	Falkirk	0

4th Round

Feb 26	Aberdeen	1	Morton	0
Feb 26	Ayr U	0	Motherwell	0
Feb 26	Celtic	4	Dundee	0
Feb 26	Dumbarton	0	Raith R	3
Feb 26	Elgin C	1	Kilmarnock	4
Feb 26	Hearts	4	Clydebank	0
Feb 26	Hibernian	2	Airdrie	0
Feb 26	St Mirren	1	Rangers	4

Replay

Mar 1	Motherwell	2	Ayr U	1

5th Round

Mar 18	Celtic	1	Hearts	1
Mar 18	Hibernian	2	Aberdeen	0
Mar 18	Motherwell	2	Rangers	2
Mar 18	Raith R	1	Kilmarnock	3

Replays

Mar 27	Hearts	0	Celtic	1
Mar 27	Rangers	4	Motherwell	2

Semi-finals

Apr 12	Celtic	3	Kilmarnock	1
	played at Hampden Park			
Apr 15	Hibernian	1	Rangers	1
	played at Hampden Park			

Replay

Apr 24	Hibernian	2	Rangers	0
	played at Hampden Park			

Final

May 6	Celtic	6	Hibernian	1
	played at Hampden Park			

League Cup results for 1971-72 are detailed on page 202.

DIVISION 1 FINAL TABLE

	P	W	D	L	F	A	Pts
Celtic	34	28	4	2	96	28	60
Aberdeen	34	21	8	5	80	26	50
Rangers	34	21	2	11	71	38	44
Hibernian	34	19	6	9	62	34	44
Dundee	34	14	13	7	59	38	41
Hearts	34	13	13	8	53	49	39
Partick T	34	12	10	12	53	54	34
St Johnstone	34	12	8	14	52	58	32
Dundee U	34	12	7	15	55	70	31
Motherwell	34	11	7	16	49	69	29
Kilmarnock	34	11	6	17	49	64	28
Ayr U	34	9	10	15	40	58	28
Morton	34	10	7	17	46	52	27
Falkirk	34	10	7	17	44	60	27
Airdrie	34	7	12	15	44	76	26
East Fife	34	5	15	14	34	61	25
Clyde	34	7	10	17	33	66	24
Dunfermline A	34	7	9	18	31	50	23

DIVISION 1

	ABERDEEN	AIRDRIE	AYR U	CELTIC	CLYDE	DUNDEE	DUNDEE U	DUNFERMLINE A	EAST FIFE	FALKIRK	HEARTS	HIBERNIAN	KILMARNOCK	MORTON	MOTHERWELL	PARTICK T	RANGERS	ST JOHNSTONE
ABERDEEN		Sep18 5-0	Apr08 7-0	Mar11 1-1	Dec11 4-1	Sep04 3-0	Dec18 3-0	Oct02 2-0	Nov13 5-0	Apr29 0-0	Nov27 2-3	Oct16 2-1	Jan29 4-2	Feb19 1-0	Mar25 4-1	Oct30 7-2	Jan15 0-0	Jan03 4-2
AIRDRIE	Jan08 1-2		Oct09 3-4	Sep25 0-5	Dec25 1-1	Apr08 4-2	Mar29 1-1	Mar04 1-0	Oct23 1-1	Mar11 2-0	Feb12 1-1	Nov13 2-2	Dec11 0-4	Jan01 2-4	Sep11 0-2	Apr22 1-1	Nov27 5-4
AYR U	Dec04 1-5	Jan29 1-1		Oct30 0-1	Oct16 0-0	Oct02 4-2	Apr15 1-1	Sep18 4-0	Mar11 0-3	Dec18 1-0	Mar25 1-2	Jan15 0-0	Jan03 1-1	Sep04 4-0	Nov13 1-1	Apr29 4-0	Nov27 1-2	Feb19 0-0
CELTIC	Nov06 1-1	Jan15 2-0	Mar04 2-0		Sep04 9-1	Oct16 3-1	Apr25 3-0	Feb19 1-0	Dec11 2-1	Nov20 2-0	Dec25 3-2	Jan29 2-1	Dec04 5-1	Sep18 3-1	Apr22 5-2	Apr01 3-1	Jan03 2-1	Oct02 0-1
CLYDE	Apr15 0-0	Apr29 0-0	Feb12 3-0	Jan01 0-7		Mar25 1-1	Oct23 0-3	Dec18 2-1	Sep25 0-1	Jan22 3-1	Oct30 0-1	Nov27 1-2	Sep11 2-0	Jan08 0-2	Apr08 1-1	Nov13 1-2
DUNDEE	Jan01 1-1	Dec04 4-1	Jan22 5-1	May01 1-1	Nov20 6-4		Sep11 4-0	Apr01 0-0	Jan08 0-0	Oct09 4-0	Sep25 0-1	Apr17 2-0	Dec18 0-1	Nov06 2-0	Mar04 0-0	Oct27 2-1	Apr10 0-1	Apr29 1-2
DUNDEE U	Apr22 2-0	Oct02 5-0	Dec11 2-2	Nov13 1-5	Feb19 3-3	Jan03 1-1		Dec25 3-2	Mar15 2-2	Oct30 3-5	Apr08 3-2	Sep18 1-4	Jan15 1-2	Jan29 2-1	Nov27 2-0	Mar11 1-0	Oct16 1-5	Sep04 3-3
DUNFERMLINE A	Jan22 1-0	Oct30 0-1	Jan08 1-1	Oct27 1-2	Apr22 2-2	Nov27 1-2	Apr29 0-1		Jan01 2-2	Sep11 0-1	Mar11 1-4	Apr18 2-1	Sep25 0-1	Dec11 2-2	Nov13 0-2	Mar25 2-1
EAST FIFE	Mar21 0-1	Feb19 1-1	Nov06 2-2	Apr15 0-3	Jan15 2-2	Sep18 2-5	Nov20 0-1	Sep04 4-1		Apr01 2-2	Mar04 2-2	Jan03 0-6	Oct16 0-1	Oct02 1-1	Dec25 2-1	Dec04 0-3	Jan29 2-1	Dec18 2-4
FALKIRK	Dec25 0-3	Nov06 1-2	Apr22 3-0	Mar25 0-1	Oct02 3-1	Jan29 1-1	Mar04 1-1	Oct16 2-1	Nov27 1-1		Dec11 2-0	Feb19 2-3	Sep04 3-1	Jan03 2-1	Apr08 3-0	Nov13 0-0	Sep18 0-3	Jan15 2-4
HEARTS	Apr01 1-0	Oct16 1-1	Nov20 1-0	Apr29 4-1	Jan29 2-0	Jan15 2-5	Jan03 3-2	Oct30 1-1	Jan03 1-1	Oct30 1-0		Sep11 0-2	Oct23 2-1	Apr15 6-1	Nov13 0-0	Mar11 0-0	Dec02 2-1	Sep18 2-1
HIBERNIAN	Feb12 2-2	Mar21 1-1	Sep25 2-3	Oct09 1-1	Mar04 1-0	Dec11 3-0	Jan08 2-0	Nov06 3-0	Sep11 2-3	Oct23 6-0	Jan01 0-0		Nov27 3-2	Apr22 1-0	Jan22 1-2	Mar25 3-2	Dec25 0-1	Apr08 7-1
KILMARNOCK	Oct09 0-3	Nov20 5-2	Sep11 1-2	Apr08 1-3	Nov06 2-1	Apr22 0-3	Sep25 2-2	Mar21 0-0	Feb12 2-3	Jan01 2-0	Oct23 2-2	Apr03 1-1		Dec25 4-2	Jan08 1-0	Jan22 1-4	Mar04 1-2	Dec11 2-0
MORTON	Oct23 0-1	Apr15 2-2	Jan01 0-3	Apr08 1-1	Apr12 4-0	Mar11 0-2	Sep29 1-2	Mar21 1-0	Jan22 3-1	Mar21 1-1	Dec18 1-1	Apr29 1-1		Sep18 3-2	Apr05 2-0	Sep09 1-0	Nov20 1-2	Oct30 0-1
MOTHERWELL	Nov20 0-4	Sep04 0-1	Mar21 2-3	Dec18 0-0	Jan03 2-0	Oct30 0-1	Apr01 1-0	Jan15 2-0	Apr29 0-1	Dec04 2-1	Nov06 1-0	Oct02 3-1	Sep18 0-3	Oct16 3-1		Apr15 2-1	Feb19 2-0	Jan29 3-1
PARTICK T	Mar04 2-0	Jan03 4-2	Dec25 0-1	Nov27 1-5	Sep18 2-2	Feb19 0-2	Nov06 3-1	Jan29 2-0	Apr08 1-0	Mar18 1-1	Apr22 2-2	Dec01 0-1	Oct02 2-2	Jan15 2-0	Dec11 8-3		Sep04 3-2	Oct16 2-1
RANGERS	Sep25 0-2	Dec18 3-0	May01 4-2	Sep11 2-3	Apr08 1-0	Nov13 2-3	Jan08 1-0	Feb27 3-4	Apr22 3-0	Sep25 3-1	Jan01 6-0	Apr29 1-2	Dec18 3-1	Mar25 1-2	Oct23 4-0	Jan01 2-1		Mar11 2-0
ST JOHNSTONE	Sep11 1-1	Apr01 3-3	Oct23 2-0	Jan22 0-3	Mar18 0-1	Dec25 0-0	Jan01 2-0	Nov20 0-0	Apr22 0-1	Sep25 3-2	Jan08 1-1	Dec04 0-2	Apr15 5-1	Mar04 1-0	Oct09 5-2	Feb12 2-1	Nov06 1-4	

The Dundee squad of 1971-72, beaten by Cup-winners Celtic in the fourth round and fifth in Division One.

DIVISION 2

	ALBION R	ALLOA	ARBROATH	BERWICK R	BRECHIN C	CLYDEBANK	COWDENBEATH	DUMBARTON	E STIRLING	FORFAR A	HAMILTON A	MONTROSE	QUEEN OF SOUTH	QUEEN'S PARK	RAITH R	ST MIRREN	STENHOUSEMUIR	STIRLING A	STRANRAER
ALBION R		Dec04 0-1	Dec18 0-3	Sep08 1-3	Feb19 1-1	Oct02 2-0	Apr29 1-2	Mar18 0-1	Oct16 1-1	Sep22 2-0	Sep04 1-0	Nov20 4-1	Nov06 0-1	Apr11 1-2	Jan03 3-1	Apr15 1-2	Jan29 1-1	Apr25 0-1	Sep18 4-0
ALLOA	Apr08 3-1		Mar25 0-3	Nov06 0-2	Sep18 1-3	Oct16 1-1	Nov27 0-4	Apr22 0-1	Apr26 0-2	Jan29 2-3	Feb19 2-2	Dec25 0-3	Dec11 1-2	Mar04 3-0	Sep22 3-2	Nov13 1-3	Sep04 2-0	Jan03 0-1	Oct02 1-3
ARBROATH	Apr22 2-0	Apr18 1-0		Dec04 2-1	Sep22 3-3	Jan15 1-2	Dec11 2-2	Mar04 3-2	Oct02 2-1	Sep04 3-0	Oct16 3-0	Nov06 2-0	Dec25 2-2	Mar18 1-0	Sep08 4-0	Apr01 3-2	Feb19 3-0	Sep18 4-3	Jan29 3-1
BERWICK R	Sep29 3-1	Mar11 2-0	Apr08 0-1		Feb05 3-0	Sep18 1-1	Jan22 2-0	Oct09 2-2	Nov27 0-1	Jan03 4-1	Feb26 1-1	Apr15 2-1	Sep15 0-3	Apr29 0-2	Oct16 0-1	Mar25 1-2	Nov13 3-0	Oct30 1-3	Feb19 0-1
BRECHIN C	Oct23 2-2	Jan08 1-1	Sep15 2-1	Apr22 3-1		Apr15 1-2	Sep25 0-2	Apr26 1-2	Nov06 1-3	Mar18 2-4	Apr01 4-1	Jan01 1-3	Oct09 0-0	Sep11 1-0	Nov20 0-4	Feb12 1-2	Mar04 2-1	Dec25 2-1	Dec04 1-4
CLYDEBANK	Jan22 3-1	Feb12 3-1	Sep25 0-0	Jan08 0-0	Dec11 1-2		Oct23 1-4	Jan01 2-3	Mar04 3-4	Nov06 2-0	Nov20 7-1	Oct09 1-2	Sep11 1-3	Sep15 1-1	Apr11 3-1	Sep29 1-3	Dec25 2-1	Apr22 0-0	Apr01 3-0
COWDENBEATH	Dec25 1-0	Apr24 3-0	Apr15 0-2	Oct02 3-2	Feb26 6-0	Feb19 0-0		Nov06 0-1	Sep22 5-0	Sep08 7-0	Jan03 1-1	Mar18 2-0	Mar04 1-1	Nov20 2-0	Sep04 2-0	Dec04 1-0	Sep18 2-0	Jan29 3-2	Oct16 0-1
DUMBARTON	Nov13 3-0	Dec18 7-1	Oct30 1-2	May03 4-2	Oct02 4-0	Sep04 2-3	Mar11 2-1		Feb19 4-0	Sep18 2-2	Sep08 2-0	Dec04 3-2	Mar25 2-0	Apr15 3-0	Apr18 5-0	Apr29 1-2	Oct16 3-2	Apr11 2-1	Jan03 2-4
E STIRLING	Feb12 4-1	Sep29 1-2	Jan22 5-0	Apr01 0-4	Mar11 2-1	Oct30 0-1	Sep15 0-0	Oct23 1-3		Dec04 1-1	Apr18 1-4	Sep25 2-1	Jan01 4-2	Jan08 3-1	Jan15 2-1	Mar25 1-0	Nov13 0-3	Apr29 3-1	
FORFAR A	Sep15 2-1	Oct09 0-4	Jan01 0-4	Sep11 0-4	Nov13 1-0	Mar11 1-4	Sep28 1-1	Jan08 1-2	Apr08 1-2		Apr29 0-0	Oct23 1-1	Feb12 0-1	Apr27 1-1	Dec18 0-3	Sep25 2-1	Nov27 0-4	Mar25 0-4	Oct30 1-1
HAMILTON A	Jan01 1-0	Oct23 0-5	Feb12 1-1	Sep25 0-2	Nov27 3-0	Mar25 0-1	Sep11 1-1	Sep29 2-6	Apr22 1-1	Dec25 2-1		Sep15 1-6	Jan08 0-3	Oct09 0-1	Mar04 1-1	Jan22 1-5	Dec11 1-3	Apr08 0-2	Nov13 1-5
MONTROSE	Mar25 2-0	Apr29 4-0	Mar11 0-0	Dec11 1-2	Sep04 2-0	Jan29 1-2	Nov13 0-2	Apr08 2-3	Jan03 2-2	Feb19 0-0	Sep22 5-0		Nov27 0-2	Feb26 4-2	Oct02 3-1	Oct30 3-1	Jan15 1-1	Oct16 2-4	Sep08 0-0
QUEEN OF SOUTH	Mar11 1-0	Apr15 4-0	Apr29 1-1	Sep22 2-2	Jan29 2-0	Jan03 0-0	Oct30 2-4	Nov20 4-2	Feb26 4-2	Oct16 3-2	Sep18 4-0	Apr01 2-1		Dec04 0-1	Feb19 1-1	Apr26 0-1	Oct02 2-0	Apr18 0-0	Sep04 5-1
QUEEN'S PARK	Nov27 2-2	Oct30 0-2	Nov13 2-1	Dec25 2-0	Jan03 5-3	Apr18 4-4	Mar20 0-2	Dec11 0-1	Sep04 0-0	Oct02 4-1	Jan29 2-0	Apr22 1-6	Apr08 0-0		Sep18 1-0	Mar11 2-1	Sep08 4-0	Feb19 0-2	Mar28 1-2
RAITH R	Sep11 3-1	Sep15 1-1	Sep29 1-1	Dec25 3-1	Mar25 0-1	Jan08 1-3	Jan01 1-1	Sep25 6-1	Dec11 3-1	Apr22 4-2	Oct30 2-1	Jan22 4-0	Oct23 1-2	Jan08 1-1		Oct09 2-0	Apr08 4-0	Nov27 2-5	Mar11 0-0
ST MIRREN	Dec11 4-0	Mar18 4-1	Nov27 0-1	Nov20 2-0	Oct16 1-1	Dec27 2-0	Apr08 3-1	Dec25 2-2	Sep18 1-2	Apr17 2-0	Oct02 6-2	Mar04 3-1	Apr22 3-0	Nov06 6-2	Jan29 2-0		Jan03 0-1	Sep04 3-2	Oct20 2-0
STENHOUSEMUIR	Oct09 2-0	Jan01 2-1	Oct23 0-1	Mar18 0-1	Oct30 2-0	Apr29 3-1	Jan08 0-0	Feb12 0-3	Nov20 1-1	Apr01 2-1	Apr15 3-1	Sep25 2-2	Jan22 1-3	Sep29 3-0	Dec04 0-1	Sep11 2-4		Mar11 0-0	Feb05 3-4
STIRLING A	Sep25 2-0	Sep11 3-2	Jan08 1-2	Mar04 2-1	Apr29 6-1	Dec18 1-1	Oct09 1-1	Sep15 2-0	Mar18 2-1	Dec04 1-1	Feb26 3-0	Dec11 1-2	Feb12 2-0	Oct23 1-1	Jan01 3-0	Jan01 3-2	Nov06 2-2		Apr15 3-0
STRANRAER	Jan08 2-2	Feb26 5-2	Oct09 4-1	Oct23 2-1	Apr08 3-2	Nov27 2-2	Feb12 1-0	Sep11 3-1	Dec25 0-3	Mar04 6-0	Mar18 4-1	Sep29 0-5	Jan01 1-1	Sep25 1-1	Nov06 2-1	Sep15 2-4	Apr22 3-1	Dec11 1-1	

DIVISION 2 FINAL TABLE

	P	W	D	L	F	A	Pts
Dumbarton	36	24	4	8	89	51	52
Arbroath	36	22	8	6	71	41	52
Stirling A	36	21	8	7	75	37	50
St Mirren	36	24	2	10	84	47	50
Cowdenbeath	36	19	10	7	69	28	48
Stranraer	36	18	8	10	70	62	44
Queen of South	36	17	9	10	56	38	43
E Stirling	36	17	7	12	60	58	41
Clydebank	36	14	11	11	60	52	39
Montrose	36	15	6	15	73	54	36
Raith R	36	13	8	15	56	56	34
Queen's Park	36	12	9	15	47	61	33
Berwick R	36	14	4	18	53	50	32
Stenhousemuir	36	10	8	18	41	58	28
Brechin C	36	8	7	21	41	79	23
Alloa	36	9	4	23	41	75	22
Forfar A	36	6	9	21	32	84	21
Albion R	36	7	6	23	36	61	20
Hamilton A	36	4	8	24	31	93	16

Season 1972-73

Rangers in 1973 with the Scottish FA Cup. Back row (left to right): D.Young, Struthers, Scott, Jackson, Hunter, McCloy, Kennedy, Forsyth, Burke, Donaldson, McNichol. Middle row: T.Craig (physiotherapist), McDonald, Hamilton, O'Hara, Conn, Smith, Johnstone, Miller, Thomson, Mathieson, Fyfe, McDougall, S.Anderson (trainer). Front row: J.Wallace (manager), Morris, McLean, MacDonald, Houston, Parlane, Greig, Jardine, Mason, Steel, Q.Young, Denny, W.Thornton (assistant manager).

DIVISION 1

(home \ away)	ABERDEEN	AIRDRIE	ARBROATH	AYR U	CELTIC	DUMBARTON	DUNDEE	DUNDEE U	EAST FIFE	FALKIRK	HEARTS	HIBERNIAN	KILMARNOCK	MORTON	MOTHERWELL	PARTICK T	RANGERS	ST JOHNSTONE
ABERDEEN		Apr07 5-1	Dec09 0-0	Feb17 1-0	Oct28 2-3	Feb20 6-0	Jan01 3-1	Mar31 0-0	Nov11 4-3	Oct14 2-2	Jan27 3-1	Sep02 1-0	Nov18 3-0	Dec23 3-0	Sep30 7-2	Mar10 0-0	Apr21 2-2	Sep16 0-0
AIRDRIE	Dec02 1-1		Nov18 3-1	Apr28 0-1	Jan27 2-1	Oct21 2-3	Sep30 0-1	Dec30 2-2	Apr14 1-1	Mar12 0-0	Dec16 0-2	Feb10 0-4	Mar03 0-1	Nov04 0-3	Sep09 1-2	Sep23 1-3	Mar20 2-6	Mar31 1-3
ARBROATH	Apr14 1-1	Mar24 2-1		Sep23 1-1	Dec16 1-2	Jan20 2-1	Nov21 2-1	Dec02 2-4	Sep09 1-0	Mar03 5-1	Nov25 2-3	Oct07 3-3	Feb10 0-1	Apr28 0-1	Jan06 2-1	Oct21 1-2	Mar10 3-0	
AYR U	Oct21 2-3	Dec23 1-0	Jan13 2-0		Jan20 1-3	Dec09 2-0	Nov25 4-1	Mar03 2-1	Feb10 1-0	Nov18 2-0	Mar21 1-1	Apr21 1-1	Jan01 2-1	Sep16 1-1	Nov04 1-1	Oct07 2-1	Sep02 2-1	Apr07 3-1
CELTIC	Mar03 2-0	Oct07 1-1	Apr21 4-0	Sep30 1-0		Apr18 5-0	Jan13 3-1	Nov04 3-0	Oct21 4-0	Mar31 4-2	Nov18 1-1	Dec23 6-2	Sep02 1-0	M06 1-0	Apr03 2-0	Feb10 1-1	Sep16 3-1	F28 4-0
DUMBARTON	Sep23 1-2	Mar07 3-5	Sep30 0-0	Apr14 1-1	Dec02 1-6		Oct14 2-2	Apr28 4-1	Mar10 0-0	Sep06 0-0	Jan06 0-2	Oct28 2-2	Dec16 4-2	Nov18 2-2	Dec16 0-0	Apr14 4-2	Mar31 1-2	Jan27 1-1
DUNDEE	Sep09 0-0	Feb19 1-1	Mar21 6-0	Mar31 2-1	Sep23 2-0	Feb10 2-1		Jan06 3-0	Dec02 4-0	Apr14 5-3	Apr28 2-2	Sep06 1-0	Oct21 6-0	Mar03 2-0	Dec30 2-0	Dec16 4-1	Nov04 1-1	Nov18 3-0
DUNDEE U	Nov25 3-2	Sep02 3-1	Apr07 1-1	Oct28 2-1	Mar10 2-2	Dec23 3-2	Sep16 2-1		Mar24 1-1	Mar07 1-0	Oct14 3-2	Jan13 1-0	Apr21 2-1	Sep30 1-0	Jan27 1-2	Nov11 0-3	Dec09 1-4	Jan01 5-1
EAST FIFE	Mar27 0-1	Dec09 3-0	Jan01 2-0	Oct14 2-2	Feb17 2-2	Nov04 2-1	Apr07 0-1	Nov18 1-0		Jan27 1-2	Sep30 1-0	Sep16 0-1	Jan13 3-0	Sep02 4-3	Mar31 3-1	Oct21 0-1	Dec23 0-4	Apr21 2-2
FALKIRK	Feb10 0-0	Sep16 1-1	Sep02 3-1	Mar24 1-2	Nov25 2-3	Feb06 2-0	Dec09 2-2	Oct21 1-2	Oct07 3-4		Nov04 1-3	Apr07 1-0	Dec23 3-2	Apr21 2-0	Mar03 0-1	Jan20 0-3	Jan13 2-4	Nov11 0-0
HEARTS	Oct07 2-1	Apr21 0-1	Oct28 3-0	Nov11 3-0	Mar24 0-2	Sep16 1-0	Dec23 1-2	Feb10 0-2	Jan20 1-1	Mar10 1-0		Jan01 0-7	Dec09 0-0	Mar12 0-0	Oct21 0-0	Apr07 2-0	0-1	Sep02 1-0
HIBERNIAN	Dec30 3-2	Oct14 5-2	Mar31 0-0	Dec16 8-1	Apr28 0-3	Mar03 5-0	Jan06 1-1	Sep23 3-1	Jan06 1-0	Dec02 3-0	Sep09 2-0		Nov04 4-1	Mar17 2-1	Apr14 0-1	Nov18 1-2	Sep30 3-2	
KILMARNOCK	Mar24 0-2	Oct28 3-1	Jan27 2-0	Sep09 1-0	Feb07 0-4	Nov11 1-1	Feb27 0-6	Dec16 2-1	Sep23 1-3	Apr28 2-2	Apr14 1-2	Mar10 2-2		Mar31 2-1	Jan06 1-0	Dec02 2-3	Sep30 2-1	Oct14 1-4
MORTON	Apr28 1-2	Mar10 4-0	Oct14 1-1	Jan06 1-1	Sep02 0-2	Mar24 1-1	Oct28 5-2	Feb21 2-0	Dec30 3-1	Dec16 1-1	Sep23 2-4	Nov11 0-3	Nov25 2-1		Dec02 1-0	Apr14 5-0	Jan27 1-2	Feb17 3-0
MOTHERWELL	Feb07 2-0	Jan01 2-0	Dec23 2-0	Mar10 1-2	Nov11 0-5	Apr21 0-2	Sep02 2-2	Oct07 1-4	Nov25 0-1	Dec16 1-1	Feb19 2-2	Apr10 1-1	Sep16 2-0	Apr07 3-0		Mar24 0-0	Oct14 0-2	Jan13 1-1
PARTICK T	Nov04 0-2	Jan13 1-2	Sep16 1-2	Jan27 1-2	Oct14 0-4	Sep02 4-1	Apr21 1-1	Mar21 2-1	Mar03 1-1	Sep30 3-1	Mar31 1-0	Oct21 1-3	Apr07 1-1	Dec09 1-0	Nov18 0-3		Jan01 0-1	Dec23 1-1
RANGERS	Dec16 0-0	Nov11 1-0	Feb19 5-0	Dec30 2-1	Jan06 2-1	Nov25 3-1	Mar10 3-1	Apr14 4-1	Apr28 2-1	Sep23 2-0	Dec02 1-0	Mar24 0-1	Jan20 1-0	Oct07 4-0	Feb10 1-1	Sep09 2-1		Oct28 5-1
ST JOHNSTONE	Mar07 1-0	Nov25 1-1	Nov04 5-2	Dec02 3-0	Apr14 1-3	Oct07 0-2	Mar24 4-1	Sep09 1-3	Dec16 4-2	Mar17 2-1	Dec30 3-2	Feb21 1-3	Feb10 2-2	Oct21 3-1	Sep23 2-2	Apr28 1-3	Mar03 1-2	

DIVISION 2

(home \ away)	ALBION R	ALLOA	BERWICK R	BRECHIN C	CLYDE	CLYDEBANK	COWDENBEATH	DUNFERMLINE A	E.STIRLING	FORFAR A	HAMILTON A	MONTROSE	QUEEN OF SOUTH	QUEEN'S PARK	RAITH R	ST MIRREN	STENHOUSEMUIR	STIRLING A	STRANRAER
ALBION R		Feb21 2-2	Oct14 0-2	Sep16 2-1	Jan13 0-3	Oct28 4-1	Mar24 2-2	Sep27 1-5	Sep13 3-2	Nov25 2-2	Jan01 2-2	Jan20 1-3	Oct07 1-2	Nov11 1-1	Sep02 0-2	Mar10 1-3	Dec23 0-2	Apr21 1-1	Dec09 0-2
ALLOA	Oct21 4-0		Oct28 0-2	Apr10 1-0	Dec09 0-0	Mar10 1-0	Nov25 2-0	Dec23 1-1	Sep16 2-1	Feb03 1-1	Apr07 4-0	Oct07 0-3	Feb10 2-1	Mar24 0-0	Sep27 0-1	Nov11 0-1	Jan01 4-1	Sep13 0-2	Sep02 2-1
BERWICK R	Feb10 1-0	Mar03 3-1		Dec09 3-1	Sep30 0-2	Mar17 1-0	Dec30 1-0	Apr07 2-0	Nov04 1-0	Apr28 3-0	Oct07 1-1	Mar24 0-2	Sep06 2-0	Mar28 1-3	Feb24 0-1	Sep20 0-0	Oct21 2-1	Sep16 0-0	Nov25 0-3
BRECHIN C	Jan06 5-1	Apr28 0-0	Apr14 0-3		Oct21 1-3	Sep06 3-1	Nov20 0-2	Mar03 0-5	Oct07 2-0	Dec02 2-0	Nov25 1-4	Sep09 1-4	Apr25 2-3	Sep23 2-2	Nov04 4-6	Dec30 3-3	Jan20 2-4	Feb10 1-2	Mar24 2-2
CLYDE	Sep23 3-1	Apr14 1-0	Jan20 1-0	Feb20 4-1		Feb24 1-0	Dec02 2-1	Jan27 2-1	Mar24 1-1	Sep20 3-2	Mar10 0-0	Dec30 2-2	Jan06 4-1	Sep09 1-1	Oct14 3-0	Nov11 5-1	Nov25 1-3	Oct28 3-0	
CLYDEBANK	Mar03 1-2	Nov04 2-3	Nov11 1-2	Sep27 2-1	Apr21 0-1		Apr18 3-0	Jan13 0-4	Jan01 1-1	Oct07 4-1	Apr25 1-2	Feb10 0-4	Oct21 1-0	Nov25 1-1	Sep16 1-1	Mar24 1-2	Sep13 0-3	Sep02 4-2	Apr07 4-2
COWDENBEATH	Nov18 2-1	Feb24 0-2	Dec02 5-0	Sep13 2-1	Apr07 1-1	Sep30 2-0		Jan01 1-0	Dec09 2-1	Mar03 4-1	Sep16 3-2	Mar17 1-3	Oct14 0-2	Apr21 3-0	Jan27 1-1	Sep27 0-2	Mar24 3-1	Jan13 1-1	Dec23 4-1
DUNFERMLINE A	Feb07 3-0	Dec16 5-0	Dec02 1-2	Oct28 8-0	Oct07 2-3	Apr28 3-3	Sep09 0-2		Nov25 3-2	Sep23 3-1	Nov11 7-2	Apr14 4-1	Dec30 6-1	Sep20 5-1	Apr25 1-0	Nov04 1-1	Jan06 1-1	Apr11 4-0	Mar10 3-0
E.STIRLING	Sep19 0-2	Jan06 2-0	Mar10 1-2	Jan27 2-0	Nov18 0-5	Sep09 4-2	Apr14 1-0	Mar31 0-2		Sep06 2-2	Feb20 0-4	Dec02 1-5	Sep23 3-2	Dec30 2-1	Sep30 0-3	Mar20 2-1	Oct28 2-1	Mar17 4-3	Oct14 2-2
FORFAR A	Mar31 1-0	Sep30 2-1	Apr07 0-1	Apr07 2-1	Sep12 0-2	Jan27 0-3	Oct28 1-1	Feb24 0-6	Sep26 1-0		Sep02 1-0	Apr28 1-1	Sep20 1-1	Nov18 1-2	Feb17 1-2	Jan01 1-2	Oct14 1-2	Sep16 0-4	Apr07 1-0
HAMILTON A	Sep09 3-3	Dec02 0-3	Jan27 4-1	Mar31 5-1	Nov04 2-4	Sep23 3-0	Jan06 2-1	Mar17 1-3	Oct21 5-2	Dec30 4-0		Apr28 2-0	Sep20 2-0	Sep06 0-3	Nov18 1-2	Feb10 0-0	Apr14 3-2	Mar03 3-0	Sep30 3-0
MONTROSE	Sep30 4-0	Jan27 3-0	Nov18 2-2	Jan01 3-2	Sep02 0-1	Oct14 1-3	Mar10 2-2	Dec09 3-2	Apr07 3-5	Nov11 1-0	Dec23		Mar31 2-1	Oct28 3-2	Sep13 1-4	Feb17 2-0	Apr21 4-1	Sep27 2-2	Apr18 4-1
QUEEN OF SOUTH	Jan27 0-0	Oct14 3-1	Dec23 1-1	Apr21 1-0	Sep16 0-0	Nov11 2-0	Sep02 4-1	Feb24 0-2	Mar24 0-1	Sep13 2-1	Nov25 4-3			Dec16 0-1	Oct28 1-1	Apr21 4-2	Dec09 1-2	Apr07 0-0	Jan01 2-2
QUEEN'S PARK	Mar20 3-2	Nov18 3-3	Apr21 1-1	Feb24 1-3	Jan01 2-2	Mar31 1-3	Feb10 1-0	Sep11 1-1	Sep02 2-0	Oct21 1-2	Sep27 0-1	Apr09 0-1	Nov04 0-2		Apr14 0-1	Sep30 2-3	Apr06 0-0	Dec23 2-1	Sep16 1-0
RAITH R	Dec27 4-0	Mar28 1-1	Sep23 8-1	Mar10 3-1	Feb10 0-0	Feb28 2-0	Dec16 2-2	Oct21 1-2	Jan20 2-2	Sep09 3-2	Mar24 2-0	Sep20 1-0	Apr28 2-0	Dec08 2-1		Dec02 3-0	Nov25 0-2	Oct07 1-1	Nov11 5-1
ST MIRREN	Nov04 4-0	Mar17 4-2	Sep13 3-1	Sep02 5-1	Dec23 0-1	Nov18 4-0	Apr21 6-3	Sep16 0-1	Apr21 1-3	Dec09 0-0	Oct21 7-1	Mar03 2-2	Feb20 2-1	Apr07 0-1	Feb24 1-1		Jan01 4-1		Sep27 5-1
STENHOUSEMUIR	Apr28 3-0	Sep09 0-0	Apr17 1-2	Sep30 1-1	Mar17 1-1	Feb03 0-1	Sep06 0-2	Nov18 0-2	Mar03 0-0	Jan06 0-1	Oct14 0-3	Apr24 0-2	Apr14 1-4	Dec02 1-1	Mar31 0-1	Sep23		Nov04 3-1	Jan27 1-2
STIRLING A	Mar28 3-0	Apr18 0-1	Jan06 2-0	Oct14 3-0	Mar31 3-1	Sep20 3-0	Sep30 1-0	Nov11 0-0	Apr14 3-4	Oct28 2-1	Sep06 3-2	Dec02 4-0	Apr28 2-2	Jan27 1-2	Sep09 3-1	Mar10 1-0			Mar14 4-2
STRANRAER	Apr14 1-0	Dec30 2-0	Mar31 5-4	Nov18 1-3	Mar03 1-2	Dec02 4-0	Apr28 2-4	Nov04 1-0	Feb10 2-1	Apr11 4-2	Sep23 1-0	Jan06 3-6	Mar17 1-0	Sep06 3-1	Oct07 1-4	Oct21 1-4			

DIVISION 1 FINAL TABLE

	P	W	D	L	F	A	Pts
Celtic	34	26	5	3	93	28	57
Rangers	34	26	4	4	74	30	56
Hibernian	34	19	7	8	74	33	45
Aberdeen	34	16	11	7	61	34	43
Dundee	34	17	9	8	68	43	43
Ayr U	34	16	8	10	50	51	40
Dundee U	34	17	5	12	56	51	39
Motherwell	34	11	9	14	38	48	31
East Fife	34	11	8	15	46	54	30
Hearts	34	12	6	16	39	50	30
St Johnstone	34	10	9	15	52	67	29
Morton	34	10	8	16	47	53	28
Partick T	34	10	8	16	40	53	28
Falkirk	34	7	12	15	38	56	26
Arbroath	34	9	8	17	39	63	26
Dumbarton	34	6	11	17	43	72	23
Kilmarnock	34	7	8	19	40	71	22
Airdrie	34	4	8	22	34	75	16

DIVISION 2 FINAL TABLE

	P	W	D	L	F	A	Pts
Clyde	36	23	10	3	68	28	56
Dunfermline A	36	23	6	7	95	32	52
Stirling A	36	19	9	8	70	39	47
Raith R	36	19	9	8	73	42	47
St Mirren	36	19	7	10	79	50	45
Montrose	36	18	8	10	82	58	44
Cowdenbeath	36	14	10	12	57	53	38
Hamilton A	36	16	6	14	67	63	38
Berwick R	36	16	5	15	45	54	37
Stenhousemuir	36	14	8	14	44	41	36
Queen of South	36	13	8	15	45	52	34
Alloa	36	11	11	14	45	49	33
E Stirling	36	12	8	16	52	69	32
Queen's Park	36	9	12	15	44	61	30
Stranraer	36	13	4	19	56	78	30
Forfar A	36	10	9	17	50	78	29
Clydebank	36	9	6	21	48	72	24
Albion R	36	5	8	23	35	83	18
Brechin C	36	5	4	27	46	99	14

League Cup results for 1972-73 are detailed on page 203.

SFA Cup

1st Round
Dec 15 Berwick R ....0 Albion R 0
Dec 24 E Stirling ....0 Clydebank 0
Dec 15 Hamilton A ......0 Alloa 0
Dec 15 Lossiemouth ....3 Fraserburgh 3
Dec 17 Queen's Park ....1 Edinburgh Univ .. 0

Replays
Dec 19 Albion R ....2 Berwick R 0
Dec 19 Fraserburgh .....6 Lossiemouth 0
Dec 19 Alloa ....4 Hamilton A 1
Dec 25 Clydebank ......1 E Stirling 0

2nd Round
Jan 5 Brechin C ....5 Stenhousemuir ...1
Jan 5 Clacknacuddin ...1 Clydebank 1
Jan 5 Cowdenbeath ....4 Fraserburgh 1
Jan 5 Ferranti T ....1 Civil Service 0
Jan 5 Queen of South ..1 Albion R 0
Jan 5 Queen's Park ....6 Hawick RA 1
Jan 5 Ross Co ....1 Forfar A 2
Jan 5 Stranraer ....1 Alloa 0

Replays
Jan 12 Clydebank ......3 Clacknacuddin 2

3rd Round
Jan 27 Aberdeen ....0 Dundee 2
Jan 26 Arbroath ....1 Dumbarton 0
Jan 27 Celtic ....6 Clydebank 1
Jan 27 Cowdenbeath .....0 Ayr U 5

Jan 26 Dundee U ....4 Airdrie 1
Jan 27 Falkirk ....2 Dunfermline A 2
Jan 27 Forfar A ....1 St Johnstone 6
Jan 26 Hearts ....3 Clyde 1
Jan 26 Hibernian ....5 Kilmarnock 2
Jan 27 Montrose ....1 Stirling A 1
Jan 27 Motherwell ......2 Brechin C 0
Jan 27 Partick T ....6 Ferranti T 1
Jan 27 Queen of South ..1 East Fife 0
Jan 27 Raith R ....2 Morton 2
Jan 26 Rangers ....8 Queen's Park ...0
Jan 26 Stranraer ....1 St Mirren 1

Replays
Jan 29 Morton ....0 Raith R 0
Jan 29 St Mirren ....1 Stranraer 1
Jan 30 Dunfermline A ...1 Falkirk 0
Jan 30 Stirling A ......3 Montrose 1
Feb 3 Morton ....1 Raith R 0
played at Tynecastle
Feb 4 St Mirren ....2 Stranraer 3
played at Somerset Park

4th Round
Feb 16 Arbroath ....1 Motherwell 3
Feb 17 Celtic ....6 Stirling A 1
Feb 17 Dundee U ....1 Morton 0
Feb 17 Dunfermline A ...1 Queen of South ..0
Feb 16 Hearts ....1 Partick T 1
Feb 17 Rangers ....0 Dundee 3
Feb 16 St Johnstone ....1 Hibernian 3
Feb 16 Stranraer ....1 Ayr U 7

Replay
Feb 19 Partick T ....1 Hearts 4

5th Round
Mar 10 Celtic ....2 Motherwell 2
Mar 10 Dunfermline A ...1 Dundee U 1
Mar 9 Hearts ....1 Ayr U 1
Mar 9 Hibernian ....3 Dundee 3

Replays
Mar 12 Dundee U ....4 Dunfermline A ...0
Mar 13 Ayr U ....1 Hearts 2
Mar 13 Motherwell ......0 Celtic 1
Mar 18 Dundee ....3 Hibernian 0

Semi-finals
Apr 3 Celtic ....1 Dundee 0
played at Hampden Park
Apr 6 Dundee U ....1 Hearts 1
played at Hampden Park

Replay
Apr 9 Dundee U ....4 Hearts 2
played at Hampden Park

Final
May04 Celtic ....3 Dundee U 0
played at Hampden Park

League Cup results for 1973-74 are detailed on pages 203-204.

DIVISION 1 FINAL TABLE

	P	W	D	L	F	A	Pts
Celtic	34	23	7	4	82	27	53
Hibernian	34	20	9	5	75	42	49
Rangers	34	21	6	7	67	34	48
Aberdeen	34	13	16	5	46	26	42
Dundee	34	16	7	11	67	48	39
Hearts	34	14	10	10	54	43	38
Ayr U	34	15	8	11	44	40	38
Dundee U	34	15	7	12	55	51	37
Motherwell	34	14	7	13	45	40	35
Dumbarton	34	11	7	16	43	58	29
Partick T	34	9	10	15	33	46	28
St Johnstone	34	9	10	15	41	60	28
Arbroath	34	10	7	17	52	69	27
Morton	34	8	10	16	37	49	26
Clyde	34	8	9	17	29	65	25
Dunfermline A	34	8	8	18	43	65	24
East Fife	34	9	6	19	26	51	24
Falkirk	34	4	14	16	33	58	22

DIVISION 1

	ABERDEEN	ARBROATH	AYR U	CELTIC	CLYDE	DUMBARTON	DUNDEE	DUNDEE U	DUNFERMLINE A	EAST FIFE	FALKIRK	HEARTS	HIBERNIAN	MORTON	MOTHERWELL	PARTICK T	RANGERS	ST JOHNSTONE
ABERDEEN		Apr27 2-2	Apr24 2-1	Apr29 0-0	Jan19 1-1	Feb09 3-0	Sep08 0-0	Oct27 3-1	Oct20 0-0	Mar30 2-0	Mar16 6-0	Nov17 3-1	Oct06 1-1	Mar09 0-0	Dec29 0-0	Apr13 2-0	Apr17 1-1	Jan05 0-1
ARBROATH	Dec22 1-3		Nov17 1-1	Dec01 1-2	Feb09 1-2	Sep22 2-1	Oct20 2-4	Apr20 1-2	Jan05 3-1	Mar16 1-2	Mar02 0-0	Nov03 2-3	Apr13 3-2	Jan19 2-1	Sep08 0-2	Mar30 0-3	Oct06 1-2	Dec29 3-1
AYR U	Apr06 0-0	Mar23 1-2		Nov10 0-1	Sep22 2-2	Jan05 0-1	Mar02 4-2	Nov24 1-1	Feb10 3-1	Dec22 1-0	Dec08 2-1	Apr20 1-1	Jan19 1-1	Sep08 1-0	Oct20 1-0	Apr03 0-0	Dec29 0-0	Oct06 3-2
CELTIC	Apr20 2-0	Apr06 1-0	Mar16 4-0		Sep08 5-0	Mar30 3-3	Feb10 1-2	Dec08 3-3	Dec29 6-0	Nov03 4-2	Dec22 6-0	Mar02 1-0	Oct20 1-1	Apr30 1-1	Oct06 2-0	Nov17 7-0	Jan05 1-0	Jan19 3-0
CLYDE	Sep29 1-3	Oct13 3-2	Jan12 1-3	Jan01 0-2		Mar09	Oct27 0-3	Apr17 0-2	Feb02 1-2	Nov10 1-0	Sep01 2-0	Sep15 0-0	Apr24 2-0	Mar23 1-1	Apr13 0-3	Feb23 1-0	Nov24 0-2	Apr27 0-1
DUMBARTON	Oct13 0-1	Jan12 5-2	Sep15 0-2	Nov24 0-2	Mar09		May10 2-0	Sep01 1-2	Apr24 1-0	Feb16 1-1	Jan02 1-5	Feb23 0-1	Apr06 3-3	Jan19 1-0	Nov03 3-0	Sep29 2-0	Dec22 0-2	Nov17 2-1
DUNDEE	Jan01 1-1	Feb23 5-2	Oct27 2-1	Oct13 0-1	Apr20 6-1	Nov10 2-1		Sep15 0-1	Nov24 1-5	Feb09 0-1	Sep01 4-0	May06 0-0	Apr10 0-1	Apr06 2-1	Jan19 0-1	Oct20 4-1	Feb03 2-3	Apr22 2-2
DUNDEE U	Mar03 0-3	Apr17 3-1	Mar30 2-1	Jan05 0-2	Oct06 4-0	Dec29 6-0	Jan05 1-2		Apr27 0-1	Nov21 0-0	Mar16 2-1	Mar16 3-3	Apr10 1-4	May10 4-2	Jan19 0-1	Apr24 1-1	Oct20 1-3	Sep08 2-0
DUNFERMLINE A	Feb24 0-0	Sep15 1-1	Oct13 0-4	Sep01 2-3	Mar16 3-2	Apr13 1-5	Mar30 2-3	Dec22 2-3		Jan01 0-1	Sep29 0-1	Apr17 2-3	Dec15 2-4	Mar03 1-1	Nov17 1-2	Jan12 1-1	Nov03 0-3	Apr10 2-1
EAST FIFE	Nov24 2-2	Nov10 0-2	Apr13 0-1	Apr17 1-6	Dec29 1-0	Oct06 0-1	Jan19 0-3	Mar23 0-2	Sep08 0-1		Apr06 1-2	Dec08 0-0	Jan05 0-3	Oct20 0-1	Apr20 1-0	Oct27 2-1	Feb09 0-3	Sep22 1-2
FALKIRK	Nov10 1-3	Oct27 2-2	Apr13 1-1	Apr27 1-1	May04 3-0	Oct20 2-3	Sep22 3-3	Nov10 0-1	Oct06 0-1	Apr13 1-1		Nov24 4-1	Mar30 0-2	Dec08 0-0	Oct06 1-1	Sep22 1-1	Mar09 0-0	Oct27 0-1
HEARTS	Mar23 0-0	Apr02 4-1	Dec15 0-0	Oct27 0-0	May04 0-0	Oct20 2-2	Sep22 2-0	Nov10 3-0	Oct06 2-2	Apr13 3-0	Nov24 4-1		Sep08 1-1	Dec29 2-0	Jan05 3-1	Apr27 2-4	Jan19 0-2	Feb09 2-1
HIBERNIAN	Feb02 3-1	Apr23 2-1	Sep29 4-2	Feb23 2-4	Nov03 5-0	Apr17 3-0	Nov17 2-1	Jan12 3-1	Apr20 1-1	Sep15 2-1	Oct13 1-0	Jan01 3-1		Dec22 5-0	Apr15 1-0	Sep01 2-1	Mar02 3-1	Mar30 3-3
MORTON	Nov03 2-0	Sep29 1-1	Jan01 1-0	Nov06 0-0	Dec15 2-2	Jan19 3-1	Oct13 0-1	Oct27 1-2	Feb03 1-0	Feb02 0-3	Sep01 2-3		Mar30 4-3			Apr24 2-3		Jan01 1-1
MOTHERWELL	Sep01 0-0	Jan02 1-1	Feb24 0-1	Feb02 0-0	Dec12 2-2	Apr09 1-0	Apr27 1-0	Sep29 0-1	Mar23 3-1	Dec15 2-1	Apr17 0-3	Sep15 2-3	Nov10 0-3	Nov24 4-3		Oct13 1-2	Apr06 1-4	Oct27 0-1
PARTICK T	Apr08 2-0	Nov24 2-3	Nov03 3-0	Mar23 2-0	Oct20 1-3	Jan19 0-0	Oct06 1-0	Apr29 2-1	Sep22 1-1	Mar02 0-1	Apr20 2-2	Dec22 1-3	Dec29 1-0	Jan05 0-0	Feb09 1-0		Sep08 0-1	Mar16 0-1
RANGERS	Jan12 1-1	Feb02 2-3	Sep01 0-0	Sep15 0-1	Mar30 4-0	Apr13 3-1	Feb24 1-2	Apr20 3-1	Apr06 3-0	Oct13 0-1	Sep29 2-1	Nov10 0-3	Apr24 4-0	Jan01 1-0	Oct27 2-1	Jan01 1-1		Dec15 5-1
ST JOHNSTONE	Sep15 1-2	Sep01 0-0	Feb02 1-1	Sep29 2-1	Dec22 1-1	Mar23 3-3	Nov03 1-4	Jan02 2-0	Apr06 1-1	Mar09 1-3	Feb23 2-0	Oct13 0-2	Nov24 0-2	Apr03 1-4	Mar02 0-1	Nov10 2-2	Apr20 1-3	

Rangers, 1973-74: Back row (left to right): Smith, Henderson, Forsyth, Jackson, Kennedy, McCloy, Hunter, Scott, Conn, Parlane, Sharp. Middle row: Mathieson, Boyd, Jardine, Armour, Miller, Johnstone, Hamilton, Farrell, O'Hara, McNicol, J. Mason (assistant trainer). Front row: J.Wallace (manager), Denny, Morris, Fife, McDougal, Greig, McDonald, Steel, McLean, Young, T.Craig (physiotherapist).

DIVISION 2

	AIRDRIE	ALBION R	ALLOA	BERWICK R	BRECHIN C	CLYDEBANK	COWDENBEATH	E.STIRLING	FORFAR A	HAMILTON A	KILMARNOCK	MONTROSE	QUEEN OF SOU'	QUEEN'S PARK	RAITH R	ST MIRREN	STENHOUSEMU	STIRLING A	STRANRAER
AIRDRIE		Sep19 0-0	Apr20 5-2	Mar02 2-0	Jan19 8-0	Dec22 4-1	Nov03 5-0	Oct06 2-0	Sep08 4-0	Apr06 4-1	Feb09 0-0	Apr29 2-0	Nov17 3-0	Sep22 4-0	Dec29 6-1	Mar16 1-0	Sep05 3-0	Jan05 3-1	Oct20 3-1
ALBION R	Apr01 0-1		Sep29 2-2	Sep01 0-3	Apr27 3-1	Feb24 3-0	Feb03 0-0	Mar09 3-3	Apr09 1-2	Jan01 1-3	Nov21 3-4	Apr17 1-4	Oct13 0-2	May01 0-1	Mar23 0-1	Sep25 2-3	Oct27 1-1	Nov10 2-0	Apr06 0-2
ALLOA	Apr16 0-1	Jan19 1-0		Nov17 1-1	Sep19 2-1	Apr29 0-1	Mar30 0-2	Dec29 2-2	Apr24 2-0	Apr27 0-1	Oct06 0-1	Oct27 3-1	Apr13 0-1	Mar09 2-1	Feb09 0-4	Sep08 3-1	Sep08 2-0	1-0	Mar23 3-2
BERWICK R	Oct27 3-1	Dec29 1-0	Jan26 1-0		Sep22 2-2	Nov24 0-0	Apr13 3-3	Jan05 1-1	Oct06 0-0	Mar10 0-0	Sep05 0-1	Nov10 3-0	Apr27 1-1	Jan19 2-0	Oct20 1-0	Apr17 3-2	Sep19 2-1	Sep08 0-1	Feb09 0-1
BRECHIN C	Sep29 0-3	Dec22 0-0	Sep12 0-4	Jan12 2-0		Oct13 0-1	Sep01 2-4	Nov10 0-3	Apr20 2-1	Feb23 0-4	Apr06 0-4	Jan01 0-4	Sep24 0-3	Oct27 1-5	Nov24 0-4	Sep15 2-4	Mar09 2-1	Mar23 2-5	Apr24 2-2
CLYDEBANK	Apr27 2-1	Oct20 0-1	Nov10 1-2	Mar30 1-2	Feb09 2-0		Apr24 2-2	Sep08 1-3	Feb16 3-3	Oct27 1-1	Dec29 1-2	Mar09 3-0	Apr17 0-1	Mar23 2-0	Sep22 1-1	Apr13 1-1	Jan19 1-1	Sep19 2-0	Oct06 5-0
COWDENBEATH	Mar09 0-1	Oct06 3-4	Nov24 2-1	Apr30 1-1	Dec29 2-0	Apr06 0-2		Sep19 3-5	Feb09 3-2	Nov10 2-3	Jan19 2-4	Mar23 4-3	Oct27 1-1	Apr02 2-2	Sep08 0-0	Oct20 3-0	Sep05 1-4		Sep22 2-2
E.STIRLING	Feb02 0-2	Nov03 1-2	Sep01 2-3	Sep15 1-0	Mar16 2-0	Jan01 5-1	Sep12 0-1		Mar02 0-1	Sep29 1-1	Apr20 1-3	Sep25 3-1	Feb23 0-1	Nov24 1-2	Feb16 0-1	Oct13 1-0	Nov17 1-2	Apr06 1-0	Dec22 1-3
FORFAR A	Jan01 0-7	Apr13 4-0	Sep25 1-1	Feb02 1-1	Dec15 1-2	Sep15 0-2	Oct13 1-2	Oct27 2-1		Sep01 1-2	Mar23 3-5	Feb23 2-3	Jan12 1-2	May06 3-1	Nov10 1-4	Jan19 0-1	Apr27 0-2	Mar09 1-7	Nov17 1-1
HAMILTON A	Dec01 0-0	Sep08 2-0	Dec22 2-0	Nov03 0-4	Oct20 3-1	Mar03 3-0	Mar16 4-1	Jan19 1-0	Dec29 2-1		Apr30 2-2	Apr20 2-0	Mar30 2-0	Apr13 3-2	Sep05 1-1	Nov17 4-2	Jan26 2-1	Oct06 1-2	Sep19 1-1
KILMARNOCK	Oct13 4-0	Mar30 3-1	Feb02 8-2	Oct02 2-3	Dec01 3-1	Sep01 3-2	Sep29 4-3	Apr09 0-4	Nov17 5-1	Jan12 3-1		Sep15 2-1	Apr24 1-0	Apr16 5-0	Oct27 1-1	Jan01 1-1	Apr13 1-3	Apr27 2-1	Mar16 4-1
MONTROSE	Apr13 2-1	Sep22 3-1	Mar02 4-0	Mar16 1-0	Sep08 3-2	Apr03 1-3	Nov17 4-1	Apr23 4-2	Oct20 5-1	Feb16 1-0	Jan05 0-2		Dec01 2-2	Apr27 2-0	Oct06 1-3	Mar30 5-0	Feb09 0-0	Dec22 2-2	Jan19 2-2
QUEEN OF SOUTH	Mar23 2-1	Feb09 5-2	May04 1-0	Dec22 3-3	Sep05 2-1	Apr20 0-1	Mar02 5-0	Feb16 3-1	Sep22 3-2	Nov24 1-2	Sep19 1-2	Apr06 5-0		Dec29 2-0	Apr10 3-3	Nov03 5-3	Oct06 5-1	Jan19 3-2	Sep08 1-2
QUEEN'S PARK	Jan12 1-3	Apr20 3-1	Nov03 0-2	Sep29 1-0	Mar02 2-1	Nov17 1-0	Sep15 6-0	Mar30 0-3	Apr29 0-2	Apr11 0-2	Dec22 0-3	Sep01 0-2			Sep19 1-0	Feb02 0-0	Mar16 1-3	Feb09 0-0	Sep05 1-3
RAITH R	Sep01 0-4	Nov17 3-0	Oct13 3-2	Feb23 1-1	Mar30 1-1	May01 2-2	Jan01 1-2	Apr13 5-0	Mar16 4-1	Sep25 0-3	Mar02 2-1	Feb02 2-2	Sep15 3-0	Apr23 3-1		Sep29 2-4	Apr02 3-0	Apr16 5-4	Nov03 1-0
ST MIRREN	Nov10 3-5	Apr23 3-1	Apr06 1-0	Apr20 0-1	Feb16 2-0	Mar27 0-0	Dec22 2-0	Feb09 0-2	Sep19 3-1	Sep08 2-1	Mar23 2-2	Nov24 0-0	Mar09 3-4	Oct06 0-0	Jan05 0-0		Sep22 4-1	Oct20 3-3	Dec29 1-2
STENHOUSEMUIR	Sep25 2-3	Mar03 1-0	Jan01 4-0	Sep12 2-1	Nov03 0-3	Jan19 4-2	Feb23 1-2	Mar23 0-1	Dec22 3-2	Sep15 1-1	Feb16 1-1	Oct13 3-3	Feb02 0-4	Nov10 3-0	Apr06 0-1	Jan12 3-1		Nov24 0-3	Apr16 4-1
STIRLING A	Sep15 0-2	Mar16 7-1	Jan12 1-0	Jan01 0-2	Nov17 5-0	Apr09 3-0	Sep25 6-1	May01 6-0	Nov03 2-0	Feb02 1-3	Dec22 1-1	Sep01 4-3	Oct13 1-0	Apr20 3-2	Feb23 1-1	Mar30 1-1			Apr02 1-0
STRANRAER	Feb23 1-6	Dec01 1-2	Sep15 1-3	Oct13 1-4	Apr13 3-0	Feb02 1-0	Jan12 5-2	Apr27 3-0	Mar30 4-2	Sep12 2-4	Nov10 2-2	Sep29 3-1	Jan01 5-5	Sep25 1-1	Mar09 2-3	Sep01 0-2	Apr20 1-0	Oct27 2-0	

DIVISION 2 FINAL TABLE

	P	W	D	L	F	A	Pts
Airdrie	36	28	4	4	102	25	60
Kilmarnock	36	26	6	4	96	44	58
Hamilton A	36	24	7	5	68	38	55
Queen of South	36	20	7	9	73	41	47
Berwick R	36	16	13	7	53	35	45
Raith R	36	18	9	9	69	48	45
Stirling A	36	17	6	13	76	50	40
Montrose	36	15	7	14	71	64	37
Stranraer	36	14	8	14	64	70	36
Clydebank	36	13	8	15	47	48	34
St Mirren	36	12	10	14	62	66	34
Alloa	36	15	4	17	47	58	34
Cowdenbeath	36	11	9	16	59	85	31
Queen's Park	36	12	4	20	42	64	28
Stenhousemuir	36	11	5	20	44	59	27
E Stirling	36	9	5	22	47	73	23
Albion R	36	7	6	23	38	72	20
Forfar A	36	5	6	25	42	94	16
Brechin C	36	5	4	27	33	99	14

SFA Cup

1st Round

Dec 14	Clacknacuddin	...8	Gala Fairydean	...1
Dec 14	Montrose	...5	Selkirk	...1
Dec 14	Ross Co	...2	Brechin C	...0
Dec 14	St Cuthbert's	...1	Albion R	...4
Dec 14	Stenhousemuir	...2	E Stirling	...2

Replays

Dec 18	E Stirling	...3	Stenhousemuir	...1

2nd Round

Jan 4	Alloa	...1	Albion R	...1
Jan 4	Clacknacuddin	...4	Stirling A	...3
Jan 4	Cowdenbeath	...0	Clydebank	...2
Jan 4	E Stirling	...2	St Mirren	...1
Jan 4	Forfar A	...2	Ross Co	...3
Jan 4	Inverness C	...2	Inverness T	...0
Jan 4	Stranraer	...2	Queen's Park	...4
Jan 4	Vale of Leithen	...0	Montrose	...12

Replays

Jan 8	Albion R	...2	Alloa	...0

3rd Round

Jan 25	Aberdeen	...1	Rangers	...1
Jan 28	Airdrie	...0	Morton	...0
Jan 25	Arbroath	...1	E Stirling	...0
Jan 25	Ayr U	...1	Queen's Park	...2
Jan 25	Clyde	...0	Dundee	...1

Jan 28	Clydebank	...2	Dunfermline A	...1
Jan 29	Dumbarton	...2	Clacknacuddin	...1
Feb 4	Dundee U	...1	Berwick R	...1
Jan 29	Hearts	...2	Kilmarnock	...0
Jan 25	Hibernian	...0	Celtic	...2
Jan 25	Inverness C	...0	Albion R	...1
Jan 27	Montrose	...0	Hamilton A	...0
Jan 25	Motherwell	...0	Partick T	...0
Jan 25	Queen of South	...2	Raith R	...0
Jan 30	Ross Co	...1	Falkirk	...5
Jan 29	St Johnstone	...1	East Fife	...0

Replays

Feb 3	Hamilton A	...3	Montrose	...0
Feb 3	Morton	...0	Airdrie	...3
Feb 3	Partick T	...0	Motherwell	...1
Feb 5	Berwick R	...0	Dundee U	...1
Feb 10	Rangers	...1	Aberdeen	...2

4th Round

Feb 15	Airdrie	...2	Falkirk	...0
Feb 15	Arbroath	...2	Albion R	...0
Feb 15	Celtic	...4	Clydebank	...1
Feb 19	Dundee U	...0	Aberdeen	...1
Feb 15	Hamilton A	...0	Dumbarton	...1
Feb 15	Motherwell	...4	Queen's Park	...0
Feb 15	Queen of South	...0	Hearts	...2
Feb 15	St Johnstone	...0	Dundee	...1

5th Round

Mar 8	Aberdeen	...0	Motherwell	...1

Mar 8	Arbroath	...2	Airdrie	...2
Mar 8	Dumbarton	...1	Celtic	...2
Mar 8	Hearts	...1	Dundee	...1

Replays

Mar 12	Dundee	...3	Hearts	...2
Mar 12	Airdrie	...3	Arbroath	...0

Semi-finals

Apr 5	Airdrie	...1	Motherwell	...1
	played at Hampden Park			
Apr 2	Celtic	...1	Dundee	...0
	played at Hampden Park			

Replay

Apr 9	Airdrie	...1	Motherwell	...0
	played at Hampden Park			

Final

May 3	Airdrie	...1	Celtic	...3
	played at Hampden Park			

League Cup results for 1974-75 are detailed on pages 204-205.

DIVISION 1 FINAL TABLE

	P	W	D	L	F	A	Pts
Rangers	34	25	6	3	86	33	56
Hibernian	34	20	9	5	69	37	49
Celtic	34	20	5	9	81	41	45
Dundee U	34	19	7	8	72	43	45
Aberdeen	34	16	9	9	66	43	41
Dundee	34	16	6	12	48	42	38
Ayr U	34	14	8	12	50	61	36
Hearts	34	11	13	10	47	52	35
St Johnstone	34	11	12	11	41	44	34
Motherwell	34	14	5	15	52	57	33
Airdrie	34	11	9	14	43	55	31
Kilmarnock	34	8	15	11	52	68	31
Partick T	34	10	10	14	48	62	30
Dumbarton	34	7	10	17	44	55	24
Dunfermline A	34	7	9	18	46	66	23
Clyde	34	6	10	18	40	63	22
Morton	34	6	10	18	31	62	22
Arbroath	34	5	7	22	34	66	17

DIVISION 1

	ABERDEEN	AIRDRIE	ARBROATH	AYR U	CELTIC	CLYDE	DUMBARTON	DUNDEE	DUNDEE U	DUNFERMLINE A	HEARTS	HIBERNIAN	KILMARNOCK	MORTON	MOTHERWELL	PARTICK T	RANGERS	ST JOHNSTONE
ABERDEEN		Sep28 1-0	Oct26 5-1	Oct12 3-0	Mar12 3-2	Apr19 4-1	Feb22 1-1	Jan01 4-0	Mar29 2-0	Dec21 1-1	Feb01 2-2	Aug31 2-3	Jan11 4-0	Nov16 3-3	Apr23 2-2	Nov09 1-1	Dec07 1-2	Sep14 3-1
AIRDRIE	Mar04 2-2		Nov09 1-0	Oct26 1-2	Mar22 1-0	Oct12 0-3	Mar18 1-1	Aug31 0-1	Oct05 1-1	Apr15 5-2	Feb22 1-1	Dec07 0-0	Apr19 2-2	Sep14 3-1	Jan01 2-0	Nov23 1-0	Dec21 4-3	Feb10 1-1
ARBROATH	Mar01 1-2	Mar15 3-1		Mar29 1-3	Feb08 2-2	Sep14 2-0	Sep28 0-3	Jan11 2-2	Nov02 1-3	Jan01 1-3	Nov16 3-1	Dec21 0-2	Apr05 0-0	Aug31 0-2	Oct05 1-1	Oct19 2-0	Apr19 1-2	Dec07 0-0
AYR U	Feb08 2-0	Mar01 1-0	Nov23 1-0		Jan18 1-5	Jan11 1-0	Mar22 1-3	Dec07 2-1	Oct19 1-1	Apr19 3-2	Nov02 3-3	Apr05 2-1	Jan01 1-1	Dec21 0-4	Sep14 5-2	Oct05 1-1	Aug31 1-1	Nov09 1-0
CELTIC	Nov02 1-0	Nov16 6-0	Oct12 1-0	Sep28 5-3		Jan01 5-1	Feb11 2-2	Apr19 1-2	Mar15 0-1	Dec07 2-1	Mar29 4-1	Oct19 5-0	Aug31 5-0	Apr05 1-1	Jan11 2-3	Mar01 3-2	Sep14 1-2	Dec21 3-1
CLYDE	Dec14 1-1	Feb08 2-1	Jan04 3-1	Sep21 1-0	Sep07 2-4		Dec28 1-3	Mar18 0-1	Apr12 1-2	Oct05 2-2	Nov30 2-2	Mar22 0-3	Feb18 4-2	Nov09 1-2	Apr26 0-0	Feb22 2-2	Dec21 1-2	Oct26 2-2
DUMBARTON	Oct19 2-3	Nov02 2-0	Feb19 5-1	Nov16 1-2	Oct05 1-3	Aug31 0-0		Nov23 1-2	Mar01 1-1	Sep14 0-1	Mar15 2-3	Apr19 1-1	Feb26 0-0	Jan01 0-1	Dec21 0-1	Feb08 1-5	Jan11 1-0	Apr05 0-0
DUNDEE	Sep07 0-1	Dec28 1-0	Sep21 0-1	Apr12 2-3	Dec14 0-6	Nov02 4-1	Mar29 2-1		Jan04 2-0	Mar01 2-0	Apr23 2-0	Oct05 0-0	Feb08 4-1	Oct19 3-0	Feb10 4-1	Nov30 1-0	Mar12 1-2	Nov16 4-0
DUNDEE U	Nov27 4-0	Feb01 1-0	Mar19 3-1	Mar05 3-1	Nov09 0-0	Dec07 3-3	Oct26 3-3	Sep14 3-0		Sep28 1-0	Oct12 5-0	Jan11 1-3	Dec21 3-4	Apr19 1-0	Aug31 5-0	Apr05 2-1	Apr05 2-2	Jan02 1-1
DUNFERMLINE A	Apr26 2-2	Nov30 3-1	Sep07 0-2	Mar08 1-3	Apr12 1-1	Feb01 3-0	Jan04 3-1	Oct26 1-2	Feb11		Sep21 2-2	Nov09 1-1	Mar22 1-1	Nov23 0-1	Mar12 1-2	Dec28 1-6	Oct12 2-3	Feb26 2-3
HEARTS	Oct05 1-4	Oct19 2-1	Mar22 0-0	Mar19 1-0	Nov23 1-1	Apr05 2-1	Nov09 0-0	Dec21 3-1	Feb08 1-0	Jan11		Jan01 0-0	Sep14 1-1	Dec07 3-1	Apr19 4-1	Jan18 3-1	Oct26 1-1	Aug31 1-2
HIBERNIAN	Dec28 0-1	Apr26 6-1	Feb01 2-1	Nov30 2-1	Feb26 2-1	Nov16 1-0	Dec14 2-0	Feb01 2-1	Sep21 3-0	Mar18 5-1	Sep07 2-1		Mar01 0-2	Nov02 5-0	Oct12 6-2	Jan04 2-2	Jan29 1-1	Sep28 0-1
KILMARNOCK	Sep21 1-0	Dec14 3-3	Nov30 2-2	Sep07 3-0	Dec28 0-1	Mar29 2-0	Apr12 1-2	Oct12 1-1	Apr26 2-4	Nov16 2-4	Jan04 1-1	Nov13 1-1		Mar15 1-1	Feb22 1-1	Mar08 0-6	Sep28 1-1	Feb01 1-1
MORTON	Mar22 0-3	Jan04 3-0	Dec28 3-2	Apr26 1-1	Nov30 0-1	Sep28 0-1	Sep07 1-1	Feb22 1-2	Dec14 0-6	Mar29 0-2	Apr12 0-0	Mar08 0-1	Nov09 2-3		Oct26 0-3	Sep21 3-1	Feb01 1-1	Oct12 1-1
MOTHERWELL	Nov30 2-1	Sep07 1-3	Feb01 3-1	Jan04 5-1	Sep21 1-2	Mar15 1-1	Apr26 3-1	Sep28 0-1	Dec28 0-1	Nov02 1-2	Dec14 1-3	Feb08 4-1	Oct19 2-0	Mar01 3-0		Apr12 0-0	Nov16 0-5	Mar29 3-4
PARTICK T	Mar15 1-0	Mar29 1-3	Feb22 1-0	Feb01 2-2	Nov06 1-2	Dec21 2-2	Oct12 1-2	Apr05 2-2	Nov16 2-0	Aug31 1-1	Sep28 2-1	Sep14 2-1	Nov02 1-0	Jan11 2-1	Dec07		Jan01 0-4	Apr19 0-2
RANGERS	Apr12 3-2	Apr26 0-1	Dec14 3-0	Dec28 3-0	Jan04 3-0	Oct19 3-1	Sep21 3-2	Nov09 1-0	Nov30 4-2	Feb08 2-0	Mar01 2-1	Nov23 0-1	Feb15 1-3	Oct05 3-0	Mar22 3-2	Sep07		Mar08 1-0
ST JOHNSTONE	Jan04 1-1	Sep21 0-1	Apr12 3-2	Mar15 0-0	Apr26 2-1	Mar01 1-0	Nov30 3-0	Mar22 3-1	Sep07 2-0	Oct19 2-1	Dec28 2-3	Jan18 1-2	Oct05 2-2	Feb08 2-0	Nov23 0-1	Dec14 1-3	Nov02 1-2	

Celtic's Paul Wilson (above), scored six goals in four Hampden Cup Finals in 1974-75; Sandy Jardine (right), ever-present as Rangers regained the League title after nine years.

DIVISION 2

Home \ Away	ALBION R	ALLOA	BERWICK R	BRECHIN C	CLYDEBANK	COWDENBEATH	EAST FIFE	E.STIRLING	FALKIRK	FORFAR A	HAMILTON A	MEADOWBANK T	MONTROSE	QUEEN OF SOUTH	QUEEN'S PARK	RAITH R	ST MIRREN	STENHOUSEMUIR	STIRLING A	STRANRAER
ALBION R		Apr16 3-2	Feb08 3-2	Apr21 3-0	Nov16 1-3	Apr09 2-0	Mar25 2-1	Sep17 6-2	Oct19 4-1	Sep21 5-3	Sep07 1-2	Oct19 0-1	Apr12 3-0	Apr26 1-1	Mar29 1-2	Nov02 2-1	Mar15 2-4	Nov30 0-0	Sep28 1-4	Mar01 4-0
ALLOA	Aug31 1-1		Apr05 0-0	Mar29 1-0	Apr19 1-0	Oct12 0-0	Oct26 0-1	Feb22 2-1	Nov16 0-1	Dec21 3-1	Sep28 0-0	Sep18 8-1	Sep04 0-2	Mar08 0-4	Feb01 3-0	Dec07 0-2	Nov09 3-1	Jan01 0-0	Sep14 2-2	Jan11 1-3
BERWICK R	Oct12 2-0	Nov30 3-0		Aug31 2-1	Sep14 2-0	Oct26 4-1	Mar08 2-0	Jan01 1-0	Mar29 1-2	Jan11 1-1	Sep18 0-1	Nov09 3-0	Mar22 2-2	Apr12 0-3	Apr26 0-2	Sep28 2-1	Sep04 1-5	Feb22 4-2	Feb01 2-1	Dec14 3-0
BRECHIN C	Apr19 3-2	Nov23 2-2	Dec28 0-1		Oct05 0-0	Mar08 3-1	Jan04 3-2	Mar22 1-0	Jan18 0-3	Sep11 4-1	Apr26 1-3	Oct12 0-1	Sep07 1-2	Feb22 0-4	Oct26 2-1	Apr05 1-1	Sep21 2-6	Dec14 4-5	Oct26 1-2	Dec21 2-2
CLYDEBANK	Mar22 2-0	Dec14 4-1	Apr30 2-1	Feb01 3-1		Nov30 2-1	Sep21 0-1	Nov09 0-3	Apr26 2-2	Sep28 1-0	Apr12 3-0	Sep07 0-0	Oct12 3-0	Dec28 0-0	Feb22 3-2	Mar29 0-0	Oct26 1-1	Sep18 0-0	Mar08 0-0	Sep04 0-3
COWDENBEATH	Sep14 1-5	Feb08 1-1	Mar01 0-0	Nov02 1-2	Apr05 0-3		Apr02 0-2	Feb15 1-1	Mar15 1-4	Jan01 2-1	Oct19 1-1	Sep28 5-0	Sep11 1-0	Nov16 0-2	Apr19 2-0	Aug31 0-2	Mar29 1-4	Dec21 0-3	Dec07 4-5	Oct05 0-0
EAST FIFE	Oct05 5-0	Mar01 3-2	Nov02 2-1	Jan11 3-0	Sep25 1-0	Sep22 2-2		Sep28 1-0	Oct19 0-1	Aug31 2-1	Mar15 1-0	Apr05 4-1	Sep11 0-4	Oct12 1-1	Nov16 1-0	Jan01 2-1	Feb08 1-2	Dec07 1-1	Apr19 1-1	Dec21 4-1
E.STIRLING	Sep11 1-0	Oct19 4-0	Sep07 0-2	Nov16 1-2	Mar15 1-0	Sep21 2-1	Jan18 2-0		Oct05 2-0	Mar01 4-0	Feb08 0-3	Sep13 3-1	Dec28 2-3	Apr15 1-2	Sep23 2-4	Nov02 1-0	Apr26 5-0	Nov30 1-1	Mar29 1-1	Apr12 0-3
FALKIRK	Jan11 3-1	Mar22 2-0	Nov23 3-0	Sep28 3-1	Dec21 0-1	Nov09 5-0	Feb22 4-0	Feb01 6-1		Dec07 2-0	Apr23 2-1	Mar08 2-0	Oct26 3-2	Oct12 1-2	Aug31 5-1	Apr19 1-0	Sep18 4-0	Sep14 2-0	Jan01 1-2	Apr05 3-0
FORFAR A	Feb22 0-5	Apr26 0-3	Sep21 2-3	Jan18 1-3	Sep18 0-2	Sep07 1-2	Dec28 1-2	Oct26 2-3	Apr12 0-2		Mar19 0-2	Nov30 1-3	Mar08 0-4	Feb01 2-3	Nov23 2-2	Sep25 2-0	Dec14 1-1	Oct12 0-3	Nov09 0-4	Mar22 1-4
HAMILTON A	Jan01 0-0	Apr30 1-0	Jan04 1-0	Dec21 1-1	Dec07 0-1	Feb22 0-0	Nov09 3-4	Oct12 0-2	Apr16 3-4	Sep14 8-0		Dec14 2-0	Apr19 2-0	Oct26 2-0	Apr05 0-1	Oct05 1-1	Mar08 3-1	Aug31 1-1	Jan11 3-1	Nov23 6-2
MEADOWBANK T	Dec07 3-1	Sep11 0-1	Mar15 1-1	Feb08 0-0	Dec30 1-0	Jan18 1-6	Nov22 2-1	Mar25 0-2	Nov02 1-0	Apr05 0-0	Nov16 0-4		Oct05 1-2	Sep25 0-2	Mar01 0-3	Jan11 1-0	Oct19 2-4	Apr19 0-2	Dec21 1-1	Dec28 1-0
MONTROSE	Dec21 0-1	Sep25 2-1	Nov16 2-0	Jan01 3-0	Feb08 1-1	Sep18 3-0	Nov30 3-1	Aug31 4-3	Nov02 0-0	Apr07 2-1	Feb01 2-0				Mar15 2-0	Jan11 0-0	Sep14 0-0	Apr29 2-1	Sep28 2-1	Oct19 3-1
QUEEN OF SOUTH	Nov23 1-1	Nov02 1-1	Dec07 1-3	Oct19 3-0	Aug31 3-2	Mar22 2-0	Sep18 2-0	Apr19 1-0	Feb08 7-0	Oct05 0-0	Mar01 3-0	Sep04 1-0	Nov09 0-3		Sep14 0-2	Dec21 1-1	Jan18 0-1	Jan11 2-1	Apr05 3-0	Jan01 4-2
QUEEN'S PARK	Mar08 1-4	Oct05 0-2	Dec21 1-2	Apr12 3-0	Oct19 1-0	Dec14 1-1	Mar22 0-0	Sep04 1-2	Dec28 0-2	Mar29 4-0	Nov30 0-3	Apr14 1-1	Sep21 1-2	Apr21 0-3		Feb08 1-1	Sep07 0-0	Nov09 1-1	Sep18 1-2	Mar11 2-1
RAITH R	Nov09 1-2	Apr12 3-1	Jan18 2-0	Nov30 5-2	Nov23 1-2	Dec28 1-0	Sep07 0-2	Mar08 1-1	Dec14 1-0	Apr23 2-0	Feb01 1-0	Apr26 3-1	Feb15 0-4	Oct12 2-2			Mar22 1-2	Oct26 2-0	Feb22 3-0	Sep18 2-1
ST MIRREN	Apr05 1-1	Mar15 5-1	Sep25 0-1	Jan11 6-1	Mar01 2-0	Nov23 1-1	Oct12 0-3	Dec21 2-0	Apr30 0-0	Apr19 2-0	Nov02 0-1	Feb22 4-0	Dec07 1-2	Sep28 0-5	Jan01 0-3	Nov16 0-1		Feb01 4-1	Aug31 3-0	Sep14 4-0
STENHOUSEMUIR	Apr01 6-1	Sep07 0-0	Oct19 2-0	Sep24 2-0	Sep11 1-2	Apr26 1-0	Apr12 0-1	Apr05 0-1	Jan04 0-1	Feb08 5-0	Dec28 2-3	Feb15 1-0	Nov23 0-1	Sep21 1-0	Mar15 1-3	Mar01 1-0	Oct05 4-4		Nov16 2-1	Nov02 0-0
STIRLING A	Sep25 3-2	Feb15 2-2	Oct05 2-0	Sep21 5-0	Nov02 3-3	Apr12 0-2	Dec14 1-3	Nov23 0-0	Sep07 0-2	Mar15 2-0	Sep21 1-2	Jan18 4-1	Nov30 3-0	Sep07 3-0	Oct19 2-1	Dec28 1-1	Mar22 0-1			Feb08 2-0
STRANRAER	Oct26 1-1	Sep21 0-4	Apr19 2-2	Mar15 0-0	Sep25 2-1	Feb01 2-1	Apr26 2-1	Dec07 1-0	Nov30 3-4	Nov16 0-0	Mar29 1-4	Aug31 3-1	Feb22 2-2	Sep07 2-1	Sep28 0-0	Sep11 0-0	Jan25 2-1	Mar08 0-0	Oct12 1-2	

DIVISION 2 FINAL TABLE

	P	W	D	L	F	A	Pts
Falkirk	38	26	2	10	76	29	54
Queen of South	38	23	7	8	77	33	53
Montrose	38	23	7	8	70	37	53
Hamilton A	38	21	7	10	69	30	49
East Fife	38	20	7	11	57	42	47
St Mirren	38	19	8	11	74	52	46
Clydebank	38	18	8	12	50	40	44
Stirling A	38	17	9	12	67	55	43
Berwick R	38	17	6	15	53	49	40
E Stirling	38	16	8	14	56	52	40
Stenhousemuir	38	14	11	13	52	42	39
Albion R	38	16	7	15	72	64	39
Raith R	38	14	9	15	48	44	37
Stranraer	38	12	11	15	47	65	35
Alloa	38	11	11	16	49	56	33
Queen's Park	38	10	10	18	41	54	30
Brechin C	38	9	7	22	44	85	25
Meadowbank T	38	9	5	24	26	87	23
Cowdenbeath	38	5	11	22	39	76	21
Forfar A	38	1	7	30	27	102	9

Season 1975-76

SFA Cup

1st Round

Dec 13	Albion R 0	Hawick RA....... 0	
Dec 13	Brechin C 1	Berwick R 1	
Dec 13	E Stirling 0	Alloa 5	
Dec 13	Elgin C 0	Forres Mechanic . 1	
Dec 13	Peterhead 0	Raith R 2	
Dec 13	Stranraer 1	Queen's Park 0	

Replays

Dec 18	Hawick RA 0	Albion R 3
Dec 20	Berwick R 3	Brechin C 3
Dec 22	Berwick R 0	Brechin C 1

2nd Round

Jan 10	Albion R 1	Glasgow Univ 1
Jan 10	Cowdenbeath ...2	Selkirk 0
Jan 10	Forfar A 2	Meadowbank T ...1
Jan 10	Forres Mechanic . 1	Alloa 2
Jan 10	Raith R 3	Clydebank 1
Jan 10	Stenhousemuir ... 2	Brechin C 2
Jan 10	Stirling A 4	Civil Service 0
Jan 10	Stranraer 2	Keith 3

Replays

Jan 14	Brechin C 0	Stenhousemuir ... 1
Jan 14	Glasgow Univ 0	Albion R 1

3rd Round

Jan 24	Albion R 1	Partick T 2
Jan 24	Alloa 0	Aberdeen 4
Jan 24	Ayr U 4	Airdrie 2
Jan 24	Cowdenbeath 3	St Mirren 0
Jan 24	Dumbarton 2	Keith 0
Jan 24	Dundee 1	Falkirk 2
Jan 24	Dundee U 4	Hamilton A 0
Jan 24	Hearts 2	Clyde 2
Jan 24	Hibernian 3	Dunfermline A ...2
Jan 24	Motherwell 3	Celtic 2
Jan 24	Morton 1	Montrose 3
Jan 24	Queen of South .3	St Johnstone 2
Jan 24	Raith R 1	Arbroath 0
Jan 24	Rangers 3	East Fife 0
Jan 24	Stenhousemuir ...1	Kilmarnock 1
Jan 24	Stirling A 2	Forfar A 1

Replays

Jan 28	Clyde 0	Hearts 1
Jan 28	Kilmarnock 1	Stenhousemuir ... 0

4th Round

Feb 14	Ayr U 2	Queen of South ..2
Feb 14	Cowdenbeath 0	Motherwell 2
Feb 14	Hearts 3	Stirling A 0
Feb 14	Hibernian 1	Dundee U 1
Feb 14	Kilmarnock 3	Falkirk 1
Feb 14	Montrose 2	Raith R 1
Feb 14	Partick T 0	Dumbarton 0
Feb 14	Rangers 4	Aberdeen 1

Replays

Feb 18	Queen of South .. 5	Ayr U 4
Feb 25	Dumbarton 1	Partick T 0
Feb 25	Dundee U 0	Hibernian 2

5th Round

Mar 6	Dumbarton 2	Kilmarnock 1
Mar 6	Montrose 2	Hearts 2
Mar 6	Motherwell 2	Hibernian 2
Mar 6	Queen of South ..0	Rangers 5

Replays

Mar 9	Hearts 2	Montrose 2
Mar 10	Hibernian 1	Motherwell 1
Mar 15	Hibernian 1	Motherwell 2
	played at Ibrox	
Mar 16	Hearts 2	Montrose 1
	played at Muirton Park	

Semi-finals

Apr 3	Dumbarton 0	Hearts 0
	played at Hampden Park	
Mar 31	Motherwell 2	Rangers 3
	played at Hampden Park	

Replay

Apr 14	Dumbarton 0	Hearts 3
	played at Hampden Park	

Final

May 1	Hearts 1	Rangers 3
	played at Hampden Park	

After-match celebrations at Hampden as Rangers complete the treble of League and both Cups in 1975-76.

PREMIER

	ABERDEEN	AYR U	CELTIC	DUNDEE	DUNDEE U	HEARTS	HIBERNIAN	MOTHERWELL	RANGERS	ST JOHNSTONE
ABERDEEN		Sep27 3-1 / Jan31 2-1	Oct11 1-2 / Feb21 0-1	Nov01 2-0 / Mar13 0-1	Sep13 1-3 / Jan10 5-3	Nov22 0-0 / Apr07 0-3	Dec27 2-2 / Apr24 3-0	Sep06 2-2 / Jan03 0-0	Dec06 1-0 / Apr14 0-0	Oct18 2-0 / Feb28 3-0
AYR U	Nov29 1-0 / Apr10 1-1		Nov12 2-7 / May01 3-5	Sep20 2-1 / Jan17 3-1	Dec06 2-2 / Apr14 1-0	Nov15 1-1 / Apr21 0-1	Nov15 1-3 / Mar27 2-0	2-0 / Feb21 0-1	Oct11 3-0 / Jan03 2-0	Sep06 1-0
CELTIC	Dec13 0-2 / Apr17 1-1	Dec27 3-1 / Apr24 1-2		Sep06 4-0 / Jan03 3-3	Sep27 2-1 / Jan31 2-1	Oct04 3-1 / Feb07 2-0	Dec10 1-1 / Feb28 4-0	Nov15 0-2 / Apr26 4-0	Nov22 3-2 / Apr03 1-0	
DUNDEE	Aug30 3-2 / Jan01 1-3	Nov22 2-2 / Apr03 1-2	Nov08 1-0 / Mar20 0-1		Dec20 0-0 / Apr21 2-1	Sep13 2-3 / Jan10 4-1	Dec06 2-0 / Apr14 1-1	Oct25 3-6 / May01 1-0	Sep27 0-0 / Jan31 1-1	Oct11 4-3 / 3-0
DUNDEE U	Nov15 1-2 / Mar27 1-0	Oct04 3-2 / Mar03 5-0	Nov08 1-3 / Apr10 3-2	Oct18 1-2 / Feb28 1-0		Dec13 0-1 / Apr17 2-0	Sep06 1-0 / Apr28 2-0	Sep20 2-0 / Jan17 1-4	Dec27 0-0 / Apr24 0-1	Nov01 0-1 / Mar31 1-1
HEARTS	Sep20 2-2 / Jan17 3-3	Oct18 2-1 / Feb28 1-0	Dec06 0-1 / Jan03 1-0	Nov15 1-1 / Mar27 3-0	Oct11 1-0 / Feb21 0-1		Nov01 1-1 / Mar13 0-1	Nov29 3-3 / Apr10 1-2	Sep06 0-2 / Jan03 1-2	Dec27 2-0 / Apr24 1-0
HIBERNIAN	Oct25 3-1 / Mar31 3-2	Sep13 1-0 / Jan10 3-0	Dec20 1-3 / Apr21 2-0	Oct04 1-1 / Feb07 4-0	Nov08 1-1 / Mar20 0-1	Aug30 1-0 / Jan01 3-0		Dec13 1-0 / Apr17 2-0	Nov22 2-1 / Apr03 0-3	Sep27 4-2 / Jan31 5-0
MOTHERWELL	Nov08 0-3 / Mar20 2-1	Aug30 1-1 / Jan01 1-0	Sep13 1-1 / Jan10 1-1	Dec27 3-2 / Apr24 1-0	Nov22 2-1 / Apr03 0-1	Sep27 1-1 / Jan31 2-0	Oct11 1-1 / Feb21 1-1		Oct18 1-0 / Feb28 2-0	Dec06 4-2 / Apr14 2-0
RANGERS	Oct04 1-0 / Feb07 2-1	Dec13 3-0 / Apr17 2-1	Aug30 2-1 / Jan17 1-0	Nov29 1-3 / Apr10 3-0	Nov12 4-1 / May04 3-0	Nov08 1-2 / Mar31 2-0	Sep20 1-1 / Jan17 3-1	Dec20 1-1 / Apr20 2-0		Sep13 2-0 / Jan10 4-0
ST JOHNSTONE	Dec20 1-1 / Apr21 2-0	Nov08 0-1 / Mar20 1-2	Sep20 1-2 / Jan17 3-4	Dec13 0-0 / Apr17 1-1	Aug30 0-1 / Jan01 1-1	Oct25 3-4 / Apr26 0-0	Nov29 2-1 / Apr10 4-0	Oct04 0-1 / Feb07 1-3	Nov15 1-5 / Mar27 0-3	

DIVISION 1

	AIRDRIE	ARBROATH	CLYDE	DUMBARTON	DUNFERMLINE A	EAST FIFE	FALKIRK	HAMILTON A	KILMARNOCK	MONTROSE	MORTON	PARTICK T	QUEEN OF SOUTH	ST MIRREN
AIRDRIE		Nov29 2-2	Dec13 2-1	Oct04 3-0	Feb07 1-1	Oct25 1-0	Feb07 2-0	Sep06 2-2	Nov08 3-4	Sep06 2-2	Nov15 2-2	Jan17 2-1	Dec20 2-4	Feb21 1-3
ARBROATH	Sep27 3-0		Feb28 3-0	Nov01 1-5	Jan17 1-0	Dec06 3-1	Feb07 0-1	Oct11 2-1	Dec20 2-0	Sep06 1-2	Jan03 0-1	Oct25 0-0	Sep20 3-2	Nov15 4-1
CLYDE	Oct11 2-2	Nov08 5-2		Aug30 1-2	Sep20 0-2	Dec20 0-2	Dec06 3-4	Feb21 0-0	Nov29 0-2	Oct25 3-0	Feb14 1-2	Jan01 1-2	Jan17 1-3	Sep13 3-0
DUMBARTON	Dec06 0-0	Feb21 3-2	Feb07 1-0		Nov08 2-0	Sep27 5-5	Dec06 1-4	Jan17 5-1	Oct11 3-0	Oct11 0-6	Oct25 0-2	Feb21 2-3	Oct11 2-1	Dec20 2-0
DUNFERMLINE A	Aug30 3-3	Nov22 0-1	Feb18 5-1	Feb28 0-3		Jan01 1-1	Oct25 2-2	Sep13 0-4	Nov15 1-0	Dec20 1-0	Dec06 1-0	Feb21 0-3	Dec11 0-0	Sep27 2-2
EAST FIFE	Dec27 1-1	Oct04 3-1	Oct18 4-3	Nov29 2-1	Sep06 5-1		Jan03 2-1	Sep20 2-4	Feb07 1-7	Nov08 2-2	Jan10 1-1	Feb21 2-0	Feb21 2-0	Dec13 0-2
FALKIRK	Jan31 1-1	Aug30 1-0	Nov01 1-2	Jan01 3-2	Dec27 4-1	Sep13 0-1		Oct21 1-0	Nov01 0-1	Nov29 2-0	Mar03 3-3	Nov15 0-0	Nov15 1-0	Jan01 1-1
HAMILTON A	Feb28 2-1	Dec13 1-0	Nov01 0-1	Mar15 0-3	Jan03 1-1	Nov22 3-2	Dec20 1-1		Feb07 1-1	Feb23 3-3	Sep20 2-0	Oct04 0-4	Sep06 2-2	Oct25 0-1
KILMARNOCK	Jan01 2-1	Oct18 2-1	Sep27 3-0	Nov22 1-0	Jan10 4-0	Jan31 2-1	Feb21 1-0	Aug30 4-2		Dec13 1-1	Dec27 3-2	Sep13 0-1	Nov08 2-0	Oct04 3-1
MONTROSE	Jan10 1-0	Jan01 3-5	Apr03 4-3	Dec13 3-2	Feb28 2-2	Aug30 3-0	Sep27 2-1	Nov22 1-1	Oct11		Feb21 1-1	Dec06 2-1	Dec06 2-1	Jan31 1-1
MORTON	Nov22 1-0	Sep13 2-2	Nov15 1-1	Dec13 1-1	Oct04 1-1	Feb28 3-0	Sep27 2-1	Jan31 2-3	Oct25 1-4	Nov01 1-3		Aug30 0-0	Dec20 0-1	Jan01 1-1
PARTICK T	Oct18 0-1	Dec27 2-0	Sep06 2-0	Jan31 0-0	Nov01 1-1	Nov15 5-0	Oct11 3-2	Jan03 2-0	Feb28 2-0	Feb07 4-1	Feb07 2-0		Sep27 2-1	Nov22 2-1
QUEEN OF SOUTH	Sep13 1-3	Jan31 2-1	Nov15 1-3	Dec27 4-2	Oct18 5-2	Dec13 1-1	Nov01 3-2	Jan10 2-2	Feb28 2-1	Oct04 2-1	Oct18 0-1	Nov29 1-1		Aug30 2-2
ST MIRREN	Nov01 2-2	Feb14 0-0	Jan03 3-0	Oct18 3-2	Nov29 2-0	Oct11 1-0	Nov08 2-2	Dec27 0-0	Dec06 3-1	Sep20 2-2	Sep06 2-3	Jan17 0-2	Feb07	

DIVISION 2

	ALBION R	ALLOA	BERWICK R	BRECHIN C	CLYDEBANK	COWDENBEATH	E STIRLING	FORFAR A	MEADOWBANK T	QUEEN'S PARK	RAITH R	STENHOUSEMUIR	STIRLING A	STRANRAER
ALBION R		Sep27 0-1	Dec06 2-2	Apr26 4-0	Oct11 0-4	Feb25 1-1	Sep13 2-1	Nov01 4-0	Nov22 4-0	Feb28 0-0	Dec27 1-2	Aug30 2-2	Oct18 1-1	Jan01 2-1
ALLOA	Nov29 2-0		Oct18 1-0	Jan31 1-0	Apr06 4-0	Feb28 1-1	Oct04 3-3	Nov15 1-0	Aug30 1-1	Nov01 3-3	Mar31 1-0	Jan01 1-1	Dec27 2-1	Sep13 3-3
BERWICK R	Oct04 0-1	Feb18 0-3		Sep13 2-1	Sep27 2-1	Feb21 1-2	Aug30 3-3	Oct25 1-0	Jan01 1-1	Feb14 1-3	Nov15 1-1	Jan31 1-1	Nov22 3-2	Nov08 1-2
BRECHIN C	Nov15 2-0	Sep20 2-3	Apr24 1-0		Feb07 1-2	Oct25 1-2	Nov29 2-2	Sep06 2-1	Feb14 0-3	Oct04 1-0	Jan17 0-4	Nov01 1-1	Feb28 2-3	Apr17 0-4
CLYDEBANK	Feb14 2-2	Nov22 3-1	Nov29 0-1	Aug30 2-1		Sep13 3-0	Nov01 0-1	Feb28 2-0	Dec13 1-1	Oct25 1-2	Oct04 1-0	Oct18 1-1	Jan01 0-1	Jan31 2-1
COWDENBEATH	Sep20 3-0	Nov08 0-1	Nov01 3-2	Dec27 5-2	Jan03 1-1		Oct18 0-1	Feb07 2-2	Nov29 2-0	Jan17 2-2	Sep06 1-1	Mar09 3-1	Apr17 2-1	Oct04 2-1
E STIRLING	Jan03 0-0	Dec06 0-3	Nov01 1-1	Sep27 1-0	Feb21 0-1	Dec20 4-2		Oct11 1-1	Oct25 3-0	Sep20 2-1	Nov08 1-3	Jan03 0-0	Jan31 0-0	Jan24 3-1
FORFAR A	Feb21 1-0	Feb24 4-3	Jan01 1-3	Jan01 0-1	Nov22 0-2	Aug30 2-3	Feb14 1-2		Jan31 1-1	Oct18 4-1	Nov29 1-0	Oct04 0-0	Sep13 3-1	Nov22 2-2
MEADOWBANK T	Jan17 4-1	Feb07 1-2	Sep16 2-6	Oct11 0-4	Nov15 0-1	Sep27 1-4	Dec27 2-0	Sep20 2-0		Jan03 1-0	Oct18 0-1	Nov08 1-1	Dec06 1-0	Feb21 2-3
QUEEN'S PARK	Nov08 2-2	Feb21 3-1	Oct11 1-0	Dec06 0-2	Dec27 0-2	Nov22 4-1	Jan01 1-0	Dec20 4-0	Sep13 1-1		Sep20 2-3	Feb24 0-3	Aug30 3-1	Nov29 2-0
RAITH R	Oct25 1-1	Oct11 1-0	Mar17 3-0	Nov22 1-1	Dec06 1-0	Jan01 2-0	Feb28 2-2	Sep27 2-2	Dec20 3-2	Jan31 0-2		Sep13 2-0	Nov01 1-0	Aug30 3-3
STENHOUSEMUIR	Feb07 4-2	Sep06 1-1	Sep20 2-1	Feb21 4-1	Dec20 2-1	Oct11 0-2	Jan17 1-2	Dec06 2-1	Feb28 2-2	Nov15 2-2	Jan03 0-3		Sep27 0-1	Oct25 1-2
STIRLING A	Dec20 1-1	Oct25 2-2	Jan17 2-0	Nov08 1-1	Sep06 0-1	Nov15 5-2	Sep20 3-2	Dec13 2-0	Oct04 5-0	Feb07 1-3	Mar06 0-1	Nov29 1-2		Oct11 3-0
STRANRAER	Sep06 1-2	Jan03 0-1	Feb28 1-2	Oct18 4-2	Sep20 0-1	Dec06 2-4	Nov15 2-1	Jan17 4-0	Nov01 5-1	Sep27 1-1	Feb07 1-3	Dec27 3-1	Apr24 1-0	

League Cup results for 1975-76 are detailed on pages 206-207.

PREMIER DIVISION FINAL TABLE

	P	W	D	L	F	A	Pts
Rangers	36	23	8	5	60	24	54
Celtic	36	21	6	9	71	42	48
Hibernian	36	18	7	11	55	43	43
Motherwell	36	16	8	12	57	49	40
Hearts	36	13	9	14	39	45	35
Ayr U	36	14	5	17	46	59	33
Aberdeen	36	11	10	15	49	50	32
Dundee U	36	12	8	16	46	48	32
Dundee	36	11	10	15	49	62	32
St Johnstone	36	3	5	28	29	79	11

DIVISION 1 FINAL TABLE

	P	W	D	L	F	A	Pts
Partick T	26	17	7	2	47	19	41
Kilmarnock	26	16	3	7	44	29	35
Montrose	26	12	6	8	53	43	30
Dumbarton	26	12	4	10	53	46	28
Arbroath	26	11	4	11	41	39	26
St Mirren	26	9	8	9	37	37	26
Falkirk	26	10	5	11	38	35	25
Airdrie	26	7	11	8	44	41	25
Hamilton A	26	7	10	9	37	37	24
Queen of South	26	9	6	11	41	47	24
Morton	26	7	9	10	31	40	23
East Fife	26	8	7	11	39	53	23
Dunfermline A	26	5	10	11	30	51	20
Clyde	26	5	4	17	34	52	14

DIVISION 2 FINAL TABLE

	P	W	D	L	F	A	Pts
Clydebank	26	17	6	3	44	13	40
Raith R	26	15	10	1	45	22	40
Alloa	26	14	7	5	44	28	35
Queen's Park	26	10	9	7	41	33	29
Cowdenbeath	26	11	7	8	44	29	29
Stirling A	26	9	7	10	39	32	25
Stranraer	26	11	3	12	49	43	25
E Stirling	26	8	8	10	33	33	24
Albion R	26	7	10	9	35	38	24
Stenhousemuir	26	9	5	12	39	44	23
Berwick R	26	7	5	14	32	44	19
Forfar A	26	4	10	12	28	48	18
Brechin C	26	6	5	15	28	51	17
Meadowbank T	26	5	6	15	24	53	16

SFA Cup

1st Round

Dec 19 Clacknacuddin . . . 1 Inverness T 2
Dec 22 Cowdenbeath . . . . 3 Clydebank 4
Dec 28 Elgin C . . . . 4 Vale of Leithen . . . 0
Dec 27 Inverness C . . . . . 3 Stenhousemuir . . . 2
Dec 18 St Cuthbert's . . . .0 Brechin C 1
Dec 18 Stranraer . . . . 1 Berwick R 0

2nd Round

Jan 8 Albion R . . . . 2 Raith R 1
Jan 8 Brechin C . . . . 0 Inverness T 0
Jan 8 Clydebank . . . . . 2 Selkirk 0
Jan 8 Forfar A . . . . .0 Elgin C 2
Jan 8 Girvan . . . . .0 Queen's Park 3
Jan 8 Inverness C . . . . . 1 Alloa 1
Jan 8 Meadowbank T . . . 1 E Stirling 2
Jan 8 Stranraer . . . . . . .0 Stirling A 0

Replays

Jan 15 Inverness T . . . . . .1 Brechin C 3
Jan 16 Alloa . . . . .3 Inverness C 1
Jan 24 Stirling A . . . . . . 2 Stranraer 1

3rd Round

Jan 29 Airdrie . . . . .1 Celtic 1
Jan 29 Arbroath . . . . . . .1 Brechin C 0
Jan 29 Dunfermline A . . . 0 Aberdeen 1
Jan 29 East Fife . . . . 2 Clyde 1
Jan 29 E Stirling . . . . . . .0 Albion R 3
Feb 2 Hamilton A . . . . . .0 Clydebank 0
Jan 29 Hearts . . . . .1 Dumbarton 1
Feb 6 Hibernian . . . . . . 3 Partick T 0
Jan 29 Morton . . . . .0 Ayr U 1
Jan 29 Motherwell . . . . . . 3 Kilmarnock 0
Jan 29 Queen of South . .3 Montrose 2
Jan 29 Queen's Park . . . .0 Alloa 0
Jan 29 Rangers . . . . 3 Falkirk 1
Feb 7 St Johnstone . . . .1 Dundee 1
Jan 29 St Mirren . . . . . . 4 Dundee U 1
Jan 29 Stirling A . . . . . . .1 Elgin C 1

Replays

Feb 2 Celtic . . . . 5 Airdrie 0
Feb 2 Dumbarton . . . . . .0 Hearts 1
Feb 2 Elgin C . . . . 3 Stirling A 2
Feb 6 Alloa . . . . .1 Queen's Park . . . 0
Feb 7 Clydebank . . . . . 3 Hamilton A 0
Feb 8 Dundee . . . . 4 St Johnstone 2

4th Round

Feb 26 Arbroath . . . . .1 Hibernian 1
Feb 27 Celtic . . . . 1 Ayr U 1
Feb 26 Dundee . . . . . . .0 Aberdeen 0
Feb 26 East Fife . . . . 2 Albion R 1
Feb 26 Hearts . . . . .1 Clydebank 0
Feb 26 Motherwell . . . . . 2 St Mirren 1
Feb 26 Queen of South . .2 Alloa 1
Feb 26 Rangers . . . . 3 Elgin C 0

Replays

Mar 2 Aberdeen . . . . . . .1 Dundee 2
Mar 2 Ayr U . . . . .1 Celtic 3
Mar 2 Hibernian . . . . . .1 Arbroath 2

5th Round

Mar 12 Arbroath . . . . . . .1 Dundee 3
Mar 13 Celtic . . . . .5 Queen of South . .1
Mar 12 Hearts . . . . .0 East Fife 0
Mar 12 Rangers . . . . 2 Motherwell 0

Replays

Mar 15 East Fife . . . . 2 Hearts 3

Semi-finals

Apr 6 Celtic . . . . 2 Dundee 0
      played at Hampden Park

Mar 30 Hearts . . . . .0 Rangers 2
      played at Hampden Park

Final

May 7 Celtic . . . . .1 Rangers 0
      played at Hampden Park

PREMIER

	ABERDEEN	AYR U	CELTIC	DUNDEE U	HEARTS	HIBERNIAN	KILMARNOCK	MOTHERWELL	PARTICK T	RANGERS
ABERDEEN		Nov24 1-0 Mar26 0-2	Oct23 2-1 Mar05 2-0	Oct30 3-2 Mar12 0-1	Sep04 2-2 Jan03 4-1	Nov27 1-0 Apr09 0-0	Sep18 2-0 Feb07 2-0	Nov02 3-1 Mar23 2-1	Jan12 1-1 Apr16 0-2	Jan19 3-3 Apr30 2-1
AYR U	Sep11 0-5 Jan08 0-0		Oct16 0-2 Feb19 2-4	Sep18 1-4 Feb07 1-4	Dec11 0-3 Apr23 1-1	Oct23 2-1 Mar05 1-2	Jan01 4-1 Apr13 1-1	Nov27 2-1 Apr09 3-2	Nov06 1-1 Mar19 1-1	Oct02 1-1 Feb05 0-2
CELTIC	Dec26 2-2 Apr20 4-1	Dec18 3-0 Apr30 2-0		Oct20 5-1 Mar26 2-0	Sep18 2-2 Feb07 4-2	Nov27 1-1 Feb05 1-0	Oct30 2-1 Apr09 2-2	Feb12 2-0 Mar16 1-0	Dec18 2-2 Mar09 2-1	Sep04 2-2 Jan11 1-0
DUNDEE U	Mar16 3-2 Apr13 2-3	Nov20 2-2 Apr02 0-1	Sep11 1-0 Jan08 1-2		Dec27 1-1 Apr20 1-2	Nov06 2-1 Mar19 1-0	Nov03 3-0 Feb19 4-0	Oct02 2-0 Feb16 1-1	Sep25 2-1 Mar01 0-0	Mar08 0-0 Apr23 0-1
HEARTS	Nov10 2-1 Mar19 1-1	Oct09 2-2 Apr06 1-2	Nov20 3-4 Apr02 0-3	Oct23 1-2 Mar05 1-1		Jan26 0-1 Apr13 2-2	Oct02 2-2 Feb05 4-0	Dec18 2-1 Apr30 3-2	Sep11 2-1 Jan08 1-0	Nov27 0-1 Apr09 1-3
HIBERNIAN	Sep25 0-0 Jan22 0-0	Dec18 1-0 Apr20 4-2	Mar30 1-1 Apr16 2-0	Sep04 1-2 Jan05 1-2	Oct30 1-1 Mar23 3-1		Mar09 2-0 Apr23 0-0	Nov24 0-2 Mar26 1-1	Oct16 1-1 Feb19 0-0	Sep18 1-1	
KILMARNOCK	Nov20 1-2 Apr02 1-2	Oct30 6-1 Mar12 0-1	Sep25 0-4 Jan22 1-3	Dec18 1-0 Apr30 1-2	Feb15 2-1 Apr16 2-2	Oct26 1-1 Feb12 0-1		Sep04 1-1 2-2	Dec27 0-0 Apr20 1-3	Nov13 0-4 Mar26 1-0
MOTHERWELL	Oct02 3-1 Apr23 1-3	Sep25 4-1 Jan22 2-4	Apr13 3-0 May10 2-2	Apr17 2-0 May04 1-1	Oct16 2-1 Feb19 2-1	Sep11 1-1 Jan08 1-1	Nov06 5-4 Mar19 2-0		Nov20 3-0 Apr02 1-1	Oct23 0-2 Mar05 0-2
PARTICK T	Oct02 2-2 Feb05 2-1	Sep04 0-2 Feb16 2-1	Feb22 2-4 Apr23 1-1	Nov27 1-5 Apr09 0-0	Nov30 2-1 Mar26 2-3	Dec18 1-1 Apr30 3-1	Oct23 2-1 Mar05 0-0	Sep18 2-0 Mar30		Oct30 2-1 Mar15 4-3
RANGERS	Oct16 1-0 Feb19 1-0	Mar23 1-1 Apr16 5-1	Nov24 0-1 Mar19 2-2	Nov09 3-0 Feb12 2-3	Sep25 4-2 Jan22 3-2	Nov20 1-1 Apr02 2-1	Sep11 0-0 Jan08 1-0	Dec26 1-0 Apr20 4-1	Jan01 1-0	

DIVISION 1

	AIRDRIE	ARBROATH	CLYDEBANK	DUMBARTON	DUNDEE	EAST FIFE	FALKIRK	HAMILTON A	MONTROSE	MORTON	QUEEN OF SOUTH	RAITH R	ST JOHNSTONE	ST MIRREN
AIRDRIE		Sep29 3-0 Apr30 2-0	Sep11 1-1 Mar02 0-2	Mar26 1-2	Sep21 2-2 Apr02 2-2	Mar30 0-0	Dec18 4-3	Mar16 2-1	Oct02 2-2 Feb05 1-2	Sep18 2-0 Feb09 1-1	Nov06 3-3	Oct23 1-1 Mar05 3-3	Nov27 3-0	Oct12 2-3 Apr23 2-2
ARBROATH	Oct06 1-0		Nov06 0-2	Sep08 1-0 Apr23 1-2	Mar19 1-0	Sep22 1-1 Apr09 1-2	Dec11 4-0	Sep11 1-1 Jan08 1-1	Nov27 2-1	Dec18 2-1 Feb05 1-1	Oct02 0-1	Nov20 2-1	Oct23 1-1 Mar05 2-1	Sep25 0-0 Jan22 1-2
CLYDEBANK	Nov13 1-0	Sep04 3-0 Jan03 8-1		Oct30 2-0 Mar12 4-2	Oct16 2-1 Feb19 3-0	Oct02 2-1 Feb05 5-1	Sep29 4-1	Mar07 2-0	Nov27 1-2	Apr02 2-3	Mar26 2-0	Sep07 3-0 Apr23 2-0	Sep18 1-0 Feb16 2-0	Dec25 2-2
DUMBARTON	Sep14 1-3 Mar19 2-1	Apr16 2-3	Jan01 1-1		Nov10 1-1	Oct05 5-1 Apr30 3-3	Oct20 4-0	Sep25 2-1 Jan22 1-1	Sep11 2-1 Jan08 2-2	Oct09 2-3 Feb12 0-4	Oct23 3-3 Mar05 2-0	Feb23 2-0	Apr06 2-4	Nov20 0-1
DUNDEE	Apr09 3-1	Sep15 2-1 Mar26 5-2	Apr12 2-3	Sep04 2-1 Mar23 4-0		Apr16 2-2	Nov27 2-0	Sep29 5-1	Nov13 6-1 Mar05 3-2	Sep18 1-1 Feb15 0-2	Jan01 1-0 Feb12 4-0	Oct30 1-0 Mar15 2-0	Apr19 0-4	
EAST FIFE	Oct09 0-4 Feb23 2-1	Apr02 1-0	Dec04 0-6	Sep29 2-3	Sep08 2-4 Apr23 0-2		Oct23 1-1 Mar05 1-0	Nov20 1-1	Dec18 1-0	Sep25 0-1 Jan22 0-2	Sep11 2-1 Jan08 1-1	Jan01 1-1 Mar26 1-1	Sep15 1-1	Nov06 3-3
FALKIRK	Oct16 1-0 Feb19 1-1	Oct09 1-3 Feb12 1-0	Oct12 0-4 Apr30 2-4	Apr02 1-3	Sep25 1-6 Jan22 0-8	Dec22 1-1		Mar23 1-1 Mar19 0-1	Nov20 0-1	Sep15 3-5	Mar02 2-0	Nov06 1-2	Apr16 0-0	Sep11 2-0 1-1
HAMILTON A	Oct30 0-4 Mar12 0-0	Nov13 0-1	Oct09 3-2 Feb12 2-0	Nov27 0-1	Oct06 4-2 Apr30 0-3	Sep18 3-1 Feb16 1-2	Oct02 1-2 Feb05 2-2		Apr16 0-2	Dec26 2-2	Sep22 2-2 Apr09 0-3	Dec18 3-2	Sep04 3-2 Feb27 6-0	Mar26 0-4
MONTROSE	Feb26 3-1	Oct30 1-2 Mar16 3-2	Sep25 2-2 Jan22 3-3	Nov13 2-1	Dec27 0-1	Oct16 2-0 Feb19 2-2	Sep18 3-2 Feb09 1-1	Sep08 1-0 Apr23 3-0		Sep04 0-0 Jan03 1-3	Mar30 2-2	Sep15 2-0 Mar26 2-1	Apr09 2-2	Oct04 2-4
MORTON	Nov20 1-3	Oct16 4-1 Feb19 1-0	Oct27 0-0 Apr09 2-2	Feb26 3-0	Sep11 2-0 Jan08 2-3	Nov27 2-0	Mar26 1-0	Oct23 3-0 Mar05 1-1	Nov06 3-0		Sep08 0-2 Apr23 3-1	Sep29 3-1	Oct02 3-1 Feb05 2-0	Jan01 1-3 6-1 Mar12 3-0
QUEEN OF SOUTH	Sep04 2-2 Mar23 3-0	Dec04 0-1	Sep15 1-2 Mar19 2-2	Dec27 1-2	Nov20 2-2	Nov13 3-1	Oct30 3-0 Mar16 3-2	Apr02 0-1	Oct09 4-2 Feb12 0-4	Apr16 0-4		Sep25 1-0 Jan22 3-3	Sep29 0-1 Apr30 1-4	Oct16 1-1 Feb19 0-4
RAITH R	Feb16 2-2	Sep18 1-0 Feb08 0-1	Apr16 2-1	Oct02 1-1	Dec15 1-2	Oct30 1-0 Mar23 2-1	Sep04 1-1 Jan22 1-3	Oct16 0-2 Feb19 3-0	Mar19 1-0	Oct06 3-3 Apr30 3-4	Nov27 1-2		Nov13 1-1	Sep22 1-1 Apr09 1-3
ST JOHNSTONE	Sep25 0-2 Jan22 1-2	Dec27 2-1	Nov20 0-0	Oct16 1-1 Feb19 0-2	Mar30 0-0	Mar19 3-1	Sep08 2-1 Apr23 1-0	Nov06 1-1 Apr02 2-3	Sep22 1-1	Feb23 1-1	Oct06 2-2	Sep11 2-2 Jan25 3-3		Oct09 1-1 Feb12 0-5
ST MIRREN	Apr16 3-0	Nov27 3-0	Oct23 0-0 Mar05 3-1	Sep18 2-1 Feb07 3-2	Oct02 4-0 Feb05 3-1	Sep04 1-1 Mar02 2-0	Nov13 5-2 Mar19 1-0	Sep14 5-2 Apr30 2-2	Sep29 2-1	Oct30 5-1	Dec18 2-1	Apr02 2-0	Mar08 1-1	

DIVISION 2

DIVISION 2	ALBION R	ALLOA	BERWICK R	BRECHIN C	CLYDE	COWDENBEATH	DUNFERMLINE A	E STIRLING	FORFAR A	MEADOWBANK T	QUEEN'S PARK	STENHOUSEMUIR	STIRLING A	STRANRAER
ALBION R		Nov13 2-2	Nov20 0-1	Sep25 2-2 / Apr18 4-0	Sep04 1-4 / Mar23 3-1	Apr20 4-2	Apr11 2-2	Feb12 3-2	Sep28 1-1 / Apr16 1-1	Mar19 3-0	Sep15 1-1 / Apr09 2-0	Oct16 0-1 / Feb19 2-0	Dec27 4-4	Oct30 5-2 / Mar12 2-1
ALLOA	Sep11 2-2 / Apr30 2-2		Sep25 5-1 / Jan22 0-0	Apr20 6-0	Apr16 2-0	Dec25 2-1	Nov20 3-3	Nov06 4-1	Sep22 5-0 / Mar19 2-2	Oct06 2-0	Oct16 1-1 / Mar29 0-1	Mar12 2-1 / Apr25 2-1	Feb12 3-0 / Apr06 0-1	Apr09 1-1
BERWICK R	Sep18 1-3 / Jan15 1-0	Nov27 2-0		Nov11 3-1 / Apr30 4-1	Apr20 1-1	Sep04 0-0 / Jan03 1-0	Oct23 0-2 / Feb26 0-1	Apr02 1-0	Oct09 2-2	Oct30 2-3 / Mar12 0-0	Oct02 0-3 / Feb05 3-2	Apr23 1-0	Mar19 0-3 / Apr27 1-0	Sep08 0-1
BRECHIN C	Nov27 1-3 / Feb05 1-3	Oct02 1-2	Sep11 1-1			Sep08 1-1 / Mar26 1-2	Apr02 4-1	Nov06 2-3	Sep22 0-0 / Mar05 0-1	Mar12 1-2	Oct23 3-1 / Feb26 1-1	Nov20 3-2 / Apr05 1-1	Oct09 3-3 / Apr13 0-4	Sep15 0-4 / Apr23 3-1
CLYDE	Nov06 3-2 / Apr02 2-0	Mar16 1-3 / Feb19 2-3	Oct16 1-0	Oct06 2-1			Jan08 4-1	Mar19 3-2	Sep11 2-2 / Apr30 4-0	Nov20 0-1	Sep14 1-1 / Apr23 3-0	Jan01 3-3	Sep25 1-2 / Jan22 0-0	Oct23 4-2 / Feb26 2-2
COWDENBEATH	Mar26 2-4 / Mar30 3-1	Oct23 0-2 / Mar09 2-3	Nov06 0-1	Sep29 2-1 / Apr16 1-4	Oct09 4-3 / Feb12 2-0		Apr06 1-0	Sep15 2-1 / Apr23 1-2	Sep11 3-0	Jan22 1-2	Mar19 1-2	Nov20 0-1	Sep25 1-1 / Feb26 0-1	Apr13 1-1
DUNFERMLINE A	Oct02 2-1 / Feb05 3-1	Sep18 0-2 / Mar23 1-2	Jan08 1-0	Sep22 1-1 / Jan03 1-0	Sep04 4-0 / Mar05 2-0	Oct30 1-1		Oct16 1-0 / Feb19 1-0	Apr09 3-1	Nov27 1-1	Apr27 1-0	Apr02 1-0	Apr20 1-0	Nov13 2-0 / Apr30 3-0
E STIRLING	Oct09 1-1 / Apr06 3-1	Sep04 2-2 / Apr27 0-1	Sep29 0-0 / Apr16 2-2	Mar19 1-1	Nov13 1-3	Apr09 2-0	Mar30 0-1		Oct23 1-0 / Feb26 2-1	Feb05 3-2	Sep25 3-0 / Nov27 1-3	Sep07 2-1	Oct30 0-3 / Mar12 0-2	Sep18 2-1
FORFAR A	Apr02 2-1	Mar05 1-2	Jan29 1-0 / Apr11 1-2	Oct30 1-0 / Feb01 0-4	Sep18 1-3 / Apr05 1-2	Nov13 1-3 / Apr30 1-2	Sep15 1-1 / Apr23 0-2	Dec27 4-1		Sep04 0-0 / Apr20 0-0	Sep08 1-2 / Mar29 4-0	Oct16 0-2 / Feb19 1-2	Feb15 0-0	Sep25 2-4
MEADOWBANK T	Dec18 1-3 / Mar05 0-0	Sep08 1-1 / Mar26 1-1	Jan26 2-0	Apr09 1-1	Apr09 3-3	Oct16 3-1 / Feb19 1-2	Sep25 1-1 / Jan22 1-0	Oct02 3-1 / Mar16 1-4	Nov06 3-2		Apr16 1-1	Sep10 1-2 / Apr06 0-0	Nov20 1-2	Oct09 2-1 / Mar23 3-1
QUEEN'S PARK	Apr23 3-0	Apr12 1-1	Feb23 1-0	Sep18 3-1	Oct30 0-4 / Mar12 4-0	Sep22 0-1 / Mar05 1-0	Oct09 0-0 / Feb12 3-0	Jan22 2-0	Oct06 3-0 / Mar26 2-2	Sep29 1-0 / Apr02 2-3		Apr20 1-1	Nov13 2-1	Sep04 1-3 / Jan03 4-2
STENHOUSEMUIR	Apr28 1-3	Oct30 3-0	Sep15 2-1 / Apr09 0-0	Mar16 3-1	Nov27 3-0	Sep18 0-2 / Jan15 0-1	Sep29 2-1 / Apr16 1-0	Oct12 0-1 / Feb05 0-1	Oct02 1-0 / Feb26 2-1	Nov13 1-0	Oct23 1-0		Sep04 0-2 / Feb22 0-3	Mar19 1-2
STIRLING A	Oct23 2-1 / Mar16 0-0	Oct09 2-1	Mar05 0-0	Apr09 1-1	Oct02 3-2 / Feb05 3-0	Nov27 4-1	Sep08 2-0 / Mar26 1-0	Mar09 1-1	Feb15 0-0	Sep18 2-2 / Mar30 1-0	Sep11 0-3 / Apr30 1-1	Nov06 2-1		Sep29 2-0 / Apr02 0-1
STRANRAER	Jan01 0-1	Sep15 3-0 / Apr23 1-1	Oct06 4-1 / Mar26 5-1	Oct16 3-1 / Feb19 5-1	Dec27 1-1	Oct02 2-0 / Feb05 3-1	Sep11 3-0 / Jan15 1-0	Nov20 3-0 / Jan22 3-2	Nov27 2-1	Dec11 2-0	Nov06 2-2	Sep22 2-1 / Mar05 4-0	Apr16 0-1	

PREMIER DIVISION FINAL TABLE

	P	W	D	L	F	A	Pts
Celtic	36	23	9	4	79	39	55
Rangers	36	18	10	8	62	37	46
Aberdeen	36	16	11	9	56	42	43
Dundee U	36	16	9	11	54	45	41
Partick T	36	11	13	12	40	44	35
Hibernian	36	8	18	10	34	35	34
Motherwell	36	10	12	14	57	60	32
Ayr U	36	11	8	17	44	68	30
Hearts	36	7	13	16	49	66	27
Kilmarnock	36	4	9	23	32	71	17

DIVISION 1 FINAL TABLE

	P	W	D	L	F	A	Pts
St Mirren	39	25	12	2	91	38	62
Clydebank	39	24	10	5	89	38	58
Dundee	39	21	9	9	90	55	51
Morton	39	20	10	9	77	52	50
Montrose	39	16	9	14	61	62	41
Airdrie	39	13	12	14	63	58	38
Dumbarton	39	14	9	16	63	68	37
Arbroath	39	17	3	19	46	62	37
Queen of South	39	11	13	15	58	65	35
Hamilton A	39	11	10	18	44	59	32
St Johnstone	39	8	13	18	42	64	29
East Fife	39	8	13	18	40	71	29
Raith R	39	8	11	20	45	68	27
Falkirk	39	6	8	25	36	85	20

DIVISION 2 FINAL TABLE

	P	W	D	L	F	A	Pts
Stirling A	39	22	11	6	59	29	55
Alloa	39	19	13	7	73	45	51
Dunfermline A	39	20	10	9	52	36	50
Stranraer	39	20	6	13	74	53	46
Queen's Park	39	17	11	11	65	51	45
Albion R	39	15	12	12	74	61	42
Clyde	39	15	11	13	68	64	41
Berwick R	39	13	10	16	37	51	36
Stenhousemuir	39	15	5	19	38	49	35
E Stirling	39	12	8	19	47	63	32
Meadowbank T	39	8	16	15	41	57	32
Cowdenbeath	39	13	5	21	46	64	31
Brechin C	39	7	12	20	51	77	26
Forfar A	39	7	10	22	43	68	24

League Cup results for 1976-77 are detailed on pages 207-208.

Celtic's Doyle gets the better of a Partick Thistle defender in his side's 2-0 victory in February 1977.

SFA Cup
1st Round
Dec 17 Brechin C . . . . 2 Falkirk 0
Dec 17 Burntisland . . . . . . 1 Berwick R 4
Dec 17 Civil Service . . . . . 4 Selkirk 3
Dec 17 Dunfermline A . . . .0 Clyde 0
Dec 17 Inverness C . . . . . 5 Inverness T 0
Dec 17 Raith R . . . . .1 Stenhousemuir . . . 0
Replays
Dec 21 Clyde . . . . .0 Dunfermline A . . . 3

2nd Round
Jan 7 Albion R . . . . 1 Buckie T 0
Jan 7 Berwick R . . . . . . 6 Raith R 0
Jan 7 Brechin C . . . . 1 Dunfermline A . . . 0
Jan 7 Inverness C . . . .4 Civil Service 0
Jan 7 Meadowbank T . . . 2 E Stirling 1
Jan 7 Peterhead . . . . 1 Cowdenbeath 1
Jan 7 Stranraer . . . . . . .0 Queen's Park 1
Jan 7 Vale of Leithen . . . 4 Forfar A 1
Replays
Jan 14 Cowdenbeath . . . . 5 Peterhead 0

3rd Round
Feb 6 Aberdeen . . . . 2 Ayr U 0
Feb 6 Airdrie . . . . .2 Hearts 3
Feb 5 Albion R . . . . .0 Morton 1
Jan 29 Alloa . . . . .2 Dumbarton 2
Jan 28 Arbroath . . . . .0 Motherwell 4
Jan 28 Berwick R . . . . . . 2 Rangers 4
Feb 6 Celtic . . . . .7 Dundee 1
Jan 28 Hamilton A . . . . . .1 Dundee U 4
Jan 28 Hibernian . . . . . . .4 East Fife 0
Jan 28 Meadowbank T . . . 2 Inverness C 1
Feb 5 Partick T . . . . .1 Cowdenbeath 1
Jan 28 Queen of South . . 2 Montrose 2
Feb 7 St Johnstone . . . . 1 Brechin C 0
Feb 6 St Mirren . . . . 1 Kilmarnock 2
Feb 7 Stirling A . . . . . . .3 Clydebank 0
Feb 4 Vale of Leithen . . .0 Queen's Park 1
Replays
Feb 6 Dumbarton . . . . . . 2 Alloa 1
Feb 6 Montrose . . . . 1 Queen of South . . . 3
Feb 27 Cowdenbeath . . . . .0 Partick T 1

4th Round
Feb 27 Aberdeen . . . . 3 St Johnstone 0
Feb 27 Celtic . . . . .1 Kilmarnock 1
Feb 18 Dumbarton . . . . . . 1 Hearts 1
Feb 27 Dundee U . . . . . . .3 Queen of South . . 0
Mar 4 Hibernian . . . . . . .0 Partick T 0
Feb 18 Morton . . . . .3 Meadowbank T . . . 0
Feb 27 Motherwell . . . . . .1 Queen's Park 3
Feb 18 Rangers . . . . 1 Stirling A 0
Replays
Feb 27 Hearts . . . . 0 Dumbarton 1
Mar 6 Kilmarnock . . . . . .1 Celtic 0
Mar 7 Partick T . . . . . . .2 Hibernian 1

5th Round
Mar 11 Aberdeen . . . . 2 Morton 2
Mar 11 Dundee U . . . . . . .2 Queen's Park 0
Mar 11 Partick T . . . . 2 Dumbarton 1
Mar 11 Rangers . . . . .4 Kilmarnock 1
Replays
Mar 15 Morton . . . . .1 Aberdeen 2

Semi-finals
Apr 12 Aberdeen . . . . 4 Partick T 2
         played at Hampden Park
Apr 5 Dundee U . . . . . . .0 Rangers 2
         played at Hampden Park

Final
May 6 Aberdeen . . . . . . .1 Rangers 2
         played at Hampden Park

League Cup results for 1977-78 are detailed on page 208.

PREMIER

	ABERDEEN	AYR U	CELTIC	CLYDEBANK	DUNDEE U	HIBERNIAN	MOTHERWELL	PARTICK T	RANGERS	ST MIRREN
ABERDEEN		Nov12 0-0 Mar25 4-1	Sep17 2-1 Jan14 2-1	Oct29 1-1 Mar21 2-0	Aug27 2-0 Jan02 1-0	Oct15 0-0 Feb25 3-0	Dec03 4-1 Apr15 5-0	Sep24 2-1 Apr04 2-1	Aug13 3-1 Mar24 4-0	Dec10 3-1 Apr22 4-2
AYR U	Sep10 0-1 Jan07 1-1		Aug20 2-0 Dec31 2-1	Oct15 2-0 Feb25 0-0	Dec10 0-2 Feb04 0-1	Nov19 1-1 Apr22 2-0	Oct22 1-2 Apr01 1-3	Nov26 0-5 Mar15 2-5	Nov05 3-2 Apr08 0-1	
CELTIC	Nov19 3-2 Apr01 2-2	Oct29 3-2 Mar11 3-0		Sep24 1-0 Apr17 5-2	Aug13 0-0 Dec24 4-1	Oct01 3-1 Apr05 2-0	Aug27 0-1 Jan02 2-1	Dec10 3-0 Apr22 4-2	Nov12 1-1 Mar25 2-1	Oct15 1-2 Feb25 1-2
CLYDEBANK	Aug20 1-3 Dec21 0-1	Dec17 0-2 Apr29 0-2	Apr08 3-2 Apr26 1-1		Sep17 0-3 May02 2-0	Nov05 1-0 Mar18 0-3	Oct08 1-1 Mar11 0-2	Sep10 0-4 Jan07 2-0	Feb19 0-3 Apr15 0-2	Oct22 2-2 Mar04 2-2
DUNDEE U	Nov05 0-1 Mar18 0-0	Apr15 4-0 Apr26 3-1	Oct22 1-1 Mar04 0-1	Nov19 4-0 Apr12 1-1		Sep10 2-0 Jan07 1-1	Sep24 3-2 Mar29 1-1	Dec17 2-2 Apr29 5-2	Oct08 0-1 Apr19 0-1	Aug20 2-1 Oct31 2-1
HIBERNIAN	Dec17 2-0 Apr29 1-1	Oct08 1-2 Mar22 4-1	Apr12 1-1 Apr15 2-1	Aug27 2-0 Jan02 0-1	Nov12 0-0 Mar25 2-0		Aug13 0-0 Dec24 2-1	Nov19 2-3 Apr01 3-1	Oct29 0-1 Mar29 1-1	Sep24 2-0 Mar11 5-1
MOTHERWELL	Oct01 1-1 Feb04 0-0	Sep17 5-0 Jan14 3-0	Nov05 2-1 Mar22 2-1	Dec10 0-0 Apr22 0-1	Nov26 1-0 Apr08 0-1	Oct22 1-0 Mar15 2-4		Aug20 3-0 Dec31 2-0	Oct15 1-4 Feb25 3-5	Sep10 0-3 Jan07 1-0
PARTICK T	Nov26 1-0 Apr08 0-2	Aug13 2-2 Dec24 4-1	Oct08 1-0 Mar29 0-4	Nov12 1-0 Mar25 0-0	Oct15 2-1 Feb25 2-1	Sep17 1-0 Apr19 2-3	Oct29 1-0 Mar18 2-3		Aug27 0-4 Jan02 1-2	Sep10 2-1 Apr26 5-0
RANGERS	Oct22 3-1 May04 0-3	Sep24 2-0 Aug12 1-1	Sep10 3-2 Jan07 3-1	Oct01 4-1 Feb04 1-0	Dec10 2-0 Apr22 3-0	Aug20 0-2 Dec31 2-0	Dec17 3-1 Apr29 2-1	Nov05 3-3 Mar21 2-0		Nov19 2-1 Apr01 1-1
ST MIRREN	Oct08 0-4 Mar29 1-2	Aug27 2-0 Jan02 2-3	Dec17 3-3 Apr29 3-1	Aug13 1-1 Dec24 2-0	Oct29 0-1 Apr15 2-0	Nov26 3-0 Apr08 3-0	Nov12 0-1 Apr25 1-1	Oct01 2-1 Feb04 1-1	Sep17 3-3 Jan14 0-2	

DIVISION 1

	AIRDRIE	ALLOA	ARBROATH	DUMBARTON	DUNDEE	EAST FIFE	HAMILTON A	HEARTS	KILMARNOCK	MONTROSE	MORTON	QUEEN OF SOUTH	ST JOHNSTONE	STIRLING A
AIRDRIE		Oct19 3-1 Mar18 2-1	Sep28 1-1 Apr15 2-1	Apr04 0-2	Oct22 3-0 Mar04 3-3	Nov05 2-1 Dec31 0-0	Sep10 1-1	Dec17 2-4	Nov26 1-2	Aug20 0-3 Jan07 4-3	Oct01 0-1 Feb28 2-3	Apr08 2-1 Apr29 2-0	Dec10 1-1	Sep17 0-1
ALLOA	Mar25 3-3		Aug13 1-1 Mar04 0-0	Dec24 3-5 Apr08 3-0	Sep14 3-2 Apr15 1-5	Nov26 3-2	Dec10 2-2	Mar11 0-2	Oct15 1-2	Oct01 1-3 Apr05 3-0	Oct29 1-3 Jan07 0-5	Sep17 2-2	Aug27 1-3 Jan02 0-0	Nov12 1-0
ARBROATH	Mar11 1-0	Oct22 2-0		Aug20 2-2 Jan07 1-1	Mar18 0-0	Oct01 2-2 Feb04 3-0	Nov05 2-1 Dec31 1-0	Sep24 0-7 Apr29 3-0	Nov22 2-2 Apr01 1-0	Sep10 0-3	Oct15 1-2 Feb25 2-2	Sep24 3-1 Apr22 0-1	Sep14 2-2	Dec10 1-3
DUMBARTON	Sep14 2-1 Apr22 2-1	Apr29 2-0	Oct29 1-0		Nov19 0-0 Apr12 2-1	Mar22 3-0	Oct15 1-0 Feb25 1-1	Aug13 2-2	Dec10 2-2	Sep24 4-0 Apr19 2-2	Nov12 1-1 Jan02 1-4	Aug27 2-0 Dec31 1-1	Oct01 5-1 Feb04 2-1	Mar25 2-2
DUNDEE	Aug13 3-0	Jan14 6-0	Oct19 2-3 Mar25 2-0	Sep17 2-1		Oct15 2-1 Feb25 2-0	Nov26 3-0	Oct19 1-1	Oct01 4-1 Mar22 5-2	Dec10 3-1	Dec24 3-0 Apr08 1-1	Mar11 3-0 Nov12 2-3 Apr22 3-0	Nov12 5-3 Jan02 3-4	Aug27 0-1
EAST FIFE	Aug27 2-3	Sep24 2-2 Mar08 1-2	Dec03 0-0	Sep28 3-1 Apr15 1-0	Dec17 0-3		Mar18 0-0	Nov12 2-0 Jan02 1-2	Dec24 2-3 Apr08 0-0	Sep03 1-0	Nov19 0-0	Oct08 1-0 Mar12 2-0	Oct29 1-2 Jan07 1-3	Aug13 1-1 Mar04 0-1
HAMILTON A	Nov12 4-0 Jan02 0-0	Oct08 4-1 Feb28 0-1	Aug27 3-1	Dec17 3-3	Sep24 1-1 Mar08 0-1	Oct19 5-3 Mar25 3-2		Apr02 0-2	Sep14 2-1 Apr22 1-3	Nov19 4-1 Apr01 2-1	Mar21 0-0	Oct29 4-3	Aug13 0-1	Dec24 1-1 Apr29 3-1
HEARTS	Oct15 3-2 Feb25 3-0	Sep28 1-0 Apr22 2-1	Apr08 3-2	Oct22 2-1 Mar04 1-1	Aug20 3-0 Jan07 2-2	Sep10 4-1	Oct01 0-2 Feb04 1-0		Nov05 1-2 Dec31 3-0	Mar18 2-2	Dec10 1-1	Jan14 1-0	Sep17 3-0	Nov26 2-0
KILMARNOCK	Sep24 0-0 Jan21 1-1	Dec17 3-1 Feb25 4-0	Sep17 3-0	Oct08 2-2 Feb11 0-1	Dec03 1-0	Apr29 0-0	Jan14 1-1	Aug27 1-1		Mar15 5-1 Apr15 1-0	Aug13 0-3	Nov12 1-1 Jan02 1-2	Oct19 0-1 Mar25 1-1	Oct23 2-3
MONTROSE	Oct29 1-2	Dec03 1-2 Jan02 1-0	Nov12 2-1	Nov26 2-2	Oct08 1-2 Mar01 0-3	Jan14 2-0 Apr22 2-1	Sep17 1-2	Oct19 3-1 Mar25 0-0	Sep28 0-0		Aug27 0-1	Aug13 0-0 Mar04 5-2 Apr08 3-2	Dec24 1-2	Oct15 2-2
MORTON	Apr26 3-1	Aug13 4-2	Dec17 1-2	Sep10 0-0	Apr29 2-3	Sep17 3-0	Sep28 0-1	Oct08 5-3 Apr12 5-0	Oct22 0-2 Apr15 3-0	Nov05 2-2 Aug08 0-1 Mar04 2-0		Oct19 0-1 Mar25 1-1	Apr05 4-1	Sep14 4-2 Jan14 2-0
QUEEN OF SOUTH	Dec24 2-2	Nov19 1-0 Apr01 1-0	Nov26 1-2 Feb15	Nov05 1-0	Sep28 0-2	Dec10 3-3	Sep14 2-1 Jan07 1-1	Aug20 3-3 Apr15	Sep10 1-0	Oct22 2-1	Mar18 2-3		Oct15 2-2 Feb25 2-2	Oct11 2-3 Mar08 1-4
ST JOHNSTONE	Oct08 2-1 Mar07 0-1	Nov05 0-1 Dec31 3-0	Mar22 2-1	Dec03 0-2	Sep10 1-2	Aug20 3-0	Oct22 1-0 Mar04 1-1	Nov19 0-1	Mar18 2-0	Apr29 1-0 Apr19 0-1	Sep24 1-3	Dec17 1-2		Sep28 0-0 Apr15 1-3
STIRLING A	Nov19 0-1 Apr01 2-0	Sep10 1-1	Oct08 0-0 Feb28 0-0	Oct19 2-3 Mar18 2-2	Nov05 0-2 Dec31 2-3	Oct22 4-1	Apr08 1-0	Sep24 2-4 Mar15 1-2	Aug20 3-5 Jan07 1-1	Dec17 1-2 Feb25 4-2	Apr22 1-2	Mar22 5-1	Mar11	

Season 1977-78

DIVISION 2

	ALBION R	BERWICK R	BRECHIN C	CLYDE	COWDENBEATH	DUNFERMLINE A	E STIRLING	FALKIRK	FORFAR A	MEADOWBANK T	QUEEN'S PARK	RAITH R	STENHOUSEMUIR	STRANRAER
ALBION R		Apr05 3-3	Oct29 2-0	Aug13 0-0	Feb25 4-3	Oct08 3-0 / Apr25 0-1	Sep13 0-1	Oct15 0-2 / Dec24 1-1	Sep24 2-0 / Apr18 1-1	Nov12 3-2	Oct22 3-3 / Apr22 3-4	Mar18 1-2	Nov19 3-1 / Apr27 2-0	Aug27 1-2 / Jan02 4-0
BERWICK R	Oct01 2-0 / Feb04 3-3		Dec10 3-2 / Apr26 5-3	Nov12 0-0	Oct19 4-0 / Mar18 1-1	Aug13 2-2	Nov19 1-1 / Apr01 2-0	Oct29 1-1	Oct22 4-1 / Apr22 2-1	Aug27 2-1 / Jan02 3-0	Dec24 1-0	Sep14 0-0 / Apr15 1-2	Sep24 2-2	Mar04 2-2
BRECHIN C	Aug20 1-2 / Mar11 0-1	Oct08 2-3		Nov19 1-2 / Apr17 0-2	Dec31 1-2	Sep14 0-1 / Apr15 1-2	Feb25 3-2	Apr12 3-1	Nov05 0-0	Sep24 0-5 / Apr19 0-1	Sep10 3-1 / Mar29 2-2	Oct22 4-0	Apr29 2-1	Oct01 0-2 / Apr05 2-2
CLYDE	Dec31 3-0 / Apr08 4-0	Sep10 3-1 / Mar22 3-1	Sep17 2-0		Sep14 3-2 / Mar29 4-1	Sep28 2-0 / Mar04 4-2	Oct22 2-2	Jan07 2-1	Jan14 2-1 / Mar18 0-0	Apr05 7-0	Nov05 0-1	Oct08 0-0 / Apr26 0-1	Aug20 3-0	Apr29 4-0
COWDENBEATH	Sep28 3-4 / Mar04 7-1	Apr12 2-1	Aug13 2-1 / Apr08 0-2	Apr15 1-2		Aug27 3-1 / Jan02 1-1	Sep24 1-2 / Apr18 1-2	Mar25 2-1	Nov19 1-4	Oct15 1-1 / Dec24 4-0	Oct08 4-3 / Apr26 1-3	Oct29 1-2	Mar08 1-2	Nov12 1-0 / Dec17 1-3
DUNFERMLINE A	Dec10 2-1	Dec31 0-0 / Apr08 1-1	Mar22 6-1	Feb25 1-1	Nov05 3-3		Oct19 1-0	Sep17 0-1 / May02 2-0	Oct01 2-0 / Apr10 1-1	Oct22 3-0 / Apr22 7-1	Aug20 4-0 / Apr18 0-0	Apr29 0-2	Sep10 2-1 / Mar15 4-1	Nov26 2-0
E STIRLING	Jan14 1-0 / Apr15 2-1	Sep17 2-7	Sep28 1-0 / Mar04 1-0	Mar25 1-1 / Apr22 2-1	Nov26 3-1	Mar18 1-0 / Apr12 1-0		Aug27 0-2 / Jan02 0-2	Oct15 0-1 / Dec24 3-4	Aug13 1-2	Oct01 1-1	Nov12 1-2 / Jan28 2-2	Apr25 2-1	Oct22 2-1
FALKIRK	Apr29 1-2	Aug20 2-1 / Mar11 0-0	Oct19 1-0 / Mar18 2-0	Sep24 2-1 / Jan28 1-0	Oct22 2-2 / Apr22 2-2	Nov19 0-0	Nov05 2-3		Sep10 1-2	Dec10 1-1 / Apr25 2-4	Feb25 0-3 / Apr04 2-2	Oct01 2-2 / Apr08 1-0	Dec31 1-1	Apr18 1-0
FORFAR A	Nov26 3-1	Mar25 1-0	Aug27 4-1 / Jan02 4-1	Oct19 1-2	Sep17 1-3 / Apr01 2-1	Apr05 0-1	Apr29 3-3	Nov12 2-0 / Mar22 2-2		Aug20 2-0	Dec17 3-1 / Apr15 0-3	Aug13 1-0 / Mar04 1-1	Sep28 4-1 / Apr25 3-1	Oct08 3-2
MEADOWBANK T	Sep10 1-2 / Dec17 0-3	Nov04 0-2	Nov26 0-0	Oct01 0-1 / Feb04 1-1	Apr28 2-3	Mar24 2-4	Dec30 2-4 / Apr08 1-1	Oct08 1-2	Oct29 1-0 / Mar10 1-1		Sep17 1-1 / Nov19 1-3	Mar04 0-0	Jan14 2-3	Oct19 2-2 / Apr12 2-1
QUEEN'S PARK	Mar25 1-1	Oct15 0-0 / Apr29 2-3	Nov12 0-2 / Jan20 0-1	Aug27 1-1	Dec10 2-1	Oct29 1-1	Dec03 3-2 / Feb08 0-0	Sep28 1-2 / Mar04 1-1	Sep13 2-1	Apr01 1-1		Sep24 0-3 / Mar21 0-0	Oct19 1-0 / Apr11 1-0	Aug13 0-2 / Apr08 2-0
RAITH R	Oct19 1-1 / Apr12 2-0	Jan14 7-1	Mar25 3-1 / Apr22 1-0	Dec10 1-1	Aug20 2-2 / Mar11 2-2	Oct15 2-1 / Dec24 0-1	Sep10 1-1	Mar29 1-1 / Apr08 2-0	Dec31 1-2 / Feb25 4-0	Sep28 1-0	Nov26 1-1		Nov05 3-0	Sep17 1-1
STENHOUSEMUIR	Sep17 2-4	Nov26 0-0 / Apr18 1-1	Oct15 2-2 / Dec24 2-2	Oct29 2-2 / Mar11 1-0	Oct01 1-3 / Feb04 0-4	Nov12 2-0	Oct08 4-1 / Dec10 1-1	Aug13 1-1	Feb25 1-0	Sep14 2-2 / Apr15 3-1	Mar18 0-2	Aug27 1-1 / Jan02 2-2		Mar25 1-0
STRANRAER	Nov05 3-5	Sep28 0-1 / Feb25 0-1	Feb04 1-1	Oct15 2-1 / Dec24 2-1	Sep10 3-1 / Jan21 0-2	Sep24 1-1 / Mar11 0-2	Aug20 3-2 / Apr15 3-0	Sep14 0-2	Dec10 4-1	Mar18 4-1	Dec31 1-1	Nov19 1-4 / Apr01 1-0	Oct22 3-0 / Apr22 1-2	

PREMIER DIVISION FINAL TABLE

	P	W	D	L	F	A	Pts
Rangers	36	24	7	5	76	39	55
Aberdeen	36	22	9	5	68	29	53
Dundee U	36	16	8	12	42	32	40
Hibernian	36	15	7	14	51	43	37
Celtic	36	15	6	15	63	54	36
Motherwell	36	13	7	16	45	52	33
Partick T	36	14	5	17	52	64	33
St Mirren	36	11	8	17	52	63	30
Ayr U	36	9	6	21	36	68	24
Clydebank	36	6	7	23	23	64	19

DIVISION 1 FINAL TABLE

	P	W	D	L	F	A	Pts
Morton	39	25	8	6	85	42	58
Hearts	39	24	10	5	77	42	58
Dundee	39	25	7	7	91	44	57
Dumbarton	39	16	17	6	65	48	49
Stirling A	39	15	12	12	60	52	42
Kilmarnock	39	14	12	13	52	46	40
Hamilton A	39	12	12	15	54	56	36
St Johnstone	39	15	6	18	52	64	36
Arbroath	39	11	13	15	42	55	35
Airdrie	39	12	10	17	50	64	34
Montrose	39	10	9	20	55	71	29
Queen of South	39	8	13	18	44	68	29
Alloa	39	8	8	23	44	84	24
East Fife	39	4	11	24	39	74	19

DIVISION 2 FINAL TABLE

	P	W	D	L	F	A	Pts
Clyde	39	21	11	7	71	32	53
Raith R	39	19	15	5	63	34	53
Dunfermline A	39	18	12	9	64	41	48
Berwick R	39	16	16	7	68	51	48
Falkirk	39	15	14	10	51	46	44
Forfar A	39	17	8	14	61	55	42
Queen's Park	39	13	15	11	52	51	41
Albion R	39	16	8	15	68	68	40
E Stirling	39	15	8	16	55	65	38
Cowdenbeath	39	13	8	18	75	78	34
Stranraer	39	13	7	19	54	63	33
Stenhousemuir	39	10	10	19	43	67	30
Meadowbank T	39	6	10	23	43	89	22
Brechin C	39	7	6	26	45	73	20

SFA Cup
1st Round
Dec 16 Dunfermline A .... 2 Albion R 2
Dec 16 Falkirk ....2 Keith 0
Dec 16 Gala Fairydean ...1 Cowdenbeath 3
Dec 16 Meadowbank T ...1 Inverness C 1
Dec 16 Threave R ....0 E Stirling 2
Dec 16 Vale of Leithen ...1 Forfar A 4

Replays
Dec 19 Albion R ....2 Dunfermline A ...3
Dec 23 Inverness C ......0 Meadowbank T ...3

2nd Round
Jan 17 Cowdenbeath .....0 Alloa 0
Jan 16 East Fife ....2 Brechin C 1
Jan 21 E Stirling ....2 Spartans 3
Jan 22 Forfar A ....1 Berwick R 2
Feb 22 Inverness T ......0 Falkirk 4
Jan 16 Meadowbank T ...2 Stenhousemuir ...1
Jan 17 Peterhead ....2 Queen's Park 3
Jan 13 Stranraer ....1 Dunfermline A 1

Replays
Jan 21 Alloa ....2 Cowdenbeath 0
Jan 22 Dunfermline A ....1 Stranraer 0

3rd Round
Jan 27 Arbroath ....0 Airdrie 1
Feb 12 Ayr U ....4 Queen of South ...0
Jan 31 Clyde ....1 Kilmarnock 5
Jan 31 Clydebank ....3 Queen's Park 3
Feb 19 Dumbarton ....1 Alloa 0
Feb 25 Dundee ....1 Falkirk 0
Feb 26 Dundee U ....0 St Mirren 2
Jan 28 Dunfermline A ....1 Hibernian 1
Jan 27 East Fife ....0 Berwick R 1
Jan 27 Hamilton A ....0 Aberdeen 2
Jan 31 Meadowbank T ...2 Spartans 1
Jan 31 Montrose ....2 Celtic 4
Feb 19 Morton ....1 St Johnstone 1
Jan 27 Raith R ....0 Hearts 2
Feb 12 Rangers ....3 Motherwell 1
Feb 19 Stirling A ....0 Partick T 2

Replays
Feb 12 Hibernian ....2 Dunfermline A ... 0
Feb 12 Queen's Park ......0 Clydebank 1
Feb 26 St Johnstone .....2 Morton 4

4th Round
Feb 21 Aberdeen ....6 Ayr U 2
Feb 26 Celtic ....3 Berwick R 0
Feb 24 Dumbarton ......3 Clydebank 1
Mar 3 Dundee ....4 St Mirren 1
Mar 3 Hearts ....1 Morton 1
Feb 21 Meadowbank T ....0 Hibernian 6
Feb 24 Partick T ....3 Airdrie 0
Feb 21 Rangers ....1 Kilmarnock 1

Replays
Feb 26 Kilmarnock ......0 Rangers 1
Mar 5 Morton ....0 Hearts 1

5th Round
Mar 10 Aberdeen ....1 Celtic 1
Mar 10 Dumbarton ....0 Partick T 1
Mar 10 Hibernian ....2 Hearts 1
Mar 10 Rangers ....6 Dundee 3

Replays
Mar 14 Celtic ....1 Aberdeen 2

Semi-finals
Apr 11 Aberdeen ....1 Hibernian 2
        played at Hampden Park

League Cup results for 1978-79 are detailed on page 208.

PREMIER

	ABERDEEN	CELTIC	DUNDEE U	HEARTS	HIBERNIAN	MORTON	MOTHERWELL	PARTICK T	RANGERS	ST MIRREN
ABERDEEN		Oct07 4-1 Mar03 0-1	Nov04 1-0 Mar17 0-2	Oct21 1-2 May02 5-0	Nov25 4-1 Apr07 0-0	Aug19 3-1 Dec30 1-2	Sep09 4-0 Mar26 8-0	Sep30 1-1 Feb28 2-1	Nov18 0-0 Apr25 2-1	Dec16 1-1 Apr28 1-2
CELTIC	Dec09 0-0 Apr21 1-1		Dec16 1-1 Apr28 2-1	Aug19 4-0 May14 1-0	Sep16 0-1 May02 3-1	Oct21 0-0 Mar28 3-0	Nov04 1-2 Mar17 2-1	Nov25 1-0 Apr07 2-0	Sep09 3-1 May21 4-2	Sep30 2-1 Apr25 2-1
DUNDEE U	Aug26 1-1 May05 2-2	Oct14 1-0 Apr11 2-1		Sep30 3-1 Apr25 2-1	Aug12 0-0 Dec23 2-1	Sep09 1-2 Mar10 4-1	Nov18 2-1 Mar14 2-1	Oct28 2-0 Apr21 1-2	Dec16 3-0 Oct21 1-2	Nov25 1-1 2-0
HEARTS	Aug12 1-4 Dec23 0-0	Oct28 2-0 Apr18 0-3	Apr04 2-0 Apr14 0-3		Aug26 1-1 Mar28 1-2	Sep16 3-2 May07 0-1	Nov11 0-1 Apr07 3-0	Oct14 0-0 Apr11 0-2	Feb24 3-2	Feb10 1-2
HIBERNIAN	Sep23 2-1 Jan20 1-1	Nov18 2-2 Mar31 2-1	Oct21 1-1 Mar03 1-0	Nov04 1-2 Mar17 1-1		Sep30 1-1 Apr28 1-1	Dec09 2-2 Apr28 4-0	Dec16 0-0 Apr28 1-0	Aug19 0-0 May31 2-1	Sep09 1-0 Apr04 0-2
MORTON	Oct28 2-1 Apr04 0-1	Aug12 1-2 Dec23 1-0	Nov11 2-1 Mar24 3-1	Nov18 0-0 Mar31 2-2	Apr14 3-0 Apr18 3-0		Oct14 1-2 Mar14 6-0	Oct07 1-0 Feb17 2-2	Sep23 2-3 Jan20 0-2	Aug26 1-0 Apr11 1-0
MOTHERWELL	Nov11 1-1 Apr18 1-1	Aug26 1-5 Apr04 3-4	Sep16 0-1 Mar07 0-4	Sep09 0-1 Jan20 3-2	Oct07 2-3 Feb10 3-0	Dec16 1-1 Aug28 3-3		Aug12 0-1 Dec23 1-1	Apr14 1-2 May02 1-2	Dec16 1-2 Mar10 3-1
PARTICK T	Apr14 0-1 May11 1-2	Sep23 2-3 May07 1-2	Aug19 1-1 Mar28 1-2	Sep09 3-2 May05 2-0	Oct14 2-1 Apr25 6-1	Dec09 2-1 Apr21 2-1	Oct21 2-0 0-0		Nov04 1-0 Mar17 0-2	Nov18 2-1 3-1
RANGERS	Sep16 1-1 May07 2-0	Nov11 1-1 May05 1-0	Oct07 1-1 Feb10 1-0	Dec16 5-3 Apr28 4-0	Oct28 1-1 Mar14 1-0	Nov25 4-1 Apr07 1-1	Sep30 0-0 Apr10 3-0	Aug26 0-0 May23 1-0		Aug12 1-0 Dec23 1-0
ST MIRREN	Oct14 2-1 Feb24 2-2	Apr14 0-1 May11 0-2	Sep23 1-3 Jan20 2-1	Dec09 4-0 Apr21 2-1	Nov11 1-0 Mar24 2-3	Nov04 0-0 Mar17 3-1	Sep16 0-1 Feb17 1-0	Sep16 0-1 May02 1-1	Oct21 0-1 Mar27 1-2	

DIVISION 1

	AIRDRIE	ARBROATH	AYR U	CLYDE	CLYDEBANK	DUMBARTON	DUNDEE	HAMILTON A	KILMARNOCK	MONTROSE	QUEEN OF SOUTH	RAITH R	ST JOHNSTONE	STIRLING A
AIRDRIE		Oct14 1-1 Feb28 2-0	Sep06 2-4 Apr28 2-0	Dec09 2-2	Sep27 1-1 Apr07 1-3	Nov11 3-6	Dec23 0-2 Apr21 2-4	Aug26 4-1 Mar14 2-1	Oct20 4-1	Apr18 1-1 Apr05 8-2	Aug12 4-1	Sep16 0-1	Nov25 0-1 Apr04 0-1	Sep30 2-1
ARBROATH	Dec16 3-3		Mar24 4-1 Apr07 2-3	Oct21 0-2 Apr21 1-1	Apr28 1-1	Aug12 1-1 Mar03 1-1	Oct28 0-1	Nov11 3-0	Dec09 3-2 Feb10 Feb21 1-1	Aug26 1-3	Sep13 1-1	Sep10 0-5	Sep16 3-0 Apr04 3-1	Nov25 1-0 Jan20
AYR U	Mar10 0-0	Sep27 3-0		Nov25 2-0	Oct21 4-3	Sep16 2-5 Apr18 1-0	Aug12 0-1 Mar31 1-2	Sep13 1-2 Apr21 2-1	Aug26 0-0 Mar07 2-1	Dec16 5-0 Feb24 5-0	Oct28 1-1	Nov11 3-0	Sep30 1-0 Apr14 4-2	Dec09 0-1 Feb10 2-0
CLYDE	Oct07 2-1 Mar07 2-3	Dec23 1-0	Sep23 2-1 Feb28 0-5		Dec02 1-2 Apr14 0-1	Sep13 1-0	Nov18 2-1	Oct14 2-3	Sep26 2-1 Apr07 0-1	Oct28 2-4	Aug26 3-0 Feb21 3-0	Aug12 3-1 Mar31 1-1	Nov11 6-4	Mar10 0-0
CLYDEBANK	Mar24 4-1	Sep06 5-2 Mar10 2-2	Dec23 3-1 Apr21 0-1	Sep30 1-4		Aug26 1-1 Apr25 3-1	Nov25 2-1	Sep16 4-1 Feb17 1-2	Aug12 2-1 Mar31 3-1	Nov11 1-0	Oct14 2-0 Feb28 2-1	Oct28 2-1	Mar07 3-0 Apr18 1-1	Sep13 5-2
DUMBARTON	Sep09 1-1 May02 0-1	Mar31 0-1	Nov04 2-0	Mar17 3-0 Apr04 0-0	Nov04 1-2		Sep27 0-0 Apr07 3-2	Sep23 2-0 Apr16 3-0	Mar13 0-3 Apr28 1-3	Sep30 4-1	May05 4-1	Dec09 1-3 Mar28 3-1	Oct14 2-0	Aug19 0-1 May07 0-2
DUNDEE	Oct21 1-0	Aug19 2-0 May06 0-2	May10 2-2	Sep16 3-0 Apr18 4-0	Sep23 2-0 Feb21 2-1	Mar24		Dec02 1-1 Apr14 4-3	Nov11 0-0	Sep06 1-1 Apr28 1-0	Oct07 5-0 Apr04 4-0	May08 2-0	Nov04 1-1	Dec16 2-1
HAMILTON A	Nov04 2-0	Sep09 3-1 Mar07 2-0	Feb03 3-1	Dec16 3-3 Feb24 2-0	Nov18 1-0	Nov25 5-0	Sep30 1-2		Oct21 2-3 Apr21 1-0	Dec09 3-1	Sep27 3-2 Mar24 0-0	Sep06 1-1	Aug19 2-1 Dec30 2-1	Mar03 1-1 Mar31 2-0
KILMARNOCK	Aug19 2-0 Apr11 1-0	Oct07 3-1	Nov04 1-2	Mar24 2-1	Mar03 0-0	Sep06 0-0	Sep09 1-1 Apr25 2-1	Dec23 4-0		Sep23 2-2 Jan20 4-1	Dec02 0-0 Apr14 3-1	Oct14 3-0 Feb24 2-1	Feb03 3-2 3-1	Nov18 5-0
MONTROSE	Sep13 2-2	Nov04 3-0	Oct14 4-6	Aug19 2-2 Apr11 4-0	Sep09 1-3 Mar28 1-2	Apr14 2-1 May09 0-2	Mar14 0-2	Oct07 1-1 Feb28 2-4	Nov28 0-4		Mar07 6-1	Dec23 1-3 Apr21 1-1	Mar03 1-3	Sep27 2-1 Mar24 0-2
QUEEN OF SOUTH	Mar03 1-3 Mar31 1-5	Feb24 1-1 Mar17 2-2	Aug19 1-0 Dec30 0-1	Mar03 3-0	Dec16 2-1	Oct21 0-2 Apr21 1-3	Dec09 3-1	Apr07 3-3	Sep30 2-1	Sep16 1-3 Nov18 2-1		Nov25 2-1	Sep06 1-1 Apr28 1-2	Sep12 1-2 May02 1-3
RAITH R	Nov18 2-0	Apr14 1-2 Apr18 1-0	Sep09 0-1 Mar14 2-0	Mar03 1-2	Aug19 4-2 May02 1-2	Oct07 0-0	Sep13 2-4 Apr11 1-2	Mar10 0-1 Apr28 2-0	Dec16 1-3	Oct21 3-1	Sep23 4-0 Jan20 3-0		Apr25 0-0	Nov04 1-2
ST JOHNSTONE	Sep23 0-2 Mar27 1-3	Nov18 1-1	May05 4-2	Sep07 2-3 Mar14 0-1	Dec16 1-1 Mar20 2-2	Aug26 0-1 May02 3-2	Oct28 0-0	Sep13 0-0	Aug12 0-0 Mar31 4-0	Mar10 5-2	Sep27 0-0 Apr07 3-0			Oct21 0-0 Apr21 0-2
STIRLING A	Apr14 2-1 Apr25 1-2	Sep23 2-1	Oct07 0-1 Apr28 3-2	Sep06 1-4 Mar17 0-0	Mar13 2-3	Oct28 1-1 Mar28 0-1	Oct14 1-0	Aug12 0-0	Sep16 1-4 Apr04 0-0	Apr07 0-1	Nov11 4-1	Aug26 0-1 Mar07 3-0	Dec23 1-5	

146

Apr 4 Partick T ....0 Rangers 0
played at Hampden Park

Replay
Apr 16 Partick T ....0 Rangers 1
played at Hampden Park

Final
May 12 Hibernian ....0 Rangers 0
played at Hampden Park

Replay
May 16 Hibernian ....0 Rangers 0
played at Hampden Park

May 28 Hibernian ....2 Rangers 3
played at Hampden Park

Derek Johnstone (right), scored twice for Rangers in the Scottish Cup Final. Roy Aitken (far right), was ever-present when Celtic regained the League title.

PREMIER DIVISION FINAL TABLE

	P	W	D	L	F	A	Pts
Celtic	36	21	6	9	61	37	48
Rangers	36	18	9	9	52	35	45
Dundee U	36	18	8	10	56	37	44
Aberdeen	36	13	14	9	59	36	40
Hibernian	36	12	13	11	44	48	37
St Mirren	36	15	6	15	45	41	36
Morton	36	12	12	12	52	53	36
Partick T	36	13	8	15	42	39	34
Hearts	36	8	7	21	39	71	23
Motherwell	37	5	7	24	33	86	17

DIVISION 1 FINAL TABLE

	P	W	D	L	F	A	Pts
Dundee	39	24	7	8	68	36	55
Kilmarnock	39	22	10	7	72	35	54
Clydebank	39	24	6	9	78	50	54
Ayr U	39	21	5	13	71	52	47
Hamilton A	39	17	9	13	62	60	43
Airdrie	39	16	8	15	72	61	40
Dumbarton	39	14	11	14	58	50	39
Stirling A	39	13	9	17	43	55	35
Clyde	39	13	8	18	54	65	34
Arbroath	39	11	11	17	50	61	33
Raith R	39	12	8	19	48	55	32
St Johnstone	39	10	11	18	57	66	31
Montrose	39	8	9	22	55	92	25
Queen of South	39	8	8	23	43	93	24

DIVISION 2 FINAL TABLE

	P	W	D	L	F	A	Pts
Berwick R	39	22	10	7	82	44	54
Dunfermline A	39	19	14	6	66	40	52
Falkirk	39	19	12	8	66	37	50
East Fife	39	17	9	13	64	53	43
Cowdenbeath	39	16	10	13	63	58	42
Alloa	39	16	9	14	57	62	41
Albion R	39	15	10	14	57	56	40
Forfar A	39	13	12	14	55	52	38
Stranraer	39	18	2	19	52	66	38
Stenhousemuir	39	12	8	19	54	58	32
Brechin C	39	7	14	16	49	65	32
E Stirling	39	12	8	19	61	87	32
Queen's Park	39	8	12	19	46	57	28
Meadowbank T	39	8	8	23	37	74	24

DIVISION 2

	ALBION R	ALLOA	BERWICK R	BRECHIN C	COWDENBEATH	DUNFERMLINE A	EAST FIFE	E STIRLING	FALKIRK	FORFAR A	MEADOWBANK T	QUEEN'S PARK	STENHOUSEMUIR	STRANRAER
ALBION R		Sep23 1-2, May10 2-1	Apr25 0-2	Oct07 3-2, May03 2-2	Mar13 1-1	Mar10 1-1, Apr28	Mar31 2-0	May08 1-1	Aug19 1-1, May01 0-0	Sep13 3-0	Sep09 1-2, Apr03 2-0	Apr14 1-0, Apr18 4-0	Oct21 0-1	Nov04 2-1
ALLOA	Nov25 2-6		Sep13 2-1	Aug19 1-1, Apr19 1-0	Sep16 2-4, Nov18 4-0	Sep09 1-1, May05 2-0	Oct21 0-0, Apr21 4-3	Dec09 2-2	Mar10 3-3, Apr28 2-0	Feb24 2-0	Sep30 1-1	Sep27 1-0, Mar24 1-1	Nov04 2-1	Mar03 3-1, Mar31 0-1
BERWICK R	Sep16 2-0, Mar28 5-1	Feb03 0-1, Mar17 3-2		Nov25 2-0, Apr04 1-0	Sep27 4-1	Oct14 2-2, Feb24 0-0	Sep09 1-2	Sep30 5-2, Apr14 5-1	Mar31 1-1	Dec09 2-4, Feb10 1-0	Aug26 0-0	Mar10 1-1	Aug19 6-1, Apr10 3-2	Oct21 1-1
BRECHIN C	Dec09 1-1	Oct28 4-2	Sep23 1-2			Aug12 1-1, Mar31 2-1	Mar07 1-6, Apr16 0-0	Apr07 1-1	Sep16 1-1, Dec06 3-1	Sep13 1-4	Aug26 3-2, Apr23 1-0	Oct21 2-2, Apr28 2-1	Mar28 1-3, Apr21 1-1	Apr11 1-2, Apr30 2-1
COWDENBEATH	Oct14 4-1, Feb24 3-1	Apr04 5-1	Apr07 1-3, Mar02 1-2	Mar03 0-0		Nov04 1-1	Sep23 1-0, Nov25 1-1	Mar05 1-2, May10 2-1	Apr21 1-1	Sep30 2-1	Aug19 2-1, Apr25 4-1	Dec09 2-2	Sep09 1-2	Sep06 2-0, Apr28 3-1
DUNFERMLINE A	Sep06 2-1	Nov11 2-2	May13 1-0	Sep13 1-1	Aug26 3-0, Apr18 2-0		Oct07 5-1, Mar28 1-1	Oct28 2-1	May16 1-1	Apr07 2-1, May02 2-2	Oct21 2-1, Feb28 1-0	Aug12 0-3, Mar03 2-2	Mar13 1-1, Apr14 2-1	Sep16 6-1, Mar18 3-0
EAST FIFE	Aug12 0-2, Mar03 1-2	Dec23 3-0	Nov11 2-4, Dec16 2-1	Sep27 0-0, Mar24 1-0	Jan20 0-1	Dec09 2-1		Sep06 5-0	Oct14 1-0	Oct28 1-2, Nov18 2-3	Sep16 2-2, Apr10 2-1	Aug26 3-2	Feb03 3-0	Sep30 2-0, Apr14 0-2
E STIRLING	Sep26 3-3, Apr07 0-1	Oct07 3-2, Feb10 3-1	Apr19 1-4	Feb28 3-2	Sep13 4-1	Aug19 1-1, Apr12 0-2	Mar10 0-1, Apr29 2-1			Nov04 1-1	Oct21 1-1, Apr21 3-1	Nov25 4-1	Sep09 4-2, Apr03 4-2	Mar31 1-3, Jan27 4-1
FALKIRK	Oct28 2-1	Sep06 1-0	Aug12 6-0, Mar03 1-1	Apr14 3-0, Apr25 2-0	Oct21 2-1, May08 0-3	Sep23 2-1, Nov25 4-1	Feb28 2-0, Apr18 2-5	Aug26 2-0, Mar28 1-1		Nov11 1-0	Oct07 6-0	Mar14 1-0, Mar20 1-1	Sep16 1-0	Mar24 2-0
FORFAR A	Apr16 1-1, May06 1-1	Oct14 2-1, Mar28 2-0	Oct07 2-2	Nov04 2-2	Dec02 4-2, Apr14 2-0	Sep26 1-2	Dec23 3-1, Mar06 1-1	Sep09 4-0, Apr04 1-4			Mar31 2-3	Nov18 2-1	Sep06 1-1, Mar10 0-0	Sep23 1-3, Mar14 2-0
MEADOWBANK T	Nov11 2-0	Dec02 0-1, Apr14 1-1	Nov03 0-5, Mar07 0-1	Mar10 0-3	Oct28 0-2	Apr21 1-3	Mar20 1-3	Sep23 3-1, Jan20 3-1	Dec09 1-2, Feb10 1-1	Aug12 0-0, Mar03 1-0		Oct14 0-4	Sep27 2-0, Mar24 1-2	Sep13 0-1
QUEEN'S PARK	Sep30 2-0	Apr07 0-1	Sep06 0-1, Apr28 1-1	Dec23 1-1	Oct07 1-1, Apr30 1-2	Mar30 0-1	Nov04 1-1	Nov10 4-0	Sep13 0-3, Mar17 1-2	Sep16 1-1, Apr25 0-1	Feb24 1-1, Mar27 3-0		Nov25 0-0	Aug19 0-1, Dec16 2-1
STENHOUSEMUIR	Dec23 3-2, Apr21 2-3	Aug26 0-2, Mar06 0-1	Oct28 0-2	Oct14 4-2	Nov11 1-1, Feb28 0-0	Sep30 1-2	Sep13 1-2, Apr24 5-0	Aug12 0-2, Mar03 2-2	Nov18 1-2	Apr28 2-0	Apr07 2-0	Sep23 1-2, Jan20 5-1		Dec09 4-1, Apr03 1-2
STRANRAER	Aug26 3-1, Feb17 0-1	Aug12 4-0	Dec23 0-0, Apr21 1-5	Sep09 1-0, Nov11 4-2	Mar10 2-4	Apr24 1-0	Dec02 2-4	Oct14 1-0, Feb24 6-2	Sep27 1-0, Apr07 2-1	Nov25 0-3	Feb03 3-1	Oct28 0-2, Mar17 1-0	Oct07 0-1	

SFA Cup

1st Round
Dec 15 Annan A ....1 Stranraer 3
Dec 15 Cowdenbeath ....3 Albion R 1
Dec 15 E Stirling ......1 Brechin C 1
Dec 15 Queen of South ..1 Falkirk 1
Dec 15 Spartans ....1 Forfar A 2
Dec 15 Stenhousemuir ...4 Queen's Park 2

Replays
Dec 19 Brechin C ....1 East Stirling 1
Dec 26 Brechin C ....1 E Stirling 0
played at Muirton Park
Dec 26 Falkirk ....0 Queen of South ...4

2nd Round
Jan 9 Alloa ....1 East Fife 0
Jan 7 Brechin C ....1 Montrose 1
Jan 5 Buckie T ....0 Brora R 0
Jan 12 Coldstream ......1 Queen of South ...1
Jan 5 Cowdenbeath ....3 Forfar A 2
Jan 5 Stenhousemuir ...0 Peterhead 0
Jan 5 Stranraer ....1 Meadowbank T ...1
Jan 5 Threave R ....2 Keith 3

Replays
Jan 12 Brora R ....1 Buckie T 2
Jan 12 Meadowbank T ...2 Stranraer 1
Jan 12 Peterhead ....2 Stenhousemuir ...0
Jan 14 Montrose ....3 Brechin C 4
Jan 14 Queen of South ..4 Coldstream 0

3rd Round
Jan 30 Airdrie ....3 St Johnstone 1
Jan 30 Alloa ....0 Hearts 1
Jan 26 Arbroath ....1 Aberdeen 1
Jan 26 Berwick R ....3 Peterhead 1
Jan 26 Celtic ....2 Raith R 1
Jan 26 Clyde ....2 Rangers 2
Jan 26 Clydebank ......1 Stirling A 1
Jan 26 Dumbarton ......1 Ayr U 2
Jan 30 Dundee U ....5 Dundee 1
Jan 30 Dunfermline A ...2 Buckie T 0
Jan 26 Hamilton A ......2 Keith 3
Jan 30 Kilmarnock ......0 Partick T 1
Jan 26 Meadowbank T ...0 Hibernian 1
Jan 26 Morton ....1 Cowdenbeath 0
Jan 26 Queen of South ..2 Motherwell 0
Jan 26 St Mirren ....3 Brechin C 1

Replays
Jan 30 Aberdeen ....5 Arbroath 0
Jan 30 Rangers ....2 Clyde 0
Jan 30 Stirling A ....1 Clydebank 1
Feb 11 Clydebank ......0 Stirling A 1
played at Brockville

4th Round
Feb 16 Aberdeen ....8 Airdrie 0
Feb 16 Celtic ....1 St Mirren 1
Feb 16 Hearts ....2 Stirling A 0
Feb 17 Hibernian ....2 Ayr U 0
Feb 16 Keith ....1 Berwick R 2
Feb 16 Morton ....5 Dunfermline A ...0
Feb 16 Queen of South ..1 Partick T 3
Feb 16 Rangers ....1 Dundee U 0

Replays
Feb 20 St Mirren ....2 Celtic 3

League Cup results for 1979-80 are detailed on page 209.

PREMIER

	ABERDEEN	CELTIC	DUNDEE	DUNDEE U	HIBERNIAN	KILMARNOCK	MORTON	PARTICK T	RANGERS	ST MIRREN
ABERDEEN		Sep22 1-2 / Jan19 0-0	Mar19 3-0 / Apr07 2-1	Nov03 0-3 / Mar15 2-1	Aug18 3-0 / Apr16 1-1	Oct13 3-1 / Feb23 1-2	Nov10 1-2 / Mar22 1-0	Oct20 1-1 / Mar01 1-1	Sep15 3-1 / Jan12 3-2	Dec15 2-0 / Apr26 2-0
CELTIC	Apr05 1-2 / Apr23 1-3		Oct13 3-0 / Feb23 2-2	Sep08 2-2 / Jan20 1-0	Nov17 3-0 / Apr16 4-0	Aug25 5-0 / Apr26 2-0	Aug11 3-2 / Dec22 3-1	Dec15 5-1 / Apr22 2-1	Oct27 1-0 / Apr26 1-0	Sep29 3-1 / Mar12 2-0
DUNDEE	Sep29 0-4 / Feb02 1-3	Apr19 5-1 / Apr30 0-2		Oct20 1-0 / Mar01 1-1	Nov03 2-1 / Mar15 3-0	Dec15 3-1 / Apr26 0-2	Sep15 4-3 / Dec12 1-0	Sep08 2-2 / Jan05 1-1	Nov24 2-2 / Apr05 1-4	Aug18 4-1 / Apr12 1-3
DUNDEE U	Aug25 1-3 / Apr29 1-1	Nov10 0-1 / Apr08 3-0	Aug11 3-0 / Dec22 0-0		Oct13 2-0 / Feb23 1-0	Oct27 4-0 / Mar08 0-0	Apr12 2-0 / Apr23 2-0	Oct06 0-0 / Mar12 0-0	Nov17 0-0 / Mar19 0-0	Nov01 0-0 / Mar29 0-0
HIBERNIAN	Oct27 1-1 / May03 0-5	Sep15 1-3 / Jan12 1-1	Aug25 5-2 / Mar25 2-0	Apr02 0-2 / Apr19 0-2		Nov01 1-1 / Apr21 1-2	Oct06 2-1 / Feb09 3-2	Dec01 1-1 / May02 2-1	Aug11 1-3 / Dec22 2-1	Sep22 0-2 / Apr29 2-1
KILMARNOCK	Apr01 0-4 / Apr19 1-3	Nov03 2-0 / Mar15 1-1	Oct06 1-0 / Feb09 1-1	Aug18 1-0 / Dec29 0-0	Sep08 3-1 / Jan05 3-1		Mar12 1-1 / Apr05 0-2	Nov17 0-1 / Mar29 0-1	Sep29 1-0 / Apr23 1-0	Oct20 1-1 / Mar01 1-1
MORTON	Sep08 3-2 / Jan05 1-0	Oct20 1-0 / Mar01 0-1	Nov17 2-0 / Mar29 2-0	Sep29 4-1 / May01 0-2	Dec15 2-0 / Apr26 2-1	Sep22 2-1 / Jan19 1-0		Aug18 2-1 / Dec29 1-3	Dec08 0-1 / Apr19 0-1	Nov03 0-0 / Mar15 2-1
PARTICK T	Aug11 1-0 / May07 1-1	Oct06 0-0 / Feb09 1-1	Nov10 2-3 / Apr13 3-0	Nov28 1-1 / Apr05 2-2	Sep29 2-1 / Apr23 1-0	Sep15 0-0 / Jan12 1-1	Oct27 1-4 / Apr02 0-1		Aug25 2-1 / May03 4-3	Apr09 1-1 / Apr19 1-2
RANGERS	Nov17 0-1 / Mar29 2-2	Aug18 2-2 / Dec29 1-1	Sep22 2-2 / Mar12 1-0	Dec15 2-1 / Apr26 2-1	Oct20 2-1 / Mar01 1-0	Dec01 2-2 / Apr30 1-0	Oct13 2-1 / Feb23 3-1	Nov03 2-1 / Mar15 0-0		Sep08 3-1 / Jan05 1-2
ST MIRREN	Oct06 2-2 / Feb09 1-1	Dec01 2-1 / May03 0-0	Oct27 4-2 / Mar08 2-1	Sep15 3-2 / Jan12 2-1	Nov24 2-1 / Apr05 2-1	Aug11 2-2 / Apr12 2-1	Aug25 0-3 / Jan01 3-1	Oct13 1-2 / Feb23 2-2	Nov10 2-1 / May07 4-1	

DIVISION 1

	AIRDRIE	ARBROATH	AYR U	BERWICK R	CLYDE	CLYDEBANK	DUMBARTON	DUNFERMLINE A	HAMILTON A	HEARTS	MOTHERWELL	RAITH R	ST JOHNSTONE	STIRLING A
AIRDRIE		Sep08 4-1 / Jan05 5-2	Sep05 6-2 / Apr26 2-1	Mar01 3-1 / Mar29 2-1	Dec08 1-2	Mar15 1-0 / Feb20 3-1	Sep15 1-0 / Nov17 0-0	Sep29 5-1	Nov03 1-0	Apr05 0-1	Oct20 4-0 / Apr19 3-1	Aug18 0-0 / Dec29 0-3	Nov24 4-2	Dec15 1-2
ARBROATH	Nov10 1-0		Dec22 1-1	Dec01 1-1 / Apr12 1-0	Oct13 3-2 / Feb23 0-0	Sep19 3-2	Apr05 4-1	Sep15 1-1 / Jan12 1-3	Sep05 1-2 / Apr26 2-5	Aug11 1-2	Oct27 3-1	Oct06 3-1	Aug25 2-2 / Jan01 1-3	Mar05 1-3 / Mar15 1-1
AYR U	Mar08 1-2	Oct20 2-1		Sep19 3-2 / Mar25 1-0	Aug25 0-0 / Mar12 2-1	Nov17 2-2	Aug11 1-2 / Mar29 1-0	Sep11 3-0	Sep08 0-3 / Jan05 4-1	Oct27 2-0	Dec15 0-0 / Feb23 0-5	Dec01 3-0	Sep22 5-1 / Apr05 2-2	Oct06 0-0
BERWICK R	Aug11 2-2	Sep29 7-2	Nov24 2-4		Dec22 1-1 / Apr19 0-2	Oct13 2-3 / Feb23 2-1	Feb02 0-1 / Mar15 3-0	Oct27 1-1	Dec08 1-1	Aug25 2-2 / Nov03 0-0	Nov10 2-2	Sep05 1-2 / Apr26 3-3	Sep15 1-3 / Jan12 5-0	Sep22 2-1 / Apr05 1-1
CLYDE	Oct06 2-3 / Feb09 1-3	Dec15 0-2	Nov03 3-3	Oct20 1-2		Aug18 1-0 / Dec29 0-2	Sep05 0-2 / Apr26 1-2	Nov10 1-0	Sep15 4-0	Dec01 2-2 / Jan12 2-2	Sep22 0-1 / Apr13 2-2	Mar01 0-4 / Apr16 1-0	Mar15 1-3	Apr09 1-2
CLYDEBANK	Sep11 2-2 / Feb16 3-1	Jan19 5-1	Sep15 1-0 / Jan12 1-0	Dec15 0-0	Oct27 2-2		Aug25 2-1 / Apr02 2-2	Mar19 3-1 / Apr09 0-1	Oct20 4-0 / Apr19 2-0	Nov10 1-1	Aug11 1-1 / Mar01 1-2	Mar25 1-0 / Apr05 0-3	Sep29 1-2	Apr26 0-1
DUMBARTON	Jan12 0-0	Sep22 1-0 / Mar25 2-3	Mar01 0-3	Sep01 4-1	Mar08 3-1	Nov03 1-0		Nov24 2-1	Aug18 3-2 / Dec29 4-0	Oct06 1-1 / Feb09 2-0	Dec01 2-2 / Apr12 1-0	Oct13 4-2	Feb16 0-1 / Apr19 5-2	Sep08 1-2 / Jan05 0-1
DUNFERMLINE A	Dec01 1-0 / Apr12 3-3	Nov17 1-1	Mar05 2-2 / Mar15 1-3	Aug18 1-2 / Dec29 2-1	Sep08 1-1 / Jan05 0-1	Oct06 1-3	Sep19 1-3 / Mar12 0-2		Apr05 0-0	Mar25 3-2	Sep05 2-0		Oct13 3-2 / Feb23 1-0	Mar01 1-0
HAMILTON A	Aug25 4-3 / Mar25 1-3	Mar08 1-0	Nov10 0-0	Oct06 1-2 / Feb09 4-0	Nov28 3-1	Dec22 3-0	Oct27 1-0	Sep22 2-0 / Apr15 4-0		Oct13 3-1	Sep11 3-2	Sep19 1-3 / Jan19 1-1	Aug11 2-2 / Mar29 1-1	Dec01 1-1 / Apr12 3-0
HEARTS	Sep22 2-2 / Apr30 1-0	Mar01 2-1 / Mar29 1-0	Aug18 0-1 / Apr01 0-1	Apr23 1-1	Sep29 2-1	Sep08 4-1	Dec08 2-1 / Jan05 3-3	Oct20 1-0 / Apr19 0-0	Dec15 1-0 / Feb23 1-0		Nov24 2-1	Apr09 2-2	Sep05 2-1	Sep15 / Nov17 1-0
MOTHERWELL	Dec22 2-1	Sep29 3-0 / Oct29 0-0	Oct13 0-2	Mar19 1-1	Apr05 3-0	Mar29 3-2	Sep29 3-0	Mar08 1-1 / Apr26 4-2	Sep19 1-1 / Jan19 0-0	Mar03 4-2		Nov17 1-2	Dec08 3-0 / Feb09 2-2	Mar05 1-0
RAITH R	Oct27 1-2	Dec08 1-1 / Feb09 2-1	Sep29 2-2 / Apr12 2-0	Mar19 2-1	Aug11 0-0 / Mar29 1-1	Sep22 2-4	Dec15 0-1 / Feb23 4-0	Sep25 0-0 / Jan01 1-0	Feb16 2-1	Sep11 3-2 / Mar15 1-2	Sep15 5-2 / Jan12 0-1		Nov10 1-2	Oct20 1-1
ST JOHNSTONE	Sep19 1-1 / Mar19 1-2	Nov03 3-0	Aug23 1-0	Nov17 3-3	Sep11 1-1 / Apr02 1-2	Dec01 0-1 / Apr12 3-1	Oct20 2-0	Dec15 1-3	Mar01 0-1	Apr16 1-0 / Apr26 0-3	Oct06 1-3 / Mar08 2-2	Sep08 2-2		Aug18 3-0 / Mar12 0-0
STIRLING A	Oct13 0-0 / Feb23 0-3	Sep11 1-1	Dec08 1-1 / Feb09 0-2	Apr16 1-1	Sep19 2-0 / Nov24 2-1	Sep05 2-0 / Mar08 2-0	Nov10 2-3	Aug11 4-0 / Mar29 1-0	Sep29 2-2	Jan12 0-1	Aug25 2-0 / Mar19 0-1	Apr02 0-1 / Apr19 0-0	Oct27 1-2	

5th Round

Mar 8	Berwick R 0	Hibernian 0	
Mar 8	Celtic 2	Morton 0	
Mar 8	Partick T 1	Aberdeen 2	
Mar 8	Rangers 6	Hearts 1	

Replay

Mar 12 Hibernian ....1 Berwick R 0

Semi-finals

Apr 12 Aberdeen ....0 Rangers 1
played at Celtic Park

Apr 12 Celtic ....5 Hibernian 0
played at Hampden Park

Final

May 10 Celtic ....1 Rangers 0
played at Hampden Park

Morton's Andy Ritchie on the attack during his side's 1-0 victory over Celtic in October 1979. The Celtic player is full-back Andy Lynch.

DIVISION 2

	ALBION R	ALLOA	BRECHIN C	COWDENBEATH	EAST FIFE	E STIRLING	FALKIRK	FORFAR A	MEADOWBANK T	MONTROSE	QUEEN OF SOUTH	QUEEN'S PARK	STENHOUSEMUIR	STRANRAER
ALBION R		Sep11 2-0 / Feb09 1-0	Feb16 4-0 / Apr28 1-1	Sep08 2-1 / Jan19 1-0	Mar08 5-1 / Apr26 4-0	Mar04 1-4	Dec13 2-2	Nov03 5-0	Nov18 3-1	Dec29 1-1	Mar29 5-1	Aug18 3-0 / Jan01 2-2	Sep29 1-2	Sep22 1-3 / Apr05 2-2
ALLOA	Mar15 1-1		Aug11 8-3 / Mar29 1-4	Oct06 1-0 / Feb16 2-1	Sep22 1-0	Mar26 2-3	Sep08 3-2 / Mar11 1-2	Dec01 0-3 / Apr12 1-1	Sep19 4-0 / Mar04 2-1	Aug25 0-1 / Jan12 2-1	Dec29 0-1	Apr26 0-1	Oct27 1-1	Nov17 1-1
BRECHIN C	Oct06 2-0	Mar01 1-1		Nov17 1-3	Dec22 1-0	Mar08 2-0 / Apr26 1-1	Apr23 1-1	Aug18 2-0 / Mar26 0-1	Sep08 3-1 / Jan19 1-1	Sep19 1-2 / Mar12 2-3	Dec01 3-0 / Apr12 4-1	Nov03 4-1	Oct20 2-3	Sep11 2-1 / Apr02 2-3
COWDENBEATH	Nov10 2-2	Dec08 2-1	Sep15 1-0 / Apr16 2-3		Oct27 2-2	Aug25 2-2 / Feb20 0-1	Nov24 0-0	Sep22 1-0 / Apr05 0-1	Sep05 1-2 / Apr26 0-1	Aug11 4-2	Oct13 3-1 / Feb23 2-2	Sep29 1-0	Mar04 3-1 / Mar15 1-1	Mar25 2-0 / Apr19 2-1
EAST FIFE	Sep05 1-0	Dec15 2-1 / Apr05 1-0	Oct13 0-1 / Feb23 2-1	Aug18 4-0 / Jan01 2-1		Dec29 0-3	Jan12 1-0 / Mar15 0-1	Mar01 2-2	Nov03 2-2	Dec01 1-1 / Apr12 2-0	Oct06 1-2	Nov17 1-1	Sep19 1-1 / Mar25 1-3	Sep08 1-0 / Jan19 1-1
E STIRLING	Sep18 2-0 / Jan05 1-1	Oct13 1-0 / Feb23 1-2	Sep05 2-1	Nov03 0-1	Oct20 2-1 / Aug19 1-0		Aug18 2-3 / Jan01 2-1	Nov28 2-1	Apr01 4-1	Apr16 3-1	Sep08 0-1 / Jan19 0-1	Mar01 0-0 / Mar29 1-3	Feb16 1-1	Sep29 3-1
FALKIRK	Dec22 4-0 / Feb23 1-0	Nov10 2-0	Sep22 3-2 / Apr05 0-0	Sep19 3-0 / Apr09 0-0	Sep11 0-0	Oct27 1-2		Oct06 1-2	Dec01 2-2	Mar08 0-0 / Apr26 2-1	Nov17 3-1	Oct20 3-0 / Apr19 4-1	Aug11 0-1 / Mar29 2-1	Aug25 3-0 / Jan26 0-0
FORFAR A	Aug25 6-2 / Jan12 2-2	Sep29 0-2	Oct27 1-1	Apr21 2-1	Aug11 1-0 / Mar29 0-4	Sep15 1-2 / Jan26 1-1	Dec08 2-1 / Feb16 2-0		Dec29 5-3 / Apr19 0-0	Oct13 1-1 / Feb23 1-2	Sep05 3-1 / Mar08 0-0	Sep10 2-1	Nov10 2-3	Nov24 3-0
MEADOWBANK T	Sep15 1-2 / Apr22 1-1	Nov24 2-1	Nov10 0-1	Mar08 0-2	Aug24 2-0 / Jan30 3-1	Sep11 0-3 / Mar15 0-1	Sep29 0-3 / Apr12 0-5	Oct20 1-0		Oct27 2-1	Sep22 2-1	Feb16 0-2 / Mar19 1-2	Dec22 0-1 / Feb23 0-1	Aug11 2-1 / Mar29 0-3
MONTROSE	Oct20 0-2 / Apr19 1-4	Nov24 2-0	Nov24 2-2	Mar01 1-1 / Mar29 2-1	Sep29 1-1	Sep22 1-3 / Apr05 2-1	Sep05 1-4	Aug18 1-4	Aug18 3-0 / Jan01 3-3		Feb09 1-3 / Mar15 3-2	Sep08 2-1 / Jan19 1-3	Sep15 0-2 / Nov17 5-0	Dec08 6-3
QUEEN OF SOUTH	Aug11 2-1 / Mar01 3-3	Oct20 0-1 / Apr19 0-0	Sep29 1-1	Dec22 2-2	Dec08 2-4 / Mar19 1-0	Nov10 1-2	Sep15 2-0 / Mar25 0-2	Apr26 2-3	Apr05 0-2 / Apr15 5-0	Sep11 1-2		Nov24 3-2 / Mar04 2-1	Aug25 2-1 / Mar12 1-1	Oct27 1-2
QUEEN'S PARK	Oct27 2-2	Sep05 7-0 / Mar08 2-2	Aug25 1-3 / Jan12 4-0	Nov28 1-1 / Apr01 0-2	Sep15 1-2 / Jan26 3-1	Aug11 2-0	Dec29 2-2	Feb09 1-0 / Mar15 0-1	Oct06 0-1	Nov10 1-0	Sep18 2-1		Apr05 1-1	Oct13 0-2 / Feb23 2-0
STENHOUSEMUIR	Dec01 1-3 / Apr12 0-1	Aug18 3-1 / Mar19 2-0	Apr08 0-1 / Apr19 2-0	Sep11 4-1	Nov24 2-0	Oct06 0-1 / Dec08 1-0	Mar01 1-1	Sep08 4-0 / Jan19 1-5	Oct13 0-1	Jan26 2-1	Nov03 2-1	Sep22 0-1 / Apr22 1-3		Mar08 6-1
STRANRAER	Apr16 2-0	Sep15 1-0 / Apr09 4-0	Mar15 1-1	Oct20 0-2	Nov10 4-2	Dec01 1-2 / Apr12 0-0	Nov03 1-2	Sep19 0-1 / Feb02 2-0	Mar01 1-2	Oct06 1-2 / Feb16 1-1	Aug18 5-1 / Jan01 1-1	Dec22 0-4	Sep05 1-0 / Apr26 2-1	

PREMIER DIVISION FINAL TABLE

	P	W	D	L	F	A	Pts
Aberdeen	36	19	10	7	68	36	48
Celtic	36	18	11	7	61	38	47
St Mirren	36	15	12	9	56	49	42
Dundee U	36	12	13	11	43	30	37
Rangers	36	15	7	14	50	46	37
Morton	36	14	8	14	51	46	36
Partick T	36	11	14	11	43	47	36
Kilmarnock	36	11	11	14	36	52	33
Dundee	36	10	6	20	47	73	26
Hibernian	36	6	6	24	29	67	18

DIVISION 1 FINAL TABLE

	P	W	D	L	F	A	Pts
Hearts	39	20	13	6	58	39	53
Airdrie	39	21	9	9	78	47	51
Ayr U	39	16	12	11	64	51	44
Dumbarton	39	19	6	14	59	51	44
Raith R	39	14	15	10	59	46	43
Motherwell	39	16	11	12	59	48	43
Hamilton A	39	15	10	14	60	59	40
Stirling A	39	13	13	13	40	40	39
Clydebank	39	14	8	17	58	57	36
Dunfermline A	39	11	13	15	39	57	35
St Johnstone	39	12	10	17	57	74	34
Berwick R	39	8	15	16	57	64	31
Arbroath	39	9	10	20	50	79	28
Clyde	39	6	13	20	43	69	25

DIVISION 2 FINAL TABLE

	P	W	D	L	F	A	Pts
Falkirk	39	19	12	8	65	35	50
E Stirling	39	21	7	11	55	40	49
Forfar A	39	19	8	12	63	51	46
Albion R	39	16	12	11	73	56	44
Queen's Park	39	16	9	14	59	47	41
Stenhousemuir	39	16	9	14	56	51	41
Cowdenbeath	39	14	12	13	54	52	40
Brechin C	39	15	10	14	61	59	40
Montrose	39	14	10	15	60	63	38
East Fife	39	12	9	18	45	57	33
Stranraer	39	12	8	19	51	65	32
Meadowbank T	39	12	8	19	42	70	32
Queen of South	39	11	9	19	51	69	31
Alloa	39	11	7	21	44	64	29

SFA Cup

1st Round

Dec 13	Alloa 1	Stenhousemuir ... 1
Dec 13	Brechin C 2	Keith 1
Dec 13	East Fife 2	Civil Service 1
Dec 13	Meadowbank T ..2	Buckie T 2
Dec 13	Queen's Park 2	Montrose 2
Dec 13	Whitehill Welfare . 1	Hawick RA 1

Replays

Dec 17	Hawick RA 4	Whitehill Welfare ..1
Dec 17	Montrose 2	Queen's Park 0
Dec 17	Stenhousemuir ... 3	Alloa 2
Dec 20	Buckie T 3	Meadowbank T ...2

2nd Round

Jan 12	Albion R 1	Arbroath 1
Jan 3	Forfar A 0	Brechin C 2
Jan 3	Hawick RA 2	Cowdenbeath 2
Jan 3	Inverness T 2	Montrose 0
Jan 10	Queen of South ...1	East Fife 2
Jan 3	Rothes 1	Clyde 5
Jan 3	Stenhousemuir ...0	Spartans 0
Jan 3	Stranraer 2	Buckie T 2

Replays

Jan 7	Spartans 1	Stenhousemuir ...2
Jan 10	Buckie T 3	Stranraer 2
Jan 12	Cowdenbeath 3	Hawick RA 0
Jan 14	Arbroath 1	Albion R 0

3rd Round

Jan 24	Airdrie 0	Rangers 5
Jan 24	Arbroath 1	Cowdenbeath 1
Jan 24	Berwick R 0	Celtic 2
Jan 24	Brechin C 1	Dundee U 2
Jan 24	Buckie T 1	Stirling A 3
Jan 24	East Fife 0	Clydebank 0
Jan 24	E Stirling 4	Inverness T 1
Jan 24	Falkirk 1	Dundee 0
Jan 24	Hamilton A 0	St Johnstone 3
Jan 24	Hibernian 1	Dunfermline A 1
Jan 24	Kilmarnock 2	Ayr U 1
Jan 24	Morton 0	Hearts 0
Jan 24	Partick T 2	Clyde 2
Jan 24	Raith R 1	Aberdeen 2
Jan 24	St Mirren 0	Dumbarton 2
Jan 24	Stenhousemuir ...1	Motherwell 1

Replays

Jan 28	Clyde 2	Partick T 4
Jan 28	Clydebank 5	East Fife 4
Jan 28	Cowdenbeath 4	Arbroath 0
Jan 28	Dunfermline A ...1	Hibernian 2
Jan 28	Hearts 1	Morton 3
Jan 28	Motherwell 2	Stenhousemuir ...1

4th Round

Feb 14	Celtic 3	Stirling A 0
Feb 14	Cowdenbeath 1	E Stirling 2
Feb 14	Dundee U 1	Partick T 0
Feb 14	Hibernian 1	Falkirk 0
Feb 14	Kilmarnock 0	Clydebank 0
Feb 14	Morton 1	Aberdeen 0
Feb 14	Motherwell 2	Dumbarton 1
Feb 14	St Johnstone 3	Rangers 3

Replays

Feb 18	Clydebank 1	Kilmarnock 1
Feb 18	Rangers 3	St Johnstone 1
Feb 23	Clydebank 1	Kilmarnock 0
	played at Love Street	

5th Round

Mar 8	Celtic 2	E Stirling 0

League Cup results for 1980-81 are detailed on page 209.

PREMIER

	ABERDEEN	AIRDRIE	CELTIC	DUNDEE U	HEARTS	KILMARNOCK	MORTON	PARTICK T	RANGERS	ST MIRREN
ABERDEEN		Nov01 4-1 Apr18 3-0	Sep27 2-2 Dec27 4-1	Aug16 1-1 Dec30 1-1	Mar07 4-1 Apr11 1-0	Oct11 2-0 May02 0-2	Sep06 6-0 Feb07 0-1	Nov15 2-1 Apr01 3-1	Dec13 2-0 Apr22 0-0	Oct18 3-2 Feb28 1-2
AIRDRIE	Aug23 0-4 Feb21 0-0		Nov15 1-4 Mar21 1-2	Sep13 0-0 Jan31 0-5	Oct25 3-0 Apr25 1-2	Sep27 1-1 Mar11 3-0	Oct11 1-0 May02 3-2	Nov29 1-0 Mar07 2-0	Aug09 0-1 Jan03 1-1	Dec06 1-2 Apr04 2-1
CELTIC	Nov08 0-2 Mar28 1-1	Sep20 1-1 Dec20 2-1		Oct04 2-0 Jan10 2-1	Oct25 3-2 Apr01 6-0	Aug09 2-1 Apr25 1-1	Sep06 4-1 Jan03 3-0	Oct18 1-2 Mar18 4-1	Dec13 2-1 Feb21 3-1	Nov22 1-1 Mar14 7-0
DUNDEE U	Oct25 1-3 Apr25 0-0	Dec13 1-0 Apr29 4-1	Nov29 0-3 Apr22 2-3		Sep27 1-1 Dec27 4-1	Aug09 2-2 Jan03 7-0	Aug23 1-1 Feb21 1-0	Oct11 0-0 Feb07 3-2	Sep06 2-4 May02 2-1	Nov15 2-0 Mar21 1-2
HEARTS	Oct04 0-1 Jan10 0-2	Aug16 0-2 Jan01 2-3	Sep13 0-2 Jan31 0-3	Nov08 0-3 Mar28 0-4		Dec06 2-0 Apr06 1-0	Sep20 0-1 Dec20 0-0	Oct18 1-0 Feb28 1-1	Nov22 0-1 Mar14 1-2	Nov01 1-1 Apr18 1-2
KILMARNOCK	Nov22 1-1 Mar14 1-0	Nov08 1-1 Mar28 0-1	Aug16 0-2 Jan01 1-4	Oct18 0-1 Feb28 2-0	Sep06 0-1 Mar24 2-0		Dec13 3-3 Apr15 0-1	Nov01 3-2 Apr18 0-1	Sep20 1-8 Dec20 1-1	Oct14 1-6 Jan10 2-3
MORTON	Dec06 1-0 Apr04 1-3	Nov22 3-1 Mar14 0-1	Oct18 2-3 Feb28 0-3	Nov01 0-2 Apr18 2-0	Nov15 2-2 Mar01 3-0	Sep13 2-0 Jan31 1-0		Sep27 1-2 Dec27 2-0	Oct04 2-2 Jan10 0-2	Aug16 1-4 Jan01 1-3
PARTICK T	Sep20 0-1 Dec20 1-1	Oct04 2-1 Jan10 1-0	Dec06 0-1 Apr05 0-2	Nov22 0-1 Mar14 0-2	Aug09 2-1 Jan03 1-0	Aug23 0-1 Feb21 1-1	Nov06 2-2 Mar28 3-1		Oct25 1-1 Apr25 1-1	Sep13 1-0 Jan31 0-0
RANGERS	Sep13 1-1 Jan31 1-0	Oct18 0-0 Feb28 2-1	Nov01 3-0 Apr18 1-0	Mar18 1-4 Apr04 May02 0-3	Oct11 3-1 May02 0-0	Nov15 2-0 Mar21 0-0	Nov29 0-1 Apr01 1-1	Aug16 4-0 Jan01		Sep27 1-1 Apr15 1-0
ST MIRREN	Aug09 0-1 Jan03 1-1	Sep06 2-2 Mar14 2-1	Oct11 0-2 May02 3-1	Sep20 2-0 Dec20 3-3	Aug23 1-3 Feb21 2-1	Nov29 2-0 Mar07 1-1	Oct25 1-1 Apr25 2-0	Dec13 1-0 Apr11 3-2	Nov08 0-0 Mar28 2-1	

DIVISION 1

	AYR U	BERWICK R	CLYDEBANK	DUMBARTON	DUNDEE	DUNFERMLINE A	E STIRLING	FALKIRK	HAMILTON A	HIBERNIAN	MOTHERWELL	RAITH R	ST JOHNSTONE	STIRLING A
AYR U		Nov01 4-1 Feb21 4-1	Nov15 1-0 Apr25 1-2	Dec13 0-0	Dec27 1-0	Sep27 2-0 Mar07 2-1	Jan03 3-3	Nov29 3-1	Sep17 2-1	Sep13 1-3 Mar28	Aug09 5-0	Oct01 1-0	Oct11 1-1 Jan17 3-3	Aug23 0-0 Apr18 1-0
BERWICK R	Sep06 1-2 Mar14 1-1		Dec06 0-1	Nov08 2-2	Oct25 0-1	Aug16 1-1 Apr04 1-0	Nov22 1-2	Dec20 0-4 Apr18 1-2	Jan10 1-0	Jan01 0-2 Jan31 0-0	Sep20 3-2 Feb07 2-2	Oct18 1-4	Sep09 0-1	Oct04 1-0 Feb28 1-0
CLYDEBANK	Sep20 2-2	Oct11 2-1 Apr11 2-0		Aug23 1-4 May02 0-0	Sep06 3-0	Dec13 2-3	Aug09 2-3 Apr25 2-0	Oct25 2-1	Oct04 3-1 Feb28 1-2	Nov22 1-1	Sep09 2-1 Mar21 0-0	Apr22 3-0	Nov08 0-2 Mar24 1-3	Jan03 1-1
DUMBARTON	Oct18 0-1	Sep17 2-0 Feb21 1-1	Jan01 1-1		Nov29 1-2	Dec20 1-0 Apr18 2-1	Sep13 2-2 Jan31 1-0	Jan10 0-1	Nov01 2-1 Apr04 1-0	Nov08 2-0 Mar21 1-4	Sep27 1-2 Apr08 0-0	Nov15 2-2	Aug16 0-3	Dec06 2-0
DUNDEE	Aug16 0-0 Jan31 2-4	Sep13 2-2 Mar28 0-0	Nov01 2-1 Apr18 1-0	Oct04 3-1 Mar11 2-1		Mar18 2-0	Oct18 2-0	Sep20 4-0	Oct14 2-0	Sep09 1-2 Dec20 1-0	Nov08 2-1	Mar14 3-1 Apr01 2-1	Jan01 2-2 Apr01 4-1	Nov22 5-1
DUNFERMLINE A	Nov22 2-3	Apr22 1-1	Oct18 1-1 Apr01 2-1	Sep09 1-1	Aug09 0-0 Apr11 1-1		Nov01 1-0	Nov08 0-1 Mar04 0-1	Dec06 2-1	Oct04 0-2 Feb28 0-5	Mar28 1-3 Apr15 2-1	Aug23 0-2	Sep20 0-2	Sep13 2-0 Jan31 0-1
E STIRLING	Oct13 0-2 Apr04 1-3	Sep27 5-1 Apr07 0-0	Apr29 2-2	Oct25 2-1	Dec13 0-2 May02 0-0	Sep06 0-4 Mar21 1-1		Jan01 0-0 Feb21 1-1	Aug16 1-1	Nov08 1-1	Oct11 0-1	Mar24 0-1	Dec20 1-1 Apr18 1-1	Sep20 2-0 Apr01 1-1
FALKIRK	Oct04 3-1 Feb28 2-1	Sep03 6-0	Sep13 3-2 Jan31 0-0	Aug09 0-5 Apr11 1-3	Nov15 0-3 Apr25 1-2	Sep17 2-1	Aug23 1-1		Oct18 2-3 Mar14 2-1	Dec06 0-2	Mar18 0-1	Jan03 1-0	Nov22 0-3	Nov01 0-0 Mar21 0-0
HAMILTON A	Nov08 1-0 Mar04 0-0	Aug09 9-1 Apr25 4-1	Nov29 3-0	Sep06 1-1	Jan03 2-2 Mar21 1-3	Oct11 4-2 Feb14 1-4	Dec27 2-2 Mar28 2-2	Dec13 0-1		Sep20 1-1 Apr18 1-2	Aug23 0-3 Mar07 0-2	Sep27 0-3	Oct25 0-0	Sep09 2-0
HIBERNIAN	Oct25 1-0	Aug23 3-0 Apr15 3-0	Sep27 4-1	Jan03 1-0	Feb07 0-0	Nov29 1-0	Sep17 2-2 Apr11 1-2	Oct11 2-0 Jan17 4-0	Nov15 3-3 Feb21		Sep06 1-1	Aug09 0-1 Apr18 2-0	Dec13 4-0 Mar18 1-2	Dec27 3-0 Apr04 2-2
MOTHERWELL	Jan10 3-2 Apr11 1-0	Nov15 2-1	Dec20 3-0	Nov22 4-2	Sep17 3-2 Feb21 4-1	Oct01 2-0	Dec06 1-1 Mar14 2-1	Aug16 3-0 Apr04 1-0	Jan01 1-3 Aug25 1-1	Nov01 2-0		Sep13 1-1 Jan31 0-0	Oct04 2-2 Feb28 3-2	Oct18 2-1
RAITH R	Dec20 2-1 Mar21 1-1	Dec13 3-0 Feb14 1-0	Aug16 0-4 Apr04 1-0	Sep20 4-1 Feb07 1-0	Oct11 0-0	Jan01 Apr25 1-0	Oct04 2-0 Feb28 0-0	Sep09 2-1 Mar28 0-0	Nov22 1-0	Jan10 2-0	Oct25 2-0		Sep06 0-0	Nov08 3-0
ST JOHNSTONE	Dec06 1-0 Mar21 6-2	Jan03 1-0 Apr02	Sep17 1-1 Mar28 2-1	Oct27 2-0	Aug23 1-0	Nov15 2-4 Feb21 4-1	Oct25 0-2	Sep06 0-0 Mar07 1-0	Oct11 1-2 Jan31	Sep13 1-2	Oct18 2-2 Apr11 1-0	Nov01 0-3		Aug09 0-1 Apr25 1-0
STIRLING A	Jan01 1-1	Nov29 1-0	Oct01 0-0 Mar28 0-0	Oct11 0-1 Mar14 0-0	Aug27 1-1 Mar24 0-1	Oct25 3-3	Nov15 4-2	Sep06 1-0	Mar11 0-2 Apr11 0-1	Aug16 0-2	Dec13 2-0 May02 0-3	Sep17 0-2 Feb21 0-1	Jan10 0-1	

Mar 7 Dundee U ......6 Motherwell 1
Mar 11 Morton ....0 Clydebank 0
Mar 7 Rangers ....3 Hibernian 1

Replays
Mar 16 Clydebank ....0 Morton 6

Semi-finals
Apr 11 Celtic ....0 Dundee U 0
played at Hampden Park
Apr 11 Morton ....1 Rangers 2
played at Celtic Park

Replays
Apr 15 Celtic ....2 Dundee U 3
played at Hampden Park

Final
May09 Dundee U ....0 Rangers 0
played at Hampden Park

Replay
May12 Dundee U ......1 Rangers 4
played at Hampden Park

John MacDonald celebrates Cooper's opening goal against Dundee in the 1980-81 SFA Cup Final. Davie Cooper died suddenly in 1995 after a brain haemorrhage.

PREMIER DIVISION FINAL TABLE

	P	W	D	L	F	A	Pts
Celtic	36	26	4	6	84	37	56
Aberdeen	36	19	11	6	61	26	49
Rangers	36	16	12	8	60	32	44
St Mirren	36	18	8	10	56	47	44
Dundee U	36	17	9	10	66	42	43
Partick T	36	10	10	16	32	48	30
Airdrie	36	10	9	17	36	55	29
Morton	36	10	8	18	36	58	28
Kilmarnock	36	5	9	22	23	65	19
Hearts	36	6	6	24	27	71	18

DIVISION 1 FINAL TABLE

	P	W	D	L	F	A	Pts
Hibernian	39	24	9	6	67	24	57
Dundee U	39	22	8	9	64	40	52
St Johnstone	39	20	11	8	64	45	51
Raith R	39	20	10	9	49	32	50
Motherwell	39	19	11	9	65	51	49
Ayr U	39	17	11	11	59	42	45
Hamilton A	39	15	7	17	61	57	37
Dumbarton	39	13	11	15	49	50	37
Falkirk	39	13	8	18	39	52	34
Clydebank	39	10	13	16	48	59	33
E Stirling	39	6	17	16	41	56	29
Dunfermline A	39	10	7	22	41	58	27
Stirling A	39	6	11	22	18	48	23
Berwick R	39	5	12	22	31	82	22

DIVISION 2 FINAL TABLE

	P	W	D	L	F	A	Pts
Queen's Park	39	16	18	5	62	43	50
Queen of South	39	16	14	9	66	53	46
Cowdenbeath	39	18	9	12	63	48	45
Brechin C	39	15	14	10	52	46	44
Forfar A	39	17	9	13	63	57	43
Alloa	39	15	12	12	61	54	42
Montrose	39	16	8	15	66	55	40
Clyde	39	14	12	13	68	63	40
Arbroath	39	13	12	14	58	54	38
Stenhousemuir	39	13	11	15	63	58	37
East Fife	39	10	15	14	44	53	35
Albion R	39	13	9	17	59	72	35
Meadowbank T	39	11	7	21	42	64	29
Stranraer	39	7	8	24	36	83	22

DIVISION 2

	ALBION R	ALLOA	ARBROATH	BRECHIN C	CLYDE	COWDENBEATH	EAST FIFE	FORFAR A	MEADOWBANK T	MONTROSE	QUEEN OF SOUTH	QUEEN'S PARK	STENHOUSEMUIR	STRANRAER
ALBION R		Nov22 3-1	Oct04 1-6, Feb28 2-4	Sep20 2-3	Jan10 3-3	Sep13 2-0, Mar28 0-2	Nov08 0-0, Feb14 3-2	Sep24 2-4, Apr11 2-1	Aug24 3-1, Jan01 2-1	Nov01 2-1	Sep10 0-4, Mar14 1-0	Oct18 2-2	Apr18 0-2	Dec06 1-3, Mar17 5-0
ALLOA	Sep27 1-0, Mar11 0-1		Oct25 1-1	Oct11 5-0, Feb07 0-2	Sep06 2-0	Aug16 1-1	Dec20 2-1, Jan31 0-0	Sep09 1-0, Apr04 0-1	Jan10 2-1	Nov15 0-4, Feb21 1-0	Mar04 1-3, Apr18 1-5	Nov19 5-2	Jan01 3-2, Mar14 0-0	Sep17 3-1
ARBROATH	Dec13 2-2	Sep13 1-1, Mar28 0-3		Sep27 2-2, Mar07 0-0	Dec20 2-2	Mar04 0-1	Oct11 1-1	Aug23 2-3, Mar14 0-0	Nov01 0-1	Sep03 1-4	Dec27 1-2, Apr25 1-1	Sep17 1-4, Feb14 0-0	Apr11 1-1, May02 2-0	Nov15 3-1, Feb21 1-0
BRECHIN C	Nov15 2-2, Feb21 2-1	Dec06 1-1	Nov22 5-1		Dec27 3-1, Mar14 2-1	Nov01 0-2, Apr04 2-1	Oct04 0-1	Sep17 1-1, Feb14 0-0	Apr11 0-0, May02 2-1	Aug23 1-1, Jan01 3-1	Mar24 2-1, Apr14 1-0	Sep13 0-0	Sep03 2-1	Oct18 1-0
CLYDE	Oct01 1-1, Mar21 4-0	Nov01 0-3, Apr11 0-0	Oct18 0-2, Jan31 1-0	Aug16 3-0		Dec06 2-2	Aug09 3-1, Apr25 6-2	Sep27 2-1, Mar07 3-1	Nov15 2-1, Feb22 1-4	Sep13 4-3, Mar28 6-0	Apr01 1-4	Mar04 1-1	Sep15 2-2	May02 3-3
COWDENBEATH	Oct25 2-1	Mar21 5-2, Apr15 4-2	Aug09 2-1, Apr18 1-0	Sep06 4-2, Mar18 2-0	Oct11 4-2		Jan01 1-1	Apr01 1-2	Sep27 1-0, Apr29 1-0	Sep17 2-1	Jan31 1-1	May02 1-2	Nov15 0-1, Feb21 1-2	Sep03 1-1, Mar24 3-0
EAST FIFE	Sep17 1-1	Oct18 1-1	Dec06 2-1, Feb07 0-2	Nov29 0-2, Feb28 2-2	Mar24 0-1	Aug23 3-2, Mar14 1-0		Dec27 0-0	Sep03 2-1	Apr11 1-1, May02	Sep27 1-1	Nov15 0-2, Feb21 1-1	Nov01 1-1	Sep13 3-1, Mar11 2-1
FORFAR A	Aug09 1-1	May02 4-1	Apr08 2-1	Nov08 0-0	Nov22 3-2	Oct04 1-2, Mar11 1-0	Aug16 3-2, Mar21 1-2			Sep13 3-2, Mar28 3-1	Oct18 0-4	Sep20 1-2, Dec13 3-4	Sep03 1-1, Apr18 1-2	Nov01 3-0
MEADOWBANK T	Apr04 2-1, Jan24 0-4	Aug09 0-3, Mar21 1-2	Aug20 1-4	Sep09 2-0	Sep20 0-2	Nov22 1-4	Feb11 1-3, Apr18 1-0	Oct25 4-2			Oct04 0-2, Feb28 2-1	Nov08 0-2, Feb14 0-0	Dec06 1-1, Jan31 1-0	Dec27 0-1
MONTROSE	Sep06 0-1, Apr25 1-1	Sep20 2-1	Jan10 1-2, Apr04 0-3	Apr18 3-2	Oct25 1-0	Nov08 3-2, Apr22 3-1	Sep09 1-0	Jan31 4-0, Mar24 0-0	Mar18 1-2		Oct11 1-1	Aug16 1-3	Sep13 1-3, Mar11 2-1	Aug09 0-0, Apr08 6-1
QUEEN OF SOUTH	May02 3-0	Sep02 1-1	Aug16 2-2	Aug09 3-2	Oct04 1-3, Feb28 0-0	Oct18 1-0, Apr08 2-2	Nov22 1-1, Mar07 2-1	Nov15 1-1	Sep17 1-1, Feb07 4-1	Dec06 1-5		Nov01 0-3, Jan24 1-0	Sep13 4-4, Mar21 0-2	Jan01 3-0
QUEEN'S PARK	Dec20 2-0, Jan31 3-1	Oct04 1-1, Feb28 2-1	Nov08 2-2	Oct25 1-0, Mar28 4-0	Aug23 2-1, Apr04 1-1	Sep09 2-1, Apr25 1-1	Sep20 1-3	Jan10 1-3, Jan03 1-1	Oct11 5-1, Apr01 1-0	Mar14	Sep06 5-1		Aug09 2-1	Nov22 1-0
STENHOUSEMUIR	Aug16 3-1, Feb24 0-3	Aug23 1-1	Sep09 1-2	Mar18 0-3, Apr25 1-3	Nov08 3-0, Feb14 1-3	Sep20 1-1	Sep06 2-0, Apr04 0-3	Oct11 0-1	Mar31 1-1	Nov22 1-2	Oct25 1-1	Feb10 2-2, Mar21		Oct04 1-2, Feb28 2-1
STRANRAER	Oct11 1-4, Feb14 2-2	Nov08 1-3	Sep20 0-2	Dec20 0-1, Jan31 1-1	Sep09 1-0, Apr18 1-1	Apr11 3-2	Mar28 1-1	Sep06 0-4, Apr25 0-3	Aug16 1-3, Mar14 1-0	Jan24 0-3	Aug23 1-0, Apr04 1-2	Sep27 2-1, Mar07 1-1	Nov29 2-5	

PREMIER

	ABERDEEN	AIRDRIE	CELTIC	DUNDEE	DUNDEE U	HIBERNIAN	MORTON	PARTICK T	RANGERS	ST MIRREN
ABERDEEN		Nov28 0-0 / Apr24 2-0	Sep05 1-3 / Jan30 1-3	Oct24 2-1 / Feb27 0-0	Oct31 1-1 / Mar20 2-1	Sep19 1-0 / Mar10 3-1	Oct03 1-0 / Feb06 0-0	Nov14 2-1 / May03 3-1	Apr21 3-1 / May15 4-0	Apr14 4-1 / May08 5-1
AIRDRIE	Sep26 0-4 / Feb20 0-3		Oct31 1-3 / Apr14 1-5	Oct10 4-2 / Mar13 0-2	Sep19 3-1 / Feb09 2-0	Nov14 3-1 / Apr03 0-2	Feb13 1-1 / May06 1-1	Oct24 1-1 / Feb27 0-1	Dec05 2-2 / Apr17 0-1	Sep05 3-4 / Apr21 0-2
CELTIC	Nov07 2-1 / Mar27 0-1	Aug29 5-2 / Mar20 2-0		Dec05 3-1 / Apr17 4-2	Oct17 1-1 / Apr21 3-1	Feb02 0-0 / May01 6-0	Sep12 2-1 / Mar03 1-0	Sep26 2-0 / Feb20 2-2	Nov03 3-3 / Apr10 2-1	May03 0-0 / May15 3-0
DUNDEE	Mar17 0-3 / May01 0-5	Dec12 3-1 / May15 1-0	Oct03 1-3 / Feb06 1-3		Nov14 1-3 / Apr03 0-2	Oct31 0-4 / Mar20 2-2	Nov28 4-1 / Apr25 2-1	Sep05 4-2 / Apr21 1-2	Oct11 2-3 / Apr14 3-1	Sep19 3-0 / Jan30 0-2
DUNDEE U	Aug29 4-1 / May05 1-2	Nov21 4-0 / Apr10 0-0	Mar31 0-2 / May08 3-0	Sep12 5-2 / Mar10 1-1		Dec05 1-0 / Apr17 0-1	Nov07 3-0 / Mar27 5-0	Oct10 0-0 / Mar13 1-1	Nov11 2-0 / Feb20 5-1	Oct24 0-2 / Feb27 1-1
HIBERNIAN	Nov21 1-1 / Apr10 0-3	Sep12 1-1 / Jan16 1-0	Oct24 1-0 / Feb27 1-0	Aug29 2-0 / Jan02 2-1	Oct03 1-1 / Feb06 0-1		Oct10 4-0 / Mar13 2-2	Dec19 3-0 / May08 1-1	Nov07 1-2 / Mar27 0-0	Nov28 0-0 / Apr24 2-1
MORTON	Dec05 2-1 / Apr17 2-1	Oct17 3-0 / Mar06 1-0	Nov14 1-1 / Apr03 1-1	Sep26 2-0 / Feb20 2-0	Sep05 1-0 / Apr07 1-1	Apr14 2-1 / May15 0-0		Sep19 1-0 / Jan30 0-0	Mar17 0-0 / May01 1-3	Oct31 0-2 / Mar20 0-1
PARTICK T	Sep12 0-2 / Feb03 0-0	Apr07 4-1 / May01 0-0	Nov28 0-2 / Apr24 0-3	Nov07 1-2 / Mar27 0-2	Apr14 2-3 / May15 1-2	Oct17 1-0 / Mar06 1-2	Nov21 2-2 / Apr10 4-0		Aug29 0-1 / Feb17 2-0	Oct03 1-1 / Feb06 0-0
RANGERS	Oct10 0-0 / Mar13 1-3	Oct03 4-1 / Mar31 1-0	Sep19 0-2 / Jan09 1-0	Dec19 2-1 / May08 4-0	Jan16 2-0 / Apr24 1-1	Sep05 2-2 / Jan30 1-1	Oct24 1-1 / Feb27 3-0	Oct31 0-2 / Mar20 4-1		Nov14 4-1 / May05 3-0
ST MIRREN	Oct17 1-2 / May12 0-2	Nov07 1-1 / Mar27 3-0	Oct10 1-2 / Mar13 2-5	Nov21 4-0 / Apr10 0-1	Feb03 1-0 / May01 2-2	Sep26 0-1 / Feb20 2-2	Aug29 2-0 / Jan03 2-2	Dec05 2-1 / Apr17 3-1	Sep12 1-1 / Mar10 2-3	

League Cup results for 1981-82 are detailed on pages 209-210.

DIVISION 1

	AYR U	CLYDEBANK	DUMBARTON	DUNFERMLINE A	E STIRLING	FALKIRK	HAMILTON A	HEARTS	KILMARNOCK	MOTHERWELL	QUEEN OF SOUTH	QUEEN'S PARK	RAITH R	ST JOHNSTONE
AYR U		Feb06 2-1	Sep30 3-2	Oct24 1-1	Oct17 5-1 / Mar27 1-1	Nov14 4-1 / Apr10 1-1	Sep05 2-0 / Apr24 3-2	Sep23 0-0 / Feb20 0-3	Mar17 1-1	Mar13 1-0 / Apr14 4-3	Jan26 1-0 / May08 5-2	Sep26 2-0	Dec05 2-0	Sep16 1-1
CLYDEBANK	Oct31 2-1 / May15 2-0		Feb17 3-0	Sep16 4-1 / May01 1-0	Jan30 2-1 / Feb27 0-2	Sep26 1-1 / Apr14 1-5	Oct20 2-1	Mar27 2-1	Sep08 0-0	Oct17 1-7	Dec05 2-1 / Mar20 5-1	Nov14 2-1 / Mar10 1-0	Feb03 0-1 / Apr17 0-0	Sep05 2-3
DUMBARTON	Mar06 3-1 / Apr07 3-1	Sep12 1-3 / Mar13 0-2		Feb23 0-1 / Mar20 0-0	Aug29 0-3	Feb06 1-2 / May08 1-0	Oct10 3-1	Nov28 3-1	Oct24 0-6 / Apr24 0-2	Sep19 0-6	Nov07 4-1 / Apr17 3-1	Apr14 1-0	Nov21 1-1 / Apr03 0-2	Oct03 2-1 / Feb20 2-0
DUNFERMLINE A	Feb03 0-0 / Apr03 2-2	Nov21 3-6	Oct17 2-2 / Mar20 0-0		Nov07 2-1 / May15 1-1	Sep23 1-1	Feb10 1-3 / Feb27 1-1	Aug29 1-1 / Apr24 1-2	Dec05 1-2	Sep26 1-2	Sep12 1-1	Feb17 2-1	Feb06 2-3	Oct31 1-1 / Apr17 1-0
E STIRLING	Feb10 2-1	Oct24 0-0 / Apr10 0-1	Nov14 1-1 / Feb27 2-2	Sep05 1-2		Sep08 2-2	Feb17 1-5 / May08 2-1	Feb06 0-1	Sep29 2-1 / May01 1-5	Dec05 0-6 / Apr03 0-2	Sep23 3-1	Sep16 0-1	Mar03 0-1 / Mar20 2-1	Oct10 1-1
FALKIRK	Aug29 1-2	Nov28 3-0	Oct31 1-1	Feb13 2-0 / Mar13 1-0	Feb20 2-0 / Apr07 0-3		Oct03 3-0	Sep12 2-2 / Mar06 3-1	Feb17 1-1 / Apr17 1-3	Nov21 1-1	Oct17 0-0	Jan30 0-0 / May15 1-1	Nov07 3-0 / Apr24 3-2	Sep19 1-0 / Mar27 2-1
HAMILTON A	Nov07 1-0	Sep12 0-2 / Feb20 3-1	Apr21 0-0 / May15 1-0	Sep19 0-2	Sep12 1-1 / May01 0-2	Dec05 2-0		Nov21 0-2 / Apr10 0-2	Oct17 1-2	Feb13 1-0	Sep26 2-3	Oct31 1-0 / Apr03 0-0	Aug29 1-0	Jan30 0-0 / Mar13 2-0
HEARTS	Apr21 2-1	Sep19 1-0	Sep26 2-1 / May01 2-5	Nov14 1-1	Oct31 0-1 / Apr27 2-0	Feb09 3-0	Sep16 2-1		Sep05 0-1	Jan30 0-3 / May15 4-1	Feb17 2-0	Dec05 1-1 / Mar20 2-0	Oct07 3-1 / Feb27 4-0	Oct17 3-1 / Apr03 3-0
KILMARNOCK	Sep12 1-1 / Feb27 1-1	Apr03 0-0 / Apr21 2-0	Jan30 1-1 / Mar10 2-0	Oct03 0-1	Nov28 2-0	Oct10 2-2 / Mar20 4-1	Jan16 2-2 / Apr17 0-0	Nov07 0-0		Aug29 2-0	Nov21 1-0 / May15 6-0	Sep19 0-0	Oct31 1-1	Dec12 0-2
MOTHERWELL	Oct10 1-1	Jan19 3-1 / Apr24 0-0	Mar03 1-1 / Apr10 1-0	Nov28 6-1 / May08 2-2	Oct03 3-2	Sep16 3-2 / Mar20 3-2	Sep08 2-2	Oct24 2-2 / Mar27 3-2	Nov07 0-0		Feb06 2-1 / Feb27 3-0	Sep05 3-0	Sep23 2-2	Feb17 2-2
QUEEN OF SOUTH	Sep19 1-2	Oct03 2-1	Sep05 0-4	Feb20 2-3 / Apr14 0-3	Feb13 1-1 / Mar06 4-0	Jan19 0-4 / Apr03 1-1	Nov28 2-4 / Mar27 0-3	Oct10 1-2 / Mar13 1-5	Sep16 1-1	Oct31 0-2 / May01 2-5		Sep08 1-1 / Apr24 1-2	Jan30 2-3	Nov14 3-3
QUEEN'S PARK	Nov24 2-0 / Apr17 0-0	Aug29 2-2	Sep23 3-0 / Mar27 2-0	Oct10 0-1 / Apr10 2-1	Nov21 2-1 / Mar13 3-0	Oct24 2-2	Feb06 2-0	Oct03 1-0	Feb20 0-2 / Mar30 2-3	Nov07 0-1	Feb02 1-1		Sep12 0-0 / May08 2-0	Mar16 3-2 / May01 2-1
RAITH R	Oct03 0-1 / May01 1-0	Oct10 0-2	Sep16 1-3 / Mar27 0-1	Sep08 1-0	Sep19 0-3	Nov14 2-0 / Mar06 3-3	Mar31 0-3 / Apr06 0-1	Mar13 2-0 / Apr21 1-2	Feb20 0-2 / Apr10 1-2	Oct24 2-1	Feb09 1-0			Nov28 0-4 / Mar15 0-1
ST JOHNSTONE	Nov21 2-0 / Mar20 3-2	Nov07 1-3 / May08 3-3	Dec05 5-2	Mar31 2-1	Mar24 3-2 / Apr24 7-1	Mar10 2-0	Oct24 1-1	Feb23 2-1	Sep23 0-2 / Apr10 1-3	Sep12 1-3 / Mar06 3-2	Aug29 1-0 / Feb27 3-3	Oct17 2-0	Sep26 2-0	

PREMIER DIVISION FINAL TABLE

	P	W	D	L	F	A	Pts
Celtic	36	24	7	5	79	33	55
Aberdeen	36	23	7	6	71	29	53
Rangers	36	16	11	9	57	45	43
Dundee U	36	15	10	11	61	38	40
St Mirren	36	14	9	13	49	52	37
Hibernian	36	11	14	11	38	40	36
Morton	36	9	12	15	31	54	30
Dundee	36	11	4	21	46	72	26
Partick T	36	6	10	20	35	59	22
Airdrie	36	5	8	23	31	76	18

DIVISION 1 FINAL TABLE

	P	W	D	L	F	A	Pts
Motherwell	39	26	9	4	92	36	61
Kilmarnock	39	17	17	5	60	29	51
Hearts	39	21	8	10	65	37	50
Clydebank	39	19	8	12	61	53	46
St Johnstone	39	17	8	14	69	60	42
Ayr U	39	15	12	12	56	50	42
Hamilton A	39	16	8	15	52	49	40
Queen's Park	39	13	10	16	41	41	36
Falkirk	39	11	14	14	49	52	36
Dunfermline A	39	11	14	14	46	56	36
Dumbarton	39	13	9	17	49	61	35
Raith R	39	11	7	21	31	59	29
E Stirling	39	7	10	22	38	77	24
Queen of South	39	4	10	25	44	93	18

DIVISION 2 FINAL TABLE

	P	W	D	L	F	A	Pts
Clyde	39	24	11	4	79	38	59
Alloa	39	19	12	8	66	42	50
Arbroath	39	20	10	9	62	50	50
Berwick R	39	20	8	11	66	38	48
Brechin C	39	18	10	11	61	43	46
Forfar A	39	15	15	9	59	35	45
East Fife	39	14	9	16	48	51	37
Cowdenbeath	39	11	13	15	51	57	35
Stirling A	39	12	11	16	39	44	35
Montrose	39	12	8	19	49	74	32
Albion R	39	13	5	21	52	74	31
Meadowbank	39	10	10	19	49	62	30
Stenhousemuir	39	11	6	22	41	65	28
Stranraer	39	7	6	26	36	85	20

SFA Cup

1st Round

Dec 12 Arbroath ....0 Meadowbank T ...2
Jan 21 Civil Service .....3 Cowdenbeath 3
Dec 30 Fraserburgh .....1 Clacknacuddin 1
Jan 21 Stenhousemuir ...2 Berwick R 5
Jan 20 Stirling A ....1 Clyde 2
Dec 23 Stranraer ....1 East Fife 1

Replays

Jan 4 East Fife ....4 Stranraer 1
Jan 25 Clacknacuddin ...3 Fraserburgh 2
Jan 25 Cowdenbeath ....6 Civil Service 1

2nd Round

Jan 30 Albion R ....2 Clacknacuddin 1
Jan 23 Alloa ....4 Hawick RA 1
Jan 23 Clyde ....0 Berwick R 0
Jan 23 Coldstream .....0 Meadowbank T ...2
Jan 30 Cowdenbeath ....1 Gala Fairydean ...1
Jan 18 East Fife ....2 Forfar 3
Jan 24 Inverness C .....1 Brechin C 3
Jan 20 Montrose ....0 Elgin C 0

Replays

Jan 25 Elgin C ....0 Montrose 0
Jan 26 Berwick R ....1 Clyde 3
Feb 3 Gala Fairydean ...3 Cowdenbeath 2
Feb 1 Elgin C ....1 Montrose 2
played at Keith

3rd Round

Jan 23 Airdrie ....1 Queen's Park 2
Jan 30 Alloa ....2 Ayr U 1
Jan 30 Brechin C ....2 Dundee U 4
Jan 23 Celtic ....4 Queen of South ..0
Jan 30 Clyde ....2 Meadowbank T ...2
Jan 23 Clydebank ......2 Dunfermline A 1
Jan 23 Dundee ....1 Raith R 0
Jan 27 E Stirling ....1 Hearts 4
Feb 6 Gala Fairydean ...1 St Johnstone 2
Jan 23 Hamilton A ......0 Forfar A 0
Jan 23 Hibernian ....2 Falkirk 0
Feb 6 Kilmarnock ......1 Montrose 0
Jan 23 Motherwell ......0 Aberdeen 1
Jan 24 Partick T ....1 Dumbarton 2
Feb 6 Rangers ....6 Albion R 2
Jan 23 St Mirren ....2 Morton 1

Replays

Jan 27 Forfar A ....3 Hamilton A 2
Feb 3 Meadowbank T ...4 Clyde 2

4th Round

Feb 13 Aberdeen ....1 Celtic 0

Feb 13 Clydebank ....0 St Mirren 2
Feb 14 Dundee ....3 Meadowbank T ...0
Feb 13 Dundee U ....1 Hibernian 1
Feb 13 Hearts ....0 Forfar A 1
Feb 13 Kilmarnock .....3 St Johnstone 1
Feb 13 Queen's Park ...2 Alloa 0
Feb 13 Rangers ....4 Dumbarton 0

Replays

Feb 17 Hibernian ......1 Dundee U 1
Feb 22 Dundee U ....3 Hibernian 0
played at Easter Road

5th Round

Mar 6 Aberdeen ....4 Kilmarnock 2
Mar 6 Queen's Park ....1 Forfar A 2
Mar 6 Rangers ....2 Dundee 0
Mar 6 St Mirren ....1 Dundee U 0

Semi-finals

Apr 3 Aberdeen ....1 St Mirren 1
played at Celtic Park
Apr 3 Forfar ....0 Rangers 0
played at Hampden Park

Replays

Apr 7 Aberdeen ....3 St Mirren 2
played at Dens Park
Apr 6 Forfar ....1 Rangers 3
played at Hampden Park

Final

May 22 Aberdeen ....4 Rangers 1
played at Hampden Park

DIVISION 2

	ALBION R	ALLOA	ARBROATH	BERWICK R	BRECHIN C	CLYDE	COWDENBEATH	EAST FIFE	FORFAR A	MEADOWBANK T	MONTROSE	STENHOUSEMUIR	STIRLING A	STRANRAER
ALBION R		Oct31 1-5 Mar20 1-1	Sep22 2-0	Oct03 1-3	Jan23 1-2 Apr17 1-2	Feb10 0-1 May01 2-3	Aug29 2-0	Mar17 1-0	Oct17 3-3	Mar31 2-0	Nov07 0-2 Feb27 2-2	Nov21 1-4 May15 2-0	Nov28 1-0 Apr10 1-0	Sep12 4-0
ALLOA	Feb17 1-0		Oct03 2-1 Feb20 2-2	Oct10 1-0 Mar06 1-1	Oct24 1-3	Mar27 2-2 Apr21 0-3	Nov21 3-1 May08 2-2	Feb02 1-2	Aug29 1-2	Nov28 4-3 Apr10 2-0	Mar22 5-0	Sep12 1-0	Nov07 0-0	Sep23 3-2 May01 1-1
ARBROATH	Dec19 4-0 Apr24 2-0	Dec05 2-1			Oct24 2-1	Sep19 1-1	Oct17 1-1	Sep12 3-1 Apr10 0-5	Feb13 3-1 Feb27 3-0	Jan02 1-1 May01 1-1	Apr29 3-2 Mar27 2-0	Nov21 1-0	Jan23 3-0 Mar13 1-0	Nov07 4-1
BERWICK R	Dec05 6-1 Mar13 4-1	Apr07 2-0	Feb06 3-0 Apr03 2-2		Oct17 3-1	Oct31 4-0	Sep26 1-2	Sep30 2-1 Mar27 3-0	Nov07 1-1 Feb27 2-2	Sep12 3-1	Aug29 4-0 Apr24 0-2	Feb23 1-0	Nov21 1-0 Apr17 2-0	Feb17 0-0
BRECHIN C	Oct10 3-2	Feb06 0-4 Mar13 0-1	Feb17 2-2 May08 0-2	Feb03 2-0 May01 1-0		Oct20 2-2	Oct31 0-1	Oct03 2-1 Apr10 1-1	Nov21 0-0	Nov07 3-0	Sep12 3-0	Feb10 1-1 Mar27 0-1	Aug29 2-1	Nov28 3-0 Feb27 3-0
CLYDE	Oct24 1-2	Sep19 1-1	Mar17 1-1 Mar20 1-2	Feb13 3-1 Apr14 1-0	Apr03 3-1 Apr17 2-0		Nov07 1-1 Mar13 1-0	Oct10 3-2 Mar30 3-3	Sep12 1-1 May08 1-1	Nov28 3-0	Aug29 3-0	Sep23 2-0	Mar17 3-0	Oct10 1-1
COWDENBEATH	Nov14 2-0 Feb23 2-3	Sep16 1-2	Mar24 1-2	Nov28 2-1	Feb13 0-0 Apr10 2-0	Sep05 0-4 May15 0-2		Sep08 2-2 Mar06 1-2	Oct24 1-1	Mar03 2-2 Mar27 3-2	Oct03 6-0	Sep23 3-1 May01 2-0	Mar17 0-0	Oct10 1-1
EAST FIFE	Sep19 3-0 May08 1-1	Oct17 1-2 Apr03 0-2	Oct31 0-1	Jan30 0-1 Apr25 1-1	Dec05 2-2	Feb06 2-2	Jan02 1-1		Sep26 0-4 Feb27 1-0	Nov21 2-0 Mar13 1-0	Feb10 0-1	Nov07 3-2 Apr17 1-0	Sep12 3-0 Mar20 1-2	Aug29 0-2
FORFAR A	Apr14 3-1 Apr28 3-0	Nov14 0-0 May15 1-1	Sep08 6-0 Apr21 1-1	Sep05 2-1	Oct27 1-1 Apr24 0-0	Feb20 2-2 Mar24 1-3	Feb06 4-0	Nov28 1-0		Oct10 1-1 May01 0-0	Mar17 2-1	Oct31 2-0 Mar20 3-0	Sep12 3-1	Oct03 3-1
MEADOWBANK T	Sep08 3-2 Mar06 0-2	Sep26 1-1	Nov14 1-2	Mar17 2-1	Sep05 1-0 Feb20 2-0	Dec05 2-3 May15 1-3	Oct17 1-1 Mar20 1-0	Sep16 1-1 Apr17 2-5	Feb23 1-1		Sep23 2-2	Feb06 6-1	Oct31 2-1 May08 0-1	Mar10 4-1 Apr03 1-1
MONTROSE	Sep05 4-2	Sep08 2-0 Apr17 0-3	Sep16 2-1	Nov14 0-2 Feb20 0-0	Jan02 2-2 Mar22 1-4	Sep26 0-3 Mar06 4-1	Dec05 2-2	Oct24 2-1 May15 1-2	Sep19 2-1	Dec19 1-0 Apr24 1-0		Jan23 2-1	Oct17 1-1 Apr03 1-2	Feb13 1-2
STENHOUSEMUIR	Sep15 2-2 Mar30 0-1	Feb27 2-2 Mar20 0-2	Nov28 1-3	Sep19 1-1	Sep08 0-4	Nov14 0-3 Apr20 2-1	Apr03 3-0	Sep05 2-0 Apr10 1-0	Feb17 0-0 May01 0-1	Oct24 1-2 May08 2-1	Oct10 2-4		Oct03 0-0	Jan30 1-0
STIRLING A	Sep26 1-0 Apr24 3-2	Sep05 0-0 Apr17 3-1	Oct10 0-1 Mar15 0-0	Sep16 0-1 Mar06 0-2	Nov14 5-0	Sep08 1-2	Sep19 0-0	Apr07 0-2	Mar10 0-0	Feb17 1-0 Mar27 2-0	Jan30 1-1	Dec05 2-3 Feb20 3-1		Oct24 1-0 Mar13 2-1
STRANRAER	Jan02 0-1 Mar27 1-4	Feb23 0-4	Sep05 4-0 May15 1-3	Sep08 2-4	Sep26 0-6	Sep16 0-2	Jan23 1-4 Apr24 1-0	Nov14 0-3 Feb20 1-2	Dec05 2-1	Sep19 0-1 Apr10 2-0	Oct31 3-5 Mar06 0-1	Oct17 2-1	Feb06 2-2	

PREMIER

League Cup results for 1982-83 are detailed on pages 210-211.

PREMIER	ABERDEEN	CELTIC	DUNDEE	DUNDEE U	HIBERNIAN	KILMARNOCK	MORTON	MOTHERWELL	RANGERS	ST MIRREN
ABERDEEN		Dec11 1-2 / Apr23 1-0	Oct16 1-0 / Feb26 3-1	Nov06 5-1 / Mar19 1-2	Jan01 2-0 / May14 5-0	Dec27 2-0 / May04 5-0	Sep11 4-1 / Jan08 2-1	Oct02 2-1 / Feb08 5-1	Sep25 1-2 / Jan22 2-0	Nov20 4-0 / Apr02 0-1
CELTIC	Oct09 1-3 / Feb12 1-3		Sep04 2-0 / Jan03 2-2	Apr06 0-2 / 2-3	Sep25 2-0 / Apr20 4-1	Oct16 2-1 / Feb22 4-0	Dec27 5-1 / May07 2-0	Sep11 3-1 / Apr02 3-0	Nov20 3-2 / Mar23 0-0	Nov13 5-0 / 1-1
DUNDEE	Dec18 0-2 / Apr30 0-2	Nov06 2-3 / Mar19 2-1		Jan01 0-2 / May14 1-2	Oct09 5-2 / Feb22 0-1	Nov27 2-0 / Apr09 0-0	Sep18 3-1 / Jan08 1-0	Nov02 1-0 / May03 2-1	Oct23 1-1 / Mar05 2-5	2-5
DUNDEE U	Sep04 2-0 / Jan03 0-3	Oct02 2-2 / Feb05 1-1	Dec11 1-0 / Mar12 5-3		Nov20 3-0 / Mar26 3-3	Dec11 7-0 / Apr23 6-0	Dec27 6-0 / Feb26 5-0	Nov13 4-0 / May07 4-0	Apr04 4-0	Sep25 3-0 / Jan22 3-2
HIBERNIAN	Oct30 1-1 / May02 0-0	Nov27 2-3 / Apr09 0-3	Dec11 1-1 / Apr23 0-0	Sep18 0-0 / Jan15 0-0		Nov13 2-2 / Apr02 8-1	Oct02 1-2 / Feb26 2-0	Oct16 1-0 / May07 1-1	Dec27 0-0 / Mar19 1-2	Sep04 0-0 / Jan03 1-1
KILMARNOCK	Oct23 0-2 / Mar05 1-2	Dec18 0-4 / Mar30 0-5	Sep25 0-0 / Jan22 2-0	Oct09 1-1 / Feb12 1-0	Sep11 1-1 / Jan08 0-2		Nov06 3-1 / Mar19 4-0	Jan01 0-2 / May14 1-1	Nov20 2-2 / Mar26 0-1	Dec04 2-2 / Apr27 2-2
MORTON	Mar13 1-1 / Mar26 1-2	Oct23 1-2 / Mar05 0-3	Nov06 1-2 / Apr07 0-4	Dec18 1-2 / Apr30 0-4	Dec04 0-0 / Apr16 3-0	Sep04 0-0 / Jan03 3-0		Sep25 3-1 / Jan22 0-1	Oct09 0-0 / Feb12 0-5	Jan01 2-0 / May14 0-2
MOTHERWELL	Dec04 0-2 / Apr27 0-3	Sep18 0-7 / Jan15 2-1	Nov13 1-0 / Mar26 1-1	Oct23 0-2 / Mar05 1-4	Dec18 0-1 / Apr30 2-0	Oct30 4-1 / Mar12 3-1	Nov27 3-1 / Apr09 4-1		Sep04 2-2 / Jan03 3-0	Oct09 2-0 / Mar01 0-1
RANGERS	Nov27 0-1 / Apr09 2-1	Jan01 1-2 / May14 2-4	Oct02 1-1 / Feb05 1-1	Sep11 2-1 / 2-1	Oct23 1-1 / Mar05 2-1	Sep18 2-0 / Jan15 1-1	Dec11 1-1 / Apr23 2-0	Nov06 4-0 / Mar19 1-0		Dec18 1-0 / Apr30 4-0
ST MIRREN	Jan15 1-1 / Sep18 1-1	Sep11 1-2 / Jan08 0-1	Dec27 0-0 / May09 2-1	Nov27 0-2 / Apr09 1-2	Nov06 3-0 / Mar19 3-0	Oct02 3-2 / Feb05 2-0	Oct30 1-1 / Mar16 2-3	Dec11 3-0 / Apr23 4-0	Oct16 2-2 / Feb26 1-0	

DIVISION 1

DIVISION 1	AIRDRIE	ALLOA	AYR U	CLYDE	CLYDEBANK	DUMBARTON	DUNFERMLINE A	FALKIRK	HAMILTON A	HEARTS	PARTICK T	QUEEN'S PARK	RAITH R	ST JOHNSTONE
AIRDRIE		Nov13 2-1 / May14 0-1	Oct23 3-1 / Mar15 1-0	Oct16 3-4	Nov27 2-2	Sep04 1-2	Oct02 1-1	Dec11 3-1 / Feb26 0-2	Sep15 2-0	Jan03 0-1 / Apr02 4-2	Sep18 1-3	Jan22 0-1	Dec27 1-2 / Apr16 2-0	Jan15 2-0 / Apr30 1-1
ALLOA	Sep08 1-2		Feb19 0-0 / Apr16 3-0	Feb08 1-3	Sep11 2-0 / Feb12 1-2	Oct30 2-0 / Mar19 0-0	Nov06 2-2 / Mar26 1-1	Jan01 0-2	Sep25 4-2	Jan15 0-0 / Apr23 1-1	Oct16 2-1	Dec04 4-1 / Mar05 3-1	Sep22 3-0	Nov20 0-2 / May07 1-1
AYR U	Feb05 1-0 / Mar19 1-1	Sep04 2-1		Jan30 2-0	Oct02 1-3 / Mar05 0-1	Nov13 0-1 / Apr02 0-2	Dec11 1-0 / Apr09 2-3	Jan15 4-0	Sep18 1-1	Dec27 0-3	Sep15 2-1	Nov27 2-2 / Apr30 0-4	Oct30 0-4 / May07 3-2	Oct16 1-0 / Feb26 0-1
CLYDE	Jan08 2-1	Oct23 2-0 / Apr09 3-3	Nov06 3-1 / May14 3-2		Sep18 3-5	Oct02 0-4 / Mar05 1-0		Sep04 0-1	Jan22 5-2	Dec11 2-3	Nov27 1-3 / Feb26 0-2	Jan01 0-1 / Mar19 3-3	Oct09 0-2 / Apr30 0-1	Sep11 1-3 / Apr16 0-1
CLYDEBANK	Sep22 0-4 / Apr23 2-0	Dec27 2-2	Dec04 0-1	Nov20 2-2 / Apr02 2-1			Sep15 5-1 / Feb26 1-1	Oct16 1-1	Feb05 0-2	Jan03 2-1	Nov13 0-3 / May14 1-2	Jan15 1-3	Sep25 2-0	Oct30 1-0 / Mar12 6-1
DUMBARTON	Feb23 0-0 / Mar26 1-1	Jan22 1-2	Sep29 1-0	Dec04 1-3	Jan01 0-4		Nov20 0-3		Sep11 1-1 / Mar12 1-3	Oct09 1-5 / Apr16 1-1	Nov27 1-1 / May07 4-2	Oct23 2-1 / Feb12 2-1	Nov06 1-1 / Apr02 2-1	Sep25 4-1
DUNFERMLINE A	Dec04 1-0 / Apr05 0-4	Jan03 2-0	Sep05 1-0	Sep08 1-1 / Apr23 0-0	Feb23 1-1 / Mar19 1-1				Oct30 0-0 / May10 2-2	Dec27 1-1	Feb09 2-1	Nov13 0-4 / Mar05 1-1	Oct09 1-2 / Apr16 2-0	Sep22 2-4
FALKIRK	Sep25 1-3	Sep15 0-1 / Apr30 2-1	Oct09 1-1 / Mar12 2-0	Nov13 1-0 / Mar23 1-2	Oct23 0-2 / Apr09 0-2	Dec27 2-1 / May14 1-2	Jan22 1-0			Nov27 1-0 / Mar26 1-1	Sep18 1-1	Sep29 1-1	Jan08 2-0	Dec04 0-1
HAMILTON A	Jan01 0-4 / May05 0-3	Dec11 1-1 / Apr02 1-2	Nov20 1-1 / Apr23 0-1	Oct30 1-0 / May07 4-1	Nov06 0-2	Jan15 4-1 / Feb26 2-1	Sep22 2-1			Oct16 1-3 / Apr09 1-3	Oct02 2-2	Sep08 2-2 / Mar19 0-5	Feb05 2-2	Dec18 1-1
HEARTS	Nov06 2-4	Oct09 3-0	Sep11 1-1 / Feb12 5-1	Sep25 1-0 / Apr16 3-1	Sep29 4-1 / Apr30 2-2	Oct06 1-1	Oct23 4-1 / Mar01 3-4	Nov20 3-1 / Apr30 3-3	Jan08 2-1 / Mar14 1-2		Jan22 0-1 / Mar19 4-0	Dec04 2-0 / Apr06 2-0		Jan01 1-0
PARTICK T	Nov20 1-0 / May07 0-1	Jan08 1-1 / Mar15 1-2	Jan01 2-2 / Mar26 3-1	Oct05 2-1	Sep29 0-1	Feb05 3-2	Sep04 1-1	Apr06 1-1 / Apr16 4-2	Dec04 1-1	Oct30 1-1		Sep11 2-3 / Mar22 1-0	Sep25 2-1 / Apr02 2-1	Nov06 3-1
QUEEN'S PARK	Oct30 1-1 / Apr09 4-3	Oct02 1-2	Sep22 0-0	Sep14 0-0	Dec11 2-2	Jan03 2-1	Jan15 2-2	Oct02 1-3 / Apr02 0-2	Nov13 1-2 / Mar15 1-2	Sep04 1-2 / Feb26 0-1	Dec27 1-4 / Apr23 3-1		Nov20 2-2	Feb05 1-2
RAITH R	Sep11 0-3	Nov27 0-1 / Feb26 3-1	Jan22 0-1	Jan15 1-2	Dec18 0-3 / Mar26 1-3	Oct16 3-0 / Apr09 0-0	Jan01 6-0	Nov06 2-1 / Apr23 0-3	Oct23 4-1	Oct02 1-0 / Mar29 0-3	Dec11 2-2	Sep18 3-1 / May14 2-2		Sep08 0-3
ST JOHNSTONE	Oct09 1-0	Sep18 3-1	Jan08 2-0	Dec27 2-1	Jan22 0-1	Dec11 1-0 / Apr23 0-0	Nov27 2-0 / May14 1-0	Oct02 3-0 / Mar19 0-2	Sep04 3-0 / Feb12 0-1	Sep15 1-1 / Mar29 2-1	Jan03 1-0	Oct23 4-1 / Mar26 2-1	Nov13 2-1 / Mar05 0-1	

SFA Cup

1st Round
Dec 11	Brechin C	2	Cowdenbeath	0
Dec 11	Meadowbank T	1	Elgin C	2
Dec 18	Peterhead	0	Forfar A	5
Dec 11	Selkirk	0	Brora R	2
Dec 18	Stirling A	1	E Stirling	0
Dec 18	Vale of Leithen	0	Stranraer	0

Replays
Dec 20	Stranraer	2	Vale of Leithen	0

2nd Round
Jan 8	Albion R	1	Stranraer	0
Jan 8	Berwick R	2	Stirling A	0
Jan 8	Brora R	0	Montrose	0
Jan 8	East Fife	1	Brechin C	0
Jan 8	Elgin C	5	Gala Fairydean	2
Jan 8	Forfar A	3	Inverness C	0
Jan 8	Queen of South	3	Hawick RA	0
Jan 8	Stenhousemuir	1	Arbroath	0

Replays
Jan 15	Montrose	1	Brora R	1
Jan 17	Brora R	5	Montrose	2
	played at Inverness			

3rd Round
Jan 29	Alloa	1	Morton	2
Jan 29	Ayr U	1	Albion R	2
Jan 29	Clyde	0	Motherwell	0
Jan 29	Clydebank	1	Celtic	3
Jan 29	Dumbarton	0	Airdrie	1
Jan 29	Dundee	2	Brora R	1
Jan 29	Dunfermline A	5	Elgin C	0
Jan 29	East Fife	1	Raith R	0
Jan 29	Falkirk	0	Rangers	2
Jan 29	Forfar A	2	Berwick R	1
Jan 30	Hamilton A	0	St Johnstone	1
Jan 29	Hibernian	1	Aberdeen	4
Jan 29	Partick T	1	Kilmarnock	1
Jan 29	Queen of South	1	Hearts	1
Jan 29	Queen's Park	4	Stenhousemuir	1
Jan 29	St Mirren	1	Dundee U	0

Replays
Feb 2	Hearts	1	Queen of South	0
Feb 2	Kilmarnock	0	Partick T	0
Feb 2	Motherwell	3	Clyde	4
Feb 7	Partick T	2	Kilmarnock	2
	played at Firhill Park			
Feb 9	Kilmarnock	0	Partick T	1
	played at Rugby Park			

4th Round
Feb 19	Aberdeen	1	Dundee	0
Feb 19	Albion R	0	Airdrie	3
Feb 19	Celtic	3	Dunfermline A	0
Feb 20	Hearts	2	East Fife	1
Feb 19	Morton	0	St Mirren	2
Feb 19	Partick T	2	Clyde	2
Feb 19	Queen's Park	1	St Johnstone	0
Feb 19	Rangers	2	Forfar A	1

Replays
Feb 23	Clyde	1	Partick T	1
	Abandoned in Extra-time			
Feb 28	Clyde	0	Partick T	6

5th Round
Mar 12	Airdrie	0	St Mirren	5
Mar 12	Celtic	4	Hearts	1
Mar 12	Partick T	1	Aberdeen	2
Mar 12	Queen's Park	1	Rangers	2

Semi-finals
Apr 16	Aberdeen	1	Celtic	0
	played at Hampden Park			
Apr 16	Rangers	1	St Mirren	1
	played at Hampden Park			

Replay
Apr 19	Rangers	1	St Mirren	0
	played at Hampden Park			

Final
May 21	Aberdeen	1	Rangers	0
	played at Hampden Park			

DIVISION 2

Results grid (home team in left column, result listed as home team's score first):

	ALBION R	ARBROATH	BERWICK R	BRECHIN C	COWDENBEATH	EAST FIFE	E STIRLING	FORFAR A	MEADOWBANK T	MONTROSE	QUEEN OF SOUTH	STENHOUSEMUIR	STIRLING A	STRANRAER
ALBION R	—	Jan15 1-3 / Apr23 0-2	Mar02 0-1 / May14 2-1	Oct09 0-0	Sep25 0-2 / Apr13 2-0	Sep11 1-0 / Mar26 1-1	Dec04 3-1	Nov02 0-1 / Mar19 1-0	Apr05 4-0 / Apr16 1-3	Nov20 2-1	Sep22 3-1	Jan01 2-1	Sep08 3-0	Nov09 2-3 / Mar05 1-2
ARBROATH	Sep04 3-1	—	Nov13 0-2 / Mar19 3-1	Jan03 0-3 / Apr16 1-1	Oct30 1-0	Dec18 3-1	Sep18 4-1 / Apr09 2-2	Sep15 2-1 / Feb23 3-3	Jan29 2-2	Oct16 3-1	Dec27 3-2	Nov27 0-0 / May07 5-2	Oct02 1-0 / May05 1-0	Feb05 3-0 / Apr30 3-2
BERWICK R	Oct23 4-0	Sep08 2-1	—	Jan22 1-1 / Mar12 1-1	Oct09 2-1 / Apr30 1-1	Nov06 1-0	Feb12 0-3 / Apr23 1-3	Nov27 1-2	Jan01 0-0	Sep25 1-1 / Mar26 3-1	Dec04 0-4 / Feb26 1-0	Jan15 2-4	Sep18 2-2 / Apr09 0-3	Sep11 2-2
BRECHIN C	Feb23 3-0 / Apr09 3-0	Nov06 3-1	Oct30 2-0	—	Sep22 1-1 / Mar19 4-1	Sep08 0-0	Sep25 3-0	Oct16 1-1 / Apr30 1-0	Nov20 1-1 / May07 1-1	Jan01 2-3 / Mar05 3-1	Mar09 2-3 / Mar26 1-0	Dec04 5-2	Sep11 1-2 / Feb19 3-1	Jan15 4-2
COWDENBEATH	Mar09 1-1	Jan22 2-1 / Feb26 3-2	Feb05 2-0	Dec01 1-3	—	Jan01 2-4	Oct23 1-1 / Mar12 3-1	Oct02 2-1	Jan15 3-1 / May14 0-1	Sep11 2-3	Oct16 2-1 / Apr09 2-3	Sep18 2-0 / Mar26 1-1	Nov06 0-0	Sep29 2-1 / Apr27 4-0
EAST FIFE	Dec27 4-3	Sep25 2-2 / May14 4-0	Jan03 0-1 / Apr02 3-0	Nov13 1-2 / Apr23 1-2	Sep15 1-1 / Mar05 0-2	—		Sep04 3-1	Mar09 0-2	Dec04 5-0	Sep22 0-1 / Mar19 4-0	Nov20 0-0	Oct09 1-1	Oct30 2-2 / Feb23 3-0
E STIRLING	Oct02 1-1 / Apr30 1-3	Nov20 1-3	Oct16 0-4	Mar15 0-3 / Apr02 2-2	Mar01 2-0	Jan15 0-3 / May07 1-1	—		Feb05 1-4 / Mar05 0-1	Sep11 1-3 / Mar19 1-2	Sep08 0-0 / Feb19 3-1	Nov03 1-2 / Apr16 0-1	Nov06 2-1	Jan01 2-1 / Sep22 1-2
FORFAR A	Jan22 2-0	Jan01 1-1	Sep22 2-2 / May07 1-1	Mar02 2-1	Dec04 0-0 / Apr16 2-2	Oct23 4-1 / Feb26 0-0	Oct09 5-1	—		Sep08 0-1 / Apr02 0-3	Nov06 2-2	Sep25 2-2	Sep11 0-0 / Mar12 2-2	Nov20 5-1
MEADOWBANK T	Oct16 4-3	Oct23 2-1 / Mar26 0-3	Sep15 4-2 / Feb19 5-0	Sep18 2-1	Sep14 2-0	Oct02 0-2 / Apr30 0-3	Dec27 0-0	Nov13 1-0	—	Feb05 5-0 / Apr09 2-0	Jan04 1-0 / Mar05 1-2	Jan22 3-1 / Apr23 1-1	Nov27 3-1	Apr13 1-0
MONTROSE	Sep18 3-3 / Feb26 1-2	Feb16 2-1 / Mar12 0-3	Dec18 1-0	Sep15 1-2	Dec27 0-4 / May07 1-1	Nov27 0-2	Nov13 1-2	Jan03 1-2 / May13 1-2	Oct09 0-1	—	Sep04 1-5	Oct23 1-2 / Apr16 0-1	Jan22 0-1	Oct02 3-1 / Apr02 1-0
QUEEN OF SOUTH	Nov27 5-0 / May07 2-0	Sep11 2-1 / Apr02 1-1	Oct02 1-2	Oct23 3-1	Feb16 0-0	Sep18 1-5 / Dec11 1-2	Jan22 2-2	Mar29 1-1 / Apr23 6-0	Nov06 1-1	Mar02 4-0 / Apr30 6-0	—	Sep08 1-2 / Feb19 2-2	Oct09 1-0 / Mar19 2-2	Jan01 6-3
STENHOUSEMUIR	Sep14 1-0 / Apr02 1-0	Sep22 1-6	Sep04 0-0 / Mar05 0-1	Oct02 2-2 / May14 0-0	Nov20 2-2	Feb09 3-2 / Apr09 0-2	Jan03 2-2 / Feb19 1-1	Dec27 0-1	Oct30 1-2	Feb23 3-1	Nov13 2-3	—	Mar09 0-0 / Apr30 0-4	Oct16 2-3 / Mar19 1-1
STIRLING A	Nov13 2-2 / Mar12 1-2	Dec04 1-0	Nov20 3-1	Dec27 1-1	Jan03 2-2 / Apr02 3-1	Oct16 2-2 / Apr16 2-2	Sep15 2-0 / May14 3-1	Sep04 2-0	Sep22 1-1 / Feb26 2-0	Oct30 2-3 / Apr23 1-0	Feb05 4-1	Sep25 1-0	—	Jan29 1-0
STRANRAER	Jan03 1-5	Oct09 0-1	Dec27 1-0 / Apr16 0-3	Sep04 1-2 / Feb26 1-3	Nov13 2-0	Jan22 2-2	Nov27 2-1 / Mar26 1-0	Sep25 2-1 / Apr09 1-2	Sep18 1-2 / Mar12 0-2	Dec04 3-3	Sep15 0-3 / May14 0-0	Feb12 2-0 / May10 0-1	Nov23 1-1	—

PREMIER DIVISION FINAL TABLE

	P	W	D	L	F	A	Pts
Dundee U	36	24	8	4	90	35	56
Celtic	36	25	5	6	90	36	55
Aberdeen	36	25	5	6	76	24	55
Rangers	36	13	12	11	52	41	38
St Mirren	36	11	12	13	47	51	34
Dundee	36	9	11	16	42	53	29
Hibernian	36	7	15	14	35	51	29
Motherwell	36	11	5	20	39	73	27
Morton	36	6	8	22	30	74	20
Kilmarnock	36	3	11	22	28	91	17

DIVISION 1 FINAL TABLE

	P	W	D	L	F	A	Pts
St Johnstone	39	25	5	9	59	37	55
Hearts	39	22	10	7	79	38	54
Clydebank	39	20	10	9	72	49	50
Partick T	39	20	9	10	66	45	49
Airdrie	39	16	7	16	62	46	39
Alloa	39	14	11	14	52	52	39
Dumbarton	39	13	10	16	50	59	36
Falkirk	39	15	6	18	45	55	36
Raith R	39	13	8	18	64	63	34
Clyde	39	14	6	19	55	66	34
Hamilton A	39	11	12	16	54	66	34
Ayr U	39	12	8	19	45	61	32
Dunfermline A	39	7	17	15	39	69	31
Queen's Park	39	6	11	22	44	80	23

DIVISION 2 FINAL TABLE

	P	W	D	L	F	A	Pts
Brechin C	39	21	13	5	77	38	55
Meadowbank T	39	23	8	8	64	45	54
Arbroath	39	21	7	11	78	51	49
Forfar A	39	18	12	9	58	38	48
Stirling A	39	18	10	11	57	41	46
East Fife	39	16	11	12	68	43	43
Queen of South	39	15	12	12	75	55	42
Cowdenbeath	39	13	12	14	54	53	38
Berwick R	39	13	10	16	47	60	36
Albion R	39	14	6	19	55	66	34
Stenhousemuir	39	7	15	17	43	66	29
Stranraer	39	10	7	22	46	79	27
E Stirling	39	7	9	23	41	79	23
Montrose	39	8	6	25	37	86	22

Aberdeen parade the Scottish Cup, along with the European Cup-winners' Cup, which they also won that year.

SFA Cup

1st Round
Dec 10 Cowdenbeath .3 Vale of Leithen ..0
Dec 10 Dalbeattie Star 1 Arbroath 5
Dec 10 E Stirling .....1 Stenhousemuir .0
Dec 10 Elgin C ......0 Queen's Park ...2
Dec 10 Forfar A .....4 Spartans 1
Dec 10 Inverness C ...2 Albion R 1

2nd Round
Jan 7 Arbroath .....0 Stirling 0
Jan 7 Cowdenbeath .2 Montrose 1
Jan 9 Dunfermline A .1 Forfar A 0
Jan 7 E Stirling ....3 Fraserburgh 1
Jan 7 Gala Fairydean 0 Inverness C 2
Jan 7 Peterhead ....1 East Fife 5
Jan 7 Stranraer ....1 Queen's Park ...2

Replays
Feb 6 Stirling A ....0 Arbroath 0
Feb 8 Arbroath .....1 Stirling A 2
played at Arbroath

3rd Round
Feb 13 Aberdeen ....1 Kilmarnock 1
Feb 13 Airdrie ......1 St Johnstone ...0
Jan 28 Berwick R ....0 Celtic 4
Feb 8 Clydebank ....0 Brechin C 0
Feb 8 Cowdenbeath .0 Dundee 2
Feb 6 Dundee U ....1 Ayr U 0
Feb 6 Falkirk ....1 Clyde 2
Feb 2 Hamilton A ...3 Alloa 1
Feb 6 Hearts ......2 Partick T 0
Jan 28 Hibernian ....0 East Fife 0
Feb 11 Inverness C ...0 Stirling A 0
Jan 28 Meadowbank T 0 St Mirren 0
Feb 6 Morton ......2 E Stirling 0
Feb 6 Motherwell ...3 Queen's Park ...0
Feb 6 Raith R ......1 Dumbarton 4
Jan 28 Rangers .....2 Dunfermline A ..1

Replays
Jan 31 East Fife .....2 Hibernian 0
Feb 6 St Mirren ....2 Meadowbank T .2
Feb 13 Brechin C ....0 Clydebank 3
Feb 15 Kilmarnock ...1 Aberdeen 3
Feb 15 Meadowbank T 1 St Mirren 2
played at Meadowbank
Feb 15 Stirling A ....1 Inverness C 2

4th Round
Feb 18 Clyde ....0 Aberdeen 2
Feb 19 Dundee .....2 Airdrie 1
Feb 18 Dundee U ....2 Hearts 1
Feb 18 East Fife .....0 Celtic 6
Feb 18 Inverness C ...0 Rangers 6
Feb 18 Morton ......2 Dumbarton 1
Feb 18 Motherwell ...3 Clydebank 1
Feb 18 St Mirren ....2 Hamilton A 1

5th Round
Mar 17 Aberdeen ....0 Dundee U 0
Mar 10 Dundee .....2 Rangers 2
Mar 17 Motherwell ...0 Celtic 6
Mar 10 St Mirren ....4 Morton 3

Replay
Mar 17 Rangers .....2 Dundee 3
Mar 28 Dundee U ....0 Aberdeen 1

Semi-finals
Apr 14 Aberdeen ....2 Dundee 0
played at Tynecastle
Apr 14 Celtic ....2 St Mirren 1
played at Hampden Park

Final
May 19 Aberdeen ....2 Celtic 1
played at Hampden Park

League Cup results for 1983-84 are detailed on page 211.

PREMIER

	ABERDEEN	CELTIC	DUNDEE	DUNDEE U	HEARTS	HIBERNIAN	MOTHERWELL	RANGERS	ST JOHNSTONE	ST MIRREN
ABERDEEN		Oct22 3-1 / Feb04 1-0	Aug20 3-0 / Dec31 5-2	Sep24 1-2 / Apr18 1-1	Nov19 2-0 / Apr02 1-1	Dec17 2-1 / May05 2-2	Dec03 3-1 / Apr07 0-0	Nov12 3-0 / May09 2-1	Sep03 5-0 / Mar30 1-0	Oct08 5-0 / Mar03 2-0
CELTIC	Dec10 0-0 / Mar31 1-0		Nov26 1-0 / Apr24 3-0	Dec27 1-1 / May12 1-0	Oct15 5-1 / Feb25 4-1	Oct29 4-0 / Apr28 3-2	Nov12 4-0 / Apr10 4-2	Sep03 5-2 / Apr02 3-0	Sep10 2-1 / Feb11 5-2	Oct01 1-1 / Feb14 2-0
DUNDEE	Oct29 1-3 / Apr28 0-1	Sep24 2-6 / Mar20 3-2		Sep03 1-4 / Apr02 2-5	Sep17 1-2 / Jan07 4-1	Dec10 0-3 / Mar31 1-2	Nov19 2-0 / Apr18 1-0	Oct15 0-1 / Feb25 1-3	Dec27 2-2 / May12 2-0	Dec26 2-2 / Apr07 2-5
DUNDEE U	Nov26 0-2 / May07 0-0	Oct08 2-1 / Mar03 0-1	Nov05 0-1 / Apr21 3-1		Oct22 1-0 / Mar11 3-1	Sep10 5-0 / Feb11 2-0	Nov19 4-0 / Dec31 2-1	Oct01 0-2 / May14 1-2	Nov12 7-0 / Apr14 3-0	Apr30 2-0 / May05 2-2
HEARTS	Oct01 0-2 / May02 0-1	Dec17 1-3 / May05 1-1	Nov13 0-0 / May09 0-0	Dec10 0-0 / Mar31 0-0		Sep03 3-2 / Jan02 1-1	Oct08 0-3 / Mar03 2-1	Sep10 0-1 / Feb11 2-2	Oct29 2-0 / Apr28 2-2	Nov26 2-2 / Mar24 2-1
HIBERNIAN	Oct15 2-1 / Feb25 0-2	Aug20 1-2 / Dec31 1-1	Oct22 0-2 / Feb29 3-1	Dec03 2-1 / Apr07 1-0	Nov05 3-1 / Apr21 0-0		Sep24 2-1 / Mar10 1-2	Dec27 0-2 / May12 0-0	Nov19 4-1 / Mar18 1-2	Sep17 3-1 / Jan07 1-1
MOTHERWELL	Sep10 1-1 / Feb11 0-4	Sep17 0-3 / Jan07 1-1	Oct01 1-3 / Mar28 2-1	Oct29 2-2 / Apr28 1-3	Dec26 1-1 / May12 0-1	Nov26 1-2 / Mar24 0-1		Dec10 0-3 / Mar31 0-3	Oct15 0-1 / Feb25 1-0	Nov05 0-0 / Apr21 1-0
RANGERS	Sep17 0-2 / Jan07 1-1	Nov05 1-2 / Apr21 1-0	Dec17 2-1 / May05 2-2	Nov19 0-0 / May02 2-2	Dec03 3-0 / Apr07 0-0	Oct08 1-0 / Mar03 0-0	Oct22 1-2 / Feb04 2-1		Sep24 6-3 / Jan21 2-0	Aug20 1-1 / Dec31 1-1
ST JOHNSTONE	Nov05 0-5 / Apr21 0-0	Dec03 0-3 / Apr07 0-0	Oct08 0-2 / Mar03 1-2	Sep17 1-2 / Jan07 1-2	Aug20 2-0 / Dec31 1-2	Oct01 1-4 / Feb18 1-1	Dec17 0-1 / May05 3-1	Nov26 0-1 / Mar06 1-4		Oct22 2-3 / Mar31 4-2
ST MIRREN	Dec24 0-3 / May12 3-2	Nov19 4-2 / Apr18 2-4	Sep10 0-0 / Feb11 4-0	Nov22 4-0 / Feb25 2-2	Sep24 0-1 / Mar17 1-1	Nov12 2-1 / Mar21 3-1	Sep03 1-1 / Jan03 2-1	Oct29 3-0 / Apr28 1-1	Dec10 1-2 / Feb04 1-1	

DIVISION 1

	AIRDRIE	ALLOA	AYR U	BRECHIN C	CLYDE	CLYDEBANK	DUMBARTON	FALKIRK	HAMILTON A	KILMARNOCK	MEADOWBANK T	MORTON	PARTICK T	RAITH R
AIRDRIE		Nov26 1-0 / Apr14 1-0	Nov19 1-0 / Mar03 1-2	Sep09 0-4	Dec10 1-0 / Mar31 3-3	Sep14 1-0 / May05 1-4	Nov05 0-1	Sep28 0-1	Jan03 1-0 / Feb25 0-1	Oct15 1-0 / Mar17 3-0	Dec27 1-2	Oct10 0-3	Feb22 / Apr21 1-0	Jan07 1-0
ALLOA	Oct08 1-0 / May12 0-0		Dec03 0-0	Sep28 4-1	Nov05 1-1 / Mar10 0-0	Nov19 0-2	Feb21 2-1	Aug20 0-1 / Feb11 3-1	Oct01 2-1 / Mar24 2-2	Dec10 0-4	Sep03 0-1	Jan07 1-3	Sep14 3-4 / Apr07 2-2	Oct15 1-2 / Apr21 2-2
AYR U	Sep17 2-2	Oct01 4-2 / Mar17 3-1		Dec10 1-1	Dec26 1-0 / Feb25 2-1	Nov26 2-2	Sep03 1-2	Oct15 0-1 / Apr28 1-2	Nov05 1-1 / Apr21 1-1	Aug20 0-2	Jan21 2-2	Nov12 2-2	Jan07 2-1 / Mar31 1-2	Sep28 2-2 / Mar14 1-5
BRECHIN C	Dec31 3-1 / Feb25 1-1	Dec17 1-0 / Mar10 4-1	Sep24 2-1		Sep17 3-0 / Apr10 2-2	Mar13 0-0 / May12 2-2	Nov12 1-0 / Apr21 0-3	Oct29 1-0	Mar06 1-0	Nov26 3-2	Oct22 0-0	Sep10 3-1	Oct01 2-0 / Apr07 1-2	Aug20 1-1
CLYDE	Sep24 1-1 / Apr07 1-1	Feb04 2-2	Sep10 1-1	Nov19 2-2		Dec31 2-2 / Mar03 1-1	Feb29 2-1	Oct22 1-2 / May05 1-2	Sep14 1-0 / May12 2-2	Oct01 0-1 / Apr21	Oct17 2-1 / Mar17 3-2	Oct29 2-3	Aug20 1-2	Nov26 5-0
CLYDEBANK	Nov12 2-4	Sep17 2-7 / Apr14 1-0	Oct08 4-1 / Feb11 1-2	Nov05 1-0	Sep03 1-0		Jan02 0-2	Jan07 3-1 / Mar24 1-2	Feb21 1-1	Sep28 4-0 / Feb25 3-0	Dec03 3-0 / Apr21 1-1	Oct15 3-3 / Apr28 1-1	Dec10 1-0	Dec26 1-1 / Mar10 4-3
DUMBARTON	Feb04 4-2 / Mar31 2-0	Oct29 1-1 / May12 0-3	Dec31 1-2	Sep14 1-2 / Apr28 2-2	Oct15 1-2 / Apr07 2-1	Aug20 3-0		Dec10 3-0	Sep28 2-0 / Mar03 2-0	Jan07 4-3	Nov19 1-0	Nov26 0-1	Sep10 1-2	Oct01 / Mar17 3-0
FALKIRK	Dec17 2-0 / Mar10 1-1	Feb29 1-1	Feb18 2-1	Oct15 3-3 / Mar17 1-1	Nov12 0-1	Oct22 1-1	Sep24 4-1		Sep17 4-1 / Mar31 2-0	Sep24 1-3 / Feb25 1-4	Dec31 2-1 / Apr21 0-1	Nov05 0-2 / May12 1-2	Sep03 2-1 / Apr14 1-1	
HAMILTON A	Aug20 1-1 / Apr14 3-2	Sep10 1-0	Feb04 0-0 / Apr24 4-1	Oct15 3-3 / Mar17 0-1	Jan07 1-2 / Feb11 1-3	Oct29 1-0 / Apr07 2-0	Dec17 4-1	Oct01 1-2		Sep17 0-1 / Mar03 1-1	Sep24 1-1 / May05 1-2	Dec31 1-1	Nov26 3-1	Nov12 0-0
KILMARNOCK	Jan14 4-1	Sep24 2-0 / Apr28 2-0	Jan03 1-0 / May05 3-0	Oct08 4-1 / Feb11 1-1	Dec03 1-2	Dec17 0-1 / Mar10 0-0	Oct22 2-1	Sep10 2-1	Nov19 2-1		Sep14 3-1 / Apr07 1-1	Feb04 0-1	Dec31 1-2	Oct22 0-0 / Mar24 1-2
MEADOWBANK T	Sep10 1-0 / Apr28 0-4	Dec31 4-0 / Mar03 2-1	Oct29 1-5 / Mar24 2-2	Jan07 2-1 / Mar31 2-2	Dec03 1-1 / Apr14 1-1	Sep17 1-3	Sep17 0-2	Nov26 0-1	Dec10 2-0	Nov12 2-1		Aug20 1-4 / Feb11 1-1	Oct15 2-1	Feb04 1-3 / May12 1-3
MORTON	Dec03 3-2 / Mar24 2-1	Oct22 1-0 / Apr18 3-0	Sep14 2-3	Dec26 0-0 / Apr14 2-0	Feb21 2-1	Feb29 1-2 / Apr14 2-0	Oct08 2-2 / Mar03 0-0	Nov19 3-1	Sep03 1-1	Nov05 2-2 / Mar17 2-1	Jan02 4-0 / May12 3-2		Sep28 1-2	Dec10 0-0
PARTICK T	Oct29 2-1	Nov12 5-0	Oct22 4-3 / Apr28 1-1	Dec03 2-0 / Feb11 1-2	Jan02 1-0 / May05 1-1	Sep24 1-2 / Mar24 0-0	Dec26 1-0	Feb04 3-1 / Mar31 1-2	Oct08 0-1 / Apr14 2-1	Sep03 4-1 / Mar10 2-1	Feb18 3-1	Dec17 1-0		Sep17 2-0
RAITH R	Oct22 0-0 / Feb11 2-3	Feb17 1-1	Dec17 1-3 / Apr07 5-0	Jan02 1-1 / May05 6-0	Oct08 2-1 / Mar31 2-2	Sep10 0-0	Dec31 1-2 / Apr28 0-2	Sep14 1-2	Feb29 2-1 / Mar03 3-1	Nov05 3-1 / Mar17 0-2	Sep24 1-3	Nov19 1-2		

Pictured at the start of the 1983-84 season with the League Cup, won the previous year, Celtic went on to pick-up all three runners-up spots, losing to Aberdeen in the League and Scottish Cup, and to Rangers in the League Cup.

DIVISION 2

	ALBION R	ARBROATH	BERWICK R	COWDENBEATH	DUNFERMLINE A	EAST FIFE	E STIRLING	FORFAR A	MONTROSE	QUEEN OF SOUTH	QUEEN'S PARK	STENHOUSEMUIR	STIRLING A	STRANRAER
ALBION R		Nov12 3-0	Feb14 4-4	Mar13 2-0	Sep17 1-1	Oct22 1-2	Sep24 2-3 May05 0-1	Oct29 2-2	Sep10 0-2 Mar24 0-4	Dec17 1-1 Feb25 1-4	Nov26 1-4 Apr07 0-0	Aug20 1-2 Apr21 1-1	Oct01 1-1 Mar10 1-4	Dec31 2-1
ARBROATH	Aug27 3-0 May12 0-1		Oct22 1-1	Sep03 3-2 Mar10 0-1	Feb21 3-0	Nov19 0-2 Apr28 0-1	Feb04 3-2	Jan02 0-1	Dec17 2-1 Feb25 1-1	Sep24 1-2 Apr21 6-3	Oct01 2-0 Mar31 0-5	Nov26 1-1	Mar20 2-1	Oct29 3-1
BERWICK R	Oct15 4-3 Apr14 0-0	Feb28 0-0 Mar17 2-0		Oct29 0-0	Nov12 1-1 May12 2-0	Dec17 1-0 Mar31 2-1	Dec31 1-2	Oct01 1-2 Mar10 0-1	Sep24 4-0	Feb04 2-0	Aug20 3-0	Sep10 3-0 Apr28 6-1	Nov26 1-1	Sep17 0-1 Feb18 2-0
COWDENBEATH	Nov05 0-1 Mar31 2-3	Dec31 0-1	Feb21 2-1 Apr07 0-1		Aug20 0-1 Mar17 1-2	Dec03 0-0 Mar03 1-2	Sep17 2-1	Mar06 0-1	Nov12 5-2 May05 1-2	Oct08 0-0 Apr28 1-0	Sep10 3-1	Dec26 1-1 Feb18 0-0	Sep28 0-4	Oct15 2-2
DUNFERMLINE A	Feb11 1-2 Apr28 5-0	Oct15 0-1 Apr07 2-0	Sep14 1-0	Mar20 0-0		Sep03 1-1 Apr21 1-1	Oct29 1-1	Sep28 1-2 Mar10 1-2	Feb08 1-1 Apr09 3-1	Nov19 1-0	Feb21 2-2	Oct01 2-0	Dec26 1-1	Nov26 1-1 Feb25 1-0
EAST FIFE	Jan14 1-0 Feb21 1-4	Sep17 0-1	Sep28 1-2	Oct01 2-1	Dec31 3-1		Nov12 2-1 Apr14 2-0	Nov26 2-3 Feb25 0-0	Aug20 1-0	Oct29 1-2 Mar10 0-0	Dec26 3-1 May05 3-0	Feb04 1-2 Apr07 3-1	Oct15 1-0 Mar24 4-2	Sep10 1-0
E STIRLING	Dec26 2-2	Nov05 0-3 Mar03 0-1	Sep03 0-2 Mar24 1-1	Nov19 3-1 May12 3-4	Feb15 0-2	Sep14 1-4		Feb11 3-1 Feb18 2-1	Oct08 1-3 Apr07 1-3	Dec03 1-0	Sep28 1-2 Apr28 2-2	Oct15 1-3	Aug20 0-1	Mar14 1-1
FORFAR A	Feb28 2-1 Mar17 1-0	Aug20 4-1 Feb18 1-1	Dec03 4-1	Oct22 1-0	Dec17 1-0	Oct08 3-1 Apr21 4-3	Sep10 0-0		Dec31 4-0 May12 2-0	Feb21 2-0 Apr28 3-0	Nov12 4-1 Mar03 0-0	Sep17 1-0	Nov05 1-1	Sep24 2-0 Apr07 5-3
MONTROSE	Nov19 3-1	Sep28 0-4 May05 2-1	Dec10 0-1	Sep14 1-2 Mar31 2-0	Nov05 0-1 Mar03 1-1	Jan02 0-1 Mar17 0-1	Nov26 2-3	Sep03 0-1		Feb11 1-0 Apr07 2-1	Oct15 1-2 Mar18 2-1	Feb15 0-0	Mar14 1-1 Apr21 0-0	Oct01 1-5
QUEEN OF SOUTH	Sep28 4-0	Dec24 2-1 Mar03 2-1	Nov05 1-1 Apr14 0-2	Nov26 1-0 Feb18 1-0	Sep10 2-1	Dec10 0-0 Mar31 1-0	Oct01 2-1	Oct15 1-1	Sep17 1-2		Dec31 2-1 Mar17 2-0	Nov12 2-0	Feb29 2-2	Aug20 3-1 Feb05 0-0
QUEEN'S PARK	Oct08 1-1	Dec03 2-1 Apr21 1-1	Jan02 1-0 Mar27 0-4	Feb11 4-3 Apr17 1-2	Oct22 3-1	Sep24 5-2 Jan28 1-1	Dec17 5-4	Sep14 0-1	Nov06 3-0	Sep03 0-2		Oct29 1-1 May12 3-1	Nov19 0-1 Apr28 3-1	Feb04 0-1 Mar10 1-0
STENHOUSEMUIR	Feb07 1-1	Oct08 0-0 Apr14 1-0	Feb11 3-2	Sep24 2-0 Feb25 0-1	Dec03 0-0 May05 2-1	Nov05 3-1	Mar06 1-1	Nov19 2-1 Mar31 0-4	Oct22 1-2 Mar10 0-0	Sep14 0-3 Mar24 2-2	Mar14 4-2		Sep03 4-3	Dec17 2-0
STIRLING A	Dec03 3-1 May05 0-1	Sep10 2-1 Feb25 0-2	Oct08 0-2	Dec17 4-1	Sep24 2-1 Mar17 1-2	Mar06 0-0	Feb21 0-0 Apr14 1-1	Oct22 2-0 May12 3-1	Sep17 1-0	Dec31 0-0 Mar03 0-3				Nov12 2-1 Mar31 0-2
STRANRAER	Sep03 3-1 Mar03 2-0	Feb15 0-1 Mar24 2-1	Nov19 1-0	Jan21 1-1 Apr21 1-1	Oct08 1-1	Feb11 1-0 May12 1-2	Oct22 1-1	Dec26 1-3 Apr14 0-0	Dec03 2-1	Jan02 2-1	Nov05 1-1	Aug27 2-0	Sep14 1-1	

PREMIER DIVISION FINAL TABLE

	P	W	D	L	F	A	Pts
Aberdeen	36	25	7	4	78	21	57
Celtic	36	21	8	7	80	41	50
Dundee U	36	18	11	7	67	39	47
Rangers	36	15	12	9	53	41	42
Hearts	36	10	16	10	38	47	36
St Mirren	36	9	14	13	55	59	32
Hibernian	36	12	7	17	45	55	31
Dundee	36	11	5	20	50	74	27
St Johnstone	36	10	3	23	36	81	23
Motherwell	36	4	7	25	31	75	15

DIVISION 1 FINAL TABLE

	P	W	D	L	F	A	Pts
Morton	39	21	12	6	75	46	54
Dumbarton	39	20	11	8	66	44	51
Partick T	39	19	8	12	67	50	46
Clydebank	39	16	13	10	62	50	45
Brechin C	39	14	14	11	56	58	42
Kilmarnock	39	16	6	17	57	53	38
Falkirk	39	16	6	17	46	54	38
Clyde	39	12	13	14	53	50	37
Hamilton A	39	11	14	14	43	46	36
Airdrie	39	13	10	16	45	53	36
Meadowbank T	39	12	10	17	49	79	34
Ayr U	39	10	12	17	56	70	32
Raith R	39	10	11	18	53	62	31
Alloa	39	8	10	21	41	64	26

DIVISION 2 FINAL TABLE

	P	W	D	L	F	A	Pts
Forfar A	39	27	9	3	73	31	63
East Fife	39	20	7	12	57	42	47
Berwick R	39	16	11	12	57	38	43
Stirling A	39	14	14	11	51	42	42
Arbroath	39	18	6	15	51	46	42
Queen of South	39	16	10	13	51	46	42
Stenhousemuir	39	14	11	14	47	57	39
Stranraer	39	13	12	14	47	47	38
Dunfermline A	39	13	10	16	44	45	36
Queen's Park	39	14	8	17	58	63	36
E Stirling	39	10	11	18	54	66	31
Montrose	39	12	7	20	36	59	31
Cowdenbeath	39	10	9	20	44	58	29
Albion R	39	8	11	20	46	76	27

SFA Cup

1st Round
Dec 8	Berwick R 3	Albion R 1	
Dec 8	Dunfermline A 1	E Stirling 3	
Dec 8	Queen of South ...2	Arbroath 1	
Dec 8	Stenhousemuir 2	Whitehill Welfare ...1	
Dec 8	Stirling A 20	Selkirk 0	
Dec 8	Stranraer 2	Gala Fairydean ...2	

Replays
Dec 15 Gala Fairydean 0   Stranraer 1

2nd Round
Jan 5	Alloa 2	E Stirling 1	
Jan 5	Berwick R 1	Inverness C 1	
Jan 5	Cowdenbeath 2	Stirling A 1	
Jan 5	Inverness T 1	Spartans 1	
Jan 5	Keith 2	Brora R 0	
Jan 5	Queen of South 3	Montrose 0	
Jan 5	Queen's Park 0	Raith R 0	
Jan 5	Stranraer 0	Stenhousemuir 0	

Replays
Jan 12	Inverness C 3	Berwick R 3	
Jan 21	Raith R 1	Queen's Park 0	
Feb 2	Spartans 1	Inverness T 2	
Feb 4	Stenhousemuir 0	Stranraer 2	
Jan 21	Berwick R 0	Inverness C 3	

played at Bayview Park

3rd Round
Jan 30	Aberdeen 5	Alloa 0	
Feb 4	Airdrie 0	Falkirk 3	
Jan 26	Ayr U 3	Keith 1	
Jan 26	Brechin C 1	East Fife 1	
Feb 4	Cowdenbeath 0	St Mirren 4	
Feb 4	Dundee U 3	Hibernian 0	
Feb 4	Forfar A 1	Clydebank 0	
Jan 30	Hamilton A 1	Celtic 2	
Jan 30	Hearts 6	Inverness C 0	
Feb 9	Inverness T 3	Kilmarnock 0	
Jan 30	Meadowbank T 4	Partick T 2	
Jan 26	Morton 3	Rangers 3	
Jan 30	Motherwell 4	Dumbarton 0	
Jan 26	Raith R 2	Clyde 2	
Feb 5	St Johnstone 1	Dundee 1	
Feb 9	Stranraer 4	Queen of South ...6	

Replays
Jan 29	East Fife 0	Brechin C 4	
Jan 30	Rangers 3	Morton 1	
Feb 4	Clyde 1	Raith R 2	
Feb 6	Dundee 2	St Johnstone 1	

4th Round
Feb 16	Ayr U 0	St Mirren 1	
Feb 16	Brechin C 1	Hearts 1	
Feb 16	Celtic 6	Inverness T 0	
Feb 16	Forfar A 2	Falkirk 1	
Feb 20	Meadowbank T 0	Motherwell 2	
Feb 16	Queen of South 0	Dundee U 3	
Feb 16	Raith R 1	Aberdeen 2	
Feb 16	Rangers 0	Dundee 1	

Replays
Feb 20 Hearts 1   Brechin C 0

5th Round
Mar 9	Dundee 1	Celtic 1	
Mar 9	Hearts 1	Aberdeen 1	
Mar 9	Motherwell 4	Forfar A 1	
Mar 9	St Mirren 1	Dundee U 4	

Replay
Mar 13	Aberdeen 1	Hearts 0	
Mar 13	Celtic 2	Dundee 1	

Semi-finals
Apr 13	Aberdeen 0	Dundee U 0	played at Tynecastle
Apr 13	Celtic 1	Motherwell 1	played at Hampden Park

Replay
Apr 17	Aberdeen 1	Dundee U 2	played at Tynecastle
Apr 17	Celtic 3	Motherwell 0	played at Hampden Park

Final
May 18 Celtic 2   Dundee U 1   played at Hampden Park

League Cup results for 1984-85 are detailed on page 212.

PREMIER

	ABERDEEN	CELTIC	DUMBARTON	DUNDEE	DUNDEE U	HEARTS	HIBERNIAN	MORTON	RANGERS	ST MIRREN
ABERDEEN		Dec08 4-2, Apr27 1-1	Nov24 1-0, Apr20 4-0	Aug11 3-2, Dec15 0-0	Dec22 4-2, Mar30 4-2	Sep29 4-0, Feb09 2-2	Sep01 4-1, Jan05 2-0	Nov10 5-0, Jan12 5-0	Sep15 0-0, Jan19 5-1	Oct20 4-0, Mar02 3-0
CELTIC	Oct06 2-1, Feb23 2-0		Nov10 2-0, May11 2-0	Dec01 5-1, May04 1-2	Aug18 1-1, Dec29 3-2	Sep15 1-0, Mar20 3-2	Oct13 3-0, Mar16 0-1	Sep01 5-0, Feb19 1-1	Dec22 1-1, May01 1-1	Nov24 7-1, Apr24 4-2
DUMBARTON	Sep22 0-2, Feb02 0-2	Sep08 1-1, Apr03 0-2		Aug25 2-1, Jan01 1-0	Dec08 2-2, Apr27 0-2	Nov03 0-1, Mar23 1-3	Nov17 2-2, Apr06 0-2	Oct13 3-1, Dec26 1-0	Aug18 1-2, Mar16 2-4	Sep22 0-1, Feb09 1-1
DUNDEE	Oct13 1-2, Mar16 0-4	Sep29 2-3, Feb09 2-0	Oct27 1-0, Apr13 1-0		Nov10 0-2, May11 1-0	Nov24 2-1, Apr20 3-0	Aug18 0-1, Dec29 2-0	Dec08 5-1, Apr27 0-0	Sep01 0-2, Jan05 2-2	Sep15 2-0, Feb20 1-0
DUNDEE U	Aug25 0-2, Jan02 2-1	Oct20 1-3, Mar02 0-0	Oct06 3-4, Feb23 4-0	Sep08 0-0, Apr03 4-0		Aug11 2-0, Dec15 5-2	Sep21 2-1, Feb02 2-0	Nov17 7-0, Apr06 2-0	Dec01 1-1, May04 3-2	Sep15 3-2, Mar23 3-1
HEARTS	Dec01 1-2, May04 0-3	Nov17 1-5, Apr06 0-2	Sep01 1-0, Jan05 5-1	Sep22 0-2, Mar16 3-3	Oct13 0-0		Oct27 0-0, Apr02 2-2	Aug18 1-2, Dec29 1-0	Oct06 1-0, Feb23 2-0	Sep08 1-2, Jan12 1-2
HIBERNIAN	Nov06 0-3, Mar23 0-5	Aug11 2-3, Dec15 0-1	Sep15 2-0, Jan19 3-1	Oct20 1-0, Mar02 0-1	Nov24 2-0, Apr20 1-1	Aug25 1-2, Jan01 1-2		Sep29 3-1, Feb09 5-1	Nov10 3-1, May11 1-0	Dec08 0-4, Apr27 0-4
MORTON	Sep08 0-3, May11 1-2	Nov03 2-1, Mar23 2-7	Aug11 2-1, Dec15 2-4	Oct06 1-1, Feb23 0-1	Sep15 0-3, Mar13 1-0	Oct20 2-3, Mar02 0-1	Dec01 4-0, May04 1-2		Nov24 1-3, Apr20 0-3	Oct27 2-1, Mar16 0-2
RANGERS	Nov17 1-2, Apr06 1-2	Aug25 0-0, Jan01 1-2	Oct20 0-0, Mar02 3-1	Nov03 0-0, Mar23 1-3	Sep29 1-0, Feb09 0-0	Dec08 1-1, Apr27 3-1	Sep08 2-0, Jan12 1-2	Sep22 2-0, Feb02 2-0		Aug11 0-0, Dec15 2-0
ST MIRREN	Aug18 1-2, Dec29 2-2	Sep22 0-0, Feb02 0-2	Dec01 2-1, May04 1-0	Nov17 1-0, Apr06 4-2	Sep01 1-0, Jan05 1-0	Nov10 2-3, May11 5-2	Oct06 0-2, Feb23 2-1	Oct27 2-1, Apr02 2-3	Oct13 0-2, Mar16 2-1	

DIVISION 1

	AIRDRIE	AYR U	BRECHIN C	CLYDE	CLYDEBANK	EAST FIFE	FALKIRK	FORFAR A	HAMILTON A	KILMARNOCK	MEADOWBANK T	MOTHERWELL	PARTICK T	ST JOHNSTONE
AIRDRIE		Mar26 1-2	Dec22 2-2	Oct13 4-3, Apr20 1-2	Aug18 1-0	Nov05 2-3, May04 2-4	Sep22 1-0, Mar02 2-1	Mar13 1-2, Apr06 2-4	Sep08 1-2	Dec01 2-1	Dec29 5-0, Mar23 3-5	Oct06 2-0	Nov17 4-1	Sep01 2-1, Feb23 2-0
AYR U	Oct20 0-2, Apr13 5-1		Nov24 2-1, Feb23 0-1	Sep15 0-0	Dec15 4-4, Apr27 3-2	Oct27 2-1, Mar16 1-2	Aug25 1-1	Aug11 1-0	Jan02 1-1	Mar30 0-0, May11 1-1	Feb02 1-1	Mar02 2-0	Sep29 3-2	Mar06 1-3
BRECHIN C	Aug25 3-0, Apr27 0-0	Sep22 0-2		Dec29 1-0	Nov03 2-2	Sep08 2-2, Feb09 1-1	Oct06 2-3, May11 0-2	Aug18 0-2	Nov21 0-1, Mar16 2-0	Dec15 3-2, Mar02 2-1	Oct20 4-1, Apr20 1-2	Feb26 0-2	Jan19 0-4, Apr09 1-3	Dec01 1-0
CLYDE	Feb16 0-0	Nov17 1-3, Mar09 1-0	Aug11 1-1, Apr06 2-2		Sep08 2-0	Sep22 1-1	Dec01 1-2	Nov03 4-2	Jan19 1-3, Apr13 2-1	Aug25 4-1	Sep01 0-0, Apr27 0-1	Oct20 3-3, Mar23 1-0	Jan01 1-0, Feb09 2-3	Oct06 2-3
CLYDEBANK	Jan01 1-0, Apr03 1-1	Oct06 2-1	Feb02 0-2	Nov10 1-2		Dec01 1-0	Dec22 1-3	Mar05 1-1	Sep01 0-0, Feb23 2-1	Sep15 5-0	Oct27 2-1	Nov24 2-1	Oct20 0-2, Mar23 1-2	Aug11 3-0, Mar02 2-1
EAST FIFE	Feb02 3-1	Sep01 1-1	Nov10 2-0	Nov24 1-1, Feb23 0-1	Sep29 4-4, May11 0-0		Aug11 2-4	Dec08 0-0	Dec22 0-1, Mar23 3-2	Oct13 0-1	Sep15 1-1, Apr20 0-2	Oct27 1-2	Jan12 3-1, Jan19 1-2	Jan01 3-0, Apr27 0-1
FALKIRK	Nov24 4-2	Feb26 3-0	Dec08 3-0, May04 0-1	Sep29 2-0, Mar16 1-0	Aug25 0-2, Mar09 0-0	Dec29 1-2		Oct20 4-6	Nov03 3-2	Mar13 3-3, Apr20 0-0	Aug18 1-0, Feb09 0-2	Sep15 0-3	Dec15 5-1	Nov10 1-3, Apr03 2-0
FORFAR A	Oct27 0-0, Feb09 0-5	Dec22 4-2, Mar19 1-0	Jan01 2-1	Feb02 1-1, Apr20 1-0	Oct06 0-0, Apr09 1-0	Jan05 1-0, Apr27 0-2			Dec01 0-0	Nov10 1-1	Nov24 4-1, May11 0-0	Sep01 2-1	Aug11 1-2, Mar16 4-0	Sep15 4-0
HAMILTON A	Nov01 1-1, Feb09 1-3	Dec29 3-1, Mar23 1-4	Sep15 0-1, Mar23 1-0	Oct27 0-2, Apr13 1-0	Dec15 0-1	Aug25 2-4, Apr13 2-1	Feb02 0-0, Mar02 0-1	Sep29 3-1, Mar02 2-1		Nov24 1-0	Jan12 0-0, Apr27 1-1	Aug18 2-0, May11 1-1	Dec09 1-0	Oct20 3-2
KILMARNOCK	Sep29 0-5, May11 1-4	Aug18 0-0	Sep01 2-0, Feb26 2-0	Dec22 1-1	Nov17 1-1, May04 0-3	Jan05 1-1, Apr06 1-0	Oct13 2-0	Sep08 1-2, Mar23 1-1	Sep22 1-2, Mar09 2-0		Dec08 2-1	Dec29 0-0	Nov03 1-1, Apr13 2-0	Jan19 3-2
MEADOWBANK T	Apr11 0-3	Nov07 3-0	Jan05 2-4, Dec15 1-1	Sep01 0-0, Apr09 0-3	Jan19 1-3, Apr13 1-1	Nov17 0-3	Dec18 1-1	Sep22 1-3, Feb23 1-3	Oct06 2-0	Oct13 2-0, Mar16 0-2		Dec01 4-0, May04 4-2	Sep08 1-1, Mar09 0-2	Dec22 1-1
MOTHERWELL	Dec08 1-1, Mar20 2-0	Sep08 1-1, May04 2-1	Oct13 2-0, Mar16 1-0	Jan05 0-0	Sep22 0-1, Feb23 2-2	Apr06 5-0	Nov17 2-3, Apr03 0-1	Dec15 2-0	Jan02 3-0	Aug11 2-0	Sep29 3-1, Mar16 2-1		Aug25 2-1	Nov03 0-2, Apr24 4-0
PARTICK T	Sep15 0-1, Mar16 1-1	Dec01 2-0, Apr06 3-2	Oct27 1-2	Aug18 1-1	Feb20 0-1, Feb23 0-1	Oct13 0-0	Sep01 0-1, May04 1-1	Dec29 2-3	Oct06 2-0	Feb02 1-0	Nov10 2-0, Apr27 0-1	Dec22 2-1		Nov24 3-7, Mar02 6-2
ST JOHNSTONE	Dec15 2-1, Apr20 0-2	Oct13 2-1, Mar23 1-1	Sep29 0-1	Dec08 1-2, Mar09 3-1	Feb16 1-1	Aug18 3-4	Sep08 0-2, Apr06 1-2	Nov17 1-1, Apr27 2-4	Jan05 1-2	Oct27 0-1	Aug25 3-2, Feb26 0-2	Nov03 0-2	Sep22 0-1	

Season 1984-85

DIVISION 2

	ALBION R	ALLOA	ARBROATH	BERWICK R	COWDENBEATH	DUNFERMLINE A	E STIRLING	MONTROSE	QUEEN OF SOUTH	QUEEN'S PARK	RAITH R	STENHOUSEMUIR	STIRLING A	STRANRAER
ALBION R		Sep15 0-1 / Apr13 4-1	Nov10 1-0 / Feb16 3-0	Nov06 1-0 / Mar16 3-2	Aug11 1-0 / May11 1-2	Oct20 0-2 / Apr16 1-1	Feb19 1-0	Feb02 1-4	Aug25 3-4	Mar05 3-3	Apr02 0-6 / Apr27 2-4	Jan01 0-1	Dec01 0-4	Sep29 1-2 / Mar09 2-0
ALLOA	Nov17 4-0		Nov03 3-0		Sep29 1-0 / Apr23 0-0	Feb26 1-3 / May04 0-0		Dec29 2-1	Sep08 3-1	Sep22 1-1	Aug11 2-0 / Mar09 2-1	Oct13 1-1	Aug25 0-0	Jan02 2-1 / Dec01 1-2 / Mar06 1-2
ARBROATH	Sep08 1-2	Jan26 0-0 / May11 0-1		Dec15 0-5 / Feb23 2-0	Oct27 1-1	Oct06 0-2 / Mar09 1-3	Oct20 2-2 / Apr27 3-0	Aug18 0-3	Jan12 3-0	Nov17 1-2	Dec29 2-1	Feb02 2-1 / Apr20 1-1	Sep22 2-0 / Mar16 0-1	Aug25 1-2 / Apr10 3-1
BERWICK R	Apr10 0-1	Oct20 0-0	Oct29 2-1		Jan01 0-2 / Apr20 0-4	Sep08 0-1	Dec01 0-0 / Mar09 0-0	Sep22 0-1 / Apr16 0-0	Feb02 0-1 / Mar23 4-0	Aug25 4-1 / Feb26 1-0	Aug11 2-1	Oct27 2-2	Nov17 1-1 / Apr27 0-2	Dec29 2-2
COWDENBEATH	Jan12 0-0	Dec15 2-1	Feb26 3-2 / Mar23 2-0	Aug18 1-0			Nov17 0-1	Feb02 5-1	Oct06 0-1	Oct20 4-1 / Apr13 0-0	Sep08 2-3 / Apr10 0-0	Aug25 5-1 / Feb23 0-0	Mar09 0-1 / Apr03 2-0	Sep22 2-1 / Apr27 4-0
DUNFERMLINE A	Feb09 1-1	Oct27 2-2	Dec01 1-2	Nov10 1-0 / May11 2-1	Sep15 2-1 / Mar02 1-2			Mar19 2-0	Dec22 1-1 / Apr20 0-0	Sep29 1-1 / Apr27 4-0	Oct13 4-0	Jan02 1-2 / Apr23 2-3	Nov24 1-1 / Mar23 0-0	Sep01 1-0 / Feb16 2-2 / Aug11 5-0
E STIRLING	Sep22 2-3 / May04 0-0	Sep01 1-2	Feb09 2-0	Oct06 1-2	Oct13 3-0 / Apr06 0-0	Nov03 2-0 / Apr13 0-0		Nov17 0-1	Sep08 0-2 / Mar16 0-0	Dec26 3-2 / Mar06 0-0	Dec15 1-3 / Mar23 0-1	Aug11 1-1 / Mar02 0-2	Dec22 2-2	Feb25 3-2
MONTROSE	Oct13 1-0 / Apr23 0-0	Nov10 2-1 / Mar23 2-0	Jan01 2-1 / Mar02 3-0	Nov24 1-1	Dec01 1-4 / Feb16 2-1	Aug25 2-4	Sep15 4-2		Feb20 2-2	Apr27 1-4	Feb09 2-0	Sep29 1-0 / May04 0-0	Aug11 1-0	Nov03 0-0 / Apr13 2-1
QUEEN OF SOUTH	Dec22 3-2 / Apr20 1-2	Nov24 1-2 / Feb23 0-2	Aug11 1-1 / May04 1-0	Oct13 3-0	Mar13 1-1	Dec15 0-0	Nov10 0-1	Sep01 3-1 / Mar09 1-1		Oct06 2-2	Nov03 3-5 / Mar16 3-0	Sep15 1-2 / Mar30 1-1	Feb26 0-1 / May11 2-1	Jan01 0-0
QUEEN'S PARK	Sep01 5-1 / Feb23 1-1	Jan12 0-0	Sep15 0-1 / Apr06 1-1	Dec22 1-0	Nov10 1-1	Feb02 4-1	Aug18 4-1 / Mar16 2-1	Oct27 0-1	Dec01 0-1 / Jan19 2-1 / Mar02 1-2		Nov24 1-1 / Apr20 1-2	Jan26 1-0	Sep29 1-2	Oct20 0-2
RAITH R	Oct27 3-0	Feb02 1-2 / Apr09 2-0	Aug25 2-0 / Apr13 2-1	Feb20 2-1 / May04 3-0	Dec22 0-3	Aug18 1-3	Sep29 2-0	Oct20 0-1 / May11 1-3	Mar26 3-0	Sep22 0-2		Dec01 3-0	Sep08 1-1 / Mar06 1-1	Nov17 1-2 / Mar09 2-4
STENHOUSEMUIR	Aug18 1-1 / Mar02 2-1	Dec22 0-3 / Apr27 2-4	Oct13 1-2	Mar20 2-1 / Apr13 1-1	Sep01 0-4	Sep22 1-0 / Feb23 0-0	Feb16 1-2	Dec15 1-0	Nov17 1-0	Nov03 3-2 / May11 2-0	Oct06 1-1		Feb09 1-1	Sep08 1-1 / Apr10 3-0
STIRLING A	Oct06 2-3 / Mar23 4-1	Aug18 0-1 / Mar02 2-3	Nov24 1-1	Sep15 1-1 / May04 3-0	Mar06 1-1	Dec29 2-2 / Apr03 3-1	Aug25 2-2 / Mar12 3-1	Sep22 3-1	Oct27 2-0 / Apr13 1-0	Dec15 3-0	Nov10 1-1	Oct20 1-2		Feb02 2-2
STRANRAER	Mar26 2-3	Oct06 2-3	Dec22 7-1	Sep01 2-0 / Mar02 1-2	Nov24 4-2	Feb23 0-1 / Apr03 0-2	Oct27 1-1 / May11 0-2	Jan26 0-3	Aug18 1-0 / Apr06 1-2	Mar20 2-1 / May04 0-0	Sep15 1-2 / Mar23 1-4	Nov10 2-4	Oct13 2-0 / Apr20 1-0	

PREMIER DIVISION FINAL TABLE

	P	W	D	L	F	A	Pts
Aberdeen	36	27	5	4	89	26	59
Celtic	36	22	8	6	77	30	52
Dundee U	36	20	7	9	67	33	47
Rangers	36	13	12	11	47	38	38
St Mirren	36	17	4	15	51	56	38
Dundee	36	15	7	14	48	50	37
Hearts	36	13	5	18	47	64	31
Hibernian	36	10	7	19	38	61	27
Dumbarton	36	6	7	23	29	64	19
Morton	36	5	2	29	29	100	12

DIVISION 1 FINAL TABLE

	P	W	D	L	F	A	Pts
Motherwell	39	21	8	10	62	36	50
Clydebank	39	17	14	8	57	37	48
Falkirk	39	19	7	13	65	54	45
Hamilton A	39	16	11	12	48	49	43
Airdrie	39	17	8	14	70	59	42
Forfar A	39	14	13	12	54	49	41
Ayr U	39	15	9	15	57	52	39
Clyde	39	14	11	14	47	48	39
Brechin C	39	14	9	16	49	57	37
East Fife	39	12	12	15	55	56	36
Partick T	39	13	9	17	50	55	35
Kilmarnock	39	12	10	17	42	61	34
Meadowbank T	39	11	10	18	50	66	32
St Johnstone	39	10	5	24	51	78	25

DIVISION 2 FINAL TABLE

	P	W	D	L	F	A	Pts
Montrose	39	22	9	8	57	40	53
Alloa	39	20	10	9	58	40	50
Dunfermline A	39	17	15	7	61	36	49
Cowdenbeath	39	18	11	10	68	39	47
Stenhousemuir	39	15	15	9	45	43	45
Stirling A	39	15	13	11	62	47	43
Raith R	39	18	6	15	69	57	42
Queen of South	39	10	14	15	42	56	34
Albion R	39	13	8	18	49	72	34
Queen's Park	39	12	9	18	48	55	33
Stranraer	39	13	6	20	52	67	32
E Stirling	39	8	15	16	38	53	31
Berwick R	39	8	12	19	36	49	28
Arbroath	39	9	7	23	35	66	25

Danny McGrain passes the trophy back as Celtic embark on their lap of honour after beating Dundee United in the 1984 Final.

SFA Cup

1st Round
Dec 7	Albion R	8	Gala Fairydean	1
Dec 7	Berwick R	0	Cowdenbeath	0
Dec 7	Dunfermline A	2	Raith R	0
Dec 7	Meadowbank T	3	East Stirling	2
Dec 7	Queen's Park	3	Buckie T	0
Dec 7	St Johnstone	1	Queen of South	0

Replays
Dec 11	Cowdenbeath	0	Berwick R	2

2nd Round
Jan 4	Fort William	0	Stirling A	0
Jan 11	Hawick RA	1	St Johnstone	2
Jan 11	Nairn Co	1	Meadowbank T	1
Jan 11	Peterhead	1	Arbroath	2
Jan 4	Queen's Park	2	Albion R	1
Jan 4	Stenhousemuir	0	Whitehill Welfare	0
Jan 4	Stranraer	1	Berwick R	2
Jan 4	Threave R	0	Dunfermline A	5

Replays
Jan 11	Stirling A	6	Fort William	0
Jan 11	Whitehill Welfare	2	Stenhousemuir	3
Jan 13	Meadowbank T	1	Nairn Co	2

3rd Round
Feb 5	Aberdeen	4	Montrose	1
Jan 25	Airdrie	0	Partick T	0
Jan 25	Arbroath	0	Clyde	0
Jan 25	Ayr U	1	Stenhousemuir	0
Jan 25	Berwick R	2	Alloa	3
Jan 25	Celtic	2	St Johnstone	0
Jan 25	Clydebank	0	Falkirk	0
Jan 25	Dundee U	4	Morton	0
Jan 25	East Fife	1	St Mirren	1
Feb 3	Hamilton A	2	Forfar A	1
Jan 25	Hearts	3	Rangers	2
Jan 26	Hibernian	2	Dunfermline A	0
Jan 25	Kilmarnock	1	Stirling A	0
Jan 25	Motherwell	1	Brechin C	1
Jan 25	Nairn Co	0	Dundee	7
Jan 25	Queen's Park	1	Dumbarton	0

Replays
Feb 3	Clyde	1	Arbroath	2
Feb 3	Falkirk	1	Clydebank	0
Feb 3	Partick T	1	Airdrie	2
Feb 4	St Mirren	3	East Fife	1
Feb 11	Brechin C	1	Motherwell	1
Feb 12	Brechin C	0	Motherwell	2
	played at Tannadice Park			

4th Round
Mar 5	Alloa	1	Motherwell	2
Feb 15	Arbroath	0	Aberdeen	1
Feb 15	Celtic	2	Queen's Park	1
Feb 19	Dundee	2	Airdrie	0
Feb 15	Dundee U	1	Kilmarnock	1
Mar 3	Hamilton A	1	Hearts	2
Feb 16	Hibernian	1	Ayr U	0
Mar 4	St Mirren	1	Falkirk	1

Replays
Feb 19	Kilmarnock	0	Dundee U	1
Mar 5	Falkirk	0	St Mirren	3

5th Round
Mar 8	Dundee	2	Aberdeen	2
Mar 9	Hearts	4	St Mirren	1
Mar 8	Hibernian	4	Celtic	3
Mar 8	Motherwell	0	Dundee U	0

Replay
Mar 12	Aberdeen	2	Dundee	1

Semi-finals
Apr 5	Aberdeen	3	Hibernian	0
	played at Dens Park			
Apr 5	Dundee U	0	Hearts	1
	played at Hampden Park			

Final
May 10	Aberdeen	3	Hearts	0
	played at Hampden Park			

League Cup results for 1985-86 are detailed on page 212.

PREMIER

	ABERDEEN	CELTIC	CLYDEBANK	DUNDEE	DUNDEE U	HEARTS	HIBERNIAN	MOTHERWELL	RANGERS	ST MIRREN
ABERDEEN		Nov02 4-1 Apr12 0-1	Oct05 3-1 Feb08 4-1	Nov09 4-1 Mar22 0-0	Oct19 3-2 Apr16 0-1	Sep07 3-0 Jan18 4-0	Aug10 3-0 Dec14 0-3	Aug24 1-1 Apr09 3-2	Feb19 1-0 Apr26 1-1	Sep21 1-1 Jan04 3-1
CELTIC	Sep14 2-1 Jan11 1-1		Nov16 2-0 Dec28 2-0	Apr02 2-1 Apr26 2-0	Oct26 0-3 Feb15 1-1	Oct12 0-1 Feb22 1-1	Nov23 1-1 Apr19 2-0	Aug17 2-1 Jan11 3-2	Aug31 1-1 Jan01 1-1	Oct05 2-0 Feb08 3-1
CLYDEBANK	Dec10 2-1 May03 0-6	Aug24 0-2 Mar29 0-5		Aug17 4-0 Dec23 0-0	Nov23 1-2 Apr19 1-1	Sep28 1-0 Feb01 1-1	Oct30 2-4 Mar15 1-3	Oct12 1-1 Apr05 1-1	Sep14 1-1 Apr12 2-1	Nov13 3-0 Mar22 0-2
DUNDEE	Aug31 1-3 Jan01 0-0	Sep28 0-2 Feb01 1-3	Oct19 2-0 Mar01 4-0		Nov16 0-3 Mar29 0-1	Dec07 1-1 May03 3-1	Sep14 3-1 Jan11 4-0	Nov23 3-2 Apr19 2-1	Mar15 2-3 Dec14 0-0	Aug10 2-1
DUNDEE U	Aug17 1-1 Dec21 2-1	Dec23 1-0 Jan04 4-2	Sep07 2-1 Jan18 4-0	Aug24 2-0 Dec28		Nov02 1-1 Apr12 0-3	Oct05 2-2 Feb08 4-0	Nov09 3-0 Apr22 4-0	Oct12 1-1 Feb22 1-1	Apr08 5-0 Apr26 1-2
HEARTS	Oct30 1-0 Apr20 1-1	Aug10 1-1 Dec14 1-1	Nov30 3-0 Apr26 1-0	Oct05 1-2 Feb08 3-1	Sep14 1-2 Jan11 1-1		Aug31 2-1 Jan01 3-1	Nov23 3-0 Mar15 2-0	Nov16 3-0 Mar29 3-1	Oct19 3-0 Mar25 3-0
HIBERNIAN	Oct12 1-1 Feb22 0-1	Sep07 0-5 Jan18 2-2	Oct01 5-0 Jan04 2-3	Nov02 2-1 Apr12 1-2	Oct26 0-1 May03 2-0	Nov09 0-0 Mar22 1-2		Sep28 1-0 Feb01 4-0	Aug17 1-3 Dec21 0-1	Aug24 2-3 Mar12 1-1
MOTHERWELL	Nov16 1-1 Mar29 0-1	Oct19 1-2 Apr30 0-2	Aug10 0-0 Dec14 3-0	Sep07 1-3 Mar22 2-2	Aug31 0-1 Jan18 2-0	Sep21 2-1 Jan04 1-3	Mar18 2-0 Apr12 3-1		Oct05 0-3 Feb08 1-0	Nov02 3-1 Apr12 1-2
RANGERS	Sep28 0-3 Feb01 1-1	Nov09 3-0 Mar22 4-4	Nov02 0-0 Jan11 4-2	Sep21 3-0 Jan04 5-0	Aug10 3-0 Dec14 1-1	Aug24 0-0 Dec28 0-2	Oct19 1-2 Mar01 3-1	Dec07 2-1 May03 2-0		Sep07 3-0 Jan18 2-0
ST MIRREN	Nov23 1-0 Mar15 1-1	Apr05 1-2 May03 0-5	Aug31 0-2 Jan01 3-0	Oct12 1-0 Feb22 1-2	Sep28 1-0 Feb01 1-1	Aug17 6-2 Dec21 0-1	Nov16 1-3 Mar29 0-2	Oct26 4-1 Jan11 1-0	Sep14 2-1 Apr19 2-1	

DIVISION 1

	AIRDRIE	ALLOA	AYR U	BRECHIN C	CLYDE	DUMBARTON	EAST FIFE	FALKIRK	FORFAR A	HAMILTON A	KILMARNOCK	MONTROSE	MORTON	PARTICK T
AIRDRIE		Mar19 3-0 Apr05 2-2	Oct12 4-1 Apr19 2-1	Sep21 1-2 Mar08 4-2	Oct05 3-0	Aug10 0-2 Apr12 2-1	Nov30 1-2	Sep07 1-1	Nov16 0-0	Mar24 0-4 May03 1-2	Oct26 1-2 Mar22 1-0	Dec21 1-1	Feb01 1-2	Aug24 2-2 Feb22 0-0
ALLOA	Aug17 0-0		Sep07 1-1	Oct05 2-3	Oct19 1-1	Feb04 2-4 Apr15 1-3	Sep24 1-1 Apr26 1-2	Aug31 4-0 Mar08 0-2	Nov30 4-5 May03 2-2	Dec14 1-4	Jan11 1-1	Feb01 Apr08 1-3	Oct26 May05 2-0	Nov16 1-1 Mar22 2-2
AYR U	Dec14 0-4	Nov09 1-3 Apr12 1-1		Sep14 1-3	Jan11 1-0 Mar08 2-0	Sep28 0-1	Oct19 1-0	Aug17 0-3 Apr26 1-2	Dec21 0-0 Mar12 2-0	Jan18 1-1 Mar22 0-1	Aug31 3-0	Nov23 2-1	Dec07 0-3	Nov02 1-3 Apr05 2-3
BRECHIN C	Nov23 0-2	Mar25 1-1 Apr22 3-1	Nov19 4-1 Apr08 1-1		Apr15 1-2 Apr26 2-2	Oct26 4-0 Apr05 1-1	Aug10 1-1	Feb01 1-0	Aug31 1-0 Mar22 0-3	Apr12 1-3	Sep28 2-4	Sep07 3-1 Mar18 4-2	Oct12 1-1	Dec21 2-0
CLYDE	Dec07 3-2 Apr02 1-1	Apr19 0-0 Apr28 4-2	Aug10 0-0	Aug24 2-0		Oct12 0-0	Mar05 3-4 Mar22 0-0	Nov16 0-4 Feb08 1-1	Jan18 1-1	Nov02 1-1 Apr12 4-2	Nov23 0-1 Apr05 1-3	Sep28 2-0	Sep07 2-1	Mar12 2-2
DUMBARTON	Mar12 3-0 Apr09 1-0	Aug24 4-0	Feb19 1-1 Mar05 2-0	Jan18 4-1	Dec14 1-1 Mar15 0-0		Oct05 2-1 Mar01 3-4	Sep21 2-0 Mar29 2-1	Nov02 1-1 Apr09 0-2	Sep07 2-2 Apr26 1-4	Oct19 1-0	Nov16 2-2	Jan01 1-2	Aug17 1-2
EAST FIFE	Sep28 1-1 Mar29 2-0	Nov23 1-0	Dec21 1-3 Mar15 0-0	Jan11 4-2 Apr12 1-0	Aug17 2-2	Dec07 1-0		Oct26 0-1	Sep07 1-1 Mar08 3-0	Nov16 2-2 Apr16 4-0	Feb01 1-1	Jan01 0-0 Apr19 2-0	Aug24 4-4	Oct12 1-1
FALKIRK	Nov09 0-1 Mar15 1-1	Jan01 3-1	Mar19 1-2 Apr19 2-1	Nov02 0-1	Sep14 0-0	Nov23 1-0	Jan18 1-0 May03 2-2		Oct12 5-3 Apr05 1-0	Aug10 0-0	Dec07 0-1 Mar25 1-1	Aug24 2-1	Dec21 1-1 Apr12 2-3	Sep28 2-3 Apr02 2-2
FORFAR A	Sep14 2-0 Apr15 1-1	Sep28 0-4	Aug24 1-0	Apr01 2-0	Oct26 2-1 Mar29 2-1	Feb01 4-0	Nov09 0-2	Dec14 2-1		Oct19 2-2 Apr22 2-0	Aug17 0-0 Apr12 1-0	Jan11 1-2 Mar15 1-2	Nov23 2-0	Dec07 1-1 Apr19 2-1
HAMILTON A	Aug31 3-1	Oct12 1-2 Apr02 1-1	Oct26 2-0	Aug17 3-0 Mar15 1-0	Feb01 3-0	Nov09 6-1	Sep14 2-1	Jan11 2-0 Apr09 0-3	Dec21 1-0		Dec28 4-1 Mar08 3-2	Dec07 4-2 Apr05 1-0	Sep28 5-0 Apr19 2-1	Nov23 2-2
KILMARNOCK	Jan18 0-2	Aug10 3-0 Mar15 0-1	Jan01 1-2 May03 3-2	Nov30 3-1 Mar29 1-2	Sep21 1-1	Dec21 1-4 Apr19 0-9	Nov02 2-2 Apr09 2-0	Oct05 1-1	Jan04 1-0	Aug24 1-0		Oct12 0-0 Mar01 3-0	Nov16 3-0 Feb08 5-0	Sep07 5-0
MONTROSE	Oct19 1-0 Apr26 2-1	Nov02 1-1 Mar29 1-0	Sep25 2-2	Nov09 3-1	Nov30 0-0 Mar25 1-1	Sep14 0-3 May03 0-0	Aug31 1-0	Mar11 1-2 Mar22 1-1	Aug10 1-2	Oct05 4-1	Dec14		Jan04 1-1 Mar08 2-1	Jan18 3-1 Apr12 0-1
MORTON	Nov02 1-4 Apr09 1-0	Jan18 2-0	Oct05 2-2 Mar01 0-1	Dec14 2-2 Feb22 3-2	Nov09 4-3 May03 3-2	Aug31 0-0 Mar25 1-0	Dec28 0-3 Apr05 2-2	Oct19 2-3	Sep23 2-3 Apr26 2-0	Nov30 0-1	Sep14 3-0	Aug17 1-2		Jan11 3-1
PARTICK T	Mar05 1-0	Sep14 1-2	Feb01 2-2	Oct19 1-3 May03 2-2	Mar08 1-2 Apr09 2-2	Dec14 1-2 Apr19 2-2	Nov30 0-3 Mar25 0-1	Oct05 0-3	Sep21 1-2 Mar29 0-2	Nov09 1-1 Apr26 2-0	Oct26 2-0	Aug10 1-1 Mar15 3-3		

Skipper Danny McGrain hugs St Mirren's Hugh Abercromby after Celtic pulled off an amazing last match of the season victory to rob Hearts of the championship. Hearts were beaten 2-0 by Dundee and lost out on goal difference.

DIVISION 2

DIVISION 2	ALBION R	ARBROATH	BERWICK R	COWDENBEATH	DUNFERMLINE A	E STIRLING	MEADOWBANK T	QUEEN OF SOUTH	QUEEN'S PARK	RAITH R	ST JOHNSTONE	STENHOUSEMUIR	STIRLING A	STRANRAER
ALBION R		Oct12 0-0	Jan11 0-0	Nov09 2-1	Mar31 0-3	Sep14 1-2 Apr29 2-1	Jan18 3-2 Apr26 0-2	Nov23 1-5 Mar25 2-2	Aug31 0-2 Mar29 1-1	Sep28 2-0	Dec14 2-4	Mar15 0-0 May06 0-1	Aug17 1-3 Apr08 0-2	Nov02 2-3
ARBROATH	Mar04 1-1 Apr05 2-0		Mar01 5-1	Sep14 0-5 Feb22 0-1	Aug10 3-3	Nov23 2-1	Aug17 3-0 Dec21 2-2	Feb01 2-2 Apr19 0-1	Oct26 1-0 Apr09 0-2	Dec14 2-2 Mar15 2-1	Aug31 1-0	Nov09 1-4	Oct19 1-0	Sep28 1-0
BERWICK R	Aug10 0-0 Mar08 1-2	Aug24 0-2 May03 0-4		Nov23 1-1	Dec21 4-4 Apr26 0-4	Sep28 1-1	Jan01 0-0	Dec14 0-1	Jan18 0-5	Oct12 4-3 Mar29 1-0	Feb01 3-1 Mar22 1-1	Sep14 1-1 Apr09 1-1	Oct26 1-0	Nov09 2-2 Mar04 4-0
COWDENBEATH	Sep07 3-0 Mar18 0-2	Nov16 1-0	Sep24 4-2 Apr22 1-0		Mar05 0-1	Nov02 1-1 Mar15 0-2	Aug10 3-1 May03 1-1	Apr29 3-3	Oct05 2-2 Apr05 1-0	Aug24 1-4	Mar11 1-3 Apr09 2-1	Oct19 2-0	Nov30 1-2 Apr26 0-1	Mar25 5-0
DUNFERMLINE A	Oct26 6-0 Apr12 4-0	Mar22 0-0 Apr22 2-0	Aug17 4-2	Aug31 3-2		Jan18 2-1 Apr19 4-0	Oct12 1-1	Nov09 2-1	Jan11 3-2 Mar08 0-0	Sep14 3-3	Nov23 4-0 Apr16 0-0	Sep28 3-2	Feb01 2-3	Dec14 1-0 Mar29 4-1
E STIRLING	Nov16 5-1	Sep21 1-2 Apr26 1-1	Mar18 0-2 Apr02 4-2	Feb01 2-1	Oct19 0-4		Oct05 1-3 Mar22 2-3	Aug17 0-0	Sep07 2-1	Oct26 0-2	Mar05 1-3	Aug31 0-2 Mar08 2-0	Dec28 0-2 Mar08 1-0	Jan11 3-1 Apr09 1-2
MEADOWBANK T	Oct19 1-1	Apr15 2-1	Aug31 0-3 Apr19 3-1	Dec28 1-1	Mar18 2-2 Apr08 4-0	Dec14 2-1		Oct26 0-0 Mar29 1-0	Feb01 2-1 Mar15 1-1	Nov09 6-0 Mar05 0-3	Sep28 4-1	Nov23 3-1 May03 1-0	Feb19 1-2 Mar08 4-1	Sep14 1-1
QUEEN OF SOUTH	Sep21 5-2 Mar15 2-1	Nov02 2-0	Oct05 2-0 Mar08 3-0	Oct12 6-1 Apr05 3-1	Sep07 0-0 Apr12 3-1	Jan04 2-1	Feb08 1-0		Feb05 0-1 Mar11 0-3	Jan18 2-0	Feb19 2-1	Aug10 2-0	Nov16 3-1	Aug31 1-1 Apr26 1-2
QUEEN'S PARK	Jan01 2-0	Feb08 1-2	Oct19 2-0 Apr12 5-0	Dec14 2-0 Apr19 0-1	Aug24 3-1	Nov09 1-0 Feb22 4-2	Nov02 2-1	Sep28 1-2		Nov23 0-0	Sep14 1-1 Mar01 2-0	Dec21 3-2 Apr04 1-1	Mar22 1-0 Apr01 2-0	Aug10 2-1 Dec28 2-1
RAITH R	Feb04 1-0 May03 5-2	Oct05 2-1	Feb18 3-1	Jan11 0-1 Mar22 2-1	Nov16 1-2 Feb15 3-3	Mar25 1-4 Apr05 2-0	Sep07 1-1	Oct19 0-1 Apr09 0-2	Sep24 3-1 Apr26 2-1		Aug10 0-2	Nov02 9-2	Aug31 1-1	Mar11 1-0 Apr22 4-1
ST JOHNSTONE	Oct05 7-1 Apr19 1-0	Jan04 1-0 Mar29 4-1	Nov02 3-2	Aug17 0-0	Sep24 1-2 Mar15 1-1	Oct12 3-0 Apr12 1-3	Apr01 1-0 May03 1-1	Aug24 0-3	Nov16 1-0	Dec28 4-1 Mar08 1-3		Mar25 1-3	Sep07 2-0 Mar18 0-2	Jan18 4-0
STENHOUSEMUIR	Aug24 4-2	Sep07 1-1 Mar18 2-1	Nov16 3-1	Jan18 1-0 Mar29 2-1	Mar12 1-1 Apr29 0-0	Apr22 4-3	Sep24 1-5	Mar22 1-2 Apr02 1-0	Aug17 4-0	Feb01 2-0 Apr12 2-0	Oct26 3-2 Apr26 0-0		Oct05 2-5	Oct12 1-2
STIRLING A	Dec21 2-0	Jan18 1-0 Apr12 1-0	Mar24 2-0 Apr05 2-2	Sep28 0-0	Nov02 0-1 May03 3-2	Aug10 0-1	Aug24 1-2	Sep14 2-2 Apr22 3-1	Oct12 0-0	Apr15 1-1 Apr19 3-1	Nov09 0-2	Dec14 1-0 Mar04 4-0		Nov23 3-0 Mar15 2-2
STRANRAER	Feb01 0-2 Mar22 2-3	Dec07 1-6 Mar08 1-5	Sep07 2-0	Oct26 1-2 Apr12 1-1	Oct05 1-3	Aug24 0-1	Nov16 0-1 Feb15 1-2	Jan01 0-2	May03 2-1	Aug17 3-2	Oct19 0-2 Apr05 1-2	Feb05 2-0 Apr19 0-1	Sep25 3-2	

PREMIER DIVISION FINAL TABLE

	P	W	D	L	F	A	Pts
Celtic	36	20	10	6	67	38	50
Hearts	36	20	10	6	59	33	50
Dundee U	36	18	11	7	59	31	47
Aberdeen	36	16	12	8	62	31	44
Rangers	36	13	9	14	53	45	35
Dundee	36	14	7	15	45	51	35
St Mirren	36	13	5	18	42	63	31
Hibernian	36	11	6	19	49	63	28
Motherwell	36	7	6	23	33	66	20
Clydebank	36	6	8	22	29	77	20

DIVISION 1 FINAL TABLE

	P	W	D	L	F	A	Pts
Hamilton A	39	24	8	7	77	44	56
Falkirk	39	17	11	11	57	39	45
Kilmarnock	39	18	8	13	62	49	44
Forfar A	39	17	10	12	51	43	44
East Fife	39	14	15	10	54	46	43
Dumbarton	39	16	11	12	59	52	43
Morton	39	14	11	14	57	63	39
Partick T	39	10	16	13	53	64	36
Airdrie	39	12	11	16	51	50	35
Brechin C	39	13	9	17	58	64	35
Clyde	39	9	17	13	49	59	35
Montrose	39	10	14	15	43	54	34
Ayr U	39	10	11	18	41	60	31
Alloa	39	6	14	19	49	74	26

DIVISION 2 FINAL TABLE

	P	W	D	L	F	A	Pts
Dunfermline A	39	23	11	5	91	47	57
Queen of South	39	23	9	7	71	36	55
Meadowbank T	39	19	11	9	68	45	49
Queen's Park	39	19	8	12	61	39	46
Stirling A	39	18	8	13	57	53	44
St Johnstone	39	18	6	15	63	55	42
Stenhousemuir	39	16	8	15	55	63	40
Arbroath	39	15	9	15	56	50	39
Raith R	39	15	7	17	67	65	37
Cowdenbeath	39	14	9	16	52	53	37
E Stirling	39	11	6	22	49	69	28
Berwick R	39	7	11	21	45	80	25
Albion R	39	8	8	23	38	86	24
Stranraer	39	9	5	25	41	83	23

SFA Cup

1st Round
Dec 6	Albion R 2	Arbroath 1
Dec 6	Ayr U 3	Annan A 1
Dec 13	Forres Mechanic 0	Berwick R 1
Dec 6	Inverness C 2	Alloa 2
Dec 6	Peterhead 1	E Stirling 0
Dec 6	Stirling A 3	Cowdenbeath ..0

Replays
Dec 13	Alloa 0	Inverness C 1

2nd Round
Feb 4	Albion R 1	Whitehill Welfare 2
Jan 19	Inverness C 5	Spartans 0
Jan 26	Raith R 4	Vale of Leithen ..0
Jan 10	Rothes 1	Peterhead 3
Jan 26	St Johnstone ..4	Queen's Park ...1
Jan 26	Stenhousemuir ..0	Berwick R 0
Jan 21	Stirling A 0	Meadowbank T .1
Jan 10	Stranraer 1	Ayr U 1

Replays
Jan 21	Ayr U 2	Stranraer 0
Jan 28	Berwick R 2	Stenhousemuir .0

3rd Round
Feb 1	Aberdeen 2	Celtic 2
Jan 31	Berwick R 0	Morton 2
Jan 31	Brechin C 2	Dumbarton ...2
Feb 3	Dundee 2	East Fife 2
Jan 31	Dundee U 1	Airdrie 1
Feb 3	Falkirk 0	Clydebank 0
Jan 31	Hearts 0	Kilmarnock ...0
Jan 31	Hibernian 2	Dunfermline A ..0
Feb 3	Meadowbank T ..2	Ayr U 0
Jan 31	Montrose 1	Forfar A 2
Feb 3	Motherwell 3	Partick T 1
Jan 31	Peterhead 2	Clyde 0
Jan 31	Queen of South .0	Raith R 1
Jan 31	Rangers 0	Hamilton A ...1
Feb 7	St Johnstone ...4	Whitehill Welfare 0
Jan 31	St Mirren 3	Inverness C 0

Replays
Feb 4	Celtic 0	Aberdeen 0
Feb 4	Dumbarton 2	Brechin C 3
Feb 4	Kilmarnock 1	Hearts 1
Feb 9	Airdrie 1	Dundee U 2
Feb 9	Aberdeen 0	Celtic 1
	played at Dens Park	
Feb 9	Clydebank 3	Falkirk 1
Feb 9	East Fife 1	Dundee 4
Feb 9	Kilmarnock 1	Hearts 3

4th Round
Feb 21	Brechin C 0	Dundee U 1
Feb 21	Clydebank 1	Hibernian 0
Feb 21	Dundee 1	Meadowbank T .1
Feb 21	Hamilton A 1	Motherwell 2
Feb 21	Hearts 1	Celtic 0
Feb 21	Morton 2	St Mirren 3
Feb 21	Raith R 2	Peterhead 2
Feb 21	St Johnstone ...1	Forfar A 2

Replays
Feb 25	Meadowbank T ..1	Dundee 1
Feb 25	Peterhead 3	Raith R 3
Mar 2	Dundee 2	Meadowbank T .0
Mar 2	Peterhead 0	Raith R 3
	played at Gayfield Park	

PREMIER

	ABERDEEN	CELTIC	CLYDEBANK	DUNDEE	DUNDEE U	FALKIRK	HAMILTON A	HEARTS	HIBERNIAN	MOTHERWELL	RANGERS	ST MIRREN
ABERDEEN		Nov26 1-1 Mar14 1-0	Nov19 5-0 Apr11 1-1	Aug30 2-0 Jan01 1-1	Oct11 2-0 Feb28 2-1	Dec03 1-0 May09 3-1	Aug16 2-0 Dec27 0-0	Sep13 0-1 Jan21 1-1	Aug13 4-0 Dec13 1-0	Oct04 2-2 Feb07 1-1	Nov22 1-0 May02 1-1	Nov08 0-0 Mar28 0-1
CELTIC	Aug23 1-1 Dec20 1-1		Oct29 6-0 Mar21 3-0	Aug09 1-0 Dec06 2-0	Nov15 1-0 Apr18 1-1	Nov22 4-2 May02 1-2	Sep06 4-1 Jan03 8-3	Sep13 2-0 Feb14 1-1	Oct08 5-1 Mar07 1-0	Sep20 3-1 Apr04 3-1	Nov01 1-1 Apr04 3-0	Oct14 2-0 Feb07 3-0
CLYDEBANK	Sep20 1-3 Jan27 0-5	Aug16 0-1 Dec27 1-1		Oct04 0-2 Feb07 1-1	Aug13 1-0 Dec13 1-2	Aug30 1-4 Jan01 2-1	Oct11 0-3 Feb28 2-3	Nov08 0-3 Mar28 1-1	Dec03 0-3 May09 1-2	Nov22 1-0 May02 0-0	Nov15 1-0 Apr18 0-3	Oct25 2-1 Mar24 2-1
DUNDEE	Nov01 0-2 Apr04 1-1	Oct11 0-3 Feb28 4-1	Nov29 3-3 Apr25 4-1		Sep06 0-2 Mar10 1-1	Oct25 3-0 Mar25 4-0	Dec03 3-3 May09 1-2	Sep27 0-0 Jan24 7-2	Nov08 3-0 Dec27 0-0	Nov15 1-1 Apr18 3-1	Sep20 1-0 Mar17 1-2	Aug13 2-1 Dec13 6-3
DUNDEE U	Aug09 2-1 Dec06 0-0	Sep13 2-2 Mar21 3-2	Oct18 2-0 Mar07 1-1	Nov08 0-3 Mar28 1-1		Oct04 2-0 Feb07 2-1	Nov19 3-0 Apr28 2-1	Aug23 1-0 Dec20 3-1	Nov22 1-0 Feb14 2-1	Oct08 4-0 Mar21 2-0	Oct29 0-0 Jan06 0-1	Aug30 3-0 Jan06 2-0
FALKIRK	Oct08 3-3 Feb21 0-3	Sep27 0-1 Jan24 1-2	Nov01 0-1 Apr04 0-0	Aug23 0-3 Apr21 0-0	Nov29 0-1 Apr25 1-2		Sep13 0-0 Feb25 0-2	Oct29 2-0 Mar21 0-0	Sep06 1-5 Jan03 1-3	Aug09 1-1 Dec06 1-2	Oct18 1-1 Mar07 1-2	Nov19 0-1 Apr14 0-0
HAMILTON A	Oct25 0-1 Mar21 0-2	Nov08 0-1 Mar28 2-3	Sep06 0-1 Dec06 1-0	Oct08 0-3 Feb14 1-1	Sep20 1-5 Apr14 0-0	Nov15 1-2 Apr18 1-0		Oct18 1-3 Mar07 0-1	Aug30 1-4 Feb07 4-2	Aug23 0-3 Jan01 0-0	Aug23 1-2 Dec20 2-0	Nov22 1-1 May02 1-0
HEARTS	Nov15 2-1 Apr18 1-1	Dec03 1-0 May09 0-1	Sep06 2-1 Jan03 3-0	Nov22 3-1 May02 1-3	Oct25 2-2 May11 1-1	Aug16 1-0 Dec27 4-0	Aug13 1-0 Dec13 7-0		Nov01 1-1 Apr04 2-1	Sep20 4-0 Feb25 1-1	Oct04 1-1 Feb07 2-5	Oct11 0-0 Feb14 1-0
HIBERNIAN	Oct18 1-1 Mar07 1-1	Nov19 0-1 Apr11 1-4	Oct08 1-3 Feb14 4-1	Oct29 0-2 Mar21 2-2	Sep27 2-1 Jan24 0-2	Nov08 1-3 Mar28 2-0	Nov29 1-3 Apr25 2-2	Sep30 1-3 Jan06 2-2		Sep23 0-0 Dec20 0-1	Aug09 2-1 Dec06 0-0	Sep13 1-1 Jan10 1-0
MOTHERWELL	Nov29 0-1 Apr25 0-2	Aug13 0-4 Dec13 1-1	Sep27 0-1 Jan24 2-3	Sep13 0-0 Jan27 1-1	Dec03 0-2 May09 1-2	Oct11 2-2 Feb28 3-2	Nov01 1-1 Apr04 1-2	Nov19 2-3 Apr15 0-1	Oct25 4-1 Mar24 1-0		Sep06 0-2 Jan06 0-1	Dec03 1-1 Dec27 1-2
RANGERS	Sep27 2-0 Jan24 0-0	Aug31 1-0 Jan10 2-0	Sep13 4-0 Jan10 5-0	Nov19 2-1 Apr14 2-0	Sep16 2-3 Dec27 4-0	Aug13 1-0 Mar14 2-0	Jan17 2-0 May29 0-1	Nov29 3-0 Apr25 1-1	Oct11 3-0 Mar28 1-0	Nov08 0-1		Dec03 2-0 May09 1-0
ST MIRREN	Sep06 1-1 Feb25 1-0	Nov29 0-0 Apr25 1-3	Aug23 1-1 Dec20 3-1	Oct18 0-1 Mar07 0-1	Nov01 0-1 Apr04 2-1	Sep20 1-0 Jan27 1-0	Sep27 0-1 Jan24 0-1	Aug09 1-1 Dec06 0-0	Nov15 0-1 Apr18 1-1	Oct29 0-1 Mar21 1-1	Oct08 1-3 Feb14 1-3	

DIVISION 1

	AIRDRIE	BRECHIN C	CLYDE	DUMBARTON	DUNFERMLINE A	EAST FIFE	FORFAR A	KILMARNOCK	MONTROSE	MORTON	PARTICK T	QUEEN OF SOUTH
AIRDRIE		Aug13 4-0 Dec13 3-1	Nov05 0-2 Apr11 3-2	Aug16 1-0 Dec27 1-0	Nov22 3-0 May02 2-1	Oct11 0-3 Mar14 0-0	Sep20 3-1 Feb24 3-1	Sep13 3-2 Apr18 4-3	Nov08 3-0 Mar28 4-1	Nov29 1-2 May09 1-0	Sep06 1-0 Jan03 1-1	Oct04 1-3 Feb28
BRECHIN C	Oct08 1-2 Mar07 0-2		Sep30 2-1 Feb14 0-1	Nov01 3-1 Apr04 1-2	Sep13 1-4 Feb24 0-2	Oct29 2-2 Apr11 3-2	Aug30 0-1 Jan01 1-1	Sep20 2-2 Feb17 1-0	Aug09 0-0 Dec06 2-3	Aug23 2-5 Dec20 1-3	Nov22 0-1 May02 1-1	Oct18 2-1 Mar11 1-2
CLYDE	Sep16 1-1 Feb21 1-0	Nov29 4-1 May09 2-1		Sep20 2-1 Jan24 1-2	Oct11 3-3 Mar14 0-1	Aug16 2-3 Dec27 0-1	Oct25 0-1 Apr18 1-2	Nov22 1-2 May02 0-1	Sep06 3-3 Feb25 0-0	Oct04 0-0 Feb28 1-1	Nov08 3-3 Mar28 1-1	Aug13 2-1 Dec13 2-1
DUMBARTON	Oct18 2-1 Mar21 2-2	Sep06 3-1 Mar31 1-1	Nov15 1-1 Apr25		Aug13 0-1 Dec13 1-2	Oct29 2-1 Feb07 1-1	Aug23 3-2 Dec20 0-2	Oct29 1-0 Apr11 2-0	Sep13 2-1 Feb21 1-0	Nov08 0-1 Mar28 3-0	Oct04 2-2 Feb28 2-3	Nov29 1-1 May09 0-0
DUNFERMLINE A	Sep27 0-0 Feb07 1-1	Oct25 4-0 Apr18 0-2	Aug23 2-0 Feb10 2-0	Oct08 0-1 Mar07 1-0		Aug30 2-4 Jan01 1-1	Aug09 1-0 Dec06 0-1	Nov01 1-0 Apr04 2-0	Sep30 1-0 Mar03 1-2	Oct18 1-1 Mar21 1-2	Sep16 2-0 Feb21 2-1	Nov15 2-2 May09 1-0
EAST FIFE	Aug23 1-1 Dec20 0-0	Sep16 0-1 Jan27 2-2	Oct18 0-0 Mar21 1-1	Nov22 2-1 May02 2-1	Nov08 0-0 Mar28 1-1		Sep30 1-2 Feb14 0-0	Aug09 1-4 Dec06 2-1	Oct08 2-2 Mar07 3-1	Sep06 1-0 Jan07 2-1	Sep20 1-0 Jan24 1-1	Oct25 1-1 Apr18 5-0
FORFAR A	Nov15 3-1 Apr25 1-0	Nov08 1-0 Mar28 0-4	Sep13 2-1 Mar31 3-1	Oct11 3-5 Mar17 0-3	Oct04 3-3 Feb28 1-1	Nov29 1-1 May09		Aug16 3-1 Dec27 1-1	Aug09 3-0 Apr11 4-1	Sep27 2-2 Feb07 3-3	Aug13 1-9 Dec13 1-2	Sep06 1-1 Jan03 1-1
KILMARNOCK	Oct25 2-0 Jan24 2-1	Nov15 0-1 Apr25 1-1	Sep27 0-0 Feb07 0-1	Sep16 2-1 Jan27 2-1	Sep06 1-2 Jan03 2-2	Oct04 1-1 Feb21 3-1	Oct18 3-0 Mar21 2-0		Aug23 3-0 Dec20 1-0	Aug13 2-2 Dec13 2-0	Nov29 3-2 May09 1-0	Nov08 3-2 Apr11 2-2
MONTROSE	Aug30 1-2 Jan01 0-1	Oct04 0-3 Feb28 1-1	Nov01 2-1 Apr04 2-1	Oct25 0-3 Apr18 2-0	Nov29 1-0 May09 1-0	Aug13 1-0 Dec13 2-1	Sep16 1-1 Feb10 0-1	Oct11 0-1 Mar14 1-1		Nov15 0-3 Apr25 1-4	Aug16 3-1 Dec27 0-0	Sep27 3-4 Feb07 3-0
MORTON	Sep20 2-1 Feb14 2-1	Oct11 2-3 Mar14 3-1	Aug30 3-0 Dec06 4-2	Aug09 0-3 Jan01 3-2	Aug16 0-0 Dec27 4-1	Sep20 1-1 Apr04 2-2	Nov22 0-0 May02 6-1	Oct08 2-0 Mar11	Sep20 0-2 Jan24		Oct25 1-2 Apr18 1-2	Sep06 5-2 Jan01 2-0
PARTICK T	Nov01 2-0 Apr04 2-2	Sep27 1-0 Feb07 0-0	Aug30 0-0 Dec06 0-2	Aug09 1-1 Jan01 0-2	Oct29 0-1 Apr11 4-0	Nov15 3-3 Feb21 2-0	Oct08 1-1 Mar03 2-1	Sep30 1-0 Mar21 2-0	Oct18 5-0 Feb10 1-3	Sep13 2-5		Aug23 1-1 Jan27 3-0
QUEEN OF SOUTH	Aug09 0-0 Dec05 0-1	Aug16 1-1 Dec27 2-0	Oct08 1-3 Mar11 4-1	Sep30 1-1 Feb14 0-4	Sep20 1-1 Jan24 1-2	Sep13 0-5 Feb21 0-1	Nov01 1-1 Apr04 1-4	Aug30 0-3 Jan01 1-2	Nov22 2-0 May02 0-0	Oct29 2-3 Apr11 2-3	Oct11 1-1 Mar14 0-1	

Season 1986-87

5th Round
Mar 14 Clydebank . . . .0 Dundee 4
Mar 14 Dundee U . . . .2 Forfar A 2
Mar 14 Hearts . . . . . . .1 Motherwell 1
Mar 14 Raith R . . . . . .0 St Mirren 2

Replay
Mar 17 Motherwell . . .0 Hearts 1
Mar 24 Forfar A . . . . .0 Dundee U 2

Semi-finals
Apr 11 Dundee . . . . . .2 Dundee U 3
    played at Tynecastle
Apr 11 Hearts . . . . . . .1 St Mirren 2
    played at Hampden Park

Final
May 16 Dundee . . . . . .0 St Mirren 1
    played at Hampden Park

Ally McCoist, Rangers' leading scorer in another title success.

> League Cup results for 1986-87 are detailed on page 213.

League Cup results for 1986-87 are detailed on page 213.

DIVISION 2

Column key: ALB = Albion R, ALL = Alloa, ARB = Arbroath, AYR = Ayr U, BER = Berwick R, COW = Cowdenbeath, EST = E Stirling, MEA = Meadowbank T, QPK = Queen's Park, RAI = Raith R, STJ = St Johnstone, STE = Stenhousemuir, STA = Stirling A, STR = Stranraer

	ALB	ALL	ARB	AYR	BER	COW	EST	MEA	QPK	RAI	STJ	STE	STA	STR
ALBION R	—	Aug30 1-2	Sep06 3-0 / Mar07 0-1	Sep27 3-2 / Mar21 0-1	Oct04 2-0 / Apr04 2-1	Nov15 4-1 / May09 0-1	Feb24 1-1	Mar10 1-1	Jan01 0-0	Nov01 2-4	Nov22 0-2 / Apr18 1-2	Aug16 1-4 / Mar03 3-4	Feb10 1-1	Oct18 1-1 / Apr25 2-0
ALLOA	Nov29 1-3 / Mar28 0-1	—	Nov15 2-3 / Apr11 0-3	Aug23 1-0	Jan24 1-2	Aug16 2-1 / Feb28 1-0	Nov01 1-0	Feb10 0-0 / May09 0-1	Oct04 2-1	Oct18 2-2 / Feb14 2-4	Sep20 3-3	Sep06 2-0 / Mar21 0-1	Jan01 2-1 / Apr25 2-1	Jan28 2-0
ARBROATH	Jan03 1-1	Aug09 2-4	—	Nov29 2-5 / Feb14 2-0	Feb03 3-0 / May02 1-1	Jan17 0-1	Oct04 0-0 / Apr04 0-3	Sep27 1-2	Nov08 4-1	Dec20 2-1 / Jan31 1-4	Sep13 1-1 / Feb28 1-1	Aug23 3-1 / Mar21 0-1	Oct18 0-1 / Apr18 0-1	Nov01 1-1
AYR U	Jan24 3-1 / Feb21 2-0	Nov22 1-0	Aug30 2-1	—	Sep06 4-2 / Apr18 2-0	Dec13 1-3	Sep20 2-1 / Mar07 0-1	Oct25 2-0	Aug09 1-0	Nov08 3-3 / Apr25 0-0	Dec27 0-2 / Mar14 3-1	Oct11 1-0 / Apr04 3-1	Jan01 4-2 / May09 2-3	
BERWICK R	Feb07 0-1 / Mar14 1-1	Sep27 1-2	Oct11 2-0	Jan03 0-2	—	Oct25 1-3 / Apr25 1-6	Aug23 2-2 / Mar07 0-1	Sep13 1-1 / Apr11 0-1	Dec27 2-1 / Mar28 1-0	Feb10 1-0	Dec16 1-2	Nov15 2-3	Aug16 0-2	Nov29 3-0 / Feb14 2-3
COWDENBEATH	Aug09 0-2	Nov08 1-0	Sep20 2-0 / Mar28 1-3	Oct18 3-1 / Apr11 1-3	Jan06 3-1	—	Nov29 1-1 / Feb21 1-1	Oct04 0-2 / May02 1-1	Jan31 1-2 / Mar14 3-3	Sep13 1-2 / Mar07 2-2	Feb03 4-3	Nov01 4-1	Aug23 0-2	Jan24 2-1
E STIRLING	Oct11 1-2 / Apr11 1-0	Dec27 1-0 / May02 0-1	Feb07 1-2	Jan28 1-2	Nov22 0-1	Sep30 0-1	—	Dec13 4-4 / Mar10 2-2	Oct25 2-0	Sep27 0-5	Aug16 1-1 / Mar25 2-2	Jan01 0-1	Nov15 1-1	Sep06 0-0
MEADOWBANK T	Sep20 5-0 / Feb28 3-0	Oct11 4-0	Jan24 2-1 / Mar14 2-1	Dec20 2-2	Dec30 1-0	Feb07 1-0	Oct18 1-0	—	Sep06 0-0	Aug23 0-1 / Apr04 1-0	Nov15 1-1 / Apr25 2-1	Nov29 5-0	Nov01 0-1 / Apr18 2-1	Aug16 1-0 / Mar17 4-2
QUEEN'S PARK	Sep13 1-2 / Feb21 0-0	Feb07 1-1 / Apr18 1-1	Aug16 5-1 / Apr25 2-0	Nov15 1-1 / Feb28 0-0	Nov01 3-1	Oct11 2-2	Dec20 2-1 / Mar21 1-3	Jan06 2-2	—	Nov29 2-2	Jan24 0-0	Oct18 0-0	Sep20 0-0	Aug23 3-2 / Apr04 1-1
RAITH R	Dec27 2-0	Dec17 0-0	Oct25 3-0 / Mar17 2-2	Aug16 5-0	Sep20 1-1	Jan01 2-2	Jan24 2-0 / Mar21 3-2	Nov22 2-3	Aug30 2-2 / Mar28 1-1	—	Oct11 2-2 / Dec13 1-1	Feb07 1-0 / Apr11 1-1	Sep06 0-0 / Feb28 2-2	Nov15 2-1
ST JOHNSTONE	Aug23 1-2	Mar07 1-3 / Mar17 2-1	Jan01 2-0	Nov01 2-2	Oct18 3-2 / Feb24 2-0	Sep06 1-0 / Mar21 1-0	Nov08 3-0	Aug09 1-5 / Apr11 0-2	Sep27 3-0	May02 1-1	—	Dec20 1-0 / Apr25 0-1	Nov29 2-1	Oct04 0-3 / Mar28 0-1
STENHOUSEMUIR	Nov08 0-0 / May02 2-3	Jan31 2-1	Nov22 0-1	Feb11 0-4	Aug09 0-0 / May09 3-1	Dec27 0-1 / Apr18 1-0	Sep13 3-2 / Feb14 3-1	Aug30 0-1 / Mar14 0-2	Dec13 0-1	Oct04 1-2	Oct25 1-1	—	Jan24 1-1 / Mar28 1-2	Sep20 1-3 / Mar07 0-0
STIRLING A	Oct25 0-2 / Mar14 0-0	Sep13 1-2	Dec13 2-2	Oct04 0-1	Nov08 2-2 / Apr18 2-2	Nov22 4-1 / Feb21 2-1	Aug09 3-0 / May02 1-2	Dec27 2-0	Mar07 1-0	Feb03 1-1	Aug30 1-0 / Mar17 4-1	Sep27 1-1	—	Feb24 2-0 / Apr04 1-1
STRANRAER	Dec13 1-0 / Apr04 1-2	Oct25 0-1 / May02 1-3	Dec27 1-0 / Feb28 0-1	Sep13 0-0 / Mar21 0-0	Aug30 2-1 / Feb14 1-2	Sep27 1-1 / May09 1-4	Jan03 0-3 / Apr11 0-3	Nov08 2-0	Nov22 2-3	Aug09 1-1	Mar11 1-1	Feb04 1-1	Oct11 1-1	—

PREMIER DIVISION FINAL TABLE

	P	W	D	L	F	A	Pts
Rangers	44	31	7	6	85	23	69
Celtic	44	27	9	8	90	41	63
Dundee U	44	24	12	8	66	36	60
Aberdeen	44	21	16	7	63	29	58
Hearts	44	21	14	9	64	43	56
Dundee	44	18	12	14	74	57	48
St Mirren	44	12	12	20	36	51	36
Motherwell	44	11	12	21	43	64	34
Hibernian	44	10	13	21	44	70	33
Falkirk	44	8	10	26	31	70	26
Clydebank	44	6	12	26	35	93	24
Hamilton A	44	6	9	29	39	93	21

DIVISION 1 FINAL TABLE

	P	W	D	L	F	A	Pts
Morton	44	24	9	11	88	56	57
Dunfermline A	44	23	10	11	61	41	56
Dumbarton	44	23	7	14	67	52	53
East Fife	44	15	21	8	68	55	51
Airdrie	44	20	11	13	58	46	51
Kilmarnock	44	17	11	16	62	53	45
Forfar A	44	14	15	15	61	63	43
Partick T	44	12	15	17	49	54	39
Clyde	44	11	16	17	48	56	38
Queen of South	44	11	12	21	50	71	34
Brechin C	44	11	10	23	44	72	32
Montrose	44	9	11	24	37	74	29

DIVISION 2 FINAL TABLE

	P	W	D	L	F	A	Pts
Meadowbank T	39	23	9	7	69	38	55
Raith R	39	16	20	3	73	44	52
Stirling A	39	20	12	7	55	33	52
Ayr U	39	22	8	9	70	49	52
St Johnstone	39	16	13	10	59	49	45
Alloa	39	17	7	15	48	50	41
Cowdenbeath	39	16	8	15	59	55	40
Albion R	39	15	9	15	48	51	39
Queen's Park	39	9	19	11	48	49	37
Stranraer	39	9	11	19	41	59	29
Arbroath	39	11	7	21	46	66	29
Stenhousemuir	39	10	9	20	37	58	29
E Stirling	39	6	11	22	33	56	23
Berwick R	39	8	7	24	40	69	23

SFA Cup

1st Round

Dec 5	Albion R 1	St Johnstone ...1
Dec 12	Inverness C ...1	E Stirling 1
Dec 5	Montrose 0	Ayr U 2
Dec 5	Stirling A 1	Cowdenbeath ...2
Dec 5	Threave R 0	Stranraer 6
Dec 5	Vale of Leithen 2	Brechin C 3

Replays

Dec 8	St Johnstone ..2	Albion R 0
Dec 21	E Stirling 2	Inverness C 1

2nd Round

Jan 10	Alloa 0	Cowdenbeath ...1
Jan 9	Berwick R 0	Brechin C 1
Jan 9	Buckie T 2	E Stirling 3
Jan 9	Fraserburgh ..2	St Johnstone ..5
Jan 9	Gala Fairydean 3	Civil Service 0
Jan 9	Queen's Park ..2	Ayr U 3
Jan 9	Stenhousemuir 1	Arbroath 1
Jan 9	Stranraer 6	Keith 2

Replays

Jan 12	Arbroath 1	Stenhousemuir .1
Jan 18	Arbroath 1	Stenhousemuir .0
	played at Muirton Park	

3rd Round

Jan 30	Arbroath 0	Dundee U 7
Jan 30	Celtic 1	Stranraer 0
Jan 30	Clyde 0	Cowdenbeath ...0
Jan 30	Dumbarton ...0	Hibernian 0
Jan 30	Dundee 0	Brechin C 0
Jan 30	Dunfermline A .1	Ayr U 1
Jan 30	East Fife 1	Airdrie 2
Jan 30	Falkirk 1	Hearts 3
Feb 3	Forfar A 1	Partick T 1
Jan 30	Gala Fairydean 3	E Stirling 5
Jan 31	Hamilton A ...2	Meadowbank T .0
Jan 30	Motherwell ...0	Kilmarnock 0
Jan 30	Queen of South 1	Morton 2
Feb 8	Raith R 0	Rangers 0
Jan 30	St Johnstone ..0	Aberdeen 1
Jan 30	St Mirren 0	Clydebank 3

Replays

Feb 2	Hibernian 3	Dumbarton 0
Feb 3	Ayr U 0	Dunfermline A ..2
Feb 3	Brechin C 0	Dundee 3
Feb 3	Cowdenbeath .0	Clyde 1
Feb 3	Kilmarnock ...1	Motherwell 3
Feb 10	Partick T 3	Forfar A 0
Feb 10	Rangers 4	Raith R 1

4th Round

Feb 20	Airdrie 0	Dundee U 2
Feb 21	Celtic 0	Hibernian 0
Feb 20	Clydebank 2	Partick T 2
Feb 20	Dundee 2	Motherwell 0
Feb 20	Dunfermline A .2	Rangers 0
Feb 20	E Stirling 2	Clyde 3
Feb 20	Hamilton A ...0	Aberdeen 2
Feb 20	Hearts 2	Morton 0

Replays

Feb 23	Partick T 4	Clydebank 1
Feb 23	Hibernian 0	Celtic 1

PREMIER

	ABERDEEN	CELTIC	DUNDEE	DUNDEE U	DUNFERMLINE A	FALKIRK	HEARTS	HIBERNIAN	MORTON	MOTHERWELL	RANGERS	ST MIRREN
ABERDEEN		Oct31 0-1 Mar19 0-1	Oct10 0-0 Feb27 1-0	Aug29 1-1 Jan02 0-0	Oct03 3-0 Jan16 1-0	Dec09 3-1 Mar23 2-0	Nov14 0-0 Apr23 0-0	Nov24 1-1 May04 0-2	Aug12 3-1 Jan23 4-0	Nov21 1-0 May07 0-0	Aug15 2-0 Feb06 1-2	Sep12 2-0 Dec16 2-1
CELTIC	Sep19 2-2 Dec19 0-0		Nov14 5-0 Apr23 3-0	Oct24 1-2 Mar26 0-0	Nov21 3-2 May07 1-0	Oct28 3-1 Mar05 2-0	Aug12 4-1 Dec12 2-2	Oct03 3-1 Jan16 2-1	Oct10 4-1 Feb27 2-0	Aug15 1-0 Feb06 1-0	Aug29 1-0 Jan02 2-0	Nov25 1-0 Apr05 2-0
DUNDEE	Aug08 1-1 Dec05 1-2	Oct07 1-1 Feb13 0-2		Oct03 1-1 Jan16 2-0	Aug29 5-0 Jan01 2-0	Sep19 3-1 Apr16 4-2	Nov21 2-1 Dec19 2-1	Oct28 1-0 Apr30 2-1	Sep19 1-0 Mar05 2-0	Jan06 0-1 Apr06 3-1	Aug06 0-3 Mar26 2-1	Aug22 2-0 Mar01 1-0
DUNDEE U	Oct17 0-0 Mar19 0-2	Sep05 0-0 Dec26 1-2	Nov28 1-3 Apr02 1-0		Nov14 1-0 2-2	Sep26 3-0 0-0	Nov18 0-3 May07 0-2	Sep12 1-2 Dec16 1-2	Aug15 3-1 Feb06 2-0	Aug12 1-1 Dec12 3-1	Oct10 1-0 Feb27 1-1	Oct31 2-3 May 5-1
DUNFERMLINE A	Nov28 0-3 Apr02 1-1	Aug22 2-1 Mar02 0-4	Oct17 1-0 Mar19 6-1	Oct06 0-1 Feb13 0-3		Nov17 0-0 Apr30 0-1	Sep26 3-3 Jan09 0-4	Aug08 4-1 Dec05 1-0	Sep19 1-1 Dec19 1-1	Sep05 0-1 Dec26 0-3	Oct28 1-0 Mar05 0-3	Nov07 1-1 Apr16 2-1
FALKIRK	Sep05 2-2 Dec26 0-2	Sep12 0-1 Dec22 0-2	Aug12 0-3 Dec12 0-6	Nov24 4-1 May04 1-2	Aug15 0-0 Feb06 1-0		Oct10 1-5 Feb27 2-0	Oct31 1-1 Mar12 0-1	Nov14 2-0 Apr23 0-0	Nov21 3-0 Mar19 2-0	Oct03 0-1 May07 0-5	Oct03 1-3 Jan16 3-0
HEARTS	Oct07 2-1 Feb13 2-2	Nov07 1-1 Apr16 3-1	Oct31 4-2 Mar30 2-0	Aug22 4-1 Feb03 1-1	Nov24 3-2 Apr13 2-1	Aug08 4-2 Dec05 1-0		Aug29 1-0 Jan02 0-0	Oct24 3-0 Dec16 2-0	Sep12 0-0 Jan16 1-1	Oct03 0-0 Apr30 1-1	Nov21 0-0 0-1
HIBERNIAN	Sep26 0-2 Jan09 0-0	Nov28 1-1 Apr02 0-2	Aug15 2-1 Feb06 2-1	Oct28 4-0 Mar05 0-0	Oct10 1-0 Feb27 2-0	Sep19 1-2 Dec19 2-0	Oct17 0-0 Mar19 0-0		Nov18 3-1 May07 1-1	Nov14 0-2 Apr23 0-2	Aug12 0-2 Dec12 0-0	Sep05 0-0 Dec26 0-0
MORTON	Nov07 0-4 Apr16 0-2	Aug08 0-4 Dec05 0-4	Sep12 4-3 Dec16 1-7	Nov21 0-1 Apr30 0-4	Oct31 1-2 Mar23 0-3	Oct07 4-1 Feb16 1-1	Sep05 1-2 Dec26 0-2	Aug22 3-3 Jan23		Oct03 1-1 Jan16 0-2	Nov24 0-3 Apr09 0-2	Oct17 0-0 Mar19 0-2
MOTHERWELL	Aug22 0-1 Jan23 2-1	Nov17 0-2 Apr30 0-1	Sep26 0-2 Jan09 3-3	Nov07 2-1 Apr16 4-2	Oct24 3-2 Mar26 3-2	Aug29 1-2 Jan01 0-0	Oct27 0-3 Mar08 0-1	Oct06 1-0 Feb13 0-2	Nov28 1-0 1-0		Sep19 0-1 Dec19 0-2	Aug08 2-1 Apr 2-1
RANGERS	Nov17 0-1 Apr30 0-1	Oct17 2-2 Mar20 1-2	Sep05 1-1 Dec26 0-2	Aug08 4-0 Dec05 0-2	Sep12 4-0 Dec15 2-2	Aug22 3-1 Jan23 3-1	Nov28 1-2 Apr02 1-2	Nov07 1-0 Apr16 1-1	Sep26 7-0 Jan09 5-0	Oct31 1-0 Mar12 1-0		Oct06 1-1 Feb13 4-0
ST MIRREN	Oct28 1-3 Mar05 0-0	Sep26 0-1 Jan09 1-1	Nov17 1-2 May07 1-0	Sep19 2-0 Dec19 0-1	Aug11 1-1 Dec12 4-1	Nov28 2-2 Apr02 0-0	Aug15 1-1 Feb06 0-6	Oct24 2-2 Mar26 1-1	Oct10 2-1 Jan02 0-0	Oct31 1-0 Feb27 0-0	Nov14 2-2 Apr23 0-3	

DIVISION 1

	AIRDRIE	CLYDE	CLYDEBANK	DUMBARTON	EAST FIFE	FORFAR A	HAMILTON A	KILMARNOCK	MEADOWBANK T	PARTICK T	QUEEN OF SOUTH	RAITH R
AIRDRIE		Sep15 4-3 Dec19 0-2	Oct31 0-2 Mar19 1-0	Aug22 0-1 Feb06 1-1	Aug08 1-0 Nov28 2-1	Sep28 0-3 Feb13 3-0	Aug29 0-3 Jan02 1-4	Sep19 3-2 Jan09 3-3	Oct17 0-0 Mar05 0-1	Nov11 3-1 Apr30 1-0	Oct24 5-1 Apr09 1-1	Nov21 3-0 Apr16 1-2
CLYDE	Oct20 1-0 Apr22 4-2		Sep12 5-1 Dec12 0-1	Aug08 5-0 Nov28 3-4	Aug22 3-3 Feb24 0-4	Oct07 2-2 Apr30 0-1	Oct24 0-3 Apr02 0-4	Nov21 0-0 Apr16 0-0	Sep19 4-1 Jan26 2-2	Aug29 2-3 Jan01 1-2	Sep29 2-3 Mar01 2-1	Oct31 3-2 Mar19 1-2
CLYDEBANK	Sep05 2-3 Dec26 1-1	Oct17 2-0 Mar05 1-2		Nov07 3-1 Mar26 1-0	Sep29 2-1 Mar01 2-0	Oct24 1-0 Apr09 3-2	Oct06 2-0 Apr30 3-1	Sep15 2-1 Dec19 3-1	Nov21 2-1 Apr16 1-0	Aug22 0-2 Nov28 0-3	Aug08 1-1 Feb06 1-1	Sep12 1-2 Jan09 3-1
DUMBARTON	Oct10 0-0 Apr02 0-1	Oct03 1-1 Feb27 0-1	Aug29 1-1 Jan02 1-3		Nov14 1-1 Apr23 0-0	Sep12 1-1 Dec12 0-1	Oct31 1-3 Mar19 1-1	Aug15 2-3 Jan23 0-1	Aug11 4-2 Dec05 0-1	Oct20 2-2 Apr22 1-2	Sep26 2-2 Jan16 1-2	Oct27 1-3 May07 3-0
EAST FIFE	Oct03 1-3 Feb27 3-1	Oct10 0-2 Apr09 2-0	Oct28 1-2 May07 1-1	Sep19 1-2 Jan09 3-4		Oct20 2-3 Mar12 4-0	Nov21 0-1 Apr16 1-1	Aug12 2-1 Dec05 2-1	Aug15 3-3 Feb06 2-1	Oct31 2-1 Mar19 2-0	Sep12 1-1 Dec12 2-2	Aug29 2-1 Jan02 1-2
FORFAR A	Oct27 4-4 May07 3-0	Aug11 3-5 Dec05 4-2	Aug15 3-0 Jan27 2-2	Oct17 0-2 Mar05 4-0	Sep15 4-0 Dec19 1-1		Sep19 1-1 Jan09 1-1	Oct10 2-0 Apr02 1-1	Aug29 0-0 Jan01 1-2	Nov22 1-4 Apr16 1-1	Oct31 3-1 Mar19 1-2	Oct03 3-0 Feb27 2-2
HAMILTON A	Nov07 2-2 Mar26 1-1	Aug15 3-2 Feb06 2-0	Aug11 3-2 Dec05 4-0	Sep05 2-1 Dec26 2-0	Sep26 0-1 Jan16 1-0	Nov14 1-1 Apr23 0-1		Oct03 1-1 Feb27 1-0	Oct27 1-5 May07 1-1	Sep12 5-0 Dec12 1-0	Oct20 2-2 Mar12 1-2	Oct10 0-2 Apr09 2-1
KILMARNOCK	Nov14 1-0 Apr23 4-1	Sep26 2-0 Jan16 3-1	Oct28 1-3 Mar12 2-2	Nov21 1-0 Apr09 3-1	Oct06 2-2 Apr30 2-3	Aug08 2-2 Feb06 2-1	Aug02 0-2 Nov28		Oct31 2-4 Mar19 0-0	Sep29 1-1 Feb13 0-0	Aug29 0-2 Jan02 1-1	Sep12 3-4 Dec12 1-1
MEADOWBANK T	Sep12 1-2 Dec12 1-1	Nov14 0-2 Apr23 0-1	Sep26 0-0 Jan16 3-2	Oct07 1-0 Apr30 2-4	Oct24 0-3 Apr02 2-1	Nov07 2-3 Feb13 3-0	Sep29 1-1 Dec26 1-3	Sep05 2-1		Aug08 3-2 Jan23 3-1	Aug22 1-0 Nov28 5-0	Oct20 4-3 Mar12 3-0
PARTICK T	Aug11 2-2 Dec05 2-0	Nov07 1-0 Mar26 1-0	Oct03 1-2 Feb27 3-0	Sep15 3-3 Dec19 1-3	Sep05 1-1 Dec26 4-2	Sep26 1-1 Jan16 0-1	Oct17 3-3 Mar05 0-0	Nov03 1-1 May07 0-1	Oct10 1-1 Apr09 2-1		Nov14 3-3 Apr23 0-3	Aug15 0-9 Feb06 5-0
QUEEN OF SOUTH	Aug15 2-2 Jan26 1-2	Oct28 3-1 May07 0-1	Oct10 2-0 Apr02 1-2	Nov21 2-0 Apr16 3-3	Oct17 1-1 Mar05 0-0	Aug08 1-1 Dec26 1-1	Sep29 0-3 Dec19 1-0	Nov07 1-4 Mar26 0-0	Nov07 0-2 Feb27 1-0	Sep19 0-0 Jan09		Aug12 0-3 Dec05 1-5
RAITH R	Sep26 3-2 Jan16 2-2	Sep05 1-3 Dec26 2-0	Nov14 1-0 Apr23 2-3	Sep29 4-1 Feb13 1-1	Nov07 7-1 Mar26 0-1	Aug08 1-4 Nov28 0-0	Aug22 1-2 Mar02 0-1	Oct17 0-2 Mar05 2-2	Sep15 2-0 Dec19 4-0	Oct24 4-3 Apr02 1-2	Oct07 3-1 Apr30 4-2	

5th Round
Mar 12 Aberdeen ....5 Clyde 0
Mar 12 Dundee ......0 Dundee U 0
Mar 12 Hearts ....3 Dunfermline A ..0
Mar 12 Partick T .....0 Celtic 3

Replay
Mar 15 Dundee U ....2 Dundee 2
Mar 28 Dundee ......0 Dundee U 3
     played at Dens Park

Semi-finals
Apr 9 Aberdeen ....0 Dundee U 0
     played at Dens Park
Apr 9 Celtic ....2 Hearts 1
     played at Hampden Park

Replay
Apr 13 Aberdeen ....1 Dundee U 1
     played at Dens Park
Apr 20 Aberdeen ....0 Dundee U 1
     played at Dens Park

Final
May 14 Celtic ....2 Dundee U 1
     played at Hampden Park

Andy Walker of Celtic joyfully grabs the ball from the back of Hearts' net and Celtic are through to the Scottish Cup Final after being 1-0 down with only three minutes to play in this Hampden Park semi-final.

DIVISION 2

	ALBION R	ALLOA	ARBROATH	AYR U	BERWICK R	BRECHIN C	COWDENBEATH	E STIRLING	MONTROSE	QUEEN'S PARK	ST JOHNSTONE	STENHOUSEMUIR	STIRLING A	STRANRAER
ALBION R		Sep26 1-0 / Apr23 1-2	Dec26 1-1	Dec12 1-1	Jan30 0-2	Jan23 2-0 / Mar12 1-5	Nov28 0-0	Aug15 1-1	Nov14 0-1 / Feb27 1-4	Aug29 0-4 / Apr09 3-1	Oct24 1-1	Oct31 3-2 / Feb20 0-4	Sep12 2-1 / Apr02 3-1	Oct10 2-1
ALLOA	Nov21 2-0		Sep19 3-1	Mar01 0-2 / Apr16 1-3	Oct24 1-0 / Feb13 3-0	Aug08 0-1 / Mar26 0-3	Aug22 5-2	Sep12 1-2 / May07 0-1	Dec12 1-0	Nov07 0-3 / Feb27 1-0	Feb17 1-1 / Apr19 1-1	Oct10 1-1	Aug29 4-0	Dec30 2-0 / Mar22 1-1
ARBROATH	Sep05 3-0 / Mar05 4-0	Nov28 1-1 / Feb20 1-1		Jan16 2-4	Sep26 3-1	Oct24 1-2 / Mar26 0-3	Feb09 2-1 / Apr30 0-0	Oct03 1-1	Sep12 0-0 / Apr09 1-1	Aug08 3-1 / Mar12 1-2	Jan02 0-2	Dec12 3-0	Aug22 3-2	Nov07 3-2
AYR U	Sep15 3-0 / Mar19 6-2	Oct17 2-1	Oct10 2-0 / Apr02 3-0		Nov14 2-0	Nov28 1-2 / Mar05 5-0	Dec19 3-1 / Apr23 1-1	Feb06 2-0	Aug15 3-1 / Feb20 1-1	Sep26 4-1	Oct31 0-3	Jan23 3-0	Dec26 4-0	Aug29 5-1 / Apr09 3-1
BERWICK R	Oct17 0-3 / Apr30 1-3	Feb23 1-2	Nov21 3-3 / May07 4-0	Aug22 0-2 / Feb13 0-1		Nov07 0-2 / Feb27 0-0	Aug29 2-2	Jan19 1-1	Sep19 2-1	Dec26 0-1	Oct10 0-4 / Apr09 0-2	Sep12 1-3 / Mar19 1-3	Jan23 0-4	Aug08 0-1 / Mar26 2-0
BRECHIN C	Oct03 2-1	Oct31 3-1	Feb16 1-1	Sep19 0-3 / May07 2-1	Aug15 4-0		Dec26 1-0 / Mar19 1-0	Jan16 2-3 / Apr09 1-0	Aug29 2-0 / Mar08 0-1	Sep12 1-1 / Apr02 2-0	Nov14 2-1	Oct17 2-0	Dec12 1-2 / Apr30 2-0	Nov21 2-0 / Feb20 4-1
COWDENBEATH	Sep19 3-3 / Mar26 1-0	Nov14 2-2 / Apr09 0-1	Oct17 3-5	Sep12 1-6 / Apr23 3-0	Jan02 5-3	Sep05 1-1		Oct31 0-0 / Mar12 0-0	Jan16 1-1 / May07 2-1	Oct03 2-4	Aug15 0-3 / Feb20 1-0	Feb06 1-1	Nov21 2-4 / Feb27 1-0	Dec12 2-0
E STIRLING	Nov07 2-2	Dec19 3-1	Jan23 1-1 / Mar19 2-1	Oct24 0-2	Sep15 1-0 / Mar01 2-1	Oct10 0-0	Aug08 0-1		Dec26 2-2 / Apr30 3-2	Nov28 0-1	Sep26 0-2	Aug29 2-0 / Mar26 1-2	Feb02 2-1 / Apr16 1-3	Aug22 1-1 / Mar05 2-0
MONTROSE	Aug22 1-2 / Feb13 0-0	Sep15 2-0 / Mar28 0-2	Dec29 1-1	Nov07 2-4 / Mar12 1-1	Nov28 4-0 / Apr16 1-0	Jan02 0-1	Oct10 2-1	Sep05 0-3		Oct24 0-2 / Apr23 1-2	Feb23 0-1	Sep26 1-0 / Feb27 1-1	Aug08 1-3	Jan23 3-1
QUEEN'S PARK	Jan02 1-1	Aug15 2-0	Oct31 1-1	Nov21 0-2	Sep05 3-2 / Mar05 2-0	Dec19 2-0	Jan23 3-2 / Apr16 1-1	Sep19 2-1 / Feb13 1-2	Feb06 1-1		Sep15 0-1 / Mar26 2-1	Nov14 0-2 / May07 2-1	Oct10 1-1 / Mar19 1-2	Oct17 3-0 / Feb16 2-0
ST JOHNSTONE	Feb06 4-1 / May07 2-0	Oct03 2-1	Aug29 3-1 / Apr16 4-0	Aug08 0-0 / Feb27 2-0	Jan16 2-1	Aug22 1-1 / Apr23 2-0	Nov07 0-1	Nov21 3-1 / Apr02 0-0	Oct17 1-1 / Mar19 5-1	Dec12 2-0		Dec26 4-1	Sep19 1-1 / Mar01 1-0	Sep12 1-0
STENHOUSEMUIR	Aug08 3-1	Jan16 0-1 / Mar12 0-0	Sep15 1-1 / Feb13 1-1	Oct03 0-6 / Apr30 2-1	Dec19 1-0	Feb24 2-1 / Apr16 2-1	Oct24 2-3 / Apr02 2-0	Jan02 0-2	Nov21 2-3 / Mar05 3-0	Aug22 0-0	Sep05 0-0		Aug15 0-0	Sep19 0-2
STIRLING A	Dec19 1-1	Jan02 2-0 / Mar05 4-1	Nov14 3-0 / Apr23 3-0	Sep05 1-1 / Mar26 1-1	Oct03 1-0 / Mar12 2-1	Sep26 2-1	Oct17 3-0	Oct31 0-2 / Feb20 3-2	Jan16 2-2	Nov28 0-6	Nov07 0-3 / Apr04 3-2			Feb06 2-0 / May07 2-0
STRANRAER	Jan16 1-2 / Apr16 2-2	Sep05 0-3	Aug15 3-1 / Feb27 0-3	Jan02 1-2	Oct31 0-2	Sep26 1-1 / Feb24 0-4	Sep15 2-2	Nov14 3-3	Oct03 1-3 / Apr02 1-1	Apr30 1-4	Dec19 1-2 / Mar12 1-3	Nov28 2-3 / Apr23 2-1	Oct24 0-0	

PREMIER DIVISION FINAL TABLE

	P	W	D	L	F	A	Pts
Celtic	44	31	10	3	79	23	72
Hearts	44	23	16	5	74	32	62
Rangers	44	26	8	10	85	34	60
Aberdeen	44	21	17	6	56	25	59
Dundee U	44	16	15	13	54	47	47
Hibernian	44	12	19	13	41	42	43
Dundee	44	17	7	20	70	64	41
Motherwell	44	13	10	21	37	56	36
St Mirren	44	10	15	19	41	64	35
Falkirk	44	10	11	23	41	75	31
Dunfermline A	44	8	10	26	41	84	26
Morton	44	3	10	31	27	100	16

DIVISION 1 FINAL TABLE

	P	W	D	L	F	A	Pts
Hamilton A	44	22	12	10	67	39	56
Meadowbank T	44	20	12	12	70	51	52
Clydebank	44	21	7	16	59	61	49
Forfar A	44	16	16	12	67	58	48
Raith R	44	19	7	18	81	76	45
Airdrie	44	16	13	15	65	68	45
Queen of South	44	14	15	15	56	67	43
Partick T	44	16	9	19	60	64	41
Clyde	44	17	6	21	73	75	40
Kilmarnock	44	13	11	20	55	60	37
East Fife	44	13	10	21	61	76	36
Dumbarton	44	12	12	20	51	70	36

DIVISION 2 FINAL TABLE

	P	W	D	L	F	A	Pts
Ayr U	39	27	7	5	95	31	61
St Johnstone	39	25	9	5	74	24	59
Queen's Park	39	21	9	9	64	44	51
Brechin C	39	20	8	11	56	40	48
Stirling A	39	18	10	11	60	51	46
E Stirling	39	15	13	11	51	47	43
Alloa	39	16	8	15	50	46	40
Montrose	39	12	11	16	45	51	35
Arbroath	39	10	14	15	54	66	34
Stenhousemuir	39	12	9	18	49	58	33
Cowdenbeath	39	10	13	16	51	66	33
Albion R	39	10	11	18	45	75	31
Berwick R	39	6	4	29	32	77	16
Stranraer	39	4	8	27	34	84	16

League Cup results for 1987-88 are detailed on page 213.

SFA Cup

1st Round
Dec 3 Berwick R ....1 Alloa 1
Dec 3 East Fife .....4 Spartans 1
Dec 3 East Stirling ..1 Gala Fairydean ..0
Dec 3 Inverness T ...0 Dumbarton 0
Dec 3 Montrose ....2 Arbroath 0
Dec 3 Stranraer ....2 Stirling A 2

Replays
Dec 7 Alloa ....2 Berwick 1
Dec 10 Dumbarton ...2 Inverness T 1
Dec 10 Stirling A ....0 Stranraer 1

2nd Round
Jan 7 Annan A .....1 Queen's Park ...5
Jan 7 Caledonian T ..1 Brechin C 1
Jan 7 Coldstream ...1 Albion R 1
Jan 7 Cowdenbeath .1 Stenhousemuir .1
Jan 7 East Stirling ..1 Montrose 2
Jan 7 Elgin C ......2 Dumbarton 2
Jan 7 Forres Mechanic1 Alloa 1
Jan 7 Stranraer ....2 East Fife 1

Replays
Jan 14 Albion R .....1 Coldstream 0
Jan 14 Alloa ....2 Forres Mechanic 0
Jan 14 Brechin C ....2 Caledonian T ...1
Jan 14 Dumbarton ....4 Elgin C 0
Jan 14 Stenhousemuir 3 Cowdenbeath ..2

3rd Round
Jan 28 Alloa ....3 Albion R 1
Jan 28 Celtic ......2 Dumbarton 0
Jan 28 Clydebank ....2 Montrose 1
Jan 28 Dundee ......1 Dundee U 2
Jan 28 Dunfermline A .0 Aberdeen 1
Jan 28 Falkirk ....1 Motherwell 1
Jan 28 Forfar A .....1 Clyde 1
Jan 28 Hearts ......4 Ayr U 1
Jan 28 Hibernian ....1 Brechin C 0
Jan 29 Meadowbank T 2 Hamilton A ...0
Jan 28 Morton ......0 Airdrie 0
Jan 28 Partick T .....0 St Mirren 0
Jan 28 Queen of South 2 Kilmarnock 2
Jan 28 Queen's Park .0 Stranraer 0
Jan 28 Raith R ......1 Rangers 1
Jan 28 St Johnstone .2 Stenhousemuir .0

Replays
Jan 31 Clyde ....0 Forfar A 1
Jan 31 St Mirren ....1 Partick T 3
Feb 1 Aberdeen ....3 Dunfermline A .1
Feb 1 Airdrie ......0 Morton 1
Feb 1 Kilmarnock ...0 Queen of South .1
Feb 1 Motherwell ...2 Falkirk 1
Feb 1 Rangers .....3 Raith R 0
Feb 1 Stranraer ....1 Queen's Park ...0

4th Round
Feb 18 Aberdeen ....1 Dundee U 0
Feb 18 Celtic ......4 Clydebank 1
Feb 18 Hearts ......2 Partick T 0
Feb 18 Hibernian ....2 Motherwell 0
Feb 18 Meadowbank T 0 Morton 1
Feb 18 Queen of South 0 Alloa 0
Feb 18 Rangers .....8 Stranraer 0
Feb 18 St Johnstone .2 Forfar A 1

Replays
Feb 22 Alloa ....4 Queen of South .2
Feb 22 Dundee U ....1 Aberdeen 1
Feb 27 Dundee U ....1 Aberdeen 0

5th Round
Mar 18 Celtic ......2 Hearts 1
Mar 18 Hibernian ....1 Alloa 0
Mar 22 Morton ......2 St Johnstone ..2
Mar 21 Rangers .....2 Dundee U 2

Replay
Mar 27 Dundee U ....0 Rangers 1
Mar 27 St Johnstone .3 Morton 2

League Cup results for 1988-89 are detailed on page 214.

PREMIER

	ABERDEEN	CELTIC	DUNDEE	DUNDEE U	HAMILTON A	HEARTS	HIBERNIAN	MOTHERWELL	RANGERS	ST MIRREN
ABERDEEN	—	Nov02 2-2 / Apr29 0-0	Nov16 2-0 / Apr11 2-0	Nov12 1-0 / Apr01 1-0	Dec03 2-0 / Apr15 3-0	Sep24 0-0 / Feb25 3-0	Sep03 1-1 / Jan07 2-0	Nov19 0-0 / May06 0-0	Oct08 1-1 / Jan14 1-2	Aug20 1-1 / Dec17 3-1
CELTIC	Sep17 1-3 / Dec10 0-0	—	Oct29 2-3 / Apr22 2-1	Oct12 1-0 / Mar25 0-0	Sep03 2-1 / Jan07 1-0	Aug13 1-0 / Dec31 4-2	Sep03 1-0 / May06 1-0	Nov12 3-1 / Feb11 1-2	Oct08 7-1 / Jan14 1-2	Apr01 1-2
DUNDEE	Aug13 1-1 / Dec31 2-0	Sep24 1-0 / Feb25 0-3	—	Sep03 0-3 / Jan07 0-1	Nov02 5-2 / Apr07 1-0	Dec03 1-1 / Apr15 2-1	Oct08 2-1 / Jan14 2-1	Oct12 1-1 / Apr29 2-1	Nov19 0-0 / May06 1-2	Nov01 0-1 / Apr01 2-1
DUNDEE U	Aug27 2-2 / Jan03 1-1	Aug20 1-0 / Dec17 2-0	Nov05 2-0 / Apr08 2-1	—	Nov26 1-0 / May13 0-1	Oct01 1-1 / Jan21 0-0	Sep17 0-1 / Dec10 4-1	Oct29 1-1 / Apr22 1-1	Sep27 0-1 / Feb11 1-1	Oct22 1-1 / Mar11 1-4
HAMILTON A	Sep27 0-1 / Feb14 0-2	Nov05 0-8 / Apr08 2-0	Sep17 1-0 / Dec10 2-0	Oct08 0-4 / Jan14 0-1	—	Oct11 0-4 / Mar25 0-2	Oct29 0-3 / Apr22 0-3	Sep24 1-0 / Jan03 2-0	Aug13 0-2 / Dec31 1-1	Nov19 2-4 / May06 0-6
HEARTS	Oct29 1-1 / Apr22 1-0	Oct22 0-2 / Mar11 0-1	Sep28 1-1 / Feb11 3-1	Nov19 0-0 / May06 0-0	Aug20 3-2 / Dec17 2-0	—	Nov12 1-2 / Apr01 2-1	Oct08 2-2 / Dec10 0-0	Sep17 1-2 / Jan07 2-0	Sep03 1-2
HIBERNIAN	Nov05 1-2 / Apr08 1-2	Oct01 3-1 / Jan21 1-3	Nov26 1-1 / May13 1-2	Nov02 0-1 / Apr29 1-2	Sep24 2-1 / Mar01 2-1	Aug27 1-0 / Jan04 1-0	—	Aug13 / Dec31 2-0	Oct12 / Mar25 0-1	Dec03 / Apr19 1-0
MOTHERWELL	Oct01 1-1 / Jan21 0-2	Dec03 1-3 / Apr12 2-2	Aug20 1-1 / Dec17 1-1	Sep24 1-2 / Mar14 1-0	Nov12 1-1 / Apr01 1-1	Nov26 2-0 / May13 1-1	Oct22 1-1 / Mar11 0-0	—	Sep24 0-2 / Jan07 2-1	Nov01 1-2 / Apr29 4-0
RANGERS	Nov26 1-0 / May13 0-3	Aug27 5-1 / Jan03 4-1	Oct01 2-0 / Jan21 3-1	Dec03 0-1 / Jan21 2-0	Nov16 3-1 / May02 3-0	Nov01 3-0 / Apr29 4-0	Aug20 0-0 / Dec17 1-0	Nov05 2-1 / Apr08 1-0	—	Sep24 2-1 / Feb25 3-1
ST MIRREN	Oct12 1-1 / Mar25 1-3	Nov26 2-3 / May13 0-1	Aug27 0-0 / Jan03 1-1	Aug13 1-1 / Dec31 0-1	Oct01 1-0 / Jan21 1-0	Nov05 1-1 / Apr08 1-1	Sep28 1-1 / Feb21 3-1	Sep17 2-1 / Dec10 2-1	Oct29 0-2 / Apr22 0-2	—

DIVISION 1

	AIRDRIE	AYR U	CLYDE	CLYDEBANK	DUNFERMLINE A	FALKIRK	FORFAR A	KILMARNOCK	MEADOWBANK T	MORTON	PARTICK T	QUEEN OF SOUTH	RAITH R	ST JOHNSTONE
AIRDRIE	—	Nov05 2-1	Oct15 1-1 / Mar11 1-1	Dec17 1-1	Jan21 0-2	Jan14 2-0 / Apr29 3-0	Dec10 0-3 / Feb11 1-1	Sep10 5-1	Oct01 0-0	Aug20 1-1 / Mar25 1-1	Sep24 5-1	Aug27 3-0 / Apr01 3-0	Nov19 3-1	Dec31 1-0 / Apr24 1-1
AYR U	Jan07 1-4 / May06 3-1	—	Oct29 1-1	Aug13 3-2 / Apr08 2-4	Oct15 2-2 / Apr22 1-2	Sep10 3-4	Sep03 2-1	Jan03 4-1 / Mar11 2-1	Dec03 2-2 / Feb25 3-2	Dec17 1-3	Nov19 1-3	Oct08 1-1 / Mar25 2-2	Feb04 1-1	Sep24 2-1
CLYDE	Dec27 0-0	Dec10 4-2 / Mar04 1-0	—	Sep10 0-5 / Feb28 1-1	Oct01 1-1	Sep24 1-2	Aug20 0-2	Nov19 0-2	Jan21 1-2	Jan17 0-1 / Apr08 1-1	Aug27 0-1 / Apr29 2-1	Nov05 3-1 / Mar28 0-0	Dec31 0-1 / Apr22 2-1	Oct22 2-4 / May13 2-0
CLYDEBANK	Oct22 3-3 / May13 4-1	Jan18 5-1	Nov12 3-2	—	Sep17 2-1 / Mar04 0-1	Aug20 2-2 / Mar25 3-2	Oct01 2-2	Sep03 2-2 / May06 3-2	Nov26 2-1	Jan03 1-1	Jan21 3-2 / Apr22 2-3	Dec10 4-2 / Feb14 3-0	Dec31 3-1	Nov05 2-0 / Apr01 2-2
DUNFERMLINE A	Oct08 1-0 / Apr08 1-1	Dec24 5-1 / May06 1-1	Feb04 3-0	Nov19 2-2	—	Dec31 3-0	Nov05 2-1	Sep24 3-0 / Mar25 0-0	Oct22 1-3 / May13 1-1	Dec10 2-1 / Apr15 1-1	Jan14 3-2	Sep10 4-2	Aug27 2-1 / Mar11 0-1	Aug20 1-0 / Feb11 1-0
FALKIRK	Aug13 0-0 / Mar28 2-0	Nov12 1-0 / Apr15 3-1	Nov26 2-1	Dec03 3-1	Sep03 2-1 / Mar07 4-0	—	Oct22 1-2	Jan07 2-0	Jan03 0-1	Sep17 0-1 / Mar04 0-0	Dec24 0-1	Feb07 2-0 / May06 7-1	Oct29 2-0 / Apr08 3-0	Oct08 2-1
FORFAR A	Oct29 1-1 / Apr01 0-0	Dec31 1-2	Dec03 2-1	Feb04 2-4 / Apr15 2-1	Jan07 2-1 / Apr29 1-0	Dec17 0-0 / May13	—	Oct08 2-2	Aug13 1-0 / Mar25 2-1	Oct15 0-1 / Feb25	Sep10 3-2	Nov19 2-2	Sep24 1-1	Dec10 1-1
KILMARNOCK	Nov12 0-3 / Mar04 1-1	Aug27 2-0 / Feb18 0-0	Sep17 1-2	Dec31 1-0	Nov26 2-2	Oct05 0-2 / Apr01 0-0	Jan21 2-1 / Mar18 2-2	—	Dec24 1-0	Oct01 3-4	Aug20 0-1 / Apr29 0-0	Jan14 2-1 / Apr15 1-2	Oct22 1-1	Dec10 0-3
MEADOWBANK T	Feb04 3-2 / Apr22 3-1	Aug20 1-2	Oct08 2-1	Sep24 1-0 / Mar18 2-0	Dec17 0-1 / Mar11 1-1	Aug27 2-1	Jan14 1-1	Oct15 0-2 / Apr08 1-2	—	Jan07 2-1	Dec10 0-2	Dec31 1-2 / Feb11 1-3	Sep10 2-1 / May06 2-1	Nov19 1-1
MORTON	Dec03 0-2	Oct22 2-0	Aug13 1-0 / Apr04 1-0	Aug27 2-2	Oct01 1-0	Nov19 1-5 / Feb21 2-2	Dec24 1-1	Mar01 2-2 / Apr22 3-0	Nov05 2-0 / Apr01 0-2	—	Dec31 1-0	Sep24 1-0	Oct08 0-1 / May06 0-1	Nov01 1-1
PARTICK T	Nov26 0-2 / Mar18 1-0	Sep17 2-2 / Feb14 4-1	Jan03 0-0	Oct08 1-1	Aug13 1-2 / Apr01 0-0	Oct15 1-3 / Mar11 4-1	Nov12 1-2 / May06 4-1	Dec03 0-1	Oct29 1-1 / Apr08	Sep03 1-4	—	Dec17 2-1	Jan07 1-1	Feb08 2-0
QUEEN OF SOUTH	Jan03 2-4	Jan21 3-3 / Apr15 1-2	Jan07 0-3	Oct29 0-3	Nov12 1-0 / Mar21 0-2	Oct01 2-1 / May13 0-6	Sep17 2-2	Aug13 2-0	Sep03 0-1 / Mar11 1-2	Nov26 2-3 / Apr29 1-4	Oct22 2-1 / Feb25 2-4	—	Dec03 0-1	Dec24 1-1
RAITH R	Sep17 1-2 / Mar01 1-1	Oct01 0-0 / Apr01 1-1	Sep03 0-0 / Apr29 0-2	Oct15 1-3	Jan03 1-3	Jan21 1-3 / Apr22 2-3	Nov26 2-1	Dec17 1-0	Nov12 1-0		Nov05 5-3 / Apr13 2-1	Aug20 2-1 / Mar04 1-1	—	Jan14 1-1 / Apr05 0-2
ST JOHNSTONE	Sep03 2-1	Nov26 2-0	Dec17 0-0 / Apr29 0-1	Jan07 2-0	Dec03 0-1 / Apr22 0-1	Jan21 2-1 / Feb25 2-2	Jan02 2-1	Oct29 2-0	Sep17 0-0	Nov12 4-2	Oct01 2-1 / Mar11 0-1	Oct15 3-1 / Apr08 1-1	Aug13 3-1 / Mar25 3-1	—

Season 1988-89

Roy Aitken of Celtic holds the SFA Cup aloft after Celtic defeated Rangers in the all-Glasgow clash at Hampden Park in 1989.

Semi-finals

Apr 16 Celtic . . . . . . .3 Hibernian 1
played at Hampden Park
Apr 15 Rangers . . . . .0 St Johnstone . . .0
played at Celtic Park

Replay

Apr 18 Rangers . . . . .4 St Johnstone . . .0
played at Celtic Park

Final

May 20 Celtic . . . . . . .1 Rangers 0
played at Hampden Park

PREMIER DIVISION FINAL TABLE

	P	W	D	L	F	A	Pts
Rangers	36	26	4	6	62	26	56
Aberdeen	36	18	14	4	51	25	50
Celtic	36	21	4	11	66	44	46
Dundee U	36	16	12	8	44	26	44
Hibernian	36	13	9	14	37	36	35
Hearts	36	9	13	14	35	42	31
St Mirren	36	11	7	18	39	55	29
Dundee	36	9	10	17	34	48	28
Motherwell	36	7	13	16	35	44	27
Hamilton A	36	6	2	28	19	76	14

DIVISION 1 FINAL TABLE

	P	W	D	L	F	A	Pts
Dunfermline A	39	22	10	7	60	36	54
Falkirk	39	22	8	9	71	37	52
Clydebank	39	18	12	9	80	55	48
Airdrie	39	17	13	9	66	44	47
Morton	39	16	9	14	46	46	41
St Johnstone	39	14	12	13	51	42	40
Raith R	39	15	10	14	50	52	40
Partick T	39	13	11	15	57	58	37
Forfar A	39	10	16	13	52	56	36
Meadowbank T	39	13	10	16	45	50	36
Ayr U	39	13	9	17	56	72	35
Clyde	39	9	16	14	40	52	34
Kilmarnock	39	10	14	15	47	60	34
Queen of South*	39	2	8	29	38	99	10

DIVISION 2 FINAL TABLE

	P	W	D	L	F	A	Pts
Albion R	39	21	8	10	65	48	50
Alloa	39	17	11	11	66	48	45
Brechin C	39	15	13	11	58	49	43
Stirling A	39	15	12	12	64	55	42
East Fife	39	14	13	12	55	54	41
Montrose	39	15	11	13	54	55	41
Queen's Park	39	10	18	11	50	49	38
Cowdenbeath*	39	13	14	12	48	52	38
E Stirling	39	13	11	15	54	58	37
Arbroath	39	11	15	13	56	63	37
Stranraer	39	12	12	15	58	63	36
Dumbarton	39	12	10	17	45	55	34
Berwick R	39	10	13	16	50	59	33
Stenhousemuir	39	9	11	19	44	59	29

*2 points deducted for breach of rules.

DIVISION 2

	ALBION R	ALLOA	ARBROATH	BERWICK R	BRECHIN C	COWDENBEATH	DUMBARTON	EAST FIFE	E STIRLING	MONTROSE	QUEEN'S PARK	STENHOUSEMUIR	STIRLING A	STRANRAER
ALBION R		Feb11 3-2	Oct15 3-1 / May06 2-2	Oct08 3-1 / May13 2-1	Sep10 1-1	Dec10 3-1 / Apr08 2-1	Sep03 2-1 / Apr22 2-0	Nov12 2-0 / Mar04 1-2	Aug13 1-0	Oct29 2-1 / Mar07 2-2	Sep24 1-1	Dec24 1-0	Jan31 1-0	Jan03 3-0 / Mar18 2-2
ALLOA	Oct01 3-1 / Apr29 2-0		Jan03 3-3 / Mar01 3-0	Oct15 2-1	Nov19 2-2	Aug20 2-1 / Mar25 2-1	Dec17 2-0	Nov26 2-1	Sep17 2-2	Jan31 1-0 / Apr22 4-0	Dec31 0-0	Sep03 1-2 / Mar04 2-0	Feb04 3-2 / Apr08 4-0	Nov05 1-1
ARBROATH	Jan21 0-3	Aug27 2-2		Jan14 1-2 / Feb25 0-3	Aug20 1-2	Dec31 0-1	Feb04 1-1 / Apr29 1-3	Dec17 1-3 / Mar18 1-3	Oct22 3-3 / Apr22 2-2	Nov26 0-0	Nov05 2-2	Sep17 5-1 / Apr08 2-1	Oct01 2-1 / May13 0-4	Nov19 1-0 / Mar11 4-3
BERWICK R	Feb04 2-1	Jan21 1-1 / Mar22 1-0	Sep03 0-3		Dec31 4-4	Nov05 0-1 / Apr15 0-0	Oct01 1-0	Oct22 1-2	Nov26 0-5 / Mar04 2-0	Sep17 1-2 / May06 1-1	Nov19 1-1 / Apr01 1-1	Dec17 1-0	Jan07 0-0 / Feb18 2-2	Aug20 0-1
BRECHIN C	Nov26 0-2 / Apr01 2-1	Aug13 2-1 / Mar07 1-2	Nov12 1-0 / Mar15 3-4	Oct29 2-0 / Apr22 0-2		Oct08 0-1	Sep17 1-1	Dec24 1-0 / May06 1-0	Dec17 2-2	Jan03 2-2	Feb11 1-0	Feb01 3-1 / Mar18 1-1	Sep03 2-3	Oct15 2-2
COWDENBEATH	Sep17 1-1	Nov12 1-1	Oct29 1-1 / Apr01 1-1	Dec24 3-3 / Apr29 0-2	Feb08 3-3 / Mar04 1-1		Oct22 2-0	Jan03 1-1	Oct01 2-1	Aug13 2-6	Jan21 2-2 / Mar18 3-1	Nov26 2-0 / Feb18 2-1	Dec17 1-1	Sep03 1-0 / Apr22 1-1
DUMBARTON	Apr04 1-0	Sep24 1-1 / May13 0-2	Oct08 1-4	Mar07 2-2 / Apr08 0-4	Dec13 3-0 / Apr15 1-0	Jan31 3-0		Aug13 3-1 / Feb18 4-0	Oct29 3-0	Dec24 3-2 / Mar28 0-3	Aug27 0-3 / Mar11 0-2	Nov12 0-2 / May06 2-0	Oct15 1-2	Sep10 0-2
EAST FIFE	Aug20 1-2	Sep10 2-0 / Mar11 1-0	Sep24 0-0	Jan28 2-2 / Apr29 1-1	Nov05 1-0	Aug27 4-1 / Feb25 1-0	Nov19 1-1		Jan14 2-2	Oct08 1-1 / May13 1-4	Dec24 2-2	Oct15 2-1 / Apr15 1-1	Dec31 2-0 / Mar25 3-0	Feb11 1-2 / Apr08 2-1
E STIRLING	Nov19 3-4 / Mar11 0-1	Dec10 2-1 / Apr15 2-0	Jan28 0-3	Sep10 3-2	Sep24 4-3 / Feb18 1-1	Mar15 1-0 / May13 0-2	Dec31 0-1 / Mar25 1-0	Sep03 2-2 / Apr01 4-2		Oct15 1-0	Aug20 2-1 / Apr29 2-1	Jan03 0-3	Nov05 2-2	Oct08 1-2
MONTROSE	Dec31 1-0	Oct22 1-0	Sep10 0-1 / Apr15 1-1	Dec10 2-1	Aug27 0-2 / Mar25 1-1	Nov19 0-2 / Mar11 2-1	Nov05 1-1	Feb04 2-2	Jan21 0-1 / Apr08 2-1		Jan14 1-1	Oct01 3-1	Aug20 3-2 / Apr29 0-6	Sep24 4-2 / Feb22 1-0
QUEEN'S PARK	Dec17 0-0 / Feb18 3-2	Oct29 0-2 / May06 0-2	Dec24 2-0 / Mar25 1-1	Aug13 2-0	Oct01 1-1 / Apr08 1-2	Oct15 1-1	Jan03 2-1	Sep17 1-0 / Apr22 1-2	Nov12 0-0	Sep03 2-0 / Mar04 1-2		Feb04 1-1	Nov26 2-0	Feb07 4-3
STENHOUSEMUIR	Nov05 2-3 / Mar25 1-2	Jan24 2-0	Dec10 0-0	Sep24 3-2 / Mar11 0-0	Oct22 0-2	Sep10 0-0	Aug20 3-1	Jan21 1-1	Aug27 1-1 / Mar06 1-0	Mar01 0-1 / Apr01 2-3	Oct08 0-0 / May13 1-1		Nov19 1-1 / Apr22 4-2	Dec31 3-4 / Apr29 2-0
STIRLING A	Oct22 4-2 / Apr15 0-0	Oct08 3-1	Feb11 1-1	Aug27 2-1	Jan18 2-2 / Mar11 0-0	Sep24 2-3 / May06 0-1	Jan21 3-1 / Apr01 3-1	Oct29 1-0	Dec24 3-2 / Mar18 2-1	Nov12 2-0	Sep10 3-2 / Feb27 0-0	Aug13 2-0		Dec14 0-3
STRANRAER	Aug27 3-1	Dec24 2-2 / Apr01 1-4	Aug13 0-1	Nov12 2-2 / Mar25 1-2	Jan25 0-1 / May13 2-1	Jan25 2-0	Nov26 2-2 / Feb25 1-1	Oct22 2-2	Feb04 1-2 / May06 0-0	Dec17 1-0	Oct22 3-1 / Apr15 3-3	Oct29 2-1	Sep17 1-1 / Mar04 1-4	

SFA Cup

1st Round
Dec 9 Berwick R ....1 Stenhousemuir .1
Dec 9 Brechin C .....3 Montrose 1
Dec 9 Elgin C ....2 Arbroath 1
Dec 9 Queen of South 2 Cove R 1
Dec 9 Queen's Park .1 Dumbarton 2
Dec 9 Stirling A .....4 Coldstream 0

Replays
Dec 12 Stenhousemuir .1 Berwick R 0

2nd Round
Dec 30 Dumbarton ....0 Cowdenbeath ...2
Dec 30 Elgin C ....2 Brechin C 2
Dec 30 Gala Fairydean .2 Inverness C 2
Jan 7 Ross Co ......1 East Fife 4
Dec 30 Stenhousemuir .0 Queen of South .1
Dec 30 Stirling A .....3 Whitehill Welfare 0
   played at Firs Park
Dec 30 Stranraer .....1 Kilmarnock 1
Dec 30 Vale of Leithen .1 E Stirling 3

Replays
Jan 6 Brechin C .....8 Elgin C 0
Jan 6 Inverness C ...4 Gala Fairydean ..1
Jan 6 Kilmarnock ....0 Stranraer 0
   Penalties 3-4

3rd Round
Jan 20 Airdrie ....2 Inverness C 2
Jan 20 Albion R ......0 Clydebank 2
Jan 20 Ayr U ....0 St Mirren 0
Jan 20 Brechin C .....0 Hibernian 2
Jan 20 Cowdenbeath ..3 Stranraer 1
Jan 20 Dundee ......0 Dundee U 0
Jan 20 Dunfermline A .0 Hamilton A 0
Jan 20 East Fife .....3 Meadowbank T .1
Jan 29 E Stirling .....0 Stirling A 1
Jan 20 Forfar A ......1 Celtic 2
Jan 20 Hearts ....2 Falkirk 0
Jan 20 Morton ....2 Raith R 2
Jan 20 Motherwell ...7 Clyde 0
Jan 20 Partick T .....2 Aberdeen 6
Jan 20 Queen of South 0 Alloa 0
Jan 20 Rangers ......3 St Johnstone ..0

Replays
Jan 23 Dundee U .....1 Dundee 0
Jan 24 Inverness C ...1 Airdrie 1
   Penalties 5-4
Jan 24 St Mirren .....2 Ayr U 1
Jan 29 Alloa ....2 Queen of South .3
Jan 29 Raith R ......1 Morton 3
Jan 31 Hamilton A ....0 Dunfermline A ..1

4th Round
Feb 24 Aberdeen .....2 Morton 1
Feb 25 Celtic ....1 Rangers 0
Feb 27 Cowdenbeath ..1 Dumbarton 2
Feb 26 Dundee U .....2 Queen of South .1
Feb 24 Hearts ....4 Motherwell 0
Feb 24 Hibernian .....5 East Fife 1
Feb 28 St Mirren .....1 Clydebank 1
Feb 28 Stirling A .....6 Inverness C 2

League Cup results for 1989-90 are detailed on page 214.

PREMIER

PREMIER	ABERDEEN	CELTIC	DUNDEE	DUNDEE U	DUNFERMLINE A	HEARTS	HIBERNIAN	MOTHERWELL	RANGERS	ST MIRREN
ABERDEEN		Sep30 1-1 / Feb17 1-3	Aug26 1-0 / Jan02 5-2	Dec09 2-0 / Apr18 1-0	Sep16 2-1 / Jan13 4-1	Oct14 1-3 / Feb03 2-0	Aug12 1-0 / Dec26 1-2	Oct28 1-0 / Mar24 2-0	Nov22 1-0 / Apr08 2-0	Nov25 5-0 / Apr28 2-0
CELTIC	Dec02 1-0 / May02 1-3		Dec16 4-1 / Apr21 1-1	Nov18 0-1 / Mar03 3-0	Aug19 1-0 / Dec30 0-2	Oct21 2-1 / Mar10 1-1	Oct04 3-1 / Jan27 0-1	Sep23 1-1 / Jan02 0-1	Aug26 1-1 / Apr07 0-3	Nov22 1-1
DUNDEE	Nov04 1-1 / Mar31 1-1	Oct14 1-3 / Feb03 0-0		Aug19 1-1 / Dec30 1-1	Oct21 1-2 / Mar10 1-1	Sep09 2-2 / Jan06 0-1	Sep23 0-0 / Jan27 2-0	Dec02 1-1 / May05 1-2	Nov18 2-1 / Mar03 2-2	Dec09 3-3 / Apr14 1-2
DUNDEE U	Oct04 2-0 / Feb10 1-1	Sep16 2-2 / Jan13 0-0	Oct28 0-0 / Mar24 1-1		Aug26 2-1 / Jan03 2-1	Sep16 2-1 / Apr28 1-0	Nov08 1-0 / Apr07 1-1	Aug12 1-1 / Dec23 0-1	Dec16 1-1 / Apr21 1-0	Sep30 0-0 / Feb17 1-0
DUNFERMLINE A	Oct18 0-3 / Mar03 2-4	Oct28 2-0 / Mar24 0-0	Aug12 2-1 / Dec26 1-0	Nov04 1-1 / Mar31 0-1		Dec09 0-2 / Apr14 0-1	Dec02 0-2 / May05 1-1	Sep09 1-1 / Jan06 0-5	Sep23 1-1 / Jan27 0-1	Oct14 5-1 / Feb03 1-0
HEARTS	Dec20 1-1 / Apr21 1-0	Aug12 1-1 / Dec26 0-0	Nov11 6-3 / Apr04 0-0	Sep23 1-2 / Jan27 3-2	Oct04 2-1 / Feb10 2-0		Aug26 1-0 / Jan01 2-0	Nov18 3-0 / Mar03 2-0	Dec02 1-2 / May05 1-1	Oct28 1-1 / Mar24 0-0
HIBERNIAN	Oct25 0-3 / Mar10 3-2	Dec09 0-3 / Apr17 1-1	Nov25 3-2 / Apr28 1-0	Sep09 2-0 / Jan06 1-1	Sep30 2-2 / Feb17 1-1	Nov04 1-1 / Mar31 0-2		Oct14 3-2 / Feb03 1-2	Aug19 2-0 / Dec30 1-2	Sep16 3-1 / Jan13 0-0
MOTHERWELL	Aug19 0-0 / Dec30 2-2	Nov25 0-0 / Apr28 1-1	Sep30 3-0 / Feb17 3-1	Oct21 3-2 / Mar10 0-1	Nov08 1-1 / Apr07 1-3	Sep16 1-3 / Jan13 0-3	Jan09 0-2 / Apr21 1-0		Oct03 1-0 / Feb10 1-1	Aug26 3-1 / Jan02 2-0
RANGERS	Sep09 1-0 / Jan06 2-0	Nov04 1-0 / Apr01 3-0	Sep16 1-0 / Jan13 3-0	Oct14 2-2 / Feb03 3-1	Nov25 3-0 / Apr28 0-0	Sep30 1-0 / Feb17 0-0	Oct28 3-0 / Mar24 1-1	Dec09 3-0 / Apr14 2-1		Aug12 0-1 / Dec23 1-0
ST MIRREN	Sep23 0-2 / Jan27 1-0	Sep09 0-2 / Jan06 0-2	Oct04 3-2 / Feb10 0-0	Dec13 1-0 / May05 0-0	Jan10 2-0 / Apr21 1-2	Aug19 1-2 / Dec30 0-0	Nov18 0-0 / Mar03 0-1	Nov04 2-2 / Mar31 0-1	Oct25 0-2 / Mar17 0-0	

DIVISION 1

DIVISION 1	AIRDRIE	ALBION R	ALLOA	AYR U	CLYDE	CLYDEBANK	FALKIRK	FORFAR A	HAMILTON A	MEADOWBANK T	MORTON	PARTICK T	RAITH R	ST JOHNSTONE
AIRDRIE		Aug26 1-0	Sep30 1-1 / Mar24 3-1	Dec09 1-1 / Feb10 6-0	Dec26 1-0	Jan30 2-2 / Apr03 3-4	Sep05 1-1	Oct28 4-1	Aug19 3-1 / May05 3-1	Oct14 0-0 / Apr14 1-1	Jan06 4-1	Nov25 3-2 / Feb17 2-1	Nov11 3-2 / Apr21 0-1	Sep16 2-2
ALBION R	Jan02 0-2 / Mar03 1-2		Nov04 1-1	Aug12 3-1		Sep23 2-0	Sep02 3-4 / May05 2-2	Dec02 2-1 / Feb03 2-2	Oct07 0-2 / Apr07 2-2	Jan09 0-0	Oct21 1-1	Jan13 5-4 / Mar31 4-2	Dec30 2-2 / Apr28 2-2	Nov18 1-3 / Mar10 2-5
ALLOA	Dec02 0-2 / Mar27 3-4	Sep05 4-1		Sep23 1-1 / May05 0-0	Nov11 1-1 / Apr28 1-0	Oct28 1-4 / Apr20 0-0	Aug26 1-1	Dec23 0-2 / Mar31 1-1	Jan06 0-2	Dec30 0-1	Nov18 1-1	Feb28 1-0	Oct07 2-0 / Apr14 0-4	Aug12 0-1
AYR U	Oct07 1-3	Dec26 2-0 / Apr14 0-2	Nov25 3-0		Jan06 1-0 / Mar14 1-1	Sep16 3-2 / Mar24 1-1	Nov11 3-1 / Feb28 1-1	Aug19 1-0	Aug26 2-1	Jan13 0-0	Sep05 2-3	Sep30 1-0 / Feb03 2-1	Dec16 1-0	Oct21 2-0 / Apr28 0-2
CLYDE	Aug12 1-0 / Feb03 0-1	Nov29 0-0 / Apr04 2-1	Sep09 2-4	Sep02 2-2		Nov04 2-0 / Mar27 2-2	Oct28 2-0 / Apr28 0-0	Sep16 0-0	Sep30 1-1	Dec09 0-3	Dec30 1-1	Jan02 3-3	Mar17 1-0 / Mar21 2-1	Oct14 0-2
CLYDEBANK	Oct21 0-3	Jan06 1-3	Jan13 3-1	Nov18 4-1 / Mar03 0-1	Sep05 2-1 / Apr07 2-1		Dec23 3-3 / Feb10 3-2	Nov11 3-2	Oct07 2-2 / Mar27 2-1	Sep23 1-1 / Apr28 0-1	Aug26 3-1	Aug12 1-2	Dec02 3-1 / Mar24 2-2	Dec23 4-0
FALKIRK	Nov04 3-1 / Apr07 3-1	Sep30 6-0	Jan02 1-0	Sep09 0-1	Jan13 3-0	Oct14 4-0 / Feb21 0-1		Dec26 4-0 / Apr21 2-2	Sep16 3-3	Sep02 1-1 / Mar31 2-0	Sep21 1-0 / Mar17 2-0	Dec09 1-1	Aug19 0-2	Nov25 1-0 / Feb10 1-0
FORFAR A	Jan13 1-1 / Mar10 2-3	Dec09 3-0	Oct14 3-3 / Mar03 3-3	Dec30 1-0	Nov18 1-1 / Mar31 2-2	Sep09 2-2	Aug12 1-2		Oct21 0-1 / Apr28 2-0	Nov04 1-3	Dec02 0-1	Sep02 0-3 / Apr14 1-1	Sep23 2-2 / Feb03 2-3	Jan02 1-5
HAMILTON A	Apr07 3-2	Oct14 0-0 / Apr21 1-2	Sep02 1-0 / Mar17 2-1	Jan02 4-0	Dec02 0-1	Dec09 2-1 / Feb03 1-3	Nov18 1-0 / Mar03 2-2	Feb14 1-1		Aug12 2-0 / Apr14 2-0	Sep23 2-2	Sep09 1-4	Oct28 3-2	Nov04 3-3 / Mar24 2-3
MEADOWBANK T	Dec20 0-1	Jan27 3-2 / Apr07 1-1	Aug19 1-0 / Apr21 1-0	Oct28 1-1	Oct07 2-1	Nov25 1-1 / May05 1-0	Jan06 1-1 / Mar17 0-3	Sep05 3-1 / Feb10 1-0	Dec23 1-0		Nov11 0-0 / Mar03 1-0	Sep16 1-1 / Mar24 1-1	Aug26 1-2	Sep30 1-3
MORTON	Sep02 0-1 / Apr28 1-1	Oct28 0-0 / Mar17 3-0	Sep16 3-2 / Feb03 2-0	Nov04 1-1 / Apr07 1-1	Aug19 0-1 / May05 2-0	Jan03 2-2	Jan27 0-2	Sep30 1-1 / Mar27 2-0	Nov25 0-0	Sep09 0-0		Oct14 2-2	Dec23 1-1	Dec09 0-0 / Feb27 1-2
PARTICK T	Sep23 2-1	Aug19 4-0 / Apr21 1-0	Oct21 3-3 / Mar23 0-3	Dec02 1-2	Aug26 2-2 / Mar31 4-0	Dec26 1-1 / Mar14 3-0	Oct07 1-0	Jan06 0-1 / Mar14 4-1	Nov11 1-1	Nov18 2-0 / Feb10 0-1	Jan09 1-0		Sep05 3-1 / May05 1-1	Jan13 2-1 / Apr07 0-2
RAITH R	Sep09 0-4	Sep16 2-1 / Feb10 3-2	Dec09 1-1	Oct14 2-0 / Mar31 5-2	Oct21 2-0	Sep30 1-0 / Apr28 1-1	Nov25 1-3	Jan13 1-1 / Apr07 0-0	Jan02 2-0 / Feb28 3-0	Aug12 1-1 / Mar10 2-1	Nov04 0-0			Sep02 0-2
ST JOHNSTONE	Nov18 1-2 / Mar31 3-1	Sep09 2-1	Dec26 3-0 / Mar17 6-0	Jan27 4-0 / Apr21 1-1	Dec16 2-0 / Apr17 1-3	Aug19 2-1	Sep23 2-0 / May05 1-0	Aug26 3-1	Sep05 3-0 / Feb03 1-2	Dec02 1-0	Oct07 1-1	Oct28 2-1 / Mar03 0-0	Jan06 1-2	

Replays
Mar 12 Clydebank ....3 St Mirren 2

5th Round
Mar 17 Aberdeen .....4 Hearts 1
Mar 17 Clydebank ....1 Stirling A 1
Mar 17 Dundee U .....1 Hibernian 0
Mar 17 Dunfermline A .0 Celtic 0

Replay
Mar 21 Celtic ....3 Dunfermline A ..0
Mar 21 Clydebank ....1 Stirling A 0
    played at Brockville Park

Semi-finals
Apr 14 Aberdeen .....4 Dundee U 0
    played at Tynecastle
Apr 14 Celtic ....2 Clydebank 0
    played at Hampden Park

Final
May 12 Aberdeen .....0 Celtic 0
    Penalties 9-8
    at Hampden Park

Trevor Steven's goal clinches the 1990 title for Rangers with Dundee United's Alan Main well beaten.

PREMIER DIVISION FINAL TABLE

	P	W	D	L	F	A	Pts
Rangers	36	20	11	5	48	19	51
Aberdeen	36	17	10	9	56	33	44
Hearts	36	16	12	8	54	35	44
Dundee U	36	11	13	12	36	39	35
Celtic	36	10	14	12	37	37	34
Motherwell	36	11	12	13	43	47	34
Hibernian	36	12	10	14	32	41	34
Dunfermline A	36	11	8	17	37	50	30
St Mirren	36	10	10	16	28	48	30
Dundee	36	5	14	17	41	65	24

DIVISION 1 FINAL TABLE

	P	W	D	L	F	A	Pts
St Johnstone	39	25	8	6	81	39	58
Airdrie	39	23	8	8	77	45	54
Clydebank	39	17	10	12	74	64	44
Falkirk	39	14	15	10	59	46	43
Raith R	39	15	12	12	57	50	42
Hamilton A	39	14	13	12	52	53	41
Meadowbank T	39	13	13	13	41	46	39
Partick T	39	12	14	13	62	53	38
Clyde	39	10	15	14	39	46	35
Ayr U	39	11	13	15	41	62	35
Morton	39	9	16	14	38	46	34
Forfar A*	39	8	15	16	51	65	29
Albion R	39	8	11	20	50	78	27
Alloa	39	6	13	20	41	70	25

* 2 points deducted for breach of rules

DIVISION 2 FINAL TABLE

	P	W	D	L	F	A	Pts
Brechin C	39	19	11	9	59	44	49
Kilmarnock	39	22	4	13	67	39	48
Stirling A	39	20	7	12	73	50	47
Stenhousemuir	39	18	8	13	60	53	44
Berwick R	39	18	5	16	66	57	41
Dumbarton	39	15	10	14	70	73	40
Cowdenbeath	39	13	13	13	58	54	39
Stranraer	39	15	8	16	57	59	38
East Fife	39	12	12	15	60	63	36
Queen of South	39	11	14	14	58	69	36
Queen's Park	39	13	10	16	40	51	36
Arbroath	39	12	10	17	47	61	34
Montrose	39	10	12	17	53	63	32
E Stirling	39	8	10	21	34	66	26

DIVISION 2

	ARBROATH	BERWICK R	BRECHIN C	COWDENBEATH	DUMBARTON	EAST FIFE	E STIRLING	KILMARNOCK	MONTROSE	QUEEN OF SOUTH	QUEEN'S PARK	STENHOUSEMUIR	STIRLING A	STRANRAER
ARBROATH		Oct28 1-0	Nov11 0-1 Feb27 0-2	Jan27 0-0 Apr21 0-1	Oct07 2-1	Jan31 3-0	Nov25 2-0	Aug19 1-1 Feb17 2-4	Sep16 2-2 Mar17 3-0	Jan13 1-0 Apr07 1-0	Sep30 2-2 Mar24 1-1	Aug26 2-1	Dec26 1-2	Dec20 2-0
BERWICK R	Feb03 3-1 May05 5-0		Oct21 1-1 Apr28 1-0	Aug12 2-0	Nov11 1-2 Mar31 3-2	Sep09 1-1 Mar10 2-0	Apr14 1-0	Nov25 3-2 Feb24	Sep30 2-0	Mar03 1-1	Jan06 2-0	Oct14 0-2 Feb10 1-0	Aug26 1-1	Jan16 3-1 Apr07 2-1
BRECHIN C	Sep02 2-2	Jan27 1-0		Dec02 1-0 Feb10 1-3	Aug19 4-0 Mar31 3-0	Nov25 2-1	Oct14 2-1 May05 0-0	Dec26 3-1	Jan01 1-1 Mar24 2-2	Sep16 3-1	Nov04 1-0 Mar03 1-0	Sep30 1-2	Jan13 3-1 Apr07 1-5	Oct28 1-0 Apr21 0-0
COWDENBEATH	Nov21 1-1	Dec26 2-1 Mar27 3-1	Nov07 1-1		Sep30 1-5	Aug26 0-1 Feb17 2-2	Feb03 4-0 Apr28 3-3	Jan13 2-1	Aug19 0-1 Apr07 2-4	Dec20 4-2 Mar07 2-1	Nov25 0-0	Jan06 0-1	Sep16 4-3 Mar13 1-1	Nov11 3-4
DUMBARTON	Dec02 0-0 Apr24 2-0	Sep02 1-5	Dec23 1-1	Nov18 2-2 Apr14 1-1		Apr21 3-1	Mar20 3-0 Apr17 2-1	Mar24 0-2 Apr03 1-3	Nov04 3-2	Aug12 2-1	Oct14 2-1	Oct21 1-0	Sep23 2-2 Apr28 1-2	Sep09 5-2 Apr10 1-1
EAST FIFE	Nov04 3-0 Mar03 2-3	Jan13 2-2	Sep23 3-1 Apr14 1-3	Jan02 0-0	Sep16 2-2 Mar14 3-1			Dec26 1-1 Mar17 1-1	Jan10 4-2	Oct28 4-1	Oct07 2-2 Mar24 1-2	Sep02 1-1 Feb10 3-2	Aug19 2-3	Nov18 1-2
E STIRLING	Sep23 1-1 Feb10 1-0	Oct07 3-1 Dec02 2-1	Jan10 2-0	Oct28 1-1	Aug26 1-2	Aug12 0-2		Nov11 2-1	Oct21 0-2 Mar14 1-1	Nov18 1-0	Dec23 1-0	Sep09 0-3 Apr11 4-2	Jan06 0-2 Apr27 0-2	Apr04 0-3 Apr24 0-1
KILMARNOCK	Dec23 3-0	Sep23 2-0	Aug12 0-2 Mar31 2-2	Sep09 0-0 May05 2-1	Oct28 3-0	Oct14 1-0 Apr07 2-0	Sep02 2-0 Mar03 2-0		Dec02 1-1	Nov04 2-0 Apr21 4-1	Jan02 2-0 Mar10 3-0	Jan20 2-0	Nov18 1-2 Mar06 1-0	Jan27 0-1
MONTROSE	Jan20 4-2	Nov18 2-1 Feb28 0-2	Aug26 0-1	Dec23 2-0	Jan06 2-2 Mar27 1-2	Feb03 2-2 Mar31 0-2	Apr21 3-0	Oct07 0-1 Apr28 1-3		Sep23 0-0 May05 1-1	Sep09 4-1 Apr14 0-1	Nov11 0-2 Mar10 1-1	Dec20 3-3	Aug12 2-2
QUEEN OF SOUTH	Sep09 2-2	Aug19 4-2 Dec23 3-2	Feb07 3-1 Mar10 2-2	Oct14 2-4	Jan10 1-4 Feb10 1-1	Dec02 5-1	Sep30 2-2 Mar31 1-1	Mar13 2-1	Nov25 3-2		Oct21 3-1 Apr28 0-0	Feb03 1-3 Apr14 0-4	Nov11 3-1	Aug26 2-2
QUEEN'S PARK	Nov18 1-2	Sep16 3-1 Apr21 0-3	Jan17 0-3	Sep23 0-0 Mar17 3-1	Dec16 2-2 May05 1-0	Nov11 2-1	Aug19 3-2 Apr07 2-1	Aug26 1-0	Jan13 2-1	Jan27 0-0		Dec26 0-0 Feb27 1-1	Oct28 2-1 Mar31 3-1	Oct07 0-2 Feb20 3-0
STENHOUSEMUIR	Jan02 3-0 Mar31 1-0	Jan09 1-3	Nov18 2-0 Feb20 1-1	Nov04 3-1 Mar03 2-1	Jan27 4-3 Apr07 1-3	Dec23 2-2 Apr28 1-2	Jan13 2-0	Sep16 1-0 Mar17 2-1	Sep02 1-3	Oct28 1-3	Aug12		Oct07 2-1	Sep23 0-2
STIRLING A	Aug12 2-3 Apr14 3-2	Jan02 3-2 Apr04 4-0	Sep09 2-0	Feb07 1-1	Nov25 4-1	Oct21 3-1 May05 2-0	Nov04 4-0	Sep30 0-1	Sep16 2-0 Mar03 2-3	Sep02 5-0 Feb17 1-1	Feb03 1-0	Dec02 1-1 Apr21 1-1		Dec23 1-0 Mar24 2-1
STRANRAER	Oct14 2-1 Apr28 2-1	Nov04 1-3	Feb03 2-4	Sep02 3-1 Mar31 1-2	Jan13 4-4	Sep30 1-1 Feb28 0-2	Sep16 1-1	Oct21 1-0 Apr14 2-1	Dec26 1-2 Feb10 2-0	Jan02 0-2 Mar17 3-0	Dec02 0-1	Nov25 2-2 May05 4-1	Aug19 0-2	

169

SFA Cup

1st Round

Dec 8	E Stirling 1	Queen of South .3	
Dec 8	Fraserburgh .3	Vale of Leithen ..1	
Dec 11	Montrose 0	Dumbarton 0	
Dec 8	Ross Co 1	Alloa 1	
Dec 15	Threave R 1	Spartans 2	
Dec 15	Whitehill Welfare 0	East Fife 4	

Replays

Dec 15 Alloa ....1 Ross Co 3
Dec 17 Dumbarton ...1 Montrose 4

2nd Round

Dec 29 Berwick R ....1 Albion R 0
Dec 29 Fraserburgh ..1 Cove R 4
Jan 5 Inverness T ...1 East Fife 1
Dec 29 Montrose ....0 Arbroath 2
Dec 29 Queen's Park .1 Stranraer 2
Jan 23 Ross Co .....2 Queen of South .2
Jan 9 Spartans ....0 Cowdenbeath ...0
Dec 29 Stirling A ....2 Stenhousemuir .0

Replays

Jan 7 East Fife .....1 Inverness T 0
Jan 21 Cowdenbeath .2 Spartans 0
Jan 28 Queen of South 2 Ross Co 6

3rd Round

Jan 26 Aberdeen ....0 Motherwell 1
Jan 26 Airdrie ......2 Hearts 1
Jan 28 Clyde ....0 Hibernian 2
Jan 26 Clydebank ....0 Ayr U 1
Jan 26 Cove R ......1 Cowdenbeath ...2
Jan 26 Dundee ......1 Brechin C 0
Jan 26 East Fife ....1 Dundee U 1
Jan 26 Forfar A ....0 Celtic 2
Jan 26 Kilmarnock ...3 Arbroath 2
Jan 26 Partick T ....0 Falkirk 0
Jan 26 Raith R ......0 Hamilton A 1
Jan 29 Rangers .....2 Dunfermline A ..0
Feb 23 Ross Co .....1 Meadowbank T .6
Jan 26 St Johnstone .0 Berwick R 0
Jan 26 Stirling A ....0 Morton 1
Jan 26 Stranraer ....1 St Mirren 5

Replays

Jan 29 Dundee U ....2 East Fife 1
Jan 30 Berwick R ....3 St Johnstone ...4
Jan 30 Falkirk ....4 Partick T 3

4th Round

Feb 23 Ayr U ....0 Hamilton A 0
Feb 26 Celtic ......3 St Mirren 0
Feb 23 Dundee .....2 Kilmarnock 0
Feb 23 Dundee U ....2 Airdrie 0
Mar 2 Morton .....3 Meadowbank T .0
Feb 23 Motherwell ..4 Falkirk 2
Feb 23 Rangers .....5 Cowdenbeath ..0
Feb 23 St Johnstone ..2 Hibernian 1

Replays

Feb 27 Hamilton A ...2 Ayr U 3

League Cup results for 1990-91 are detailed on page 214.

PREMIER

	ABERDEEN	CELTIC	DUNDEE U	DUNFERMLINE A	HEARTS	HIBERNIAN	MOTHERWELL	RANGERS	ST JOHNSTONE	ST MIRREN
ABERDEEN		Nov03 3-0 Apr06 1-0	Sep15 1-1 Jan02 0-1	Dec01 3-2 Mar13 0-0	Oct20 3-0 Feb02 5-0	Aug25 2-0 Apr20 3-0	Dec15 1-1 Jan12 1-0	Oct06 0-0 May04 2-1	Nov17 0-0 Apr06 1-0	Sep22 2-1 Dec26 1-0
CELTIC	Sep01 0-3 Jan19 1-0		Oct20 0-0 Feb02 1-0	Dec15 2-1 Apr20 5-1	Sep22 0-0 Dec29 1-1	Sep08 3-1 Jan05 1-1	Nov06 1-2 Mar30 1-2	Nov25 0-0 Mar24 3-0	Oct06 0-0 Mar02 3-1	Nov17 4-1 May05 1-0
DUNDEE U	Nov24 2-3 Mar23 1-2	Dec08 3-1 Apr13 2-1		Oct10 3-0 Mar02 2-1	Nov17 1-1 May04 0-0	Oct13 2-1 Feb09 2-1	Sep01 2-1 Jan19 1-3	Sep22 1-2 Dec29 2-1	Oct27 1-1 Mar30 2-1	Sep08 2-1 Jan05 3-2
DUNFERMLINE A	Sep08 1-1 Jan05 1-4	Oct13 1-1 Mar06 0-1	Dec22 1-0 May11 1-0		Sep01 2-0 Feb23 3-1	Sep29 1-1 Mar16 1-1	Nov10 3-3 Apr27 2-5	Nov20 0-1 Mar23 0-1	Nov24 1-2 Mar23 3-2	Dec11 0-0 Apr21 2-2
HEARTS	Dec08 1-0 Apr13 1-4	Nov11 0-1 Apr27 0-1	Sep29 2-1 Feb16 2-1	Ncv03 0-1 Apr06 4-1		Nov24 1-1 Mar23 3-1	Dec22 3-2 May11 2-1	Sep08 1-3 Jan05 0-1	Oct13 2-3 Mar06 2-1	Aug25 2-1 Jan12 2-0
HIBERNIAN	Oct27 1-1 Mar30 2-4	Dec01 0-3 Mar09 0-2	Dec15 0-0 Apr20 1-4	Nov17 1-1 May04 3-0	Sep15 0-3 Jan02 1-4		Oct20 1-0 Feb02 1-1	Sep01 0-0 Jan19 0-2	Sep22 1-0 Dec29 3-0	Oct06 1-1 Mar02 2-1
MOTHERWELL	Oct13 0-0 Mar05 0-2	Aug25 2-0 Jan30 1-1	Nov03 0-2 Apr16 2-1	Sep22 2-0 Feb17 1-0	Oct06 1-1 Mar02 1-3	Dec11 4-1 Apr13 1-0		Nov17 2-4 May04 3-0	Sep08 3-0 Jan05 2-2	Nov24 1-1 Mar23 3-1
RANGERS	Dec22 2-2 May11 2-0	Sep15 1-1 Jan02 2-0	Nov10 1-2 Apr24 1-0	Aug25 3-3 Jan12 2-0	Dec01 4-0 Mar09 2-1	Nov03 4-0 Apr06 0-0	Sep29 2-0 Feb16 2-0		Dec08 4-1 Apr13 3-0	Oct13 5-0 Feb09 1-0
STJOHNSTONE	Sep29 5-0 Feb13 0-1	Dec22 3-2 May11 2-3	Aug25 1-3 Feb19 0-1	Sep22 3-2 Jan02 2-0	Oct06 2-1 Apr20 0-1	Nov10 1-1 Apr27 1-4	Dec01 2-1 Mar09 1-1	Oct20 0-0 Feb26 1-1		Nov03 0-1 Apr09 2-1
ST MIRREN	Nov10 0-4 Apr27 0-1	Sep29 2-3 Mar12 0-2	Dec01 1-1 Mar09 0-1	Oct20 0-1 Feb19 2-2	Oct27 2-1 Mar30 0-0	Dec22 1-0 May11 1-1	Sep15 1-0 Jan02 2-2	Dec15 1-0 Apr20 0-1	Sep01 0-3 Jan19 0-1	

DIVISION 1

	AIRDRIE	AYR U	BRECHIN C	CLYDE	CLYDEBANK	DUNDEE	FALKIRK	FORFAR A	HAMILTON A	KILMARNOCK	MEADOWBANK	MORTON	PARTICK T	RAITH R
AIRDRIE		Sep22 4-0	Sep08 3-0	Dec08 2-2 Apr20 1-1	Oct06 2-2	Nov24 0-1 Mar02 0-1	Oct27 1-3 Mar30 0-3	Jan19 1-1 Apr27 2-1	Jan02 2-1	Nov10 2-0 Mar16 2-0	Sep18 2-0	Aug25 4-0 Apr23 3-0	Mar12 0-0	Oct20 1-5
AYR U	Dec15 2-2 Apr13 0-1		Jan19 4-0	Oct20 4-1 Apr06 0-1	Oct27 1-1	Oct06 2-4	Nov24 1-1	Aug25 1-1	Nov20 2-2 Mar26 1-2	Jan02 1-2 May11 1-0	Sep08 1-0 Apr27 0-1	Dec29 1-0 Apr10 1-1	Sep18 0-1	Sep29 2-0 Mar02 5-3
BRECHIN C	Feb05 1-2 Feb16 1-1	Sep15 1-2 Mar23 2-2		Feb02 0-2 Mar30 2-0	Jan29 3-2	Oct27 1-3	Sep22 0-2	Oct13 2-1	Dec11 0-1 Mar02 2-2	Oct06 0-2	Jan05 1-3	Nov24 0-1 Apr20 1-3	Nov10 2-2 Apr27 1-2	Aug25 0-4
CLYDE	Sep29 1-4	Mar09 1-0 Apr02 2-2	Nov13 1-1		Aug25 0-1 Mar12 3-1	Mar23 4-2 Apr30 0-1	Oct06 1-3	Sep08 1-1 Apr06 0-1	Nov24 0-2	Feb26 1-1 Apr27 2-1	Dec15 1-0	Oct27 1-3 May11 0-1	Oct13 2-4 Apr13 1-0	Nov10 1-2
CLYDEBANK	Dec01 5-2 Mar09 1-3	Dec22 0-2	Nov03 3-4 Mar16 1-0	Nov17 2-1		Sep08 1-3 Mar30 1-1	Sep01 3-1 Feb27 2-2	Oct10 2-2	Oct20 3-1 Apr27 1-3	Sep18 1-3 Apr20 0-0	Sep29 2-2	Jan02 2-4	Jan19 2-3 May11 7-1	Dec15 1-1
DUNDEE	Oct09 0-1	Dec01 1-0 Mar05 4-0	Dec22 2-2 Mar09 0-1	Sep15 3-1	Feb05 1-0		Oct20 2-2	Dec18 4-1 Mar16 1-0	Feb02 3-2	Sep29 1-1	Nov03 1-1 Apr20 4-0	Nov20 1-1 Apr06 1-0	Aug25 1-1	Jan01 2-1 Apr27 2-0
FALKIRK	Dec22 1-1 May08 4-1	Oct09 1-2 Apr06 2-1	Dec15 3-0 Mar02 2-1	Dec01 2-0	Nov10 5-1	Jan05 1-0 Apr13 0-0		Sep29 1-0	Oct13 0-1 Mar16 3-0	Jan19 2-2 May11 2-1	Sep18 2-1	Sep08 0-2		Dec15 7-1 Feb16 0-2
FORFAR A	Sep15 1-4 Apr20 1-1	Nov17 3-1 May11 4-1	Mar05 0-0 Mar23 2-2	Feb23 1-3	Nov24 0-3	Sep22 1-1	Dec12 1-2 Apr02 0-0		Dec29 0-0	Oct27 2-3 Mar16 1-1	Sep01 3-2 Feb20 2-0	Oct20 5-1 May04 2-2	Oct06 0-1	Feb02 3-1
HAMILTON A	Oct13 0-1 Mar23 1-1	Sep01 0-0	Sep29 0-1 May04 3-1	Oct10 1-0	Jan05 2-0	Sep18 1-0 May11 1-2	Nov17 0-2	Nov03 2-0 Mar20 0-1		Sep08 3-1	Mar09 1-1 Mar13 2-1	Nov10 1-1	Dec15 2-0 Apr06 0-1	Dec01 2-0 Apr20 1-2
KILMARNOCK	Sep01 3-4	Oct13 3-1	Dec01 2-1 Apr13 2-2	Nov03 2-1	Feb02 3-0	Dec08 2-1 May04 0-0	Sep15 1-1 Mar23 1-1	Dec22 1-0	Jan12 1-0 Mar30 1-1		Nov17 2-3	Sep22 3-1 Mar09 2-1	Jan05 2-3 Feb16 1-1	Oct19 1-1
MEADOWBANK T	Apr06 0-1 Apr03 2-4	Jan12 1-0 May04 1-1	Oct20 6-1 Mar26 1-1	Sep22 0-2 Apr13 2-3	Dec08 0-3	Dec29 0-1	Mar20 0-1	Nov10 2-2	Oct27 1-1	Aug25 1-0 Apr10 1-8		Oct31 1-1	Nov24 1-1	Sep15 1-1 Mar23 4-1
MORTON	Nov17 1-0	Nov03 2-1	Oct09 3-3	Mar05 0-0	Oct13 0-0 Apr02 2-2	Sep01 0-1 Apr27 0-1	Feb02 1-1	Mar26 1-1	Sep15 0-1	Dec15 3-0 Feb16 1-1	Dec01 0-4 Apr13 1-1		Sep29 4-0 Mar23 1-1	Mar30 4-0 Apr16 1-2
PARTICK T	Nov03 1-1 May04 0-2	Mar30 0-0 Apr23 2-0	Sep01 3-3	Apr16 2-0	Sep15 0-1	Nov17 1-3 Mar26 1-0	Mar05 2-0 Apr20 1-1	Sep22 0-1	Nov17 3-2 Mar02 2-4	Oct20 2-2	Nov06 1-1 Mar16 2-4	Dec08 2-2		Feb23 0-3
RAITH R	Jan05 1-1 May11 0-1	Dec08 3-0	Nov17 1-2 Feb19 1-0	Sep01 1-1 May04 1-0	Sep22 2-0	Oct13 1-1	Dec29 1-4	Sep18 2-1 Apr13 1-2	Oct06 1-0	Nov24 1-1 Apr06 1-2	Mar06 1-3	Sep08 1-0	Oct27 0-0 Mar09 1-5	

Season 1990-91

5th Round

Mar 17 Celtic . . . . . . .2 Rangers 0
Mar 13 Dundee U . . . .3 Dundee 1
Mar 16 Motherwell . . .0 Morton 0
Mar 16 St Johnstone . .5 Ayr U 2

Replay

Mar 19 Morton . . . . . .1 Motherwell 1
        Penalties 4-5

Semi-finals

Apr 3 Celtic . . . . . . .0 Motherwell 0
       played at Hampden Park
Apr 6 Dundee U . . . .2 St Johnstone . . .1
       played at East End Park

Replay

Apr 9 Celtic . . . . . . .2 Motherwell 4
       played at Hampden Park

Final

May 18 Dundee U . . . .3 Motherwell 4
        played at Hampden Park

Ally McCoist acknowledges the crowd as Rangers leave the field after beating Celtic in the 1991 Skol Cup. Rangers went on to clinch the League title for the third year running.

PREMIER DIVISION FINAL TABLE

	P	W	D	L	F	A	Pts
Rangers	36	24	7	5	62	23	55
Aberdeen	36	22	9	5	62	27	53
Celtic	36	17	7	12	52	38	41
Dundee U	36	17	7	12	41	29	41
Hearts	36	14	7	15	48	55	35
Motherwell	36	12	9	15	51	50	33
St Johnstone	36	11	9	16	41	54	31
Dunfermline A	36	8	11	17	38	61	27
Hibernian	36	6	13	17	24	51	25
St Mirren	36	5	9	22	28	59	19

DIVISION 1 FINAL TABLE

	P	W	D	L	F	A	Pts
Falkirk	39	21	12	6	70	35	54
Airdrie	39	21	11	7	69	43	53
Dundee	39	22	8	9	59	33	52
Partick T	39	16	13	10	56	53	45
Kilmarnock	39	15	13	11	58	48	43
Hamilton A	39	16	10	13	50	41	42
Raith R	39	14	9	16	54	64	37
Clydebank	39	13	10	16	65	70	36
Morton	39	11	13	15	48	55	35
Forfar A	39	9	15	15	50	57	33
Meadowbank T	39	10	13	16	56	68	33
Ayr U	39	10	12	17	47	59	32
Clyde	39	9	9	21	41	61	27
Brechin C	39	7	10	22	44	80	24

DIVISION 2 FINAL TABLE

	P	W	D	L	F	A	Pts
Stirling A	39	20	14	5	62	24	54
Montrose	39	20	6	13	54	34	46
Cowdenbeath	39	18	9	12	64	50	45
Stenhousemuir	39	16	12	11	56	42	44
Queen's Park	39	17	8	14	48	42	42
Stranraer	39	18	4	17	61	60	40
Dumbarton	39	15	10	14	49	49	40
Berwick R	39	15	10	14	51	57	40
Alloa	39	13	11	15	51	46	37
East Fife	39	14	9	16	57	65	37
Albion R	39	11	13	15	48	63	35
Queen of South	39	9	12	18	46	62	30
E Stirling	39	9	11	19	36	71	29
Arbroath	39	8	11	20	41	59	27

DIVISION 2

	ALBION R	ALLOA	ARBROATH	BERWICK R	COWDENBEATH	DUMBARTON	EAST FIFE	E.STIRLING	MONTROSE	QUEEN OF SOUTH	QUEEN'S PARK	STENHOUSEMUIR	STIRLING A	STRANRAER
ALBION R		Nov17 3-1	Oct09 1-1 Mar09 1-3	Jan19 1-1 Apr27 4-2	Sep01 3-1	Sep15 3-2	Nov24 0-2 Feb23 3-1	Jan05 4-0	Oct27 0-3	Dec22 1-0 Apr06 0-0	Oct13 1-0	Sep18 1-4 Mar16 0-0	Mar23 2-2	Sep29 0-1 Apr13 1-4
ALLOA	Aug25 1-0 May04 1-2		Sep18 2-1 Apr06 2-2	Nov10 5-0 Apr20 1-1	Oct30 1-2	Oct20 0-1 Mar16 2-1	Mar12 3-6	Feb26 0-1	Dec01 1-0 Mar02 1-0	Sep08 4-1	Oct27 1-1	Jan22 1-0 Feb19 1-1	Sep29 0-1	Feb02 0-1
ARBROATH	Jan12 0-0	Jan29 1-1		Aug25 4-2 Feb23 0-1	Sep22 1-2	Nov10 2-1 Apr20 0-1	Feb09 1-1 0-1	Oct06 3-0 Mar16 0-1	Jan02 0-1	Oct27 1-1	Dec22 3-0	Dec01 0-0 Mar30 0-2	Sep08 2-3 Mar02 0-1	Oct20 3-0 May11 1-5
BERWICK R	Oct06 3-0	Sep01 1-0	Nov17 1-1		Jan12 0-1 Mar09 1-1	Dec15 2-1	Oct20 1-0	Feb02 2-2 Mar30 0-1	Sep08 2-1 Apr13 3-3	Dec01 2-0 Feb26 2-3	Sep18 1-2 Mar16 2-1	Sep29 0-1	Dec08 1-1 May04 0-0	Nov03 3-2
COWDENBEATH	Nov10 2-0 Mar02 2-2	Mar06 1-1 May11 1-0	Feb02 0-1 4-2	Oct10 0-1			Nov24 4-2 Feb27 1-3	Mar26 2-0	Sep18 2-1	Oct20 0-1	Sep29 2-1	Dec01 0-1 Apr06 2-1	Nov03 3-3 May04 1-1	Aug25 0-2	Dec15 2-3 Mar16 2-0
DUMBARTON	Dec01 2-2 Feb16 0-2	Jan26 0-0	Sep01 1-1	Oct27 1-1 Mar23 2-0	Sep08 1-3		Nov17 3-2 Mar02 2-1	Oct13 2-1	Dec22 1-1 Mar30 2-2	Jan12 0-2 May04 2-0	Sep29 1-0 May11 1-0	Feb02 0-0 Apr13 2-1	Oct06 0-0	Sep18 0-1
EAST FIFE	Sep08 2-2	Nov03 2-2 Apr27 1-3	Sep29 2-0	Feb19 4-1 May11 0-5	Oct13 1-1 Apr20 0-1	Aug25 2-1			Dec11 1-1	Jan12 1-3 Mar16 2-2	Sep18 2-0	Feb02 2-1	Oct06 1-1 Mar09 1-0	Nov10 1-2 Mar30 1-2
E.STIRLING	Oct20 0-3 May11 1-1	Oct09 0-0 Feb23 1-6	Jan19 1-1	Sep22 0-4	Jan29 1-3 Mar23 0-0	Jan22 2-1 Apr27 2-0	Oct27 3-1 Apr06 5-1		Sep29 0-1	Nov17 1-0 Apr20 1-1	Nov24 1-3 Mar09 1-1	Sep01 2-2	May05 0-1	Sep15 0-2
MONTROSE	Dec15 5-0 Apr20 3-0	Sep15 2-4	Oct13 3-0 Mar23 1-0	Nov24 1-2	Feb05 2-0 Feb16 1-0	Nov03 1-2	Oct09 0-2	Feb09 2-2 May04 2-0		Feb02 0-0	Sep01 1-0	Nov17 2-3	Oct23 1-1 Apr06 0-1	Jan19 3-0 Mar12 2-1
QUEEN OF SOUTH	Nov03 1-1 Mar09 0-0	Nov24 1-3 Apr27 6-1	Dec15 1-0	Sep15 2-0 Mar30 2-2	Feb09 2-4	Oct10 1-2 Apr13 1-3	Mar06 3-0	Aug25 1-2 May11 0-3	Sep22 2-1		Jan26 3-2	Oct20 3-2	Nov10 0-0 Mar16 0-0	Jan02 1-1 Feb23 1-2
QUEEN'S PARK	Jan02 1-1 Mar30 0-0	Dec18 1-0 Apr13 3-1	Nov03 2-1 Feb16 0-0	Feb05 2-1	Sep15 1-0	Feb09 1-1	Sep22 0-2 Mar23 2-0	Sep08 4-0	Nov10 0-0 Apr27 0-3	Oct06 3-1 Mar02 3-0		Jan12 1-0	Oct20 0-0	Aug25 3-1
STENHOUSEMUIR	Jan26 2-0	Oct13 1-0	Sep15 2-0	Mar05 2-0 Apr06 1-3	Dec22 2-1	Sep22 1-4	Feb27 1-1	Nov10 4-1 Mar02 0-0	Aug25 0-1 Feb23 0-1	Feb05 2-1 Mar23 0-1	Oct09 4-2 Apr20 4-1		Oct27 2-2 May11 2-1	Nov24 3-2 Apr27 2-0
STIRLING A	Sep22 2-0 Feb13 3-0	Feb09 2-0 Mar30 1-2	Nov24 3-1	Oct13 4-1	Nov17 5-1 Apr27 0-0	Jan19 2-0 Mar09 0-0	Sep15 1-2 Aug13	Nov03 3-0	Sep01 3-0	Jan05 0-0 Feb23	Sep01 0-1 1-1	Dec15 1-1		Oct09 3-1
STRANRAER	Feb09 2-1	Sep22 2-0 Mar23 0-0	Jan16 2-3	Dec22 1-2 Mar02 4-1	Oct27 1-3	Jan30 2-1 Apr10 1-4	Sep01 2-2	Dec01 1-2 Feb16 2-0	Oct06 1-0	Oct13 4-1	Nov17 2-1 May04 1-3	Sep08 1-2	Jan12 1-4 Apr20 0-0	

171

SFA Cup

1st Round
Dec 7	Albion R	0	Arbroath	2
Dec 7	Alloa	7	Hawick	1
Dec 7	East Fife	6	Queen's Park	0
Dec 7	East Stirling	0	Dumbarton	2
Dec 14	Gala Fairydean	2	Ross Co	2
Dec 7	Vale of Leithen	1	Stranraer	2

Replay
Dec 16	Ross Co	3	Gala Fairydean	0

2nd Round
Jan 4	Alloa	0	Dumbarton	2
Jan 4	Berwick	7	Ross Co	4
Jan 4	Brechin	0	East Fife	0
Jan 14	Clyde	2	Arbroath	0
Jan 4	Huntly	4	Civil Service S	2
Jan 4	Peterhead	1	Cowdenbeath	1
Jan 4	Stenhousemuir	1	Caledonian T	4
Jan 4	Stranraer	4	Queen of South	1

Replays
Jan 11	Cowdenbeath	6	Peterhead	1
Jan 14	East Fife	3	Brechin	1

3rd Round
Jan 22	Aberdeen	0	Rangers	1
Jan 25	Airdrie	2	Stranraer	1
Jan 25	Ayr	1	Motherwell	1
Jan 25	Caledonian T	3	Clyde	1
Jan 25	Celtic	6	Montrose	0
Jan 25	Clydebank	3	Cowdenbeath	1
Jan 25	Dumbarton	0	Huntly	2
Feb 3	Dundee	1	Stirling A	1
Jan 26	Dundee U	6	Berwick	0
Jan 25	Forfar	0	Dunfermline A	0
Jan 25	Hamilton	0	Falkirk	1
Jan 25	Hibernian	2	Partick	0
Jan 25	Meadowbank	1	Kilmarnock	1
Jan 25	Morton	4	East Fife	2
Jan 25	Raith	0	St Johnstone	2
Jan 25	St Mirren	0	Hearts	0

Replays
Feb 4	Kilmarnock	1	Meadowbank	1
Feb 4	Motherwell	4	Ayr	1
Feb 5	Dunfermline A	3	Forfar	1
Feb 5	Hearts	3	St Mirren	0
Feb 5	Stirling A	0	Dundee	1

4th Round
Feb 15	Caledonian T	2	St Johnstone	2
Feb 11	Celtic	2	Dundee U	1
Feb 15	Clydebank	1	Hibernian	5
Feb 15	Dunfermline A	1	Hearts	2
Feb 15	Falkirk	0	Dundee	0
Feb 15	Huntly	1	Airdrie	3
Feb 15	Morton	2	Meadowbank	2
Feb 15	Rangers	2	Motherwell	1

Replays
Feb 24	Dundee	0	Falkirk	1
Feb 26	Meadowbank	2	Morton	3
Feb 26	St Johnstone	3	Caledonian T	0

5th Round
Mar 7	Celtic	3	Morton	0
Mar 8	Hearts	3	Falkirk	1
Mar 7	Hibernian	0	Airdrie	2
Mar 3	St Johnstone	0	Rangers	3

Semi-finals
Apr 4	Airdrie	0	Hearts	0
	played at Hampden Park			
Mar 31	Celtic	0	Rangers	1
	played at Hampden Park			

Replay
Apr 14	Airdrie	1	Hearts	1
	played at Hampden Park			
	Penalties 4-2			

Final
May 9	Airdrie	1	Rangers	2
	played at Hampden Park			

PREMIER

	ABERDEEN	AIRDRIE	CELTIC	DUNDEE U	DUNFERMLINE	FALKIRK	HEARTS	HIBERNIAN	MOTHERWELL	RANGERS	STJOHNSTONE	ST MIRREN
ABERDEEN		Oct12 3-1 Mar28 1-0	Aug24 1-0 Dec28 2-2	Nov02 0-1 Mar21 0-2	Aug17 3-0 Feb01 1-1	Nov30 1-1 Apr25 1-1	Nov20 0-2 Mar18 2-0	Sep21 1-1 Feb08 0-1	Oct30 3-1 Apr11 2-0	Dec04 3-1 May02 0-2	Sep07 2-3 Dec14 4-1	Oct05 4-1 Jan04 0-0
AIRDRIE	Aug10 1-2 Dec07 2-0		Nov02 0-3 Apr18 0-0	Oct26 1-3 Mar17 2-0	Nov12 3-1 Apr11 3-2	Nov02 0-0 Mar21 2-2	Nov02 2-3 Jan18 2-1	Sep01 0-1 Jan18 0-0	Aug24 0-1 Dec14 2-0	Oct05 0-4 Dec28 0-0	Aug31 1-2 Jan04 0-3	Oct19 4-1 Apr21 1-1
CELTIC	Nov09 2-1 Mar14 1-0	Sep21 3-1 Feb08 2-0		Oct12 4-1 Mar28 3-1	Nov30 1-0 Apr25 2-0	Aug17 4-1 Feb01 2-0	Oct05 3-1 1-2	Dec04 0-0 May02 1-2	Nov20 2-2 Mar17 4-1	Aug31 0-2 Apr11 1-3	Oct30 4-0 Apr11 3-2	Sep07 0-0 Dec14 4-0
DUNDEE U	Aug31 0-0 Jan01 4-0	Oct08 3-4 Jan11 2-1	Aug10 0-0 Dec07 1-1		Sep07 3-0 Dec14 0-0	Nov16 2-1 Dec29 2-1	Nov23 1-1 Apr18 2-0	Nov09 2-1 Mar14 1-0	Sep28 1-2 Feb22 2-2	Oct29 3-2 Apr11 1-2	Oct19 1-2 Apr04 2-1	Aug13 4-1 Jan18 1-3
DUNFERMLINE A	Oct19 0-0 Apr04 0-0	Sep14 1-2 Jan15 0-0	Aug13 1-3 Jan18 0-1	Nov06 1-2 Mar07 0-1		Oct08 0-4 Jan11 1-0	Aug10 1-2 Dec07 2-0	Nov16 1-2 Feb29 0-0	Nov23 0-0 Apr18 3-1	Nov03 0-5 Mar14 1-3	Aug31 0-0 Jan01 0-0	Sep28 1-4 Feb22 0-0
FALKIRK	Aug14 0-1 Jan18 2-2	Aug31 3-2 Jan01 0-3	Oct19 4-3 Apr04 0-3	Oct05 0-4 Jan04 1-3	Nov20 0-1 Apr11 2-0		Sep28 1-2 Mar04 1-2	Nov12 3-2 Apr11 2-3	Aug10 1-1 Dec07 0-1	Sep07 0-2 Dec14 1-3	Nov23 2-3 Apr18 2-0	Nov09 3-0 Mar14 1-0
HEARTS	Oct09 1-0 Jan11 0-4	Nov30 3-1 Apr25 2-2	Nov16 1-1 Feb29 1-2	Sep21 1-1 Feb08 1-0	Oct12 1-0 Mar28 1-0	Dec04 2-0		Aug31 0-0 Jan01 1-1	Sep07 2-0 Dec14 3-1	Aug17 0-1 Feb01 0-1	Nov09 2-1 Mar14 2-0	Oct30 1-0 Apr11 0-0
HIBERNIAN	Nov03 1-0 Apr18 1-1	Nov05 2-2 Apr07 1-2	Sep28 1-1 Feb22 0-2	Aug24 1-0 Dec28 3-2	Oct05 3-0 Jan04 1-2	Sep14 2-2 Dec21 1-2	Nov02 1-1 Mar21 1-2		Oct19 0-0 Apr04 2-3	Nov19 0-3 Mar10 1-2	Aug13 4-1 Jan18 1-3	Aug13 4-1 Dec07 1-1
MOTHERWELL	Sep14 0-1 Jan14 3-3	Nov09 1-2 Mar14 0-3	Oct08 0-2 Jan11 0-0	Dec03 1-1 May02 1-2	Sep21 3-0 Feb08 1-2	Oct12 4-2 Mar28 0-1	Oct26 0-1 Apr07 1-1	Aug17 1-1 Feb01 1-1		Nov30 0-2 Apr23 1-2	Nov16 1-1 Feb29 3-1	Aug31 1-0 Jan01 3-0
RANGERS	Sep28 0-2 Feb25 0-0	Nov16 4-0 Feb29 5-0	Nov02 1-1 Mar21 0-2	Sep14 1-1 Dec21 2-0	Aug24 2-0 Dec28 2-1	Oct26 1-1 Apr07 4-1	Oct19 4-2 Apr28 1-1	Oct08 2-0 Jan11 2-0	Aug13 2-0 Jan18 2-0		Aug10 6-0 Dec07 3-1	Nov23 0-1 Apr18 4-0
STJOHNSTONE	Oct26 1-3 Apr08 0-0	Dec04 1-0 May02 1-1	Sep14 1-0 Jan08 0-1	Nov02 1-1 Feb01 1-0	Nov02 3-2 Mar21 1-2	Sep21 2-3 Feb08 1-2	Aug24 0-1 Dec28 1-1	Nov30 0-1 Apr25 1-0	Oct05 0-1 Jan04 1-0	Oct12 2-3 Mar28 1-1		Nov20 1-0 Mar07 1-2
ST MIRREN	Nov16 0-1 Feb29 0-2	Aug17 1-2 Feb01 4-1	Oct26 0-5 Apr08 1-1	Nov30 1-1 Apr25 0-1	Dec04 0-0 May02 3-1	Aug24 0-0 Dec28 0-1	Sep14 2-3 Dec21 1-0	Oct12 0-1 Mar28 1-1	Nov02 1-2 Mar21 1-2	Sep21 1-2 Feb08 1-2	Oct09 1-1 Jan11 1-5	

DIVISION 1

	AYR U	CLYDEBANK	DUNDEE	FORFAR A	HAMILTON A	KILMARNOCK	MEADOWBANK T	MONTROSE	MORTON	PARTICK T	RAITH R	STIRLING A
AYR U		Aug17 3-0 Feb01 3-1	Oct29 4-1 Apr11 0-0	Oct12 0-2 Mar28 1-0	Nov19 0-3 Mar07 2-0	Nov02 0-2 Mar21 0-2	Sep21 7-0 Apr25 0-0	Nov30 2-0 May02 0-0	Dec03 1-3 Dec14 0-2	Sep07 1-0 Dec28 1-1	Aug24 0-2 Dec28 1-1	Oct05 1-2 Jan04 1-2
CLYDEBANK	Oct19 3-2 Apr04 1-0		Aug10 1-2 Dec07 2-2	Oct29 3-3 Apr11 0-0	Nov23 1-1 Apr18 2-2	Sep07 1-1 Dec14 2-3	Oct05 1-1 Jan04 0-2	Sep24 4-1 Dec28 1-1	Nov02 3-1 Mar21 2-3	Nov09 0-6 Mar10 0-2	Aug13 0-2 Jan18 1-1	Sep28 0-1 Feb26 1-0
DUNDEE	Sep14 3-1 Jan07 1-1	Oct12 4-0 Mar28 3-0		Nov30 4-0 Apr25 3-1	Aug24 4-1 Dec28 1-2	Sep21 2-1 Feb08 1-1	Aug17 3-1 Feb01 2-1	Dec03 1-0 May02 1-2	Oct26 0-1 Apr07 1-0	Oct05 1-2 Jan04 3-2	Nov02 1-1 Mar21 1-5	Nov19 0-0 Mar07 5-0
FORFAR A	Aug10 2-3 Nov26 0-1	Sep14 2-1 Jan07 1-3	Aug13 0-3 Jan18 0-3		Oct26 1-3 Apr07 1-3	Oct05 2-4 Jan04 0-0	Nov19 0-9 Mar07 1-0	Nov02 2-0 Mar21 2-0	Aug24 0-9 Dec28 1-5	Sep28 2-4 Feb22 0-0	Oct19 0-1 Apr04 1-2	Nov23 1-1 Apr18 1-1
HAMILTON A	Oct09 3-1 Jan11 2-1	Sep21 0-0 Feb08 1-1	Nov09 1-3 Mar14 1-3	Sep07 4-0 Dec14 1-1		Nov30 2-2 Apr25 0-1	Oct12 2-0 May02 2-0	Aug17 1-1 Mar28 2-2	Nov23 1-1 Feb01 0-0	Oct12 4-1 Jan01 3-1	Nov16 4-1 Feb29 1-1	Oct30 3-1 Apr11 1-1
KILMARNOCK	Aug31 1-1 Jan01 1-1	Oct26 2-1 Apr07 1-0	Nov23 1-2 Apr18 2-0	Nov16 4-2 Jan29 2-0	Aug13 1-2 Jan18 0-2		Nov09 1-0 Mar14 2-1	Sep14 0-0 Jan11 5-1	Oct08 0-1 Jan11 0-1	Oct19 2-3 Apr04 1-3	Sep28 1-0 Feb26 1-0	Aug10 0-0 Dec07 2-0
MEADOWBANK T	Nov23 1-1 Apr18 0-1	Nov16 1-1 Feb29 2-0	Oct19 0-0 Apr04 0-0	Oct09 3-3 Jan11 2-0	Sep28 2-3 Feb22 1-2	Aug24 1-0 Dec28 1-0		Oct26 0-0 Apr08 0-1	Sep14 1-1 Feb12 0-0	Aug12 0-1 Jan18 0-0	Aug10 1-0 Dec07 0-1	Nov02 1-0 Mar21 1-0
MONTROSE	Aug13 1-3 Jan18 1-0	Nov09 1-3 Mar14 2-1	Sep28 1-2 Feb22 0-3	Aug31 2-1 Jan01 2-1	Nov09 2-2 Dec17 1-1	Oct29 2-2 Apr11 4-2	Sep07 2-2 Dec14 1-0		Nov16 1-1 Feb29 0-1	Nov23 0-2 Apr18 1-0	Oct03 0-3 Jan11 1-2	Oct19 4-1 Apr04 2-2
MORTON	Aug13 3-4 Mar17 2-0	Nov09 1-7 Dec14 5-0	Sep28 3-0 Mar14 0-0	Aug31 1-3 Nov09 1-1	Sep07 1-0 Oct19 1-1	Nov09 1-0 Nov19 0-1	Oct29 0-1 Mar24 0-0	Oct05 2-1 Jan04 3-1		Aug10 2-1 Dec07 0-1	Nov23 0-2 Apr18 0-1	Aug13 2-1 Jan18 2-0
PARTICK T	Oct26 3-0 Feb15 4-1	Oct08 1-0 Jan11 2-1	Nov16 1-1 Feb29 2-0	Dec03 3-4 May02 0-0	Nov02 1-1 Mar21 0-0	Aug17 2-1 Feb01 2-1	Nov30 5-0 Apr25 1-2	Sep21 1-3 Feb08 3-0	Oct12 4-2 Mar28 1-0		Sep14 5-0 Dec21 0-1	Aug24 1-0 Dec28 0-1
RAITH R	Nov09 0-0 Mar14 2-4	Nov30 4-0 Apr25 1-0	Aug13 0-1 Jan01 1-0	Sep07 2-0 Feb01 2-0	Oct05 1-3 Jan04 1-2	Dec03 1-1 May02 5-0	Oct12 1-1 Mar28 2-0	Sep21 2-1 Mar07 1-2	Sep07 1-1 Feb08 0-1	Oct29 1-0 Apr11 1-2		Sep07 1-0 Dec14 1-2
STIRLING A	Nov16 0-0 Feb29 1-2	Dec03 3-0 May02 2-0	Oct08 1-1 Jan11 0-3	Sep21 1-3 Feb08 4-1	Sep14 0-1 Jan08 3-0	Oct12 0-3 Mar28 1-0	Aug31 2-3 Jan01 0-0	Aug17 2-2 Feb01 4-1	Nov30 2-2 Apr25 4-3	Nov09 1-1 Mar14 1-1	Oct26 1-3 Apr07 1-2	

172

Season 1991-92

DIVISION 2

	ALBION R	ALLOA	ARBROATH	BERWICK R	BRECHIN C	CLYDE	COWDENBEATH	DUMBARTON	EAST FIFE	E.STIRLING	QUEEN OF SOUTH	QUEEN'S PARK	STENHOUSEMUIR	STRANRAER
ALBION R		Aug17 2-1 Mar10 1-3	Aug10 0-1	Jan11 1-2	Sep28 0-3 Apr18 1-2	Oct12 2-2 May02 0-2	Nov23 0-4 Apr04 1-2	Dec26 0-3 Feb15 1-1	Feb01 0-1	Sep17 1-1 Feb24 1-3	Aug24 1-1	Jan04 1-1 Mar21 3-4	Oct26 1-1	Sep14 2-1
ALLOA	Nov09 1-0		Jan18 0-0	Dec28 2-1	Nov05 1-0 Feb08 6-1	Nov16 4-2	Feb25 4-2 May02 0-0	Oct05 1-2	Nov30 0-0 Apr25 1-2	Oct19 0-1 Apr11 1-0	Nov23 3-1 Mar28 3-1	Jan25 1-0 Mar14 2-1	Mar03 1-0	Dec14 3-1 Feb29 0-0
ARBROATH	Nov02 2-1 Mar14 1-1	Sep28 2-2 Apr18 1-3		Nov16 1-1	Sep21 3-2	Nov30 0-0 Feb08 3-0	Aug31 2-1 Mar28 1-0	Dec28 1-0	Jan11 0-0	Sep07 3-3	Oct12 2-3 Apr11 0-3	Oct26 2-2 Feb22 2-1	Feb01 2-0	Aug17 1-0
BERWICK R	Oct05 3-1 Feb29 1-1	Sep17 0-1 Feb15 0-1	Aug24 0-0 Apr25 3-2		Sep07 1-1	Jan01 2-1	Jan18 1-3	Nov09 2-2 Mar28 1-5	Oct26 1-2 May02 1-4	Feb18 1-0	Dec21 1-1	Feb25 1-3	Aug10 0-0 Apr04 0-1	Oct19 0-0 Mar14 1-2
BRECHIN C	Jan18 1-2	Aug10 0-2	Jan01 1-1 Apr04 1-0	Nov23 2-2 Mar07 2-2		Sep17 1-0 Feb29 1-2	Oct05 0-1	Sep14 0-4	Aug24 4-4 Mar21 0-1	Jan07 0-0	Oct26 7-1 Feb15 1-1	Oct19 2-0 Apr25 1-1	Nov09 1-0 May02 0-0	Feb04 2-1
CLYDE	Feb04 6-2 Apr04 0-1	Aug24 2-0	Sep14 1-1 Mar03 0-1	Sep10 2-0	Dec28 0-0		Oct19 4-0	Nov23 0-1	Aug10 2-1 Feb15 4-0	Oct26 2-3	Dec07 2-3 Mar17 2-1	Oct05 3-1	Jan21 0-0 Apr18 4-0	Jan18 4-2 Mar21 1-1
COWDENBEATH	Sep07 1-0	Oct12 1-1	Feb18 3-1 Mar21 4-1	Sep28 2-1 Apr11 2-1	Feb12 2-1 Mar14 3-1	Feb01 0-3		Oct26 2-1	Sep21 3-3 Feb29 3-1	Nov09 3-2 Feb15 4-0	Aug10 0-1 Apr25 3-1	Nov30 0-2	Aug24 2-0	Dec28 2-0
DUMBARTON	Aug31 4-3	Jan11 2-2 Mar21 1-1	Sep17 2-1 May02 1-1	Aug17 1-1	Nov30 3-0 Feb25 1-3	Sep07 0-0 Apr11 2-1	Dec14 0-0 Apr18 2-1		Sep28 1-2	Jan14 1-1 Mar17 0-1	Feb01 3-1	Nov02 3-1	Oct12 1-0	Nov16 1-0 Feb08 0-0
EAST FIFE	Oct19 3-2 Mar28 3-1	Sep14 0-0	Oct05 2-2 Mar07 3-1	Dec14 3-1	Nov16 2-1	Nov02 1-2	Jan01 1-0	Jan18 2-2 Apr02 0-2		Feb04 2-2 Apr18 1-1	Sep17 4-1 Feb22 5-1	Aug17 2-0 Feb08 2-2	Nov23 4-4	Aug31 2-1
E.STIRLING	Dec28 2-1	Feb01 2-1	Nov23 1-1 Feb29 0-5	Sep14 4-1 Feb08 0-4	Aug31 3-3 Mar14 0-0	Dec14 2-3 Apr25 2-1	Aug17 1-2	Sep21 1-2	Oct12 4-2		Jan11 2-1	Nov16 2-1	Sep28 2-1 Mar28 0-3	Nov02 2-2 Apr04 2-2
QUEEN OF SOUTH	Nov16 2-4 Feb08 3-0	Sep07 1-3	Jan25 0-2 Apr18 0-3	Aug24 0-3	Dec14 4-2	Aug17 1-2	Nov02 3-3 Mar14 1-2	Oct19 2-4 Mar21 2-3	Dec28 3-1 Mar21 2-3	Oct05 5-1		Jan18 2-2 Apr04 5-3	Sep14 2-1 Feb29 1-3	Sep21 0-2
QUEEN'S PARK	Sep23 1-1	Aug31 2-1	Dec14 1-0 Apr11 4-1	Oct12 3-2	Feb01 0-1 Mar28 1-0	Jan11 1-1 Feb29 1-2	Sep14 2-3 Feb29 0-0	Aug10 0-3 May02 1-1	Nov09 1-0	Aug24 4-2	Sep28 1-4		Dec28 2-1 Feb15 2-0	Nov23 0-1 Apr18 5-2
STENHOUSEMUIR	Dec14 1-1 Apr11 4-0	Sep21 4-0 Jan01 1-1	Oct19 2-1 Mar21 1-0	Nov02 0-2	Aug17 1-2	Aug31 1-3	Nov16 1-0	Feb04 2-1 Feb08 2-4	Sep07 2-1 Apr25 0-1	Jan18 1-3 Mar14 1-2	Nov30 1-3	Sep17 1-3		Oct05 0-1
STRANRAER	Nov30 1-2 Apr25 2-0	Oct26 1-0	Nov09 2-0 Feb15 1-0	Feb01 2-2	Oct12 1-3 Mar28 1-1	Sep28 2-0	Sep17 2-2 Feb22 1-0	Aug24 2-1	Jan08 0-2 Apr11 1-1	Aug10 3-5	Jan01 0-2 May02 1-3	Sep07 2-1	Jan11 3-2 Mar11 1-1	

PREMIER DIVISION FINAL TABLE

	P	W	D	L	F	A	Pts
Rangers	44	33	6	5	101	31	72
Hearts	44	27	9	8	60	37	63
Celtic	44	26	10	8	88	42	62
Dundee U	44	19	13	12	66	50	51
Hibernian	44	16	17	11	53	45	49
Aberdeen	44	17	14	13	55	42	48
Airdrie	44	13	10	21	50	70	36
St Johnstone	44	13	10	21	52	73	36
Falkirk	44	12	11	21	54	73	35
Motherwell	44	10	14	20	43	61	34
St Mirren	44	6	12	26	33	73	24
Dunfermline A	44	4	10	30	22	80	18

DIVISION 1 FINAL TABLE

	P	W	D	L	F	A	Pts
Dundee	44	23	12	9	80	48	58
Partick T	44	23	11	10	52	36	57
Hamilton A	44	22	13	9	72	48	57
Kilmarnock	44	21	12	11	59	37	54
Raith R	44	21	11	12	59	42	53
Ayr U	44	18	11	15	63	55	47
Morton	44	17	12	15	66	59	46
Stirling A	44	14	13	17	50	57	41
Clydebank	44	12	12	20	59	77	36
Meadowbank T	44	7	16	21	37	59	30
Montrose	44	5	17	22	45	85	27
Forfar A	44	5	12	27	36	85	22

DIVISION 2 FINAL TABLE

	P	W	D	L	F	A	Pts
Dumbarton	39	20	12	7	65	37	52
Cowdenbeath	39	22	7	10	74	52	51
Alloa	39	20	10	9	58	38	50
East Fife	39	19	11	9	72	57	49
Clyde	39	18	7	14	61	43	43
E Stirling	39	15	11	13	61	70	41
Arbroath	39	14	11	14	49	48	38
Brechin C	39	13	12	14	54	55	38
Queen's Park	39	14	7	18	59	63	35
Stranraer	39	13	9	17	46	56	35
Queen of South	39	14	5	20	71	86	33
Berwick R	39	10	11	18	50	65	31
Stenhousemuir	39	11	8	20	46	57	30
Albion R	39	5	10	24	42	81	20

League Cup results for 1991-92 are detailed on page 214.

SFA Cup
1st Round
Dec 8	Cove R 2	Peterhead 0	
Dec 8	Forfar 5	Albion R 0	
Dec 5	Huntly 4	Stranraer.......2	
Dec 5	Inverness T ..3	Civil Service S ...1	
Dec 5	Queen of South 3	Spartans 0	
Dec 5	Queen's Park ..0	Clyde 1	

2nd Round
Dec 19	Clyde 3	Brechin 1
Dec 19	Cove R 2	Montrose 0
Dec 19	East Fife 1	Alloa 1
Dec 19	Gala Fairydean .1	Arbroath 1
Jan 4	Huntly 2	Queen of South .1
Dec 26	Inverness T ..0	Berwick 1
Dec 28	Stenhousemuir .2	Forfar 3
Dec 19	Vale of Leithen .2	East Stirling 2

Replays
Jan 28	Alloa 1	East Fife 1
	Penalties 5-6	
Jan 28	Arbroath 2	Gala Fairydean ...0
Jan 28	East Stirling ...3	Vale of Leithen ..2

3rd Round
Jan 9	Aberdeen 4	Hamilton 1
Jan 9	Airdrie 0	Clydebank 0
Jan 9	Arbroath 3	Morton 0
Jan 9	Clyde 0	Celtic 0
Jan 9	Cove R 2	East Stirling ...2
Jan 10	Dundee 2	Dumbarton 0
Jan 9	Dundee U 3	Meadowbank 1
Jan 9	Dunfermline A .1	Ayr 2
Jan 27	Falkirk 5	Berwick 2
Jan 9	Hearts 6	Huntly 0
Jan 9	Hibernian 5	St Mirren 2
Jan 9	Kilmarnock ...5	Raith 0
Jan 9	Motherwell ...0	Rangers 2
Jan 9	Partick 0	Cowdenbeath ...1
Jan 9	St Johnstone ..6	Forfar 0
Jan 9	Stirling A 1	East Fife 2

Replays
Jan 19	Clydebank 2	Airdrie 0
Jan 20	Celtic 1	Clyde 0
Jan 25	East Stirling ...2	Cove R 1

4th Round
Feb 7	Aberdeen 2	Dundee U 0
Feb 6	Arbroath 0	East Fife 0
Feb 6	Ayr 0	Rangers 2
Feb 6	Cowdenbeath ..0	Hibernian 0
Feb 6	East Stirling ...1	Clydebank 2
Feb 6	Falkirk 2	Celtic 0
Feb 6	Hearts 2	Dundee 0
Feb 6	Kilmarnock 0	St Johnstone ...0

Replays
Feb 10	Hibernian 1	Cowdenbeath ...0
Feb 10	St Johnstone ..1	Kilmarnock ...0
Feb 16	East Fife 1	Arbroath 4

5th Round
Mar 6	Aberdeen 1	Clydebank 1
Mar 6	Arbroath 0	Rangers 3
Mar 6	Hearts 2	Falkirk 0
Mar 6	Hibernian 2	St Johnstone ...0

Replay
Mar 16	Clydebank 3	Aberdeen 4

Semi-finals
Apr 3	Aberdeen 1	Hibernian 0
	played at Tynecastle	
Apr 3	Hearts 1	Rangers 2
	played at Hampden Park	

Final
May 29	Aberdeen 1	Rangers 2
	played at Hampden Park	

PREMIER

	ABERDEEN	AIRDRIE	CELTIC	DUNDEE	DUNDEE U	FALKIRK	HEARTS	HIBERNIAN	MOTHERWELL	PARTICK T	RANGERS	ST. JOHNSTONE
ABERDEEN		Sep02 0-0 Jan16 7-0	Aug05 1-1 Feb13 1-1	Aug22 2-1 Jan02 0-0	Oct03 0-1 Feb24 0-0	Oct17 3-1 Mar13 2-2	Nov28 6-2 Mar13 3-2	Aug01 3-0 Dec19 2-0	Nov11 2-0 Mar27 1-0	Sep19 2-0 Mar02 1-0	Feb02 0-1 May12 1-0	Dec05 3-0 May08 1-1
AIRDRIE	Oct31 1-2 Apr10 1-1		Aug29 1-1 Jan23 0-1	Aug08 0-0 Jan30 2-2	Sep12 1-2 Mar06 1-3	Aug22 2-0 Jan02 0-1	Sep26 2-0 Feb20 0-0	Nov21 1-3 Apr20 3-1	Dec12 0-2 May15 1-2	Oct10 2-2 Mar09 2-2	Dec01 1-1 May01 0-1	Nov14 0-2 Apr27 1-1
CELTIC	Dec02 2-2 May01 1-0	Oct24 2-0 Apr06 4-0		Dec12 1-0 May15 2-0	Aug15 2-0 Dec26 0-1	Nov21 3-2 Apr20 1-0	Oct17 1-1 Mar10 2-1	Sep12 2-3 Mar16 1-0	Aug08 1-1 Jan30 3-1	Sep26 2-1 Feb20 0-0	Nov07 0-1 Mar20 0-0	Sep02 2-0 Feb03 5-1
DUNDEE	Nov07 1-2 Mar20 0-4	Oct17 2-0 Mar13 0-1	Oct03 0-1 Feb23 0-1		Nov21 1-3 Apr20 2-1	Aug01 1-2 Dec19 0-4	Sep01 1-3 May03 2-1	Dec05 2-1 May08 1-0	Sep12 0-2 Mar06 0-3	Oct24 4-3 Apr26 1-3	Aug15 0-1 Dec26 1-0	Aug04 1-1 Feb13 1-0
DUNDEE U	Dec12 2-2 May15 1-4	Nov28 0-0 Apr17 3-0	Nov11 1-1 Mar27 2-3	Sep19 0-1 Feb27 1-0		Aug29 2-0 Jan23 2-1	Aug08 1-1 Jan30 0-1	Oct31 2-1 Apr13 0-3	Oct07 2-1 Apr09 0-0	Dec01 1-1 May01 3-1	Sep26 0-4 Feb20 0-0	Aug22 2-1 Jan02 1-2
FALKIRK	Aug08 0-1 Jan30 1-4	Nov07 5-1 Mar20 0-1	Nov11 4-5 Feb27 0-3	Sep19 0-1 Mar10 1-0	Oct10 2-2 Apr03 1-0		Dec02 2-1 May01 6-0	Aug15 2-1 Dec26 3-3	Sep26 0-1 Feb20 4-2	Sep12 1-2 Feb02 1-2	Dec19 1-2 May15 2-2	Nov28 2-2 Apr17 2-2
HEARTS	Sep12 1-0 May05 1-2	Dec05 1-3 May08 1-1	Aug01 0-1 Dec19 1-0	Oct31 1-0 Apr10 0-0	Oct17 1-0 Mar13 1-0	Aug05 3-0 Feb13 3-1		Nov07 1-0 Mar20 1-0	Aug29 1-0 Mar28 0-0	Aug15 2-1 Feb26 1-1	Nov21 1-1 Apr14 2-3	Oct03 1-1 Jan20 2-0
HIBERNIAN	Oct07 1-3 Mar09 1-2	Sep19 2-2 Feb27 3-1	Nov28 1-2 Apr17 3-1	Sep26 0-0 Feb20 1-3	Sep02 0-1 Jan16 2-1	Nov14 1-1 Mar27 1-1	Aug22 2-0 Jan02 0-0		Dec01 2-2 May01 1-0	Dec12 1-0 May15 0-1	Aug08 2-2 Jan30 3-4	Oct24 0-0 Apr06 2-2
MOTHERWELL	Aug15 2-1 Dec26 0-2	Oct03 2-0 Feb06 0-0	Oct17 1-3 Apr03 1-2	Nov28 1-3 Apr17 1-2	Aug01 0-1 Feb02 2-0	Dec05 0-1 May08 1-1	Oct24 1-3 Apr20 0-1	Aug04 1-2 Feb13		Nov07 0-2 Mar20 2-3	Sep02 1-4 Feb23 0-4	Sep19 3-3 Feb27 1-1
PARTICK T	Nov24 0-7 Apr20 1-3	Aug01 1-0 Dec19 1-1	Dec05 2-3 May08 0-1	Aug29 6-3 Jan27 2-0	Aug05 0-1 Feb13 0-4	Oct31 1-2 Apr10 0-1	Nov10 1-1 Apr10 1-1	Oct03 2-2 Feb16 0-3	Aug22 2-2 Jan02 0-1		Sep12 1-4 May04 3-0	Oct17 1-0 Mar13 1-1
RANGERS	Aug29 3-1 Mar30 2-0	Aug04 2-0 Feb13 2-2	Aug22 1-1 Jan02 1-0	Nov11 3-1 Mar27 3-0	Jan05 3-2 May08 1-0	Oct03 4-0 Feb09 5-0	Sep19 2-1 Feb27 2-1	Oct17 1-0 Mar13 3-0	Oct31 4-2 Apr10 1-0	Nov28 3-0 Apr17 3-1		Aug01 1-0 Dec19 2-0
STJOHNSTONE	Sep26 0-3 Feb20 0-2	Aug15 3-0 Dec26 1-0	Oct31 0-0 Apr10 1-1	Dec02 4-4 May01 1-1	Nov07 2-0 Mar20 1-1	Sep12 3-2 Mar16 1-4	Aug29 1-1 May15 1-0	Nov24 1-1 Jan23 3-1	Aug08 1-1 Apr24 2-0	Oct07 1-5 Jan30 0-0		

DIVISION 1

	AYR U	CLYDEBANK	COWDENBEATH	DUMBARTON	DUNFERMLINE A	HAMILTON A	KILMARNOCK	MEADOWBANK T	MORTON	RAITH R	ST MIRREN	STIRLING A
AYR U		Oct17 2-1 Mar13 0-0	Sep12 0-1 Mar06 3-1	Nov21 5-3 Apr24 0-0	Aug01 1-1 Dec12 1-0	Oct31 0-0 Apr10 1-0	Aug22 2-0 Jan02 0-1	Aug04 1-2 Feb13 1-0	Sep05 0-2 Feb09 0-0	Nov07 1-1 May08 0-0	Dec05 2-0 Jan26 3-3	Oct03 2-1 Jan26 2-2
CLYDEBANK	Aug08 1-1 Jan30 1-1		Oct10 4-1 Mar09 5-0	Aug22 0-1 Jan02 3-1	Oct31 1-0 Apr10 2-1	Sep26 3-1 Feb20 1-1	Sep05 1-1 Feb16 0-1	Nov28 0-2 Apr17 3-1	Dec19 3-0 May01 2-2	Dec01 2-2 May15 4-1	Nov07 1-2 Mar27 0-3	Sep19 4-1 Feb27 1-1
COWDENBEATH	Dec08 2-2 Apr17 0-1	Aug01 3-3 Dec12 1-3		Sep05 0-1 Feb23 0-2	Aug05 2-5 Feb13 1-2	Nov07 0-3 Mar27 1-1	Dec05 2-3 May08 1-1	Aug22 1-5 Jan20 2-2	Oct31 1-3 Apr10 0-1	Sep19 0-3 Feb27 2-2	Oct03 1-2 Jan27 1-0	Oct17 1-1 Mar13 1-1
DUMBARTON	Sep19 0-3 Feb27 2-0	Nov14 3-1 Mar20 0-2	Oct24 1-0 Apr03 0-0		Dec05 0-1 May00 2-0	Nov28 2-2 Apr17 2-0	Aug04 1-3 Feb13 1-0	Oct03 3-2 Dec01 0-1	Aug15 0-1 Feb06 3-1	Aug29 1-2 Mar13 1-2	Oct17 4-2 Dec12 1-2	Aug01 4-3 Mar13 0-3
DUNFERMLINE A	Oct10 1-3 Mar10 1-1	Aug29 1-3 Feb02 2-0	Dec19 3-2 May01 0-2	Sep26 2-2 Feb20 2-2		Aug08 2-1 Jan30 2-1	Nov07 1-3 Mar27 2-2	Sep19 2-2 Feb27 3-2	Dec02 0-1 May15 1-2	Aug22 0-0 Jan02 0-0	Nov28 1-2 Apr17 1-2	Oct24 0-1 Apr03 0-1
HAMILTON A	Aug29 1-1 Mar02 1-3	Dec08 3-0 May08 2-1	Aug15 2-0 Dec26 4-0	Sep12 3-2 Mar06 0-2	Oct17 2-1 Mar13		Oct03 1-1 Jan27 1-2	Aug01 1-3 Jan06 2-2	Nov24 3-1 Apr24 0-0	Oct24 2-2 Apr03 2-0	Aug05 0-0 Feb13 2-2	Nov14 1-0 Mar20 2-0
KILMARNOCK	Nov14 3-0 Mar20 1-1	Oct24 3-3 Apr03 6-0	Sep26 3-0 Feb20 1-1	Dec19 1-0 May01 1-0	Aug15 0-1 Dec26 2-3	Dec01 1-0 May15		Aug29 1-0 Jan16 5-0	Oct10 3-0 Mar09 2-2	Aug08 1-1 Jan30 3-0	Sep19 1-2 Feb27 1-1	Nov28 1-0 Apr17 3-0
MEADOWBANK T	Dec19 1-0 May01 1-2	Sep12 1-0 Mar31 0-1	Nov14 2-3 Mar20 3-1	Jan27 3-2 May15 2-1	Nov21 3-2 Apr24 0-1	Oct10 1-0 Mar10 1-2	Oct31 4-2 Apr14 1-1		Aug08 0-3 Jan30 1-1	Sep26 0-2 Feb20 1-1	Sep05 1-1 Feb03 1-2	Aug15 0-0 Feb06 1-1
MORTON	Oct24 2-1 Apr03 1-0	Aug04 5-1 Feb13 2-0	Aug29 1-0 Feb02 0-0	Oct03 1-2 Mar27 1-1	Nov28 0-1 Feb06 2-0	Oct03 2-1 Feb27 1-0	Aug01 2-1 Dec29 1-3	Oct17 4-1 Mar13		Nov28 3-4 Apr17 1-1	Aug22 0-1 Jan02 1-1	Sep19 2-2 May08 1-3
RAITH R	Aug15 1-0 Dec26 1-1	Oct03 2-2 Jan26 4-2	Nov21 3-0 Apr24 4-1	Oct31 4-1 Apr20 2-0	Nov14 1-0 Mar20 2-0	Sep05 2-1 Feb02 1-1	Oct17 1-1 Mar13 1-1	Dec05 5-0 May08 3-2	Sep12 2-1 Mar06 2-0		Aug01 7-0 Dec12 3-1	Aug04 0-0 Feb13 2-0
ST MIRREN	Sep26 2-0 Feb20 1-0	Aug15 0-0 Dec26 3-2	Dec02 4-0 May15 1-2	Aug08 2-1 Jan30 1-2	Sep12 0-2 Mar06 0-1	Dec19 2-1 May01 2-1	Nov21 1-1 Apr24 1-2	Oct24 2-3 Apr03 2-0	Nov14 1-1 Mar20 1-1	Oct10 1-0		Aug29 1-1 Jan16 1-0
STIRLING A	Dec01 0-0 May15 1-1	Nov21 0-1 Apr24 2-3	Aug08 2-1 Feb16 2-1	Oct10 1-2 Mar09 1-0	Oct15 0-4 Feb09 1-2	Sep05 0-5 Jan01 0-0	Sep12 0-2 May06 2-2	Oct17 0-1 Mar27 2-2	Nov07 4-1 Feb20 0-2	Sep26 1-1 May01 2-1	Dec29 0-3	

174

Rangers' Hateley and McCoist celebrate an own-goal by Aberdeen in the 1992 Skol Cup.

DIVISION 2

	ALBION R	ALLOA	ARBROATH	BERWICK R	BRECHIN C	CLYDE	EAST FIFE	E.STIRLING	FORFAR A	MONTROSE	QUEEN OF SOUTH	QUEEN'S PARK	STENHOUSEMUIR	STRANRAER
ALBION R		Oct03 0-1	Feb13 0-1 May01 1-2	Sep05 1-1 Mar13 0-2	Nov07 1-4	Dec12 1-2	Oct31 0-5 Apr03 4-2	Jan30 2-2	Oct17 2-1	Sep12 2-2	Jan09 2-1 Mar27 1-3	Aug15 3-2	Feb16 0-0 Apr24 0-2	Nov21 1-1 Feb27 1-2
ALLOA	Dec26 4-0 Feb20 1-0		Sep12 0-2 Apr03 0-3	Aug08 2-0 Mar20 0-2	Sep26 3-2	Aug29 1-5 Apr24 1-1	Jan02 0-2	Nov21 1-0	Nov14 1-1	Jan26 3-0 Mar13 3-1	Feb06 2-2	Oct24 0-0	Aug22 2-1 May01 0-2	Oct10 1-4
ARBROATH	Oct10 2-0	Nov28 0-0		Jan05 0-1 Apr10 1-2 6-0	Aug08 0-0 Feb20 2-0	Nov14 1-1	Sep19 1-3	Aug22 4-5 May08 3-0	Jan02 2-3 Mar16 0-0	Sep26 3-4 May15 0-0	Oct24 0-0	Aug29 2-1	Feb10 3-2 Mar27 2-1	Jan20 2-1 Apr24 1-4
BERWICK R	Nov14 1-1	Dec12 2-2	Oct03 5-1		Feb06 0-2 Apr03 2-1	Jan16 0-3 Mar06 0-1	Jan30 3-0	Oct17 2-5 May01 0-0	Feb13 2-1	Nov07 3-0 Mar27 2-1	Nov28 1-4 Feb20 2-0	Sep19 1-0 Apr24 3-0	Jan02 1-1	Oct24 1-2
BRECHIN C	Aug29 2-0 May08 2-0	Jan30 4-2 Mar27 1-0	Dec12 2-0	Aug22 5-1		Oct24 2-1	Oct17 1-0	Oct03 2-1 Apr10 5-0	Feb02 1-2 Apr24 0-1	Aug15 3-1 Feb27 0-0	Nov14 3-0	Feb13 1-0	Nov21 2-2	Sep12 1-1 Mar13 0-1
CLYDE	Aug08 2-0 Apr17 4-0	Nov07 1-1	Sep05 2-0 Mar09 2-0	Oct31 2-0	Feb23 0-1 May15 1-2		Aug22 2-2	Jan02 5-1 Mar27 2-1	Sep19 0-1 May01 3-2	Oct10 1-2 Apr10 2-1	Feb16 2-1	Nov28 4-1 Feb20 2-3	Sep26 0-0	Feb06 0-0
EAST FIFE	Jan16 5-0	Aug15 2-0 Mar06 2-2	Nov21 1-3	Sep26 4-2 May15 1-2	Feb09 1-0 May01 1-2	Jan16 1-1 Feb27 2-3		Sep12 2-2	Aug29 0-3	Oct24 2-3 Apr24 0-0	Oct10 2-5	Nov14 2-1	Aug08 1-1 Apr10 2-1	Dec01 0-1 Mar27 2-1
E.STIRLING	Sep26 1-1 May15 0-1	Sep19 4-2 Feb27 0-2	Feb23 1-2	Feb10 2-0	Dec26 0-0	Aug15 1-2	Nov28 1-6 Mar20 1-3		Oct24 1-0 Mar13 0-2	Aug08 0-2 May08 0-0	Aug29 1-2 Apr24 1-2	Feb02 2-2 Apr03 4-1	Oct10 3-7	Nov14 1-2
FORFAR A	Feb06 3-2 Apr10 5-2	Sep05 1-1 May08 1-1	Aug15 1-1 Apr17 0-2	Oct10 5-3	Oct31 0-1	Nov21 2-4	Nov07 2-2 Feb20 1-2	Jan23 5-1		Jan19 4-3	Aug08 5-1	Jan26 2-0 Mar27 2-2	Sep12 2-2 Mar06 1-0	Sep26 4-1
MONTROSE	Nov28 2-1 Mar06 1-1	Oct31 1-4 Apr17 2-0	Jan30 1-1	Aug29 1-3	Jan02 0-2	Feb13 1-2	Jan23 1-3	Dec12 4-1	Oct03 0-0 Mar20 1-3		Sep19 5-1 Apr03 0-1	Oct17 0-2 May15 0-3	Sep05 0-1 Feb20 0-0	Oct03 0-2 May01 0-2
QUEEN OF SOUTH	Aug22 0-3	Oct17 1-2 May15 0-7	Feb02 0-1 Mar20 2-3	Sep12 1-0	Sep05 0-0 Mar06 1-2	Oct03 3-1 May08 2-3	Feb13 1-1 Apr17 2-0	Nov07 1-2	Dec12 1-1 Feb27 2-4	Nov21 0-1		Jan30 5-2	Oct31 0-1	Jan02 2-0 Apr10 3-3
QUEEN'S PARK	Jan02 1-0 Mar20 1-1	Feb09 0-3 Apr10 2-2	Nov07 4-0 Feb27 2-1	Nov21 1-0	Oct10 1-2 Apr17 1-0	Sep12 1-6	Sep05 1-3 Mar13 2-2	Oct31 4-2	Aug22 1-2	Feb06 3-1	Sep26 1-2 May01 1-1		Dec26 2-2	Aug08 1-1
STENHOUSEMUIR	Oct24 2-0	Feb02 0-1	Oct17 1-3	Aug15 1-3 Feb27 0-0	Sep19 2-4 Mar20 3-0	Oct03 0-2 Apr03 3-0	Dec12 3-1 Apr17 2-0	Feb13 1-2	Nov28 2-0	Nov14 2-0	Jan26 1-1 Mar13 2-1	Oct03 2-0 May08 3-0		Aug29 1-2 May15 2-5
STRANRAER	Sep19 1-1	Feb13 1-2 Apr17 3-3	Oct31 1-0	Jan23 1-3 May08 3-1	Nov28 0-0	Oct17 1-1 Mar20 1-1	Oct03 2-1	Sep05 4-1 Feb20 0-0	Jan30 2-0 Apr03 3-1	Jan09 3-1	Aug15 2-2	Dec12 1-1 Mar06 4-2	Nov07 0-0	

PREMIER DIVISION FINAL TABLE

	P	W	D	L	F	A	Pts
Rangers	44	33	7	4	97	35	73
Aberdeen	44	27	10	7	87	36	64
Celtic	44	24	12	8	68	41	60
Dundee U	44	19	9	16	56	49	47
Hearts	44	15	14	15	37	35	44
St Johnstone	44	10	20	14	52	66	40
Hibernian	44	12	13	19	54	64	37
Partick T	44	12	12	20	50	71	36
Motherwell	44	11	13	20	46	62	35
Dundee	44	11	12	21	48	68	34
Falkirk	44	11	7	26	60	86	29
Airdrie	44	6	17	21	35	70	29

DIVISION 1 FINAL TABLE

	P	W	D	L	F	A	Pts
Raith R	44	25	15	4	85	41	65
Kilmarnock	44	21	12	11	67	40	54
Dunfermline A	44	22	8	14	64	47	52
St Mirren	44	21	9	14	62	52	51
Hamilton A	44	19	12	13	65	45	50
Morton	44	19	10	15	65	56	48
Ayr U	44	14	18	12	49	44	46
Clydebank	44	16	13	15	71	66	45
Dumbarton	44	15	7	22	56	71	37
Stirling A	44	11	13	20	44	61	35
Meadowbank T	44	11	10	23	51	80	32
Cowdenbeath	44	3	7	34	33	109	13

DIVISION 2 FINAL TABLE

	P	W	D	L	F	A	Pts
Clyde	39	22	10	7	77	42	54
Brechin C	39	23	7	9	62	32	53
Stranraer	39	19	15	5	69	44	53
Forfar A	39	18	10	11	74	54	46
Alloa	39	16	12	11	63	54	44
Arbroath	39	18	8	13	59	50	44
Stenhousemuir	39	15	10	14	59	48	40
Berwick R	39	16	7	16	56	64	39
East Fife	39	14	10	15	70	64	38
Queen of South	39	12	9	18	57	72	33
Queen's Park	39	8	12	19	51	73	28
Montrose	39	10	7	22	46	71	27
E Stirling	39	8	9	22	50	85	25
Albion R	39	6	10	23	36	76	22

League Cup results for 1992-93 are detailed on page 215.

SFA Cup
1st Round
Dec 11	Albion R 0	Huntly 0
Dec 11	Cowdenbeath .1	Queen's Park ...1
Dec 11	East Fife 5	Rothes 0
Dec 11	Forfar 8	Queen of South .3
Dec 11	Ross Co 11	St Cuthbert's ...0
Dec 11	Stranraer 3	Whitehill 3

Replays
Dec 14	Queen's Park ..2	Cowdenbeath ...3
Dec 18	Whitehill 0	Stranraer 4
Jan 15	Huntly 5	Albion R 3

2nd Round
Jan 15	Alloa 4	Gala 0
Jan 8	Berwick 1	East Fife 0
Jan 15	Cowdenbeath .1	Stenhousemuir .0
Jan 8	E.Stirling 4	Cove R 1
Jan 8	Forfar 0	Ross Co 4
Jan 8	Meadowbank ..1	Montrose 2
Jan 15	Selkirk 0	Arbroath 3
Jan 22	Huntly 1	Stranraer 2

3rd Round
Jan 29	Airdrie 1	Dunfermline A ..1
Feb 8	Alloa 2	Ross Co 0
Jan 29	Arbroath 2	Dundee U 3
Jan 29	Clydebank 1	Dundee 1
Feb 8	E.Stirling 1	Aberdeen 3
Jan 29	Hibernian ...2	Clyde 1
Jan 29	Kilmarnock ..2	Ayr 1
Jan 29	Morton 2	Cowdenbeath ...2
Jan 29	Motherwell ...1	Celtic 0
Jan 29	Partick 0	Hearts 1
Jan 29	Raith 2	Brechin 0
Jan 29	Rangers 4	Dumbarton 1
Jan 29	St Johnstone .2	Hamilton 0
Jan 29	St Mirren 2	Montrose 0
Jan 29	Stirling A 1	Berwick 0
Jan 29	Stranraer 2	Falkirk 1

Replays
Feb 8	Cowdenbeath .1	Morton 2
Feb 8	Dunfermline A .1	Airdrie 3
Feb 9	Dundee 2	Clydebank 1

4th Round
Feb 19	Aberdeen 1	Raith 0
Feb 19	Airdrie 1	Stranraer 0
Feb 20	Dundee 3	St Mirren 1
Feb 19	Dundee U 2	Motherwell 2
Feb 20	Hibernian 1	Heats 2
Feb 19	Morton 0	Kilmarnock 1
Feb 19	Rangers 6	Alloa 0
Feb 28	St Johnstone ..3	Stirling A 3

Replays
Mar 1	Motherwell 0	Dundee U 1
Mar 1	Stirling A 0	St Johnstone ...2

5th Round
Mar 12	Airdrie 0	Dundee U 0
Mar 12	Kilmarnock ...1	Dundee 0
Mar 12	Rangers 2	Hearts 0
Mar 12	St Johnstone ..1	Aberdeen 1

Replays
Mar 15	Aberdeen 2	St Johnstone ...0
Mar 15	Dundee U 2	Airdrie 0

Semi-finals
Apr 9	Aberdeen 1	Dundee U 1
	played at Hampden Park	
Apr 10	Kilmarnock ...0	Rangers 0
	played at Hampden Park	

PREMIER

	ABERDEEN	CELTIC	DUNDEE	DUNDEE U	HEARTS	HIBERNIAN	KILMARNOCK	MOTHERWELL	PARTICK T	RAITH R	RANGERS	ST JOHNSTONE
ABERDEEN		Nov09 1-1 May14 1-1	Oct30 1-0 Apr30 1-1	Oct23 2-0 Mar26 1-0	Oct05 0-0 Mar05 0-1	Nov27 1-1 Mar29 2-3	Aug14 0-0 Dec18 3-1	Nov13 0-1 Apr16 0-0	Dec14 1-0 Apr23 2-0	Sep25 4-1 Feb12 4-0	Sep18 2-0 Jan22 0-0	Aug28 0-1 Jan19 1-1
CELTIC	Sep04 0-1 Jan19 2-2		Oct09 2-1 Apr06 1-1	Sep18 1-1 Jan22 0-2	Nov20 0-0 Apr09 1-1	Aug14 1-1 Dec18 0-2	Oct02 0-0 Mar01 4-0	Nov24 3-0 Mar26 3-0	Nov06 2-0 May07 1-3	Nov27 0-0 Mar30 2-1	Oct05 0-0 Jan01 1-1	Dec04 1-0 Apr27 1-1
DUNDEE	Aug21 1-1 Jan11 0-1	Dec11 1-1 Apr23 0-2		Dec07 1-2 Mar24 1-1	Oct02 2-0 Mar01 0-2	Nov06 3-2 May07 4-0	Oct23 1-0 Dec18 3-0	Aug14 1-2 Dec26 1-3	Oct05 0-1 Mar05 1-0	Sep18 1-1 Jan22 2-2	Sep04 1-1 Jan15 1-1	Nov20 0-1 Apr09 0-1
DUNDEE U	Aug28 1-1 Dec27 0-1	Nov30 1-0 Apr02 1-3	Sep11 1-0 Feb05 1-1		Aug28 2-0 Jan08 3-0	Nov13 0-2 Apr16 3-0	Dec04 2-2 Apr26 1-3	Sep25 0-0 Feb12 1-2	Oct16 2-2 Mar19 2-3	Nov09 1-3 May14 0-0	Oct09 0-0 Apr05 0-0	Oct30 2-0 Apr30 0-0
HEARTS	Dec04 1-1 Apr27 1-1	Sep25 1-0 Feb12 0-2	Nov13 1-2 Apr16 0-2	Nov06 1-1 Apr07 2-0		Aug21 1-0 Jan12 0-1	Sep18 0-1 Jan22 1-0	Dec15 2-3 Mar30 2-2	Sep04 2-1 Jan15 0-1	Aug14 1-0 Dec18 0-2	Nov03 2-2 Mar26 1-0	Oct09 1-1 Apr06 1-1
HIBERNIAN	Sep11 2-1 Feb05 3-1	Oct16 1-1 Mar19 0-0	Aug28 2-0 Jan08 2-0	Oct02 2-0 Feb26 0-1	Oct30 0-2 Apr20 0-0		Nov09 2-1 May14 0-0	Dec11 3-2 Apr23 0-2	Aug07 0-0 Dec27 5-1	Oct05 3-2 Mar05 3-0	Nov20 0-0 May03 1-0	Nov30 0-0 Apr02 0-0
KILMARNOCK	Oct16 1-1 Mar19 2-3	Nov13 1-2 Apr16 2-0	Aug07 1-1 Jan04 1-0	Oct05 0-1 Mar05 1-1	Nov30 1-1 Apr02 0-1	Sep04 0-1 Jan15 0-0		Aug21 3-1 Jan01 1-0	Sep25 1-0 Feb12 0-0	Dec11 1-0 Apr23 0-0	Nov06 0-2 May07 1-0	Sep11 1-1 Feb05 0-0
MOTHERWELL	Oct02 0-0 Mar08 1-1	Aug07 2-2 Jan11 2-3	Oct16 1-0 Mar19 1-1	Nov20 2-0 May03 0-1	Sep11 2-0 Feb05 2-1	Oct09 0-2 Mar12 2-1	Oct30 2-2 Apr30		Nov30 1-0 Apr02 2-2	Aug28 4-1 Jan25 3-1	Dec04 0-2 Apr26 2-1	Nov30 1-0 May14 0-1
PARTICK T	Oct09 3-2 Apr05 1-1	Aug28 0-1 Jan08 1-0	Dec04 3-2 Apr26 1-0	Aug14 1-2 Dec18 1-0	Oct23 0-0 May14 0-1	Nov02 2-2 Mar26 0-1	Nov20 0-1 Apr19 1-0	Sep18 1-0 Jan22 0-0		Oct30 1-1 Apr30 2-2	Nov27 1-1 Mar29 1-2	Oct02 4-1 Mar22 0-0
RAITH R	Dec07 1-1 May03 0-2	Sep11 1-4 Feb05 0-0	Nov30 2-1 Apr02 0-1	Sep04 2-1 Jan15 1-1	Oct16 1-0 Mar19 2-2	Dec04 2-2 Apr26 1-1	Oct09 0-3 Mar15 3-2	Aug21 2-2 May07 3-3			Oct02 1-1 Feb26 1-2	Aug07 1-1 Jan19 1-1
RANGERS	Nov30 2-0 Apr02 1-1	Oct30 1-2 Apr30 0-1	Nov10 3-1 May14 0-0	Dec11 0-3 Apr23 2-0	Aug07 2-1 Dec27 2-2	Sep25 2-1 Feb12 2-0	Aug28 1-2 Jan08 1-1	Oct06 1-2 Apr05 4-0	Sep11 1-1 Feb05	Nov13 2-2 Apr16		Oct16 2-0 Mar19
ST JOHNSTONE	Nov06 1-1 May07 0-1	Oct16 2-1 Mar05 0-1	Sep25 2-1 Feb12 1-1	Aug21 1-1 Jan25 1-1	Dec11 2-0 Apr23 0-0	Sep18 1-3 Jan22 2-2	Nov27 0-1 Jan22 0-1	Sep04 3-0 Feb08 2-1	Nov13 1-3 Apr16 1-0	Oct23 1-1 Dec16 2-0	Aug14 1-2 Dec11 0-4	

DIVISION 1

	AIRDRIE	AYR U	BRECHIN C	CLYDE	CLYDEBANK	DUMBARTON	DUNFERMLINE A	FALKIRK	HAMILTON A	MORTON	ST MIRREN	STIRLING A
AIRDRIE		Oct02 1-1 Feb12 0-0	Aug14 2-1 Jan22 0-1	Sep14 1-1 Dec18 3-2	Nov30 1-1 Apr26 0-0	Nov20 1-1 Apr16 1-1	Nov06 1-1 May07 1-0	Oct23 1-0 Apr02 0-0	Aug21 4-0 Jan18 0-1	Sep04 2-0 Feb01 2-2	Oct09 1-1 Mar26 0-2	Sep18 3-2 Mar05 3-0
AYR U	Nov13 1-2 Apr09 2-3		Oct23 1-0 Apr02 0-0	Oct30 1-0 Apr30 1-1	Oct09 1-1 Mar26 0-1	Aug28 0-1 Jan08 1-4	Sep25 0-3 Mar12 0-3	Sep14 1-4 Dec18 1-0	Dec04 1-1 Apr23 2-1	Sep28 2-2 Mar01 3-1	Oct09 0-1 May14 2-1	Aug14 2-1 Jan22 3-1
BRECHIN C	Dec11 0-2 Mar29 0-2	Sep11 0-2 Feb05 1-4		Nov30 4-2 Apr26 0-1	Sep18 1-0 Mar05 0-1	Oct16 0-3 Mar19 0-0	Aug21 1-0 Jan04 0-0	Oct02 1-0 Feb12 0-2	Aug07 1-2 Jan11 0-0	Nov06 0-3 May07 1-2	Nov20 1-4 Apr16 1-2	Sep04 1-2 Jan15 2-1
CLYDE	Oct16 0-2 Mar19 0-1	Aug21 1-1 Jan11 0-0	Sep25 Mar12 1-0		Nov06 0-2 May07 1-1	Dec11 1-0 Mar29 1-2	Sep04 2-0 Feb19 0-1	Nov23 2-0 Apr16 1-1	Sep11 2-1 Feb05 0-2	Aug07 0-1 Feb22 0-0	Dec04 1-1 Mar23 3-0	Oct02 2-1 Feb12 0-0
CLYDEBANK	Sep25 1-2 Mar22 0-2	Aug07 1-0 Jan04 0-2	Dec04 3-2 Apr23 2-1	Aug28 2-1 Jan08 0-2		Oct30 2-0 Apr30	Dec11 0-3 Mar29 1-2	Sep04 1-1 May14 1-3	Nov23 2-2 Mar19 1-0	Oct16 0-0 Feb05 0-0	Sep11 1-1 Feb12 0-3	Nov20 2-1 Apr16 2-1
DUMBARTON	Sep28 0-1 Mar01 0-0	Nov06 1-1 May07 1-1	Sep14 1-0 Dec18 3-1	Aug14 3-0 Jan22 1-1	Aug21 2-4 Jan18 2-2		Nov13 1-5 Apr12 0-2	Sep18 0-1 Mar05 0-1	Sep04 0-0 Jan15 0-1	Nov27 2-0 Apr26 0-4	Oct23 3-3 Mar26 2-3	Oct09 1-2 Mar26 0-0
DUNFERMLINE A	Aug28 3-2 Jan25 0-0	Dec14 6-1 Apr26 1-0	Oct30 4-0 Apr30 2-1	Nov09 4-0 May14 5-0	Aug14 0-2 Jan22 2-0	Oct02 4-1 Feb12 3-2		Oct09 1-0 Mar26 1-1	Dec07 4-0 Apr16 2-1	Sep18 4-3 Mar05 3-0	Sep14 3-4 Dec18 4-2	Oct23 3-0 Apr02 2-1
FALKIRK	Sep11 2-1 Feb05 0-0	Oct16 2-0 Mar19 2-0	Nov13 2-0 Apr09 4-2	Sep29 0-5 Mar01 1-2	Sep04 0-4 Jan15 0-0	Dec04 1-1 Apr23 4-0	Nov06 3-3 May07 3-1		Jan11 5-1 Mar29 2-0	Sep25 2-0 Mar12 2-0	Aug21 2-0 Feb15 1-3
HAMILTON A	Oct30 3-2 Apr30 1-0	Sep18 2-1 Mar05 2-1	Oct09 5-0 Mar26 9-1	Oct23 2-0 Apr02 2-1	Sep15 2-3 Dec18 1-0	Nov10 2-0 May14 2-1	Sep29 0-2 Jan08 1-1	Aug28 1-1		Nov13 4-1 Apr13 3-2	Aug14 0-0 Jan22 0-0	Feb02 0-1 Apr27 0-1
MORTON	Nov09 0-0 May14 1-3	Nov20 0-0 Apr16 0-1	Aug28 0-0 Jan08 1-1	Oct09 3-1 Mar26 2-0	Oct23 0-0 Apr02 1-1	Sep25 0-0 Mar12 0-0	Dec04 3-1 Apr23 2-2	Aug14 1-5 Jan22 1-1	Oct02 1-2 Feb12 2-2		Oct30 1-2 Apr30 1-2	Sep14 1-2 Dec18 0-1
ST MIRREN	Aug07 0-1 Jan11 3-0	Sep04 0-1 Jan25 1-3	Sep28 2-0 Feb26 1-1	Sep18 2-1 Mar05 1-0	Nov13 1-0 Apr09 0-0	Sep11 0-1 Feb05 2-0	Oct16 1-2 Mar19 0-3	Jan03 3-1 Apr26 0-2	Nov03 1-0 Mar29 1-5	Aug21 2-2 Jan18		Nov06 4-0 May07 4-0
STIRLING A	Dec04 0-4 Apr23 1-1	Dec11 0-0 Mar29 1-3	Nov09 2-1 May14 0-3	Nov13 1-1 Apr09 0-1	Sep28 0-3 Feb26 1-2	Aug07 2-0 Jan11 0-0	Sep11 2-0 Feb05 1-0	Oct30 3-4 Apr30 1-0	Sep25 3-1 Mar12 0-1	Oct16 1-1 Mar19 0-3	Aug28 1-0 Jan08 3-0	

Replays
Apr 12 Aberdeen 0   Dundee U 1
  played at Hampden Park
Apr 13 Kilmarnock ...1   Rangers 2
  played at Hampden Park

Final
May 21 Dundee U 1   Rangers 0
  played at Hampden Park

Two 'English' players came home to Scotland to join Rangers in search of honours and furthering their international careers, midfielder Stuart McCall and defender Richard Gough, via Everton and Tottenham Hotspur respectively.

League Cup results for 1993-94 are detailed on page 215.

DIVISION 2

	ALBION R	ALLOA	ARBROATH	BERWICK R	COWDENBEATH	EAST FIFE	E. STIRLING	FORFAR A	MEADOWBANK T	MONTROSE	QUEEN OF SOUTH	QUEEN'S PARK	STENHOUSEMUIR	STRANRAER
ALBION R		Aug07 0-2; Apr30 1-1	Oct09 0-1	Feb12 0-2	Nov13 0-1; Apr09 1-0	Jan29 1-1	Dec04 1-5	Nov06 3-4	Oct16 0-0; Feb19 3-1	Jan25 1-3; Apr23 1-3	May14 0-2; Mar05 0-1	Sep25 1-1	Aug21 2-0; Mar19 1-1	Sep11 1-2; Jan08 1-2
ALLOA	Dec18 1-1		Jan22 1-2	Oct23 1-0	Aug14 0-1; Apr16 0-0	Jan18 2-2; May14 1-1	Aug21 0-0; Mar05 0-1	Dec07 1-1; May07 1-3		Oct02 1-0	Sep25 0-1	Nov13 1-0; Mar15 0-1	Oct30 1-1; Apr12 1-2	Sep11 1-0; Mar26 1-1
ARBROATH	Nov27 1-1; May07 1-0	Oct16 2-3; Mar12 0-0			Jan26 0-4	Oct02 2-2	Dec29 3-2	Feb02 1-1	Aug21 1-1	Nov20 3-2; Mar26 1-1	Nov06 2-0; Feb26 0-0	Aug07 2-5; Apr09 0-3	Sep11 2-0; Apr23 2-1	Feb12 0-0
BERWICK R	Sep04 1-1; Apr16 3-0	Feb01 1-1; Mar19 1-1	Aug28 2-0; May14 5-0			Feb05 3-2	Aug07 0-1; Mar05 1-3	Nov06 2-2	Nov30 0-2; Apr09 2-2	Jan11 2-2	Oct16 3-3	Jan18 1-2; Oct09 6-0	Dec04 2-1; Apr30 3-0	Sep18 2-1; Feb23 1-0
COWDENBEATH	Sep18 0-1	Nov06 1-1	Dec04 0-1; Apr02 1-0	Sep11 1-2; Mar26 2-0			Aug21 1-2; Apr23 1-2	Oct09 1-3	Jan18 1-2	Aug07 1-2; Mar05	Mar22 0-1	Oct16 3-3; May14 1-1	Feb12 3-4; Apr30 1-1	Nov01 1-2; Mar16 1-1
EAST FIFE	Oct23 1-1; Apr02 3-1	Aug28 4-1	Oct30 1-0; Apr30 1-2	Dec18 1-1	Jan11 2-0		Sep25 0-1; Mar26 1-0	Oct02 3-2; Feb26 1-1	Feb05 0-2	Nov27 5-2	Sep04 0-2; Apr16 0-1	Nov13 5-5; Mar12 1-0	Aug14 3-0	Jan25 1-1
E. STIRLING	Oct02 1-4	Jan11 0-1	Oct23 2-4; Mar19 2-0	Aug14 2-1; May07 4-0	Nov27 3-2; Mar12 1-5	Nov20 2-1		Sep18 1-2	Aug28 0-2; Mar15 1-0	Sep04 2-3	Feb05 0-0	Jan22 0-2; Apr09 2-2	Dec18 0-2; Apr09 2-3	Oct23 1-0; Apr23 2-3
FORFAR A	Aug14 3-0	Oct09 0-3	Jan11 1-4; Mar05 3-2	Sep25 1-1	Oct30 3-2; Mar02 2-1	Dec04 1-0; Apr16 0-2	Nov13 1-1		Sep04 0-2; Apr02 0-0	Sep11 1-1; May14	Aug28 1-2; Mar19 4-4	Dec18 4-0	Jan22 1-1	Oct23 0-1; Apr30 1-3
MEADOWBANK T	Jan22 4-2	Dec04 1-1; Mar02 3-2	Sep25 3-0	Aug21 1-1; Apr23 1-2	Dec18 1-1; Apr09 2-2	Sep11 1-0	Jan15 1-1; Mar15 1-0	Feb12 4-2		Nov13 5-3	Oct09 0-0; May07 2-1	Oct23 1-1	Oct30 3-1; Mar19 1-0	Aug14 1-3; Mar12 1-1
MONTROSE	Oct30 1-0	Nov20 1-2; Apr23 2-2	Aug14 0-0	Jan22 2-3; Mar12 3-1	Oct23 1-2; Mar19 1-1	Oct09 0-1; Feb19 3-0	Feb12 2-2; Apr02 2-0	Feb05 1-1	Sep18 0-3; Apr30 2-0		Dec04 2-1	Jan15 1-2	Aug21 2-0	Jan04 0-2
QUEEN OF SOUTH	Nov20 1-2; Mar12 1-2	Sep18 0-1	Dec18 6-0; Apr02 0-0	Oct30 2-5	Jan22 1-2	Feb12 0-0; Apr30 1-1	Sep11 5-0; Mar26 1-0	Jan15 1-0	Nov30 5-1	Oct02 1-0		Aug14 5-2; Feb19 3-0	Oct23 1-2	Aug21 0-1
QUEEN'S PARK	Jan01 2-0	Dec27 2-1	Feb05 2-1	Nov27 0-0; Mar01 1-3	Sep04 1-3	Sep18 4-2	Oct16 1-1	Aug07 3-2	Jan29 2-1; May14 2-0	Aug28 2-1; Mar26 3-2	Nov06 3-1; Apr16 1-3		Nov20 1-2; Mar05 2-4	Oct02 1-0; Apr02 1-1
STENHOUSEMUIR	Feb05 5-1; Mar26 0-0	Sep04 1-1; Apr02 1-0	Nov13 4-0; Feb19	Oct02 2-1	Aug28 1-1; May07 1-1	Nov06 0-1	Aug07 3-1; Mar12	Oct16 2-1; Apr16 2-0	Jan25 1-1	Jan18 3-0	Feb08 2-0	Sep25 2-0		Nov30 2-2
STRANRAER	Aug28 2-1; Feb26 2-1	Feb05 1-1; Apr16 1-0	Sep04 2-1; May07 1-0	Nov13 3-0	Sep25 4-0; Mar19 2-1	Oct16 3-2	Dec27 1-0	Nov06 2-0	Aug07 3-1	Jan01 2-4; Apr13 1-0	Dec04 1-2; Mar05 3-3	Oct09 1-0; May14 0-1	Nov30	

PREMIER DIVISION FINAL TABLE

	P	W	D	L	F	A	Pts
Rangers	44	22	14	8	74	41	58
Aberdeen	44	17	21	6	58	36	55
Motherwell	44	20	14	10	58	43	54
Celtic	44	15	20	9	51	38	50
Hibernian	44	16	15	13	53	48	47
Dundee U	44	11	20	13	47	48	42
Hearts	44	11	20	13	37	43	42
Kilmarnock	44	12	16	16	36	45	40
Partick T	44	12	16	16	46	57	40
St Johnstone	44	10	20	14	35	47	40
Raith R	44	6	19	19	46	80	31
Dundee	44	8	13	23	42	57	29

DIVISION 1 FINAL TABLE

	P	W	D	L	F	A	Pts
Falkirk	44	26	14	4	81	32	66
Dunfermline A	44	29	7	8	93	35	65
Airdrie	44	20	14	10	48	38	54
Hamilton A	44	19	12	13	66	54	50
Clydebank	44	18	14	12	56	48	50
St Mirren	44	21	8	15	61	55	50
Ayr U	44	14	14	16	42	52	42
Dumbarton	44	11	14	19	48	59	36
Stirling A	44	13	9	22	41	68	35
Clyde	44	10	12	22	35	58	32
Morton	44	6	17	21	44	75	29
Brechin C	44	6	7	31	30	81	19

DIVISION 2 FINAL TABLE

	P	W	D	L	F	A	Pts
Stranraer	39	23	10	6	63	35	56
Berwick R	39	18	12	9	75	46	48
Stenhousemuir	39	19	9	11	62	44	47
Meadowbank T	39	17	13	9	62	48	47
Queen of South	39	17	9	13	69	48	43
East Fife	39	15	11	13	58	52	41
Alloa	39	12	17	10	41	39	41
Forfar A	39	14	11	14	58	58	39
E Stirling	39	13	11	15	54	57	37
Montrose	39	14	8	17	56	61	36
Queen's Park	39	12	10	17	52	76	34
Arbroath	39	12	9	18	42	67	33
Albion R	39	7	10	22	37	66	24
Cowdenbeath	39	6	8	25	40	72	20

PREMIER

	ABERDEEN	CELTIC	DUNDEE U	FALKIRK	HEARTS	HIBERNIAN	KILMARNOCK	MOTHERWELL	PARTICK T	RANGERS
ABERDEEN		Dec26 0-0 Apr15 2-0	Oct29 3-0 May06 2-1	Aug20 2-2 Jan07 0-0	Aug13 3-1 Dec31 3-1	Nov09 0-0 Mar18 0-0	Dec03 0-1 Apr01 0-1	Oct15 0-1 Feb25 0-2	Sep17 1-1 Jan14 3-1	Sep24 2-2 Feb12 2-0
CELTIC	Oct08 0-0 Mar05 2-0		Aug20 2-1 Jan07 1-1	Oct22 0-2 Dec31 2-0	Jan11 1-1 Apr19 0-1	Sep24 2-0 Feb11 1-1	Sep17 1-1 Jan14 2-1	Dec03 2-2 Apr01 0-1	Nov09 0-0 May02 1-1	Oct30 1-3 May07 3-0
DUNDEE U	Aug27 2-1 Jan01 0-0	Nov05 2-2 May13 0-1		Sep24 1-0 Feb21 1-0	Nov19 5-2 Mar21 1-0	Oct22 0-0 Apr29 1-2	Dec26 2-2 Apr15 1-1	Sep10 1-1 Jan21 6-1	Oct15 0-1 Feb25 2-0	Dec04 0-3 Apr01 0-1
FALKIRK	Nov05 2-1 May13 0-2	Aug13 1-1 Apr29 1-2	Nov26 1-3 Apr08 3-1		Oct01 2-1 Feb04 2-0	Oct15 0-0 May06 1-0	Nov08 3-3 Mar25 2-0	Dec26 0-1 Apr15 3-0	Aug27 2-1 Jan17 1-3	Sep17 0-2 Jan14 2-3
HEARTS	Oct22 2-0 Apr29 1-2	Oct15 1-0 Feb25 1-1	Sep17 2-1 Jan14 2-0	Dec03 1-0 Apr01 0-1		Aug27 0-1 Jan18 2-0	Sep24 3-0 Feb11 2-2	Nov05 1-1 May13 1-3	Dec26 3-0 Apr15 0-1	Nov09 1-1 Mar18 2-1
HIBERNIAN	Sep10 2-2 Jan21 4-2	Nov30 1-1 May10 1-1	Aug13 5-0 Dec31 4-0	Dec10 2-2 Apr19 0-2	Oct29 2-1 May06 3-1		Aug20 0-0 Jan07 2-1	Nov19 2-2 Mar22 2-0	Oct01 0-0 Feb04 1-2	Oct08 1-2 Mar04 1-1
KILMARNOCK	Oct01 2-1 Feb04 3-1	Nov19 0-0 Mar21 0-1	Oct08 0-2 Mar04 2-0	Sep10 1-1 Jan21 2-1	Nov26 3-1 Apr12 3-2	Nov05 0-0 May13 1-2		Aug27 0-1 Jan17 2-0	Oct22 2-0 Apr29 0-0	Dec10 1-2 Apr20 0-1
MOTHERWELL	Dec10 0-1 Apr18 2-1	Oct01 1-1 Feb04 1-0	Nov08 1-1 Mar18 2-1	Oct08 5-3 Mar07 1-2	Aug20 1-1 Jan08 0-0	Sep17 1-1 Jan13 2-0	Oct29 3-2 May06 3-3		Nov26 3-1 Apr08 1-2	Oct22 2-1 Dec31 1-3
PARTICK T	Nov19 2-1 Mar11 2-2	Sep10 1-2 Jan21 0-0	Mar07 2-0 Apr18 1-3	Oct29 1-2 May06 0-0	Oct08 0-1 Apr04 3-1	Dec03 2-2 Apr01 2-2	Aug13 2-0 Dec31 2-2	Sep24 2-2 Mar14 0-0		Aug20 0-2 Jan07 1-1
RANGERS	Nov25 1-0 Apr08 3-2	Aug27 0-2 Jan04 1-1	Oct01 3-0 Feb04 1-1	Nov19 2-0 Mar11 2-2	Sep11 2-0 Jan21 1-0	Dec26 2-0 Apr16 3-1	Oct15 2-1 Feb25 3-0	Aug13 3-0 Apr29 0-2	Nov05 1-1 May13 1-1	

DIVISION 2

	BERWICK R	BRECHIN C	CLYDE	DUMBARTON	EAST FIFE	MEADOWBANK T	MORTON	QUEEN OF SOUTH	STENHOUSEMUIR	STIRLING A
BERWICK R		Nov05 2-1 May13 1-1 2-0	Nov19 1-1 Mar25 1-2 1-1	Sep10 2-1 Feb04 0-0 1-2	Oct01 0-1 Feb25 1-0 0-0	Oct08 1-3 Mar04 3-4 1-0	Oct22 2-2 Apr29 3-1 3-4	Aug27 2-1 Jan10 0-0 3-1	Nov26 1-0 Apr08 0-0 0-0	Dec31 1-0 Apr22 0-0 0-0
BRECHIN C	Aug20 1-2 Jan21 1-0		Dec31 0-2 Apr22 0-0 0-0	Oct01 1-2 Feb25 0-0 0-1	Oct29 2-0 May06 0-0 1-5	Aug13 1-5 Jan14 3-1 1-1	Nov19 1-3 Mar18 1-1 0-1	Oct01 0-1 Apr08 2-0 1-1	Sep10 1-1 Feb14 0-2 2-1	Oct08 1-1 Mar04 2-1
CLYDE	Sep03 3-4 Feb11 1-3	Oct15 4-0 Mar11 1-3		Nov26 3-1 Apr08 1-0 1-0	Nov12 1-1 Mar18 4-1	Oct01 2-1 Feb25 1-3	Dec26 0-0 Apr15 3-2 2-2	Nov05 2-2 Jan21 2-6	Oct22 0-1 Apr29 3-2 2-2	Aug27 1-2 Jan17 2-0
DUMBARTON	Nov12 3-2 Mar21 1-0	Dec03 6-0 Apr01 4-1	Sep24 2-1 Feb18 2-2		Dec26 4-0 Apr15 2-0	Sep03 0-1 Feb11 4-0	Aug27 2-1 Jan24 2-4	Oct22 0-0 Apr29 2-2	Oct15 1-2 Mar14 5-1	Nov05 1-0 Jan21 2-2
EAST FIFE	Dec03 3-0 Apr01 0-1	Aug27 1-1 Jan02 4-0	Sep10 2-3 Feb04 1-3	Oct08 2-3 Mar04 0-2		Dec31 2-1 Apr22 1-1	Sep24 1-3 Feb28 1-1	Nov05 2-3 Mar25 3-1	Nov05 4-3 Jan21 0-2	Oct22 4-3 Apr29 1-2
MEADOWBANK T	Dec10 1-1 Apr15 0-3	Oct22 2-1 Apr29 2-1	Dec03 0-1 Apr01 0-1	Nov19 1-0 Mar25 1-0	Oct15 1-3 Mar11 1-3		Aug20 0-1 Jan21 1-0	Sep10 0-1 Feb04 1-2	Aug27 3-0 May05 1-0	Sep24 1-2 Mar08 0-3
MORTON	Aug13 1-1 Jan14 2-1	Sep10 0-2 Feb04 1-2	Oct08 0-0 Mar14 4-1	Oct29 3-0 May06 1-1	Nov26 3-0 Apr08 1-2	Nov05 4-0 May13 1-1		Dec31 1-1 Apr22 0-0	Oct01 3-2 Feb25 2-2	Nov12 1-1 Mar25 2-2
QUEEN OF SOUTH	Oct29 5-4 May06 2-0	Sep24 0-2 Feb18 1-0	Aug20 1-2 May13 1-0	Aug13 4-1 Jan14 0-0	Sep03 0-2 Feb14 3-3	Nov12 0-0 Mar18 2-0	Oct15 3-0 Mar11 1-0		Dec26 1-2 Apr15 1-2	Dec03 0-1 Apr01 1-3
STENHOUSEMUIR	Sep24 1-1 Mar07 2-2	Nov19 2-0 Mar25 3-0	Aug13 1-0 Jan14 2-2	Dec31 1-0 Apr22 0-2	Aug20 1-1 May13 2-1	Oct29 1-1 Jan10 0-1	Dec03 0-0 Apr01 1-1	Oct08 0-0 Mar21 2-2		Sep10 3-0 Feb04 0-2
STIRLING A	Oct15 3-2 Mar11 2-2	Dec24 2-0 Apr15 2-0	Oct29 1-1 May06 2-2	Aug20 1-1 May13 0-2	Aug13 1-1 Jan14 3-0	Nov26 2-3 Apr08 2-1	Sep03 2-0 Feb11 0-3	Oct01 3-0 Feb25 1-1	Nov12 0-2 Mar18 3-1	

DIVISION 1

	AIRDRIE	AYR U	CLYDEBANK	DUNDEE	DUNFERMLINE A	HAMILTON A	RAITH R	ST JOHNSTONE	ST MIRREN	STRANRAER
AIRDRIE		Sep10 0-0 Jan24 2-2	Sep24 2-0 Feb14 1-2	Nov19 2-1 Mar25 0-3	Aug13 0-0 Dec31 0-0	Oct29 1-0 May06 0-1	Oct08 0-0 Mar06 1-2	Aug20 0-0 Jan07 0-2	Jan10 2-0 Apr22 1-0	Dec03 8-1 Apr01 2-1
AYR U	Nov12 0-3 Mar18 0-2		Dec26 1-1 Apr15 1-0	Sep24 3-2 Feb11 1-0	Oct15 0-0 Feb25 1-2	Aug13 3-2 Dec31 1-2	Dec03 3-4 Apr01 0-1	Sep03 1-1 Jan14 1-3	Aug20 2-0 Jan07 2-0	Oct29 1-1 May06 3-0
CLYDEBANK	Nov26 0-1 Apr11 1-1	Oct08 3-0 Mar11 1-1		Sep10 5-2 Jan21 0-1	Aug20 0-0 Jan07 0-3	Jan10 1-0 Apr22 1-2	Nov19 0-3 Apr04 1-4	Oct01 0-0 Feb04 1-2	Oct29 2-0 May06 0-1	Aug13 3-1 Dec31 2-3
DUNDEE	Sep03 1-1 Jan14 0-1	Nov26 1-1 Apr08 1-1	Nov12 2-0 Mar18 3-2		Oct01 4-4 Feb04 2-3	Dec10 2-0 Mar04 4-0	Oct29 2-1 Apr22 2-1	Aug13 1-0 May06 0-4	Aug13 1-1 Dec31 4-0	Aug20 3-1 Jan07 3-0
DUNFERMLINE A	Oct22 2-2 Apr29 3-0	Dec10 6-0 Apr22 0-3	Nov05 4-1 May13 0-2	Dec03 0-1 Apr01 1-1		Sep10 4-0 Jan21 2-1	Aug27 1-0 Jan11 1-1	Oct08 3-0 Mar11 1-1	Nov19 1-0 Mar25 1-1	Sep24 1-0 Feb14 3-1
HAMILTON A	Aug27 2-6 Jan02 3-0	Oct22 2-0 Apr29 1-0	Oct15 0-0 Feb25 0-1	Dec26 0-0 Apr15 1-4	Nov12 3-1 Mar22 1-3		Nov05 0-3 May13 0-0	Nov26 3-1 Apr08 1-0	Oct01 2-2 Feb04 1-0	Sep03 1-0 Jan14 1-0
RAITH R	Dec26 3-2 Apr15 0-1	Oct01 3-0 Feb04 2-1	Sep03 1-1 Jan14 1-0	Oct15 2-5 Feb25 0-0	Oct29 1-1 May06 0-0	Aug20 1-1 Jan07 2-0		Aug13 1-1 Dec31 2-1	Dec06 1-1 Apr08 2-1	Nov12 4-2 Mar18 1-1
ST JOHNSTONE	Nov12 4-0 May13 2-1	Nov19 1-0 Mar25 1-1	Dec03 1-1 Apr01 1-0	Aug27 0-3 Jan11 2-2	Dec26 3-2 Apr15 1-1	Feb18 3-0	Apr29 1-2		Sep10 1-1 Jan21 5-1	Oct15 3-0 Feb25 3-0
ST MIRREN	Oct15 0-1 Feb25 1-0	Nov05 1-0 May13 1-1	Aug27 2-1 Jan02 0-1	Oct22 1-2 Apr29 0-1	Sep03 1-1 Jan14 1-0	Dec03 0-1 Apr01 0-1	Sep24 1-2 Feb11 3-2	Nov12 2-2 Mar21 1-2		Dec26 1-0 Apr15 2-0
STRANRAER	Oct01 0-1 Feb04 1-4	Aug27 2-1 Jan02 2-0	Oct22 0-1 Apr29 0-5	Nov23 0-2 May13 0-1	Nov26 0-0 Apr08 0-1	Nov19 2-0 Mar25 0-5	Sep10 0-0 Jan24 2-4	Dec10 2-2 Apr22 2-6	Oct08 1-1 Mar11 1-3	

DIVISION 3

	ALBION R	ALLOA	ARBROATH	CALEDONIAN T	COWDENBEATH	E. STIRLING	FORFAR A	MONTROSE	QUEEN'S PARK	ROSS Co
ALBION R		Aug13 0-4 Jan14 0-1 0-1	Oct08 1-2 Apr15 1-1 1-2	Sep03 0-1 Feb11 1-2 2-0	Sep24 2-4 Feb18 2-0 1-2	Nov12 0-2 Apr05 3-1 0-3	Dec03 0-1 Apr01 0-3 1-2	Aug20 2-4 Mar22 1-4 1-4	Oct29 3-2 May06 0-2	Dec31 0-1 Apr22 1-2
ALLOA	Oct22 1-0 Apr29 5-0		Sep10 3-1 Feb04 3-2	Sep24 1-1 Feb18 1-0	Dec03 1-0 Apr01 2-1	Aug27 1-3 Feb07 0-1	Nov05 0-1 Jan24 0-2	Oct08 1-1 Mar28 0-1	Dec31 2-3 Apr22 0-1	Nov19 1-1 Mar25 1-1
ARBROATH	Dec24 0-1 Mar04 2-0	Nov12 1-2 Mar18 2-1		Oct22 1-2 Apr29 2-0	Nov05 0-3 Jan21 0-3	Oct15 1-1 Mar11 5-2	Aug27 0-3 Jan28 1-1	Oct01 0-3 Feb25 4-1	Sep03 1-1 Feb15 3-1	Nov26 0-1 Apr08 0-1
CALEDONIAN T	Nov19 2-1 Apr11 0-2	Nov26 2-2 Apr08 1-0	Aug13 5-2 Jan14 2-0		Oct08 0-3 Mar04 1-1	Oct01 3-3 Feb25 0-4	Sep10 1-0 Feb04 0-0	Aug27 0-4 Apr22 3-0	Aug20 0-4 May13 0-1	Oct29 1-0 May06 3-0
COWDENBEATH	Nov26 2-2 Apr08 2-0	Oct01 1-3 Feb25 1-3	Aug20 6-2 May13 3-1	Dec26 1-1 Apr15 1-1		Sep03 1-1 Mar22 1-4	Oct15 1-0 Mar11 1-3	Oct29 1-1 May06 1-3	Nov12 2-0 Mar18 2-0	Aug13 0-2 Jan14 0-2
E. STIRLING	Sep10 4-0 Mar07 3-0	Oct29 1-2 May06 1-0	Dec31 1-0 Apr22 0-2	Dec03 2-0 Apr01 1-0	Nov19 0-2 Mar18 1-0		Sep24 3-1 Feb18 1-2	Oct22 1-2 Mar15 0-3	Oct08 3-2 Apr18 3-2	Aug20 2-2 Jan21 0-2
FORFAR A	Oct01 1-1 Feb25 4-0	Aug20 3-0 May13 0-0	Oct29 3-1 May06 2-1	Nov12 2-1 Mar18 4-1	Dec31 1-1 Apr22 2-2	Nov26 3-2 Apr08 1-0		Sep03 1-0 Apr04 1-3	Oct22 2-0 Jan14 3-0	Oct08 1-0 Mar04 4-2
MONTROSE	Nov05 4-1 May13 4-1	Dec24 1-2 Apr15 0-0	Dec03 3-0 Apr01 5-0	Oct15 0-3 Mar11 0-1	Aug27 2-0 Jan02 1-2	Aug13 2-0 Apr29 1-0	Nov19 2-0 Mar25 1-2		Sep24 1-1 Feb18 2-2	Sep10 0-2 Feb04 1-1
QUEEN'S PARK	Aug20 2-1 Jan02 0-0	Oct15 1-0 Mar11 0-4	Sep10 0-2 Mar25 0-3	Nov12 0-3 Jan21 2-3	Dec26 2-3 Feb04 1-2	Aug13 1-2 Apr15 4-1	Nov26 1-1 Apr29 1-1	Nov26 1-1 Apr11		Oct01 3-1 Feb25 1-2
ROSS Co	CO 3-0 Mar29 4-1	Oct15 3-3 Feb11 6-0	Sep03 1-4 Feb18 0-1	Sep24 1-3 Jan02 3-1	Aug27 4-0 Apr29 2-0	Oct22 1-4 May13 2-3	Nov05 2-1 Apr15 0-1	Jan11 0-1 Apr19 0-3	Nov12 2-0 Apr01 1-0	Dec03

League Cup results for 1994-95 are detailed on page 215.

SFA Cup
1st Round
Dec 26 Albion R .....2 Montrose 5
Dec 17 Caledonian T ..1 Queen of South .2
Dec 17 Dumbarton ...3 Stirling A 3
Dec 17 Stenhousemuir 3 E.Stirling 0

Replay
Dec 19 Stirling A .....3 Dumbarton 0

2nd Round
Jan 7 Alloa ....2 Ross Co 3
Jan 7 Brechin ......2 Stirling A 3
Jan 7 Buckie ....1 Berwick 3
Jan 7 Burntisland ...6 St Cuthbert's ...2
Jan 7 Cove R .....2 Cowdenbeath ..1
Jan 7 Forfar A ......0 Meadowbank T .1
Jan 7 Gala Fairydean .2 East Fife 6
Jan 7 Keith ....2 Huntly 2
Jan 7 Queen of South 0 Clyde 2
Jan 9 Queen's Park ..2 Morton 2
Jan 7 Stenhousemuir 4 Arbroath 0
Jan 7 Whitehill Welfare 0 Montrose 0

Replays
Jan 14 Huntly ......3 Keith 1
Jan 14 Montrose .....5 Whitehill 2

Jan 17 Morton .....2 Queen's Park ..1

3rd Round
Jan 28 Aberdeen .....1 Stranraer 0
Jan 28 Celtic ....2 St Mirren 0
Feb 1 Clydebank ....1 Hearts 1
Jan 28 Cove R .....0 Dunfermline A ..4
Jan 29 Dundee .....2 Partick 1
Jan 28 Dundee U ....0 Clyde 0
Feb 1 East Fife ......1 Ross Co 0
Feb 6 Falkirk ....0 Motherwell 2
Feb 6 Hamilton .....1 Rangers 3
Jan 28 Huntly ....7 Burntisland 0
Jan 28 Kilmarnock ...0 Morton 0
Feb 6 Meadowbank ..1 Berwick 1
Jan 28 Montrose .....0 Hibernian 2
Jan 28 Raith ....1 Ayr 0
Jan 31 St Johnstone ..1 Stenhousemuir .1
Feb 1 Stirling A .....1 Airdrie 2

Replays
Jan 31 Morton ......1 Kilmarnock 2
Feb 7 Berwick R ....3 Meadowbank ..3
      Penalties 6-7
Feb 7 Clyde ....1 Dundee U 5
Feb 7 Hearts ....2 Clydebank 1
Feb 7 Stenhousemuir 4 St Johnstone ..0

4th Round
Feb 18 Airdrie ....2 Dunfermline A ..0
Feb 18 Celtic ....3 Meadowbank ..0
Feb 18 Dundee ......1 Raith 2
Feb 20 Hearts ....4 Rangers 2
Feb 18 Hibernian .....2 Motherwell 0
Feb 18 Huntly ......1 Dundee U 3
Feb 18 Kilmarnock ...4 East Fife 0
Feb 18 Stenhousemuir 2 Aberdeen 0

5th Round
Mar 10 Celtic ....1 Kilmarnock 0
Mar 12 Hearts ....2 Dundee U 1
Mar 11 Raith ....1 Airdrie 4
Mar 11 Stenhousemuir 0 Hibernian 4

Semi-finals
Apr 8 Airdrie ....1 Hearts 0
Apr 7 Celtic ....0 Hibernian 0

Replays
Apr 11 Celtic ....3 Hibernian 1

Final
May 27 Airdrie ....0 Celtic 1
      played at Hampden Park

Mark Hateley (far left) and Brian Laudrup (left) were just two of the many foreign imports Rangers acquired in the quest for European glory, culminating in the 1995 close season with the purchase of Paul Gascoigne from Lazio, of Italy.

PREMIER DIVISION FINAL TABLE

	P	W	D	L	F	A	Pts
Rangers	36	20	9	7	60	35	69
Motherwell	36	14	12	10	50	50	54
Hibernian	36	12	17	7	49	37	53
Celtic	36	11	18	7	39	33	51
Falkirk	36	12	12	12	48	47	48
Hearts	36	12	7	17	44	51	43
Kilmarnock	36	11	10	15	40	48	43
Partick T	36	10	13	13	40	50	43
Aberdeen	36	10	11	15	43	46	41
Dundee U	36	9	9	18	40	56	36

DIVISION 1 FINAL TABLE

	P	W	D	L	F	A	Pts
Raith R	36	19	12	5	54	32	69
Dunfermline A	36	18	14	4	63	32	68
Dundee	36	20	8	8	65	36	68
Airdrie	36	17	10	9	50	33	61
St Johnstone	36	14	14	8	59	39	56
Hamilton A	36	14	7	15	42	48	49
St Mirren	36	8	12	16	34	50	36
Clydebank	36	8	11	17	33	47	35
Ayr U	36	6	11	19	31	58	29
Stranraer	36	4	5	27	25	81	17

DIVISION 2 FINAL TABLE

	P	W	D	L	F	A	Pts
Morton	36	18	10	8	55	33	64
Dumbarton	36	17	9	10	57	35	60
Stirling A	36	17	7	12	54	43	58
Stenhousemuir	36	14	14	8	46	39	56
Berwick R	36	15	10	11	52	46	55
Clyde	36	14	10	12	53	48	52
Queen of South	36	11	11	14	46	51	44
East Fife	36	11	10	15	48	56	43
Meadowbank T*	36	11	5	20	32	54	35
Brechin C	36	6	6	24	22	60	24

*3 Points deducted

DIVISION 3 FINAL TABLE

	P	W	D	L	F	A	Pts
Forfar A	36	25	5	6	67	33	80
Montrose	36	20	7	9	69	32	67
Ross Co	36	18	6	12	59	44	60
E Stirling	36	18	5	13	61	50	59
Alloa	36	15	9	12	50	45	54
Caledonian T	36	12	9	15	48	61	45
Arbroath	36	13	5	18	51	62	44
Queen's Park	36	12	6	18	46	57	42
Cowdenbeath	36	11	7	18	48	60	40
Albion R	36	5	3	28	27	82	18

Scottish League Cup Results

DIV 1 SECTION A

	Clyde	Hearts	Kilmarnock	Partick T
Clyde		Sep21 1-2	Oct05 3-2	Oct19 3-1
Hearts	Oct12 2-1		Sep28 3-1	Oct26 1-1
Kilmarnock	Oct26 1-2	Oct19 2-0		Sep21 3-2
Partick T	Sep28 2-2	Oct05 4-4	Oct12 1-3	

DIV 1 SECTION B

	Morton	Queen's Park	Rangers	St Mirren
Morton		Sep21 2-1	Oct26 0-2	Oct19 6-1
Queen's Park	Oct12 0-6		Sep28 2-4	Oct05 2-2
Rangers	Oct05 3-0	Oct19 1-0		Sep21 4-0
St Mirren	Sep28 2-3	Oct26 2-0	Oct12 0-4	

DIV 1 SECTION C

	Celtic	Hamilton A	Hibernian	T Lanark
Celtic		Oct26 3-1	Oct12 1-1	Sep28 0-0
Hamilton A	Oct05 2-2		Sep28 3-6	Oct12 3-0
Hibernian	Sep21 4-2	Oct19 2-0		Oct05 1-2
T Lanark	Oct19 2-3	Sep21 3-5	Oct26 1-2	

DIV 1 SECTION D

	Aberdeen	Falkirk	Motherwell	Queen of South
Aberdeen		Sep21 4-3	Oct05 2-3	Oct19 1-0
Falkirk	Oct12 0-1		Sep28 1-1	Oct26 2-1
Motherwell	Oct26 3-0	Oct19 5-3		Sep21 0-1
Queen of South	Sep28 2-5	Oct05 0-2	Oct12 4-3	

DIV 2 SECTION A

	Alloa A	Dunfermline A	East Fife	St Johnstone
Alloa		Oct26 2-1	Oct19 0-2	Sep21 0-0
Dunfermline A	Oct05 3-1		Sep21 0-2	Oct19 3-2
East Fife	Sep28 6-0	Oct12 7-0		Oct26 3-0
St Johnstone	Oct12 1-0	Sep28 6-2	Oct05 0-2	

DIV 2 SECTION B

	Dundee	Raith R	Stenhousemuir
Dundee		Oct12 3-1	Sep28 4-0
Raith R	Sep21 0-2		Oct26 2-4
Stenhousemuir	Oct19 0-4	Oct05 1-2	

DIV 2 SECTION C

	Arbroath	Cowdenbeath	Dumbarton	Dundee U
Arbroath		Oct19 3-3	Sep21 4-1	Oct05 1-3
Cowdenbeath	Sep28 5-2		Oct26 2-3	Oct05 4-1
Dumbarton	Oct12 8-0	Oct05 0-4		Sep28 0-3
Dundee U	Oct26 3-2	Sep21 2-0	Oct19 2-1	

DIV 2 SECTION D

	Airdrie	Albion R	Ayr U
Airdrie		Sep28 6-1	Oct26 3-0
Albion R	Oct19 1-5		Sep21 5-4
Ayr U	Oct05 2-1	Oct12 4-3	

DIV 2 Section A

	P	W	D	L	F	A	Pts
East Fife	6	6	0	0	22	0	12
St Johnstone	6	2	1	3	9	10	5
Dunfermline A	6	2	0	4	9	20	4
Alloa	6	1	1	4	3	13	3

DIV 2 Section B

	P	W	D	L	F	A	Pts
Dundee	4	4	0	0	13	1	8
Raith R	4	1	0	3	5	10	2
Stenhousemuir	4	1	0	3	5	12	2

DIV 2 Section C

	P	W	D	L	F	A	Pts
Dundee U	6	5	0	1	14	8	10
Cowdenbeath	6	3	1	2	18	11	7
Dumbarton	6	2	0	4	13	15	4
Arbroath	6	1	1	4	12	23	3

DIV 2 Section D

	P	W	D	L	F	A	Pts
Airdrie	4	3	0	1	15	4	6
Ayr U	4	2	0	2	10	12	4
Albion R	4	1	0	3	10	19	2

DIV 1 Section A

	P	W	D	L	F	A	Pts
Hearts	6	3	2	1	12	10	8
Clyde	6	3	1	2	12	10	7
Kilmarnock	6	3	0	3	12	11	6
Partick T	6	0	3	3	11	16	3

DIV 1 Section B

	P	W	D	L	F	A	Pts
Rangers	6	6	0	0	18	2	12
Morton	6	4	0	2	17	9	8
St Mirren	6	1	1	4	7	19	3
Queen's Park	6	0	1	5	5	17	1

DIV 1 Section C

	P	W	D	L	F	A	Pts
Hibernian	6	4	1	1	16	9	9
Celtic	6	2	3	1	11	10	7
Hamilton A	6	2	1	3	14	16	5
T Lanark	6	1	1	4	8	14	3

DIV 1 Section D

	P	W	D	L	F	A	Pts
Aberdeen	6	4	0	2	13	11	8
Motherwell	6	3	1	2	15	11	7
Falkirk	6	2	1	3	11	12	5
Queen of South	6	2	0	4	8	13	4

Quarter-finals
Mar 1 Airdrie ....4 Hibernian 4
Mar 5 Hibernian ....1 Airdrie ....0 Agg 5-4
Mar 1 Dundee ....0 Aberdeen 1
Mar 5 Aberdeen ....3 Dundee ......2 Agg 4-2
Mar 1 Hearts ....0 East Fife 1
Mar 5 East Fife ......2 Hearts ....5 Agg 3-5
Mar 1 Rangers ....2 Dundee U 1
Mar 5 Dundee U ....1 Rangers ......1 Agg 2-3

Semi-finals
Mar 22 Aberdeen ....6 Hearts 2
played at Easter Road
Mar 22 Hibernian ....1 Rangers 3
played at Hampden Park

Final
Apr 5 Aberdeen ....0 Rangers 4
played at Hampden Park

DIV 1 SECTION A

	Aberdeen	Motherwell	Queen of South	St Mirren
Aberdeen		Aug16 2-0	Sep13 9-0	Aug30 2-0
Motherwell	Sep06		Aug09 4-0	Aug23 3-1
Queen of South	Aug23 1-2	Aug30 0-1		Aug16 8-1
St Mirren	Aug09 0-1	Sep13 0-3	Sep06 7-1	

DIV 1 SECTION B

	Falkirk	Morton	Partick T	Queen's Park
Falkirk		Sep06 5-0	Aug09 5-6	Sep13 4-1
Morton	Aug16 1-2		Aug23 2-1	Aug30 3-1
Partick T	Aug30 3-3	Sep13 4-1		Aug16 3-1
Queen's Park	Aug23 0-4	Aug09 4-1	Sep06 4-3	

DIV 1 SECTION C

	Celtic	Dundee	Rangers	T Lanark
Celtic		Aug16 1-1	Aug30 2-0	Aug23 3-1
Dundee	Sep06 4-1		Sep13 1-1	Aug09 5-0
Rangers	Aug09 2-0	Aug23 3-0		Sep06 3-0
T Lanark	Sep13 3-2	Aug30 5-1	Aug16 1-3	

DIV 1 SECTION D

	Airdrie	Clyde	Hearts	Hibernian
Airdrie		Aug30 3-1	Aug16 3-2	Aug23 1-0
Clyde	Aug09 4-2		Sep13 5-2	Sep06 3-4
Hearts	Sep06 1-0	Aug23 1-0		Aug09 2-1
Hibernian	Sep13 5-0	Aug16 5-1	Aug30 1-2	

DIV 2 SECTION A

	Alloa A	Dunfermline A	Hamilton A	Raith R
Alloa		Sep13 1-1	Aug09 1-2	Sep06 1-2
Dunfermline A	Aug23 1-0		Sep06 1-3	Aug09 0-2
Hamilton A	Aug30 9-0	Aug16 3-2		Sep13 6-1
Raith R	Aug16 4-2	Aug09 6-1	Aug23 3-1	

DIV 2 SECTION B

	Albion R	Cowdenbeath	Dundee U	Leith A
Albion R		Sep06 4-1	Aug09 3-0	Sep13 1-1
Cowdenbeath	Aug16 2-3		Sep13 1-0	Aug30 0-1
Dundee U	Aug30 2-1	Aug23 0-2		Aug16 2-2
Leith A	Aug23 2-2	Aug09 2-1	Sep06 3-1	

DIV 2 SECTION C

	Arbroath	Dumbarton	St Johnstone	Stenhousemui
Arbroath		Aug16 1-3	Aug30 1-2	Sep13 5-1
Dumbarton	Sep06 4-2		Sep13 1-6	Aug09 5-5
St Johnstone	Aug09 5-1	Aug23 1-0		Sep06 0-1
Stenhousemuir	Aug23 2-0	Aug30 2-1	Aug16 3-2	

DIV 2 SECTION D

	Ayr U	East Fife	Kilmarnock	Stirling A
Ayr U		Aug23 2-5	Aug09 2-2	Sep06 3-2
East Fife	Sep13 5-0		Sep06 1-3	Aug09 3-2
Kilmarnock	Aug30 1-2	Aug16 0-0		Sep13 3-2
Stirling A	Aug16 1-5	Aug30 2-5	Aug23 5-3	

DIV 1 Section A
	P	W	D	L	F	A	Pts
Aberdeen	6	5	0	1	16	3	10
Motherwell	6	5	0	1	13	3	10
St Mirren	6	1	0	5	9	18	2
Queen of South	6	1	0	5	10	24	2

DIV 1 Section B
	P	W	D	L	F	A	Pts
Falkirk	6	4	1	1	23	11	9
Partick T	6	3	1	2	20	16	7
Queen's Park	6	2	0	4	11	18	4
Morton	6	2	0	4	8	17	4

DIV 1 Section C
	P	W	D	L	F	A	Pts
Rangers	6	4	1	1	12	4	9
Dundee	6	2	2	2	12	11	6
Celtic	6	2	1	3	9	11	5
T Lanark	6	2	0	4	10	17	4

DIV 1 Section D
	P	W	D	L	F	A	Pts
Hearts	6	4	0	2	10	10	8
Hibernian	6	3	1	2	17	9	7
Airdrie	6	2	1	3	9	14	5
Clyde	6	2	0	4	14	17	4

DIV 2 Section A
	P	W	D	L	F	A	Pts
Hamilton A	6	5	0	1	24	8	10
Raith R	6	5	0	1	18	11	10
Dunfermline A	6	1	1	4	6	15	3
Alloa	6	0	1	5	5	19	1

DIV 2 Section B
	P	W	D	L	F	A	Pts
Leith A	6	3	3	0	11	7	9
Albion R	6	3	2	1	14	8	8
Cowdenbeath	6	2	0	4	7	10	4
Dundee U	6	1	1	4	5	12	3

DIV 2 Section C
	P	W	D	L	F	A	Pts
Stenhousemuir	6	4	1	1	14	13	9
St Johnstone	6	4	0	2	16	7	8
Dumbarton	6	2	1	3	14	17	5
Arbroath	6	1	0	5	10	17	2

DIV 2 Section D
	P	W	D	L	F	A	Pts
East Fife	6	4	1	1	19	9	9
Ayr U	6	3	1	2	14	16	7
Kilmarnock	6	2	2	2	12	12	6
Stirling A	6	1	0	5	14	22	2

Quarter-finals
Sep 27 Aberdeen ....8 Leith A 2
Sep 27 Falkirk ....3 Hamilton A ..1
Sep 27 Hearts ....3 East Fife 4
Sep 27 Rangers ....2 Stenhousemuir ..0

Semi-finals
Oct 11 Aberdeen ....0 East Fife 1
played at Dens Park
Oct 11 Falkirk ....1 Rangers 0
played at Hampden Park

Final
Oct 25 East Fife ....0 Falkirk 0
played at Hampden Park

Replay
Nov 1 East Fife ....4 Falkirk 1
played at Hampden Park

Season 1948-49

DIV 1 SECTION A

	Celtic	Clyde	Hibernian	Rangers
Celtic		Oct09 3-6	Sep11 1-0	Sep25 3-1
Clyde	Sep18 0-2		Oct16 1-4	Oct02 1-3
Hibernian	Oct02 4-2	Sep25 4-0		Sep18 0-0
Rangers	Oct16 2-1	Sep11 1-1	Oct09 1-0	

DIV 1 SECTION B

	Albion R	Dundee	Falkirk	Motherwell
Albion R		Oct02 2-3	Oct16 2-1	Sep18 0-1
Dundee	Sep11 2-1		Oct09 4-2	Oct16 0-1
Falkirk	Sep25 2-1	Sep18 2-3		Oct02 1-0
Motherwell	Oct09 8-3	Sep25 0-1	Sep11 1-0	

DIV 1 SECTION C

	East Fife	Hearts	Partick T	Queen of South
East Fife		Sep18 4-0	Oct16 3-0	Oct02 3-1
Hearts	Oct09 6-1		Sep11 2-2	Oct16 4-0
Partick T	Sep25 2-5	Oct02 3-1		Sep18 9-0
Queen of South	Sep11 0-4	Sep25 2-3	Oct09 3-2	

DIV 1 SECTION D

	Aberdeen	Morton	St Mirren	T Lanark
Aberdeen		Sep25 3-1	Sep11 3-1	Oct09 2-4
Morton	Oct16 3-1		Oct09 0-3	Sep11 2-1
St Mirren	Oct02 1-1	Sep18 1-1		Sep25 4-0
T Lanark	Sep18 1-1	Oct02 2-2	Oct16 4-2	

DIV 2 SECTION A

	Cowdenbeath	Dunfermline A	Raith R	Stirling A
Cowdenbeath		Sep18 0-2	Oct02 0-6	Sep25 3-3
Dunfermline A	Oct09 3-2		Oct16 1-0	Sep11 1-1
Raith R	Sep11 3-3	Sep25 2-1		Oct09 6-2
Stirling A	Oct16 5-2	Oct02 4-3	Sep18 1-7	

DIV 2 SECTION B

	Alloa	E Stirling	Kilmarnock	Queen's Park
Alloa		Sep18 1-0	Oct16 2-0	Oct02 1-0
E Stirling	Oct09 1-3		Sep11 2-1	Oct16 1-1
Kilmarnock	Sep25 4-3	Oct02 4-1		Sep18 3-3
Queen's Park	Sep11 4-1	Sep25 2-0	Oct09 2-2	

DIV 2 SECTION C

	Dundee U	Hamilton A	St Johnstone	Stenhousemuir
Dundee U		Sep25 1-2	Oct02 4-2	Sep18 4-2
Hamilton A	Oct16 6-3		Sep18 2-2	Oct02 3-0
St Johnstone	Sep11 1-1	Oct09 0-0		Sep25 2-1
Stenhousemuir	Oct09 2-1	Sep11 1-1	Oct16 3-4	

DIV 2 SECTION D

	Airdrie	Arbroath	Ayr U	Dumbarton
Airdrie		Oct09 3-2	Sep25 6-1	Sep11 8-1
Arbroath	Sep18 2-3		Oct02 1-1	Sep25 4-2
Ayr U	Oct16 1-4	Sep11 2-1		Oct09 2-1
Dumbarton	Oct02 0-5	Oct16 1-1	Sep18 1-2	

DIV 1 Section A
	P	W	D	L	F	A	Pts
Rangers	6	3	2	1	8	6	8
Hibernian	6	3	1	2	12	5	7
Celtic	6	3	0	3	12	13	6
Clyde	6	1	1	4	9	17	3

DIV 1 Section B
	P	W	D	L	F	A	Pts
Dundee	6	5	0	1	13	8	10
Motherwell	6	4	0	2	11	5	8
Falkirk	6	2	0	4	8	11	4
Albion R	6	1	0	5	9	17	2

DIV 1 Section C
	P	W	D	L	F	A	Pts
East Fife	6	5	0	1	20	9	10
Hearts	6	3	1	2	16	12	7
Partick T	6	2	1	3	18	14	5
Queen of South	6	1	0	5	6	25	2

DIV 1 Section D
	P	W	D	L	F	A	Pts
St Mirren	6	2	2	2	12	9	6
Aberdeen	6	2	2	2	11	11	6
T Lanark	6	2	2	2	12	13	6
Morton	6	2	2	2	9	11	6

DIV 2 Section A
	P	W	D	L	F	A	Pts
Raith R	6	4	1	1	24	8	9
Dunfermline A	6	3	1	2	11	9	7
Stirling A	6	2	2	2	16	22	6
Cowdenbeath	6	0	2	4	10	22	2

DIV 2 Section B
	P	W	D	L	F	A	Pts
Alloa	6	4	0	2	11	9	8
Queen's Park	6	2	3	1	12	8	7
Kilmarnock	6	2	2	2	14	13	6
E Stirling	6	1	1	4	5	12	3

DIV 2 Section C
	P	W	D	L	F	A	Pts
Hamilton A	6	3	3	0	14	7	9
St Johnstone	6	2	3	1	11	11	7
Dundee U	6	2	1	3	14	15	5
Stenhousemuir	6	1	1	4	9	15	3

DIV 2 Section D
	P	W	D	L	F	A	Pts
Airdrie	6	6	0	0	29	7	12
Ayr U	6	3	1	2	11	15	7
Arbroath	6	1	2	3	12	14	4
Dumbarton	6	0	1	5	6	22	1

Quarter-finals
Oct 30 Dundee ....1 Alloa 1
Oct 30 Hamilton A ....1 Airdrie 1
Oct 30 Raith R ....5 East Fife 3
Oct 30 Rangers ....1 St Mirren 0

Replays
Nov 3 Airdrie ....1 Hamilton A 1
Nov 3 Alloa ....1 Dundee 3
Nov 8 Airdrie ....0 Hamilton A 1
played at Celtic Park

Semi-finals
Nov 20 Dundee ....1 Rangers 4
played at Hampden Park
Nov 20 Hamilton A ....0 Raith R 2
played at Celtic Park

Final
Mar 12 Raith R ....0 Rangers 2
played at Hampden Park

Season 1949-50

DIV 1 SECTION A

	Aberdeen	Celtic	Rangers	St Mirren
Aberdeen		Aug17 4-5	Sep03 1-1	Aug27 1-0
Celtic	Aug31 1-3		Aug13 3-2	Sep03 4-1
Rangers	Aug20 4-2	Aug27 2-0		Aug17 5-1
St Mirren	Aug13 3-1	Aug20 1-0	Aug30 1-1	

DIV 1 SECTION B

	Falkirk	Hibernian	Queen of South	T Lanark
Falkirk		Aug27 2-1	Aug17 1-0	Aug20 1-2
Hibernian	Aug13 1-0		Sep03 5-3	Aug31 4-2
Queen of South	Aug31 0-0	Aug20 1-2		Aug13 2-4
T Lanark	Sep03 3-0	Aug17 0-2	Aug27 1-1	

DIV 1 SECTION C

	Clyde	Dundee	Motherwell	Partick T
Clyde		Aug27 2-0	Aug20 2-2	Aug17 1-2
Dundee	Aug13 1-1		Aug31 0-1	Aug20 5-2
Motherwell	Sep03 1-1	Aug17		Aug27 1-1
Partick T	Aug31 3-1	Sep03 4-2	Aug13 2-0	

DIV 1 SECTION D

	East Fife	Hearts	Raith R	Stirling A
East Fife		Sep03 4-3	Aug27 3-2	Aug17 3-1
Hearts	Aug20 1-1		Aug17 5-1	Aug27 4-5
Raith R	Aug13 0-3	Aug31 1-2		Aug20 6-2
Stirling A	Aug31 0-3	Aug13 1-5	Sep03 4-1	

DIV 2 SECTION A

	Albion R	Forfar A	Hamilton A	Stenhousemuir
Albion R		Sep03 2-2	Aug17 1-0	Aug27 2-2
Forfar A	Aug20 3-2		Aug27 3-0	Aug17 2-2
Hamilton A	Aug31 1-1	Aug13 0-1		Aug20 0-0
Stenhousemuir	Aug13 0-1	Aug31 3-1	Sep03 3-0	

DIV 2 SECTION B

	Airdrie	Arbroath	Dumbarton	Dundee U
Airdrie		Aug31 3-1	Aug20 2-2	Aug13 5-2
Arbroath	Aug17 1-2		Aug27 3-1	Aug20 2-4
Dumbarton	Sep03 0-4	Aug13 5-1		Aug31 3-1
Dundee U	Aug27 6-0	Sep03 4-1	Aug17 5-1	

DIV 2 SECTION C

	Alloa	Ayr U	Cowdenbeath	Morton
Alloa		Aug17 2-2	Aug27 1-4	Aug20 0-4
Ayr U	Aug31 4-0		Aug20 2-2	Aug13 3-4
Cowdenbeath	Aug13 2-0	Sep03 2-0		Aug31 2-0
Morton	Sep03 7-1	Aug27 3-3	Aug17 1-0	

DIV 2 SECTION D

	Dunfermline A	Kilmarnock	Queen's Park	St Johnstone
Dunfermline A		Aug20 5-1	Aug27 3-0	Aug17 1-2
Kilmarnock	Sep03 2-4		Aug17 2-0	Aug27 2-0
Queen's Park	Aug13 0-1	Aug31 3-1		Aug20 2-0
St Johnstone	Aug31 2-3	Aug13 3-2	Sep03 2-3	

DIV 1 Section A

	P	W	D	L	F	A	Pts
Rangers	6	3	2	1	15	8	8
Celtic	6	3	0	3	13	13	6
Aberdeen	6	2	1	3	12	14	5
St Mirren	6	2	1	3	7	12	5

DIV 1 Section B

	P	W	D	L	F	A	Pts
Hibernian	6	5	0	1	15	8	10
T Lanark	6	3	1	2	12	10	7
Falkirk	6	2	1	3	4	7	5
Queen of South	6	0	2	4	7	13	2

DIV 1 Section C

	P	W	D	L	F	A	Pts
Partick T	6	4	1	1	14	10	9
Motherwell	6	2	3	1	7	6	7
Clyde	6	1	3	2	8	9	5
Dundee	6	1	1	4	8	12	3

DIV 1 Section D

	P	W	D	L	F	A	Pts
East Fife	6	5	1	0	17	7	11
Hearts	6	3	1	2	20	13	7
Stirling A	6	2	0	4	13	22	4
Raith R	6	1	0	5	11	19	2

DIV 2 Section A

	P	W	D	L	F	A	Pts
Forfar A	6	3	2	1	12	9	8
Stenhousemuir	6	2	3	1	10	6	7
Albion R	6	2	3	1	9	8	7
Hamilton A	6	0	2	4	1	9	2

DIV 2 Section B

	P	W	D	L	F	A	Pts
Airdrie	6	4	1	1	16	12	9
Dundee U	6	4	0	2	22	12	8
Dumbarton	6	2	1	3	12	16	5
Arbroath	6	1	0	5	9	19	2

DIV 2 Section C

	P	W	D	L	F	A	Pts
Cowdenbeath	6	4	1	1	12	4	9
Morton	6	4	1	1	19	9	9
Ayr U	6	1	3	2	14	13	5
Alloa	6	0	1	5	4	23	1

DIV 2 Section D

	P	W	D	L	F	A	Pts
Dunfermline A	6	5	0	1	17	7	10
Queen's Park	6	3	0	3	8	9	6
St Johnstone	6	2	0	4	9	13	4
Kilmarnock	6	2	0	4	10	15	4

Quarter-finals

Sep 17 Airdrie ....3 Dunfermline A 4
Sep 20 Dunfermline A .....0 Airdrie ....0 Agg 4-3
Sep 17 Forfar A ....1 East Fife 3
Sep 21 East Fife ....5 Forfar A ....1 Agg 8-2
Sep 17 Partick T ....4 Hibernian 2
Sep 21 Hibernian ....4 Partick T ....0 Agg 6-4
Sep 17 Rangers ....2 Cowdenbeath 3
Sep 21 Cowdenbeath ......1 Rangers ....3 Agg 4-5

Semi-finals

Oct 8 Dunfermline A .....2 Hibernian 1
played at Tynecastle
Oct 8 East Fife ....2 Rangers 1
played at Hampden Park

Final

Oct 29 Dunfermline A .....0 East Fife 3
played at Hampden Park

Celtic in 1949-50, when they failed to qualify in their Section 'A' League Cup Group that included St Mirren, Aberdeen and Rangers. In the semi-final Rangers were to lose to East Fife, who collected the trophy that year. Rangers gained revenge later that season when they beat East Fife 3-0 in the SFA Cup. Rangers were also League champions for the second year running.

Season 1950-51

DIV 1 SECTION A

	Celtic	East Fife	Raith R	T Lanark
Celtic		Aug12 2-0	Aug19 2-1	Aug30 3-1
East Fife	Aug26 1-1		Aug16 3-3	Aug19 2-5
Raith R	Sep02 2-2	Aug30 1-4		Aug12 3-2
T Lanark	Aug16 1-2	Sep02 3-3	Aug26 1-0	

DIV 1 SECTION B

	Dundee	Falkirk	Hibernian	St Mirren
Dundee		Aug16 1-2	Aug26 0-2	Aug19 3-1
Falkirk	Aug30 1-2		Aug19 4-5	Aug12 1-1
Hibernian	Aug12 2-0	Sep02 4-0		Aug30 5-0
St Mirren	Sep02 3-1	Aug26 2-0	Aug15 0-6	

DIV 1 SECTION C

	Airdrie	Hearts	Motherwell	Partick T
Airdrie		Sep02 1-3	Aug26 2-6	Aug16 2-3
Hearts	Aug19 3-2		Aug16 4-1	Aug26 2-0
Motherwell	Aug12 3-1	Aug30 3-2		Aug19 2-1
Partick T	Aug30 3-1	Aug12 1-1	Sep02 2-3	

DIV 1 SECTION D

	Aberdeen	Clyde	Morton	Rangers
Aberdeen		Aug12 4-3	Sep02 6-1	Aug30 2-0
Clyde	Aug26 4-1		Aug16 3-3	Sep02 1-5
Morton	Aug19 0-2	Aug30 4-4		Aug12 1-2
Rangers	Aug16 1-2	Aug19 4-0	Aug26 6-1	

DIV 2 SECTION A

	Ayr U	Dumbarton	Dunfermline A	Kilmarnock
Ayr U		Aug26 3-0	Aug19 1-0	Aug16 2-2
Dumbarton	Aug12 1-4		Aug30 1-1	Aug19 1-0
Dunfermline A	Sep02 2-5	Aug16 4-1		Aug26 5-4
Kilmarnock	Aug30 0-1	Sep02 0-0	Aug12 3-1	

DIV 2 SECTION B

	Cowdenbeath	Dundee U	St Johnstone	Stenhousemuir
Cowdenbeath		Aug19 2-2	Aug12 0-2	Aug30 5-1
Dundee U	Sep02 4-1		Aug30 4-1	Aug12 2-1
St Johnstone	Aug26 2-2	Aug16 2-5		Aug19 6-2
Stenhousemuir	Aug16 2-2	Aug26 3-2	Sep02 1-2	

DIV 2 SECTION C

	Hamilton A	Queen of South	Queen's Park	Stirling A
Hamilton A		Aug26 1-1	Aug16 2-1	Sep02 3-0
Queen of South	Aug12 3-2		Sep02 4-3	Aug30 2-2
Queen's Park	Aug30 3-1	Aug19 2-2		Aug12 1-0
Stirling A	Aug19 1-0	Aug16 1-3	Aug26 2-2	

DIV 2 SECTION D

	Albion R	Alloa	Arbroath	Forfar A
Albion R		Aug19 1-3	Aug12 3-2	Aug30 1-2
Alloa	Sep02 2-2		Aug30 3-1	Aug12 6-0
Arbroath	Aug26 1-0	Aug16 1-1		Aug19 3-0
Forfar A	Aug16 0-2	Aug26 3-1	Sep02 4-1	

DIV 1 Section A	P	W	D	L	F	A	Pts
Celtic	6	4	2	0	12	6	10
T Lanark	6	2	1	3	13	13	5
East Fife	6	1	3	2	13	15	5
Raith R	6	1	2	3	10	14	4

DIV 1 Section B	P	W	D	L	F	A	Pts
Hibernian	6	6	0	0	24	4	12
St Mirren	6	2	1	3	7	16	5
Dundee	6	2	0	4	7	11	4
Falkirk	6	1	1	4	8	15	3

DIV 1 Section C	P	W	D	L	F	A	Pts
Motherwell	6	5	0	1	18	12	10
Hearts	6	4	1	1	15	8	9
Partick T	6	2	1	3	10	11	5
Airdrie	6	0	0	6	9	21	0

DIV 1 Section D	P	W	D	L	F	A	Pts
Aberdeen	6	5	0	1	17	9	10
Rangers	6	4	0	2	18	7	8
Clyde	6	1	2	3	15	21	4
Morton	6	0	2	4	10	23	2

DIV 2 Section A	P	W	D	L	F	A	Pts
Ayr U	6	5	1	0	16	5	11
Dunfermline A	6	2	1	3	13	15	5
Kilmarnock	6	1	2	3	9	10	4
Dumbarton	6	1	2	3	4	12	4

DIV 2 Section B	P	W	D	L	F	A	Pts
Dundee U	6	4	1	1	19	10	9
St Johnstone	6	3	1	2	15	14	7
Cowdenbeath	6	1	3	2	12	13	5
Stenhousemuir	6	1	1	4	10	19	3

DIV 2 Section C	P	W	D	L	F	A	Pts
Queen of South	6	3	3	0	15	11	9
Queen's Park	6	2	2	2	12	11	6
Hamilton A	6	2	1	3	9	9	5
Stirling A	6	1	2	3	6	11	4

DIV 2 Section D	P	W	D	L	F	A	Pts
Alloa	6	3	2	1	16	8	8
Forfar A	6	3	0	3	9	14	6
Albion R	6	2	1	3	9	10	5
Arbroath	6	2	1	3	9	11	5

Quarter-finals
Sep 16 Aberdeen . . . . .4 Hibernian 1
Sep 20 Hibernian . . . . .4 Aberdeen . . . . . . .1 Agg 5-5
Sep 16 Ayr U . . . . .3 Dundee U 0
Sep 20 Dundee U . . . . .1 Ayr U . . . . .2 Agg 1-5
Sep 16 Celtic . . . . .1 Motherwell 4
Sep 20 Motherwell . . . . . . .0 Celtic . . . . .1 Agg 4-2
Sep 16 Queen of South . . . .1 Alloa 0
Sep 20 Alloa . . . . .2 Queen of South . .2 Agg 2-3

Replays
Oct 2 Aberdeen . . . . .1 Hibernian 1
played at Ibrox
Oct 3 Aberdeen . . . . .1 Hibernian 5
played at Hampden Park

Semi-finals
Oct 7 Ayr U . . . . .3 Motherwell 4
played at Ibrox
Oct 7 Hibernian . . . . .3 Queen of South . .1
played at Tynecastle

Final
Oct 28 Hibernian . . . . .0 Motherwell 3
played at Hampden Park

Season 1951-52

DIV 1 SECTION A

	Airdrie	Celtic	Morton	T Lanark
Airdrie		Aug15 1-1	Aug25 1-3	Aug18 2-1
Celtic	Aug29 2-0		Aug18 2-0	Aug11 1-1
Morton	Aug11 2-1	Sep01 2-0		Aug29 5-2
T Lanark	Sep01 5-0	Aug25 0-1	Aug15 2-0	

DIV 1 SECTION B

	Hibernian	Motherwell	Partick T	Stirling A
Hibernian		Aug15 0-4	Aug25 5-1	Aug18 4-2
Motherwell	Aug29 1-0		Sep01 3-2	Aug11 6-4
Partick T	Aug11 4-2	Aug18 0-0		Aug29 2-0
Stirling A	Sep01 1-1	Aug25 3-2	Aug15 0-1	

DIV 1 SECTION C

	Dundee	Hearts	Raith R	St Mirren
Dundee		Aug15 2-1	Aug18 5-0	Aug25 0-1
Hearts	Aug29 5-2		Aug11 1-0	Sep01 3-1
Raith R	Sep01 1-3	Aug25 2-0		Aug15 3-2
St Mirren	Aug11 2-2	Aug18 5-5	Aug29 2-0	

DIV 1 SECTION D

	Aberdeen	East Fife	Queen of South	Rangers
Aberdeen		Sep01 2-3	Aug11 5-4	Aug29 2-1
East Fife	Aug18 3-0		Aug29 1-0	Aug11 0-0
Queen of South	Aug25 2-0	Aug15 3-2		Aug18 0-3
Rangers	Aug15 2-1	Aug25 4-1	Sep01 5-2	

DIV 2 SECTION A

	Cowdenbeath	Dundee U	Falkirk	Stenhousemuir
Cowdenbeath		Aug25 2-0	Aug15 0-5	Aug18 2-3
Dundee U	Aug11 1-1		Sep01 0-1	Aug29 4-2
Falkirk	Aug29 6-1	Aug18 3-0		Aug11 3-1
Stenhousemuir	Sep01 3-1	Aug15 1-1	Aug25 2-5	

DIV 2 SECTION B

	Alloa	Dunfermline A	Hamilton A	Queen's Park
Alloa		Aug25 2-2	Sep01 1-2	Aug15 2-0
Dunfermline A	Aug11 4-1		Aug29 3-0	Sep01 2-1
Hamilton A	Aug18 0-1	Aug15 1-4		Aug25 2-3
Queen's Park	Aug29 2-1	Aug18 2-0	Aug11 1-2	

DIV 2 SECTION C

	Albion R	Arbroath	Clyde	St Johnstone
Albion R		Sep01 5-4	Aug29 0-2	Aug11 3-4
Arbroath	Aug18 0-1		Aug11 2-3	Aug29 2-2
Clyde	Aug15 4-0	Aug25 5-2		Sep01 0-1
St Johnstone	Aug25 0-1	Aug15 4-0	Aug18 3-2	

DIV 2 SECTION D

	Ayr U	Dumbarton	Forfar A	Kilmarnock
Ayr U		Aug15 5-0	Aug18 2-3	Aug25 1-2
Dumbarton	Aug29 1-3		Aug11 3-4	Aug18 1-0
Forfar A	Sep01 3-0	Aug25 1-1		Aug15 2-1
Kilmarnock	Aug11 3-0	Sep01 2-0	Aug29 1-0	

DIV 1 Section A

	P	W	D	L	F	A	Pts
Celtic	6	3	2	1	7	4	8
Morton	6	4	0	2	12	8	8
T Lanark	6	2	1	3	11	9	5
Airdrie	6	1	1	4	5	14	3

DIV 1 Section B

	P	W	D	L	F	A	Pts
Motherwell	6	4	1	1	16	9	9
Partick T	6	3	1	2	10	10	7
Hibernian	6	2	1	3	12	13	5
Stirling A	6	1	1	4	10	16	3

DIV 1 Section C

	P	W	D	L	F	A	Pts
Dundee	6	3	1	2	14	10	7
Hearts	6	3	1	2	15	12	7
St Mirren	6	2	2	2	13	13	6
Raith R	6	2	0	4	6	13	4

DIV 1 Section D

	P	W	D	L	F	A	Pts
Rangers	6	4	1	1	15	6	9
East Fife	6	3	1	2	10	9	7
Queen of South	6	2	0	4	11	16	4
Aberdeen	6	2	0	4	10	15	4

DIV 2 Section A

	P	W	D	L	F	A	Pts
Falkirk	6	6	0	0	23	4	12
Stenhousemuir	6	2	1	3	12	16	5
Dundee U	6	1	2	3	6	10	4
Cowdenbeath	6	1	1	4	7	18	3

DIV 2 Section B

	P	W	D	L	F	A	Pts
Dunfermline A	6	4	1	1	15	7	9
Queen's Park	6	3	0	3	9	9	6
Alloa	6	2	1	3	8	10	5
Hamilton A	6	2	0	4	7	13	4

DIV 2 Section C

	P	W	D	L	F	A	Pts
St Johnstone	6	4	1	1	14	8	9
Clyde	6	4	0	2	16	8	8
Albion R	6	3	0	3	10	14	6
Arbroath	6	0	1	5	10	20	1

DIV 2 Section D

	P	W	D	L	F	A	Pts
Forfar A	6	4	1	1	13	8	9
Kilmarnock	6	4	0	2	9	4	8
Ayr U	6	2	0	4	11	12	4
Dumbarton	6	1	1	4	6	15	3

Quarter-finals

Sep 15 Celtic .....4 Forfar A 1
Sep 19 Forfar A .....1 Celtic .....1 Agg 2-5
Sep 15 Dunfermline A .....1 Rangers 0
Sep 19 Rangers .....3 Dunfermline A .....1 Agg 3-2
Sep 15 Falkirk .....0 Dundee 0
Sep 19 Dundee .....2 Falkirk .....1 Agg 2-1
Sep 15 St Johnstone .....0 Motherwell 4
Sep 19 Motherwell .....3 St Johnstone .....0 Agg 7-0

Semi-finals

Oct 13 Celtic .....0 Rangers 3
played at Hampden Park
Oct 13 Dundee .....5 Motherwell 1
played at Ibrox

Final

Oct 27 Dundee .....3 Rangers 2
played at Hampden Park

Season 1952-53

DIV 1 SECTION A

	Celtic	Hibernian	Partick T	St Mirren
Celtic		Aug16 2-0	Aug13 2-5	Aug23 3-1
Hibernian	Aug30 3-0		Aug23 3-1	Aug13 5-2
Partick T	Aug27 0-1	Aug09 1-5		Aug30 2-2
St Mirren	Aug09 0-1	Aug27 3-1	Aug16 5-1	

DIV 1 SECTION B

	East Fife	Falkirk	Queen of South	T Lanark
East Fife		Aug27 4-1	Aug09 2-0	Aug16 0-1
Falkirk	Aug13 3-3		Aug30 2-3	Aug23 2-1
Queen of South	Aug23 2-3	Aug16 2-2		Aug13 0-3
T Lanark	Aug30 2-0	Aug09 2-4	Aug27 3-1	

DIV 1 SECTION C

	Aberdeen	Hearts	Motherwell	Rangers
Aberdeen		Aug13 2-4	Aug23 0-1	Aug30 1-2
Hearts	Aug27 1-1		Aug16 0-1	Aug09 5-0
Motherwell	Aug09 5-2	Aug30 1-2		Aug27 3-3
Rangers	Aug16 3-1	Aug23 2-0	Aug13 2-0	

DIV 1 SECTION D

	Airdrie	Clyde	Dundee	Raith R
Airdrie		Aug23 4-0	Aug13 1-3	Aug16 0-1
Clyde	Aug09 1-1		Aug30 3-3	Aug27 6-1
Dundee	Aug27 3-2	Aug16 2-2		Aug09 2-1
Raith R	Aug30 1-1	Aug13 4-3	Aug23 1-2	

DIV 2 SECTION A

	Alloa	Arbroath	Dunfermline A	Kilmarnock
Alloa		Aug13 3-1	Aug16 2-2	Aug23 0-1
Arbroath	Aug27 1-1		Aug09 0-5	Aug16 2-0
Dunfermline A	Aug30 4-3	Aug23 3-1		Aug13 3-4
Kilmarnock	Aug09 3-1	Aug30 4-0	Aug27 3-2	

DIV 2 SECTION B

	Ayr U	Dumbarton	Dundee U	Stirling A
Ayr U		Aug13 11-1	Aug16 4-1	Aug23 1-2
Dumbarton	Aug27 1-1		Aug09 3-1	Aug30 2-1
Dundee U	Aug30 2-1	Aug23 1-0		Aug13 2-6
Stirling A	Aug09 2-0	Aug16 3-0	Aug27 6-1	

DIV 2 SECTION C

	Cowdenbeath	Forfar A	Hamilton A	Morton
Cowdenbeath		Aug09 2-0	Aug27 0-1	Aug16 2-3
Forfar A	Aug23 3-1		Aug30 1-1	Aug09 0-2
Hamilton A	Aug13 2-0	Aug16 2-2		Aug23 2-3
Morton	Aug30 2-2	Aug27 5-2	Aug09 4-1	

DIV 2 SECTION D

	Albion R	Queen's Park	St Johnstone	Stenhousemuir
Albion R		Aug09 2-0	Aug27 2-4	Aug30 4-4
Queen's Park	Aug23 2-0		Aug16 0-0	Aug13 1-3
St Johnstone	Aug13 6-3	Aug30 3-4		Aug23 1-0
Stenhousemuir	Aug13 1-0	Aug27 0-1	Aug09 1-5	

DIV 1 Section A

	P	W	D	L	F	A	Pts
Hibernian	6	4	0	2	17	9	8
Celtic	6	4	0	2	9	9	8
St Mirren	6	2	1	3	13	13	5
Partick T	6	1	1	4	10	18	3

DIV 1 Section B

	P	W	D	L	F	A	Pts
T Lanark	6	4	0	2	12	7	8
East Fife	6	3	1	2	12	9	7
Falkirk	6	2	2	2	14	15	6
Queen of South	6	1	1	4	8	15	3

DIV 1 Section C

	P	W	D	L	F	A	Pts
Rangers	6	4	1	1	12	10	9
Hearts	6	3	1	2	12	7	7
Motherwell	6	3	1	2	11	9	7
Aberdeen	6	0	1	5	7	16	1

DIV 1 Section D

	P	W	D	L	F	A	Pts
Dundee	6	4	2	0	15	10	10
Clyde	6	1	3	2	15	15	5
Raith R	6	2	1	3	9	14	5
Airdrie	6	1	2	3	9	9	4

DIV 2 Section A

	P	W	D	L	F	A	Pts
Kilmarnock	6	5	0	1	15	8	10
Dunfermline A	6	3	1	2	19	13	7
Alloa	6	1	2	3	10	12	4
Arbroath	6	1	1	4	5	16	3

DIV 2 Section B

	P	W	D	L	F	A	Pts
Stirling A	6	5	0	1	20	6	10
Ayr U	6	2	1	3	18	9	5
Dumbarton	6	2	1	3	7	18	5
Dundee U	6	2	0	4	8	20	4

DIV 2 Section C

	P	W	D	L	F	A	Pts
Morton	6	5	1	0	19	9	11
Hamilton A	6	2	2	2	9	10	6
Forfar A	6	1	2	3	8	13	4
Cowdenbeath	6	1	1	4	7	11	3

DIV 2 Section D

	P	W	D	L	F	A	Pts
St Johnstone	6	4	1	1	19	10	9
Queen's Park	6	3	1	2	8	7	7
Stenhousemuir	6	2	1	3	8	12	5
Albion R	6	1	1	4	11	17	3

Quarter-finals

Sep 13 Morton .....0 Hibernian 6
Sep 17 Hibernian .....6 Morton .....3 Agg 12-3
Sep 13 Rangers .....2 T Lanark 0
Sep 17 T Lanark .....0 Rangers .....2 Agg 0-2
Sep 13 St Johnstone .....1 Kilmarnock 3
Sep 17 Kilmarnock .....4 St Johnstone .....1 Agg 7-2
Sep 13 Stirling A .....3 Dundee 1
Sep 17 Dundee .....5 Stirling A .....0 Agg 6-3

Semi-finals

Oct 4 Dundee .....2 Hibernian 1
played at Tynecastle
Oct 4 Kilmarnock .....1 Rangers 0
played at Hampden Park

Final

Oct 25 Dundee .....2 Kilmarnock 0
played at Hampden Park

Season 1953-54

DIV 1 SECTION A

	Falkirk	Hibernian	Queen of South	St Mirren
Falkirk		Aug26 1-2	Aug29 4-0	Aug08 1-1
Hibernian	Aug12 4-1		Aug22 2-1	Aug29 3-2
Queen of South	Aug15 1-4	Aug08 0-4		Aug26 1-0
St Mirren	Aug22 1-1	Aug15 2-2	Aug12 3-2	

DIV 1 SECTION B

	Aberdeen	Airdrie	Celtic	East Fife
Aberdeen		Aug12 2-0	Aug22 5-2	Aug29 3-4
Airdrie	Aug26 4-3		Aug15 2-1	Aug08 4-1
Celtic	Aug08 0-1	Aug29 2-0		Aug26 0-1
East Fife	Aug15 2-0	Aug22 5-1	Aug12 1-1	

DIV 1 SECTION C

	Hamilton A	Hearts	Raith R	Rangers
Hamilton A		Aug22 1-1	Aug12 1-2	Aug29 0-5
Hearts	Aug08 5-0		Aug15 2-0	Aug26 1-1
Raith R	Aug26 2-0	Aug29 3-1		Aug08 0-4
Rangers	Aug15 5-1	Aug12 4-1	Aug22 3-1	

DIV 1 SECTION D

	Clyde	Dundee	Partick T	Stirling A
Clyde		Aug12 2-4	Aug22 2-3	Aug15 4-1
Dundee	Aug26 4-2		Aug15 1-1	6-1
Partick T	Aug08 4-1	Aug29 4-0		Aug26 3-0
Stirling A	Aug29 3-3	Aug22 0-2	Aug12 3-0	

DIV 2 SECTION A

	Alloa	Cowdenbeath	St Johnstone	T Lanark
Alloa		Aug26 3-1	Aug29 0-3	Aug08 0-10
Cowdenbeath	Aug12 2-1		Aug22 2-1	Aug15 4-2
St Johnstone	Aug15 2-0	Aug08 2-4		Aug26 4-1
T Lanark	Aug22 3-1	Aug29 7-0	Aug12 2-0	

DIV 2 SECTION B

	Albion R	Ayr U	Queen's Park	Stenhousemuir
Albion R		Aug12 1-4	Aug22 1-1	Aug29 2-2
Ayr U	Aug26 3-0		Aug29 3-1	Aug08 2-1
Queen's Park	Aug08 4-0	Aug15 0-0		Aug26 2-0
Stenhousemuir	Aug15 4-0	Aug22 4-2	Aug12 3-2	

DIV 2 SECTION C

	Dundee U	Kilmarnock	Morton	Motherwell
Dundee U		Aug29 0-3	Aug22 2-2	Aug12 0-5
Kilmarnock	Aug15 4-1		Aug12 1-0	Aug22 4-1
Morton	Aug08 5-3	Aug26 0-2		Aug29 2-3
Motherwell	Aug26 3-1	Aug08 3-0	Aug15 2-0	

DIV 2 SECTION D

	Arbroath	Dumbarton	Dunfermline A	Forfar A
Arbroath		Aug29 4-0	Aug22 3-1	Aug12 0-0
Dumbarton	Aug15 3-0		Aug12 1-3	Aug22 0-0
Dunfermline A	Aug08 2-1	Aug26 6-1		Aug29 3-0
Forfar A	Aug26 1-2	Aug08 2-1	Aug15 2-1	

DIV 1 Section A

	P	W	D	L	F	A	Pts
Hibernian	6	5	1	0	17	7	11
Falkirk	6	2	2	2	12	9	6
St Mirren	6	1	3	2	9	10	5
Queen of South	6	1	0	5	5	17	2

DIV 1 Section B

	P	W	D	L	F	A	Pts
East Fife	6	4	1	1	14	9	9
Aberdeen	6	3	0	3	14	12	6
Airdrie	6	3	0	3	11	14	6
Celtic	6	1	1	4	6	10	3

DIV 1 Section C

	P	W	D	L	F	A	Pts
Rangers	6	5	1	0	22	4	11
Hearts	6	2	2	2	11	9	6
Raith R	6	3	0	3	8	11	6
Hamilton A	6	0	1	5	3	20	1

DIV 1 Section D

	P	W	D	L	F	A	Pts
Partick T	6	4	1	1	15	7	9
Dundee	6	4	1	1	17	10	9
Clyde	6	1	1	4	14	19	3
Stirling A	6	1	1	4	8	18	3

DIV 2 Section A

	P	W	D	L	F	A	Pts
T Lanark	6	4	0	2	25	9	8
Cowdenbeath	6	4	0	2	13	16	8
St Johnstone	6	3	0	3	12	9	6
Alloa	6	1	0	5	5	21	2

DIV 2 Section B

	P	W	D	L	F	A	Pts
Ayr U	6	4	1	1	14	7	9
Stenhousemuir	6	3	1	2	14	10	7
Queen's Park	6	2	2	2	10	7	6
Albion R	6	0	2	4	4	18	2

DIV 2 Section C

	P	W	D	L	F	A	Pts
Kilmarnock	6	5	0	1	14	5	10
Motherwell	6	5	0	1	17	7	10
Morton	6	1	1	4	9	13	3
Dundee U	6	0	1	5	7	22	1

DIV 2 Section D

	P	W	D	L	F	A	Pts
Dunfermline A	6	4	0	2	16	8	8
Arbroath	6	3	1	2	12	10	7
Forfar A	6	2	2	2	5	7	6
Dumbarton	6	1	1	4	6	15	3

Quaretr-finals

Sep 12 East Fife . . . . .6 Dunfermline A . . .2
Sep 16 Dunfermline A . . . . .2 East Fife . . . . . . .3 Agg 4-9
Sep 12 Kilmarnock . . . . .4 Partick T 3
Sep 16 Partick T . . . . .4 Kilmarnock . . . . . .0 Agg 7-4
Sep 12 Rangers . . . . .4 Ayr U 2
Sep 16 Ayr U . . . . .3 Rangers . . . . . . .2 Agg 5-6
Sep 12 T Lanark . . . . .0 Hibernian 4
Sep 16 Hibernian . . . . .4 T Lanark . . . . . . .0 Agg 8-0

Semi-finals

Oct 10 East Fife . . . . .3 Hibernian 2
played at Tynecastle
Oct 10 Partick T . . . . .2 Rangers 0
played at Hampden Park

Final

Oct 24 East Fife . . . . .3 Partick T 0
played at Hampden Park

Celtic were still awaiting success in the Scottish League Cup, having yet to even reach the Final. Here is the team that gained both the other domestic honours in 1953-54. Back row (left to right): Haughney, Meecham, Bonner, Evans, Stein, Peacock. Front row: Higgins, Fernie, Fallon, Tully, Mochan.

DIV 1 SECTION A

	Kilmarnock	Motherwell	Raith R	St Mirren
Kilmarnock		Sep01 0-1	Aug14 3-2	Aug21 2-2
Motherwell	Aug18 4-0		Aug21 1-1	Aug28 3-1
Raith R	Aug28 0-1	Sep04 3-0		Aug18 2-2
St Mirren	Sep04 3-2	Aug14 4-4	Sep01 3-1	

DIV 1 SECTION B

	Aberdeen	East Fife	Hibernian	Queen of South
Aberdeen		Sep04 5-1	Sep01 1-1	Aug14 4-0
East Fife	Aug21 0-3		Aug14 3-1	Sep01 3-0
Hibernian	Aug18 2-0	Aug28 1-2		Aug21 3-1
Queen of South	Aug28 3-0	Aug18 1-4	Sep04 3-5	

DIV 1 SECTION C

	Clyde	Partick T	Rangers	Stirling A
Clyde		Aug28 2-0	Sep04 1-2	Aug18 0-1
Partick T	Aug14 3-2		Sep01 1-2	Sep04 9-1
Rangers	Aug21 1-3	Aug18 1-1		Aug28 2-0
Stirling A	Sep01 3-2	Aug21 0-2	Aug14 0-5	

DIV 1 SECTION D

	Celtic	Dundee	Falkirk	Hearts
Celtic		Sep01 0-1	Aug14 3-0	Aug21 1-2
Dundee	Aug18 3-1		Aug21 3-1	Aug28 4-1
Falkirk	Aug28 2-2	Sep04 4-0		Aug18 2-6
Hearts	Sep04 3-2	Aug14 3-1	Sep01 4-1	

DIV 2 SECTION A

	Forfar A	Hamilton A	St Johnstone	Stenhousemuir
Forfar A		Aug28 2-2	Sep04 3-3	Aug18 2-3
Hamilton A	Aug14 2-0		Sep01 0-0	Sep04 4-2
St Johnstone	Aug21 4-2	Aug18 2-0		Aug28 3-1
Stenhousemuir	Sep01 5-1	Aug21 4-3	Aug14 2-4	

DIV 2 SECTION B

	Ayr U	Brechin C	Dundee U	Dunfermline A
Ayr U		Aug18 2-2	Aug28 3-1	Sep04 3-1
Brechin C	Sep01 2-4		Aug21 2-0	Aug14 1-1
Dundee U	Aug14 2-5	Sep04 0-1		Sep01 3-1
Dunfermline A	Aug21 4-0	Aug28 2-1	Aug18 3-1	

DIV 2 SECTION C

	Airdrie	Cowdenbeath	Queen's Park	T Lanark
Airdrie		Aug18 2-1	Aug28 5-4	Aug21 2-0
Cowdenbeath	Sep01 1-2		Sep04 5-3	Aug14 1-0
Queen's Park	Aug14 2-4	Aug21 4-1		Sep01 1-2
T Lanark	Sep04 1-2	Aug28 4-0	Aug18 2-0	

DIV 2 SECTION D

	Albion R	Alloa	Arbroath	Morton
Albion R		Sep01 2-2	Sep04 3-1	Aug14 1-0
Alloa	Aug18 0-0		Aug28 3-3	Sep04 1-0
Arbroath	Aug21 3-1	Aug14 2-3		Sep01 2-2
Morton	Aug28 3-0	Aug21 3-0	Aug18 5-2	

DIV 1 Section A	P	W	D	L	F	A	Pts
Motherwell	6	3	2	1	13	9	8
St Mirren	6	2	3	1	15	14	7
Kilmarnock	6	2	1	3	8	12	5
Raith R	6	1	2	3	9	10	4

DIV 1 Section B	P	W	D	L	F	A	Pts
East Fife	6	4	0	2	13	11	8
Aberdeen	6	3	1	2	13	7	7
Hibernian	6	3	1	2	13	10	7
Queen of South	6	1	0	5	8	19	2

DIV 1 Section C	P	W	D	L	F	A	Pts
Rangers	6	4	1	1	13	6	9
Partick T	6	3	1	2	16	8	7
Clyde	6	2	0	4	10	10	4
Stirling A	6	2	0	4	5	20	4

DIV 1 Section D	P	W	D	L	F	A	Pts
Hearts	6	5	0	1	19	11	10
Dundee	6	4	0	2	12	10	8
Celtic	6	1	1	4	9	11	3
Falkirk	6	1	1	4	10	18	3

DIV 2 Section A	P	W	D	L	F	A	Pts
St Johnstone	6	4	2	0	16	8	10
Hamilton A	6	2	2	2	11	10	6
Stenhousemuir	6	3	0	3	17	17	6
Forfar A	6	0	2	4	10	19	2

DIV 2 Section B	P	W	D	L	F	A	Pts
Ayr U	6	4	1	1	17	12	9
Dunfermline A	6	3	1	2	12	9	7
Brechin C	6	2	2	2	9	9	6
Dundee U	6	1	0	5	7	15	2

DIV 2 Section C	P	W	D	L	F	A	Pts
Airdrie	6	6	0	0	17	9	12
T Lanark	6	3	0	3	9	6	6
Cowdenbeath	6	2	0	4	9	15	4
Queen's Park	6	1	0	5	14	19	2

DIV 2 Section D	P	W	D	L	F	A	Pts
Morton	6	3	1	2	13	6	7
Alloa	6	2	3	1	9	10	7
Albion R	6	2	2	2	7	9	6
Arbroath	6	1	2	3	13	17	4

Quarter-finals

Sep 22 Ayr U ....2 Airdrie 1
Sep 25 Airdrie ....6 Ayr U ....1 Agg 7-3
Sep 22 Morton ....2 East Fife 2
Sep 25 East Fife ....2 Morton ......0 Agg 4-2
Sep 22 St Johnstone ...0 Hearts 5
Sep 25 Hearts ....2 St Johnstone ...0 Agg 7-0
Sep 22 Motherwell ....2 Rangers 1
Sep 25 Rangers ....1 Motherwell ....1 Agg 2-3

Semi-finals

Oct 9 Airdrie ....1 Hearts 4
        played at Easter Road
Oct 9 East Fife ....1 Motherwell 2
        played at Hampden Park

Final

Oct 23 Hearts ....4 Motherwell 2
        played at Hampden Park

Section 1

	Airdrie	Dundee	Kilmarnock	St Mirren
Airdrie		Aug13 4-0	Sep03 3-3	Aug31 2-4
Dundee	Aug27 2-2		Aug17 1-2	Aug20 2-0
Kilmarnock	Aug20 2-0	Aug31 0-0		Aug13 0-0
St Mirren	Aug17 3-2	Sep03 0-3	Aug27 3-0	

Section 2

	East Fife	Hearts	Partick T	Raith R
East Fife		Aug20 1-0	Aug17 2-3	Aug27 0-2
Hearts	Sep03 4-0		Aug27 2-1	Aug17 5-0
Partick T	Aug31 2-1	Aug13 0-2		Aug20 4-0
Raith R	Aug13 2-4	Aug31 0-2	Sep03 0-1	

Section 3

	Aberdeen	Clyde	Dunfermline A	Hibernian
Aberdeen		Aug20 3-2	Aug17 3-2	Aug27 2-1
Clyde	Sep03 1-2		Aug27 3-2	Aug17 2-2
Dunfermline A	Aug31 2-2	Aug13 4-2		Sep03 1-3
Hibernian	Aug13 0-1	Aug31 2-1	Aug20 3-1	

Section 4

	Celtic	Falkirk	Queen of South	Rangers
Celtic		Aug20 5-1	Aug13 4-2	Aug31 0-4
Falkirk	Sep03 1-1		Aug31 4-0	Aug13 0-5
Queen of South	Aug17 0-2	Aug27 0-3		Aug20 1-2
Rangers	Aug27 1-4	Aug17 4-3	Sep03 6-0	

Section 5

	Alloa	Arbroath	Cowdenbeath	Hamilton A
Alloa		Aug13 5-3	Aug31 5-3	Sep03 2-2
Arbroath	Aug27 1-2		Sep03 1-1	Aug17 1-2
Cowdenbeath	Aug17 5-3	Aug20 5-1		Aug27 1-2
Hamilton A	Aug20 1-1	Aug31 7-0	Aug13 6-1	

Section 6

	Ayr U	Queen's Park	St Johnstone	Stirling A
Ayr U		Aug17 3-2	Sep03 3-2	Aug27 2-2
Queen's Park	Aug31 2-0		Aug20 1-2	Aug13 3-0
St Johnstone	Aug13 5-1	Sep03 3-0		Aug31 3-2
Stirling A	Aug20 3-1	Aug27 1-0	Aug17 0-1	

Section 7

	Albion R	Dundee U	Forfar A	Motherwell
Albion R		Aug27 3-3	Aug17 1-0	Aug20 0-2
Dundee U	Aug13 1-3		Sep03 3-2	Aug31 0-2
Forfar A	Aug31 2-1	Aug20 2-5		Aug13 1-6
Motherwell	Sep03 4-0	Aug17 7-1	Aug27 2-1	

Section 8

	Brechin C	Morton	Stenhousemuir	T Lanark
Brechin C		Sep03 4-0	Aug31 3-3	Aug13 2-1
Morton	Aug20 7-1		Aug13 3-1	Aug31 2-0
Stenhousemuir	Aug17 2-0	Aug27 2-4		Aug20 1-1
T Lanark	Aug27 1-4	Aug17 1-0	Sep03 3-0	

Section 9

	Berwick R	Dumbarton	E Stirling	Montrose	Stranraer
Berwick R				Sep03 1-2	Aug17 2-0
Dumbarton	Aug13 2-0		Sep03 6-1		
E Stirling	Aug27 3-2				Aug20 5-2
Montrose		Aug20 0-2	Aug17 2-5		
Stranraer		Aug27 3-3		Aug13 3-2	

DIV 1 Section 1	P	W	D	L	F	A	Pts
St Mirren	6	3	1	2	10	9	7
Kilmarnock	6	2	3	1	7	7	7
Dundee	6	2	2	2	8	8	6
Airdrie	6	1	2	3	13	14	4

DIV 1 Section 2	P	W	D	L	F	A	Pts
Hearts	6	5	0	1	15	2	10
Partick T	6	4	0	2	11	7	8
East Fife	6	2	0	4	8	13	4
Raith R	6	1	0	5	4	16	2

DIV 1 Section 3	P	W	D	L	F	A	Pts
Aberdeen	6	5	1	0	13	8	11
Hibernian	6	3	1	2	11	8	7
Dunfermline A	6	1	1	4	12	16	3
Clyde	6	1	1	4	11	15	3

DIV 1 Section 4	P	W	D	L	F	A	Pts
Rangers	6	5	0	1	22	8	10
Celtic	6	4	1	1	16	9	9
Falkirk	6	2	1	3	12	15	5
Queen of South	6	0	0	6	3	21	0

DIV 2 Section 5	P	W	D	L	F	A	Pts
Hamilton A	6	4	2	0	20	6	10
Alloa	6	3	2	1	18	15	8
Cowdenbeath	6	2	1	3	16	18	5
Arbroath	6	0	1	5	7	22	1

DIV 2 Section 6	P	W	D	L	F	A	Pts
St Johnstone	6	5	0	1	16	7	10
Stirling A	6	2	1	3	8	10	5
Ayr U	6	2	1	3	10	16	5
Queen's Park	6	2	0	4	8	9	4

DIV 2 Section 7	P	W	D	L	F	A	Pts
Motherwell	6	6	0	0	23	3	12
Dundee U	6	2	1	3	13	19	5
Albion R	6	2	1	3	8	12	5
Forfar A	6	1	0	5	8	18	2

DIV 2 Section 8	P	W	D	L	F	A	Pts
Morton	6	4	0	2	16	9	8
Brechin C	6	3	1	2	14	14	7
T Lanark	6	2	1	3	7	9	5
Stenhousemuir	6	1	2	3	9	14	4

DIV 2 SECTION 9	P	W	D	L	F	A	Pts
Dumbarton	4	3	1	0	13	4	7
E Stirling	4	3	0	1	14	12	6
Stranraer	4	1	1	2	8	12	3
Berwick R	4	1	0	3	5	7	2
Montrose	4	1	0	3	6	11	2

Play-offs

Sep 6 Dumbarton ....2 Morton 1
Sep 8 Morton ....0 Dumbarton ......1 Agg 1-3

Quarter-finals

Sep 14 St Mirren ....5 Dumbarton 1
Sep 17 Dumbarton ......1 St Mirren ......1 Agg 2-6
Sep 14 Aberdeen ....5 Hearts 3
Sep 17 Hearts ....2 Aberdeen ......4 Agg 5-9
Sep 14 St Johnstone ....1 Motherwell 2
Sep 17 Motherwell ......0 St Johnstone ..1 Agg 2-2
Sep 14 Hamilton A ....1 Rangers 2
Sep 17 Rangers ....8 Hamilton A ....0 Agg 10-1

Replay

Sep 21 Motherwell ....2 St Johnstone ...0
played at Ibrox

Semi-finals

Oct 1 Aberdeen ....2 Rangers 1
played at Hampden Park
Oct 1 Motherwell ....3 St Mirren 3
played at Ibrox

Replay

Oct 8 Motherwell ....0 St Mirren 2
played at Celtic Park

Final

Oct 22 Aberdeen ....2 St Mirren 1
played at Hampden Park

The jubilant Aberdeen players tour the city in a 'make-do' open-top bus, with Paddy Buckley rising to the occasion after the Dons' 1956 League Cup success.

Section 1

	Airdrie	Dundee	Motherwell	Raith R
Airdrie		Sep01 1-7	Aug15 1-3	Aug25 3-1
Dundee	Aug18 3-1		Aug25 2-1	Aug15 1-0
Motherwell	Aug29 6-1	Aug11 0-1		Sep01 0-1
Raith R	Aug11 4-2	Aug29 2-2	Aug18 4-2	

Section 2

	Aberdeen	Celtic	East Fife	Rangers
Aberdeen		Aug11 1-2	Aug29 4-1	Aug18 2-6
Celtic	Aug25 3-2		Aug18 2-1	Aug15 2-1
East Fife	Aug15 2-1	Sep01 0-1		Aug25 1-4
Rangers	Sep01 4-1	Aug29 0-0	Aug11 3-0	

Section 3

	Dunfermline A	Kilmarnock	Queen of South	St Mirren
Dunfermline A		Aug25 5-1	Aug15 2-1	Sep01 2-0
Kilmarnock	Aug11 0-0		Aug18 2-3	Aug29 1-4
Queen of South	Aug29 1-1	Sep01 0-2		Aug11 0-0
St Mirren	Aug18 2-0	Aug15 2-2	Aug25 1-1	

Section 4

	Falkirk	Hearts	Hibernian	Partick T
Falkirk		Sep01 1-1	Aug29 4-0	Aug11 0-2
Hearts	Aug18 5-0		Aug11 6-1	Aug29 2-2
Hibernian	Aug15 0-1	Aug25 1-2		Sep01 2-2
Partick T	Aug25 2-0	Aug15 3-1	Aug18 4-1	

Section 5

	Alloa	Brechin C	Dumbarton	Hamilton A
Alloa		Aug29 1-3	Sep01 1-3	Aug11 3-1
Brechin C	Aug15 3-1		Aug25 3-4	Sep01 2-0
Dumbarton	Aug18 1-1	Aug11 1-8		Aug29 3-4
Hamilton A	Aug25 3-2	Aug18 1-1	Aug15 5-3	

Section 6

	Berwick R	Cowdenbeath	Morton	Stranraer
Berwick R		Aug15 0-3	Aug25 1-1	Sep01 2-0
Cowdenbeath	Aug29 3-1		Aug18 0-1	Aug11 1-1
Morton	Aug11 1-1	Sep01 0-1		Aug29 1-1
Stranraer	Aug18 5-2	Aug25 1-3	Aug15 1-4	

Section 7

	Clyde	Queen's Park	St Johnstone	Stirling A
Clyde		Aug29 2-2	Sep01 5-1	Aug11 2-1
Queen's Park	Aug15 0-1		Aug25 0-2	Sep01 2-0
St Johnstone	Aug18 1-6	Aug11 2-1		Aug29 1-0
Stirling A	Aug25 0-3	Aug18 0-2	Aug15 0-0	

Section 8

	Ayr U	Dundee U	Stenhousemuir	T Lanark
Ayr U		Aug25 1-1	Sep01 3-1	Aug15 3-3
Dundee U	Aug11 6-1		Aug29 3-4	Sep01 2-1
Stenhousemuir	Aug18 1-1	Aug15 3-2		Aug25 2-1
T Lanark	Aug28 1-5	Aug18 1-2	Aug11 8-2	

Section 9

	Albion R	Arbroath	E Stirling	Forfar A	Montrose
Albion R		Aug11 2-1	Aug18 9-2		
Arbroath				Aug18 3-0	Sep01 6-1
E Stirling		Aug25 0-3		Aug15 3-0	
Forfar A	Aug15 4-2		Sep01 0-1		
Montrose	Aug25 3-5			Aug11 2-3	

League Tables

Section 1
	P	W	D	L	F	A	Pts
Dundee	6	5	1	0	16	5	11
Raith R	6	3	1	2	12	10	7
Motherwell	6	2	0	4	12	10	4
Airdrie	6	1	0	5	9	24	2

Section 2
	P	W	D	L	F	A	Pts
Celtic	6	5	1	0	10	5	11
Rangers	6	4	1	1	18	6	9
Aberdeen	6	1	0	5	11	18	2
East Fife	6	1	0	5	5	15	2

Section 3
	P	W	D	L	F	A	Pts
Dunfermline A	6	3	2	1	10	5	8
St Mirren	6	2	3	1	9	6	7
Queen of South	6	1	3	2	6	8	5
Kilmarnock	6	1	2	3	8	14	4

Section 4
	P	W	D	L	F	A	Pts
Partick T	6	4	2	0	15	6	10
Hearts	6	3	2	1	17	8	8
Falkirk	6	2	1	3	6	10	5
Hibernian	6	0	1	5	5	19	1

Section 5
	P	W	D	L	F	A	Pts
Brechin C	6	4	1	1	20	8	9
Hamilton A	6	3	1	2	14	14	7
Dumbarton	6	2	1	3	15	22	5
Alloa	6	1	1	4	9	14	3

Section 6
	P	W	D	L	F	A	Pts
Cowdenbeath	6	4	1	1	11	4	9
Morton	6	2	3	1	8	5	7
Stranraer	6	1	2	3	9	13	4
Berwick R	6	1	2	3	7	13	4

Section 7
	P	W	D	L	F	A	Pts
Clyde	6	5	1	0	19	5	11
St Johnstone	6	3	1	2	7	12	7
Queen's Park	6	2	1	3	7	7	5
Stirling A	6	0	1	5	1	10	1

Section 8
	P	W	D	L	F	A	Pts
Dundee U	6	3	1	2	16	11	7
Ayr U	6	2	3	1	14	13	7
Stenhousemuir	6	3	1	2	13	18	7
T Lanark	6	1	1	4	15	16	3

Section 9
	P	W	D	L	F	A	Pts
Arbroath	4	3	0	1	13	3	6
Albion R	4	3	0	1	18	10	6
Forfar A	4	2	0	2	7	8	4
E Stirling	4	2	0	2	6	12	4
Montrose	4	0	0	4	6	17	0

Play-offs
Sep 3 Arbroath ....2 Dundee U 0
Sep 5 Dundee U ....5 Arbroath ....0 Agg 5-2

Quarter-finals
Sep 12 Brechin C ....3 Clyde 2
Sep 15 Clyde ....3 Brechin C ....1 Agg 5-4
Sep 12 Dundee ....7 Dundee U 3
Sep 15 Dundee U ....2 Dundee ....1 Agg 5-8
Sep 12 Celtic ....6 Dunfermline A ...0
Sep 15 Dunfermline A ...3 Celtic ....0 Agg 3-6
Sep 12 Cowdenbeath .....1 Partick T 2
Sep 15 Partick T ....2 Cowdenbeath ....1 Agg 4-2

Semi-finals
Oct 6 Celtic ....2 Clyde 0
played at Hampden Park
Oct 6 Dundee ....0 Partick T 0
played at Ibrox

Replay
Oct 9 Dundee ....2 Partick T 3
played at Ibrox

Final
Oct 27 Celtic ....0 Partick T 0
played at Hampden Park

Replay
Oct 31 Celtic ....3 Partick T 0
played at Hampden Park

Celtic in 1957, showing off their League Cup trophy. Back row (left to right): Goldie, Fallon, Beattie, McPhail, Fernie, Evans. Front row: W.Johnstone (trainer), Tully, Collins, Peacock, Wilson, Mochan, J.McGrory (manager).

Season 1957-58

Section 1

	Aberdeen	Falkirk	Motherwell	Queen of S'h
Aberdeen		Aug28 2-1	Aug31 5-3	Aug10 5-1
Falkirk	Aug14 3-4		Aug24 1-3	Aug17 3-0
Motherwell	Aug17 2-3	Aug10 1-4		Aug28 2-1
Queen of South	Aug24 2-3	Aug31 1-1	Aug14 3-0	

Section 2

	Partick T	Raith R	Rangers	St Mirren
Partick T		Aug24 1-4	Aug14 0-1	Aug31 0-2
Raith R	Aug10 1-0		Aug31 4-3	Aug10 4-1
Rangers	Aug28 0-3	Aug17 4-3		Aug10 6-0
St Mirren	Aug17 1-0	Aug13 1-0	Aug24 0-4	

Section 3

	Airdrie	Celtic	East Fife	Hibernian
Airdrie		Aug24 1-2	Aug31 9-1	Aug14 4-1
Celtic	Aug10 3-2		Aug28 6-1	Aug31 2-0
East Fife	Aug17 1-3	Aug14 1-4		Aug24 2-2
Hibernian	Aug28 5-1	Aug17 3-1	Aug10 4-0	

Section 4

	Dundee	Hearts	Kilmarnock	Queen's Park
Dundee		Aug20 2-2	Aug14 0-3	Aug24 1-1
Hearts	Aug31 4-2		Aug24 1-1	Aug14 9-2
Kilmarnock	Aug28 1-1	Aug10 2-1		Aug17 3-1
Queen's Park	Aug10 2-5	Aug28 0-0	Aug31 2-2	

Section 5

	Clyde	Dumbarton	Dundee U	Stranraer
Clyde		Aug17 7-1	Aug24 8-1	Aug14 10-0
Dumbarton	Aug31 1-4		Aug14 2-4	Aug24 10-3
Dundee U	Aug10 1-4	Aug28 0-3		Aug31 3-0
Stranraer	Aug28 0-5	Aug10 3-1	Aug17 2-4	

Section 6

	Ayr U	Brechin C	Cowdenbeath	Dunfermline A
Ayr U		Aug24 4-2	Aug31 3-2	Aug14 4-1
Brechin C	Aug10 5-2		Aug28 7-1	Aug17 2-1
Cowdenbeath	Aug17 1-1	Aug14 1-1		Aug24 2-5
Dunfermline A	Aug28 3-0	Aug31 3-1	Aug10 1-1	

Section 7

	Morton	Stenhousemuir	Stirling A	T Lanark
Morton		Aug17 7-5	Aug10 0-1	Aug28 3-3
Stenhousemuir	Aug31 1-2		Aug28 4-0	Aug10 3-3
Stirling A	Aug24 1-3	Aug14 0-1		Aug31 0-1
T Lanark	Aug14 1-0	Aug24 3-0	Aug17 2-0	

Section 8

	Albion R	Arbroath	Hamilton A	St Johnstone
Albion R		Aug17 2-0	Aug28 1-1	Aug10 2-4
Arbroath	Aug31 4-1		Aug10 1-1	Aug28 3-1
Hamilton A	Aug14 3-2	Aug3 3-0		Aug31 4-1
St Johnstone	Aug24 6-2	Aug14 1-2	Aug17 0-3	

Section 9

	Alloa	Berwick R	E Stirling	Forfar A	Montrose
Alloa		Aug17 5-0	Aug14 3-3		
Berwick R				Aug10 3-5	Aug24 1-3
E Stirling		Aug31 5-1			Aug10 3-1
Forfar A	Aug24 2-3		Aug17 2-1		
Montrose	Aug31 3-1			Aug14 4-1	

Tables

Section 1	P	W	D	L	F	A	Pts
Aberdeen	6	6	0	0	22	12	12
Falkirk	6	2	1	3	13	11	5
Motherwell	6	2	0	4	11	17	4
Queen of South	6	1	1	4	8	14	3

Section 2	P	W	D	L	F	A	Pts
Rangers	6	4	0	2	18	10	8
Raith R	6	4	0	2	16	10	8
St Mirren	6	3	0	3	5	14	6
Partick T	6	1	0	5	4	9	2

Section 3	P	W	D	L	F	A	Pts
Celtic	6	5	0	1	18	8	10
Hibernian	6	3	1	2	15	10	7
Airdrie	6	3	0	3	20	13	6
East Fife	6	0	1	5	6	28	1

Section 4	P	W	D	L	F	A	Pts
Kilmarnock	6	3	3	0	12	6	9
Hearts	6	2	3	1	17	9	7
Dundee	6	1	3	2	11	13	5
Queen's Park	6	0	3	3	8	20	3

Section 5	P	W	D	L	F	A	Pts
Clyde	6	6	0	0	38	4	12
Dundee U	6	3	0	3	13	19	6
Dumbarton	6	2	0	4	18	21	4
Stranraer	6	1	0	5	8	33	2

Section 6	P	W	D	L	F	A	Pts
Brechin C	6	3	1	2	18	12	7
Dunfermline A	6	3	1	2	14	10	7
Ayr U	6	3	1	2	14	14	7
Cowdenbeath	6	0	3	3	8	18	3

Section 7	P	W	D	L	F	A	Pts
T Lanark	6	4	2	0	13	6	10
Morton	6	3	1	2	15	12	7
Stenhousemuir	6	2	1	3	14	15	5
Stirling A	6	1	0	5	2	11	2

Section 8	P	W	D	L	F	A	Pts
Hamilton A	6	4	2	0	15	5	10
Arbroath	6	3	1	2	10	9	7
St Johnstone	6	2	0	4	13	16	4
Albion R	6	1	1	4	10	18	3

Section 9	P	W	D	L	F	A	Pts
Montrose	4	3	0	1	11	6	6
E Stirling	4	2	1	1	12	7	5
Alloa	4	2	1	1	12	8	5
Forfar A	4	2	0	2	10	11	4
Berwick R	4	0	0	4	5	18	0

Play-offs
Sep 2 Montrose ....1 Hamilton A 0
Sep 4 Hamilton A ....3 Montrose ......0 Agg 3-1

Quarter-finals
Sep 11 Celtic ....6 T Lanark 1
Sep 14 T Lanark ....0 Celtic ....3 Agg 1-9
Sep 11 Kilmarnock ....2 Rangers 1
Sep 14 Rangers ....3 Kilmarnock ....1 Agg 4-3
Sep 11 Aberdeen ....1 Clyde 2
Sep 14 Clyde ....4 Aberdeen ......2 Agg 6-3
Sep 11 Hamilton A ....2 Brechin C 4
Sep 14 Brechin C ....1 Hamilton A ....0 Agg 5-2

Semi-finals
Sep 28 Celtic ....4 Clyde 2
played at Ibrox
Sep 28 Brechin C ....0 Rangers 4
played at Hampden Park

Final
Oct 19 Celtic ....7 Rangers 1
played at Hampden Park

Celtic retain the League Cup in emphatic style as Mochan beats Niven of Rangers for Celtic's second of seven goals.

Season 1958-59

Section 1

	Hearts	Raith R	Rangers	T Lanark
Hearts		Aug30 3-1	Aug23 2-1	Aug13 3-0
Raith R	Aug16 1-3		Aug13 3-1	Aug23 3-1
Rangers	Aug09 3-0	Aug27 6-0		Aug16 2-2
T Lanark	Aug27 4-5	Aug09 4-2	Aug30 0-3	

Section 2

	Airdrie	Celtic	Clyde	St Mirren
Airdrie		Aug27 1-2	Aug16 2-3	Aug09 3-4
Celtic	Aug13 3-3		Aug23 2-0	Aug16 3-0
Clyde	Aug30 3-1	Aug09 1-4		Aug27 6-1
St Mirren	Aug23 3-2	Aug30 6-3	Aug13 1-2	

Section 3

	Dundee	Motherwell	Partick T	Queen of South
Dundee		Aug27 2-3	Aug09 2-3	Aug30 2-0
Motherwell	Aug13 1-2		Aug16 2-5	Aug23 4-0
Partick T	Aug23 3-2	Aug30 1-1		Aug13 5-1
Queen of South	Aug16 1-0	Aug09 1-2	Aug27 3-0	

Section 4

	Aberdeen	Falkirk	Hibernian	Kilmarnock
Aberdeen		Aug16 5-1	Aug13 1-2	Aug23 0-2
Falkirk	Aug30 1-1		Aug23 0-4	Aug13 1-3
Hibernian	Aug27 4-2	Aug09 3-2		Aug16 0-3
Kilmarnock	Aug09 1-2	Aug27 1-2	Aug30 2-1	

Section 5

	Brechin C	Dunfermline A	East Fife	Stirling A
Brechin C		Aug30 1-2	Aug13 0-3	Aug23 2-5
Dunfermline A	Aug16 4-1		Aug23 5-2	Aug13 6-1
East Fife	Aug27 5-1	Aug09 1-3		Aug30 5-2
Stirling A	Aug09 3-2	Aug27 1-3	Aug16 1-0	

Section 6

	Cowdenbeath	Dundee U	Morton	St Johnstone
Cowdenbeath		Aug27 6-1	Aug09 2-1	Aug30 2-1
Dundee U	Aug13 1-3		Aug16 1-4	Aug23 5-3
Morton	Aug23 0-0	Aug30 6-1		Aug13 1-3
St Johnstone	Aug16 1-2	Aug09 1-2	Aug27 2-0	

Section 7

	Alloa	Arbroath	Dumbarton	Queen's Park
Alloa		Aug23 2-5	Aug13 1-3	Aug30 2-2
Arbroath	Aug09 3-1		Aug16 6-3	Aug27 4-0
Dumbarton	Aug27 3-1	Aug30 0-1		Aug09 3-3
Queen's Park	Aug16 5-2	Aug13 2-1	Aug23 0-3	

Section 8

	Ayr U	Forfar A	Hamilton A	Montrose
Ayr U		Aug16 4-0	Aug23 3-1	Aug13 7-1
Forfar A	Aug30 1-1		Aug13 1-0	Aug23 4-1
Hamilton A	Aug09 3-1	Aug27		Aug30 3-0
Montrose	Aug27 1-2	Aug09 2-2	Aug16 2-3	

Section 9

	Albion R	Berwick R	E Stirling	Stenhousemuir	Stranraer
Albion R			Aug23 4-1	Aug13 0-4	
Berwick R	Aug30 2-2		Aug13 3-2		
E Stirling				Aug09 0-5	Aug16 1-2
Stenhousemuir		Aug16 0-1			Aug27 3-4
Stranraer	Aug09 4-1	Aug23 2-1			

Section 3

	P	W	D	L	F	A	Pts
Partick T	6	4	1	1	17	11	9
Motherwell	6	3	1	2	13	11	7
Dundee	6	2	0	4	10	11	4
Queen of South	6	2	0	4	6	13	4

Section 4

	P	W	D	L	F	A	Pts
Kilmarnock	6	4	0	2	12	6	8
Hibernian	6	4	0	2	14	10	8
Aberdeen	6	2	1	3	11	11	5
Falkirk	6	1	1	4	7	17	3

Section 5

	P	W	D	L	F	A	Pts
Dunfermline A	6	6	0	0	23	7	12
East Fife	6	3	0	3	16	12	6
Stirling A	6	3	0	3	13	18	6
Brechin C	6	0	0	6	7	22	0

Section 6

	P	W	D	L	F	A	Pts
Cowdenbeath	6	5	1	0	15	5	11
Morton	6	2	1	3	12	9	5
St Johnstone	6	2	0	4	11	12	4
Dundee U	6	2	0	4	11	23	4

Section 7

	P	W	D	L	F	A	Pts
Arbroath	6	5	0	1	20	8	10
Dumbarton	6	3	1	2	15	12	7
Queen's Park	6	2	2	2	12	15	6
Alloa	6	0	1	5	9	21	1

Section 8

	P	W	D	L	F	A	Pts
Ayr U	6	4	1	1	18	7	9
Hamilton A	6	4	0	2	12	7	8
Forfar A	6	2	2	2	8	10	6
Montrose	6	0	1	5	7	21	1

Section 9

	P	W	D	L	F	A	Pts
Stranraer	4	4	0	0	12	6	8
Berwick R	4	2	1	1	7	6	5
Stenhousemuir	4	2	0	2	12	5	4
Albion R	4	1	1	2	7	11	3
E Stirling	4	0	0	4	4	14	0

Play-offs

Sep 1 Stranraer ....3 Arbroath 4
Sep 3 Arbroath ....1 Stranraer ......0 Agg 5-3

Quarter-finals

Sep 10 Ayr U ....1 Hearts 5
Sep 17 Hearts ....3 Ayr U ....1 Agg 8-2
Sep 10 Celtic ....2 Cowdenbeath 0
Sep 17 Cowdenbeath ......1 Celtic ....8 Agg 1-10
Sep 10 Kilmarnock ....4 Dunfermline A ..1
Sep 16 Dunfermline A ....3 Kilmarnock .....3 Agg 4-7
Sep 10 Partick T ....2 Arbroath 1
Sep 17 Arbroath ....1 Partick T ......1 Agg 2-3

Semi-finals

Oct 1 Celtic ....1 Partick T 2
    played at Ibrox
Oct 1 Hearts ....3 Kilmarnock 0
    played at Easter Road

Final

Oct 25 Hearts ....5 Partick T 1
    played at Hampden Park

Section 1

	P	W	D	L	F	A	Pts
Hearts	6	5	0	1	16	10	10
Rangers	6	3	1	2	16	7	7
Raith R	6	2	0	4	10	18	4
T Lanark	6	1	1	4	11	18	3

Section 2

	P	W	D	L	F	A	Pts
Celtic	6	4	1	1	17	11	9
Clyde	6	4	0	2	15	11	8
St Mirren	6	3	0	3	15	19	6
Airdrie	6	0	1	5	12	18	1

Season 1959-60

Section 1

	Airdrie	Celtic	Partick T	Raith R
Airdrie		Aug15 4-2	Aug22 4-0	Aug12 2-3
Celtic	Aug29 2-2		Aug12 1-2	Aug22 1-0
Partick T	Aug08 0-0	Aug26 0-2		Aug29 1-3
Raith R	Aug26 3-0	Aug08 2-1	Aug15 2-0	

Section 2

	Clyde	Dunfermline A	St Mirren	T Lanark
Clyde		Aug08 0-0	Aug15 4-2	Aug26 2-2
Dunfermline A	Aug22 1-4		Aug12 3-0	Aug29 2-3
St Mirren	Aug29 2-1	Aug26 1-2		Aug08 2-3
T Lanark	Aug12 2-0	Aug15 6-1	Aug22 3-1	

Section 3

	Aberdeen	Hearts	Kilmarnock	Stirling A
Aberdeen		Aug26 1-4	Aug29 2-4	Aug08 3-1
Hearts	Aug12 2-2		Aug22 2-0	Aug29 2-2
Kilmarnock	Aug15 2-3	Aug08 0-4		Aug26 5-0
Stirling A	Aug22 2-5	Aug15 1-2	Aug12 2-2	

Section 4

	Dundee	Hibernian	Motherwell	Rangers
Dundee		Aug12 4-3	Aug22 1-4	Aug29 2-3
Hibernian	Aug26 1-3		Aug15 1-3	Aug08 1-6
Motherwell	Aug08 4-2	Aug29 4-2		Aug26 2-1
Rangers	Aug15 2-0	Aug22 5-1	Aug12 1-2	

Section 5

	Ayr U	Berwick R	Falkirk	Hamilton A
Ayr U		Aug22 1-1	Aug12 1-1	Aug29 5-2
Berwick R	Aug08 2-3		Aug15 0-2	Aug26 2-2
Falkirk	Aug26 1-1	Aug29 3-0		Aug08 3-2
Hamilton A	Aug15 1-0	Aug12 3-3	Aug22 2-3	

Section 6

	Albion R	Arbroath	Dumbarton	Stenhousemuir
Albion R		Aug29 4-1	Aug26 1-0	Aug08 1-2
Arbroath	Aug15 0-3		Aug08 2-0	Aug26 1-0
Dumbarton	Aug12 3-3	Aug22 3-4		Aug29 1-2
Stenhousemuir	Aug22 3-0	Aug12 2-3	Aug15 0-2	

Section 7

	Brechin C	East Fife	Forfar A	Queen of South
Brechin C		Aug08 0-0	Aug26 6-1	Aug29 2-1
East Fife	Aug22 3-0		Aug29 4-1	Aug12 4-0
Forfar A	Aug12 2-2	Aug15 0-3		Aug22 4-4
Queen of South	Aug15 2-2	Aug26 0-2	Aug08 1-1	

Section 8

	Alloa	Cowdenbeath	Morton	St Johnstone
Alloa		Aug29 1-1	Aug08 4-2	Aug26 1-3
Cowdenbeath	Aug15 4-3		Aug26 3-1	Aug08 3-1
Morton	Aug22 0-1	Aug12 0-2		Aug15 2-4
St Johnstone	Aug12 6-3	Aug22 3-3	Aug29 3-1	

Section 9

	Dundee U	E Stirling	Montrose	Queen's Park	Stranraer
Dundee U		Aug08 2-0			Aug15 2-0
E Stirling			Aug15 5-1	Aug12 1-2	
Montrose	Aug12 1-1			Aug22 0-2	
Queen's Park	Aug29 0-4				Aug08 4-1
Stranraer		Aug22 2-1	Aug29 4-2		

Section 1

	P	W	D	L	F	A	Pts
Raith R	6	5	0	1	13	5	10
Airdrie	6	2	2	2	12	10	6
Celtic	6	2	1	3	9	10	5
Partick T	6	1	1	4	3	12	3

Section 2

	P	W	D	L	F	A	Pts
T Lanark	6	5	1	0	19	8	11
Clyde	6	2	2	2	11	9	6
Dunfermline A	6	2	1	3	9	14	5
St Mirren	6	1	0	5	8	16	2

Section 3

	P	W	D	L	F	A	Pts
Hearts	6	4	2	0	16	6	10
Aberdeen	6	3	1	2	16	15	7
Kilmarnock	6	2	1	3	13	13	5
Stirling A	6	0	2	4	8	19	2

Section 4

	P	W	D	L	F	A	Pts
Motherwell	6	6	0	0	19	8	12
Rangers	6	4	0	2	18	8	8
Dundee	6	2	0	4	12	17	4
Hibernian	6	0	0	6	9	25	0

Section 5

	P	W	D	L	F	A	Pts
Falkirk	6	4	1	1	13	7	9
Ayr U	6	3	2	1	12	8	8
Hamilton A	6	1	2	3	12	16	4
Berwick R	6	0	3	3	8	14	3

Section 6

	P	W	D	L	F	A	Pts
Arbroath	6	4	0	2	11	12	8
Albion R	6	3	1	2	12	9	7
Stenhousemuir	6	3	0	3	9	8	6
Dumbarton	6	1	1	4	9	12	3

Section 7

	P	W	D	L	F	A	Pts
East Fife	6	5	1	0	16	1	11
Brechin C	6	2	3	1	12	9	7
Queen of South	6	0	3	3	8	15	3
Forfar A	6	0	3	3	9	20	3

Section 8

	P	W	D	L	F	A	Pts
Cowdenbeath	6	4	2	0	16	9	10
St Johnstone	6	4	1	1	20	13	9
Alloa	6	2	1	3	13	16	5
Morton	6	0	0	6	6	17	0

Section 9

	P	W	D	L	F	A	Pts
Dundee U	4	3	1	0	9	1	7
Queen's Park	4	3	0	1	8	6	6
Stranraer	4	2	0	2	7	9	4
E Stirling	4	1	0	3	7	7	2
Montrose	4	0	1	3	4	12	1

Play-offs
Aug 31 Falkirk ....1 Dundee U 1
Sep 2 Dundee U ....0 Falkirk ....3 Agg 1-4

Quarter-finals
Sep 9 Cowdenbeath ......3 East Fife 1
Sep 16 East Fife ....1 Cowdenbeath ....2 Agg 2-5
Sep 9 Motherwell ....1 Hearts 1
Sep 16 Hearts ....6 Motherwell .....2 Agg 7-3
Sep 9 Raith R ....2 Arbroath 2
Sep 16 Arbroath ....2 Raith R ....1 Agg 4-3
Sep 9 T Lanark ....2 Falkirk 1
Sep 16 Falkirk ....0 T Lanark ...3 Agg 1-5

Semi-finals
Oct 7 Arbroath ....0 T Lanark 3
played at Ibrox
Oct 7 Cowdenbeath ......3 Hearts 9
played at Easter Road

Final
Oct 24 Hearts ....2 T Lanark 1
played at Hampden Park

Season 1960-61

Section 1

	Clyde	Hearts	Motherwell	St Mirren
Clyde		Aug17 2-0	Aug27 1-1	Aug20 4-0
Hearts	Aug31 6-2		Sep03 2-1	Aug13 1-1
Motherwell	Aug13 4-4	Aug20 2-3		Aug31 5-2
St Mirren	Sep03 0-0	Aug27 3-1	Aug17 0-4	

Section 2

	Celtic	Partick T	Rangers	T Lanark
Celtic		Aug31 1-2	Sep03 1-2	Aug13 2-0
Partick T	Aug17 1-1		Aug27 1-4	Sep03 0-4
Rangers	Aug20 2-3	Aug13 3-1		Aug31 3-2
T Lanark	Aug27 1-3	Aug20 3-1	Aug17 2-1	

Section 3

	Airdrie	Dunfermline A	Hibernian	Kilmarnock
Airdrie		Aug27 4-2	Sep03 3-1	Aug17 0-2
Dunfermline A	Aug13 5-2		Aug31 3-1	Sep03 2-0
Hibernian	Aug20 6-1	Aug17 3-0		Aug27 2-2
Kilmarnock	Aug31 2-0	Aug20 2-1	Aug13 4-2	

Section 4

	Aberdeen	Ayr U	Dundee	Raith R
Aberdeen		Aug13 4-3	Aug20 1-4	Aug31 3-0
Ayr U	Aug27 1-1		Aug17 1-2	Sep03 1-2
Dundee	Sep03 6-0	Aug31 3-0		Aug13 5-0
Raith R	Aug17 4-1	Aug20 1-1	Aug27 0-3	

Section 5

	Albion R	Montrose	Queen of South	Queen's Park
Albion R		Aug31 2-1	Aug13 0-3	Aug20 3-1
Montrose	Aug17 3-1		Sep03 1-2	Aug27 2-0
Queen of South	Aug27 5-2	Aug20 5-2		Aug17 2-0
Queen's Park	Sep03 0-1	Aug13 0-2	Aug31 0-1	

Section 6

	Arbroath	Falkirk	Hamilton A	St Johnstone
Arbroath		Aug27 2-2	Aug20 0-4	Aug17 0-0
Falkirk	Aug13 2-2		Aug31 2-1	3-2
Hamilton A	Sep03 1-0	Aug17 4-1		Aug27 3-2
St Johnstone	Aug31 2-2	Sep03 7-1	Aug13 2-3	

Section 7

	Alloa	Berwick R	Dumbarton	Morton
Alloa		Sep03 2-1	Aug31 1-5	Aug13 1-2
Berwick R	Aug20 1-2		Aug13 2-2	Aug31 3-1
Dumbarton	Aug17 0-0	Aug27 3-0		Sep03 3-3
Morton	Aug27 3-2	Aug17 2-2	Aug20 1-3	

Section 8

	Brechin C	Dundee U	Stenhousemuir	Stirling A
Brechin C		Aug31 2-1	Aug13 1-3	Aug20 1-2
Dundee U	Aug17 2-1		Aug20 3-3	Aug27 2-1
Stenhousemuir	Aug27 2-1	Sep03 1-1		Aug17 2-0
Stirling A	Sep03 4-2	Aug13 1-2	Aug31 2-2	

Section 9

	Cowdenbeath	East Fife	E Stirling	Forfar A	Stranraer
Cowdenbeath			Aug20 3-0	Aug17 3-1	
East Fife	Aug13 2-5			Sep03 4-3	
E Stirling		Aug27 4-1			Aug17 1-3
Forfar A			Aug13 2-2		Aug27 5-1
Stranraer	Sep03 3-1	Aug20 2-2			

Section 1

	P	W	D	L	F	A	Pts
Clyde	6	2	3	1	13	11	7
Hearts	6	3	1	2	13	11	7
Motherwell	6	2	2	2	17	12	6
St Mirren	6	1	2	3	6	15	4

Section 2

	P	W	D	L	F	A	Pts
Rangers	6	4	0	2	15	10	8
Celtic	6	3	1	2	11	8	7
T Lanark	6	3	0	3	12	10	6
Partick T	6	1	1	4	6	16	3

Section 3

	P	W	D	L	F	A	Pts
Kilmarnock	6	4	1	1	12	7	9
Dunfermline A	6	3	0	3	13	12	6
Hibernian	6	2	1	3	15	13	5
Airdrie	6	2	0	4	10	18	4

Section 4

	P	W	D	L	F	A	Pts
Dundee	6	6	0	0	23	2	12
Aberdeen	6	2	1	3	10	18	5
Raith R	6	2	1	3	7	14	5
Ayr U	6	0	2	4	7	13	2

Section 5

	P	W	D	L	F	A	Pts
Queen of South	6	6	0	0	18	5	12
Montrose	6	3	0	3	11	11	6
Albion R	6	3	0	3	9	13	6
Queen's Park	6	0	0	6	2	11	0

Section 6

	P	W	D	L	F	A	Pts
Hamilton A	6	5	0	1	16	7	10
Falkirk	6	2	2	2	11	18	6
St Johnstone	6	1	2	3	15	12	4
Arbroath	6	0	4	2	6	11	4

Section 7	P	W	D	L	F	A	Pts
Dumbarton	6	3	3	0	16	7	9
Morton	6	2	2	2	12	14	6
Alloa	6	2	1	3	8	12	5
Berwick R	6	1	2	3	9	12	4

Section 8	P	W	D	L	F	A	Pts
Stenhousemuir	6	3	3	0	13	8	9
Stirling A	6	3	1	2	12	9	7
Dundee U	6	2	2	2	9	11	6
Brechin C	6	1	0	5	8	14	2

Section 9	P	W	D	L	F	A	Pts
Cowdenbeath	4	3	0	1	12	6	6
Stranraer	4	2	1	1	9	9	5
Forfar A	4	1	1	2	11	10	3
E Stirling	4	1	1	2	7	9	3
East Fife	4	1	1	2	9	14	3

Play-offs
Sep 5 Dumbarton ....3 Cowdenbeath 0
Sep 7 Cowdenbeath .....2 Dumbarton ....1 Agg 2-4
Sep 12 Clyde ....2 Hearts 1

Quarter-finals
Sep 14 Clyde ....1 Kilmarnock 2
Sep 21 Kilmarnock ......3 Clyde ....1 Agg 5-2
Sep 14 Hamilton A ......4 Stenhousemuir 0
Sep 21 Stenhousemuir ....5 Hamilton A ....4 Agg 5-8
Sep 14 Queen of South ...2 Dumbarton 0
Sep 21 Dumbarton ....2 Queen of South ....1 Agg 2-3
Sep 14 Rangers ....1 Dundee 0
Sep 21 Dundee ....3 Rangers ......4 Agg 3-5

Semi-finals
Oct 12 Hamilton A ....1 Kilmarnock 5
played at Ibrox
Oct 19 Queen of South ....0 Rangers 7
played at Celtic Park

Final
Oct 29 Kilmarnock ....0 Rangers 2
played at Hampden Park

Brand of Rangers draws goalkeeper Brown out before scoring against Kilmarnock in the 1960-61 Scottish League Cup Final as the Killies went down 2-0 at Hampden.

Season 1961-62

Section 1

	Celtic	Hibernian	Partick T	St Johnstone
Celtic		Sep02 2-1	Aug26 3-2	Aug16 0-1
Hibernian	Aug19 2-2		Aug16 2-1	Aug26 4-1
Partick T	Aug12 2-3	Aug30 2-1		Aug19 0-0
St Johnstone	Aug30 2-0	Aug12 1-1	Sep02 4-3	

Section 2

	Aberdeen	Dundee U	Dunfermline A	Motherwell
Aberdeen		Sep02 2-2	Aug26 0-0	Aug16 3-4
Dundee U	Aug19 5-3		Aug16 0-0	Aug26 0-2
Dunfermline A	Aug12 1-2	Aug30 3-0		Sep02 2-0
Motherwell	Aug30 2-1	Aug12 5-3	Aug19 1-1	

Section 3

	Airdrie	Dundee	Rangers	T Lanark
Airdrie		Aug26 0-5	Aug19 1-2	Aug16 2-2
Dundee	Aug12 2-0		Aug30 1-1	Sep02 2-2
Rangers	Sep02 4-1	Aug16 4-2		Aug26 5-0
T Lanark	Aug30 3-1	Aug19 3-2	Aug12 0-2	

Section 4

	Hearts	Kilmarnock	Raith R	St Mirren
Hearts		Aug30 2-0	Aug12 1-0	Sep02 3-1
Kilmarnock	Aug16 1-2		Sep02 4-1	Aug26 6-1
Raith R	Aug26 3-1	Aug19 1-7		Aug16 0-3
St Mirren	Aug19 1-0	Aug12 1-0	Aug30 0-2	

Section 5

	Alloa	Berwick R	Stirling A	Stranraer
Alloa		Sep02 4-4	Aug12 2-3	Aug30 2-0
Berwick R	Aug19 3-1		Aug30 0-2	Aug12 2-1
Stirling A	Aug26 3-1	Aug16 4-2		Aug19 4-1
Stranraer	Aug16 1-1	Aug26 1-2	Sep02 3-0	

Section 6

	Clyde	Hamilton A	Montrose	Stenhousemuir
Clyde		Aug30 2-3	Aug19 3-2	Aug12 3-0
Hamilton A	Aug16 3-2		Aug26 2-0	Sep02 3-1
Montrose	Sep02 4-0	Aug12 2-2		Aug30 4-0
Stenhousemuir	Aug26 2-4	Aug19 1-3	Aug16 1-4	

Section 7

	Arbroath	Brechin C	East Fife	Queen of South
Arbroath		Sep02 4-1	Aug16 1-4	Aug26 1-0
Brechin C	Aug19 1-2		Aug26 2-8	Aug16 0-4
East Fife	Aug30 6-0	Aug12 3-1		Sep02 1-0
Queen of South	Aug12 1-0	Aug30 5-1	Aug19 1-3	

Section 8

	Ayr U	Cowdenbeath	Dumbarton	Falkirk
Ayr U		Aug30 3-1	Aug12 3-1	Aug19 1-1
Cowdenbeath	Aug16 2-3		Aug19 4-3	Aug26 1-1
Dumbarton	Aug26 1-2	Sep02 2-1		Aug16 0-1
Falkirk	Sep02 4-4	Aug12 2-2	Aug30 3-0	

Season (top continuation)

Section 9

	Albion R	E Stirling	Forfar A	Morton	Queen's Park
Albion R		Aug12 5-2		Sep02 3-1	
E Stirling			Aug26 1-0	Aug19 4-1	
Forfar A	Aug19 3-5				Aug12 1-3
Morton			Aug16 2-1		Aug26 1-3
Queen's Park	Aug16 1-3	Sep02 7-2			

Section 1

	P	W	D	L	F	A	Pts
St Johnstone	6	3	2	1	9	8	8
Celtic	6	3	1	2	10	10	7
Hibernian	6	2	2	2	11	9	6
Partick T	6	1	1	4	10	13	3

Section 2

	P	W	D	L	F	A	Pts
Motherwell	6	4	1	1	14	10	9
Dunfermline A	6	2	3	1	7	3	7
Aberdeen	6	1	2	3	11	14	4
Dundee U	6	1	2	3	10	15	4

Section 3

	P	W	D	L	F	A	Pts
Rangers	6	5	1	0	18	5	11
Dundee	6	2	2	2	14	10	6
T Lanark	6	2	2	2	10	14	6
Airdrie	6	0	1	5	5	18	1

Section 4

	P	W	D	L	F	A	Pts
Hearts	6	4	0	2	9	6	8
Kilmarnock	6	3	0	3	18	8	6
St Mirren	6	3	0	3	7	11	6
Raith R	6	2	0	4	7	16	4

Section 5

	P	W	D	L	F	A	Pts
Stirling A	6	5	0	1	16	9	10
Berwick R	6	3	1	2	13	13	7
Alloa	6	1	2	3	11	14	4
Stranraer	6	1	1	4	7	11	3

Section 6

	P	W	D	L	F	A	Pts
Hamilton A	6	5	1	0	16	8	11
Montrose	6	3	1	2	16	8	7
Clyde	6	3	0	3	14	14	6
Stenhousemuir	6	0	0	6	5	21	0

Section 7

	P	W	D	L	F	A	Pts
East Fife	6	6	0	0	25	5	12
Queen of South	6	3	0	3	11	6	6
Arbroath	6	3	0	3	8	13	6
Brechin C	6	0	0	6	6	26	0

Section 8

	P	W	D	L	F	A	Pts
Ayr U	6	4	2	0	16	10	10
Falkirk	6	2	4	0	12	8	8
Cowdenbeath	6	1	2	3	11	14	4
Dumbarton	6	1	0	5	7	14	2

Section 9

	P	W	D	L	F	A	Pts
Albion R	4	4	0	0	16	7	8
Queen's Park	4	3	0	1	14	7	6
E Stirling	4	2	0	2	9	13	4
Morton	4	1	0	3	5	11	2
Forfar A	4	0	0	4	5	11	0

Play-offs
Sep 4 East Fife ......4 Albion R 1
Sep 6 Albion R ......1 East Fife ......2 Agg 2-6

Quarter-finals
Sep 13 Ayr U ......4 Stirling A 2
Sep 20 Stirling A ......3 Ayr U ......0 Agg 5-4
Sep 13 Hamilton A ......1 Hearts 2
Sep 20 Hearts ......2 Hamilton A ......0 Agg 4-1
Sep 13 Motherwell ......3 St Johnstone 3
Sep 20 St Johnstone ......1 Motherwell ......1 Agg 4-3
Sep 13 Rangers ......3 East Fife 1
Sep 20 East Fife ......1 Rangers ......3 Agg 2-6

Semi-finals
Oct 11 Hearts ......2 Stirling A 1
played at Easter Road
Oct 11 Rangers ......3 St Johnstone 2
played at Celtic Park

Final
Oct 28 Hearts ......1 Rangers 1
played at Hampden Park

Replay
Dec 18 Hearts ......1 Rangers 3
played at Hampden Park

Season 1962-63

Section 1

	Airdrie	Dunfermline A	Kilmarnock	Raith R
Airdrie		Aug18 2-4	Aug25 0-4	Aug15 1-1
Dunfermline A	Sep01 4-1		Aug15 3-3	Aug25 1-1
Kilmarnock	Aug11 4-0	Aug29 3-2		Sep01 3-1
Raith R	Aug29 3-1	Aug11 2-2	Aug18 2-3	

Section 2

	Celtic	Dundee	Dundee U	Hearts
Celtic		Aug29 3-0	Aug18 4-0	Aug11 3-1
Dundee	Aug15 1-0		Aug25 2-1	Aug18 0-2
Dundee U	Sep01 0-0	Aug11 3-2		Aug29 2-0
Hearts	Aug25 3-2	Sep01 2-0	Aug15 3-1	

Section 3

	Aberdeen	Falkirk	Motherwell	Partick T
Aberdeen		Aug18 3-0	Aug15 4-0	Aug25 0-3
Falkirk	Sep01 1-2		Aug25 0-1	Aug15 1-3
Motherwell	Aug29 4-1	Aug11 9-1		Sep01 0-1
Partick T	Aug11 1-2	Aug29 3-1	Aug18 1-1	

Section 4

	Hibernian	Rangers	St Mirren	T Lanark
Hibernian		Aug11 1-4	Aug18 2-0	Aug18 3-2
Rangers	Aug25 0-0		Sep01 4-0	Aug15
St Mirren	Aug15 3-3	Aug18 2-1		Aug25 1-1
T Lanark	Sep01 1-4	Aug29 2-5	Aug11 1-2	

Section 5

	Ayr U	Berwick R	E Stirling	Hamilton A
Ayr U		Aug15 2-2	Aug25 2-1	Sep01 3-2
Berwick R	Aug29 1-1		Sep01 2-0	Aug11 4-1
E Stirling	Aug11 4-1	Aug18 3-2		Aug29 0-1
Hamilton A	Aug18 4-4	Aug25 0-2	Aug15 4-4	

Section 6

	Clyde	Cowdenbeath	St Johnstone	Stranraer
Clyde		Aug25 1-0	Aug15	Sep01
Cowdenbeath	Aug11 1-2		Aug18 0-7	Aug29 3-0
St Johnstone	Aug29 1-0	Sep01 4-1		Aug11 1-0
Stranraer	Aug18 3-5	Aug15 2-1	Aug25 1-4	

Section 7

	East Fife	Montrose	Queen of South	Queen's Park
East Fife		Aug15 0-5	Aug25 1-0	Sep01 5-4
Montrose	Aug29 0-1		Sep01 0-0	Aug11 3-1
Queen of South	Aug11 3-1	Aug18 2-1		Aug29 4-4
Queen's Park	Aug18 3-0	Aug25 1-1	Aug15 0-4	

Section 8

	Alloa	Arbroath	Morton	Stirling A
Alloa		Sep01 2-2	Aug15 2-3	Aug25 2-1
Arbroath	Aug18 3-0		Aug25 3-3	Aug15 3-2
Morton	Aug29 5-2	Aug11 2-2		Sep01 2-0
Stirling A	Aug11 1-1	Aug29 2-3	Aug18 1-4	

Section 9

	Albion R	Brechin C	Dumbarton	Forfar A	Stenhousemuir
Albion R			Aug11 3-5		Sep01 1-2
Brechin C	Aug25 0-4		Aug18 3-5		
Dumbarton				Aug25 1-0	Aug15 1-1
Forfar A	Aug15 0-0	Sep01 1-1			
Stenhousemuir		Aug11 2-1		Aug18 2-3	

Section 1

	P	W	D	L	F	A	Pts
Kilmarnock	6	5	1	0	20	8	11
Dunfermline A	6	2	3	1	16	12	7
Raith R	6	1	3	2	10	11	5
Airdrie	6	0	1	5	5	20	1

Section 2

	P	W	D	L	F	A	Pts
Hearts	6	4	0	2	11	8	8
Celtic	6	3	1	2	12	5	7
Dundee U	6	2	1	3	7	11	5
Dundee	6	2	0	4	5	11	4

Section 3

	P	W	D	L	F	A	Pts
Partick T	6	4	1	1	12	5	9
Aberdeen	6	4	0	2	12	9	8
Motherwell	6	3	1	2	15	8	7
Falkirk	6	0	0	6	4	21	0

Section 4

	P	W	D	L	F	A	Pts
Rangers	6	4	1	1	19	7	9
Hibernian	6	3	2	1	13	10	8
St Mirren	6	2	2	2	8	12	6
T Lanark	6	0	1	5	5	20	1

Section 5

	P	W	D	L	F	A	Pts
Berwick R	6	3	2	1	12	8	8
Ayr U	6	2	3	1	13	14	7
E Stirling	6	2	1	3	12	12	5
Hamilton A	6	1	2	3	13	16	4

Section 6

	P	W	D	L	F	A	Pts
St Johnstone	6	5	0	1	18	7	10
Clyde	6	5	0	1	17	7	10
Stranraer	6	1	0	5	7	18	2
Cowdenbeath	6	1	0	5	6	16	2

Section 7	P	W	D	L	F	A	Pts
Queen of South	6	3	2	1	13	7	8
Montrose	6	2	2	2	10	5	6
East Fife	6	3	0	3	8	15	6
Queen's Park	6	1	2	3	13	17	4

Section 8	P	W	D	L	F	A	Pts
Morton	6	4	2	0	19	10	10
Arbroath	6	3	3	0	16	11	9
Alloa	6	1	2	3	9	15	4
Stirling A	6	0	1	5	7	15	1

Section 9	P	W	D	L	F	A	Pts
Dumbarton	4	3	1	0	12	7	7
Stenhousemuir	4	2	1	1	7	6	5
Forfar A	4	1	2	1	4	4	4
Albion R	4	1	1	2	8	7	3
Brechin C	4	0	1	3	5	12	1

Play-offs
Sep 3 Dumbarton ....0 Berwick R 0
Sep 5 Berwick R ....1 Dumbarton ....2 Agg 1-2

Quarter-finals
Sep 12 Dumbarton ....1 Rangers 3
Sep 19 Rangers ....1 Dumbarton ...1 Agg 4-2
Sep 12 Morton ....0 Hearts 3
Sep 19 Hearts ....3 Morton ......1 Agg 6-1
Sep 12 Partick T ....1 Kilmarnock ...2
Sep 19 Kilmarnock ......3 Partick T .....1 Agg 5-2
Sep 12 Queen of South .....1 St Johnstone ...0
Sep 19 St Johnstone ......4 Queen of South ...1 Agg 4-2

Semi-finals
Oct 10 Hearts ....4 St Johnstone ...0
played at Easter Road
Oct 10 Kilmarnock ....3 Rangers 2
played at Hampden Park

Final
Oct 27 Hearts ....1 Kilmarnock 0
played at Hampden Park

Season 1963-64

Section 1

	Falkirk	Hearts	Motherwell	Partick T
Falkirk		Aug24 0-3	Aug17 0-6	Aug14 2-2
Hearts	Aug10 6-2		Aug28 0-0	Aug31 2-2
Motherwell	Aug31 4-0	Aug14 3-0		Aug24 2-0
Partick T	Aug28 3-2	Aug17 2-2	Aug10 0-2	

Section 2

	Aberdeen	Dundee U	Hibernian	St Mirren
Aberdeen		Aug24 2-0	Aug31 0-2	Aug14 2-2
Dundee U	Aug10 1-1		Aug28 2-4	Aug31 3-2
Hibernian	Aug17 2-2	Aug14 3-2		Aug24 3-0
St Mirren	Aug28 0-3	Aug17 2-3	Aug10 1-1	

Section 3

	Airdrie	Dundee	Dunfermline A	T Lanark
Airdrie		Aug28 4-1	Aug10 0-1	Aug17 2-3
Dundee	Aug14 2-1		Aug17 4-1	Aug24 3-2
Dunfermline A	Aug24 3-2	Aug31 3-4		Aug14 2-3
T Lanark	Aug31 2-1	Aug10 1-2	Aug28 0-3	

Section 4

	Celtic	Kilmarnock	Queen of South	Rangers
Celtic		Aug28 2-0	Aug17 1-1	Aug10 0-3
Kilmarnock	Aug14 0-0		Aug24 2-0	Aug17 1-4
Queen of South	Aug31 2-3	Aug10 1-4		Aug28 2-5
Rangers	Aug24 3-0	Aug31 2-2	Aug14 5-2	

Section 5

	Albion R	Alloa	Cowdenbeath	Stirling A
Albion R		Aug31 0-1	Aug24 2-0	Aug14 3-2
Alloa	Aug17 0-2		Aug14 1-2	Aug24 2-4
Cowdenbeath	Aug10 2-3	Aug28 1-0		Aug17 1-2
Stirling A	Aug28 2-0	Aug10 3-3	Aug31 3-2	

Section 6

	Ayr U	Clyde	Morton	Stranraer
Ayr U		Aug28 2-4	Aug10 0-1	Aug31 1-2
Clyde	Aug14 3-4		Aug31 0-4	Aug24 4-1
Morton	Aug24 5-2	Aug17 3-1		Aug14 5-0
Stranraer	Aug17 2-1	Aug10 0-2	Aug28 1-2	

Section 7

	E Stirling	Hamilton A	Queen's Park	St Johnstone
E Stirling		Aug31 1-0	Aug10 2-0	Aug28 2-1
Hamilton A	Aug17 2-3		Aug28 1-0	Aug10 2-3
Queen's Park	Aug24 0-1	Aug14 2-1		Aug17 0-3
St Johnstone	Aug14 3-1	Aug24 5-0	Aug31 1-0	

Section 8

	Arbroath	Dumbarton	East Fife	Raith R
Arbroath		Aug10 1-1	Aug28 1-1	Aug31 2-0
Dumbarton	Aug24 1-2		Aug17 2-3	Aug31 3-0
East Fife	Aug14 3-0	Aug31 4-2		Aug24 3-0
Raith R	Aug17 3-4	Aug28 1-2	Aug10 1-1	

Section 9

	Berwick R	Brechin C	Forfar A	Montrose	Stenhousemuir
Berwick R		Aug17 4-1	Aug24 3-1		
Brechin C				Aug24 2-2	Aug14 1-1
Forfar A		Aug31 3-3		Aug14 1-2	
Montrose	Aug10 3-0				Aug17 2-3
Stenhousemuir	Aug31 2-4		Aug10 2-2		

Section 1	P	W	D	L	F	A	Pts
Motherwell	6	5	1	0	17	0	11
Hearts	6	2	3	1	13	9	7
Partick T	6	1	3	2	9	12	5
Falkirk	6	0	1	5	6	24	1

Section 2	P	W	D	L	F	A	Pts
Hibernian	6	4	2	0	15	7	10
Aberdeen	6	2	3	1	10	7	7
Dundee U	6	2	1	3	11	14	5
St Mirren	6	0	2	4	7	15	2

Section 3	P	W	D	L	F	A	Pts
Dundee	6	5	0	1	16	12	10
Dunfermline A	6	3	0	3	13	13	6
T Lanark	6	3	0	3	11	13	6
Airdrie	6	1	0	5	10	12	2

Section 4	P	W	D	L	F	A	Pts
Rangers	6	5	1	0	22	7	11
Kilmarnock	6	2	2	2	9	9	6
Celtic	6	2	2	2	6	9	6
Queen of South	6	0	1	5	8	20	1

Section 5	P	W	D	L	F	A	Pts
Stirling A	6	4	1	1	16	11	9
Albion R	6	4	0	2	10	7	8
Cowdenbeath	6	2	0	4	8	11	4
Alloa	6	1	1	4	7	12	3

Section 6	P	W	D	L	F	A	Pts
Morton	6	6	0	0	20	4	12
Clyde	6	3	0	3	14	14	6
Stranraer	6	2	0	4	6	15	4
Ayr U	6	1	0	5	10	17	2

Section 7	P	W	D	L	F	A	Pts
St Johnstone	6	5	0	1	16	5	10
E Stirling	6	5	0	1	10	6	10
Hamilton A	6	1	0	5	6	14	2
Queen's Park	6	1	0	5	2	9	2

Section 8	P	W	D	L	F	A	Pts
East Fife	6	4	2	0	15	6	10
Arbroath	6	3	2	1	10	9	8
Dumbarton	6	2	1	3	11	11	5
Raith R	6	0	1	5	5	15	1

Section 9	P	W	D	L	F	A	Pts
Berwick R	4	3	0	1	11	7	6
Montrose	4	2	1	1	9	6	5
Stenhousemuir	4	1	2	1	8	9	4
Brechin C	4	0	3	1	7	10	3
Forfar A	4	0	2	2	7	10	2

Play-offs
Sep 2 St Johnstone ......2 Berwick R 2
Sep 4 Berwick R ....4 St Johnstone ....2 Agg 6-4

Quarter-finals
Sep 11 Dundee ....3 Hibernian 3
Sep 18 Hibernian ......2 Dundee ....0 Agg 5-3
Sep 11 East Fife ....1 Rangers 1
Sep 18 Rangers ....2 East Fife ......1 Agg 3-1
Sep 11 Motherwell ....0 Morton 0
Sep 18 Morton ....2 Motherwell ....0 Agg 2-0
Sep 11 Stirling A ....2 Berwick R 2
Sep 18 Berwick R ....4 Stirling A ......3 Agg 6-5

Semi-finals
Oct 2 Berwick R ....1 Rangers 3
played at Hampden Park
Oct 7 Hibernian ....1 Morton 1
played at Ibrox

Replay
Oct 14 Hibernian ....0 Morton 1
played at Ibrox

Final
Oct 26 Morton ....0 Rangers 5
played at Hampden Park

Section 1

	Aberdeen	Rangers	St Johnstone	St Mirren
Aberdeen		Aug22 3-4	Aug12 2-1	Aug29 2-2
Rangers	Aug08 4-0		Aug29 3-1	Aug26 6-2
St Johnstone	Aug26 1-1	Aug15 1-9		Aug08 1-2
St Mirren	Aug15 3-3	Aug12 0-0	Aug22 2-0	

Section 2

	Airdrie	Dunfermline A	Hibernian	T Lanark
Airdrie		Aug08 1-4	Aug29 1-4	Aug26 1-2
Dunfermline A	Aug22 3-0		Aug12 2-0	Aug15 3-1
Hibernian	Aug15 5-0	Aug26 1-1		Aug08 3-0
T Lanark	Aug12 5-2	Aug29 0-1	Aug22 0-2	

Section 3

	Celtic	Hearts	Kilmarnock	Partick T
Celtic		Aug26 6-1	Aug15 4-1	Aug08 0-0
Hearts	Aug12 0-3		Aug22 0-1	Aug29 4-3
Kilmarnock	Aug29 2-0	Aug08 1-1		Aug26 4-0
Partick T	Aug22 1-5	Aug15 2-1	Aug12 0-0	

Section 4

	Dundee	Dundee U	Falkirk	Motherwell
Dundee		Aug08 2-3	Aug15 4-1	Aug26 6-0
Dundee U	Aug22 2-1		Aug12 3-0	Aug29 2-1
Falkirk	Aug29 1-3	Aug26 5-2		Aug08 1-1
Motherwell	Aug12 3-0	Aug15 0-1	Aug22 3-1	

Section 5

	East Fife	Montrose	Queen of South	Raith R
East Fife		Aug15 4-2	Aug12 5-0	Aug22 1-5
Montrose	Aug29 0-5		Aug22 1-6	Aug12 2-4
Queen of South	Aug26 1-1	Aug08 2-0		Aug15 1-1
Raith R	Aug08 1-4	Aug26 7-0	Aug29 2-3	

Section 6

	Clydebank	Hamilton A	Stenhousemuir	Stranraer
Clydebank		Aug15 2-4	Aug08 2-2	Aug26 3-3
Hamilton A	Aug22 0-0		6-0	2-2
Stenhousemuir	Aug22 1-2	Aug12 1-2		Aug15 3-3
Stranraer	Aug12 2-2	Aug22 2-1	Aug29 1-0	

Section 7

	Albion R	Arbroath	Clyde	Queen's Park
Albion R		Aug22 1-3	Aug15 0-5	Aug12 0-1
Arbroath	Aug08 1-3		Aug26 1-2	Aug29 2-2
Clyde	Aug29 5-1	Aug12		Aug22 4-1
Queen's Park	Aug26 0-2	Aug15 1-3	Aug08	

Section 8

	Ayr U	Berwick R	Dumbarton	Morton
Ayr U		Aug22 6-0	Aug15 2-1	Aug12 0-1
Berwick R	Aug08 3-1		Aug26 0-0	Aug15 0-5
Dumbarton	Aug29 2-1	Aug12 3-2		Aug22 1-1
Morton	Aug26 1-1	Aug29 5-2	Aug08 1-1	

Section 9

	Alloa	Brechin C	Cowdenbeath	Forfar A	Stirling A
Alloa			Aug12 0-0		Aug29 2-1
Brechin C	Aug15 3-5				Aug08 1-4
Cowdenbeath		Aug29 2-3		Aug08 1-2	
Forfar A	Aug22 3-0	Aug12 4-1			
Stirling A			Aug22 4-0	Aug15 1-2	

Section 1

	P	W	D	L	F	A	Pts
Rangers	6	5	1	0	26	7	11
St Mirren	6	2	3	1	11	12	7
Aberdeen	6	1	3	2	11	15	5
St Johnstone	6	0	1	5	5	19	1

Section 2

	P	W	D	L	F	A	Pts
Dunfermline A	6	5	1	0	14	3	11
Hibernian	6	4	1	1	15	4	9
T Lanark	6	2	0	4	8	12	4
Airdrie	6	0	0	6	5	23	0

Section 3

	P	W	D	L	F	A	Pts
Celtic	6	4	1	1	18	5	9
Kilmarnock	6	3	2	1	9	5	8
Partick T	6	1	2	3	6	14	4
Hearts	6	1	1	4	7	16	3

Section 4

	P	W	D	L	F	A	Pts
Dundee U	6	5	0	1	13	9	10
Dundee	6	3	0	3	16	10	6
Motherwell	6	2	1	3	8	11	5
Falkirk	6	1	1	4	9	16	3

Section 5

	P	W	D	L	F	A	Pts
East Fife	6	4	1	1	20	9	9
Queen of South	6	3	2	1	13	10	8
Raith R	6	3	1	2	20	11	7
Montrose	6	0	0	6	5	28	0

Section 6

	P	W	D	L	F	A	Pts
Hamilton A	6	3	2	1	15	7	8
Stranraer	6	2	4	0	13	11	8
Clydebank	6	1	4	1	11	12	6
Stenhousemuir	6	0	2	4	7	16	2

Section 7

	P	W	D	L	F	A	Pts
Clyde	6	4	2	0	17	4	10
Arbroath	6	2	2	2	11	10	6
Albion R	6	2	0	4	7	15	4
Queen's Park	6	1	2	3	5	11	4

Section 8

	P	W	D	L	F	A	Pts
Morton	6	3	3	0	14	5	9
Dumbarton	6	2	3	1	8	7	7
Ayr U	6	2	1	3	11	8	5
Berwick R	6	1	1	4	7	20	3

Section 9

	P	W	D	L	F	A	Pts
Forfar A	4	4	0	0	11	3	8
Alloa	4	2	1	1	7	7	5
Stirling A	4	2	0	2	10	5	4
Brechin C	4	1	0	3	8	15	2
Cowdenbeath	4	0	1	3	3	9	1

Play-offs
Aug 31 Forfar A 4 East Fife 3
Sep 2 East Fife 4 Forfar A 1 Agg 7-5

Quarter-finals
Sep 9 Clyde 0 Morton 3
Sep 16 Morton 0 Clyde 2 Agg 3-2
Sep 9 Dundee U 8 Hamilton A 0
Sep 16 Hamilton A 1 Dundee U 2 Agg 1-10
Sep 9 East Fife 2 Celtic 0
Sep 16 Celtic 6 East Fife 0 Agg 6-2
Sep 14 Dunfermline A 0 Rangers 3
Sep 16 Rangers 2 Dunfermline A 2 Agg 5-2

Semi-finals
Sep 29 Celtic 2 Morton 0
  played at Ibrox
Sep 30 Dundee U 1 Rangers 2
  played at Hampden Park

Final
Oct 24 Celtic 1 Rangers 2
  played at Hampden Park

Section 1

	Celtic	Dundee	Dundee U	Motherwell
Celtic		Aug21 0-2	Aug28 3-0	Aug18 1-0
Dundee	Sep04 1-3		Aug18 0-0	Aug28 1-2
Dundee U	Aug14 2-1	Sep01 1-3		Aug21 4-1
Motherwell	Sep01 2-3	Aug14 1-0	Sep04 3-2	

Section 2

	Aberdeen	Clyde	Hearts	Rangers
Aberdeen		Aug28 2-0	Aug18 1-1	Aug21 2-0
Clyde	Aug14 1-2		Sep04 1-2	Sep01 1-3
Hearts	Sep01 2-0	Aug21 1-2		Aug14 4-2
Rangers	Sep04 4-0	Aug18 3-0	Aug28 1-0	

Section 3

	Dunfermline A	Kilmarnock	Partick T	St Johnstone
Dunfermline A		Aug21 1-3	Aug28 6-2	Aug18 5-1
Kilmarnock	Sep04 0-1		Aug18 2-0	Aug28 3-0
Partick T	Aug14 0-0	Sep01 1-2		Aug21 0-1
St Johnstone	Sep01 3-1	Aug14 0-1	Sep04 2-0	

Section 4

	Falkirk	Hibernian	Morton	St Mirren
Falkirk		Aug14 3-1	Sep01 3-2	Aug21 0-1
Hibernian	Aug28 3-1		Sep04 3-0	Aug18 1-2
Morton	Aug18 1-1	Aug21 2-4		Aug28 0-1
St Mirren	Sep04 2-3	Sep01 0-3	Aug14 1-2	

Section 5

	Berwick R	Cowdenbeath	Hamilton A	T Lanark
Berwick R		Aug21 6-1	Sep01 1-1	Aug14 4-1
Cowdenbeath	Sep04 3-2		Aug14 1-1	Sep01 0-1
Hamilton A	Aug18 1-1	Aug28 0-1		Aug21 2-2
T Lanark	Aug28 3-2	Aug18 1-1	Sep04 5-1	

Section 6

	Arbroath	Queen's Park	Raith R	Stirling A
Arbroath		Aug28 3-0	Aug18 2-2	Aug21 1-3
Queen's Park	Aug14 2-2		Aug21 1-1	Sep01 2-1
Raith R	Sep01 4-2	Sep04 3-0		Aug14 3-1
Stirling A	Sep04 4-1	Aug18 0-2	Aug28 1-2	

Section 7

	Airdrie	Albion R	Queen of South	Stranraer
Airdrie		Aug18 6-1	Aug21 5-1	Aug28 3-0
Albion R	Sep01 8-2		Aug14 1-1	Sep04 2-1
Queen of South	Sep04 2-3	Aug28 2-0		Aug18 1-2
Stranraer	Aug14 1-3	Aug21 0-0	Sep01 1-1	

Section 8

	Alloa	Dumbarton	East Fife	E Stirling
Alloa		Aug21 2-1	Aug14 3-2	Sep01 2-1
Dumbarton	Sep04 4-1		Sep01 6-1	Aug14 2-1
East Fife	Aug28 1-2	Aug18 3-2		Aug21 4-1
E Stirling	Aug18 1-0	Aug28 1-0	Sep04 6-2	

Section 9

	Ayr U	Brechin C	Forfar A	Montrose	Stenhousemuir
Ayr U				Aug21 5-0	Aug14 5-2
Brechin C	Aug28 0-1		Aug21 1-0		
Forfar A	Sep04 1-3			Aug14 4-1	
Montrose	Aug18 2-0				Aug28 1-3
Stenhousemuir	Sep04 1-0	Aug18 2-1			

Section 1

	P	W	D	L	F	A	Pts
Celtic	6	4	0	2	11	7	8
Motherwell	6	3	0	3	9	11	6
Dundee	6	2	1	3	7	7	5
Dundee U	6	2	1	3	9	11	5

Section 2

	P	W	D	L	F	A	Pts
Rangers	6	4	0	2	13	7	8
Hearts	6	3	1	2	10	7	7
Aberdeen	6	3	1	2	7	8	7
Clyde	6	1	0	5	5	13	2

Section 3

	P	W	D	L	F	A	Pts
Kilmarnock	6	5	0	1	11	3	10
Dunfermline A	6	3	1	2	14	9	7
St Johnstone	6	3	0	3	7	10	6
Partick T	6	0	1	5	3	13	1

Section 4

	P	W	D	L	F	A	Pts
Hibernian	6	5	0	1	15	6	10
Falkirk	6	3	1	2	11	10	7
St Mirren	6	2	0	4	5	9	4
Morton	6	1	1	4	7	13	3

Section 5

	P	W	D	L	F	A	Pts
T Lanark	6	3	2	1	13	10	8
Berwick R	6	2	2	2	16	10	6
Cowdenbeath	6	2	2	2	7	11	6
Hamilton A	6	0	4	2	6	11	4

Section 6

	P	W	D	L	F	A	Pts
Raith R	6	4	2	0	15	7	10
Queen's Park	6	2	2	2	7	10	6
Stirling A	6	2	0	4	10	11	4
Arbroath	6	1	2	3	11	15	4

Section 7

	P	W	D	L	F	A	Pts
Airdrie	6	5	0	1	22	13	10
Albion R	6	2	2	2	12	12	6
Queen of South	6	1	2	3	8	12	4
Stranraer	6	1	2	3	5	10	4

Section 8

	P	W	D	L	F	A	Pts
Alloa	6	4	0	2	10	10	8
Dumbarton	6	3	0	3	15	9	6
E Stirling	6	3	0	3	11	10	6
East Fife	6	2	0	4	13	20	4

Section 9

	P	W	D	L	F	A	Pts
Ayr U	4	4	0	0	14	3	8
Stenhousemuir	4	3	0	1	8	7	6
Forfar A	4	1	0	3	6	7	2
Montrose	4	1	0	3	4	12	2
Brechin C	4	1	0	3	1	4	2

Play-offs
Sep 6 T Lanark ....1 Ayr U 2
Sep 8 Ayr U ....1 T Lanark ....0 Agg 3-1

Quarter-finals
Sep 15 Airdrie ....1 Rangers 5
Sep 22 Rangers ....4 Airdrie ....0 Agg 9-1
Sep 15 Alloa ....0 Hibernian 2
Sep 22 Hibernian ......11 Alloa ....2 Agg 13-2
Sep 15 Kilmarnock .....2 Ayr U 0
Sep 22 Ayr U ....2 Kilmarnock ...2 Agg 2-4
Sep 15 Raith R ....1 Celtic 8
Sep 22 Celtic ....4 Raith R ....0 Agg 12-1

Semi-finals
Oct 4 Celtic ....2 Hibernian 2
played at Ibrox
Oct 6 Kilmarnock .....4 Rangers 6
played at Hampden Park

Replay
Oct 18 Celtic ....4 Hibernian 0
played at Ibrox

Final
Oct 23 Celtic ....2 Rangers 1
played at Hampden Park

It's the first for Celtic as big John Hughes sends Rangers' goalkeeper Billy Ritchie the wrong way in the 1965-66 League Cup Final.

Section 1

	Aberdeen	Dundee	Dundee U	St Johnstone
Aberdeen		Aug31 2-0	Aug20 4-1	Aug13 3-0
Dundee	Aug17 3-4		Aug27 1-1	Aug20 2-0
Dundee U	Sep03 3-4	Aug13 2-0		Aug31 5-3
St Johnstone	Aug27 0-3	Sep03 2-2	Aug17 1-1	

Section 2

	Hibernian	Kilmarnock	Rangers	Stirling A
Hibernian		Aug17 2-1	Aug27 3-2	Sep03 3-0
Kilmarnock	Aug31 3-0		Sep03 0-1	Aug13 2-0
Rangers	Aug13 1-0	Aug20 0-0		Aug31 1-1
Stirling A	Aug20 2-4	Aug27 0-0	Aug17 0-8	

Section 3

	Dunfermline A	Falkirk	Motherwell	Partick T
Dunfermline A		Aug20 2-2	Aug13 2-1	Aug31 3-2
Falkirk	Sep03 1-2		Aug31 0-2	Aug13 0-0
Motherwell	Aug27 4-3	Aug17 2-2		Aug20 4-0
Partick T	Aug17 0-3	Aug27 1-0	Sep03 0-0	

Section 4

	Celtic	Clyde	Hearts	St Mirren
Celtic		Aug17 6-0	Aug27 3-0	Aug20 8-2
Clyde	Aug31 1-3		Sep03 1-3	Aug13 1-0
Hearts	Aug13 0-2	Aug20 4-3		Aug31 3-1
St Mirren	Sep03 0-1	Aug27 0-1	Aug17 0-0	

Section 5

	Ayr U	Berwick R	Cowdenbeath	Raith R
Ayr U		Aug27 2-0	Aug20 2-2	Aug17 0-0
Berwick R	Aug13 1-1		Aug31 1-1	Aug20 1-1
Cowdenbeath	Sep03 0-3	Aug17 0-0		Aug27 2-1
Raith R	Aug31 3-1	Sep03 2-0	Aug13 1-2	

Section 6

	Arbroath	East Fife	Morton	T Lanark
Arbroath		Aug31 2-1	Aug20 0-0	Aug13 2-0
East Fife	Aug17 0-0		Aug27 0-1	Aug20 2-2
Morton	Sep03 2-0	Aug13 2-1		Aug31 3-2
T Lanark	Aug27 1-1	Sep03 2-3	Aug17 0-1	

Section 7

	Airdrie	Dumbarton	Queen of South	Queen's Park
Airdrie		Aug13 3-0	Aug31 1-1	Sep03 3-2
Dumbarton	Aug27 1-2		Aug20 1-1	Aug17 1-2
Queen of South	Aug17 0-3	Sep03 4-2		Aug27 6-1
Queen's Park	Aug20 1-3	Aug31 0-3	Aug13 1-5	

Section 8

	Albion R	Alloa	Hamilton A	Montrose
Albion R		Aug27 1-0	Aug17 0-0	Aug20 0-0
Alloa	Aug13 4-0		Aug20 3-1	Aug31 1-0
Hamilton A	Aug31 3-0	Sep03 1-0		Aug13 1-3
Montrose	Sep03 2-2	Aug17 2-1	Aug27 2-0	

Section 9

	Brechin C	Clydebank	E Stirling	Forfar A	Stenhousemuir	Stranraer
Brechin C		Aug20 3-1			Aug13 4-0	
Clydebank			Aug13 3-0		Sep03 3-2	
E Stirling	Aug17 0-4				Aug27 1-1	Aug20 0-0
Forfar A	Aug27 1-1	Aug17 2-1	Sep03 5-1			
Stenhousemuir			Aug20 1-3			Aug17 1-1
Stranraer	Sep03 1-2	Aug27 1-0	Aug13 2-1			

Bobby Lennox slips the ball past Rangers' Ronnie McKinnon for the only goal of the game as the Parkhead boys retain the League Cup in 1966-67.

Section 1	P	W	D	L	F	A	Pts
Aberdeen	6	6	0	0	20	7	12
Dundee U	6	2	2	2	13	13	6
Dundee	6	1	2	3	8	11	4
St Johnstone	6	0	2	4	6	16	2

Section 2	P	W	D	L	F	A	Pts
Rangers	6	3	2	1	13	4	8
Hibernian	6	4	0	2	12	9	8
Kilmarnock	6	2	2	2	6	3	6
Stirling A	6	0	2	4	3	18	2

Section 3	P	W	D	L	F	A	Pts
Dunfermline A	6	4	1	1	15	10	9
Motherwell	6	3	2	1	13	7	8
Partick T	6	1	2	3	3	10	4
Falkirk	6	0	3	3	5	9	3

Section 4	P	W	D	L	F	A	Pts
Celtic	6	6	0	0	23	3	12
Hearts	6	3	1	2	10	10	7
Clyde	6	2	0	4	7	16	4
St Mirren	6	0	1	5	3	14	1

Section 5	P	W	D	L	F	A	Pts
Ayr U	6	2	3	1	9	6	7
Cowdenbeath	6	2	3	1	7	8	7
Raith R	6	2	2	2	8	6	6
Berwick R	6	0	4	2	3	7	4

Section 6	P	W	D	L	F	A	Pts
Morton	6	5	1	0	9	3	11
Arbroath	6	2	3	1	5	4	7
East Fife	6	1	2	3	7	9	4
T Lanark	6	0	2	4	7	12	2

Section 7	P	W	D	L	F	A	Pts
Airdrie	6	5	1	0	15	5	11
Queen of South	6	3	2	1	17	9	8
Dumbarton	6	1	1	4	8	12	3
Queen's Park	6	1	0	5	7	21	2

Section 8	P	W	D	L	F	A	Pts
Montrose	6	3	2	1	9	5	8
Alloa	6	3	0	3	9	5	6
Hamilton A	6	2	1	3	6	8	5
Albion R	6	1	3	2	3	9	5

Section 9	P	W	D	L	F	A	Pts
Brechin C	5	4	1	0	14	3	9
Forfar A	5	3	1	1	12	6	7
Stranraer	5	2	2	1	5	4	6
Clydebank	5	2	0	3	8	8	4
Stenhousemuir	5	0	2	3	5	12	2
E Stirling	5	0	2	3	2	13	2

Play-offs

Sep 5 Brechin C ....1 Morton 2
Sep 7 Morton ....5 Brechin C .....2 Agg 7-3

Quarter-finals

Sep 14 Ayr U ....1 Rangers 1
Sep 21 Rangers ....3 Ayr U ....0 Agg 4-1
Sep 14 Celtic ....6 Dunfermline A .3
Sep 21 Dunfermline A .....1 Celtic ....3 Agg 4-9
Sep 14 Montrose ....3 Airdrie 3
Sep 21 Airdrie ....5 Montrose ......1 Agg 8-4
Sep 14 Morton ....3 Aberdeen 1
Sep 21 Aberdeen ....3 Morton ....0 Agg 4-3

Semi-finals

Oct 19 Aberdeen ....2 Rangers 2
played at Hampden Park
Oct 17 Airdrie ....0 Celtic 2
played at Hampden Park

Replay

Oct 24 Aberdeen ....0 Rangers 2
played at Hampden Park

Final

Oct 29 Celtic ....1 Rangers 0
played at Hampden Park

More action from the Final as Rangers' Alex Smith is foiled by Ronnie Simpson and Bobby Murdoch of Celtic, as they search for an equaliser.

Section 1

	Airdrie	Dunfermline A	Kilmarnock	Partick T
Airdrie		Aug19 2-3	Aug16 1-2	Aug26 2-1
Dunfermline A	Sep02 2-1		Aug26 1-3	Aug16 1-1
Kilmarnock	Aug30 0-0	Aug12 2-2		Aug19 4-0
Partick T	Aug12 0-1	Aug30 3-2	Sep02 1-0	

Section 2

	Aberdeen	Celtic	Dundee U	Rangers
Aberdeen		Sep02 1-5	Aug30 2-2	Aug12 1-1
Celtic	Aug19 3-1		Aug12 1-0	Aug30 3-1
Dundee U	Aug16 5-0	Aug26 0-1		Sep02 0-3
Rangers	Aug26 3-0	Aug16 1-1	Aug19 1-0	

Section 3

	Clyde	Dundee	Hibernian	Motherwell
Clyde		Aug16 1-2	Sep02 0-2	Aug26 2-1
Dundee	Aug30 1-0		Aug12 0-0	Aug19 2-1
Hibernian	Aug19 3-1	Aug26 2-4		Aug16 1-0
Motherwell	Aug12 2-2	Sep02 2-5	Aug30 2-1	

Section 4

	Falkirk	Hearts	St Johnstone	Stirling A
Falkirk		Aug19 0-2	Aug30 0-3	Aug12 0-2
Hearts	Sep02 3-1		Aug12 1-2	Aug19 4-1
St Johnstone	Aug16 0-0	Aug26 3-2		Aug19 2-1
Stirling A	Aug26 1-1	Aug16 0-1	Sep02 1-0	

Section 5

	Ayr U	Berwick R	St Mirren	Stranraer
Ayr U		Sep02 2-1	Aug16 2-0	Aug26 1-0
Berwick R	Aug19 2-1		Aug26 1-3	Aug16 2-0
St Mirren	Aug30 1-2	Aug12 2-2		Sep02 2-1
Stranraer	Aug12 1-4	Aug30 1-0	Aug19 1-3	

Section 6

	Cowdenbeath	Hamilton A	Montrose	Queen's Park
Cowdenbeath		Aug30 0-0	Aug19 3-0	Aug12 0-2
Hamilton A	Aug16 0-1		Aug26 3-1	Aug19 1-0
Montrose	Sep02 2-1	Aug12 2-3		Aug30 0-1
Queen's Park	Aug26 1-0	Sep02 1-1	Aug16 2-1	

Section 7

	Dumbarton	Morton	Queen of South	Raith R
Dumbarton		Sep02 1-3	Aug16 1-2	Aug26 1-1
Morton	Aug19 6-0		Aug26 3-2	Aug16 3-1
Queen of South	Aug30 3-1	Aug12 0-4		Sep02 3-2
Raith R	Aug12 2-0	Aug30 2-3	Aug19 2-5	

Section 8

	Albion R	Alloa	Arbroath	East Fife
Albion R		Sep02 4-3	Aug30 1-1	Aug12 2-4
Alloa	Aug19 1-4		Aug12 1-2	Aug30 0-2
Arbroath	Aug16 1-3	Aug26 1-1		Aug19 4-3
East Fife	Aug26 1-0	Aug16 3-1	Sep02 3-0	

Section 9

	Brechin C	Clydebank	E Stirling	Forfar A	Stenhousemuir
Brechin C			Aug19 2-1	Aug26 2-1	
Clydebank	Aug12 2-0				Aug19 2-1
E Stirling		Aug16 0-1			Aug26 3-3
Forfar A	Sep02 1-2	Aug12 4-0			
Stenhousemuir	Sep02 2-4		Aug16 3-1		

Section 1	P	W	D	L	F	A	Pts
Kilmarnock	6	3	2	1	11	5	8
Dunfermline A	6	2	2	2	11	12	6
Airdrie	6	2	1	3	7	8	5
Partick T	6	2	1	3	6	10	5

Section 2	P	W	D	L	F	A	Pts
Celtic	6	5	1	0	14	4	11
Rangers	6	3	2	1	10	5	8
Dundee U	6	1	1	4	7	8	3
Aberdeen	6	0	2	4	5	19	2

Section 3	P	W	D	L	F	A	Pts
Dundee	6	5	1	0	14	6	11
Hibernian	6	3	1	2	9	7	7
Motherwell	6	1	1	4	8	13	3
Clyde	6	1	1	4	6	11	3

Section 4	P	W	D	L	F	A	Pts
St Johnstone	6	4	1	1	10	5	9
Hearts	6	4	0	2	13	7	8
Stirling A	6	2	1	3	6	8	5
Falkirk	6	0	2	4	2	11	2

Section 5	P	W	D	L	F	A	Pts
Ayr U	6	5	0	1	12	5	10
St Mirren	6	3	1	2	11	9	7
Berwick R	6	2	1	3	8	9	5
Stranraer	6	1	0	5	4	12	2

Section 6	P	W	D	L	F	A	Pts
Queen's Park	6	4	1	1	7	3	9
Hamilton A	6	3	2	1	8	5	8
Cowdenbeath	6	2	1	3	5	5	5
Montrose	6	1	0	5	6	13	2

Section 7	P	W	D	L	F	A	Pts
Morton	6	6	0	0	22	6	12
Queen of South	6	4	0	2	15	13	8
Raith R	6	1	1	4	10	15	3
Dumbarton	6	0	1	5	4	17	1

Section 8	P	W	D	L	F	A	Pts
East Fife	6	5	0	1	16	7	10
Albion R	6	3	1	2	14	11	7
Arbroath	6	2	2	2	9	12	6
Alloa	6	0	1	5	7	16	1

Section 9	P	W	D	L	F	A	Pts
Clydebank	4	4	0	0	7	2	8
Brechin C	4	3	0	1	8	6	6
Stenhousemuir	4	1	1	2	9	10	3
Forfar A	4	1	0	3	7	7	2
E Stirling	4	0	1	3	4	10	1

Play-offs
Sep 4 Ayr U ....1 Clydebank 1
Sep 6 Clydebank ....2 Ayr U ....4 Agg 3-5

Quarter-finals
Sep 13 Celtic ....6 Ayr U 2
Sep 27 Ayr U ....0 Celtic ....2 Agg 2-8
Sep 13 East Fife ....0 Dundee 1
Sep 20 Dundee ....4 East Fife ......0 Agg 5-0
Sep 13 Morton ....3 Kilmarnock 2
Sep 27 Kilmarnock ......1 Morton ....3 Agg 3-5
Sep 13 Queen's Park .....0 St Johnstone ...5
Sep 27 St Johnstone .....3 Queen's Park ....1 Agg 8-1

Semi-finals
Oct 11 Celtic ....7 Morton 1
played at Hampden Park
Oct 11 Dundee ....3 St Johnstone 1
played at Tannadice

Final
Oct 28 Celtic ....5 Dundee 3
played at Hampden Park

Section 1

	Falkirk	Hibernian	Raith R	St Johnstone
Falkirk		Aug31 0-2	Aug10 1-1	Aug28 2-2
Hibernian	Aug17 2-0		Aug28 3-0	Aug10 0-1
Raith R	Aug24 4-2	Aug14 0-1		Aug31 2-1
St Johnstone	Aug14 2-3	Aug24 2-2	Aug17 0-0	

Section 2

	Airdrie	Dundee	Hearts	Kilmarnock
Airdrie		Aug31 0-3	Aug10 2-3	Aug28 2-0
Dundee	Aug17 1-1		Aug28 4-0	Aug10 4-0
Hearts	Aug24 0-2	Aug14 2-1		Aug31 0-0
Kilmarnock	Aug14 0-3	Aug24 2-2	Aug17 3-3	

Section 3

	Aberdeen	Clyde	Dundee U	Dunfermline A
Aberdeen		Aug24 0-2	Aug17 4-1	Aug14 1-0
Clyde	Aug10 4-1		Aug28 0-4	Aug31 3-0
Dundee U	Aug31 1-0	Aug14 2-3		Aug24 2-1
Dunfermline A	Aug28 1-2	Aug17 2-1	Aug10 3-2	

Section 4

	Celtic	Morton	Partick T	Rangers
Celtic		Aug14 4-1	Aug17 4-0	Aug24 1-0
Morton	Aug28 0-3		Aug10 1-3	Aug31 0-5
Partick T	Aug31 1-6	Aug24 2-0		Aug14 1-5
Rangers	Aug10 0-2	Aug17 2-0	Aug28 2-1	

Section 5

	Arbroath	Ayr U	Cowdenbeath	Stirling A
Arbroath		Aug17 1-1	Aug28 2-0	Aug10 2-1
Ayr U	Aug31 3-1		Aug10 3-1	Aug28 1-0
Cowdenbeath	Aug14 1-1	Aug24 0-2		Aug31 3-6
Stirling A	Aug24 1-0	Aug14 2-4	Aug17 2-1	

Section 6

	Berwick R	Clydebank	East Fife	Queen of South
Berwick R		Aug28 3-0	Aug31 1-4	Aug10 1-1
Clydebank	Aug14 2-4		Aug24 1-3	Aug31 1-1
East Fife	Aug17 1-0	Aug10 2-0		Aug28 1-1
Queen of South	Aug24 2-0	Aug17 1-2	Aug14 1-1	

Section 7

	Hamilton A	Montrose	Motherwell	St Mirren
Hamilton A		Aug31 2-0	Aug10 2-1	Aug28 2-1
Montrose	Aug17 0-2		Aug28 2-1	Aug10 1-2
Motherwell	Aug24 0-0	Aug14 1-2		Aug17 6-0
St Mirren	Aug14 3-0	Aug24 1-0	Aug31 2-0	

Section 8

	Albion R	Dumbarton	Forfar A	Queen's Park
Albion R		Aug24 5-0	Aug17 2-4	Aug14 3-2
Dumbarton	Aug10 0-4		Aug28 5-1	Aug17 4-3
Forfar A	Aug31 2-2	Aug14 1-0		Aug24 0-2
Queen's Park	Aug28 2-3	Aug31 1-0	Aug10 4-0	

Section 9

	Alloa	Brechin C	E Stirling	Stenhousemuir	Stranraer
Alloa				Aug10 0-1	Aug31 0-1
Brechin C	Aug14 2-3		Aug31 3-0		
E Stirling	Aug24 2-2			Aug17 3-0	
Stenhousemuir		Aug24 1-0			Aug14 1-3
Stranraer	Aug17 1-2	Aug10 2-1			

Section 1

	P	W	D	L	F	A	Pts
Hibernian	6	4	1	1	10	3	9
Raith R	6	2	2	2	7	8	6
St Johnstone	6	1	3	2	8	9	5
Falkirk	6	1	2	3	8	13	4

Section 2

	P	W	D	L	F	A	Pts
Dundee	6	3	2	1	15	5	8
Airdrie	6	3	1	2	10	7	7
Hearts	6	2	2	2	8	12	6
Kilmarnock	6	0	3	3	5	14	3

Section 3

	P	W	D	L	F	A	Pts
Clyde	6	4	0	2	13	9	8
Dundee U	6	3	0	3	12	11	6
Aberdeen	6	3	0	3	8	9	6
Dunfermline A	6	2	0	4	7	11	4

Section 4

	P	W	D	L	F	A	Pts
Celtic	6	6	0	0	20	2	12
Rangers	6	4	0	2	14	5	8
Partick T	6	2	0	4	8	18	4
Morton	6	0	0	6	2	19	0

Section 5

	P	W	D	L	F	A	Pts
Ayr U	6	5	1	0	14	5	11
Stirling A	6	3	0	3	12	11	6
Arbroath	6	2	2	2	7	7	6
Cowdenbeath	6	0	1	5	6	16	1

Section 6

	P	W	D	L	F	A	Pts
East Fife	6	4	2	0	12	4	10
Queen of South	6	1	4	1	7	6	6
Berwick R	6	2	1	3	9	10	5
Clydebank	6	1	1	4	6	14	3

Section 7

	P	W	D	L	F	A	Pts
Hamilton A	6	4	1	1	8	5	9
St Mirren	6	4	0	2	9	9	8
Montrose	6	2	0	4	5	9	4
Motherwell	6	1	1	4	9	8	3

Section 8

	P	W	D	L	F	A	Pts
Albion R	6	4	1	1	19	10	9
Queen's Park	6	3	0	3	14	10	6
Forfar A	6	2	1	3	8	15	5
Dumbarton	6	2	0	4	9	15	4

Section 9

	P	W	D	L	F	A	Pts
Stranraer	4	3	0	1	7	4	6
Brechin C	4	2	0	2	7	5	4
Stenhousemuir	4	2	0	2	3	6	4
E Stirling	4	1	1	2	6	7	3
Alloa	4	1	1	2	5	6	3

Play-offs
Sep 2 Stranraer 3 Albion R 3
Sep 4 Albion R 0 Stranraer 2 Agg 3-5

Quarter-finals
Sep 11 Ayr U 0 Clyde 1
Sep 25 Clyde 2 Ayr U 0 Agg 3-0
Sep 11 Celtic 10 Hamilton A 0
Sep 25 Hamilton A 2 Celtic 4 Agg 2-14
Sep 11 East Fife 1 Hibernian 4
Sep 25 Hibernian 2 East Fife 1 Agg 6-2
Sep 11 Stranraer 0 Dundee 4
Sep 25 Dundee 6 Stranraer 0 Agg 10-0

Semi-finals
Oct 9 Celtic 1 Clyde 0
played at Hampden Park
Oct 9 Dundee 1 Hibernian 2
played at Tynecastle

Final
Apr 5 Celtic 6 Hibernian 2
played at Hampden Park

Season 1969-70

Section 1

	Airdrie	Celtic	Raith R	Rangers
Airdrie		Aug23 0-3	Aug13 3-1	Aug16 0-3
Celtic	Aug09 6-1		Aug16 5-0	Aug20 1-0
Raith R	Aug20 2-1	Aug27 2-5		Aug09 2-3
Rangers	Aug27 3-0	Aug13 2-1	Aug23 3-3	

Section 2

	Aberdeen	Clyde	Dunfermline A	Hibernian
Aberdeen		Aug20 3-0	Aug09 2-2	Aug16 2-2
Clyde	Aug13 0-0		Aug27 0-0	Aug23 3-1
Dunfermline A	Aug23 0-1	Aug16 0-0		Aug13 3-1
Hibernian	Aug27 0-0	Aug09 4-1	Aug20 2-0	

Section 3

	Dundee	Kilmarnock	Partick T	St Johnstone
Dundee		Aug16 0-0	Aug13 4-0	Aug23 1-2
Kilmarnock	Aug27 1-0		Aug23 6-0	Aug13 2-3
Partick T	Aug20 0-1	Aug09 0-2		Aug16 1-8
St Johnstone	Aug09 3-1	Aug20 2-1	Aug27 4-0	

Section 4

	Dundee U	Hearts	Morton	St Mirren
Dundee U		Aug09 2-3	Aug20 0-2	Aug27 2-1
Hearts	Aug23 1-0		Aug16 0-1	Aug13 0-0
Morton	Aug13 4-1	Aug27 0-2		Aug23 1-2
St Mirren	Aug16 0-1	Aug20 1-0	Aug09 1-1	

Section 5

	Albion R	East Fife	Montrose	Motherwell
Albion R		Aug19 2-1	Aug09 0-1	Aug27 2-4
East Fife	Aug13 1-1		Aug16 4-1	Aug23 0-0
Montrose	Aug23 1-1	Aug27 1-3		Aug13 1-4
Motherwell	Aug16 5-1	Aug09 2-0	Aug20 3-2	

Section 6

	Ayr U	E Stirling	Queen of South	Queen's Park
Ayr U		Aug20 0-0	Aug16 4-1	Aug09 2-0
E Stirling	Aug13 0-1		Aug23 0-0	Aug27 2-0
Queen of South	Aug27 2-1	Aug09 2-0		Aug20 2-1
Queen's Park	Aug23 0-1	Aug16 7-2	Aug13 1-4	

Section 7

	Clydebank	Cowdenbeath	Dumbarton	Stranraer
Clydebank		Aug16 3-1	Aug09 1-3	Aug20 3-2
Cowdenbeath	Aug27 2-1		Aug20 2-3	Aug09 2-2
Dumbarton	Aug23 1-0	Aug13 2-3		Aug27 2-0
Stranraer	Aug13 1-1	Aug23 3-3	Aug16 2-2	

Section 8

	Arbroath	Falkirk	Forfar A	Stirling A
Arbroath		Aug27 1-3	Aug09 1-0	Aug09 2-3
Falkirk	Aug16 1-2		Aug09 3-1	Aug20 4-3
Forfar A	Aug13 2-1	Aug23 1-1		Aug16 0-3
Stirling A	Aug23 4-1	Aug13 2-3	Aug27 1-2	

Section 9

	Alloa	Berwick R	Brechin C	Hamilton A	Stenhousemuir
Alloa			Aug20 2-0	Aug09 0-3	
Berwick R	Aug23 1-2			Aug16 2-0	
Brechin C		Aug09 1-0			Aug16 2-1
Hamilton A		Aug13 1-2			Aug23 2-0
Stenhousemuir	Aug12 3-3	Aug26 3-3			

Section 1

	P	W	D	L	F	A	Pts
Celtic	6	5	0	1	21	5	10
Rangers	6	4	1	1	14	7	9
Raith R	6	1	1	4	10	20	3
Airdrie	6	1	0	5	5	18	2

Section 2

	P	W	D	L	F	A	Pts
Aberdeen	6	2	4	0	8	4	8
Hibernian	6	2	2	2	10	9	6
Dunfermline A	6	1	3	2	5	6	5
Clyde	6	1	3	2	4	8	5

Section 3

	P	W	D	L	F	A	Pts
St Johnstone	6	6	0	0	22	6	12
Kilmarnock	6	3	1	2	12	5	7
Dundee	6	2	1	3	7	6	5
Partick T	6	0	0	6	1	25	0

Section 4

	P	W	D	L	F	A	Pts
Morton	6	3	1	2	9	6	7
Hearts	6	3	1	2	6	4	7
St Mirren	6	2	2	2	5	5	6
Dundee U	6	2	0	4	6	11	4

Section 5

	P	W	D	L	F	A	Pts
Motherwell	6	5	1	0	18	6	11
East Fife	6	2	2	2	9	7	6
Albion R	6	1	2	3	7	13	4
Montrose	6	1	1	4	7	15	3

Section 6

	P	W	D	L	F	A	Pts
Ayr U	6	4	1	1	9	3	9
Queen of South	6	4	1	1	11	7	9
E Stirling	6	1	2	3	4	10	4
Queen's Park	6	1	0	5	9	13	2

Section 7

	P	W	D	L	F	A	Pts
Dumbarton	6	4	1	1	13	8	9
Cowdenbeath	6	2	2	2	13	14	6
Clydebank	6	2	1	3	9	10	5
Stranraer	6	0	4	2	10	13	4

Section 8

	P	W	D	L	F	A	Pts
Falkirk	6	4	1	1	15	10	9
Stirling A	6	3	0	3	16	12	6
Forfar A	6	2	1	3	6	10	5
Arbroath	6	2	0	4	8	13	4

Section 9

	P	W	D	L	F	A	Pts
Brechin C	4	3	0	1	5	4	6
Alloa	4	2	1	1	7	7	5
Hamilton A	4	2	0	2	6	4	4
Berwick R	4	1	1	2	6	6	3
Stenhousemuir	4	0	2	2	7	10	2

Play-offs
Sep 1 Brechin C ....1 Dumbarton 1
Sep 3 Dumbarton ....5 Brechin C ......2 Agg 6-3

Quarter-finals
Sep 10 Aberdeen ....0 Celtic 0
Sep 24 Celtic ....2 Aberdeen ....1 Agg 2-1
Sep 10 Dumbarton ....1 Ayr U 4
Sep 24 Ayr U ....1 Dumbarton ....0 Agg 5-1
Sep 10 Morton ....3 Motherwell 0
Sep 24 Motherwell ......3 Morton ....0 Agg 3-3
Sep 10 St Johnstone .....5 Falkirk 1
Sep 24 Falkirk ....2 St Johnstone ...6 Agg 3-11

Replay
Sep 30 Morton ....0 Motherwell 1
    played at Ibrox

Semi-finals
Oct 8 Ayr U ....3 Celtic 3
    played at Hampden Park
Oct 1 Motherwell ....0 St Johnstone 2
    played at Hampden Park

Replay
Oct 13 Ayr U ....1 Celtic 2
    played at Hampden Park

Final
Oct 25 Celtic ....1 St Johnstone ...0
    played at Hampden Park

Season 1970-71

Section 1

	Celtic	Clyde	Dundee U	Hearts
Celtic		Aug12 5-3	Aug15 2-2	Aug22 4-2
Clyde	Aug19 0-2		Aug08 1-1	Aug26 1-5
Dundee U	Aug26 2-2	Aug22 1-1		Aug12 2-1
Hearts	Aug08 1-2	Aug15 1-2	Aug19 0-0	

Section 2

	Dunfermline A	Morton	Motherwell	Rangers
Dunfermline A		Aug12 0-2	Aug26 1-1	Aug22 0-6
Morton	Aug19 3-2		Aug08 1-4	Aug26 0-2
Motherwell	Aug15 3-0	Aug22 0-2		Aug12 0-2
Rangers	Aug08 4-1	Aug15 0-0	Aug19 2-0	

Section 3

	Ayr U	Dundee	Kilmarnock	St Mirren
Ayr U		Aug12 1-2	Aug22 0-0	Aug15 2-2
Dundee	Aug19 4-1		Aug15 2-0	Aug08 1-0
Kilmarnock	Aug08 1-0	Aug26 2-1		Aug19 2-0
St Mirren	Aug26 1-2	Aug22 0-2	Aug12 1-3	

Section 4

	Aberdeen	Airdrie	Hibernian	St Johnstone
Aberdeen		Aug22 7-3	Aug15 1-1	Aug12 2-1
Airdrie	Aug08 1-1		Aug19 2-4	Aug26 1-0
Hibernian	Aug26 4-0	Aug12 3-2		Aug22 1-1
St Johnstone	Aug19 0-1	Aug15 0-1	Aug08 1-3	

Section 5

	East Fife	Partick T	Queen of South	Stirling A
East Fife		Aug15 1-1	Aug22 2-1	Aug12 1-1
Partick T	Aug26 1-3		Aug12 4-1	Aug22 1-1
Queen of South	Aug08 1-1	Aug19 0-0		Aug26 1-1
Stirling A	Aug19 2-1	Aug08 2-3	Aug15 2-2	

Section 6

	Alloa	Berwick R	Brechin C	Dumbarton
Alloa		Aug19 0-1	Aug26 2-0	Aug08 1-3
Berwick R	Aug12 1-1		Aug22 4-1	Aug15 0-2
Brechin C	Aug15 1-3	Aug08 2-3		Aug19 1-3
Dumbarton	Aug22 5-2	Aug26 3-2	Aug12 2-2	

Section 7

	Cowdenbeath	E Stirling	Montrose	Raith R
Cowdenbeath		Aug08 1-1	Aug19 3-0	Aug15 3-1
E Stirling	Aug22 1-4		Aug15 1-2	Aug12 2-0
Montrose	Aug12 3-2	Aug26 2-1		Aug22 4-1
Raith R	Aug26 0-2	Aug19 2-1	Aug08 1-0	

Section 8

	Albion R	Arbroath	Clydebank	Falkirk
Albion R		Aug15 2-1	Aug12 2-2	Aug22 0-3
Arbroath	Aug26 5-3		Aug22 4-0	Aug15 1-4
Clydebank	Aug19 5-1	Aug08 4-1		Aug15 0-3
Falkirk	Aug08 5-0	Aug19 2-1	Aug26 1-1	

Section 9

	Forfar A	Hamilton A	Queen's Park	Stenhousemuir	Stranraer
Forfar A		Aug15 1-2		Aug08 2-1	
Hamilton A			Aug19 1-1		Aug08 2-3
Queen's Park	Aug12 1-1				Aug15 2-1
Stenhousemuir		Aug12 3-2	Aug22 1-4		
Stranraer	Aug22 1-0		Aug19 4-0		

Section 1

	P	W	D	L	F	A	Pts
Celtic	6	4	2	0	17	10	10
Dundee U	6	1	5	0	8	7	7
Clyde	6	1	2	3	8	15	4
Hearts	6	1	1	4	10	11	3

Section 2

	P	W	D	L	F	A	Pts
Rangers	6	5	1	0	16	1	11
Morton	6	3	1	2	8	8	7
Motherwell	6	2	1	3	8	8	5
Dunfermline A	6	0	1	5	4	19	1

Section 3

	P	W	D	L	F	A	Pts
Dundee	6	5	0	1	12	4	10
Kilmarnock	6	4	1	1	8	4	9
Ayr U	6	1	2	3	6	10	4
St Mirren	6	0	1	5	4	12	1

Section 4

	P	W	D	L	F	A	Pts
Hibernian	6	4	2	0	16	7	10
Aberdeen	6	3	2	1	12	10	8
Airdrie	6	2	1	3	10	15	5
St Johnstone	6	0	1	5	3	9	1

Section 5

	P	W	D	L	F	A	Pts
Partick T	6	2	3	1	10	8	7
East Fife	6	2	3	1	9	7	7
Stirling A	6	1	4	1	9	9	6
Queen of South	6	0	4	2	6	10	4

Section 6

	P	W	D	L	F	A	Pts
Dumbarton	6	5	1	0	18	8	11
Berwick R	6	3	1	2	11	9	7
Alloa	6	2	1	3	9	11	5
Brechin C	6	0	1	5	7	17	1

Section 7

	P	W	D	L	F	A	Pts
Cowdenbeath	6	4	1	1	15	6	9
Montrose	6	4	0	2	11	9	8
Raith R	6	2	0	4	5	12	4
E Stirling	6	1	1	4	7	11	3

Section 8

	P	W	D	L	F	A	Pts
Falkirk	6	5	1	0	18	3	11
Clydebank	6	2	2	2	12	12	6
Arbroath	6	2	0	4	13	15	4
Albion R	6	1	1	4	8	21	3

Section 9

	P	W	D	L	F	A	Pts
Stranraer	4	3	0	1	9	4	6
Queen's Park	4	2	2	0	8	4	6
Hamilton A	4	1	1	2	7	8	3
Forfar A	4	1	1	2	4	5	3
Stenhousemuir	4	1	0	3	5	12	2

Play-offs
Aug 31 Partick T ....2 Stranraer 1
Sep 2 Stranraer ....2 Partick T ....2 Agg 3-4

Quarter-finals
Sep 9 Dundee ....2 Celtic 2
Sep 23 Celtic ....5 Dundee ....1 Agg 7-3
Sep 9 Falkirk ....0 Cowdenbeath 1
Sep 23 Cowdenbeath ......0 Falkirk ....0 Agg 1-0
Sep 9 Hibernian ....1 Rangers 3
Sep 23 Rangers ....3 Hibernian ......1 Agg 6-2
Sep 9 Partick T ....3 Dumbarton 3
Sep 23 Dumbarton ....3 Partick T ....2 Agg 6-5

Semi-finals
Oct 7 Celtic ....0 Dumbarton 0
    played at Hampden Park
Oct 14 Cowdenbeath .....0 Rangers 2
    played at Hampden Park

Replay
Oct 12 Celtic ....4 Dumbarton 3
    played at Hampden Park

Final
Oct 24 Celtic ....0 Rangers 1
    played at Hampden Park

Season 1971-72

Section 1

Section 1	Dundee U	Hibernian	Kilmarnock	Motherwell
Dundee U		Aug25 1-4	Aug14 1-0	Aug21 2-2
Hibernian	Aug18 2-0		Aug21 3-1	Aug28 2-1
Kilmarnock	Aug28 4-2	Sep01 0-0		Aug18 2-1
Motherwell	Sep01 1-3	Aug14 0-3	Aug25 2-0	

Section 2

Section 2	Aberdeen	Clyde	Dundee	Falkirk
Aberdeen		Aug25 5-0	Aug14 1-1	Aug21 1-0
Clyde	Aug18 0-2		Aug21 0-1	Aug28 0-1
Dundee	Aug28 3-1	Sep01 3-0		Aug18 2-2
Falkirk	Sep01 3-1	Aug14 5-2	Aug25 1-0	

Section 3

Section 3	Airdrie	Dunfermline A	Hearts	St Johnstone
Airdrie		Aug28 1-0	Aug18 1-3	Aug21 1-3
Dunfermline A	Aug14 2-1		Aug21 1-0	Aug25 0-2
Hearts	Aug25 1-2	Sep01 4-0		Aug14 4-1
St Johnstone	Sep01 0-1	Aug18 1-1	Aug28 1-0	

Section 4

Section 4	Ayr U	Celtic	Morton	Rangers
Ayr U		Aug21 0-3	Aug14 1-0	Aug25 0-4
Celtic	Aug30 4-1		Aug25 0-1	Aug14 2-0
Morton	Aug28 2-0	Aug18 0-1		Sep01 0-1
Rangers	Aug18 4-0	Aug28 0-3	Aug21 2-0	

Section 5

Section 5	Berwick R	Clydebank	Cowdenbeath	Queen's Park
Berwick R		Aug14 2-2	Aug25 0-1	Aug21 2-3
Clydebank	Aug28 5-0		Aug21 2-1	Aug18 3-2
Cowdenbeath	Aug18 2-2	Sep01 3-4		Aug28 1-1
Queen's Park	Sep01 0-1	Aug25 1-1	Aug14 1-0	

Section 6

Section 6	Dumbarton	Queen of South	Stenhousemuir	Stirling A
Dumbarton		Sep01 1-3	Aug25 1-2	Aug14 1-1
Queen of South	Aug21 1-0		Aug14 3-2	Aug25 1-2
Stenhousemuir	Aug18 2-3	Aug28 1-0		Aug21 1-3
Stirling A	Aug28 3-2	Aug18 2-1	Sep01 3-1	

Section 7

Section 7	Arbroath	East Fife	Partick T	Raith R
Arbroath		Aug21 2-2	Aug28 2-4	Aug18 4-0
East Fife	Sep01 0-2		Aug18 2-3	Aug28 1-1
Partick T	Aug14 4-0	Aug25 1-1		Sep01 5-0
Raith R	Aug25 1-1	Aug14 2-1	Aug21 1-1	

Section 8

Section 8	Albion R	Montrose	St Mirren	Stranraer
Albion R		Aug25 0-2	Sep01 2-1	Aug14 2-1
Montrose	Aug18 1-1		Aug28 0-1	Aug21 2-2
St Mirren	Aug21 1-0	Aug14 4-1		Aug25 3-0
Stranraer	Aug28 2-0	Sep01 2-4	Aug18 2-0	

Section 9

Section 9	Alloa	Brechin C	E Stirling	Forfar A	Hamilton A
Alloa		Aug21 1-1			Aug14 3-0
Brechin C			Aug25 1-4	Aug28 2-1	
E Stirling	Aug18 1-1				Aug28 2-6
Forfar A	Aug25 0-0		Aug14 2-2		
Hamilton A		Aug18 2-2		Aug21 1-4	

Standings

Section 1	P	W	D	L	F	A	Pts
Hibernian	6	5	1	0	14	3	11
Kilmarnock	6	2	1	3	7	9	5
Dundee U	6	2	1	3	9	13	5
Motherwell	6	1	1	4	7	12	3

Section 2	P	W	D	L	F	A	Pts
Falkirk	6	4	1	1	12	6	9
Dundee	6	3	2	1	10	5	8
Aberdeen	6	3	1	2	11	7	7
Clyde	6	0	0	6	2	17	0

Section 3	P	W	D	L	F	A	Pts
St Johnstone	6	3	1	2	8	7	7
Hearts	6	3	0	3	12	6	6
Airdrie	6	3	0	3	7	9	6
Dunfermline A	6	2	1	3	4	9	5

Section 4	P	W	D	L	F	A	Pts
Celtic	6	5	0	1	13	2	10
Rangers	6	4	0	2	11	5	8
Morton	6	2	1	3	4	5	5
Ayr U	6	0	1	5	2	18	1

Section 5	P	W	D	L	F	A	Pts
Clydebank	6	4	2	0	17	9	10
Queen's Park	6	2	2	2	8	8	6
Cowdenbeath	6	1	2	3	8	10	4
Berwick R	6	1	2	3	7	13	4

Section 6	P	W	D	L	F	A	Pts
Stirling A	6	5	1	0	14	7	11
Queen of South	6	3	0	3	9	8	6
Stenhousemuir	6	2	0	4	9	13	4
Dumbarton	6	1	1	4	8	12	3

Section 7	P	W	D	L	F	A	Pts
Partick T	6	4	2	0	18	6	10
Arbroath	6	2	2	2	11	11	6
Raith R	6	1	3	2	5	13	5
East Fife	6	0	3	3	7	11	3

Section 8	P	W	D	L	F	A	Pts
St Mirren	6	4	0	2	10	5	8
Montrose	6	2	2	2	10	10	6
Stranraer	6	2	1	3	9	11	5
Albion R	6	2	1	3	5	8	5

Section 9	P	W	D	L	F	A	Pts
Alloa	4	1	3	0	5	2	5
Forfar A	4	1	2	1	7	5	4
E Stirling	4	1	2	1	9	10	4
Brechin C	4	1	2	1	6	8	4
Hamilton A	4	1	1	2	9	11	3

Play-offs
Sep 6 Partick T ....4 Alloa 1
Sep 8 Alloa ....1 Partick T ....1 Agg 2-5

Quarter-finals
Sep 8 Clydebank ....0 Celtic 5
Sep 22 Celtic ....6 Clydebank ......2 Agg 11-2
Sep 8 Falkirk ....2 Hibernian 0
Sep 22 Hibernian ....1 Falkirk ....0 Agg 1-2
Sep 20 St Johnstone ......2 Partick T 1
Sep 22 Partick T ....5 St Johnstone ....1 Agg 5-3
Sep 8 St Mirren ....2 Stirling A 0
Sep 22 Stirling A ....0 St Mirren ....3 Agg 0-5

Semi-finals
Oct 6 Celtic ....3 St Mirren 0
   played at Hampden Park
Oct 4 Falkirk ....0 Partick T 2
   played at Hampden Park

Final
Oct 23 Celtic ....1 Partick T 4
   played at Hampden Park

In 1971-72 Celtic, in the middle of a 14-year unbroken run of reaching the League Cup Final, were soundly beaten by unfancied Partick Thistle, who had just gained promotion to the First Division the previous season. Here, Lou Macari and Bobby Murdoch leave the field together with Partick's Alex Forsyth (right). Celtic successfully defended their League and SFA Cup trophies though.

Season 1972-73

Section 1

	Cowdenbeath	Morton	Partick T	Stranraer
Cowdenbeath		Aug19 1-0	Aug12 1-5	Aug23 0-2
Morton	Aug30 7-2		Aug23 0-0	Aug12 1-5
Partick T	Aug26 2-2	Aug16 0-0		Aug30 2-0
Stranraer	Aug16 3-0	Aug26 1-3	Aug19 0-2	

Section 2

	Aberdeen	Hibernian	Queen of South	Queen's Park
Aberdeen		Aug16 4-1	Aug26 2-1	Aug19 5-1
Hibernian	Aug23 2-1		Aug19 3-0	Aug12 4-2
Queen of South	Aug12 0-4	Aug30 1-3		Aug23 1-0
Queen's Park	Aug30 0-3	Aug26 0-1	Aug16 1-2	

Section 3

	Ayr U	Clydebank	Rangers	St Mirren
Ayr U		Aug23 5-0	Aug30 1-2	Aug12 2-1
Clydebank	Aug16 1-0		Aug26 0-5	Aug30 3-3
Rangers	Aug19 2-1	Aug12 2-0		Aug23 1-4
St Mirren	Aug26 0-3	Aug16 4-2	Aug19 0-4	

Section 4

	Dundee U	Dunfermline A	Kilmarnock	Stenhousemuir
Dundee U		Aug12 2-0	Aug23 2-1	Aug19 5-0
Dunfermline A	Aug26 0-1		Aug30 1-0	Aug16 2-2
Kilmarnock	Aug16 2-3	Aug19 2-1		Aug26 3-1
Stenhousemuir	Aug30 2-0	Aug23 5-2	Aug12 1-1	

Section 5

	Falkirk	Montrose	Raith R	St Johnstone
Falkirk		Aug26 3-0	Aug19 1-0	Aug16 1-2
Montrose	Aug12 3-4		Aug23 2-1	Aug30 0-3
Raith R	Aug30 1-0	Aug16 1-2		Aug26 3-0
St Johnstone	Aug23 6-1	Aug19 4-1	Aug12 2-0	

Section 6

	Airdrie	Berwick R	Dumbarton	Hearts
Airdrie		Aug12 0-0	Aug30 2-1	Aug23 2-1
Berwick R	Aug26 1-4		Aug16 1-0	Aug19 1-1
Dumbarton	Aug19 4-1	Aug23 2-2		Aug12 1-0
Hearts	Aug16 0-0	Aug30 3-0	Aug26 1-1	

Section 7

	Clyde	Dundee	E Stirling	Motherwell
Clyde		Aug23 0-1	Aug19 3-1	Aug12 2-2
Dundee	Aug16 2-1		Aug26 3-0	Aug30 2-1
E Stirling	Aug30 0-2	Aug12 2-8		Aug23 1-5
Motherwell	Aug26 1-1	Aug19 1-3	Aug16 1-0	

Section 8

	Arbroath	Celtic	East Fife	Stirling A
Arbroath		Aug19 0-5	Aug26 3-0	Aug16 1-2
Celtic	Aug28 3-3		Aug16 1-1	Aug26 3-0
East Fife	Aug12 2-1	Aug23 2-3		Aug19 0-0
Stirling A	Aug23 2-1	Aug12 0-3	Aug30 0-2	

Section 9

	Albion R	Alloa	Brechin C	Forfar A	Hamilton A
Albion R			Aug19 3-0	Aug26 2-1	
Alloa	Aug16 4-3				Aug26 2-0
Brechin C		Aug23 1-2		Aug16 2-1	
Forfar A		Aug12 2-1			Aug19 1-0
Hamilton A	Aug22 4-3		Aug12 1-0		

Section 1	P	W	D	L	F	A	Pts
Partick T	6	3	3	0	11	3	9
Stranraer	6	3	0	3	11	8	6
Morton	6	2	2	2	11	9	6
Cowdenbeath	6	1	1	4	6	19	3

Section 2	P	W	D	L	F	A	Pts
Aberdeen	6	5	0	1	19	5	10
Hibernian	6	5	0	1	14	8	10
Queen of South	6	2	0	4	5	13	4
Queen's Park	6	0	0	6	4	16	0

Section 3	P	W	D	L	F	A	Pts
Rangers	6	5	0	1	16	6	10
Ayr U	6	3	0	3	12	6	6
St Mirren	6	2	1	3	12	15	5
Clydebank	6	1	1	4	6	19	3

Section 4	P	W	D	L	F	A	Pts
Dundee U	6	5	0	1	13	5	10
Stenhousemuir	6	2	2	2	11	13	6
Kilmarnock	6	2	1	3	9	9	5
Dunfermline A	6	1	1	4	6	12	3

Section 5	P	W	D	L	F	A	Pts
St Johnstone	6	5	0	1	17	6	10
Falkirk	6	3	0	3	10	12	6
Raith R	6	2	0	4	6	7	4
Montrose	6	2	0	4	8	16	4

Section 6	P	W	D	L	F	A	Pts
Airdrie	6	3	2	1	9	7	8
Dumbarton	6	2	2	2	9	7	6
Hearts	6	1	3	2	6	5	5
Berwick R	6	1	3	2	5	10	5

Section 7	P	W	D	L	F	A	Pts
Dundee	6	6	0	0	19	5	12
Motherwell	6	2	2	2	11	9	6
Clyde	6	2	2	2	9	7	6
E Stirling	6	0	0	6	4	22	0

Section 8	P	W	D	L	F	A	Pts
Celtic	6	4	2	0	18	6	10
East Fife	6	2	2	2	7	8	6
Stirling A	6	2	1	3	4	10	5
Arbroath	6	1	1	4	9	14	3

Section 9	P	W	D	L	F	A	Pts
Alloa	4	3	0	1	9	6	6
Albion R	4	2	0	2	11	9	4
Forfar A	4	2	0	2	5	5	4
Hamilton A	4	2	0	2	5	6	4
Brechin C	4	1	0	3	3	7	2

Play-offs
Sep 4 Alloa ....0 Ayr U 0
Sep 6 Ayr U ....0 Alloa ....1 Agg 0-1
Sep 4 Motherwell ......4 Albion R 1
Sep 6 Albion R ....0 Motherwell ....4 Agg 1-8

2nd Round
Sep 20 Aberdeen ....8 Falkirk 0
Oct 4 Falkirk ....3 Aberdeen ......2 Agg 3-10
Sep 20 Dumbarton ....3 Dundee 0
Oct 4 Dundee ....4 Dumbarton ....0 Agg 4-3
Sep 20 Dundee U ......2 Hibernian 5
Oct 4 Hibernian ......0 Dundee U .....0 Agg 5-2
Sep 20 East Fife ....1 Partick T 0
Oct 4 Partick T ....0 East Fife ......0 Agg 0-1
Sep 20 Motherwell .....0 Airdrie 1
Oct 4 Airdrie ....1 Motherwell ....1 Agg 2-1
Sep 20 St Johnstone ...2 Alloa 0
Oct 3 Alloa ....0 St Johnstone ...1 Agg 0-3
Sep 20 Stenhousemuir ....0 Rangers 5
Oct 4 Rangers ....1 Stenhousemuir .2 Agg 6-2
Sep 20 Stranraer ....1 Celtic 2
Oct 4 Celtic ....5 Stranraer ......2 Agg 7-3

Quarter-finals
Oct 11 Aberdeen ....3 East Fife 0
Nov 1 East Fife ....1 Aberdeen ......4 Agg 1-7
Oct 11 Airdrie ....2 Hibernian 6
Nov 1 Hibernian ......4 Airdrie ....1 Agg 10-3
Oct 11 Dundee ....1 Celtic 0
Nov 1 Celtic ....3 Dundee ....2 Agg 3-3
Oct 11 Rangers ....1 St Johnstone 1
Nov 1 St Johnstone ......0 Rangers ....2 Agg 1-3

Replay
Nov 20 Celtic ....4 Dundee 1
played at Hampden Park

Semi-finals
Nov 27 Aberdeen ....2 Celtic 3
played at Hampden Park
Nov 22 Hibernian ....1 Rangers 0
played at Hampden Park

Final
Dec 9 Celtic ....1 Hibernian 2
played at Hampden Park

Season 1973-74

Section 1

	Arbroath	Celtic	Falkirk	Rangers
Arbroath		Aug29 1-3	Aug18 3-1	Aug15 1-2
Celtic	Aug11 2-1		Aug22 2-1	Aug25 1-3
Falkirk	Aug25 2-3	Aug15 0-2		Aug29 1-5
Rangers	Aug22 3-0	Aug18 1-2	Aug11 3-1	

Section 2

	Ayr U	Dumbarton	Hibernian	Morton
Ayr U		Aug11 2-0	Aug22 0-2	Aug25 2-1
Dumbarton	Aug29 1-0		Aug25 4-1	Aug15
Hibernian	Aug15 1-0	Aug18 1-0		Aug29 2-1
Morton	Aug18 3-2	Aug22 1-0	Aug11 1-4	

Section 3

	Dundee	Hearts	Partick T	St Johnstone
Dundee		Aug18 2-1	Aug22 4-0	Aug11 1-0
Hearts	Aug25 0-0		Aug11 2-0	Aug22 4-1
Partick T	Aug15 0-3	Aug29 0-0		Aug25 1-3
St Johnstone	Aug29 1-1	Aug15 2-1	Aug18 5-1	

Section 4

	Aberdeen	Dundee U	East Fife	Motherwell
Aberdeen	—	Aug22 0-2	Aug18 1-1	Aug11 3-1
Dundee U	Aug15 0-0	—	Aug29 5-2	Aug25 0-3
East Fife	Aug25 0-2	Aug11 1-2	—	Aug22 3-0
Motherwell	Aug29 0-0	Aug18 4-0	Aug15 5-0	—

Section 5

	E Stirling	Hamilton A	Kilmarnock	Queen's Park
E Stirling	—	Aug18 2-0	Aug11 3-2	Aug22 1-3
Hamilton A	Aug25 0-0	—	Aug22 0-4	Aug11 2-2
Kilmarnock	Aug29 4-0	Aug15 0-0	—	Aug18 2-0
Queen's Park	Aug15 0-1	Aug29 1-3	Aug25 1-1	—

Section 6

	Cowdenbeath	Queen of South	Raith R	Stirling A
Cowdenbeath	—	Aug11 0-1	Aug27 1-0	Aug25 1-5
Queen of South	Aug29 5-1	—	Aug25 1-2	Aug15 2-1
Raith R	Aug15 5-1	Aug18 2-2	—	Aug29 1-0
Stirling A	Aug18 4-1	Aug22 2-0	Aug11 1-0	—

Section 7

	Airdrie	Alloa	Clyde	Montrose
Airdrie	—	Aug11 3-0	Aug22 1-1	Aug25 6-4
Alloa	Aug29 0-2	—	Aug25 0-2	Aug15 3-1
Clyde	Aug15 0-2	Aug18 1-0	—	Aug29 2-1
Montrose	Aug18 2-2	Aug22 3-0	Aug11 2-2	—

Section 8

	Berwick R	Dunfermline A	St Mirren	Stenhousemuir
Berwick R	—	Aug22 1-2	Aug11 1-1	Aug25 3-1
Dunfermline A	Aug15 3-2	—	Aug18 5-1	Aug29 2-2
St Mirren	Aug29 2-1	Aug25 2-1	—	Aug15 2-0
Stenhousemuir	Aug18 0-1	Aug11 1-0	Aug22 1-2	—

Section 9

	Albion R	Brechin C	Clydebank	Forfar A	Stranraer
Albion R	—	Aug18 4-1	Aug15 3-1		
Brechin C		—	Aug25 2-2	Aug15 1-0	
Clydebank			—	Aug22 0-1	Aug18 3-0
Forfar A	Aug11 1-1			—	Aug25 2-1
Stranraer	Aug22 4-0	Aug11 2-1			—

Section 1

	P	W	D	L	F	A	Pts
Rangers	6	5	0	1	17	6	10
Celtic	6	5	0	1	12	7	10
Arbroath	6	2	0	4	9	13	4
Falkirk	6	0	0	6	6	18	0

Section 2

	P	W	D	L	F	A	Pts
Hibernian	6	5	0	1	11	6	10
Dumbarton	6	2	1	3	6	6	5
Morton	6	2	1	3	8	11	5
Ayr U	6	2	0	4	6	8	4

Section 3

	P	W	D	L	F	A	Pts
Dundee	6	4	2	0	11	2	10
St Johnstone	6	3	1	2	12	9	7
Hearts	6	2	2	2	8	5	6
Partick T	6	0	1	5	2	17	1

Section 4

	P	W	D	L	F	A	Pts
Motherwell	6	3	1	2	13	6	7
Aberdeen	6	2	3	1	6	4	7
Dundee U	6	3	1	2	9	10	7
East Fife	6	1	1	4	7	15	3

Section 5

	P	W	D	L	F	A	Pts
Kilmarnock	6	3	2	1	13	4	8
E Stirling	6	3	1	2	7	9	7
Hamilton A	6	1	3	2	5	9	5
Queen's Park	6	1	2	3	7	10	4

Section 6

	P	W	D	L	F	A	Pts
Stirling A	6	4	0	2	13	5	8
Raith R	6	3	1	2	10	6	7
Queen of South	6	3	1	2	11	8	7
Cowdenbeath	6	1	0	5	5	20	2

Section 7

	P	W	D	L	F	A	Pts
Airdrie	6	4	2	0	16	7	10
Clyde	6	3	2	1	8	6	8
Montrose	6	1	2	3	13	15	4
Alloa	6	1	0	5	3	12	2

Section 8

	P	W	D	L	F	A	Pts
St Mirren	6	4	1	1	10	9	9
Dunfermline A	6	3	1	2	13	9	7
Berwick R	6	2	1	3	9	9	5
Stenhousemuir	6	1	1	4	5	10	3

Section 9

	P	W	D	L	F	A	Pts
Albion R	4	2	1	1	8	7	5
Forfar A	4	2	1	1	4	3	5
Stranraer	4	2	0	2	7	6	4
Clydebank	4	1	1	2	6	6	3
Brechin C	4	1	1	2	5	8	3

Play-offs

Sep 3 Albion R ....1 E Stirling 0
Sep 5 E Stirling ....0 Albion R ....0 Agg 0-1
Sep 3 Clyde ....4 Forfar A 0
Sep 5 Forfar A ....1 Clyde ....3 Agg 1-7

2nd Round

Sep 12 Aberdeen ....3 Stirling A 0
Oct 10 Stirling A ....0 Aberdeen ....3 Agg 0-6
Sep 11 Albion R ....3 Airdrie 0
Oct 10 Airdrie ....0 Albion R ....1 Agg 0-4
Sep 12 Clyde ....1 St Mirren 0
Oct 10 St Mirren ....4 Clyde ....5 Agg 4-6
Sep 12 Dunfermline A .....2 Dundee 3
Oct 10 Dundee ....2 Dunfermline A ..2 Agg 5-4
Sep 12 Hibernian ....3 Raith R 2
Oct 10 Raith R ....0 Hibernian .....2 Agg 2-5
Sep 12 Motherwell ....1 Celtic 2
Oct 10 Celtic ....0 Motherwell .....1 Agg 2-2
Sep 12 Rangers ....6 Dumbarton 0
Oct 10 Dumbarton ....1 Rangers ....2 Agg 1-8
Sep 12 St Johnstone .....1 Kilmarnock 0
Oct 10 Kilmarnock ....3 St Johnstone ....1 Agg 3-2

Replay

Oct 29 Celtic ....3 Motherwell 2

Quarter-finals

Oct 30 Albion R ....2 Kilmarnock 0
Nov 24 Kilmarnock ....5 Albion R ....2 Agg 5-4
Oct 31 Celtic ....3 Aberdeen 2
Nov 21 Aberdeen ....0 Celtic ....0 Agg 2-3
Oct 31 Dundee ....1 Clyde 0
Nov 21 Clyde ....2 Dundee ....2 Agg 2-3
Oct 31 Rangers ....2 Hibernian 0
Nov 21 Hibernian ....0 Rangers ....0 Agg 0-2

Semi-finals

Dec 5 Celtic ....3 Rangers 1
played at Hampden Park
Dec 3 Dundee ....1 Kilmarnock 0
played at Hampden Park

Final

Dec 15 Celtic ....0 Dundee 1
played at Hampden Park

Season 1974-75

Section 1

	Arbroath	Clyde	Dumbarton	Partick T
Arbroath	—	Aug17 2-0	Aug14 3-3	Aug28 0-2
Clyde	Aug24 2-1	—	Aug28 1-1	Aug14 2-2
Dumbarton	Aug21 0-2	Aug10 2-3	—	Aug24 3-1
Partick T	Aug10 4-0	Aug21 3-1	Aug17 1-2	—

Section 2

	Dundee	Hibernian	Rangers	St Johnstone
Dundee	—	Aug14 2-1	Aug17 0-2	Aug28 6-1
Hibernian	Aug21 4-2	—	Aug10 3-1	Aug17 4-0
Rangers	Aug24 4-0	Aug28 0-1	—	Aug07 3-2
St Johnstone	Aug10 2-1	Aug24 1-3	Aug14 3-6	—

Section 3

	Aberdeen	Dunfermline A	Hearts	Morton
Aberdeen	—	Aug24 3-0	Aug10 0-1	Aug21 4-0
Dunfermline A	Aug17 1-1	—	Aug21 2-1	Aug10 1-1
Hearts	Aug28 2-1	Aug14 2-3	—	Aug24 2-0
Morton	Aug14 3-1	Aug28 1-1	Aug17 0-5	—

Section 4

	Ayr U	Celtic	Dundee U	Motherwell
Ayr U	—	Aug14 3-2	Aug28 2-2	Aug17 0-3
Celtic	Aug21 5-2	—	Aug17 1-0	Aug10 2-1
Dundee U	Aug10 3-1	Aug24 0-1	—	Aug21 1-0
Motherwell	Aug24 5-0	Aug28 2-2	Aug14 0-0	—

Section 5

	Berwick R	Hamilton A	Queen of South	Raith R
Berwick R	—	Aug28 0-2	Aug17 0-0	Aug14 2-0
Hamilton A	Aug10 4-0	—	Aug21 2-1	Aug17
Queen of South	Aug24 1-0	Aug14 0-2	—	Aug28 2-0
Raith R	Aug21 1-0	Aug24 2-1	Aug10 1-1	—

Section 6

	Kilmarnock	Montrose	Queen's Park	Stranraer
Kilmarnock	—	Aug10 2-0	6-0	2-0
Montrose	Aug28 1-1	—	Aug14 0-0	Aug24 0-2
Queen's Park	Aug17 0-2	Aug21 2-3	—	Aug10 0-0
Stranraer	Aug14 0-5	Aug17 2-4	Aug28 0-0	—

Section 7

	Airdrie	Clydebank	St Mirren	Stirling A
Airdrie		Aug10 4-0	Aug17 0-1	Aug21 3-2
Clydebank	Aug28 1-2		Aug14 2-0	Aug17 3-1
St Mirren	Aug24 0-6	Aug21 1-0		Aug10 3-2
Stirling A	Aug14 2-1	Aug24 5-2	Aug28 0-4	

Section 8

	Alloa	Cowdenbeath	East Fife	Falkirk
Alloa		Aug21 1-0	Aug10 1-2	Aug17 0-1
Cowdenbeath	Aug14 0-0		Aug24 2-0	Aug28 1-3
East Fife	Aug28 5-1	Aug17 2-1		Aug14 1-4
Falkirk	Aug24 3-0	Aug10 4-0	Aug21 1-0	

Section 9

	Albion R	Brechin C	E Stirling	Forfar	Meadowbank T	Stenhousemuir
Albion R		Aug14 6-1				Aug24 5-1
Brechin C				Aug17 1-1		Aug10 2-2
E Stirling	Aug17 1-2	Aug24 3-2			Aug14 3-1	
Forfar A	Aug21 1-5		Aug10 3-3		Aug24 2-1	
Meadowbank T	Aug09 0-1	Aug28 1-4				
Stenhousemuir			Aug28 0-2	Aug14 3-0	Aug17 2-1	

Section 1

	P	W	D	L	F	A	Pts
Partick T	6	3	1	2	13	8	7
Dumbarton	6	2	2	2	11	11	6
Clyde	6	2	2	2	9	11	6
Arbroath	6	2	1	3	8	11	5

Section 2

	P	W	D	L	F	A	Pts
Hibernian	6	5	0	1	16	6	10
Rangers	6	4	0	2	16	9	8
Dundee	6	2	0	4	11	14	4
St Johnstone	6	1	0	5	9	23	2

Section 3

	P	W	D	L	F	A	Pts
Hearts	6	4	0	2	13	6	8
Dunfermline A	6	2	3	1	8	9	7
Aberdeen	6	2	1	3	10	7	5
Morton	6	1	2	3	5	14	4

Section 4

	P	W	D	L	F	A	Pts
Celtic	6	4	1	1	13	8	9
Motherwell	6	2	2	2	11	5	6
Dundee U	6	2	2	2	6	5	6
Ayr U	6	1	1	4	8	20	3

Section 5

	P	W	D	L	F	A	Pts
Hamilton A	6	5	0	1	12	3	10
Queen of South	6	2	2	2	5	5	6
Raith R	6	2	1	3	4	7	5
Berwick R	6	1	1	4	2	8	3

Section 6

	P	W	D	L	F	A	Pts
Kilmarnock	6	5	1	0	18	1	11
Montrose	6	3	2	1	10	7	8
Queen's Park	6	0	3	3	2	11	3
Stranraer	6	0	2	4	2	13	2

Section 7

	P	W	D	L	F	A	Pts
Airdrie	6	4	0	2	16	6	8
St Mirren	6	4	0	2	9	10	8
Stirling A	6	2	0	4	12	16	4
Clydebank	6	2	0	4	8	13	4

Section 8

	P	W	D	L	F	A	Pts
Falkirk	6	6	0	0	16	2	12
East Fife	6	3	0	3	10	10	6
Cowdenbeath	6	1	1	4	4	10	3
Alloa	6	1	1	4	3	11	3

Section 9

	P	W	D	L	F	A	Pts
Albion R	5	5	0	0	19	4	10
E Stirling	5	3	1	1	12	8	7
Stenhousemuir	5	2	1	2	8	10	5
Brechin C	5	1	2	2	10	13	4
Forfar A	5	1	2	2	7	13	4
Meadowbank T	5	0	0	5	4	12	0

Play-offs

Sep 2 Albion R . . . . .1 Falkirk 2
Sep 4 Falkirk . . . . .6 Albion R . . . . . .1 Agg 8-2

Quarter-finals

Sep 11 Celtic . . . . .2 Hamilton A 0
Sep 25 Hamilton A . . . . . .2 Celtic . . . . .4 Agg 2-6
Sep 11 Hearts . . . . .0 Falkirk 0
Sep 25 Falkirk . . . . .1 Hearts . . . . . . .0 Agg 1-0
Sep 11 Kilmarnock . . . . . . .3 Hibernian 3
Sep 25 Hibernian . . . . . . .4 Kilmarnock . . . .1 Agg 7-4
Sep 11 Partick T . . . . .2 Airdrie 5
Sep 25 Airdrie . . . . .1 Partick T . . . . . .1 Agg 6-3

Semi-finals

Oct 9 Airdrie . . . . .0 Celtic 1
      played at Hampden Park
Oct 9 Falkirk . . . . .0 Hibernian 1
      played at Tynecastle

Final

Oct 26 Celtic . . . . .6 Hibernian 3
      played at Hampden Park

Celtic gain revenge for their 1972-73 League Cup Final defeat at the hands of Hibernian as goalkeeper McArthur is beaten by Celtic's Paul Wilson for their third goal in the 6-3 victory at Hampden Park, giving them the 'hat-trick' of domestic honours for that season.

The triumphant Rangers team in the dressing room after their 1-0 victory in the 1975-76 League Cup Final.

Section 1

	Airdrie	Clyde	Motherwell	Rangers
Airdrie		Aug16 2-1	Aug13 2-1	Aug27 1-2
Clyde	Aug23 2-1		Aug27 1-2	Aug13 0-1
Motherwell	Aug20 2-0	Aug09 2-0		Aug23 2-2
Rangers	Aug09 6-1	Aug20 6-0	Aug16 1-1	

Section 2

	Ayr U	Dundee	Dunfermline A	Hibernian
Ayr U		Aug16 1-1	Aug27 2-2	Aug13 2-1
Dundee	Aug23 2-4		Aug13 4-0	Aug27 1-2
Dunfermline A	Aug09 1-1	Aug20 1-1		Aug23 0-4
Hibernian	Aug20 2-1	Aug09 2-0	Aug16 3-0	

Section 3

	Aberdeen	Celtic	Dumbarton	Hearts
Aberdeen		Aug27 0-2	Aug13 2-0	Aug16 1-2
Celtic	Aug09 1-0		Aug16 3-1	Aug20 3-1
Dumbarton	Aug20 0-1	Aug23 0-8		Aug09 2-1
Hearts	Aug23 1-0	Aug13 2-0	Aug27 6-2	

Section 4

	Dundee U	Kilmarnock	Partick T	St Johnstone
Dundee U		Aug16 2-0	Aug20 1-2	Aug09 2-1
Kilmarnock	Aug23 1-0		Aug09 1-3	Aug20 1-0
Partick T	Aug13 3-1	Aug27 2-1		Aug23 3-0
St Johnstone	Aug27 1-2	Aug13 2-1	Aug16 2-4	

Section 5

	Falkirk	Hamilton A	Queen of South	Stirling A
Falkirk		Aug09 0-1	Aug16 0-0	Aug20 2-1
Hamilton A	Aug27 2-2		Aug13 0-2	Aug16 0-0
Queen of South	Aug23 0-1	Aug20 0-3		Aug09 2-0
Stirling A	Aug13 3-0	Aug23 1-0	Aug27 2-3	

Section 6

	East Fife	Montrose	Raith R	St Mirren
East Fife		Aug23 1-1	Aug27 2-2	Aug13 2-0
Montrose	Aug16 4-0		Aug27 2-1	Aug13 1-1
Raith R	Aug20 0-2	Aug09 2-1		Aug16 1-0
St Mirren	Aug09 2-1	Aug20 1-2	Aug23 1-1	

Section 7

	Arbroath	Berwick R	Clydebank	E Stirling
Arbroath		Aug23 2-0	Aug09 4-0	Aug20 3-1
Berwick R	Aug16 1-0		Aug20 0-1	Aug09 1-2
Clydebank	Aug27 1-0	Aug13 3-2		Aug16 1-1
E Stirling	Aug13 0-4	Aug27 2-2	Aug23 0-1	

Section 8

	Albion R	Morton	Stenhousemuir	Stranraer
Albion R		Aug09 0-1	Aug20 0-1	Aug23 2-1
Morton	Aug27 2-1		Aug16 4-1	Aug13 2-5
Stenhousemuir	Aug13 0-0	Aug23 2-1		Aug27 3-2
Stranraer	Aug16 3-2	Aug20 2-1	Aug09 0-0	

Section 9

	Alloa	Brechin C	Cowdenbeath	Forfar A	Meadowbank T	Queen's Park
Alloa			Aug09 1-3			Aug16 1-2
Brechin C	Aug23 2-1			Aug09 1-1		
Cowdenbeath		Aug13 5-2		Aug27 6-2	Aug16 0-2	
Forfar A	Aug13 2-1	Aug16 4-0				
Meadowbank T	Aug18 0-1			Aug23		Aug13 1-2
Queen's Park		Aug27 1-2	Aug23 0-1	Aug09 5-0		

Section 1

	P	W	D	L	F	A	Pts
Rangers	6	4	2	0	18	5	10
Motherwell	6	3	2	1	10	6	8
Airdrie	6	2	0	4	7	14	4
Clyde	6	1	0	5	4	14	2

Section 2

	P	W	D	L	F	A	Pts
Hibernian	6	5	0	1	14	4	10
Ayr U	6	2	3	1	11	9	7
Dundee	6	1	2	3	9	10	4
Dunfermline A	6	0	3	3	4	15	3

Section 3

	P	W	D	L	F	A	Pts
Celtic	6	5	0	1	17	4	10
Hearts	6	4	0	2	13	8	8
Aberdeen	6	2	0	4	4	6	4
Dumbarton	6	1	0	5	5	21	2

Section 4

	P	W	D	L	F	A	Pts
Partick T	6	6	0	0	17	6	12
Dundee U	6	3	0	3	8	8	6
Kilmarnock	6	2	0	4	5	9	4
St Johnstone	6	1	0	5	6	13	2

Section 5

	P	W	D	L	F	A	Pts
Queen of South	6	3	1	2	7	6	7
Hamilton A	6	2	2	2	6	5	6
Falkirk	6	2	2	2	5	6	6
Stirling A	6	2	1	3	7	7	5

Section 6

	P	W	D	L	F	A	Pts
Montrose	6	3	2	1	11	6	8
East Fife	6	2	2	2	8	9	6
Raith R	6	2	2	2	7	6	6
St Mirren	6	1	2	3	5	8	4

Section 7

	P	W	D	L	F	A	Pts
Clydebank	6	4	1	1	7	7	9
Arbroath	6	4	0	2	13	3	8
E Stirling	6	1	2	3	6	12	4
Berwick R	6	1	1	4	4	10	3

Section 8

	P	W	D	L	F	A	Pts
Stenhousemuir	6	3	2	1	7	7	8
Stranraer	6	3	1	2	13	10	7
Morton	6	3	0	3	11	11	6
Albion R	6	1	1	4	5	8	3

Section 9

	P	W	D	L	F	A	Pts
Cowdenbeath	5	4	0	1	15	7	8
Queen's Park	5	3	0	2	10	5	6
Meadowbank T	5	2	1	2	8	5	5
Brechin C	5	2	1	2	7	12	5
Forfar A	5	2	0	3	9	16	4
Alloa	5	1	0	4	5	9	2

Play-offs

Sep 2 Cowdenbeath ......0 Clydebank 2
Sep 3 Clydebank ....2 Cowdenbeath ....0 Agg 4-0

Quarter-finals Agg

Sep 10 Hibernian ....1 Montrose 0
Sep 24 Montrose ....3 Hibernian ......1 Agg 3-2
Sep 10 Partick T ....4 Clydebank 0
Sep 24 Clydebank ....1 Partick T ....1 Agg 1-4
Sep 10 Rangers ....1 Queen of South ..0
Sep 24 Queen of South ..2 Rangers ....2 Agg 2-3
Sep 10 Stenhousemuir ....0 Celtic 2
Sep 24 Celtic ....1 Stenhousemuir ..0 Agg 3-0

Semi-finals

Oct 6 Celtic ....1 Partick T 0
played at Hampden Park
Oct 8 Montrose ....1 Rangers 5
played at Hampden Park

Final

Oct 25 Celtic ....0 Rangers 1
played at Hampden Park

Season 1976-77

Section 1

	Dundee	Hearts	Motherwell	Partick T
Dundee		Sep01 3-2	Aug18 2-1	Aug21 0-2
Hearts	Aug14 2-0		Aug21 2-1	Aug25 3-3
Motherwell	Aug25 3-3	Aug28 1-4		Aug14 1-1
Partick T	Aug28 0-1	Aug18 0-2	Sep01 2-0	

Section 2

	Aberdeen	Ayr U	Kilmarnock	St Mirren
Aberdeen		Aug21 1-0	Aug14 2-0	Aug25 4-0
Ayr U	Aug28 1-1		Aug25 3-1	Aug14 2-1
Kilmarnock	Sep01 2-1	Aug18 2-0		Aug21 1-1
St Mirren	Aug18 2-3	Sep01 2-2	Aug28 1-0	

Section 3

	Arbroath	Celtic	Dumbarton	Dundee U
Arbroath		Aug21 0-5	Sep01 0-3	Aug18 1-3
Celtic	Aug28 2-1		Aug18 3-0	Sep01 1-1
Dumbarton	Aug14 2-0	Aug25 3-3		Aug21 1-2
Dundee U	Aug25 2-0	Aug14 0-1	Aug28 1-1	

Section 4

	Hibernian	Montrose	Rangers	St Johnstone
Hibernian		Sep01 0-0	Aug18 1-1	Aug28 9-2
Montrose	Aug14 0-1		Aug28 0-3	Aug25 5-1
Rangers	Aug25 3-0	Aug21 4-0		Aug14 5-0
St Johnstone	Aug21 1-2	Aug18 0-0	Sep01 0-1	

Section 5

	Airdrie	Clyde	Queen's Park	Raith R
Airdrie		Aug28 1-0	Aug14 3-1	Aug25 7-1
Clyde	Aug21 2-3		Aug25 1-2	Aug14 1-1
Queen's Park	Sep01 2-1	Aug18 3-5		Aug28 0-4
Raith R	Aug18 1-4	Sep01 1-1	Aug21 0-1	

Section 6

	East Fife	Falkirk	Hamilton A	Stranraer
East Fife		Aug28 1-5	Aug25 3-0	Aug14 3-0
Falkirk	Aug21 1-2		Aug14 1-0	Aug25 5-1
Hamilton A	Aug18 5-0	Sep01 1-2		Aug21 6-1
Stranraer	Sep01 5-0	Aug18 5-0	Aug28 3-3	

Section 7

	Cowdenbeath	E Stirling	Morton	Stirling A
Cowdenbeath		Aug14 2-1	Aug28 0-0	Aug25 0-1
E Stirling	Sep01 4-0		Aug18 1-1	Aug28 0-6
Morton	Aug21 7-1	Aug25 1-1		Aug14 1-0
Stirling A	Aug18 0-0	Aug21 1-1	Sep01 3-2	

Section 8

	Alloa	Clydebank	Dunfermline A	Queen of South
Alloa		Aug14 1-0	Aug25 4-0	Aug28 1-0
Clydebank	Sep01 1-0		Aug28 2-0	Aug18 1-0
Dunfermline A	Aug18 3-0	Aug21 0-1		Sep01 0-0
Queen of South	Aug21 2-2	Aug25 1-4	Aug14 1-0	

Section 9

	Albion R	Berwick R	Brechin C	Forfar A	Meadowbank T	Stenhousemuir
Albion R				Aug18 1-0	Aug21 0-0	
Berwick R	Aug14 1-1		Aug21 1-1			
Brechin C	Aug28 0-2	Aug18 3-1				Aug21 2-0
Forfar A			Aug25 0-2		Aug28 2-3	Aug14 0-3
Meadowbank T			Aug25 1-1	Aug14 0-0		
Stenhousemuir	Aug25 1-3	Aug28 0-0			Aug18 1-1	

Section 1

	P	W	D	L	F	A	Pts
Hearts	6	4	1	1	15	8	9
Dundee	6	3	1	2	9	10	7
Partick T	6	2	2	2	8	7	6
Motherwell	6	0	2	4	7	14	2

Section 2

	P	W	D	L	F	A	Pts
Aberdeen	6	4	1	1	12	5	9
Ayr U	6	2	2	2	8	8	6
Kilmarnock	6	2	1	3	6	8	5
St Mirren	6	1	2	3	7	12	4

Section 3

	P	W	D	L	F	A	Pts
Celtic	6	4	2	0	15	5	10
Dundee U	6	3	2	1	9	5	8
Dumbarton	6	2	2	2	10	9	6
Arbroath	6	0	0	6	2	17	0

Section 4

	P	W	D	L	F	A	Pts
Rangers	6	5	1	0	17	1	11
Hibernian	6	3	2	1	13	7	8
Montrose	6	1	2	3	5	9	4
St Johnstone	6	0	1	5	4	22	1

Section 5

	P	W	D	L	F	A	Pts
Airdrie	6	5	0	1	19	7	10
Queen's Park	6	3	0	3	9	14	6
Clyde	6	1	2	3	10	11	4
Raith R	6	1	2	3	8	14	4

Section 6

	P	W	D	L	F	A	Pts
Falkirk	6	4	0	2	14	10	8
Hamilton A	6	2	2	2	16	8	6
Stranraer	6	2	1	3	15	17	5
East Fife	6	2	1	3	7	17	5

Section 7

	P	W	D	L	F	A	Pts
Stirling A	6	3	2	1	11	4	8
Morton	6	2	3	1	12	6	7
E Stirling	6	1	3	2	8	11	5
Cowdenbeath	6	1	2	3	3	13	4

Section 8

	P	W	D	L	F	A	Pts
Clydebank	6	5	0	1	9	2	10
Alloa	6	3	1	2	8	6	7
Queen of South	6	1	2	3	4	8	4
Dunfermline A	6	1	1	4	3	8	3

Section 9

	P	W	D	L	F	A	Pts
Albion R	5	3	2	0	7	2	8
Brechin C	5	3	1	1	7	3	7
Meadowbank T	5	1	4	0	5	4	6
Stenhousemuir	5	1	2	2	5	6	4
Berwick R	5	0	4	1	4	6	4
Forfar A	5	0	1	4	3	10	1

Play-offs
Sep 6 Airdrie ....3 Albion R 2
Sep 8 Albion R ....3 Airdrie ....1 Agg 5-4

Quarter-finals
Sep 22 Aberdeen ....1 Stirling A 0
Oct 6 Stirling A ....1 Aberdeen ....0 Agg 1-1
Sep 22 Albion R ....0 Celtic 1
Oct 6 Celtic ....5 Albion R ......0 Agg 6-0
Sep 22 Hearts ....1 Falkirk 1
Oct 6 Falkirk ....4 Hearts ....3 Agg 5-7
Sep 22 Rangers ....3 Clydebank 3
Oct 6 Clydebank ....1 Rangers ....1 Agg 4-4

Replays
Oct 18 Aberdeen ....2 Stirling A 0
played at Dens Park
Oct 18 Rangers ....0 Clydebank 0
Oct 19 Clydebank ....1 Rangers 2
played at Firhill Park

Semi-finals
Oct 27 Aberdeen ....5 Rangers 1
played at Hampden Park
Oct 25 Celtic ....2 Hearts 1
played at Hampden Park

Final
Nov 6 Aberdeen ....2 Celtic 1
played at Hampden Park

1st Round
Aug 17 Aberdeen ....3 Airdrie 1
Aug 24 Airdrie ....0 Aberdeen ....2 Agg 1-5
Aug 17 Alloa ....5 Stranraer 3
Aug 24 Stranraer ....3 Alloa ....0 Agg 6-5
Aug 17 Clydebank ....5 East Fife 0
Aug 24 East Fife ....0 Clydebank .....1 Agg 0-6
Aug 17 Dundee U ....5 Albion R 0
Aug 23 Albion R ....1 Dundee U ......5 Agg 1-10
Aug 17 Hibernian ....1 Queen of South .2
Aug 24 Queen of South ...0 Hibernian ......0 Agg 2-1
Aug 17 Montrose ....1 Dundee 3
Aug 24 Dundee ....1 Montrose ......0 Agg 4-1

2nd Round
Aug 31 Aberdeen ....5 Cowdenbeath 0
Sep 3 Cowdenbeath .....0 Aberdeen ....5 Agg 0-10
Aug 30 Ayr U ....1 Queen's Park ...0
Sep 3 Queen's Park ....1 Ayr U ....0 Agg 1-1
Penalties 2-4
Aug 31 Celtic ....0 Motherwell 0
Sep 3 Motherwell ....2 Celtic ....4 Agg 2-4
Aug 29 Clyde ....0 Dunfermline A ..0
Sep 3 Dunfermline A ...2 Clyde ....1 Agg 2-1
Aug 31 Clydebank ....0 Stranraer 0
Sep 3 Stranraer ....0 Clydebank .....1 Agg 0-1
Aug 31 Dumbarton ....4 Hamilton A 1
Sep 3 Hamilton A ......6 Dumbarton .....0 Agg 7-4
Aug 31 Dundee ....4 Berwick R 0
Sep 3 Berwick R ....1 Dundee ....1 Agg 1-5

Aug 31 E Stirling ....0 Stirling A 1
Sep 3 Stirling A ....0 E Stirling ....0 Agg 1-0
Aug 29 Hearts ....1 Stenhousemuir ..0
Sep 3 Stenhousemuir ....0 Hearts ....5 Agg 0-6
Aug 31 Kilmarnock ....0 St Mirren 0
Sep 3 St Mirren ....1 Kilmarnock .....1 Agg 2-1
Aug 31 Meadowbank T ....2 Forfar A 2
Sep 3 Forfar A ....2 Meadowbank T ..0 Agg 4-2
Aug 31 Morton ....0 Falkirk 1
Sep 3 Falkirk ....2 Morton ....3 Agg 2-3
Penalties 4-2
Aug 31 Partick T ....0 Dundee U 0
Sep 3 Dundee U ....1 Partick T ......0 Agg 1-0
Aug 31 Queen of South ...2 Brechin C 0
Sep 3 Brechin C ....2 Queen of South .2 Agg 2-4
Aug 31 Raith R ....0 Arbroath 1
Sep 3 Arbroath ....3 Raith R ....1 Agg 4-1
Aug 24 Rangers ....3 St Johnstone 1
Sep 3 St Johnstone .....0 Rangers ....3 Agg 1-6

3rd Round
Oct 5 Arbroath ....0 Dundee U 4
Oct 26 Dundee U ....2 Arbroath ....1 Agg 6-1
Oct 5 Ayr U ....2 Forfar A 1
Oct 26 Forfar A ....0 Ayr U ....1 Agg 4-3
Oct 5 Dundee ....0 Queen of South ..0
Oct 26 Queen of South ...6 Dundee ....0 Agg 6-0
Oct 5 Dunfermline A ....2 Clydebank 0
Oct 26 Clydebank ....2 Dunfermline A ..2 Agg 2-4
Oct 5 Hamilton A ....0 St Mirren 2
Oct 26 St Mirren ....1 Hamilton A ....2 Agg 3-2

Oct 5 Hearts ....3 Morton 0
Oct 26 Morton ....2 Hearts ....0 Agg 2-3
Oct 5 Rangers ....2 Aberdeen 1
Oct 26 Aberdeen ....3 Rangers ....1 Agg 4-7
Oct 5 Stirling A ....1 Celtic 2
Oct 26 Celtic ....1 Stirling A ......1 Agg 3-2

4th Round
Nov 9 Dundee U ....3 Hearts 1
Nov 16 Hearts ....2 Dundee U ......0 Agg 3-3
Penalties 4-2
Nov 8 Queen of South ...3 Forfar A 3
Nov 16 Forfar A ....1 Queen of South ..0 Agg 4-3
Nov 9 Rangers ....3 Dunfermline A ..1
Nov 16 Dunfermline A ....1 Rangers ....3 Agg 2-6
Nov 9 St Mirren ....1 Celtic 3
Nov 16 Celtic ....2 St Mirren ......0 Agg 5-1

Semi-finals
Mar 1 Celtic ....2 Hearts 0
played at Hampden Park
Feb 27 Forfar A ....2 Rangers 5
played at Hampden Park

Final
Mar 18 Celtic ....1 Rangers 2
played at Hampden Park

1st Round
Aug 16 Alloa ....4 Stirling A 1
Aug 23 Stirling A ....0 Alloa ....1 Agg 1-5
Aug 16 Berwick R ....2 St Johnstone ...0
Aug 23 St Johnstone .....0 Berwick R ......0 Agg 0-2
Aug 16 Celtic ....3 Dundee 1
Aug 23 Dundee ....0 Celtic ....3 Agg 1-6
Aug 16 Dumbarton ....0 St Mirren 0
Aug 23 St Mirren ....2 Dumbarton .....0 Agg 2-0
Aug 16 Montrose ....4 Queen of South .0
Aug 23 Queen of South ...0 Montrose ......1 Agg 0-5
Aug 16 Rangers ....3 Albion R 0
Aug 23 Albion R ....0 Rangers ....1 Agg 0-4

2nd Round
Aug 30 Airdrie ....3 Dunfermline A ..0
Sep 2 Dunfermline A ....0 Airdrie ....5 Agg 0-8
Aug 30 Ayr U ....1 Stranraer 0
Sep 2 Stranraer ....1 Ayr U ....3 Agg 1-4
Aug 30 Berwick R ....1 St Mirren 3
Sep 2 St Mirren ....5 Berwick R ......1 Agg 8-2
Aug 30 Brechin C ....0 Hibernian 3
Sep 2 Hibernian ....6 Brechin C ......0 Agg 6-1
Aug 30 Clyde ....3 Motherwell 1
Sep 2 Motherwell ....0 Clyde ....0 Agg 4-3
Aug 30 Cowdenbeath .....3 Hamilton A 0
Sep 2 Hamilton A ....2 Cowdenbeath ...0 Agg 4-3
Aug 30 Dundee U ....2 Celtic 3
Sep 2 Celtic ....1 Dundee U ......0 Agg 4-2
Aug 30 East Fife ....0 Arbroath 1

Sep 2 Arbroath ....1 East Fife ......0 Agg 2-0
Aug 30 Hearts ....1 Morton 3
Sep 2 Morton ....4 Hearts ....1 Agg 7-2
Aug 30 Kilmarnock ....2 Alloa 0
Sep 2 Alloa ....1 Kilmarnock .....1 Agg 1-3
Aug 30 Meadowbank T ....0 Aberdeen 5
Sep 2 Aberdeen ....4 Meadowbank T ..0 Agg 9-0
Aug 28 Montrose ....0 E Stirling 1
Sep 2 E Stirling ....0 Montrose ......2 Agg 1-3
Aug 30 Partick T ....1 Falkirk 1
Sep 2 Falkirk ....2 Partick T ......2 Agg 3-3
Penalties
Aug 30 Raith R ....4 Queen's Park ...2
Sep 2 Queen's Park .....4 Raith R ....2 Agg 6-6
Penalties
Aug 30 Rangers ....3 Forfar A 0
Sep 2 Forfar A ....1 Rangers ....4 Agg 1-7
Aug 30 Stenhousemuir ...1 Clydebank 0
Sep 2 Clydebank ....4 Stenhousemuir ..1 Agg 4-2

3rd Round
Oct 4 Arbroath ....1 Airdrie 1
Oct 10 Airdrie ....3 Arbroath ....2 Agg 2-3
Oct 4 Celtic ....0 Motherwell 1
Oct 11 Motherwell ....1 Celtic ....4 Agg 2-4
Oct 4 Falkirk ....0 Ayr U 2
Oct 11 Ayr U ....1 Falkirk ....1 Agg 3-1
Oct 4 Hamilton A ....0 Aberdeen 1
Oct 11 Aberdeen ....7 Hamilton A ....1 Agg 8-1
Oct 4 Hibernian ....1 Clydebank 0

Oct 11 Clydebank ....1 Hibernian ......1 Agg 1-2
Oct 4 Kilmarnock ....2 Morton 2
Oct 11 Morton ....5 Kilmarnock ....2 Agg 5-4
Oct 4 Raith R ....3 Montrose 0
Oct 11 Montrose ....5 Raith R ....1 Agg 5-4
Oct 4 Rangers ....3 St Mirren 2
Oct 11 St Mirren ....0 Rangers ....0 Agg 2-3

4th Round
Nov 8 Ayr U ....3 Aberdeen 3
Nov 15 Aberdeen ....3 Ayr U ....1 Agg 6-4
Nov 8 Montrose ....1 Celtic 3
Nov 15 Celtic ....3 Montrose ......1 Agg 4-2
Nov 8 Montrose ....1 Hibernian 0
Nov 15 Hibernian ....2 Morton ....0 Agg 2-1
Nov 8 Rangers ....1 Arbroath 0
Nov 15 Arbroath ....1 Rangers ....2 Agg 1-3

Semi-finals
Dec 13 Aberdeen ....1 Hibernian 0
played at Dens Park
Dec 13 Celtic ....2 Rangers 3
played at Hampden Park

Final
Mar 31 Aberdeen ....1 Rangers 2
played at Hampden Park

208

Season 1979-80

1st Round
Aug 15 Aberdeen ....4 Arbroath 0
Aug 22 Arbroath ....2 Aberdeen ....1 Agg 2-5
Aug 15 Dumbarton ....1 St Johnstone 1
Aug 22 St Johnstone .....3 Dumbarton ....2 Agg 4-3
Aug 15 E Stirling ....1 Albion R 1
Aug 27 Albion R ....4 E Stirling ....1 Agg 5-2
Aug 15 Forfar A ....3 Berwick R 2
Aug 22 Berwick R ....2 Forfar A ....2 Agg 4-5
Aug 15 Kilmarnock ....2 Alloa 1
Aug 22 Alloa ....1 Kilmarnock .....1 Agg 2-3
Aug 15 Stranraer ....0 Dunfermline A ...0
Aug 22 Dunfermline A ....2 Stranraer ......4 Agg 2-4

2nd Round
Aug 29 Airdrie ....2 Dundee U 1
Sep 1 Dundee U ....2 Airdrie ....0 Agg 3-2
Sep 1 Ayr U ....2 Hearts 2
Sep 3 Hearts ....0 Ayr U ....1 Agg 2-3
Aug 29 Clyde ....1 Rangers 2
Sep 1 Rangers ....4 Clyde ....0 Agg 6-1
Aug 29 Clydebank ....0 Hamilton A 0
Sep 2 Hamilton A ....1 Clydebank ......0 Agg 1-0
Sep 1 Dundee ....3 Cowdenbeath ....1 Agg 7-2
Aug 29 Cowdenbeath .....1 Dundee 4
Aug 29 Falkirk ....1 Celtic 2
Sep 1 Celtic ....4 Falkirk ....2 Agg 6-2
Aug 29 Hibernian ....2 Montrose 1
Sep 1 Montrose ....1 Hibernian ......1 Agg 2-3
Aug 29 Kilmarnock ....2 Forfar A 0
Sep 1 Forfar A ....1 Kilmarnock .....1 Agg 1-3

Aug 29 Meadowbank T ....0 Aberdeen 5
Sep 1 Aberdeen ....2 Meadowbank T ...2 Agg 7-2
Aug 29 Motherwell ......1 Queen's Park 4
Sep 1 Queen's Park .....0 Motherwell ....2 Agg 4-3
Aug 29 Partick T ....0 Albion R 2
Sep 1 Albion R ....0 Partick T ......1 Agg 2-3
Aug 29 Queen of South ...0 Morton 1
Sep 1 Morton ....4 Queen of South .0 Agg 5-0
Aug 29 Raith R ....1 East Fife 0
Sep 1 East Fife ....0 Raith R ....2 Agg 0-3
Aug 29 St Johnstone .....3 Stranraer 1
Aug 28 Stenhousemuir ...1 St Mirren 4
Sep 1 St Mirren ....4 Stenhousemuir ..2 Agg 8-3
Aug 29 Stirling A ....3 Brechin C 1
Sep 1 Brechin C ....0 Stirling A ......1 Agg 1-4

3rd Round
Sep 26 Aberdeen ....3 Rangers 1
Oct 10 Rangers ....0 Aberdeen ....2 Agg 1-5
Sep 26 Dundee ....2 Ayr U 1
Oct 10 Ayr U ....0 Dundee ....1 Agg 1-3
Sep 26 Hamilton A ....1 St Mirren 3
Oct 10 St Mirren   0 Hamilton A .....2 Agg 3-3
Penalties 2-4
Sep 26 Hibernian ....1 Kilmarnock 2
Oct 10 Kilmarnock ....2 Hibernian ......1 Agg 4-2
Sep 26 Partick T ....0 Morton 1
Oct 10 Morton ....4 Partick T ......1 Agg 5-1
Sep 26 Queen's Park .....0 Dundee U 3
Oct 10 Dundee U ....2 Queen's Park ...1 Agg 5-1

Sep 26 Raith R ....1 St Johnstone 1
Oct 10 St Johnstone .....1 Raith R ....3 Agg 2-4
Sep 26 Stirling A ....1 Celtic 2
Oct 10 Celtic ....2 Stirling A ......0 Agg 4-1

4th Round
Oct 31 Aberdeen ....3 Celtic 2
Nov 24 Celtic ....0 Aberdeen ....1 Agg 2-4
Oct 31 Dundee U ....0 Raith R 0
Nov 14 Raith R ....0 Dundee U ....1 Agg 0-1
Oct 31 Hamilton A ....3 Dundee 1
Nov 14 Dundee ....1 Hamilton A .....0 Agg 2-3
Oct 31 Morton ....3 Kilmarnock 2
Nov 24 Kilmarnock ....3 Morton ....2 Agg 5-5
Penalties 4-5

Semi-finals
Dec 1 Aberdeen ....2 Morton 1
played at Hampden Park
Nov 24 Dundee U ....6 Hamilton A 2
played at East End Park

Final
Dec 8 Aberdeen ....0 Dundee U 0
played at Hampden Park

Replay
Dec 12 Aberdeen ....0 Dundee U 3
played at Dens Park

Season 1980-81

1st Round
Aug 13 Ayr U ....1 Morton 2
Aug 20 Morton ....0 Ayr U ....2 Agg 2-3
Aug 13 East Fife ....2 Dundee U 5
Aug 20 Dundee U ....4 East Fife ......0 Agg 9-2
Aug 13 Kilmarnock ....1 Airdrie 0
Aug 20 Airdrie ....0 Kilmarnock .....1 Agg 0-2
Aug 13 Queen's Park .....1 E Stirling 0
Aug 19 E Stirling ....0 Queen's Park ...4 Agg 0-5
Aug 13 Raith R ....3 Falkirk 2
Aug 20 Falkirk ....2 Raith R ....2 Agg 2-5
Aug 13 St Johnstone .....0 Clydebank 2
Aug 20 Clydebank ....0 St Johnstone ...0 Agg 2-0

2nd Round
Aug 27 Aberdeen ....8 Berwick R 1
Aug 30 Berwick R ....0 Aberdeen ....4 Agg 1-12
Aug 26 Albion R ....1 St Mirren 2
Aug 30 St Mirren ....5 Albion R ....0 Agg 7-1
Aug 27 Alloa ....0 Hibernian 2
Aug 30 Hibernian ....1 Alloa ....0 Agg 3-1
Aug 27 Brechin C ....0 Clyde 0
Aug 30 Clyde ....2 Brechin C ......1 Agg 2-1
Aug 27 Dumbarton ....0 Raith R 1
Aug 30 Raith R ....1 Dumbarton ......1 Agg 2-1
Aug 26 Dundee ....2 Arbroath 0
Aug 30 Arbroath ....0 Dundee ....3 Agg 0-5
Aug 27 Dundee U ....4 Cowdenbeath 0
Aug 30 Cowdenbeath ......1 Dundee U ....4 Agg 1-8
Aug 27 Forfar A ....0 Rangers 2

Aug 30 Rangers ....3 Forfar A ....1 Agg 5-1
Aug 27 Hamilton A ....5 Stranraer 1
Aug 30 Stranraer ....0 Hamilton A .....2 Agg 1-7
Aug 27 Hearts ....0 Montrose 1
Aug 30 Montrose ....1 Hearts ....3 Agg 2-5
Aug 27 Kilmarnock ....0 Dunfermline A ...0
Aug 30 Dunfermline A ....1 Kilmarnock .....2 Agg 1-2
Aug 27 Meadowbank T ....1 Clydebank 2
Aug 30 Clydebank ....2 Meadowbank T ...1 Agg 4-2
Aug 27 Partick T ....3 Queen's Park ...1
Aug 30 Queen's Park .....1 Partick T ......1 Agg 2-4
Aug 27 Queen of South ...1 Ayr U 2
Aug 30 Ayr U ....1 Queen of South .0 Agg 3-1
Aug 27 Stenhousemuir ....0 Motherwell 1
Aug 30 Motherwell ....6 Stenhousemuir ..1 Agg 6-1
Aug 27 Stirling A ....1 Celtic 0
Aug 30 Celtic ....6 Stirling A ......1 Agg 6-2

3rd Round
Sep 3 Clyde ....0 Hibernian 2
Sep 24 Hibernian ....2 Clyde ....1 Agg 4-1
Sep 3 Dundee ....0 Kilmarnock 0
Sep 24 Kilmarnock ....0 Dundee ....0 Agg 0-0
Penalties 3-5
Sep 22 Hamilton A ....1 Celtic 3
Sep 24 Celtic ....4 Hamilton A .....1 Agg 7-2
Sep 3 Hearts ....2 Ayr U 3
Sep 24 Ayr U ....4 Hearts ....0 Agg 7-2
Sep 3 Motherwell ....2 Dundee U 1
Sep 24 Dundee U ....4 Motherwell ....2 Agg 5-4

Sep 3 Partick T ....2 St Mirren 0
Sep 24 St Mirren ....0 Partick T ......0 Agg 0-2
Sep 3 Raith R ....0 Clydebank 1
Sep 24 Clydebank ....1 Raith R ....0 Agg 2-0
Sep 3 Rangers ....1 Aberdeen 0
Sep 24 Aberdeen ....3 Rangers ....1 Agg 3-2

4th Round
Oct 8 Ayr U ....2 Hibernian 2
Oct 22 Hibernian ....0 Ayr U ....2 Agg 2-4
Oct 8 Clydebank ....2 Dundee U 1
Oct 29 Dundee U ....4 Clydebank ......1 Agg 5-3
Oct 8 Dundee ....0 Aberdeen 0
Oct 29 Aberdeen ....0 Dundee ....1 Agg 0-1
Oct 8 Partick T ....0 Celtic 1
Oct 20 Celtic ....2 Partick T ......1 Agg 3-1

Semi-finals
Nov 5 Ayr U ....1 Dundee 1
Nov 19 Dundee ....3 Ayr U ....2 Agg 4-3
Nov 12 Dundee U ....1 Celtic 1
Nov 19 Celtic ....0 Dundee U ....3 Agg 1-4

Final
Dec 6 Dundee ....0 Dundee U 3
played at Dens Park

Season 1981-82

Section 1

Section 1	Celtic	Hibernian	St Johnstone	St Mirren
Celtic		Aug15 4-1	Aug19 4-1	Aug08 1-3
Hibernian	Aug26 1-4		Aug08 1-2	Aug19 0-1
St Johnstone	Aug12 2-0	Aug22 1-2		Aug15 2-3
St Mirren	Aug22 1-5	Aug12 0-0	Aug26 2-0	

Section 2

Section 2	Dundee	Morton	Raith R	Rangers
Dundee		Aug15 1-2	Aug08 1-2	Aug19 1-2
Morton	Aug26 3-2		Aug19 2-0	Aug08 1-1
Raith R	Aug22 1-1	Aug12 2-5		Aug26 1-3
Rangers	Aug12 4-1	Aug22 1-0	Aug15 8-1	

Section 3

Section 3	Aberdeen	Airdrie	Hearts	Kilmarnock
Aberdeen		Aug15 3-0	Aug19 3-0	Aug08 3-0
Airdrie	Aug26 0-0		Aug08 0-1	Aug19 0-1
Hearts	Aug12 1-0	Aug22 2-3		Aug15 1-1
Kilmarnock	Aug22 0-3	Aug12 1-1	Aug26 2-0	

Section 4

Section 4	Ayr U	Dundee U	Motherwell	Partick T
Ayr U		Aug15 3-4	Aug19 1-0	Aug15 1-0
Dundee U	Aug22 2-1		Aug26 1-1	Aug12 2-0
Motherwell	Aug12 2-3	Aug15 1-2		Aug22 0-1
Partick T	Aug26 1-5	Aug19 1-2	Aug08 2-0	

Section 5

Section 5	Brechin C	Cowdenbeath	Dumbarton	Queen of South
Brechin C		Aug12 2-0	Aug15 2-1	Aug22 1-2
Cowdenbeath	Aug19 4-0		Aug08 2-0	Aug15 1-2
Dumbarton	Aug26 1-3	Aug22 3-0		Aug12 1-0
Queen of South	Aug08 1-3	Aug26 2-2	Aug19 3-2	

Section 6

Section 6	Alloa	Falkirk	Forfar A	Stirling A
Alloa		Aug12 1-1	Aug22 0-2	Aug15 4-3
Falkirk	Aug19 3-0		Aug15 1-0	Aug08 4-1
Forfar A	Aug08 4-1	Aug26 3-2		Aug19 1-0
Stirling A	Aug26 2-2	Aug22 0-0	Aug12 0-1	

Section 7 (1981-82)

	Berwick R	Clyde	Clydebank	Queen's Park
Berwick R		Aug08 2-1	Aug19 3-1	Aug26 3-0
Clyde	Aug22 2-2		Aug15 3-0	Aug12 0-3
Clydebank	Aug12 2-2	Aug26 1-0		Aug22 4-1
Queen's Park	Aug15 2-0	Aug19 1-0	Aug08 1-0	

Section 8

	Dunfermline A	E Stirling	Hamilton A	Montrose
Dunfermline A		Aug15 2-1	Aug22 2-3	Aug12 2-1
E Stirling	Aug26 0-1		Aug12 0-2	Aug22 1-2
Hamilton A	Aug08 2-0	Aug19 1-0		Aug26 4-2
Montrose	Aug19 0-1	Aug08 1-0	Aug15 1-2	

Section 9

	Albion R	Arbroath	East Fife	Meadowbank T	Stenhousemuir	Stranraer
Albion R			Aug13 1-1		Aug15 5-2	
Arbroath	Aug22 4-0				Aug08 3-0	Aug15 4-0
East Fife		Aug19 1-1		Aug15 0-1		
Meadowbank T	Aug08 2-2	Aug12 1-3				Aug19 1-1
Stenhousemuir			Aug22 2-3			Aug12 2-3
Stranraer	Aug19 2-0		Aug08 1-3	Aug22 1-2		

Section 1	P	W	D	L	F	A	Pts
St Mirren	6	4	1	1	10	8	9
Celtic	6	4	0	2	18	9	8
St Johnstone	6	2	0	4	8	12	4
Hibernian	6	1	1	4	5	12	3

Section 2	P	W	D	L	F	A	Pts
Rangers	6	5	1	0	19	5	11
Morton	6	4	1	1	13	7	9
Raith R	6	1	1	4	7	20	3
Dundee	6	0	1	5	7	14	1

Section 3	P	W	D	L	F	A	Pts
Aberdeen	6	4	1	1	12	1	9
Kilmarnock	6	2	2	2	5	8	6
Hearts	6	2	1	3	5	9	5
Airdrie	6	1	2	3	4	8	4

Section 4	P	W	D	L	F	A	Pts
Dundee U	6	5	1	0	13	7	11
Ayr U	6	4	0	2	14	9	8
Partick T	6	2	0	4	5	10	4
Motherwell	6	0	1	5	4	10	1

Section 5	P	W	D	L	F	A	Pts
Brechin C	6	4	0	2	11	9	8
Queen of South	6	3	1	2	10	10	7
Cowdenbeath	6	2	1	3	9	9	5
Dumbarton	6	2	0	4	8	10	4

Section 6	P	W	D	L	F	A	Pts
Forfar A	6	5	0	1	11	4	10
Falkirk	6	3	2	1	11	5	8
Alloa	6	1	2	3	8	15	4
Stirling A	6	0	2	4	6	12	2

Section 7	P	W	D	L	F	A	Pts
Berwick R	6	3	2	1	12	8	8
Queen's Park	6	4	0	2	8	7	8
Clydebank	6	2	1	3	8	10	5
Clyde	6	1	1	4	6	9	3

Section 8	P	W	D	L	F	A	Pts
Hamilton A	6	6	0	0	14	5	12
Dunfermline A	6	4	0	2	8	7	8
Montrose	6	2	0	4	7	10	4
E Stirling	6	0	0	6	2	9	0

Section 9	P	W	D	L	F	A	Pts
Arbroath	5	4	1	0	15	2	9
East Fife	5	2	2	1	8	6	6
Meadowbank T	5	2	2	1	7	7	6
Albion R	5	1	2	2	8	11	4
Stranraer	5	2	0	3	7	11	4
Stenhousemuir	5	0	1	4	4	15	1

Play-offs
Aug 31 Arbroath ....1 Forfar A 2
Sep 2 Forfar A ....2 Arbroath ....2 Agg 4-3

Quarter-finals
Sep 2 Aberdeen ....5 Berwick R 0
Sep 23 Berwick R ....0 Aberdeen ....3 Agg 0-8
Sep 2 Brechin C ....0 Rangers 4
Sep 23 Rangers ....1 Brechin C ....0 Agg 5-0
Sep 16 Forfar A ....1 St Mirren 1
Sep 23 St Mirren ....6 Forfar A ......0 Agg 7-1
Sep 2 Hamilton A ....0 Dundee U 4
Sep 23 Dundee U ....5 Hamilton A ......0 Agg 9-0

Semi-finals
Oct 7 Dundee U ....0 Aberdeen 1
Oct 28 Aberdeen ....0 Dundee U ....3 Agg 1-3
Oct 7 St Mirren ....2 Rangers 2
Oct 28 Rangers ....2 St Mirren ......1 Agg 4-3

Final
Nov 28 Dundee U ....1 Rangers 2
played at Hampden Park

Season 1982-83

Section 1

	Alloa	Arbroath	Celtic	Dunfermline A
Alloa		Aug28 0-1	Aug18 0-5	Sep01 3-0
Arbroath	Aug14 1-2		Aug21 0-3	Aug25 1-0
Celtic	Aug25 4-1	Sep01 4-1		Aug14 6-0
Dunfermline A	Aug21 2-1	Aug18 0-0	Aug28 1-7	

Section 2

	Aberdeen	Dumbarton	Dundee	Morton
Aberdeen		Aug21 3-0	Aug14 3-3	Aug25 3-0
Dumbarton	Sep08 1-2		Aug25 2-3	Aug14 1-3
Dundee	Aug28 1-5	Aug18 3-2		Sep01 3-3
Morton	Aug11 2-2	Aug28 4-1	Aug21 4-1	

Section 3

	Airdrie	Clydebank	Hibernian	Rangers
Airdrie		Aug14 1-3	Sep01 3-1	Aug25 1-2
Clydebank	Aug28 1-2		Aug18 0-2	Aug21 1-4
Hibernian	Aug21 1-1	Aug25 1-1		Aug14
Rangers	Aug18 3-1	Sep01 3-2	Aug28 0-0	

Section 4

	Dundee U	Falkirk	Raith R	St Johnstone
Dundee U		Aug25 4-0	Aug21 5-1	Aug14 3-0
Falkirk	Aug18 0-4		Aug28 2-0	Aug21 1-6
Raith R	Sep01 1-3	Aug14 1-0		Aug25 3-3
St Johnstone	Aug28 0-3	Sep01 1-0	Aug18 5-0	

Section 5

	Clyde	Forfar A	Hearts	Motherwell
Clyde		Aug28 0-1	Aug21 1-7	Aug18 3-3
Forfar A	Aug14 2-0		Aug25 0-2	Sep01 2-1
Hearts	Sep01 3-0	Aug18 2-1		Aug28 1-0
Motherwell	Aug25 3-1	Aug21 1-1	Aug14 2-1	

Section 6

	Ayr U	Queen of South	St Mirren	Stirling A
Ayr U		Aug21 0-2	Aug28 2-1	Aug18 0-0
Queen of South	Sep01 1-4		Aug18 0-1	Aug28 0-2
St Mirren	Aug14 3-1	Aug25 6-0		Sep01 0-0
Stirling A	Aug25 1-1	Aug14 2-0	Aug21 0-3	

Section 7

	Brechin C	East Fife	E Stirling	Partick T
Brechin C		Aug28 4-0	Aug18 4-0	Sep01 1-1
East Fife	Aug14 0-0		Aug21 0-1	Aug25 0-3
E Stirling	Aug25 1-1	Sep01 0-0		Aug14 0-4
Partick T	Aug21 0-0	Aug18 0-0	Aug28 4-2	

Section 8

	Berwick R	Hamilton A	Kilmarnock	Queen's Park
Berwick R		Aug21 0-1	Aug28 2-1	Aug18 1-0
Hamilton A	Sep01 0-1		Aug18 0-0	Aug28 1-2
Kilmarnock	Aug14 4-0	Aug25 1-0		Sep01 5-1
Queen's Park	Aug25 2-1	Aug14 1-1	Aug21 0-2	

Section 9

	Albion R	Cowdenbeath	Meadowbank T	Montrose	Stenhousemuir	Stranraer
Albion R				Aug28 1-2	Aug21 0-0	Aug14 2-2
Cowdenbeath	Aug25 2-1			Aug14 0-1	Aug28 1-1	
Meadowbank T	Aug18 3-2	Aug21 0-1				
Montrose		Aug25 0-1				Aug21 1-0
Stenhousemuir		Aug14 1-1	Aug18 2-2			Aug25 0-4
Stranraer	Aug18 1-3	Aug28 0-2				

Section 1	P	W	D	L	F	A	Pts
Celtic	6	6	0	0	29	3	12
Arbroath	6	2	1	3	4	9	5
Alloa	6	2	0	4	7	13	4
Dunfermline A	6	1	1	4	3	18	3

Section 2	P	W	D	L	F	A	Pts
Aberdeen	6	4	2	0	18	7	10
Morton	6	3	2	1	16	11	8
Dundee	6	2	2	2	14	19	6
Dumbarton	6	0	0	6	7	18	0

Section 3	P	W	D	L	F	A	Pts
Rangers	6	4	2	0	13	6	10
Hibernian	6	1	4	1	6	6	6
Airdrie	6	2	1	3	9	11	5
Clydebank	6	1	1	4	8	13	3

Section 4	P	W	D	L	F	A	Pts
Dundee U	6	6	0	0	22	2	12
St Johnstone	6	3	1	2	15	10	7
Falkirk	6	1	1	4	3	15	3
Raith R	6	0	2	4	5	18	2

Section 5	P	W	D	L	F	A	Pts
Hearts	6	5	0	1	16	4	10
Motherwell	6	3	2	1	10	7	8
Forfar A	6	2	1	3	5	6	5
Clyde	6	0	1	5	5	19	1

Section 6	P	W	D	L	F	A	Pts
St Mirren	6	4	1	1	14	3	9
Stirling A	6	2	3	1	5	4	7
Ayr U	6	2	2	2	8	8	6
Queen of South	6	1	0	5	3	15	2

Section 7

	P	W	D	L	F	A	Pts
Partick T	6	3	3	0	12	3	9
Brechin C	6	2	4	0	10	2	8
E Stirling	6	1	2	3	4	13	4
East Fife	6	0	3	3	0	8	3

Section 8

	P	W	D	L	F	A	Pts
Kilmarnock	6	4	1	1	13	3	9
Berwick R	6	3	0	3	5	8	6
Queen's Park	6	2	1	3	6	11	5
Hamilton A	6	1	2	3	3	5	4

Section 9

	P	W	D	L	F	A	Pts
Meadowbank T	5	3	1	1	7	4	7
Cowdenbeath	5	3	1	1	7	4	7
Montrose	5	3	1	1	6	4	7
Stenhousemuir	5	0	4	1	4	8	4
Stranraer	5	1	1	3	7	8	3
Albion R	5	0	2	3	6	9	2

Play-offs
Sep 1 Cowdenbeath ......3 Meadowbank T ..0
Sep 6 Kilmarnock ....1 Cowdenbeath 0
Sep 8 Cowdenbeath ......1 Kilmarnock 0
Penalties 3-4

Quarter-finals
Sep 22 Aberdeen ....1 Dundee U 3
Oct 6 Dundee U ....1 Aberdeen ......0 Agg 4-2
Sep 15 Celtic ....4 Partick T 0
Sep 22 Partick T ....0 Celtic ....3 Agg 0-7
Sep 22 Kilmarnock ....1 Rangers 6
Oct 6 Rangers ....6 Kilmarnock ....0 Agg 12-1
Sep 15 St Mirren ....1 Hearts 1
Sep 22 Hearts ....2 St Mirren .....1 Agg 3-2

Semi-finals
Oct 27 Celtic ....2 Dundee U 0
Nov 10 Dundee U ....2 Celtic ....1 Agg 2-3
Oct 27 Rangers ....2 Hearts 0
Nov 10 Hearts ....1 Rangers ....2 Agg 1-4

Final
Dec 4 Celtic ....2 Rangers 1
played at Hampden Park

Season 1983-84

1st Round
Aug 13 Albion R ....0 Queen of South ..4
Aug 17 Queen of South ...2 Albion R ....1 Agg 6-1
Aug 13 Arbroath ....0 East Fife 1
Aug 17 East Fife ....1 Arbroath ....1 Agg 2-1
Aug 13 Berwick R ....2 Stranraer 0
Aug 17 Stranraer ....1 Berwick R ......1 Agg 1-3
Aug 13 Forfar A ....1 Stenhousemuir ..0
Aug 17 Stenhousemuir ....2 Forfar A ....2 Agg 2-3
Aug 13 Montrose ....1 E Stirling 0
Aug 17 E Stirling ....1 Montrose ....2 Agg 1-3
Aug 15 Stirling A ....1 Cowdenbeath 1
Aug 17 Cowdenbeath ......2 Stirling A .....0 Agg 3-1

2nd Round
Aug 24 Aberdeen ....9 Raith R 0
Aug 27 Raith R ....0 Aberdeen ....3 Agg 0-12
Aug 24 Airdrie ....2 Clyde 0
Aug 27 Clyde ....1 Airdrie ....0 Agg 1-2
Aug 24 Ayr U ....1 Clydebank 2
Aug 27 Clydebank ....1 Ayr U ....0 Agg 3-1
Aug 24 Brechin C ....0 Celtic 1
Aug 27 Celtic ....0 Brechin C ......0 Agg 1-0
Aug 24 Cowdenbeath ......0 Hearts 1
Aug 27 Hearts ....1 Cowdenbeath ....1 Agg 1-1
Penalties 4-2
Aug 24 Dundee U ....6 Dunfermline A ...1
Aug 27 Dunfermline A ....0 Dundee U ....2 Agg 1-8
Aug 24 East Fife ....1 St Johnstone ...2
Aug 27 St Johnstone .....6 East Fife ......3 Agg 8-4
Aug 24 Falkirk ....2 Alloa 4
Aug 27 Alloa ....2 Falkirk ....2 Agg 6-4
Aug 24 Hamilton A ....2 Morton 1
Aug 27 Morton ....3 Hamilton A .....1 Agg 4-3
Aug 24 Hibernian ....5 Dumbarton 0
Aug 27 Dumbarton ....1 Hibernian ......2 Agg 1-7
Aug 23 Meadowbank T .....2 Partick T 1
Aug 27 Partick T ....1 Meadowbank T ..2 Agg 2-4
Aug 23 Montrose ....1 Dundee 3
Aug 27 Dundee ....4 Montrose ....1 Agg 7-2
Aug 24 Motherwell ....2 Berwick R 0
Aug 27 Berwick R ....0 Motherwell .....2 Agg 0-4
Aug 24 Queen's Park .....3 Kilmarnock 2
Aug 27 Kilmarnock ....3 Queen's Park ...1 Agg 5-4
Aug 24 Rangers ....4 Queen of South ..0
Aug 27 Queen of South ...1 Rangers ....4 Agg 1-8
Aug 24 St Mirren ....1 Forfar A 0
Aug 27 Forfar A ....2 St Mirren ......2 Agg 2-3

3rd Round

Section 1

	Alloa	Dundee U	Morton	Motherwell
Alloa		Nov09 2-4	Nov30 1-0	Sep07 1-2
Dundee U	Aug30 5-0		Oct26 3-0	Oct05 4-2
Morton	Oct05 2-4	Sep07 1-1		Nov09 4-2
Motherwell	Oct26 2-2	Nov30 0-3	Aug31 3-0	

Section 2

	Clydebank	Hearts	Rangers	St Mirren
Clydebank		Nov30 0-3	Nov09 0-3	Sep07 2-0
Hearts	Oct05 1-1		Sep07 0-3	Nov09 3-1
Rangers	Aug31 4-0	Oct26 2-0		Oct05 5-0
St Mirren	Oct26 3-3	Aug31 2-2	Nov30 0-1	

Section 3

	Aberdeen	Dundee	Meadowbank T	St Johnstone
Aberdeen		Oct05 0-0	Aug31 4-0	Oct26 1-0
Dundee	Nov30 1-2		Oct25 1-1	Aug31 2-1
Meadowbank T	Nov09 1-3	Sep07 0-1		Nov30 0-0
St Johnstone	Sep07 0-1	Nov09 0-3	Oct04 1-2	

Section 4

	Airdrie	Celtic	Hibernian	Kilmarnock
Airdrie		Aug31 1-6	Nov30 1-3	Oct26 1-2
Celtic	Nov09 0-0		Sep07 5-1	Oct05 1-1
Hibernian	Oct05 0-0	Oct26 0-0		Aug31 2-0
Kilmarnock	Sep07 3-0	Nov30 0-1	Nov09 3-1	

Section 1

	P	W	D	L	F	A	Pts
Dundee U	6	5	1	0	20	5	11
Motherwell	6	2	1	3	11	14	5
Alloa	6	2	1	3	10	15	5
Morton	6	1	1	4	7	14	3

Section 2

	P	W	D	L	F	A	Pts
Rangers	6	6	0	0	18	0	12
Hearts	6	2	2	2	9	9	6
Clydebank	6	1	2	3	6	14	4
St Mirren	6	0	2	4	6	16	2

Section 3

	P	W	D	L	F	A	Pts
Aberdeen	6	5	1	0	11	2	11
Dundee	6	3	2	1	8	4	8
Meadowbank T	6	1	2	3	4	10	4
St Johnstone	6	0	1	5	2	9	1

Section 4

	P	W	D	L	F	A	Pts
Celtic	6	3	3	0	13	3	9
Kilmarnock	6	3	1	2	9	6	7
Hibernian	6	2	2	2	7	9	6
Airdrie	6	0	2	4	3	14	2

Semi-finals
Feb 22 Aberdeen ....0 Celtic 0
Mar 10 Celtic ....1 Aberdeen ....0 Agg 1-0
Feb 14 Dundee U ....1 Rangers 1
Feb 22 Rangers ....2 Dundee U ......0 Agg 3-1

Final
Mar 25 Celtic ....2 Rangers 3
played at Hampden Park

Rangers pictured in 1984. Back row (left to right): Prytz, D.Ferguson, McFarlane, Kennedy, McPherson, McClelland, Paterson, McAdam, Mitchell, E.Ferguson, Munro, Fleck. Middle row: Stan Anderson (youth-team coach), Lindsay, Davies, Durrant, S.Fraser, Walker, McCloy, Bruce, Burns, McKinnon, Leeman, Connor, Bob Findlay (physiotherapist). Front row: Redford, Dawson, I.Ferguson, Williamson, Cooper, Alex Totton (first-team coach), Jock Wallace (manager), John Hagart (reserve coach), Clark, C.Fraser, McCoist, Russell, MacDonald.

Season 1984-85

1st Round

Aug 14 Albion R ....2 Montrose 0
Aug 15 Dunfermline A ....4 Arbroath 0
Aug 15 E Stirling ....1 Berwick R 1
Penalties 4-3
Aug 15 Queen of South ...2 Queen's Park 1
Aug 15 Stirling A ....2 Stenhousemuir ...0
Aug 15 Stranraer ....0 Cowdenbeath 3

2nd Round

Aug 22 Airdrie ....3 Aberdeen 1
Aug 22 Ayr U ....1 Motherwell 0
Aug 21 Cowdenbeath .....3 Partick T 0
Aug 22 Dundee ....3 Hamilton A 0
Aug 21 Dundee U ....5 Forfar A 0
Aug 22 Dunfermline A ....2 Celtic 3
Aug 22 Hearts ....4 E Stirling 0
Aug 22 Hibernian ....1 East Fife 0
Aug 22 Kilmarnock ....1 Alloa 1
Penalties 3-2

Aug 21 Meadowbank T ....2 Morton 1
Aug 22 Queen of South ....1 Dumbarton 2
Aug 21 Raith R ....2 Clydebank 0
Aug 22 Rangers ....1 Falkirk 0
Aug 22 St Johnstone .....2 Albion R 1
Aug 22 St Mirren ....1 Clyde 0
Aug 22 Stirling A ....3 Brechin C 4

3rd Round

Aug 29 Airdrie ....0 Celtic 4
Aug 29 Brechin C ....2 St Johnstone 4
Aug 29 Cowdenbeath .....2 St Mirren 0
Aug 29 Dumbarton ......0 Dundee U 4
Aug 29 Dundee ....1 Kilmarnock 1
Penalties 3-2
Aug 29 Hearts ....1 Ayr U 0
Aug 29 Hibernian ....1 Meadowbank T ..2
Aug 29 Rangers ....4 Raith R 0

4th Round

Sep 5 Cowdenbeath ......1 Rangers 3
Sep 4 Dundee ....0 Hearts 1
Sep 5 Dundee U ....2 Celtic 1
Sep 5 Meadowbank T ....2 St Johnstone 1

Semi-finals

Sep 26 Hearts ....1 Dundee U 2
Oct 10 Dundee U ....3 Hearts ....1 Agg 5-2
Sep 26 Rangers ....4 Meadowbank T ..0
Oct 9 Meadowbank T ....1 Rangers ....1 Agg 1-5
played at Tynecastle

Final

Oct 28 Dundee U ....0 Rangers 1
played at Hampden Park

Season 1985-86

1st Round

Aug 14 Berwick R ....1 Cowdenbeath ...3
Aug 19 Dunfermline A ....4 Stenhousemuir ..0
Aug 14 E Stirling ....1 Raith R 3
Aug 14 Queen of South ...3 Arbroath 0
Aug 14 Queen's Park .....1 Stirling A 2
Aug 14 Stranraer ....3 Albion R 0

2nd Round

Aug 21 Aberdeen ....5 Ayr U 0
Aug 21 Alloa ....0 Dundee U 2
Aug 21 Brechin C ....3 Falkirk 1
Aug 21 Clydebank ....7 Raith R 2
Aug 20 Hamilton A ....2 East Fife 0
Aug 21 Hibernian ....6 Cowdenbeath ...0
Aug 20 Meadowbank T ....2 Forfar A 3
Aug 20 Montrose ....1 Hearts 3
Aug 21 Morton ....2 Dunfermline A ...2
Penalties 4-3

Aug 21 Motherwell ....1 Partick T 0
Aug 21 Queen of South ....1 Celtic 4
Aug 21 Rangers ....5 Clyde 0
Aug 21 St Johnstone .....1 Airdrie 0
Aug 20 St Mirren ....3 Kilmarnock 1
Aug 21 Stranraer ....2 Dundee 3
Aug 21 Stirling A ....1 Dumbarton 1
Penalties 4-2

3rd Round

Aug 28 Celtic ....7 Brechin C 0
Aug 28 Dundee U ....2 Clydebank 0
Aug 27 Forfar A ....2 Rangers 2
Penalties 5-6
Aug 28 Hamilton A ....2 Dundee 1
Aug 27 Hearts ....2 Stirling A 1
Aug 28 Hibernian ....6 Motherwell 1
Aug 28 Morton ....1 St Mirren 4
Aug 28 St Johnstone .....0 Aberdeen 2

4th Round

Sep 4 Aberdeen ....1 Hearts 0
Sep 4 Dundee ....2 St Mirren 1
Sep 4 Hamilton A ....1 Rangers 2
Sep 4 Hibernian ....4 Celtic 4
Penalties 4-3

Semi-finals

Sep 25 Dundee U ....0 Aberdeen 1
Oct 9 Aberdeen ....1 Dundee U ......0 Agg 2-0
Sep 25 Hibernian ....2 Rangers 0
Oct 9 Rangers ....1 Hibernian ......0 Agg 1-2

Final

Oct 27 Aberdeen ....3 Hibernian 0
played at Hampden Park

Aberdeen made two appearances at Hampden in 1985-86 and were victorious on both occasions, by the same scoreline of 3-0, beating their Edinburgh opponents Hearts in the SFA Cup and Hibernian in the League Cup. Here they are celebrating after their win against Hearts.

1st Round
Aug 12 Albion R . . . . .3 Berwick R 1
Aug 13 Arbroath . . . . .2 Raith R 1
Aug 13 Cowdenbeath . . . . . .0 St Johnstone 1
Aug 13 Meadowbank T . . . . .1 Stirling A 4
Aug 13 Stenhousemuir . . . .1 Queen's Park 0
Aug 13 Stranraer . . . . .0 E Stirling 2

2nd Round
Aug 20 Aberdeen . . . . .4 Alloa 0
Aug 20 Albion R . . . . .2 Forfar A 2
  Penalties 1-3
Aug 19 Brechin C . . . . .0 Hamilton A 1
Aug 20 Celtic . . . . .2 Airdrie 0
Aug 19 Clyde . . . . .2 Falkirk 1
Aug 20 Clydebank . . . . . . .3 St Johnstone 0
Aug 20 Dumbarton . . . . . . .1 Stirling A 0
Aug 20 Dunfermline A . . . . .0 St Mirren 2
Aug 19 Hearts . . . . .0 Montrose 2

Aug 20 Hibernian . . . . .1 E Stirling 0
Aug 20 Kilmarnock . . . . .1 Ayr U 2
Aug 20 Morton . . . . .2 Dundee 5
Aug 20 Motherwell . . . . .4 Arbroath 0
Aug 20 Partick T . . . . .0 East Fife 1
Aug 20 Queen of South . . . .0 Dundee U 1
Aug 20 Stenhousemuir . . . . .1 Rangers 4

3rd Round
Aug 27 Aberdeen . . . . .3 Clyde 1
Aug 27 Ayr U . . . . .0 Dundee U 3
Aug 27 Celtic . . . . .3 Dumbarton 0
Aug 27 Dundee . . . . .4 Montrose 0
Aug 27 East Fife . . . . .0 Rangers 0
  Penalties 4-5
Aug 27 Forfar A . . . . .5 St Mirren 1
Aug 27 Hamilton A . . . . .0 Hibernian 1
Aug 27 Motherwell . . . . .2 Clydebank 0

4th Round
Sep 3 Aberdeen . . . . .1 Celtic 1
  Penalties 2-4
Sep 3 Hibernian . . . . .0 Dundee U 2
Sep 3 Motherwell . . . . .2 Forfar A 1
Sep 3 Rangers . . . . .3 Dundee 1

Semi-finals
Sep 23 Celtic . . . . .2 Motherwell 2
  Penalties 5-4
  played at Hampden Park
Sep 24 Dundee U . . . . .1 Rangers 2
  played at Hampden Park

Final
Oct 26 Celtic . . . . .1 Rangers 2
  played at Hampden Park

As the tie went into a penalty competition, Aberdeen's Peter Nicholas blasts his spot-kick over the bar against Rangers in the 1987-88 Scottish League Cup Final.

Season 1987-88

1st Round
Aug 12 Arbroath . . . . .1 Ayr U 3
Aug 12 Berwick R . . . . . . .1 Stirling A 2
Aug 12 Cowdenbeath . . . . .1 Queen's Park 3
Aug 12 St Johnstone . . . . .4 Alloa 1
Aug 11 Stenhousemuir . . . .1 E Stirling 3
Aug 12 Stranraer . . . . .0 Albion R 3

2nd Round
Aug 19 Aberdeen . . . . . . .5 Brechin C 1
Aug 19 Albion R . . . . .1 East Fife 1
  Penalties 5-3
Aug 19 Ayr U . . . . .0 Dumbarton 1
Aug 19 Celtic . . . . .3 Forfar A 1
Aug 19 Dundee U . . . . . . .4 Partick T 1
Aug 18 E Stirling . . . . .1 Dunfermline A . . .3
Aug 19 Hearts . . . . .6 Kilmarnock 1
Aug 18 Hibernian . . . . .3 Montrose 2

Aug 18 Meadowbank T . . . . .1 Hamilton A 0
Aug 19 Morton . . . . .1 Clyde 5
Aug 19 Motherwell . . . . . . .3 Airdrie 1
Aug 18 Queen of South . . . .2 Falkirk 1
Aug 18 Queen's Park . . . . . .0 Dundee 3
Aug 19 Raith R . . . . .2 Clydebank 1
Aug 18 St Mirren . . . . .0 St Johnstone 1
Aug 19 Stirling A . . . . .1 Rangers 2

3rd Round
Aug 26 Aberdeen . . . . .3 St Johnstone 0
Aug 26 Dumbarton . . . . . . .1 Celtic 5
Aug 26 Dunfermline A . . . . .1 Rangers 4
Aug 25 Hearts . . . . .2 Clyde 0
Aug 25 Hibernian . . . . .3 Queen of South . .1
Aug 26 Meadowbank T . . . . .0 Dundee 3
Aug 26 Motherwell . . . . . . .4 Albion R 0
Aug 25 Raith R . . . . .1 Dundee U 2

4th Round
Sep 1 Aberdeen . . . . .1 Celtic 0
Sep 2 Dundee . . . . .2 Dundee U 1
Sep 1 Motherwell . . . . .1 Hibernian 0
Sep 2 Rangers . . . . .4 Hearts 1

Semi-finals
Sep 23 Aberdeen . . . . .2 Dundee 0
  played at Tannadice
Sep 23 Motherwell . . . . . . .1 Rangers 3
  played at Hampden Park

Final
Oct 25 Aberdeen . . . . .3 Rangers 3
  Penalties 3-5
  played at Hampden Park

Season 1988-89

1st Round
Aug 10 Alloa ....2 Stirling A 4
Aug 10 Brechin C ....3 Montrose 1
Aug 10 Cowdenbeath ......0 Albion R 0
　　　　Penalties 3-4
Aug 11 E Stirling ......0 Arbroath 1
Aug 10 Queen's Park ......1 Stranraer 2
Aug 10 Stenhousemuir ....3 Berwick R 0

2nd Round
Aug 17 Aberdeen ....4 Arbroath 0
Aug 17 Airdrie ....0 Motherwell 1
Aug 16 Albion R ....2 Hamilton A 4
Aug 17 Brechin C ....0 Morton 2
Aug 17 Celtic ....4 Ayr U 1
Aug 17 Clyde ....0 Rangers 3
Aug 17 Clydebank ....2 Stenhousemuir ..0
Aug 16 Dumbarton ....1 St Mirren 3

Aug 17 Dundee ....5 Queen of South ...1
Aug 17 East Fife ....1 Dunfermline A ...1
　　　　Penalties 3-4
Aug 17 Falkirk ....1 Raith R 1
　　　　Penalties 9-8
Aug 17 Hearts ....5 St Johnstone 0
Aug 17 Hibernian ....4 Stranraer 0
Aug 17 Kilmarnock ....1 Forfar A 0
Aug 16 Meadowbank T ......2 Stirling A 1
Aug 16 Partick T ....0 Dundee U 2

3rd Round
Aug 24 Celtic ....7 Hamilton A 2
Aug 24 Dundee ....2 Falkirk 1
Aug 24 Dunfermline A ......2 Motherwell 1
Aug 23 Hibernian ....1 Kilmarnock 0
Aug 23 Meadowbank T ......0 Hearts 2
Aug 23 Morton ....1 Aberdeen 2

Aug 24 Rangers ....6 Clydebank 0
Aug 24 St Mirren ....1 Dundee U 3

4th Round
Aug 31 Dundee U ....2 Celtic 0
Aug 31 Dunfermline A .....1 Hearts 4
Aug 31 Hibernian ....1 Aberdeen 2
Aug 31 Rangers ....4 Dundee 1

Semi-finals
Sep 20 Aberdeen ....2 Dundee U 0
　　　　played at Dens Park
Sep 21 Hearts ....0 Rangers 3
　　　　played at Hampden Park

Final
Oct 23 Aberdeen ....2 Rangers 3
　　　　played at Hampden Park

Season 1989-90

1st Round
Aug 9 Arbroath ....1 E Stirling 0
Aug 9 Cowdenbeath ......0 Montrose 4
Aug 8 Dumbarton ....3 Stenhousemuir ..0
Aug 9 East Fife ....2 Queen's Park ...2
　　　　Penalties 6-7
Aug 9 Stirling A ....0 Berwick R 3
Aug 9 Stranraer ....3 Brechin C 4

2nd Round
Aug 15 Airdrie ....4 Forfar A 0
Aug 16 Albion R ....0 Aberdeen 2
Aug 15 Ayr U ....0 Hamilton A 1
Aug 15 Berwick R ....0 St Mirren 3
Aug 16 Brechin C ....0 Falkirk 3
Aug 16 Clydebank ....3 Meadowbank T ..1
Aug 15 Dumbarton ....0 Celtic 3
Aug 15 Dundee ....5 Clyde 1

Aug 16 Dundee U ....1 Partick T 0
Aug 15 Dunfermline A .....3 Raith R 0
Aug 16 Hearts ....3 Montrose 0
Aug 15 Hibernian ....2 Alloa 0
Aug 15 Kilmarnock ....1 Motherwell 4
Aug 16 Queen of South ....1 St Johnstone ...0
Aug 15 Queen's Park ......0 Morton 1
Aug 15 Rangers ....4 Arbroath 0

Aug 23 St Mirren ....1 Motherwell 0

3rd Round
Aug 23 Aberdeen ....4 Airdrie 0
Aug 22 Celtic ....2 Queen of South ..0
Aug 23 Dunfermline A .....1 Dundee 0
Aug 23 Falkirk ....0 Hearts 4
Aug 23 Hamilton A ....2 Dundee U 1
Aug 22 Hibernian ....0 Clydebank 0
　　　　Penalties 5-3
Aug 23 Morton ....1 Rangers 2

4th Round
Aug 30 Aberdeen ....3 St Mirren 1
Aug 30 Hamilton A ....0 Rangers 3
Aug 30 Hearts ....2 Celtic 2
　　　　Penalties 1-3 ....
Aug 29 Hibernian ....1 Dunfermline A ...3

Semi-finals
Sep 20 Aberdeen ....1 Celtic 0
　　　　played at Hampden Park
Sep 19 Dunfermline A .....0 Rangers 5
　　　　played at Hampden Park

Final
Oct 22 Aberdeen ....2 Rangers 1
　　　　played at Hampden Park

Season 1990-91

1st Round
Aug 14 E Stirling ....2 Dumbarton 2
　　　　Penalties 4-1
Aug 15 Montrose ....1 Queen of South ..2
Aug 14 Queen's Park ......3 East Fife 3
　　　　Penalties 5-4
Aug 14 Stenhousemuir .....0 Cowdenbeath ...2
Aug 15 Stirling A ....1 Arbroath 2
Aug 15 Stranraer ....4 Berwick R 3

2nd Round
Aug 21 Airdrie ....1 Stranraer 2
Aug 21 Alloa ....0 Dundee U 3
Aug 21 Brechin C ....0 Hamilton A 2
Aug 22 Celtic ....4 Ayr U 0
Aug 22 Cowdenbeath ......0 Hearts 2
Aug 21 Dunfermline A .....4 Albion R 0
Aug 22 Falkirk ....1 Partick T 1
　　　　Penalties 1-4

Aug 21 Forfar A ....1 Raith R 2
Aug 21 Kilmarnock ....3 Clydebank 2
Aug 22 Meadowbank T .....0 Hibernian 1
Aug 21 Motherwell ....4 Morton 3
Aug 21 Queen of South ...2 Dundee 2
　　　　Penalties 4-1
Aug 21 Queen's Park ......1 Aberdeen 2
Aug 21 Rangers ....5 E Stirling 0
Aug 21 St Johnstone ......0 Clyde 2
Aug 22 St Mirren ....1 Arbroath 0

3rd Round
Aug 29 Aberdeen ....4 Stranraer 0
Aug 28 Dunfermline A .....1 Queen of South ..2
Aug 29 Hamilton A ....0 Celtic 1
Aug 28 Motherwell ....4 Clyde 1
Aug 28 Partick T ....1 Dundee U 3
Aug 29 Raith R ....1 Hibernian 0
Aug 28 Rangers ....1 Kilmarnock 0

Aug 29 St Mirren ....0 Hearts 1

4th Round
Sep 5 Aberdeen ....3 Hearts 0
Sep 5 Celtic ....2 Queen of South ..1
Sep 4 Dundee U ....2 Motherwell 0
Sep 4 Rangers ....6 Raith R 2

Semi-finals
Sep 26 Aberdeen ....0 Rangers 1
　　　　played at Hampden Park
Sep 25 Celtic ....2 Dundee U 0
　　　　played at Hampden Park

Final
Oct 28 Celtic ....1 Rangers 2
　　　　played at Hampden Park

Season 1991-92

1st Round
Aug 13 Alloa ....0 Stranraer 0
　　　　Penalties 8-7 ....
Aug 14 Berwick R ....0 Dumbarton 1
Aug 21 Cowdenbeath ......1 Arbroath 0
Aug 13 East Fife ....2 E Stirling 2
　　　　Penalties 2-4
Aug 13 Queen of South ....0 Albion R 4
Aug 13 Queen's Park ......4 Stenhousemuir ..2

2nd Round
Aug 20 Brechin C ....3 St Mirren 3
　　　　Penalties 4-5
Aug 21 Clyde ....0 Aberdeen 4
Aug 26 Cowdenbeath ......0 Kilmarnock 1
Aug 20 Dumbarton ....3 Airdrie 2
Aug 21 Dundee ....2 Ayr U 4
Aug 20 Dundee U ....3 Montrose 2
Aug 20 Dunfermline A .....4 Alloa 1

Aug 20 Falkirk ....3 E Stirling 0
Aug 20 Hamilton A ....2 Forfar A 0
Aug 20 Hearts ....3 Clydebank 0
Aug 21 Meadowbank T .....0 St Johnstone ...2
Aug 21 Morton ....2 Celtic 4
Aug 20 Partick ....2 Albion R 0
Aug 20 Raith R ....4 Motherwell 1
Aug 20 Rangers ....6 Queen's Park ...0
Aug 20 Stirling A ....0 Hibernian 3

3rd Round
Aug 28 Aberdeen ....0 Airdrie 1
Aug 27 Ayr U ....2 St Johnstone ...0
Aug 27 Celtic ....3 Raith R 1
Aug 28 Dundee U ....1 Falkirk 0
Aug 28 Dunfermline A .....1 St Mirren 1
　　　　Penalties 3-2
Aug 28 Hamilton A ....0 Hearts 2
Aug 28 Kilmarnock ....2 Hibernian 3

Aug 28 Partick ....0 Rangers 2

4th Round
Sep 3 Airdrie ....0 Celtic 2
　　　　Penalties 4-2
Sep 3 Ayr U ....0 Hibernian 2
Sep 3 Dunfermline A .....3 Dundee U 1
Sep 4 Hearts ....0 Rangers 1

Semi-finals
Sep 24 Airdrie ....1 Dunfermline A ...1
　　　　played at Tynecastle
　　　　Penalties 2-3
Sep 25 Hibernian ....1 Rangers 0
　　　　played at Hampden Park

Final
Oct 27 Dunfermline A .....0 Hibernian 2
　　　　played at Hampden Park

Season 1992-93

1st Round
Aug 4 Brechin C . . . . .2 Albion R 1
Aug 1 E Stirling . . . . .0 Alloa 1
Aug 4 Queen of South . . . .3 Berwick R 0
Aug 4 Queen's Park . . . . . .1 Clyde 3
Aug 1 Stenhousemuir . . . . .2 Arbroath 3
Aug 1 Stranraer . . . . .0 East Fife 0
    Penalties 5-4

2nd Round
Aug 11 Airdrie . . . . .2 Stranraer 3
Aug 11 Alloa . . . . .1 St Johnstone 3
Aug 12 Arbroath . . . . .0 Aberdeen 4
Aug 11 Brechin C . . . . .4 Hamilton A 2
Aug 11 Dumbarton . . . . . . .0 Rangers 5
Aug 11 Dundee U . . . . .6 Queen of South . .0
Aug 12 Falkirk . . . . .4 Forfar A 1
Aug 12 Hearts . . . . .1 Clydebank 0
Aug 12 Hibernian . . . . .4 Raith R 1

3rd Round
Aug 11 Meadowbank T . . . .0 Dundee 3
Aug 12 Montrose . . . . .0 Dunfermline A . . .6
Aug 11 Morton . . . . .2 Kilmarnock 3
Aug 11 Motherwell . . . . . . .4 Clyde 2
Aug 11 Partick T . . . . .2 Ayr U 0
Aug 12 St Mirren . . . . .1 Cowdenbeath 0
Aug 12 Stirling A . . . . .0 Celtic 3

3rd Round
Aug 19 Aberdeen . . . . .1 Dunfermline A . . .0
Aug 19 Brechin C . . . . .1 Hearts 2
Aug 19 Celtic . . . . .1 Dundee 0
Aug 18 Dundee U . . . . .3 St Mirren 0
Aug 18 Kilmarnock . . . . . . .3 Hibernian 1
Aug 19 Motherwell . . . . . . .0 Falkirk 1
Aug 19 St Johnstone . . . . . .2 Partick T 2
    Penalties 4-3
Aug 19 Stranraer . . . . .0 Rangers 5

4th Round
Aug 25 Kilmarnock . . . . . . .1 St Johnstone . . .3
Aug 26 Dundee U . . . . .2 Rangers 3
Aug 26 Falkirk . . . . .1 Aberdeen 4
Aug 26 Hearts . . . . .1 Celtic 2

Semi-finals
Sep 23 Aberdeen . . . . .1 Celtic 0
    played at Hampden Park
Sep 22 Rangers . . . . .3 St Johnstone 1
    played at Hampden Park

Final
Oct 25 Aberdeen . . . . .1 Rangers 2
    at Hampden Park

Season 1993-94

1st Round
Aug 3 Alloa . . . . .1 Berwick R 0
Aug 3 East Fife . . . . .1 Albion R 2
Aug 4 Montrose . . . . .0 E Stirling 1
Aug 4 Queen of South . . . .1 Stranraer 2
Aug 3 Queen's Park . . . . . .0 Arbroath 1
Aug 3 Stenhousemuir . . . . .3 Forfar A 1

2nd Round
Aug 10 Aberdeen . . . . .5 Clydebank 0
Aug 10 Airdrie . . . . .2 Cowdenbeath 1
Aug 11 Albion R . . . . .1 Partick T 11
Aug 10 Ayr U . . . . .0 Motherwell 6
Aug 10 Brechin C . . . . .0 St Mirren 1
Aug 11 Clyde . . . . .1 St Johnstone 2
Aug 11 Dunfermline A . . . . .2 E Stirling 0
Aug 10 Hamilton A . . . . . . .0 Dundee U 1
Aug 10 Hearts . . . . .2 Stranraer 0
Aug 10 Hibernian . . . . .2 Alloa 0

3rd Round
Aug 10 Kilmarnock . . . . .1 Morton 2
Aug 10 Meadowbank T . . . .1 Dundee 1
    Penalties
Aug 11 Raith R . . . . .1 Arbroath 2
Aug 11 Rangers . . . . .1 Dumbarton 0
Aug 10 Stenhousemuir . . . . .1 Falkirk 2
Aug 10 Stirling A . . . . .0 Celtic 2

3rd Round
Aug 24 Aberdeen . . . . .5 Motherwell 2
Aug 25 Arbroath . . . . .1 Celtic 9
Aug 24 Dunfermline A . . . . .0 Rangers 2
Aug 25 Hearts . . . . .0 Falkirk 1
Aug 24 Hibernian . . . . .2 Dundee 1
Aug 24 Morton . . . . .0 Partick T 1
Aug 25 St Johnstone . . . . . .0 Airdrie 2
Aug 24 St Mirren . . . . .0 Dundee U 1

4th Round
Aug 31 Celtic . . . . .1 Airdrie 0
Aug 31 Dundee U . . . . .3 Falkirk 3
    Penalties 4-2
Aug 31 Partick T . . . . .2 Hibernian 2
    Penalties 2-3
Sep 1 Rangers . . . . .2 Aberdeen 1

Semi-finals
Sep 21 Dundee U . . . . .0 Hibernian 1
    played at Hampden Park
Sep 22 Rangers . . . . .1 Celtic 2
    played at Hampden Park

Final
Oct 24 Hibernian . . . . .1 Rangers 2
    played at Hampden Park

Season 1994-95

1st Round
Aug 10 Arbroath . . . . .1 Alloa 1
    Penalties 5-4
Aug 9 Berwick R . . . . .0 Montrose 0
    Penalties 2-3
Aug 9 East Fife . . . . .1 Forfar A 0
Aug 9 E Stirling . . . . .0 Caledonian T 2
Aug 10 Queen of South . . . .2 Albion R 0
Aug 10 Ross . . . . .3 Queen's Park 2
Aug 9 Stenhousemuir . . . . .0 Meadowbank T . .4
Aug 10 Stranraer . . . . .2 Cowdenbeath 2
    Penalties 4-2

2nd Round
Aug 17 Aberdeen . . . . .1 Stranraer 0
Aug 17 Airdrie . . . . .1 Rangers 6
Aug 16 Ayr U . . . . .0 Celtic 1
Aug 16 Dumbarton . . . . . . .0 Hearts 4
Aug 17 Dundee . . . . .3 Caledonian T 0
Aug 17 Dunfermline A . . . . .4 Meadowbank T . .1
Aug 16 Falkirk . . . . .1 Montrose 1
    Penalties 5-4

3rd Round
Aug 17 Hamilton A . . . . . . .3 Clyde 0
Aug 17 Kilmarnock . . . . . . .4 East Fife 1
Aug 16 Morton . . . . .1 Airdrie 1
    Penalties 3-5
Aug 16 Motherwell . . . . . . .3 Clydebank 1
Aug 16 Partick T . . . . .5 Brechin C 0
Aug 17 Queen of South . . . .0 Hibernian 3
Aug 17 Ross . . . . .0 Raith R 5
Aug 16 St Mirren . . . . .0 Dundee U 1
Aug 17 Stirling A . . . . .0 St Johnstone 2

3rd Round
Aug 31 Dundee . . . . .1 Celtic 2
Aug 31 Hamilton A . . . . . . .1 Dundee U 1
    Penalties 3-5
Aug 30 Hibernian . . . . .2 Dunfermline A . . .0
Aug 31 Hearts . . . . .2 St Johnstone 4
Aug 31 Motherwell . . . . . . .1 Airdrie 2
Aug 30 Partick T . . . . .0 Aberdeen 5
Aug 31 Raith R . . . . .3 Kilmarnock 2
Aug 31 Rangers . . . . .1 Falkirk 2

4th Round
Sep 21 Celtic . . . . .1 Dundee U 0
Sep 21 Falkirk . . . . .1 Aberdeen 4
Sep 21 Hibernian . . . . .1 Airdrie 2
Sep 20 St Johnstone . . . . . .1 Raith R 3

Semi-finals
Oct 25 Airdrie . . . . .1 Raith R 1
    Penalties 4-5
    played at Hampden Park
Oct 26 Celtic . . . . .1 Aberdeen 0
    played at Hampden Park

Final
Nov 27 Celtic . . . . .2 Raith R 2
    Penalties 5-6
    played at Ibrox